PLANT HARDINESS ZONES

KEY

0a	4a
0b	4b
1a	5a
1b	5b
2a	6a
2b	6b
3a	7a
3b	7b
	8a

Davis Strait

Foxe Basin

Iqaluit

Hudson Strait

LABRADOR SEA

D

A

Hudson Bay

Caniapiscau

0a

NEWFOUNDLAND & LABRADOR

Churchill

Labrador City

St. John's

James Bay

La Grande Rivière

Newfoundland

Corner Brook

Albany

QUEBEC

0b

Gulf of St. Lawrence

ARIO

Harricana

1a

Lac Mistassini

1b

PRINCE EDWARD ISLAND

Charlottetown

Jonquière Chicoutimi

Saguenay

NEW BRUNSWICK

NOVA SCOTIA

St. Maurice

Moncton

2a

Charlesbourg

Fredericton

Lake Superior

2b Trois-Rivières

Québec

Dartmouth

Ottawa

3a

St. Lawrence

Saint John

Halifax

3b

Laval

Sherbrooke

Sudbury

4a

Gatineau 4b

Montréal

Sault Ste.Marie

North Bay

OTTAWA

5a

ATLANTIC OCEAN

Peterborough Kingston

Lake Huron

Oshawa

Lake Ontario

Kitchener

Toronto

Lake Michigan

Hamilton St.Catharines

London 5b

Sarnia

6a

Windsor

6b *Lake Erie*

CANADIAN ENCYCLOPEDIA OF
GARDENING

CANADIAN ENCYCLOPEDIA OF
GARDENING
REVISED & UPDATED

EDITOR-IN-CHIEF CHRISTOPHER BRICKELL
EDITOR-IN-CHIEF FOR CANADA TREVOR COLE

REVISED AND UPDATED EDITION 2013

Senior Editors Helen Fewster, Caroline Reed, Rebecca Warren
Senior Art Editors Joanne Doran, Elaine Hewson
Canadian Editor Barbara Campbell
Consultant Fern Marshall Bradley
Editors May Corfield, Jill Hamilton, Christine Heilman,
Kate Johnsen, Margaret Parrish
Designer Alison Shackleton
Pre-Production Producers Marc Staples, George Nimmo
Senior Pre-Production Producer Tony Phipps
DK Images Romaine Werblow
Picture Research Susie Peachey
Jacket Designer Rosie Levine
Senior Producers Jen Lockwood, Seyhan Esen
Managing Editor Penny Warren
Managing Art Editor Alison Donovan
Publisher Mary Ling

DK INDIA

Senior Editor Nidhilekha Mathur
Senior Art Editor Balwant Singh
Editor Divya Chandhok
Art Editor Vandna Sonkariya
Assistant Editor Ekta Sharma
Senior DTP Designer Pushpak Tyagi
Managing Editor Glenda Fernandes
Managing Art Editor Navidita Thapa
CTS/DTP Manager Sunil Sharma
Picture Researcher Nivisha Sinha

This revised and updated edition published in 2013.

DK Publishing is represented in Canada by
Tourmaline Editions Inc.
662 King Street West, Suite 304
Toronto, Ontario M5V 1M7

Published in Great Britain in 1992 by Dorling Kindersley Limited, London

13 14 15 10 9 8 7 6 5 4 3 2 1
001 – 191912 – Apr/2013

Library and Archives Canada Cataloguing in Publication
    Canadian encyclopedia of gardening / editor-in-chief, Christopher
Brickell ; editor-in-chief for Canada, Trevor Cole. -- Rev. and updated ed.

Includes index.
ISBN 978-1-55363-195-8

    1. Gardening--Canada. I. Brickell, Christopher II. Cole, Trevor J.

SB453.3.C2C35 2013   635.0971   C2012-906346-0

DK books are available at special discount when purchased in bulk for
corporate sales, sales promotions, premiums, fund-raising, or educational
use. For details, please contact: specialmarkets@tourmaline.ca

Printed and bound in China by Toppan
See our complete catalog at
www.dk.com

CONTENTS

SPECIAL FEATURES

THE EDITOR-IN-CHIEF

CHRISTOPHER BRICKELL was Director General of the Royal Horticultural Society for many years, representing its interests all over the world. He is the author of several books, has contributed to a number of horticultural and botanical reference works, and is Editor-in-Chief of DK's *Encyclopedia of Plants and Flowers* and *A–Z Encyclopedia of Garden Plants*. Christopher Brickell was awarded the Society's prestigious Victoria Medal of Honor. He is also Chairman of the International Commission for the Nomenclature of Cultivated Plants, and is a past President of the International Society for Horticultural Science.

THE EDITOR-IN-CHIEF FOR CANADA

TREVOR COLE is an expert on Canadian horticulture. After graduating from the Royal Botanic Gardens in Kew, Trevor immigrated to Canada and worked as a horticultural technician for Agricultural Canada in the study of native plants, eventually becoming the Curator of the Dominion Arboretum. He is the author or editor of many books, including DK's *A–Z Encyclopedia of Garden Plants, Great Canadian Plant Guide, What Grows Where in Canadian Gardens,* and *What Grows When in Canadian Gardens.*

THE CONTRIBUTORS

ROGER AYLETT *Dahlias*
BILL BAKER *Lilies*
LARRY BARLOW (WITH **W.B. WADE**) *Chrysanthemums*
CAROLINE BOISSET *Climbing Plants*
DENI BOWN *Growing Herbs*
ALEC BRISTOW (WITH **WILMA RITTERSHAUSEN**) *Orchids*
ROY CHEEK (WITH **GRAHAM RICE** AND **ISABELLE VAN GROENINGEN**) *Perennials*
TREVOR COLE (WITH **MICHAEL POLLOCK**) *Cold and Wind Protection*
KATH DRYDEN AND CHRISTOPHER GREY-WILSON (WITH **JOHN WARWICK**) *Rock, Scree, and Gravel Gardening; Alpine Houses and Frames*
JACK ELLIOTT *Irises; Bulbous Plants; Tulips and Daffodils*
COLIN ELLIS (WITH **MERVYN FEESEY**) *Bamboos*
RAYMOND EVISON *Clematis*
JOHN GALBALLY (WITH **EILEEN GALBALLY**) *Carnations and Pinks*
JIM GARDINER *Ornamental Trees; Dwarf Conifers; Topiary; Hedges and Screens; Ornamental Shrubs*
MICHAEL GIBSON (WITH **PETER HARKNESS**) *Roses, Roses for Display and Exhibtion*
GEORGE GILBERT *Growing Fruit*
RICHARD GILBERT *Hydroculture*
WILL GILES *Hardy Palms and the Exotic Look*
RUPERT GOLBY *Garden Planning and Design*
DEENAGH GOOLD-ADAMS (WITH **RICHARD GILBERT**) *Indoor Gardening*
DIANA GRENFELL *Hostas*
JOHN HACKER (WITH **GEOFF STEBBINGS**) *The Lawn*
ANDREW HALSTEAD AND PIPPA GREENWOOD (WITH **CHRIS PRIOR, LUCY HALSALL** AND **BEATRICE HENRICOT**) *Plant Problems*
LIN HAWTHORNE *Meadow Gardening*
ARTHUR HELLYER (WITH **GRAHAM RICE**) *Annuals and Biennials*
CLIVE INNES (WITH **TERRY HEWITT**) *Cacti and Other Succulents;* (WITH **RICHARD GILBERT**) *Bromeliads*
DAVID JOYCE *Container Gardening, Balconies and Roof Gardens, Water Gardens in Containers*
TONY KENDLE *Soils and Fertilizers*
HAZEL KEY (WITH **URSULA KEY-DAVIS**) *Ferns, Annual Geraniums*
JOY LARKCOM (WITH **MICHAEL POLLOCK**) *Growing Vegetables*
KEITH LOACH (WITH **DAVID HIDE**) *Principles of Propagation;* (WITH **MICHAEL POLLOCK**) *Basic Botany*
BILL MAISHMAN (WITH **JEFF BRANDE**) *Sweet Peas*
PETER MARSTON *Conservatory Gardening*
PETER MCHOY (WITH **GEOFF STEBBINGS**) *Tools and Equipment; Greenhouses and Cold Frames; Structures and Surfaces*
MICHAEL POLLOCK *Climate and the Garden; The Bed System*
DAVID PYCRAFT *Weeds*
PETER ROBINSON *Water Gardening; Water Lilies; Water Conservation and Recycling*
DON TINDALL *Tender Vegetables and Fruits*
ISABELLE VAN GROENINGEN *Perennial Groundcovers*
JOHN WRIGHT (WITH **GEORGE BARTLETT**) *Fuchsias*
Willow Walls: TEXT AND PICTURES COURTESY OF *The Garden Magazine*

PREFACE

DK's beautifully illustrated and authoritative *Canadian Encyclopedia of Gardening* has now been revised and updated. In the years since its original publication, it has become the definitive guide to all aspects of practical gardening in Canada for both home enthusiasts and horticultural students alike. Whether you want to grow your own vegetables and fruits, design and install a water garden, enhance your home landscape with trees and shrubs, or reduce the time you spend on routine garden maintenance, you'll find in-depth techniques, plant lists, and care recommendations to help you on your way.

This new edition includes expanded coverage of popular trends in gardening, such as planting to encourage pollinators, and the greening of roofs and walls. New features on cultivating vegetables and fruit in containers provide advice on how to grow your own edible crops even in the smallest spaces. With awareness increasing of the current and predicted impact of climatic changes on gardening practices, there are features throughout with information and practical advice for gardeners on how to respond to this new challenge. The Plant Problems section is a great resource, fully updated with a valuable visual guide to help ease the diagnosis of ailing plants in your garden.

All of these improvements have been made to ensure that this edition of the *Canadian Encyclopedia of Gardening* continues to fulfill DK's commitment to make the best and most comprehensive gardening resource available. DK would like to thank Editor-in-Chief Christopher Brickell, Editor-in-Chief for Canada Trevor Cole, Fern Marshall Bradley, and all the other contributors for their continued support of this essential reference book on gardening techniques.

INTRODUCTION

Every gardener who keeps an eye on the weather is aware of the gradual changes to the climate that have occurred over the last few decades. There is little, if any, doubt that extreme weather events of recent years—storms, periods of drought, and floods—are a consequence of global warming, due primarily to higher levels of greenhouse gases such as carbon dioxide in the atmosphere.

Climate change is a continuous process and, because plants are often sensitive to altered conditions, it is likely to present us with both challenges and opportunities. We may have to adapt both our plant choices and our techniques in order to maintain our gardens in the hot, dry summers and warm, wet winters that scientists predict will become the norm. Adventurous gardeners may enjoy experimenting with an expanded range of plants, but those who love tradition may struggle to maintain their lawn and established garden beds.

Gardeners should not, however, be discouraged: the oxygen released into the atmosphere as a byproduct of photosynthesis (the process by which green plants take in carbon dioxide and release oxygen to generate the energy needed for growth) will alleviate some of the effects of climate change. Therefore simply by growing more plants and encouraging tree planting in our local communities we can help to address the impact of global warming. And if we adopt more organic practices, reducing or avoiding the use of synthetic fertilizers and pesticides, we can reap wider environmental benefits as we continue to pursue this pleasurable hobby—no matter what the weather brings.

Low-maintenance shrubs for year-round foliage and structure
Densely planted evergreens, including *Aucuba japonica* and *Euonymus*, form a lush and harmonious backdrop to the natural stone steps and walls, yet they are all drought-tolerant shrubs where hardy. Large pots with clipped boxwood and bay add structural interest, and grasses introduce an element of light and movement. As a final touch, bowls of pansies provide a welcome splash of seasonal color in this small urban garden.

What is organic gardening?

The term "organic gardening" is often used simplistically to describe the cultivation of gardens without the aid of synthetically produced fertilizers, pesticides, or other chemicals in order to produce healthy, vigorous plants. This approach relies instead on using manures and fertilizers derived only from plant or animal residues to improve and maintain soil fertility.

Organic gardening also encompasses a wider holistic approach that not only stresses the avoidance of polluting activities but also works to conserve natural resources and encourage biodiversity. These range from conserving scarce resources—for instance, by saving and storing water, and recycling, reusing, or composting as much waste as possible—to being aware of the source and treatment of wood used for decks or furniture,

and seeking alternatives to styrofoam seed trays, which are not compostable. Some dedicated organic gardeners also prefer not to use natural materials—such as peat-based composts—that have been transported long distances when more local alternatives are available. The result is a more sustainable way of gardening that recognizes the importance of biological and genetic diversity, advocates preventive methods for pest and disease control, and encourages wildlife.

Implementing completely organic principles can be a considerable challenge, and is a matter of choice. However, using synthetic products and chemicals to grow ornamentals, fruit, and vegetables does not rule out adopting other organic practices such as composting and integrated pest management.

Chemical-free pest control
Grow marigolds as companion plants to deter soil pests; discourage bird pests with improvised bird-scarers; hoe regularly to keep weeds down; and welcome ladybugs into the garden to control aphids.

Organic soil management and composting

A successful organic garden depends on biologically active soil, supplemented as required by incorporating bulky materials such as composts, animal manures, leaf mold, or green manures. These organic soil improvers help to feed the soil organisms that break them down, providing plants with essential foods and trace elements. If necessary, natural fertilizers such as bonemeal, alfalfa meal, fish meal, kelp meal, and rock phosphate can be applied when and where appropriate.

It takes a few years to develop and maintain a high level of soil fertility, and ensure that the soil structure, which allows the free passage of air and water through the soil particles, is not impaired. Clay soil in particular can become compacted, restricting airflow and drainage, if walked on during cultivation, especially during cold, wet weather. It is always advisable to use a board or plank to distribute your weight when sowing seeds or planting seedlings.

Although working the soil breaks up compaction, helps improve drainage and root penetration, aerates the soil, and provides an opportunity to incorporate

bulky manures, it is often best to keep digging to a minimum. Some organic gardeners prefer not to dig at all: undisturbed soil loses less moisture through evaporation, provides a good environment for beneficial organisms, and may help to preserve soil structure. Regular mulching with organic soil improvers insulates the soil surface against water evaporation, improves the structure, and suppresses weeds.

Garden compost acts both as a soil improver and as a source of environmentally friendly plant food, and a compost bin is an excellent recycling facility for kitchen, garden, and other organic waste: no garden should be without at least one pile or bin. Compost is nature's way of recycling waste, and increases the soil's ability to retain water. As well as supporting a community of microbes and soil organisms, the pile provides shelter for creatures like toads and ground beetles—which eat slugs and other pests.

Waste not, want not
Every garden has room for a compost bin to provide a free mulch, and some bins can be very attractive. Compost may be forked into the soil, but other organic soil improvers such as hay work best when applied as a mulch.

Making wildlife work
Attracting wildlife is a very satisfying method of pest control. A pond may reward you with hungry frogs, a pile of logs or leaves will shelter toads, and both will compete for a slug dinner. A pond will also provide drinking and bathing water for birds. Nectar-rich flowers draw bees, butterflies, and lacewings, as well as many other beneficial pollinating insects.

Wildlife gardening

By their nature, gardens provide numerous habitats where wildlife can flourish. With the increase in urban development and loss of natural habitat taking their toll, these garden refuges are more important than ever. Private gardens form a natural "bridge" between built-up and open areas, which allows wildlife to move between them easily. The presence of birds, butterflies, bumblebees, honey bees, moths, and hoverflies enhances the garden, and attracting wildlife is a very effective method of controlling pests. Natural predators and pollinating insects are much more likely to visit plants and be more active in gardens where no pesticides are used.

There are many ways of making your garden attractive to wildlife. For example, planting beds and borders with ornamentals that provide nectar, pollen, seeds, and fruit will encourage bees, ladybugs, lacewings, bluebirds, and other birds that also feed on insect pests. Wildlife-attracting planting should also include species that provide birds with fruit or seeds in the fall and winter; for example, sunflowers, purple coneflowers, and black-eyed Susans will produce ample winter fare for seed-eating birds. Evergreen climbers and large shrubs create safe nesting sites for birds, and small trees can provide useful vantage points from

which to check for approaching predators. Log piles, long grass, and compost piles can provide homes for invertebrates, which are a vital source of food for many birds.

Water and shelter are also important for wildlife: water features, however small, add to the biodiversity of the garden by encouraging slug- and snail-eating amphibians to spawn, as well as providing birds and mammals with water. Birds, mammals, and insects will appreciate areas to live and breed; hedges provide excellent habitats, but specially built boxes for bats and butterflies may also help add to the range of wildlife and alleviate the loss of biodiversity in developed areas.

Naturalistic and meadow styles

Developing an area of a garden to emulate the richly diverse flora that occurs naturally in meadows, prairies, and other natural settings has considerable attractions for gardeners, particularly those who want to provide habitats for wildlife. Even in relatively small yards, it is often possible to have a designated area where wildflowers are encouraged to flower and seed naturally, for the benefit of bees, butterflies, and other insects, as well as small mammals and seed-eating birds.

If you want to enjoy close-up views of a meadow or prairie garden, it is a good idea to maintain some mown pathways among the flowers. Parts of the meadow may be left uncut occasionally into September so that late-flowering species can seed. Leave some patches or edges uncut through winter to provide winter refuge for insects. Meadow gardens are often devoted to growing native species, but you can extend the season and create a longer span of interest by naturalizing early- and late-flowering bulbs such as spring and fall crocuses, snake's-head fritillaries, and colchicums.

In contrast to habitat plantings that used primarily or only native plants, "naturalistic gardens" may include many non-natives. The intent is to reproduce the extraordinarily colorful displays of wild plants in places such as parts of South Africa, California, and Australia, and countries bordering the Mediterranean. Here, predominantly sandy areas are ablaze in spring with a kaleidoscope of annuals, perennials, and bulbs that repeat their displays every year.

Relaxed meadow style
Drifts of annuals and perennials—including purple loosestrife, fennel, campanulas, and ox-eye daisies—appear to roam through grassland to create a flowering meadow. The result looks entirely natural, but in fact is carefully designed to achieve a pleasing mix of color, and ensure that no one species dominates. Later in the year, dramatic seed heads add a beauty of their own.

Reproducing the conditions in which these species grow is not always easy, and it is important to research all the candidates for a naturalistic garden to avoid plants that may escape cultivation and spread into neighboring natural areas, where they may out-compete native vegetation.

Sustainable gardening

As the effects of climate change become more apparent it is important that as gardeners we seriously consider the sustainability of the way in which we use natural resources, and the effects that fertilizers and other chemicals have on the environment as a whole. The use of peat in horticultural products is a well-publicized example. Peat is used as a base for potting mixes, as a soil improver, and for mulching, and there are large areas of natural peat beds in North America that are being harvested in an ecological way. Only a comparatively small area is used for production at a given time, the peat is removed to a pre-determined depth, then the area is replanted with the native species. Even so, gardeners who wish to avoid peat-based products can now try alternatives such as leaf mold, composted bark, or coir (coconut fiber).

Ways with water

As climate change results in seasonal temperatures and rainfall patterns becoming more variable, it is probable that hotter summers, less rain in the fall, and more frequent periods of drought will lead to serious water shortages. It is essential that we counter the adverse impact this will have by introducing water-saving techniques as standard gardening practice.

Ensure a good supply of water for the garden during periods of drought by collecting and storing rainwater running off the house and other building roofs in rain barrels. Gray water siphoned from washing machines or baths may be another source on a small scale, provided it does not contain high levels of cleaning products; however, gray water use is regulated in some communities.

Try simple cultivation techniques to reduce the evaporation of water from the soil surface—for example, by preparing beds during fall and winter, rather than in spring or summer when warm temperatures increase evaporation, or by spreading mulches after rain to retain moisture. Prioritize the garden's needs—it is not necessary to water the lawn in a drought—and water thoroughly but less often because this is more beneficial to plants.

The ethical approach

Reusing and recycling materials can play an important role in conserving resources as part of a sustainable gardening regime. Where possible vegetative material—prunings, lawn mowings, leaves, and vegetable waste—should be composted and used to improve soil structure, feed plants, and as a mulch. Burning garden wastes is usually prohibited, and is inadvisable in any case because it releases greenhouse gases into the environment. You can also develop an ethical approach to gardening by ensuring that wood used for structures or furniture comes from a sustainable source: look for forest certification labeling. Alternatively consider using reclaimed or recycled lumber.

The practice of "greening" the exterior surfaces of both domestic and commercial buildings is a relatively recent innovation that provides a number of environmental benefits. The most popular example is installing a green roof, but the concept may be applied equally successfully to other structures such as walls and fences (see LIVING ROOFS AND WALLS, pp.50–51). Consider using climbing plants to clothe structures and surfaces that are not robust enough to support the weight of plants in a growing medium: the overall effect is similar, and by selecting appropriate plants you can encourage birds and other wildlife to come to the garden.

Endangered species
It may seem astonishing that plants at risk of extinction in the wild include popular garden favorites such as *Cyclamen repandum* (top) as well as orchids like *Lycaste deppei* (above). You can help discourage the practice of over-collection from the wild by ensuring that your plants come from cultivated sources.

Avoiding chemicals and working with nature

By taking a few simple steps to create a more wildlife-friendly environment you can acquire a biological "police force" that limits the damage to plants by encouraging pest predators to remain in your garden all year. Choose food plants for birds and insects, and wait until spring to clear leaf litter and decaying vegetation that may house overwintering aphid predators like ladybugs and lacewings. Ground beetles and toads will thank you for shelter and winter hibernation sites, such as log piles or permanently mulched areas, such as at the base of a hedge, by feasting on slugs and snails.

Many pests and diseases can be kept in check by encouraging their natural predators, by introducing parasites, or by applying products based on bacterial or fungal diseases of the pests. Although they sound drastic, these biological weapons are highly selective, targeting specific pests without harming other species—unlike chemical controls, which often need to be applied several times in a season. Some "natural" biological controls are available commercially, including the

Water, water everywhere
Covered rain barrels and storage tanks help keep the garden watered in time of drought, but we also need strategies to cope with downpours that drop so much water that it causes flooding and waterlogging. Constructing a permeable driveway, using gravel or porous block paving, will absorb as much as 90 percent of the water that falls on its surface, easing the strain on drainage systems and providing all the benefits associated with plant growth.

Increasing diversity

A range of plants including achilleas, campanulas, veronicas, and *Thalictrum* may be used to create planting designs that are not only pleasing to the human eye but also attract insects (right). Colorful pollinators like bees (above) enliven your garden, and the larvae of some, such as hoverflies (top) feed on aphids, thrips, and other plant-sucking pests.

bacterium *Bacillus thuringiensis,* which is sprayed on plants subject to damage by chewing caterpillars, nematodes to control beetle grubs, and a range of others for use in the greenhouse (see also p.643).

Conserving our plant heritage

Many ornamental plants are now endangered in the wild—partly due to over-collection—so gardeners are advised to check the source of plants they acquire. It is important to purchase seeds and plants that are of known cultivated origin to help stop any illegal trade in plants listed under the Convention on International Trade in Endangered Species of Wild Fauna and Flora (CITES) regulations—including popular groups of plants like cacti, orchids, snowdrops (*Galanthus*), cyclamen, and cycads.

It is also vital that we conserve older plants raised in gardens in the past, many of which have been replaced by newer cultivars. Old garden varieties are valuable for breeding new flowers, fruits, and vegetable crops; they can also pass on resistance to pests and diseases. Consider joining one of the many plant conservation organizations that are working to maintain the great diversity of our garden plants for future generations, such as the Seeds of Diversity, Seed Savers Exchange, and the New England Wildflower Society.

PART ONE

CREATING THE GARDEN

HOW TO APPLY THE PRINCIPLES OF DESIGN, CHOOSE AND CULTIVATE
EVERY TYPE OF PLANT, AND CREATE AND PLANT GARDEN FEATURES

GARDEN PLANNING AND DESIGN

TO NURTURE A GARDEN OVER A PERIOD OF TIME—SEEING IT DEVELOP AND MATURE THROUGH THE SEASONS—IS A REWARDING EXPERIENCE FOR ITS CREATOR.

For a garden to be successful, however, it needs careful and considered thought from the very beginning. A garden with simple lines and a natural flow, effortlessly summoning up a relaxed charm, may appear to have received little design input, yet it is almost certainly underpinned by intelligent planning. The design process is conspicuous in a garden of geometric formality, but the same input is required for seemingly artless informal plantings if they are to combine the necessary qualities of unity, balance, and proportion, and be in harmony with their surroundings.

Why do we garden?

Where does the motivation come from to cultivate a piece of ground, altering its appearance for our own benefit? Perhaps we still have an instinctive need to grow food to survive, or to make a mark on a territory that defines a specific area as our own, or to raise a defensive boundary around it. Once within the garden gate, we can leave behind our demanding and often stressful working lives, and retreat to the safety of our private space. Whatever the underlying motivation, that first small spark of interest can easily grow into a lifelong passion and a source of real enjoyment.

Hard and soft A pleasing blend of hard edges and soft planting.

Climate and surroundings

In the majority of cases a yard will surround a house, creating fundamental practical reasons to tame the environment. The need for entry by foot and by vehicle necessitates making clear paths and drives that allow easy access to the house in all weather throughout the year. Similarly basic is the need for light: plant growth near windows and doors must be controlled.

At a greater distance, planting a windbreak of trees and shrubs can provide invaluable protection against damaging winds, sheltering both buildings and less robust plantings. Such windbreaks of trees will also prevent snow from drifting into the yard. Conversely, in hot climates, trees and shrubs bring shade and coolness to the house and its immediate surroundings. Strategic plantings of shrubs and trees can also help preserve soil, by preventing erosion by wind and water.

Creating the right setting

The yard should never be viewed in isolation, removed from its context and setting. Property boundaries define and protect our private space, limiting the influence of the outside world on the place we call home. They make it possible to screen, and thus ignore nearby unsightly features, as well as increasing privacy. Conversely, if your yard backs onto fields, boundaries can be designed to open up the view and bring the countryside into the back yard, while still keeping grazing animals away. Garden hedges and trees can also baffle intrusive noise from a neighboring property or busy road.

A garden retreat can be used as an extension of the living areas within the home, making an imperceptible transition from house to garden. Paved terraces, plant-covered structures, and open-fronted verandas all blur the hard interface between indoors and outdoors. They create safe outdoor play areas for children—especially welcome in a modestly sized house—as well as providing space for enjoying meals *al fresco*.

Enhancing our environment

Beyond the fulfillment of our basic living requirements, there is of course one obvious role that a home landscape performs, and that is to improve the appearance of the house, whether for our own private enjoyment or to enhance the street or neighborhood we live in. Community spirit is not, however, incompatible with a competitive tendency between neighbors, often generating passions and levels of gardening expertise rarely seen in professional horticulture.

To create a beautiful landscape around the confines of a house and use the spaces to maximum advantage is a challenge that many gardeners relish. Draw inspiration from the style of your house and its construction materials, and let your planting complement the look. The ultimate goal is to achieve a harmonious whole. This may look effortless, but those directly involved can appreciate the hard work, vision, and imagination required.

Planning and designing a garden is a real opportunity to express your individual tastes and creativity, and to allow your personality to come through in the finished concept, design, color, and plant combinations. Unlike interior design or painting a picture, a garden is a living thing that constantly changes, and

Defining boundaries Land adjoining the garden may not need to be screened for protection or privacy. Make the most of an attractive backdrop and incorporate it visually to blend with and extend your garden, leaving gaps in your planting and boundaries to provide vantage points to nearby features.

Harmonious setting This beautifully designed English-cottage garden is perfectly in keeping with the style of house. The planting softens the lines between the house and garden.

each passing season will present new rewards and challenges. Although often hard work, the practical nature of the majority of the tasks involved and the visual reward so readily offered, make gardening a great tonic, as well as providing beneficial exercise for those who spend the majority of their time working indoors or in an office.

Homegrown produce

A yard does not have to be large to be productive; even a modest area can provide a variety of vegetables, fruit, and herbs for the kitchen as well as an abundance of flowers for the home. Traditionally, the garden always incorporated a good-sized vegetable plot for reasons of economy and to guarantee a steady supply of fresh food. Today, despite year-round availability of fruit and vegetables, many people are concerned about the overuse of pesticides and fertilizers and prefer to grow their own produce using organic methods. Although the yield from an organically grown crop may be slightly lower, many consider the taste and quality to be superior, and there is frequently less waste.

Security and access

The safety and security of your home can be improved significantly by the way the landscape is designed and laid out. Open spaces around a house prevent unseen access, and are particularly important if you have security cameras, which require a clear field of vision around all sides of a building. Footsteps are readily heard on gravel surfaces—a great deterrent to burglars, especially when a dog is alerted by the noise. Impenetrable hedges of prickly and thorny material, such as hawthorn

(*Crataegus monogyna*), holly (*Ilex aquifolium*), and firethorn (*Pyracantha*), are also very effective. Climbing plants and wall shrubs that potentially offer easy access to second-floor windows should be avoided.

For visitors and deliveries, the everyday accessibility of a house can be greatly improved by the careful planning of the landscape, the avoidance of too many level changes, a comfortable width of paths, and the provision of vehicular access to at least one external door of the house.

ENVIRONMENTAL CONCERNS

Gardening according to environmentally sound principles is a goal that many gardeners today are contemplating. To exclude all harmful chemicals, including synthetic insecticides, herbicides, and fungicides, as well as artificial fertilizers, from the yard is a valiant and practical first step toward creating a home landscape that is synchronized with the wider natural habitat.

There are also many other gardening practices that enhance and protect the environment rather than depleting and destroying it. Water conservation, recycling organic matter to produce garden compost, collecting fall leaves to make leaf mold, using peat-free potting mixtures, and

buying nursery stock (particularly bulbs) that have been raised in cultivation rather than collected from the wild are all relatively easy measures to adopt.

If you would like to develop your yard further along environmentally sound lines, consider creating a wildlife-friendly landscape that includes plants that are food sources for birds and insects, shrubs and trees for nesting, and water for aquatic creatures. By avoiding the use of chemicals, you will also encourage more pollinating insects to visit your yard, generally improve plant performance and productivity, and thus considerably enrich the whole environment.

Multidimensional planting This delightful planting design provides a subtle combination of colors and more strongly contrasting textures, shapes, and forms.

The importance of landscape design

The term "landscape design" has connotations of formality and, for many, implies the rigid application of strict rules and complicated formulas. Fortunately, this is not the case. But there is, however, one overriding principle that should always be observed—that adequate thought and consideration of all the alternatives are needed well in advance of any intended work. Making changes to the design once work has started can be costly and may compromise the success of the plan. Many beautiful landscapes have been and are created without the implementation of grand planting plans. They have developed organically from a starting point: a favorite tree planted in an open place; a natural path between road and house; or a previous owner's layout. Evolving year after year, possibly in a rather haphazard way with much left to chance, a garden of great charm can indeed come about, but opportunities may have been missed and a lack of cohesion is all too often apparent.

Design awareness

We live in a designed society. There is a great awareness and appreciation today of well-designed products, and yards have not escaped the attentions of designers or the media. Beautifully illustrated books and magazines, as well as informative television programs, have created a growing interest in styles, products, and plants, reaching a wider audience than ever before. For the first time, designers have been able to demonstrate the advantages of planning a landscape and then to communicate clearly, using photographs of each stage, the development of a design.

A designer's fresh and experienced eye can realize the potential of a plot, drawing out its strengths while respecting and taking inspiration from the site. Most importantly, a good designer will not impose his or her own ideas on the site without first considering the owner's wishes, needs, and lifestyle.

A professional designer can, of course, be employed to execute the entire project but at a considerable cost. However, a single visit, early in the planning process, to offer advice, guidance, and an unbiased opinion can be invaluable and is certainly less expensive, with the option of consultations at a later stage as the project progresses.

Skilled design An experienced designer will be able to make best use of the space and can incorporate many different features, such as habitat for wildlife, within the same area.

Garden types and styles

Categorizing gardens into particular types or styles is very difficult because every garden is different. Many yards are comprised of a series of disparate themes loosely linked together, while others do not fit readily into any single category because they incorporate several styles. All divisions, therefore, are somewhat arbitrary and should be regarded only as very general guidelines.

Developing a style

When starting to develop a new look or reshaping an old one, a common theme, even if adapted and personalized, is generally adopted. Plucked from a magazine article or a book, or inspired by a visit to a garden, a particular look can reflect a house interior or evolve from the style of house and its surroundings. A building and its locality have a great deal to communicate to any receptive landscape designer, contributing many simple common-sense details to the plan.

All yards should exude a sense of place and of belonging. A yard designed and built in a style that is very alien to the house or landscape may not sit well there, however much it is desired and however great the resources spent on its creation. Developing and refining a design that reflects the sense of place almost invariably gives more harmonious results, especially where relaxation and calm are desired.

Design variations

Within any broad landscape style, you can incorporate variations that reflect a personal interest, a lifestyle, or even the age group using the area. A desire to attract wildlife into the yard or to grow large quantities of herbs will add another dimension to the design. Or you might want to achieve a purely visual effect by introducing a particular flower color or luxuriant foliage that blends with the house colors or nearby vegetation.

Personal preferences and the way in which you use your yard at various times of the year all have a bearing on what is required. A yard that looks particularly striking in midsummer, for example, may be wanted if the space is used mainly for outdoor entertaining. A yard for relaxation that requires minimal upkeep but has appeal throughout the year may be an attractive idea, or you may wish to shut out the world and create a secluded haven where you can cultivate specialty plants in peace.

Planting considerations

The choice of plants growing within the framework of the landscape will significantly influence its style. Large-leaved, rich-textured foliage gives depth and luxuriance, while a predominance of fine, silver- and gray-leaved plants will provide a lighter feel. Of equal influence is the degree of maintenance required in the yard. An efficiently

Low maintenance In this design, stepped rectangular gravel- and slate-filled containers house small bubble fountains, while a mix of granite setts, gravel, and slabs provide a foil for minimalist planting.

maintained landscape with a well-defined layout will look surprisingly different from a yard of similar design that has been poorly or erratically maintained.

High and low maintenance

Generally speaking, it is possible to make a distinction between two different styles of landscape in terms of their function. A yard may have been designed for visual impact, or the creation of a restful ambience may be a priority. A yard for relaxation should be low maintenance, leaving as much time as possible to enjoy it. In contrast, the pleasure for the plant enthusiast with a specialty collection of plants comes from the hours spent nurturing and maintaining them. In a prized collection, plants are not purely decorative; they have an integrity, a personality, and a history, particularly where a botanical collection has been established.

Interestingly, both approaches to gardening can lead to an extended social life. The low-maintenance garden is ideal for outdoor entertaining, while for the plant enthusiast there are opportunities to contact and compare notes with like-minded collectors.

Enhancing buildings

The yard presents a wonderful opportunity to change the appearance of a house without expensive or major alterations. Plants can be used to soften an unsympathetic roof line or to disguise the inappropriate use of ugly and incompatible building materials. An unremarkable structure, too, can be greatly improved by the addition of striking, climbing or architectural plants, which will strengthen the appearance of the building and add character. In both cases, the built structure and planted landscape can come together and complement each other. With the exception of very few architecturally significant buildings whose façades are better left unadorned, the majority of houses are greatly improved by allowing plants to stand close by or to clamber partway across the front—by appearing to bring the garden to the house.

Formal garden styles

Formal gardens are characteristically well proportioned, usually symmetrical and geometrically balanced in layout, and impart a tangible sense of restraint. They usually derive an inherent strength of line from an underlying backbone in the form of walls, paths, or terracing, around which planting is firmly controlled. Formal planting traditionally contains very few different plants, but these are used in quantity to lend a uniformity of texture and color. The whole emphasis is one of an overriding sense of control.

Ordered layouts

The underlying philosophy of the formal garden is to present a strong, simple statement of a very obvious control of nature. Intricately clipped parterres that form a filigree of crisply shaped evergreens when set against fine gravel, or a flat, closely mown lawn that is framed by neatly trimmed hedges, are good examples of this philosophy in practice.

Historically, the formal style was chosen to convey a sense of power over the wider landscape and, on a large scale, this achieved an intimidating effect that was an intentional expression of wealth and status. A similar impression was conveyed even on a more modest scale, since such layouts required regular, labor-intensive, and costly maintenance.

Ancient inspiration

The grand formal gardens of 17th- and 18th-century Italy and France, which influenced garden styles throughout Europe, were themselves inspired by the gardens of ancient Greece and Rome. In these, the sharply defined proportions and scale of the buildings were mirrored by the strong architectural and symmetrical design of the gardens that surrounded them.

These sumptuous but controlled landscapes were frequently laid out as a series of terraces connected by grand flights of steps, and featured water cascades, canals, and fountains amid hedged and tree-lined walkways, ornamented with classical statuary and potted plants.

Classical gardens

Greek and Roman features that still inspire modern formal gardens include neatly mown and edged lawns, tightly clipped hedges and topiary, and planted borders framed by low, trimmed hedges. Straight paths and a network of vistas that terminate in a view or focal point may be lined by *allées* and avenues of identical, regularly spaced specimen plants. Ornamentation is added with restraint and, where several decorative items are used, either they are designed to form a matching set or a single design is replicated to form a sequence of repeated features.

Plants for formal gardens

Whether clipped and trained as hedging or topiary, shaped plants are an important element in the formal garden. The striking profiles of evergreen topiary lend height, form, and dramatic sculptural interest to an otherwise two-dimensional layout. Slow-growing evergreens, such as boxwood (*Buxus sempervirens*), yew (*Taxus baccata*), and English holly all withstand the necessary regular trimming over many years. See also TOPIARY, p.108, and HEDGES AND SCREENS, p.82.

Pleached trees and stilt hedges make attractive internal divisions within a formal garden. Their regimented forms and colonnaded trunks provide a sense of rhythm and order when used to flank walkways and *allées*. Lindens (*Tilia*) and hornbeam (*Carpinus betulus*) are the most frequently used species for this type of feature. Such plantings can also be introduced in a highly functional way. Trained and pleached lindens, for example, can be used as a garden boundary to create a living wall that gives privacy and an intimate sense of enclosure. See also "Pleached trees," p.75.

Knots and parterres

Knot gardens and parterres are a highly developed type of formal gardening in which control of the planting is absolute. In knot gardens, intricate planting patterns are confined by an edging of dwarf, clipped evergreen shrubs such as boxwood (*Buxus sempervirens*). Traditional knots were inspired by 16th-century needlework and decorative plaster ceilings. In parterres, colored gravel or low plantings fill compartments created by low, trimmed hedging. Both knots and parterres offer year-round structure that is of particular value in winter, especially when located near the house.

Unity and contrast

Elements of naturalistic plantings among otherwise formal layouts create an element of contrast that can sharpen the underlying formality. The lax and free growth of herbs, for example, planted among clipped lavender (*Lavandula*), rosemary (*Rosmarinus*), bay laurel (*Laurus nobilis*), or boxwood (*Buxus sempervirens*) can be used to create such contrasts. Similarly, containers on a deck planted with a set of trimmed Portugal laurel (*Prunus lusitanica*) can bring an element of order and uniformity close to the house that could contrast with less structured planting elsewhere in the landscape.

Eastern formality

The gardens of China, which can be traced back more than 3,000 years, were created as sublimely peaceful places for contemplation and meditation. They drew inspiration from their dramatic surrounding landscapes, which were replicated in miniature within walled enclosures. Plantings were formal and restrained, often clipped or trained, and usually highly stylized. Each tree or shrub had a symbolic meaning that was intended to stimulate contemplation.

Traditional Japanese gardens borrowed Chinese design ideas more than 1,200 years ago. With a similarly naturalistic inspiration, they used richer, more diverse plantings, symbolically shaped and sited rocks, and raked gravel or sand. Such a garden was based on formal principles of balance, simplicity, and symbolism.

Structured layout
The partitioned squares of this boxwood-edged parterre bring order and year-round structure to an otherwise informal medley of plantings. Its strong lines lead the eye to a series of focal points beyond the low wall.

Simple shapes
Weight and substance are conferred on a design by the imposing forms of mature topiary sculptures, however simple or elaborate the clipped shapes are. Here several boxwoods (*Buxus sempervirens*), trimmed into differently sized globes, temper the robust horizontal lines of the adjacent wall and paving. Their trimmed formality is also brought into relief by the informally planted borders around them.

Statuary
Pleasingly proportioned, carefully sited and framed ornaments, used with discretion, can often be a great asset to the general garden scene.

Pleached lindens
High-level screening by a stilt hedge of linden (*Tilia*) encloses yet does not oppress this small knot garden. In winter when the linden leaves fall, the skillful training of the branch framework offers yet more to be admired.

Formal still water
Mirrored reflections double the impact of a symmetrical design. The random drifting of floating plants on the surface of the dark water adds interest and movement to the serenity of this formal garden.

Informal garden styles

Informal gardens, at their best, often look as though nature has played a part in their design. There is an irregularity and a softness in their lines that, although manufactured, could conceivably have occurred naturally. Even though informal gardens may appear slightly out of control, their success depends on strong design and on the firm hand of the gardener to retain a degree of order among what might otherwise become chaos.

Elements of informality

A garden with an air of informality offers a relaxed ambience that can provide a sanctuary from the pressures of modern life. In contrast to the hard-edged geometry of the formal style, an informal garden is created with flowing curves and gentle contours. Hard surfaces are softened by plants that spread over their margins, and borders are stocked with billowing mounds of plants that mingle together, apparently at random. Climbing plants scramble freely over walls or through trees and shrubs. While shrubs may be pruned to ensure good health and productivity, they are allowed to assume natural shapes and are rarely clipped in a restrictive way, as they are in strictly formal situations.

Informal elements within a garden can produce a sense of maturity in a relatively short time—for example, when plantings are used to disguise unsightly features with a mantle of growth.

Great charm can be given to the most unpromising site if softening growth disguises the hard angles or harsh colors of a building. Even the most uniform, rectangular garden acquires an element of mystery when its stark outlines are masked by layer upon layer of informal planting.

Informal styles

The style and degree of informality of a garden is influenced partly by the nature of the site and partly by individual preference. At one end of the spectrum, it may be possible to augment an existing woodland or prairie area simply by planting more of the natural flora that already grows there. Alternatively, the creation of an informal garden may entail the remodeling of border edges to form curving, sinuous lines, perhaps with a relaxation of the mowing regimen and a reduction in border maintenance to permit self-sown plants to thrive. At the other end of the spectrum is a totally new garden, for which there is a range of informal styles to choose from.

Cottage gardens

The traditional cottage garden was essentially a working garden in which to grow ornamental and edible crops. Fruits, vegetables, herbs, and flowers, such as peonies, larkspurs, and columbines, were all combined. The flowers ensured a thriving population of beneficial insects to aid pollination of crop flowers, control harmful insects, and encourage a bird population, all of which helped produce vigorous and healthy crops.

The quaint, homespun appearance of a cottage garden can be created using rustic items such as tree-branch arches or woven willow supports for climbers. Brick-patterned or cobbled paths edged with found or reclaimed materials, such as pebbles or tiles, also help define the style.

Wild and woodland gardens

Informal gardens in a more naturalistic style not only provide a beautiful and relaxed type of garden but also offer a lifeline to flora and fauna whose habitats may have become threatened elsewhere.

Areas of grass, for example, where bulbs are naturalized for an early display, can be left uncut so that grasses and meadow flowers can bloom (see MEADOW GARDENING, p.401). An area of water, however small, attracts a range of wildlife into the garden, particularly if edged with waterside plantings to provide safe shelter for birds and amphibians alike. See also "Wildlife ponds," p.284.

Small trees or an area of woodland, especially if underplanted with shrubs and festooned with climbers, provide nesting places for birds and hibernating sites for insects and small mammals. Even in more controlled areas of the garden, seed heads of herbaceous plants, if retained through winter, will provide excellent food for birds when other sources are low.

Controlled chaos

Plants can be ruthlessly competitive and the strongest may smother and eventually kill the weakest. They must be controlled to prevent this. It may be necessary, for example, to divide vigorous herbaceous plants regularly to keep them in check, to thin or reduce oversized shrubs, or to remove colonies of self-sown seedlings. These tasks help to maintain a balance in wild and informal gardens, and will prevent their natural style from degenerating into a wild and unkempt state.

Woodland
In the shade of trees, woodland plants must be selected to tolerate low light levels and the extremes of dry and excessively wet soil conditions.

Grass border
An airy and elegant selection of grasses catches the fall sunlight and makes a dramatic statement in the garden. This inspirational planting relies on a variety of heights, colors, and shapes to avoid the monotonous appearance sometimes found in all-grass planting schemes.

Cultivated and self-sown mixture (left)
A shimmering profusion of nectar-rich flowers, in billowing swaths of color, creates a feature of great beauty and provides an immensely valuable food source in summer for bees, butterflies, and other beneficial insects. Careful management is essential for year-to-year success.

Self-sown (below)
Melianthus major and Jacob's rod (*Asphodeline lutea*), planted here at the foot of a wall, simulate a self-sown planting. In a mature garden, such combinations may occur naturally—and to great effect.

Potager (above)
California poppies (*Eschscholzia californica*) jostle with herbs, Brussels sprouts, and zucchini in cottage-garden tradition, where not even the smallest space is wasted.

Marginal planting (above, center)
Even the smallest pond offers the opportunity to blur the distinction between land and water with a range of garden plants. Native wildlife will benefit greatly from the cool, sheltered conditions.

Cottage garden style (right)
Roses, delphiniums, and climbers are skillfully planted to mingle in the border and spill from supports in a generous, relaxed style.

Mixed maintenance (far right)
While fruit trees must be well kept for good yields, the relaxation of the mowing regimen here gives this small orchard a charming air of informality.

People-oriented gardens

A yard to be enjoyed by a family almost certainly needs to be a multipurpose space. To ensure that the design serves the needs of all its potential users, spend some time identifying what these might be. They may include a deck for dining and entertaining, or areas for children to play safely and experiment with growing their own plants. The yard may have to accommodate herb and vegetable gardens to provide kitchen produce, or borders for cut flowers to decorate the home.

As well as fulfilling its functional requirements, a yard such as this can also be highly decorative. An arbor clothed with scented climbers, for example, is not only ornamental but could also provide shade for a favorite place for midsummer dining. By installing outdoor lighting, its usefulness can be extended to include evening entertaining, perhaps with a barbecue. It may also display ornaments that are highly individual, such as presents from friends or souvenirs from memorable vacations. The style of planting is very much a matter of personal choice, whether highly traditional or more experimental. Sources of design inspiration have never been more plentiful, from online videos and television shows to the variety of gardens, both private and public, that are open to visitors.

Gardens for living
Just as the interior of a home is designed to meet the requirements of those living there, so can yards and gardens be tailored to suit the needs of the household. This often means extending indoor living to outdoors, using the yard as an extra room. If, for example, entertaining is high on the list of priorities, there should be a flat, clean, all-weather surface close enough to the kitchen to make outdoor dining convenient. To make access safe and easy, avoid steps, slopes, or changes of level between the house and eating area. On a very sunny deck, deciduous (rather than evergreen) climbers trained above head height will provide comfortable shade in midsummer, but little or none in spring and fall, when warmth and light levels are lower.

Where a suitable sheltered, warm site for an outdoor room does not exist, consider creating one by enclosing an area with hedges or scented-leaved shrubs. They will help trap warm air and provide shelter from cool evening breezes.

To maximize use of the space and to create a pleasant ambience, install subtle lighting for the evenings. Bear in mind that the route to and from the dining area should also be well lit.

Special interests
If the yard as a whole is planned with minimal maintenance in mind, this will allow the development of areas for specific activities. A simple grass lawn, for example, surrounded by robust, low-maintenance plantings, can offer a child-friendly play area for younger family members, or an oasis of calm for the adults. Around this, areas of more focused activity can evolve. These might include a small kitchen garden to produce unusual fruits, vegetables, and herbs that are hard to find in stores. If a kitchen garden is small, tending it will not be a chore; it will give satisfaction to the gardener, and it can even be a learning experience if children are encouraged to participate.

Another special-interest area might be a border for cut flowers, to provide material for floral arrangements throughout the year. It might include shrubs such as forsythias and Oregon grape for early spring and the bright stems of Tatarian dogwood (*Cornus alba*) for winter decoration. To allow uninhibited cutting during summer and fall, set aside a patch for perennials, supplementing them with annuals and biennials to supply flowers for many months.

Special needs
For those in the family who are less mobile or who have limited strength, a garden of raised containers or an entire raised bed removes the strain of bending while still satisfying the desire to garden. Permanently sited containers can be set at a suitable height and regularly reinvigorated with colorful annuals. A row of outdoor tomatoes planted in pots on top of a sunny wall, or a raised herb garden enjoying a sunny exposure and well-drained soil, will give endless pleasure and produce worthwhile quantities of useful crops.

Looking to the future
With a little foresight, some areas of the yard can be designed to evolve with a family's changing needs. A wooden playhouse, for example, could in later years become a tool shed or chicken coop. An irregularly shaped or formal rectangular sandbox, if positioned carefully when the yard is laid out, may be transformed into a small pond once the children are old enough to understand the dangers of water. A playset of smooth lumber could, later on, become an interesting support over which climbing plants scramble to create a dramatic effect.

MAKING ROOM FOR WILDLIFE

One of the delights of developing a garden is finding that the local wildlife is also happy to visit. Food and shelter are all that is needed to attract birds and insects, and it is easy to include suitable habitats and wildlife-friendly features.

Position bird feeders so that activity may be observed from the house, especially during winter. Birdhouses may need to be placed on posts, walls, or fences with different exposures, according to the preferences of the species you want to attract. A shallow bowl of water provides small mammals and birds with a drink, while a pond will attract a great diversity of wildlife, particularly amphibians and insects such as dragonflies.

Mulches, wood piles, and even your compost pile are also great resources for wildlife, providing nooks and crannies in which to forage, nest, and hibernate. Hedges offer shelter and nesting sites, and fruits and seeds from informal mixtures of dense shrubs and climbers like highbush cranberry, bayberry, wild roses, and Virginia creeper help keep the natural pantry well stocked. Choose plants that are rich in nectar and pollen (see p.179), and your garden will soon find favor with bees, moths, and butterflies.

Well-designed terrace
This seating area with its all-weather patio floor, shelter from wind, and overhead shade provision encourages maximum use of the terrace over a long season.

Family-friendly features (right)
A yard mirrors the lifestyle of its occupants and the layout will be dictated by their interests. Here, an imaginative design, incorporating areas for planting, entertainment, relaxation, and play, maximizes the uses of this small suburban yard.

Safe water features (below)
Even the smallest and most shallow of ponds can pose a danger to young children. This small fountain, however, has a strong metal grid over its concealed reservoir.

Play area (below, center)
A lawn, surrounded by robust, thornless plantings, makes an ideal spot for children to enjoy many types of games.

Elevated gardening (above)
A raised bed makes gardening comfortable for those with limited mobility. An ideal display setting is created where plant detail can be appreciated close up. The use of containers allows those plants in need of attention (here including some developing topiary shapes) to be brought within reach, and for seasonal changes to be made.

Dual purpose (left)
Here, in late summer, flowers for indoor decoration are grown alongside plants with ripening fruits, to great ornamental effect. This cheerfully haphazard mixture has been planted solely with the needs of the house in mind, yet the result is as decorative as any other type of themed border.

Plant-oriented gardens

In a plant-oriented garden, the plants take center stage, rather than being used simply as "soft" design materials. Owners of such a garden can collect and grow a specific range of botanical or exhibition-quality plants. Some plant groups need much more maintenance than others, because they are extremely picky about their growing conditions. A garden's soil or microclimate might especially suit one specialty group of plants, but more often than not, additional work will be needed to provide the appropriate soil, light, moisture, and shelter.

Pure gardening

The garden that is inspired by plants first and foremost is perhaps the purest form of gardening. There are many and diverse avenues of interest within this type of garden, but all follow a love for plants.

It is the fascination of collecting, cultivating to perfection, pollination, and propagation that holds the attention and further develops a gardener's interest in horticulture. The search for rare or newly discovered forms can become a lifelong occupation. In such a "pure" garden, skill and expertise are obvious at every turn, and demonstrate the gardener's dedication to a wide range of tasks.

Sources for ideas

The site itself may be the inspiration for the plant-oriented garden. Perhaps a dark and damp, north-facing slope will spark an interest in an extensive collection of ferns. Alternatively, a dry, stony, south-facing bank may encourage the planting of Mediterranean natives— such as a collection of *Cistus* species.

Turning what might appear to be a disadvantage into a positive attribute, an area of overgrown woods may appear lost to cultivation, yet with careful management it can present a wealth of unusual planting possibilities. A collection of shade-loving, woodland-floor natives that is unique to such a site should thrive beneath a deciduous canopy.

Where the conditions provided are substandard, plants will grow poorly, never realizing their full potential. Such poor conditions, however, can often be rectified. Soil conditions can be modified by adding organic matter or improving drainage; shelter can be increased by the use of windbreaks and shelterbelts (see HEDGES AND SCREENS, p.82, and BAMBOOS, pp.120–121); and light levels can be increased by thinning or lifting the canopies of surrounding trees.

Themed collections

An herbaceous border in matching colors, textures, and forms is one way to display a collection that depends solely on good design skills. Many subtly or dramatically different variations are possible. A historical approach may be taken to recreate an early-20th-century border, for example. This border

Specialty plants
The display of a very specific plant collection need not be devoid of all aesthetic qualities. Here, many forms of potted auricula primroses are attractively placed on tiered stands.

would contain tall herbaceous plants that are very dependent on traditional forms of staking with willow twigs or hazel branches. Color-themed borders are another possibility for a themed collection (see "Planting for texture, structure, and color," pp.46–47).

A more modern interpretation might be a mixed border that is dominated by drifts of shrub roses and self-supporting perennials, self-sown annuals, and swaths of ornamental grasses. Alternatively, such a border, particularly in a sheltered situation, might include lush foliage plants and tender bedding perennials in vibrant colors to give a tropical flavor (see also HARDY PALMS AND THE EXOTIC LOOK, p.60).

Collections with style

The plant-oriented garden may take a very different course from the refinements of the mixed border. A hobby of growing exhibition plants may develop, where perhaps dahlias (see p.250) or roses (see p.147) are grown to perfection, to the exclusion of any aesthetic value their arrangement in the garden might offer. Alternatively, such a

well-defined collection could be arranged with every possible attention paid to aesthetics. A fruit garden, for example, with trees trained in particular forms could provide structural boundaries and internal divisions within the garden as a whole (see GROWING FRUIT, "Trained forms," p.419). Such a display would pay tribute to meticulous, long-term pruning as the trees slowly develop great character, eventually creating an almost timeless ambience.

A collector of trees may be fortunate to have sufficient space to create an arboretum, but this need not be a sterile collection of solitary trees arranged in rows. Groupings of trees in clumps and groves create a landscape style that is beautiful in its own right (see also ORNAMENTAL TREES, "Trees as design elements," p.54).

A collection of plants indigenous to a particular region may require the controlled conditions of a greenhouse or alpine house. But plants need not be set on gravel-covered, featureless beds or benches. With a little imagination, they can be arranged in a simulation of their native terrain.

Natural plant collections
A specific collection can readily be incorporated into a garden setting. Here, a cheerful group of crocuses flourish in a lawn.

Restricted color (above)
A white border, tiered in height and with every shade of green, white, and silver, is a classic, timeless design theme. The dignified purity of the scheme demands meticulous staking, deadheading, and weeding.

Single-season display (above)
Some garden designers seek to exploit every plant type, shape, form, and color so that they perform and peak at the same time— in this case, as a color-coordinated collage.

Tropical style (left)
A warm, sheltered area with fertile soil provides an opportunity to experiment with tender exotics through the summer months. Many will need careful lifting and storage over winter, but amply repay such attention.

Stylized gardens

A highly stylized garden can be seen as a refined work of art of purely aesthetic value in which plants fulfill a design function of tight and often strictly limited criteria. Such a garden might serve as a backdrop to a collection of contemporary sculpture, for example, or form a calm and unobtrusive foreground to an architecturally important house. This style of garden demands a high degree of coordination and planning to distill the essence of the style required. The colors, textures, and finishes of all the materials are of utmost importance. Here, plants are used as a furnishing—their qualities being assessed and employed for their utility rather than for their individual beauty as living plants.

Mass bedding
When plants are used as basic building elements to construct an effect, the results can be dramatic. This softly textured landscape has a sculptural quality, which transcends the form of any one individual plant.

Dominant themes

When a designer's sole aim is to create a highly stylized image, the approach is similar to that of an artist painting a picture, or a designer contriving a theatrical stage set. The result can be breathtaking, because all attention has been focused toward maximum visual impact, undiluted by sentiment or an interest in individual plants. Selecting plants only for their color, form, and texture, and arranging them in an almost abstract, pictorial composition, ensures that the finished arrangement forms a cohesive whole of complementary materials.

While this approach is commonly used by landscape architects in large-scale projects, it might equally well be adapted to smaller, more intimate situations. It avoids the problem of using too many different materials in a confined site, which can look busy and distracting. In contrast, minimal materials give an impression of strength and unity.

Such essentially sophisticated designs all have an innate simplicity that is their most telling factor.

Even in gardens of traditional layout, this straightforwardness can underlie the development of an overall concept or theme: for example, a garden based on a restricted color range, comprising plants only in shades of green, with red or white flowers. A more radical alternative is a garden that is almost free of plants, consisting only of sweeping grass mounds to be mown in different directions and at varying lengths according to the texture required.

Another alternative that lends style and drama is when a single plant is introduced in great quantity, especially if the plant in question is unusual. Blocks of a hundred or more can be a revelation. A mass planting of peonies, tree poppies (*Romneya coulteri*), or many of the euphorbias can provide a spectacular sight. Less radically, gardens of a practical nature can

be given stylistic treatment. A working kitchen garden can be designed as a decorative potager. While still providing edible crops, there is greater emphasis on an attractive display of color and texture within the strict confines of its highly structured layout.

Coordinated designs

In domestic situations, one of the greatest challenges is to match a highly stylized garden with the house or region. One way of doing this is to use plants and materials from the area, but in a very different form. For example, locally abundant trees and shrubs (if they withstand clipping) can be used to create trimmed hedges and feature trees that are then arranged in a

tightly regimented design within the garden (see ORNAMENTAL TREES, "Pleached trees", p.75, and HEDGES AND SCREENS, p.82). Local stone and gravel could form paving and mulches beneath plantings to create a thoroughly modern reinterpretation of the formal garden.

Small city gardens, especially if framed by boundary walls, are ideal for stylized gardens. Since they are usually seen from only one viewpoint—the house windows—they present unusual possibilities. A truly theatrical, almost two-dimensional garden can be created, with an odd or false sense of perspective achieved by the angles of hard surfaces and by the choice of their colors, shapes, and placement.

Planting arrangements
With skill, knowledge, and care, a series of well-planned "vignettes" may be constructed. Harmonious colors and contrasting leaf forms and shapes can be positioned with all the accuracy and poise of a staged floral design.

Modern style
Even the most familiar garden plants can be used in a stylized way. Here, the effect of trailing plants is transformed by planting them in custom-built containers arranged on different levels.

Modern design
Squares of baby's tears (*Soleirolia soleirolii*), forming tight, ground-hugging cushions of growth, alternate with blue glass chips in a contemporary scheme that plays upon geometry and color blocks.

Japanese raked garden
In this uncompromisingly simple abstract arrangement of rocks and raked gravel, the eye is drawn only to pure line and the effortless balance of mass and space.

Modern sculpture
A "habitat" created as a setting for a piece of modern water sculpture enables an otherwise alien artifact to become a believable part of the general garden scene.

Succulents
Strongly architectural plants, such as *Agave americana* 'Mediopicta' and *A. attenuata*, create a dramatic impression in this warm and sunny, well-drained bed, alongside summer-flowering perennials.

Assessing an existing landscape

Whether you are remodeling your own landscape or tackling one inherited from a previous owner, one of the most difficult tasks is to visualize how to transfer your ideas and aspirations onto what is there. Everything that makes up an existing garden must be scrutinized and assessed in order to determine the components that make a positive contribution to the overall effect, and those that offer least or are farthest removed from your preferred style and taste. No aspect of a landscape should escape this scrutiny, for even those factors that might be considered impossible to change can be influenced and modified by skillful design and planting. Nothing can alter the shape and size of a backyard, for example, yet there are any number of design solutions that can make narrow areas appear wider, open sites become more sheltered, and awkward shapes flow more freely.

Separating materials from their context
Even if you do not like a feature, or its design makes it awkward to garden around, consider whether its materials might be used elsewhere.

A time for reflection

The inspiration for your new design may be held entirely in your imagination—or be the result of visiting other gardens or poring over books and magazines. Before beginning to make even the roughest preliminary sketch, however, a period of time spent in the yard doing nothing more than simply mulling over possibilities will be well repaid. The earliest planning stage of a garden should be a period of calm, cool observation; a critical scrutiny of both what exists and what is desired. If insufficient time is given to important decisions, the result will be poor long-term planning.

The landscape's development over an extended period of time needs a vision, seeing beyond the clutter of existing features. It should also at this stage be free of the distractions of budgets, labor, time, and other practical constraints. Defining a goal, and the means to that goal, can be the realization of a dream that will bestow a style and a personality—your own personality—on the property as a whole. Even if a master plan has to be tackled piecemeal, having such a plan firmly in mind will permit a greater degree of control over the ongoing development of the garden.

Weighing the elements

As you appraise the existing landscape, you will begin to form a broad idea of the scale of remodeling that a new design will involve. It is worth considering at this stage whether you intend to implement the new design in a single operation, or spread the work and expense over several years.

Carry a notebook with you, in which to enter thoughts and ideas about all of the elements your yard contains, set against what you desire. As the wealth of possibilities is distilled into a concept that could work, many ideas will be dispensed with, refining only those that are appropriate to site and scale, style, and local conditions of soil and weather.

A methodical "audit" of structures, surfaces, features, and plantings, with a view to deciding which you will keep, which you will redesign or relocate, and which are superfluous, can be tremendously useful. Examples of the kinds of questions that should be asked and factors that should be considered are detailed in the pages that follow.

WATER-SAVING BY DESIGN

The increasing need to save water is a difficult issue for gardeners, but by building water storage and water-saving tactics into the design, you can balance the need for water conservation with your gardening interests. Ensure that your house and garage, as well as any substantial outbuildings with sloping roofs, have gutters and downspouts feeding rain barrels or covered tanks; if space allows, position them in tandem so that two (or more) can be filled during a heavy rain. In a greenhouse, covered tanks may be sunk in the ground under benches to store water from the roof. You can also consider channeling water runoff from patios and hard surfaces directly into borders (see p.585). A rain garden can soak up rainfall from a house roof and support a range of moisture-loving plants.

Deciding on priorities
An existing yard may contain many elements that meet your own requirements, such as a seating area or raised beds, even if the materials or finishes used are not exactly to your taste. Just as plants can be judiciously retained or reshaped to preserve the structure of borders, much can also be done to adapt and personalize the hardscape.

USING PHOTOGRAPHS

Difficult decisions can often be simplified and clarified by the use of photographs. A set of pictures portraying the whole yard will help to put all of its features into context, and allow carefully considered conclusions to be drawn. Curiously, a photograph has a focusing and simplifying effect, removing the distractions of a live situation , and throwing strengths and weaknesses into high relief. The frozen image is easier to analyze, and clearly reveals the underlying composition and workings of the landscape. This detachment seems to allow decisions to be made with greater freedom. The dominance of an oversized evergreen shrub, the poorly flowing line of the front of a border, or any weak, jumbled plantings are more vividly displayed in static images, and these can then be rectified in the new design.

Contemplating existing plants
If at all possible, never discard a beautiful, mature, and healthy plant just because it is in a less than perfect setting. This *Trachycarpus* is a fine specimen; it would be well worth adjusting plans to accommodate it; in fact, it could suggest the theme of a new planting scheme.

Appraising your own yard

Sentimentality can often play a significantly negative role in a backyard long established by its owners. Plants that really have no place in a well-designed and practical layout are preserved and overlooked; geriatric, diseased, or inappropriately-sized plants are retained, particularly when they commemorate an event or were a gift, a reminder of a dear friend or relative. With the passing of a property to new owners, such anomalies tend to be addressed more objectively—a silver maple planted as a seedling years ago, for example, which now completely overshadows a formerly sunny deck, may be removed without so much as a backward glance.

However, individuality—the lifeblood of interesting gardens—often stems from quirks of personal sentiment. Although unconventional, it may be these features that give the garden a unique character, so, again, deep thought before action is essential. The clean sweep or makeover approach may have unexpectedly negative consequences. The removal of a conifer simply because it is "unfashionable," for example, may also mean the loss of useful screening from neighbors, or perhaps a well-placed nesting site, visible from the house, to which birds will no longer return in spring.

Appraising a landscape new to you

A new owner will almost certainly wish to make changes to an existing landscape. An eager gardener will probably waste little time before introducing personal preferences or old friends in the form of plants or ornaments, but if the garden, or parts of it, is not fundamentally to your individual taste, then a broader perspective is required.

In many ways, the would-be designer tackling a virgin site—for example, in a new subdivision—or even a completely neglected, featureless plot has an easier task, with a blank canvas on which to project the new vision. To appreciate fully the complexities of an inherited, well-kept landscape requires time and patience. The most valuable advice is not to make any hurried changes; an old garden that has evolved over many years may contain features of great worth, which have stood the test of time. To retain and perhaps reinterpret some existing plants and structures is greatly preferable to clearing the site and beginning from a sterile piece of ground.

These existing elements in a garden, laid out by the previous owners, may summon up a certain atmosphere, which it is important to retain. The overenthusiastic tidying up of such gardens can suddenly remove any charm or mystery. Such a quality is a rare commodity to be nurtured rather than swept aside. A unique richness

Taking inspiration from shapes
This aging tree cloaked in ivy (far left) may need to be removed, but its overarching low branch creates a pleasing frame for the elements beyond, which might suggest the addition of an arch in its place.

may be found within a garden cultivated over several generations, layer upon layer of plantings creating microclimates of mutual benefit, evolving beautifully tiered structures of some complexity. With the passing of time, plants and structures can attain a character that takes them beyond mere furnishings.

Watching the landscape unfold

The landscape should be monitored during as many seasons as possible (ideally, a full year), during which time observations of factors such as shade cast, prevailing wind, areas of warmth, and seasonal value of plantings can be made. Paths and decks can be used in all seasons, the effectiveness of privacy afforded by screening shrubs can be checked—summer and winter—and the maintenance requirements of the entire yard and its plantings can be gauged.

Letting plants show their worth

Only within specific seasons may the reason for certain plantings be revealed: a cherry tree with low sweeping branches, which bursts into flower in spring in partnership with drifts of bulbs beneath it, will immediately justify its existence and unconventional stature.

All too easily, mistakes can be made: a "laurel," planted for some reason up against the south-facing wall of a house, may be hastily cut to the ground and discarded only to discover later that this was a fine *Magnolia grandiflora* of considerable age. If you find plants difficult to identify, advice may be sought from a local nursery, garden club, or botanical garden to avoid the unintentional removal of valuable plants.

Once the identities of all important plants are known, do not be hasty in removing any of them. Retaining some plants of obvious age and maturity as a permanent or temporary measure will prevent the complete loss of scale within the reworked landscape, offer shelter to young, vulnerable plants, and give privacy while other plantings are gradually establishing.

Surfaces, paths, and level changes

Lawns/grassed areas

Assess what you have

- Is the lawn level, composed of good-quality grass, and weed-free?
- Is the lawn in poor condition, shaded by the house or trees, and becoming mossy due to insufficient light or poor drainage?
- Is it large enough to accommodate a tent or to be used for games?
- Are there any trees?
- Would the area be better paved, graveled, or incorporated into a planted bed?
- Does a closely mown lawn cover an extensive area? Perhaps the far end could be mown less frequently to provide a fringe of meadow grass.
- Is your lawn too small? This is rare, but it is possible for a yard without a lawn to feel overly designed or even a little frenzied. A lawn's level green surface has a calming effect.

What to consider

Access There must be adequate access to the lawn not only for pedestrians but for a mower or wheelbarrow, too. It's best to use a mulching mower, but if not, a route will need to be kept clear for disposal of grass clippings. When a lawn is to replace a hard surface that acts as a path, it is advisable to retain a hard strip on one side for use in bad weather.

Central role Even a relatively small lawn plays a scene-setting role—it provides an open foreground across which to view a scenic background. This role may be important enough to justify the removal or reduction of existing planted borders to give an adequate area of grass.

For more information, see:
THE LAWN, pp.384–400

Patios and decks

Assess what you have

- Is the patio or deck large enough?
- Is it sunny, or cold and gloomy?
- Does it lie at a junction of paths, making it difficult to position permanent furniture?
- Is it close to the house? A patio at the far end of the yard might catch the last rays of the setting sun but may not be practical for outdoor eating and entertainment.
- Is the surface in good condition, with a slight slope away from the house to prevent standing water?
- What is the patio made of? Gravel is an uneven surface for chairs and tables. A flat paved surface is better, or poured concrete with the aggregate exposed to make it nonslip and add texture.

What to consider

Hard surface A hardscaped area in a yard is invaluable both as a working area and for entertaining outdoors.

Aspect and positioning Patios and decks need separate areas of sun and shade in which you can sit at various times of the day and during different seasons. Consider both the view and the exposure.

Surrounding materials Paving often looks best when it matches the color and texture of surrounding building materials. Decide whether you prefer a surface that is of one color and uniform texture, or highly decorative in design.

Access Provide clear access between house and patio—without steps, if possible. This minimizes accidents when carrying drinks or food.

For more information, see:
"Patios and decks," p.585

Paths

Assess what you have

- Are paths in good repair and wide enough for walking or pushing a wheelbarrow?
- Are there any broken or uneven surfaces? These can be hazardous and should be repaired or replaced.
- Do paths follow natural movement lines through the yard, free of temptations to take shortcuts?
- Do the paths add both landscape interest and structure? They should create visual links from one area to another. If any routes appear to be unnecessary, remove them.
- How often are the paths used? Grass paths are attractive but soft thoroughfares: overuse will result in damage.

What to consider

Routes Paths should follow the most logical and scenic route. Avoid the spaghetti effect of too many paths.

Covering material Gravel paths are cheaper and softer on the eye than paved ones, particularly when curves and sweeps are to be negotiated—straight-edged materials can be difficult to accommodate.

Base material A well-prepared base of compacted stone chips will ensure good drainage and an even surface; the path should retain its good line over time.

Width Paths should be broad enough for two people to walk abreast. If appropriate, the width should be sufficient to allow passage of a lawn tractor and trailer.

For more information, see:
"Paths and steps," p.593

Steps and slopes

Assess what you have

- Would any sloping sites function better if redesigned to form a series of terraces linked by steps?
- Do existing changes of level divide the yard into workable plots?
- Within the confines of a small yard, would a slight change in level either add importance to an area or provide an opportunity for a change in materials or theme?
- Could a flight of steps physically and visually draw areas together?
- Do retaining walls and planted or grass banks contribute horizontal divisions? Do they have the potential to mark a change in style or detail between levels?

What to consider

Visual impact However cleverly it is interpreted, a flat landscape will not possess the liveliness of one that exploits a hillside or the undulation of rolling terrain.

Retaining walls These can be used to exaggerate a slight variation in land heights.

Accentuating features Changes in height can be exploited to display plants and water. A series of pools on different levels, linked by waterfalls, makes a lively composition.

Users and visitors Steps might not be appropriate for the young or elderly.

Step detail Steps should be well built and even in rise and tread width. If the sides are planted, a central area of sufficient width must be left uncluttered.

For more information, see:
"Paths and steps," p.593

Boundaries and structures

Walls and fences

Assess what you have

- Are existing walls safe? If in doubt, seek expert advice. If work is needed on old garden walls, contact an experienced stonemason or builder familiar with local building techniques so repairs will be done sensitively.
- Are the fences in good condition? In particular, inspect the base of fence posts for rot and fungal growth. Individual panels and posts can often be replaced without rebuilding the entire structure.
- Are walls and fences aesthetic or merely practical? The easiest option for an ugly wall or fence is to disguise it with climbers or shrubs.
- Does the soil at the base need improvement before planting?
- Are mortars or plasters lime-based? If old walls shed detritus containing lime, soil may become inhospitable to acid-loving plants such as camellias.

What to consider

Cost Traditional brick or stone walls are challenging and expensive to build. A more cost-effective option is a block wall rendered in plaster. Do not skimp on workmanship if the wall is to be of any height.
Height Restrictions on height usually apply to walls or fences forming the boundary to a neighboring property.
Materials Use robust fencing for garden boundaries. Lighter structures such as screens, trellises, or even woven willow walls (see p.85) make softer, more pleasing internal divisions.

For more information, see:
"Walls," p.596
"Fences," p.600

Hedges

Assess what you have

- Are existing hedges in the right position in the yard? They may filter the wind and provide shelter, but equally may obscure views and create excessive shade.
- Have existing hedges grown too wide or tall for the yard?
- Do you have the right type of hedges for your yard? Evergreen ones sometimes prove oppressive and overly dominant, while deciduous hedges tend to let more light into the yard on dark winter days.
- How long have the hedges been in place? Old hedges can become thin at their base; reducing the height and width of the upper part will encourage regrowth lower down.

What to consider

Shape A hedge need not have the angular rigid lines that are associated with walls and fences, and can trace a sweeping curve to frame an informal border.
Material The hedging material can be varied and mixed in different combinations to offer textures and degrees of formality or informality.
Aesthetics Hedges bearing colorful flowers, fruits, or berries add interest.
Shade from trees Overhanging trees create shade that stifles the growth of hedging plants. Overcome this by planting a mixed hedge using shade-tolerant species beneath trees.
Formal hedges These add structure to a landscape design. Clipped hedges act as walls for garden "rooms." Cut windows and archways to create vistas and passageways between rooms.

For more information, see:
HEDGES AND SCREENS, p.82

Outbuildings

Assess what you have

- Is the building in good repair?
- Does it stand in the best position for its purpose? An outbuilding—whatever its function—should not dominate the yard. If necessary, consider moving the structure to another location.
- Does the building blend in with its surroundings? One option is to camouflage it using climbers or shrubs. Buildings could be painted a different color or refaced with a more attractive material.
- Would a building be more useful if refitted for a different role? A shed or summerhouse could be used to store garden furniture or tools, and a conservatory could double as a greenhouse for plants.

What to consider

Secondary role Buildings may either form part of the landscape, adding a modest architectural element, or be hidden by climbers and shrubs.
Siting Strike a balance between a building's practical use and its aesthetic quality. A summerhouse, conservatory, or greenhouse requires a position with a favorable exposure for its occupants, whether human or plant. A garden shed, however, can be sited in a shady corner. All buildings should be readily accessible, ideally from a hard surface.
Materials All structures should be constructed from strong materials that are easy to maintain; they must also have adequate foundations.

For more information, see:
CONSERVATORY GARDENING, p.356
GREENHOUSES AND FRAMES, pp.566–583
"Garden sheds," p.605

Arbors and arches

Assess what you have

- Is the structure structurally sound? It must safely bear both the weight of the plants and the overhead structure.
- Is the structure able to withstand the wind resistance created by the plant canopy?
- Are there any weaknesses in existing structures? Check and repair lumber and metalwork, if necessary; sound surfaces should be cleaned and treated with preservative or paint. It may be advisable to employ a structural engineer or qualified builder to inspect large structures.
- Are any plantings out of control? They should be drastically cut back to allow light and air into the canopy.
- Are any plants looking tired? Old, twisted, and gnarled specimen climbers should be retained for their character, and carefully pruned.

What to consider

Architectural element An arbor or series of arches may define the main axis of a landscape, directing the flow or marking a transition from one section to another.
Materials and design These may be dictated by those already used in the garden or house.
Framework A range of weights can be used for different effects, from a skeletal metalwork frame to a heavy brick and timber construction. In winter, deciduous plants will no longer conceal their supports, so structures need to be elegant.

For more information, see:
"Arbors and rustic work," p.603

Ornamental plantings

Trees

Assess what you have

- How mature are the trees? Mature or semimature trees are a great asset. Their scale cannot readily be acquired, and the shadows they cast give a special quality to a landscape.
- Do you wish to add a favorite tree? Small trees are ideal in confined spaces. In larger yards they will, if positioned correctly, enhance the landscape effect provided by larger "specimen" trees.
- Do the existing trees dominate? New landscapes are often planted heavily for immediate results; this may later require the removal of some trees or the reduction of their canopies.
- Do trees encroach on a view or cut out light? They must be controlled with appropriate pruning. The same applies if leaves from trees near the house block gutters and downspouts.

What to consider

Function A single tree can fulfill many roles. It may have an elegant form, with flowers, fruit, good fall color, and attractive bark, providing almost year-round interest.
Continuity This can be achieved by using lots of one species or cultivar.
Development A mixture of trees can be planted for short- and longer-term effect; part of the enjoyment is watching a tree develop.
Placement Tree roots, especially those of fast-growing species, can damage sewer pipes and foundations. Take care when choosing sites for trees to allow adequate clearance around buildings.

For more information, see:
ORNAMENTAL TREES, pp.52–85

Shrubs

Assess what you have

- Do existing shrubs give decorative value over a long period of time?
- Are they performing well, or are they straggly and undernourished, or perhaps starved of light?
- Are they overgrown, or too large for the position? Not all shrubs respond well to pruning; identify the plants before removing or reducing growth.
- Have grafted shrubs developed suckers from the rootstock? Left in place they may overpower the plant; remove them cleanly at their source.
- Do you require a low-maintenance yard? Shrubs that need regular attention may have to be replaced.
- Have variegated shrubs produced green-leaved stems? Cut these off.

What to consider

Seasonal features For every month there is a shrub that provides color and scent, even in the dark days of winter. Some are dual-purpose— flowering, then fruiting later. Many shrubs are also suitable for cutting for indoor arrangements.
Shape and form These differ from shrub to shrub, and give the yard a softer edge, reducing the predictably angular lines of the average property.
Dividing role Where a hedge or fence would create too strong a division across the garden, a cluster of shrubs can be a better choice. They tend to be covered with foliage to ground level, and evergreens will retain their leaves throughout winter.
Wildlife Shrubs can provide habitats for nesting birds or food for overwintering creatures.

For more information, see:
ORNAMENTAL SHRUBS, pp.86–121
ROSES, pp.146–169

Climbing plants

Assess what you have

- Do existing climbers enhance the yard, allowing plant growth to flow up, over, and around buildings and walls?
- Are plants too vigorous for their supporting structures, whether a tree, wall, arch, or arbor? A plant that outgrows its space will need considerable pruning, which may then reduce flowering and fruiting.
- Are wall-trained shrubs planted too close to buildings? This can damage their foundations. Dense climbers may retain moisture or obscure light from windows.
- Are climbers so overgrown that they are blocking gutters or working their way under roof shingles? Offending plants must be removed or regularly pruned.

What to consider

Camouflage Carefully chosen climbing plants can redeem the most mundane or ugly building, disguising it with a thin veil of foliage and softening lines and construction materials.
Use on walls Some climbers cling tightly to the angles of walls while others blur the edges, transforming sharp corners into flowing curves.
Maintenance The amount of time you can invest in climbing plants will dictate their appearance. A rampant, trailing climber will, if left unchecked, festoon a building in a few seasons. The same climber, pruned regularly and precisely tied, can offer a neatly tailored, formal layout of well-secured branches.

For more information, see:
"Wall shrubs," p.91
CLIMBING PLANTS, pp.122–45

Herbaceous borders

Assess what you have

- Is the scale, coloring, and content of the border to your liking?
- Will the border look spectacular for one month but nondescript for the rest of the year?
- Have vigorous plants swamped other more delicate species and spoiled the design and balance?
- Do any plants need rejuvenating? After lifting and dividing, replant only young, vigorous sections.
- Is the border overrun with perennial weeds (see p.670) such as goutweed (*Aegopodium podagraria*) or quackgrass (*Elymus repens*)?
- Could borders be reduced in size or the planting simplified for easy maintenance?

What to consider

Color The primary purpose of herbaceous plantings is to provide uplifting color.
Positioning Borders that run parallel to a house will be critically observed at close quarters; they may look empty for much of the year. It is better to position borders so you look down their length: the planting will always appear to be full, and gaps will be less noticeable.
Themes A border can adopt a theme, such as a particular color or season, or a favorite plant genus. Plant foliage could harmonize with the color or texture of a hedge or material used as an edging, path, or wall.

For more information, see:
PERENNIALS, pp.170–205
ANNUALS AND BIENNIALS, pp.204–23
BULBOUS PLANTS, pp.224–51

Garden features

Kitchen garden

Assess what you have

- Does the current site have the best soil in the yard, a warm, sheltered spot, and good light? If there is another spot with more suitable growing conditions, consider relocating the garden to this area.
- Do you intend to keep an existing kitchen garden area? Always assess the condition of the soil before deciding what to grow (see "Soil and its structure," p.616). It may need improvement or deep cultivation.
- Are existing fruit trees and bushes productive, or old and neglected? Old specimens may need pruning to restore them to productivity, or may be better replaced. Consider, too, your family's needs and any specific likes and dislikes.

What to consider

Priority crops Decide on your main requirement—this might be salad crops, unusual produce that is not available at the supermarket, or a year-round supply of organic vegetables and fruit.
Time available Growing vegetables requires an investment of time and occasional hard physical work. Keep this in mind when deciding how big your garden should be.
Space available Where space is limited and smaller crops are required, vegetables and fruits can be integrated throughout the entire yard. This may actually reduce the incidence of pest problems, and it will look attractive, too.

For more information, see:
Growing Fruit, pp.416–89
Growing Vegetables, pp.490–548

Herb garden

Assess what you have

- Does an inherited herb garden include plants that are important to you? With such a wide range of plants available, the contents of the herb garden are a personal matter; it may be necessary to discard some of the existing herbs, and replanning and replanting may be required.
- Have fast-spreading herbs, such as mints, come to dominate and smother less vigorous ones? Such plants should be cut back, but this may not be a permanent solution; consider growing more delicate herbs in the safety of containers, or confining rampant growers to pots sunk into the soil.

What to consider

Site and soil To grow well, herbs require very well-drained soil, which need not be particularly rich, and a very sunny site that receives maximum light and warmth.
Location Ideally, an herb garden should be located near the house and within easy reach of the kitchen for use throughout the year. Large quantities of herbs required for culinary or other purposes, such as making potpourri, may be grown in specific areas to be harvested and stored for use out of season.
Planting combinations If desired, you can group culinary, aromatic, and medicinal plants. The herb garden theme may be extended throughout the cultivated areas of the yard. Flowers, fruit, vegetables, and herbs may be combined, using an extended range of fragrances and color, as well as flower and leaf shapes and textures.

For more information, see:
Growing Herbs, pp.402–15

Water features

Assess what you have

- Are the water features in the yard well maintained or in need of repair? Before adopting any existing ponds, fountains, or streams, their overall condition should be assessed and any problems addressed.
- Has a pond site become overshadowed by trees, leaving the water too shaded or perhaps full of debris?
- Is the scale of the area of water in relation to that of the yard as a whole inappropriate? Ponds require considerable time and effort to keep them in good condition. If this commitment cannot be fulfilled, they may be better removed.
- Is the water feature properly protected? Safety must be a primary consideration in family gardens. The smallest pond can pose a threat to children, especially those unfamiliar with the yard.

What to consider

Safety If the safety of small children is a concern, reduce the depth of small ponds by partially filling them with rounded pebbles. Ledges around pool sides will help older children scramble out. Sloping pond margins also allow for escape from deeper water, and may save the lives of pets or small garden mammals.
Scale The smallest amount of water brings movement, sound, and life into a garden, whatever its size. A patio may host a small spout and basin; a backyard may have a modest pond with native plants; and a landscape may have a series of interconnected pools and water courses—each one is at an appropriate scale for its setting.

For more information, see:
Water Gardening, pp.280–303

Ornaments and pots

Assess what you have

- When moving to a new property, is there a chance of acquiring long-established decorative garden items? If so, seize the opportunity. However, it is rare to inherit statues and large architectural containers with a house and garden. Ornaments are usually removed along with the house contents or sold.
- How well placed are the existing ornaments? A garden that benefits from well-positioned ornaments will be weakened by their removal or replacement. Conversely, an overembellished garden will confuse the eye—it must be controlled to restore balance and bring order to the scene.

What to consider

Garden design Well-placed containers and ornaments can be used to enhance existing garden styles. Ornaments should comply with local factors—scale, style, material, and general appropriateness.
Personal taste Statues and pots can be a reflection of personal taste. The art they introduce to the garden may be traditional or contemporary, representational or abstract. A distinctive individuality can be achieved with the use of commissioned pieces of sculpture or plant containers.
Focal points Ornaments may act as signposts within the garden by encouraging visitors to move through it or to pause to admire a view; they enhance certain points and draw together disconnected areas.

For more information, see:
Container Gardening, pp.304–35

Sketching out a plan

Before accurately measuring a yard and formulating any new garden design, a preliminary sketch or sketches will help you assess the overall layout of the existing landscape. This will form the basis of a detailed scale plan (see p.36), on which you will be able to mark those features and plants that are to be retained, and the elements to be added (see p.38).

These sketches should comprise rough ground plans on which to note the many practical factors that will affect the final layout and choice of plants. With accompanying notes, they should detail elements particular to the site, such as climate, soil type, views to consider, shade cast, and the orientation of yard and house, as well as the shape and size of the area—factors that cannot be changed. They should also include utilities relating to the house as well as to the yard and its maintenance, such as outside faucets and sheds. Such items may currently be poorly positioned.

Climate and exposure

The climate of the general locality and that found specifically within the yard are key determining factors, influencing its layout and the choice and placing of plants (see CLIMATE AND THE GARDEN, pp.606–615). Information on the climatic conditions of the locality, annual rainfall, average temperatures, and quantities of sunlight should be sought and studied. These general conditions will be influenced by the particular terrain within the yard. A low-lying site may be sheltered from strong winds but it may also form a frost

pocket, while a hilltop site may remain several degrees colder than a neighboring, protected, south-facing slope. A property near the sea can also be affected by strong winds, possibly salt-laden, but the maritime influence will prevent extreme fluctuations in temperature compared with inland regions.

Within one yard, pockets of particular conditions will exist, forming microclimates of warmth or cold, humidity or dryness, each suiting a different range of plants (see "Microclimate", p.611). The orientation of the yard, and of the house within it, will affect the warmth or coldness of the house walls, and where shadows will create deep or partial shade. These factors will affect not only your choice of plants but also decisions on where seating areas should be positioned.

Assessing your soil type

The soil found within a yard is a crucial factor to take into account. The type, texture, and level of acidity or alkalinity (the pH) of the soil are important to recognize (see "Soil and its structure," p.616). Soils vary greatly from region to region, from heavy clay to light sandy loam, and alkaline soil to acidic peat.

Gaining perspective
An upstairs window may afford a good view when sketching the boundaries and any irregularities in a yard. It is also an ideal vantage point from which to observe and map changing patterns of sun and shade.

Each variation in soil will suit a different plant range. Those happily accommodated will thrive, while those planted in an inappropriate soil type will struggle to survive. Moisture retention and drainage will vary with soil type, as will ease of cultivation, which can be severely hindered by badly drained, heavy soil.

Poor drainage is a factor that may affect more than plant choice. A soft, boggy site will be unsuitable for any substantial building work unless the problem can be alleviated by installing drainage (see "Improving drainage," p.623). If large areas of rubble or subsoil

have been left behind after building and construction work, it may be simpler to work with them rather than attempt an overhaul. They may be used to form the foundations of a terraced area or perhaps a gravel garden; this type of site provides ideal conditions for plants that prefer fast-draining soil (see "Gravel beds and paving," p.256).

Utilities and access

Other fixed features within the property should be noted on the plan, including driveways and sidewalks, and important yet irritating features to be worked around, such as utility covers, electrical junction boxes, and air conditioner units that require certain amounts of access space. There may also be meter inspection points and septic tanks to be marked. A propane tank is often an ugly but unavoidable component of a yard in a rural area; it may be possible to relocate it, but screening is obviously an easier option. A woodpile, however, can look charming in the right spot, and is also an attractive wildlife habitat.

Any overhead power or telephone lines need to be marked on the site plan, because tall-growing trees must not be planted where they will interfere with the lines. It is also inadvisable to plant twining climbers on a house wall where cables enter the building, because the plants will use the wires as a climbing frame. Such points on the house wall are often inaccessible, too, and attempts to prune or pull away growth can be hazardous.

Garden topography
An area of water increases not only soil moisture but also the humidity of the surrounding air, to the benefit of many plants. However, water often occupies a low-lying spot, which is very likely to be a frost pocket (see p.607). Plants may need to be selected for their hardiness as well as their suitability for the soil and conditions.

A rough site plan

Sketch the layout of the yard and the position of the house. Then add substantial structural plantings such as trees and hedges, the outlines of areas of pavement and lawns, the route of paths, and any internal garden divisions and buildings such as sheds, screens, and walls. At this point, more generally planted borders and areas may be indicated simply by shading. In this garden, the diagonal hatching represents shade cast by the sun taking its highest, midsummer route across the sky.

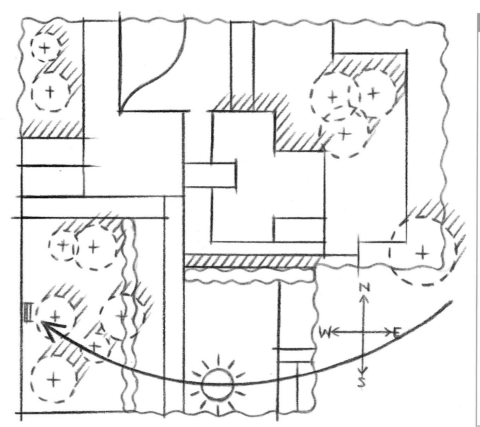

THINKING AHEAD

While your plans may be at an embryonic stage, ideas for major changes—for example, removal of a tree or construction of a building such as a greenhouse—may already be germinating. Right from the start there are certain legal aspects worth investigating, or you may run the risk of unpleasant surprises thwarting your plans later. These include local building and planning regulations, the possible existence of tree preservation ordinances, the responsibility for, and delineation between, boundaries separating neighboring properties, and any statutory environmental protection for your area. Any necessary permissions should be sought as early as possible, even if you eventually do not follow the ideas through, because reaching agreements or getting variances can take considerable amounts of time.

Other practicalities

There are certain practicalities that few yards can be without, and a checklist can be compiled to determine whether the existing yard is equipped to suit your needs. Mark the position of outside faucets, and consider whether these may need to be moved. To inherit a yard with an established compost pile is a plus, but this can easily be moved elsewhere, as can other potentially useful structures such as cold frames and small sheds.

Draw the current position of these onto the plan, together with garages, sheds, and storage areas, and consider whether the capacity these offer is adequate, not only for garden tools but also for general family clutter such as folding chairs, toys, and bicycles.

What lies beyond

Elements quite literally beyond your control should still be noted for consideration on the plan. The immediate surrounds of the property, where views may be taken advantage of or ugly buildings concealed by carefully positioned trees, will enable an enterprising gardener to exploit the site to the fullest. Privacy and security at the boundaries of the yard should be examined and noted for their existing effectiveness. Weigh up possible loss of views or sunlight if extra privacy and shelter are required, and ensure that any changes will not annoy your neighbors. Security can often be improved by opening up the yard, rather than reinforcing enclosure; consider whether driveways and sheds might perhaps be better brought into view.

The impact of a busy road passing the property, perhaps with an intersection where car headlights sweep the yard, can be reduced or lost if the boundary gaps are filled. Dense, clipped hedges can also act as a useful noise baffle (see also HEDGES AND SCREENS, p.82).

Views to obscure

An unwelcome reminder of urban life in the form of a distant parking lot intrudes into this otherwise charming yard. Planting a narrow, upright tree, or raising the height of the rear wall slightly with trellises on which a climber could be trained, would restore seclusion. Consider local fencing laws and your neighbors' wishes before implementing changes that could block light.

Lengthening a vista

Reshaping this border and introducing more height in the foreground would open up and lengthen a vista toward the conifer, and lead on to views of the countryside beyond. Lowering the hedge would also add distance, but its presence, together with the trees behind it, suggests a windbreak. Prevailing winds should be investigated—this site could be very exposed.

Making a scale plan

Choose a mild, dry day for compiling a scale plan of your landscape, and allow yourself enough time to take accurate measurements. The assistance of a second person will greatly ease the task, as will a good-sized sketch pad or a clipboard and paper, two 100ft (30m) measuring tapes, a pencil, an eraser, and a compass. With a small yard, a single "field plan" can be made of the entire site. Larger yards can be broken into separate areas, mapped, then the individual plans joined together as one master plan.

Making a start

The lot lines of the property should be measured and marked on the plan, with heights of any boundary walls, hedges, or fences marked alongside their lengths. Then the house and other buildings must be plotted within the property lines. This may be achieved by measuring from two known fixed points on the boundary, such as corners, gate posts, or tree trunks, to a corner or fixed point on the house. If three or four such points are established around the house, then an accurate location will be found for the building. Surrounding decks or patios can be relatively easily measured from the house to their edges, checking that they run parallel to the house and, if not, gauging the discrepancy.

Plotting positions

When plotting outlying features that cannot be related easily to a nearby boundary or house wall, you must create an artificial line from which measurements can be taken. A long measuring tape pulled straight out between known and pinpointed features in the yard, such as a central door in the house and a fence post on the far boundary, provides a "datum line." From this, use a second tape to identify the position of features, such as a tree, sundial, or utility cover, by measuring at a right angle from the first, datum-line tape. Note the measurement on the first tape where the second crosses it, and the distance from this point to the feature.

Once a datum line has been established, any number of items can be measured using coordinates to the left or right of the line. A number of such datum lines may

Measuring from a datum line
Except in the tiniest yards, it is almost impossible to position elements such as trees and small buildings on a plan by taking measurements between them and their nearest boundaries. Using a central datum line makes the job much easier. Here, a line in the pavers running parallel to the house has provided a useful starting point for a datum line that will run to a fixed, traceable point at the far end of the garden.

Measuring the existing layout
Using a datum line, or lines, enables you to build up a plotted plan of the yard by making a series of offset measurements to the right and to the left of the line. The running, or incremental, measurements taken along the datum line are also a valuable way of confirming the site's dimensions.

Measuring tapes 1 measures down the yard from a fixed point (here, one corner of the house)

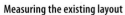

Measuring tape 2 is used to make the cross-measurements

House

0m

4.4m

4m

4.8m

7.98m

3m

9.2m

5.8m

8.4m

7.65m

7.35m

8.3m

9.9m

10.2m

5.1m

11.3m

3m

5.1m

7.6m

15.1m

Triangulation

Where a feature such as a tree cannot be directly related to existing straight sight lines, measure against two fixed points to establish its position. To transfer to a plan, scale down the two distances appropriately, and use each as the radius of a circle drawn with a compass around the fixed points—here the two corners of the garage. The point at which the circles intersect will be the location of the feature (here a tree). The compass can also be used to describe the tree's canopy.

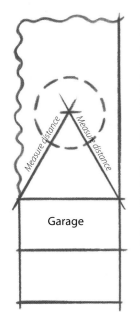

Garage

Measure distance *Measure distance*

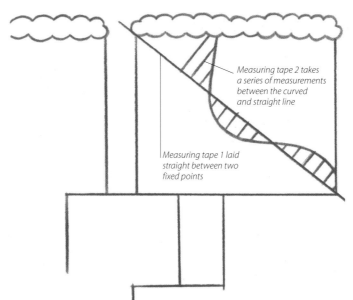

Measuring tape 2 takes a series of measurements between the curved and straight line

Measuring tape 1 laid straight between two fixed points

Establishing an irregular curve

Two measuring tapes must be used for this: one to lie straight and flat across the curve (or curves) between two given measured and plotted points, the second to be used to measure the curve at regular intervals from the first tape. For example, at 20in (50cm) intervals along the first tape, the second tape is laid across it at right angles and the distance to the edge of the curve measured and recorded as a series of coordinates.

be necessary to plot all features within a large yard. To pinpoint a single, isolated feature, such as a tree in a lawn, the technique known as triangulation (see above) may be used. While straight edges are easy to measure and plot, the curved edge of a drive or generous sweep of a border may take more time to replicate precisely on paper (see above, right).

Adding more dimensions

As linear measurements are taken, other useful information can be gathered. Measure and mark the positions of all entrances to the property, and all doors and windows of the house. Heights of internal garden divisions such as screens and hedges should be recorded, together with the height and canopy spread of trees, arbors, or arches.

Changes in level should also be recorded. These are critical factors that may necessitate terracing, retaining walls, steps, and slopes in future plans for the yard where awkward level changes prevail. Simple slopes and slight changes can be calculated relatively easily, but an undulating site of various levels and cross-falls will require the hiring of a professional surveyor. A large yard, which is more difficult to plot and coordinate than a small one, may also be better left to a professional.

Transferring the field plan

With the "fieldwork" statistics accurately gathered, including a number of additional cross-measurements made as a check to the detail and to the overall plan, the information can be committed to paper or entered into a garden design software program. If working on paper, keep in mind that a plan created at too small a

TRANSFERRING THE FIELD PLAN TO GRAPH PAPER

Establish the scale of the plan using the largest dimensions possible on a sheet of paper that will accommodate them; if necessary, tape several sheets together to produce a large, clear plan. A general landscape plan, such as the one below, showing basic outlines and features can be drawn at a scale of 1:100. Mark everything on the plan, including features you may not want to keep. This plan, together with your visual memory of what already exists in each area, will help in both imagining and deciding on the scale of new outlines and features (see p.38).

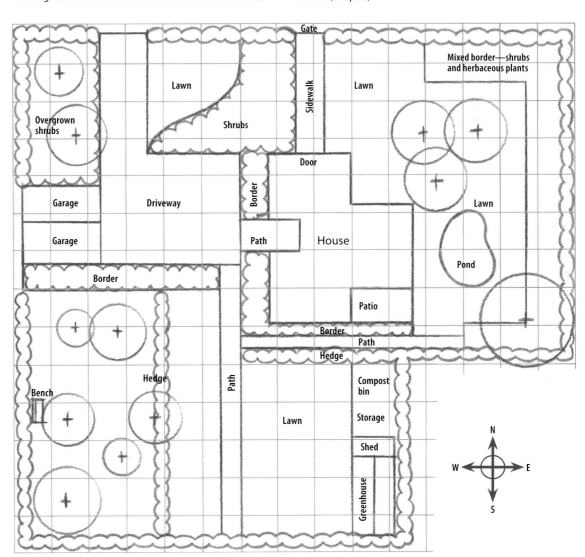

scale will be difficult to draw and awkward to read. As large a scale as possible should be adopted so that every detail can be recorded. Graph paper will allow the easy transfer of measurements from field notes to plan, although designs on blank paper using a scale rule, once mastered, will give greater flexibility. A general landscape plan detailing all the items and features may be drawn at a scale of 1:100, but a more detailed one of plants within a border (see also p.45) requires a scale of 1:50 or 1:40 for a readable depiction.

When using graph paper, a decision on how many squares are to represent one square yard (square meter) must be made. The biggest scale that the paper can afford should first be calculated by penciling in the greatest measurement, because if this can be accommodated then the entire drawing will fit. Art and design supply stores stock paper in larger sizes that may be difficult to find in other stores.

Putting pencil to paper

The design novice will almost certainly require several attempts at plotting a scale plan, and even a professional will work only in pencil at this stage. The principal features should be entered onto the plan first, starting with the property lines and any gateways or openings within them. From these points, the house with its doorways and windows can be positioned. These openings are important as often a sight line or vista will be revealed from a doorway or window. Once the outer and "inner" perimeters of the yard are established, small details around the house can be arranged. From here you can draw in paths and driveways, establishing between them areas of lawn, pavement, and gardens. These will facilitate the positioning of more isolated features, such as specimen trees, sheds, and greenhouses.

Omit only those features that will definitely not be retained in the final design. At this stage all else must appear on the plan, even elements that may be removed later. The drawing can then be made permanent by inking the lines. A thin line should be used to depict all of the existing detail, to permit the overlay of new ideas and the blocking in or heightening of old features. Thus you will create a new design that includes worthy existing elements enhanced by proposals, suggestions, and experiments new to the site.

Imposing the new design

The original master copy of the plan should remain unmarked. Either make photocopies on which to work, or use tracing paper laid across the original. With a known scale and an accurate drawing, there are endless possibilities that can be tried on the plan. Different sizes and positions for decks, driveways, and ponds can be considered (see STRUCTURES AND SURFACES, pp.584–605, and WATER GARDENING, pp.280–303). Cutting out paper shapes representing plantings, ornaments, ponds, or buildings to place and move around the plan helps envision the impact these features will have on the site.

This preliminary planning period, although rather abstract and divorced from the physical practicalities of making a garden, is an essential one, as all those thoughts, ideas, and dreams of what your personal garden should comprise must be described, considered, applied, and then adopted or rejected. Many rough drawings should be made to expose all the design possibilities.

Any working drawings that follow the thought process should be kept—frequently a discarded idea may be resurrected in a different guise. The possibility of two ideas combining and working together when one of the ideas in isolation would be rejected is sufficient reason for retaining every idea and drawing until the project has been completed.

Rounding out the vision

When a design has been rigorously scrutinized, experimented with, and passed such tests as practicality, accessibility, and suitability for the site, then the foundations of a new approach to the landscape are beginning to be laid. Areas of the plan could be shaded or colored to give a more powerful representation of the differing elements, aiding final decisions of proportion and scale.

You will also begin to appreciate the proportions of hardscaping to "soft"—that is, plantings—in your design, and adjust them if needed. You may already have ideas about building materials, and the nature of the main planting elements—even the identities of individual structural plants (see also "Principles of planting," pp.42–45). A scrapbook or collage of photographs, or elements of photographs, cut out of magazines and catalogs will add color and texture to your vision, and serve as a reminder of items to order and buy to complete your design.

BUILDING THE NEW DESIGN ON THE EXISTING PLAN

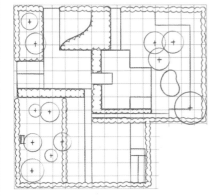

Having created an accurately plotted field plan (see p.37, and above), use copies of it, or tracing paper, to begin experimenting with your new design. The advantage of using tracing paper is that features and outlines that are to be discarded can simply be left out of the drawing, to produce a much cleaner and clearer picture. In the overlay on the right, elements to be retained from the existing yard—including much of the fine mature hedges, and the most desirable of the trees—have been marked in blue. The driveway has been given a softer profile; more space has been allocated to borders; a potager-style kitchen garden replaces a decrepit orchard; and the family room of the house now enjoys a serene vista of a sunken garden with a formal pool.

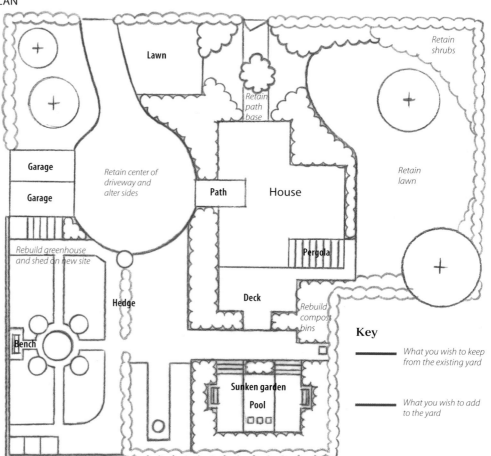

Lawn

Retain shrubs

Retain path base

Garage

Retain center of driveway and alter sides

Path

House

Retain lawn

Garage

Rebuild greenhouse and shed on new site

Pergola

Deck

Rebuild compost bins

Hedge

Bench

Sunken garden

Pool

Key

—— What you wish to keep from the existing yard

—— What you wish to add to the yard

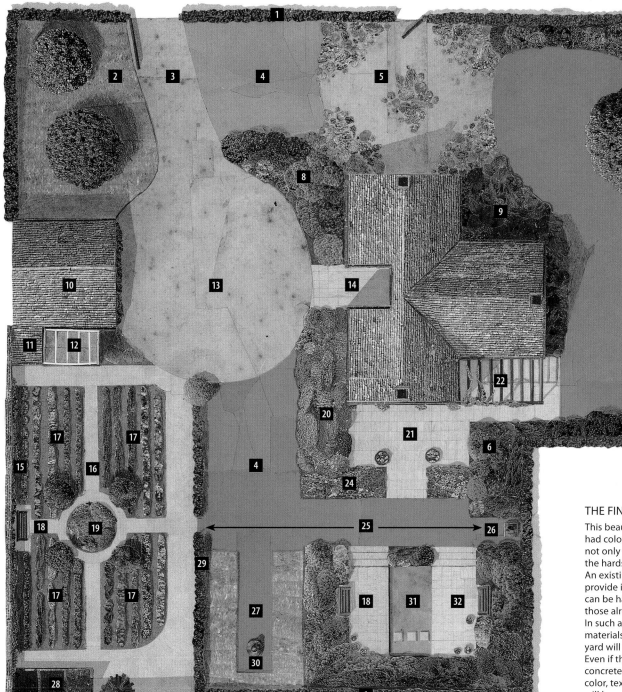

THE FINISHED DESIGN

This beautifully realized plan has had color, detail, and texture added, not only in planted areas but also in the hardscaped areas such as the patio. An existing garden and house may provide inspiration where materials can be harmoniously linked with those already found on the property. In such a case, a seamless flow of materials from the house into the yard will produce a pleasing design. Even if the identical brick, stone, or concrete cannot be found, a similar color, texture, and scale of material will be perfectly satisfactory.

A garden devoid of existing hardscaping offers the opportunity to introduce new materials. Local colors and textures should still be respected, yet within the design a particular paver, brick, or block can be selected. Small-scale, intricately patterned materials are appropriate in small, confined spaces but can look complicated and busy on a large scale, while bigger units offer a calmer feeling.

Lumber for arbors, gates, fences, or decks and gravel for terraces, paths, or a driveway must all be chosen for their suitability for the site, aesthetic appeal, and durability. The color of a fence, whether natural or painted, can alter the appearance of an entire yard, as can the color and size of gravel or stone chips used as loose surfaces.

KEY

1 Evergreen hedge
2 Long grass with bulbs and woodland plants
3 Gravel drive with timber edging
4 Standard mown lawn
5 Rose garden
6 Mixed shrub planting
7 Specimen tree
8 Planting with year-round interest
9 Border of shade-loving plants
10 Two-car garage
11 Storage shed
12 Greenhouse
13 Gravel courtyard with enough space for turning a vehicle
14 Flagstone walkway to front door
15 Raspberry bushes
16 Permanent paths
17 Vegetables, cut flowers, fruit, and herbs
18 Garden bench
19 Central herb garden
20 Mixed border
21 Flagstone terrace
22 Arbor with table and chairs
23 Tree screening neighboring house
24 Bed of colorful annuals
25 Axial vista
26 Sculpture
27 Central mown grass path flanked by meadow grass and bulbs
28 Compost and wood piles
29 Deciduous hedge
30 Urn ornament
31 Formal pool bridged by stepping stones
32 Sunken garden with steps

Putting the plan into practice

In the same way that the existing yard has been recorded on paper, you must now translate your new design onto the site. Often it is during this process of measuring and marking out the proposed plan that problems with the design become apparent. You may have been overambitious with the available space, for example, or mistaken about the most practical route for a path. Only by standing at proposed vantage points to contemplate imaginary vistas may an unwelcome eyesore be revealed.

Using props

A design can be laid out *in situ* using whatever comes to hand to simulate temporarily the key elements of the design. You must work around features that are probably destined to be removed—however inconvenient this may be—because the experimental layout may show that these are actually valuable elements that are worth keeping after all.

Stakes, containers, hoses, string, pots, cardboard boxes, and trash cans can be used to assume roles such as path and border edges, stair treads, specimen trees, ponds, or rows of repeating shrubs across the front of an imaginary terrace. Heavy wooden tree stakes driven into an open lawn will readily confirm or rule out a location for a broad, spreading tree, where neighboring plantings, buildings, and views may all be important considerations.

Where possible, props should be left in place for their impact to be experienced over a few days and at different times of day. Lay

out the edges of garden beds with stakes and twine. Then use spray paint or a line of sand trickled from a bottle to mark the layout, and remove the twine and stakes.

Photographs taken of the garden with its props in place may prove invaluable when determining the eventual placement or removal of features. These final decisions should not be hurried; allow enough time to consider and even reconsider. At this point, indecision is a strength—holding onto an original concept doggedly in the light of subsequent modifications is foolhardy. Opportunities available now will not present themselves again, and matters of construction are more easily resolved on the drawing board than on site with an impatient contractor.

Order of work

A carefully orchestrated schedule of work is needed to coordinate and implement a new landscape plan. There are many different

Transferring the design
Formal, symmetrical designs can be as simple to mark out on the proposed site as they are to plot on paper. A grid may be created using string guides that correspond with the scale on the plan, allowing the entire design to be transferred onto the ground with relative ease. It is important that all of the measurements and angles are correctly taken and carefully checked.

elements and skills involved, and each should be undertaken in a logical sequence to provide a smooth-running program and keep disruption to a minimum.

A fundamental decision must be made as to whether the plan of improvements is to be undertaken as a single operation or in stages over a number of weeks, months, or years. It's best to have all hardscaping work completed in a single phase, because this

eliminates the need for contractors and delivery trucks to return and create a second period of dust, noise, and inconvenience (see STRUCTURES AND SURFACES, pp.584–605). Timing the operations is important to enable construction work to be completed in favorable weather, allowing fall or spring for planting, sowing, and laying sod.

Remodeling in stages

It is often the case, whether because of time limits or budget constraints, or simply the need to retain a usable outdoor area of some sort at all times, that a reworking of the yard can only be implemented piecemeal. A strategy for change must be drawn up. For some time the desired landscape will overlay the existing layout, which may look odd, with permanently retained features, temporarily kept items, and new plantings and features all present. The evolving hybrid will require intricate planning to ensure a smooth transition to the new design.

To assist with a phased series of changes, an essential first step is to label all plantings and features with written or color-coded tags indicating plants and materials to stay, to be moved, to remain temporarily, or to be removed immediately. Although decisions have been made, a period of final deliberation is useful, during which the labeled plants may be reassessed to avoid any later confusion and irrevocable errors.

Setting the scene
By arranging and rearranging items gleaned from the house and yard, you can simulate the key features of the proposed design. Here, bamboo tepees indicate the position of obelisks planted with climbers; inverted tubs stand in for shrubs; and the slats and landscape fabric form a terraced area flanked by massed plantings of lavender. To complete the effect, a specimen tree in the lawn and an undulating border edging of boxwood have been added.

Hiring professionals

Once the scale of operations has been identified, the amount of assistance needed to implement the plans can be gauged. It may be possible over a period of time to make all the changes yourself, or some help may be needed to execute, say, construction work or tree removal. On the other hand, a landscape contractor may be hired to implement the entire design. Where assistance is being sought, it is important to state accurately what is required and to obtain a detailed price quotation. Good references or, ideally, personal recommendations for the firm are also highly desirable.

Professional advice may also be sought to assess the condition of trees, walls, and outbuildings. With their good condition confirmed (or otherwise), the appropriate action can then be taken. Even if some elements are unaffected by the current work, examine their condition early on; to invite arborists or landscapers back into the finished yard could be disruptive and damaging.

Coping with limited access

A row house or townhouse without access from street to backyard should ideally have work scheduled to coincide with house remodeling, because materials must be carried through the house itself, creating possible damage to the interior. Materials can be lifted over

Hardscaping
Because of the inevitable soil compaction involved, built features should always take priority over new planting. Where only part of the yard is being remodeled, as above, clear an area large enough for you to work comfortably. Conduits laid under paving at the construction stage (right) may be useful in the future to carry utilities such as wiring.

adjoining walls, but at some cost and effort. If it's not possible to bring a dumpster into the yard, you may have to apply for permission to place one at curbside.

Excavations and rubble

When excavations produce large quantities of soil to be taken off-site, remember to discard subsoil, but keep topsoil. Where ground level is being lowered, this will involve taking off and reserving the topsoil, digging out and removing subsoil, and then replacing the topsoil, so that the best soil does not leave the property. When holes are to be dug, ask your utility companies to locate and mark buried water lines, phone and electric cables, and gas pipes. Many provinces have a call-before-you-dig central contact number. Never start digging until this critical step is carried out.

Clearing the area

The first stage of the landscape refurbishment is the removal of all unwanted materials and structures. Hire a qualified, insured arborist if trees need to be cut down and taken away. Stumps must also be removed; leaving them to rot in the soil increases the danger of fungal infections (see p.660). High-quality materials in good condition, such as old bricks and paving stones, will have a resale value that justifies taking the trouble to find a reputable dealer. Those materials

that are eventually to be reused should be cleaned and carefully stacked in a safe place off-site.

In a large yard, the area to be worked on should be fenced off, restricting potential damage and accumulation of materials to one place. Paving and steps to be retained should also be protected by covering them with plywood while heavy materials are being maneuvered. Sod can be stripped and carefully stacked for a short time before reuse or cleared for new sod to take its place.

Plants left in place

Plants to be left *in situ* can be carefully wrapped in sheets and tied for a brief period if, say, surrounding walls are being repaired. Large shrubs, too big for their locations yet too interesting and attractive to remove, could be thinned or reduced, or even cut hard to the ground to encourage regeneration (see "Renovation," p.107). Before cutting them back, some plants can be propagated as an extra safety measure: in the right season, take cuttings of plants such as roses, hollies, or clematis, to ensure the variant survives (see PRINCIPLES OF PROPAGATION, "Cuttings," p.632).

Clumps of many perennials will tolerate being lifted, divided, and potted if kept well watered in a sheltered, shady corner (see PERENNIALS, "Lifting and dividing," p.194). Taking cuttings or collecting seeds (see "Collecting and storing seeds," p.629) is another way of preserving such plants to incorporate into the new garden.

Creating the landscape

With unwanted materials out of the way, the cleared site should then have any pernicious weeds, such as goutweed and bindweed,

Correct timing
Never delay the installation of new sod. The timing of delivery is crucial—if left rolled (as below) for more than a day or two, the sod will swiftly deteriorate. Laying sod in fall allows bulbs to be planted at the same time, to flower in spring; nothing gives a new lawn an air of maturity like a scattering of bulbs, such as crocuses (left).

eradicated (see "Controlling weeds," p.645). At this stage any adjustments to levels can also be made, as well as any excavations for services such as power for garden lighting, or irrigation systems. Wall footings or sidewalk bases can now be excavated, and solid foundations built (see "Paths and steps," p.593, and "Walls," p.596). Construction of walls and structures can then take place (see STRUCTURES AND SURFACES, pp.584–605, and "Erecting the greenhouse," p.571). To add the finishing touches before planting, fences and lumber may be treated or painted, and trellises or support wires put up on walls and fences for climbers.

Ready to plant

Where larger, more mature plants are being used in a design, it may be necessary to plant them while the hardscape is being constructed—at a later stage it may not be possible to maneuver them into place. However, the task of reintegrating any preserved plant material into new designs, and introducing new plants, generally begins once the hardscape is completed and services installed or reconnected.

Before plants are introduced, however, any soil compaction should be remedied, and the soil improved by the addition of well-rotted organic matter (see "Improving soil structure," p.621).

Any protection given to shrubs and hard surfaces can now be removed, and surfaces cleaned using a high-pressure hose. With the potentially dirty tasks complete, loose surfaces can have their final layers applied, with clean gravel or bark chips laid on top. After that, new planting plans (see p.42) can begin to take shape.

Principles of planting

Once the general layout of the yard is in place, the greatest enjoyment comes from selecting plants. The impact plant choice can make on a landscape is extraordinary. Plants give a setting style, charm, character, depth, and warmth—to mention but a few of their qualities. An adjacent street may be enhanced by an overhanging tree, which softens rigid lines and brings seasonal color and texture to an urban landscape. A sheltered courtyard with high surrounding walls may appear like a prison yard, yet the decorative effect of a climber, such as a wisteria, trained over it will transform the space into a welcoming retreat.

The flowing form and mellowing tones of plants bring a calming effect to a landscape. Like curtains or drapes in a house, plants help to muffle harsh noise. It is also increasingly accepted that, allergy sufferers notwithstanding, the presence of plants improves the atmosphere around us, possibly alleviating the effects of pollution, and certainly increasing the oxygen and moisture content of the air.

Ensuring that plants succeed
Successful plant choice can quite literally make a garden; it might even be said that until plants and flowers are established and growing well, a garden does not really exist. The garden's therapeutic powers, which can soothe the mind and alleviate tension, derive mainly from its thriving plants, and perhaps also from the presence of water and the use of harmonious building materials. The element of quiet combined with charm and style can turn a small backyard into a sanctuary. Even the most elementary of plantings, such as a well-kept lawn that has replaced a hard surface within a built environment, will bring life, color, and softness to an otherwise harsh and alien site.

Selecting plants for success
The wealth of different plants available can be bewildering, but the choice will never be as limitless as it may seem. Within the various categories of trees, shrubs, perennials, and so on, many plants can be dismissed immediately as inappropriate on numerous grounds: for example, incompatible soil type, climate, size, or growth rate. Once the most suitable plants have been identified, personal preference for certain colors and shapes will narrow and refine the choice still further.

The manner and frequency of planned use will help dictate the range of plants, too: for example, an area that is used only in summer will be planted to perform best in that season. Plantings around a house and along a driveway will also place greater demands on the choice of plant material, because year-round interest of some description will be expected. A carefully selected combination of plants that will provide a display of flowers in each season is needed. Alternatively, group plants together that combine other attributes— mix evergreens with some fruiting trees or shrubs, add plants with attractive stems or bark, and include bulbs and annuals to inject some welcome color and interest at dull times of the year.

Defining a style of planting
In every yard there are so many variables that each one is unique. So to talk about a particular or specific planting style may appear to impose false categories and divisions. However, there are two extremes between which all plantings fall. These are the formal and informal styles. Deciding on the degree of formality or informality required will greatly assist the initial selection of plants and the diversity of plant material used. A very formal garden, for example, may have an extremely restricted palette of plants compared to a more informal arrangement.

Formal planting

Great strength and order can be given to a landscape by using only a small selection of plants but in quantity. The planting, however, does not necessarily need to be arranged in an angular and regimented fashion, or within precisely designated areas. Some formality can be achieved using sweeps of single plants in broad blocks, creating tranquility in

Contrasting planting styles
The style of planting within a yard or an area of it can be broadly categorized as either formal or informal. Some plants lend themselves more to one style than the other. The labor involved in maintaining the formal garden (far right) is evident, but an informal planting, such as this border (right), does not necessarily involve less work: a great deal of skill and care is needed to maintain a balance between the needs and vigor of different plants when growing in close proximity.

"Editing" nature
Careful plant choices, to suit the surroundings and compete successfully with less desirable plants, produce a pleasingly naturalistic woodland scene.

uniformity. Even relatively informal plants grown *en masse* can assume an orderly role—an expanse of ornamental grasses or bamboos planted to create a solid platform of texture can impose order and structure, for example.

The strongly architectural quality of the conventional formal garden conveys a powerful image—one of careful symmetry and balance, precision, and accuracy. Plants may be interpreted as strong structural elements, more closely aligned to walls and other built elements. The sheared, trimmed, and pruned formal landscape owes as much of its visual impact to the selection of appropriate plants as it does to their subsequent control and maintenance. Formal plantings will impact a view, summer or winter. In winter—with all else laid bare—their angular simplicity in clear bright sunshine can be most appealing. See also TOPIARY, p.108.

Formality often requires restraint, which can pose a dilemma for those who would like to design with the widest possible variety of plants. Faced with a spacious driveway approach flanked by mown lawns, for example, some gardeners may find it hard to resist the temptation to choose 20 different species of trees. Yet far greater formal impact would be achieved by repeating a single species, in regular blocks or in a continuous double line, to form a well-designed avenue.

Softening the effect
Strongly formal plantings and landscape plans can be varied in a number of ways, all with equal effect. Extreme forms of topiary,

knot gardens, and parterres can be planted with or alongside free-flowing informal mixtures of plants to create a marked contrast of styles. This combination changes with the seasons and will reduce the stark impact of the formal plantings. A landscape clearly divided into distinct units can also be planted with an area of marked formality to contrast with an adjacent, informal one.

The juxtaposition of styles presents a lively and stimulating set of surprises at each turn of house corner, hedge, or shrub. Formality can also blend with informality when formal features are allowed to relax toward the informal. A finely clipped hedge of yew (*Taxus baccata*) can be planted in a serpentine line and pruned to simulate clouds; flowering shrubs planted at regular intervals along the whole length of a broad border, will grow to form large mounds of equally spaced and sized yet irregularly shaped forms. Thus, a degree of formality underpins a broadly informal planting arrangement.

Informal planting

A planting that appears informal may in fact comprise a wealth of different plants: trees, shrubs, herbaceous perennials, and annuals, their diversity, richness, and profusion all skillfully combined to bring the color, texture, shape, and form of unrelated plants together with dramatic effect.

As with a formal style, there are as many—if not more—variations on the theme of informality.

An artificial environment
Select plants suitable for the growing conditions: a roof may not be a natural planting site, but these hardy, sun-loving, wind-resistant plants are thriving here.

A cottage-style garden of organized chaos, where garden plants are combined in a seemingly haphazard concoction, can soon become truly chaotic—an overgrown wilderness in which many plants will not survive the inherent crowding and competition. To preserve and maintain the plant content of such a garden requires expertise, and considerable time spent controlling the different plants and keeping their growth in check.

This informality of planting may be taken a few stages further by choosing a combination of plants that will grow together in harmony, whose strengths are well matched, and whose climate and soil requirements are met. Herbaceous plants that require little or no support provide a good example. Cultivated garden plants can be combined to create the impression of a wild meadow, or native species can be planted to create a "natural" meadow (see MEADOW GARDENING,

p.401). In fact, an entire habitat can be made up of plants that would naturally occur in the locality. Native plants will also attract wildlife to your garden by providing a welcome source of food and nesting sites.

For many people this approach may be taking informal gardening too far, but by studying the local environment and taking note of which plants thrive in it, the planting plan can be adapted to cultivated garden plants. Planting a light canopy of trees allows sufficient daylight penetration for an understory of shrubs to be grown. Beneath this, shade-tolerant herbaceous plants will thrive after spring-flowering bulbs have faded away. This layered community of plants may appear crowded, yet they will all flourish if the chosen plants are given the appropriate light and conditions at each level of the undergrowth, throughout the growing season.

How to make planting plans

To map out plant groups, selections, and numbers accurately, first draw a plan to scale, using graph paper if this is helpful. A box drawn to represent 1sq yd (1sq m) and another to represent 4sq yd (4sq m) is a useful guide to the area covered by a clump of herbaceous plants and the area covered by a shrub or small tree, respectively. Always use a scale that is large enough to represent the plants clearly. This may, in fact, require two scales of plans: a large-scale plan to show the general garden area (see pp.36–37) and a smaller one to detail the composition of a border. The simpler the plan, the better, both for reading by others and for subsequent alterations. Numbers, symbols, or code initials can be used to indicate individual plants, but where space permits, enter the full plant names for clear and instant identification.

Making the most of plants

The majority of gardens benefit from areas of calm, so the temptation to cram them with plants should be resisted. Another common planning mistake is to select as many different plants as possible: using a wide range can weaken the design, whereas the repetition of a few key plants ties the whole plan together.

On the planting plan, shade in any areas where evergreens are to be planted, and work out how much cover will remain during winter. Also indicate where plants with colored foliage or strong, bright flowers are to be sited in a border. This helps to assess the proportions of each color, allowing you to maintain an even distribution, and also to calculate the number of green-leaved plants to balance the display.

Finalizing the plan

After indicating which plants are to be retained, enter key specimens onto the plan. These are plants that frame a view, end a view, give height or weight, and in essence anchor the whole planting plan. In the early stages such plants need not be specified; an idea of the general height and spread of the plant is all that is necessary. Make a list of suitable plants and have photographs collected from books, catalogs, and magazines on hand—but aim to be flexible and do not fixate too rigidly on a particular plant. A meticulously planned layout can lead to an overdesigned, predictable garden where heights, colors, and spacings are too accurately

Contrasting border styles

Two borders of similar proportions and background, consisting largely of herbaceous plants in a similarly tiered array of ascending heights, nevertheless look strikingly different thanks to the choice of plant material. The mixed flower border above faces onto a mown lawn, with a strip of bricks along the border edge for easy mowing, where plants spill over; the border below, planted thickly with grasses, is complemented by an informal gravel path.

determined. A few surprises should be "planned" to add spontaneity and liveliness with height occurring at close quarters or a bold color introduced as a sharp contrast.

Grouping and planting distances

Groupings of odd numbers of plants—generally threes, fives, or sevens—create satisfactory blocks and can be used to create winding, shallow drifts. Choosing plants that flower at different times in the drifts will also bring interest to the garden over a long period. Alternatively, a more random planting, repeating single varieties in many small groups of no fewer than three plants, will produce a lighter, checkerboard effect.

Unlike the interior design of a room, a planting that initially makes little impact can create a truly spectacular effect in just a few years. When designing and planning a garden, take account of time scale. You will need to decide if you wish to thin out the planting

in the short or long term, and whether temporary fillers are to be inserted between permanent plantings to give a little fullness to an otherwise thinly planted area.

A garden planted with semimature plants for an instant effect of fullness and scale can, by its very nature, present problems several years later, when those same plants are outgrowing their positions in the garden. If more space is required, valuable plant material may then need to be sacrificed to save the most treasured specimens.

One solution is to purchase a mixture of a few large but costly specimens, which will give scale, along with quite a few smaller, less expensive plants. A younger plant will frequently grow more quickly and eventually overtake one that was larger and more mature when originally planted, so you need to exercise a little patience.

To calculate planting distances, you need to know the mature spread of the plant or plants.

Close spacing
The exceptions to calculating planting distance based on eventual spread are: when using hedging and edging plants; where a dense effect is needed; and when planting out bedding, since bedding plants have a short life and will tolerate cramped conditions.

Consult labels, study reference books, or seek advice from nursery staff to obtain accurate information. The last source may well be the most reliable, especially if the nursery is local, because plant performance varies between different regions. Equally valuable is advice on the time plants take to reach maturity, because this will help

you to decide whether to include either annual or longer-term perennial "filler" plants.

The distance required between two very similar plants is equal to the spread of one of them. To help calculate the space needed between two different plants, simply add their mature spreads together and divide the number by two.

If possible set out all your plants on the ground, *in situ*, before planting according to the plan. Minor adjustments may be necessary to accommodate differing sizes of specimens and the ground plan may change if you come across buried pipes, for example, or a large boulder that must be concealed by evergreens. Once the plants have been placed satisfactorily, they should be carefully planted out and mulched with a weed-suppressing, moisture-retentive organic medium (see SOILS AND FERTILIZERS, "Organic mulches," p.626). Always ensure that the plants are nurtured carefully during their first all-important year, while they are becoming fully established.

Size and scale
In a small area (as at right), be careful not to overplant: start with the heights and spreads your plants are likely to achieve when mature, then map out a pattern of overlapping disks that fill, but will not crowd, the available space. With experience, you can estimate how plants will perform in your garden in terms of vigor and size, and, space permitting, begin to sketch in bolder groupings or drifts of plants, as shown in the section of a classic English border (below). To create an annual border requires a slightly different technique: areas are mapped out for sowing, either directly onto the soil (see also p.215) or using a preliminary plan.

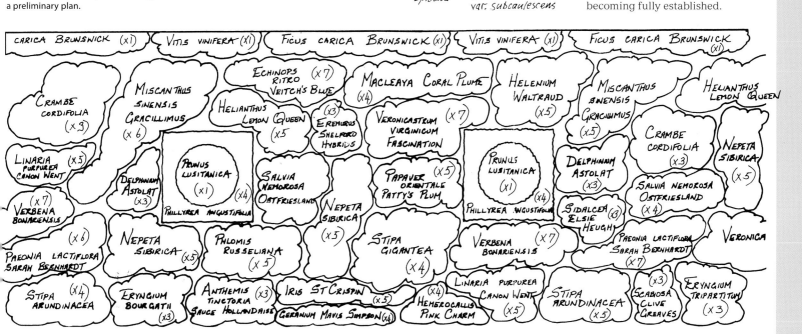

Planting for texture, structure, and color

When selecting plants, their flowers, fruits, or fall colors are often the main consideration, although they may last for just a few weeks of the year. In contrast, shape, form, and eventual size influence a landscape throughout the year and are equally or even more important. To create an enduring planting design, select a small number of plants with attractive forms for year-round interest, and choose others that offer seasonal color at different times. Plants are best seen first-hand, and visiting gardens is an ideal way to appreciate their more subtle qualities.

Architectural plants

Plants with bold foliage or a strong form are described as architectural or accent plants. These make ideal garden specimens, creating impact when used on their own as focal points, or to contrast with their neighbors. The toothed leaves of *Melianthus major* or the plumelike flowerheads of *Miscanthus sinensis* are good examples of structural plants; while upright shrubs, such as *Aralia elata,* and the tiered branches of *Cornus controversa* have excellent architectural appeal.

Altering outlooks

Planting can be used to highlight landscape features or disguise eyesores. For example, an ugly, boxy building will retain its unsightly silhouette if a clinging creeper, such as *Parthenocissus,* is grown over it, but if a more interesting climber, such as wisteria, is used, then the outline will be masked beneath twisted branches and pendulous flowers.

Similarly, a visual barrier, such as a retaining wall that marks a level change, can be lost if a mound-forming or tiered plant is grown on the lower level. *Viburnum plicatum* or *Euonymus alatus* would both work well in this situation.

An area of lawn can be enhanced by a specimen tree. When selecting one, the lawn's size and proximity to the house are important factors to consider, as are soil type and local climate. A specimen tree also needs to look right in its setting. One with a rounded canopy will sit well on a lawn, whereas a tall spire can resemble a rocket on a launch pad in such an open area.

Natural strength

Soothing greens and an attractive structure can help to create a restful scene. A classic example of this is a fern garden, where beautiful shapes and forms provide interest without the distraction of bright colors (see FERNS, p.203).

Grasses add a graceful, refined structure, and the sound and movement of their rustling leaves makes them indispensable. Even in winter their skeletal forms play an important role in an otherwise bleak landscape. Planted alongside broad-leaved *Macleaya cordata,* the elegant grasses *Stipa gigantea* and *Helictotrichon sempervirens* are very eye-catching.

A backdrop of large evergreens will provide color and form when all deciduous plants have been left bare in winter. Not only do they present foliage interest and strong shapes throughout the year, but they also protect wildlife in bad weather, and can be used to create permanent screens and privacy.

Evergreens that grow into naturally neat shapes resemble formal topiary, giving the garden a sculptural appearance without the need for training and trimming. Globes of many dwarf conifers make excellent accent plants along the front of a border, while *Choisya ternata* and *Viburnum dentatum* BLUE MUFFIN both grow into large orbs of tight foliage.

Pruning into shapes

A plant's natural structure can be enhanced by pruning. When some willows (*Salix*) and dogwoods (*Cornus*) are pruned to the ground, or coppiced, every two years, they produce a flush of colorful, straight stems. Lindens (*Tilia*) and sycamores (*Platanus*) may be pollarded: if the branches are pruned back to the same point every year or two, they produce swollen "fists" at the pruning points. Both pruning methods create strong architectural forms that can greatly enhance a garden design. (See "Coppicing and pollarding shrubs," p.104.)

Enduring forms
Trees create permanent structure in a garden setting. Look for those with interesting leaf shapes, such as mountain ash (*Sorbus*), with its divided foliage, and the deeply lobed leaves of Japanese maples (*Acer palmatum*). Both trees have excellent fall color and beautiful architectural outlines in winter and early spring.

Plants for focal points
The striking, spiky foliage of this variegated yucca is further accentuated by placing it in a tall, rounded terra-cotta urn.

Spot color (far left)
Dark red *Knautia macedonica* is thrown into sharp focus when grown against the pale hues of the foxgloves and fennel.

Cool greens (above, center)
Every shade of green in the garden plays a role in calming and harmonizing the design.

Peeling bark (above)
The paperbark maple, *Acer griseum*, has wonderful copper-colored, peeling bark, which stands out in a winter landscape.

Traditional palette (left)
This classic combination of white, pink, and blue is perfect for this romantic garden.

Using color

When using color in the garden, personal taste can be allowed to reign almost unhindered. Yet a totally unlimited palette of colors, where every hue and tone are set against a contrasting shade, may produce an overwhelming medley that would challenge even the greatest champion of color as a tool of garden design. Restraint should be used to limit the range and quantity of color. For example, a backdrop of muted greens will calm a busy foreground of mixed colors and allow the vivid shades to shine.

Color and distance

Bright, light colors such as lemon yellows and whites are better reflectors of sunlight than darker hues, which from a distance may be lost or appear muted. Such light colors used in the foreground will visually jump forward from their positions. These shades introduced at a distance will also appear closer, foreshortening the perceived length of a garden, usually detrimentally.

Traditionally, colors with depth, such as blues, mauves, purples, and silvers, are used to create a sense of distance at the farther reaches of a garden, with paler shades of yellow, white, cream,

and pink occupying the foreground. Reds, oranges, and deep yellows are best planted in the middle of a bed; at a distance they are lost, while close up they dominate the scene.

The influence of light

Location is an important factor to consider when choosing plant color schemes. In strong, direct sunlight, the more powerful yellows, oranges, and reds become almost luminous, and can produce a vibrant picture. If, however, you wish to cool down a seating area in a hot, sunny corner, silver and gray foliage and blue flowers will create a more restful setting.

A mix of pastel colors, such as soft blue, pink, creamy yellow, and silver, will create a beautiful composition in low light conditions. A deck or patio used during the evenings for entertaining, and planted with white flowers and pale or white-variegated foliage, will, in minimal light, reflect back atmospheric ghostly hues. Equally effective would be a dull courtyard enlivened by bright shades.

Combining colors

One of the most challenging areas of good garden design is creating effective color combinations. Blue

and white make elegant partners, giving a cool, clean look that is hard to rival, although for sheer purity green and white are unbeatable, especially when on the same flower, such as a snowdrop (*Galanthus*) or *Dicentra spectabilis* 'Alba'.

These subtle and refined planting combinations will be heightened if other schemes display a less restricted palette. Orange and purple, two dominant colors of equal strength, are shockingly brilliant when used together— bright orange calendulas set against the leaden purple foliage of ornamental cabbages makes for an eye-catching arrangement. Blue and yellow also create a sharp contrast; the bold intensity of each introduces a lively juxtaposition of colors. When an acid yellow tulip or *Fritillaria imperialis* 'Maxima Lutea' is mixed with the clear blue of forget-me-nots (*Myosotis*) or *Ceanothus*, the interplay between them can be truly electric.

Adding texture

Many plants exhibit rich foliage texture, and interesting effects can be achieved when they are planted in broad swaths. A sweep of lavender (*Lavandula*) or rosemary (*Rosmarinus*), clipped annually,

will grow into soft mounds of dense aromatic growth, equal in beauty to any herbaceous flower border.

Even plants of little decorative interest individually can be useful in groups. The shrubby honeysuckle, *Lonicera nitida*, and many of the taller bamboos provide masses of textural variations, and make excellent hedging and screening (see BAMBOOS, pp.120–121).

A play of different textures creates subtle interest, even with a single plant. A yew (*Taxus*), for example, clipped neatly below but allowed to spread out at the top to form long, loose stems, provides a wonderful textural contrast. A layered look can be achieved with mixed plantings; for example, the feathery fronds of ostrich fern (*Matteuccia struthiopteris*) set off by the vast flat leaves of *Gunnera manicata*, in turn backed by white-stemmed birch (*Betula*).

Tree stems have tactile qualities that should not be overlooked. Old European chestnuts (*Castanea sativa*) develop deep, furrowed bark that contrasts well with smooth, horizontal shapes, while shrubs such as *Hydrangea quercifolia*, *Physocarpus opulifolius*, and *Euonymus alatus* also develop eye-catching bark over time.

Planting for seasonal and year-round interest

The art of planting the well-planned garden is for each season to bring new richness and interest. All too often, from late spring to midsummer, a garden builds up week after week to a peak, but then deteriorates rapidly into a flowerless wasteland in fall and winter. With more than half the year remaining and some late mild weather still to come, it is important to plan for these often-forgotten months.

A landscape should contain a well-chosen collection of plants to carry interest throughout these seasons of reduced light and growth. A permanent framework of plantings, formed by trees, shrubs, and hedges, will create the basic skeleton onto which a series of interwoven layers—climbers, herbaceous plants, bedding plants, and bulbs—can be used to provide beauty and interest throughout each season.

Spring

Late winter and early spring are not only a time for flowers but also a season for sweet scents. Shrubs, such as Christmas box (*Sarcococca confusa*), winter honeysuckle (*Lonicera x purpusii*), wintersweet (*Chimonanthus praecox*), and the many beautiful species of *Daphne* fill the air with their powerful perfumes. Bulbs offer early color, when aconites (*Eranthis hyemalis*) and snowdrops (*Galanthus*) compete to be the first to flower, followed by crocuses, daffodils, and tulips. The bulbs are joined by the earliest-flowering perennials, such as hellebores, and later, as the bulbs die down, other herbaceous plants fill in the gaps.

Summer

Early summer heralds an explosion of color from the herbaceous perennials, with every shade, shape, and form working together to create a luxuriance unrivaled throughout the rest of the year. Peonies, delphiniums, campanulas, and lupines give a spectacular display, while roses perform alongside deutzias, mallows (*Lavatera*), and mock orange in the shrub border. As summer peaks, large-flowered clematis can be used to scramble over spring-flowering shrubs, such as forsythia. Later on, annuals like *Nicotiana* and *Cosmos* fill gaps between shrubs; tender or marginally hardy perennials, such as penstemons and diascias, brighten bed or border color schemes.

Fall

The well-maintained garden, where regular deadheading and careful interplanting have been carried out, can often reach a peak in this season. As well as the spillover of summer blooms, late-flowering perennials like Japanese anemones, crocosmias, and New York asters (*Aster novi-belgii*) perform throughout the fall. As the light

Seasonal sunlight
Not only do landscape plantings ebb and flow with the seasons, but sunlight can also be used throughout the year to highlight evolving shapes and forms. Here, the weak winter sun casts long shadows that stretch over a colorful carpet of *Cyclamen coum*, the flowers of which open as light filters through the leafless trees.

pales, clusters of dark pink blooms open on *Clerodendrum bungei*, scenting the cool air with its rich sweet fragrance.

Foliage tints begin to fire up in fall, with trees such as maples and *Parrotia persica* slowly turning every shade of yellow, orange, purple, and red. The large leaves

of *Vitis coignetiae* also provide spectacular color before they fall. Berries and fruits contribute to the richness of autumnal hues, with viburnums, crabapples, and many others decorating the garden with their jeweled displays. Flowering bulbs and corms, such as cyclamen and colchicums, contribute to the fall display, too.

Winter

The depths of winter are the most testing times in the landscape, when color and interest are most difficult to achieve. It is now that permanent structures take center stage. The stems of deciduous shrubs and trees, such as silver birch (*Betula*) and colorful dogwoods (*Cornus*), stand out vibrantly in the weak winter sunlight.

The texture, form, and shape of evergreens furnish the winter scene when all else is bare. Pines, spruces, firs, junipers, cedars, cypresses, and arborvitaes give substance to otherwise "empty" borders. Meanwhile, some evergreen shrubs, such as *Skimmia japonica* and *Viburnum tinus*, put on displays of beadlike flower buds. These are accompanied by the highly scented flowers of *Viburnum x bodnantense*, which will break into bloom at the first hint of milder weather.

Extended interest
Crocosmia 'Lucifer' is invaluable for its long-lasting interest. In spring, swordlike, architectural leaves emerge, followed in late summer by sprays of scarlet flowers (right). The seed heads look striking, too, when dusted with frost (above).

Early to mid-spring

Among the first flowers to bloom in early spring are the bulbs. Here, bold swaths of daffodils have been planted to brighten up the borders with their nodding heads of golden-yellow flowers and straplike foliage. These are accompanied by spikes of spurge (*Euphorbia*) and emerging perennials, the foliage of which is now pushing its way through the soil.

Late spring

As spring progresses and light levels increase, borders rapidly fill out with lush foliage and early flowers, which help to camouflage the fading blooms and leaves of early bulbs. Here, blue geraniums and wavy-edged, rounded-leaved lady's mantle (*Alchemilla mollis*) dominate in the foreground, while similarly tinted flowers thrive toward the end of the garden.

High summer

A profusion of flowers, including the blue geraniums that are still in bloom, heralds the height of summer. Pastel blues, soft yellows, and creamy whites create a cool border that takes the heat out of the sun. These colors also give the illusion of extended perspective, making the border look longer and leading the eye to the seating area at the far end.

Summer into fall

The pale pastels have given way to splashes of fiery red designed to mirror tree and shrub foliage that will soon be taking on vibrant fall hues. This border design shows how planting can be used to change the color and mood, and alter perspectives, in the garden as the seasons progress, building up to a crescendo as summer turns to fall.

Living roofs and walls

Roof gardens have long been popular with urban gardeners, but recently more innovative approaches to green structures and surfaces have been promoted on a wider scale. The concept of growing plants directly on pitched roofs or solid external walls is becoming increasingly widespread—especially on buildings in crowded cities where the environmental impact is particularly beneficial. Green roofs and walls absorb rainwater, insulate buildings, reduce noise levels, and provide all the benefits associated with plant growth, such as improving air quality and increasing biodiversity by creating wildlife habitats.

What is a green roof?

Living or green roofs are quite simply roofs on which vegetation is growing. Sometimes lichens, mosses, grasses, or seed-blown wildflowers naturally colonize the roofs of houses, garages, sheds, and outbuildings, but in recent years green roofs have been developed artificially for aesthetic, ecological, and environmental reasons, particularly in urban areas.

Two types of green roof, which differ in their basic concepts, are generally recognized. Intensive green roofs—often known simply as roof gardens—are designed and constructed on flat roofs that have been strengthened to accommodate a range of traditional garden plants—from alpines to shrubs and small trees. Plants are generally grown in containers, but may also be planted in beds filled with soil or a soil mix. Roof gardens are often constructed on office buildings, hospitals, or schools. See also BALCONIES AND ROOF GARDENS, pp.316–317.

Extensive roof gardens usually require less maintenance. They are constructed using a base of sod or thin layers of soil or soil mix in which a range of plants will thrive—such as low-growing sedums, thyme, thrift, and wildflowers. Extensive green roofs are easier for gardeners to develop on the flat or gently sloping roofs of houses or outbuildings, such as garages and sheds, but are also frequently seen on the roofs of commercial buildings, as well as on schools and stores.

Reaping the benefits

Green roofs have a positive impact on the environment in more ways than one. Plants have antipollutant qualities: they filter carbon dioxide, acid rain, and heavy metals from the atmosphere, improving air quality in urban and industrial areas, and decreasing the impact of noise pollution. In addition, the vegetation on a green roof retains a high percentage of rainwater runoff that would otherwise be lost through the drainage system. A green roof also provides a degree of insulation, reducing heat loss during winter and reflecting heat away in summer, which may reduce the cost of heating and cooling the building. In addition, it is thought that the lifespan of some roofs may be extended because the soil and vegetation protect the roof from sunlight, ultraviolet radiation, and temperature fluctuations.

A further benefit, particularly in towns and cities, is to increase the biodiversity of the area. Green roofs provide many insects with breeding grounds, especially if there are opportunities to glean nectar and pollen from plants nearby, and also create new nesting sites—as well as a source of food—for birds.

Attracting pollinators
The different varieties of sedums on this living roof provide a splash of color, and their flowers attract bees, butterflies, flower flies, and other insects into the garden.

Constructing and maintaining a living roof

The installation of a green roof on a house or on other buildings usually requires a building permit and is often best undertaken by a qualified contractor.

It is important to make sure the existing roof and the building are both strong enough to bear the weight of the materials used to construct the green roof before work begins on development. For sheds or similar buildings with traditional roofs it may be necessary to provide extra

Weather protection
A green or living roof helps to retain rainwater that would otherwise be lost, and provides some protection to the structure below. Here, wildflowers grow on a converted shipping container.

Grass above, grass below
Using grass to cover roofs is an idea that has been in use for hundreds of years and is now making a resurgence. A permit is usually required before installing a green roof.

PLANTS FOR LIVING STRUCTURES AND SURFACES

Armeria maritima

Festuca glauca

Thymus vulgaris

Acaena saccaticupula
'Blue Haze'

Stachys byzantina

Delosperma nubigenum

Sempervivum
'Mrs. Giuseppi'

Artemisia schmidtiana
'Nana'

Sedum spathulifolium
'Cape Blanco'

Dianthus deltoides

Useful growing areas
Vertical areas such as fences and walls can be utilized for cultivating herbs or ther plants. Here, a variety of herbs are grown in planting pockets attached to a sturdy fence.

support because of the additional weight of the layers required for drainage and planting.

The initial layer should be a waterproof membrane. This first layer is then covered by a root-barrier membrane, and topped by a drainage membrane before the area is covered to the required depth with the growing medium.

The depth of the growing medium or substrate layer will depend on the type of plants to be grown. *Sedum* and *Sempervivum* species or turf and wildflowers are frequently used because they grow well in substrate depths of only 1½–2¼in (4–6cm), while larger perennials like *Alyssum*, *Dianthus*, and *Thymus* require a layer up to 4in (10cm) deep.

A wide range of different plants that may be used successfully on green roofs are raised commercially

as plug plants. Alternatively, for large-scale designs, plants may be grown on "vegetation mats," and laid directly onto the growing medium being used.

Green roof plants will require a degree of maintenance once they are established so it is important to ensure there is easy access to the roof. Some weeding can be necessary and occasional feeding may be needed as well as watering in drought conditions—although many of the plants commonly used, like sedums, are drought tolerant.

Vertical gardening

Also referred to as green or living walls, the concept of vertical gardening has largely developed during the last 25 years. The

benefits provided to the environment are similar to those attributed to living roofs. The idea is that the vertical wall spaces of houses, garages, and other buildings can be used to grow and display ornamental plants as well as for the cultivation of herbs and salad crops. While it is particularly useful for those with small or no gardens, it also has a wide appeal to gardeners generally.

Before making a green wall, it is important to ensure that the surface is sufficiently sturdy to support the vertical framework on which the plants will be grown—whether brick, concrete, or wood. It may sometimes be necessary to protect the surface with a waterproofing product.

The young plants that will form the wall are planted in a free-draining soil mix in pockets or pouches made of propagation felt, or similar material, which are attached to the vertical framework. This is then attached to the wall or fence but may also be developed as a freestanding structure to use elsewhere in a garden. If practical, it is preferable to install a drip-irrigation or similar automatic watering system so that all the plants are watered evenly.

A considerable range of vertical planters using slightly different techniques is now available, and some include automatic irrigation systems. In large designs the plants are grown hydroponically, without

soil in an inert medium, receiving their water and nutrients in a diluted solution.

Good choices for planting along green walls include bedding plants—*Impatiens*, *Calibrachoa*, petunias, and geraniums, as well as a variety of herbs and salad crops, such as lettuce.

PLANTS FOR LIVING ROOFS

1½–2¼in (4–6cm) substrate

Acaena caesiiglauca, A. microphylla
Chiastophyllum oppositifolium
Rosularia aizoon
Saxifraga callosa, S. cotyledon,
  S. paniculata
Sedum acre, S. acre 'Aureum',
  S. album, S. cauticola,
  S. 'Ruby Glow'
Sempervivum arachnoideum,
  S. tectorum

2¼–4½in (6–12cm) substrate

Alyssum saxatilis
Antennaria dioica and cultivars
Armeria maritima
Aubrieta
Dianthus deltoides
Prunella vulgaris

4–6in (10–15cm) substrate

Achillea chrysocoma
Ajuga reptans
Alchemilla alpina
Bergenia purpurascens
Stachys byzantina

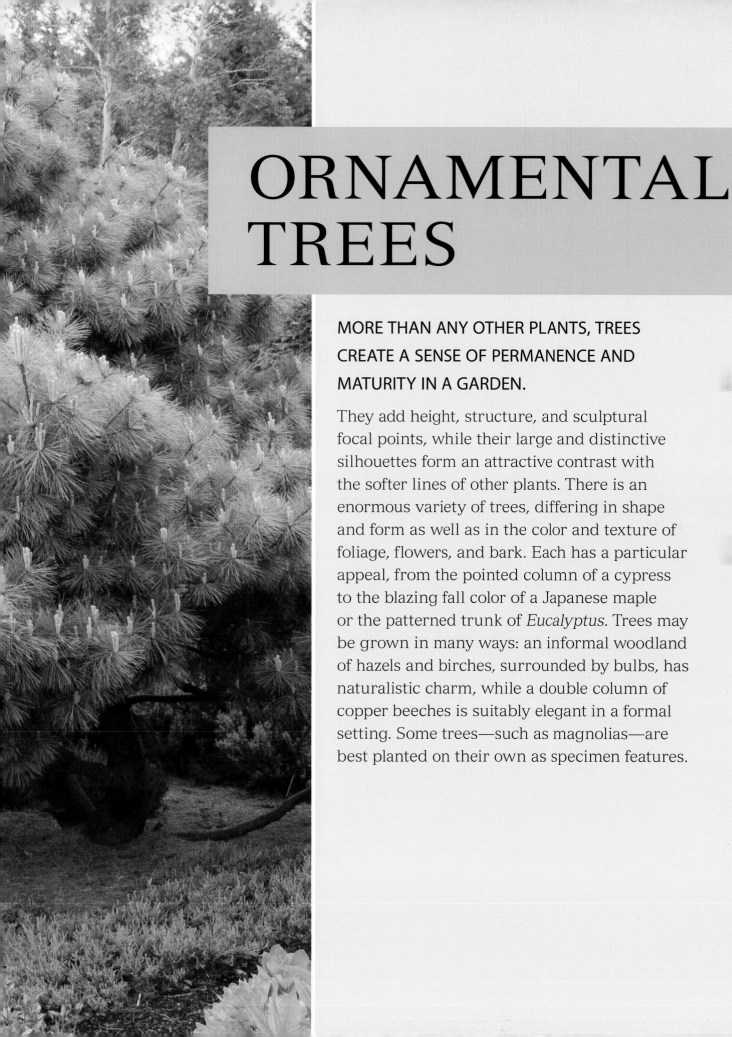

ORNAMENTAL TREES

MORE THAN ANY OTHER PLANTS, TREES CREATE A SENSE OF PERMANENCE AND MATURITY IN A GARDEN.

They add height, structure, and sculptural focal points, while their large and distinctive silhouettes form an attractive contrast with the softer lines of other plants. There is an enormous variety of trees, differing in shape and form as well as in the color and texture of foliage, flowers, and bark. Each has a particular appeal, from the pointed column of a cypress to the blazing fall color of a Japanese maple or the patterned trunk of *Eucalyptus*. Trees may be grown in many ways: an informal woodland of hazels and birches, surrounded by bulbs, has naturalistic charm, while a double column of copper beeches is suitably elegant in a formal setting. Some trees—such as magnolias—are best planted on their own as specimen features.

Trees for the garden

Ornamental trees are grown for the beauty of their flowers, foliage, bark, or decorative fruit, with several that exhibit more than one quality, rather than for their edible produce or wood. Many fruiting trees, however, are graced by beautiful flowers, and a few ornamental trees, such as crabapples (*Malus*), bear rich crops of fruits for preserving. The distinction between trees and shrubs is similarly blurred; the former usually, but not always, with a single trunk and the latter, for example, lilacs (*Syringa*), multistemmed, although sometimes reaching treelike proportions.

Double color Crabapples bear colorful flowers and fruit.

Choosing trees

Trees are generally the largest and longest-lived garden plants, and selecting and siting them are major design decisions. The fewer trees a garden can accommodate, the more important careful choice and siting become; in a one-tree landscape these points are crucial to the success of the design. The general appearance and special features of a tree obviously matter, but its suitability for a garden's soil, climate, and exposure, and its ultimate height, spread, and growth rate, are equally important. Once a tree is chosen, the design process continues, by deciding where to plant it (see "Choosing a planting site," p.63). Garden centers stock a limited range of the most popular ornamental trees throughout the year; specialty nurseries, some with a mail-order service, offer a wider choice, although the trees are generally only available bare-root in fall and winter.

Heights range from about 3ft (1m) for some dwarf conifers to the massive 300ft (90m) of a redwood (*Sequoia*). Growth rates vary from 1in (2.5cm) or less a year for dwarf conifers to 3ft (1m) or more for some poplars (*Populus*). A young tree in a garden center gives little indication of its potential size and some species, particularly conifers, include both miniature and very large cultivars. Select cultivars with care and, if you are offered substitutes, make sure that they will be equally appropriate for your requirements.

Trees as design elements

Trees create a strong visual impact in the same way as do hard landscaping features. They also help to form the permanent framework of a garden, around which the more temporary elements may come and go.

Trees may be used as living sculptures (see "Specimen trees," p.55): a simple, contrasting setting is most likely to enhance a tree used in this way. A tree with pale or variegated foliage looks very striking seen against a neat hedge of dark green yew (*Taxus baccata*), for example, while the bold winter tracery of bare branches stands out particularly well when viewed in front of a white-painted wall.

Used structurally, trees can also define or enclose space. A stately row or an informal clump of trees can mark the boundary of a property, separate one part of the garden from another, or emphasize a path. A pair of trees might act as a verdant frame for a distant view or create an attractive living arch through which the garden is entered.

Shape and form

The shape and form of a tree are as important as its size—in setting the mood and style as well as in practical considerations of space. Some trees, such as many ornamental cherries (*Prunus*), are small and charming, while others, such as cedars (*Cedrus*), are grand and monumental. Most can be formal or informal, according to the setting and treatment. *Rhus typhina* has a striking architectural form, which is ideal for a modern, paved area, while the arching fronds of many palms bring lushness to a courtyard or conservatory. Mountain ash (*Sorbus aucuparia*) and hollies (*Ilex*) are typical English-cottage garden trees; Japanese maples (*Acer palmatum*) and the large *Salix babylonica* var. *pekinensis* 'Tortuosa' are suitable for Asian gardens; native species are ideal for wild gardens.

Trees in the garden
A carefully chosen tree in a border, such as this *Cornus controversa* 'Variegata', can make a strong, bold design statement. When combined with contrasting forms and colors, it provides a structure around which to build.

Narrow, upright trees, such as *Malus tschonoskii*, are suitable for small gardens but have a formal, almost artificial appearance. Round-headed or wide-spreading trees seem more informal but cast much more shade and rain shadow, making underplanting difficult, while those with an irregular, open-branch framework have a natural-looking appeal. Neat cone- or pyramid-shaped trees have a solid sculptural effect, while weeping trees have a softer silhouette.

Consider how long the tree takes to develop its characteristic shape—in some cases, it can be decades. *Prunus* 'Kanzan', for example, has a stiff growth habit when young, with awkwardly angled branches; yet after ten years its branches begin to arch, and by 30 years the tree has a graceful, rounded crown.

Where space allows, combining contrasting tree shapes can create a dynamic effect, but planting many differently shaped trees may simply appear disjointed and uncoordinated.

Specimen trees

A specimen tree is grown on its own to allow it to develop and display its full natural beauty without the physical or aesthetic competition from any neighboring trees. Depending on the climate, Chinese dogwood (*Cornus kousa* var. *chinensis*), weeping willow (*Salix* x *sepulcralis* var. *chrysocoma*), various ornamental cherries (*Prunus*), and palms, such as *Howea* and *Phoenix*, are popular specimen trees. A specimen tree can be effective as a focal point in all types of surroundings, although you should select a tree that is the right size for its setting—tiny specimen trees look lost in large gardens and outsized ones can appear overbearing in confined spaces. Specimen trees, particularly in formal gardens, are traditionally placed in the center of a lawn. Siting a specimen tree to one side, however, can add a sense of liveliness and informality to a landscape, as well as allowing a view in the garden. Other options include planting a specimen tree next to a gate or back yard entrance, or at the bottom or top of a flight of stairs, in order to mark the transition from one space or level in the yard to another.

Planting in a swathe of gravel or among groundcover plants, such as English ivy (*Hedera*) or periwinkle (*Vinca*), provides a complementary foil for a specimen tree. In a mixed border, use a tree as the keystone around which to build the color and form of the surrounding groups of plants. A specimen tree may be reflected in a garden pond or offset by a statue or white-painted bench beneath it, so that each element enhances the other.

Grouping trees

If space permits, plant three or more trees of the same species in informal clumps, or combine different species of similar size.

TREE SHAPES

Spreading
Prunus x *yedoensis* (Yoshino cherry)

Weeping
Salix caprea 'Kilmarnock' (Kilmarnock willow)

Pyramidal
Carpinus betulus 'Fastigiata' (Upright common hornbeam)

Conical
Populus x *canadensis* 'Robusta' (Canadian poplar)

Round-headed
Malus 'Magdeburgensis' (Crabapple)

Arching
Archontophoenix alexandrae (King palm)

Columnar
Acer rubrum 'Columnare' (Red maple)

A group of trees also creates a more substantial, curtainlike frame than a single tree for one or both sides of a view.

Clumps of large trees, such as oaks (*Quercus*) or beeches (*Fagus*), make focal points on a very grand scale, as exemplified in the landscapes of the great 18th-century English landscape gardener, Capability Brown. In warmer climates, stands of tall, bare-trunked palms can be equally impressive on their own in grass or gravel, or interplanted with lower-growing or multistemmed species.

On a smaller scale, a modest group of deciduous trees with light foliage, such as birches (*Betula pendula*) or maples (*Acer*), can form the backbone of a miniature woodland. The dappled shade and leafy soil beneath the canopy are perfect for growing daffodils, bluebells (*Hyacinthoides non-scripta*), and primroses (*Primula vulgaris*). Trees in informal groups can be planted more closely than the combined potential spread of their crowns. Relatively tall, narrow, or asymmetrical growth

may result but the effect can be pleasantly informal, with intermingled branches forming an attractive tracery against the sky.

Features of interest

Although trees are most often valued for their architectural qualities, they also provide interest through particular features, such as flowers, foliage, berries, and bark. Site a tree so that its attractive characteristics are shown off to advantage (see also "Successional interest," p.57).

Leaves

For sheer mass and duration of display, leaves are by far the most important feature. Their shape, size, and color offer infinite variation, from the delicate, golden, ferny foliage of *Gleditsia triacanthos* 'Sunburst' to the huge, architectural leaves of palms, such as *Phoenix*. Surface texture affects how light

is reflected, with glossy leaves adding a bright touch. The density of the canopy ranges from opaque to airy, an important factor if considering underplanting around a tree.

Trees with colored or variegated foliage, such as the reddish-purple of *Prunus virginiana* 'Schubert' or the yellow-edged leaves of *Ligustrum lucidum* 'Excelsum Superbum', provide a mass of color that contrasts well with green-leaved trees.

Some leaves, such as those of *Eucalyptus*, are pleasantly aromatic, while others, such as those of an aspen, quiver in the slightest breeze, adding the extra pleasure of sound.

Flowers

Flowers have a fleeting but memorable presence and range from modest to opulent. Fall, winter, and early spring flowers are especially valuable when there may be less interest from other plants in the yard.

Flower color should complement the larger landscape plan. Pale flowers stand out against dark leaves, while dark flowers show up best in a pale setting. By training climbers, such as clematis or roses, up mature trees, you can easily extend the floral display by up to several weeks.

Few trees are scented, and fragrance is best considered a bonus, ranging from the subtle, winter perfume of *Acacia dealbata* to the heady, summer scent of the Japanese big-leaf magnolia (*Magnolia obovata*) and frangipani (*Plumeria rubra* f. *acutifolia*). For flowers and fragrance, a sheltered situation is best.

Fruit, berries, and pods

These can rival or exceed flowers in beauty, ranging from the bright red, strawberrylike fruits of *Arbutus* and the yellow crabapples

Foliage color and texture Here the fall foliage of a deciduous tree is offset by the blue-green mass of a conifer, creating a tableau of color, texture, and shape. The green and silver leaves from the groundcover perennials below add further contrast, although they will die back as the fall progresses.

Color from flowers The spectacular, vivid pink flowers of *Malus* 'Liset' stand out against the purple leaves and dark stems and are a welcome sight in the spring garden.

of *Malus* 'Golden Hornet' to the sculptural seed pods of magnolias. In warm climates, trees like lemons and figs may be laden with eye-catching edible fruit. Certain trees, such as hollies (*Ilex*), need cross-pollination to fruit; others fruit only when mature or when particular climatic conditions are met. Birds find some ornamental berries, such as those of Mountain ash (*Sorbus aucuparia*), tempting and may strip them when barely ripe, but you can choose trees with less appealing berries. Other fruiting trees, such as *Crataegus* x *lavallei* 'Carrierei', ripen late in the season and therefore their fruit persist well into spring. Ask garden center staff for advice.

Bark and branches

Bark can provide color and textural interest, especially in winter when the covering veil of leaves has fallen. Options include the mahogany-red, silky sheen of *Prunus serrula*, the ghostly white bark of *Betula utilis* var. *jacquemontii*, and the exotic-looking *Eucalyptus pauciflora* subsp. *niphophila* with its pythonlike, green, gray, and white bark.

The scarlet willow (*Salix alba* var. *vitellina* 'Britzensis') bears scarlet-orange young branches, brilliant when lit from behind, and the golden willow (*S. alba* var. *vitellina*) has rich yellow shoots. These fast-growing trees are best pruned regularly to produce new shoots because these have the strongest color. Some trees have showy bark only when mature; others color well when young.

Successional interest

Plants that change character and appearance with the seasons give a yard a more lively tempo. With careful choice and planning,

Herald of spring Before the leaves begin to show, the hanging yellow male catkins of *Betula papyrifera*, the paper birch, are displayed against the white beauty of the bark.

orchestrate their display as foliage, flowers, fruits, berries, and pods come and go against a permanent framework of branches and bark. By planting trees that flower successively, such as a Judas tree (*Cercis siliquastrum*) for spring, *Catalpa bignonioides* for summer, *Eucryphia* x *nymansensis* for early fall, and *Prunus subhirtella* 'Autumnalis' for winter, ongoing interest is maintained, with the focal point altering as the seasons change. Some trees provide interest all year round, either from their evergreen foliage, such as holly (*Ilex*) and most conifers, or from their fine or distinctive shapes.

Deciduous trees offer the greatest scope to exploit seasonal changes, especially in spring, when many ornamental cherries (*Prunus*) are covered with beautiful blossoms, and in fall, when many maples (*Acer*) have brilliantly colored foliage. Evergreen trees, on the other hand, provide a useful sense of continuity rather than change. Selecting and planting a mixture of deciduous and evergreen trees provides lasting interest in the landscape that changes with the seasons to create a dynamic rather than a static effect.

Spring and summer

In spring, emerging leaves and flower buds bring fresh life to the bare branches of deciduous trees. Some—such as the silver-leaved *Sorbus aria* 'Lutescens'—have particularly fine young foliage. As the reawakening trees come fully into leaf, they take on their characteristic outlines while their developing canopies provide striking blocks of color and texture, as well as shade.

In late spring and summer, flowers, ranging in color and form from the trailing, yellow chains of *Laburnum* to the upright cream or reddish-pink candles of horse chestnuts (*Aesculus*), add extra color and interest to lighten the dense effect of the massed leaves.

Fall and winter

When most herbaceous plants die down in the fall and deciduous shrubs have lost their leaves, the color provided by trees is particularly welcome, whether from leaves turning from green through shades of yellow, orange, and red to brown, or from the bright flecks of color from fruits or berries. Ornamental members of the Rosaceae family, especially those from the genera *Cotoneaster*, *Crataegus*, *Malus*, and *Sorbus*, include many species, cultivars, and hybrids that have an attractive display in the fall; in some cases, the fruits will remain on the tree right through the winter months.

In winter, many trees stand out most effectively with little else in the yard to compete with them. Their skeletons or silhouettes become most noticeable and create greater sculptural impact. The color and texture provided by coniferous and broadleaved evergreens may be used to complement and soften the architectural, "hard" look of nearby deciduous trees, while

TREES WITH ORNAMENTAL BARK

Acer capillipes

Betula utilis **var.** *jacquemontii*

Prunus serrula

Eucalyptus dalrympleana

Acer griseum

Acer pensylvanicum

patterned, textured, or peeling bark adds an extra point of interest. A few conifers, such as forms of Japanese cedar (*Cryptomeria japonica*), have foliage that takes on attractive russet overtones during winter.

Trees for small yards

For small yards, trees that do not reach more than about 20ft (6m) in height are the most suitable. There may only be space for just one tree (see "Specimen trees," p.55), so those that provide more than one season of interest are especially valuable. A Japanese crabapple (*Malus floribunda*), for example, produces masses of crimson buds, then pale pink or white flowers, and finally small red or yellow fruits, on arching branches.

A deciduous tree's appearance when leafless is particularly important in a small yard, because the tree may be bare for six months each year and visible from every window facing the garden. Good choices include *Rhus typhina*, fig (*Ficus carica*), and *Pyrus salicifolia* 'Pendula'. None has showy flowers but all have handsome foliage and winter silhouettes with character.

Heavily thorned or prickly trees, such as hawthorns (*Crataegus*) or hollies (*Ilex*), may be unsuitable in a very small yard; they may restrict access on either side, while those such as some lindens (*Tilia*) that drip sticky honeydew should not be sited where they will overhang sitting areas. If underplanting, choose a light-foliaged, deep-rooted tree, such as *Gleditsia* or *Robinia*, because small plants seldom compete successfully with the shallow, greedy roots of ornamental cherries (*Prunus*), for example.

Small-yard tree The modest stature of this *Robinia pseudoacacia* 'Frisia' makes it a good choice for a small garden, casting minimal shade so other plants can grow around it.

Trees for broad streets

Primarily used in formal settings, broad streets rely on the uniformity of trees and spacing for their grand effect. The longer and straighter the street, the more impact the rhythm of the trees and their shadows has on the landscape. Trees should be sited so that they lead the eye to an impressive feature or focal point; large trees are often used on either side of a driveway to line the route to the house. Long-lived, forest trees, such as beeches (*Fagus*) and horse chestnuts (*Aesculus*), are traditionally used for boulevards, while the strong shapes of conifers may be more striking in a contemporary design. Trees such as whitebeam (*Sorbus aria*) or the evergreen Chinese privet (*Ligustrum lucidum*) are suitable for smaller landscapes.

Informal streetscapes may also be created, perhaps with the young trees bent and tied over each side to form a living arch over a walkway. The spacing used may be less rigid than for a formal avenue to avoid creating a heavily regimented appearance.

Training for effect

Trees may be pleached to create an elegant formality. The side branches are trained to meet in horizontal, parallel lines and other growth is cut back or interwoven to form a vertical screen. Beeches, lindens (*Tilia*), hornbeams (*Carpinus*), and planes (*Platanus*) are traditional trees for pleaching and, in the fruit garden, espaliered apples and pears provide a variation of this technique.

Pollarding involves regularly lopping back the entire crown to short stumps that produce dense, thin branches and a single, tight ball of foliage. It achieves a formal, if artificial, effect and is useful in urban areas where a natural crown would cast too much shade or impede traffic. Some willows (*Salix*) are often pollarded or coppiced (cut back to ground level) for their colorful young shoots. Coppiced trees look appropriate in a naturalistic or informal setting, such as a woodland garden or on the banks of a pond.

Trees for screens and shelter belts

Large-scale tree planting can screen buildings and roads, deaden noise, and provide shelter from wind and frost. A single, straight row of fast-growing Lombardy poplars (*Populus nigra* 'Italica') is often planted to screen eyesores, but their great height and fingerlike shape often tend to highlight what they are intended to conceal. Looser stands of mixed deciduous and evergreen trees are usually more natural-looking and effective. Hedges are the most compact for screening, and their size can be controlled (see HEDGES AND SCREENS, pp.82–85).

Trees planted *en masse* can filter wind, reducing potential damage more effectively than solid barriers, which often create wind

Pleached trees In this small formal scheme, pleached limes are used to define a seating area and to mark the boundary with the surrounding landscape.

swirl on the leeward side. A windbreak or group of trees can protect vulnerable plants from cold, especially in spring.

Trees in containers

Growing trees in large pots greatly extends their design potential. In courtyard or patio designs, several trees in containers is the quickest way to create a finished appearance, adding height and structure to the look.

Use trees in large pots to frame a doorway that is surrounded by hard paving or to flank wide steps; these locations are particularly appropriate for topiary (see TOPIARY, pp.108–109). Trees too tender to overwinter outside may be grown in containers, displayed outdoors in summer, and moved to a frost-free place as cold weather approaches. Annuals and tender plants, such as petunias, fuchsias, or trailing nasturtiums (*Tropaeolum*), may be included in the container for seasonal color and interest, or English ivy (*Hedera*) for permanent groundcover.

Container-grown trees are long-term features, so use containers that are both durable and attractive. A wide range of sizes, styles, and materials is available, (see CONTAINER GARDENING, "Choosing containers," p.320). Make sure that the containers you choose are frost-proof if they are to be permanent features in an area of the yard that is subject to cold during the winter.

PLANTER'S GUIDE TO TREES

TREES FOR SMALL GARDENS

Acer capillipes ♠,
  A. × *conspicuum* 'Silver Vein' ♠,
  A. griseum ♠, *A. palmatum*,
  A. palmatum 'Sango-kaku',
  A. pseudoplatanus
  'Brilliantissimum' ♠
Amelanchier lamarckii
Arbutus × *andrachnoides*
Betula albosinensis
  var. *septentrionalis* ♠,
  B. ermanii ♠, *B. pendula* ♠,
  B. pendula 'Dalecarlica' ♠,
  B. utilis var. *jacquemontii* ♠
Catalpa bignonioides 'Aurea'
Cercidiphyllum japonicum ♠
Cercis siliquastrum
Cinnamomum
  C. camphora
Cornus kousa
Crataegus laevigata 'Paul's Scarlet',
  C. × *lavallei* 'Carrierei',
Cydonia oblonga
Eucalyptus pauciflora subsp.
  niphophila ♠
Eucryphia × *nymansensis* 'Numansay'
Fagus sylvatica 'Dawyck Gold' ♠
Gleditsia triacanthos 'Sunburst' ♠
Grevillea robusta ♠
Hoheria lyallii
Laburnum × *watereri* 'Vossii'
Maackia amurensis ♠
Magnolia 'Elizabeth',
  M. × *loebneri* 'Merrill' ♠
  M. salicifolia
Malus 'Dartmouth', *M. floribunda*,
  M. 'Golden Hornet',
  M. tschonoskii ♠
Melia azedarach
Mespilus germanica ♠
Phoenix dactylifera ♠
Prunus – many including
  P. 'Okame', *P.* 'Pandora',
  P. 'Spire', *P.* × *subhirtella*,
  P. × *yedoensis*
Pyrus calleryana 'Chanticleer',
  P. salicifolia 'Pendula'
Sorbus aria (some forms),
  S. aucuparia (some forms),
  S. cashmiriana,
  S. commixta 'Embley',
  S. vilmorinii
Stewartia pseudocamellia
Vitex agnus-castus

WINTER INTEREST

Decorative flowers

Acacia dealbata
Magnolia campbellii
  'Charles Raffill', (and forms),
Prunus mume,
  P. × *subhirtella* 'Autumnalis',
  P. × *subhirtella* 'Autumnalis Rosea'

Golden foliage

Chamaecyparis lawsoniana
  'Lanei Aurea',
  C. lawsoniana 'Stewartii',
× *Cupressocyparis leylandii*
  'Castlewellan',
Cupressus macrocarpa 'Goldcrest',
Juniperus chinensis 'Aurea'

Gray foliage

Cedrus atlantica f. *glauca*
Chamaecyparis lawsoniana
  'Pembury Blue'
Cupressus glabra 'Pyramidalis'
Eucalyptus pauciflora
Tsuga mertensiana 'Glauca'

Decorative bark

Acer capillipes,
  A. × *conspicuum* 'Silver Vein',
  A. davidii,
  A. griseum,
  A. grosseri var. *hersii*,
  A. palmatum 'Sango-kaku',
  A. pensylvanicum
  (and forms),
Arbutus × *andrachnoides*,
  A. menziesii
Betula albo-sinensis
  var. *septentrionalis*,
  B. 'Jermyns',
  B. pendula,
  B. utilis var. *jacquemontii*
Eucalyptus dalrympleana,
Pinus bungeana
Prunus maackii 'Amber Beauty',
  P. serrula
Salix acutifolia 'Blue Streak',
  S. alba var. *vitellina* 'Britzensis',
  S. daphnoides,
  S. 'Erythroflexuosa'
Stewartia pseudocamellia

TREES FOR CONTAINERS

Acacia dealbata
Acer palmatum cvs
Araucaria heterophylla
Chamadorea
Citrus limon,
  C. medica
  C. × *paradisi*
Cordyline australis
Cupressus macrocarpa 'Goldcrest',
  C. sempervirens
Eriobotrya japonica
Ficus benjamina
Howea
Jacaranda mimosifolia
Juniperus scopulorum
  'Skyrocket'
Lagerstroemia indica
Laurus nobilis
Olea europaea
Phoenix
Prunus 'Amanogawa',
  P. 'Kiku-shidare-zakura'
Sabal minor
Salix caprea 'Kilmarnock'
Taxus baccata 'Standishii'
Washingtonia

TWO OR MORE SEASONS OF INTEREST

Spring/Fall

Amelanchier lamarckii
Crataegus × *lavallei*
  'Carrierei'
Malus 'Golden Hornet'
Prunus 'Okame',
  P. sargentii

Winter/Spring

Acer negundo

Summer/Fall

Catalpa bignonioides
Cladrastis lutea
Cornus kousa,
  C. kousa var. *chinensis*
Eucryphia glutinosa
Fagus sylvatica 'Dawyck Gold'
Liriodendron tulipifera
Stewartia pseudocamellia
Tilia 'Petiolaris'

Fall/Winter

Acer capillipes,
  A. davidii,
  A. griseum,
  A. palmatum 'Sango-kaku',
  A. pensylvanicum
Stewartia pseudocamellia

All year

Acacia dealbata
Arbutus × *andrachnoides*,
  A. menziesii
Betula albo-sinensis
  var. *septentrionalis*,
  B. ermanii,
  B. 'Jermyns',
  B. utilis var. *jacquemontii*
Ilex × *altaclerensis*
  'Golden King'
Magnolia grandiflora

SPECIMEN TREES

Abies magnifica,
  A. procera
Acer pensylvanicum,
  A. pseudoplatanus,
  A. rubrum
Aesculus hippocastanum
Alnus cordata
Betula 'Jermyns',
  B. pendula 'Dalecarlica'
Cedrus
Eucalyptus coccifera,
  E. dalrympleana
Fraxinus angustifolia
  'Raywood'
Liquidambar styraciflua,
  L. styraciflua 'Lane Roberts'
Liriodendron tulipifera
Livistona
Magnolia campbellii,
  M. campbellii
  'Charles Raffill'
Metasequoia glyptostroboides
Nothofagus alpina
Nyssa sylvatica
Phoenix
Picea breweriana,
  P. omorika
Pinus nigra,
  P. radiata,
  P. sylvestris,
  P. wallichiana
Platanus × *hispanica*
Roystonea
Salix × *sepulcralis*
  var. *chrysocoma*

Sequoiadendron giganteum
Tilia 'Petiolaris',
  T. platyphyllos
Tsuga heterophylla
Zelkova carpinifolia

TREES FOR WINDY SITES

Acer pseudoplatanus
Betula pendula,
  B. pubescens
Crataegus × *lavallei*,
  C. monogyna
Fraxinus excelsior
Laburnum (spp. and cvs)
Picea abies
Pinus contorta
Quercus robur
Salix alba
Sorbus aria

POLLUTION-TOLERANT TREES

Acer platanoides (and cvs),
  A. pseudoplatanus (and cvs),
  A. saccharinum (and cvs)
Aesculus hippocastanum
Betula pendula
Carpinus betulus (and cvs)
Catalpa bignonioides
Corylus colurna
Ginkgo biloba
Ilex × *altaclerensis*
Malus
Populus
Pyrus
Salix
Sophora japonica
Taxus baccata,
  T. × *media*

Key

♠ May grow to 20ft (6m) or more

Acer pseudoplatanus 'Brilliantissimum'

Hardy palms and the exotic look

In the past, in frost-prone regions, many beautiful tropical and subtropical plants were grown in the protected environment of heated greenhouses. As the costs of maintenance—particularly heating—soared during the 20th century, the cultivation of these "exotics" declined. Recently, however, a new style of gardening has emerged that recreates the visual impact of tropical and subtropical plants in sheltered, outdoor gardens in mild-winter regions. This style makes use of hardy, marginally hardy, and some tender plants with striking shapes, distinctive textures, handsome, large foliage, and vivid flowers.

In frost-prone climates, most of the plants used should be hardy enough to survive year-round. Planting plans can then be varied during the warmer months by integrating marginally hardy or tender, container-grown exotics into the design (see also p.61). These can be used as accents and focal points, or placed strategically within the overall framework of the planting to create seasonal interest. Such displays require careful planning, of course, as well as the use of a frost-free greenhouse or other well-lit space in which the plants can be overwintered.

Marginally hardy plants may be planted permanently outside, but they will need to be bundled up in straw, burlap, or other coverings in severe weather, to protect them from cold winds and temperature shifts that would otherwise desiccate evergreen foliage. Equally important is to ensure that such plants are grown in fast-draining soil, to avoid root decay, particularly during very cold spells. Exotic planting designs of this type are most likely to succeed in coastal or sheltered city gardens in Zone 7 and warmer, but variations on this theme may be well worth trying in colder areas.

Key framework plants

Exotic-style plants seldom grow as large in temperate climates as they do in their native regions, although they can still make handsomely sized, vigorous garden plants for outdoor cultivation in the appropriate situation. Plants to use as treelike, structural elements in the exotic style of gardening can be divided roughly into three groups: palms and palmlike plants, tree ferns, and bananas. Each contains plants with imposing, attractive foliage, and under favorable conditions the palms and bananas may flower. These tropical-looking plants can be blended with more-familiar large foliage plants, such as elegant bamboos (see pp. 120–121), *Rheum*, and *Gunnera*.

Palms and palmlike plants

Several species of palms are grown successfully outdoors in mild-winter areas, the most familiar being the Chusan palm (*Trachycarpus fortunei*) from the Himalayas. This withstands temperatures of 5°F (-15°C) or below, if grown in a reasonably sheltered position. The closely related *T. wagnerianus* has stiffer, more wind-tolerant leaves. Another suitable palm for a garden setting is the Mediterranean dwarf fan palm (*Chamaerops humilis*). Although it originates in hot, dry regions, it will tolerate 14°F (-10°C) or below when grown in a sheltered spot. Forms with silvery-blue leaves (*C. humilis* var. *argentea*) are particularly attractive.

Blue hesper palm (*Brahea armata*) from Mexico and California is occasionally grown in very sheltered sites outdoors; in cold areas, it is also an excellent container plant for summer garden displays. The jelly palm (*Butia capitata*), although Brazilian and Uruguayan in origin, is also surprisingly tough and of similar stature and hardiness to *Brahea*.

Known to survive outdoors and develop to about 15ft (5m) in mild-winter areas, the Chilean wine palm (*Jubaea chilensis*), with its delicate feathery foliage, is another fine candidate for the exotic style, as is the Canary island date palm (*Phoenix canariensis*). Its delightful dwarf relative, *P. roebelenii*, is better grown in a container in a conservatory and moved outside in summer.

Unless large specimens are obtained from specialty nurseries, borderline hardy palms should be grown initially in containers until well established. They can then be planted out in well-drained soil that is reasonably moisture-retentive. As the palm stems thicken with age, the plants become more tolerant of lower temperatures, although winter protection is usually advisable.

Palmlike plants, such as cabbage palm (*Cordyline*) and *Yucca*, are also valuable constituents of an

Bold foliage contrast
Huge, paddle-shaped banana leaves here contrast strikingly with the palmate foliage of a castor bean plant (*Ricinus*) to provide a strong focal point.

Resistance to cold
Frosted fans of a Chusan palm (*Trachycarpus fortunei*) demonstrate the surprising hardiness of this plant.

Tree fern
A nearby tree offers shade and shelter for this tree fern (*Dicksonia*). It has been carefully planted just beyond the range of the tree's leafy canopy, beneath which the soil would be too dry for it to flourish.

A RANGE OF EXOTICS

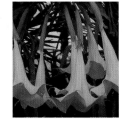

Melianthus major

Brugmansia suaveolens

Hedychium gardnerianum

Tibouchina urvilleana

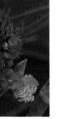

Ricinus communis
'Zanzibariensis'

Passiflora caerulea

Canna 'Rosemond Coles'

Hibiscus schizopetalus

Agave americana

Euphorbia mellifera

Exotic gardens
Striking subtropical plants originating in all parts of the globe will flourish in the warmth of sheltered gardens in mild-winter areas such as southern British Columbia.

placed in a shaded site, because the developing fronds may burn if exposed to bright sun.

Although *D. antarctica* will withstand at least 23°F (-5°C), its crown and trunk should be insulated where more severe freezes can be expected (see also "Frost protection," p.613). Slightly more tender are the New Zealand species *D. fibrosa* and *D. squarrosa*. Both are best grown as container plants, which can be given a summer outing. Another tree fern that requires similar cultivation and sheltered conditions is the spectacular sago fern (*Cyathea medullaris*).

the foliage has been cut off. A board across the pot top will keep rain out and prevent the straw from rotting. Older plants can be protected with a 6in (15cm) mulch of straw placed around each trunk. The old foliage will die off in winter, and new shoots should appear in mid-spring.

Given suitable overwintering conditions, *Musa*, *Ensete*, and many other banana genera are among the best of all foliage plants for inclusion in exotic planting designs.

exotic garden. The New Zealand cabbage or Torbay palm (*C. australis*) can be grown outdoors in mild-winter areas, where it reaches up to 20–40ft (6–12m) in height. Green-leaved *C. australis* grows without protection in sheltered gardens but in severe winters may lose some of its foliage, although it often recovers in spring. Variants with colored or variegated leaves are not always tolerant if the temperature drops below freezing for several days.

Species of *Yucca*, such as Adam's needle (*Y. filamentosa*) and Spanish dagger (*Y. gloriosa*), also provide an exotic feel in a garden and can be used as permanent residents within the planting design. Both will withstand temperatures down to as low as 5°F (-15°C).

Tree ferns
Several species of *Dicksonia* and *Cyathea* are becoming increasingly popular for conservatories and in sheltered gardens. The woolly tree fern (*Dicksonia antarctica*), for example, grows well in humid shade, a habitat that mimics its native temperate rainforests in Australia.

If not already containerized, tree ferns should be planted with the sawn-off "trunk" at least 1ft (30cm) into the ground in a shaded, humid, wind-sheltered site. It is very important, particularly in the first year, to keep the plants moist—they must not be allowed to dry out. A drip irrigation system (see p.561) to maintain a high level of humidity around the plants will simulate the natural conditions in which they grow. Sometimes it is better to establish tree ferns in containers

Bananas
The two main genera of bananas grown as ornamentals are *Musa* (including *Musella*) and *Ensete*— an impressive giant African genus with enormous architectural foliage. Both should be grown in moist, fertile soil, and mulched with well-rotted manure. Bananas need sun and a sheltered site, to prevent their large, paddle-like leaves from tearing in the wind, as well as plenty of water and frequent applications of fertilizer during the growing season.

A few *Musa* species, including *M. basjoo*, are reasonably cold-hardy and will withstand temperatures down to 18°F (-8°C). However, even in sheltered gardens, it is always advisable to provide some winter protection. Young plants should have a deep, straw-filled pot—a tall can is ideal—fitted over the crown after

OTHER PLANTS WITH A TROPICAL LOOK

Acanthus mollis,
Aralia elata,
  A. elata 'Variegata'
Arundo donax
Astelia chathamica
Beschorneria
  yuccoides
Blechnum chilense
Cycas
Dahlia coccinea,
  D. imperialis
Echium candicans,
  E. pininana
Eryngium agavifolium
Fatsia japonica
Gunnera tinctoria
Impatiens tinctoria
Phormium
Phyllostachys
Rheum palmatum
  (and cvs)
Solenostemon

Dwarf conifers

Greatly valued for their ease of maintenance, dwarf conifers are particularly suitable for a small, modern landscape, whether grown in compact beds or in containers. Colors range from rich golds through brilliant greens to pale blues and silvers, and shapes include globose, pyramidal, and slender, spire-shaped forms. Habits are diverse, with prostrate, mound-forming, erect, and weeping types; the variation in foliage texture ranges from soft and feathery to dense and spiky. With careful planning, this rich variety of color, form, and texture can provide interest throughout the year. For details on cultivation, routine care, and propagation, see ORNAMENTAL TREES, pp.63–81.

Selecting plants

When selecting conifers for a small space, it is important to recognize the true dwarf and slow-growing species and cultivars; sometimes so-called "dwarf" conifers are simply slower-growing variants of large trees. Conifers can be very difficult to identify when young— their juvenile foliage often differs widely from adult foliage. Check that the plants are correctly named when buying them to avoid any that will rapidly outgrow their allotted space; if in any doubt, seek advice from a specialized supplier.

Designing with dwarf conifers

Dwarf conifers are suitable for a wide range of situations in a garden. They may be planted individually to form a feature, or collectively to create a band of harmonious year-round color; and they may be used either to complement other plants or to provide effective groundcover. Rock gardens, mixed borders, and ornamental containers are also excellent locations for growing all types of dwarf conifers.

Enhancing conifers
To display dwarf conifers to the best advantage, add other evergreens, such as heathers and boxwoods, for flower and foliage contrasts.

Specimen plants
Some of the slow-growing conifers are suitable for use as specimen plants. Spreading forms, for example, may be used to soften the edges of paths and patios, while columnar specimens create a focal point.

Group planting
If space allows, a collection of dwarf conifers can make a very attractive feature. The color spectrum in conifers may also be used to highlight areas at different times of year; blues and silvers, for example, are at their most beautiful in the cool light of winter, while golds and greens appear at their freshest in spring.

Steep slopes and banks, which often prove difficult to plant sucessfully, can make striking landscape features when planted with bold drifts of prostrate conifers. Once plants are established, these often problematic areas are easy to maintain and are more or less weed-free.

Planting combinations
Dwarf conifers associate well with other groups of plants that are similar in character. They are often used as components of heather gardens to extend the season of interest and provide contrast in color and form with the foliage and color variants of *Calluna*, *Daboecia*, and *Erica* cultivars. Other complementary plants include dwarf azaleas, boxwood (*Buxus sempervirens*), and the smaller cotoneaster species and cultivars.

Rock gardens
In the rock garden, dwarf conifers provide the framework for other associated but less permanent

plants. The complete repertoire of colors, textures, and shapes can be used, but take care to select plants that will not become too large or dominant. The smaller species and cultivars, such as *Juniperus communis* 'Compressa', are ideal for the miniature landscapes of compact, raised beds as well as troughs, sink gardens, and other ornamental containers.

Groundcover
Many dwarf conifers make excellent weed-smothering groundcover, either by forming dense mats, as with *Juniperus horizontalis* and its cultivars, or by growing taller and spreading to exclude light beneath their canopy. Some Pfitzer junipers are particularly useful for screening utility meters or for softening paved areas. See SHRUBS FOR GROUNDCOVER, p.94.

Specimen planting
Ideal for a focal point, the golden yew, *Taxus baccata* 'Aurea', has golden foliage all year round.

A RANGE OF DWARF CONIFERS

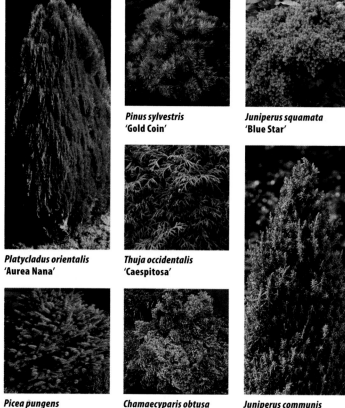

Platycladus orientalis 'Aurea Nana'

Pinus sylvestris 'Gold Coin'

Juniperus squamata 'Blue Star'

Thuja occidentalis 'Caespitosa'

Picea pungens 'Montgomery'

Chamaecyparis obtusa 'Nana Aurea'

Juniperus communis 'Compressa'

Soil preparation and planting

Once planted, a tree may remain in place for decades or even centuries, so it is essential to provide it with the best possible growing conditions. Climate, soil type, and the amount of light and shelter available all affect a tree's growth, so take these factors into account when deciding on a planting location. Careful preparation and planting as well as aftercare are vital in helping a tree to establish quickly and grow well.

Climate considerations

Before selecting a tree, check if it will flourish in the temperature range, rainfall, and humidity levels of the site. Special local factors, such as strong winds on exposed hilltop sites, should also influence your choice. Even within a species, different cultivars may be more suited to certain conditions, so one plant may thrive while another may not: various cultivars of *Magnolia grandiflora*, for example, tolerate minimum temperatures ranging from 10–43°F (-12–6°C).

In areas subject to spring frost, choose trees that come into leaf late because frost frequently damages young growth. In cold areas, trees that are not fully hardy may be grown outdoors, but they may need protection from frost during winter (see FROST AND WIND PROTECTION, pp.612–613) and should be planted in a sheltered site. If growing tender or tropical species in temperate areas, keep them under cover or grow them in containers so that they can be brought indoors for the winter.

Trees rarely grow well in regions where the annual rainfall is less than 10in (250mm), and most prefer at least four times this amount. Most trees do not require irrigation, however, except when newly planted, because they obtain enough water from rain and, in some areas, from heavy mists condensing on their foliage.

Choosing a planting site

When planting a tree, try to choose the best location for it within the yard, because the microclimate may vary considerably from one part of the yard to another. Make sure that the selected site will provide an appropriate amount of light and shelter: many large-leaved trees, for example, will thrive in a sheltered, partially shaded location but may

CHOOSING TREES

Container-grown tree

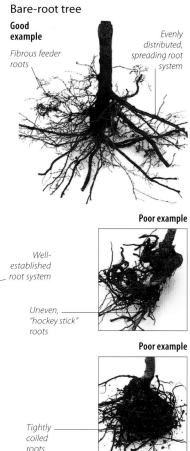

Good example

Well-balanced branch framework

Good example

Well-established root system

Poor example

Tightly wound, congested roots

Bare-root tree

Good example

Fibrous feeder roots

Evenly distributed, spreading root system

Poor example

Uneven, "hockey stick" roots

Poor example

Tightly coiled roots

Balled-and-burlapped tree

Good example

x *Cupressocyparis leylandii*

Firm root ball with the covering intact

not grow well in an exposed site where the foliage would be subjected to strong winds and high light levels.

In coastal areas, choose a planting site that is sheltered because sea spray and salt-laden winds (even a few miles inland) may scorch foliage and cause damage to the growth buds. Some trees, however, tolerate coastal conditions (see *Trees for Exposed or Windy Sites*, p.67), and may be planted as windbreaks to help screen other, more vulnerable, plants from strong winds. Similarly, if trees are being planted on a slope, remember that sensitive trees are more likely to succeed halfway down, where it is usually more sheltered than at either the top or the bottom (see also "Frost pockets and damage," p.607).

It is best not to plant trees very close to walls or buildings, otherwise, when young, the trees may suffer from reduced light and moisture as a result of the "rain shadow" effect (see *Rain Shadow*, p.608). Ideally they should be planted half their mature height away from any structure.

In addition, the strong, fibrous roots of some trees, such as poplars (*Populus*) and willows (*Salix*), may damage drains and the foundations of buildings as they develop (see "Tree roots and buildings," p.70). Tender species can be planted near a warm wall; there they will benefit from the wall's retained heat and so may survive in an area where they would fail in more open conditions.

When choosing a site, ensure that the trees will not interfere with overhead wires and underground pipes, which may obstruct trees or be damaged by them.

Selecting a tree

Trees may be bought container-grown, bare-root, or balled-and-burlapped, although conifers and palms are rarely available bare-root. They may be purchased in a variety of sizes and stages of maturity, from seedlings through to semimature trees. Young trees tend to become established more quickly than older trees, while the latter create a strong and immediate impact in the garden but are more

GROW YOUR OWN LEAF MOLD

An additional benefit of planting deciduous trees and shrubs is that they can provide a rich organic source of humus— leaf mold—from the decaying leaves shed each fall. Leaf mold has good consistency and moisture retention, and contains some disease-combating microbes, making it an excellent soil-improver, and a useful ingredient of seed and potting composts. All you have to do is collect the leaves and wait a couple of years for them to decay (see p.628).

Use only leaves from deciduous trees and shrubs, such as beech, oak, or ash; ideally, avoid those from trees with prominent, hard-veined foliage, such as some species of maples (*Acer*), which decay slowly. Evergreen and most conifer foliage takes longer to decompose and is unsuitable for making leaf mold.

expensive. Whichever type you choose, check that the tree has healthy, vigorous top growth and roots with no sign of pests, disease, or damage. Both the branch and root systems should be well developed and evenly balanced around the stem. The top growth, however, must not be overlarge for the root system, otherwise the roots cannot absorb the nutrients and moisture needed to create new growth, and the tree may fail to establish. The spread of a container-grown tree, for example, should be no more than three or four times the width of its container.

Trees that have been allowed to flower or fruit prematurely, so that they look seemingly impressive to buyers, should also be avoided. Such growth may well have been at the expense of basic root development.

Container-grown trees

These are widely available and may be bought and planted throughout the growing season, except when the soil is very dry or very wet; container-grown trees are usually more expensive than bare-root or balled-and-burlapped specimens of a comparable size. This is the best method of buying trees that do not establish easily when transplanted, such as magnolias and *Eucalyptus*, because there is less disturbance to the roots. Such difficult-to-establish trees should also be bought and planted when they are still small. Exotic and less common trees are usually sold in pots.

Before buying a tree, remove it from its container, if possible, so that you can see the roots clearly: do not buy a potbound tree with a mass of congested roots or one with thick roots protruding through the drainage holes. Such trees may not establish well. Equally, if the compost does not cling to the root ball when the tree is removed from its container, do not buy it because its root system is not sufficiently established. Make sure that the container is large enough in relation to the tree: as a guide, the pot's diameter should be at least one-sixth of the tree's height. A tall tree growing in a small container will almost certainly be potbound.

The potting medium is also important: trees that are in containers in soil-based potting composts establish more quickly in open ground than those grown in other types of composts, because they have less of an adjustment to make to the surrounding soil.

Bare-root trees

Trees sold bare-root, which are almost always deciduous, are grown in open ground, then lifted with virtually no soil around the roots. As soon as they are exposed to the air, however, the fine feeder roots begin to dry out. A reputable nursery will remove any ragged ends as well as prune away any lopsided, overlong, or damaged roots.

It is essential to buy bare-root trees when they are dormant, preferably in fall or early spring; they are unlikely to survive transplanting if purchased and planted when in leaf. Ash (*Fraxinus*), poplars (*Populus*), and many rosaceous trees, such as crabapples (*Malus*), are often sold bare-root.

Make sure that the tree you choose has well-developed roots spreading evenly in all directions.

A number of small roots about 1/16–1/4 in (2–5mm) in diameter is a good sign. It indicates that they have been undercut every year or so, a technique that encourages sturdy growth and vigorous root systems. Examine the roots to check that they are free from damage and disease and that there is no sign of dryness that may have been caused by exposure to wind. Do not buy trees with "hockey stick" roots, where all the growth is on one side; these will not establish well.

Balled-and-burlapped trees

These trees are also grown in open ground but, when lifted, the roots and surrounding soil are wrapped in burlap or netting to hold the root ball together and stop the roots from drying out. Deciduous trees over 12ft (4m) and many evergreens, especially conifers and palms of more than 5ft (1.5m), are often sold in this way.

Buy and plant balled-and-burlapped trees when dormant, in fall or early spring, following the same criteria as for bare-root and container-grown trees. Check that the root ball is firm and its wrapping is intact before purchase: if there is any sign of drying out or root damage, the tree is less likely to establish well and, because the resulting root system is unstable and not well anchored, the tree will be susceptible to wind-rock, especially when mature.

STAKING

Root systems of newly planted trees need one or more growing seasons to anchor firmly in the soil, so staking against strong winds may so be necessary. Drive the stake in about 24in (60cm) below soil level so that it is completely stable. After two or three years, the tree should be sufficiently established for the stake to be removed. The method of support chosen depends on the tree, the proposed planting site, and personal preference.

Traditionally, a tall, vertical stake has been used, placed on the side of prevailing wind and long enough to reach to just below the crown. A low stake is now preferred: it allows the tree to move naturally in the wind.

With flexible-stemmed trees, such as crabapples, use a tall stake in the first year after planting, cut it down to the lower level in the second year, and remove the stake in the third year.

For container-grown and balled-and-burlapped trees, a low stake angled into the prevailing wind is preferable since it can be driven safely even after the tree has been planted. Alternatively, space two or three vertical, low stakes evenly around the tree outside the area of the root ball.

In windy sites or for trees more than 12ft (4m) tall, insert two vertical stakes when planting, one on either side of the root ball. Large trees are often secured by guy ropes attached to low stakes. Covering the guys with pieces of garden hose or with white tape makes them more visible and reduces the risk of tripping over them.

Tall stake
Drive in a single tall stake before planting. Secure the tree to the stake using two padded or buckle-and-spacer ties.

Low stake
A low stake allows the tree's stem some movement; insert it so that only about 20in (50cm) protrudes above ground level.

Angled stake
A low, angled stake may be added after planting. Drive it into the ground at a 45° angle, so it is leaning into the prevailing wind.

Two stakes
Insert two stakes so that they are on opposite sides of the tree, and secure them to the tree with heavy-duty rubber ties.

TREE TIES

Ties must be secure, long-lasting, and able to accommodate the tree's girth as it grows without cutting into the bark. Commercial ties are available, or you can make them from nylon webbing or rubber tubing. Prevent stakes from chafing the bark by using spacers, or form a padded tie into a figure eight and nail it to the stake. When using two or three stakes, secure the tree with heavy-duty rubber or plastic strips. If supporting a large tree with guy ropes, use multistrand wire or nylon rope.

Buckle-and-spacer tie
Thread the tie through the spacer, around the tree, and back through the spacer; buckle it so that it is taut but will not damage the bark.

Rubber tie
If using a rubber or plastic tie without a buckle, nail it to the stake to prevent bark damage caused by friction.

Seedlings, transplants, and whips

Seedlings up to one year old are available from specialty nurseries. Transplants are seedlings or cuttings transplanted in the nursery and are up to four years old. They make sturdy, bushy plants and are usually 2–4ft (60cm–1.2m) tall. The age and treatment may be given in shorthand: "1+1" denotes a seedling left for one year in the seedbed and then transplanted for a further season; "1 u 1" means that it was undercut (see "Bare-root trees," p.64) after the first year and remained *in situ* for a further year. Whips are single, whiplike shoots sold by height; they are 3–6ft (1–2m) tall and will have been transplanted at least once.

Feathered trees

These have a single main leader with a spread of lateral branches ("feathers") down to ground level. They will have been transplanted at least once and are usually 6–8ft (2–2.5m) tall.

HEELING IN

If planting is delayed, heel in the tree in a sheltered position. First, prepare a trench, then set the tree in it. Angle the tree so that the trunk is supported. Cover the roots and base of the trunk with moist, friable soil and do not allow the roots to dry out.

Size standards for trees

The American Nursery and Landscape Association has set standards for sizing trees sold by nurseries. The standards describe how tree size, root-ball size, and container size are measured and described. For shade and flowering trees, the height of the tree and the caliper (diameter of the trunk) are measured; the amount of branching is also considered. Bare-root trees are sized by minimum root spread, balled-and-burlapped trees by minimum root-ball diameter. Trees are also grouped into types according to speed of growth and expected mature height, and described according to their plant form, such as "narrow," "broad," and "clumping."

Transportation shock

Many trees falter or die of stress and desiccation as a result of being transported on a roof rack, stuck

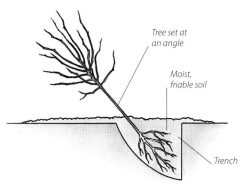

Tree set at an angle

Moist, friable soil

Trench

through an opening in a car roof, or exposed on an open truck, where they may be buffeted in the wind.

Trees may also experience a setback in their growth rate because their environment has suddenly changed, from one of protected, close planting at the nursery to isolation and exposure to strong winds, hot sun, or hard frosts within the garden.

When to plant

It is best to plant trees as soon as possible after purchase, although container-grown and balled-and-burlapped trees may be stored in frost-free conditions for a few weeks if kept moist.

Container-grown trees may be planted at any time of year, except during drought or cold; deciduous bare-root trees should be planted between mid-fall and mid-spring (avoiding periods of severe cold). Plant hardy evergreens and hardy deciduous trees with fleshy roots in mid-fall or mid- to late spring, and half-hardy trees in mid-spring. Balled-and-burlapped trees are best planted in early to mid-fall or mid- to late spring; if deciduous, they may be planted out in winter in mild conditions.

Fall planting allows tree roots to become established before winter sets in. This helps the tree withstand hot, dry spells the following summer. In cold regions, planting in spring may allow trees to establish more successfully. If planting in winter, the ground may be lifted by subsequent cold spells; if so, the soil should be refirmed once it has thawed.

Soil preparation

Preparing the site in advance allows the soil to settle and minimizes the delay between buying and planting a tree. Choose a well-drained site; one that is poorly drained may need to be improved before planting (see "Improving drainage," p.623). Remove all plant growth in the immediate area to eliminate competition for nutrients and water in the soil, then dig the soil, adding organic matter as you work.

Most trees require a soil depth of 20in–3ft (50cm–1m) to grow well. Some may grow on soils only 6 in (15 cm) deep, although they are then less stable and less drought-tolerant.

TREES FOR ACID SOIL

Abies
Arbutus menziesii
Cercidiphyllum japonicum
Cornus nuttallii
Cryptomeria
Embothrium coccineum
Fagus grandifolia
Magnolia acuminata,
   M. campbellii (and cvs)
Michelia
Oxydendrum arboreum
Picea (most spp.)
Pseudolarix amabilis
Pseudotsuga
Rhodoleia championii
Sciadopitys verticillata
Stewartia
Styrax japonicus
Tsuga heterophylla

TREES FOR VERY ALKALINE SOIL

Acer campestre,
   A. cappadocicum subsp. *lobelii*
   A. negundo (and cvs),
   A. platanoides (and cvs)
Aesculus
Carpinus betulus
Cedrus libani
Cercis siliquastrum
Chamaecyparis
   lawsoniana (and cvs)
Crataegus
x *Cupressocyparis leylandii*
   (and cvs)
Cupressus glabra
Fagus sylvatica (and cvs)
Fraxinus excelsior,
   F. ornus
Juniperus
Malus
Morus nigra
Ostrya carpinifolia
Phillyrea latifolia
Pinus nigra
Populus alba
Prunus avium 'Plena',
   P. sargentii
Pyrus (spp. and cvs)
Robinia (spp. and cvs)
Sorbus aria (and cvs)
Taxus baccata (and cvs)
Thuja
Tilia tomentosa

Prunus sargentii

Planting trees

Once the site has been prepared, dig the planting hole, between two and four times the width of the tree's root ball, depending on the type of tree planted. If doing this in advance, backfill it loosely until ready to plant the tree so that the soil remains warm. Do not improve the soil that has been removed because this inhibits the tree roots from growing beyond the planting hole, especially on poor soils. Fork over the sides and base of the hole to break up the surrounding soil and allow the tree roots to spread into it more easily; this is particularly important in heavy, clay soils. If you are using a single stake, drive it into the hole just off-center before planting the tree to ensure that the root ball is not damaged later (see also *Staking*, p.64).

Container-grown trees

Thoroughly moisten the pot—if it is very dry, stand the container in water for an hour or two until the soil mix is moist throughout. Then remove the container, cutting it away if necessary. Gently tease out the roots to encourage them to grow into the surrounding soil; this is essential with a potbound plant. Trees with a full but not potbound root system could, alternatively, have the outer surface scored with a garden knife, by making two or four shallow vertical cuts, from below, on the root ball before planting. Trim any broken or damaged roots with pruners.

It is important to check that the planting depth is correct: if a tree is planted too deeply, its roots may not receive enough oxygen and it may slow down in growth or even die; if planted too shallowly, the

TREES FOR SANDY SOIL

Abies grandis
Acacia dealbata
Acer negundo (and cvs)
Agonis flexuosa
Banksia serrata
Betula pendula (and cvs)
Castanea sativa
Celtis australis
Cercis siliquastrum
Cupressus glabra
Eucalyptus ficifolia
Gleditsia triacanthos
Juniperus
Larix decidua
Melia azedarach
Nothofagus obliqua
Phoenix canariensis
Pinus pinaster,
  P. radiata
Quercus ilex
Schinus molle
Tabebuia chrysotricha
Thuja occidentalis
  (and cvs)

TREES FOR CLAY SOIL

Acer platanoides (and cvs)
Castanospermum australe
Crataegus laevigata (and cvs)
Fraxinus
Juglans nigra
Malus
Metasequoia
  glyptostroboides
Nyssa sylvatica
Pinus strobus
Populus
Pterocarya fraxinifolia
Pyrus calleryana 'Chanticleer'
Quercus palustris,
  Q. robur
Salix
Taxodium distichum

*Juniperus
communis*

PLANTING A CONTAINER-GROWN TREE

1 Soak the root ball of the potted tree in a bucket of water for 1–2 hours. Mark the area of the hole to be dug—about 3 or 4 times the diameter of the tree's root ball. Lift any turf or weeds, then dig out the hole to about 1½ times the depth of the root ball.

2 Scarify the sides and bottom of the hole with a fork. There is no need to improve the soil.

3 If using one stake, hammer it into the hole, just off-center and on the windward side.

4 Lay the tree on its side and slide it out of the pot. Gently tease out the roots without breaking up the root ball and remove any weeds from the soil mix.

5 Hold the tree next to the stake and spread out the roots. Lay a stake across the hole to check the planting depth. Adjust this by adding or removing some soil.

6 Backfill around the tree with more topsoil, working it down the root ball, then build a ring of soil around the hole to form a water-catching moat.

7 Cut back damaged stems, long sideshoots, and lower feathers. Mulch 2–3in (5–7cm) deep around the tree.

roots may dry out. Place the tree in the hole and locate the soil mark—a dark mark near the base of the stem indicating the soil level when the tree was growing at the nursery. Place a stake across the hole alongside the stem and add or remove soil from beneath the root ball, if necessary, so that the soil mark is level with the stake. On free-draining soil, a section of 4in (10cm) diameter perforated drainage pipe can be inserted into the planting hole—the top end should be just above ground level, while the lower one should rest among the tree's roots. During subsequent hot weather, water can be poured down this pipe, direct to the tree's roots.

Backfill the hole, firming the soil in stages to remove any air pockets; take care not to firm too heavily on clay soils because this may compact the ground and impede drainage. On sandy soils, a shallow moat around the tree helps to channel water to the roots. Conversely, on clay soils, a slight mound around the stem drains water away from the root ball.

Lightly prune the topgrowth to balance it with the root system (see "Formative pruning," p.71),

PLANTING A BALLED-AND-BURLAPPED TREE

1 Dig a planting hole 2–3 times the diameter of the tree's root ball. Mix the removed soil with well-rotted organic matter, then place the tree in the hole and untie the wrapping.

2 Tilt the tree to one side and roll the material up under the root ball, then tilt the tree the other way and carefully pull out the material. Backfill the hole, firm, mulch, and water well.

then secure the tree to the stake with one or more ties (see *Tree Ties,* p.65). Water thoroughly and apply a thick mulch (see "Mulching," p.68).

Bare-root trees
Prepare the site in the same way as for container-grown trees, ensuring that the planting hole is wide enough for the tree's roots to be spread out fully; trim back any damaged roots to healthy growth.

If using a single stake, drive it in just off-center of the planting hole, and spread the tree's roots around it. Adjust the planting depth if necessary, then partly backfill the hole and gently shake the stem to settle the soil. Firm the backfilled soil in stages, taking care not to damage the roots. Finally, water the tree well; mulch the area around it.

Balled-and-burlapped trees
The method of planting balled-and-burlapped trees is very similar to that used for container-grown trees. The planting hole should be twice the width of the root ball, however, or, in heavy, clay soils, three times the width. Place the tree in the hole at the correct depth, then remove the burlap or netting surrounding the root ball. If using an angled stake or two stakes, one on either side of the root ball, drive them in; they should rest firmly against the root ball without piercing it.

In heavy, clay soils, it is possible to improve drainage by planting so that the top of the root ball is slightly above soil level, and covering the exposed part with 2–3in (5–7cm) of friable soil, leaving a gap of 1–2in (2.5–5cm) around the stem. Water thoroughly and mulch.

Aftercare
For the first two or three years after planting, it is important to provide trees with plenty of water, particularly in dry spells. Failure to do this may impede establishment, or the tree may even die. Keep the surrounding area clear of grass and weeds, and feed and mulch regularly (see "Routine care," pp.68–70).

Some trees need extra protection from frost and wind; evergreens in an exposed site should be protected initially from drying winds with windbreaks, for example (see Frost and Wind Protection, pp.612–613).

PROTECTING THE STEM

In many regions, it is necessary to protect young trees from damage caused by rabbits or other animals that strip bark. Either surround the tree with a barrier of chicken wire or wire netting secured in place with several stakes, or place a commercial tree guard around the tree trunk. There are many types of guard available from garden centers and nurseries, including spiral, wrap-around guards made of flexible plastic,

as well as those made from heavy-duty plastic or wire mesh. Biodegradable, plastic-net tree guards are also available in a range of heights from 2ft (60cm) up to 6ft (2m).

In exposed sites, such as on hillsides, tree shelters may be used to assist young transplants and whips to become well established; these biodegradable plastic structures are up to 4ft (1.2m) long, and between 3in (8cm) and 6 in (15 cm) across.

| A | B | C | D |

Protect the bark of newly planted trees from animal damage with a barrier of wire mesh or plastic netting secured to the ground with stakes (A), a rigid, plastic tree shelter (B), a heavy-duty rubber or plastic stem guard (C), or a spiral, wrap-around, plastic guard (D).

TREES FOR EXPOSED OR WINDY SITES

Those marked ✿ are not suitable for coastal sites

Acer pseudoplatanus
Betula pendula ✿,
  B. pubescens ✿
Crataegus x *lavallei,*
  C. monogyna
Eucalyptus gunnii,
  E. pauciflora (and subsp.)
Fraxinus excelsior
Ilex altaclerensis (and cvs)
Picea abies ✿, *P. sitchensis* ✿
Pinus contorta, P. nigra,
  P. radiata, P. sylvestris
Quercus robur
Salix alba
Sorbus aria, S. aucuparia
  (and cvs)

TREES THAT TOLERATE POLLUTED AIR

Acer platanoides (and cvs),
  A. pseudoplatanus (and cvs),
  A. saccharinum (and cvs)
Aesculus hippocastanum
Alnus cordata, A. glutinosa
Betula pendula
Carpinus betulus (and cvs)
Catalpa bignonioides
Corylus colurna
Crataegus
x *Cupressocyparis leylandii*
Fraxinus
Ginkgo biloba
Gleditsia
Ilex x *altaclerensis*
Liriodendron
Magnolia grandiflora
Malus
Nyssa
Platanus
Populus
Pyrus
Quercus x *hispanica* (and cvs),
  Q. ilex, Q. x *turneri*
Robinia
Salix
Styphnolobium japonicum
Sorbus aria, S. aucuparia,
  S. intermedia
Taxus baccata,
  T. x *media*
Tilia x *euchlora,*
  T. x *europaea,*
  T. platyphyllos (and cvs)

Sorbus aucuparia

Routine care

The amount of maintenance that a tree needs largely depends on the species, microclimate, soil type, and site. Most trees require watering, feeding, and a clear, weed-free area during the first few years if they are to establish well; container-planted trees should also be regularly topdressed and occasionally repotted. In addition, other procedures such as removing suckers or controlling pests or diseases are sometimes necessary, while in certain circumstances—for example, if a tree is not thriving— the best solution may be either to cut down the tree or to transplant it.

Watering

Most trees need plenty of water to grow well, especially on light, sandy soil or if they have been planted within the previous two or three years. As a general guide, apply approximately 10–15 gallons/ sq yd (50–75 liters/sq m) of water per tree each week in dry weather during the growing season. Once they have become well established, most trees only need to be irrigated during spells of drought.

Fertilizing

All trees will benefit from feeding, particularly on soils that are low in nutrients and during the first few years after planting. However, older trees usually require feeding only occasionally. Trees grown for their flowers and fruit generally require more potassium and phosphorus than do trees grown for their foliage, which need more nitrogen.

TOPDRESSING

Trees in pots exhaust supplies of nutrients faster than they do in the open ground because their roots are restricted. You can replenish supplies by topdressing in spring. Use a trowel or your hands to remove mulch and the top 2in (5cm) of soil. Replace it with fresh potting mix mixed with compost or slow-release fertilizer. Water the mix well, and mulch.

Organic fertilizers such as well-rotted manure or compost are usually applied as a mulch: in fall, or during any frost-free period in the dormant season, spread the material in a layer 2–3in (5–8cm) deep around the tree, keeping a clear area immediately around the trunk. When feeding a young tree, extend the mulch to the "drip line"—the ground beneath the outer edge of the canopy; an area 10–12ft (3–4m) in diameter is appropriate for a larger tree.

Commercial fertilizers are usually applied in spring. Broadcast the fertilizer around the base of the tree, at the recommended rate, or mix it with compost and insert it into small holes dug 6ft (2m) apart around the drip line. Alternatively, apply a commercial liquid fertilizer around the tree.

Trees planted in lawns may need to be fed every year if they are not thriving. The grass between the trunk and the drip line may be removed by hand or with chemicals and a nutrient-rich mulch applied.

Trees in containers

Container-planted trees generally require watering and feeding more frequently than those planted in open ground, because the small amount of soil in which they are growing can store only limited reserves of water and nutrients. During hot, dry weather, they may need to be watered at least twice a day. Apply an annual mulch of bark chips or similar material on top of the soil to help retain moisture. In addition, topdress the tree each spring before it starts

into growth. This involves replacing some of the old soil with fresh soil enriched with fertilizer. At the same time, prune back any dead, damaged, weak, or straggly stems to rejuvenate the tree and ensure that it produces healthy, vigorous growth.

Every three to five years, repot the tree completely either into the same container or, preferably, into a larger one. To do this, first remove the tree carefully from the container, then tease out the roots, cutting back by up to a third any that are large and coarse. Soak the root system well, if dry, then repot the tree into fresh potting mix (see "Planting trees in containers," p.334). If using the same container, wash it out before adding fresh potting mix and repotting.

Mulching

Mulching around a tree keeps weeds under control, reduces the effect of temperature extremes around the roots, and cuts down moisture loss from the soil surface. In general, organic materials such as shredded bark look most attractive, and they can be used to cover a biodegradable mulch mat. Black plastic is also effective, but do not use clear plastic, because heat is rapidly transferred to the soil and may damage surface roots. Mulches that are rich in nutrients are generally used only if a tree needs feeding.

Mulches are best applied in spring but, provided the soil is moist, they may be spread at any time except during cold or drought. Apply mulch over an area 12–18in (30–45cm) larger than the tree's root system. Top off every year or two under young trees.

Weeding

The area beneath a tree's canopy should be kept clear of weeds and grass, as this ensures that the fibrous feeder roots of the tree do not have to compete for a limited supply of water and nutrients. However, if a tree's growth is too rapid, retaining or establishing grass around it will help to reduce its vigor by competing for food and water.

Some weedkillers may be used around trees because they do not affect tree roots. Mulching, however, should make weeding largely unnecessary. For treatment of weeds, see "Weeds and Lawn Weeds", pp.645–649.

Suckers and water sprouts

Suckers and water sprouts will divert nutrients from the main shoots of the tree if they are left to develop unchecked. Remove them as soon as they appear.

Stem and root suckers

A tree may produce both stem and root suckers: a stem sucker is a shoot that appears just beneath the graft union on the rootstock of a grafted tree, a root sucker is one that develops directly from the roots. Suckers of a grafted plant may quickly grow larger than the top growth, or even replace it within a few years, so that the rootstock species predominates rather than the grafted cultivar.

Trees that are particularly vigorous or that have roots near the soil surface, such as poplars (*Populus*) and ornamental cherries (*Prunus*), may form root suckers if the root system is damaged. They

Using pruners, cut off the suckers as close to the trunk as possible, then pare over the cut surface with a knife; rub out any regrowth as soon as it appears.

may be used for propagation, but are a nuisance if they come up in lawns and paths.

Cut or pull off the suckers as close to the base as possible, digging down to where the sucker joins the root, if necessary. For some genera such as *Prunus*, painting the cuts on the roots with an herbicide may prevent regrowth; seek advice from an expert source before trying this.

Water sprouts

Epicormic or water sprouts may grow directly out of the trunk, often around pruning wounds. Rub them out with your fingers or thumb as soon as they appear, or cut them back to the base and rub them out as they regrow.

Frost and wind

Trees can be damaged by strong winds, and severe frosts may affect young growth, so provide protection such as windbreaks, particularly in exposed sites. Windbreaks may be constructed, such as fencing, or natural, such as hedges (see also "How a windbreak works," p.609). The soil around newly planted trees may be lifted by frost; if this occurs, refirm it after thawing so that the roots do not dry out (see Frost and Wind Protection, pp.612–613).

In regions with severe winters, trees frequently develop vertical cracks on the south or west side of the trunk. These become more

pronounced in the succeeding winter and may eventually lead to areas of bark lifting completely. The cracks are caused by the sun warming the sap under the bark followed by a rapid freezing and are most common where a shadow moves across the tree in late afternoon, causing a rapid temperature change. They can be prevented by tying a plank against the southern side of the tree for the winter, to shade the bark and prevent it from warming in the sunlight.

Tree problems

Lack of vigor is a reliable indicator that there is a problem with a tree. As well as checking for pests and diseases, make sure that the tree has not been too deeply planted or that the roots and stems have not been damaged; these are possible causes of poor growth and dieback.

The most common pests are aphids (p.654) and spider mites (p.670). A wide range of diseases attacks trees; most are specific to a few species. Some including fire blight (p.660), may be lethal.

Transplanting a tree

It is best to prepare the tree a year in advance before transplanting, because this will greatly increase its chances of reestablishing.

Cut back to the base with pruners any water sprouts that may grow through the bark or sprout at the edges of a wound where a branch has been removed.

CUTTING DOWN A SMALL TREE

Tree felling can be undertaken at any time of year. It is a skilled and potentially dangerous operation; if the tree is over 15ft (5m), it should be tackled by an arborist. Ensure the tree, if on a boundary, legally belongs to you; if not, seek written permission from your neighbor to remove it.

Make sure there is space for the tree to fall safely and that there is an escape route at right angles to the proposed fall line.

A tree is usually taken down in stages, and you must always wear protective gloves. First remove any large branches in sections (see *Removing a Branch*, p.71), and then the rest of the trunk.

You may choose to remove the stump, but keep in mind that decomposing tree stumps provide habitat and food for wildlife. Dig out the stump and any large roots with a spade. Sever tough roots with an ax. If you have a large stump, employ a contractor to grind it or winch it out.

Alternatively, cover the stump with a tarp to retain moisture, or drill holes in the trunk and add some nitrogen fertilizer. These techniques speed up the rotting process.

1 On the side the tree is to fall, make an angled cut just over one-third of the trunk diameter, about 3ft (1m) above ground. Cut out a wedge by sawing horizontally to meet the base of the cut. Remove the wedge to ensure the tree falls in the right direction.

2 On the opposite side of the trunk, make the final cut just above the base of the wedge cut. Push the tree in the right direction as it starts to fall. If felling a large tree, tie ropes around the trunk to guide its fall.

3 Remove the remaining stump by digging a wide trench around it, loosening the roots with a fork or spade, and then winching or digging it out.

Unless the tree is very young, it may be difficult to transplant and may not adjust well; if taller than 8ft (2.5m), the tree may be difficult to establish in its new location. Large trees may need to be transplanted by trained arborists.

Preparation

In early fall the year before the planned move, while the soil is still warm and the tree roots are in active growth, mark the optimal root ball diameter for the tree—about one-third of the tree's height. Dig a trench about 12in (30cm) wide and 24in (60cm) deep just outside the marked area and mix the removed soil with plenty of well-rotted organic matter.

Using a sharp spade, undercut the root ball as far as possible to sever any large, coarse roots. This has the effect of stimulating the growth of fibrous feeder roots, which will help the tree to develop and grow successfully after transplanting. Then replace the mixture of soil and organic matter in the trench.

Lifting the tree

Transplant the tree the following fall (see "When to plant," p.65), first pruning out any thin branches and reducing the tree to a well-balanced framework. Then carefully tie the remaining branches to the central stem to protect them and to increase the working space around the tree.

Dig a trench just outside the one made the previous year and of similar dimensions, and gradually fork away the excess soil until the root ball is of a manageable size and weight; be careful not to damage the fibrous roots. In sandy soil, thoroughly soak the ground before starting to dig, to make the root ball firmer. Then cut with a spade through any roots underneath the root ball to separate it completely from the surrounding soil. To hold the root ball together and stop the roots from drying out while the tree is removed from the hole, it should be securely wrapped in some burlap or plastic. This can be tricky to do, but the easiest way is to tilt the tree first one way and then the other, so that each side of the root ball is raised and the burlap slipped under it. Use rope to secure the wrapping around the root ball. Then maneuver the tree onto a ramp and transport it to its new location.

Replanting

Well before the tree reaches its new site, prepare the planting hole (see *Planting a Balled-and-Burlapped Tree*, p.67). When the tree arrives, lower it into the hole and adjust the planting depth until the dark mark on the tree stem is at soil level. Then undo the root-ball ties and, carefully tilting the tree, remove the burlap covering around the root ball. Backfill the hole, working the soil around and over the root ball and firming it in stages, until the soil is level with the dark mark on the tree stem.

It may be necessary to reduce the crown by 25–30 percent, to minimize water loss and stimulate regrowth the following spring. Until it is well established, support the tree with guy ropes secured to angled stakes in the ground. Water the tree well, then spread a thick mulch about 4in (10cm) deep on the surrounding soil, to retain moisture and suppress weeds. If it is impossible to replant the tree immediately, give it the same care as you would a newly purchased tree (see *Heeling in*, p.65).

TREE ROOTS AND BUILDINGS

Many trees, especially large, forest-sized ones in an urban area, grow too large for their surroundings and/or too near buildings. It may be the legal responsibility of the land owner to rectify any damage that their roots or branches may cause.

Tree roots, for example, may crack building foundations, especially if these are less than 20in (0.5m) deep and sited on clay soils. Walls are particularly vulnerable in times of drought, because soil shrinks as the tree roots absorb the moisture needed to survive. Roots may also block drains, which burst and so cause unstable, wet areas underground.

Roots and suckers may disturb paving slabs on pavement or sidewalks, so they become a hazard to pedestrians, and falling branches may damage roofs, gutters, fences, power lines, or even nearby vehicles.

HOW TO MOVE A YOUNG TREE

1 Prepare the tree for transplanting a year ahead. To transplant, start by tying the branches to the main stem to protect them from damage while working around the tree. Then, keeping outside the area of the root ball, dig a trench about 12in (30cm) wide and 24in (60cm) deep around the tree.

2 Carefully fork away the soil from around the root ball, removing a small amount at a time to avoid damaging the roots.

3 Undercut the root ball with a spade and cut back with pruners any awkward roots protruding from the root ball.

4 Roll up a length of burlap (or plastic) and, tilting the tree to raise one side of the root ball, slide the burlap underneath.

5 Carefully tilt the tree back the other way and pull the burlap through underneath; the root ball should now be resting on the center of the burlap.

6 Pull the burlap up around the root ball so that it is completely covered. Tie it securely in place with rope to keep the root ball intact while the tree is being moved.

7 Tilt the tree to one side and slide two planks underneath it to act as a ramp. Ease the tree up the ramp and then transport it to the new planting site.

Pruning and training

Correct pruning and training helps maintain a tree's health and vigor, regulate its shape and size, and, in some instances, improve ornamental qualities. It is important to prune young trees correctly to develop a strong framework of evenly spaced branches.

The degree of pruning and training depends on the type of tree and the desired effect: relatively little is required to produce a well-balanced tree while creating a pleached avenue with interwoven branches demands much more work and expertise.

When to prune

Most deciduous trees are best pruned when dormant in late fall or winter; they may also be pruned at other times, except in late winter or early spring when many trees "bleed" (exude sap) if cut. Maples (*Acer*), horse chestnuts (*Aesculus*), birches (*Betula*), walnuts (*Juglans*), and cherries (*Prunus*) all bleed extensively, even toward the end of their dormant season; prune

these in mid- to late summer after new growth has matured. Evergreens need little or no pruning except for the removal of dead or diseased branches in late summer.

The principles of pruning

Always wear strong protective gloves when pruning. The first stage is to remove any dead, diseased, or damaged wood on the tree, and to cut out weak or straggly shoots. Then assess the remaining framework and decide which branches should be pruned back or removed for well-balanced growth. Take care not to impair the natural growth habit of a tree by pruning unless aiming to produce a certain shape or form, such as an espalier. Hard pruning stimulates vigorous growth, while light pruning produces only limited growth.

It is important to make pruning cuts accurately and cleanly to minimize damage to the tree. If cutting back a stem, cut just

CUTTING BACK A STEM

Alternate buds
To prune trees with alternate buds, make a clean, angled cut just above a healthy, outward-facing bud.

Opposite buds
To prune trees with opposite buds, make a clean, straight cut directly above a strong pair of buds.

above a healthy bud, a pair of buds, or a sideshoot pointing in the required direction of growth. For example, if thinning out congested stems, cut back to a bud or shoot that is growing outward so that it will not rub against another stem as it grows. Cut neither too far from

the bud, which leaves a stub that provides an entry point for disease, nor too close, which could damage the bud itself.

When pruning trees with opposite buds, make a straight cut with sharp pruners directly above a pair of buds; for trees with alternate buds, make a sloping cut 1/8–1/4in (3–5mm) above a bud so that the base of the cut is just level with the top of the bud, on the opposite side of the stem.

If pruning back a branch completely, cut just outside the branch collar—the slight swelling on the branch where it joins the trunk. This is where the callus is formed that will eventually cover the wound. Never cut flush with the main stem because this damages the tree's natural protective zone, making it more vulnerable to disease. The branch collar on dead branches may extend some way along the branch, but it is still important to make any cut outside it.

REMOVING A BRANCH

If removing whole branches of less than 1in (2.5cm) diameter, make a single cut with a pruning saw or pruners. For branches thicker than this, first remove the bulk of the weight: partially undercut the branch at least 12in (30cm) from the trunk, then a little farther out, saw through from above. If no undercut is made, the branch may break off in midcut, ripping the bark back to the trunk so making it vulnerable to infection.

To remove the remaining stub, undercut it just outside

the branch collar, then cut through from above. If you find it difficult to locate the branch collar, cut through the stub at a short distance from the trunk, making the cut so that it slopes outward away from the tree.

If the angle between the branch and the trunk is very acute, it may be easier to cut through the stub from beneath. Do not apply a wound paint or dressing: there is no clear evidence that they speed up the healing process or prevent disease.

WHERE TO CUT

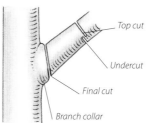

Top cut
Undercut
Final cut
Branch collar

When removing a branch, take care not to damage the branch collar: first remove the bulk of the branch with two cuts, then cut off the stub just outside the collar.

Formative pruning

Young trees benefit from formative pruning to ensure that they develop a strong, well-balanced framework of evenly spaced branches. At its simplest, this involves the removal of dead, damaged, and diseased wood, as well as any weak or crossing branches.

Formative pruning may also be used to determine the tree's shape as it grows: for example, a young feathered tree may be pruned over several years to form a standard, or trained against a wall as an espalier. The extent of the pruning depends on both the type of tree selected and the required shape when mature.

1 When making the final cut, first make a cut on the underside of the branch, close to the collar—about 1 1/4in (3cm) from the trunk. Stop cutting when you are a third of the way through.

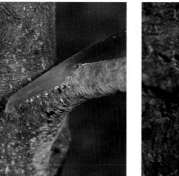

2 Make the second cut directly above the first, or a little closer to the collar. Ensure that the two cuts meet exactly to achieve a smooth, clean wound that will heal quickly.

3 The cut surface should be as small as possible, minimizing the area through which diseases can enter the plant. Smooth any rough edges with a sharp pruning knife.

As with all types of pruning, care should be taken not to spoil the tree's natural growth characteristics.

It is particularly important to prune young tropical trees—their growth rate is very rapid and the girth of both main stems and branches develops extremely quickly; provided that they have been pruned correctly during the first few years after planting, they may then be left to grow naturally. Most other evergreens, on the other hand, will develop naturally into well-shaped specimens with little or no attention; pruning is usually restricted to the removal of dead, damaged, or crossing stems, and badly placed laterals.

The formative pruning of ornamental garden trees depends on the type of tree bought or required. Feathered trees have a single, central leader and laterals along the whole length of the stem. Central-leader standards have a clear length of stem at the base, while branched-head standards also have a clear stem but have their central leader removed to encourage the formation of vigorous lateral branches—as commonly seen in many Japanese cherries (*Prunus*).

Feathered trees
Feathered trees may either be simply pruned to enhance their natural shape or more extensively pruned to train them into standards. This process also occurs naturally sometimes. Although many feathered trees retain their lower branches, these die back in some species and the tree ultimately becomes a central-leader standard; other trees may also lose their central-leader dominance and so become branched-head standards.

Early training is straightforward, however, regardless of the eventual habit of the tree. First remove any competing shoots to leave a single main leader. Then take out any small, weak, and poorly placed laterals, so that the framework of branches around the main stem is evenly spaced and well balanced.

Central-leader standards
Feathered whips may be pruned over two to three years to form a standard; a technique called "feathering" is often used because it also channels food to the main stem, which thickens and becomes sturdier. Initially, prune a feathered whip to remove any competing leaders or weak laterals. Then, on the lowest third of the tree, cut back all the feathers to the main stem; on the middle third, reduce the feathers by about half; leave the

PRUNING AND TRAINING YOUNG TREES

Feathered tree

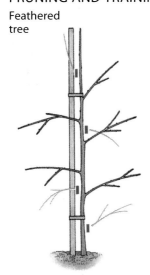

Remove congested and crossing shoots, then cut out any laterals that are small, spindly, or badly positioned, to achieve a well-balanced framework of branches.

Central-leader standard

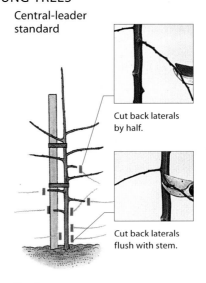

Cut back laterals by half.

Cut back laterals flush with stem.

Year 1
On the lowest third of the tree, cut back laterals to the main stem; on the middle third, cut back laterals by half. Remove any weak or competing leaders.

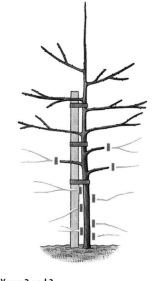

Years 2 and 3
Continue the pruning process, removing the lowest laterals completely and cutting back by about half those laterals that are on the middle third of the tree.

Branched-head standard

Cut back central leader

Remove crossing branches

Remove lower feathers and watersprouts

Remove crossing laterals and any growths on the lower third of the tree. Cut back the leader to a healthy bud or shoot.

Weeping tree

Remove any awkwardly placed shoots that spoil the shape.

Cut back laterals on main stem

Cut back crossing or vertical branches that spoil the symmetry of the tree. Remove any growths on the main stem.

Cut upward-growing shoots back to a downward-pointing bud.

Cut out crossing, rubbing, or congested growth.

top third unpruned, but remove any vigorous, upright shoots that might form a competing leader.

In late fall or early winter, cut back the pruned laterals flush with the main stem. Repeat the procedure over the next two or three years to form a tree with approximately 6ft (1.8m) of clear stem.

Branched-head standards
To form a branched-head standard, train the tree initially as a central-leader standard to achieve the desired length of clear stem. Then, in mid- to late fall, cut back the leader to a strong, healthy bud or shoot to leave a framework of four or five strong, well-placed lateral branches. At this stage, also remove

any crossing or congested laterals and any that spoil the balance of the branch framework.

In subsequent years, prune the tree as much as necessary to keep the crown well balanced and with an open center; remove any vigorous, vertical shoots that may grow into a new leader; and cut back any feathers to the main stem as soon as possible. Some branched-head standards can be formed by topworking (or topgrafting) as for weeping standards.

Weeping standards
A weeping standard is formed by grafting one or two scions of a weeping cultivar onto a stock plant with a clear stem of about 6ft (1.8m).

This is known as topworking or topgrafting, a technique that is most commonly used for fruit trees (see "Topworking," p.443) but also for weeping ash (*Fraxinus excelsior* 'Pendula'), the Kilmarnock willow (*Salix caprea* 'Kilmarnock'), and a large number of other weeping ornamental trees. Young, pendulous branches start to develop once the grafts have taken.

Pruning is best restricted to the removal of crossing and vertical branches as well as any that spoil the overall symmetry of the framework. Although upward-growing branches are usually removed, leave some semiupright stems to develop naturally because they often grow downward later and produce tiers of weeping branches. If growths appear on the main stem, rub or pinch them out as soon as they appear.

Espalier- and fan-trained trees

The aim of both espalier- and fan-training is to form a symmetrical, attractive network of branches in a single plane by pruning and training a young tree over several years. These techniques are occasionally used for growing ornamental trees against fences or walls, but they are more commonly associated with growing fruit trees.

Pruning times vary according to the selected species: for example, *Magnolia grandiflora,* which flowers from mid- to late summer, should be pruned at the start of growth in spring, while the spring-flowering *Acacia dealbata* should be pruned directly after flowering. For full instructions on the pruning techniques, see GROWING FRUIT, "Espalier," p.442, and "Fan," p.441.

Pruning established deciduous trees

Once a deciduous tree is well established, there is little need for further pruning. Major pruning of a mature tree is best carried out by a tree surgeon or arborist because the work is both skilled and dangerous, and, if poorly executed, may ruin the tree.

Many branched-head trees become overcrowded in the center as they mature, restricting the amounts of air and light that reach the central branches. Cut out inward-growing shoots and any branches that spoil the balance of the framework.

If a tree has grown too large for its situation, do not attempt to restrict its size by cutting back all new growth each year; this "haircut" pruning produces an unsightly, congested cluster of shoots each season that spoils the tree's natural appearance and reduces flower and fruit production. The correct treatment is as for the renovation of old trees (see p.74).

As a result of hard pruning or the removal of large branches, a tree may produce a mass of epicormic or watersprouts; rub or cut these out immediately (see p.69).

If the central leader is damaged, select a strong shoot close to the top of the main stem and train it vertically as a replacement leader. Tie the selected shoot to a stake or stake secured high on the main stem, and prune out any potential competing shoots. Once the shoot

REMOVING A COMPETING LEADER

Prune out a competing leader by making a clean cut at the base with pruners or loppers, taking care not to damage the remaining leader.

has developed into a strong, dominant growth, the stake can be removed.

If a tree develops two or more competing leaders, remove all but the strongest shoot. The very narrow angle between rival leaders is a source of structural weakness and the tree could split open at this point in a high wind.

Vigorous, upright shoots may develop on young, branched-head trees. If left, these will quickly grow into competing leaders and so it is important to remove them entirely as soon as possible.

Pruning established evergreen trees

Broadleaved evergreens need only minimal pruning. Provided that the trees have an established leader and that any badly placed laterals have been cut out when young, it is only necessary to remove any dead, damaged, or diseased wood.

Conifers require only basic pruning once established, except when they are grown as a hedge (see HEDGES AND SCREENS, pp.82–85). On some pines (*Pinus*), silver firs (*Abies*), and spruces (*Picea*), the terminal bud on the leader may die; if this occurs, train in the best placed lateral as a replacement leader (see above) and cut out any competing, upright shoots. Established palms require no pruning apart from the removal of dead leaves, which should be cut back to the main stem.

Root pruning

If an established tree is growing vigorously, but producing very few flowers or fruit, pruning the roots may help slow down growth and stimulate better overall performance. In early spring, dig a trench just outside the extent of the tree canopy. Then prune back any thick

roots to the inner edge of the trench, using a pruning saw, pruners, or loppers. Retain any fibrous roots at the inner edge of the trench, backfill the soil, and firm. For further details, see GROWING FRUIT, "Root pruning," p.430. In some instances, it may be necessary to support the tree with stakes or guy ropes if it seems unstable afterward (see *Staking*, p.64). For root pruning of trees in containers, see "Trees in containers," p.68.

Pruning container-planted trees

Container-planted trees should be pruned annually, following the same principles as for other trees, to regulate their shape and size and maintain a balanced framework of evenly spaced branches.

Coppicing and pollarding

Coppicing is the regular pruning of a tree close to the ground to encourage strong, basal shoots

HOW TO COPPICE A TREE

Coppicing may be used to restrict a tree's size, enlarge leaves, or enhance stem color.

Use pruning loppers to cut back all stems to 3in (7cm); do not cut into the swollen, woody base of the tree.

TRAINING A NEW LEADER

Replace a damaged leader by training in a strong shoot vertically. Attach a stake to the top of the main stem and tie the shoot to the stake. Prune out the old, damaged leader. Remove the stake once the new leader is dominant and growing strongly.

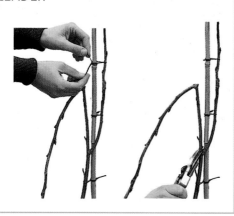

to grow. Pollarding is the pruning of a tree back to its main stem or branch framework, stimulating new shoots at this level. Traditionally, both techniques were practiced to give a regular supply of firewood or pliable stems for basketwork and fencing. Now they are used in gardens to enhance leaf color and the size or the color of ornamental stems, or to restrict tree size.

Coppicing

Trees should be coppiced in late winter or early spring; some willows, when grown for their colored or glaucous stems, may be left until mid-spring, however, and pruned just before or very shortly after bud break. Cut back all stems to the base, leaving the swollen basal wood unpruned because all new growth occurs here. Less vigorous trees should be coppiced over two years, cutting half the stems during the first year and the remaining old ones in the second.

Pollarding

To form a pollard, plant a young, branched-head standard (see opposite). When its trunk has reached 6ft (2m), or the desired

Propagation

Trees may be propagated from cuttings, seed, layering, or grafting. Taking cuttings is probably the most common method of propagation because it is fairly simple and provides new plants relatively quickly, while raising trees from seed or layering is easy but very slow. Grafting is rarely used by amateur gardeners because it requires considerable expertise to grow new plants successfully this way.

Tree species can be propagated from seed but hybrids and cultivars rarely come true to type. Vegetative methods of propagation, such as taking cuttings, layering, and grafting, may be used for hybrids and cultivars as well as species; however, some care in the selection of plant material is required in order to be successful.

Hardwood cuttings

Many deciduous trees can be propagated from hardwood, or dormant, cuttings. In early fall, prepare the ground for the cuttings while it is still warm. In areas with long, harsh winters, cuttings usually die if left outside; root them in deep boxes in a basement or frost-free root cellar.

Cuttings of trees that root easily, such as willows (*Salix*), may be inserted directly into a trench, while those that are more difficult to root, such as *Metasequoia*, should be inserted in a sand bed and then transplanted into a trench early the next spring. In either case, make the trench narrow and with one side vertical so that the cuttings are held upright while they root. The depth of the trench will depend on the type of plant required: for multistemmed trees, it should be 1in (2.5cm) shallower than the length of the cuttings; for single-stemmed trees, it should be the same depth as the cuttings so that the top bud is barely covered and the lack of light inhibits the growth of all other buds.

For best results, dig the trench in friable, well-drained soil; in heavy, clay soil, add some coarse sand to the base. If preparing a few trenches, space them 12–15in (30–38cm) apart in open ground, or about 4in (10cm) apart in a cold frame.

SLOW-ROOTING HARDWOOD CUTTINGS

1 For species that do not root easily (here, *Metasequoia*), tie cuttings into bundles. Dip the ends in hormone rooting powder.

2 Insert the bundles of cuttings in a sand bed and leave in a cold frame over winter. In spring, insert them individually in a trench in a prepared site outside.

Preparing and inserting the cuttings
Select the cuttings just after leaf fall: choose strong, vigorous shoots of the current season's growth and remove them by cutting just above a bud or pair of buds at the junction between the current and the previous season's growth. Trim down the cuttings as shown and dip the basal cuts in hormone rooting powder to encourage them to root. Place the cuttings against the vertical side of the trench at the correct depth, and backfill with soil. Then firm in gently and water well.

For species that do not root easily, tie the cuttings into small bundles of no more than ten and then plunge them in a sand bed (see p.638) in a cold frame for the winter, where they should callus or root before being transplanted.

FAST-ROOTING HARDWOOD CUTTINGS

1 To prepare the trench, push the spade vertically into the soil, then press it forward slightly to form a flat-backed trench about 7in (19cm) deep.

2 Select strong, straight stems with healthy buds (right); avoid soft, spindly, old, or damaged stems (left). Remove about 12in (30cm) of the stem, cutting just above a bud.

3 Remove any leaves. Trim the cuttings to about 8in (20cm): make an angled cut just above the proposed top bud and a horizontal cut below the bottom one.

4 Insert the cuttings in the trench 4–6in (10–15cm) apart, and at the correct depth depending on whether a single- or a multistemmed tree is desired.

PLANTING DEPTHS

Multistemmed trees
For multistemmed trees, insert cuttings with the top 1–1½in (2.5–3cm) above the soil surface.

Single-stemmed trees
The top bud of each cutting should be just below the soil surface.

5 Firm the soil around the cuttings, rake the surface, and label. Space other rows 12–15in (30–38cm) apart.

6 Lift the rooted cuttings the following fall. Then pot them up individually or transplant them into open ground in their final locations.

Aftercare

Label the cuttings and leave them until the following fall. During winter, the ground may be lifted by frost; refirm the soil around the cuttings if this occurs. By fall, the cuttings should be well rooted and may then be transplanted individually into open ground or into containers, as required. If they have been kept in a cold frame, harden them off in the first spring, then transplant outside; the following spring, pot them up or move them to their final spots in open ground.

Semiripe cuttings

Many conifers, as well as certain broadleaved evergreens such as *Magnolia grandiflora* and *Prunus lusitanica*, may be propagated readily from semiripe cuttings. These cuttings are taken in late summer or fall from stems that have nearly ripened—that is, when they have thickened and become harder (see also ORNAMENTAL SHRUBS, "Semiripe cuttings," p.111).

Selecting the cuttings

In a closed case, at 70°F (21°C), or in a cold frame, prepare a suitable rooting medium for the cuttings. For example, this might consist of equal parts of grit and compost or peat (see also "Standard propagation mix," p.565). Using a sharp knife, take heel cuttings from healthy sideshoots, including a sliver of hardened wood from the main stem (see ORNAMENTAL SHRUBS, "Heel cuttings," p.112). Alternatively, take 4–6in (10–15cm) long cuttings from leaders or sideshoots and trim immediately below a node.

For cuttings from conifers, choose leaders or sideshoots that are characteristic of the parent plant, because conifer shoots vary considerably in their growth patterns. It is particularly important to select cutting material carefully from slow-growing (dwarf)

conifers; some plants may produce reverted or uncharacteristic shoots, but only use shoots that typify what you want to propagate.

Preparing and inserting the cuttings

For all semiripe cuttings, cut off the lower pair of leaves with a sharp knife and reduce the remaining leaves by a third or a half to minimize the loss of moisture; if the cutting tips are soft, pinch them out. To encourage the cuttings to root, use the tip of the knife to make two shallow, vertical wounds, about 1in (2.5cm) long, on opposite sides of each cutting down to the base. Alternatively, make a longer wound along the side of each cutting with a knife, and remove a sliver of bark as well. In either case, dip the basal cut, including the wound, in hormone rooting powder.

Insert the bottom third of each cutting in the rooting medium, being careful to leave enough space between the cuttings so that they do not overlap; this allows air to circulate freely around them. Then firm the medium and water it thoroughly. Be sure to label everything clearly.

Aftercare

Check the cuttings periodically, watering them only to keep them from drying out. Remove any fallen leaves as soon as they appear— these may rot and spread disease to the cuttings. During cold spells, cold frames should be insulated with burlap or a similar covering.

If the cuttings are being kept in a closed case with bottom heat, they should root by early spring. Cuttings in a cold frame are usually left until the following fall, although it is preferable to leave them in the frame for a second winter and pot them up the following spring.

During the summer, mist-spray the cuttings frequently to keep them from drying out. If the cuttings are in strong, direct sunlight, they risk being scorched and it may be necessary to shade them; apply a greenhouse shading

paint or place shading material over the frame (see p.576). Once the cuttings root, lift them out carefully with a hand fork and transplant them into individual pots, then harden them off (see p.637) before potting them again or planting them out in open ground. Rooted cuttings in a cold frame may be hardened off while still in the frame by raising the frame cover for short, then longer, periods. Once they are sufficiently well rooted, pot them or transplant them outside. If there may be a delay before potting, give a liquid feed to the rooted cuttings in the interim.

Softwood cuttings

This method of propagation is suitable for birch (*Betula*), *Metasequoia*, some ornamental cherries (*Prunus*), and a few other tree species, although it is more commonly used for shrubs. Softwood cuttings are taken in spring from the fast-growing tips of new shoots and usually root very easily. They wilt rapidly, however, so it is vital to prepare and insert them as quickly as possible after removing them from the parent plant.

Preparing and inserting the cuttings

In spring, before taking the cuttings, prepare containers by filling them with an appropriate propagation mix and then firming to just below the rim. Take the cuttings by removing the new growth from stem tips, cutting just above a bud or leaf joint with pruners or a sharp knife. To reduce any moisture loss, immerse the cuttings in water right away or place them in an opaque, plastic bag and seal it. Even a small loss of water will hinder the development of new roots.

Prepare the cuttings by trimming them with a sharp knife to about 2½in (6cm), cutting just below a leaf joint. Remove the lower leaves. The base of each cutting can be dipped in hormone rooting powder to encourage rooting. Insert the cuttings into the prepared pots of compost, label them clearly, and water the posts well.

To encourage rapid rooting, place the containers in a mist unit or closed case at 70–75°F (21–24°C), preferably with basal heat. Water with a fungicide once a week to protect against rotting and disease. Once they are rooted, the cuttings may be hardened off gradually before they are transplanted carefully into individual pots.

PREPARING A SEMIRIPE CUTTING

Cut a shoot 4–6in (10–15cm) long from a leader or sideshoot and trim immediately below a node. Strip off the lower leaves (here, of *Chamaecyparis obtusa* 'Nana Aurea') and pinch out the tip if it is soft. Make a wound, about 1in (2.5cm) long, down the side of the cutting and dip it in rooting hormone.

TREES TO PROPAGATE FROM CUTTINGS

Hardwood
Cordyline
Ficus
Metasequoia glyptostroboides
Morus
Platanus
Populus
Salix

Semiripe
Austrocedrus ▽
Calocedrus ▽
Chamaecyparis ▽
Cinnamomum ▽
x *Cupressocyparis* ▽
Cupressus ▽
Drimys winteri
Eucryphia
Grevillea
Hoheria
Ilex
Juniperus ▽
Ligustrum lucidum
Magnolia grandiflora ▽
Metrosideros excelsa,
  M. robusta,
  M. umbellata
Michelia ▽
Nothofagus dombeyi
Podocarpus, some ▽
Prunus lusitanica
Quercus ilex ▽,
  Q. myrsinifolia▽,
  Q. semecarpifolia▽
Schefflera
Taxus
Thuja ▽
Thujopsis ▽
Trochodendron aralioides ▽
Tsuga ▽
Weinmannia

Softwood
Acer cappadocicum
Betula
Catalpa
Celtis occidentalis
Cotinus coggygria
Eucryphia lucida
Ginkgo biloba
Halesia
Koelreuteria paniculata
Lagerstroemia, some
Liquidambar styraciflua
Metasequoia glyptostroboides
Pistacia
Prunus
Ulmus

Key
▽ Take cuttings with a heel

Catalpa bignonioides

Raising trees from seed

Tree species may be propagated from seed because their seedlings usually retain the distinctive characteristics of the parent plant; hybrids and cultivars rarely come true to type. Raising a tree from seed is a relatively simple process; it is, however, a slow method if a tree is being grown mainly for its flowers—the tree will take several years to reach flowering size.

Extracting seed

The protective covering of some seeds should be removed first. The method for this varies, depending on the type of seed coat. The coating on winged seeds can be removed simply by rubbing it between finger and thumb. Some cones disintegrate naturally and the scales may then be separated. Place pine and spruce cones in a paper bag and keep them in a warm, dry place until the cone scales open and shed the seed into the bag; immerse cedar cones in hot water and leave them to soak until the scales open.

The method of extracting seed from fruits or berries depends on the seed size and type of flesh. Large fruit, such as those of crabapples (*Malus*), can be cut open and the seeds extracted. Soak smaller fruit, such as those of *Sorbus*, in warm water for several days. Viable seed will sink. Discard the pulp, soak again until the seed can be removed, and pick off any remaining flesh.

Storing

Once the seed has been extracted, dry it if necessary and place it in a sealed and labeled plastic bag. If planning to sow the seed within a few days, store it at room temperature; for longer-term storage, keep it on the top shelf of a refrigerator so that it is cool but not frozen.

CLEANING FLESHY SEEDS

1 Remove the fleshy seeds with your fingers. Immerse them in warm water, and soak for 1–2 days. Once the fleshy coating has softened and split, drain off the water.

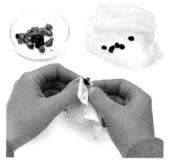

2 Pick off the remaining coating and wipe the seeds dry. Sow the seeds fresh or store in a plastic bag in a refrigerator for no more than a few weeks.

Breaking seed dormancy

Some seeds have a natural period of dormancy to prevent germination in adverse climatic conditions that would threaten the survival of the seedlings; this has to be overcome before the seed will germinate. Several kinds of dormancy occur, sometimes combined, which vary according to the species: most commonly, dormancy is achieved either by a hard, thick seed coat, which prevents water from being taken up, or by a chemical inhibitor, which delays germination until there is a significant temperature change. In most cases, dormancy can be broken artificially by wearing away the seed coat or by chilling the seed.

Scarification

Before sowing seeds with an impermeable coating, scarify them to allow germination to occur: large seeds with a particularly hard covering, such as oaks (*Quercus*), may be nicked with a sharp knife, or a section of the seed coat filed away to let in moisture; smaller seeds that are not easily nicked, such as those of pines, may be shaken in a jar that has been lined with sandpaper or partly filled with sharp grit, or they may be filed individually with an emery board. Seed from legumes (for example *Acacia* and *Robinia*) should simply be left to soak in a container of hot water for approximately 24 hours in a ratio of three parts hot water to one part seed.

Stratification

Dormancy in seed of trees from temperate climates is commonly overcome by chilling or "stratification." Seed may either be sown outside so that it is chilled naturally during winter or, more reliably, stratified artificially by being stored in a refrigerator.

If refrigerating seed, first mix it with moistened vermiculite, peat substitute, or peat. Place it in a clear plastic bag, then seal the bag and put it in a refrigerator. Check the seed regularly through the unopened bag—it should be sown as soon as there are signs of germination.

The length of chilling time required varies considerably: as a guideline, many deciduous species require about six to eight weeks of chilling at 33–34°F (0.5–1°C), while conifers need only about three weeks. Some seeds only germinate after they have been sown and once chilling has ceased. In such cases, sow batches of seed at intervals—for example, after four, eight, and twelve weeks of chilling. This should ensure that at least some seeds germinate.

Sowing seed in containers

This is a simple way of raising a small number of seedlings. Thoroughly clean any work surfaces and containers to be used before sowing the seed to avoid contamination from soil-borne pests and diseases. First fill the pots, pans, or seed flats with seed compost up to the rim.

Large seeds or those that produce seedlings with long taproots, such as oaks (*Quercus*), should be sown about 3in (8cm) apart in deep seed flats or packs, or in flexible root trainers. Using a presser board, press the seeds into unfirmed potting mix, then cover them to their own depth with more mix and firm to about ¼in (5mm) below the rim (see below).

Sow very large seeds, for example those of horse chestnut (*Aesculus*), singly in 4–6in (10–15cm) pots. Insert the seed in firmed potting mix, so that just the top of the seed is exposed above the surface.

Small seeds, for example those of *Sorbus*, may be either scattered evenly or, if sufficiently large, individually pressed into prepared pots or flats of firmed potting mix. They should then be barely covered with sifted potting mix, followed by a layer of fine grit ¼in (5mm) deep.

SOWING IN CONTAINERS

1 Sow fine seed (here, *Sorbus*) in containers of firmed seed starter mix, making sure they are scattered evenly; keep your hand low to stop them from bouncing.

2 Hold a sieve containing propagation mix over the flat, then tap the side of the sieve until the seeds are just covered to their own depth with the sifted soil.

3 Cover the sown seeds with a ¼in (5mm) deep layer of horticultural grit. Label and water the seeds, using a watering can fitted with a fine rose.

4 Once the seedlings are large enough to handle, gently prick them out into individual pots, being careful not to crush the delicate stems or roots.

SOWING LARGE SEEDS

1 Press large seeds and those of trees with long taproots into propagation mix in individual pots. Cover with more mix.

2 Sowing in deep pots allows the taproot (see inset) of each seedling (here, *Quercus*) to develop without any restriction.

After sowing, thoroughly water all seeds from above, then label. Place the containers in a cold frame or, within a greenhouse, in a closed propagation case or under a pane of glass. Temperate species are best kept at 54–59°F (12–15°C), and warm-temperate and tropical species at 70°F (21°C) to stimulate germination. After germination, ensure good air circulation to discourage damping off (see p.658).

Pricking out

When the seedlings are large enough to be handled by their seed leaves, prick them out so that they have more space to grow. This can be done by knocking the container sides to loosen the soil, and then lifting and transplanting the seedlings into individual pots. Alternatively, remove all the seedlings and soil mix together from the container so that the seedlings may be separated with minimal root disturbance. After transplanting, firm the soil mix gently around the seedlings, then level it by gently tapping the pot on the work surface.

Aftercare

Water and label the seedlings, and keep them out of direct sunlight in a temperature similar to that needed for germination until established. Gradually harden them off (see p.637) over a few weeks, feeding them regularly. Do not overwater, but make sure that the soil mix does not dry out. Once hardened off, they may be planted out if there is no danger of frost.

Sowing seed outdoors

If raising a large number of seedlings, seed may be sown in an outdoor seedbed; with this method, the seedlings require less regular attention and their growth is less restricted than if sown in containers, but a special bed must be prepared. If possible, do this a few months before sowing by thoroughly digging the area to a spade's depth (see "Single digging," p.619), incorporating organic matter and some coarse grit. Keep the ground clear of weeds.

When ready to sow, rake the soil down to a fine tilth, then broadcast small seeds or station sow larger ones individually. (For depth of sowing, see "Sowing seed in containers," opposite.) Lightly rake over the seeds, cover the bed evenly with a ¼–½in (0.5–1cm) layer of grit, and firm with a presser. If the soil is dry, water thoroughly; then label with the plant name and sowing date.

In exposed sites, young seedlings may need to be protected with windbreak netting (see p.613) or with a floating row cover (see p.582). If the seeds are well spaced, disease should not be a problem and the seedlings may be grown on *in situ* for 12 months before being pricked out. Water the seedlings as needed and check them regularly in case treatment is needed for pests such as aphids (see "Aphids," p.654) and spider mites (p.670).

Layering

Layering can be used to propagate hybrids and cultivars as well as species. This method of propagation occurs naturally in some plants, when a low-growing stem roots itself in the ground; once this happens, the stem can be removed from the parent plant and planted out. Air layering, where the shoot remains above ground, may be used for trees without low-growing stems.

The advantage of layering is that the layered stem needs very little attention while the roots become established. It is a slow method, however, because in order

SIMPLE LAYERING

Cut a 2in (5cm) tongue 12–18in (30–45cm) behind the tip of a vigorous shoot, or remove a narrow ring of bark at this point. Brush the wound with hormone rooting powder and peg the shoot into a shallow hole. Tie the shoot to a supporting stake and backfill the hole.

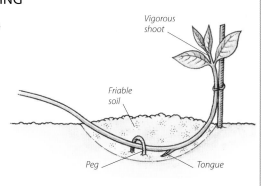

Vigorous shoot

Friable soil

Peg

Tongue

to obtain suitable material, the plant must be prepared a year in advance, and the layered stem may take a year or more to root.

Simple layering

In this method, a shoot is pegged down into the ground until it has rooted and is then cut off from the parent plant (see also *Propagating a Shrub by Simple Layering*, p.115).

Prepare the parent plant a year before layering is to take place: in late winter or early spring, prune a low branch to stimulate new, young shoots that will root easily. In early spring the following year, select a vigorous shoot and make a small wound 12–18in (30–45cm) from the tip. Brush this with hormone rooting powder to encourage rooting. Add plenty of leaf mold or similar organic matter and sharp grit to the soil where the shoot touches the ground and peg it down into a shallow hole, tying it to a vertical stake.

Backfill the hole and firm the soil well, leaving the shoot tip exposed, then water thoroughly and, if necessary, protect the shoot from rabbits and other animals with wire netting. About 12 months later, check to see whether the shoot has rooted; if it has, sever it from the parent and either plant it in open ground or pot it; if it has not rooted, leave it in place and check a month later.

Air layering

The principle of air layering is the same as simple layering, except that the layered shoot roots above the ground rather than in it (see also *Air Layering a Shrub*, p.116). In spring, select a strong stem that has ripened in the previous year, and remove any leaves 12–18in (30–45cm) behind the growing tip. Prepare the stem either by cutting a tongue 2in (5cm) long in the bark, 9–12in (22–30cm) behind its tip, or by removing a ¼–⅜in (6–8mm) wide ring of bark from the stem at this point; in either case, brush the wound with hormone rooting powder.

Surround the cut stem with a moist rooting medium and seal it in. To do this, first make a plastic sleeve by cutting off the sealed end of a plastic bag, then slide it along the stem until it surrounds the cut, and secure the lower end with string or tape. Moisten some well-aerated rooting medium (such as sphagnum moss or a mix of equal parts of peat substitute or peat and perlite), then use it to wedge open the tongue; add more medium around the stem inside the sleeve and seal the top.

If the layer has rooted by the next spring, sever the stem from the parent plant, remove the sleeve, and pot up; if not rooted, it should be left in place for another year.

TREE SEEDS REQUIRING STRATIFICATION

Acer (some)
Betula
Carya
Fagus
Sorbus

TREES TO BE LAYERED
Simple layering
Cercidiphyllum
Chionanthus retusus
Corylus
Davidia
Dipteronia
Eucryphia
Halesia
Hoheria lyallii
Laurus
Magnolia campbellii,
 M. grandiflora, M. obovata

Air layering
Ficus
Magnolia campbellii,
 M. grandiflora

Davidia involucrata

Grafting

Grafted plants, unlike cuttings, have the benefit of a developed root system so they establish relatively quickly. Part of a stem (the scion), taken from the plant to be propagated, is joined to a compatible rootstock of another plant, usually of the same genus. In some cases, the rootstock may confer a desirable characteristic, such as a particular growth habit or high resistance to disease, on the resulting plant.

Grafting methods include side-veneer, chip-budding, apical-wedge, whip-and-tongue, and basal whip.

For details of basal whip and whip-and-tongue types, see PRINCIPLES OF PROPAGATION, p.636. Check that the rootstocks and scions are compatible.

Side-veneer grafting

This is the most common grafting technique used for ornamental trees; a one-year-old stem is used for the scion and grafted onto the side of the prepared rootstock. It is usually carried out just before leaf break, in mid- to late winter, although for maples (*Acer*) summer-grafting is sometimes more successful.

Prepare the rootstocks a year in advance by potting up one- or two-year-old seedlings in the fall and establishing them in an open frame. About three weeks before grafting, bring them into a cool greenhouse to force them gently into growth. Keep the stocks dry, particularly those from trees that "bleed" sap, such as birches (*Betula*) and conifers. Excessive sap may prevent a successful union with the scions.

For the scions, collect strong, one-year-old stems from the tree to be propagated; they should have a diameter similar to the rootstock stems, if possible. Trim them down to 6–10in (15–25cm), cutting just above a bud or pair of buds, and place them in a plastic bag in a refrigerator until ready to graft.

Either cut back the top growth of the stocks to about 2–3in (5–7cm) or leave some top growth above the graft and cut this back in stages later (see "Aftercare," opposite).

Prepare the stocks and scions, one pair at a time, with compatible cuts. It is important to unite the rootstock and scion as soon as they have been cut; if they are allowed to dry out even slightly, this is likely to impede successful union. If the scion is narrower than the stock, align one edge to ensure that at least one side of the cambium layer unites. Tie the scion in position with clear plastic grafting tape, raffia, or a rubber strip, then wax

---

TREES TO BE GRAFTED

Chip-budding

Crataegus
Laburnum
Magnolia
Malus
Prunus
Pyrus
Sorbus

Apical-wedge

Aesculus
Catalpa
Cercis
Fagus

Side-veneer

Abies
Acer
Betula
Carpinus
Cedrus
Cupressus
Fagus
Fraxinus
Ginkgo
Gleditsia
Larix
Magnolia
Picea
Pinus
Prunus
Robinia
Sorbus

Whip-and-tongue

Fraxinus
Gleditsia
Robinia

Ginkgo biloba

PROPAGATING TREES BY SIDE-VENEER GRAFTING

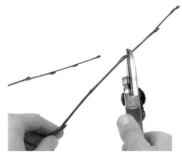

1 Trim the scion to a length of 6–10in (15–25cm), cutting just above a bud or pair of buds. Place it in a plastic bag and refrigerate until ready to graft.

2 Using a sharp knife, make a short, downward, inward nick about 1in (2.5cm) from the top of the rootstock.

3 Starting near the top of the stock, make a sloping, slightly inward cut down to meet the inner point of the first cut. Remove the resulting sliver of wood.

4 Make the final cut on the stock by slicing straight up with the knife from the first cut below. This leaves a flat cut on one side of the stock (see inset).

5 Now prepare the scion: make a shallow, sloping cut about 1in (2.5cm) long down to the base; then make a short, angled cut at the base, on the opposite side (see inset).

Growth visible from buds

8 A few weeks later, if the graft has taken, the buds of the scion will show signs of growth. Remove any suckers that may have appeared on the rootstock or they will divert growth away from the scion.

6 Fit the base of the scion into the cut in the rootstock (see inset). Starting at the top, wrap a piece of grafting tape around the union to secure it.

7 Brush grafting wax over the external cut surfaces on both the stock and the scion. In addition, wax the top of the scion if it has been trimmed back.

and late summer (see *Formal, Clipped Hedges*, p.82). Most formal hedges are cut with shears or an electric trimmer. Use a straight edge or a garden line as a guide when trimming the hedge to shape.

Informal hedges also need regular pruning to shape. Remove misplaced growths, and cut back within the required bounds. Flowering or fruiting hedges must be pruned only at the appropriate season (see *Informal and Flowering Hedges*, p.83). Informal hedges and those with large evergreen leaves should, where practical, be pruned with pruners to avoid unsightly damage to the leaves.

Renovation

A number of hedging species, notably hornbeam (*Carpinus*), honeysuckle (*Lonicera*), and yew (*Taxus baccata*), respond well to renovation even where hedges have been neglected and have become overgrown. For best results, deciduous hedges should be renovated in winter, and evergreen ones in mid-spring.

If drastic pruning is required, alternate sides should be cut back in subsequent seasons. If the renovation is to be successful, it is most important to feed and mulch the plants in the season before pruning, and then again after cutting back to encourage healthy new growth.

Willow walls

Weaving with willow (*Salix*) stems has a long and distinguished history. Woven barriers have been used for fencing since prehistoric times, and, when coated with thick layers of mud, clay, and dung, were a major building material in many parts of the world: wattle and daub. Living willow, used as sculpture, is a new form of horticultural art. The contrast between the lines of the stems and exuberant, fresh young growth gives even functional items such as seats, screens, arbors, and arches an inherent sculptural quality, which many gardeners are becoming eager to incorporate into their own personal landscapes.

Suitable plants

The species or cultivar of willow must be matched to the size and nature of the proposed living structure. Vigor, physical strength, and esthetic qualities are the main points to be taken into consideration. Most willows are flexible enough for weaving with the exception of the brittle *Salix*

fragilis. Cultivars of *S. alba* are especially suitable because their brightly colored stems look spectacular in winter.

Preparation

Planting and weaving should be carried out in winter, when the plants are dormant. Willow can be inserted as normal hardwood cuttings of the current year's growth, about 15in (38cm) long and set 12in (30cm) deep, which are then allowed to grow on site, or as long rods that can be woven together immediately. Rods can establish just as successfully as cuttings provided the ground is well prepared, and they are freshly cut and kept well watered. Another option is to use multistemmed plants, which are easy to develop from nursery-grown stock, hard-pruned to encourage the growth of two or more stems.

Plan the shape and height of the screen; it can follow a straight or curved baseline. Mark the outline before planting, bearing in mind willows need bright light to thrive.

Work out how many rods of what length will be needed. Rods should be planted at least 6in (15cm) apart,

and should be more widely spaced for tall screens using more vigorous cultivars. At 6in (15cm) apart, a 40ft (12m) screen would need 80 rods.

Weaving and tying

Once a row of evenly spaced rods has been planted, weaving can begin so an attractive diamond pattern is created. It is best to try and weave to the desired height all at once to keep the main lines straight. New shoots can be used to continue the structure upward, but will not follow the original rods exactly. The weaving itself will hold the stems together to some extent, but crossing points should be tied firmly with tarred twine. For simple screens, tie only every third or fourth crossing point.

The twine will biodegrade over about two years, but grafts may form more quickly than this. Check the tied crossing points regularly, and, if the stems have united, remove the tie.

Where long rods have been planted, remove sideshoots as they appear, so growth is restricted to the stem tips. This will encourage

extension growth and the formation of the pressure grafts. Once the stems have united, allow sideshoots to develop and use them to fill in as required, again weaving them over and under the main stems. When structures are established, trim back or weave in new shoots regularly.

Weaving horizontal and vertical stems to form a screen of squares is more difficult. Horizontal living stems cannot be established initially, as they would have to be bent through 90 degrees. Dead stems can be woven in as horizontals until the verticals produce sideshoots that can take their place, but the screen will take longer to establish. Training shoots horizontally also lowers their sap flow and reduces vigor.

More complex structures

The other main weaving technique, which is used to form arches and tunnels, is to bend and twist the stems around one another. The twisted stems need to be tied to hold them together. Extra stability is also provided by planting large rods deeper than 12in (30cm); this does not affect their ability to root successfully.

HOW TO SHAPE A LIVING WILLOW WALL

1 Plant a row of evenly spaced rods. Then weave together by angling them at 45 degrees from the vertical and alternately crisscrossing over and under each rod.

2 Tie the crossing points securely with tarred twine. This will force the stems together as they expand and so unite their cambium layers, forming pressure grafts to hold the structure.

3 At the top of a screen, join the last row of crossing points with rubber plant ties. These allow the rods to move slightly in the wind and prevent their tops from breaking.

Green trellis
Screens of living willow make excellent garden sculptures. They have even been employed on a scale large enough to shield entire English villages from the sights and sounds of heavy traffic.

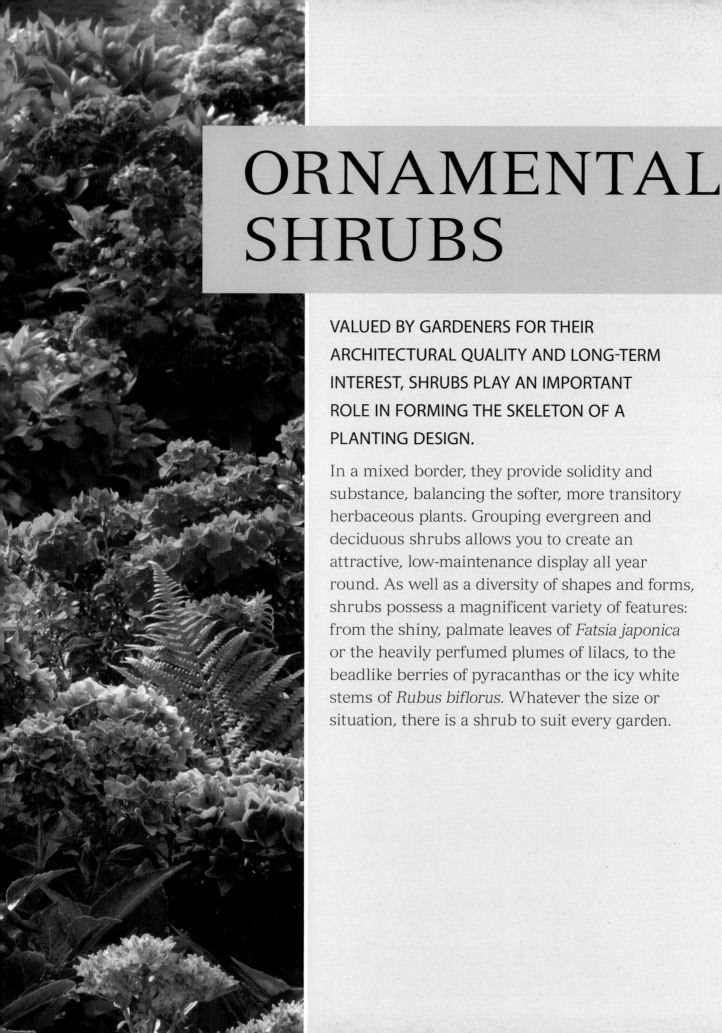

ORNAMENTAL SHRUBS

VALUED BY GARDENERS FOR THEIR ARCHITECTURAL QUALITY AND LONG-TERM INTEREST, SHRUBS PLAY AN IMPORTANT ROLE IN FORMING THE SKELETON OF A PLANTING DESIGN.

In a mixed border, they provide solidity and substance, balancing the softer, more transitory herbaceous plants. Grouping evergreen and deciduous shrubs allows you to create an attractive, low-maintenance display all year round. As well as a diversity of shapes and forms, shrubs possess a magnificent variety of features: from the shiny, palmate leaves of *Fatsia japonica* or the heavily perfumed plumes of lilacs, to the beadlike berries of pyracanthas or the icy white stems of *Rubus biflorus*. Whatever the size or situation, there is a shrub to suit every garden.

Designing with shrubs

Shrubs are woody-stemmed plants that typically produce a framework of branches from the base, unlike the single trunk of most trees. The division between shrubs and trees is not a rigid one, however. Some shrubs (such as fuchsias) can be trained as standards with a single trunk, and many trees are multistemmed. Similarly, the difference in scale is not a clear demarcation. Some shrubs grow larger than some trees. Numerous shrubs are available for planting in home landscapes of any size or style. Species from many genera collected worldwide have given rise to a wide range of ornamental cultivars.

Choosing shrubs

Shrubs are invaluable in landscapes and gardens for many reasons; perhaps most important of all, they impart shape, structure, and substance to a design, and provide a framework. They are far from being purely functional keystones, however, for they are also endowed with a variety of ornamental qualities, including fragrant and colorful flowers, evergreen or variegated foliage, attractive fruits, and colored or shapely stems.

These decorative attributes are a major consideration when choosing plants. There are, however, important practical considerations to be taken into account when deciding which shrubs to grow in your yard.

Compatibility with the natural or adapted growing conditions is essential for their well-being, (see "Matching shrubs to the site," right), while a shrub's growth rate, habit, and eventual height and spread also determine whether it is suitable for a particular site.

Form and size

In size, shrubs range from extreme dwarfs, such as the mat-forming *Penstemon newberryi* at only 6–8in (15–20cm) tall, that are suitable for the rock garden, to much more substantial plants that are 15–20ft (5–6m) tall. These include some of the handsome, evergreen rhododendrons, which can be regarded as almost treelike in scale.

Shrubs have many different forms and habits, including rounded, arching, and vertical. Some—for example, *Yucca glauca*, with its explosive spray of swordlike leaves and erect panicles of flowers—are worth growing for their form alone. Others, like *Chaenomeles japonica*, have a sprawling habit that often looks better if wall-trained. Most are invaluable in low-maintenance landscapes, especially low-growing shrubs used as groundcover, surrounded by mulch.

Shrubs as design features

When selecting shrubs, consider how they will associate with nearby plants and structural elements, such as the house or deck. If they are to form part of the design framework, shrubs with distinctive, sculptural silhouettes are usually most suitable—for example, the spreading, wavelike form of *Juniperus squamata* 'Blue Carpet' or the bold, upright mass of *Mahonia* x *media*. Think of them as abstract shapes that may be used singly or in combination to create a balanced design of contrasting and complementary forms.

Foundation planting

Shrubs are often used as foundation planting to link the house with the landscape, forming a transition between the rigid lines of the building and the softer shapes and textures of border plants and lawn.

This type of planting is effective when used to mark the entrance to the house; symmetrical groups or rows of shrubs could flank the drive or the doorway, for example, or an informal curved bed might border a winding path to the door.

Design the planting so that it complements the style, color, and scale of the building. Evergreen shrubs are often chosen for their continuous display but, especially in an informal setting, including deciduous plants as well creates a greater variety of interest while still providing mass and structure.

Matching shrubs to the site

To ensure that shrubs flourish and give pleasure for a long time, it is essential to invest in plants that will thrive in the particular conditions in your yard. Even in a small yard, these growing conditions

often vary considerably. Because there are so many shrubs from which to make a selection, there is no need to grow plants that are unsuited to the chosen site.

Soil types

The character of the soil should be the first consideration; in many cases, it may be improved to widen the range of plants that can be grown satisfactorily. It is particularly important to make heavy soils more open and faster-draining and light soils more moisture-retentive, as well as to moderate any excessive acidity or alkalinity that may be a problem.

Successful planting must take into account the soil's underlying character, however. Even for relatively extreme conditions, there are a number of plants to choose from: dogwoods (*Cornus*) and willows (*Salix*) like moist soil, while broom (*Cytisus/Genista*) and lavender (*Lavandula*) thrive in well-drained soil. Rhododendrons and other ericaceous plants require acidic conditions; but many shrubs do well in alkaline soil, including *Deutzia*, *Hypericum*, and *Philadelphus*.

Aspect and microclimate

A plant's preference for sun or shade should also be kept in mind. Sun-lovers will become straggly if not planted in full sun, but many shrubs tolerate or even prefer some shade. The latter are often ideal for urban settings, where instead of dappled light filtering through trees, they are subjected to both full sun and deep shade cast by buildings.

SHRUBS IN A CHANGING CLIMATE

While climate change and global warming are regarded as having many serious drawbacks, gardeners have found that one of the benefits has been to extend the range of shrubs that may be grown outside. A popular shrub classically listed as hardy only to Zone 7b, such as crepe myrtle (*Lagerstroemia indica*), may now be worth planting in a Zone 6 yard, especially if you can provide a somewhat sheltered site. And glossy abelia (*Abelia x grandiflora*), which loses some of its leaves in the colder part of the range, may not serve reliably as an evergreen that retains its foliage throughout the year.

If you want to challenge your zone in terms of shrub selection, start small with one or two plants. Remember, climate change may bring extremes of cold weather some years even in the midst of an overall warming trend.

Planting combinations
A successful shrub border relies on choosing plants that perform well in the same growing conditions and provide a long period of interest.

The hardiness of shrubs is another factor to consider. The temperature range, altitude, degree of shelter, sun exposure, and distance from the sea all affect what may be grown. The sea moderates temperature, but salt-laden winds can damage many plants in coastal gardens. There are, however, shrubs (such as *Escallonia* and *Genista*) that benefit from mild conditions and tolerate salt spray. Plants of borderline hardiness for the area that might well succumb in the open garden are more likely to thrive as wall-trained specimens in a more sheltered position.

Successional interest

When selecting shrubs, consider their season of interest and whether it is continuous, as from evergreen foliage, or transitory, as from a burst of summer blooms. For an unbroken display, plant shrubs with a brief period of interest near others that peak shortly afterward.

Spring

Spring-flowering shrubs are valued for the color and vitality that they bring. Combine them to provide interest all season long—from the early *Salix melanostachys*, with its black catkins borne on dark red twigs, to *Jasminum nudiflorum*, treasured for its yellow flowers on arching, green stems.

Summer

The wide choice of summer-flowering shrubs makes it easy to form a continuous display. Invaluable shrubs such as *Potentilla* 'Elizabeth' and *Syringa microphylla* 'Superba' offer a flowering period that often extends from late spring until early fall.

RECOMMENDED SHRUBS FOR ACIDIC SOIL

Camellia x williamsii 'Donation'

Erica x williamsii 'P. D. Williams'

Eucryphia milliganii

Gaultheria mucronata 'Wintertime'

Gaultheria shallon

Kalmia latifolia

Rhododendron 'Homebush'

Rhododendron wardii

Vaccinium parvifolium

Zenobia pulverulenta

Fall

This is the season when many deciduous shrubs come to the fore, with colorful foliage providing an eye-catching spectacle. Shrubs for fall interest include *Euonymus alatus*, with its intense red leaves, and the various cultivars of *Cotinus coggygria*, with yellow, red, or purple foliage. Color from berries, such as the orange clusters of *Pyracantha* 'Mohave' or the shiny red fruits of *Cotoneaster divaricatus*, is also valuable.

Winter

Shrubs are vital elements in the winter garden, with a rich variety of features. Evergreen foliage probably makes the greatest contribution, providing bold masses of color and texture. Flowers also play their part, however, with a choice ranging from the sculptural *Mahonia japonica*, with its spreading, yellow sprays, to the spiderlike, red flowers borne by *Hamamelis* x *intermedia* 'Diane', while other fragrant shrubs such as *Viburnum* x *bodnantense* may be welcome. Also common are shrubs with ornamental stems, such as *Cornus sericea* 'Flaviramea', which has vivid, lime-green shoots.

Shrub borders

One of the most satisfactory ways of using shrubs in the landscape is to grow them in a border on their own. From the large range available that will be suitable for the soil, climate, and site, a selection may be made that will give a succession of color and interest throughout the year. The aim is to create a balanced design, taking into account the shape, form, height, and spread of each shrub, as well as its ornamental qualities and any seasonal changes in appearance.

The planting may rely almost entirely on a blend of foliage textures and colors, but other features may also play a part. Include shrubs with interesting shapes, for example, and others with colorful berries or stems to maintain year-long interest. Resist the temptation to rely on flowers, since their display may be impressive but transitory. By careful selection, however, it is possible to sustain a long succession of flowers.

Some shrubs may be regarded as long-term plants, while others tend to mature and fade quickly. When planning a border, space out the long-term shrubs so that they will not need thinning or drastic pruning to keep them in check once mature. Fast-growing shrubs may also be included, but they should be thinned as soon as they threaten to crowd out the core planting of shrubs.

Herbaceous perennials, annuals, and other plants may be interplanted initially, so that in the short term the shrub border might have

Mixed planting In this design, evergreen rhododendrons and laurel provide permanent structure and texture, while herbaceous grasses and perennials give summer color.

similar components to a mixed border. Dense planting, including groundcover, may help to keep down weeds, although mulching is advisable to reduce weeds and water loss while the plants are becoming established.

Mixed borders

The idea of a mixed border is to combine a framework planting of shrubs with a variety of herbaceous plants to reap the benefits of both. Its main advantage is that the shrubs provide long-term, sometimes year-round, interest and a background to a succession of other plants. As the shrubs provide height and structure, there is less need to grow tall perennials that require staking than in a traditional herbaceous border.

The mixed border may be designed to suit various settings. If situated next to a wall, the planting may include a combination of wall-trained and other shrubs at the back as

well as climbers, other plants being introduced in loosely shaped niches between shrubs in the foreground. In an island bed, shrubs are normally used to form an irregular core at the center, surrounded by other plants arranged in irregular clumps or flowing drifts.

Managing a mixed border is sometimes more complex than caring for a shrub one, because the various plants have diverse needs. It is, however, one of the most effective ways of bringing together the wide-ranging qualities of different plant groups.

Specimen shrubs

Shrubs that are particularly attractive—perhaps because of their fine shape or a special characteristic, such as exquisite flowers or striking foliage—may be best planted as individual specimens, sited so that they can be better appreciated from various different angles and viewing points.

Standout choices

A shrub grown as a specimen clearly stands out in the garden, so it is important that its appearance warrants its prominent position. Shrubs with shapely silhouettes are especially suitable, such as the dense symmetrical cone of *Picea glauca* var. *albertiana* 'Conica'. A flowering shrub such as *Camellia japonica* 'Mathotiana' would also be an impressive focal point when in full flower during spring.

When selecting a plant to be grown as a specimen, its long-term interest is an important consideration. In a large yard, a relatively short but magnificent display may be sufficient for your needs, because there will be many shrubs to enjoy at other times. A shrub that occupies a prime spot in a small yard, on the other hand, needs to justify its presence by contributing color and form throughout the year, or by having more than one interesting phase—attractive flowers and good fall foliage, for example.

Siting a specimen shrub

When deciding where to site a specimen shrub, make sure its size will be in keeping with its position in the landscape and that it relates well to the overall design. Often the best location is at the focal point of a view from a main window of the house or at the meeting point of two vistas. The background is as important as the shrub itself; usually, a uniform texture and color, as provided by a dense, evergreen hedge or the green swath of a lawn, forms the most complementary foil.

There is, however, scope for experimenting with the positioning of specimen shrubs, particularly in combination with other garden features, such as a pond that creates appealing reflections. Before planting, roughly assess the effect of the shrub's scale and position in the design by substituting stakes or a similar prop of the same height and width.

Wall shrubs

A border at the foot of a warm, sheltered wall is a prime site for many plants; although it frequently tends to be somewhat dry, if the plants are adequately watered, the conditions are suitable for various shrubs that might otherwise be too tender to grow in more open or exposed areas of the garden.

Training shrubs against a wall is often the best option for lax types such as *Forsythia suspensa* which produce tangled growth unless supported. For a number of shrubs, it is the best way of displaying their ornamental features, such as the orange or red berries of pyracanthas. Some hardy shrubs, such as *Chaenomeles*, that may also be grown freestanding, look attractive wall-trained, and complement the clean background.

Sometimes no training is needed: shrubs such as myrtle (*Myrtus*) may simply be planted close to the foot of a wall to benefit from the warmth and shelter. Other shrubs such as *Buddleja crispa* do require training to flower well.

Dwarf and groundcover shrubs

Planting low shrubs, such as many *Hebe* cultivars or *Daphne blagayana*, within raised beds or containers makes it very easy to appreciate them at close quarters, as well as providing structure and long-term interest in the overall planting. On a large scale, use low-growing shrubs to balance against contrasting, rounded, or upright forms in beds and borders.

These shrubs are also excellent where interest is needed at ground level; *Helianthemum* cultivars and a vast array of colorful heathers (*Calluna, Daboecia,* and *Erica*) brighten up the front of a mixed border or soften the hard edges of a path.

Wall-trained shrubs *Euphorbia mellifera* and *Carpenteria californica* are tender and benefit from the warmth and protection when grown against a wall.

Some spread into an attractive carpet that forms a fine foil for other planting. Those that are relatively fast-growing may be used as groundcover (see p.94). Groundcover shrubs present one of the best solutions for sites such as steep banks that are difficult to cultivate; even in the unpromising, shady areas directly beneath trees, shrubs such as *Mahonia repens* and *Taxus canadensis* grow well.

Foliage

The substance and the seasonal continuity of a landscape depend to a large extent on foliage. Evergreen shrubs, in particular, unify the scene all through the year. The leaves of deciduous shrubs—from spring growth to autumn leaf—also give a longer period of interest than most flowers.

Color

Much may be made of foliage color, which includes not only every shade of green but also silvers and grays, reds and purples, as well as yellow, gold, and variegated forms. The boldest leaf colors, such as the gold and red of *Spiraea japonica* 'Goldflame', the red of the young growth of some *Pieris*, or the white-splashed green of *Clethra alnifolia* 'Creels Calico' may be used in much the same way as flower color.

Shape and texture

There are many other attributes of shrub foliage that are worth exploiting in an ornamental display. Large or distinctively shaped leaves, such as those of Japanese Aralia (*Fatsia japonica),* are particularly striking, and changes of texture, from smooth and glossy to matt and felted, also provide satisfying contrasts.

Flowers

Ranging from the tiny, pealike flowers of many brooms (*Cytisus/Genista*) to the large, heavy panicles of lilacs (*Syringa*), there is an impressive diversity of shrub flowers.

Color and form

Shrubs have flowers in every color, with endless variations of each; for example, shades of pink range from the pale pinkish-white blooms of *Magnolia* 'Pinkie' to the crimson of *Rhododendron* 'Hinodegiri'.

Sometimes it is the sheer mass of flowers that appeals, as with the dense blue clusters of *Ceanothus* or the sprays of starlike, yellow flowers of forsythias, while other shrubs—such as the exquisite but short-lived flowers of *Paeonia suffruticosa*—seduce by the sumptuous beauty of their individual blooms.

In an extensive landscape it does not much matter that a plant's star turn is only brief; in a small yard, this may be a serious drawback, so consider a plant's form and foliage, too, if its floral display is very short.

Scent

While the appeal of some flowers lies largely in their color and form, those that are scented give a planting another dimension. The flowers may be showy and also deliciously fragrant, as are many mock oranges (*Philadelphus*), or, like the minute flowers of *Sarcococca*, more muted in appearance but casting their fragrance through the yard.

Berries

Berrying shrubs are valuable for sustaining color from late summer into winter, and also for attracting birds. On evergreens such as pyracanthas, bright berries framed by green foliage make an attractive contrast, while those on deciduous shrubs such as *Viburnum opulus* are seen against a changing backdrop of fall foliage followed by bare winter stems. Orange and red berries are common, but there are other colors—from yellow *Cotoneaster* 'Rothschildianus' to pretty pink *Gaultheria mucronata* 'Sea Shell'.

Bear in mind that with some species of shrubs, male and female flowers are borne on separate plants. Thus, satisfactory fruiting is only achieved when male and female plants are grown near each other.

Bark and stems

In winter, the silhouettes of bare stems may be very striking. As well as their sculptural simplicity, some, such as dogwoods (*Cornus*), are strongly colored, while others—for example, *Salix irrorata*—are overlaid with an attractive, glaucous bloom.

Group a few shrubs of the same type together to reap the benefit of their massed

Colored stems The bare stems of *Cornus alba* 'Sibirica' provide a vivid display in winter. To produce vigorous growth each year, prune stems hard in early spring.

stems, or site a single fine specimen against a simple background. Imagine the brilliant red stems of *Cornus alba* 'Sibirica' offset by a plain white wall, or the chalky white skeleton of *Rubus biflorus* by a dark one.

The delicate tracery of fine stems is often overlooked unless it is highlighted by vivid coloring, but unusual shapes and heavily thorned or contorted shoots provide added interest. The bizarrely twisted stems of *Corylus avellana* 'Contorta' and *Salix* 'Erythroflexuosa' make them interesting curiosities to set against a plain wall or plants of more familiar growth pattern.

Regular pruning is advisable for many shrubs grown for their stems because the new wood that is most eye-catching (see "Coppicing and pollarding shrubs," p.104).

Shrubs in containers

Provided that they are watered regularly, many shrubs adapt happily to life in containers: grown in this way, they make versatile as well as ornamental features. Use them as living sculptures to provide strong shapes and a framework to offset other planting. An evergreen shrub or dwarf conifer forms a fine centerpiece in a planter all year round, which may be complemented by bulbs in spring and colorful and trailing annuals in summer.

A container-grown shrub is particularly valuable in a small yard or on a patio or balcony. It may be used alone or combined with a changing display of other plants in containers. In a larger setting, a handsomely potted shrub may make a more striking focal point than a piece of garden statuary. Container-grown shrubs may introduce a formal note simply, as a pair flanking an archway, or, more elaborately, marking an avenue in grander designs.

Selecting plants

The most suitable shrubs are those with a long season of interest. Good examples for containers include evergreen camellias and rhododendrons, which remain attractive even after their flowers have faded. For valuable foliage effects, consider the tender *Chamaerops humilis*, which has huge, palm-like, glossy fans, and conifers with their wide range of colors and textures.

Deciduous foliage can change from spring to fall and, in the case of Japanese maples (*Acer palmatum*), an intricate pattern of delicate stems remains when all the leaves have fallen. Shrubs such as *Spiraea japonica* 'Goldflame', with its strikingly colored leaves and heads of rose-pink flowers, often look particularly fine grown in an ornamental pot.

Practical advantages

An advantage of growing shrubs in containers is that tender plants, such as *Nerium oleander* and palms, may be used to give the garden a Mediterranean or subtropical look in the summer, and then moved to a protected site for winter, and scented shrubs can be positioned near seating areas or windows when in bloom. It is also an excellent way of including shrubs that would not otherwise tolerate the soil of the open ground: for example, given soft water and acidic potting mix, camellias and rhododendrons may be grown in pots or other containers even in alkaline areas.

Container shrubs Japanese maples (*Acer palmatum*) perform well in containers and make an elegant feature in the landscape, especially when planted in attractive containers.

PLANTER'S GUIDE TO SHRUBS

EXPOSED SITES

Shrubs that tolerate exposed or windy sites; those marked 🍃 are not suitable for coastal sites

Acer tataricum subsp. Ginnala
Amorpha fruticosa
Arctostaphylos uva-ursi
Calluna vulgaris (and cvs)
Caragana
Cistus
Cornus stolonifera
Cotoneaster (dwarf spp.),
  C. horizontalis
Elaeagnus angustifolia
Erica carnea (and cvs) 🍃
Escallonia
Euonymus alatus
Euonymus fortunei (and cvs)
Fuchsia magellanica (and cvs)
Gaultheria shallon 🍃
Genista
Halimodendron halodendron
Hebe
Hippophäe rhamnoides
Ilex aquifolium
Lavatera
Myrica gale
Phormium
Prunus spinosa
Pyracantha
Rhamnus alaternus
Rhododendron ponticum 🍃
Salix
Senecio
Spartium
Spiraea
Tamarix
Ulex
Yucca

SHELTERED SITES

Shrubs that prefer sheltered sites

Abelia floribunda
Abutilon
Acer palmatum (cvs)
Aucuba japonica
Buxus microphylla
Camellia hybrids
Citrus
Coprosma
Cornus florida
Datura
Dendromecon rigida
Euryops pectinatus
Musa basjoo
Nerium
Pieris
Rhododendron maddenii,
  R. Section Vireya
Taxus
Viburnum plicatum

WALL SHRUBS

Abelia
Abutilon
Acacia dealbata
Buddleja crispa
Callistemon
Camellia

Ceanothus
Chaenomeles
Cotoneaster horizontalis
Daphne bholua
Euonymus fortunei (and cvs)
Fremontodendron
Itea ilicifolia
Pyracantha
Solanum crispum 'Glasnevin',
  S. laxum

AIR POLLUTION

Shrubs that tolerate polluted air

Aucuba
Berberis
Buddleja davidii
Camellia japonica (and cvs)
Cornus sericea
Cotoneaster
Elaeagnus
Euonymus japonicus
Fatsia japonica
Fuchsia magellanica
  (and cvs)
Garrya
Ilex x altaclerensis,
  I. aquifolium
Ligustrum
Lonicera pileata
Magnolia grandiflora
Mahonia aquifolium
Osmanthus
Philadelphus
Salix
Spiraea
Viburnum

DRY SHADE

Shrubs that tolerate dry shade

Aucuba
Cornus canadensis
Daphne laureola
Euonymus fortunei,
  E. japonicus
Fatsia japonica
Hedera
Ilex aquifolium
Pachysandra

MOIST SHADE

Shrubs that prefer moist shade

Aucuba
Buxus sempervirens
Camellia japonica
Cornus canadensis
Daphne laureola
Euonymus fortunei,
  E. japonicus
Fatsia japonica
Ilex aquifolium
Lonicera pileata
Mahonia aquifolium
Osmanthus
Rubus tricolor
Sarcococca
Skimmia
Vinca

TWO OR MORE SEASONS OF INTEREST

All year round

Ardisia japonica
Convolvulus cneorum
Elaeagnus x ebbingei
  'Gilt Edge'
Lavandula stoechas

Winter/Spring

Berberis temolaica
Corylus avellana 'Contorta'
Salix irrorata

Spring/Summer

Calycanthus occidentalis
Pieris 'Forest Flame'

Spring/Fall

Cornus 'Eddie's White
  Wonder'

Summer/Fall

Citrus 'Meyer'
Cornus mas 'Variegata'
Cotinus 'Flame'
Cotoneaster conspicuus
Dipelta yunnanensis
Hydrangea quercifolia
  'Snowflake'
Lonicera korolkowii
Myrtus communis,
  M. communis subsp. tarentina
Neillia thibetica
Phlomis chrysophylla
Pyracantha
Rosa 'Fru Dagmar Hastrup',
  R. moyesii 'Geranium'

Fall/Winter

Arbutus unedo
Berberis temolaica
Cornus mas 'Variegata'

FRAGRANT FLOWERS

Abeliophyllum distichum
Buddleja alternifolia
Camellia sasanqua
Chimonanthus praecox
  'Luteus'
Choisya 'Aztec Pearl',
  C. ternata
Clethra alnifolia 'Paniculata'
Colletia hystrix 'Rosea'
Daphne bholua,
  D. blagayana,
  D. cneorum,
  D. odora
Elaeagnus
Erica lusitanica
Hamamelis x intermedia
  'Pallida'
Lonicera x purpusii 'Winter Beauty',
  L. standishii
Luculia gratissima
Magnolia sieboldii,
  M. x thompsoniana
Mahonia japonica
Osmanthus delavayi
Philadelphus (many)
Pittosporum tobira

Rhododendron auriculatum,
  R. edgeworthii,
  R. 'Fragrantissimum',
  R. Ghent hybrids,
  R. Loderi Group,
  R. luteum, R. occidentale (and
  hybrids), R. 'Polar Bear',
  R. Rustica hybrids,
  R. viscosum
Ribes odoratum
Rosa (many)
Sarcococca
Viburnum (many)

AROMATIC FOLIAGE

Calycanthus
Caryopteris
Perovskia
Ruta graveolens
Santolina
Skimmia x confusa

ARCHITECTURAL SHRUBS

Agave
Aralia elata 'Aureovariegata'
Buddleja alternifolia
Chamaerops
Corylus avellana 'Contorta'
Fatsia japonica
Hydrangea quercifolia
Phormium
Sabal
Yucca

Erica carnea

Groundcover shrubs

Covering the ground with a dense carpet of flowering or foliage plants is a planting technique designed primarily to minimize weeding among ornamental plants. Groundcover can also reduce evaporation from exposed, freely draining soils. A dense planting of drought-resistant evergreens, such as *Cistus* x *hybridus* or the pink-flowered *C.* x *skanbergii*, and most cultivars of rosemary (*Rosmarinus*) and lavender (*Lavandula*), will shade the soil and keep it cool, and their slowly decomposing leaf litter also acts as a mulch.

Steep banks subject to erosion by rain and wind may be planted with groundcover shrubs such as *Juniperus squamata* 'Blue Carpet' or *Cotoneaster dammeri*. Their low, spreading habit, evergreen foliage, and vigorous rooted layers combine to form a stable cover that prevents erosion of topsoil.

In a wildlife garden, groundcover can be used to attract bees and butterflies: the low, creeping thymes, such as *Thymus praecox* and its cultivars, for example, are extremely attractive to bees.

Once established, groundcover plants will smother most weed seedlings that attempt to grow beneath their canopy by depriving them of light, as well as by competing with them for water and nutrients. In the wild, this is frequently a natural process; nature may be imitated in the garden to create attractive, integrated plantings that require very little aftercare.

In large gardens, evergreen groundcover shrubs can act as low boundary markers. Their branches also trap windblown debris, which can be raked out readily and removed.

Textural carpet
A vigorous dwarf juniper, *Juniperus squamata* 'Blue Carpet', provides a spreading mat of color and texture up to 10ft (3m) wide.

Selecting plants

Choose attractive, vigorous plants that will quickly cover their allotted space with close, dense growth. Low-growing shrubs with a spreading habit are among the most useful. Evergreens are a good choice for year-round visual interest, especially if, like *Euonymus fortunei* 'Sunspot' with its golden-variegated, dark green leaves, they will brighten a dark corner.

Plants should be selected to suit the location—for example, wet or dry, shady, or hot and sunny situations. They should be easy to care for, routinely requiring either no pruning or perhaps annual clipping and fertilizing. Choose long-lived plants that should remain healthy for five to ten years or more. Finally, look for species, cultivars, and forms that will provide attractive foliage and habit, with flowers and fruits as a bonus.

Combining plants

Massed groupings of a single plant give a unified "carpeting" effect, but plants can be combined provided they are of similar vigor. Groundcover plants with various colors, textures, and forms may be mixed to make garden features in their own right, or provide an attractive linking element in a design. A low carpet of shrubs also makes an excellent, low-maintenance background for naturalized bulbs such as daffodils, and, unlike grass, will not need mowing as the bulb foliage fades.

Some shrubs are particularly useful in providing medium-height cover, or as an undercanopy below trees. *Cotoneaster conspicuus*, with bright scarlet berries, dense and spreading *Prunus laurocerasus* 'Otto Luyken', and *Viburnum davidii* and *V. tinus* with their glossy, dark green leaves and showy winter buds, cover the ground well and provide interest, even in winter.

General cultivation

Once the ground has been thoroughly prepared, there are several ways of planting groundcover shrubs to ensure quick cover: plant them at spacings recommended for the species or cultivar concerned and cover the soil with 2in (5cm) of a loose organic mulch; in hot, humid climates where mulch breaks down more quickly, up to 5in (12cm) may be needed. Another option is to plant them more densely than usual.

The choice of method will depend on the type and cost of plants used, the climate and soil conditions, and how long you are willing to wait for the final effect.

Fast-growing plants in favorable conditions and at recommended spacings will generally fill in within two to three years.

Once established, many shrubby plants benefit from an occasional trim, to keep them compact, as well as the removal of dead or damaged shoots. A few need more intrusive, annual pruning: for example, shrubs such as *Vinca* and *Hypericum calycinum*, which become rather straggly after a few years, and those such as *Santolina*, which tend to open out, revealing their center.

MULCHING GROUNDCOVERS

When groundcover plants have been newly planted at the correct distance, the ground between them will still be bare. Until the plants have begun to spread over the surrounding area, it is advisable to apply mulch in the gaps around them. This will help to retain moisture in the soil, and will also discourage the growth of weeds. A loose mulch such as bark chips is ideal for the purpose, and should be applied to a depth of about 2in (5cm).

To preserve moisture between new plants (here *Erica carnea*), apply a loose mulch 2in (5cm) deep. Every spring, renew the mulch around established plants.

PRUNING GROUNDCOVERS

Santolina
Some bushy plants need hard pruning. In spring, cut back to just above where new growth is breaking on the main stems.

Hypericum calycinum
In spring, cut the previous season's shoots back hard.

Soil preparation and planting

A wide range of shrubs can be grown in most gardens, even if the soil falls short of ideal—which is a fertile, well-drained but moisture-retentive loam. Improving the drainage of wet soils and, by the addition of humus, the structure and moisture-holding properties of dry soils greatly increases the range of shrubs that may be grown. The soil acidity or alkalinity, another factor limiting the range of plants that can be grown, may also be modified. Important though these improvements may be, garden soil will still naturally tend toward being moist or dry, heavy or light, and acidic or alkaline. The best shrubs for your garden are those suitable for the growing conditions available.

Selecting shrubs

Shrubs may be bought direct from garden centers, nurseries, and nonspecialist outlets, such as supermarkets. Some nurseries also sell shrubs by mail order or online; plants are normally dispatched during their dormant period. They are sold in containers, balled-and-burlapped, or bare-root.

Shrubs on sale should be accurately labeled, healthy, undamaged, and free of pests and diseases. When buying direct, inspect the plants thoroughly and select a specimen with evenly distributed branches close to ground level or, with standard shrubs, at the head of a clear stem of the desired height. Shrubs sold in the warm, dry atmosphere of a supermarket have a short shelf life. Reliable suppliers may give a year's guarantee to replace the shrub if it is not true to name or if it dies within the first year, provided that it has been given reasonable care.

Shrubs in containers

Shrubs are most commonly sold as container-grown specimens, the containers ranging from rigid pots to plastic bags. Most shrubs sold in this way have been container-grown throughout their lives. Some are field-grown and potted up (containerized) in the season before sale to prolong their sale life. The two are difficult to distinguish, although container-grown shrubs normally have better-established root systems (often visible through the drainage holes of the pot).

If possible, slide the shrub out of its container; the roots should show healthy, white tips and the

SELECTING A SHRUB
Container-grown shrubs

Good example

Vigorous, well-balanced top growth

Prostanthera cuneata

Well-established, fibrous root system

Poor example

Twiggy, sparse stems showing little new growth

Potbound roots

Renovating a poor example

Tease out potbound roots and cut back any that are very long or damaged

Good example

Well-developed, even branch framework

Viburnum farreri

Healthy, vigorous growth, free from damage and disease

Balled-and-burlapped shrub

Wrapping is intact, not split or damaged

Check that the root ball is firm

root system, if well established, will retain all or most of the medium from the pot. Reject plants with poorly developed root systems and those that are potbound (with roots protruding from the container), because these rarely grow well.

A major advantage of container-grown shrubs is that they may be bought and planted out at any time, except when there are extremes of temperature or drought. Containerized shrubs can be safely planted out in winter, but at other times may be slow to establish unless they have a well-developed root system.

Bare-root shrubs

Deciduous shrubs that are easily propagated are sometimes lifted from the open ground during

their dormant season and sold with their roots bare of soil. The buying season for these bare-root shrubs is from fall to spring. To prevent desiccation, they are normally heeled into the ground until they are sold. Before purchasing, check that bare-root shrubs have an evenly developed, fibrous root system.

Balled-and-burlapped shrubs

These shrubs, usually available in fall or early spring, have been grown in open ground, then lifted with soil around their root balls; the root balls are wrapped in burlap or netting. Conifers are often sold in this way. Always check that the wrapping is intact, or the roots may have been exposed to drying wind, and that the root ball is firm.

PLANTER'S GUIDE TO SHRUBS FOR SANDY SOIL

Berberis empetrifolia
Calluna vulgaris (and cvs)
Ceanothus thyrsiflorus
Cistus × *cyprius*
Clethra alnifolia
Cytisus scoparius
Erica arborea, E. cinerea
Fuchsia magellanica (and cvs)
Genista tinctoria
Hakea lissosperma
Halimodendron halodendron
Helianthemum
Helichrysum
Hippophäe
Lavandula
Olearia
Ozothamnus
Phlomis
Phormium
Spartium junceum
Tamarix
Ulex europaeus
Yucca gloriosa

SHRUBS FOR WELL-DRAINED CLAY SOIL

Amelanchier
Aralia
Aronia arbutifolia
Aucuba
Berberis
Chaenomeles × *superba* (and cvs)
Cornus alba 'Sibirica'
Cotinus
Cotoneaster
Deutzia
Forsythia
Garrya
Hippophäe
Kalmia latifolia
Lonicera
Mahonia × *media*
Philadelphus
Potentilla
Pyracantha
Salix caprea
Sambucus racemosa
Spiraea
Taxus
Viburnum opulus
Weigela

Philadelphus

When to plant

Fall to spring is the planting season for bare-root and balled-and-burlapped shrubs, and the optimal time for container-grown shrubs; however, those of borderline hardiness should be planted out in spring. Fall planting allows the roots to establish while the ground is still warm, so the shrub should be growing vigorously before dry weather the next summer.

Planting may be carried out during mild weather in winter, but not when the ground is frozen. Roots will not grow away in very cold soil, and there is a risk that they may freeze and be killed.

The major disadvantage of spring planting is that top growth is likely to develop before the roots establish and, if there is an early spell of dry weather, watering may be required to help the plants survive.

Soil preparation

Many shrubs are potentially long-lived, so the ground needs to be thoroughly prepared before planting. The aim should be to cultivate an area well beyond the planting site for an individual shrub and, preferably, the entire bed.

The best seasons for cultivation are late summer and fall. Remove or kill all weeds first, taking care to eradicate perennials (see "Weeds and lawn weeds," pp.645–649). Double dig (see p.620), mixing in a 3–4in (8–10cm) layer of well-rotted organic matter into the lower trench. If this is impractical, work large quantities of organic matter into the top 12–18in (30–45cm) of soil. Add fertilizer if appropriate (see "Soil nutrients and fertilizers," pp.624–625).

How to plant

The planting hole for a shrub must be wide enough to accommodate the shrub's root ball. For container-grown or balled-and-burlapped plants, make the hole twice the width of the contained root mass, or as much as three times the width if planting in clay soils. For bare-root shrubs, the hole must be large enough to allow the roots to be spread out fully. The hole must also be sufficiently deep to allow the shrub to be planted at the same level as it was in its container or in the open ground. This is indicated by the soil mark—a dark mark near the base of the stem. A stake laid across the top of the planting hole provides a guide to the depth of planting. Treatment of a shrub in a container depends on how developed the root system is when removed from the pot. If the soil mix falls away, plant as for a bare-root shrub; if it does not, treat as if container-grown. Tease out the root system if at all rootbound. Remove the burlap or netting surrounding a balled-and-burlapped shrub after it is in the hole. When backfilling the hole, shake a bare-root plant gently to settle the soil. Firm the soil in stages—do not compact clay soils. To improve drainage around

PLANTING A WALL SHRUB

1 Dig a hole at least 9in (22cm) away from the wall. Plant the shrub (here, a pyracantha) and tie in the supporting stake to a wire.

2 Firm back the soil. Secure lateral bamboo stakes to the central stake and to the wires, so that the sideshoots can be supported and tied in (see inset).

PLANTING A CONTAINER-GROWN SHRUB

1 Dig a hole about twice the width of the shrub's root ball (here, a *Viburnum*). Mix the removed soil with well-rotted organic matter. Fork over the base and sides of the hole.

2 Placing one hand on top of the soil mix and around the shrub to support it, carefully ease the plant out of its container. Place the shrub upright into the prepared hole.

3 Lay a stake alongside to check that the soil level is the same as before. Adjust the planting depth, if necessary, by adding or removing topsoil beneath the shrub's roots.

4 Backfill around the shrub with the removed soil and well-rotted organic matter mixture, firming the soil in stages to prevent air pockets from forming.

5 Once the hole has been filled to the original level with the planting mixture, carefully firm the soil around the shrub.

6 Prune any diseased or damaged wood back to healthy growth and cut back any inward-growing or crossing stems to an outward-growing shoot or bud. You should also remove any very long, weak, or straggly stems, or those that spoil the overall balance of the shrub's framework.

7 Water the shrub thoroughly; apply a mulch of well-rotted compost or shredded bark about 2–3in (5–7cm) deep and 12–18in (30–45cm) wide around the shrub.

shrubs to be grown in clay soils, plant the shrub slightly above the soil level and mound soil around the exposed section of the root ball up to the level of the soil mark. On sandy soils, plant the shrub in a slight trench to channel water around the plant's roots. Water the shrub and mulch.

Planting wall shrubs

Some shrubs may be trained on wires fixed to a wall or fence. Plant these at least 9in (22cm) from the wall, leaning the plant in toward the wall. Support the main stem and laterals of the shrub with stakes, which are then tied into the wires (see also "Wall shrubs," pp.105–106).

Staking

Shrubs do not normally need staking, except for large, root-bound specimens and standards. The former, which ideally should not be selected, will almost certainly need some support in their first year or two at least, until their roots begin to spread out and they become stable.

The best method for any shrub that branches from near ground level is to brace the shrub with guy ropes fixed to three stakes spaced evenly around a circle with a radius of about 3ft (1m) centered on the shrub. To prevent any bark damage, it is advisable to cover the guy ropes where they touch the branches with rubber or similar material (see also ORNAMENTAL TREES, *Staking*, p.64).

For standards, insert the stake in the planting hole before planting to avoid damaging the root system. The top of the stake should be just below the first branches. Secure the stem to the stake, using a

USING A WATERING RING

To help retain water, create a shallow depression with a low wall of soil around the shrub. After several waterings, push the wall into the depression, then mulch.

STAKING A STANDARD SHRUB

1 Drive a stake into the hole just off-center; the top of the stake should be just below the head of the shrub after planting. Plant the shrub next to the stake.

2 If the depth is correct, backfill and firm in. On free-draining soil, form a dip around the shrub to retain moisture. Secure the stem with a suitable tie (see inset).

---

commercial tie with a spacer or a homemade figure-eight tie to prevent chafing.

Protecting newly planted shrubs

Newly planted shrubs may suffer from desiccation or cold if not protected. Broadleaved evergreens and conifers in exposed locations are particularly vulnerable.

A screen of burlap or mesh significantly reduces the drying force of cold winds. Erect a strong, wooden framework 12in (30cm) away from the windward side of the shrub needing protection. Tack the burlap or the mesh to the frame, which should extend at least 12in (30cm) above and either side of the shrub. More complete protection is given by surrounding individual plants with a four-sided framework to which burlap or mesh is tacked.

Another measure, which may be used either alone or in addition to screening, is to spray the plants with an antidesiccant product to reduce water loss. Apply a thin film of spray to both sides of the leaves.

A mulch spread around the base of the shrub will help protect the roots from ground frost. It is best to spread the mulch during periods of mild weather, when the ground is reasonably warm and damp.

In areas of heavy snow, particularly vulnerable evergreen shrubs may need added protection. This is best provided by a lumber and chicken wire cage. Dislodge any heavy accumulations of snow promptly. More extreme measures may be needed to protect half-hardy and tender shrubs (see FROST

AND WIND PROTECTION, pp.612–613). When removing the insulation in spring, check for pests and diseases that may have benefited from the winter protection.

Planting shrubs in containers

Late summer to fall is the main period for planting shrubs in containers (see also CONTAINER GARDENING, "Shrubs," p.315). When transplanting a shrub, the new container should be 2in (5cm) larger in depth and diameter than the previous one. If using an old container, scrub its inside surface thoroughly before filling. Heavy containers should be placed in position before planting. Stand the container on bricks or blocks to allow free drainage. Place a piece of screening over drainage holes, then add a 1in (2.5cm) layer of drainage material, such as coarse gravel.

A soil-based potting mix, which is rich in nutrients, is preferable to a peat-based mix, which contains limited added nutrients and dries out more rapidly. Shrubs grown in peat-based mix will therefore require frequent feeding. Use an acidic soil mix for rhododendrons and other lime-haters, or to obtain blue flowers on hydrangeas. After placing the plant in the pot, spread its roots out evenly and work soil around them. Ensure that the soil mark is level with the surface of the soil mix. Topdressing the soil with a covering of grit or bark chips ensures that it does not form a crust. This type of mulch also looks decorative.

SHRUBS FOR ACID SOIL

Andromeda
Arbutus (most spp.)
Arctostaphylos
  (some spp.)
Calluna
Camellia
Clethra
Cornus canadensis
Corylopsis (most spp.)
Desfontainia spinosa
Enkianthus
Erica (most spp.)
Fothergilla
Gaultheria
Hakea
Kalmia
Leucothöe
Menziesia
Philesia magellanica
Pieris
Rhododendron (most spp.)
Styrax officinalis
Telopea speciosissima
Vaccinium
Zenobia pulverulenta

SHRUBS FOR VERY ALKALINE SOIL

Aucuba japonica (and cvs)
Berberis darwinii
Buddleja davidii (and cvs)
Buxus
Chamaerops
Choisya ternata
Cistus
Cotoneaster
Cytisus
Deutzia
Euonymus
Forsythia
Hebe
Hibiscus
Hypericum
Ligustrum
Lonicera
Nerium oleander
Philadelphus
Phlomis fruticosa
Photinia
Potentilla (all shrubby spp.)
Rosa rugosa
Rosmarinus
Senecio
Syringa
Viburnum tinus
Vitex agnus-castus
Weigela
Yucca aloifolia

Pieris

Routine care

The following guidelines for maintenance are generally applicable, although not all shrubs have the same requirements. Newly planted shrubs usually need watering and feeding, while those planted in containers should also be periodically topdressed or repotted. In addition, deadheading, removing suckers, weeding, and controlling pests and diseases may all be necessary.

Feeding

Most shrubs benefit from regular applications of organic or synthetic fertilizers, especially if pruned regularly. A wide range of organic-based fertilizers is now available as well as fast-acting and slow-release ones. They are best applied in early spring. Some slow-release fertilizers release their nutrients only when temperatures are high enough for plants to use them. A standard rate of application is 2oz/sq yd (60g/sq m) (see also SOILS AND FERTILIZERS, "Types of fertilizer," p.624).

Quick-release powder fertilizers are useful to boost growth as it commences in spring. Liquid fertilizers work even faster than powders—these should be applied once the shrub is growing.

Fertilizers in granular or powder form should be worked into the soil over an area slightly wider than the spread of the top growth of the shrub. With surface-rooting shrubs, allow the fertilizer to leach in naturally or water it in to avoid the risk of the roots being injured by forking. The application of fertilizers may affect the soil's pH level; most synthetic, nitrogen fertilizers, for example, make the soil more acidic (see also SOILS AND FERTILIZERS, "Soil nutrients and fertilizers," pp.624–625).

Watering

Established shrubs require watering only in periods of prolonged drought, but young specimens may need regular watering. Apply the water to the ground around the shrub, soaking the soil. Do not water often and lightly, because this will encourage root growth close to the surface, and shallow roots make shrubs vulnerable in drought conditions. The best time to water is in the evening, when evaporation is minimal.

Mulching

Mulching with well-rotted, bulky manures helps soil conserve moisture and, if nutrient-rich, improves soil fertility. It also moderates extremes of temperature around the roots and inhibits weeds.

Apply the mulch around newly planted shrubs over an area about 18in (45cm) wider in diameter than the plant's root system. The mulch around established shrubs should extend beyond the area of top growth by 6–12in (15–30cm). A mulch of bark chips, wood chips, or leaf mold should be 2–4in (5–10cm) deep but kept clear of the stems. Do not apply any mulch in cold weather or when soil is dry.

Weeding

Weeds compete for nutrients and moisture, so it is essential to clear the ground of all weeds before planting. The area around newly planted groundcover shrubs needs weeding until the plants form dense growth that suppresses competition. For treatment, see "Weeds and lawn weeds," pp.645–649.

Removing suckers

Some grafted shrubs, especially roses, are prone to producing growths, or suckers, beneath the graft union, from either stems or roots. Rub out suckers between finger and thumb as soon as they are noticed. If too large to treat in this way, cut them off as close as possible to the stems or roots from which they are growing. Pulling them off helps to remove any dormant growth buds, but take care not to damage the stem or root. Watch for further growth.

Reversion and mutation

Many variegated shrubs are propagated from green-leaved plants that have produced mutated branches, known as sports. From time to time, branches of variegated shrubs revert to the original foliage of the parent plant or mutate to plain cream or yellow leaves. These branches are usually more vigorous, so they eventually crowd out those showing variegation, and therefore should be cut out.

Deadheading

Some shrubs, including rhododendrons, lilacs (*Syringa*), and *Kalmia*, benefit if their faded flower heads are promptly removed, where practical, before seed sets. Removing old flowers diverts energy into growth, improving the flowering potential for the following season, but it is not essential for the health of a shrub.

DEADHEADING A RHODODENDRON

Before new buds have fully developed, snap each dead flower head off at the base of its stem. Take care not to damage any young growth.

To avoid damage to new buds, deadhead as soon as the flowers fade, using fingers and thumb to pick off each one where it joins the stem. With lilacs, remove the old flower heads back to the first pair of leaves with pruners.

Shrubs in containers

Container-grown shrubs need more care than those grown in the ground, because they have less access to moisture and nutrients. Until shrubs reach maturity, repot them every year or two in spring, then topdress. When mature, just replace the top 2–4in (5–10cm) of potting mix each spring. (See also CONTAINER GARDENING, "Maintaining shrubs and trees in containers," pp.333–334.)

HOW TO REMOVE SUCKERS

Sucker removal
Pull or cut off the sucker (here on a *Hamamelis*) at the base; if it is pulled off, pare back the wound to leave a clean cut (see inset).

Recognizing suckers
A sucker can usually be distinguished by its leaves: a normal stem from the top growth, left; a sucker from the root, right.

REMOVING NONVARIEGATED AND REVERTED SHOOTS

Nonvariegated shoot
With variegated shrubs (here, *Euonymus fortunei* 'Emerald 'n' Gold'), cut any plain shoots back to the variegated growth.

Reverted shoot
Cut back reverted shoots (here, on *E. fortunei* 'Emerald Gaiety') to the main stem. If necessary, remove the entire stem.

Moving an established shrub

Careful selection and siting of a shrub should make transplanting unnecessary, although sometimes it may be desirable or unavoidable. Thin out growth of deciduous shrubs by up to a third to compensate for root disturbance. The younger the shrub, the more likely it is to reestablish well.

When to transplant

Most deciduous young shrubs can be lifted bare-root when dormant. Established shrubs that have large root systems should be lifted with a ball of soil around the roots before being moved. Fall is the best time to do this. Evergreens should be transplanted in spring, just before new growth occurs, carefully digging up the whole root ball.

Balling-and-burlapping a shrub

Most often, it is best to ball-and-burlap a shrub so that root damage is kept to a minimum. Prepare the new planting site first before lifting the shrub.

Dig a trench around the shrub just beyond the spread of its branches. Cut through woody roots but leave fibrous ones intact. If necessary, use a fork to loosen the soil around the root ball and reduce its size. Then undercut it with a spade, using pruners to sever any woody taproots.

Once the root ball is free, work a sheet of burlap or similar material underneath it. Tie the burlap firmly around the ball, lift the shrub from the hole, and transplant it. Remove or untie the burlap before replanting.

Transplanted shrubs require the same treatment as those that have been planted for the first time, although they may take longer to reestablish (see p.96).

Shrub problems

Plants are less likely to succumb to pest attack or disease if they are given good growing conditions and care. Many problems originate from poor drainage, lack of moisture, planting too deeply, compaction of the soil, or exposure to temperature extremes in an unsuitable site.

Physical damage

Wounds caused by a jagged pruning cut, a badly placed cut, or pruning at the wrong time may allow disease fungi to establish. This may also cause dieback. Mechanical wounding—for example, by a lawnmower grazing a stem—also provides a convenient entry point for disease.

Pests and diseases

Maintaining good garden hygiene minimizes the chance of pests and diseases establishing a foothold. As shrubs age, however, they lose vigor and become more prone to pests and diseases. Old or diseased shrubs that have lost their vigor are rarely worth saving and should be replaced.

Pests and diseases most likely to affect shrubs are aphids (p.654), spider mites (p.670), black vine weevils (p.655), *Phytophthora* stem rots (see "*Phytophthora* root rots," p.666), and powdery mildew (p.667). Be alert to the signs of a problem, which include streaking and changes of foliage color, drooping leaves, loss of leaves, distorted growth, and the development of mushrooms.

Cold and wind

When selecting and siting shrubs, it is vital to take account of the general weather pattern of the area as well as the garden's individual microclimate; it is almost impossible, however, to take precautions against freak extremes of temperature or exceptional winds.

There is a wide range of hardy shrubs available, and many gardeners choose to rely on these rather than risk the loss of more tender specimens. If growing shrubs that are of marginal hardiness for your area, then it is worth using the appropriate cold and wind protection methods (see pp.612–613).

Container-grown shrubs are more vulnerable to extremes of weather than those grown in the open garden. In areas where temperatures only occasionally fall below freezing, most container-grown hardy shrubs can be overwintered outdoors (except those, such as camellias, that are root-tender). In colder areas, however, move shrubs indoors to where the ambient daytime temperature is about 45–55°F (7–13°C) or higher, according to the species.

TRANSPLANTING A SHRUB

1 Before moving a large shrub, it can be helpful to thin out growth. This will make handling easier and help the shrub to reestablish. Then, using a spade, mark out a circle around the perimeter of the shrub's branches (here, *Ilex aquifolium* 'Golden Milkboy'). Tie in any trailing stems or wrap the shrub in burlap to prevent damage.

2 Dig a trench around the circle, then use a fork to loosen the soil around the root ball. Take care not to damage any fibrous roots.

3 Continue to carefully fork away soil from around the shrub's root ball to reduce its size and weight.

4 Undercut the root ball with a spade, cutting through woody roots if necessary to separate them from the surrounding soil.

5 Roll up a length of burlap. Tilt the shrub to one side and unroll the burlap beneath the root ball. Tilt the root ball the other way, and unroll the rest of the burlap.

6 Pull the burlap up around the root ball and tie it securely. Remove shrub from its hole and transport it to its new position.

7 Remove the burlap and replant the shrub in the new, prepared hole with the soil mark at the same level as before. Firm, water well, and mulch.

Pruning and training

Some shrubs, particularly evergreens of naturally compact habit such as *Sarcococca*, make attractive plants with little or no pruning or training. They may require no more than the removal of dead, damaged, and diseased wood. If left untreated, this will be unsightly and may threaten the health of the shrub. Many shrubs need pruning or a combination of pruning and training to realize their full ornamental potential.

Aims and effects of pruning and training

The most common requirement is for formative pruning that creates a vigorous and well-shaped shrub. Many shrubs also need a regular schedule of pruning to maintain the ornamental quality of their flowers, fruit, foliage, or stems. The timing of this, which may be critical, varies depending on the growth pattern of the shrub and the effect desired.

Pruning can also be a way of bringing neglected and overgrown plants back to healthy, manageable growth. It is a matter of judgment whether a shrub warrants being rescued. Replacement is often the best course when a shrub requires regular cutting back.

Shrubs grown as topiary or hedges require specialized pruning from their formative stage. For further information see TOPIARY, pp.108–109, and HEDGES AND SCREENS, pp.82–85.

PRUNING FOR WILDLIFE

Most pruning aims to encourage vigorous growth and to maximize flower and fruit production. But left unpruned, or lightly pruned, many ornamental shrubs afford excellent habitats for wildlife.

Densely branched shrubs like pyracanthas, old-fashioned and species roses, some cotoneasters, euonymus, and viburnums are among a range of shrubs valued for flowers and fruit that come into this category: they provide food and shelter for small birds, and the flowers attract butterflies, bees, and other insects. Left unpruned (apart from the removal of dead, damaged, or diseased growth), these shrubs will continue to bloom and fruit freely, if sometimes less prolifically than more manicured specimens.

In training, the gardener plays an active role in directing plant growth. Most shrubs grown in the open require no training at all. Shrubs grown against supports, however, normally need a combination of pruning and training to form a well-spaced framework of branches.

Principles of pruning and training

Pruning normally stimulates growth. The terminal shoot or growth bud of a stem is often dominant, inhibiting the growth of buds or shoots below it. Pruning that removes the ends of stems affects the control mechanism, resulting in more vigorous development of lower shoots or growth buds.

Hard or light pruning

Hard pruning promotes more vigorous growth than light pruning; this needs to be kept in mind when correcting the shape of an unbalanced shrub. Hard cutting back of vigorous growth often encourages even stronger growth. Prune weak growth hard but strong growth only lightly.

How to prune

Pruning wounds, like other injuries that a shrub might suffer, are possible entry points for disease. The risk is reduced by making well-placed, clean cuts with sharp tools.

Stems with alternate or whorled arrangements of growth buds should be cut just above a bud pointing in the desired direction of growth—for example, an outward-facing bud that will not cross another shoot as its growth develops. Use an angled cut, starting opposite a healthy growth bud, and slant the cut so that it finishes slightly above the bud. If the cut is too close, the bud may die; if too far, the stem itself may die back.

With shrubs that have buds in opposite pairs, cut straight across the shoot just above a pair of healthy buds. Both buds will develop, resulting in a forked branch system.

In the past, gardeners have often been advised to use a wound paint on pruning cuts, but research now suggests that wound paints are not generally an effective way of controlling diseases and in some cases may even encourage them.

Pruning alone will not promote vigorous new growth. Shrubs that are renovated or regularly cut back benefit from fertilizing and mulching. Apply a general-purpose

fertilizer at the beginning of the growing season according to manufacturer's recommendations and mulch to a depth of 2–4in (5–10cm) with well-rotted organic material in spring, when the ground has warmed up a little.

Training

The growth of lower buds or shoots on a stem may also be modified by training. When a stem is allowed to grow upright, the lower shoots on the stem usually grow weakly.

With stems that are trained more horizontally, however, the lower shoots and buds grow more vigorously. Training branches near the horizontal can substantially increase the amount of flower and fruit that a shrub is able to produce. Wall-trained shrubs should be tied in to supports as growth develops. As stems ripen and turn woody, they become far less flexible and are therefore more difficult to train successfully.

Formative pruning

The aim of formative pruning is to ensure that a shrub has a

Cutting back hard for vigor
Promote vigorous growth by hard pruning. Using sharp, clean loppers or pruners, cut back a number of the main stems right to the base of the shrub.

WHERE TO CUT

Opposite shoots
Prune stems with opposite buds to just above a strong pair of buds or shoots, using a clean, straight cut.

Alternate shoots
For shrubs with alternate buds, prune to just above a bud or shoot, using a clean, angled cut.

An angled cut
Angle the cut so that its lowest point is opposite the base of the bud and the top just clears the bud.

framework of well-spaced branches so that it will develop according to its natural habit. The amount of formative pruning required depends very much on the type of shrub and on the quality of the plants available. When buying shrubs, therefore, you should look for sturdy specimens with a well-balanced branch formation, as well as healthy roots.

Evergreen shrubs generally need little formative pruning. Excessive growth resulting in a lopsided, unbalanced shape should be lightly pruned in mid-spring, after the shrub has been planted.

Deciduous shrubs are much more likely to require formative pruning than evergreen shrubs. This should be carried out in the dormant season, between mid-fall and mid-spring, either at or after planting.

The following guidelines apply to most deciduous shrubs. If a vigorous shoot distorts the framework, cut it back lightly rather than severely, to encourage relatively weak growth. If the shrub does not have a well-spaced, branch framework, cut it back hard to promote strong growth.

In the case of most shrubs, remove completely any spindly and crossing or rubbing branches that clutter the framework. An exception is made for a handful of slow-growing deciduous shrubs, in particular Japanese maples (*Acer japonicum* and *A. palmatum*), which generally need no pruning at all.

Sometimes an apparently good specimen will have too much top growth in relation to the size of its root system. Reducing the number of stems by up to a third, and then shortening the stems that remain, also by a third, will help create a more stable plant.

FORMATIVE PRUNING

After planting a young shrub (here, *Philadelphus*), cut out any dead, damaged, and weak stems, and remove crossing and congested stems to form a well-balanced framework with an open center.

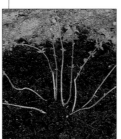

Prune back crossing or congested shoots to an outward-facing bud, or right back to the base.

Prune out weak and spindly, or long and straggly stems, cutting them back to the base.

Remove awkward stems that spoil the shape, leaving an evenly branching framework.

Deciduous shrubs

These may be divided into four groups: those requiring minimal pruning; those pruned in spring, which usually flower on the current season's growth; those pruned after flowering in summer, which usually flower on the previous season's wood; and those of suckering habit. Two important factors are the degree to which shrubs produce replacement growths and the age of the flower-bearing wood.

Minimal pruning

Once established, shrubs that do not regularly produce vigorous growth from the base or lower branches need little or no pruning; simply remove dead, diseased, and damaged wood, and cut out weak or crossing growth. Do this just after flowering. Fertlize and mulch in spring. Japanese maples and other shrubs prone to heavy bleeding if pruned in spring, should be pruned in mid- to late summer, when their sap is least active.

Pruning in spring

Left unpruned, deciduous shrubs that bear flowers on the current season's growth tend to become congested, and flower quality deteriorates. When pruned in spring, these shrubs often produce vigorous shoots that flower in

summer or early fall. Shorten flowered stems in fall, to minimize the risk of wind-rock.

Some large shrubs, such as deciduous *Ceanothus*, develop a woody framework. In their first spring, lightly prune the main stems of less vigorous shrubs and, in the second spring, reduce the previous season's growth by half. In late winter or early spring of subsequent years, prune hard to leave only one to three pairs of buds of the previous season's growth. Prune framework branches to slightly different heights to encourage flower production at all levels. On mature specimens, cut out some of the oldest wood as part of the annual pruning operation to prevent congestion. For pruning *Buddleja davidii*, see p.102.

Some subshrubs, for example *Perovskia*, may form a woody base that allows them to be pruned hard back to a 6–12in (15–30cm) high framework. Cut back the previous season's growth annually in spring, leaving one or two buds.

A few shrubs, such as *Prunus triloba*, that flower in late winter or early spring on wood produced in the previous season are best pruned hard in spring after flowering, and so may be treated as other shrubs in this group. In the first spring after planting, shorten the main stems by about half to form a basal framework. After flowering in subsequent years, cut back all

MINIMAL PRUNING OF DECIDUOUS SHRUBS

If pruning is needed, which may not be every year, do it immediately after flowering, taking out any dead wood, weak stems, and congested growth to maintain a balanced, open-centered framework on shrubs, such as *Hamamelis*.

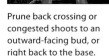

Using pruners, cut back any crossing or rubbing shoots to clear congested growth, especially from the center of the shrub.

Cut back any weak, straggly, wayward, or misshapen shoots to the main stems.

SHRUBS THAT ARE PRUNED IN SPRING

Shrubs (here, *Spiraea japonica*) that flower on wood produced in the current season should be pruned in spring to encourage new, flowering stems.

Prune out stems of the previous year's growth to within 2–4 buds of old wood.

Prune out dead or damaged stems back to healthy growth or cut them right back to the base.

Cut back some of the main stems to the base of the shrub, as well as any weak, twiggy, or spindly growth.

PRUNING DECIDUOUS SHRUBS

Minimal pruning

Amelanchier
Aronia
Buddleja globosa
Caragana
Chimonanthus
Clethra (deciduous spp.)
Cornus alternifolia 'Argentea'
Corokia
Corylopsis
Daphne (deciduous spp.)
Decaisnea
Disanthus
Enkianthus
Eucryphia (deciduous spp.)
Fothergilla
Hoheria (deciduous spp.)
Lindera
Magnolia (deciduous spp.)
Poncirus
Potentilla
Ptelea
Pterostyrax
Rhamnus (deciduous spp.)
Viburnum (deciduous spp.)
Zenobia

Prune in spring

Abutilon
Aloysia
Buddleja davidii
Caryopteris x clandonensis
Ceanothus x delileanus (cvs)
Ceratostigma willmottianum
Colquhounia
Cotinus
Datura
Forsythia (after flowering)
Fuchsia (hardy cvs)
Hibiscus syriacus
Hydrangea
Hypericum
Indigofera
Lavatera
Leycesteria
Perovskia
Prunus triloba (after flowering)
Sorbaria (some spp.)
Spiraea douglasii,
  S. japonica
Tamarix ramosissima
Zauschneria

Lavatera trimestris
'Ruby Regis'

PRUNING *BUDDLEJA DAVIDII*

Because it is very vigorous, *Buddleja davidii* needs more drastic formative pruning than most other shrubs that flower on new wood. At the back of a border, where a tall plant is required, prune to leave a woody framework 3–4ft (90–120cm) high. In another location, however, this may be no more than 2ft (60cm) high.

In the first spring after planting, shorten main stems by a half to three quarters, pruning to pairs of shoots or buds. Cut out growths other than main stems. In early to mid-spring of subsequent years, cut back the previous season's growth and shorten new growth from the base.

To keep the shrub from becoming congested, cut out one or two of the oldest branches as part of the annual pruning regime.

Using loppers, cut back some of the woody spurs to clear congested growth and produce an open, balanced framework.

Using pruners, cut back all the main shoots that flowered the previous year to within 1–3 buds of the old wood.

HYDRANGEAS

For pruning purposes, hydrangeas (excluding climbing species such as *Hydrangea anomala* subsp. *petiolaris*) fall into three groups.

The first group (for example, *H. paniculata*) flowers from midsummer on the current season's growth, and these plants should be treated in the same way as other shrubs that require hard pruning in spring (see p.101).

In early spring of the first year after planting, cut out all but two or three strong stems, pruning back to a healthy pair of buds about 18in (45cm) above ground level. If it is in an exposed site, where summer temperatures will not ripen stems sufficiently to withstand very cold winters, prune to just above ground level. Apply a quick-release fertilizer at a rate of about 4oz/sq yd (120g/sq m) and a 4in (10cm) deep mulch in a 24in (60cm) circle around the shrub. In early spring of subsequent years, cut back the previous year's growth to one or two strong pairs of growth buds, fertilize, and mulch.

The second group, comprising mophead and lacecap hydrangeas (*H. macrophylla*), also flowers from midsummer but on shoots made during the previous growing season. Lightly prune the young plants in early spring, cutting out any thin, twiggy growth and any old flower heads.

Once the plant is established and about three or four years old, remove some of the oldest wood annually in early spring. Cut out stems that are more than three years old and shorten the other stems that flowered in the previous season, cutting back to a strong pair of buds 6–12in (15–30cm) from the base. Then fertilize and mulch.

Other species, like *H. aspera*, and related forms constitute a third group and require only minimal pruning in spring.

In spring, prune back all flowered stems, also damaged and weak growth, and cut back some older wood to the base.

Hydrangea macrophylla

Cut back any dead wood to healthy growth or right back to the base of the plant, if necessary.

Prune out all flowered stems, making a straight cut above a strong pair of growth buds.

growth to two to three buds of the framework stems. In areas where annual growth is limited by cool summers, cut back only a third of shoots near to ground level, and the others to 6–12in (15–30cm).

For all shrubs in this group, apply fertilizer just after pruning. In mid-spring, mulch the area matching the spread of the shrub before pruning.

Shrubs pruned in summer after flowering

Many deciduous shrubs that flower in spring or early summer carry their flowers on wood produced in the previous growing season. Sometimes, flowers are formed on last year's wood, as with *Chaenomeles*. Other shrubs bear flowers on short lateral growth produced from last year's wood, for example, *Deutzia*, *Philadelphus*, *Syringa*, and *Weigela*.

Without pruning to encourage the development of vigorous, young growths from close to ground level, shrubs in this group can become densely twiggy and topheavy, and the quantity and quality of flowers deteriorate. Removing spent flower heads prevents shrubs from expending energy in seed production.

When planting a shrub in this group, cut out weak or damaged growth and trim back the main shoots to a healthy bud or pair of buds, to encourage the development of a strong framework. If flowers are produced in the first year, prune again immediately after flowering. Cut back flowered shoots to a strong bud or pair of buds and remove any spindly growth. After pruning, lightly work in fertilizer and apply a mulch around the shrub.

Follow this procedure immediately after flowering in subsequent years. Although it is desirable to cut back flowered wood to the strongest buds, do not adhere to this rigidly—it is also important to maintain a well-balanced shape. Feed and mulch as a matter of course after pruning.

As plants mature, more drastic pruning may be needed to encourage growth. After the third year, up to one-fifth of the oldest stems may be cut back annually to within 2–3in (5–8cm) of the ground.

Use discretion when following these guidelines because harsh pruning of young specimens in this group, like forsythias, may result in an awkward and unnatural shape.

Other shrubs in this group, especially when grown as freestanding rather than as wall shrubs, require very little pruning. *Chaenomeles*, for example, has a naturally twiggy habit, with numerous crossing branches, and mature specimens need little pruning. Spur pruning encourages heavier flowering (see Growing Fruit, "Winter pruning," p.438); shorten spurs and sideshoots to three to five leaves in midsummer.

Particular care must be taken in pruning shrubs such as lilacs (*Syringa*) that come into growth during flowering. The new shoots that form below the flowers can be easily damaged when the old flower heads are cut, and this reduces flowering in the next year.

Flowering shrubs of suckering habit

A few shrubs grown for their flowers produce flowers on wood of the previous year but make most of their new growth from ground level. These shrubs spread by suckers and are pruned differently from shrubs that form a permanent woody framework.

After planting, prune suckering shrubs by cutting out weak growth but retain vigorous stems and their sideshoots. The following year, immediately after flowering, remove any weak, dead, or damaged stems, then cut back flowered stems hard to a strong bud or pair of buds.

From the third year, annually cut back a quarter to a half of all flowered stems to 2–3in (5–8cm) above ground level and prune others by about half to vigorous, replacement shoots, then feed and mulch.

SHRUBS TO PRUNE IN SUMMER

Buddleja alternifolia
Deutzia
Dipelta
Exochorda
Holodiscus discolor
Jasminum humile
Kolkwitzia
Neillia
Philadelphus
Photinia villosa
Ribes sanguineum
Rubus deliciosus, R.'Tridel'
Spiraea 'Arguta',
  S. prunifolia,
  S. thunbergii
Stephanandra
Syringa
Weigela

Minimal pruning

Calycanthus
Chaenomeles
Cotoneaster (deciduous spp.)
Magnolia x *soulangeana*,
  M. stellata
Rhododendron
  (deciduous spp.)

Syringa vulgaris 'Mrs. Edward Harding'

PRUNING SHRUBS IN SUMMER

After shrubs such as *Weigela* have flowered, cut back flowered shoots and remove dead and spindly stems. Also prune out some old, main stems.

Using pruners, cut any dead wood right back to healthy growth.

Cut out up to one-fifth of the oldest wood to within 2–3in (5–8cm) of the ground.

Before

Cut out any very weak, twiggy, or straggly stems back to the base just above soil level.

After

Continue cutting out weak or crossing stems to form an open-centered, well-balanced shrub.

PRUNING A DECIDUOUS SUCKERING SHRUB

After flowering, prune back all flowered stems on deciduous suckering shrubs (here, *Kerria*), most by about half, the remainder almost to the ground. Cut out any weak, dead, or damaged growth.

Prune flowered stems by about half their length, cutting back to strongly growing, new shoots.

Cut back up to half of the flowered stems to within 2–3in (5–8cm) of the ground. Also cut to the ground any dead or damaged shoots.

SHRUBS FOR COPPICING AND POLLARDING

Coppicing

Cornus alba 'Aurea',
 C. alba 'Elegantissima',
 C. alba 'Kesselringii',
 C. alba 'Sibirica',
 C. alba 'Spaethii',
 C. alba 'Variegata',
 C. sericea 'Flaviramea'
Corylus maxima 'Purpurea'
Cotinus coggygria,
 C. 'Grace'
Hydrangea paniculata 'Floribunda',
 H. paniculata 'Grandiflora',
 H. paniculata 'Unique'
Rubus biflorus,
 R. cockburnianus,
 R. thibetanus
Salix alba var. *vitellina* 'Britzensis',
 S. daphnoides,
 S. 'Flame',
 S. irrorata
Sambucus racemosa
 'Plumosa Aurea'

Pollarding

Eucalyptus
Salix acutifolia

Cornus alba 'Sibirica'

EVERGREENS THAT MAY BE PRUNED HARD

Aucuba
Berberis darwinii
Buxus
Choisya ternata
Citrus
Escallonia 'Donard Seedling'
Euonymus fortunei,
 E. japonicus
Hibiscus rosa-sinensis
Ilex x *altaclerensis*, *I. aquifolium*
Ligustrum japonicum
Lonicera nitida, *L. pileata*
Nerium oleander
Osmanthus
Phillyrea
Prunus laurocerasus, *P. lusitanica*
Rhododendron ponticum,
 R. Subsection Triflora
Santolina
Sarcococca hookeriana
 var. *humilis*
Taxus
Viburnum tinus

*Hibiscus
rosa-sinensis*

Coppicing and pollarding shrubs

A number of deciduous shrubs grown for the ornamental value of their stems or leaves require severe pruning in spring. Most of these shrubs flower on shoots formed the previous season but, when grown for their stems or leaves, their flowers are sacrificed. The method of hard pruning used on these shrubs is an adaptation of traditional methods of managing trees and shrubs to give a constant and renewable supply of wood for firewood and fencing. In coppicing, shrubs and trees are cut back regularly to near ground level. In pollarding, growth is cut back each year to a permanent framework of a single stem or several stems.

Coppicing shrubs such as *Cornus alba* ensures a regular supply of young branches, which are more strikingly colored than older wood and effective in winter. On shrubs such as *Sambucus racemosa* 'Plumosa Aurea', grown for their foliage, hard pruning usually results in larger leaves. Just before growth commences in early to mid-spring, coppice vigorous shrubs such as *Salix alba* subsp. *vitellina* 'Britzensis' (syn. *S. alba* 'Chermesina') by pruning all shoots to within about 2–3in (5–8cm) of ground level. It may be preferable to vary the height to which stems are cut back to avoid a rigid, uniform effect. Weaker shrubs such as *Cornus alba* 'Sibirica' may be cut back less severely by coppicing only about a third to a half of the stems. Then apply a quick-release fertilizer and mulch liberally, covering a circle of 24in (60cm) radius around the shrub.

Shrubs that have been trained so that they have one or more clean, main stems are pruned back—or

POLLARDING A EUCALYPTUS

Establish a framework by cutting back a young shrub to one or more main stems (below). Each subsequent spring, cut the previous year's growth back hard, either to within 2–3in (5–8cm) of the framework or to the base, because *Eucalyptus* can regenerate from ground level (right).

pollarded—to this stem framework each season. The aim of pruning in the first year is to establish the framework; after planting, before growth commences in spring, cut back a young plant to form a standard with a single stem of 1–3ft (30–90cm). Alternatively, leave three, five, or seven stems, depending on the size of plant required and the space available. Apply a quick-release fertilizer and mulch around the stem (or stems), as for shrubs that are coppiced.

During the plant's first growing season, restrict the number of shoots growing from below the cut to only four or five, rubbing out other shoots, and any that develop low down on the main stem. Continue this process for the next year or two; this allows

the main stem to thicken so that it can support heavier top growth. In spring of the second and subsequent years, reduce the previous season's growths to above a bud within 2–3in (5–8cm) of the framework (see also *Pollarding a Eucalyptus*, above). For larger specimens, prune only a half or one-third of the stems. Feed and mulch.

Evergreen shrubs

The appropriate method for pruning and training evergreens depends on the size they are expected to reach when mature. All evergreen shrubs that show signs of dieback after a hard winter should be treated in the same way, regardless of size.

In mid-spring, prune out dead wood to where the shrub has begun to regenerate and thin out the new shoots if they are overcrowded or crossing. If a shrub shows no sign of life by mid-spring, nick the bark to see if there is any live, green wood beneath. Some shrubs remain dormant for a whole growing season.

Small shrubs up to 3ft (90cm)

Low-growing evergreens are divided into two groups, requiring different pruning regimes. The first group includes several short-lived shrubs that flower profusely, if they are trimmed annually and are not overly-mature, such as lavender cotton (*Santolina chamaecyparissus*), lavender (*Lavandula*), and most heathers (*Calluna, Daboecia,* and *Erica,* but not tree heaths). These shrubs are best replaced every

COPPICING A SHRUB FOR WINTER STEM EFFECT

With shrubs that have colored stems (here, a *Cornus sericea* cultivar) cut back hard all the shrub's stems to about 2–3in (5–8cm) from the base before growth begins in spring (see inset). Apply fertilizer around the shrub to promote new growth, and then mulch. Coppicing stimulates the growth of new, vigorous stems whose color is especially strong.

PRUNING EVERGREEN SHRUBS

After flowering, prune evergreen shrubs (here, *Prunus lusitanica*) by removing damaged or dead wood and cutting back flowered stems and any awkward or straggly stems that mar the shape.

Cut back flowered stems to a main stem. Cut out thickly congested and crossing stems.

Cut back awkwardly growing stems to well-placed, healthy, outward-growing shoots.

Cut out any dead or damaged wood back to healthy growth or, if necessary, to the base.

FAN-TRAINING ORNAMENTAL SHRUBS

A few shrubs, such as ornamental peaches (for example, *Prunus persica* 'Klara Meyer'), are suitable for fan-training like fruit trees. In the first spring after planting, cut back the plant 15–18in (38–45cm) above the graft union, retaining three or four strong shoots. Train the shoots on stakes tied to horizontal wires. Toward the end of the growing season, remove the central shoot if three strong shoots were retained; if four shoots were kept, space these out to form a fan. In winter, reduce all shoots by half their length.

The following growing season, select two or four new shoots on each stem; attach each of these to a stake tied to the wires. Then, in midsummer, remove all other shoots. In the third year, immediately after flowering, cut back all framework shoots by a quarter to a third. Tie in two or three new shoots on each framework stem. Remove unwanted shoots in midsummer. If there are gaps in the fan, prune back adjacent shoots by a third after flowering has finished to encourage new growth. Cut back all other extension growths to 2–3in (5–8cm) to encourage flowering on one-year-old spurs. For full details, see GROWING FRUIT, "Fan," p.453.

Here, *Prunus mume* 'Beni-chidori' is trained to develop an evenly spaced branch framework, using the same method as fan-trained fruit trees.

five to ten years. Also replace plants that have not been pruned for several years because they become weak and leggy and rarely flower or regenerate well.

In mid-spring, use pruners or garden shears to cut out weak growth or flowering shoots on newly planted shrubs. This ensures new growth is generated from basal shoots in the center of the plant. Each subsequent year in mid-spring, remove the old flower heads, and any dead, diseased, or damaged shoots. Some heathers have attractive winter foliage and these, as well as other evergreens, are sometimes deadheaded in fall. In very cold areas, there is a risk of dieback after fall deadheading and, for this reason pruning may be delayed until mid-spring. After pruning, apply slow-release fertilizer at a rate of 2oz/sq yd (60g/sq m) and mulch to a depth of 2in (5cm).

The second group comprises slow-growing shrubs—dwarf cotoneasters and hebes. They require less pruning than those in the first group, the main purpose being to remove dead, diseased, or damaged shoots in mid-spring. Deadheading is unnecessary.

Medium-sized, evergreen shrubs up to 10ft (3m) tall

Most intermediate evergreen shrubs, such as *Berberis darwinii*, camellias, *Escallonia*, *Hibiscus rosa-sinensis*, and many rhododendrons, require little pruning once a well-balanced framework has been established.

In mid-spring, just before growth is about to start, remove crossing or weak shoots as well as any that affect the overall symmetry of the shrub. Fertlize and mulch. Subsequent pruning is limited to cutting out straggly growth, restricting size, and shaping the plant to suit its location. Use pruners or long-handled loppers to remove all or part of selected branches.

Winter- or spring-flowering shrubs like *Berberis darwinii* and *Viburnum tinus* should be pruned right after flowering. Prune others that flower from midsummer, such as *Escallonia*, by removing older wood at the start of growth in mid-

spring or by cutting out flowered stems in midsummer. *Hibiscus rosa-sinensis*, with its flowering season from spring to fall, is best pruned in mid-spring. Fertlize and mulch spring-pruned shrubs after pruning. Do not fertilize or mulch shrubs pruned in late summer until the following spring, to minimize damage from cold.

Large, evergreen shrubs more than 10ft (3m) tall

Large rhododendrons and other tall evergreens require little pruning but may need shaping when young to create a balanced framework. Prune before young plants start into growth or else wait until flowers have faded.

The aim is to encourage an open-centered bush with well-spaced branches. Cut out all crossing and weak branches, and fertilize and mulch after pruning. Regular pruning is generally limited to the removal of dead, damaged, and diseased wood. Some large evergreens like laurels (*Prunus laurocerasus*) may also be used for hedging (see pp.82–85).

Palmlike shrubs

The palmlike *Cordyline* and *Yucca* need pruning only if they have suffered cold-damage or if a bushy, multistemmed plant is needed. In spring, once new growth appears, cut damaged branches back to just above newly formed shoots. Feed and apply a mulch. To create a multibranched specimen, remove the growing point before growth commences, then fertilize and mulch. Both genera respond well to hard pruning and renovation: cut back to suitable sideshoots or basal shoots.

Other palmlike succulents such as *Agave* and *Phormium* require only dead leaves to be removed or faded flower stems cut out.

Wall shrubs

There are three reasons to grow shrubs against walls. First, some are too tender for the open garden in frost-prone areas, but will thrive if sheltered. Second, training shrubs, including hardy shrubs, such as pyracanthas, against a wall makes it possible to accommodate plants that might not otherwise fit. Third, some shrubs are natural ramblers (for example, *Cestrum elegans*), so they need support.

It is vital to train and prune wall shrubs early on so they are compact and "well tailored" and produce plenty of flowering shoots regularly. When training wall shrubs, make a framework to which growth can be tied, such as trellis, netting, or spaced, horizontal wires as used for wall-trained fruit trees (see p.424).

Advice for pruning freestanding shrubs also applies to wall-trained specimens, but more care is needed for formative training and pruning. Tie in shoots as they grow and cut back sublaterals growing strongly away from the wall.

Formative training and pruning

During the first growing season, train in the leader and main laterals to form a framework; prune back outward-growing laterals to encourage short sideshoots to develop close to the framework. Remove completely any laterals growing toward the wall or fence, and shoots growing outward in the wrong direction. The aim is to create a neat, vertical carpet of foliage to cover the space.

Routine pruning

In the second and following seasons, flowering laterals should form. After flowering, cut back

PRUNING CEANOTHUS

Immediately after flowering, cut back new shoots of spring-flowering *Ceanothus* to 2–3 leaves. Tie in new shoots and trim back outward-growing shoots to keep growth trained close to the wall or fence.

flowered shoots to within 3–4in (7–10cm) of the main framework. This encourages new flowering laterals to develop, providing the next season's display. Continue tying in framework shoots; trim outward-pointing laterals and remove inward-growing and other wrongly aligned shoots. Do not trim wall shrubs after midsummer, which may reduce the following year's flowering shoots; this is particularly important with *Ceanothus* and many half-hardy evergreen shrubs, which might otherwise produce soft

growth liable to cold damage. Fertlize and mulch wall-trained shrubs annually in spring to maintain healthy growth.

Shrubs, such as pyracantha, that are grown both for flowers and fruits or berries need slightly modified pruning. Shoots that have flowered are not cut back, but left to develop fruit. Trim back new laterals to two to three leaves from their base as the fruit swell, so that they are exposed to more light and ripen well. Old fruit clusters may be cut out in spring as young growth develops.

Summer- and fall-flowering wall shrubs, like some *Ceanothus*, should be trained as described earlier but pruned according to whether they flower on the previous season's wood (see "Shrubs pruned in summer after flowering," p.103), or that of the current season (see "Pruning in spring," p.101). Some half-hardy or tender shrubs—particularly *Ceanothus*—do not break readily from old wood and are difficult to renovate once neglected.

Scrambling shrubs

These also require careful training to contain their flexible shoots. On some, such as half-hardy *Cestrum elegans*, that produce flowers in late summer on terminal shoots or short laterals, the flowered shoots may be cut out entirely or cut back to

strong, low, lateral growths in spring. Others flower in summer mainly on lateral growths, which should be cut back after flowering to 3–4in (7–10cm) and will often produce further sublaterals that flower the same season. In spring, these laterals are pruned back again to 3–4in (7–10cm) and will flower in summer.

Training and pruning standard shrubs

Some shrubs, for example, fuchsias and *Buddleja alternifolia*, may be grown as standards. The height of the stem varies according to the vigor of the plant and the effect required. For details on training a standard fuchsia, see p.119; for pruning a standard rose, see p.162.

To train a shrub such as *Buddleja alternifolia* as a standard, tie a strong stem to a stake in the first growing season. Pinch all sideshoots back to two or three leaves, leaving a few growing near the stem tip. As the stem grows, continue to pinch out the tips. When the clear stem is at the desired height, stop the terminal shoot to encourage shoots to form the head. In early spring of the following year, shorten the branches of the head to about 6in (15cm). Retain two or three of the

PRUNING AND TRAINING A YOUNG WALL SHRUB

In the first year, prune the shrub (here, a pyracantha) to build up a balanced framework, tying in main stems. In subsequent years, tie in new growth in spring; in midsummer, cut back inward- and outward-growing shoots to form a vertical carpet; remove entirely dead, damaged, or spindly growth.

Using pruners, cut back any weak, spindly stems as well as any dead or damaged wood.

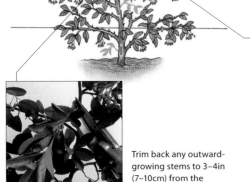

Trim back any outward-growing stems to 3–4in (7–10cm) from the framework in midsummer.

Check and replace any broken ties. Use garden twine tied in a figure-eight loop to resecure the stem to the wire.

PRUNING AN ESTABLISHED WALL SHRUB

Prune mature plants (here, pyracantha) to maintain a well-balanced framework of stems and expose the fruits on berrying shrubs. In late summer, remove outward-growing shoots and, with the exception of shrubs grown for fruits or berries, cut back flowered shoots to promote dense growth. Also check and replace ties where necessary. Tie in new shoots in spring.

Cut back young shoots to 2–3 leaves from their base to expose the ripening berries.

Using pruners, cut back any damaged or dead wood to healthy growth.

shoots each produces. Fertilize and mulch. Prune subsequently as for other shrubs pruned in summer after flowering (see p.103).

Some pendulous cultivars are grafted onto a rootstock. Remove any suckers (see p.103) and treat as for roses (see "Suckers and how to deal with them," p.159).

Root pruning

Root pruning is sometimes used to control the top growth of vigorous shrubs and to make them flower more freely; grafted specimens that are having prolific leaf growth but producing few flowers or fruit usually benefit from root pruning.

In early spring, dig a trench around the shrub to a depth of 12–24in (30–60cm) with a circumference just beyond the spread of the top growth. Use pruning loppers or a saw to cut back the thick, woody roots; as a guide, shorten them to about half the radius of the trench. Leave fibrous roots unpruned. Control further root spread by inserting a barrier of slates or polycarbonate sheets around the trench (see *Restricting the Spread of Bamboo*, pp.120–121). After backfilling, mulch the area within the trench.

Root pruning is often used to control container-grown shrubs. This is best done when repotting. Shorten up to one-fifth of woody roots by a quarter; cut back others so that they fit in the container. Repot, using fresh potting mix and a slow-release fertilizer, and water them thoroughly.

Renovation

Old, tangled, or overgrown shrubs may sometimes be renovated by extensive pruning. Shrubs that respond well usually produce young growth from the base.

It is not worth trying to salvage a shrub that is badly diseased. Some shrubs do not tolerate drastic pruning; if in any doubt, stagger a program of heavy pruning over two or three years.

Renovate deciduous shrubs, such as lilacs, after flowering or when they are dormant; for evergreens, such as *Viburnum tinus*, delay renovation until mid-spring, after flowering.

Renovating old or overgrown shrubs

Cut out all weak and crossing stems and shorten main stems to 12–18in (30–45cm) above the ground, leaving a balanced framework. Apply a slow-release fertilizer at 4oz/sq yd (120g/sq m), and mulch the area around the shrub to a depth of 2–4in (5–10cm). Keep the shrub well watered throughout summer.

In the next growing season, a mass of shoots should emerge from below the cuts on the main stems. Retain two to four of the strongest on each stem to provide the new branch framework. On deciduous shrubs, cut out extra shoots during the dormant season. On evergreens, do this in mid-spring.

In the following growing season, some secondary growth may occur where shoots have been cut. Rub out these growths.

Staggered renovation

A less drastic method is to spread the pruning over two or three years. Prune deciduous shrubs after flowering, evergreens in mid-spring. Prune half of the oldest stems to 2–3in (5–8cm) from the ground. If possible, cut back remaining stems by about half to new, vigorous, replacement shoots. Apply slow-release fertilizer, water well, and mulch. At the same time the next year, repeat the process on the remaining old stems. Thereafter, prune the shrub according to its growth and flowering habits.

GRADUAL RENOVATION

Renovate deciduous shrubs after flowering and evergreens in mid-spring. Cut back a third to a half of the oldest main stems (here, on a *Deutzia*) almost to the ground and remove dead, twiggy stems. Over the next year or two, cut back remaining old, main stems.

Cut back about half the stems to within 2–3in (5–8cm) of the base. Cut out the oldest stems and any that spoil the shape.

Cut back older stems by half to new, vigorous shoots, and remove any weak, twiggy growth or dead wood.

Prune back crossing, rubbing, or congested stems to a bud or stem that will not cause more crossing shoots.

DRASTIC RENOVATION

A shrub that produces new growth from the base (here lilac) can be renovated when dormant if it is deciduous or in mid-spring if evergreen. Cut back all main stems to within 12–18in (30–45cm) of the ground. Remove suckers by cutting them off at the base.

PRUNING AND COMPOSTING

Most gardeners need to dispose of woody waste material like hedge clippings, tree and shrub prunings, or sometimes large tree branches at least once a year. Rather than burning it, which has an adverse environmental impact, it is better to chop up—or preferably shred—the pruned woody shoots and compost them. Shredded vegetation will rot down faster than chopped clippings or prunings in a compost heap.

If practical, it is best to compost clippings and prunings from deciduous plants separately from those of evergreens—especially those with large, tough leaves like *Prunus laurocerasus* and hollies—because evergreen foliage usually takes longer to break down.

Mixing the shredded material with compost activators like grass mowings or comfrey leaves hastens the composting process. The resulting compost, which takes 3–12 months to mature, may be used as a mulch on established trees and shrubs. See also p.627.

Topiary

A form of training and pruning trees and shrubs to create attractive, boldly artificial shapes, topiary is a garden art that has been popular since Roman times. Traditionally used to produce architectural and geometric shapes in formal gardens, it has been developed to include birds, animals, and unusual, even whimsical, features such as giant chess pieces and life-sized trains.

Designing with topiary

Different styles of topiary may be used to create a variety of effects. Imaginative, living sculptures express personal style and add a humorous or bizarre touch. Using topiary for geometric shapes such as cones, obelisks, and columns provides a strong, structural element in a design. This type of topiary may be valuable both in formal gardens, perhaps to frame a vista or form an avenue, and in informal gardens, as a contrasting foil for less structured planting.

In some gardens, it may be appropriate to treat part of the hedge top as topiary, clipping it into one or more birds, spheres, or cubes, for example. Topiary can also be striking in containers; use a single container plant as a centerpiece, a pair to flank a doorway, or several to line a path. It can also be adopted to create eye-catching stem effects, such as twists and spirals, with one or more stems.

Plants for topiary

Plants to be used for topiary require dense, pliable growth, small leaves, and the ability to recover quickly from clipping. Evergreens such as boxwood (*Buxus sempervirens*), privet (*Ligustrum ovalifolium*), yew (*Taxus baccata*), *Lonicera nitida*, and *Osmanthus delavayi* are ideal in a temperate climate. *Cupressus sempervirens* can also be trained into geometric designs, but only thrives in warmer climates. Bay (*Laurus nobilis*), holly (such as *Ilex crenata* and nonspiny clones of *I. x altaclerensis*), and many other evergreens may be used, but are more difficult to train.

Ivies, such as *Hedera helix* 'Ivalace', are very adaptable and may easily be trained to grow up a frame; alternatively, several cuttings can be taken from an existing plant to grow up a moss-padded structure.

Creating a shape

Most topiary designs are best formed with the aid of a guiding framework, although some simple shapes may also be cut freehand.

Simple designs
Using young plants, select the stem or stems that will form the core of the design. The simplest shape to produce is a cone, which needs only guiding stakes. For other shapes, attach a framework made from chicken wire or single wires attached to stakes placed in the ground next to the main group of shoots. Tie in the stems to the wire framework and then pinch back the shoots to encourage them to branch and cover the form.

Train new shoots into the framework to fill in any gaps, until they meet around its perimeter. Growth will vary around the plant, depending on the sun exposure. Shoots trained downward always grow slowly.

Complex designs
Frameworks for complex designs are now generally available, although you may decide to make your own basic framework from sturdy materials such as heavy-duty fencing wire. Chicken wire or thin-gauge wire may then be intertwined to form a more precise shape. Garden stakes are also useful as a temporary

HOW TO CREATE A SIMPLE DESIGN

1 If using a young plant (here, boxwood) to form a geometric shape, first cut the plant to shape by eye.

2 The following year, make a cutting guide from stakes and wire, place over the plant, and cut the plant to shape.

3 When the plant is the desired shape, clip each year with pruners to retain a crisp outline.

A RANGE OF PLANTS SUITABLE FOR TOPIARY

Viburnum tinus 'Variegatum'

Hedera helix (small-leaved cultivars)

Laurus nobilis

Taxus baccata

Ilex x altaclerensis 'Golden King'

Buxus sempervirens 'Suffruticosa'

Ilex crenata

Lonicera nitida 'Baggesen's Gold'

Osmanthus delvayi

Clipped bird
Traditional shapes are still the most popular for topiary. This delightful bird sits on top of its nest surveying the surrounding gardens.

aid in developing and shaping a framework. Twine is good for tying shoots onto a framework, since it eventually decays.

Training stems
Young stems being trained onto a frame grow quickly, and some work is required to tie in new shoots throughout the growing season. Tie in the shoots while they are young and pliable and check previous ties to make sure that they are not broken, rubbing, or in any way restricting the shoots.

If stakes have been used in the framework, make sure that they are still firm and have not cracked, snapped, or bent. If they are defective, replace them with new ones.

Clipping

Topiary involves much more precise clipping than is required for normal hedge cutting. Take time, particularly when initially forming

topiary pieces, to cut the branchlets carefully to the required shape. Do not cut too much in one place or it may spoil the symmetry of a topiary design for a whole season until new replacement growth appears.

Even if you have a good eye for shaping plants, it is wise to use levels, plumb lines, and any other aids available to check the accuracy of a cut. Always work from the top of the plant downward and from the center outward, cutting both sides together in order to retain a balanced symmetry.

Rounded topiary pieces are easier to produce and maintain than angular, geometric shapes and may often be cut freehand. To produce a spherical shape, first trim the top of the plant and then cut a channel downward around the circumference to leave a ring. A further ring at 90° should then be cut, leaving four distinct quarters to be trimmed.

Geometric topiary that has precise, flat surfaces and angled or squared edges is difficult to form and maintain successfully and needs to be tackled with confident, accurate clipping for a well-defined shape. Such geometric designs are best cut using guidelines attached to stakes to maintain symmetry.

When to clip
Once a topiary feature is established, it will need frequent routine clipping during the growing season. The time between cuts will depend on the rate of growth. An intricate, geometric design in boxwood may need to be cut at four- to six-week intervals.

Architectural designs
Two eye-catching spiral shapes enhance the central, cone-shaped topiary along this path and complement the two dome-shaped side pieces.

Trim as soon as any new growth begins to appear uneven.

If a perfect finish is not required throughout the year, two cuts during the growing season are usually sufficient for a reasonable effect, depending on the plant used. Yew needs to be cut only once a year, boxwood (depending on the cultivar) usually needs to be cut twice, and *Lonicera nitida* three times.

Clip plants at the appropriate time of year. Do not clip bushes after early fall because the young shoots produced after the first trim need to ripen sufficiently to withstand low winter temperatures. In warm climates where growth may be almost continuous, regular trimming will be required throughout the year.

Routine care

Weeding, watering, and mulching is essential in the same way as for free-growing shrubs (see p.98). It is important, however, to apply two or three feeds of a balanced fertilizer at the recommended rate during the growing season.

Winter care
In regions where regular snowfalls occur, netting topiary pieces will help prevent the branches from breaking under the weight of snow. Knock snow off any flat surfaces; its weight may damage the framework.

Repairs and renovation
If a leader, a section, or a branch of topiary has been damaged or broken, cut it back cleanly with pruners. Manipulate nearby shoots by tying them in to fill the gap.

If topiary plants have been left unclipped for one or two years, regular clipping should restore the original form within the season. If the topiary has been neglected for years and the shape has been lost, severe pruning to restore the outline should be carried out the first spring followed by two or three seasons of more precise clipping.

Scorch and dieback
The foliage of some evergreens may be scorched in fierce winters and can die. The damaged foliage will soon be covered by new growth in spring, but cut it back where it is unsightly, taking care to follow the shape of the topiary piece. If shoots do not fill the gap, there may be a root problem, which will need to be treated.

HOW TO MAKE A COMPLEX DESIGN

1 Make frameworks for large topiary pieces from strong materials—they will be in place for several years. Clip a young plant (here, yew) as necessary to keep it within the framework.

2 As the plant grows and fills the frame, clip it once a year, following the outline of the framework and pinching out shoots to encourage bushy growth.

3 When mature, the plant will form a dense bush and cover the framework. It needs regular clipping to maintain the precise outline of the design.

Propagation

There are many ways to propagate shrubs to raise new plants, including taking cuttings, sowing seed, layering, division, and grafting.

Taking cuttings is a simple way of propagating many shrubs and, unlike seed, which may produce variable offspring, it may be used for cultivars, hybrids, and sports.

Sowing seed is both simple and inexpensive but it is relatively slow to produce plants of flowering size. Some shrubs may be divided, while others may be layered.

Grafting involves uniting a stem from the plant to be propagated with the rootstock of a compatible plant. It is not commonly used by casual gardeners because it requires more expertise and skill than other methods, but it is the most suitable method for some shrubs.

Softwood cuttings

This technique is suitable for raising several, mainly deciduous, shrubs, for example *Fuchsia* and *Perovskia*. Softwood cuttings are taken in spring from fast-growing stem tips when these are about 2½–3in (6–8cm) long. The cuttings have a soft base and a higher capacity to root than cuttings of more mature wood.

Preparing the cuttings

Take the cuttings early in the morning. Select healthy, pliable, single-stemmed shoots and seal them in an opaque plastic bag. Prepare the cuttings as soon as possible after collection: trim the cuttings just below a node and remove the lower leaves. The soft tip is generally pinched off because it is vulnerable to rotting; removing it also encourages the cutting, once rooted, to form a bushy plant. Use a propagation mix of equal parts peat substitute (or peat) and either perlite or sharp sand. With a dibber, insert them into the mix. Water them in, applying a fungicide to minimize rot, label, and place in a mist unit or propagator.

Aftercare

Softwood cuttings wilt quickly if not kept in a humid atmosphere and aftercare is very important; remove dropped leaves daily, if possible, and apply a fungicidal spray every week. Once rooted, harden off the cuttings and transplant them into individual pots or retain them in the container. If kept in the propagation mix, give a supplementary fertilize every two weeks during the growing season and pot up the rooted cuttings individually the following spring.

Greenwood cuttings

Almost all the shrubs that may be propagated by softwood cuttings may also be propagated by greenwood cuttings. Take greenwood cuttings, either nodal or heel cuttings (see p.112), from vigorous shoots in late spring or early summer, when these are firm and slightly woody at the base. Follow the method for softwood cuttings.

Remove the soft tips if the cuttings are more than 3–4in (8–10cm) long and trim off the bottom leaves. On a nodal cutting, make a straight cut with a sharp blade directly below the node. Trim

TAKING GREENWOOD CUTTINGS

Select and prepare greenwood cuttings (here, of *Philadelphus*) in late spring when growth has slowed and the new stems are firmer.

off the tail on a heel cutting. Dip the cuttings in a rooting hormone and insert them into propagation mix. Water the cuttings with a fungicidal solution before placing them in a mist unit or propagator. Remove any fallen leaves daily and apply a fungicide once a week.

Once rooted, harden off the cuttings and transplant them or grow them on in the original container. If the latter, fertilize them

---

PROPAGATING BY SOFTWOOD CUTTINGS

1 In spring, cut off young, nonflowering shoots (here, from a hydrangea) with 3–5 pairs of leaves. Seal them in an opaque plastic bag and keep shaded until they can be prepared.

2 Reduce each cutting to 3–4in (8–10cm) in length, making a straight cut just below a node (see inset). Trim off the lower leaves and pinch out the growing tip.

3 Insert the cuttings into prepared pots of propagation mix, ensuring that the leaves do not touch each other.

4 Water the cuttings with a fungicidal solution, then label and place them in a propagator. Maintain a temperature of 64–70°F (18–21°C).

5 Once the cuttings have rooted, harden them off, then remove them from the pot and carefully tease them apart.

6 Transplant the separated cuttings into individual pots and firm in. Water, label, and keep the cuttings in a shaded spot until well established.

SHRUBS FROM SOFT- OR GREENWOOD CUTTINGS

Abelia
Abutilon
Aloysia ❦
Calluna
Caryopteris
Ceanothus (deciduous spp.)
Ceratostigma ❦
Cestrum ❦
Cotoneaster (deciduous spp.)
Cytisus
Daboecia
Daphne x *burkwoodii*
Deutzia (some spp.)
Enkianthus
Erica
Forsythia
Fuchsia
Genista
Halesia
Hydrangea ❦
Kolkwitzia
Lagerstroemia ❦
Lantana ❦
Lavatera ❦
Perovskia
Philadelphus
Potentilla
Viburnum (deciduous spp.)
Weigela (some spp.)

Key
❦ Softwood cuttings only

Calluna vulgaris

regularly during the growing season and transplant them the following spring.

Semiripe cuttings

Many evergreen as well as some deciduous shrubs may be propagated from semiripe cuttings.

Suitable cuttings

The cuttings are normally taken from mid- to late summer and sometimes into the early fall. Select shoots from the current season's growth that are firm and woody near the base but still soft at the tip. Unlike softwood cuttings, they should offer some resistance when bent. Some shrubs are propagated by variations of this semiripe cuttings technique, such as mallet cuttings (see p.112) or leaf-bud cuttings (see p.112).

Preparing the rooting medium

Before collecting the cutting material from the parent shrub, fill sufficient containers of appropriate size, or a propagator (equipped with basal heating) with a suitable rooting medium: use fine-grade pine bark or a mixture of equal parts of peat substitute (or peat) and either grit or perlite.

Preparing the cuttings

Cuttings may be taken with a heel (see p.112) or as nodal cuttings. Heel cuttings should be 2–3in (5–7cm) long, trimmed at the heel; nodal cuttings should be 4–6in (10–15cm) long, taken from leaders or sideshoots, and cut with a sharp knife or pruners just below a node.

Remove the soft tips of nodal and heel cuttings. In both cases, remove the lowest pair of leaves and, with large-leaved plants, reduce the size of the remaining leaves by about a half to minimize moisture loss.

An optional step is to prepare the base of the cuttings by making a shallow wound at one side; on plants that are difficult to root, such as *Daphne sericea*, this cut should be made deeper so that a sliver of bark is also removed.

Potting up

Dip the bases of the cuttings, including the entire wound on wounded cuttings, in a rooting hormone before using a dibber to insert them in the prepared propagation mix, either directly in a propagator, or in containers.

Space the cuttings approximately 3–4in (8–10cm) apart, and make certain that their leaves do not overlap because this may create stagnant conditions in which rot

fungi thrive. Firm the propagation mix around the cuttings. Label each container and water the cuttings thoroughly with a fungicidal solution in order to protect them against damping off diseases (see p.658).

Correct temperature

Overwinter cuttings in containers in a cold frame or greenhouse. Those that have been inserted directly in a propagator should have basal heat maintained at 70°F (21°C).

Aftercare

Inspect the cuttings periodically during the winter period, removing any fallen leaves promptly. Water the containers if the propagation mix shows any signs of drying out. If the cuttings are being overwintered in a cold frame, this may need some form of insulation, such as a burlap cover or a piece of old carpet, to protect the cuttings from cold damage.

Cuttings kept in a cold frame or unheated greenhouse will almost certainly need a further growing season in their containers before rooting satisfactorily. Keep the frame closed except on very mild days. The glass should be kept clean and free of any condensation because the high moisture content of the air inside the cold frame provides ideal conditions for fungal infection to occur. In late spring and early summer, gradually open the cover for longer and longer periods to harden off the rooted cuttings. If necessary, protect them from strong, direct sunlight by covering the glass with suitable shading material.

Throughout the growing season, apply a liquid fertilizer every two weeks to all semiripe cuttings. Check them regularly, and remove any that are weak or showing signs of disease.

Transplanting

Cuttings overwintered in a propagator should have rooted by early spring because the basal heat helps speed up root development. Check that there is strong root growth before transplanting the cuttings. Ease them from their containers, separate each cutting carefully, and either pot them up individually or plant, clearly labeled, in the open ground. If some cuttings have not rooted but have formed a callus, scrape off some of the callus to stimulate rooting and reinsert the cuttings in the propagation mix.

Cuttings grown in a cold frame may be planted out in fall, if well developed, or kept in a sheltered location outside or in the cold frame until spring. They are then potted up individually or planted out.

PROPAGATING BY SEMIRIPE CUTTINGS

1 In mid- to late summer, select healthy shoots of the current season's growth for the cuttings. Sever them from the parent plant (here, *Ilex x altaclerensis* 'Golden King') just above a node. They should be semiripe: still soft at the top but firm at the base.

2 Remove the sideshoots from the main stem. Trim each sideshoot to 4–6in (10–15cm) long, cutting just below a node.

3 Trim off the soft tip of each cutting and then remove the lowest pair of leaves, cutting flush with the stem.

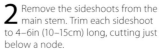

4 Stimulate rooting by wounding the cutting: carefully cut away a piece of bark about 1–1½in (2.5–4cm) long from one side of the base.

5 Dip the base of each cutting in hormone rooting powder, then insert it into propagation mix in a propagator or in pots in a cold frame.

6 Once they are well rooted, carefully lift the cuttings and plant them individually. Gradually harden them off before growing them on in their pots or transplanting them outside.

SHRUBS FROM SEMIRIPE CUTTINGS

Andromeda
Arctostaphylos
Aucuba ▽
Azara ▽
Berberis ▽
Boronia ▽
Brachyglottis
Bupleurum ▽
Buxus
Callistemon ▽
Camellia
Cantua ▽
Carmichaelia ▽
Carpenteria ▽
Cassinia ▽
Cassiope ▽
Ceanothus ▽
Choisya
Colletia ▽
Coprosma ▽
Corokia ▽
Cotoneaster ▽
Cytisus ▽
Daphne
Deutzia (some spp.)
Drimys
Elaeagnus ▽
Erica
Escallonia ▽
Garrya ▽
Gordonia ▽
Grevillea ▽
Griselinia ▽
Hibiscus rosa-sinensis
Ilex
Itea ilicifolia ▽
Lavandula
Leptospermum ▽
Leucothöe ▽
Magnolia grandiflora ▽
Mahonia
Nerium ▽
Olearia ▽
Philadelphus
Photinia ▽
Pieris ▽
Pittosporum
Prunus (evergreen spp.) ▽
Pyracantha
Rhododendron ▽
Skimmia ▽
Viburnum
Weigela

Key
▽ With a heel

Aucuba japonica
'Crotonifolia'

HEEL CUTTINGS

Heel cuttings, which may be taken from greenwood, semiripe, or hardwood stems, are vigorous sideshoots of the current season's growth. Each cutting is taken with a "heel" of old wood at its base, in which the growth hormones that assist the rooting process are concentrated.

Heel cuttings are particularly suitable for a number of evergreen shrubs such as *Pieris* and some azaleas (*Rhododendron*), deciduous shrubs that have pithy or hollow stems, such as *Berberis* and *Sambucus*, and those shrubs that have greenwood stems, such as broom (*Cytisus/Genista*).

Select as cuttings healthy sideshoots that are characteristic of the parent plant. Pull the shoot away from the main stem so that a small strip of bark from the parent shoot comes away with it. Avoid tearing too much bark off the main shoot as this may expose it to infection. Trim the heel with a sharp blade and then follow the technique for greenwood (see p.110), semiripe (see p.111), or hardwood cuttings (see right), according to the particular stem's maturity.

1 Pull away healthy sideshoots of the current season's growth (here, on *Prunus laurocerasus* 'Schipkaensis') with a heel of bark.

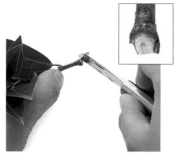

2 Using a sharp knife, trim off the "tail" at the base of the heel before inserting it in propagation mix.

Mallet cuttings
A mallet cutting, which is taken from semiripe stems, is a ripened shoot of the current season's growth attached to a piece of wood from the previous season, forming a mallet-shaped plug at its base. Mallet cuttings are often used to propagate shrubs with pithy or hollow stems, because rot fungi are less likely to affect older wood. It is particularly suitable for many *Spiraea* and deciduous *Berberis*, which produce short sideshoots on main branches.

In late summer, remove a stem of the last season's growth from the parent and cut it into sections, each containing a vigorous sideshoot of new growth. If the mallet is more than ¼in (5mm) in diameter, slit it lengthwise. Then treat the cutting as for semiripe cuttings (see p.111).

MALLET CUTTINGS

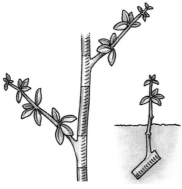

Remove a stem produced the previous year and cut it above each sideshoot and about 1in (2.5cm) below. Reduce it to 4–5in (10–13cm) and trim off lower leaves.

Leaf-bud cuttings
A leaf-bud cutting is taken from semiripe stems and comprises a short piece of stem bearing a leaf and a leaf bud. In comparison with stem cuttings, leaf-bud cuttings make much more economical use of the material from the parent plant. This method of propagation is most commonly used for camellias and mahonia.

In late summer or early fall, select a vigorous shoot of the current season's growth, bearing healthy leaves and well-developed buds. Using a sharp knife or pruners, cut the stem just above each leaf, then make a cut about ¾in (2cm) below the petiole so that the shoot is divided into several sections.

Leaf-bud cuttings do not need to be treated with hormone rooting powder before potting up, but may be wounded at the base to hasten rooting. Insert them in containers of propagation mix and treat as for semiripe cuttings (see p.111).

To save space in the cold frame or propagator, roll up any large leaves and secure them with elastic bands; a stake inserted down the middle of a rolled-up leaf will help anchor it firmly in the propagation mix. Trim compound leaves on shrubs such as mahonia by a half.

Hardwood cuttings

An easy way to raise many deciduous and some evergreen shrubs is from hardwood cuttings. Use fully ripe, vigorous growths of the current season, taken from late fall to midwinter. Take cuttings of deciduous shrubs just after leaf fall, or just before bud burst, in spring.

Preparing the ground
Cuttings are best rooted in a prepared bed or containers kept in

LEAF-BUD CUTTINGS

1 Select semiripe shoots (here, of *Camellia japonica*). Make a straight cut ¾in (2cm) below each leaf and a further cut just above.

2 Remove a ¼in (5mm) sliver of bark at the base of each cutting (see inset). Insert the cuttings in the propagation mix so that the leaf axils are just visible above the surface.

SHRUBS FROM HARDWOOD CUTTINGS

Atriplex halimus
Aucuba (some spp.)
Buddleja
Buxus (some spp.)
Cornus alba, C. sericea
Cotoneaster x *watereri*
Deutzia x *elegantissima* 'Rosealind',
    D. longifolia,
    D. x *rosea,*
    D. scabra
Forsythia
Hypericum x *moserianum*
Ligustrum ovalifolium
Philadelphus
Ribes
Rosa rugosa
Rubus
Ruta graveolens
Salix
Sambucus
Spiraea
Symphoricarpos
Tamarix
Viburnum (deciduous spp.)
Weigela

Sambucus

a cold frame, but they may also be inserted in a bed in open ground.

Prepare the bed in late summer or early fall, first working the soil until it is friable, and then digging out a flat-backed trench 5–6in (12–15cm) deep. To encourage rooting, put a 1–2in (2.5–5cm) layer of coarse sand in the base of the trench; this is essential on heavy soils. Space the trenches 15in (38cm) apart.

Preparing the cuttings

Take cuttings that are about pencil thickness, cutting at the junction of the current and the previous season's growth.

Trim deciduous cuttings into 6–9in (15–22cm) lengths, cutting at the top just above a bud or pair of buds and, at the bottom, below a bud or pair of buds; make evergreen cuttings 6in (15cm) long, cutting above and below leaves. Take heel cuttings of pithy stems (see p.112). Remove all leaves on the bottom two-thirds of evergreen cuttings and cut large leaves in half. Treat the basal cut with a rooting hormone. Removing a sliver of bark near the base may encourage difficult cuttings to root.

Insert the cuttings in containers of propagation mix, or place deciduous cuttings against the vertical side of a prepared trench,

6in (15cm) apart in open ground, or in a cold frame, 4in (10cm) apart. Leave 1–2in (2.5–5cm) of the cuttings above ground. Backfill the trench and firm in the cuttings.

Aftercare

If the ground is lifted by frost, firm it down around the cuttings. Keep the bed weed-free and well-watered during the growing season. Cuttings in a cold frame will normally root by the following spring. Harden them off (see p.638) before potting up or planting out. Those in the open ground should be left in place until the following fall and then transplanted to their permanent location.

Root cuttings

Shrubs that may be propagated from root cuttings include *Aesculus parviflora, Aralia, Clerodendrum, Myrica, Rhus,* and *Xanthorhiza simplicissima.* Lift a young plant prior to regrowth, in mid- to late winter, and tease the soil from its roots. If this is not practical, expose part of the shrub's root system. Cut off young roots at least ¼in (5mm) in diameter close to the main stem, and keep in a plastic bag until they can be prepared.

Preparing the cuttings

First remove and discard fibrous, lateral roots. Then make a straight cut on an undamaged root at the end where it was severed from the plant. At the opposite end of the root, make a slanting cut. Cuttings should be 2–6in (5–15cm) long—thinner cuttings should be longer—and several cuttings may be prepared from the same root. The colder the rooting environment and the thinner the root, the longer the cutting needs to be; cuttings to be rooted outdoors need to be at least 4in (10cm) long. Dust each cutting with fungicide but do not treat with a rooting powder, because this will tend to discourage the production of shoots.

Inserting the cuttings

Aralia and other shrubs that will reproduce readily from root cuttings may be inserted in open ground. For shrubs that root less readily, a controlled environment is preferable. Prepare containers of propagation mix large enough for several cuttings. Firm the propagation mix lightly and insert each cutting vertically 2in (5cm) apart with the slanted end down. Thinner, longer cuttings can be laid horizontally. Firm the mix so that the flat end of each cutting is just visible. Cover with ⅛in (3mm) of

grit (or vermiculite for those laid horizontally), and water. This watering may be sufficient to last until the shoots develop; excessive moisture may cause rotting.

Aftercare

Cuttings will root in ten weeks outdoors, eight weeks in a cold frame or cool greenhouse. Under cover, cuttings produce shoots in four to six weeks if they are kept at 64–75°F (18–24°C). Cuttings from shrubs that grow rapidly should be repotted as soon as they have rooted. Other root cuttings may be left in their pots for a further 12 months; apply a liquid fertilizer once or twice a month. Then pot up or plant out.

Raising shrubs from seed

Growing shrubs from seed is simple and economical. In genera whose species hybridize readily, only use seed produced by controlled pollination. Garden-raised hybrids, however, can produce interesting new plants when open-pollinated seed is used.

REMOVING SEED FROM BERRIES

1 Squash berries (here, pyracantha) between finger and thumb, removing most of the outer flesh. Wash seeds by rubbing them in warm water.

2 Dry the seeds with a tissue and place them in a clear plastic bag with coarse sand or moist vermiculite; refrigerate until ready to sow.

HARDWOOD CUTTINGS

1 Select strong, healthy, ripened shoots from this year's growth for the cuttings (see inset, left); avoid weak, thin stems (center) and older wood (right).

Healthy   Weak   Old wood

2 Remove any deciduous leaves and trim off the soft tip. Cut the stem into 6–8in (15–20cm) lengths, dipping the bases into hormone rooting powder.

3 Insert the cuttings into prepared pots of propagation mix so that approximately 1–2in (2.5–5cm) of each is visible. Label the pots and place in a cold frame.

Collecting and cleaning seed

Gather the seed capsules or fruits when ripe. Extract the seed, then clean and dry it before sowing or storing. Soak fleshy fruits in warm water or squash them so that the seed may be picked out more easily. Collect fine seed by gathering whole capsules, preferably when they have already turned brown. Place capsules in a paper bag and keep at room temperature until they split open.

Storing seed

The length of time seed is viable depends on the species and storage conditions. Daphne, *Kalmia*, and rhododendrons, for example, should be sown when fresh. Oily seeds do not store well and should be sown soon after collection. The viability of seed may be prolonged if it is stored at 37–41°F (3–5°C).

Breaking seed dormancy

The seeds of some shrubs have a form of dormancy to prevent them from germinating in adverse conditions. This dormancy may be broken artificially by scarification or stratification (see PRINCIPLES OF PROPAGATION, "How to overcome dormancy," p.629).

To allow air and moisture to penetrate large seeds with hard coats, such as camellia and peonies (*Paeonia*), scarify them by nicking the seed coat with a knife or filing away a small section before sowing. Hard-coated seeds too small to be nicked may be rubbed with sandpaper. Germination of some seeds may be aided by soaking the seed in either cold water (for example, camellia and *Pittosporum*) or hot but not boiling water (for example, *Arbutus*, *Caragana*, *Coronilla*, and *Cytisus*) for a few hours. This softens the hard seed coat allowing water to enter and germination to begin.

Seeds that need a period of chilling are stratified—*Acer palmatum*, *Amelanchier*, *Cotoneaster*, *Euonymus*, *Hippophäe*, and *Viburnum* producing seeds that need such treatment. As soon as the seed is gathered, place a piece of screening in the base of a container that has drainage holes, and scatter the seed between two layers of a sand and peat substitute (or peat) mix. Plunge the container in an open bed or place in a cold frame.

The next spring, when some of the seed may have germinated, it may be separated out and space sown. Seed of certain hardy shrubs, such as some *Viburnum*, may need further chilling in a refrigerator.

Refrigerating hardy seed may produce more reliable results. Mix the seed with moist vermiculite, peat substitute, or peat, then seal it in a clear plastic bag and refrigerate. The chilling period varies from species to species and it is best to try to sow the seed before it starts germinating in the refrigerator, that is, in mid- to late winter. For safety, keep a few extra seeds in the refrigerator, checking them each week until germination has started, then remove and sow them.

Sowing seed in containers

Seeds of hardy shrubs are sown in a cold frame in fall, or placed in a refrigerator and sown in mid- to late winter, while seeds of temperate and tender shrubs are sown in spring, in pots. Most fine, acid-loving seed is stored in the refrigerator until mid- to late winter, when it is germinated under mist at a temperature of 59°F (15°C).

Clean all containers, implements, and surfaces. Use a standard seed-starting mix, but for lime-haters use an acidic mix. Many large seeds are sown individually into their own cell pack or seed flat. Overfill a pot or tray with seed mix and gently firm before scraping off the surplus. Firm again with a presser board so that the level is ½in (1cm) below the rim of the pot or tray. Sow the seeds 2in (5cm) apart, then firm them evenly into the seed mix. Cover with a ¼in (5mm) layer of sifted seed mix and a ¼in (5mm) layer of clean grit. Label and date each container and water the seeds.

Many medium-sized seeds may also be sown in this way, but the gap between the rim and seed-starting mix should be ¼–⅜in (5–8mm). Cover seeds with sifted seed mix and then ¼in (5mm) of clean grit. Place wire netting over the container to protect the seedlings from small animals. When sowing fine seed, firm the seed mix to within ¼in (5mm) of the container rim. Water and allow the seed mix to drain before sowing, carefully shaking the seed out over the surface. Do not cover the seed or water it from above.

Aftercare for seedlings in containers

After sowing, place the containers in a propagator, greenhouse, or cold frame. Temperate species need a temperature of 54–59°F (12–15°C); warm-temperate and tropical species prefer 70°F (21°C). For seed sown in spring under cover, a constant temperature of 54–59°F (12–15°C) should be maintained. Inspect containers of seed regularly and water as necessary. Never

water fine seed from above; place the container in a shallow tub of water for a short time so that water is taken up by capillary action. When the seeds have germinated, spray the container occasionally with fungicide.

Pricking out

Once large enough to handle, prick out the seedlings. Knock the sides of the container gently against, for example, the greenhouse bench to loosen the soil mix or remove the seedlings and soil mix together and separate the seedlings, disturbing their roots as little as possible.

Transfer the seedlings into clean pots or seed flats of propagation mix, leveled but not firmed. Make a hole in the mix using a widger and insert the seedling. Level the propagation mix by tapping the top of the container and firm in, then label and water. Until the seedlings are established, place the pots out of direct sunlight in a temperature similar to that needed for germination.

Sowing seed outdoors

Open-ground seedbeds are useful for sowing large batches of seed that do not require daily attention. Such beds are generally 36–39in

(90–100cm) wide and raised 6–8in (15–20cm) above the surrounding ground, to improve drainage. Prepare the bed between six months and a year before sowing.

In fall, rake the soil to a fine tilth. Fine seed is broadcast sown over the area, while medium or large seed is sown up to 4–6in (10–15cm) apart, in rows 18in (45cm) apart. Large seeds may be sown at greater distances apart, if required.

Cover large and medium seeds to a depth of ¼–½in (0.5–1cm) but leave fine seed uncovered. Then place a ¼–½in (0.5–1cm) layer of grit over the seedbed. Firm the grit with a presser board, and label the rows.

Aftercare for seedlings outdoors

Protect seedlings from wind damage by covering them with 50 percent permeable netting, and from frost by using firmly secured row cover. If the seeds are well spaced, they should not be troubled by disease, but aphid (p.654), spider mites (p.670), and mice (see "Rodents," p.668) may be a problem.

If the spacing is adequate, the seedlings may be left in the seedbed until the following fall; they should then be either potted up or transplanted into a separate bed.

SOWING SEED IN CONTAINERS

1 Sow seeds evenly onto a prepared tray of sieved propagation mix by tapping them from a folded piece of paper.

2 Cover the seeds with a fine layer of mix, then add a ¼in (5mm) layer of grit. Label and place in a cold frame until the seeds have germinated.

3 When the seedlings are large enough to handle, prick them out, lifting them carefully with a widger and holding them gently by their leaves.

4 Transfer the seedlings into individual pots or insert 3 into a 5in (13cm) pot. After the second pair of leaves has formed, pot them up individually.

Propagation by layering

Layering is a method of propagating shrubs where a stem is encouraged to develop roots before being removed from the parent plant. Dropping and stooling, techniques that are often used commercially, are variations of layering.

Simple layering

Many deciduous and evergreen shrubs can be propagated by this method. In fall or spring, about 12 months before layering is to take place, prune a low branch on the parent plant to encourage vigorous shoots, which have a greater capacity to root. Between the following late fall and early spring, prepare the soil around the stem to be layered so that it is friable. Add grit and humus if the ground is heavy.

Retain any leaves at the tip of the selected shoot but strip off others and any sideshoots. Bring the stem down to ground level and mark the ground about 9–12in (22–30cm) behind its tip. Dig a shallow hole or trench at this point for the stem. Wound the stem at the point where it will be pegged into the hole, that is about 12in (30cm) behind its tip, either with an angled cut or by removing a ring of bark. Dust the cut with a rooting hormone, then pin the stem in the hole with bent wire, turning up the tip and securing it to a stake. Fill in the trench and firm the soil, leaving the tip exposed.

Throughout the growing season keep the area around the layer moist. The layer should have rooted by fall. In the following spring, check that there is a good root system before severing the layer from the parent plant and potting it up or planting it out in the open garden. If it has not rooted or there are only a few roots, keep it attached and in place for another growing season.

Air layering

This technique is particularly suitable for shrubs with branches that are difficult to lower to ground level. It is also good for plants growing in high humidity and rainfall and in warm-temperate areas.

In spring, choose a strong, healthy, one-year-old stem that has ripened. Trim the sideshoots or leaves to leave a clear length of stem behind the tip. Wound the stem with an angled cut and dust the cut surface with a rooting hormone. Cut off the sealed end of a black

or opaque plastic bag, about 9 x 7in (22 x 18cm). Slip it over the stem and secure the end farthest from the growing tip using tape, raffia, or string.

Moisten a well-aerated rooting medium of sphagnum moss or equal parts of perlite and peat substitute or peat so that it is wet but not sodden. Pack the moist medium into the bag around the stem's cut surface and seal the top end. Keep the bag in position for a complete season.

The following spring, check that the layer has rooted. If so, sever it immediately below the point of layering. Remove the bag and tease out the roots. Prune back any new growth on the layered stem to a leaf or bud close to the old wood. Pot up using a standard or acidic potting mix, as appropriate. Label and place the layer in a cool greenhouse or cold frame until well established. If only a few (or no) roots have developed when the bag is removed, reseal it and leave it in place for several months more. Then follow the process described above.

Tip layering

A few shrubs, mainly species and hybrids of the genus *Rubus*, root readily from the tips of stems and may be propagated in this way. In spring, select a vigorous, one-year-

old shoot and pinch out the growing point to promote sideshoots. In late spring, cultivate the soil around the shoot. Work in organic matter and grit if the soil is heavy.

In midsummer, when the tip growth has firmed slightly, bring the stem down to ground level and mark the position of the tip. At that point, dig a trench about 3–4in (7–10cm) deep, with one side vertical and the other sloping toward the parent plant. Using inverted, U-shaped wire staples, pin the growing tip at the bottom of the trench close to the vertical side. Fill in the trench, firm lightly, and water.

By late fall, well-rooted plants should have developed. Sever these at the point where the arched stem enters the trench. Lift the rooted layers and pot them or replant outdoors. (See also *Tip Layering*, p.471.)

Dropping

With this technique a plant is almost buried. It is used to raise dwarf shrubs, such as low-growing rhododendrons and heathers (*Erica, Daboecia, Calluna*), from parent plants that have become straggly.

In the dormant season, thin out branches of plants that have a mass of congested stems, to allow the remaining stems sufficient contact

---

SHRUBS SUITABLE FOR SIMPLE LAYERING

Andromeda
Aucuba
Carpenteria
Cassiope
Chaenomeles
Chionanthus
Corylopsis
Daphne blagayana
Disanthus
Elaeagnus commutata
Epigaea
Erica
Fothergilla
Gaultheria
Illicium
Kalmia
Laurus
Magnolia
Osmanthus
Rhododendron
Skimmia
Stachyurus
Syringa
Vaccinium corymbosum

Chaenomeles x superba 'Pink Lady'

▌PROPAGATING A SHRUB BY SIMPLE LAYERING

1 Select a young, pliable, low-growing stem. Bring it down to the soil and mark its position with a stake about 9–12in (22–30cm) behind the tip.

2 At the marked point, dig a hole in the prepared soil about 3in (8cm) deep, with a shallow slope on the side where the stem joins the parent plant.

3 Trim off sideshoots and leaves on the selected stem. On the underside of the stem, at a point where it touches the ground, cut a tongue or ring of bark.

4 Apply a rooting hormone to the wound on the stem. Pin down the stem with bent wire so that the stem's cut surface is held in contact with the soil.

5 Gently bend up the stem's tip vertically and secure it to the stake with a tie. Fill in the hole with more soil. Lightly firm with your fingers and water in.

6 Once rooted (see inset), lift the layered stem and cut it off the parent plant, severing it close to the new, young roots. Pot up the layer or plant it out.

AIR LAYERING A SHRUB

1 Select a healthy, horizontal stem from the previous year's growth. Trim off any leaves and sideshoots to provide a 9–12in (22–30cm) section of clear stem.

2 Slide a plastic sleeve over and along the stem; seal and secure the lower end of the sleeve to the stem with adhesive tape.

3 Fold back the plastic. Make a 1½in (4cm) diagonal cut ¼in (5mm) into the stem in the direction of growth, away from the shrub. Apply a rooting hormone.

4 Soak about 2 handfuls of sphagnum moss in water, then gently squeeze it out. With the back of the knife, pack the cut with moss, wedging it open.

5 Pull back the plastic sleeve over the cut. Carefully pack the sleeve with more moistened moss so that the moss is all around the stem.

6 Continue to pack the sleeve until the moss is about 2in (5cm) from the open end. Close the end and secure it firmly in place with adhesive tape.

7 The sealed sleeve encourages rooting by retaining moisture. Leave it in place for at least a growing season to allow new roots to develop.

8 Once the layer has rooted, remove the sleeve and cut off the layer below the roots. Pot up or plant out the new shrub (here, a rhododendron) in its new site.

STOOLING

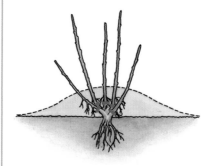

Cover shoots with free-draining soil, adding more as they grow. The shoots will root down and can be separated in fall and repotted.

with the soil to develop roots once buried. Before growth starts, but after the risk of penetrating frost has passed, dig a pit large enough to bury the plant with only the branch tips visible. If the soil is heavy, add grit and organic material.

Lift the parent plant with the root ball as complete as possible and drop it into the prepared hole. Work the soil around each stem, leaving 1–2in (2.5–5cm) of each tip exposed. Firm the soil and label the plant. In summer, keep the soil moist and, in fall, carefully move the soil around the plant to check for rooting. Sever any rooted shoots from the parent plant, and pot up or plant out, clearly labeled. If rooting has not occurred, replace the soil and leave for a further 12 months.

Stooling

Although primarily used to raise fruit tree rootstocks, stooling may also be used to propagate deciduous ornamental shrubs, such as dogwoods (*Cornus*) and lilacs (*Syringa*), from ungrafted plants.

Plant a rooted layer or other young plant in spring, label, and grow on for a season. The next spring, cut back the stem to within 3in (8cm) of the ground and apply a balanced fertilizer at 4oz/sq yd (120g/sq m). When the resulting shoots from this stem (or stool) are 6in (15cm) long, work friable soil enriched with organic matter between the shoots and bury them. Add grit if the soil is heavy. As the shoots grow, continue to mound up soil until about 9in (22cm) of each shoot is buried. Keep the soil moist in dry weather.

In fall, gently fork away the soil to ground level right after leaf fall, leaving the rooted shoots exposed. Cut them off and pot them up or plant them out. Provided that the stools are kept fertilized, the process may be repeated annually and the same stool used for propagation in subsequent years.

Magnolia 'Ricki'

French layering

This method is a form of stooling and is used to increase the stock of deciduous shrubs, such as dogwoods (*Cornus alba, C. sericea*) and *Cotinus coggygria.*

In spring, plant a rooted layer or young plant, label it, and grow it on for a season. Then, in the dormant season, cut back the stool to within 3in (8cm) of the ground. In the following spring, apply a balanced fertilizer according to manufacturer's instructions.

The following fall, cut out all but about the ten best stems; shorten the tips of these, so that they are all about the same length. With U-shaped wire staples, pin each stem to the ground, spreading them evenly around the parent stool. Each bud along the length of the stem should break evenly in spring.

When the new shoots on the pinned-down stems are about 2–3in (5–8cm) long, take out the staples and cultivate the ground around the parent stool, incorporating a balanced fertilizer at at the manufacturer's recommended rate. Space the stems evenly again, dropping each into a 2in (5cm) deep trench. Pin down each stem in the bottom of the trench and cover with soil, leaving the shoot tips exposed. Hill up all but 2–3in (5–8cm) of the new shoots as they develop, until the mound is 6in (15cm) high. Water the area well in dry weather.

After leaf fall, carefully fork away the soil from around the new shoots to expose the stems that were laid horizontally. Cut these flush with the central stool. Then cut the stems to separate the rooted sections. Pot these up or plant them out in an open bed, and label them. The same stool may be used again.

Division

Division is an easy way of increasing shrubs that produce suckers. *Ruscus*, *Kerria*, *Gaultheria*, and *Sarcococca* are all suitable for this. Shrubs must be growing on their own roots not grafted onto another rootstock.

Before growth starts in spring, lift the plant. Break the clump into sections, retaining any with vigorous shoots and well-developed roots. Prune any damaged roots, and cut back the top growth by one-third to a half to reduce water loss. Replant the divisions in the open and water in dry weather. Alternatively, simply lift a suckering root, severing it from the parent plant, and then replant it in the open.

With a few shrubs, including *Rhus*, suckering may be encouraged by digging deeply around the parent plant during summer or fall. This damages the roots and stimulates adventitious buds to develop suckers in spring. These rooted suckers may then be lifted and potted up or planted out.

Grafting

This technique is used to unite two plants so that they grow together as one. One part, known as the scion, is taken from the plant to be propagated and provides the top growth of the new plant, while the other part, known as the rootstock or stock, provides the root system. The rootstock and scion must be compatible, and they are normally of the same or closely related species.

Grafting is an important way of propagating shrubs that are difficult to root or that are unlikely to come true from seed. By using selected rootstocks, it is possible to improve a plant's vigor, disease-resistance, or tolerance to specific growing conditions, or sometimes to control its basic growth pattern.

Among the many variations of this particular technique, three that are widely used are saddle, spliced side-veneer, and apical-wedge grafting. In all cases, the stocks and scions should be joined immediately after they have been cut and the cut surfaces of each should be kept clean. All types of graft respond well to hot-pipe callusing, which speeds the formation of the callus (see Hot-pipe Callusing of Grafts, p.637).

Saddle grafting

This grafting technique is predominantly used to propagate evergreen rhododendron species and hybrids, with *Rhododendron ponticum* or *R*. 'Cunningham's White' generally serving as the rootstock. About one month before grafting is to commence, in late winter or early spring, bring the rootstock into a greenhouse maintained at a temperature of 50–54°F (10–12°C).

In late winter or very early spring, select the scion material so that it is ready for grafting. The scions selected should be about 2–5in (5–13cm) long, and taken from vigorous, nonflowering, one-year-old shoots on the plant to be propagated. If only shoots with flower buds are available, pinch these off. The scions should be labeled and stored in a plastic bag in a refrigerator.

Select a straight-stemmed rootstock of about pencil thickness and cut it back to within 2in (5cm) of the base, making a straight cut across the stem with pruners. Then, using a knife, make two slanting cuts to make an upside-down V wound on the top of the stock. Prepare the scion by making two corresponding angled cuts so that its base—the saddle—will fit snugly onto the apex of the rootstock.

Ensure that the two sections of the graft fit well together, and then bind the stock and scion together with a length of clear grafting tape. Cut back any very large leaves by half to reduce moisture loss. Label clearly, and then place the grafted plant in a propagator and shade it from direct sunlight. Check the plant daily for watering and hygiene, and spray it once a week with a fungicide solution. Union normally takes place within four to five weeks.

Once the scion is growing freely, remove the tape and gradually harden off the grafted plant—opening the propagator for longer periods each day. If the grafted plant is kept in the original pot for a season, give it some liquid fertilizer once a month.

Spliced side-veneer grafting

This grafting technique is used to propagate a variety of both evergreen and deciduous shrubs. Most spliced side-veneer grafting is carried out in midwinter, but deciduous shrubs, such as *Viburnum x burkwoodii*, may also be grafted during the summer.

For the appropriate rootstocks, choose one- to three-year-old seedlings that are compatible with the plant to be propagated. The stems should be of pencil thickness. About three weeks before grafting, bring the rootstock into the greenhouse. Water it sparingly so that the rootstock does not break dormancy too quickly, because vigorous sap movement may prevent successful grafting. If grafting in summer, use two-year-old seedlings for the rootstocks and keep them fairly dry for a month in advance.

For both summer and winter grafting, prepare and unite the stocks and scions in the same way.

Just before grafting takes place, collect vigorous, one-year-old shoots that have some mature wood to be used as scions. They should be of a similar thickness to the rootstocks onto which they will be grafted. If there is any delay, label the scions and place them in a plastic bag in a refrigerator.

When grafting, first trim the scion to a length of 5–8in (15–20cm), or 4–5in (10–12cm) for magnolias. Make a sloping cut at the base of the scion, 1–1½in (2.5–4cm) long, then turn it over and make a small wedge-shaped cut on the other side.

PROPAGATING SUCKERING SHRUBS BY DIVISION

1 Lift a root with suckers on it, without disturbing the parent plant. Check that there are fibrous roots at the base of the suckers.

2 Remove the long, suckering root by cutting it off close to the parent plant. Firm back the soil around the parent plant.

3 Cut the main root back to the fibrous roots, then divide the suckers so that each has its own roots. Cut back the top growth by about half.

4 Replant the suckers in open ground in prepared planting holes. Firm the soil around the suckers and water in. (The plant used here is *Gaultheria shallon*.)

SUCKERING SHRUBS TO DIVIDE

Amelanchier canadensis
Andromeda
Aronia
Aster albescens
Berberis buxifolia
Buxus sempervirens
Cassiope hypnoides
Ceratostigma plumbaginoides
Clerodendrum bungei
Cornus alba, C. canadensis,
  C. sericea
Danäe racemosa
Diervilla lonicera
Erica
Euonymus fortunei
Gaultheria
Itea virginica
Kerria
Mahonia repens
Menziesia ciliicalyx
Paxistima
Polygala
Rhus
Ruscus aculeatus
Sarcococca
Spiraea japonica (cvs)

Kerria japonica 'Golden Guinea'

SHRUBS TO GRAFT

Saddle

Rhododendron
  (many hybrids and species)

Spliced side-veneer

Acer palmatum (cvs)
Aralia elata 'Aureovariegata'
Arbutus unedo (cvs)
Camellia reticulata,
  C. sasanqua
Caragana arborescens
Cotoneaster
  'Hybridus Pendulus'
Daphne bholua
  D. petraea
Hamamelis
Magnolia
Pittosporum eugenioides
  'Variegatum'
Prunus glandulosa
Rhaphiolepis

Apical-wedge

Caragana arborescens
  'Walker'
Daphne arbuscula
Hibiscus, some
Syringa

Acer palmatum

SADDLE GRAFTING

1 Select vigorous, nonflowering shoots of the previous year's growth to be propagated (here a rhododendron) as scions.

2 Prepare a selected rootstock of about the same diameter as the scion by cutting it back to within about 2in (5cm) of the base.

3 Using a sharp knife, cut the stock with two upward-angled cuts so that its apex is shaped like a slightly rounded, upside-down "V".

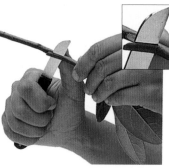

4 Make compatible, angled cuts on the scion (see inset), trimming its length to about 2–5in (5–13cm).

5 Place the cut scion (see inset) on top of the stock so that they fit together. If the scion is too narrow, place it so one side of the cambium layer meets that of the stock.

6 Bind the scion in place with plastic grafting tape or raffia. Cut back very large leaves by half. Leave the grafted plant in a propagator until union occurs.

Reduce the rootstock stem to about 12in (30cm). Make two cuts in the stock, starting 3in (8cm) above soil level, to take out a sliver of wood, leaving a cut that roughly matches that on the scion.

Place the rootstock and scion together so that the cambium layers match as closely as possible, and if necessary on one side only for stocks and scions of differing widths; tie them securely in position with grafting tape. Label the grafted plant and place it in a propagator at an even temperature of 50–59°F (10–15°C). Water the plant regularly and, once a week, spray with a fungicide.

Union should occur in four to five weeks. Harden off the grafted plant over the next four weeks, then remove it from the propagator and grow it on in a cool greenhouse.

As the scion starts to grow, gradually cut back the stem of the stock; by the end of the first growing season, all the stock above the graft union should have been cut back. During the first season, remove the initial tie and, if growth is rapid, replace it with a single tie.

On plants that have been grafted in summer, cut back the stock to just above the union before growth starts in spring. Replace the old tie with a small one around the union, because there is a tendency for the scion to be pushed off the stock. After repotting, support the leader with a stake.

Apical-wedge grafting

Apical-wedge grafting, or cleft grafting, is a comparatively straightforward technique and is suitable for the propagation of a number of shrubs, including *Caragana*, *Hibiscus*, and lilac (*Syringa*).

During midwinter, collect vigorous, one-year-old stems for use as scions. Place these in a clearly labeled plastic bag and store them in a refrigerator in order to retard their development.

Also in midwinter, select one-year-old seedlings of compatible shrubs as rootstocks. Stock and scion should both be about the thickness of a pencil. Immediately prior to grafting, lift the rootstock and wash it. Cut its stem horizontally, about 1in (2.5cm)

above the roots. With a sharp knife, make a 1in (2.5cm), vertical cut down the center of the rootstock stem.

Remove the scions from the refrigerator and select one with healthy buds of similar diameter to the rootstock. Trim it down by making a horizontal cut just above a healthy bud or buds and a similar cut 6in (15cm) below. To form the wedge, make a 1–1½in (2.5–4cm) long, sloping cut down toward the middle of the scion base, and a similar cut on the other side.

Push the scion into the prepared cut on the stock. If the scion is narrower than the stock, align one edge of the scion so it is flush with one edge of the stock. Bind them with grafting tape or moist raffia. If raffia is used, coat the union edges with grafting wax to stop moisture loss and to seal the top of the scion.

Either pot up the grafted plants or insert them in potting mix in a seed flat. Label and then, to provide basal heat, place them in a propagator at 50–59°F (10–15°C).

The union of the stock and scion should take place within about five

to six weeks. Remove the tape or raffia when there is a firm union. Pot up the plants that are in seed flats and harden them off gradually. Grow the plants on for another year in a cold frame before planting them outside into their final locations.

APICAL-WEDGE GRAFTING

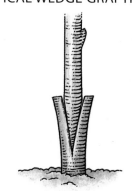

Make a simple, vertical cut down into the stock. Cut the base of the scion with 2 downward cuts into a "V" and push the base into the stock. Bind them together, pot up, and place in a propagator.

Fuchsias

Fuchsias are extremely adaptable plants, cultivated for their lovely pendent flowers, which range from modest, slender tubes to fully double, bicolored blooms with distinctive, swept-back sepals. All the species and cultivars may be used in summer bedding designs or grown in containers (see CONTAINER GARDENING, "Shrubs," p.315), and many are hardy enough to be used in permanent plantings. Those of upright habit may be trained as standards or as other formal shapes, while lax or trailing cultivars look very attractive when planted in hanging baskets and window boxes.

Routine care

Water enough to keep the soil moist but not waterlogged—at least once a day for fuchsias in hanging baskets, and every few days for those in plastic pots. Never leave containers standing in water. Most fuchsias dislike intense sun or hot greenhouse conditions; in cold areas, many may need frost protection.

Fuchsias in hanging baskets benefit from a balanced liquid fertilizer in late summer. Hardy garden fuchsias need a dressing of general fertilizer after pruning in spring and again during summer. Mature plants benefit from an occasional balanced feed in early spring and a high-potassium liquid fertilizer when flowering begins.

Black vine weevil (p.655), aphids (p.654), whiteflies (p.673), spider mites (p.670), and gray mold/ *Botrytis* (p.661) can be troublesome. At the first signs of rusts (p.668) remove infected leaves and spray with a systemic fungicide.

Propagation

Fuchsias grow easily from cuttings, and the plants are almost always superior to those raised from seed. Take cuttings at any time of year when plants have nonflowering shoots. If taken in early spring, they will have beautiful blooms by late summer; if taken in late summer, overwinter in a greenhouse for late spring flowers. Tips removed when pinching out will root, and hardwood cuttings are also successful.

Softwood cuttings

Cut the stem below a node, with the tip and three sets of leaves. Remove the lowest two sets and proceed as for other shrubs (see p.110). For several cuttings, cut a young shoot into sections, each with a group of leaves and about ½in (1cm) of stem above and below the leaves. Split these to form single-leaf cuttings if the bud in the leaf axil is intact. Bottom heat will accelerate rooting.

Keep a moist atmosphere with good air circulation to avoid damping off.

Once rooted, transplant them into 3in (7cm) pots of potting mix, and feed weekly with a high-nitrogen liquid fertilizer. Early on, avoid fertilizers high in phosphate and potassium. Pot on into 5in (13cm) pots when roots reach the outside of the soil ball. Use a general-purpose potting mix with good drainage.

Hardwood cuttings

Before severe frosts occur, cut the stem below a node, 9in (22cm) long; remove all the leaves and soft tip. Wound the base of the cutting and dip into hormone rooting powder or liquid. Insert three or four cuttings in a 3½in (9cm) pot of propagation mix, and set in a cold frame. Keep soil just moist during winter. Once roots appear, pot on or use young shoots as softwood cuttings.

Training

Fuchsias are often trained into bushes or standards. Fans and espaliers may be created in the same way as fruit trees (see pp.441–442, and "Peaches," p.453).

Bush fuchsias

To form a bush, wait until young plants have three sets of leaves, then

CUTTINGS

Stem section

Tip cutting

Stem trimmed just above and below one set of leaves

Single-leaf cutting

Stem split vertically to retain only one leaf

Cuttings may be taken at any time of the year from growing tips, when stopping the plant.

pinch out (stop) the growing tip to stimulate two to four sideshoots to grow. When these have developed two sets of leaves, stop the shoots until the plant is as bushy as needed.

Pinching out increases the potential number of blooms but delays flowering. To time flowering for exhibition purposes, stop for the last time 60 days before the show for single cultivars (four petals), 70 days for semidoubles (five to seven petals), and 80 days for doubles (eight or more petals).

Standard fuchsias

To train a standard, leave the tip of the young plant to grow and wait until sideshoots appear. Then pinch out all the sideshoots, but do not remove the leaves on the main stem. Tie the stem at intervals to a stake to provide support for the plant. Continue until the desired length of stem has been reached.

The recognized stem lengths for a standard are: "mini standard" 6–10in (15–25cm); "quarter standard" 10–18in (25–45cm); "half standard" 18–30in (45–75cm); and "full standard" reaching 30–42in (75–107cm). Allow a further three sets of leaves to grow, then pinch out the tip. After this, follow the same stopping procedures as for a bush.

It will take 18 months to achieve a full standard and about six months for a quarter or mini standard.

Overwintering

Some fuchsias are hardier than thought and often bedded-out plants, such as *Fuchsia* 'Mrs. Popple', can be left *in situ*. Take cuttings in early fall as insurance against frost damage. Always bring standards under cover in winter.

Hardy fuchsias

In areas that are cold in fall, mulch fuchsias with straw, bracken, or bark over the crowns. Even if the plants are cut back by frost, they will shoot from the crown like an herbaceous plant. Deep planting is also useful. When regrowth starts in spring, cut back to ground level.

Frost-tender fuchsias

In late fall, move cold-sensitive fuchsias into frost-free conditions. Given a minimum temperature of 46°F (8°C), they may flower through winter. Lift and pot up plants that have been bedded out. Remove green tips and leaves. Keep plants cool and not quite dry through winter. In spring, repot them into slightly smaller pots, and prune back hard.

HOW TO TRAIN A STANDARD FUCHSIA

1 When the cutting is about 6in (15cm) high, pinch out any sideshoots as they appear in the leaf axils.

2 When it is at the desired height, and has grown 3 more sets of leaves, pinch out the growing tip.

3 Pinch out the tips of the sideshoots that form at the top of the stem so that they will branch further.

4 Once the head has filled out, the leaves on the stem will usually drop off naturally, or they may be carefully removed.

Bamboos

These woody, evergreen members of the grass family are among the most versatile of plant groups. Bamboos are known to have been used for several millennia—particularly in Asian countries —as a source of material for buildings, furniture, and many other items, and several species are also cultivated for their edible young shoots. They provide gardeners with a range of useful perennial plants valued for their elegant foliage and graceful habit as well as their ability to thrive in a variety of conditions.

Choosing bamboos

Many bamboos are from tropical areas so be sure to check that any bamboo you buy will overwinter successfully in your hardiness zone. Their rhizomatous roots—which can be long and spreading or compact and clump-forming— send up woody, segmented shoots known as canes or culms that are sometimes striped along their length in a range of vibrant colors from black or red to verdant green and bright yellow. Culms are usually hollow and grow to their full height in one season, producing branches and foliage from the nodes. A few species produce grasslike flowers regularly, but most may not flower for years.

Heights vary from 20in (50cm) to 30ft (10m) and the colorful stems of species and cultivars including *Chusquea culeou, Phyllostachys rubromartinata, P. bambusoides* 'Holochrysa', *P. nigra; P. violascens and P. aureosulcata* are very attractive. This great diversity makes bamboos invaluable as specimens, in mixed plantings, as hedges or screens, or in containers.

General cultivation

Bamboos grow well in sun or shade in acidic or alkaline conditions, but perform best in moist, humus-rich, well-drained soil. Dig the planting site thoroughly, adding bone meal and well rotted compost or manure. Most bamboos are pot-grown, so loosen fibrous roots at the edges of the root ball before planting to encourage them to grow outward.

Do not allow bamboos to dry out, especially when young, and do not let their roots freeze. If plants suffer cold damage, they may recover well in spring given sufficient water. Once plants are established an annual 2in (5cm) mulch of composted bark or well-rotted leaf mold in spring and an occasional dressing of a balanced fertilizer is sufficient to maintain strong growth.

Restricting bamboo growth

A number of bamboo species can become invasive, so a physical barrier is sometimes used to keep them within their allotted space. These are usually made of plastic or rubber and should be inserted into the soil to a depth of about 2ft (60cm) around the clump and sealed at the joint(s). Rhizomes may still cross over the top of the barrier and should be removed as soon as seen. It is sometimes suggested that low-growing bamboos may be restricted by cutting them to the ground in early spring. However, while the removal of the old foliage

Clusters of canes
Fargesia robusta and other clump-forming bamboos are fine specimen plants. They can create excellent screens, hedges, or windbreaks, and may be useful in mixed plantings.

will produce more attractive young growth, the strength of the plant is not usually greatly reduced.

Pests and diseases
Bamboos are particularly vulnerable to bamboo spider mite —a sap-sucking insect that lives on the underside of leaves covered by a dense web. In some cases, foliage develops dots and dashes (like Morse code) of longitudinal, yellow variegations on the leaves. To eradicate it, remove and destroy infected leaves; if necessary, spray with an acaricide that will kill these pests. Whiteflies (p.673) and spider mites (p.670) will attack bamboo under cover but are not a problem outdoors. Aphids (p.654) are a nuisance on some species, and rabbits (p.669) and squirrels (p.671) may eat the new growth.

Pruning and crownlifting

As they mature bamboos may require some pruning. Wear thick gloves when pruning bamboo.

Thinning established clumps
Cut out the oldest culms at the base and clear away debris to let in light and air.

RESTRICTING THE SPREAD OF BAMBOO

1 Dig a narrow trench, deeper than the plant's root, all around the clump. Chop through and remove peripheral roots.

2 Insert a barrier made of non-perishable material such as slate or rigid plastic. Fill in the trench. Firm the ground well.

Prune in spring to remove dead, damaged, congested, or weak and spindly culms. Cut them out close to the base—do not shorten the culms; this may ruin their appearance.

In late summer thin out dense clumps of culms to relieve congestion at the center of the plant. Remove any weak, dead, and damaged culms, and cut out the oldest ones at the base. Clear debris to let in light and air, and allow the young culms to grow unchecked.

The term "crownlifting" is sometimes used to describe a method of pruning bamboos to display the attractive young culms of some species and cultivars, such as those of *Phyllostachys* and *Chusquea culeou*, more effectively. Crownlifting should be carried out either in spring or late summer. Remove the thin, weaker stems completely and also all the lowest branches to expose the colorful young culms.

Propagation

Bamboos in cultivation seldom produce seed so propagation is by dividing established clumps of rhizomes. The best times to do this are in early spring before the new culms are produced, so that the young growth is not damaged, or in the fall when it is cool and moist.

Single rhizomes are difficult to establish—small divisions often grow weakly—so when dividing bamboos, ensure that you replant several rhizomes together. For species with clump-forming rhizomes, use a spade or ax to cut through the colony, ensuring that there are several rhizomes in the section you remove. To propagate bamboos with long, spreading rhizomes, loosen the soil at the edge of the clump to expose the rhizomes. Use pruners to sever sections of several rhizomes from the parent plant, and keep these sections together. Although open ground divisions may succeed, it is better to pot them and keep them in a cold frame or cool glasshouse in a humid atmosphere where they will establish more quickly.

Bamboos in containers

Some clump-forming bamboos with compact rhizomes, such as x *Hibanobambusa tranquillans* 'Shiroshima', *Shibataea kumasaca*, and many fargesias, may be grown successfully as container plants. They are particularly attractive on patios and similar sites.

Glazed ceramic pots and strong flexible plastic containers with good basal drainage holes are the most suitable. Use a soil based, free-draining mix containing a slow-release balanced fertilizer and topdress the surface with grit or small pebbles to help slow down water loss. Bamboos require plenty of moisture to thrive in pots and should never be allowed to dry out. Regularly thinning out old culms before growth starts in spring will also cut down water loss. Keep the soil mix moist throughout the growing season; less water is needed in winter. Apply a liquid fertilizer once or twice a year if the bamboo is kept in the same pot for several years. Repot into a larger container after a few years, perhaps dividing the clump to produce two or three vigorous new plants.

BAMBOOS FOR ELEGANT FOLIAGE

Phyllostachys nigra

Phyllostachys flexuosa

Phyllostachys bambusoides

**Phyllostachys nigra
f. henonis**

**Pleioblastus
variegatus**

Fargesia nitida

Fargesia rufa

GUIDE TO CLUMP-FORMING BAMBOOS

Bambusa multiplex 'Alphonse Karr'
Borinda boliana
Fargesia 'Dracocephala'
Chusquea culeou
Fargesia nitida 'Nymphenburg',
  F. robusta
x *Hibanobambusa tranquillans*
  'Shiroshima'
Indocalamus tessellatus
Phyllostachys aureosulcata
  f. spectabilis,
  P. bambusoides 'Castillonis',
  P. bambusoides 'Holochrysa',
  P. variegatus 'Fortunei',
  P. vivax,
  P. vivax f. aureocaulis
Pleioblastus viridistriatus
Semiarundinaria fastuosa,
  S. fastuosa var. viridis

MAINTAINING A POT-GROWN BAMBOO

1 Container-grown bamboos lose vigor as the pots fill with roots, and must be repotted every 2 or 3 years.

2 Look for a natural line through the top growth and, using a saw, divide the plant into halves or thirds depending on size.

3 Ensure that each section has a reasonable root system, some vigorous stems, and a few new shoots visible near the surface.

4 The divided bamboo can be planted either in the old pot, or a larger one; other sections could be planted in the garden.

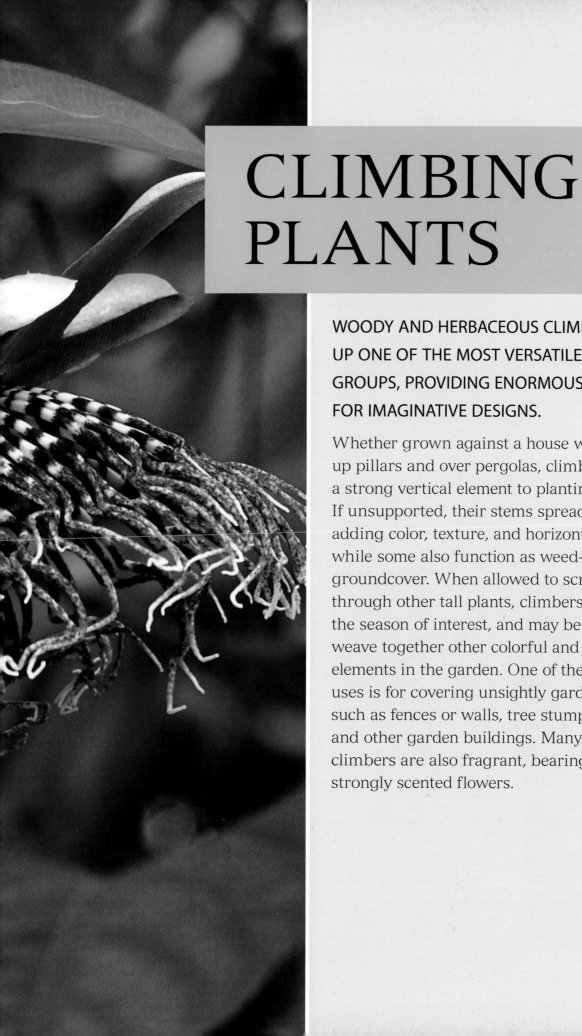

CLIMBING PLANTS

WOODY AND HERBACEOUS CLIMBERS MAKE UP ONE OF THE MOST VERSATILE PLANT GROUPS, PROVIDING ENORMOUS SCOPE FOR IMAGINATIVE DESIGNS.

Whether grown against a house wall or up pillars and over pergolas, climbers bring a strong vertical element to planting designs. If unsupported, their stems spread luxuriantly, adding color, texture, and horizontal lines, while some also function as weed-smothering groundcover. When allowed to scramble through other tall plants, climbers can extend the season of interest, and may be used to weave together other colorful and textural elements in the garden. One of their greatest uses is for covering unsightly garden features, such as fences or walls, tree stumps, sheds, and other garden buildings. Many popular climbers are also fragrant, bearing abundant strongly scented flowers.

Designing with climbers

Gardens of every size and style can benefit from climbing plants. Some, such as *Passiflora* species, are grown primarily for their beautiful flowers, while others like *Lonicera periclymenum* are equally valued for their scent. Many are grown for their handsome foliage, which may give year-round interest, or provide rich and spectacular fall color, as with *Parthenocissus* and *Vitis coignetiae*. Even when leafless, their elegant habit and architectural forms can enhance the stark winter landscape. Several climbers also bear fruits or berries that are attractive both to the gardener and to wildlife.

Siting Climbing honeysuckle prefers a sunny location.

Climbing methods and supports

In their natural habitats, climbers use various techniques to climb through host plants to gain access to the light. Plants, walls, and other features can provide support for the wide range of growth habits among climbing plants. Some climbers are self-clinging, attaching themselves to their supports either by aerial roots (adventitious rootlets), as do ivies (*Hedera*), or by adhesive tendril tips, as does Virginia creeper (*Parthenocissus quinquefolia*). These cling to any surface offering sufficient grip, including walls and tree trunks, and need no additional support except during the early stages, when they require the guidance of a stake, string, or wire until they are able to establish secure contact. Climbers with aerial roots are also particularly well-suited for use as groundcovers.

Twining species coil their stems in a spiral around their support—clockwise or counterclockwise, depending on their anatomical and morphological characteristics.

Climber support Golden-leaved hop (*Humulus lupulus* 'Aureus') is a vigorous climber that attaches itself using twining stems that are clothed with coarse, bristly hairs.

Both *Lonicera periclymenum* and *Humulus lupulus,* for instance, twine clockwise, whereas *Ceropegia sandersonii* and *Wisteria sinensis* twine counterclockwise. All twining species need permanent support, usually provided by a trellis or wire. They may also be grown up the stems and branches of a sturdy host plant (see also "Climbing through other plants," p.126).

A few climbers, such as clematis and some nasturtiums (*Tropaeolum*), attach themselves to supports by means of curling leaf stalks. Many others are tendril climbers that twine around their supports by means of contact-sensitive tendrils, which are often modified leaves or leaflets as in *Bignonia capreolata* and sweet peas (*Lathyrus odoratus*); axillary shoots as in *Passiflora*; or terminal shoots as in grapevines. In *Parthenocissus*, the tendrils develop adhesive pads at the tips once they come in contact with a support.

Scandent, scrambling, and trailing climbers, such as bougainvillea, *Quisqualis indica*, and winter jasmine (*Jasminum nudiflorum*) produce long, arching stems that attach themselves only loosely, if at all, to their supports. These plants need to be tied to a wire framework or trellis as they grow. Alternatively, they may be left to spread over walls and banks for a less formal effect. Plants in this group can also be trained across the soil surface as groundcovers, weaving in between plants and suppressing weeds.

Some species, including climbing roses and certain *Rubus* species, are equipped with hooked thorns that help them to scramble naturally through host plants. If not grown through other plants, however, these need to be tied to sturdy supports.

Site and exposure

To achieve their full potential, a number of climbers, including most clematis cultivars, prefer a sunny site with their roots in the shade, although some plants need a cooler spot. Others are less demanding and, while they prefer a sunny location, they may still tolerate shade—*Parthenocissus* and *Schizophragma* are just two examples.

Less hardy climbers will require a sheltered site, such as against a south-facing wall, in colder climates. There are numerous hardy climbers, however, that will perform perfectly well without any protection at all.

Sunny or sheltered sites

A sheltered wall can provide a suitable microclimate for growing marginally hardy or tender flowering climbers. *Lapageria rosea* and blue passionflower (*Passiflora caerulea*), among many others, should thrive with winter protection in such a position; the heat radiated by the wall helps to ripen the wood so that the plants are better able to withstand prolonged cold winter temperatures.

The wall itself also gives protection against several degrees of frost. If frost is likely to occur at flowering time, avoid planting such climbers in spots where the flower buds are exposed to early-morning sun, because the buds will often be damaged as a result of rapid thawing. Sun-loving herbaceous plants and bulbs may be planted near the base of the climbers to help keep their roots cool.

Cool or exposed sites

For shady, north-facing walls and those exposed to cold winds, vigorous, hardy climbers—Virginia creeper and some honeysuckles, in particular—are the most suitable plants. In very cold climates, using annuals will extend the range of climbers; scarlet runner beans and canary creeper (*Tropaeolum peregrinum*) are good choices.

Climbers on walls, buildings, and fences

Whether they are complementing or camouflaging their support, climbing plants make an immediate visual impact when trained against walls and buildings. Many provide strong color, while others give a more diffuse and subtle backdrop to the whole garden design. Most buildings may be enhanced by the softening effect of a climber grown against them. In the same way, garden walls and fences become decorative features when clothed with plants bearing blossoms, foliage, seed heads, and fruits.

Enhancing a building

Before planting, assess the architectural merits of a building and use the plants to emphasize its good points. A well-designed building may be complemented by climbers that have a strong visual impact with, for example, distinctively shaped or colored foliage or outstanding flowers. *Actinidia kolomikta*, with its pink- or white-tipped rounded leaves, is an excellent choice for this.

Planted obelisks Freestanding obelisks are ideal for compact climbers, such as summer-flowering clematis or annual sweet peas, and can be positioned wherever needed in the garden to create a sense of height. Use them to support two or three different climbers to provide the longest possible season of color.

A less visually pleasing building may also be made more attractive by using climbers. Regular panels of plants may be used to break up long stretches of blank wall, and may also serve to exaggerate or mitigate strong vertical or horizontal lines. Narrow panels of foliage that extend upward can make a building seem taller than it is. On the other hand, wider panels of plants allowed to grow only as high as the first floor will make a tall, narrow building appear broader. If necessary, less attractive features of the building may be disguised completely using climbers. The most suitable plants for this purpose include most species of ivy and other self-clinging root climbers, such as *Hydrangea anomala* subsp. *petiolaris* and *Schizophragma hydrangeoides*; these form rich foliage that may be pruned into the desired shape.

In a more relaxed, informal setting, vigorous climbing plants may be combined to produce a profusion of flowers and fragrance: the dark green year-round foliage and white flowers of *Clematis paniculata*, or the strongly fragrant red and yellow flowers of *Lonicera* x *americana*, combine well with many species of climbing rose, perhaps with annual sweet peas (*Lathyrus odoratus*) grown through them. This combination will be attractive all year, particularly around a window or doorway, where the flowers and scents may be best appreciated.

Screening with climbers

The more vigorous climbing plants may be used to camouflage an unattractive shed, wall, or fence remarkably quickly. Use plants such as *Clematis montana*, for its considerable mass of pink or white flowers in late spring, or sliver lace vine (*Fallopia baldschuanica*), which soon produces dense cover combined with panicles of tiny white flowers in late summer. It is known as mile-a-minute vine for a good reason—it is extremely rampant and must therefore be sited with great care, because it will swamp even reasonably vigorous neighbors. It also needs regular, severe pruning to keep it within bounds.

Where year-round cover is required, ivies may be more appropriate. Alternatively, use a combination of evergreen and deciduous plants; the bluish green, evergreen leaves of *Lonicera sempervirens*, for instance, provide the perfect foil in summer for the soft-pink blooms of the climbing rose 'New Dawn'.

Climbers on pergolas and pillars

Pergolas, pillars, and other built structures enable climbers to be viewed from all sides and, in addition, contribute strong stylistic elements to the garden design. They may be used to add height to an otherwise flat garden. Depending on materials used, they may be formal and elegant, or informal and rustic. If well designed, they can be at their most attractive when only partially covered with plants, when some of the structure remains visible. They must, however, be strong enough to bear the often considerable weight of stems and foliage and should also be durable, because the plants will need their support for many years.

Pergolas

Pergolas or arbors festooned with climbers not only provide a cool, shady sitting area in the yard but also bring a sense of seclusion and privacy to an otherwise open site. The most suitable plants to choose are those that put on their best display at the time of day or during the particular season when the structure is most often used.

If an arbor is to be used often on summer evenings, suitable plants might include common white jasmine (*Jasminum officinale*), *Lonicera periclymenum* 'Graham Thomas', or the climbing rose 'Mme. Alfred Carrière', all with beautifully fragrant blooms in pale colors that show up well in the fading light. For summer shade, use large-leaved climbers such as *Vitis coignetiae* (which also gives splendid fall color) or *V. vinifera* 'Purpurea', whose claret-colored young leaves turn dusky purple as they mature. Alternatively, use the massed floral display of *Wisteria frutescens* as a summer canopy. The flowers of this plant look beautiful when it is grown up a pergola along a walkway. Ensure that the crossbeams are high enough, however, so there is no need to stoop to avoid the flowers.

For winter interest, plant evergreen climbers, such as ivy, especially variegated forms, or, in mild areas, tender *Lardizabala biternata*. Alternatively, use deciduous plants such as *Celastrus* or wisteria, whose bare twisted stems take on beautiful sculptural qualities in winter.

Pillars

To give borders a vertical element, climbers such as clematis may be grown up pillars. Also consider using them to mark an axis or a focal point, like the corner of a bed or where levels change. Link pillars with rope swags and train climbers along them.

For an evergreen climber, or as a temporary feature, a sturdy post with mesh wrapped around it will provide adequate support. If growing a deciduous plant, which would leave the pillar visible in winter, buy a ready-made obelisk or column, which will be attractive even when it is bare of flowers.

Climbing through other plants

In the wild, many climbers grow naturally through other plants. You can copy this effect in your home landscape—although the climbers should not be too vigorous for the hosts. Always plan color combinations carefully before planting, taking flowers, foliage, and fruit into consideration; the climber may either complement or contrast with its host when the latter is putting on its best display, or extend the season of interest.

Climbers that are suitable for growing through shrubs include *Clematis viticella* hybrids and those large-flowered clematis that are cut back each year. It is also a useful method of growing most annual climbing plants and *Tropaeolum speciosum*, with its fiery red flowers and stems that are best supported by another plant.

For growing through trees, vigorous species, such as *Ampelopsis brevipedunculata* var. *maximowiczii* or *Schizophragma hydrangeoides*, produce beautiful combinations of foliage, fruit, and flower. Alternatively, try mingling the cascading blooms of *Rosa filipes* 'Kiftsgate' with the white or pink sprays of *Clematis montana*. Both produce strong, twining stems that quickly scramble into the branches of a tree.

Plant partners Summer-flowering clematis, such as 'Hagley Hybrid', can be planted to provide supplementary interest to rambling roses, which flower spectacularly but briefly.

Groundcover If grown without support, many vigorous climbers, such as annual nasturtiums (above), will form attractive, weed-suppressing groundcovers; their stems will scale any obstacles they come up against. Ivies can also be planted and grown in this way to provide a permanent evergreen groundcover.

Climbers as groundcovers

Some climbers, particularly those with aerial roots or with a scandent, trailing, or scrambling habit, may be grown without support to produce swaths of groundcovers. They are particularly useful when allowed to spread over a sloping bank or when trailing over a wall, where they will often root into the soil beneath.

Climbers that attach themselves by adhesive tendrils, like *Parthenocissus*, and those that are self-layering, are effective in suppressing weeds when grown as groundcovers. Take care when siting these plants, because if there is any other plant nearby that could serve as a support, it may be swamped. To avoid this, choose less vigorous climbing species or relocate other plants so that the climber has a free run.

Twining climbers may also be used as groundcovers if the shoots are spread evenly across the ground; wire pins may be used to keep the shoots in place. The large, deeply colored flowers of *Clematis* 'Ernest Markham' and *C.* 'Jackmanii' are eye-catching at ground level, as are the blue-green leaves and scarlet flowers of *Tropaeolum speciosum*.

Colorful climbers

Color impact varies according to light levels in different parts of the garden. In a sunny spot, bright or deep colors, which absorb light, show up more strongly than paler colors. The latter will illuminate a dark space and may be used to great effect in areas that are most often viewed in the evening.

Before planting climbers, first consider the color of the garden's permanent features. If the wall or support is already bright, use plants with subtle, complementary coloring—unless you wish to create a particularly vibrant combination.

Color combinations

Growing different climbers together or in combination with other plants adds another dimension to color schemes. Climbers can be useful for interweaving the different color components of a planting design, creating brilliant combinations with complementary colors or more subtle harmonies with closely related tones.

Flowers for color

The flowers of climbers occur in colors across the spectrum, from the deep violet of *Clematis viticella* 'Etoile Violette' to the brilliant scarlet of *Campsis radicans* to the soft, creamy-white of *Araujia sericifera*. Many of the most vividly colored climbing plants are tropical in origin, and are not always hardy in cooler temperate zones, so may they need protection.

Climbers with strongly colored flowers, such as tender bougainvillea, have a bold and exuberant appearance but these usually need

Seasonal interest Many climbers offer more than one season of interest and are especially suitable for small yards where space is limited and plants need to provide maximum interest. *Clematis tangutica* (above) flowers in late summer but also has attractive seed heads that can last well into winter.

thoughtful placement if they are not to be overwhelming. Those that have paler-colored flowers—for example, pink *Clematis montana* 'Tetrarose'—are more suitable for subtle-hued planting designs.

Foliage and fruits for color

Use the leaves of climbers as well as their flowers: the skillful use of foliage can produce beautiful effects, the leaf tone providing soothing contrasts and balancing vivid flower color. *Humulus lupulus* 'Aureus' has yellow leaves that appear almost gold if placed against a dark background. Even more striking is *Actinidia kolomikta*, which has leaves splashed with creamy-white and pink. The variegated ivies are almost as showy, especially the large-leaved forms, and being evergreen, they give a year-long display.

Other climbers bear fruits that are at least as colorful as their flowers and sometimes more so: outstanding among these are the fruits of *Lonicera sempervirens* (red), the slightly frost-tender *Billardiera longiflora* (purple-blue or white), and *Celastrus orbiculatus* (green, then black, splitting to show yellow insides with red seeds).

Interest through the seasons

For continuity of interest throughout the year, devise a planting plan in which different climbers succeed each other as the seasons progress. Choose plants that come into flower in succession, perhaps using annual climbers to fill any flowering lulls. This technique can be applied to climbers that are being grown closely together or to those in separate parts of the garden.

Spring and summer

Numerous climbing plants put on their best show during the spring and summer months. Early-flowering *Clematis macropetala* and *Lonicera periclymenum* 'Serotina', which reaches its flowering peak in midsummer, make an attractive combination when planted together. The blooms of the clematis also leave behind silvery-gray, fluffy seed heads to augment the beauty of the honeysuckle's scented tubular flowers, and often continue their eye-catching display throughout the fall months and sometimes even into early winter. See also ANNUALS AND BIENNIALS, "Climbers and trailers," p.209.

Beneficial plants Many climbing plants are as attractive to wildlife as they are to people. Scented jasmine is beautiful in the garden and acts as a magnet for pollinating insects.

Fall and winter interest

Some climbers provide glorious fall leaf color: the deeply cut, sometimes crinkled, leaves of *Parthenocissus tricuspidata* may be the most spectacular of all, turning scarlet, crimson, and deepest burgundy before they fall. Climbers that flower in winter are few and are not generally hardy; one rare exception is winter jasmine (*Jasminum nudiflorum*), hardy to 0°F (-18°C), which produces delicate yellow blooms even on a north-facing wall. The slightly tender *J. polyanthum* produces a profusion of flowers in a sheltered situation, and *Clematis cirrhosa* flowers in all areas in frost-free weather.

Evergreen climbers with unusual foliage provide interest in winter, too. Ivies are the most versatile, because most are hardy. Some are boldly variegated, too: the colorful *Hedera helix* 'Buttercup' and 'Goldheart' are good examples. Others are grown for their leaf shape—the bird's-foot ivy (*H. h.* 'Pedata'), with leaves shaped like a bird's foot, and 'Parsley Crested', with crinkly edged leaves, are two foliage plants of merit.

Scented climbers

Perfumed climbers, such as the tropical *Beaumontia grandiflora* and the sweet pea (*Lathyrus odoratus*), have special appeal. To fully appreciate their fragrance, plant sweet peas in a sunny position near doorways or windows. If planted in a border, place them close to the outer edge. They can also be grown in containers to enjoy the scent easily.

Some climbing plants release their fragrance at a particular time of day; jasmines (*Jasminum*) are often more heavily scented at night; try growing them to cover an arbor or near a terrace or patio that is used in the evening. Such night-scented climbers are ideal planted against the wall of a house, where their scent will waft in through any open windows, filling the room.

Annual climbers

Annual climbers, such as sweet peas, and those that are treated as annuals in cool-temperate climates, such as *Eccremocarpus scaber*, are particularly useful for short-term effects. Annuals provide an excellent way of introducing variety into planting plans, because they can be changed every year, if desired. They may also be used to fill gaps relatively quickly, and introduce a vertical element when trained up bamboo tepees, for example, in the border until more permanent plants become well established (see "Annuals and biennials as fillers," p.209). Most are easy to raise from seed and will flower within a month or two.

Annual color Some climbers grown as annuals, like black-eyed Susan vine (*Thunbergia alata*), are tender perennials that are best grown from seed each year.

Climbers in containers

Climbers in containers can be trained in the same way as those grown in the ground; if the support is attached to the container, the plant may be moved as desired. Some low-growing climbers, such as *Clematis macropetala*, may also be grown without support—plant these in tall containers, so that their stems trail to the ground. Ivies can also be grown this way.

If space is limited, rampant climbers, such as bougainvillea, can be grown in containers. Their growth will be checked, and regular repotting will also be needed to keep them healthy. For less hardy climbing species, simply take the containers indoors or into a heated greenhouse at the onset of fall frosts.

Temporary displays Growing climbers in containers allows them to be moved to a prime position when in bloom, then repositioned elsewhere once they are past their best.

PLANTER'S GUIDE TO CLIMBERS

NORTH-FACING WALLS

Climbers that may be grown against north-facing walls

Agapetes (some spp.)
Akebia quinata
Allamanda cathartica
Aristolochia littoralis
Berberidopsis corallina
Cissus
Clematis, some
Clerodendrum thomsoniae
Clytostoma calystegioides
Codonopsis convolvulacea
Dioscorea discolor
Epipremnum
Hardenbergia
Hedera, some
Hoya
Humulus lupulus
Hydrangea anomala
  subsp. petiolaris
Kadsura japonica
Lapageria rosea
Lathyrus latifolius
Lonicera x americana,
  L. x brownii,
  L. x heckrottii,
  L. sempervirens,
  L. x tellmanniana
Mitraria coccinea
Monstera deliciosa
Parthenocissus, some
Philodendron
Pileostegia viburnoides
Schizophragma hydrangeoides
Stigmaphyllon ciliatum
Syngonium podophyllum
Tetrastigma voinierianum
Tropaeolum speciosum
Vitis coignetiae

AIR POLLUTION

Climbers that tolerate polluted air

Campsis radicans
Clematis, some
Fallopia
Hedera, some
Hydrangea anomala
  subsp. petiolaris
Parthenocissus, some
Vitis, some

SHADE

Climbers that tolerate shade

Actinidia
Asteranthera ovata
Euonymus fortunei
Fallopia
Humulus lupulus
Parthenocissus tricuspidata
Strongylodon macrobotrys

FRAGRANT FLOWERS

Anredera cordifolia
Beaumontia grandiflora
Clematis armandii,
  C. montana
Combretum indicum
Hoya australis,
  H. carnosa

Jasminum officinale,
  J. polyanthum
Lathyrus odoratus
Lonicera spp.
  (not L. sempervirens
  or L. x tellmanniana), some
Schisandra
Solandra maxima
Stephanotis floribunda
Trachelospermum
Wisteria

CLIMBERS FOR CONTAINERS

Bougainvillea
  (prune very hard)
Cissus (some spp.)
Clematis alpina,
  C. macropetala
Dioscorea discolor
Epipremnum
Gynura aurantiaca
Hardenbergia
Hedera helix
Jasminum officinale,
  J. polyanthum
Lapageria rosea
Lophospermum erubescens
Monstera deliciosa
Philodendron (some spp.)
Senecio macroglossus
  'Variegatus'
Stephanotis floribunda
Streptosolen jamesonii
Syngonium (some spp.)
Tetrastigma voinierianum
Thunbergia alata
Wisteria (prune very hard)

EVERGREEN CLIMBERS

Allamanda
Anemopaegma
Anredera
Araujia
Argyreia
Asteranthera ovata
Beaumontia
Berberidopsis
Calceolaria pavonii
Calochone
Cissus
Clerodendrum splendens,
  C. thomsoniae
Clytostoma
Combretum grandiflorum
Decumaria sinensis
Dioscorea discolor
Distictis
Dregea sinensis
Epipremnum
Gelsemium sempervirens
Hardenbergia
Hedera
Hibbertia scandens
Holboellia
Hoya
Jacquemontia
Kennedia
Lapageria
Lardizabala
Macfadyena
Mandevilla
Merremia
Monstera

Mussaenda
Mutisia
Pandorea
Pileostegia
Podranea
Pyrostegia
Rhoicissus
Semele
Senecio confusus,
  S. macroglossus,
  S. mikanioides,
  S. tamoides
Solandra
Stauntonia
Stephanotis
Stigmaphyllon
Strongylodon
Syngonium
Tecoma
Tecomanthe
Tetrastigma
Trachelospermum

CLIMBERS TO GROW THROUGH OR OVER OTHER PLANTS

Bomarea multiflora
Bougainvillea
Celastrus
Clematis
Codonopsis convolvulacea
Humulus lupulus
Lonicera
Mutisia
Pseudogynoxys chenopodioides
Tropaeolum peregrinum,
  T. speciosum
Vitis coignetiae
Wisteria sinensis

FAST-GROWING CLIMBERS

Allamanda cathartica
Ampelopsis
Anredera cordifolia
Antigonon leptopus
Aristolochia littoralis
Clematis
Clitoria ternatea
Clytostoma callistegioides
Cobaea scandens
Combretum indicum
Epipremnum aureum
Fallopia
Humulus lupulus
Kennedia rubicunda
Parthenocissus
Passiflora
Periploca
Phaseolus coccineus
Philodendron hederaceum
Plumbago auriculata
Pyrostegia venusta
Solanum
Stigmaphyllon ciliatum
Strongylodon macrobotrys
Vitis vinifera

ANNUAL CLIMBERS

Combretum indicum
Convolvulus tricolor
Eccremocarpus scaber
Ipomoea (some spp.)

Lablab purpureus
Lathyrus odoratus
Lophospermum erubescens
Thunbergia alata
Tropaeolum peregrinum

HERBACEOUS CLIMBERS

Bomarea multiflora
Canarina canariensis
Codonopsis convolvulacea
Humulus lupulus
Lathyrus grandiflorus,
  L. latifolius
Tropaeolum speciosum,
  T. tricolor,
  T. tuberosum

CLIMBERS FOR GROUNDCOVER

Clematis
Kennedia
Mitraria
Parthenocissus
Pileostegia
Plumbago auriculata
Tecoma
Trachelospermum
Tropaeolum

Bougainvillea glabra 'Harrissii'

Soil preparation and planting

Given ideal growing conditions, climbing plants bring enduring rewards, so always ensure that they are well suited to the type of soil in which they are planted. Climbers seldom thrive in excessively damp or dry conditions. A few, such as *Agapetes* and *Mitraria*, do not tolerate alkaline conditions; others, such as clematis, thrive in alkaline soil but also grow well in all except the most acidic soil. Many climbers are vigorous and require ample nutrients, so dig and fertilize the soil well before planting (see also "Soil nutrients and fertilizers," pp.624–625).

When planting climbers, it is important to use the correct support. Choose one that will easily accommodate the eventual height, spread, and vigor of the plant.

Types of support

The three main types of support used are wooden or plastic trellis panels, wire or plastic mesh, and wires (usually plastic-covered) stretched between eye hooks or galvanized nails. Sturdy garden twine or reinforcing wire may be adequate for annuals or for herbaceous climbers if the

supports are replaced each year. Make sure that all supports are fixed securely in the correct position before planting. Do not use U-shaped metal staples to attach the stems of any plant to its support: plants rapidly outgrow these staples and the stems may become constricted and die back. Choose a support that will match the size and strength of the climber. One that is not sufficiently sturdy for a vigorous climber may quickly be engulfed and will eventually collapse. Trellises are the most reliable supports for all twining climbers, and may also be used for scramblers if they are tied in. Wires or mesh are appropriate supports for tendril climbers.

If the support is not to be a permanent structure, use climbers that are either herbaceous (*Lathyrus grandiflorus* and *L. latifolius*, for example) or cut to ground level each year (late-flowering *Clematis viticella* hybrids and cultivars), or annual climbers such as *Ipomoea hederacea*. When growing plants against a flat, freestanding trellis or over a pillar, bear in mind that climbers grow toward the light, and produce their flowers on one side of the support only, so position plants to provide their display where it will be most prominent.

Trellis and mesh

To allow air to circulate freely, fix a trellis panel or mesh so that it is held slightly away from the wall or fence and make sure that the base of the framework is approximately 12in (30cm) above soil level.

Walls are likely to need maintenance (painting, cleaning, or plastering) at some time: wherever possible, attach trellis and mesh with hooks at the top and hinges at the base, or hooks at top and bottom. Climbers with flexible stems may then be lowered from the wall or, if only hooks are used, taken down and laid flat on the ground while the wall is repaired. Alternatively, use climbers that withstand drastic cutting back. Never try to lower rigid-stemmed climbers or shrubs, such as climbing roses or pyracantha.

Wires

Wires may be stretched horizontally or vertically between eye hooks or galvanized nails. As with trellis panels, the wires should be held 2in (5cm) from the surface of the wall or fence, and must be kept taut to prevent sagging; either tighten the eye hooks with pliers or attach

VIGOROUS CLIMBERS

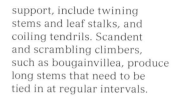

Actinidia chinensis, A. deliciosa
Akebia quinata
Aristolochia macrophylla
Beaumontia grandiflora
Bougainvillea
Campsis
Cissus
Clematis montana
Distictis buccinatoria
Fallopia baldschuanica
Humulus lupulus
Ipomoea horsfalliae
Mandevilla
Parthenocissus quinquefolia,
  P. tricuspidata
Passiflora
Petrea volubilis
Solandra maxima
Solanum wendlandii
Tetrastigma voinierianum
Vitis coignetiae
Wisteria sinensis

*Distictis
buccinatoria*

CLIMBING METHODS

Climbers attach themselves to supports by various means. Many climbers have aerial roots that readily attach to vertical surfaces without support. Other methods, all of which require some support, include twining stems and leaf stalks, and coiling tendrils. Scandent and scrambling climbers, such as bougainvillea, produce long stems that need to be tied in at regular intervals.

Aerial roots
Ivy (*Hedera*) is a self-clinging plant.

Leaf stalks
Clematis climbs using its leaf stalks.

Coiling tendrils
Passiflora attaches itself with tendrils.

Twining stems
Akebia weaves its stems in a spiral around the support.

ATTACHING A TRELLIS PANEL TO A WALL

To mount a trellis support, first securely attach vertical wooden laths at least 2in (5cm) thick to the wall and trellis. This allows the trellis to be suspended away from the wall and enables air to circulate freely. The trellis may then be permanently screwed to the laths (right); this restricts access to the wall, however. Using hooks and hinges (below) allows the plant and support to be lowered, if required. Hooking the trellis to the laths at both top and bottom allows it to be removed from the wall altogether.

Using laths
Screw the trellis to thick wooden laths.

Trellis attached at top with hook and eye

Hinge hardware at base

Using hooks and hinges
To allow access to the wall for maintenance, attach laths to both the wall and the trellis. Add hinges along the bottom of the panel with hooks at the top to hold it in place.

HOW TO SELECT CLIMBERS

Good example

Label

Healthy buds

Vigorous, sturdy stems

Honeysuckle (*Lonicera*)

Roots are visible and healthy but not coiled

Poor example

Spindly, weak growth with damaged buds

Poor example

Roots coiled tightly around the root ball

Natural support
Plant one or two seeds or plug plants—here, sweet peas (*Lathyrus odoratus*)—at the base of each leg of an obelisk or tepee so that the young plants can easily clamber up the structure as they develop.

tensioners at approximately 6ft (2m) intervals. Space the wires 12–18in (30–45cm) apart, with the lowest horizontal wire (or the base of vertical wires) 12in (30cm) above soil level.

Buying climbers

Climbing plants are usually sold container-grown, although a few (including climbing roses) may be sold bare-roots. Choose a healthy plant with a well-balanced framework of strong shoots, and reject any that show signs of pest infestation or disease. Bare-root plants should have plenty of healthy, well-developed, fibrous roots that are in proportion to the amount of top growth. For pot-grown plants, turn the pot over and check that the tips of the young roots are just showing; if so, the plant is well-rooted. Reject potbound plants—those that have tightly coiled roots around the root ball or a mass of roots protruding through the drainage holes in the pot—because they seldom grow satisfactorily.

Planting outdoors

If you choose to include marginally hardy climbers in your yard, plant them in spring, so that they are well established before their first winter. Evergreen and herbaceous climbers are more quickly established if planted in spring when the soil is warming up, but they may also be planted in fall in a protected situation. All other container-grown climbers may be planted in spring, fall, or any other time of year as long as the ground is not frozen or waterlogged. Planting during dry spells in summer is not recommended, but if this is unavoidable, cover the newly planted climber with a paper bag or a piece of burlap for the first few days, and water the plant daily while dry conditions persist.

Positioning the plant
Walls and solid fences create their own rain shadow, so plants that are to be trained against them should be planted at least 18in (45cm) from the foot of the support. In this way, once established, they normally receive sufficient rain to grow without additional watering. A pillar or freestanding trellis does not produce the same density of rain shadow and so the planting distance need be only 8–12in (20–30cm).
    When grown through another plant, the climber will compete with the host plant for food and

CLIMBERS THAT TOLERATE SANDY SOIL

Adlumia fungosa
Anredera cordifolia
Asarina
Bomarea andimarcana
Ceropegia
Clianthus puniceus
Ercilla volubilis
Gloriosa superba
Humulus
Ipomoea
Kennedia rubicunda
Maurandya
Merremia tuberosa
Mutisia oligodon
Parthenocissus
Passiflora
Petrea volubilis
Solanum wendlandii
Streptosolen jamesonii
Thunbergia alata

CLIMBERS THAT TOLERATE CLAY SOIL

Aristolochia macrophylla
Campsis
Celastrus scandens
Clematis
Distictis
Euonymus fortunei
  'Silver Queen'
Hedera
Humulus lupulus 'Aureus'
Hydrangea anomala
  subsp. *petiolaris*
Lathyrus latifolius
Lonicera
Parthenocissus
Passiflora
Schisandra
Vitis coignetiae,
  V. vinifera
Wisteria

CLIMBERS THAT REQUIRE ACIDIC SOIL

Agapetes
Asteranthera ovata
Beaumontia grandiflora
Berberidopsis corallina
Billardiera
Kennedia
Lapageria rosea
Lardizabala biternata
Mitraria coccinea
Mutisia, some

Gloriosa superba

moisture; to minimize this, plant the climber so that its roots stay as far away as possible from those of its host. If the host plant has deep roots, plant the climber fairly close to the host's main stem. If the host plant has rhizomatous or shallow roots, however, plant the climber about 18in (45cm) from the main root spread. A stake tied to the host plant, inserted just behind the climber's main stems, may be used to train the climber toward it at an angle.

Preparing the soil

Remove all weeds from the planting area (see "Weeds and lawn weeds," pp.645–649), then dig in coarse organic matter. This will improve the water retentiveness and fertility of sandy soil, or lighten the texture of heavy clay soil. Carefully fork in a dressing of slow-release fertilizer, at a rate of 2–3oz/sq yd (50–85g/sq m).

The planting hole should be at least twice the diameter of the container in which the climber was grown in order to allow the roots ample room to spread in the prepared soil. This may not be possible, however, if the climber is to be encouraged to grow through

---

CLIMBERS FOR VERY ALKALINE SOIL

Actinidia kolomikta
Akebia quinata
Asarina
Campsis x *tagliabuana*
    'Madame Galen'
Celastrus scandens
Clematis
Eccremocarpus scaber
Fallopia baldschuanica
Hedera
Hydrangea anomala
    subsp. *petiolaris*
Jasminum officinale,
    J. polyanthum
Lathyrus grandiflorus,
    L. latifolius
Lonicera
Maurandella antirrhiniflora
Parthenocissus tricuspidata
Passiflora caerulea
Schizophragma integrifolium
Solanum crispum
Trachelospermum
    jasminoides
Vitis
Wisteria sinensis

Lathyrus grandiflorus

---

a tree or shrub, in which case dig a hole large enough to accommodate the root ball and leave plenty of room for the roots to spread.

How to plant

Before removing the plant from its pot, make sure that the soil is moist—water the plant well so that the root ball is thoroughly wet and then leave it to drain for at least an hour. Remove the surface layer of soil to eliminate weed seeds, and then invert the pot, taking care to support the plant as it slides out. If the roots have begun to curl around inside the pot, gently tease them out. Any dead, damaged, or protruding roots should be cut back to the perimeter of the root ball.

Position the plant so that the top of the root ball is just level with the surrounding soil. It is advisable to plant clematis more deeply, however (see *Planting a Clematis*, p.139). Climbers that have been grafted (as is the case with most wisterias) should be planted with the graft union 2½in (6cm) below soil level. This encourages the scion itself to root, and reduces the incidence of sucker growths from the stock. For information on planting bare-root climbers, see "Planting a bush rose," p.157. When planting in a container, select a deep pot, and, if the climber is to remain outdoors in winter, it should be frost-proof. The soil mix should be moisture-retentive but free-draining; use a mixture of two parts of regular soilless potting mix and one part sharp sand. Supplement this with compost or with a packaged organic fertilizer applied according to the manufacturer's instructions. Anchor any supporting trellis into the potting mix before planting (see CONTAINER GARDENING, *Planting a Climber in a Container*, p.325).

Fill the planting hole with soil, then firm the plant in and water well. Insert stakes at the base of the plant and secure them to the support. To train the main shoots, fan them out and tie them individually to the stakes and to the support itself (if they will reach). Do not damage the stems by attaching them too tightly. Remove dead or damaged growth and cut back wayward shoots.

Tendril climbers readily attach themselves to a support, but the shoots may require gentle guidance and some tying in until they become firmly established. Twining climbers soon fasten their shoots to a support in their natural direction of growth (clockwise or counterclockwise) but may also

---

need initial tying in. Scramblers that do not support themselves should have their shoots fastened to the support at regular intervals with appropriate ties. For further information, see "Training established climbers," p.136.

Watering and mulching

Water the newly planted climber thoroughly, then cover the surface of the soil surrounding the plant with a 2–3in (5–7cm) layer of mulch to a radius of about 2ft (60cm). This is beneficial to the roots because it retains moisture throughout the area, giving the roots a chance to establish themselves. In addition, the mulch discourages the germination of weeds that would otherwise compete with the newly planted climber for nutrients and moisture.

PLANTING A CLIMBER AGAINST A WALL

1 Attach a support 12in (30cm) above the soil and 2in (5cm) from the wall. Dig a hole 18in (45cm) from the wall. Loosen the soil at the base and add compost.

2 Soak the climber's root ball well. Position it in the hole at a 45° angle, placing a stake across to check the planting level. Spread the roots away from the wall.

3 Fill in around the plant and firm and level the soil, ensuring that no air pockets remain between the roots and that the plant is fully supported.

4 Untie the stems from the central stake and select 4 or 5 strong shoots. Insert a stake for each shoot and attach it to the lowest wire. Tie in the shoots.

5 Trim back any weak, damaged, or wayward shoots to the central stem using pruners. This establishes the initial framework for the climber.

6 Thoroughly water the plant (here, *Jasminum mesnyi*). Cover the surrounding soil with a deep mulch to retain moisture and discourage weeds.

Routine care

Climbers need annual fertilizing, and the soil around their base should be kept moist. Climbers grown in containers need topdressing or repotting regularly. Adequate watering is essential. Regular deadheading helps to prolong flowering. Plants also need protection from pests, diseases, and, if tender, cold.

Feeding

Feed climbers in spring during their first two seasons with a dressing of rich compost or a balanced fertilizer. Thereafter, apply fertilizer annually at the manufacturer's recommended rate.

Watering

During dry periods, water climbers weekly. Soak thoroughly around the base of the plant; apply a 2–3in (5–7cm) mulch over the root area to keep the soil from drying out.

Deadheading and tying in

Where practical, deadhead climbers as the flowers fade. This enables the plant to concentrate its energies on producing further flowers, rather than fruits or seed heads. If fruits or seed heads are needed for ornamental purposes, deadhead only a quarter to one-third of the flowered shoots. This will be enough to encourage a continuing display of flowers.

Tie in new shoots as they develop, while still flexible, and cut back overgrown plants as needed (see "Pruning and training," pp.134–137).

Pests and diseases

Check carefully for signs of pests and diseases and treat any affected plants as recommended in PLANT PROBLEMS, pp.639–673.

Protecting tender climbers

Protect the top growth and base of marginally hardy and newly planted climbers with some sort of cover to block wind and sun and to moderate temperatures (see FROST AND WIND PROTECTION, pp.612–613).

CUTTING BACK CLIMBERS

Where a climber (here, *Hedera colchica* 'Sulphur Heart') has outgrown its allotted space, cut it back with pruners. Trim the stems irregularly for a natural effect.

MAINTAINING CONTAINER-GROWN CLIMBERS

Container-grown climbers may need to be watered once or twice a day in dry weather. When frost is likely, they may be moved indoors or plunged in the ground in a sheltered part of the garden. During the year, a climber grown in a container uses up most of the nutrients in the soil mix. The topdressing (i.e., the top layer of the soil and any mulch) should therefore be renewed annually. When the plant is watered, the fresh nutrients will gradually permeate and replenish the soil below. All but the slowest-growing climbers need to be moved into a larger container, using fresh soil mix, every two to four years. Spring-flowering plants should be repotted in fall, others in fall or spring.

Renewing the topdressing of a container-grown climber

1 In spring or early summer, scrape away and discard the top 1–2in (2.5–5cm) of soil in the container. Take care not to disturb any surface roots of the climber and the companion planting.

2 Replace the discarded soil with a layer of fresh potting mix blended with a little fertilizer. Firm gently to eliminate air pockets. Make sure that the soil level is the same as before. Water well.

3 To aid moisture retention during the summer months, cover the soil in the container with a light, decorative mulch such as cocoa shells or bark chips.

Repotting a container-grown climber

1 Every 2 to 4 years repot container-grown climbers (such as this honeysuckle) to prevent them from becoming potbound. Soak the soil well, then carefully slide the root ball out of the container.

2 Tease out the roots and trim back the thicker roots by about one-third. Leave fibrous roots intact and retain as much soil as possible around them.

3 Prune the topgrowth by a third and remove dead or damaged stems. Repot the plant in fresh, moist soil mix, adding an organic fertilizer to the top 1-2in (2.5-5cm).

4 Ensure that the final planting level is the same as before. Insert a triangle of stakes, then tie in the main stems securely but not too tightly.

WINTER PRUNING

When pruning deciduous climbers in winter, it is easy to assess the framework of the plant and train any new growth. The climber shown here is *Schisandra glaucescens*.

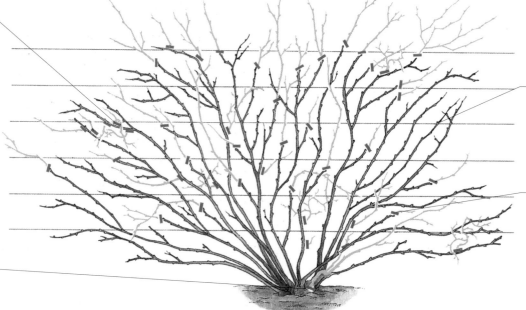

Thin out overcrowded stems, removing weak and crossing shoots.

Remove dead wood, pruning to the base of the stem if this is necessary.

Tie in new shoots, spacing them to produce a balanced framework.

To promote flowering, prune all sideshoots to about 5 buds.

Evergreen climbers

Prune evergreen climbers in spring, after all danger of frost has passed and as the plants are about to begin fresh growth. Evergreen climbers that are grown for their flowers as well as their foliage produce flowers on the previous season's wood, so delay pruning these until after flowering. In both cases, remove dead or damaged wood and trim stray shoots to shape.

Early winter pruning

Climbers that have already had at least one pruning during the previous growing season may be pruned again in winter to tidy up their appearance (see illustrations above). This is particularly useful for deciduous plants, whose frameworks can be assessed more easily when the branches are bare. Do not remove ripened wood, which will carry the next season's flowers. If winter-pruned plants are stimulated into new growth during mild spells, the new shoots may later be damaged by frost. Prune these back in spring.

Ornamental grapevines (*Vitis*) should be pruned in early winter, when the plants are dormant and pruning cuts may be made without the risk of "bleeding," or loss of sap. If the stems are cut in spring when the sap is rising, they will "bleed" profusely; this is difficult to stop and weakens the plants. (For pruning of grapevines, see pp.462–465.)

Training established climbers

Climbers that attach themselves by means of aerial roots need very little training, except in the first few years until enough aerial roots have formed to support the plant. All other climbing plants need training of new shoots each year to establish the desired shape.

Each year during the growing season, select the strongest new stems, before they become hard and woody, and train them in to continue the basic framework. Follow the shape of the allocated space and allow the leading stem to extend in a straight line until it has reached the required height. Tie all stems securely to the support at regular intervals using plastic twist-ties or twine.

PRUNING BOUGAINVILLEA

Bougainvillea is rampant and flowers reliably whether pruned or not. Prune between midwinter and early spring to keep the plant in check. Shorten sideshoots to within an inch or two of the main stems, but leave any needed to extend the main framework.

1 Trim wayward sideshoots to within 1–2in (2.5–5cm) of the main framework stems.

2 Cut cleanly, close to a healthy bud. The buds will soon produce new growth.

TRAINING CLIMBERS ON PERGOLAS AND PILLARS

To produce an even distribution of growth over a pergola or pillar, tie in the main stems throughout the growing season, spreading them out as required to fill any gaps. To promote flowering lower down a plant's stem, regularly train sideshoots of twining species around their support, making sure that the shoots are following their natural direction of growth: clockwise or counterclockwise.

After the flowering season, remove any dead or diseased shoots and prune the main stem and any leaders. This will encourage strong lateral growth to be produced in the following year.

1 Guide stray sideshoots onto the support in their natural direction of growth, then tie in.

2 In late summer, cut back all the leading stems by one-third to promote lateral growth.

Make sure that the ties are tight enough to prevent the stems from being blown around in strong winds and rubbing against the support; they should not restrict development of the plant's stems, however. The ties will need to be loosened periodically as the stems thicken with age.

Renovating an old or neglected climber

Unpruned climbers—or those that have not been trained—often become a mass of tangled, woody stems and produce a poor display of flowers. Such plants may be pruned hard to rejuvenate them. Most climbers withstand pruning close to the base or to main framework stems, but a plant in poor health may not survive this treatment. In this case, it is preferable to reduce the size of the plant gradually over a period of two or three years, in conjunction with annual feeding.

For a plant that is to be pruned to the base, cut down all existing growth in early spring to within 1–2ft (30–60cm) of the ground. To promote new growth, apply a dressing of balanced fertilizer according to label instructions.

HOW TO PRUNE HONEYSUCKLE

Climbing honeysuckles (*Lonicera*) require little pruning to flower profusely but tend, if neglected, to develop into a mass of thin, tangled stems that bear foliage and flowers only at the top of the shoots. To renovate a honeysuckle in this condition, prune it severely in late winter or early spring, at the beginning of the growing season. New shoots will soon begin to develop and these should be trained in to provide an evenly balanced framework.

If such severe pruning is not required, it is still possible to renovate the plant by removing dead or damaged shoots and stems from beneath new, young growth. Use a pair of shears, rather than pruners, for speed.

Renovation pruning
If the plant is badly overgrown, cut back all the stems with long-handled loppers to within 1–2ft (30–60cm) of ground level.

Alternative method
If it is undesirable or unnecessary to prune so severely, cut away all dead material from underneath the new, fresh growth.

Soak the root area with water, and then apply a mulch. Train all new growth as for newly planted climbers.

Renovation over a two- to three-year period (see below) is more difficult, because the stems frequently become entangled. In the spring, remove as much of the congested growth as possible,

then cut to the base one of every two (or three) main stems. Gently unravel the top growth of the severed stems. If any shoots are damaged, cut them out once the pruned main stems and their top growth have been removed. Cut out any weak, spindly shoots—these will not flower satisfactorily—and remove any dead wood. Fertilize,

water, and mulch, as you would when pruning a climber to the base, to encourage healthy new growth. Train fresh basal shoots to fill gaps, making sure they do not become entangled with old shoots. The following spring, repeat the process and fertilize, water, and mulch the plant.

RENOVATING A NEGLECTED CLIMBER

A neglected climber may be renovated gradually over two or three seasons by pruning hard each late winter or early spring.

Remove as much congested growth as possible.

Remove weak, twiggy, or damaged shoots so that only strong shoots remain.

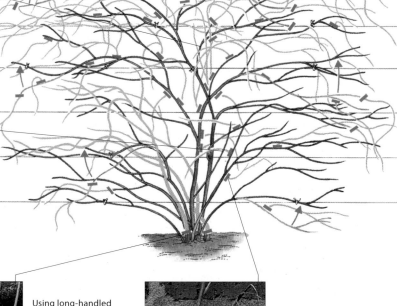

Using long-handled loppers, cut back to the base one-third to one-half of the old stems, retaining the more vigorous ones.

All dead or diseased wood should also be removed. Prune to a healthy bud, using sharp pruners.

CLIMBERS THAT MAY BE CUT TO THE GROUND

Allamanda cathartica
Anredera cordifolia
Antigonon leptopus
Aristolochia
Campsis x *tagliabuana*
Clematis (most spp.)
Clerodendrum thomsoniae
Clytostoma calystegioides
Distictis buccinatoria
Fallopia baldschuanica
Lonicera (most spp.)
Macfadyena unguis-cati
Manettia cordifolia ,
   M. luteorubra
Passiflora
Petrea volubilis
Pyrostegia venusta
Quisqualis indica
Solandra maxima
Solanum
Stigmaphyllon ciliatum
Strongylodon macrobotrys
Thunbergia
Vitis
Wisteria

Passiflora
caerulea

Clematis

Clematis grow well in almost any exposure and climate. Of all climbers, they offer the longest flowering period, with species or hybrids that bloom in almost every month of the year, many with the additional interest of silvery seed heads appearing after flowering has occurred. They are diverse in habit, varying from herbaceous plants, such as *Clematis integrifolia* and the clump-forming *C. recta*, to spreading subshrubs such as *C.* x *jouiniana*, as well as the better-known climbers.

Clematis also present a huge range of flower color and flower forms, ranging from the attractive sprays of delicate, ivory-colored bells in *C. rehderiana*, and exotic-looking, fleshy, golden lanterns in *C. tangutica*, to the simple but richly colored blooms of *C. viticella* and its many hybrids, or the more complex forms of large-flowered double clematis such as *C.* 'Proteus' and *C.* 'Vyvyan Pennell'.

Where to grow clematis

Clematis can be chosen for almost any landscape situation. The vigorous, spring-flowering species and cultivars are ideal for clothing and camouflaging unsightly buildings, fences, and walls, or for scrambling over old trees, tree stumps, and arbors, adding color and interest to otherwise dull features.

Less rampant types may be wall-trained on trellises and pergolas or allowed to cascade over terraces; more delicate species will spread horizontally at ground level, where their blooms can be best enjoyed.

Some clematis are suitable for container cultivation, on patios, or, for tender species, under glass. Others have great potential for being grown through host plants—trees, climbers, and sturdy shrubs, for example—to provide an extended season of interest or a splash of color, or to create unusual and enchanting plant associations.

Clematis groups

Clematis may be divided into three main groups, based on their flowering time and habit.

Group 1 is made up of the early-flowering species and their cultivars, and the Alpina, Macropetala, and Montana groups, which flower directly from the previous season's ripened stems. In Group 2 are the early, large-flowered cultivars, blooming on the current season's short stems, which arise from the previous season's mature wood. Groups 1 and 2 are sometimes known as "old wood"-flowering clematis. Group 3 includes the late-flowering species, large-flowered, late cultivars, and herbaceous types, which flower on the current season's growth.

Early-flowering species and cultivars

The early-flowering evergreen species and their forms are mostly from regions with warm climates and must be grown with protection in areas where marginally hardy. The hardiest evergreens are the vigorous *C. armandii* and smaller *C. cirrhosa*. Both grow best in a south- or southwest-facing site and are lovely when growing through other wall-trained plants.

The Alpina and Macropetala groups withstand very low winter temperatures and are ideal for growing through wall-trained trees and shrubs in any exposure. Do not grow them through climbing roses or other shrubs that need annual pruning, because these clematis need little or no cutting back. They are suitable for difficult sites such as northeast corners of buildings but also are superb container plants for the patio and can be trained on any support.

The members of the Montana group are hardy and vigorous, climbing 22–40ft (7–12m). These plants will cover walls and arbors and are dramatic growing through conifers or old fruit trees that are past their productive best, but may damage the foliage of evergreens with their rampant, dense growth.

Early, large-flowered cultivars

These are generally hardy, growing to 8–12ft (2.5–4m). The more compact cultivars such as *C.* 'Edith', which are normally the first to flower, are ideal for containers. The double and semidouble cultivars and the midsummer flowering types with very large flowers are best grown through the branches of other wall-trained trees or shrubs, where their flowers are protected from severe wind or heavy rain. Paler-flowered cultivars with mauve-striped or pink flowers will bleach in full sun and so are best planted in partial shade, where their flowers may be used to lighten a dark wall. The deep reds and purples are better for sunny situations because they develop better color in strong light.

Late-flowering species and cultivars

This group of clematis includes the large-flowered, late cultivars such as *C.* 'Jackmanii', small-flowered *C. viticella* and its hybrids, and a whole range of species and their forms, including the herbaceous clematis. The Jackmanii types are superb when grown through climbing roses, shrub roses, or most medium-sized shrubs (both evergreen and deciduous), whether freestanding or wall-trained. The *C. viticella* hybrids in particular are excellent for growing through groundcover plants, especially the summer- or winter-flowering heathers (*Calluna*, *Daboecia*, and *Erica*).

Of the other members in this group, *C.* x *jouiniana* makes an ideal groundcover and the miniature, tuliplike flowers of *C. texensis* and its hybrids look good against a background of low-growing evergreens. The vigorous *C. orientalis* and *C. tangutica* need a large wall or tree where they can grow unconfined and display their many flowers and their fluffy seed heads. *C. heracleifolia* var. *davidiana* and other herbaceous species do not climb and should be grown in mixed or herbaceous borders; *C. integrifolia*, for example, associates very well with cluster-flowered bush roses.

Soil preparation and planting

When using vigorous clematis to clothe trellises or pergolas, ensure that the support structure is strong and sound before planting. Similarly, when growing clematis through old trees, the branches

CLEMATIS

GROUP 1

C. montana var. rubens

C. 'Frances Rivis'

C. 'Markham's Pink'

GROUP 2

C. 'The President'

C. 'Henryi'

C. 'Nelly Moser'

GROUP 3

C. 'Ernest Markham'

C. 'Jackmanii'

C. 'Madame Julia Correvon'

must be robust enough to bear the often considerable weight. For clematis grown through other host plants, it is essential to match the vigor of the clematis with that of its host, if the host is not to be overrun. Also ensure that the pruning requirements of host and clematis are compatible.

Most climbing species can be sited in part shade or in sun, provided that the roots are cool and shaded. Either underplant them with low shrubs or plant on the shaded side of the host tree or wall. The herbaceous species thrive in a sunny situation. To grow clematis on a patio, use a container with dimensions of 18 in diameter x 18in deep (45 x 45cm).

Most clematis will thrive in any rich, fertile, and well-drained soil, especially if it is neutral or slightly alkaline. The evergreens and species such as *C. tangutica* and *C. orientalis* should not be grown in soil that remains wet during the winter months because they have fine, fibrous root systems, which quickly rot. Planting details are the same as for other climbers (see "Soil preparation and planting," pp.130–132), except that clematis should be planted about 2in (5cm) deeper than normal to encourage basal buds to develop below soil level. If the stems are damaged, the plant may then grow again from below soil level.

Routine care

Keep newly planted specimens well watered until established and mulch climbing and herbaceous species annually in spring with compost or well-rotted manure.

Fresh young growth is very susceptible to slug damage (p.669) in early spring. Clematis are prone to attack from aphids (p.654), and

PLANTING A CLEMATIS

Plant clematis 2in (5cm) deeper than the nursery planting level. This helps buds to develop below soil level and overcome clematis wilt.

the later-flowering, large-flowered cultivars may be affected by powdery mildew (p.667). Clematis wilt (p.657), a condition caused by a fungus, can attack newly planted, large-flowered clematis.

Pruning and training

Pruning requirements vary for each group, so always check before cutting back. If pruned incorrectly, the flowering wood may be unintentionally cut out.

Initial pruning and training for all groups

Clematis climb by means of leaf-stalk tendrils that attach themselves to their support. They need to be trained to reach their support and new growth will need to be tied in during spring and summer. Tie just below a node (or leaf axil bud), and space stems evenly on the support, leaving enough room for further growth to develop.

Clematis require special care in initial training and pruning. If they are left untrained, vigorous plants may produce one or two stems that are 50–60ft (15–18m) long,

resulting in a topheavy tangle of growth and a bare base. To avoid this, all newly planted clematis should be pruned hard the first spring after planting.

Unless the plant already has three or four stems growing from the base, cut back all the stems just above a strong, healthy pair of leaf buds about 12in (30cm) above soil level. If this hard pruning does not produce three or four extra stems in early spring, any new stems should be pruned again to about 6in (15cm), just above a strong pair of leaf buds.

Group 1

Many of these vigorous clematis require little, if any, regular pruning, especially if cut back hard when first planted. If restricting the size or tidying tangled growth is necessary, pruning should be done after flowering. Any dead, weak, or damaged stems can also be removed at this time. New growth will ripen during late summer and fall and provide flowers the following spring. Any excess growth may be reduced during the fall, and tied into its support, but bear in mind that this will reduce the flowering display. *C. armandii*, which produces a mass of flowers on trailing stems, may be thinned annually to avoid congestion; cut back to well-placed, young shoots immediately after flowering.

GROUP 1 – EARLY-FLOWERING SPECIES

C. alpina and cvs
C. armandii and cvs
C. cirrhosa
C. macropetala and cvs
C. montana and cvs
C. montana var. *grandiflora*
C. montana var. *rubens*

Clematis macropetala 'Maidwell Hall'

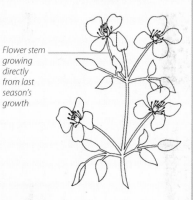

Flower stem growing directly from last season's growth

PRUNING GROUP 1 CLEMATIS

Mature stems of Group 1 clematis produce flower stems for the next season, so prune after flowering only if the plant has become overgrown.

Cut back any damaged shoots to the main stem or to a healthy pair of buds.

Thin or remove stems that are growing densely or that have outgrown the available space, cutting them back to their point of origin.

Color contrast

Clematis are excellent as companion plants and can be grown through a variety of host plants to create an unusual display. Here, the bright petals of *C.* 'Venosa Violacea' present an attractive contrast to the green of *Juniperus sabina* 'Tamariscifolia' over which it is scrambling.

Group 2

The solitary, large flowers are produced on stems of lengths varying from 6–24in (15–60cm) which arise from the previous season's growth. Prune these plants in early spring just before the new growth commences.

Remove any dead, weak, or damaged stems and cut back healthy stems on the framework to just above a strong pair of leaf buds. These buds will produce the first crop of flowers. This group may also produce a second, but smaller, flush of blooms on new shoots in late summer.

PRUNING GROUP 2 CLEMATIS

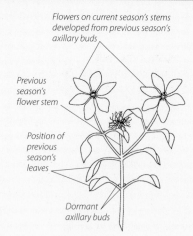

Flowers on current season's stems developed from previous season's axillary buds

Previous season's flower stem

Position of previous season's leaves

Dormant axillary buds

Group 2 clematis flower on current season's stems, so prune in early spring before growth starts.

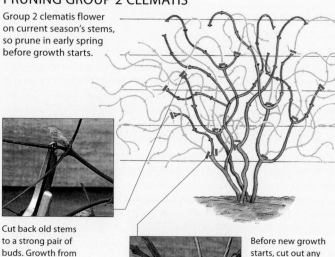

Cut back old stems to a strong pair of buds. Growth from these will produce this season's flowers.

Before new growth starts, cut out any damaged stems to their point of origin or to ground level.

Group 3

Flowers produced by this group are borne on stems of the current season's growth. Prune in early spring before new growth starts. Remove all the previous season's stems down to a strong pair of leaf buds just above the base of the previous season's growth, 6–12in (15–30cm) above soil level. As new growth appears, tie it to its support

Flowering stems on current season's new growth

PRUNING GROUP 3 CLEMATIS

Group 3 clematis produce flowers on the current season's growth, so prune in early spring before new growth begins.

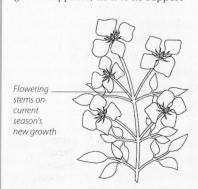

Cut just above the lowest pair of strong buds on each stem—this will be 6–12in (15–30cm) above soil level. Make a straight cut with sharp pruners, ensuring that the buds are not damaged.

or host. Take care with the soft and often brittle, new stems. Space them evenly and tie in at regular intervals.

Clematis growing over host or groundcover plants, such as heathers, should also be pruned. In late fall, remove excessive growth to keep the plant and host tidy and less prone to wind damage. When clematis are grown over winter-flowering heathers, all clematis topgrowth should be removed down to 12in (30cm) in late fall, before the heathers come into flower.

Propagation

Clematis species can be propagated by seed sown in fall and over-wintered in a cold greenhouse or cold frame (cultivars do not come true from seed). Cultivars are usually increased by softwood or semiripe cuttings (see p.632) or layering (see p.631); division (see p.378) or basal cuttings (see p.200) are used for herbaceous types.

Internodal cuttings of softwood and semiripe wood are usually preferred to nodal cuttings, but both methods may be used successfully. Take them in spring just above a node and trim the stem to 1–2in (2.5–5cm) below the node. Remove one of the pair of leaves ¼in (1cm) away from the node. Reduce the remaining leaf area by half and cut the stem above the node back to approximately ¼in (1cm). Treat the base with hormone rooting powder. Root in a closed propagating case with bottom heat. Harden off the new plants gradually (see p.638) before planting out the young clematis in spring.

INTERNODAL CUTTINGS

Node

Leaf removed

Make cuttings 2in (5cm) long by trimming just above a node and 1½in (3.5cm) below the node. Remove one leaf from each cutting.

GROUP 2 – EARLY, LARGE-FLOWERED CULTIVARS

C. 'Barbara Jackman'
C. 'Carnaby'
C. 'Daniel Deronda'
C. 'Duchess of Edinburgh'
C. 'Elsa Späth'
C. 'Général Sikorski'
C. 'Lasurstern'
C. 'Marie Boisselot', syn C. 'Mme. Le Coultre'
C. 'Mrs. N. Thompson'
C. 'Nelly Moser'
C. 'Niobe'
C. 'The President'
C. 'Vyvyan Pennell'

GROUP 3 – LATE-FLOWERING SPECIES AND CULTIVARS

C. 'Comtesse de Bouchaud'
C. 'Duchess of Albany'
C. 'Ernest Markham'
C. 'Etoile Violette'
C. florida and cvs
C. 'Hagley Hybrid'
C. 'Huldine'
C. 'Jackmanii'
C. 'Lady Betty Balfour'
C. paniculata
C. 'Perle d'Azur'
C. PETIT FAUCON ('Evisix')
C. 'Star of India'
C. tangutica and cvs
C. 'Ville de Lyon'
C. viticella and cvs

Clematis 'Ville de Lyon'

Propagation

Climbing plants may be propagated from seed, from stem or root cuttings, or by layering. Wisteria is also often propagated by grafting (for further information on this technique, see Ornamental Trees, "Grafting," p.80).

Propagation from seed is the most cost-effective way of producing large quantities of plants; it is also the only practical method for increasing annuals and the easiest method for propagating herbaceous climbers. Hybrids and cultivars, however, seldom reproduce true from seed, and it is therefore advisable to propagate these by vegetative methods, such as cuttings. Also, woody plants may take several years to reach flowering size if they are raised from seed.

Propagation from stem cuttings that are taken from soft or semiripe wood may be carried out successfully for almost all climbers and is the best method for selected cultivars. Propagation from hardwood cuttings is normally applied only to vines (*Vitis*); root cuttings may be used for a small number of plants, such as *Celastrus*. Some climbers produce new plants naturally by self-layering. If only a few plants are required, simple and serpentine layering are both straightforward methods of propagating climbers that are difficult to raise successfully from cuttings.

Propagating climbers from seed

Most species produce viable seed without any difficulty. In the case of some marginally hardy plants, however, a long, hot summer is necessary for the seed to ripen fully. To obtain seed from unisexual plants, such as *Actinidia deliciosa* and *Celastrus scandens*, plants of both sexes must be grown reasonably close together to ensure that they pollinate each other.

The sex of any seedling is unknown until the time it reaches flowering size. Named, vegetatively propagated male and female clones are available for some plants, such as *Actinidia deliciosa*. For sowing and planting annual climbers, see Annuals and Biennials, pp.214–219.

Preparing the seed

For certain climbers it may be necessary to soak the seeds in water before sowing them: *Hardenbergia* seeds should be soaked for 24 hours, and *Lapageria* seeds for 48 hours. Seeds with a hard outer coating may need to have their dormancy broken by a period of cold. To achieve this, put them in a refrigerator for at least six to eight weeks (for further information, see Principles of Propagation, "Cold stratification," p.630.)

Sowing

If sowing seed in a clay pot, first cover the drainage holes with a piece of screen (this is not necessary when plastic pots, seed flats, or pans are used), then fill the pot, flat, or pan with seed-sowing mix, firming with a presser board to ensure that there are no air spaces or hollows. Large seeds should be evenly spaced; press them gently into the mix and then cover to their own depth with a layer of sifted propagation mix that has been blended with a small amount of fine horticultural grit.

Mix tiny seeds with a little fine, dry sand so that they may be sown evenly and thinly; no extra covering of soil is needed.

Label the pot and water the propagation mix with a fine spray. Add a thin layer of fine grit or place clear plastic wrap or glass over the pot to keep the soil from drying out.

The seeds of certain climbers such as *Eccremocarpus* and *Tropaeolum peregrinum* require supplemental heat to germinate when grown in a cool climate and so should be placed in a propagator at 55–61°F (13–16°C). *Cobaea*, if grown as an annual, should be sown in late winter with heat so that the young plants are well developed by the time they are planted outside. Most other seeds should be kept in a warm place out of direct sun. Hardy climbers such as most clematis, however, germinate best in cold conditions: plunge the containers into a protected place such as a cold frame.

Pricking out

As soon as the seedlings emerge, remove the glass or plastic wrap, if used. When the first pair of true leaves has formed (the seedling's first leaves may differ significantly from the leaves of the adult plant) prick out the seedlings singly into small pots. If they are very small, however, it is best to use a flat, pricking out in rows separated by the space of about one leaf's width.

Inspect the base of the pots or flat at frequent intervals; as soon as the roots are visible through the drainage holes, pot on the seedlings. Seedlings that were germinated in a cold environment should be grown on initially in warmer conditions under cover.

Planting out

Plant out the seedlings when they are well established. Fast-growing climbers, both annual and perennial, may be planted where they are to flower. If frost is likely and the climbers are not fully hardy, either plant them under some sort of cover or delay planting out until all danger of frost has passed.

Slow-growing climbers should be potted on each time the roots begin to appear through the base of the pot. In their first season, grow them on in a sheltered position or in a nursery bed. Provide stakes to support the plants in all cases and keep the soil of pot-grown plants moist.

SOWING SEEDS

1 Harvest seed (here, clematis) from the plant when ripe—it should pull away from the seed head easily. There is no need to remove the fluffy "tails."

2 Sow thinly in a prepared flat or other container of firmed, moist, gritty seed-sowing mix.

3 Cover the seeds with a thin layer of gritty mix, add a shallow layer of fine grit, and label. Plunge in a sand bed or cold frame outdoors.

4 After germination, prick out the seedlings: use a plant label or plastic knife to loosen a clump. Lift and replant the seedlings singly, holding each gently by the leaves.

5 When the seedlings have developed their first pair of true leaves, pot them on individually in moist potting mix. Label, and place in a cold frame.

6 Grow the seedlings until well established. They are then ready for planting out in their permanent positions.

Root cuttings

A few climbers, notably *Celastrus* and *Solanum*, may be propagated from root cuttings, taken from late winter to early spring.

Taking the cuttings

Dig a hole 18–24in (45–60cm) away from the base of the plant to expose roots that are about ½in (1cm) thick; these provide the best cutting material. Remove sections of root up to 8–12in (20–30cm) long, depending on how many cuttings are required. Cut straight across the top of the root (nearest to the plant) and cut the base of the root at an angle. Place the cutting material in a clear plastic bag to prevent it from drying out.

Preparing and inserting the cuttings

Wash the sections of root to remove any soil, then cut them into smaller pieces and remove the fibrous laterals. Make a horizontal cut at the top and a slanted cut at the base. Insert the cuttings, slanted cut downward, in a pot filled with a rooting medium of equal parts peat substitute (or peat) and sand. Space them approximately 3in (7cm) apart, with the tips protruding slightly. Cover with a ½in (1cm) layer of sand. Moisten the soil thoroughly, label the pot, and place it in a cold frame or propagator, or plunge it in a trench. Keep the soil moist.

Hardening off and potting on

Buds will appear near the top of the cuttings in spring. Pot up the cuttings individually during early summer, and harden them off gradually, occasionally applying a liquid or foliar fertilizer. Stake the cuttings as they develop. Set out the new plants in their permanent positions the following fall.

PROPAGATION FROM ROOT CUTTINGS

1 Dig a hole well away from the base of the plant to expose some of the roots.

2 Cut off sections of root with pruners. The pieces should be about ½in (1cm) thick and at least 4in (10cm) long.

3 Wash the roots and divide into pieces 1½–2in (4–5cm) long, cutting horizontally at the top and obliquely at the base (see inset).

4 Insert each cutting vertically into a pot of propagation mix, so that the tips are just protruding above the surface of the soil.

5 Cover with a ½in (1cm) layer of sand. Water, label, and place in a cold frame.

6 Pot on into individual pots once the cuttings are well rooted and young shoots are 1–2in (2.5–5cm) tall.

Self-layering climbers

Many climbers have trailing shoots that root naturally where they come into contact with the surrounding soil. A shoot that has self-layered can be lifted and cut from the parent plant in fall or early spring. Choose a healthy, well-rooted layer that has fresh new growth. Lift it carefully and cut it off. Trim back the layered shoot, retaining only the piece or pieces of stem that have produced new roots and that have new buds forming. Strip off any leaves growing near the roots. Pot up the rooted layers individually into a standard propagation mix of half peat substitute or peat and half sand, and water them in well. If the layer is severed and potted in fall, leave it (particularly if evergreen) in a cold frame to establish and then plant out the following spring. Plant out other layers once they have strong roots and shoots.

Simple layering

The long, trailing shoots produced by climbers may often be propagated by simple layering

PROPAGATION OF SELF-LAYERING PLANTS

1 Select a low-growing shoot that has rooted into the ground and lift the rooted section with a hand fork.

2 Carefully sever the shoot from the parent plant (here, ivy), cutting between nodes, using a pair of sharp pruners.

3 Cut the shoot into sections, each with a healthy root system and vigorous new growth. Remove the lower leaves.

4 Replant each section of rooted shoot either into a pot of propagation mix or in its permanent position in the yard.

if they do not root naturally. A shoot is wounded and pinned down into the surrounding soil; this induces it to root at a node to provide a young plant.

Layers of many climbers that have been pinned down in spring will develop strong root systems by fall, at which time they may be separated from the parent plant. *Campsis* and *Vitis* should be layered in late fall or winter, because if the stems are wounded in spring, the layers "bleed" sap and are less likely to root.

Soil preparation

If the soil surrounding the plant to be layered is poor, fork in some organic matter at least a month before layering takes place. Alternatively, fill a pot with potting mix and plunge it into the ground in the location where the layer is to be pegged down.

Making the layer

Choose a healthy, vigorous, nonflowering shoot or stem that is long enough to trail along the ground. Trim the leaves and any sideshoots from the section of stem to be layered to provide a clear length of stem for about 12in (30cm) behind the tip of the shoot.

Gently bend the stem down to the ground and, to encourage root formation, wound the underside of the stem close to a node, making an angled cut halfway through with a sharp knife. For most climbers, apply hormone rooting powder to the wound; vigorous climbers such as wisteria, however, do not require it.

Pin the stem firmly to the ground with one or more landscape staples or U-shaped pieces of wire, and cover with not more than 3in (8cm) of soil. Attach the tip of the layered stem to a stake so that it stays upright.

Separating the rooted layer

In fall, when new shoots and roots have grown from the buried part of the stem, the rooted layer may be severed from the parent plant and potted up or planted out. Trim back the old stem before replanting, and stake the new plant. If the layer is planted in a container, it should be overwintered in a cold frame or plunged into a protected spot and mulched lightly. Repot as necessary before gradually hardening off the plant. Set out the plant in its permanent position the following year if the plant is big enough.

PROPAGATION BY SIMPLE LAYERING

1 Select a young, low-growing shoot. Trim off the leaves to provide a clear length of stem behind the tip.

2 Make an angled cut on the underside of the shoot to form a "tongue" in the center of the trimmed length of stem.

3 Using a clean brush, dust the incision with fresh hormone rooting powder (see inset) and gently shake off any surplus.

4 Pin down the shoot firmly in the prepared area, using wire staples. Cover with up to 3in (8cm) of soil.

5 The following fall, sever the layered shoot close to the parent plant. Lift with a hand fork and trim back the old stem.

6 Plant the layer in a 5in (13cm) pot of standard potting mix or into its permanent position in the yard. Then water and label.

PROPAGATION BY SERPENTINE LAYERING

Carefully bend a trailing shoot down to the prepared soil and trim off leaves and sideshoots. Make several wounds close to nodes, leaving at least one bud between each incision. Apply hormone rooting powder and pin down the wounded sections, as for simple layering. Separate plantlets in fall, when roots will have formed from each of the wounds. Trim the old stem from the new plants before replanting and staking.

Several new plants may be produced by serpentine layering. Pin down layers with wire staples (see inset).

Hoya lanceolata subsp. *bella*

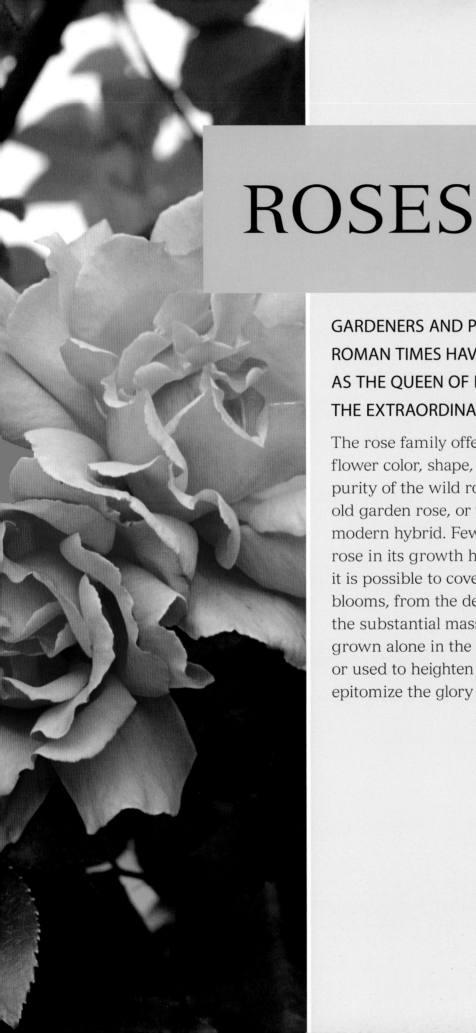

ROSES

GARDENERS AND POETS SINCE BEFORE
ROMAN TIMES HAVE REVERED THE ROSE
AS THE QUEEN OF FLOWERING PLANTS FOR
THE EXTRAORDINARY BEAUTY OF ITS BLOOMS.

The rose family offers an enormous range of
flower color, shape, and scent, from the simple
purity of the wild rose to the pastel charm of an
old garden rose, or the jewel-like brilliance of a
modern hybrid. Few plants are as varied as the
rose in its growth habit, height, foliage, and form;
it is possible to cover the whole garden in rose
blooms, from the delicacy of a tiny pot rose to
the substantial mass of a huge rambler. Whether
grown alone in the splendor of a formal garden
or used to heighten a mixed planting, roses
epitomize the glory of a summer's day.

Roses in the home landscape

Whether you choose to grow old garden roses for their grace of habit, foliage, and scent, or modern roses for their long flowering season and showy blooms, the diversity of roses (*Rosa*) makes it possible to find a plant for almost every part of the landscape, and to create any style or mood of planting, from restrained classicism to luxuriant informality.

Choosing roses

Roses are adaptable plants that grow happily in almost all parts of the world. They are most vigorous in warm, temperate regions, although some adapt well to subtropical or cold regions. In hot climates, they may flower virtually continuously throughout the year.

The number of rose cultivars available is bewildering, with many new ones added each year. Before choosing, it is certainly worth visiting some established gardens to observe as many different roses as possible growing in garden conditions. Do this over a period of time to assess the plants' habit, eventual height, health, vigor, fragrance, fastness of flower color in strong sun, and all the other desirable features of a good rose. Note, too, whether a rose produces a single flush of blooms or if it is a remontant rose, which, being a repeat- or perpetual-flowering plant, will have a greatly extended flowering period.

Many rose societies publish listings that give details of where species roses and cultivars offered by members and other nurseries may be purchased; these are often invaluable in locating suppliers of more unusual roses. In addition to their selling name, many roses now have coded cultivar names—for example, the rose sold as CASINO has the coded cultivar name 'Macca'—so you can be sure that you are buying the correct plant (see also *Plant Names*, p.677).

Flower shapes

The genus *Rosa* comprises many flower forms, from the simple, single flowers of species roses to the elegantly furled blooms of the modern rose and the cabbagelike complexity of many old rose flowers.

The main flower shapes shown at the right give a general indication of the flower shape when in its perfect state (which in some cases may be before it has fully opened). The flowers may be single (4–7 petals), semidouble (8–14 petals), double (15–20 petals), or fully double (more than 30 petals).

Framed view The mix of shrub roses and climbers here gives this walled rose garden a soft, informal look.

ROSE CLASSIFICATIONS

About 250 species roses as well as many natural hybrid roses grow in the wild. After 2,000 years of being grown as ornamentals, rose cultivars now number in the thousands. The ancestry of almost all of them is so mixed, after centuries of casual and indiscriminate breeding before cross-pollination was understood and proper records of parentage kept, that it is impossible to classify them precisely. For example, the hybridizing of miniature roses with Floribunda roses has led to the Patio roses, intermediate in stature between the parents.

Roses are continually evolving, so categories (or classes) that rose lovers devise are subject to change and should be regarded as signposts for guidance, not inflexible definitions. The Canadian Rose Society (CRS) has adopted different groupings than the World Federation of Rose Societies. The CRS groups are as follows, with equivalent World Federation names in parentheses.

Modern garden roses

Hybrid Tea and Grandiflora (Large-flowered bush) Upright, remontant (repeat-flowering) shrubs with large flowers carried one to a stem or in small clusters.

Floribunda (Cluster-flowered bush) Upright, remontant shrubs with better continuity of bloom than Hybrid Teas; the smaller flowers are borne on large sprays.

Patio (Dwarf cluster-flowered bush) Similar to Floribundas, but with a smaller, neat habit.

Miniature Tiny counterparts of Hybrid Teas and Floribundas.

Groundcover Low-growing, trailing, or spreading roses. Some flower once a year; others are remontant.

Climbing Climbing roses with long, strong shoots and large flowers borne singly or in small clusters. Some flower once a year; most are remontant. Climbing roses include a small group of roses, such as 'Albertine', which in habit are between a climber and a rambler. They were once classed as ramblers, but culturally they should be treated as climbers.

Rambler Vigorous, climbing roses with long, flexible shoots that bear small blooms in large clusters, flowering once a year.

Shrub A widely varying group impossible to classify further, ranging from low, mound-forming cultivars to wide-spreading shrubs and giant cluster-flowered bushes. Some bloom once a year; many are remontant.

Sweet Briar Hybrids from *Rosa rubiginosa* (syn. *R. eglanteria*), noted for its apple-scented leaves. Large, twiggy, prickly shrubs in pink, fawn-yellow, or purple.

Old garden roses

Alba Large, freely branching roses with flower clusters borne once in the season among abundant, gray-green foliage.

Bourbon Very vigorous, open, fully or partly remontant roses that bear double, fragrant flowers, often three to a cluster. Many grow tall and open.

Centifolia (Provence) Rather lax, thorny shrubs bearing fragrant flowers once a year. Commonly called cabbage roses.

China Small to medium remontant shrubs of twiggy, airy growth, bearing small, mainly double flowers singly or in clusters.

Damask Open shrubs bearing loose clusters of very fragrant flowers, mainly once a year.

Gallica Fairly dense shrubs that produce richly colored flowers, often three to a cluster, once a year.

Hybrid Musk Vigorous, remontant shrubs with abundant foliage and fragrant, primarily double blooms borne in clusters.

Hybrid Perpetual Vigorous, sometimes remontant, shrubs with flowers borne singly or in threes.

Moss Often lax shrubs with a furry, mosslike growth on stems and calyx. Most bloom once a year, but some are remontant.

Noisette Remontant climbing roses that bear large clusters of flowers with a slightly spicy fragrance.

Portland Upright, dense, and less vigorous (but more remontant) version of the Damask rose.

Tea Remontant shrubs and climbers bearing loose, usually double flowers that have a spicy fragrance.

Species roses

Wild, or species, roses and species hybrids (which share most characteristics of both parent species) are mainly large, arching shrubs bearing one flush of single, five-petaled flowers in spring or summer and decorative hips in fall.

Notable among the species is *Rosa rugosa*, the remontant parent of a diverse group of dense, very hardy, and disease-resistant, vigorous shrubs bearing extremely fragrant, single to semidouble blooms. A few are more open in habit, less hardy, and not as fragrant as others.

Consult local rose experts for further information suited to specific regional and garden conditions.

FLOWER SHAPES

Flat Open, usually single or semidouble, with petals that are almost flat, shown above in *Rosa moyesii* 'Geranium'

Cupped Open, single (as in this *R. rugosa* 'Rosea') to fully double, with petals curving out from the center.

Pointed Semidouble to fully double Hybrid Tea type, with high, tight centers, such as *R.* 'Silver Jubilee'.

Rounded Double or fully double, with even-sized, overlapping petals in a bowl-shaped outline (here, *R.* 'Alpine Sunset').

Pompon Small, rounded, double or fully double, usually in clusters, with many small petals, such as *R.* PINK BELLS ('Poulbells').

Rosette Flattish, double, or fully double, with slightly overlapping unevenly shaped petals (here, *R.* 'Tour de Malakoff').

Urn-shaped Classic, curved, and flat-topped, semi to fully double, Hybrid Tea type. *R.* SIMBA ('Korbelma') is a fine example.

Quartered-rosette Flattish, double, or fully double (as in this *R.* 'Gloire de Dijon'), with petals in a quartered pattern.

Fragrance

Roses have long been prized for their scent; most old garden species and some modern roses possess enchanting and diverse perfumes with hints of clove, musk, honey, lemon, spice, and even tea, as well as the "true rose" fragrance. It is not easy to be specific about rose scent, because its character and intensity may vary greatly with the time of day, the air humidity, the age of the bloom, and the "nose" of individual gardeners; some will find a particular cultivar fragrant, while others will not.

With most roses one must be quite close to smell them; they are best enjoyed by planting them near a door or a window, where their scent may drift into the house on summer evenings, around the patio or along a path, or in a sheltered position in the yard. Other roses, particularly many of the tree-climbing ramblers, are so freely scented that they can perfume the whole yard.

Flower color

Modern roses embrace virtually every color of the spectrum, from pale pastels to bold, bright reds and yellows. The blue rose remains the stuff of legend, despite the use of the word "blue" in such cultivars as 'Blue Moon', which is actually lilac. The old garden roses range in hue from white, through the palest of blush pinks, deep pink, crimson, and violet, to purple; many are striped pink and white or purple and white. Most roses look good together and with other plants, but combining too many brilliant colors, for example, bright vermilion with cerise pink, may create a discordant effect. Plant white roses

Formal garden A rose garden developed within the formal setting of clipped box hedges offset by delphiniums and other herbaceous plants will provide a long summer display. The cool green structure of the hedges allows the roses to be the star performers, while softening the hard lines.

or those with softer, pastel hues between groups of strongly toned roses to cool them down and prevent them from clashing.

Foliage color

In addition to producing a fine flowering display, some groups of roses provide color in other ways to extend the season of interest. The Alba roses and many of the species roses have pleasing foliage, from a soft gray-green to a deep, glossy blue-green, making them attractive even when the bush is not in flower. The bright green foliage of Rugosa roses has an interesting wrinkled (or rugose) texture and, if the roses are planted as a hedge, it makes a good background for other plantings. The leaves of some species are a dusky plum-purple, as in *Rosa glauca*, while the foliage of some, such as *R. virginiana*, turns in color to vivid sunset tints in fall.

Ornamental rose hips or thorns

Rugosa roses with single or semidouble flowers also develop bright red, decorative rose hips at the end of the flowering season. Some of the species roses, too, such as *R. moyesii* and its hybrids, produce ornamental and sometimes showy hips in fall that range in color from yellow and orange, through all the shades of red, to a blackish-purple.
R. sericea subsp. *omeiensis* f. *pteracantha* has huge, flat thorns that, when young, glow ruby red if the sun is behind them.

Designing with roses

One of the best settings for the beds of a rose garden is a smooth, green lawn, but the subtle gray and honey tones of stone paving can be just as attractive. A mellow brick path may complement a rose planting alongside it, especially one of soft, pale tones. Whatever the material, avoid multicolored patterns that may compete with the roses. Gravel, although pleasant in appearance and texture, can be

Fall show The red hips of this rose bring a splash of color to an otherwise green background and contrast well with the fluffy seed heads of a clematis.

troublesome to look after, because weeds can appear through it and be difficult to dig out, and the stones may gradually spread out or disappear into the soil.

Edging plants may be used to frame a rosebed. A traditional boxwood hedge makes a formal boundary, but many other plants may be used more informally, particularly those that provide gray-green or silver-gray foliage. Pearly everlasting (*Anaphalis nepalensis* var. *monocephala)* and pussy toes (*Antennaria*) with their woolly leaves, or the more dwarf forms of lavender are suitable, as is catmint (*Nepeta*) if there is room for it to sprawl over the path.

Many of the more restrained hardy geraniums, in particular those with blue flowers, are similarly appealing, and even miniature roses, in contrasting or complementary colors, may be grown on the sunny side of a bed.

Formal rose gardens

A popular way to grow roses is in a formal rose garden, devoted to displaying the glories of the rose in beds shaped to reflect the plant's classic elegance. Generally, modern cultivars grown as bushes and standards are used as permanent bedding plants, grouped in blocks of color. The stiff and upright growth of many such bushes lends itself to the formality of bedding and does not blend so well with other plants, although roses may be attractively underplanted (see p.152).

Rosebeds may be designed in any shape or size—square, oblong, triangular, or round; at the edges of paths or driveways they may be narrow and ribbonlike. Before creating new rosebeds, draw a plan on paper and experiment with different shapes and layouts of beds to decide which is the best design for the site. Do not make the beds so wide that access to the roses for spraying, mulching, and pruning is difficult.

If mixing rose cultivars in the same bed, plant no fewer than five or six plants of the same cultivar together in a regular formation for substantial clumps of color; not all cultivars reach their peak of flowering at the same time. A garden planted with variations on a color theme, for instance, pale and deep pinks with a touch of white, creates a more harmonious effect than a crowd of bright colors.

When planting, bear in mind the variations in eventual height of different cultivars. For a bed in an open area, choose cultivars of a more or less uniform height. A rosebed that is backed by a wall or hedge is more attractive if the roses at the front are shorter than those behind. Standard roses may be used to provide height. Placing a single standard in the center of a round bed that echoes the shape of the rose creates a graceful symmetry, while several standards placed at intervals of about 5ft (1.5m) along the middle of a long bed help to break up its uniformity.

Informal plantings

The charm of roses may be exploited in a wide range of informal planting designs, particularly with herbaceous plants or other shrubs. Roses suitable for virtually any site in the yard may be chosen from the multitude of shrub, miniature, climbing, and groundcover roses of varied stature and habit now available.

Roses combine happily with other plantings; for example, miniature roses give both summer color and height to a planting of rock plants that are mainly spring-flowering, and a groundcover rose may clothe a bank with fragrant flowers.

The belief that roses do not mix with other plants probably dates from the days when many commonly used cultivars were large and ungainly and did not suit the Edwardian and Victorian bedding designs. They were grown in separate walled gardens to provide cut blooms for the house. It has, however, long been recognized that roses do not have to be grown in isolation.

Roses with herbaceous plants

Growing roses in beds or raised beds with herbaceous plants both highlights the beauties of the rose in flower and provides interest when the rose itself is not blooming. The growth habit of many shrub roses, such as the light and airy China roses or the lax and open Damasks, perfectly suits the casual profusion of an informal planting.

Muted drifts of flower or foliage, for example, the haze of tiny, white *Crambe cordifolia* flowers, best complement the showy flowers of roses in the summer. At other times of the year, use more flamboyant flowering plants or some with evergreen foliage to extend the season and conceal the bare rose stems.

Many plants may enhance a planting dominated by roses. The tall spikes of purple foxgloves (*Digitalis purpurea*), white *Lilium regale*, or other white and pink lilies pushing up through a planting of lush, old garden roses, for example, make for a striking contrast, both in habit of growth and flower form.

Pleasing pastels This wall provides a very pleasing backdrop to the climbing rose, the greenery in the center, and the lavender and variegated form of *Iris pallida* in the foreground.

Warm coloring *Rosa* 'Armada' is a vigorous, hardy, spreading shrub rose with clusters of fragrant, semidouble blooms followed by rounded orange hips and is a good hedging plant.

Abundance of flower *Rosa* 'Princess Alice', a vigorous, repeat-flowering rose, produces large clusters of up to 20 golden-yellow blooms well into fall.

Roses with other shrubs

Both shrub and species roses combine well with other shrubs, as long as they receive enough sunlight. They provide abundant, beautiful, often fragrant flowers to set against the foliage of other spring-flowering shrubs, sometimes right through the summer. Many such roses have almost evergreen foliage and colored hips in the fall (see "Ornamental hips or thorns," p.150). Smaller shrub roses as well as the Gallicas, most of the Damasks, the Portland roses, and many modern cultivars of similar stature make an excellent ornamental foreground to any planting of shrubs.

Roses that have long, questing branches, such as the freely flowering 'Sea Foam' or 'Complicata', with its deep pink blooms, may scramble through and enliven a drab, evergreen shrub. Ramblers may adorn a tree's foliage with their blooms or beautify a dead tree.

The soft colors of old roses are particularly attractive when planted with subshrubs that combine gray-green leaves with blue flowers, such as the free-flowering *Caryopteris* x *clandonensis*, the ethereal fronds of *Perovskia atriplicifolia*, certain hebes, and most lavenders.

Underplanting a rosebed

The display in a rosebed may be enhanced and extended beyond the rose-flowering season by growing low, shallow-rooted plants between the roses. A wide range of plants may clothe the ground and provide the roses with a background of contrasting color, texture, and form. Violets (*Viola*) are a favorite choice: the white, soft blue, and mauve cultivars complement roses well. All such groundcover plants make mulching difficult, however. Be careful not to step on the groundcover planting when spraying the roses in a particularly wide bed.

When planting between roses, take account of the eventual heights of the various companion plants, and place them so that they will not obscure each other or the roses when mature.

The yellow-green of *Alchemilla mollis*, pink and white heads of *Armeria maritima*, and spreading, hardy geraniums also make a fine display under roses. Spring bulbs brighten up bare rosebeds early in the year: try planting blue or white *Chionodoxa*, daffodils, snowdrops (*Galanthus*), and white, starry *Tulipa turkestanica* to create a bright patchwork of color. Their only drawback is their dying foliage, which looks messy until it is removed and may make it difficult to maintain the bed for the roses.

Many fragrant, evergreen herbs are good companions for roses: use lavender cotton (*Santolina chamaecyparissus*), various thymes (*Thymus*), or sages (*Salvia*)—either the culinary kind or any that have attractive, variegated leaves. Roses are always attractive when they are contrasted with the silver foliage of perennial plants such as the fern-leaved *Artemisia ludoviciana* and *A. frigida*, or the gray, woolly leaved, mat-forming *Stachys byzantina*.

Terraces

On a steep hillside, terraces may be used to transform a difficult site into a striking showcase for roses. They provide areas sufficiently level for planting and retain moisture that the roses need. The terrace walls look best if made of weathered brick or mellow stone. Bush roses may be grown in the terrace beds, and ramblers or groundcover roses planted to tumble over the retaining walls, creating curtains of bloom.

Smaller terraced beds are ideal, too, for growing miniature roses. It is much easier to savor the beauty and scent of their neat individual flowers if they are raised some way above ground level. Each bed for miniature roses should be approximately 1½–2ft (45–60cm) wide. Place miniature standards along the top bed of the terrace to draw the eye and use some of the smaller and more dainty groundcover roses to tumble over the walls. Where winter temperatures fall to −10°F (−25°C), roses in terrace beds will probably not survive.

Specimen planting

A large shrub rose on its own makes a handsome specimen plant, perhaps in a lawn or to mark a focal point in a garden, as long as it is an outstanding rose of its type; any defects in a specimen are immediately obvious. Used in this way, weeping standard roses can be especially striking. These are formed by grafting rambler cultivars onto a 5ft or 6ft (1.5m or 2m) stem, so that their long, flexible shoots, laden with blossom in the summer, hang down all around, right to the ground. They usually flower for a limited period, unless a standard grafted from a remontant, groundcover rose is chosen.

Climbing roses grown as standards may provide a profusion of blooms throughout the entire summer, but their stiff growth does not produce the same dramatic waterfall effect as weeping standards.

Many of the larger shrub roses, with their graceful, arching habit, almost evergreen foliage, and abundant flowers, are natural choices for planting as specimens in large yards. 'Nevada', for example, which can reach 6 × 6ft (2 × 2m) or even more, is smothered with large, cream blooms in early summer, and again in late summer. Other roses, particularly species roses and their hybrids, such as 'Frühlingsgold', have no second blooming.

For a small yard where space for flowering plants is limited, use remontant roses that earn their space by blooming all summer and well into the fall, such as the strongly scented 'Frau Dagmar Hartopp'. Smaller shrub roses, such as 'Chinatown', which has masses of gold blooms tinged with pink, and 'Sally Holmes', with large, white flowers clustered above the foliage, are not quite large enough to justify being planted on their own, but are very handsome if planted in specimen groups of three.

Walls, arbors, and pergolas

Most ramblers and climbing species roses are very vigorous and produce an exuberance of bloom in midsummer. They may clothe structures such as arbors, walls, and fences, disguise unsightly features, or give height to the summer display in the landscape. Be sure to choose a rose with an eventual height that will cover the intended area well without outgrowing it.

Ramblers and climbing roses may be trained on a range of commercially available plastic-coated metal bowers, tunnels, arches, and tripod pillars. Although metal supports may not look so attractive initially as ones made from rustic poles, they have a much longer life and are soon concealed once the roses trained on them become well established. Rustic arches, even if treated, eventually rot at soil level.

Other climbing plants, such as clematis, or honeysuckle may be planted to grow through the rose, to complement the rose blooms. Those with blue flowers are particularly effective. Some of the more vigorous shrub roses, particularly Bourbons, also make excellent short climbers for a pillar or small wall.

Ramblers

Ramblers have more flexible shoots than climbers and are easier to train along complex structures, such as pergolas, arches, and trellises. When grown against walls, however, their mass of shoots may become mildewed as a result of the poor air circulation. To cover a long pergola, use one of the vigorous, small-flowered, white ramblers such as 'Trier' or 'Seagull', but remember that they can grow to 30ft (10m) or more and will overwhelm a small structure.

For a picturesque effect, try training roses along chains or ropes that are suspended between uprights to create great swags of bloom.

Climbers

The stiffer shoots of climbing roses are easier to prune than those of ramblers and happily grace walls and fences. Many of the less robust modern climbers may be grown on pillars or as freestanding shrubs with great effect. Pink 'Aloha' is beautifully scented but is too stiff and upright in habit for an arch, although it would be suitable for the pillars of a tall pergola. The Bourbon rose 'Zéphirine Drouhin', which has pink flowers and repeats well, is a favorite for growing on arches and pergolas, because it is the only currently available climber that is both thornless and fragrant. It is, however, prone to mildew.

Rose hedges and screens

Roses may, if they are carefully chosen, provide some of the most colorful and attractive plants for an informal hedge or screen. A few, for example, *R. rugosa* and its hybrids, may be shaped to some extent by gentle clipping in winter to make dense hedges while maintaining the natural outline of the shrub. No rose is fully evergreen, so few provide a screen that gives complete privacy all year, although the thorns make the hedge virtually impenetrable. For further details, see HEDGES AND SCREENS, pp.82–85.

The Hybrid Musk roses, such as the apricot 'Buff Beauty', grow into a thick, thorny screen up to 6ft (2m) in height covered in fragrant flowers all summer long—if their natural unpredictability of growth is curbed by training on horizontal wires or chain-link fencing. If a rose hedge is to line a path, use upright cultivars, because those of unpredictable growth may impede the pathway.

For a small yard, a hedge of tall Floribunda roses is preferable. These are generally upright plants with little spread and, if planted in two staggered rows (see *Planting Distances for a Rose Hedge*, p.157), cultivars such as the apricot-yellow ANNE HARKNESS ('Harkarame') rapidly form a pretty screen about 1¼ft (0.3m) tall. Some shorter-growing old garden roses, such as 'Charles de Mills', have attractive foliage and form hedges of similar height but flower only once. Their vulnerability to mildew is, however, increased by close planting.

A delightful way of dividing one part of the home landscape from another is to train climbing roses or ramblers on decorative screens formed by constructing open, wooden frameworks of the desired height. Commercially produced wooden and plastic trellis is available, but make sure that it is sturdy, since it has to support a considerable weight and last for years.

Roses in containers

Roses are invaluable for their summer color and fragrance in patio gardens where the surface is mostly paved and there are few or no beds. Containers of many kinds, including hanging baskets, are suitable as long as they are in a position that receives sun for at least half the day (see also CONTAINER GARDENING, pp.304–335). Select bushy and compact modern cultivars (see CONTAINER GARDENING, p.315)—leggy roses with bare stems at the base look unsightly. If grouping roses in a container, ensure that it is large enough for the plants to be spaced out to allow for future growth, and make sure not to underestimate how much room they will need.

Even quite vigorous climbers may, given the support of a wall, be grown in tubs or half-barrels. They should be planted and trained as other climbing roses but because the nutrients in the containers will be quickly exhausted (and the roses difficult to repot), they will require regular feeding.

Traditional companions The combination of a climbing or rambling rose on a pergola or rose arch, with a clematis weaving through it is a tried and tested way of bringing a romantic, old-fashioned look to the garden.

Groundcover roses

Low-growing roses that readily spread along the ground to form a dense and flower-filled carpet of color for long periods in the summer and fall can be very attractive groundcover. They can be used to disguise an unsightly feature such as a utility meter or to spread down a steep bank that is difficult to plant or maintain satisfactorily. They serve as a lush edging at the front of shrub beds or borders, where they provide long-lasting color.

Choosing groundcover roses

Roses have long been used as groundcovers. Historically cultivars derived from two European species —the Ayrshire rose (*Rosa arvensis*) and *R. sempervirens*—were used for this purpose, as were derivatives of the Chinese *R. wichurana*. Many of these were rambler roses; however, although they are useful for covering large areas of unused ground, they are rarely dense enough to suppress weeds.

Plenty of attention has been given to developing groundcover roses in recent years, and many of the cultivars now grown can be planted to provide masses of color on the grounds of public parks, college campuses, and office buildings. Introductions,

such as the disease-resistant FLOWER CARPET ('Heidetraum')—a small, spreading shrub with large clusters of deep pink, semidouble blooms over a long season—have proven very successful for this purpose; there are numerous variants available in different colors, such as FLOWER CARPET GOLD ('Noalesa') and FLOWER CARPET WHITE ('Noaschnee'). Additionally, there are several other roses being used successfully as groundcovers. They include double white-flowered KENT ('Poulcov'), rich apricot SUSSEX ('Poulowe'), and HAMPSHIRE ('Korhamp'), which has single bright scarlet blooms.

Newer ramblers such as PHEASANT ('Kordapt') and GROUSE ('Korimro'), which both have small, pink flowers and glossy foliage, are

excellent groundcover roses but their vigor makes them unsuitable for small yards. They grow naturally along the ground, rooting as they go, covering the soil very closely. They do, however, need strict control to stop them from spreading too far.

If you have a sunken rose garden with fairly low walls, roses such as 'Nozomi' or 'Raubritter' are good choices for planting along the top. They have the right kind of low, spreading growth to form a waterfall of flowers over the walls.

Cultivation

Groundcover roses require the same basic treatment as other roses in the garden. However you should not expect roses to suppress weeds as effectively as groundcover plants, such as pachysandra or the ornamental ivies that naturally form dense mats and outcompete just about everything in their path. It is therefore important to clear and clean the site of any annual or perennial weeds where the roses are to be grown and to mulch the area after planting. This will minimize the need to battle the thorns when weeding the area as the roses establish and grow.

If you are planting a large area of roses as groundcover, clear the ground of all perennial weeds, enrich the soil with compost or manure, then spread layers of newspaper over the surface, plant the roses through the paper, and cover the paper with bark mulch. This will minimize future maintenance without preventing rain from penetrating the soil.

ROSES FOR GROUNDCOVER

Rosa SNOW CARPET ('Maccarpe')

Rosa HAMPSHIRE ('Korhamp')

Rosa KENT ('Poulcov')

Rosa SURREY ('Korlanum') *Rosa* 'Nozomi' *Rosa* LAURA ASHLEY ('Chewharla')

PEGGING DOWN ROSES

This technique is an effective but time-consuming method of increasing flower production on Bourbon and Hybrid Perpetual roses that tend to send up long, ungainly shoots with flowers only at the tips. Rather than pruning the shoots in late summer or fall, bend them over gently, being very careful not to snap them. Peg the shoots firmly into the ground. Alternatively, tie the tips to pegs in the ground, to

wires strung between pegs, or to a low wire frame placed around the plant. Prune sideshoots on the pegged shoot to 4–6in (10–15cm).

This has much the same effect as horizontally training the shoots of climbing and rambler roses (see p.164) and produces an arching mound covered with a large number of flowering sideshoots to enjoy in the following season.

Select long, nonflowering shoots and prune the soft tips. Gently bend each shoot over and fasten it to the soil with sturdy wire hoops (see inset).

A carpet of blooms
This groundcover rose (SURREY) effectively masks an expanse of bare earth with a succession of attractive double flowers from summer to fall.

Some vigorous climbing roses also provide excellent groundcover when grown and pegged down horizontally rather than vertically. 'Adelaide d'Orleans', 'Felicite Perpetue', 'Max Graf', 'New Dawn', 'Paulii Rosea', and 'Raubritter' are old favorites suitable for growing in this way.

Pruning

The majority of groundcover roses are low-growing, spreading, modern shrub roses, so renewal-prune them as for shrub roses (see p.162). Some—mostly those related to the rambler *Rosa wichurana*—creep over the ground. Prune these only to stop them from spreading past the available space (see below).

Renewal pruning a groundcover rose
Prune shoots to well within the intended area of spread, cutting to an upward-facing bud.

PLANTER'S GUIDE TO ROSES

FRAGRANT FLOWERS
Rosa ALEC'S RED ('Cored') †
Rosa 'Arthur Bell' †
Rosa x *centifolia* cultivars
Rosa 'Climbing Etoile de Hollande'
Rosa 'Compassion' †
Rosa DOUBLE DELIGHT ('Andeli') †
Rosa FRAGRANT CLOUD ('Tanellis') †
Rosa GERTRUDE JEKYLL ('Ausbord') †
Rosa 'Korresia' †
Rosa L'AIMANT ('Harzola')
Rosa 'Madame Hardy' †
Rosa 'Madame Isaac Pereire' †
Rosa MARGARET MERRIL ('Harkuly') †
Rosa NEW ZEALAND ('Macgenev')
Rosa PERCEPTION ('Harzippee')
Rosa 'Prima Ballerina' †
Rosa 'Rose de Resht'
Rosa ROSEMARY HARKNESS ('Harrowbond') †
Rosa 'Roseraie de l'Haÿ' †
Rosa SCEPTER'D ISLE ('Ausland') †
Rosa 'Wendy Cussons'

DECORATIVE HIPS
Rosa 'Fru Dagmar Hastrup'
Rosa 'Geranium'
Rosa glauca †
Rosa rugosa 'Charles Albanel' †
R. rugosa 'Jens Munk' †
Rosa 'Scabrosa'
Rosa 'Sealing Wax'

MIXED FLOWER BORDERS
Front of border
Rosa AVON ('Poulmulti')
Rosa BABY LOVE ('Scrivluv')
Rosa 'Champlain'
Rosa 'Henry Hudson' †
Rosa KENT ('Poulcov') †
Rosa 'Morden Amorette'
Rosa PRINCESS OF WALES ('Hardinkum')
Rosa 'The Fairy' †
Rosa THE TIMES ROSE ('Korpeahn') †
Rosa 'Winnipeg Parks'

Middle ground
Rosa ANNA LIVIA ('Kormetter')
Rosa 'Ballerina' †
Rosa BETTY HARKNESS ('Harette')
Rosa BONICA ('Meidomonac') †
Rosa 'Buff Beauty' †
Rosa 'Cuthbert Grant'
Rosa ESCAPADE ('Harpade') †
Rosa 'David Thompson'
Rosa gallica 'Versicolor' †
Rosa HERITAGE ('Ausblush')
Rosa JACQUELINE DU PRÉ ('Harwanna') †
Rosa MARJORIE FAIR ('Harhero') †
Rosa 'Morden Ruby'
Rosa 'Penelope' †

Middle to rear
Rosa 'Captain Samuel Holland'
Rosa 'Cornelia'
Rosa 'Fantin-Latour' †
Rosa 'Golden Wings'
Rosa 'Louis Jolliet'
Rosa GRAHAM THOMAS ('Ausmas') †
Rosa 'Marie Victorin'
Rosa 'Roseraie de l'Haÿ' †
Rosa 'Prairie Joy'

SOUTH- OR WEST-FACING WALLS
Rosa ALTISSIMO ('Delmur')
Rosa ANTIQUE ('Antike')
Rosa BREATH OF LIFE ('Harquanne') †
Rosa CLAIR MATIN ('Meimont')
Rosa 'Compassion' †
Rosa CRIMSON CASCADE ('Fryclimbdown')
Rosa 'Danse du Feu' †
Rosa 'Dreaming Spires'
Rosa DUBLIN BAY ('Macdub') †
Rosa GOOD AS GOLD ('Chewsunbeam')
Rosa HIGH HOPES ('Haryup') †
Rosa 'Madame Alfred Carrière' †
Rosa PENNY LANE ('Hardwell') †
Rosa SUMMER WINE ('Korizont') †
Rosa 'White Cockade'

NORTH- OR EAST-FACING WALLS
Rosa 'Albéric Barbier' †
Rosa ARMADA ('Haruseful') †
Rosa 'Chinatown'
Rosa 'Cornelia'
Rosa 'Compassion' †
Rosa 'Dortmund' †
Rosa 'Morning Jewel'
Rosa 'New Dawn' †
Rosa 'Penelope' †
Rosa 'Prosperity'

ATTRACTIVE FOLIAGE
Rosa fedtschenkoana
Rosa glauca †
Rosa gymnocarpa var. *willmottiae*
Rosa nitida
Rosa primula †
Rosa sericea subsp. *omeiensis* f. *pteracantha*
Rosa virginiana

SPECIMEN SHRUB ROSES
Rosa 'Cerise Bouquet'
Rosa 'Complicata' †
Rosa 'Felicia' †
Rosa 'Fritz Nobis'
Rosa 'Marguerite Hilling' †
Rosa 'Nevada' †
Rosa 'Scabrosa'
Rosa xanthina 'Canary Bird' †

ARCHES, PILLARS, AND PERGOLAS
Rosa 'Albéric Barbier' †
Rosa 'Albertine' †
Rosa 'Alister Stella Gray'
Rosa 'Aloha'
Rosa 'Bantry Bay'
Rosa BRIDGE OF SIGHS ('Harglowing') †
Rosa CITY GIRL ('Harzorba')
Rosa 'Climbing Cécile Brünner'
Rosa 'Compassion' †
Rosa 'Dortmund' †
Rosa 'Dreaming Spires'
Rosa 'Easlea's Golden Rambler'
Rosa 'Emily Gray'
Rosa 'Félicité Perpétue' †
Rosa 'François Juranville'
Rosa 'Golden Showers' †
Rosa 'Goldfinch'
Rosa 'John Davis'
Rosa 'Leverkusen'
Rosa 'Madame Grégoire Staechelin' †
Rosa 'Maigold' †

Rosa 'Phyllis Bide'
Rosa ROSALIE CORAL ('Chewallop')
Rosa 'Sander's White Rambler'
Rosa 'Sympathie' †
Rosa 'Veilchenblau' †
Rosa WARM WELCOME ('Chewizz')

ROSES TO GROW UP TREES
Rosa 'Bobbie James'
Rosa 'Blush Rambler'
Rosa 'Emily Gray'
Rosa filipes 'Kiftsgate' †
Rosa mulliganii
Rosa 'Paul's Himalayan Musk'
Rosa 'Rambling Rector'
Rosa 'Seagull'
Rosa soulieanaw
Rosa 'Treasure Trove'

GROUNDCOVER ROSES
Rosa BLENHEIM ('Tanmurse') †
Rosa BROADLANDS ('Tanmirsch') †
Rosa DOUCEUR NORMANDE ('Meipopul') †
Rosa ESSEX ('Poulnoz') †
Rosa EYEOPENER ('Interop') †
Rosa FIONA ('Meibeluxen') †
Rosa GLENSHANE ('Dicvood') †
Rosa GROUSE2000 ('Korteilhab') †
Rosa GWENT ('Poulurt') †
Rosa HAMPSHIRE ('Korhamp') †
Rosa LAURA ASHLEY ('Chewharla') †
Rosa LOVELY FAIRY ('Spevu') †
Rosa MAGIC CARPET ('Jaclover') †
Rosa 'Morden Cardinette' †
Rosa 'Nozomi' †
Rosa OUR MOLLY ('Dicreason') †
Rosa OXFORDSHIRE ('Korfullwind') †
Rosa PARTRIDGE ('Korweirim') †
Rosa PATHFINDER ('Chewpobey') †
Rosa PHEASANT ('Kordapt') †
Rosa RED BLANKET ('Intercell') †
Rosa ROSY CUSHION ('Interall') †
Rosa 'Simon Frazer' †
Rosa SNOW CARPET ('Maccarpe') †
Rosa SWANY ('Meiburenac')

Key
† moderate or good disease-resistance

Rosa ROSEMARY HARKNESS ('Harrowbond')

Soil preparation and planting

Growing roses in the garden is not difficult if their basic needs are satisfied. They are relatively long-lived flowering plants, so it is worth investing time and effort in choosing a suitable site, properly preparing the soil, selecting cultivars appropriate to the conditions, and planting the roses correctly.

Site and exposure

All roses need a site that is open to the sun and sheltered from strong winds, with good air circulation and fertile soil. They do not thrive in deep shade, under trees, if crowded by deep-rooted plants, or in excessively dry or waterlogged soil. Most sites may be improved to meet these needs—for example, by erecting windbreaks or by draining heavy, wet soil (see SOILS AND FERTILIZERS, "Improving drainage," p.623). Planting roses in an appropriate soil mix in raised beds or containers may solve the problem of unsuitable soil.

Evaluate the site carefully before choosing a cultivar: the enormous variety of the rose family provides plants that tolerate a range of conditions. Most modern roses do not flourish in very alkaline soil, but almost all the old garden roses grow well in alkaline conditions

if given large quantities of organic matter when being planted and mulched. *Rosa rugosa* and *R. pimpinellifolia* groups do well in sandy soil. These are generalizations; even among modern roses there may be great differences between cultivars. For example, in poor soil, 'Gold Medal' and 'Maid of Honor' suffer, but 'Elina', 'Crimson Glory', and others thrive if given extra nutrients and water. Certain rootstocks may help in some circumstances: for example, *R. multiflora* tolerates and often grows well in heavy, cold soil.

Soil quality

Roses grow in most types of soil, but prefer slightly acidic conditions, about pH 6.5. A water-retentive yet well-drained soil is best of all. Always clear weeds when preparing the soil so that the young roses will not have to compete with them for light, moisture, and nutrients.

Improving the soil

The drainage of clay soil, water-retentiveness of light, sandy soil, and pH level of alkaline soil may be improved by incorporating plenty of organic matter. Excavate very shallow topsoil to about 24in (60cm) when planting, and replace some of the subsoil with extra organic

matter. For further information on how to influence the soil acidity, and on general soil preparation, see "Soil cultivation," pp.618–621. If possible, prepare the soil approximately three months before planting to allow it to settle.

Choosing roses

Where and how you purchase roses will depend to some extent on the particular cultivars that you wish to purchase. Many old roses are obtainable only from specialty nurseries, by mail order if they are not situated locally. Bear in mind that catalog photographs may not always accurately represent the color of the flower, nor is it possible to assess the quality of the plant before it arrives, although with a reputable nursery this should not be a problem. Beware of special "bargains," often advertised in mass mailings, that offer bedding or hedging roses cheaply, as the plants may be of poor quality.

Nurseries in North America use a variety of rose species as rootstocks, depending on the climate of the region where the mature plants will be grown. Rootstocks may be purchased by those wishing to bud their own roses (see also "Hybridizing," pp.168–169).

Bare-root roses

Mail-order suppliers and garden centers sell roses bare-root; local retailers usually sell them in sleeves or boxes filled with peat. The bare-root roses are in a semidormant or dormant state and their roots are essentially clean of soil. Provided that they have not dried out in transit and are planted as soon as possible after arrival, they should establish satisfactorily.

When buying a bare-root rose in a store, examine it carefully. If the environment in which the rose has been kept is too warm, the rose either dries out or starts growing prematurely, producing blanched, thin shoots that usually die after planting. Do not purchase any roses that display such symptoms.

Container-grown roses

Roses grown in containers may be planted at any time, except during periods of prolonged drought or when the ground is frozen. Many garden centers and suppliers trim the roots of unsold bare-root roses and pot them into containers for convenience, so before buying a rose in a container, check that it has not been recently potted by holding the plant by its main shoot and gently shaking it. If the rose is not firmly rooted and moves around in the soil mix, it probably has been in its container only a short time. However these roses may be acceptable provided that they are in general good health and do not have spindly, weak growth. Treat them as bare-root roses where storage and planting are concerned. If any roots are growing through the drainage holes in the container, tap the plant out of its pot and check that its roots are not thickly coiled around the root ball—a sign that the rose is potbound and has been in the container for too long.

Selecting a healthy rose

Whether bare-root or container-grown, the plant should have at least two or three strong, firm main canes and a healthy network of roots in good proportion to the top growth. Any foliage on container-grown roses should be vigorous, abundant, and free of pests and diseases. If buying a climbing rose, check that the shoots are healthy and at least 12in (30cm) long. Choose a standard rose with a balanced head because it is likely to be viewed from all sides; a straight stem is best, although a slightly crooked stem is acceptable.

SELECTING HEALTHY ROSES

A bare-root bush rose
Good example

A container-grown rose
Good example

A standard rose
Good example

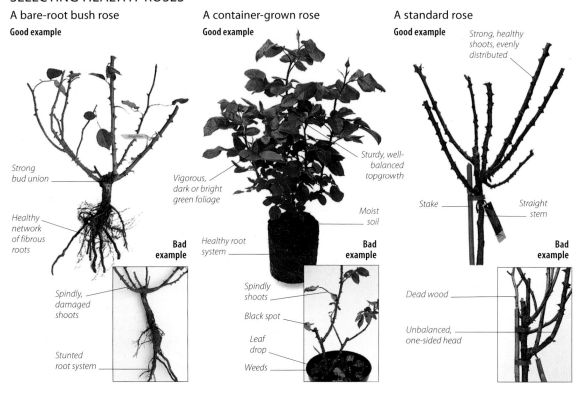

Strong bud union

Healthy network of fibrous roots

Bad example

Spindly, damaged shoots

Stunted root system

Vigorous, dark or bright green foliage

Healthy root system

Bad example

Spindly shoots

Black spot

Leaf drop

Weeds

Strong, healthy shoots, evenly distributed

Sturdy, well-balanced topgrowth

Moist soil

Stake

Straight stem

Bad example

Dead wood

Unbalanced, one-sided head

PLANTING DISTANCES FOR A ROSE HEDGE

Tall hedging roses
Plant the roses in a line 3–4ft (1–1.2 m) apart, so that, when mature, the branches intermingle to form a screen.

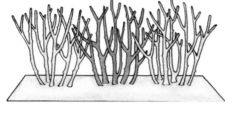

Modern bush roses
For a denser hedge, plant roses in a staggered formation in 2 rows, 18–24in (45–60cm) apart.

Preparing to plant

Following a few simple principles at the planting stage, such as observing correct planting distances and depths, handling the roots carefully, and providing proper support where necessary, avoids problems with routine care later on. Delay planting for a few days if the ground is frozen, too wet, or too dry for roots to adjust easily to the soil.

When to plant bare-root roses

Bare-root roses are best planted just before or at the beginning of their dormant period, in fall or early winter, to lessen the shock of transplanting. Early spring may be better in areas that suffer through harsh winters. Plant the roses as soon as possible after purchase. If there is any delay, perhaps because of unsuitable weather, it is best to heel them into a spare garden bed, with the roots buried in a shallow trench (see ORNAMENTAL TREES, *Heeling in*, p.65). Alternatively, store the roses in a cool and frost-free place, and keep the roots moist.

When to plant container-grown roses

These may be planted at any time of the year in suitable weather conditions. Container-grown roses, unlike bare-root roses, may be left outdoors in their containers for three weeks or more while awaiting planting, as long as they are kept properly watered. Even though most roses are quite hardy, do not expose them to prolonged cold, because the roots in the containers may suffer some damage in very cold conditions.

Spacing bedding roses

The growth habit determines the planting distances between bedding roses. A narrow, upright cultivar needs less space for healthy growth than a lax, spreading one and will tolerate closer planting. As a general rule, plant the bushes 18–24in (45–60cm) apart and about 12in (30cm) from the edge of the rose bed.

If underplanting large shrub or species roses, allow more space, about 2½–4ft (75–120cm), depending on their ultimate size and growth habit. Space miniature roses roughly 12in (30cm) apart.

Another factor to consider when spacing your plants is the length of your growing season. Plants grow larger in areas with a longer growing season, so it makes sense to allow for this by spacing your plants farther apart than would be done in an area with a shorter growing season. Generally, the farther north the garden, the closer you need to plant to fill the space adequately.

However, be aware that overly close planting makes mulching, pruning, and other care more difficult, and may create stagnant air conditions, which allow rapid spread of mildew and black spot.

Spacing roses for a hedge

The size and growth habit of the chosen cultivar governs the position of roses in forming a hedge. To gain uniformly dense growth, plant tall hedging roses such as 'Penelope' and 'Golden Wings', which reach 4ft (1.2 m) or more across, in a single line, and modern bush roses such as ALEXANDER ('Harlex') in two rows in a staggered formation.

Replanting roses

Keep in mind that new roses may not thrive if planted at the same site where roses have been growing previously for longer than two years. The new roses often succumb to rose replant disease, a phenomenon whose cause is not fully understood. The roses don't die, but they don't thrive or produce much new growth. If you must plant roses in such a site (for example, if you're replacing a rose or two in an established rose bed), dig a hole at least 18in (45cm) deep by 24in (60cm) across and exchange the soil with some from another part of your yard where roses have not grown for several years.

Planting a bush rose

The first stage in planting a rose is to prepare the plant. If the roots of a bare-root rose look dry, soak the plant in water for an hour or two until thoroughly moist. Place a container-grown rose in a pail of water until the soil mix surface appears moist. If the root ball is wrapped in plastic or burlap, cut away the wrapping carefully. Remove any loose soil mix, gently tease out the roots, and prune any damaged or diseased roots or shoots; on bare-root roses, remove any buds or hips and most remaining leaves.

Make a planting hole that is wide enough to accommodate the roots or root ball, and deep enough so that, when planted, the bud union is at the correct level for your region. The bud union is easily recognizable as a bulge at the base of the shoots. As a general guide, in Zones 4–5, plant so that the union is 1–2in (2.5–5cm) below ground level. Gardeners in Zone 6–7 should position the bud union at soil level, while in Zone 8 the union should be as much as 1in (2.5cm) above the soil surface.

Position the rose in the center of the hole and check that the planting depth is correct. If the roots of a bare-root rose all point in one direction, place the rose close to one side of the hole and fan the roots out as widely as possible. Water and backfill the hole in stages, shaking the rose a little to allow the soil to settle around the roots. Do not compact the wet soil around the rose, especially if the soil is heavy.

HOW TO PLANT A BARE-ROOT BUSH ROSE

1 Remove diseased or damaged growth. Cut out any crossing shoots and thin or straggly stems at the base to produce a balanced shape. Trim any thick roots by about one-third.

2 Dig the planting hole in a prepared bed and fork half a bucketful of compost, mixed with bonemeal or balanced fertilizer, into the bottom of the hole.

3 Place the rose in the center of the hole and spread out the roots evenly. Lay a stake across the hole to check that the bud union will be at the correct depth for the type of rose and your climate zone.

4 In 2 or 3 stages, water the hole and backfill with soil after the water has drained. After planting is complete, mound up soil or mulch temporarily to prevent the plant from drying out.

HOW TO PLANT A CLIMBING ROSE

1 Place the rose in the planting hole, leaning it toward the wall at an angle of about 45° so that the shoots reach the lowest support wire. Place a stake across the hole to check the planting depth.

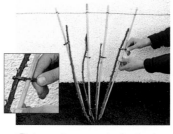

2 Use stakes to guide the shorter shoots toward the wires. Tie all the shoots to the stakes or wires with plastic ties (see inset).

Planting a climbing rose or rambler

Train climbers grown against a wall or fence along horizontal wires that are about 18in (45cm) apart and held in place by eye hooks or strong nails driven into the surface. If the brickwork or masonry of a wall is very hard, drill holes for the vine eyes with a ³⁄₁₆in (4.7mm) bit. Keep the wires 3in (7cm) away from the wall to allow air circulation and discourage disease.

The ground next to a wall is likely to be dry, because it is in a rain shadow and masonry may absorb moisture from the soil. Plant about 18in (45cm) from the wall where the soil is less dry and water from any eaves will not constantly drip on the rose.

Prepare the soil and planting hole, and trim the rose as for bush roses. Position the plant, leaning it toward the wall at 45°, and fan out its roots toward moist ground. If necessary, train the shoots along stakes pushed into the ground, but keep each stake far enough from the roots to avoid damaging them.

After planting, as for a bush rose, attach the shoots to the support wires with string, burlap ties, or

small ready-made plastic straps that are designed for tying in roses. Take care not to tighten the straps too much around the rose's stems—room must be left for the shoots to grow. Check the ties frequently, and loosen and retie them when necessary.

Prune the main shoots of a climber at this stage. For further pruning instructions, see "Climbing roses and ramblers," p.162. Keep the roots thoroughly watered and uncrowded by other plants to help them establish.

Planting a rambler by a tree

Choose a rose that will not overwhelm the host tree while scrambling up it. Plant it on the windward side of the tree so that the rose's young, flexible shoots blow toward and around the tree, rather than away from it. Dig a planting hole at least 3ft (1m) away from the trunk to increase the amount of rain that reaches the roots of the rose. Train all the new shoots toward the tree along sloping stakes, tied at their upper ends to the trunk and inserted just behind the rose. If planting in this way on a boundary, bear in mind that the blooms grow toward, and are visible from, the direction of the strongest sunlight.

Planting a standard rose

Most nurseries bud their standard roses onto stocks that have a tendency to sucker, although a few nurseries are experimenting with better rootstocks. To keep suckering to a minimum, plant the rose no deeper than the recommended depth for your area (see "Planting a bush rose,"

p.157). Deeper planting will increase sucker growth.

A standard rose needs a stake, placed on the side of the prevailing wind, to support it. Paint the whole stake with a preservative that is not toxic to plants, then allow it to dry. Insert the stake very firmly near the center of the planting hole before positioning the rose to avoid damaging the roots, as a result encouraging suckers. Position the rose next to the stake and check that it just reaches the base of the lowest branches; if necessary, adjust the height of the stake. Use a stake or rake handle to make sure the soil mark and soil surface are level.

Fill in the soil and water as for a bush rose. Secure the stem to the stake with two rose ties. These need to incorporate a buffer (such as a figure-eight tie) to prevent the stake from rubbing the stem. Do not tighten the ties fully until the rose has settled in the soil. The ties will need to be loosened at least once during the growing season as the diameter of the stem increases.

HOW TO PLANT A STANDARD ROSE

1 Position the stake in the hole so that the rose stem will be in the center. Drive the stake into the ground and check that the top is just below the head of the rose.

2 Place a stake across the hole to check the planting depth. Use the old soil mark on the stem as a guide and plant at the correct depth. Fill in the hole, then water.

3 Use a rose tie (see inset) just below the head of the rose and another halfway up the stem to attach the rose to the stake. Cut out weak or crossing shoots.

PLANTING ROSES IN CONTAINERS

The container should be at least 12–18in (30–45cm) deep for bush roses or 9–14in (23–35cm) deep for miniatures to allow for root growth. Place a piece of screening over the drainage holes and fill the container with a standard, soil-based potting mix. Plant in the same way, and at the correct depth, as for bush roses (see p.157). Take care to space them correctly.

Routine care

Roses need regular care to produce healthy, vigorous plants that are resistant to pests and diseases. Attention paid to fertilizing, watering, mulching, weeding, and maintenance will be rewarded with a fine display throughout the season.

Fertilizing

Roses are heavy feeders and quickly exhaust even a well-prepared rosebed rich in nutrients. Many essential mineral salts rapidly leach out in the rain, especially from light soil. To flourish, roses need regular fertilizing with a balanced formulation of essential nutrients (nitrogen, phosphates, and potassium) and trace elements. Many commercial rose fertilizers are available. For information on how to deal with particular nutrient deficiencies, see PLANT PROBLEMS, pp.639–673.

After pruning in the spring, and when the soil is moist, sprinkle a small handful or 1–2 oz (25–50 g) of fertilizer around each rose. Hoe or rake it in lightly and evenly, keeping it clear of the stems. Repeat the application about a month after the first bloom flush, before a second crop of bloom develops. Do not apply a general fertilizer once temperatures cool down in fall, because this encourages soft fall growth that may suffer frost damage. A dressing of potassium sulfate, however, applied at a rate of 2oz/sq yd (60g/sq m) in early fall, protects late shoots by helping them mature before the first frost.

Foliar feeding (spraying a liquid fertilizer on the leaves and bypassing the roots) is recommended for producing larger blooms and leaves, especially on exhibition roses.

Roses in containers soon use up the soil mix nutrients. Compensate for this loss by topdressing annually with a balanced fertilizer and foliar fertilizing every week or two in the growing season to maintain vigorous growth.

Watering

Roses need plenty of water for healthy growth, especially if newly planted. Watering too little and too often can be counterproductive, because it encourages roots to grow toward the surface. Give the roses enough water to soak the soil well around their roots instead. Try not to wet the leaves, because some disease organisms spread easily in surface water on foliage.

Roses are deep-rooted plants and can flourish in long, dry summers and near-drought conditions, particularly if they are well established. In such conditions, the flowers may be smaller than usual and may open very quickly. The petals may also be vulnerable to scorching by the sun. In hot, dry climates, avoid wetting the flowers in strong sun, because the blooms may spoil. Water roses in containers every other day, or daily in exceptionally hot and dry weather.

Mulching roses

A 3-in (8-cm) layer of mulch applied in early spring after pruning and feeding helps to smother any weed seeds, and maintain high moisture levels and even temperatures in the soil. Well-rotted horse manure is an

---

SUCKERS AND HOW TO DEAL WITH THEM

Suckers are shoots that grow below the bud union, directly from the rootstock onto which a cultivar has been grafted. They are usually narrower and a much lighter green than those of the cultivar, often with thorns of a different shape or color, and paler green leaves may have seven or more leaflets.

Remove suckering shoots as soon as they appear, to prevent the rootstock from wasting energy on the sucker's growth at the expense of the cultivar. Some rootstocks produce suckers more readily than others, especially if they have been planted at the wrong depth. Root damage, caused by severe frost or accidental nicks from hoes, other

implements, or a stake, may also stimulate the production of suckers.

Pull the sucker to detach it from the rootstock: this removes any dormant buds that may be present at the point where it joins the roots. Do not cut it—as this is the equivalent of pruning it and only encourages more vigorous sucker growth. However, it may sometimes be necessary to cut a sucker if it originates from beneath the rose and if pulling it off would mean damaging or lifting the rose.

Shoots on stems of standard roses are also suckers, because the stem is part of the rootstock. As with other grafted roses, any suckers will look different from the cultivar. Pare them from the stem with a knife.

On standards, pull away any suckers growing from the stem, taking care not to tear the bark.

Removing a sucker from a bush rose

1 Carefully scrape away soil to expose the top of the rootstock. Check that the suspect shoot arises from below the bud union.

2 Using a glove to protect your hand, pull the sucker away from the rootstock. Refill the hole and gently firm the soil.

How suckers grow

Sucker

The sucker (right) grows directly from the rootstock. If only cut back at ground level, it will shoot again and divert further energy from the rose.

---

ideal mulch, providing many of the nutrients that roses need, but if this proves difficult to obtain, shredded leaves are an excellent alternative. For further details, see also SOILS AND FERTILIZERS, "Topdressings and mulches," p.626.

Deadheading

Removing faded flowers stimulates the earliest possible development of new, young shoots and more blooms during the flowering season. Once a rose flower has been pollinated, it starts to fade. If left on the plant, it may delay the production of new shoots below the old flower cluster.

In some roses, a seed pod or hip forms, and this diverts energy from further flower production; remove the dead flowers regularly unless you require the hips for ornamental purposes. In late summer, even if some roses continue to bloom, stop deadheading to avoid encouraging new, soft growth, which would be damaged by the first frosts.

Moving roses

A rose may be moved at almost any age, but the older it is, the greater is the risk that it may resettle badly. The roots of older roses are thick and spread deeply, and also have fewer of the fine feeding roots that are essential for reestablishing the plant. It is not difficult to move roses that are up to three or four years old, but do not risk planting in old rose beds.

BLIND SHOOTS

These are shoots that develop without a terminal flower bud. They divert the plant's energy in the same way as a sucker (see *Suckers and How to Deal with them*, p.159), so prune any out as soon as they appear.

Cut the blind shoot by about a half to an outward-facing bud to encourage it to grow and flower. If no bud is visible, cut back to the main stem.

HOW TO DEADHEAD ROSES

1 **The central bloom** of a spray will fade first and should be cut out to maintain the display.

2 When all flowers have faded, remove the whole spray by cutting back to an emerging bud or fully formed shoot.

Hybrid Tea roses Cut back stems with faded flowers to an outward-facing bud (see inset) or fully formed shoot.

If circumstances allow, move a rose only when it is dormant and always into a well-prepared bed. First loosen the soil by cutting down on all sides with a spade at least 10in (25cm) out from the root ball. Insert a fork well away from the center of the plant and lift it, taking a good ball of soil with it and disturbing the roots as little as possible; in light soil, use a spade because the soil is likely to fall away from the roots. Trim off any coarse roots and wrap the root ball in plastic or burlap to prevent the roots from drying out; water immediately after replanting, and regularly, until the rose is established.

Fall cut-back

Strong winter winds may rock taller roses and loosen their roots, making them vulnerable to cold damage. To help stop this from happening, shorten any overly long shoots in fall.

Winter protection

In temperate climates, roses need protection during a cold winter. In heavy and poorly drained soils, any accumulated water will later freeze. The expansion of the water as it freezes lifts and breaks the roots, and it may damage the bud union—the most vulnerable part of the rose. Mound soil, brought from another part of the 6–8in (15–20cm) above the bud union. Loosely packed leaves or straw, held in place by a staked ring of chicken wire, gives an added measure of protection.

Roses that are hardy between -4 to -10°F (-20 to -23°C) include Centifolias, *Rosa californica*, and *R. wichurana*. At colder temperatures, provide protection, or choose roses that tolerate extreme cold. Hybrid Teas and Floribunda roses tolerate temperatures as low as –20°F (–29°C) for a week or so if soil is mounded over the crown. Pack the crowns of standards with straw or leaves, loosely tied in place with twine. Grow Alba, Damask, and Gallica roses, some species roses, and the various 'Morden' series hybrids in areas where the temperatures

fall to -22°F (-30°C). A few roses, such as *R. virginiana*, *R. blanda*, *R. canina*, *R. glauca*, and *R. rugosa*, survive cold as severe as -35°F (-37°C). For full instructions on protecting roses, see FROST AND WIND PROTECTION, pp.612–613.

Pests and diseases

Aphids (p.654), black spot (see "Fungal leaf spots," p.660), powdery mildew (p.667), rose dieback (p.668), and rusts (p.668) are common problems. Inspect regularly and use preventive measures whenever possible.

CUTTING BACK IN THE FALL

Before (left)
In mid- to late fall, cut back Hybrid Tea, Grandiflora, and Floribunda roses to avoid damage from wind-rock.

After (below)
Reduce the entire bush by one third to one half of its height, cutting all shoots above a bud.

Pruning and training

The purpose of pruning is to speed up the natural process of new, vigorous, disease-free shoots developing to replace the old, weakened ones, and so produce an attractive shape and the optimal display of blooms. Training a plant on supports stimulates the production of flowering sideshoots and directs new growth into the given space. The severity of pruning depends on the rose type; certain principles of pruning, however, apply to all roses.

Basic principles of pruning roses

A pair of sharp, high-quality pruners is essential; loppers and a fine-toothed pruning saw are also useful for removing gnarled, woody stumps and thicker shoots. Wear strong, protective gloves for all pruning tasks.

How to prune

Always make a clean, angled cut above a bud that faces in the direction in which the resultant new shoot should develop. This is usually an outward-facing bud, but it may face inward on a lax, sprawling rose if the center of the bush needs filling out. Cut to the appropriate height if a dormant bud is not visible, and cut out any stubs that develop later.

Remove dead and dying shoots, cutting back to disease-free, white pith, even if this means pruning almost to ground level; also cut out crossing growth that might prevent the free circulation of light and air into the center of the plants.

Opinions differ as to whether to prune bush roses further. The Royal National Rose Society in England has been conducting pruning trials to assess the merits of different pruning methods. While the traditional practice is to remove all thin, twiggy growth that seems incapable of producing flowering shoots, the trial results indicate that it may be beneficial, in fact, to leave them on the plant, because they tend to come into leaf early, and thus provide a valuable source of energy to the rose at the beginning of the growing season.

When to prune

Prune roses when they are dormant or semidormant, that is, between leaf drop in fall and when the buds are just beginning to break in the spring. Pruning a rose in active growth is sometimes necessary but severely checks growth. Do not prune in cold conditions because the growth bud below the cut may be damaged and the shoot may die back. Following a very severe winter, cut back cold-damaged shoots in spring to a healthy bud; if the winters are always severe, prune roses in spring, immediately after removing any winter protection material. Conversely, in a climate so warm that the roses flower almost continuously, prune them in the cooler months to induce dormancy and give them an artificial period of rest.

MAKING A PRUNING CUT

Position the thin blade of the pruners just above the bud. Be careful not to make the cut too far from the bud or leave a snag, because disease may enter the stem and cause dieback. If this happens, cut back the shoot as far as is necessary to reach good, healthy wood.

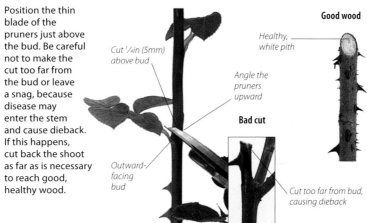

Cut ¼in (5mm) above bud

Angle the pruners upward

Outward-facing bud

Good wood

Healthy, white pith

Bad cut

Cut too far from bud, causing dieback

Pruning roses after planting

Almost all newly planted roses should be pruned hard to encourage the development of vigorous shoot and root systems. Climbing roses are the exception to this rule—give them only a light, cosmetic pruning in the first year to remove any weak, dead, or damaged shoots. Remove any weak, dead, or crossing growth from standard roses. Less severe pruning and regular fertilizing are preferable for roses grown in soils that are deficient in nutrients.

HOW TO PRUNE A HYBRID TEA ROSE

Prune the rose fairly hard, in fall or spring, by trimming off any unproductive growth and then reducing the main shoots to form a strong, balanced framework.

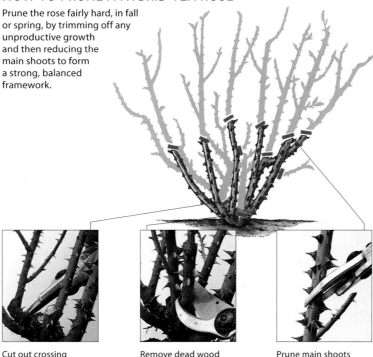

Cut out crossing and congested stems, to create an open-centered plant.

Remove dead wood and any that shows signs of damage or disease.

Prune main shoots to within about 8–10in (20–25cm) of ground level.

PRUNING A NEWLY PLANTED BUSH ROSE

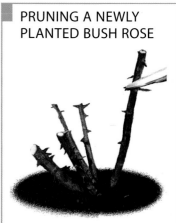

Prune a newly planted bush rose to about 3in (8cm) above ground level. Cut back to outward-facing buds and remove any cold-damaged growth.

Modern garden bush roses

Modern roses flower on new or the current season's growth, so they are pruned fairly severely to stimulate vigorous, new shoots and to produce a good display of blooms.

Hybrid Tea roses and Grandifloras (Large-flowered bush roses)

Remove dead, damaged, and diseased shoots. Twiggy shoots may be left on the plant, if desired (see "How to prune," left). Use long-handled loppers to cut away any stumps from previous prunings that, although healthy, have not subsequently produced any worthwhile new growth.

Thin out any weak or crossing shoots from the center of the bush to leave a well-balanced framework and allow free air circulation. It is not as important to produce a balanced framework with bedding roses planted close together as it is with a specimen rose, which is seen from all sides.

In temperate climates, the main shoots should then be pruned back to between 8–10in (20–25cm). In extremely mild areas, the shoots may be cut down less severely to about 18–24in (45–60cm). To achieve blooms that are of exhibition quality, cut the main shoots back hard to leave only two or three buds.

Floribundas (Cluster-flowered bush roses)

When pruning these types, cut out any unproductive wood as for Hybrid Tea roses (see above). Reduce any sideshoots by about one-third on smaller cultivars and by two-thirds on taller-growing cultivars, such as 'Fred Loads'. Cut back the main shoots to 12–15in (30–38cm), but reduce the shoots of taller cultivars by about one-third of their length. Do not prune them any harder, unless growing the roses for exhibition, because this reduces the number of blooms that will be produced in the following season.

Patio roses

These are smaller versions of the Floribunda roses, and should be pruned in fall or spring following the same principles.

Miniature roses

There are two distinct methods of pruning miniature roses. The simpler of the two is to give them only the minimum of attention: remove shoots that have died back, thin out occasionally the shoots of those cultivars that produce a dense tangle of twiggy growth, and shorten any overly vigorous shoots that may throw the whole plant out of balance.

The second method is to treat the plants as if they were miniature Hybrid Tea or Floribunda roses. Cut back all growth except the strongest shoots, and then shorten these by about one-third. This method is used satisfactorily for cultivars introduced from distant areas that do not adapt easily to their new conditions. Such plants benefit from the extra stimulus of a severe pruning and produce strong, new growth. It can also improve poor shape (see below).

Standard roses

Most standards are formed from Hybrid Tea or Floribunda bush cultivars or from small shrub roses that are budded onto a straight,

HOW TO PRUNE A FLORIBUNDA ROSE

In fall or spring, cut out unproductive growth, and prune the sideshoots. Reduce the main shoots by a proportion suitable to the height of the cultivar.

Remove crossing or congested wood back to the main stem.

Prune out all dead, damaged, or diseased wood to a healthy bud.

Prune main shoots to 12–15in (30–38cm) from ground level.

Reduce sideshoots by one- to two-thirds, cutting to a bud.

unbranched stem, usually 3½–4ft (1.1–1.2m) tall. Prune as for the bush or shrub rose equivalents, cutting back shoots by about one-third, so that they are roughly equal in length. It is especially important with a standard rose to achieve a balanced head that looks pleasing from all sides. If the head is unbalanced, prune the shoots on the thicker side less hard so that they do not produce as much new growth as those on the thinner side.

Weeping standards

These roses are usually formed from cultivars of small-flowered ramblers grafted onto especially tall standard stems of about 5ft (1.5m). The flexible shoots are pendent and require only limited pruning: remove the old, flowered wood when the blooms have faded, leaving growth from the current season intact. Repeat flowering weeping standards need only a light trim in fall and a more severe cutting back in winter.

Shrub, species, and old garden roses

Although these vary enormously in their growth habit, most modern and old garden shrub roses, and all the species roses, flower on wood that is two or more years old. They should be pruned fairly lightly to leave the flowering wood intact. Many flower freely for years without any formal pruning if allowed to develop naturally. It is necessary only to cut out any dead, damaged, diseased, or weak wood to keep the roses really healthy. Despite this, some pruning may help to increase the number and quality of the blooms.

Give mature, remontant shrub roses, including Hybrid Musk and Tea roses, a light renewal pruning each winter by cutting down some of the older, main growths to the base. This encourages the production of vigorous, new basal shoots that will flower the following summer. Over a four-year period of renewal pruning, all the shoots are replaced and, with regular fertilizing, the bushes will remain free-flowering and healthy for many years. Treat nonremontant roses similarly, but prune them immediately after flowering.

Rugosa and China roses may be given similar, annual, renewal pruning to keep them in good health.

Gallica roses

Many of these produce a twiggy tangle of shoots that should be regularly thinned out. After flowering, shorten the sideshoots only and remove any dead or diseased wood. Gently clip Gallica roses used for hedging to maintain a tidy shape. Do not attempt to shape them into a formal hedge

HOW TO RESHAPE A MINIATURE ROSE

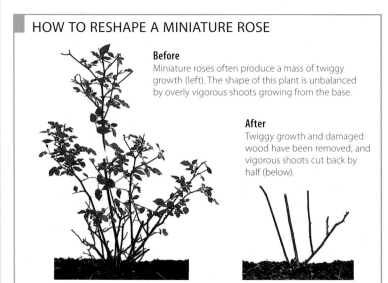

Before
Miniature roses often produce a mass of twiggy growth (left). The shape of this plant is unbalanced by overly vigorous shoots growing from the base.

After
Twiggy growth and damaged wood have been removed, and vigorous shoots cut back by half (below).

HOW TO PRUNE A STANDARD ROSE

Before
In the spring, prune a standard rose to prevent the plant from becoming too top heavy and to retain an evenly shaped head that will be able to flower freely.

After
All dead and damaged wood, and any crossing stems, have been removed to leave healthy shoots. The main shoots have been reduced to 8–10in (20–25cm) and the sideshoots by one-third.

PRUNING A GALLICA ROSE

Throughout the flowering season, thin out the rose to keep it healthy. The annual pruning after flowering involves cutting back sideshoots, unproductive wood, and some older shoots to encourage new growth.

Thin out twiggy growth regularly, and remove spent blooms by cutting back to the main shoot.

On mature roses, cut out up to one-quarter of old main shoots at the base.

Shorten sideshoots, but not the main shoots, by about two-thirds. Cut out any dead, diseased, or weak wood.

PRUNING ALBA, CENTIFOLIA, DAMASK, AND MOSS ROSES

Prune after flowering, cutting back both main shoots and sideshoots. If necessary, prune again in late summer to remove any overlong shoots that have developed.

Reduce main shoots that are old and woody by one-quarter to one-third.

LATE SUMMER

Cut back any overlong, whiplike shoots by about one-third.

Prune sideshoots to about two-thirds of their length.

---

because this would remove many of the sideshoots that will bear flowers the following year.

Species roses

Much of the charm of these roses lies in their arching shoots which, in the second and subsequent years, carry flowers all along their length, often on relatively short sideshoots.

Formative pruning is needed to establish a balanced framework of strong, new growth. Thereafter these roses need only the removal of dead and diseased wood, unless they become too dense or produce few flowers, in which case renewal prune them in the same way as nonremontant shrub roses. Severe pruning encourages strong vegetative growth but produces few, if any, flowers until the second year. If the bush becomes lopsided, reshape it after flowering, and trim back all the overlong shoots.

Alba, Centifolia, Damask, and Moss roses

After flowering, reduce both main shoots and sideshoots. At the end of the summer, cut back any vigorous, overlong shoots that might whip about in the wind and cause wind-rock damage to the roots.

Bourbon and Hybrid Perpetual roses

These are usually remontant, so prune them, and all hybrids derived from *Rosa rugosa*, in early spring as for Hybrid Tea roses (see p.161), but much more lightly.

DISBUDDING ROSES FOR DISPLAY AND EXHIBITION

Grow several bushes of the same cultivar to ensure a wide choice of blooms. Some cultivars are as good in the garden as they are on the show table, provided that they are well looked after and the foliage is kept free from pests and disease. Prune cultivars severely to produce a limited number of strong shoots with only eight or nine blooms a season from which to choose exhibition blooms. Maintain vigorous growth with extra fertilizer. Roses are often disbudded to produce exhibition quality blooms. Remove the newly formed side buds from Hybrid Tea roses so that the main bud develops strongly.

Disbudding the central bloom of Floribunda roses ensures that all the other buds open at roughly the same time.

Blooms should be of average size for the cultivar. Good, healthy foliage is also important.

Hybrid Tea roses

As soon as they are large enough to handle easily, pinch out all the side buds, leaving the main, central bud.

Terminal bud left to develop

Pinch out sidebuds

Floribunda roses

Pinch out the young, central bud of each smaller spray in the cluster for uniform flowering.

Pinch out terminal bud

Sidebuds left to develop

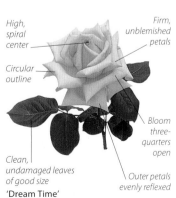

High, spiral center

Firm, unblemished petals

Circular outline

Bloom three-quarters open

Clean, undamaged leaves of good size

Outer petals evenly reflexed

'Dream Time'

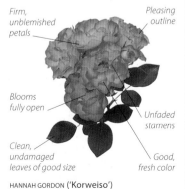

Firm, unblemished petals

Pleasing outline

Blooms fully open

Unfaded stamens

Clean, undamaged leaves of good size

Good, fresh color

HANNAH GORDON ('Korweiso')

Climbing roses and ramblers

These roses require minor pruning but regular annual training. Neither climbing nor rambler roses are self-supporting and, if trained incorrectly, may not flower freely and may become bare at their base. Some bush roses that send out large shoots at awkward angles, such as some Hybrid Musks, may also be trained against walls or other supports.

Climbing roses

In their first year, and in their second unless they have had exceptional growth, do not prune climbing roses except to remove any dead, diseased, or weak growth. Never prune climbing sports of bush roses (roses with the word "climbing" before the cultivar name, such as 'Climbing Shot Silk') in the first two years, because they may revert to the bush form if cut back hard too soon. Prune climbing miniature and Boursault roses in the same way as climbing roses.

Begin training as soon as the new shoots reach the supports; train them sideways along horizontal supports to encourage flowering. Where this is not possible, such as in a narrow area between a door and a window, choose a cultivar that is halfway between a tall shrub and a climbing rose. Many of these flower well from the plant base without special training: examples are 'Golden Showers', 'Joseph's Coat', and some more vigorous Bourbon roses.

Many climbing roses flower well for years with little pruning, except the removal of dead, diseased, or

HOW TO PRUNE AND TRAIN A CLIMBING ROSE

In the first two years after planting, restrict pruning to cutting out unproductive growth. From the third year, prune in fall after flowering.

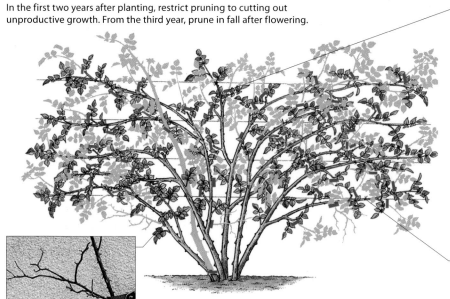

Remove any diseased, dead, or twiggy growth, cutting back to healthy wood or the main shoot.

Reduce the sideshoots by about two-thirds or about 6in (15cm), cutting above an outward-facing bud.

Tie all new shoots into horizontal wires 6–8in (15–20cm) apart: the shoots should not cross each other.

twiggy growth. Prune them in the fall, after flowering. Leave unpruned the strong main shoots unless they are exceeding their allotted space, then shorten them as appropriate. Otherwise simply shorten the sideshoots. Train in all the new season's growth to the supports while it is still flexible.

Occasional renewal pruning may be necessary if the base of a climbing rose becomes very bare. Cut back one or two of the older, main shoots to within 12in (30cm) or so above ground level to encourage vigorous new shoots to develop and replace older growths. Repeat this as required in subsequent years.

Rambler roses

Like climbing roses, ramblers flower satisfactorily for a good many years without any formal pruning. They produce much more growth from the base than most climbers and, if not carefully trained, grow into a tangle of unmanageable shoots. This results in poor air circulation, which encourages the incidence of disease and makes it extremely difficult to spray the plants thoroughly.

Prune ramblers in late summer. In the first two years, restrict pruning to cutting back all the sideshoots by about 3in (7.5cm) to a vigorous shoot; also remove dead or diseased wood. In later years, prune the rose more heavily to

maintain its framework. Untie all the shoots from their supports and, if possible, lay them on the ground. Cut no more than one-quarter to one-third of the oldest, spent shoots to ground level, leaving the new shoots and some older, but still vigorous, shoots for tying in to form a well-balanced framework.

Remove any immature wood from the tips of the main shoots and cut back any sideshoots. Cut back any wayward shoots that are outgrowing the available space or spoiling the overall shape of the rose. Train in the shoots, as close to the horizontal as possible, to encourage flowering on new, short sideshoots that will develop all along the main shoots.

Training on arches, pergolas, pillars, and trees

Climbing roses or ramblers may be trained up pillars, arches, or pergolas. Twist the main shoots around the uprights to encourage flowering shoots to form low down. Carefully train the shoots in the direction of their natural growth before they have matured and hardened. This is vital for climbers that have stiff, semirigid shoots. Tie them in using twine or plastic rose ties; these are easy to undo when pruning or to loosen as the new shoots develop. Once the main shoots reach the top of the support, regularly prune them to keep the rose within bounds.

An excess of overlong sideshoots may spoil the appearance of a pillar rose but a little additional pruning soon remedies this. Cut sideshoots back to three or four buds or by about 6in (15cm) in the spring.

HOW TO PRUNE AND TRAIN A MATURE RAMBLER ROSE

After the first two years, prune in late summer as soon as flowering is over, cutting out any dead, diseased, or weak wood. Then train in the new shoots.

Cut sideshoots down to leave between 2 and 4 healthy buds or shoots.

Cut back any old, spent shoots to ground level, using loppers.

Tie all shoots into the wires as close to the horizontal as possible. Secure any loose wires.

Propagation

Roses can be propagated in three main ways: by taking cuttings, by budding onto a rootstock, or from seed. Taking cuttings is the easiest method but it involves the longest wait: it takes about three years, except for miniature roses, for the new plant to become established. Budding needs rootstocks that have grown on in advance, but usually produces stronger and more vigorous plants. Many species roses (*Rosa glauca*, for example) readily breed true from seed. Cross hybrid roses with other hybrids, or sometimes with species, to produce new cultivars.

Hardwood cuttings

Most roses can be propagated from hardwood cuttings, in particular some cultivars that are related closely to wild species, such as rambler roses. Cuttings taken from miniature roses root so easily and develop so quickly that they are commercially propagated in this way. Hybrid Teas and others of complex parentage do not root as readily and may not be of sufficient size to sell commercially for two or three years, so they are less available on their own roots.

One advantage of roses grown from cuttings is that they do not have a different rootstock and so do not produce suckers. The disadvantages include a loss of vigor with some cultivars (although this may be useful with miniatures), and a tendency toward vigorous but nonflowering growth in the first few years, particularly with species roses.

In many climates, roses from hardwood cuttings are the most reliable, but success in rooting them is variable; it is therefore sensible to take a good number of cuttings to allow for possible failures.

Preparing the cuttings

In early fall, select material for cuttings from the current season's growth. Trim any old flower heads from the chosen shoots and put the shoots into a transparent plastic bag to stop them from drying out. Prepare the cuttings by trimming off their leaves and shortening them to 9in (23cm). Breaking off the thorns will make the cuttings easier to handle. Moisten the base of each cutting, dip it into hormone rooting powder, and shake off the excess.

Take shorter lengths of stem for miniature rose cuttings, which only need to be 2–4in (5–10cm) long.

Preparing the cutting bed

Choose an open site for the cutting bed, preferably one that is sheltered from the midday sun. Loosen the soil, firm, and rake it to produce an even surface.

Inserting the cuttings

Make a series of planting holes, 6in (15cm) deep, with a stake or dibber, and trickle a little coarse sand into the bottom of each one to improve the drainage. Alternatively, dig a narrow, slitlike trench to the same depth and trickle sand along the base. On light, sandy soil, it is sufficient to push a spade vertically into the earth along a center line, working it back and forth to widen the slit.

Insert the cuttings vertically into the holes or trench, leaving about a third of their length above ground. They should be inserted far enough apart so that, once rooted, they may be lifted individually without disturbing adjacent cuttings. Firm and water the soil around the cuttings. In any dry spells that follow, water them again; after frost, which may loosen the roots in the ground, refirm the soil.

Another option is to root hardwood cuttings in deep pots of light, sandy soil. Plunge the pots in soil or sand in a shady outdoor site, and water them as needed. Grow bags or pots in a cold frame or cool greenhouse may be more convenient for miniature rose cuttings.

Development of the cuttings

During the fall a callus should develop at the base of each cutting, from which the roots will be produced in spring. Once rooted, the young plants should develop strongly, but if flower buds form during the summer, remove them so that the plants can concentrate their energy on the production of new, strong, vegetative growth. The following fall, if they are large enough, that is about 9–12in (23–30cm), transplant the young roses to their permanent sites; if they are not yet large enough, leave them to grow for another year.

Semiripe cuttings

Semiripe cuttings may be more successful than hardwood cuttings in areas that are subject to severe winters. In the late summer after flowering, select mature sideshoots that are still green. Take 6in (15cm) lengths, cutting above a bud where the shoot is beginning to turn woody, and trim off the soft tips. Prepare cuttings about 4in (10cm) long, following the same procedure as for hardwood cuttings.

Insert them into deep pots of sandy rooting mix (equal parts peat substitute, or peat, and sand). Cover the pots with plastic bags, or put them in a propagator, to prevent the cuttings from losing moisture. Keep in a cool, frost-free place. In spring, plant out the rooted cuttings in a nursery bed.

HOW TO PROPAGATE ROSES FROM HARDWOOD CUTTINGS

1 Select a healthy, well-ripened shoot of roughly pencil thickness (here, 'Dreaming Spires'), that has flowered in the summer and is about 12–24in (30–60cm) long. Remove it, cutting at an angle, just above an outward-facing bud. Prepare the cuttings by removing the leaves and soft tip wood.

2 Cut into 9in (23cm) lengths, making an angled cut above the top bud and a straight cut below the bottom bud. Dust the base with hormone rooting powder.

3 Make a row of planting holes 6in (15cm) deep and the same distance apart. In heavy soil, put a little coarse sand to a depth of about 1in (2.5cm) in each hole.

4 Insert a cutting into each hole: make sure that it reaches the bottom and that about 6in (15cm) of the cutting is buried. Firm the soil, water, and label the cuttings.

5 A year later, lift each rooted cutting with a hand fork, taking care not to damage the roots. Plant them in a bed or put them in a cold frame to continue growing.

HOW TO BUD-GRAFT A ROSE

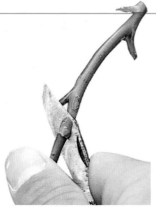

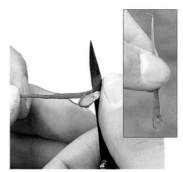

1 Select a flowered shoot about 12in (30cm) long, with 3–4 growth buds. Remove it, making an angled cut above an outward-facing bud on the parent plant.

2 Hold the budwood so that the buds point downward. Insert the knife ¼in (5mm) from a bud. With a scooping action, remove the bud with a "tail" 1in (2.5cm) long.

3 Holding the scion by the tail, peel away the coarse wood from the green bark. Discard the wood. Trim off the tail, to leave a scion about ½in (1cm) long.

4 Use the blunt side of the knife to remove the thorns from the stem of the rootstock, cleaning a section about 1½in (4cm) long.

5 Cutting just deeply enough to pierce the bark, make a T-shaped incision, with the horizontal cut about ¼in (5mm) long and the vertical cut ¾in (2cm) long.

6 Insert the tapered end of the budding knife under the flaps of the T, then ease them outward to reveal the inner, white cambium layer.

7 Hold the scion by its tail and insert it behind the bark flaps of the rootstock, sliding it well down so that the bud is held firmly in place, just below the cross-stroke of the T cut.

8 Using the knife, carefully trim away the surplus tail protruding above the T, following the line of the horizontal cut. Try to do this without damaging the wood beneath the bark. Discard the tail.

9 Attach a rubber binding tie tightly around the grafted area, pinning it on the side opposite the bud. This binds the stock and scion tightly together.

T-BUDDING ONTO A STANDARD ROOTSTOCK

To create a standard rose with a well-balanced head, graft 2 or 3 buds, 3in (8cm) apart and staggered vertically, around the rootstock stem at the desired height—generally 3½–4ft (1.1–1.2m) above ground level. Secure each bud with a rubber binding tie (right). In spring, cut back the stock just above the new shoots that are developing from the grafted buds (far right).

Bud-grafting

The budding process involves uniting plant material taken from two different roses in order to combine the virtues of both. A dormant bud (the scion) from the top growth of one plant, usually chosen for its display, is inserted under the bark and just above the roots of a rootstock, normally a rose species or a specific clone that is selected for its vigor and hardiness. Different rootstocks may be used to suit the soil conditions or climate or to promote the vigorous growth of the scion.

Choosing a suitable rootstock

Many stocks are used to suit varying conditions: the hardy and vigorous *Rosa multiflora* is widely used as a rootstock, particularly where the winters are cold; it is also suitable for use on poor soils although plants budded onto this stock are not long-lived. *R. canina* produces hardy plants and is popular where winters are severe or on heavy soils, but it suckers freely; the crimson climber 'Dr. Huey' (at one time known as 'Shafter' when used as a stock) is more often used where the dormancy period is shorter. The selected clone 'Laxa' has now largely replaced most other commercial stocks—it performs reliably in most soils and climatic conditions, is almost thornless, easy to use for budding, and rarely produces suckers. Any commercial supplier of rootstocks, or a local nursery, should be able to provide information on the best stock to use for local growing conditions.

Stocks may be obtained from wild roses growing in fields or along roadsides, but their quality is unreliable. It is better to use proven rootstocks.

Planting the rootstocks

Plant the rootstocks in fall in a nursery bed, about 12in (30cm) apart and with 30in (75cm) between the rows. For bush roses, the scions are inserted at the point where the shoots and roots join (the "neck"), so for ease of budding, plant the rootstocks at an angle of 45°, with the top of the root just at soil level. Mound soil up to the base of the shoots to keep the bark moist and supple at the point where the scion is to be inserted. Standard rootstocks must be grown to about 6–7ft (2–2.2m), and any buds rubbed off before they develop to create a straight, bare stem.

When to bud-graft

Budding should be carried out from mid- to late summer, preferably in cool, rainy conditions. If the weather is very dry in the months that precede budding, water the rootstocks regularly and thoroughly. This ensures a free flow of sap that prevents the wood from drying out, so it is possible to lift the bark from the wood without bruising the wood underneath. Speed is also important to prevent the wood of both bud and rootstock from drying out before they have been grafted together.

A budding knife, with a single, specially formed blade and a sharp, tapered end (see "Garden knives," p.555) may be used, but an ordinary horticultural knife is also suitable. Any knife used for budding must be kept scrupulously clean and sharp.

Selecting the budwood

Prepare scions from well-ripened shoots that have fat, dormant growth buds in their leaf axils. These shoots are known as the budwood. Cut off the leaves and leaf stalks; alternatively, leave the stalks as "handles" for inserting the buds later. Place the budwood in a plastic bag to prevent it from drying out before it is used.

Preparing the scion

Hold a piece of budwood upside down and, from just above the base of a bud, use the budding knife to scoop out the bud together with a thin tail. This shieldlike piece of bark, about 1in (2.5cm) long, within which the growth bud is contained, is known as the scion. Remove the woody material behind the bud, and shorten the tail so the scion is about ½in (1cm) long. If retained, the wood will prevent the bud from uniting with the rootstock or "taking." The base of the bud should then be visible as a small, circular growth. It is difficult to do this without damaging the bud if the shield has been cut too deeply from the shoot.

Preparing the rootstock

For a bush rose, clear the soil from the rootstock neck, take off the thorns, and wipe the neck clean. Using the blade of the budding knife, make a "T"-shaped cut in the neck, penetrating the bark without cutting into the wood, because this causes damage.

Grafting the bud onto the rootstock

Carefully peel back the cut bark of the rootstock with the blunt side of the knife blade, taking care not to tear the bark or the wood beneath. Gently push the scion into position in the "T" so that the

bud faces up. Trim off any of the tail that may still be visible and, if necessary, the leaf stalk. Use a rubber binding tie to hold the bud securely in place and keep the flaps of bark tightly closed to avoid moisture loss. The tie is easily pinned in place and does not inhibit the growth of the bud because it soon rots away. Inserting two scions, opposite each other on the rootstock, is sometimes recommended to produce balanced shoot growth more rapidly but is seldom practiced commercially except on standard roses.

Cutting back the rootstock

If the scion takes successfully, the bud will quickly swell and will then produce a shoot, generally by the following spring. Once the shoot develops, cut off the growth of the rootstock above the scion. If the shoot needs support, tie it to a stake, but this is not often needed.

Bud-grafting a standard rose

Budding onto a standard rootstock is performed near the top of the stem at the desired height, usually about 3½–4ft (1.1–1.2m); weeping standards are usually budded a little higher, at about 5ft (1.5m). Insert two or three buds around the stem to achieve an evenly balanced head. If using *Rosa canina* rootstocks, insert the buds into equally spaced lateral growths, close to the main stem. It is more usual to place three buds around the main stem of *R. rugosa* stock, staggered vertically.

Layering roses

Any rose that possesses shoots that are long and flexible enough to be bent over and pinned into the ground can be successfully propagated by simple layering.

In late summer after flowering, choose a shoot of healthy, mature wood and trim some of the leaves to create a clear length of stem. Work some potting mix or peat into the ground where the shoot is to be layered and pin the shoot down into the prepared ground to encourage it to root. The next spring, separate the rooted layer from the parent by cutting the shoot just behind the roots, and plant it out into its destined location to continue growing.

Ramblers and climbing roses are ideal for layering, although if they are planted in narrow beds along the base of a wall, there may not be a large enough area of exposed soil to pin down the shoots, particularly if other plants

are growing around the base of the rose. Many shrub roses, such as Damask, Centifolia, Bourbon, and most Alba and species roses, are suitable for layering because they have a lax growth habit and are likely to have more exposed soil around the base into which the selected shoots may be inserted.

Modern shrub roses, such as 'Chinatown', which are in fact very tall-growing Floribunda roses, have fairly stiff shoots, so train these shoots horizontally while they are still young and flexible to prepare for layering. Some groundcover roses lend themselves to this method of propagation. The shoots of some, such as PHEASANT ('Kordapt') or GROUSE ('Korimro'), root naturally into the soil; simply separate them from the parent and plant them out.

The modern Hybrid Tea and other roses found in the majority of gardens are mostly too stiff and upright in their habit of growth for successful layering and should be increased by taking cuttings. Only a few that are

lax, wide-spreading growers, such as 'Europeana', are easily increased by layering.

Propagation by division

If a rose is growing on its own roots, taking rooted suckers is an easy method of propagation. Most roses from nurseries are grafted onto rootstocks, however, so suckers will be from the stock and not the cultivar budded onto it.

Some species grown from seed and other roses grown from cuttings sucker naturally. In the dormant period, detach the rooted suckers or shoots from the parent and plant them out, either in a nursery bed or into permanent sites. Deep planting of budded shrub roses sometimes stimulates the cultivar shoots to produce roots. Treat these as rooted suckers.

Roses that sucker freely such as the cultivars of *Rosa pimpinellifolia*, *R. rugosa* and some Gallica roses are readily propagated in this way.

HOW TO LAYER ROSES

1 Make a 1in (2.5cm) slit on the lower side of a long, ripe, but flexible shoot. Dust the cut with hormone rooting powder and then wedge it open with a match (see inset).

2 Position the shoot in a small depression in prepared soil and pin it down firmly with a wire hoop. Cover it with soil, firm, and tie in the tip of the layered shoot to a short stake.

PROPAGATING ROSES BY DIVISION

1 In late fall or early spring, select a well-developed sucker. Scrape away the soil to expose its base. Sever it from the rootstock, with as many roots as possible.

2 Prepare a hole, wide and deep enough for the roots. Plant the sucker immediately and water and firm the soil (see inset). Trim shoots to 9–12in (23–30cm).

RAISING ROSES FROM SEED

1 Slit open a ripe hip (see inset), taken from the parent plant, with a clean, sharp knife. Take out individual seeds carefully with the back of the knife blade.

2 Place the seeds in a plastic bag of moist peat substitute or peat and keep for 2–3 days at room temperature. Then place in a refrigerator for 3–4 weeks.

3 Sow the seeds singly onto the surface of a sandy potting mix (1 part sand: 1 part peat substitute). Cover with grit, label, and put in a cold frame.

4 When the seedlings have their first pairs of true leaves, prick them out singly into 2in (5cm) pots filled with soil-based potting mix.

Propagating roses from seed

Species roses, unlike cultivars, are self-fertile and can be raised from seed in the same way as other shrubs. Although seeds are not generally available from commercial sources, it is easy to extract them from mature roses. Hybrid roses do not breed true to type from seed so they are usually propagated by bud-grafting (see p.166).

Extracting and sowing seed

In the fall, when the rose hips are swollen and ripe, extract the seeds and stratify them in a refrigerator before sowing (see "How to overcome dormancy," p.629). Stratification—the simulation of natural temperature changes—is necessary for all seeds of species roses.

Sow the rose seeds into flats, cell packs, or individual pots, which should be at least 2½in (6cm) deep. If using a seed flat, place the seeds on the potting mix about 2in (5cm) apart, and cover them to their own depth with sand or grit. Then leave the flat or packs in a cold frame to protect it from mice and other animals. The seed may take up to a year to germinate. Prick out the seedlings into individual containers as soon as the first true rose leaves have formed; the first pair, the seed leaves, are oval, unlike typical rose leaves. Care is needed in handling the seedlings because they are very fragile at this stage in their development.

Grow the young seedlings in the cold frame until they have become established in their pots. Then harden them off by moving them out of the cold frame during the day. Once acclimatized, the seedlings may be kept in the open, and potted on as necessary until large enough to be planted out.

Hybridizing

New rose cultivars are created by hybridizing, a process by which one cultivar or species is cross-pollinated with another and the new seed sown and grown on. The aim is to create a new rose that inherits the best characteristics of both parents.

Selecting the parents

Most roses are of mixed ancestry, so it is impossible to predict the results of hybridization, and the chances of producing a high quality cultivar, with distinct characteristics, are small. Knowledge of the parent roses'

genetic characteristics, in particular their chromosomal number and structure, is important in breeding.

The chromosomes are the parts of plant cells that control the inheritance of characteristics through the genes. Roses may have different chromosome numbers, although the total number per cell in each case is always a multiple of seven. Most of the species roses have 14 (diploid), 28 (tetraploid), 42 (hexaploid), or 56 (octoploid) chromosome numbers. When two roses have been cross-pollinated, equivalent chromosomes from the parents arrange themselves in pairs, which then fuse and count as one in the chromosome number of the new cultivar. Most garden roses are tetraploids and two tetraploids brought together in this fusion

HOW TO HYBRIDIZE ROSES

Preparing the seed parent

1 Select an unblemished bloom (here, 'Sun Flare') that has not fully unfolded its petals and should therefore not yet have been pollinated.

2 Remove the petals, taking off the outer ones first. Work gradually toward the center, taking care not to damage the stigmas as they become exposed.

3 Using tweezers or a small pair of scissors, remove the stamens around the stigmas and all fragments of stamens or petals.

4 Use a magnifying glass to inspect the rose and make sure that no fragments remain. If left they may decay and allow rot fungi to enter the rose hip.

5 Make a paper cone, twisting its point firmly closed (see inset). Holding back the sepals, cover the flower with the cone, and tie securely around the stem.

Alternative step
Place a clean, dry plastic bag over the flower and secure it with a twist tie. The flower is then protected from pollinating insects.

produce another tetraploid rose. A diploid (14) crossed with a tetraploid (28), however, results in 7 + 14 chromosomes, or a total of 21 (triploid) in the new rose. This is not an even number so there are seven chromosomes left without comparable chromosomes with which to pair. Triploids are often sterile and of little use in breeding. Where the chromosome count is known, it is given in the most recent edition of *Modern Roses* (published by the American Rose Society on behalf of the International Registration Authority for Roses). This also gives details of the pedigree of many roses.

Heredity is not the only factor influencing the selection of parent plants. Some hybrid roses make good pollen (male) parents, but poor seed (female) parents, and vice versa. Some are completely infertile and others almost so, and in a rose with a large number of petals, such as a Centifolia, a proportion of these may have taken the place of the stamens, so that little pollen is available for hybridizing. Crossing a nonremontant rose with a remontant one may be a problem if remontancy is one of the desired characteristics—the first generation from such a cross is always nonremontant. At least one more cross is needed before remontancy reappears in the offspring.

This is a simplification of a very complex subject, and there is a good amount of chance involved in rose breeding. However scientific an approach is taken, the result is still unpredictable. As a general rule, choose the healthiest cultivars available as parents, and start with what is perhaps the easiest cross of all, that between two different cultivars of Floribunda roses.

Controlling the growing environment

Except in a frost-free climate, use pot-grown roses in a greenhouse, because this allows greater control of temperature, humidity, insect pests, and diseases, and gives the hips a better chance of ripening properly. Precise record-keeping is essential: after crosses have been made, carefully identify all the flower stems with a dated label on which is written the names of both parent plants, giving the seed parent first, for example, 'Europeana' x 'Showbiz'.

Preparing the seed parent

First select a bloom of the rose you have chosen for the seed parent, at the stage where it is starting to unfold but before insects could have reached the stamens in the center and contaminated them with alien pollen. Carefully remove the petals and the stamens (emasculation), and make sure that no tissue is remaining that could later lead to rot in the hip. Tie a paper cone or plastic bag over the emasculated flower and leave it for one to two days to allow the stigmas to fully mature.

Preparing the pollen parent

Cut the flower that is to be the pollen parent, which should be at about the same stage as the seed parent. Stand the pollen parent in a vase of water and protect it from insects until the anthers release the tiny, orange pollen grains, usually on the day after being cut. The stigmas of the seed parent should begin to exude a sticky secretion, indicating that they are ready to receive the pollen. Pull off the petals from the pollen parent, leaving the anthers intact.

Pollinating the seed parent

Remove the protective covers and brush the stamens of the pollen parent against the stigmas of the seed parent; their sticky secretion helps the pollen adhere to the stigmas. Replace the cover on the pollinated flower and label the stem.

An alternative method is to cut off the pollen parent's anthers, place them in a small, clean container, such as a plastic pill bottle, labeled with the name of the rose, and store it in cool, dry conditions until the released pollen grains are visible in the bottle. Using a fine brush, dust pollen from the box onto the stigmas of the seed parent. If carrying out more than one cross with different roses, make sure that the brush has been thoroughly cleaned between each operation, preferably with rubbing alcohol.

If the cross has not taken successfully, the newly forming hip will shrivel quickly. If it has been successful, the sepals will begin to lift and the hip to swell; once this is evident, remove the protective cone or bag to allow the hip to grow.

The hip will continue to swell; it normally takes about two and a half months to ripen, depending on the climate. As it ripens, the hip changes its color from green to red to yellow or possibly maroon, depending on the individual rose.

Harvesting and sowing

Remove the ripened hip and carefully extract the seeds. Sow and raise the seed (see "Extracting and sowing seed," p.168). Seed resulting from hybridization, however, may be sown fresh without a stratification period.

Selection

The seedlings are likely to flower in the first year—often within a few weeks of germination in a greenhouse—but it is only in the second year that the blooms will be more or less typical of the new hybrid and it is possible to judge whether it should be kept and developed or discarded.

Promising new seedlings can be budded onto rootstocks (see "Bud-grafting," p.166) when they have stems of sufficient thickness, that is about ¼in (5mm). Even experienced hybridists, however, find this stage challenging, because it is often not easy to detect faults until a selection has been grown in trials for several years.

Preparing the pollen parent

6 Select an unblemished bloom that is not yet fully open (here, ELINA). Cut the stem of the flower at an angle just above a bud.

7 Place the chosen flower in water and keep it indoors, free from insects, until it opens fully (usually overnight).

8 When the flower is open and the anthers split, revealing the pollen, gently remove all the petals.

9 The exposed anthers are now ready to release their tiny pollen grains.

Pollinating the seed parent

10 Uncover the seed parent and brush the anthers of the pollinator across its stigmas. The pollen grains will adhere to the sticky stigmas of the seed parent.

11 Replace the protective cone over the seed parent and tie securely. Label the rose with the names of the seed parent and pollen parent, and leave it to ripen.

PERENNIALS

WITH FLOWERS IN EVERY COLOR OF THE RAINBOW, A BREATHTAKING RANGE OF SHAPES AND TEXTURES, AND OFTEN FRAGRANT SCENTS, PERENNIALS RICHLY DESERVE THEIR POPULARITY.

Their diversity makes them suitable for most gardens, while their reliability makes them a lasting source of pleasure. For many people, a traditional herbaceous border is the epitome of garden beauty, but perennials can be equally attractive in mixed borders, interplanted with shrubs, annuals, bulbs, and vegetables, or grown in containers or as groundcover. Foliage ranges from lacy fern fronds to the straplike leaves of crocosmias; and there are flowers to suit all tastes, from delicate *Gypsophila* to sumptuous peonies. Some, like many sedums, are followed by pretty seed heads. Against a more static background of woody plants, perennials provide an almost unlimited, changing planting palette.

Perennials for the garden

Although botanically speaking these plants should be referred to as herbaceous perennials, they are usually known as just "perennials." "Herbaceous" explains the fact that the part above ground dies down each year, while "perennial" refers to the fact that the root system lives for three or more years. A few perennials, such as *Helleborus foetidus*, are evergreen, and so have a valuable winter presence.

Choosing perennials

Most perennials will flower, set seed, and then die back to ground level by fall, going dormant for the winter season. Some retain a woody base, such as *Achillea filipendulina*, or fleshy shoots, such as *Sedum telephium*, while others disappear completely underground. Some perennials, such as *Doronicum orientale*, go completely dormant during the heat of summer, instead of in the cold of winter. Most perennials flower during summer, though some, such as *Liriope muscari* and *Iris unguicularis*, enliven the garden in fall and winter, while *Helleborus orientalis* and *Pulmonaria* welcome in early spring.

More than any other group of plants, perennials have an immense variety of shape, form, color, texture, and scent. Mostly valued for their flowers, many also have attractive foliage—from ribbed, unfurling hosta leaves, or swordlike straps of iris, to transparent tracery of fennel (*Foeniculum vulgare*). Particularly in a small garden, some perennials should have ornamental leaves, to extend the season of interest—the foliage usually outlasting the flowers.

Perennials range in height from the *Acaena* at just 2in (5cm) tall to the statuesque *Helianthus salicifolius*, whose feathered stems reach 8ft (2.5m) or more. Low-growing perennials are ideal for the front of borders or in between shrubs, while tall plants belong at the back of a border to give height and structure to the planting design. Perennials with an attractive structure, such as the African lily (*Agapanthus*) or some grasses, such as *Chionochloa rubra* and *Carex comans* 'Frosted Curls', are good specimen plants in a border or container.

Some perennials, such as many carnations and pinks (*Dianthus*) and highly perfumed lily-of-the-valley (*Convallaria majalis*), are worth growing for their fragrance alone. Carnations and pinks are ideal for raised beds or window boxes, while the ground-covering lily-of-the-valley thrives in shady shrubberies. Other perennials, such as *Sedum spectabile* and many of the daisy and umbel family, such as asters and *Angelica*, bear flowers that attract beneficial insects, such as bees and butterflies.

It is also possible to prolong the season of interest into fall and winter by selecting plants with interesting seed heads and winter silhouettes. Fennels, *Iris sibirica*, and *Achillea* are a few examples of flowers that will surprise you at a time of year when you least expect it. Birds will gain twofold from these seed heads: they enjoy eating the seeds, and benefit from the insects that overwinter in the cavities created by hollow stems and seed heads.

As with all plants, when choosing perennials for a planting plan, make sure that they are appropriate for the growing conditions, such as soil, microclimate, and aspect of the bed or border. Given the correct environment, plants are much more likely to flourish, and require less maintenance than those struggling in an unsuitable position (see also "Site and aspect," p.183).

Herbaceous and mixed borders

Perennials are traditionally used in borders: these are long, rectangular beds, fronted by a lawn or a path and backed by a hedge or wall, either as a single border or as double, facing borders. Popularized in the late 19th century, herbaceous borders were planted only with perennials, in groups or drifts, the shortest plants at the front, grading up with lupines, phlox, and the like, to the taller ones, such as delphiniums, at the rear. Their season of interest was restricted to the summer months, because in many gardens, the borders were but one of many areas of interest, each with a different seasonal highlight.

As gardens reduced in size during the 20th century, and space became more restricted, gardeners were forced to extend the flowering season and plant range of borders. As a result, mixed borders have become increasingly popular; they now contain a variety of plants including bedding plants, shrubs, climbers, and even small flowering trees, as well as perennials.

The advantage of a mixed border is that it can be less labor-intensive than an herbaceous one, because larger areas may be filled with less-demanding woody plants (see "Designing beds and borders," p.174). A successful border requires regular maintenance. Careful staking is needed; otherwise, the perennials may grow long and lanky as they compete for the somewhat reduced light levels caused by the close planting, and the presence of a wall or hedge in the background. Water and nutrient levels also need to be monitored regularly in any such dense planting plan.

Additional chores generated by a mixed

Informal border The stalwart backdrop of dark green yew (*Taxus baccata*) provides a contrasting foil for the informality and diversity of the softly blending perennials used here.

border involve bedding out early bulbs and annuals, followed by dahlias, cannas, and other tender plants, to extend the length of interest into early spring and fall. Plants also need to be deadheaded regularly and kept neat over the longer flowering period.

Island beds

Surrounded by lawn or paving, island beds can be seen and accessed from all sides, so the planting design should be effective from all viewpoints. As with borders, beds that are dedicated to herbaceous plants are at their most impressive in summer. For a more enduring display, interplant perennials with a variety of bulbs and perhaps one or two shrubs.

Because access to the center of the bed may be difficult, plants should be sturdy, dwarf, or compact, which should reduce the need for staking; generally, though, there will be less requirement for support because higher light levels and better air circulation promote sturdier plant growth than within borders.

Geometric, round, square, or rectangular island beds suit a formal setting; in an informal garden or one with gently undulating ground, loosely curved island beds are more appropriate. Avoid intricate shapes and tight curves, because they are awkward to maintain and may detract from the planting itself. To gain space, small gardens can be filled with island beds.

Raised island beds can provide improved growing conditions for demanding perennials, tougher alpines, and Mediterranean plants

Island bed This bed is shaped to reflect the surrounding contours. The tallest plants should be sited in the middle; the lowest ones at the edge. Here, height is provided by *Astilbe*, *Lobelia*, and *Filipendula*.

Mass and color This formal display bordering a lawn shows a relatively restricted color palette. Formality is suggested by the use of repeat planting; for example, the acid-yellow *Euphorbia* is spaced at intervals at the front to create a rhrythmic pattern that draws the eye along the border.

in gardens where the soil is poor or tends to become waterlogged. The increased bed height make it possible to tend plants with minimal stooping—which is often an important factor for gardeners who are less able or elderly.

Designing beds and borders

When designing a planting plan, the principles are broadly similar whether planning an herbaceous or mixed border or an island bed. Considerations of height, mass, scale, texture, sequential interest, form, and color are all variable factors that influence the design. Planting is a very individual issue. Everybody has favorite plants and colors, as well as set ideas as to which plants complement each other.

Imagination and personal taste will inevitably influence planting plans, but there are a few basic guidelines to follow, which may help develop an attractive border.

General principles

Herbaceous borders may be designed and planted in various styles so that they set or

strengthen the character and tone of the garden. Crisply edged, straight-lined borders backed by well-trimmed hedges create a dominant structure, which will be attractive in winter, but which can be softened by planting during summer. Irregularly shaped island beds, weaving their way through the garden, are much more relaxed, but will do little for the garden during winter. Self-contained, stately plants, such as lupines, delphiniums, and veronicas, arranged according to a restricted color scheme and planted in a rhrythmic pattern look somewhat formal. For a more relaxed approach, introduce plants with a loose, less ordered habit, such as baby's breath (*Gypsophila*) and lady's mantle (*Alchemilla mollis*), and then add key feature plants such as *Sedum* 'Herbstfreude' at random rather than at strict intervals.

Before starting a planting plan, prepare a comprehensive list of plants you want to use. This should contain any existing plants you would like to retain, as well as a thoroughly researched list of others that will cover all seasons, and are well suited to your garden. It may be easier to compile this list with the help of a good nursery catalog.

Allow sufficient room for the plants to spread as they mature, taking account of the different rates at which they develop. Slow-growing plants can be surrounded by shade-tolerant groundcover (see PERENNIALS FOR GROUNDCOVER, p.180) to fill the area while waiting for the main plant to achieve its desired height and spread.

Start by placing the key plants, such as shrubs, roses, and any imposing perennials and grasses, as well as the important feature plants, which you may wish to repeat at regular intervals to create a symmetric rhythm to the border. Position the smaller plants last. Set out the plants according to your planting plan and make any adjustments at this stage, before planting them. However carefully the design has been planned, minor adjustments are inevitable because no two gardens are alike, and plants react differently, however well you know them.

Scale of planting
Although the size of beds and borders is usually dictated by the surrounding space, the scale of planting should take account of the scale of the garden and adjacent buildings.

The extent of a border or bed will vary but, as a rough guide, the larger the garden setting, the more generous the border or bed can be. Two large beds are better than three or four little ones; they will enhance the feeling of space, and prevent the garden from looking too disjointed.

A border should be no less than 5ft (1.5m) deep, and preferably 10–15ft (3–5m), depending on a path's length and width. This will give a good planting width and will create a layered, well-balanced effect.

Large borders, seen from a great distance and flanked by a wide path, should be planted with bold groups of plants, to create sufficient visual impact. The smaller the viewing distance, the smaller the planting scale should be, so that the border remains interesting as you stroll along it (see also "Planting in groups," below).

Varying plant height

Traditionally, tall plants are placed at the back of a front-facing border, grading down the heights as they approach the front, to create a tiered effect in which no flowering plant is hidden behind another.

In an island bed, the tallest plants are placed in the center, with the smallest around the outer edge. This planting rule will create quite a formal, rigid scheme. Mystery and contrast can be added by introducing the occasional taller but translucent plant near the front; this will give a stronger undulation to the overall scheme.

Particularly slim plants such as *Verbena bonariensis* or many grasses such as *Stipa gigantea* provide extra height, while allowing the eye to wander past them and also see through them. Plant textural perennials, such as *Molinia caerulea* subsp. *arundinacea* 'Transparent' with its soft flower panicles, so that they are close enough to touch from the edge of the bed.

As a rule, later-flowering perennials tend to be the tallest because they have the longest growing period. This can result in late summer flowers towering over the dead flower stalks of earlier plants. To hide gaps where earlier flowerers, such as Oriental poppies, have vanished, plant some of the shorter late flowers, such as *Aster pilosus* var. *pringlei* 'Monte Cassino' near to the front of the bed.

Generally, the wider the bed or border, the taller the plants may be; very tall plants in narrow borders may look awkward and the angle from the tallest to the shortest may seem uncomfortably steep.

Planting in groups

Several plants of the same cultivar can successfully be massed together to create larger groups. Particularly toward the rear of a border, or the center of a bed, large clumps of one plant will create a good impact, whereas near the front smaller clumps will increase variety and interest. Depending on the scale of the scheme, always aim to plant in groups of three or more, up to a dozen or so. For a fluid, informal style, plant in odd numbers—even

numbers create a formal rigidity to a bed or border. Groups of varying sizes should also be introduced. If in doubt, create an "outline" of the plants—using bamboo stakes, brooms, or other more bulky props—to see what would fit the space.

Small-leaved perennials are more impressive when planted in large groups: small-leaved London pride (*Saxifraga* x *urbium*), for example, is best planted in groups of seven or more, while large-leaved *Bergenia* species and hybrids look effective in threes. The huge *Gunnera manicata*, however, is striking enough to be planted singly (see "Specimen planting," p.178).

Plants that have strong outlines, such as *Kniphofia caulescens* with its upright, pokerhead flowers, are more dramatic when planted in smaller groups than those of less distinct forms such as the loose-flowered *Geranium phaeum*.

Forms and outlines

Perennials have widely differing forms and silhouettes, including upright, rounded, or arching, as well as horizontally spreading outlines. Juxtapose groups of plants with contrasting forms to create a series of vignettes, which build up within a bed or border. The slim flower spikes of delphiniums or *Eremurus*, for example, act like giant, colorful exclamation marks, when viewed against the foaming, cloudlike cushions of *Gypsophila paniculata* or *Crambe cordifolia*. Contrast is introduced when the strong vertical lines of irises and other strap-leaved plants are set against the horizontal planes of the flower heads of *Achillea* 'Moonshine' or *Sedum telephium* 'Matrona'.

Some plants are two-tiered, and have their own contrasting form: a fine example is *Rheum palmatum* 'Atrosanguineum', which makes a lower layer of reddish purple leaves 3ft (1m) tall, over which tower smoky-pink plumes of tiny flowers.

Understanding plant textures

Although flowers, and to a lesser extent stems, contribute to the overall texture of a planting scheme, it is foliage that provides the strongest impact, because it is present for a much longer period of time during the year. Even when seen from a distance, it can create striking contrasts and subtle harmonies. The dainty leaves of *Coreopsis verticillata* or the filigree fronds of fennel (*Foeniculum vulgare*)

Harmonizing textures A variety of form and textures can create a lush and exotic feel in a border. The use of hot colors, such as carmines, oranges, and reds contrasts pleasantly with the greens and paler colors.

are very delicate, whereas large, individual leaves, such as those of *Hosta sieboldiana* var. *elegans*, create a bold, textural effect. Grasses, particularly, can add a wide range of textural variety to a garden. The narrow flowering stems and strap-shaped leaves tend to be very supple, yet strong, waving in the wind, bringing flowing movement into a garden, as well as a gentle rustling sound of the foliage. Many, such as *Miscanthus sinensis* 'Malepartus' or *Calamagrostis* x *acutiflora* 'Karl Foerster', are so strong that their dried flower stems will remain standing well into fall, or even throughout winter.

Texture is also affected by a leaf's surface, whether it is the matte, waxy foliage of *Sedum spectabile*, the glossy, leathery leaves of *Bergenia purpurascens*, or the wooly texture of *Lychnis coronaria*. It is important to understand how a leaf's texture will affect your planting plan: glossy surfaces, for example, reflect light, adding sparkle on a sunny day, while matte ones absorb light, creating a more somber effect.

As with form, juxtaposing groups of plants with contrasting textures increases interest; for example, the downy, pleated leaves of lady's mantle (*Alchemilla mollis*) contrast well with the spiny stems and jagged foliage of sea holly (*Eryngium*). Groundcover perennials, such as hardy *Geranium* species and cultivars and *Ajuga reptans*, are especially useful to grow as a low foil for other plants, and to fill

a gap in a planting plan, and so complete the textural tapestry (see also PERENNIALS FOR GROUNDCOVER, p.180).

Color blends and contrasts

Choosing colors is a very personal affair. Everyone has preferences as well as dislikes. It is important to select hues that you feel comfortable with, regardless of their current fashion status, or your best friend's opinion. A restricted color palette can be wonderful, but may be hard to adhere to in a small garden.

For the widest plant choice, opt for an extensive range of colors that will either appear at the same time or follow on in a seasonal succession. If you are concerned about creating too dramatic clashes, try using all but one of the colors. The most awkward ones to combine are oranges and pinks. Using one or the other with yellows, violets, blues, and reds can look very attractive. Alternatively, you could opt for complementary colors—those opposite each other in the color wheel—such as oranges and blues, yellows and violets, or greens and reds. Another possibility is to use adjacent hues in the wheel, combining the hot colors such as yellows, oranges, and reds, or the cool pinks, blues, purples, and mauves. Such combinations were frequently used by the doyenne of color schemes, Gertrude Jekyll.

In a monochrome planting design, foliage plays as important a role as flowers. Such

a one-color plan, however, not only restricts the plant range but can also prove visually boring unless there is considerable contrast and variety within the design.

When creating a white garden, for example, it is important to include different types of white, such as cream, pinkish white, and blueish white, as well as shades of green. Introducing contrasting leaf tones, shapes, and textures helps to bring tension to a scheme. Thus, in a white garden, use silver, gray, and glaucous leaves as well as light, mid-, and dark green ones.

Unusually tinted foliage plants will emphasize a color scheme, particularly in a mixed border, where golden-, silver-, or red-leaved shrubs can help to enhance flowers. They should be used as small accents, and not become the main features.

Color intensities can also play an important part in garden design. Light colors, such as white, pale pink, and pale yellow reflect higher levels of light than do darker shades—blue, red, and violet—and will be seen from farther away. They also start shimmering at dusk when light levels have dropped—causing some flowers seemingly to disappear, while others develop an almost luminous character. The latter can be used near an area where you are likely to sit in the evenings. Light colors also help enliven dark corners, or can be employed to draw attention to a focal point. Dark colors, on the other hand, are better used in the foreground, closest to the viewpoint.

Seasonal interest

Although, in a mixed border, it is possible to plan a succession of color schemes that change with the course of the seasons, to do so involves coordinating the timing of each plant's display, so that one feature smoothly follows another and fading flowers pass unnoticed, eclipsed by nearby plants coming into bloom. A plan that manages to maintain a succession of interest requires forethought, yet mistakes are easily corrected by repositioning the offenders the following fall.

The spring season may be announced as early as midwinter, when the first snowdrops (*Galanthus*) and winter aconites (*Eranthis hyemalis*) reveal their petals, soon followed by hellebores. Some winter-flowering shrubs and climbers, such as wintersweet (*Chimonanthus praecox*) and honeysuckle (*Lonicera* x *purpusii*), at the rear of mixed borders will help increase the early show. Later in the season such woody plants can support not-too-vigorous herbaceous climbers, such as the flame creeper (*Tropaeolum speciosum*) or *Clematis viticella* hybrids. In late winter and early spring, yellow is predominant, from primroses (*Primula vulgaris*), daffodils, and *Doronicum*, and pale blue, from irises and *Pulmonaria*, interspersed with grape hyacinths (*Muscari*). With tulips, spring comes to an end.

Spring colors A bright display of late spring flowers gives plenty of color from the lavender-blue of the forget-me-nots (*Myosotis*), the yellow of the California poppies (*Eschscholzia californica*), and darker blue of the bluebells (*Hyacinthoides*), before taller summer-flowering perennials take over the border.

By early summer, most of the bulbs have finished their performance, and the real season for perennials starts. There are showstoppers, such as Oriental poppies, with their short-lived but showy flowers, and the wonderfully baroque peonies as well as dainty, long-spurred *Aquilegia chrysantha* and the numerous hardy geraniums. Once there is little risk of frost, the remainder of the tender plants will gradually vie for attention, including dahlias, argyranthemums, osteospermums, and cannas. These all flower over a long period, and are invaluable for providing color until the first frosts arrive in fall. There are hundreds of plants to choose from, including lupines, old-fashioned scabious, fluffy meadow rue (*Thalictrum*), strongly scented phlox, red hot pokers (*Kniphofia*), and numerous daisy family members such as fleabanes (*Erigeron*), *Helenium*, coneflowers (*Echinacea purpurea*), sunflowers (*Helianthus*), *Rudbeckia*, chrysanthemums, and asters—the last two being vital for fall flowers.

It is sometimes possible to extend the effect of a particular plant or group by growing next to it a plant that creates a similar impression. The deep blue flower spikes of *Delphinium* 'Blue Nile', for example, could be followed by those of *Aconitum carmichaelii*, and, if the latter is planted in front, the yellowing delphinium foliage will be hidden from view. Plant perennials such as lupines (*Lupinus*) that die back early in front of plants, such as *Physostegia*, that develop later in the season, to hide any awkward gaps or fading leaves.

In mixed borders, bulbs are particularly useful for providing color in late winter and spring when perennials are starting into growth. Similarly, the new growth of the latter masks the fading foliage of the bulbs once their flowers have finished. For example, the black-purple leaves of the evergreen *Ophiopogon planiscapus* 'Nigrescens', the soft gray-blue foliage of *Acaena saccaticupula* 'Blue Haze', or the copper variants of *A. microphylla* make excellent foils for snowdrops (*Galanthus*) and continue to provide interest after the snowdrops are past their best. Daffodils and tulips, planted toward the rear of a border, will have finished flowering by the time perennials come into growth, and so hide the dying foliage.

Particularly in small gardens, shrubs are invaluable to maintain the shape and structure of the design in late fall and winter, as well as contributing color and texture. The inclusion of deciduous shrubs with attractive fall foliage (such as *Cotinus coggygria* 'Royal Purple') and those with bright fruits (such as many shrub roses) will also help distract attention from perennials with dying foliage.

Long-lasting display Having flowered since midsummer, the flat seed heads of the frosted umbels of dried *Sedum* sparkle beneath the majestic beauty of the spiky *Eryngium* towering above and behind.

Naturalistic planting styles

Particularly in a large area, sizeable drifts of perennials look good when planted in naturalistic settings. Plants should be chosen to match the given habitat—such as woodland plants for woodland conditions, and waterside plants for boggy margins—and the planting pattern should reflect each plant's natural regeneration habits. Such planting designs should be allowed to evolve gradually. Plants that increase by self-seeding in the immediate vicinity should be dotted around singly, while those with spreading rootstocks, such as asters, are best planted in drifts. All soil should be covered, either by plants or with a mulch.

In creating a matrix of vegetation, a much more natural and relaxed effect is obtained, one in which plants can evolve and change. Looking after such a garden becomes more an issue of vegetation management than gardening in the conventional way, because you need to control vegetation groups, occasionally reducing a species or cultivar if it is getting out of hand. Ideally, such a planting design is looked after by somebody who understands its aims and who knows which seedlings to leave and which ones are likely to become a threat. Maintenance is minimal, because there is little or no need for staking or deadheading, because plants are usually selected with their fall and winter appearance in mind and are allowed to retain their seed heads. Grasses play an important part in naturalistic plantings. They bring movement and are likely to remain looking good into fall and winter, especially on a frosty morning.

Cottage gardens

Traditional cottage gardens are a glorious mixture of herbs, roses, climbers, annuals, vegetables, and fruits, as well as perennials. They are noted for their simplicity of form, maximizing the space for production, with little money invested in elaborate structures,. Planting areas are intersected by narrow paths and adorned with simple structures, such as arches supporting climbers. In the past, cottagers bred plants themselves and produced enchanting perennials, such as pansies (*Viola* x *wittrockiana*), auriculas (*Primula auricula*), and scented pinks (*Dianthus*). Plants were exchanged or passed on to other gardeners because there were few plant nurseries until the late 19th century. Many of these old cultivars have now been lost, or superseded by stronger or more reliable ones. Other typical cottage plants are peonies (*Paeonia*), lupines (*Lupinus*), Madonna lilies (*Lilium candidum*), Oriental poppies, delphiniums, and phlox, while wild flowers with fragrant, double, extra-large, or unusually colored blooms, such as primulas and daisies (*Bellis perennis*), are also very appropriate.

Perennials in woodland gardens

Deciduous woodland provides conditions of shelter, light shade, and humus-rich soil suitable for many perennials. A small grove of birches (*Betula*) and other light-foliaged, deciduous trees may provide a suitable setting for a number of shade-loving plants; site the perennials where they will not face too much competition from tree roots. If such roots are unavoidable, make sure the planting area is generously mulched with a medium- to low-fertility mulch, such as leafmold, each year, to give the shallow-rooted perennials a moist rooting zone.

Woodland gardens are normally rather informal, imitating nature in their layout, structure, and planting. Therefore straight lines and sharply defined planting groups should be avoided by intermingling plant communities at the edges and scattering individual plants, such as foxgloves, through the area. Many ferns thrive in the low light levels of a woodland setting and add architectural interest to a plan, whether they are planted in bold swathes or scattered through other planting. Some of the most enchanting perennials are the small woodland plants that usher in spring. In order to grow, they make use of the light and rain that penetrate through to the woodland floor during fall, winter, and spring, and then lie dormant, having adapted to the low light levels and dry conditions that prevail in summer. For color and interest in spring, while the overhead

canopy is still leafless, plant perennials, such as cyclamen, snowdrops (*Galanthus*), primroses (*Primula vulgaris*), wood anemones (*Anemone nemorosa*), and dog's-tooth violet (*Erythronium*). Combine them with woodland bulbs and shade-loving shrubs. In cool, dry woodland shade, grow groundcover perennials, such as lily-of-the-valley (*Convallaria majalis*), Solomon's seal (*Polygonatum*) with its pearly-white flowers, and *Pulmonaria*, some of which have attractive foliage.

Among the few shade-tolerant, summer-flowering perennials are *Kirengeshoma palmata*, with its waxy, soft yellow, tubular bells, and *Aster divaricatus*, which bears white, starry flowers on lax, wiry stems.

Specimen planting

In large areas of lawn or gravel, stately perennials with an architectural form or sculptural foliage, such as *Acanthus spinosus*, may be sited on their own as specimen plants to create a striking effect. In smaller gardens,

Year-round interest This strikingly lush herbaceous border contains few flowers but provides a long season of interest. Feathery *Pennisetum alopecuroides*, strap-leaved *Phormium*, and *Sedum* 'Fall Joy' are placed to the fore, with more ornamental grasses forming part of the backdrop. This display will continue long into winter.

Moist woodland Where there is a permanent source of water, a wide range of moisture-loving perennials can be grown for a spring and early summer display. Here, *Hosta sieboldiana* and *Primula pulverulenta* 'Bartley' thrive around a pond.

a specimen perennial that is surrounded by low groundcover could be used to provide a focal point where a border projects onto a lawn or hard paving, or in a corner of a garden where two borders meet. The jutting, sword-shaped leaves and the arching, fiery-red flower stems of *Crocosmia* 'Lucifer', for example, look spectacular rising above the frothy, lime-green mass of lady's mantle (*Alchemilla mollis*) or, alternatively, a neatly cropped blanket of *Acaena microphylla* 'Kupferteppich'.

For year-round interest, evergreen perennials, such as *Phormium tenax* and *Euphorbia characias* subsp. *wulfenii*, are excellent. In sheltered areas, try *Melianthus major* with its neatly serrated, gray-green foliage. Many of the grasses will provide a long show. Especially well behaved and elegant are *Molinia caerulea* subsp. *arundinacea* 'Karl Foerster', with its slender flower spikes that arch elegantly in the rain, the tall, light panicles of *Stipa gigantea*, and the airy, silky plumes of *Miscanthus sinensis* 'Grosse Fontäne', which will be especially eye-catching through fall and well into winter, if left uncut.

Other perennials that provide a briefer display may also make spectacular accent plants because of their form, flowers, or foliage. These range from the towering, felty stems of *Verbascum olympicum* to the massive leaves of moisture-loving *Gunnera manicata* or the glorious blooms of *Paeonia lactiflora* 'Sarah Bernhardt'. Because these plants die down in winter, it may be wise to place another feature, such as a pot-grown plant, nearby to create interest during their dormant period. Specimen plants are best offset by a plain backdrop, such as a hedge, wall, or an area of lawn, so that nothing detracts from their impact.

Growing perennials in containers

Perennials are as effective in containers on a paved patio, courtyard, balcony, or roof garden as they are in open beds and borders (see also Container Gardening, p.313). Growing them in this way also makes it possible to include plants that need cover during the winter months, as well as those that require a different soil type or different

| INSECT-FRIENDLY PERENNIALS |

Colorful perennial flowers are often rich in pollen and nectar—and irresistible food sources for insects like bees, butterflies, and moths. In return they inadvertently ensure the next generation of seed is produced by transferring pollen from one plant to another. Perennials also attract predators, such as lacewings and hoverflies, whose larvae feed on aphids.

By including certain perennials in your plantings, you can entice beneficial insects into the garden throughout the growing season, from the opening of the first hellebore flowers in spring, until the asters and anemones fade in fall.

Spring insect magnets whose attractions continue into summer include geums, polemoniums, Oriental poppies, *Anchusa azurea*, and *Liatris spicata*. Campanulas, *Gypsophila paniculata*, *Sidalcea*, and *Veronica longifolia* work their charm in summer, while salvias, heleniums, rudbeckias, geraniums, and *Verbena bonariensis* provide temptations lasting into fall.

moisture levels from the garden soil, for example the ornamental rhubarb *Rheum palmatum* 'Atrosanguineum', which prefers to have its feet moist. Pots or containers are also ideal for plants that might otherwise invade a garden, for example, variegated ground elder (*Aegopodium podagraria* 'Variegatum') or *Houttuynia cordata* 'Chameleon'. A number of container-grown evergreen perennials such as *Bergenia purpurascens* and *Liriope muscari* can provide a magnificent display throughout the year, while herbaceous perennials may be better planted with an evergreen shrub or winter-flowering bulbs, such as winter aconites (*Eranthis hyemalis*), in order to extend the season of interest.

In general, containers tend to look better when they are grouped together rather than scattered around the garden, and the plants also benefit from the favorable microclimate created by one another's company.

Perennial groundcovers

Groundcover plantings are particularly suitable for areas of minimal maintenance, such as woodlands and shrub borders, or on slopes that need stabilizing with plants. It is also important in areas that would otherwise have bare soil, because groundcovers not only prevent topsoil erosion and leaching of nutrients but also reduce evaporation and weed growth.

Many groundcover perennials will cope with shady conditions, because their natural habitat is the understory in woodlands. They are therefore ideal when planted among taller perennials, shrub roses, or other shrubs, especially when such plants are young and will take several years to bulk out. The ground can be covered with shade-tolerant, early-flowering perennials such as *Viola odorata*, *Pulmonaria* 'Sissinghurst White', or *Doronicum orientale*. These can be removed and planted elsewhere when the shade becomes too dense for healthy growth.

Carpeting plants produce surface runners that root where they touch the soil. Alpine strawberries, the purple-leaved *Ajuga reptans* 'Catlins Giant', or the silver-variegated *Lamium maculatum* 'Beacon Silver' are good colonizers, often covering large areas within a few years.

The most effective type of groundcover plants produce underground roots, which send up new shoots. Good examples of these are the stately *Acanthus mollis*, goose-necked *Lysimachia clethroides*, or *Euphorbia cyparissias* 'Fens Ruby' with its fine, needlelike, glaucous foliage and dark red buds in spring. Such persistent spreaders can become problematic if they are too invasive.

Some groundcover perennials are better weed suppressants than others. The most valuable establish quickly, have dense foliage that blocks out light to prevent weed germination, and retain their leaves during the dormant season. Good examples are *Bergenia cordifolia* and *B.* 'Abendglut', with its red foliage in winter, *Epimedium*, and some of the geraniums, particularly

Leafy carpet
To the rear, *Hosta fortunei* 'Albomarginata' gives the planting a vertical accent. In front, *Viola sororia* surrounds *Epimedium* x *youngianum* 'Niveum'.

Geranium 'Tiny Monster' and *G. macrorrhizum* cultivars, which flower over a long period, have scented foliage, and provide some fall color. Clump-forming plants that bear low, spreading stems, such as *Euphorbia myrsinites*, also quickly and extensively cover the surrounding soil.

Mixing plants

To create a more harmonious effect and extend the season of interest, drifts of one plant can be interspersed with key specimens of another species, flowering at a different time. A groundcover that flowers later in summer can be interplanted with bulbs: medium-height perennials can be mixed with daffodils and bluebells, while low-growing ones look good interspersed with crocus and snowdrops. Low-growing, early-flowering species that are not too rampant can be planted with summer- and fall-flowering, sturdy perennials, such as *Persicaria polymorpha* or *Kirengeshoma palmata*, as well as a wide variety of ferns.

General cultivation

Particularly in areas where established trees and shrubs create competition for light and moisture, it is important to plant in early fall, soon after leaf drop, giving the groundcover plenty of time to become established before the trees

produce new growth and leaves. Plant groundcover perennials in well-prepared soil and water them well, especially in areas where there is considerable competition from tree roots. Additional mulching will help to keep the area weed-free, increase fertility, and retain moisture.

Most groundcover perennials need only a little routine care (see pp.192–194). *Epimedium* foliage, however, should be cut back in late winter, allowing flowering stems to come up before the new leaves.

Plants to use

A variety of perennials can be used as groundcover. Some, such as the daylily (*Hemerocallis*) or the mouse plant (*Arisarum proboscideum*), develop through underground tuberous growths, which gradually form large, dense clumps. Some of these die back quite early, so are suitable under spreading, late perennials or deciduous shrubs and trees.

ORNAMENTAL GROUNDCOVER PLANTS

Anaphalis triplinervis
Plant 20in (50cm) apart.

Sedum spurium 'Schorbuser Blut'
Plant 6in (15cm) apart.

Symphytum 'Goldsmith'
Plant 20in (50cm) apart.

Pulmonaria angustifolia subsp. azurea
Plant 12in (30cm) apart.

Tiarella cordifolia
Plant 12in (30cm) apart.

Lamium maculatum 'Beacon Silver"
Plant 12in (30cm) apart.

MORE PERENNIALS FOR GROUNDCOVER
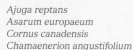

Ajuga reptans
Asarum europaeum
Cornus canadensis
Chamaenerion angustifolium
  var. *album*
Epimedium
Euphorbia cyparissias,
  E. griffithii
Fragaria vesca
Galium odoratum
Geranium
Heuchera
Hosta
Houttuynia cordata 'Chameleon'
Luzula sylvatica
Lysimachia clethroides
Persicaria
Phlox subulata
Prunella
Sedum cauticola,
  S. spathulifolium
Stachys
Tellima
Viola odorata, V. riviniana
  Purpurea Group

PLANTER'S GUIDE TO PERENNIALS

EXPOSED SITES

Perennials that tolerate exposed or windy sites

Achillea
Anaphalis
Armeria maritima
Artemisia absinthium
Calamagrostis × *acutiflora*
 'Karl Foerster'
Centaurea dealbata,
 C. hypoleuca
Centranthus ruber
Crambe maritima
Eryngium variifolium
Euphorbia characias
Festuca glauca
Lavatera maritima,
 L. thuringiaca
Limonium platyphyllum
Nepeta
Phlomis russeliana
Sedum spectabile,
 S. telephium
Stachys byzantina
Yucca filamentosa, Y. flaccida

MOIST SHADE

Perennials that prefer moist shade

Ajuga reptans
Astilbe simplicifolia
Astrantia major
Brunnera macrophylla
Carex (except *C. buchananii*
 and *C. comans*)
Convallaria majalis
Darmera peltata
Geranium sylvaticum
Hemerocallis
Hosta
Kirengeshoma palmata
Ligularia przewalskii
Milium effusum 'Aureum'
Molinia
Myrrhis odorata
Persicaria bistorta 'Superba'
Primula bulleyana,
 P. florindae,
 P. japonica,
 P. pulverulenta
Rodgersia aesculifolia, R. pinnata
Thalictrum
Trillium grandiflorum, T. sessile

DRY SHADE

Perennials that tolerate dry shade

Acanthus mollis
Aconitum carmichaelii, A. napellus
Adiantum pedatum
Anemone hupehensis, A. × *hybrida*
Aquilegia vulgaris
Asarum europaeum
Asplenium
Campanula trachelium
Dicentra
Digitalis grandiflora, D. lutea
Epimedium
Geranium
Helleborus foetidus,
 H. orientalis

Iris foetidissima
Lathyrus vernus
Luzula sylvatica 'Marginata'
Matteuccia
Ophiopogon
Saxifraga umbrosa, S. × *urbium*
Symphytum grandiflorum
Tellima grandiflora Rubra Group
Vinca minor
Viola odorata, V. riviniana

WINTER AND EARLY SPRING INTEREST

Decorative flowers

Bergenia 'Ballawley', *B. cordifolia*
Doronicum
Epimedium
Euphorbia amygdaloides var. *robbiae,*
 E. characias
Helleborus
Iris lazica, I. unguicularis
Lathyrus vernus
Pulmonaria

Decorative leaves

Arum italicum 'Marmoratum'
Carex comans bronze-leaved
Festuca glauca
Heuchera 'Chocolate Ruffles',
 H. 'Pewter Moon'
Iris foetidissima 'Variegata'
Lamium maculatum 'Beacon Silver',
 L. maculatum GOLDEN ANNIVERSARY
 ('Dellam'),
 L. maculatum 'White Nancy'
Liriope muscari 'Variegata'
Ophiopogon planiscapus 'Nigrescens'
Phormium (cvs)
Stachys byzantina 'Silver Carpet'
Tiarella polyphylla
Vinca (variegated cvs)

FRAGRANT FLOWERS

Convallaria majalis
Cosmos atrosanguineus
Dianthus, many
Dictamnus albus
Filipendula ulmaria
Galium odoratum
Hemerocallis
Hesperis matronalis
Hosta plantaginea var. *grandiflora*
Iris graminea
Oenothera odorata
Paeonia lactiflora
Phlox paniculata
Viola cornuta, V. odorata

FLOWERS FOR CUTTING

Alchemilla mollis
Allium
Alstroemeria
Aquilegia
Aster
Astrantia
Centaurea
Cephalaria
Crocosmia
Dahlia
Delphinium
Dianthus

Dicentra
Doronicum
Erigeron
Gypsophila
Helenium
Kniphofia
Monarda
Paeonia
Phlomis tuberosa 'Amazone'
Phlox
Rudbeckia
Scabiosa
Sedum spectabile,
 S. telephium
Solidago
Veronica

FLOWERS FOR DRYING

Achillea
Alchemilla mollis
Anaphalis
Aruncus dioicus
Astilbe
Catananche
Centaurea
Cynara
Echinops bannaticus,
 E. ritro
Gypsophila
Limonium
Persicaria amplexicaulis 'Firetail'
Rodgersia
Sedum spectabile,
 S. telephium
Solidago

ARCHITECTURAL PLANTS

Acanthus hungaricus, A. mollis
Angelica archangelica, A. gigas
Arundo donax var. *versicolor*
Cortaderia selloana
Crambe cordifolia
Cynara
Eupatorium maculatum
 'Atropurpureum'
Foeniculum vulgare
Gunnera manicata
Helianthus salicifolius
Helleborus argutifolius
Hosta sieboldiana var. *elegans*
Inula magnifica
Ligularia dentata 'Othello'
Lysichiton americanus
Macleaya
Melianthus major
Miscanthus sinensis
Persicaria polymorpha
Rheum palmatum
 'Atrosanguineum'
Rodgersia
Sedum telephium 'Matrona'
Stipa gigantea
Verbascum olympicum

DECORATIVE SEED HEADS

Acanthus
Achillea
Eryngium
Foeniculum vulgare
Hosta
Inula magnifica
Iris

Lunaria rediviva
Miscanthus
Molinia
Papaver orientale
Physalis alkekengi
Sedum

ATTRACTIVE TO INSECTS

Aster
Digitalis
Echinacea purpurea
Foeniculum vulgare
Helenium
Inula
Nepeta
Oenothera
Salvia
Sedum
Verbascum

FAST-GROWING PERENNIALS

Achillea filipendulina 'Gold Plate',
 A. grandifolia
Artemisia lactiflora Guizhou Group
Arundo donax 'Macrophylla'
Centaurea macrocephala
Cephalaria gigantea
Crambe cordifolia
Eupatorium maculatum
 'Atropurpureum'
Ferula communis
Gunnera manicata
Macleaya cordata
Malva alcea var. *fastigiata*
Persicaria polymorpha
Phormium tenax
Rheum palmatum
 'Atrosanguineum'
Romneya coulteri
Rudbeckia laciniata 'Goldquelle'
Salvia uliginosa
Solidago canadensis
Stipa gigantea
Thalictrum rochebruneanum
Vernonia crinita
Veronicastrum virginicum

Astrantia major

Attracting pollinating insects

Gardens are increasingly recognized as very important habitats for insects as well as other wildlife. Among the ways in which gardeners can help increase biodiversity is to grow plants that attract a wide range of visiting insects by providing pollen, which is rich in proteins, and nectar that contains high-energy sugars on which insects feed. Fortunately, there are plenty of highly decorative plants that also benefit a wide range of insects—enabling gardeners to choose plants that bring the satisfaction of developing an attractive garden at the same time as supporting a diverse range of wildlife.

Borders for butterflies and bees
Insects are attracted to plants of all colors, shapes, and sizes: tall, oval *Allium sphaerocephalon* is combined with meadow clary and sage (*Salvia* spp.).

Why insects matter

Although a few plants like grasses are wind pollinated, most of our garden plants depend on insects to transfer pollen from flower to flower so that fertilization can occur—with the subsequent production of seeds and fruit. During the last fifty or more years there has been a marked reduction in the populations of once common insects—particularly bees, wasps, flower flies, butterflies, and moths—which appears to coincide with a reduction in meadow habitats and native wildflowers. It is important to reverse this decline;

the reduction of insect activity affects not only ornamental plants but also commercial crops and homegrown fruits and vegetables such as strawberries, apples, pears, cherries, pumpkins, and zucchini.

What gardeners can do

There is now such a wide range of commercially available trees, shrubs, herbaceous perennials and alpine plants, herbs, and bulbs that attract insects that borders and beds can be designed specifically to encourage pollinating insects to

your garden in almost every season. In mild-winter areas, scented shrubs like *Sarcococca confusa* and cultivars of *Mahonia* x *media* attract bees on sunny days, as do early-flowering *Crocus tommasinianus*, single snowdrops (*Galanthus*), winter aconites (*Eranthis hyemalis*) and the early hellebores—and of course, the insects are not the only ones that benefit from an injection of scent and color in the winter period.

However it is during the spring, summer, and fall months that insects are at their busiest; if you are choosing plants to maximize the biodiversity of your garden, the ideal would be to include a range of insect-friendly plants that flower throughout that period, planning your beds and borders to include

successive blooms. Remember that plants, such as roses or dahlias with single flowers, may provide more nectar and pollen—and easier access to it—than their double-flowered relatives, and consider adding native wildflowers like coneflowers and gayfeathers to your planting design to increase the range of pollinators your garden can support. Shrubs including summersweet (*Clethra alnifolia*) and ninebark (*Physocarpus opulifolius*) are excellent landscape plants as well as good sources of nectar, living up to the common name of butterfly bush, while crops of Lima beans and runner beans attract pollinators to the vegetable garden. Finally, be sure not to undo your work: avoid using weedkillers unless as a last resort. Even then, avoid spraying blooming plants.

A RANGE OF PERENNIALS FOR POLLINATORS

***Echinacea purpurea* 'Magnus'**

Echinops ritro

***Aster amellus* 'King George'**

***Eryngium planum* 'Blue Hobbit'**

Knautia macedonica

Verbena bonariensis

***Rudbeckia fulgida* var. *sullivantii* 'Goldsturm'**

***Solidago* 'Goldenmosa'**

***Achillea millefolium* 'Paprika'**

SEASONAL PERENNIALS FOR POLLINATORS

Spring *Aubrieta deltoidea, Doronicum, Euphorbia polychroma, Hesperis matronalis, Lamium maculatum, Lunaria annua, Primula, Pulmonaria*
Summer *Aconitum, Agastache foeniculum, Aruncus dioicus, Centaurea, Echinacea, Erysimum cheiri, Geranium pratense, Geum, Heliotropium, Helianthus, Lavatera olbia, Malva moschata, Monarda, Nepeta, Origanum, Papaver orientale, Penstemon, Polemonium, Sidalcea, Stachys macrantha, Veronica, Veronicastrum*
Fall *Aster, Heliopsis, Rudbeckia, Salvia, Solidago*
Winter *Helleborus*

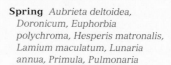
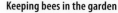

Keeping bees in the garden
Surrounding a hive with nectar-rich plants helps maintain a healthy bee population with the extra benefit of honey for the table.

Soil preparation and planting

Herbaceous perennials originate from many regions, which have widely varying climatic and soil conditions, so whether the proposed site is sheltered or exposed, fertile or stony, there is always a number of plants that will thrive. It is better to select plants that will flourish in the given growing conditions rather than struggle against nature.

Site and exposure

When deciding which plants to grow, take into account climate, exposure, and soil type, as well as the amount of sun, shade, and shelter the site receives at different times of day and from season to season. For example, the shade cast by deciduous trees is most dense in late spring and summer when the trees are in leaf.

Different areas of your yard may provide varying growing conditions: for example, a south-facing border would be ideal for plants that thrive in sun, such as sedums, while a north-facing site or a location beneath a tree would be better for shade-loving species, such as hostas, provided that they can be kept moist.

The ground next to a wall, fence, or hedge is usually fairly dry due to the effect of rain shadow, but it also tends to be warm and sheltered, so it may be a good location for plants that are not fully hardy.

Altering conditions

In small yards especially, it may be necessary to adapt some elements to create growing conditions that suit a wide range of plants. Heavy, waterlogged soil may be drained or the plants grown in raised beds or containers, while lighter soils may benefit from the addition of organic matter. Shade from trees may be reduced by judicious pruning, and shelter provided by shrubs, hedges, or windbreaks (see also FROST AND WIND PROTECTION, pp.612–613, and HEDGES AND SCREENS, pp.82–85).

Soil preparation

The ideal soil for the majority of perennial plants is fertile and well drained but retains adequate moisture. Use a commercial soil-testing kit to find out the degree of acidity or alkalinity of the soil, because this partially determines which plants will thrive there.

It is also important to check soil drainage; if much of the ground remains waterlogged in wet weather, then it will be necessary to install tile or French drains (see "Improving drainage," p.623).

Clearing the site

All weeds should be cleared from the site prior to planting because, once other plants are established, perennial weeds, in particular, are difficult to eradicate. If the ground is infested with weeds, smother them out with a covering of black plastic or heavy cardboard during the season before planting. If there are few perennial weeds, however, simply dig them out.

During the first growing season, any perennial weeds that resprout among your new plantings should be carefully removed with a hand fork as soon as they are noticed, or spot-treated with a systemic weedkiller, taking care not to harm the newly planted perennials. Annual weeds may be pulled just before planting.

Improving the soil

All soils may be improved by the addition of humus or well-rotted organic matter or by commercial soil amendments (see SOILS AND FERTILIZERS, "Soil nutrients and fertilizers," pp.624–625); this increases the water retention of light, free-draining soils and helps to open up heavy, clay soils. It also improves soil fertility. Before planting (preferably a few weeks in advance), apply a 2–4in (5–10cm) layer of well-rotted organic matter, then fork or dig it into the top layer of the soil. Allow the soil to settle. If the soil is sufficiently fertile and rich in humus, it may be unnecessary to use fertilizer, although plants may require feeding in subsequent seasons (see "Fertilizing," p.192).

CHOOSING PERENNIALS

Good example

Lupine

Strong, healthy top growth

Moist soil mix

Established, vigorous roots

Poor examples

Weak, woody top growth

Underdeveloped root system

Dry soil mix

Moss and weeds growing on the soil mix

Potbound roots

Selecting plants

Most perennials are sold container-grown, but bare-root plants are also sometimes available from fall to early spring, when they are dormant. When selecting plants, look for healthy, vigorous specimens with no sign of dieback or abnormally colored leaves that may indicate a lack of nutrients. If you are buying herbaceous plants at the beginning of the growing season, check that there are strong, emerging shoots: plants that have a few fat, healthy looking buds are better than those that have a large number of weaker ones.

One or two annual weeds growing in the soil may be removed easily enough, but do not buy any container-grown plants with perennial weeds, moss, or liverworts. These often indicate that the plant has been in its container for too long and may be starved of nutrients or that the soil mix is poorly drained, in which case the plant's roots may have rotted or died back.

When possible, remove the plant from its container and inspect the roots: do not choose a plant with a mass of tightly coiling roots or one that has large roots pushing through the drainage holes. The roots should, however, be sufficiently established to retain most of the soil mix when the plant is removed from its pot. Look for withered tips on the shoots; this can indicate that a plant has been allowed to dry out too much.

If buying bare-root plants, ensure that the root systems are strong and have not dried out, and that the young shoots are not wilting. Plant them as soon as possible after purchase, protecting them against moisture loss by wrapping them in plastic or wet newspaper until ready to plant.

Dividing large plants

When buying fibrous-rooted plants, choose large examples with healthy shoots that may be divided before planting, rather than a few smaller, cheaper specimens. Divide the plant by prying it apart with your hands or two hand forks used back-to-back, taking care that each division has its own root system and retains as much soil around the roots as possible (see also "Dividing perennials," p.198).

PREPARING THE GROUND FOR MEADOW PLANTINGS

To create meadow or prairie garden (see p.401) you may need to reduce the fertility of your soil. Developing this type of feature is easier in landscapes with sandy soil, where soil fertility is usually low. On richer soils you can reduce fertility in a number of ways:
- Do not add fertilizers or manures.
- Ensure the site is well drained.
- To create conditions for meadow species, spread a deep 4in (10cm) layer of gritty sand over the area.
- If the site is planted with grass, mow at regular intervals, removing and composting all grass cuttings.

- On rich grassland remove the top layer of turf; stack it upside down and leave it to compost into homemade potting mix.

After removing the sod, rake the soil surface well and pull out any remaining weed roots prior to sowing seed. Another option is to prepare a site by smothering out the existing plants by covering the area with black plastic, heavy cardboard weighted down with organic mulch, or a piece of old carpeting. Leave the covering in place for as long as one year.

PERENNIALS FOR SANDY SOIL

Acanthus spinosus
Achillea
Alchemilla
Armeria
Asphodeline lutea
Centranthus ruber
Dianthus, some
Echinops
Eryngium x *tripartitum*
Gaillardia x *grandiflora* (cvs)
Globularia
Limonium platyphyllum
Nepeta x *faassenii*
Origanum vulgare 'Aureum'
Papaver orientale
Romneya coulteri
Sedum, some
Sempervivum
Sisyrinchium, some

PERENNIALS FOR CLAY SOIL

Aruncus dioicus
Astilbe
Butomus ◗
Caltha ◗
Cardamine pratensis
Darmera peltatum
Dodecatheon
Eomecon
Filipendula ulmaria 'Aurea'
Gunnera manicata ◗
Hemerocallis
Hosta
Houttuynia
Lobelia cardinalis
Lysichiton ◗
Lysimachia, some
Mimulus guttatus ◗
Myosotis scorpioides ◗
Persicaria
Phormium
Pontederia ◗
Primula bulleyana,
  P. florindae,
  P. rosea
Ranunculus ficaria cultivars,
  R. flammula ◗
Rheum
Rodgersia
Sagittaria, some
Scrophularia auriculata
Trollius

Key
◗ Tolerates waterlogged soil

Achillea 'Fanal'

When to plant

Perennials grown in containers may be planted out at any time of the year when the soil is workable, but the best seasons are spring and fall. Planting in the fall helps the plants to establish quickly before the onset of winter, since the soil is still warm enough to promote root growth yet is unlikely to dry out. In cold areas, however, spring planting is preferable for perennials that are not entirely hardy or that dislike wet conditions, such as *Kniphofia, Schizostylis, Lobelia cardinalis,* and *Scabiosa caucasica.* This ensures that they are fully established before their first winter.

Bare-root specimens should be planted in spring or fall, although a few, such as hostas, may be transplanted successfully during the growing season.

Planting perennials

Plant perennials in prepared ground, being careful to position them at the right depth (see below): for example, those prone to rotting at the base are best planted higher in the soil so that excess water may drain away.

Container-grown plants
Water the plant thoroughly, preferably the night before it is to be planted. Dig a planting hole, then remove the plant from its

HOW TO PLANT A CONTAINER-GROWN PERENNIAL

1 In a prepared bed, dig a hole 1¹/₂ times wider and deeper than the plant's root ball.

2 Soak the compost in the pot before sliding the plant out (here, an *Aster*).

3 Gently scrape off the top 1¹/₂in (3cm) of soil to remove weeds and weed seeds. Carefully tease out the roots around the sides and base of the root ball.

4 Check that the plant crown is at the correct depth when planted and fill in around the root ball. Firm in around the plant and water thoroughly.

PLANTING DEPTHS

Sisyrinchium striatum 'Aunt May'

Aster

Hosta

Polygonatum

While most perennials are best planted out at the same soil level as they were in their pots, a number grow better if planted higher or deeper, depending on their individual requirements. Some prefer a raised, well-drained site while others thrive in deeper, moist conditions.

Ground-level planting
The majority of perennials should be planted so that the crown of the plant is level with the surrounding soil.

Raised planting
Set plants that are prone to rot at the base, and variegated plants that tend to revert, with their crowns slightly above the ground.

Shallow planting
Plant perennials that require a moist environment with their crowns about 1in (2.5cm) below ground level.

Deep planting
Plant perennials with rhizomatous root systems so that the crowns are about 4in (10cm) below the soil surface.

container, being careful not to damage the roots. To help the plant establish quickly, carefully loosen the sides and base of the root ball, particularly if root-bound, by teasing out the roots with your fingers or a hand fork. Place the plant at the appropriate depth in the prepared hole, backfill with soil, and firm. Loosen the surface of the soil with a hand fork and water in thoroughly.

Bare-root plants

To prevent dehydration, plant bare-root perennials as soon as possible after purchase. Prepare a hole as for container-grown plants, spread out the roots evenly, check the planting depth, work in soil between the roots, then water well.

Transplanting self-sown seedlings

A number of perennials, for example *Aquilegia* and foxgloves (*Digitalis*), regularly produce self-sown seedlings that may be moved to another area in the garden or nursery bed.

Before lifting the seedlings, prepare suitable planting holes, spacing them to allow room for the plants to develop. Then gently lift each seedling with a trowel, taking care to retain as much soil around the roots as possible, and replant it immediately. Firm it in well and water it thoroughly. Shade the plants in sunny weather, and water them regularly until they are established.

Raised beds

These beds are often used for growing acid-loving plants in a yard with alkaline soil or for providing a free-draining bed on heavy, clay soil. Plants that will only thrive in acid soil are best planted in a raised bed filled with an acidic soil mix (see also ROCK, SCREE, AND GRAVEL GARDENING, "Raised beds," p.257, and "Ericaceous plants," p.257).

Raised beds may be constructed from a variety of materials including wood, bricks, stone, and logs (see also STRUCTURES AND SURFACES, "Raised beds," p.599). Include a deep layer of coarse drainage material (such as broken bricks) in the base—about a third of the depth of the bed is ideal. Cover this with a layer of fibrous material and fill in with topsoil before planting.

Containers

As well as being a highly attractive way of displaying a number of plants, growing perennials in containers

provides an opportunity to include plants that would not flourish in the open garden, either because they are too tender, or because the soil type is not suitable. If growing different plants together in one container, take care to choose those that thrive in similar conditions.

When choosing a container, make sure that it is sufficiently deep and wide to allow room for the plants' roots to develop properly. Consider how the selected plants will look when in full growth in relation to the container to achieve a pleasing balance between them. Tall plants in deep, narrow containers and small plants in large, wide ones may seem out of proportion.

TRANSPLANTING SEEDLINGS

Lift seedlings with soil around their roots so as not to break up the root ball. Water well after planting.

▌ PLANTING IN CONTAINERS

If using a heavy container such as a stone urn or trough, wooden half-barrel, or large terra-cotta pot, place it in position before planting—it will be very cumbersome to move afterward; plastic containers are, of course, considerably lighter, but they are less stable and may be blown over in strong winds. Set the container on a support of blocks or bricks to allow free drainage.

Make sure that the container has drainage holes in the base, or low on the sides, to prevent waterlogging. Cover the holes with pieces of screening (either metal or plastic window screening, or a similar open-weave nylon mesh will do); this allows water to filter through

freely yet prevents soil mix from being washed down into the base and blocking the drainage holes.

Most potting mixes are suitable, although acid-loving plants must be planted in an acidic soil mix. All-purpose potting mix with compost or a slow-release fertilizer added (see p.323) suits most plants; those that need extra drainage (such as *Sedum* or *Achillea*) prefer a soil mix containing extra grit or sharp sand.

Before planting, arrange the plants on the surface to ensure that they have enough room to develop freely. Plant as for perennials in open ground and keep well watered until established.

Heuchera micrantha 'Palace Purple'

Penstemon 'Rich Ruby'

Artemisia 'Powis Castle'

Geranium sanguineum var. *striatum*

1 When planting in a container, group the plants while still in their pots to determine the spacing and arrangement. Then plant, firm in, and water well.

2 A few months later, the plants will have grown and developed to form a well-balanced, attractive display.

PERENNIALS FOR ACIDIC SOIL

Anigozanthos manglesii
Cypripedium reginae
Darlingtonia
Drosera, some
Gentiana, many
Pinguicula, some
Sarracenia flava
Trillium
Uvularia

PERENNIALS FOR ALKALINE SOIL

Acanthus spinosus
Achillea filipendulina 'Gold Plate'
Aconitum
Anchusa
Anemone hupehensis, *A. x hybrida*
Anthyllis
Bergenia
Berkheya, some
Brunnera
Campanula lactiflora
Catananche
Centranthus
Clematis heracleifolia, *C. recta*
Coronilla varia
Corydalis lutea
Dianthus
Doronicum
Eremurus
Eryngium, some
Galega
Geranium pratense
Gypsophila paniculata
Helenium
Helleborus, some
Heuchera
Kniphofia, some
Lathyrus vernus
Linaria purpurea
Linum narbonense
Lychnis chalcedonica
Paeonia
Salvia nemorosa
Saponaria
Scabiosa
Sidalcea
Stachys, some
Verbascum
Veronica spicata

Bergenia 'Silberlicht'

Chrysanthemums

The rich colors and luxuriant shapes of their long-lasting flower heads make the florists' chrysanthemum popular for providing displays in the garden, cuttings for the house, and for exhibiting. They prefer a sunny site and regular feeding.

Classifying chrysanthemums

The florists' chrysanthemum is derived from a number of species from eastern Asia and is of complex hybrid origin. A varied range of different flower types has been developed—these are grouped both according to the shape and arrangement of their petals and the florets within the flower heads, and by their season of flowering.

Chrysanthemums naturally form a number of flower heads on the same stem, known as "sprays." Disbudded chrysanthemums are formed by removing the lateral buds of spray types at an early stage; this leaves a single, terminal bud that will then produce a much larger flower head.

Early-flowering chrysanthemums bloom from late summer to early fall, and are grown outdoors. Late-flowering ones are grown in pots outdoors in summer and brought into a greenhouse, where they flower from fall until late winter. Cultivation is similar for early- and late-flowering types, but plants for exhibition need more time and attention. Early charms (dwarf chrysanthemums) flower from late summer to mid-fall and are grown outdoors.

Early-flowering chrysanthemums

Early-flowering cultivars may be ordered from a specialist for delivery in spring. To be sure of selecting the desired colors, it is best to see the plants at flowering time, or to choose them from an illustrated catalog.

Once established in the garden, plants that are growing vigorously and producing good, healthy blooms should be marked so that they can be used for propagating new plants from cuttings.

Disbudded chrysanthemums
The large individual blooms on this example, *Chrysanthemum* 'Hazy Days', are formed by removing all but one of the flower buds on each lateral stem.

Soil preparation and planting

Fully hardy in most areas, early-flowering chrysanthemums require a sunny but sheltered site. They prefer a well-drained, slightly acid soil that has a pH value of 6.5. For most soils, prepare the ground in late fall or early winter, incorporating plenty of well-rotted organic matter. Light soils will not need to be prepared until early spring, with the organic matter applied as a mulch in early summer.

Before planting out in late spring, insert 4ft (1.2m) stakes about 18in (45cm) apart (tie a split stake to the top to support a tall cultivar, if needed). Plant each chrysanthemum next to a stake, with the root ball just covered with soil. Tie the stem of each plant securely to the supporting stake.

Stopping

Soon after planting (refer to a growers' catalog or specialty publication for precise timing),

TYPES OF CHRYSANTHEMUM FLOWER HEADS

Incurved
Chrysanthemum 'Alison Kirk'
Fully double flower heads with incurved petals closing tightly over the crown.

Fully reflexed
C. 'Primrose West Bromwich'
Fully double flower heads with curved petals reflexing back to touch the stem.

Reflexed
C. 'Yvonne Arnaud'
Fully double flower heads with partly reflexed petals and a spiky outline.

Intermediate
C. 'Discovery'
Fully double flower heads with incurving petals and a regular shape.

Spider
C. 'Muxton Plume'
Fully double flower heads with pendent, long, fine florets with hooked or coiled tips.

Quill
C. 'Penine Flute'
Flower heads with straight, tubular florets that open at the tips to form spoon shapes.

Anemone-centered
C. 'Sally Ball'
Single flower heads each with a dome-shaped disk and flat, or occasionally spoon-shaped, petals.

Pompon
C. 'Salmon Fairie'
Fully double, dense flower heads bearing tubular florets with flat, rounded petals.

Single
C. 'Shamrock'
Flower heads with prominent central disks and five rows of flat-petaled florets.

Spoon
C. 'Pennine Alfie'
Single flower heads with straight, tubular florets. Petals open at the tips to form a spoon shape.

the plants need to be "stopped." This consists of pinching out the growing tips to encourage flower-bearing laterals.

When the laterals are about 3in (8cm) long, reduce them to the number required: four laterals to each main stem should be sufficient for a general display on cultivars grown as sprays, while four to six are needed for disbudded plants and two or three for those grown for exhibition.

About one month after stopping, hoe and water in a balanced fertilizer, at a rate of 2oz/sq yd (70g/sq m). Repeat this feed about one month later, to encourage strong growth. Remove any sideshoots that develop from the laterals as soon as possible so that all the plant's energy is concentrated on the laterals.

Disbudding

Seven or eight weeks after stopping, a main, or apical, bud, surrounded by sideshoots, should be visible at the end of each lateral.

If only one flower per stem is required, snap off all the sideshoots from each lateral. The apical buds can then develop unhindered, and each lateral will bear a single bloom (the "disbud"). To produce a spray of small, even-sized flower heads,

STOPPING AND REMOVING LATERALS

Stopping
When the cutting is 6–8in (15–20cm) high, pinch out ½in (1cm) at the tip to encourage laterals.

Removing excess laterals
About two months later, select three or four healthy, evenly spaced laterals and remove any others.

DISBUDDING

For disbuds, once the sidebuds around each apical bud have tiny stalks, pinch them out so that only the central bud develops.

pinch out the apical bud only; this allows all the sideshoots to develop and produce a spray of flowers.

Routine care

Water plants regularly, and apply a balanced liquid feed at weekly or ten-day intervals while the buds are developing. Feeding must be discontinued just before the buds show color so the blooms do not become soft and prone to damage.

Taking cuttings

Take cuttings four to six weeks after new shoots have appeared, and discard the parent plant. Select close-jointed shoots near the base of the stem, with soft but firm growth, and remove them with a knife or snap them off. Trim them to about 1½in (4cm), cutting just under a leaf node. Dip the base of each cutting in a rooting hormone, insert them in standard cutting compost, and then place the pots in a propagator, preferably with gentle bottom heat at 50°F (10°C). Rooting occurs in two to three weeks (see also *How to Propagate by Basal Stem Cuttings*, p.200).

Aftercare

Once rooted, move the cuttings from the propagator to slightly cooler conditions for about a week, then plant them in batches of six to eight to a pot or box, filled with moist soil-based or soilless potting compost. If there are just a few cuttings, pot them up individually. Keep them slightly dry for a few weeks, in frost-free conditions. Check regularly for pests and diseases, and treat them accordingly (see Plant Problems, pp.639–673). After a month or so, transfer the plants to a cold frame and gradually harden them off; protect from severe frost and provide ample ventilation.

OVERWINTERING

1 After flowering, cut back the stems, lift the plant (here a young plant is used), and wash the roots. Trim any straggly roots to leave the root ball about the size of a tennis ball.

2 Line a 4in (10cm) deep box with paper, and place plants with stems upright on a 1in (2.5cm) layer of damp potting mix. Fill around them and firm; store the box in a cool, light place.

Late-flowering chrysanthemums

Indoor or "late" chrysanthemums are grown in containers and are brought into a house or a temperate or warm greenhouse to flower. Their cultivation requirements are similar to early-flowering chrysanthemums.

Planting

Plants may be potted using moist soil-based or soilless potting compost in late spring and staked as for early-flowering cultivars. Tie stakes between support wires to hold them upright in windy weather. Stand the pots outdoors throughout the summer, in a sunny, sheltered position. Water when needed, never allowing the compost to dry out.

Stopping and disbudding

Stop the plants in midsummer; they will produce their flower buds 10–12 weeks later. Disbud and remove sideshoots in the same way as for early-flowering chrysanthemums.

Routine care

In early fall, move pots to a cool greenhouse with the temperature kept to about 50°F (10°C). The greenhouse should be shaded to keep the temperature low. Continue to feed with a balanced liquid fertilizer until the flower color just begins to show. Bring them into a warmer place to flower.

Taking cuttings

Take cuttings and root them in a propagator, as for early-flowering chrysanthemums. Cuttings of late-flowering spray cultivars do not need to be rooted until early or midsummer. Once rooted, treat the cuttings as for early-flowering cultivars. In late spring, when roots have filled the pots, pot plants on

into their final containers. Use 9in (24cm) or 10in (25cm) pots, depending on root vigor. Use moist soil-based potting mix and add slow-release fertilizer. Stake tall cultivars, as well as those with large flower heads, before final potting.

Garden mums

Also known as cushion mums, these dwarf chrysanthemums have become very popular. Plant directly in garden beds and borders, or patio pots or tubs.

Their cultivation requirements are similar to early-flowering chrysanthemums when grown outside and to late-flowering ones when container-grown, except that charms should not be disbudded.

Plant out in late spring, setting the plants 12–15in (30–38cm) apart in a bed, or insert three plants in a 12in (30cm) pot. Stop the growing points immediately, and again when lateral shoots reach 2in (5cm) long. Continue to stop container-grown garden mums, to encourage a large, well-shaped plant. Garden mums are self-supporting, so do not need to be staked. Apply a balanced fertilizer regularly (see p.192).

They can be grown in open ground year-round in mild, frost-free climates. Elsewhere, in mid-fall dig them up, place them in a soil-based potting mix in a box, and store dry in a frost-free greenhouse for winter. At the same time, bring container-grown plants into the greenhouse until spring.

Taking cuttings

In late winter or early spring, take cuttings for container-grown garden mums and root in a propagator. Take cuttings in mid-spring for planting in a garden bed. Once rooted, harden off the cuttings and pot on or plant out.

Daylilies

Although they belong to the lily family (Liliaceae), daylilies (*Hemerocallis*) are not true lilies; their common name comes from the lily-shaped flowers that, in the older selections, open in the morning and fade before sunset. Many modern cultivars stay open into the evening, whereas others open in the evening and last through the following day, especially if the weather is overcast.

Types of daylilies

There are three growth types of daylily: dormant, semievergreen, and evergreen. Daylilies range in size from compact plants that grow to only 12–15in (30–38cm) tall, to large plants that can reach heights of 5ft (1.5m) or more. Tetraploid daylilies, which have four sets of chromosomes in their cells, are larger overall than the diploids (with two sets) and produce sturdier growth. However, some enthusiasts consider them to be less graceful than the diploids.

Modern hybrids are available in a wide range of colors, from near white through shades of yellow, orange, red, pink, and purple to al-most black. Many cultivars have contrasting eye zones, washes, bands, and other markings of varied colors on the petals. The flowers may be from 1½in (4cm) to more than 9in (22cm) in diameter, and they come in a variety of forms, including single, double, spider (with long petals, often referred to as tepals) and polytepal (with more than 6 tepals).

Daylilies bloom throughout late spring into fall. Good modern cultivars flower for three to four weeks. Extended-flowering cultivars bloom longer, such as 'Stella de Oro', and there are some repeat-flowering varieties, such as 'Pardon Me'. Some species, such as *Hemerocallis liliosphodelus* and the night-blooming *H. citrina*, are strongly fragrant.

Using daylilies

With their long period of flowering, daylilies are good for a wide variety of situations. In the mixed border, daylilies make good accent plants; you might choose tall cultivars, such as 'Autumn Minaret', or *H. altissima*. Their abundant leaves may be used to hide the dying foliage of *Papaver orientale*. Daylilies are also useful as a groundcover on gentle slopes or simply to cover large areas. For containers, use fast-growing, upright cultivars, such as 'Janice Brown', 'Always Afternoon', and 'Strawberry Candy'. After flowering, container-grown daylilies featured on a patio, for example, can be moved to a less prominent position.

Cultivation

Evergreen daylilies are generally best suited to warmer climates and dormant ones to colder, whereas semievergreen types are usually suitable for both. Local nurseries should sell appropriate cultivars for your climate. All have the same cultural needs.

DAYLILY FLOWERS AND GROWTH TYPES

***Hemerocallis* 'Suzie Wong'** (dormant)

***H.* 'Moonlight Masquerade'** (semievergreen)

***H.* 'Jersey Spider'** (dormant)

***H.* 'Frans Hals'** (dormant)

***H.* 'Little Grapette'** (semievergreen)

***H.* 'Chorus Line'** (evergreen)

Site and planting

Daylilies will survive in almost any soil, except wet clay. They thrive in sun or shade but bloom best if they are in sunlight for at least half the day. When grown in shade, the blooms will be fewer and the plants taller. For details of how to plant, see "Planting perennials," p.184.

Routine care

For the greatest number of flowers, fertilize daylilies in early spring and again in summer, using a balanced fertilizer at a rate of 2oz (50g) per established plant. Water daylilies well, especially during bloom. In cold climates, lightly mulch for winter to protect the crowns.

An established clump needs dividing to maintain vigor once its flower size becomes smaller and the clump becomes congested. Division is usually necessary every three to five years in rich soil, especially for repeat-flowering cultivars, but less often in poorer soil. Divide in spring or four to six weeks after bloom.

Pests and diseases

Thrips (p.671) may feed on flower buds, causing pale streaks on the petals. Earwigs (p. 659), Japanese beetles (p.662), and spotted cucumber beetles (p.658) eat the buds, flowers, and leaves. Crown rot can cause problems in wet soils during hot, humid weather.

Propagation

The easiest method is by division (see "Fibrous-rooted plants," p.198). To make the clump easier to handle, cut the foliage down to about 8in (20cm) and trim and wash the roots before dividing the clump. Aim for plants with at least two shoots ("fans") each, although most will re-establish from a single fan

Daylilies are also easy to raise from seed (see p.196); they should come into flower from one to three years after sowing.

Daylilies in a mixed bed
Daylilies blend well with other herbaceous perennials and come in a wide range of colors from near white to dark purple.

Repeat-flowering daylilies
Cultivars such as 'Green Flutter' offer an extended flowering season.

Peonies

The exotic, often fragrant blooms of peonies are one of the delights of the garden in spring. After flowering, they maintain their attractive, deeply divided leaves into the fall, and some species, such as *Paeonia mlokosewitschii*, bear colorful seedpods.

The genus includes herbaceous perennials (common garden peonies), which often reach a height of 3ft (1m), and deciduous shrubs (tree peonies) up to 6ft (2m). Their cup-shaped or globular flowers are classified as single, double, semidouble, or anemone-form. Colors range from pure white through pink to crimson and purple, plus shades of yellow and salmon. Peonies combine easily with other perennials and woody plants. They prefer sun but tolerate light shade.

Herbaceous peonies

The spectacular blooms of some herbaceous peonies have traditionally mingled well in cottage gardens (see p.178). They may be planted as a hedge, lasting from the bronze-red shoots in spring until the foliage is cut down by fall frosts. Once established, herbaceous peonies can also be cut freely for indoor decoration and flower arranging.

Herbaceous peonies need 30–60 days with night temperatures around freezing in order to flower.

Planting

Herbaceous peonies should be planted bare-root in early fall (see p.185); if planted in spring, they may not bloom for a year or two. Space them at least 18in (45cm) apart with 2in (5cm) of soil over the buds or "eyes"; if planted too deeply, the peony may not flower, and if too shallowly, the buds may dry out. Maintain a loose, 1in (2.5cm) mulch throughout the year.

Routine care and propagation

Apply a high-phosphorus fertilizer in early spring. Support herbaceous peonies when the new shoots are ankle-high (see "Staking," p.193). For extra-large or exhibition blooms, disbud in spring by pinching out the lateral buds when they are pea sized, to concentrate growth into the central bloom. After a hard frost in fall, cut the stems to the ground. Peony wilt (p.666) and gray mold/Botrytis (p.661) may be troublesome.

Propagate by division in late summer or fall (see "Dividing peonies," p.199); peonies are slow to reestablish. Alternatively, sow seed in fall after cold stratification (see p.196); it may take three years to germinate so patience is needed.

TYPES OF PEONY

Paeonia mlokosewitschii
(single; herbaceous)

***P.* 'Bowl of Beauty'**
(anemone; herbaceous)

***P.* 'Black Pirate'**
(semidouble; tree)

***P.* 'Karl Rosenfield'**
(double; herbaceous)

***P.* 'Miss America'**
(semidouble; herbaceous)

***P.* 'Mme Louis Henri'**
(semidouble; tree)

Tree peonies

Tree peonies are often planted in front of evergreens, such as yew (*Taxus*), *Euonymus*, or holly (*Ilex*), which show off the peony blooms. They may also be used as accent shrubs in herbaceous borders and mixed borders where their flowering time coincides with *Dicentra*, candytuft (*Iberis*), irises, tulips, crabapples (*Malus*), azaleas (*Rhododendron*), and *Wisteria*. Tree peonies make perfect cut flowers if the blooms are cut as the flower buds show color and start to open.

Tree peonies are usually bought container-grown and grafted onto a readily available rootstock so that the cultivar comes into flower more quickly. Tree peonies prefer a slightly alkaline pH; prepare the soil for and plant as for other shrubs in fall (see "Soil preparation" and "How to plant," p.96). Space them at least 4ft (1.2m) from nearby plants. Bury the rootstock 4in (10cm) below soil level so that the grafted cultivar develops its own roots.

Routine care and pruning

Apply a high-phosphorus fertilizer in spring. Protect from small animals (p.669) in the first few years, and from spring frosts.

Prune tree peonies to improve their shape and, occasionally, to maintain or reduce size. In spring, cut out dead and crossing branches and any frost-damaged shoots. After flowering, cut back new growth that is straggly or unbalanced to a shoot or bud facing in the required direction.

Propagation

Propagate by semiripe cuttings in late summer (see p.111) or by apical-wedge grafting in winter (see p.118). Species may also be propagated by seed in fall (see p.113).

PRUNING A TREE PEONY

Remove any branches that overlap or cross each other.

Cut out dead wood at the base, using loppers if necessary.

Cut back frost-damaged shoots to where new growth starts.

In spring, prune tree peonies to remove any dead or frost-damaged wood and crossing branches

Cottage garden
Peonies are well suited to the cottage garden and look particularly striking against an old stone wall

Hostas

Grown primarily for their bold, sculptural foliage, many hosta species and cultivars also produce attractive white, lilac, or purple flowers. Being easy to maintain and with a long lifespan, hostas make a valuable addition to any garden.

Although there are more than 2,000 registered cultivars, there is no agreed upon formal classification system for hostas. Many nurseries, however, follow the American Hosta Society sizing, which is based on the foliage height of the clump when mature: dwarf hostas are less than 4in (10cm) tall; miniatures are 4–6in (10–15cm) tall; small 6–10in (15–25cm) tall; medium 10–18in (25–45cm) tall; large 18–28in (45–70cm) tall; and extra large taller than 28in (70cm).

Using hostas in the garden

Hostas are highly sought after as foliage plants for light to moderately shaded areas and make eye-catching displays in pots or beside ponds. The range of colors, textures, and shapes of their foliage is stunning: modern hybrids may have leaves patterned in shades of green, white, and gold, or edged in a contrasting color. Their texture may be rich and glossy or soft and velvety. Leaves may be narrow and ribbonlike, heart-shaped, or almost circular. There are hostas suitable for most degrees of shade, from light or dappled to moderate. In general, the blue-leaved hostas flourish in light shade all day, while yellow-leaved cultivars prefer some sun.

Hostas for shady places

Hostas make excellent companion plants for other shade-loving perennials. They act as a foil for bright flowers such as those of *Astilbe*, while their large leaves make a counterpoint to the finer foliage of other plants including Japanese painted fern (*Athyrium niponicum* var. *pictum*) and sedges (*Carex*). For shady places in the rock garden, choose miniature hostas such as *Hosta venusta* and *H.* 'Shining Tot'.

Consider planting a hosta to enliven a shady entrance. To make an impact, choose a variety that has striking foliage, such as the platelike *H.* 'Blue Angel' or the white-margined *H.* 'Patriot', both of which have showy flowers in midsummer. Fragrant hostas ideal for planting close to the house include *H.* 'Sugar and Cream', *H.* 'So Sweet', and *H. plantaginea*, which is one of the last to flower.

Mixed raised bed
Hostas blend well with other shade plants, acting as a foil for summer flowers and providing interest after the flowers have finished.

On a shaded patio, grow hostas in containers to contrast with more flamboyant annuals. Golden-yellow *H.* 'Richland Gold' or the yellow-centered *H.* 'June' are excellent plants for pots or other containers.

Groundcover

Hostas make particularly striking groundcover when planted as a mass. Choose cultivars carefully for continuous interest from both foliage and flowers. For example, a combination of *H.* 'Green Piecrust', *H.* 'Krossa Regal', *H.* 'Honeybells', and *H. plantaginea* makes an exotic planting that will flower for several months in succession. A more subtle effect is achieved by restricting the design to a few hostas within a limited spectrum of leaf colors. For a fast-growing, low groundcover, choose cultivars such as *H.* 'Pearl Lake' and *H.* 'Ground Master'.

Hostas in other positions

Several hostas planted together may be used as a low summer hedge that requires no clipping.

HOSTAS FOR DIFFERENT LOCATIONS

H. 'Love Pat'
Medium to large size for light shade.

H. 'Morning Light'
Medium size for light to medium shade.

H. 'Gold Standard'
Medium size prefers light shade

H. 'Halcyon'
Medium size for light shade

H. 'Buckshaw Blue'
Medium size for light to moderate shade.

H. 'Golden Tiara'
Medium size for light shade.

H. montana 'Aureomarginata'
Extra large hosta for light to medium shade

H. lancifolia
Small to medium, tolerates full sun but prefers light shade

H. 'Loyalist'
Medium size for moderate shade.

H. 'Paradise Joyce'
Medium size, tolerates full sun but prefers light shade.

H. 'Honeysong'
Medium to large size for light shade.

The lance-leaved hosta (*H. lancifolia*) is ideal for this and will take full sun in all but the hottest regions; it gives a display of slender purple bells in late summer. Most hostas will grow well in sites that are close to water; *H.* 'Sum and Substance', *H. undulata* var. *erromena*, and *H. undulata* var. *albomarginata* are especially good in soils that are moist.

Cultivation

Hostas tolerate a wide range of soils, except for unimproved heavy clay or pure sand. They grow best in good, moist soil, rich in organic matter, with a pH from 6.5 to 7.3. Prepare the soil well before planting, particularly if it is lacking in nutrients (see "Soil preparation," p.183).

Planting hostas

Bare-root hostas can be planted in spring or fall. Container-grown hostas can be planted at any time, but do not disturb the roots if planting while they are in active growth (see "Planting perennials," p.184). In spring or fall, however, unless the container is full of roots, it is better to shake off most of the potting mix and treat as a bare-root hosta.

Plant with the crown slightly below ground level (see *Planting Depths*, p.184). Do not allow any manure to come into contact with the roots when planting, because it may cause discolored foliage in the first year. Leave a slight depression around the plant at first so that when you water the moisture soaks directly down to the roots of the plant.

Routine care

Hostas take about five years to reach maturity and can then be left undisturbed for many years. Hostas do best if the soil is moist at all times.

To produce lush foliage of a good color, topdress hostas with compost or well-rotted manure; these increase the soil humus and nutrient content. In spring, apply a well-balanced fertilizer to hostas in poor soil.

Mulching

Apply a spring mulch while the soil is moist. Use only well-rotted materials in order to discourage slugs. In regions with very cold winters, apply a mulch of straw or leaves around each hosta before the ground has frozen; be careful not to cover the crown of the plant. On new, shallow-rooted plants the mulch prevents them from lifting after a severe frost, while on established plants it often reduces crown rot. If very coarse material is used as a mulch, it should be removed in the spring.

Pests and diseases

Slugs and snails (p.669) may devastate hostas, sometimes reducing leaves to tatters by the end of the season; earwigs (p.659) will also chew holes in the foliage. Crown rot (p.658) may cause problems, especially on heavy soils or in climates that are relatively humid.

Propagation

Hostas are easily increased by division (see *Dividing Hostas*, right) or cutting a slice out of a crown with a sharp shovel. Although the offspring only rarely come true to type, hostas may be raised from seed collected when the capsules turn brown. Sow in fall or winter (see p.196).

Division by topping

A practical method of propagating hostas is to top them: small cuts are made in the rootstock in spring to stimulate new buds and roots. This method is useful for hostas that are slow to increase.

By fall, the cuts will have calloused and developed new roots and dormant buds. The entire plant can then be lifted in the fall or the following spring and divided into pieces, each with its own bud. After transplanting, the new plants should be allowed to grow on for at least a year before this process is repeated.

DIVIDING HOSTAS

Large hostas with tough rootstocks should be divided using a shovel. Include several buds on each division and trim any damaged parts with a knife. Hostas that have looser, fleshy rootstocks may be separated by hand or with back-to-back forks; each division should have at least one "eye" or shoot.

Tough, fibrous roots
Divide the crown with a shovel; each section should include several developing buds.

Loose, fleshy roots
Divide small plants and those with a loose rootstock by pulling the clump apart by hand.

Groundcover
In a raised bed with dappled shade, hostas make ideal groundcover. Here, *Hosta* 'Frances Williams', with its heart-shaped, green leaves and lighter green edges, brightens up the shade, and its bold form contrasts well with the ferns behind it.

Routine care

Although most perennials will thrive with little maintenance, certain routine tasks help to keep them looking attractive and healthy. Occasional watering and feeding is necessary, and the surrounding ground should be kept clear of weeds. In addition, many perennials produce further growth and flowers if deadheaded or cut back, while dividing the plants renews vigor. Tall, fragile perennials, or those with topheavy flower heads, may also require staking, particularly in exposed gardens.

Watering

The amount of water that plants require depends on the site, climate, and the individual species; provided that they are grown in appropriate conditions, established perennials often need little or no additional irrigation. If there are prolonged dry spells during the growing season, give extra water to the plants. If they wilt or die back from lack of water, they will normally recover fully after heavy rainfall or will become dormant until the following season. The most efficient way to provide extra water is using drip or trickle irrigation, rather than an overhead spray (see also Tools and Equipment, "Watering aids," pp.560–561). Drip irrigation is especially appropriate in arid areas such as the Southwest.

Young plants need sufficient water to become established, but should not be watered once they are growing satisfactorily, except in very dry weather.

Fertilizing

In soil that has been thoroughly prepared before planting, few perennials require more than an annual topdressing of compost or a balanced fertilizer, preferably applied in early spring after rain.

If conditions are dry, first water the soil thoroughly, then work the fertilizer into the soil surface with a hand fork. Do not let the fertilizer touch the leaves because it may scorch them. Plants grown primarily for their ornamental foliage, for example Rheum and hostas, benefit from an occasional foliar feed during the growing season.

If a plant is not growing well, in spite of being in a suitable site, look to see if it has been attacked by pests or disease, and treat accordingly. Foliage

that is yellowing prematurely may indicate problems with soil drainage or a lack of certain nutrients. If appropriate drainage or feeding does not seem to improve the condition of the plant, sending a soil sample for analysis by a soil-testing lab will determine which elements are lacking (see also "Soil nutrients and fertilizers," pp.624–625).

Mulching

An annual mulch of organic matter, such as commercial mulch or bark chips, helps to suppress weed growth, reduce soil moisture loss, and improve the structure of the soil. Apply mulch when the ground is moist during spring or fall by spreading a 2–4in (5–10cm) deep layer around the crowns of the plants (see also Soils and Fertilizers, "Mulches," p.626).

Weeding

Keep beds and borders free from weeds at all times, if practical, since they compete with the ornamental plants for moisture and nutrients in the soil. Underplanting with suitable groundcover plants (see p.180) or mulching in spring helps to reduce problems with annual weeds. Any weed seedlings that do appear from wind-blown seed or seeds that have been dormant in the soil should be removed by hand before they become established.

If perennial weeds appear in the ground after initial cultivation, carefully dig them out with a hand fork. It is usually impractical to apply systemic weedkillers at this time because, to be effective, they must be applied when the weeds are in full growth, usually as they reach the flowering stage. At this point it is virtually impossible to avoid spraying the ornamental plants accidentally at the same time.

If the roots of a perennial weed have grown into those of a border plant, dig up the plant in early spring, wash the roots, and carefully pull out the weed. Then replant the border plant, ensuring that no part of the weed is left in the original site. Do not hoe around perennials because this may cause damage to any surface roots and emerging shoots. For further information on controlling weed growth, see Plant Problems, "Weeds and Lawn Weeds," pp.645–647.

APPLYING MULCH

Clear any weeds, and apply a 2–4in (5–10cm) layer of mulch to moist soil; do not damage the young shoots of the plant (here, a peony).

Improving flowering

Certain perennial plants may be cut back during growth in one of two ways to improve the number or size of their flowers or to extend the flowering season.

Thinning

Although most herbaceous plants produce numerous vigorous shoots in spring, some of these may be spindly and thin; if these weak shoots are removed at an early stage of growth, the plant then goes on to develop fewer, sturdier shoots that usually produce larger flowers. When the plant is about a quarter to a third of its eventual height, pinch out or cut back the weakest

shoots. This thinning technique may be used successfully with, for example, delphiniums, phlox, and asters.

Pinching

It is possible to increase the number of flowers on perennial plants that readily produce sideshoots, such as Helenium and Rudbeckia species and cultivars, by removing (pinching)the growing tip of each stem; this also produces sturdier growth and prevents the plant from becoming too tall and straggly. Pinching should generally be carried out when the plant is about a third of its ultimate height, and in this case 1–2in (2.5–5cm) of each shoot is pinched off with the fingers or cut back with pruners just above a node. This encourages the buds in the uppermost leaf axils of the shoot to develop.

Individual plants in a group may be pinched a few days apart; this has the added effect of producing a longer flowering season overall. For further information on how to produce fewer but larger blooms, see Dahlias, "Pinching and disbudding," p.251.

A similar technique may be used to extend the flowering season of some perennials such as heleniums, phlox, and asters. Rather than cutting shoots individually, use shears to cut all shoots on a group of plants. If all the shoots are cut back by a third to a half, this should delay flowering until later in the

HOW TO THIN AND PINCH PERENNIALS

Thinning
Thin young shoots (here, of a phlox) when they are no more than a third of their final height. Remove about one shoot in three by cutting or pinching out weaker shoots at the base.

Pinching
When the shoots (here, of an Aster) are a third of their final height, pinching out the top 1–2in (2.5–5cm) to promote bushier growth.

CUTTING BACK TO EXTEND FLOWERING

Delphinium
After flowering, cut back old stems to ground level. In colder climates, remove only part way.

Phlox
Cut back the central part of the flower head as the blooms fade to encourage the sideshoots to flower.

STAKING

Tall and fragile perennials may need stakes to support them, particularly in windy situations. Insert stakes early in the season—staking is harder to do and more likely to damage the plant when growth is more developed. Push the stakes deep into the ground so that they can be raised in stages as the plant grows.

For delphiniums and other tall, single-stemmed perennials, use sturdy stakes that are two-thirds of the stem's eventual height: push a stake firmly into the ground near the base of each shoot, taking care not to damage the roots. Secure the stem to the stake with figure-eight twine ties as it grows.

To support plants with many stems, it may be easier to use a number of stakes placed at intervals in a circle around the plant. Loop twine around the stakes at about one-third and two-thirds of the plant's height. Clump-forming plants, such as peonies (*Paeonia*), may be supported with commercial devices such as ring stakes and link stakes, or similar homemade supports constructed from large-gauge wire mesh fixed to stakes. Stems grow through the support and eventually hide it.

There are two fairly unobtrusive methods of staking. Push several twiggy stems into the soil next to the young shoots and bend them toward the center of the clump to form a sturdy cage that is soon covered by the plant as it grows. Alternatively, insert one stout stake in the center of a small group of plants or stems and radiate ties out to each stem.

summer. Alternatively, cut back half the stems at the front of the clump, which will extend the flowering season rather than delay it entirely. If you have several clumps of one plant, try cutting back a few, leaving others to prolong the overall flowering time.

Deadheading

Unless decorative seed heads are desired or the seed is to be collected to raise further plants, remove the flowers as they begin to fade. More flowering sideshoots may then develop on the plant and extend the flowering season.

With a number of perennials, for example delphiniums and lupines (*Lupinus*), cutting back the old stems to their base when the first flowers have faded may encourage new shoots to develop that will produce a second display of flowers later in the season.

Cutting back

Shrubby perennials, such as Nippon daisy (*Nipponantheum nipponicum*), should be pruned back annually in early spring. Cut the main stems with pruners to reduce the plant to less than half its former size. Also remove twiggy, weak, or unproductive growth. This encourages the growth of more compact plants that will better support the blooms throughout the flowering season.

Fall clean-up

Once perennial plants have finished flowering in fall, cut down the shoots to the base and remove

them. In cold climates, leave about 6in (15cm) of stem to trap insulating snow, and cut this back the following spring. For marginally hardy plants, all of the top growth should be left to protect the crown from frost heave; the dead top growth is then removed in spring. Some perennial plants, such as *Sedum spectabile* and many grasses, have foliage or flower heads that remain attractive even when brown, and these can be left on the plant to provide winter decoration until early spring.

Transplanting established perennials

Most perennials may be easily transplanted if you wish to change the planting design of the landscape. If possible, move them

Cutting down in the fall
In fall or early winter, cut dead stems (here, of *Rudbeckia*) to ground level, or to just above new growth.

Ring stake
Stake low, clump-forming plants (here, peony) early in the season. Raise the stake as the plant grows.

Link stakes
For taller plants such as this *Aster*, push link stakes deep into the soil, then raise them as the plant grows.

Single stake
Stake single-stemmed plants (here, delphinium) when 8–10in (20–25cm) high. Tie in the stem loosely.

Ring of stakes
Encircle weak-stemmed plants (here, *Centaurea*) with twine, looped around thin stakes to secure it.

STORING PLANTS

Perennials can be lifted and stored over winter if necessary or if replanting is to be delayed —if transplanting when moving home, for example.

Lift the plants in winter when they are dormant and place them in a box half-filled with moist bark or peat. Cover the roots with more bark or peat to keep them from drying out. Store in a cool, frost-free place.

when dormant in fall, or when just coming into growth in spring. Plants that dislike cold, wet conditions, such as *Kniphofia*, and those that are not fully hardy should be moved in spring once the soil has warmed up enough to encourage rapid growth. A few long-lived plants, notably hellebores (*Helleborus*) and peonies (*Paeonia*), do not like disturbance and take two or more years to establish after transplanting. Normally they should be lifted only if it is necessary to propagate them.

Prepare the new site as for planting, and dig a hole of suitable size. Lift the plant, keeping as much soil around the root ball as possible. It is best to divide the plant at this stage (see "Lifting and dividing," right). Remove any weeds from the clump by hand, then replant the divisions as for container-grown perennials (p.184), firming in and watering well.

Moving plants during the growing season

Occasionally, it may be necessary to move a plant while in full growth; mature plants may not transplant successfully, however, and should be treated carefully if transplanting is essential at this time.

To minimize the stress caused to the plant, soak it in a bucket of water for several hours after lifting it. Then cut back the top growth to within 3–5in (8–12cm) of the base and pot the plant into a good potting mix. Keep the plant in a cool, shaded location, spraying it lightly on a daily basis. When there are signs of healthy, fresh growth, carefully prepare a new location and replant it, keeping as much soil around the root ball as possible.

Lifting and dividing

Where it is practical, perennials in a bed or border should be lifted, then divided, and replanted every three to five years. Fast-growing, vigorous species, particularly those that have a mat-forming habit, such as *Ajuga* and *Stachys*, may need to be divided every other year. Plants that have become woody, with signs of dieback at the center, or that look congested and flower less freely than in previous years, are in need of being divided.

Lifting plants makes it possible to clear the site of any weeds, and dig over and incorporate well-rotted organic matter or fertilizer as required. Dividing a plant rejuvenates it, keeps it healthy, and checks overvigorous growth.

In late fall or early spring, lift the plant, being careful not to damage its roots, and divide it into several portions by gently pulling them away from the main plant. Use a spade or fork to split larger clumps (see below). Discard the old, woody center; each division should contain a number of healthy, young shoots and its own root system (see also "Dividing perennials," p.198). Then dig over and fertilize the original site as necessary and replant the divisions, leaving enough space between each for the plants to develop. Alternatively, replant the divisions in well-prepared ground in a new site, as desired.

Perennials in containers

Perennials planted in containers require more care than those in open ground because they have limited reserves of food and water.

Ensure that the soil mix does not dry out during the growing season: daily watering may be necessary in hot, dry weather. Plant roots should always remain moist but not wet. Water-absorbing polymers can be added to soil mix (see CONTAINER GARDENING, p.323) to help conserve soil moisture. Mulching helps to reduce water evaporation as well as suppress weeds; if using an organic mulch, replace it periodically.

Every year or two in spring or fall, divide plants and replant the most vigorous portions using fresh soil mix, otherwise they soon exhaust the available nutrients and become too large for the pot. If using the same container, wash the inside before replanting, or use a larger container (see "Repotting woody plants," p.334). Cut back roots of shrubby plants by a quarter before repotting. In cold areas, bring in half-hardy and tender plants in the fall, and protect them until danger of frost has passed (see FROST AND WIND PROTECTION, pp.612–613).

Pests and diseases

Perennial plants, if grown in fertile soil, are not usually seriously troubled by fungal diseases, insects, or other pests. Damage by slugs and snails (p.669), attack by black vine weevil (p.655), aphids (p.654), and thrips (p.671) and, with certain plants (such as *Aster novi-belgii* cultivars), infestations of powdery and downy mildew (pp.659 and 667) do occur but seldom cause concern. In the growing season, check plants for signs of attack, and treat with an appropriate control if necessary.

DIVIDING HERBACEOUS PERENNIALS

1 Select a healthy plant and water it well to ensure roots are moist. Cut down old stems so the crown is clearly visible. Dig around the clump and pry it out.

2 Shake off surplus soil. If you cannot tease the clump apart by hand, insert two forks back to back and use them to split it. Repeat until you have enough segments.

3 Replant each section in fresh, well-prepared ground before the roots dry out. Check that the plants are at the same depth as before, firm in, and water well.

Ornamental grasses

This versatile group of garden plants includes true grasses as well as sedges (*Carex*), rushes (*Juncus*), and bamboos (see pp.120–121). Their popularity is due not only to the diversity of form, color, and stature of the many species and cultivars available but also for the ease with which most can be grown and the wide range of conditions in which they will thrive.

GRASSES FOR FLOWERS AND FOLIAGE EFFECTS

Miscanthus sinensis 'Morning Light'

Pennisetum alopecuroides 'Hameln'

Stipa tenuissima

Deschampsia flexuosa 'Tatra Gold'

Grasses as garden plants

The use of grasses in borders and as bedding plants has added greatly to the ways we can enhance different areas of the home landscape. They add variety to the color palette with shades of green, gray-green, and occasionally yellow foliage—some with white-, cream-, or yellow-striped leaves—while the foliage and flower heads of others provide orange-red or bronze tints in the fall. Their varied habits, which may be arching, upright, mounded, or spreading, are an attractive addition to almost any kind of planting, including rock gardens, where blue-green *Festuca glauca* and its cultivars can provide an attractive contrast to vibrant alpines. Tall grasses like *Nassella Stipa, Pennisetum,* and *Miscanthus* are excellent as specimens grown either in pots or in the landscape.

Grasses that spread rapidly by rhizomes or self-sow freely can become a nuisance. Check on the growth habit before buying grasses, and purchase only well-behaved, clump-forming grasses.

Cultivation

Grasses are mainly sun-loving plants, and most grow well in any well-drained, reasonably fertile soil, requiring little attention during the growing season other than a light organic mulch and watering in very dry periods. Sedges and rushes usually prefer moist conditions.

When planting, ensure the crown is at soil level; deeper planting may inhibit growth. Additional feeding is rarely necessary and may cause soft growth and disease problems. Once the decorative effect of the foliage has faded in winter, cut back deciduous grasses close to the ground, and trim and tidy up the foliage of evergreen grasses before new growth appears in spring.

Propagation

Most perennial grasses are clump-forming or rhizomatous and are readily propagated by division of the rootstock. Select strong, healthy divisions from the younger, outer growths with strong fibrous roots or rhizomes and discard old, woody, or dead material in the center of the clump. Replant them as soon as possible, making sure they do not dry out. A few species may also be propagated from cuttings of the sideshoots.

For propagation purposes grasses are generally designated as cool-season or warm-season. Cool-season grasses such as *Calamagrostis, Festuca,* and *Stipa* are divided in late fall when dormant or in early spring as they are coming into growth. Warm-season grasses including *Muhlenbergia, Miscanthus,* and *Pennisetum* should only be divided from late spring to early summer as they are coming into growth. Annual grasses like *Melinis nerviglumis* may be started from seed indoors or sown directly into a garden bed in spring.

Shape and texture
Grasses have become an integral part of many herbaceous bed and border plans, where they add movement and texture, as well as being an essential component of naturalistic plantings.

ORNAMENTAL GRASSES

Andropogon gerardii
Briza media
Calamagrostis x *acutiflora* 'Karl Foerster', *C. arundinacea*
Cymbopogon citratus
Deschampsia cespitosa 'Bronzeschleier', *D. flexuosa* 'Tatra Gold'
Elymus canadensis
Festuca glauca 'Blaufuchs'
Hakonechloa macra 'Albovariegata', *H. macra* 'Aureola'
Helictotrichon sempervirens
Miscanthus nepalensis, M. sinensis 'Kleine Fontäne', *M. s.* 'Morning Light', *M. s.* 'Silberfeder'
Molinia caerulea subsp. *arundinacea, M. c.* subsp. *arundinacea* 'Karl Foerster', *M. c.* subsp. *caerulea*
Muhlenbergia lindheimeri
Panicum virgatum (many cultivars)
Pennisetum alopecuroides 'Hameln', *P. a.* 'Herbstzauber', *P. a.* 'Woodside', *P. orientale, P. setaceum*
Stipa calamagrostis, S. gigantea, S. tenuissima

PERENNIAL SEED NEEDING SPECIAL TREATMENT

Stratification

Aconitum
Adonis amurensis
Campanula
Meconopsis
Primula

Scarification

Anthyllis
Baptisia
Galega
Lathyrus
Lupinus

Sowing when fresh

Helleborus
Meconopsis
Primula

Soaking

Arum
Baptisia
Euphorbia

PERENNIALS THAT FLOWER FROM SEED WITHIN TWO YEARS

Alchemilla
Anemone
Aquilegia
Aster
Astrantia
Campanula
Catananche
Centaurea
Cuphea
Delphinium
Dianthus
Gaura
Gazania
Hemerocallus
Iris
Linaria
Lobelia
Lychnis
Malva
Meconopsis
Osteospermum
Papaver
Polemonium
Primula
Rudbeckia
Salvia (not shrubby spp.)
Scabiosa
Sidalcea
Silene
Verbascum

Helleborus orientalis
subsp. *guttatus*

Propagation

There are several ways of propagating herbaceous perennials. Growing them from seed is ideal where a large number of new plants is required. Little experience or expertise is needed to raise seedlings successfully, but this method is generally only suitable for propagating species rather than cultivars.

For many perennials, the simplest and most common propagation method is to lift them and divide clumps into separate plants, but others are better raised from seed or by vegetative means, such as cuttings or, more rarely, grafting. Vegetative methods should be used for propagating almost all named cultivars.

Seed

Raising plants from seed is a simple and inexpensive way to propagate many perennials but, apart from a few named cultivars (for example, *Aquilegia* 'Crimson Star'), most cultivars do not grow true from seed. Most species also show some variation in habit and flower color so, if collecting seed yourself, always gather it from plants with the best flower and growth characteristics.

Seed of early-flowering perennials, which ripens on the plant in early to midsummer, usually germinates quickly if sown as soon as it is ripe, producing young plants that may be overwintered successfully in open beds or in a cold frame. For most perennials, however, sow the seed immediately after it has been gathered in the fall so that it germinates early the following spring. If stored in cool, dry conditions, most seed also germinates well when sown in spring.

Seed of some herbaceous plants, however, such as peonies (*Paeonia*) and hellebores (*Helleborus*) usually remains dormant for a considerable period —peonies for up to 18 months— unless suitable conditions are provided or occur naturally to break dormancy and induce germination. Some require a period of exposure to cold or light, while others have hard seed coats that should be weakened by scarification or softened by soaking before sowing (see also PRINCIPLES OF PROPAGATION, "How to overcome dormancy," p.629).

Pregermination treatment of seeds

Seeds that need to be subjected to a cold period to break dormancy may either be sown outside in fall or winter (see also *Sowing Seed that Requires Chilling*, p.197) or chilled in a refrigerator for a few weeks before sowing in spring. This method of breaking dormancy is suitable for many genera, including *Aconitum*, *Adonis*, *Campanula*, and *Primula*. Seeds of a few plants, such as those of *Gentiana asclepiadea*, require a period of exposure to light for successful germination.

Scarifying and soaking

A number of perennials, particularly those of the pea family Papilionaceae, have seeds with hard coats that impede rapid and even germination. Just before sowing the seeds, scarify them either by rubbing them with an emery board or sandpaper or by chipping them slightly with a sharp blade to allow water to be absorbed and then germination to occur.

Alternatively, many seeds may benefit from having their hard coats softened by being soaked in hot, but not boiling, water for 12–24 hours; this allows the seed to absorb water and it is therefore easier for germination to take place. Soaking is suitable for a number of perennials, for example *Arum*, *Baptisia*, and *Euphorbia*. Once soaked, the seed should be sown immediately.

Double dormancy

Peony and *Trillium* seeds usually require two periods of cold to trigger germination of both roots and shoots. Root development from the germinating seed occurs during the first season but the shoots do not normally start to appear until the seeds have received a second period of cold weather, usually during the following winter. Sow the seeds in containers in the fall in the normal way.

Sowing seed in containers

Unless a very large number of plants is required, it is usually easiest to sow seed in containers. A plastic half-flat will accommodate as many as two or three hundred seeds, while even a large square pot will be adequate for sowing up to 50 seeds, depending on their size. Square pots fit closely together in rows and provide a greater area of propagation mix than round pots of the same width.

Fill the pot or tray with an appropriate seed-starting mix. Soil-based mixes are often preferable to peat-based ones if the young seedlings are to be kept in them for more than a short period after germination. Gently press the mix around the edges of the pot or flat, then roughly level the surface and firm it with a presser board or the base of another pot, so that the soil is about ½in (1cm) below the container rim.

COLLECTING SEED

Collect the seed as it ripens: shake it from the pods or tie the seed heads into small bunches, enclosed in paper bags, and hang them upside down so that the seeds fall into the bags. It is important to make sure that the seed is completely dry before storing it in clean paper bags or envelopes labeled with the plant name and harvesting date.

Collect ripened seed pods (here, of *Meconopsis*) when they have turned brown. Shake the seeds out of each pod onto a piece of paper and store in a cool, dry place until ready to sow.

Sowing

The seeds should always be sown thinly—about ¼in (0.5cm) apart; sowing too densely may result in thin, spindly plants that are prone to damping off (see p.658). Fine seeds, and those that require light to germinate, for example, some gentians (*Gentiana*), may be left uncovered or sprinkled with a shallow layer of fine, sifted soil mix, perlite, or vermiculite and then gently firmed with a presser board. Larger seeds, such as those of peonies, should be covered with a ¼in (0.5cm) layer of soil mix.

Aftercare

Label the containers with the seed name and sowing date, then water them using a can with a fine spray, being careful not to dislodge the seeds. Alternatively, if small seeds are being sown, stand the containers in a bowl or tray of water for a short time until they have absorbed enough to moisten the sowing mix throughout; this method prevents the seeds from being washed away. Minimize evaporation by covering the containers with glass, a piece of plastic, and place them in a cold frame, greenhouse, or sunny windowsill. In sunny weather, provide some shade with newspaper or shade netting. Once the seeds have started to germinate, remove the cover and reduce any shading.

Plunging the containers in an outdoor bed

If the containers are to be placed outside unprotected from the weather during fall and winter to break seed dormancy, add a covering of grit over the sown seeds. This prevents them from being washed out of the containers by heavy rain and, to some extent, deters mosses and liverworts from growing on the surface of the sowing mix. Cover the containers with fine-mesh chicken wire to protect the seed if rodents or birds are likely to be a problem.

Plunge the pots in an open sand bed because this provides stable, even conditions for germination. Once the seed has germinated and the seedlings are visible, place the containers in a cold frame and care for the seedlings as for those raised under cover.

Pricking out

Once the seedlings are large enough to handle, that is, when the first or second pair of true leaves has formed, they can be pricked out. Either space them evenly in seed flats with about

RAISING PLANTS FROM SEED

1 Fill a 5in (13cm) pot with moist seed-starting mix. Firm the mix to about ½in (1cm) below the rim of the container.

2 Using a clean, folded piece of paper, scatter the seeds (here, *Chrysanthemum* x *superbum*) sparingly over the mix.

3 Cover the seeds with a shallow layer of fine, sieved mix. Label and then water without displacing the seeds.

4 Cover with a piece of clear plastic to retain moisture. Place the pot in a cold frame until the seedlings develop two pairs of leaves.

5 Prick out the seedlings into pots; biodegradable pots allow planting out directly. Handle the seedlings by the leaves—the stems are easily damaged.

6 When the seedlings have developed into small plants with a good root system, plant them out or in pots, as appropriate.

SOWING SEED THAT REQUIRES CHILLING

1 In the fall, sow the seed thinly in pots of seed-starting mix, then cover with a thin layer of fine mix and topdress with fine grit.

2 Label the pots with the seed name and date of sowing, and water thoroughly. Then plunge the pots in an open sand bed outside to encourage the seeds to germinate.

30–40 in each flat or prick them out into individual containers. The latter is advisable for seedlings that do not tolerate much root disturbance. Alternatively, prick out the seedlings into cell flats. In all cases, a good, soil-based potting mix should be used. Water the seedlings thoroughly, label them, and then place them in a cold frame or cool greenhouse until they are established. They may then be potted individually or planted out in their permanent site in open beds when they are large enough.

Sowing outside in open ground

If you need large numbers of plants, it may be more convenient to sow seed outside. Prepare an area in fertile, well-drained soil by clearing the weeds and cultivating the soil to a fine tilth. Using a line or a straight-edged board as a guide, make a seed furrow using a draw hoe, onion hoe, or the point of a large label.

The depth of the furrow depends on the size of the seed: about ¼in (0.5cm) deep is adequate for small seeds, while large seeds require a drill at least ½in (1cm) deep. If the seedlings are to be transplanted when young, make the furrows 4–6in (10–15cm) apart; if, however,

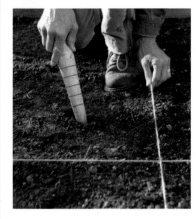

Mark off areas for sowing seeds with string lines. Larger seeds can be sown individually by making holes with a dibber.

For smaller seeds, make a furrow marked with a line and space seeds carefully, according to the seed pack instructions.

they are to be grown on in rows, allow about 6–9in (15–22cm) between them. Sow small seeds thinly so that they are about ¼in (0.5cm) apart, large seeds, such as peonies, at intervals of 1in (2.5cm) or more.

After sowing, cover the furrows by raking soil lightly over them, then label each row with the name of the seed sown and the date. Water the rows carefully, trying not to wash away the soil. For further details, see ANNUALS AND BIENNIALS, *Sowing in Furrows*, p.215.

Dividing perennials

This method is suitable for propagating many perennials that have a spreading rootstock and produce shoots from the base. It is a way of increasing stocks, and in many cases division rejuvenates the plants and keeps them vigorous, because old or unproductive parts may be discarded (see also "Lifting and dividing," p.194).

Some perennials can be divided by pulling sections apart by hand, or by using two forks back-to-back; other plants that have fleshy roots are best split with a spade or knife.

When to divide

Most plants should be divided when they are dormant, between late fall and early spring, but not in extremely cold, wet, or dry weather because these conditions may make it difficult for the divided plants to reestablish successfully.

Fleshy-rooted perennials are usually best moved in late summer in order to give them time to make new roots before winter sets in. Irises, peonies, and poppies (Papaver) are the most common fleshy-rooted perennials. Potted plants may be planted in spring.

Preparation

First lift the plant to be divided by loosening the surrounding soil, being careful not to damage the roots, then prying it out with a fork. Shake off as much loose soil from the roots as possible and remove dead leaves and stems to make it easier to see the best points for division. This allows you to identify the healthy parts of the plant to be retained and the old, unproductive parts that can be discarded.

Wash most of the soil off the roots and crowns of fleshy-rooted plants, so that all the buds are clearly visible and therefore do not become damaged inadvertently when you are dividing the plant.

Fibrous-rooted plants

Insert two hand forks back-to-back near the center of each plant so the tines are close together and the handles apart; then push the handles gently back and forth so that the prongs gradually tease the plant apart and separate the clumps into two smaller portions. Repeat this process with each portion to divide the plant into more sections, each with some new shoots.

Plants that form woody clumps or that have thick, solid roots should be cut into portions with a spade or sharp knife; make sure there are at least two growth buds or shoots on each piece. Discard the old, weak, and often woody growth from the center of the plant; the sections containing vigorous, young shoots and healthy roots tend to grow at the perimeter of the plant.

Perennial plants that have loose, spreading crowns and numerous shoots, for example phlox and asters, are easy to pull apart by hand or with two hand forks. Simply separate off single stems growing at the edges of the crown so that each has its own root system.

Fleshy-rooted plants

Plants that have bulky, almost solid, fleshy roots, such as *Rheum*, may need to be divided with a spade because it would be difficult to separate the crowns using back-to-back forks. After cleaning the plant so that the developing buds are clearly visible, slice through between them with a spade, being careful to leave two or more buds on each piece. Then trim each division neatly with a knife, discarding any old, woody material and any damaged or rotting roots.

Plants with numerous, intertwined crowns, such as *Kniphofia* and tufted ornamental grasses, may also be divided with two forks.

Replanting and aftercare

Dust any cut surfaces with an appropriate fungicide if rot has been a problem (see PRINCIPLES OF

HOW TO PROPAGATE PERENNIALS BY DIVISION

1 Lift the plant to be divided, being careful to insert the fork far enough away from the plant so that the roots are not damaged. Shake off surplus soil. The plant shown here is a *Helianthus*.

2 Separate plants with a woody center by chopping through the crown with a spade.

3 Divide the plant into smaller pieces by hand, retaining only healthy, vigorous sections, each with several new shoots.

4 Cut back the old topgrowth and replant the divided sections to the same depth as before. Firm in and water thoroughly.

ALTERNATIVE METHOD

Divide fibrous-rooted, herbaceous plants (here, *Hemerocallis*) using two forks back-to-back.

PROPAGATION, "How roots form," p.632). Replant the divisions as soon as possible. It is important that they do not dry out, so if replanting is unavoidably delayed for a couple of hours, dip the plants briefly in water and keep them in a sealed plastic bag in a cool, shady place until you are ready to replant them.

Large divisions, if replanted immediately, may still provide a good show of flowers in the same season, although the stems are often slightly shorter than those of more established plants. Very small divisions, however, are best grown for a season in pots in order to become established. In general, the divisions should be replanted at the same depth as the original plant, but those that are prone to rotting at the base are best set slightly above the surrounding soil level to keep the crowns of the plants free of excess water (see also *Planting Depths*, p.184).

When replanting, ensure that the roots are well spread out in the planting hole and the plant firmed in. Water newly planted divisions thoroughly; be careful not to expose the roots by washing away any soil.

DIVISION OF RHIZOMATOUS PLANTS

Divide plants with thick rhizomes, such as *Bergenia* and rhizomatous irises, by splitting the clump into pieces by hand, then cutting the rhizomes into sections, each with one or more buds (see right). Bamboos have tough rootstocks that either form dense clumps with short rhizomes or have long, spreading rhizomes; divide the former with a spade or use two back-to-back forks; use pruners to cut the latter into sections, each of which should have three nodes or joints (see also BAMBOOS, pp.120–121).

1 Lift the plant to be divided (here, an iris), inserting the fork well away from the rhizomes to avoid damaging them.

2 Shake the clump to remove any loose soil. Using your hands or a hand fork, split the clump into manageable pieces.

3 Discard any old rhizomes, then detach the new, young rhizomes from the clump and neatly trim off their ends.

4 Dust and trim long roots by one third. For irises, shorten the leaves to about 6in (15cm), to prevent plants from being dislodged by strong wind.

5 Plant the rhizomes about 5in (12cm) apart. The rhizomes should be half buried, with their leaves and buds upright. Firm in well and water.

DIVIDING PEONIES

Peonies should be divided with particular care because they do not transplant easily and tend to reestablish slowly. For best results, lift and divide the plants toward the end of the summer, when the swelling, red growth buds are clearly visible. Cut the crown into sections, each with a few buds, being careful not to damage the thick, fleshy roots.

1 Lift the plant in late summer, when healthy growth buds are visible on the crown. Cut it into sections, each one with several buds.

2 Dust all the cut surfaces of the divided sections with fungicide to discourage infection and rot.

3 Plant out the divided sections about 8in (20cm) apart. The buds should be just 1–3in (2.5–8cm) deep.

PERENNIALS TO DIVIDE

Achillea
Aconitum
Adenophora
Anemone hupehensis
Arum
Aster
Astilbe
Astrantia
Bergenia
Buphthalmum
Campanula
Carex
Centaurea dealbata
Clematis (herbaceous)
Coreopsis verticillata
Crambe cordifolia
Doronicum
Epilobium
Galega
Geranium
Helenium
Helianthus
Helleborus orientalis
Hemerocallis
Heuchera
Hosta
Iris (rhizomatous)
Kniphofia
Liatris
Lobelia cardinalis
Lychnis
Lysimachia
Lythrum
Maianthemum
Miscanthus
Nepeta
Oenothera fruticosa
Ophiopogon
Paeonia
Phormium
Phlox
Physostegia
Polemonium
Pulmonaria
Rheum
Rudbeckia
Salvia nemorosa, S. pratensis
Saponaria
Scabiosa caucasica
Schizostylis
Sedum spectabile
Sidalcea
Silphium
Solidago
Stachys byzantina
Symphytum
Tanacetum coccineum
Thalictrum
Tradescantia
   Andersoniana
   Group
Trollius
Veronica

Liatris spicata

PROPAGATING PERENNIALS BY STEM TIP CUTTINGS

1 Select lengths of soft wood about 3–5in (7–12cm) long from the tips of strong, healthy shoots. The plant shown here is a *Penstemon* cultivar.

2 Trim the lower end of each cutting just below a node, with a straight cut, reducing the length to 2–3in (5–7cm). Remove the lower pairs of leaves.

3 Insert the cuttings around the edge of a 6in (15cm) pot of rooting mix and water. Cover with a plastic bag, held away from the cuttings by stakes.

4 When the cuttings have rooted, gently lift them and pot them individually into 4in (10cm) pots.

PERENNIALS FROM STEM CUTTINGS

Tip
Arctotis
Argyranthemum
Calceolaria integrifolia
Cuphea
Dianthus
Diascia
Epiloblum canon
Erysimum
Felicia
Gazania
Lavatera
Lobelia cardinalis
Lotus berthelotii
Mimulus aurantiacus
Oenothera macrocarpa
Osteospermum
Parahebe
Penstemon
Salvia
Scrophularia auriculata
Sphaeralcea
Tradescantia
Trifolium pratense
Verbena
Viola

Basal
Anthemis tinctoria
Aster
Chrysanthemum
Delphinium
Lupinus
Monarda
Phlox paniculata (variegated cvs only)
Physostegia
Sedum

Argyranthemum 'Mary Wootton'

Stem tip cuttings

This method of propagation is used most commonly for herbaceous perennials that are difficult to divide successfully and for cultivars that do not grow true from seed. Cuttings may be taken at any time during the growing season provided that suitable shoots are available.

Select strong growing tips without flower buds, rejecting any that are thin, weak and leggy, or damaged. If there is likely to be any delay before inserting the cuttings, place them in a sealed plastic bag to protect them from dehydration.

Preparing and inserting the cuttings

Take cuttings with pruners or a sharp knife, cutting across the stem immediately above a node. Remove the leaves from the lowest third of each cutting, then trim the cuttings to just below a node or to 2in (5cm) long. Dip each base into hormone rooting powder or gel. Then insert the cuttings into prepared pots or flats of an appropriate propagation mix and firm in with your fingers. Leave sufficient space between the cuttings so that the leaves do not touch each other and air can circulate freely. This inhibits the spread of damping off diseases (see p.658).

Aftercare

Water the cuttings using a watering can with a fine nozzle and treat them with a fungicide if rot has been a past problem. It is important that the cuttings are maintained at a high humidity level, otherwise they will wilt, so, if possible, keep them in a mist unit or propagator. Alternatively, cover the cuttings with a plastic tent or bag; this should be supported on stakes or hooped wires to prevent the plastic from touching the leaves because any condensation forming on the foliage could encourage fungal infection. When the weather is hot, shade the cuttings with newspaper, commercial shade netting, or other semitranslucent material to prevent the leaves from scorching or wilting. The shading should be removed as soon as possible to ensure the cuttings get plenty of light.

Inspect the plants daily, removing any fallen and dead leaves and any material that is infected. Water the mix as necessary to keep it moist but not wet. After about two to three weeks, the cuttings should produce roots and may be potted into individual pots. Any healthy cuttings that have not developed roots by this stage should be reinserted and cared for as before until they have rooted.

Basal stem cuttings

This type of cutting is suitable for a number of herbaceous plants that produce clusters of new shoots at the base in spring. Short, basal cuttings of plants with hollow or pithy stems, such as lupines (*Lupinus*) and delphiniums, as well as those that have soft tissues, may

HOW TO PROPAGATE BY BASAL STEM CUTTINGS

1 Take cuttings when the shoots (here, of *Chrysanthemum*) are 3–4in (7–10cm) tall, each with a small piece of basal wood.

2 Remove the basal leaves from each cutting. Make a straight cut just below a node, if visible, or so the cuttings are 2in (5cm) long.

3 Dip the cuttings in hormone rooting powder or gel, then insert into a prepared pot of moist propagation mix. Place the pots in a propagator or plastic bag.

4 When the cuttings have rooted, separate them, retaining as much mix as possible around the roots. Pot up the cuttings individually.

be rooted successfully from sturdy shoots that are taken from plants in the mid-spring.

If required, the plants to be propagated may be lifted and grown in pots or flats in a warm greenhouse to encourage the production of basal shoots earlier than if the plants were growing in open beds. The cuttings should then be rooted, and young plants established, earlier in the season. The plants from which cuttings have been taken may then be replanted in the garden.

Preparing and inserting the cuttings

Select strong, sturdy shoots whose first leaves have just unfolded and, using a sharp knife, remove them as close to the base as possible; include part of the woody, basal tissue in the cutting. Do not use any shoots that are hollow or damaged.

Trim off the lower leaves of the cuttings, dip them in hormone rooting powder, and insert them in propagation mix, either individually or several to a pot, or in flats. Firm in the cuttings, water thoroughly, and place in a cold frame or propagator. Alternatively, cover each container with a clear plastic bag supported on wire hoops firmly inserted into the mix. Shade the cuttings from direct sunlight to prevent the leaves from scorching or wilting.

Aftercare

Check the cuttings every few days, removing any dead or decaying foliage as soon as possible to prevent the spread of rot. Ensure that the soil mix is moist, but not wet, at all times, and wipe away excess water and condensation from the glass or plastic covers. The cuttings should normally be well rooted within a month, and they may then be potted into individual pots filled with equal parts of soil, sand, and peat substitute or peat.

Root cuttings

This is a useful method of propagating perennials that have fairly thick, fleshy roots, such as *Verbascum* and *Papaver orientale* cultivars. It is also the only way of raising new, healthy plants from border phlox cultivars that are affected by nematode. The nematodes occur in the topgrowth of affected phlox but not in the roots, so taking root cuttings makes it possible to produce healthy, nematode-free plants. However, this method cannot be used for those phlox cultivars with variegated foliage, because the resulting plants produce only plain green leaves.

Be careful to minimize damage to the parent plant when cutting its roots, and replant it right after taking the cuttings. Root cuttings are most successful when they are taken during the plant's dormant period, usually in winter.

Preparation

Lift a strong, healthy plant and wash off the soil so that the roots can be seen. Select roots that are young, vigorous, and thick—these are more likely to provide successful new plants than those that are weak and thin or old, gnarled, and woody. Cut off the young roots close to the crown and replant the parent plant.

When propagating plants with thick roots, for example, *Acanthus, Anchusa, Romneya*, and *Verbascum*, choose roots that are about the thickness of a pencil and cut them into sections 2–4in (5–10cm) long. With thin-rooted perennials, cut the roots into 3–5in (7–13cm) lengths so there is sufficient food storage for the developing cuttings.

Cut each section so that the top end (that nearest the plant's stem) is cut straight across and the bottom end (nearest the root tip) is cut at an angle; this makes it easy to insert the cuttings the correct way up. Shoots will develop from the top end of the cutting and roots from the lower end. Trim off any fibrous roots before inserting the cuttings.

Inserting the cuttings

After preparing the cuttings, dust them with fungicide if rot has been a past problem. Then insert them vertically, straight ends at the top, in prepared pots or flats of propagation mix about one-and-a-half times their depth; the tops of the cuttings should be level with the surface. Cover the pots with a thin layer of fine sand or grit, label, and place them in a propagator or cold frame. Do not water the cuttings until they begin to root. Once young shoots have developed, pot them up singly into an appropriate soil mix.

Plants with thinner roots, such as *Anemone hupehensis, A.* x *hybrida, Campanula*, phlox, and *Primula denticulata*, are often treated slightly differently because their roots may be too fine to insert vertically. Lay the root cuttings flat on the surface of pots or flats of firmed propagation mix, then cover with more mix. Then treat as for standard root cuttings.

HOW TO PROPAGATE PERENNIALS BY ROOT CUTTINGS

1 Lift the plant (here, *Acanthus*) when dormant and wash the roots. Select roots of pencil thickness and slice them off with a knife, cutting close to the crown.

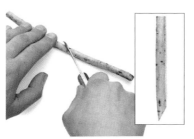

2 Trim the roots and cut each into lengths of 2–4in (5–10cm). Make a straight cut at the upper end of each cutting and an angled cut at the lower end (see inset).

3 Insert the cuttings into holes made in pots of moist propagation mix and firm. The top end of each cutting should be flush with the surface of the mix.

4 Topdress the pots of cuttings with coarse grit, label them, and place them in a cold frame until the cuttings root.

5 When the cuttings have developed young shoots, pot them into individual pots filled with soil-based potting mix. Water and label the pots (see inset).

ALTERNATIVE METHOD FOR THIN ROOTS

Place the trimmed cuttings horizontally on moist, firmed soil mix. Cover with more mix and firm lightly.

PERENNIALS FROM ROOT CUTTINGS

Acanthus
Anchusa azurea
Anemone hupehensis, A. x *hybrida*
Arnebia
Campanula
Catananche caerulea
Dodecatheon
Echinops
Erodium
Eryngium
Gaillardia
Geranium
Gypsophila
Limonium platyphyllum
Linum
Mertensia
Morisia
Papaver orientale
Phlox paniculata, P. subulata
Primula denticulata
Pulsatilla vulgaris
Romneya
Stokesi
Trollius
Verbascum

Papaver orientale

Ferns

Among the most popular of the foliage plants, ferns add texture and atmosphere to the house or garden, where they are particularly effective in settings by streams or in damp, shady corners.

Cultivation

Hardy ferns are suitable for growing in the landscape, while tender tropical ferns are best cultivated indoors in a greenhouse or conservatory, or as houseplants.

Hardy ferns

Most hardy ferns are easy to grow and are suitable for shady, moist conditions. Being very tough, they require minimal cultivation and upkeep once they become established. With the exception of *Thelypteris oreopteris* and all the *Blechnum* and *Cryptogramma* species, which require very acidic soil, ferns prefer neutral conditions. Garden soil with added organic matter suits most species.

Planting may be carried out at any time if container-grown plants are used. In dry weather, water regularly until the plants are established. Always plant in full or dappled shade; some genera, such as *Dryopteris*, will tolerate dry conditions if they are well shaded, but almost all require damp conditions to thrive.

Many ferns, such as *Athyrium*, *Cryptogramma*, and *Osmunda*, die down at the first touch of frost, but some of the *Dryopteris* retain their fronds well into winter. Leaving the old fronds

on the plant until early spring protects the crowns, but these should be removed as the young ones start to uncurl. All species and cultivars of *Asplenium*, *Cyrtomium*, *Polystichum*, and *Polypodium* make good plants for a greenhouse with a minimum daytime temperature of 41–50°F (5–10°C) and a minimum nighttime temperature of 35°F (2°C).

Tender tropical ferns

Ferns that will not withstand frost make excellent greenhouse or conservatory foliage plants, grown in pots or hanging baskets. Some also make good houseplants. Most require a winter minimum temperature of 50–60°F (10–15°C) but do not like hot, dry conditions and should be shaded from direct sunlight; a north-facing position on a bed of gravel that can be wetted down in hot weather is ideal.

Tender ferns are usually sold in very small pots and should then be repotted into 5in (13cm) or 6in (15cm) pots using a soilless potting mix. For this mix, use 3 parts peat- or peat substitute-

based potting mixture to 2 parts coarse sand or medium-grade perlite. Add a cupful of charcoal granules to every quart (liter) of mixture and, following the package instructions, a balanced granular or powdered fertilizer.

The root ball should not dry out completely; keep the plant in its pot inside a watertight outer container with about 1in (2.5cm) of sand or gravel permanently kept damp at its base. Ferns, particularly *Adiantum* species, do not like to

be sprayed or overwatered, and *Nephrolepis*, which are probably the easiest to keep as houseplants, should be nearly dry before watering. Feed the ferns occasionally with a houseplant liquid fertilizer.

Propagation

Ferns are mainly raised from spores, but may be propagated by division or, in some species, by bulbils.

Water setting
Matteuccia thrives in damp conditions by a stream and provides a striking contrast of form and texture with the *Rodgersia* in the foreground.

Rock crevice
The lance-shaped fronds of the semievergreen *Ceterach officinarum* contrast well with the rock behind that provides shade and shelter.

PROPAGATION BY BULBILS

1 Select a frond that is drooping under the weight of bulbils. The bulbils may have tiny green fronds emerging from them. Cut off the parent frond close to the base. The plant shown here is *Asplenium bulbiferum*.

2 Pin down the frond onto prepared potting mix. Make sure the frond's ribs are flat.

3 Water thoroughly, label the tray, and put it in a plastic bag. Seal the bag and leave the tray in a warm, light place until the bulbils have rooted.

4 Remove the wire pins and lift each rooted bulbil with a knife; if necessary, cut the bulbil away from the parent frond.

5 Put each bulbil into a 3in (7cm) pot of moist, soilless potting mix. Keep moist in a warm, light place until the plants are large enough to replant.

Bulbils

Asplenium bulbiferum and some of the hardy *Polystichum* species produce bulbils or small plantlets along the fronds. These may be used for propagation by pinning down the part of the frond with bulbils onto a flat of sowing or rooting medium. The bulbils soon produce rooted plantlets, which can be separated from the parent plant and repotted. Bulbils root fastest when the parent plant is actively growing. During the dormant season, rooting may take six months.

Spores

Ferns produce neither flowers nor seeds, and have a unique way of reproducing. Fronds carry on their undersurfaces very small capsules (sporangia), which release large numbers of powdery spores that, when sown on damp potting mix, produce small growths (prothalli). Each prothallus carries both the male and female organs: the male organ (antheridium) produces spermatozoids, which swim across the surface moisture of the prothallus to fertilize the "egg cell" lying within the female organ (archegonium). After fertilization, a zygote is formed, which eventually develops into a tiny new fern. In this way the normal cycle of growth is continued.

Growing ferns from spores may take 18 to 24 months from sowing the spores to planting out the mature ferns. Collect the spores by removing from the parent plant fronds that are almost ready to shed their spores. Ripe sporangia are plump and vary in color between species; many are dark brown, some blue-gray, others orange. Immature sporangia are flat and green or pale yellow. If the sporangia are dark brown and rough, they will probably already have shed their spores. Lay the fronds on a sheet of clean paper and leave them in a warm room. In a day or so the spores will be shed onto the paper, looking like brown dust. Transfer them to a labeled seed envelope.

Fill a 3in (7cm) pot with seed-starting medium; firm and smooth the surface. Sterilize the medium by carefully pouring boiling water through a piece of paper towel laid on the surface until water comes through the drainage holes. When the medium has cooled, remove the paper towel and sow spores thinly over the surface. Cover the pot, or put it in a propagator, and leave it in a warm, light place out of direct sunlight. To keep the surface constantly moist, mist-spray it regularly with previously boiled, lukewarm water. Remove the cover when the top of the pot is covered with a green, velvety "moss"; if the soil seems dry, moisten it by standing the pot in a saucer of water for a short period.

Depending on the species, it takes from 6–12 weeks for the young prothalli to cover the soil surface. Separate them out by lifting small pieces of the "moss." Space them evenly, green-side up, on the surface of other pots of sterilized sowing medium, press them down, and spray with lukewarm water that has been boiled. Cover the pots with plastic wrap or return them to the propagator. As the prothalli develop, spray them daily with lukewarm water until tiny plantlets appear. When they are large enough to handle, transplant them separately into pots of soilless potting mix and grow them on, repotting as necessary, until they are large enough to plant out.

Formal plantings
The clean, horizontal line of the golden boxwood (foreground) provides a perfect foundation for the striking shuttlecock shapes of *Matteuccia struthiopteris*.

PROPAGATION BY SPORES

1 Examine the undersides of the fronds to find one with sporangia that are ready to release their spores. Cut off the selected frond with a clean, sharp knife and place it carefully on clean, white paper to collect the spores. The plant shown here is *Adiantum raddianum* 'Fritz Lüthi'.

Not ready　　**Ready**　　**Too late**

2 Sow a few of the collected spores onto a pot of prepared sterile potting mix by tapping them from a piece of folded paper. Cover with some plastic wrap or place the pot in a propagator.

3 Mist-spray twice a week until the surface is covered with a bumpy green "moss." Lift small clumps with a knife.

4 Divide the clumps into small pieces and gently firm them down onto sterile potting mix. Spray with water and then return them to the propagator.

5 When leaflike plantlets appear, lift them carefully. Firm into cell packs or small pots of moist potting mix. Repot when they have developed small fronds.

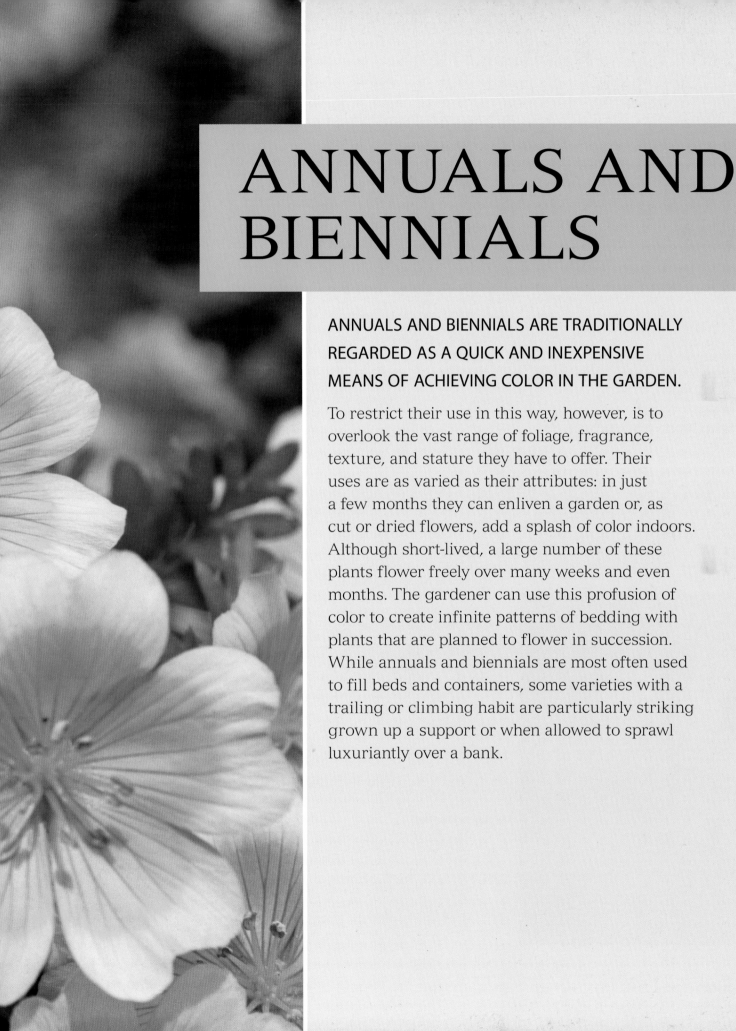

ANNUALS AND BIENNIALS

ANNUALS AND BIENNIALS ARE TRADITIONALLY REGARDED AS A QUICK AND INEXPENSIVE MEANS OF ACHIEVING COLOR IN THE GARDEN.

To restrict their use in this way, however, is to overlook the vast range of foliage, fragrance, texture, and stature they have to offer. Their uses are as varied as their attributes: in just a few months they can enliven a garden or, as cut or dried flowers, add a splash of color indoors. Although short-lived, a large number of these plants flower freely over many weeks and even months. The gardener can use this profusion of color to create infinite patterns of bedding with plants that are planned to flower in succession. While annuals and biennials are most often used to fill beds and containers, some varieties with a trailing or climbing habit are particularly striking grown up a support or when allowed to sprawl luxuriantly over a bank.

Annuals and biennials for the garden

The term "annual" describes a plant whose entire life cycle takes place within the space of one year. Those that are able to withstand some cold are hardy annuals; those that are not are half-hardy and must be raised under cover and planted out in the spring after all danger of frost has passed. Biennials require two growing seasons. In their first season they produce leaf and root growth; they then overwinter and flower in the following year.

Flowering grasses Annual grasses give subtle color.

Annual borders

Whole borders or beds devoted to annuals produce colorful displays. Ideal in a new garden, where they quickly provide a vibrant show, annuals may also be used as features in established gardens. The plants may be changed several times in a season to create different displays.

Many plants grown as annuals are actually tender perennials and will survive outdoors only where frosts do not occur.

Color effects

The most attractive annual borders are often those that exploit a limited range of colors—dazzling oranges and reds, muted pinks and purples, soft blues, and mauves. Plan the planting with a broad sweep of color, selecting tones that, when adjacent, blend together harmoniously. Grays, greens, and whites are particularly useful for providing a respite from the more vibrant reds and blues. Many annuals, such as snapdragons (*Antihinum*), pansies (*Viola x wittrockiana*), and petunias,

are available in a very wide range of colors, making it possible to select a particular plant whatever the color range required. A bed devoted to pure white flowers looks fresh and crisp, but plain green-foliaged plants prevent the planting from looking cold. Cream-colored blossoms should not be substituted for the cleaner whites or mixed with them.

Form and texture

Border compositions are often enhanced by the leaf texture or the overall plant shape as much as by color alone. Place plants with contrasting textures of either leaf or flower in adjacent groupings. Their differing characteristics will then be better appreciated. Form and texture of annuals are often overlooked, but they add greatly to the character of a planting, whether it be with the wispy foliage of *Nigella*, the bold spikes of *Salvia splendens*, or the spreading informality of the poached-egg flower (*Limnanthes douglasii*) to provide contrast. Consider adding vegetables with attractive foliage to provide boldness and solidity to annual flower plantings; purple-leaved cabbage and Brussels sprouts, and various kales are especially suitable. An annual grass that is particularly valuable to include in annual gardens is the ornamental corn *Zea mays* 'Japonica', with its variegated leaves, plumelike flowers, tassels, and ears of variously colored kernels.

Including a variety of shapes and sizes adds interest to the design. Select from, for example, the daisy-like shapes of *Gaillardia*, the golden disks of sunflowers (*Helianthus annuus*), the large bells of petunias, the feathery plumes of *Celosia cristata*, or the tiny pompons of English daisies (*Bellis perennis*) or double-flowered feverfew (*Tanacetum parthenium*).

Grouping the plants

Most annuals look their best when planted in large groups of one cultivar to give a bold block of color. Single plants can otherwise easily become isolated and weaken the structure of the planting. Sow in irregular patches so that the impact as the plants mature is similar to the interlocking drifts of flowers made by perennials in a traditional herbaceous border. The shapes and sizes of the groups should be varied to create a natural, free-flowing look.

When a border is to be viewed mainly from one direction, perhaps from a path or lawn, or is backed by a fence or hedge, arrange plants according to height. Plant the tallest plants, such as hollyhocks (*Alcea*), the taller *Amaranthus*, and tall sunflowers at the back, and use naturally low-growing species such as *Ageratum*, sweet alyssum (*Lobularia maritima*), and annual phlox to cover the front of the border. For those that are intermediate in height, juxtapose groups of slightly different heights to achieve variation. This creates a billowing, undulating informality.

Combine plants that flourish in similar conditions. For instance, species or cultivars of *Nicotiana*, which have loose clusters of scented tubular flowers on tall stems, combine well with the low-growing, flower-covered, compact shapes of *Impatiens* cultivars, because both generally prefer cool and shady sites.

Foliage plants

There are several annuals grown chiefly for their foliage to harmonize or contrast with bright flower color, and to add to the range of textures in a bed or border.

Dusty Miller (*Senecio cineraria*), with its silver-gray leaves, is easily cultivated from seed. Although frequently treated as a half-hardy annual, it is in fact a perennial, and may be kept for years if it is protected from cold where marginally hardy. A clump of castor bean plants (*Ricinus communis*), another perennial that flourishes in cooler climates when treated as a half-hardy annual, provides an eye-catching feature, with its green or purplish-bronze leaves.

The curious bright green, cuplike flowers of the annual bells-of-Ireland (*Molucella laevis*) contrast well with colorful planting designs, while selected cultivars of coleus (*Solenostemon*) and *Amaranthus* provide a range of foliage color: reds and purples, yellows and greens, and two or three colors often combined in one leaf. Some fibrous-rooted begonias are well worth growing for their attractive bronze leaves.

Some ornamental vegetables also make excellent foliage plants to use with annuals. Swiss chard cultivars such as 'Ruby Chard', with its vivid red, upright stalks, 'Bright Yellow', with its dazzling, buttercup-yellow stems, or the mixed 'Bright Lights', which

Annual display Many summer annuals, such as snapdragons (*Antirrhinum majus*), produce flowers in a bold variety of colors and can be grown as a mixture for a vibrant show.

contains six different colors, are especially vivid. The ornamental cabbages and kales (*Brassica oleracea* forms) provide low-growing, muted foliage in purples, pinks, greens, and white late in the season and some edible curly kales, such as the purple-leaved 'Redbor', are very attactive together with red cabbage and purple-leaved Brussels sprouts.

Seasonal display

Plan the planting so that the flowering periods of the annuals coincide as much as possible, as this should avoid gaps in the design. To provide interest over a long period, use annuals that bloom in succession; for specific color combinations, make sure that the chosen plants bloom at the same time.

For a spring display, choose wallflowers (*Erysimum*), forget-me-nots (*Myosotis*), daisies (*Bellis*), pansies (*Viola x wittrockiana*), and primroses (*Primula vulgaris* and *P.* [math x] *polyanthus)*. For summer and early fall, the range of flowering plants is much greater, and the combinations are seemingly limitless.

Mixed planting Growing a mixture of different annuals, along with some perennials, helps to ensure a seamless show of color throughout the summer months.

Petunias have been diversified so greatly that you can use them to create elaborate color combinations all on their own. Choose from the boldly contrasting, striped blooms, the bright, single colors, or the subtly shaded ones, using them either singly or in combination. Both the multiflora and grandiflora tkypes are excellent for use in large or small bedding designs.

Marigolds also offer a wide range of colors, from cream to deep orange to mahogany-red, and the flower heads vary from the single daisies of signet marigolds to the large globes of the African cultivars. Easy-to-grow French marigolds, derived from *Tagetes patula*, with single and double flower heads, display coloring in the full range from lemon through gold and orange to chestnut and mahogany. Many other marigolds that are intermediate between African and French types are also available.

Formal bedding designs

The wide variation of color, shape, and size, as well as the uniformity of growth characteristic of many modern cultivars of annuals, provides opportunities to create long-lasting displays from spring to fall. One of the glories of annuals is the intensity of color achieved when a single cultivar of

one of the low-growing, floriferous kinds is massed in a bed so that individual plants merge together. A scarlet carpet of geraniums or of *Salvia splendens*, for example, makes a vivid display when set into a fresh, green lawn. Patterned designs, using annuals of different colors, may produce similarly eye-catching effects. The dense growth habit and continuous flowering of many annuals make them ideal candidates for these complex, formal patterns. There is a wide range of dwarf and intermediate cultivars available. Plants may be used to add color to designs that have been delineated with bricks, gravel, or other architectural materials.

Annuals are excellent for filling in knot gardens and parterres, where small evergreen plants, such as boxwood (*Buxus*), thyme (*Thymus*), or lavender (*Lavandula*), are clipped to create permanent outlines. Vary color themes with the seasons: a winter planting of pansies that continues into spring may be followed by a summer one of dwarf zinnias, for example.

Alternatively, annuals, biennials, and other temporary plants can be used alone to create designs that are expressed in the use of contrasting colors and form. An outline of low, mound-forming plants in a single color will help to define a pattern and contain filler

plants. White always makes a crisp, clear edging—English daisies (*Bellis perennis*) in spring, sweet alyssum (*Lobularia maritima*) or white *Lobelia erinus* cultivars in summer. The fillers may be flowers with a looser, more irregular shape, such as snapdragons.

Mixed borders

A mixed border, containing shrubs, perennials, bulbs, and annuals, is one of the delights of the garden. With such a diversity of plants, it offers the greatest possible variety in terms of color, texture, season of interest, and design. Annuals and biennials warrant a place in any permanent planting plan, in which they can be sown each year or left to self-seed. If allowed to self-sow, they will produce a random profusion of flowers reminiscent of the traditional cottage garden, where all manner of plants, including salad and vegetable crops, happily jostle for space in the same informal plot.

Used as color highlights among perennials and shrubs, annuals and biennials bring life to established borders. Possibilities range from cheerful mixtures of *Clarkia* (syn. *Godetia*), *Cosmos*, and California poppies *Eschscholzia californica*), and to carefully coordinated

one-color designs. For example, flowering annuals such as crimson *Amaranthus caudatus* and *Nicotiana alata*, or scarlet begonias, geraniums, and *Verbena* cultivars will add highlights to a red border with a framework of purplish foliage.

Other annuals that can be used to fill gaps and provide extra interest include silvery-gray Scotch thistle (*Onopordum acanthium*), bright red annual poppies (*Papaver somniferum*), and Johnny-jump-ups (*Viola tricolor*). Self-sown annuals and biennials may soon become a permanent feature in a mixed border, helping to unify the planting and introducing a pleasing unpredictability. In early summer *Nigella damascena* makes a hazy web of color, filling gaps and weaving together neighboring blooms and the young leaves of later-flowering plants. The spirelike stems of biennials such as *Verbascum* and the purple and white spikes of foxgloves (*Digitalis*) add an air of informality to an otherwise structured border.

Architectural plants

Handsome leaves, eye-catching flower shapes, and striking habits of growth make certain plants stand out from their companions. Annuals or biennials with such architectural qualities can be key features in a mixed bed or border, enhancing the composition. These plants create the greatest impact when they complement—rather than dominate—the other plants in the vicinity. The large, spiny, gray leaves and tall, widely branched flower stems of the Scotch thistle (*Onopordum acanthium*), for instance, make a statuesque centerpiece in a border that features other types of silver-foliaged plants. The flower spikes of the Excelsior Series foxgloves and larkspur (*Consolida*) rise gracefully above all the neighboring plants. Shapely or unusual blooms, such as the large and complex flower heads of spider flower (*Cleome*) and floss flower (*Ageratum*), will also command attention.

Plants grown primarily for their foliage also play an architectural role. In large borders, the green or purple leaves of castor beans (*Ricinus communis*) add a strong textural quality, as do the bold leaves of the ornamental cabbages (*Brassica oleracea* forms).

Annuals and biennials as fillers

Since they grow rapidly and are relatively cheap to raise, use annuals and biennials to fill gaps that occur, either through failure of a plant or between immature perennials and recently planted shrubs in a new border. Sow seed where the plants are to flower, choosing cultivars in a height and color range to suit the permanent planting designs.

In warmer areas, at the end of the season, plant wallflowers (*Erysimum*) for their winter foliage and spring flowers. Multicolored

Architectural planting Annuals and biennials come in a range of distinctive habits, including plants to give an architectural quality to your planting. In this design, biennial foxgloves (*Digitalis purpurea*) provide a vertical backdrop to the rounded seed heads of annual poppies (*Papaver somniferum*).

Temporary groundcover Annuals planted close together or direct-sown, develop into beautiful groundcovers that also prevent young weeds from becoming established.

carpets of early-flowering pansies (*Viola* x *wittrockiana*) and primroses (*Primula vulgaris*), may be interplanted with spring-flowering bulbs, such as daffodils, hyacinths, or late-flowering tulips.

Until alpines become established, gaps in the rock garden may be filled by sun-loving annuals that enjoy the same conditions. To avoid overwhelming the alpines' delicate colors and modest stature, however, choose a selection of annuals that are on a similar scale, such as *Viola tricolor*, *Lobelia erinus*, and *Portulaca*.

Annuals and biennials as groundcovers

Some annuals and biennials may be used as temporary groundcovers, creating pools of color within an otherwise bare space. There are annuals to suit shade as well as sun, poor soil as well as rich. Single-color cultivars of sweet alyssum (*Lobularia maritima*) or annual candytufts (*Iberis*)

may be used to provide dense cover in a sunny spot. Use *Impatiens* cultivars in shade, where their spreading growth and colorful, continuous blooms will quickly cover the ground. For a more textured quality as well as lively color, sow corn poppies (*Papaver rhoeas*) or California poppies (*Eschscholzia*); both spread quickly. To create an attractive groundcover quickly, use cultivars of vinca (*Catharanthus roseus*) in white or rose, or the bushier nasturtiums in vivid reds, oranges, or yellows, some with pretty, variegated leaves.

Climbers and trailers

Vigorous annuals and biennials that climb and trail quickly may transform an expanse of wall or fence with a colorful curtain of foliage and flower, weaving a screen to provide privacy, or embellishing an existing structure such as an arch. A number of annuals have attractive leaves as well as beautiful flowers, and a few—for example, sweet peas (*Lathyrus odoratus*)—offer the additional pleasure of scent (see SWEET PEAS, pp.212–213).

Plants with a climbing or trailing habit are particularly valuable in restricted spaces such as patios and balconies, where they make use of the vertical space as well as the ground area. Moreover, many annual climbers can be grown in pots, and are ideal for furnishing new gardens, softening bleak surfaces, and disguising an unsightly view.

In addition to favorites such as sweet peas and morning glory (*Ipomoea*), an increasing range of half-hardy and tender climbers is now more widely available as seeds or young plants. Exuberant plants such as the climbing cultivars of nasturtium or black-eyed Susan vine (*Thunbergia alata*) may be used to provide an abundance of summer flowers along with more permanent perennial climbers. Particularly striking, although slower to grow initially, are *Cobaea scandens* with its large bell-shaped flowers in purple or greenish-white, and *Rhodochiton atrosanguineus*, an intriguing plant with curious, deep purple, tubular flowers in dusky maroon calyces.

Climbing annuals are intriguing when they are grown through host plants, such as ivy (*Hedera*) or conifers. Try the climbing annual canary creeper (*Tropaeolum peregrinum*), which has pale green, dissected leaves and bright yellow, fringed flowers. Another good choice is the half-hardy climber *Eccremocarpus scaber*, the fiery Chilean glory flower, which climbs by means of tendrils and has a long flowering season, with clusters of tubular flowers that glow yellow, orange, or red among small, tooth-shaped, pinnate leaves. For a dense, leafy screen, plant scarlet runner beans (*Phaseolus coccineus*), which have delicate scarlet flowers, and the bonus of edible pods. For a more exotic look, try the purple hyacinth bean (*Lablab purpureus* 'Ruby Moon') with purplish-green foliage, bright purple flowers, and shiny, deep purple pods.

Annuals for cutting and drying

Many annuals can provide excellent cut flowers for indoor arrangements. If you have enough space, it is worth growing flowers especially for cutting. They may be either integrated into borders or sown in a separate area. Taller cultivars may be particularly suitable; choose from a range including snapdragons, cornflowers (*Centaurea cyanus*), stocks (*Matthiola*), and *Gypsophila*. Sweet peas (*Lathyrus odoratus*) are particularly good as cut flowers and fill the house with their heady fragrance; if the flowers are cut regularly, the plants will continue to produce blooms for many weeks. Larkspur (*Consolida*) is also useful for cutting and is equally attractive whether fresh or dried.

Many annuals may be dried as everlasting flowers for indoor display throughout the year; they include strawflower (*Xerochrysum*), *Amaranthus caudatus*, and *Limonium*. Others such as honesty (*Lunaria*) and *Nigella* are often grown for their decorative seed heads.

Planting containers Growing annuals in containers offers an opportunity to experiment with different colors and planting combinations. Choose a mixture of plants with upright and trailing habits, and also consider smaller perennials and shrubs, such as evergreen ivies (*Hedera helix*).

Annual grasses, such as hare's tail (*Lagarus ovatus*), are also worth growing because their feature seed heads make a fine display.

Annuals in containers

Whether it is a pot, tub, or window box, any container is a potential focal point in the garden, and the plants grown in it can make an eye-catching feature. F1 hybrid annuals, with their uniform growth habit and consistent flower colors, are specifically bred to provide uniform, long-lasting displays. Most annuals, however, may be used in containers, either on their own or to complement other plants (see also CONTAINER GARDENING, p.313).

Annuals are available for a season-long display. In late spring and early summer, some cultivars of pansies and primroses will thrive in sheltered spots away from the blazing sun and heat. Protected but sunny sites on patios are also ideal for gazanias, coleus, New Guinea impatiens, and seed-raised dahlias, all of which maintain their color throughout summer and well into fall.

Compact cultivars are particularly good choices for containers because they don't need support and are less likely to blow over in the wind. For example, select dwarf snapdragon cultivars rather than tall ones. New hybrid geraniums that are intermediate in habit between trailing and bushy types are ideal for growing in containers. Try the Sensation, Breakaway, and Multibloom Series. Heliotrope's delightful perfume will waft indoors from a container placed near a window or doorway. Stocks (*Matthiola*) have wonderful scent, and the Harmony and Midget series are types that do well in pots.

Hanging baskets and window boxes
Plants with a trailing habit are ideal for growing in window boxes and hanging baskets, and appealing displays may be created by a mass of foliage and flower. Reliable performers include trailing petunias, *Lobelia erinus*, such as the Cascade Series, and *Verbena* x *hybrida* cultivars, which are available in a wide range of colors, including pure reds and scarlets as well as deep purples, crimsons, and whites. Trailing and spreading F1 geraniums, renewed annually from seed, are also good value (see also GERANIUMS, pp.220–221).

Everlasting flowers Statice (*Limonium sinuatum*) and many other colorful annuals, can easily be dried by hanging the cut stems upside down in a warm, airy place.

Vertical planting Trailing plants, such as ivy-leaf geraniums, cascade down from hanging baskets and window boxes to create a continuous curtain of color.

PLANTER'S GUIDE TO ANNUALS AND BIENNIALS

EXPOSED SITES

Annuals and biennials that tolerate exposed or windy sites (may require support)

Borago officinalis
Calendula
Catharanthus roseus
Centaurea cyanus
Cerinthe
Clarkia
Dianthus barbatus,
  D. chinensis
Echium vulgare
Erysimum
Eschscholzia
Glaucium flavum
Iberis amara,
  I. umbellata
Lavatera trimestris
Limnanthes
Linum grandiflorum
Lobularia maritima
Lunaria
Malcolmia
Malope trifida
Oenothera biennis
Papaver rhoeas,
  P. somniferum
Petunia
Rudbeckia hirta (hybrids)
Salvia viridis
Tagetes tenuifolia
Vaccaria hispanica
Verbena bonariensis
Xanthophthalmum (formerly
  Chrysanthemum) carinatum,
  X. coronarium,
  X. segetum

DRY SHADE

Annuals and biennials that tolerate dry shade

Digitalis purpurea
Matthiola longipetala
  subsp. bicornis

MOIST SHADE

Annuals and biennials that enjoy moist shade

Impatiens walleriana
Matthiola longipetala
  subsp. bicornis
Mimulus x hybridus 'Calypso',
  M. x hybridus Magic Series,
  M. Malibu Series
Oenothera biennis
Primula Polyanthus Group,
  P. vulgaris
Viola x wittrockiana

FRAGRANT FLOWERS

Amberboa moschata
Calomeria amaranthoides
Centaurea moschata
Dianthus Giant
  Chabaud Series
Exacum affine
Heliotropium
Lathyrus odoratus
Lobularia maritima

Matthiola Brompton Series,
  M. East Lothian Series,
  M. incana Ten Week Mixed
Nicotiana alata,
  N. x sanderae, N. sylvestris
Primula
Reseda odorata
Viola x wittrockiana

TRAILING PLANTS FOR CONTAINERS

Arctotis venusta
Asarina
Begonia Panorama Series
Bidens ferulifolia
Brachyscome iberidifolia
Calibrachoa (Million Bells)
Convolvulus tricolor
Heliotropium
Impatiens walleriana
Lobelia erinus Cascade Series,
  L. erinus Fountain Series,
  L. erinus Regatta Series
Lobularia maritima
  Trailing Series, L. maritima
  'Wandering Star'
Pelargonium Multibloom Series,
  P. 'Summer Showers'
  (and suitable other F1 and F2 Series)
Petunia, especially Surfinia Series
Sanvitalia procumbens
Scaevola
Tropaeolum majus semitrailing cvs
  including T. majus 'Empress of India',
  T. majus Gleam Series,
  T. majus Whirlybird Series
Verbena x hybrida (trailing types)
Viola x wittrockiana Splendid Series

FLOWERS FOR DRYING

Ageratum
Amaranthus
Ammobium alatum
Avena sterilis
Briza maxima, B. minor
Calendula
Celosia
Centaurea cyanus
Clarkia
Consolida ambigua
Gomphrena globosa
Hordeum jubatum
Lagurus ovatus
Limonium sinuatum
Lonas
Moluccella laevis
Nigella
Panicum miliaceum 'Violaceum'
Pennisetum villosum
Salvia viridis
Setaria glauca
Stipa pennata
Syncarpha

ANNUAL CLIMBERS

See list on p.129.

ARCHITECTURAL PLANTS

Alcea rosea
Amaranthus caudatus,
  A. tricolor

Bassia scoparia
  f. trichophylla
Brassica oleracea Osaka Series,
  B. oleracea 'Tokyo'
Campanula medium (tall cvs)
Canna
Cleome hassleriana
Consolida
Digitalis purpurea
  Excelsior Group
Helianthus annuus
Onopordum acanthium,
  O. nervosum
Ricinus communis
Salvia sclarea var. sclarea
Silybum marianum
Tagetes erecta (tall cvs)
Verbascum bombyciferum,
  V. densiflorum
Zea mays 'Quadricolor'

POT PLANTS

Annuals suitable for growing from seed as (greenhouse) pot plants

Antirrhinum
Begonia semperflorens
Calomeria amaranthoides
Campanula pyramidalis
Capsicum
  (ornamental fruit cvs)
Centaurea moschata
Datura (dwarf cvs)
Exacum affine
Impatiens walleriana
  (tall cvs)
Isotoma
Osteospermum
Pelargonium
  (F1 and F2 hybrids)
Pericallis x hybrida (cvs)
Petunia
Primula malacoides,
  P. obconica,
  P. sinensis
Psylliostachys suworowii
Salpiglossis
Schizanthus
Solenostemon
Thunbergia alata
Torenia fournieri
Trachelium caeruleum
Trachymene coerulea

PERENNIALS THAT MAY BE GROWN AS ANNUALS

Achillea Summer Pastels Group
Agastache aurantiaca
Alcea 'Majorette',
  A. Summer Carnival Group
Coreopsis grandiflora
  'Early Sunrise'
Delphinium Centurion Series
Dianthus 'Champion',
  D. 'Floristan'
Diascia
Leucanthemum x superbum
  'Snow Lady'
Linaria purpurea cvs
Lobelia x speciosa Fan Series,
  L. x speciosa Compliment Series
Nemesia

Penstemon Tubular Bells Series
Prunella 'Pagoda'
Ricinus communis
Veronica 'Sightseeing'

FLOWERS FOR CUTTING

Agrostemma githago 'Milas'
Antirrhinum (tall cvs)
Calendula
Callistephus (tall cvs)
Centaurea cyanus
Consolida ambigua
Coreopsis grandiflora
  'Early Sunrise'
Cosmos
Dianthus barbatus,
  D. Giant Chabaud Series,
  D. Knight Series
Erysimum cheiri
Gaillardia pulchella
Gilia capitata
Gomphrena globosa
Gypsophila elegans
Helianthus annuus,
  H. Color Fashion Series
Lathyrus odoratus
Limonium sinuatum
Lunaria annua
Matthiola Brompton Series,
  M. East Lothian Series,
  M. incana,
  M. incana Ten Week Mixed
Moluccella laevis
Nigella damascena
Papaver croceum,
  P. croceum 'Summer Breeze'
Psylliostachys suworowii
Rudbeckia hirta (hybrids)
Salvia viridis
Syncarpha
Xanthophthalmum (formerly
  Chrysanthemum) carinatum,
  X. coronarium,
  X. segetum
Xeranthemum annuum
Zinnia

Lathyrus odoratus

Sweet peas

Sweet peas (*Lathyrus odoratus*) have been dubbed "the queen of annuals" for their beautiful flowers, marvelous scent, and long flowering period. As long as you can provide the cool, moist growing conditions that sweet peas thrive in, they will provide long-lasting, colorful, and fragrant displays when trained up tepees, pillars, or stakes.

Types of sweet peas

Most familiar are the heirloom and exhibition types, which climb a supporting framework by means of leaf tendrils. Some large-flowered cultivars may grow 6–10ft (2–3m) high depending on growing conditions. Heirloom cultivars, such as 'Old Spice Mix', have smaller, "old-fashioned" flowers but they are more highly scented.

Intermediate-height sweet pea cultivars, such as 'Knee-Hi' and 'Supersnoop', reach about 3ft (1m) tall if supported, but they also serve as a colorful groundcover if left unsupported. Dwarf types include 'Little Sweetheart', 'Bijou', and 'Pink Cupid'.

Old fashioned sweet peas
Old-fashioned sweet peas are more similar to the species than most of the modern cultivars. They have delicately colored, small, highly scented flowers.

Dwarf sweet peas
Dwarf sweet peas grow to about 18in (45cm) high and need little or no support. They grow well when planted in tubs, window boxes, and hanging baskets.

Growing sweet peas from seed

Seeds may be sown in late fall in mild-winter regions. If you have cold winters but hot summers, start the seeds early indoors or in a cold frame 6–8 weeks before the last frost. Protect seedlings from being eaten by mice or chipmunks.

Sowing

Sweet pea seeds vary in color from pale buff to black. To help them germinate, nick the darker seeds with a sharp pocket knife, removing a small piece of seed coat opposite the eye. Sweet pea seeds may be soaked to achieve fast germination, although there may be a problem with rotting.

Sow the seeds in flats, cell packs, or deep 2in (5cm) pots (one, two, or three seeds per pot). Use a soilless potting mix with 20 percent grit added, or a standard seed-sowing mix.

Dark seeds germinate well in fairly damp soil, but pale ones require soil that is only just moist. Cover the containers with glass or plastic wrap and keep them at about 60°F (15°C). When the seedlings appear, transfer them to a cold frame—they like temperatures of 40–50°F (4–10°C).

Repotting

Prick out seedlings from flats and then pot them individually when plants are about 1½in (3.5cm) tall. Fill 3-in (6-cm) pots with a potting mix similar to that used for sowing. Pinch out root tips and then repot.

If you wish, you can pinch the growing tip of fall-sown sweet peas if they have failed to produce sideshoots by midwinter. Pinch spring-sown seedlings at the second pair of leaves.

Overwintering seedlings

Keep the cold frame open as much as possible during light frosts—this will help harden off the plants. If temperatures drop below 28°F (-2°C), close and insulate the frame. In heavy rain, prop open the top of the frame for ventilation. Control aphids (p.646) and give diluted liquid fertilizer in late winter.

(p.646)

BUSH SWEET PEAS

Pea stick supports
Pea sticks are the traditional means of supporting sweet peas. Insert the pea sticks when the seedlings are planted out, leaning the sticks in toward the center of the clump for extra stability.

Wire rings
Bush sweet peas may be grown up wire rings anchored with several bamboo canes. The plants will grow through the wire, hiding their supports.

Tepee
A tepee of bamboo canes secured near the top also provides a sturdy support. One seedling beside each cane is usually enough to provide a dense mass of flowers.

Hardening off spring-sown plants

This demands more care because the plants are smaller and growth is softer than on fall-sown plants. Keep the cold frame very well ventilated, but close the top if frost threatens and protect with heavyweight row cover during any very hard freezes.

Planting

Sweet peas thrive in sunny, open sites and well-drained, humus-rich soil (see "Soil structure and water content," p.620). Fortify the soil well with compost or aged manure before planting. Adding a pea inoculant to the soil can help if this is the first time peas have been grown in this location. Three weeks prior to planting, carefully rake in a balanced fertilizer at a rate of 3oz/sq yd (85g/sq m).

Plant out fall-sown sweet peas in mid-spring, spring-sown ones in late spring. Set plants 9in (23cm) apart just behind and to one side of their support, with the bottom shoot level with the soil. Water during dry spells and when flower buds appear. Foliar-feed the plants two or three times at two-week intervals from midsummer onward. Deadhead plants to encourage continuous flowering.

see "Soil structure and water content," p.620

INITIAL TRAINING OF CORDONS

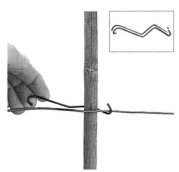

1 After setting up the wires and posts, insert 8ft (2.5m) bamboo canes 9in (23cm) apart at a slight angle along the row and attach them to the wires using V-clips.

2 About 2 weeks after planting the young sweet peas, select the strongest shoot of each plant and attach it to the cane with a wire ring loosely fastened below a leaf node.

3 At the same time, pinch or cut out all the other sideshoots to concentrate the vigor into the main shoot.

4 Keep pinching out any sideshoots or tendrils that form and any flower stems carrying fewer than 4 buds.

Bush sweet peas

Sweet peas are usually allowed to develop naturally into bushes. Support the plants with pea sticks, trellises, stakes, or rigid plastic netting. Stakes and sticks may be grouped in circles, tepee-style, or arranged in rows. A double row of pea sticks and stakes must be well supported, preferably with a post at each end and a strainer wire. Tie young plants to their supports with twine; thereafter they need little tying in. Sideshoots are left to develop, producing more flowers on short stems.

Cordon sweet peas

If you want to try growing topquality sweet peas, you can train them in a system of cordons: plants trained upright on individual stakes.

Providing supports

At each end of a row, drive in a post with an 18in (45cm) cross-piece near the top, 6ft (2m) off the ground. Stretch two parallel wires between the cross-pieces. Place 8ft (2.5m) bamboo stakes, spaced 9in (23cm) apart, at a slight angle against the wires and secure them with V-clips. Rows should run north to south to expose plants evenly to sunlight.

Initial training

Leave plants to establish for two weeks. Then pinch out the weaker shoots to leave the strongest shoot on each plant as well as the shoot immediately below the growing point in case the main leader is damaged by, for example, birds. Train the shoots up the cane, tying them with raffia, tape, or rings at each node. Remove sideshoots and tendrils as they grow. When flower stems form, remove any with fewer than four buds.

Layering

When plants are 4ft (1.2m) tall, they should be untied and trained up a new cane farther along the row (see *Layering Cordons*, right). Do this on a warm day when plants are not too sappy. They will then continue to grow and flower for several weeks.

LAYERING CORDONS

1 In early summer, when the sweet peas have reached a height of 4ft (1.2m), they are ready to be layered. This will give them more space to continue growing and flowering.

2 Carefully untie the plants from their canes and lay them on the ground to their full length. If the plants are in double rows, do this for one row at a time.

3 Attach the shoot tip to a new cane farther along the row, so that it reaches 1ft (30cm) up the cane. Work along the row until all the plants are attached to new canes.

4 Repeat for the second row of plants, if required. Flowers will then continue to be produced on the new growth stimulated by the layering method. Sweet peas can be layered again later in the season, provided the plants remain healthy and disease-free. Once they reach the top wire, untie each stem and attach the tip to a new cane farther up the row.

Sowing and planting

ANNUALS AND BIENNIALS FOR SANDY SOIL

Anchusa capensis
Argemone mexicana
Brachyscome iberidifolia
Calendula officinalis
Camissonia cheiranthifolia
Centaurea cyanus
Clarkia amoena
Coreopsis tinctoria
Dianthus
Eschscholzia californica
Glaucium flavum
Lavatera trimestris
Limnanthes douglasii
Limonium sinuatum
Linaria maroccana
Lobularia maritima
Mentzelia lindleyi
Oenothera biennis
Papaver rhoeas,
  P. somniferum
Platystemon californicus
Portulaca grandiflora
Rudbeckia hirta
Schizanthus
Tagetes
Verbascum bombyciferum
Xerochrysum bracteatum

ANNUALS AND BIENNIALS FOR VERY ALKALINE SOIL

Ageratum houstonianum
Antirrhinum majus
Calendula officinalis
Callistephus chinensis
Calomeria amaranthoides
Cosmos
Dianthus, some
Erysimum cheiri
Gomphrena globosa
Lavatera trimestris
Limonium sinuatum
Lobularia maritima
Matthiola Brompton Series,
  M. incana
Salvia viridis
Tagetes
Tropaeolum, some
Ursinia anthemoides
Xeranthemum annuum
Zinnia

Cosmos bipinnatus
Sensation Series

Annuals and biennials are among the easiest of plants to raise from seed. They may also be obtained as seedlings or young plants from nurseries or garden centers, and will provide an instant display of color in a garden border or container placed indoors or outside.

Buying seeds

Always buy fresh seeds that have been stored in cool conditions. The viability of seeds of different species varies greatly; while some, such as peas and beans, may remain viable for a few years if kept cool and dry, most start to deteriorate after a year, especially if they are stored in damp, warm conditions. Seeds in sealed foil packs last for several years; once the packs are opened, however, the seed viability deteriorates.

F1 and F2 hybrid seeds are available for many annuals and for some biennials; these produce plants that are vigorous and true to type with even growth and flower characteristics. These seeds are ideal for the gardener seeking uniformity, but for most ordinary garden purposes well-produced, open-pollinated seeds are equally satisfactory.

Pelleted and primed seeds

Seeds may be individually coated with a paste, or pelleted, to form a smooth ball. This enables them to be handled separately, so that they may be more easily spaced in containers or beds and borders. If pelleted seeds are space-sown at the correct distance for the cultivar concerned, they do not need to be thinned so, although they cost more, fewer are required. The seeds should be watered thoroughly after sowing to ensure that the moisture needed for germination to occur penetrates the seed coat as quickly as possible. Pelleted seeds are normally available in a number of hybrids and species, especially where the seed is small, as well as in some open-pollinated genera, such as *Lobelia* and *Alyssum*.

Primed seeds are pretreated so they are ready to germinate as soon as they are sown. They are very useful for species and cultivars that do not germinate easily.

Seed tapes and gels

Seed tapes are tissuelike, soluble strips with evenly spaced seeds embedded within them. The tapes are laid at the base of a furrow, then covered with a thin layer of soil. Gel kits may be purchased for fluid sowing—seeds are added to a paste so that they are suspended and therefore evenly spaced throughout. The mixture is then squeezed along a prepared furrow. It is important not to allow the mixture to dry out. Both these methods distribute the seeds evenly so that less thinning is required than for hand-sown seeds.

Buying seedlings

Seeds of some plants that germinate less readily are available from some seed firms at the chitting stage—when the seed coat has burst open and roots and seed leaves are starting to emerge. The seeds are usually sown on agar jelly and kept in a sealed plastic container. Healthy seedlings should have fresh, moist roots and seed leaves; reject any that have pale green leaves or are overcrowded. The jelly contains enough food and moisture to sustain them for a few days but the seeds should be transferred to the required growing conditions as soon as possible so the seedlings have sufficient light to develop. Seedlings of selected cultivars may be purchased as plug plants, when they have developed at least one pair of true leaves and are ready for pricking out (see p.217). This is useful for plants with very small seeds, such as begonias, which are difficult for many gardeners to germinate successfully. The plugs are sent out in a rigid transparent plastic container to keep them as fresh as possible. If pricked out within 24 hours of arrival and kept within a protected environment, they will usually grow as well as plants from home-germinated seeds.

HARDY AND HALF-HARDY ANNUALS AND BIENNIALS

Annuals complete their life cycle in a year, while biennials require two years. Horticulturally, annuals and biennials are termed hardy or half hardy. Hardy annuals are resistant to cold and so may be sown early in open beds and will be established before more frost-prone annuals. Half-hardy annuals withstand only a limited amount of cold and are killed or badly damaged at freezing temperatures; they need to be maintained in frost-free conditions of 55–70°F (13–21°C) in order to germinate and establish. Hardy biennials should be sown by midsummer to allow the plants to become well established by winter. Overwinter half-hardy biennials in a cool greenhouse or insulated cold frame.

Limnanthes douglasii

Small seedlings already well established in wedges or plugs of potting mix are also readily available. Depending on size, they can be grown on in their cell flats or be potted up individually in small pots or hanging baskets. They should be grown on in a greenhouse or cold frame, or on a sunny windowsill, until they are ready to be hardened off and planted out. They are much cheaper than bedding plants.

Sowing

When and where to sow annuals and biennials depends on when they are required to flower and the temperature they need for germination to occur.

Hardy annuals

Sow hardy annuals where they are to flower when the soil has warmed up to at least 45°F (7°C) in the spring. If sown in successive batches until midsummer, hardy annuals provide a long summer display.

Some hardy annuals, if sown *in situ* in the fall, germinate to produce small plants that overwinter satisfactorily outdoors and flower in late spring or early summer the following year. Love-in-a-mist (*Nigella*), cornflower (*Centaurea cyanus*), and poppies (*Papaver*) are some examples.

Seeds of hardy annuals may also be sown in pots or seed flats and either planted out in their final flowering locations in late fall or overwintered in a cold frame to be planted out in spring. This is a useful practice in gardens with clay soil that is slow to warm up in spring.

Hardy biennials

Most hardy biennials may be sown outdoors from late spring until midsummer. The optimal time varies: forget-me-nots (*Myosotis*) grow rapidly so should not be sown until midsummer, while Canterbury bells (*Campanula medium*) need longer to develop and should be sown in late spring or early summer.

The young plants may be transplanted to their final flowering location in fall or, if they are not crowded, the following spring. Premature flowering reduces the spring display, so pinch off any buds that form in the first season.

Half-hardy annuals and biennials

In warm climates, sow seed directly outside once the soil temperature reaches the optimum for germination. In colder regions, sow half-hardy annuals in containers in spring at 55–70°F (13–21°C), according to the particular genus. Half-hardy biennials may be sown under the same conditions in midsummer. Frost-tender perennials, such as *impatiens*, gazanias, and some *Lobelia* species, may be raised from seed in the same way as half-hardy annuals.

Many tender perennials (including *Argyranthemum* and *Osteospermum*) may be propagated by cuttings taken in fall (see PERENNIALS, "Stem tip cuttings," p.200) and be overwintered in frost-free conditions for planting out in late spring.

Sowing in beds and borders

There are two main methods of sowing outdoors *in situ*: broadcast and in furrows. For both methods, a seedbed in a sunny place should be prepared. Dig the soil to one shovel's depth, then rake it well and firm it by stepping down gently on the surface. Do not sow in soil that is too rich, because this will encourage leaf rather than flower production. In soils lacking nutrients, however, a dressing of 2oz/sq yd (70g/sq m) of a balanced fertilizer may be added before sowing (see "Soil nutrients and fertilizers," pp.624–625) in order to boost production.

Before sowing a border, prepare a plan showing the position of each cultivar, using any areas likely to be shaded to grow those that are shade-tolerant. Mark the area for each cultivar with grit or a stake so that it is easy to check the balance of colors, heights, and habits of the different plants before sowing the seed.

SOWING SEED BROADCAST

1 Prepare the soil by raking to produce a fine tilth. Scatter the seeds thinly over the prepared area by hand or from the packet.

2 Rake over the area lightly at right angles to cover the seeds so that they are disturbed as little as possible.

LAYING OUT ANNUAL BORDERS

1 Sprinkle grit or sand on the soil or score the soil with a stick to mark interlocking areas for sowing seeds.

2 The seedlings may appear too sparse at first but will blend together as they grow.

Bed and border sowing is particularly suitable for annuals that produce deep taproots such as *Clarkia*, *Gypsophila*, and poppies (*Papaver*), because they are best sown where they are to flower since they do not transplant readily.

Sowing broadcast

Sprinkle seeds thinly and evenly on the surface of the prepared seedbed and rake them in lightly. Label, then water the area with a watering can equipped with a fine nozzle.

Sowing in furrows

Seeds sown in furrows produce seedlings growing in straight rows at regular intervals so they are readily distinguished from weed seedlings, which are randomly distributed. The seedlings initially look regimented but, once thinned, form a dense and informal planting, and rows in adjoining areas can be arranged at different angles.

Using either a trowel tip or the corner of a hoe, mark out shallow furrows 3–6in (8–15cm) apart

SOWING IN FURROWS

1 Using a line of string as a guide, make a furrow about 1in (2.5cm) deep with a hoe.

2 Holding the seeds in one hand, pick up several at a time and scatter them evenly along the furrow.

ALTERNATIVE STEP

If the seeds are pelleted, place them individually in the base of the furrow.

3 Rake the soil back over the furrow without dislodging the seeds. After labeling the row, water the soil using a watering can with a fine nozzle.

SELF-SEEDING ANNUALS AND BIENNIALS

Annuals and biennials that self-seed either true to type or with minor variations if closely related cultivars are not growing nearby

Agrostemma githago
Borago officinalis
Calendula officinalis
Centaurea cyanus
Clarkia amoena
Collinsia bicolor
Digitalis purpurea
Eschscholzia californica
Hesperis matronalis
Limnanthes douglasii
Linaria maroccana
Lobularia maritima
Lunaria annua
Malcolmia maritima
Myosotis sylvatica
Nicotiana langsdorffii
Nigella damascena
Oenothera biennis
Omphalodes linifolia
Onopordum acanthium,
  O. nervosum
Papaver rhoeas, P. somniferum
Platystemon californicus
Silene armeria
Silybum marianum
Tanacetum parthenium
Tropaeolum majus
Vaccaria hispanica
Verbascum (some sp.)
Viola (many spp.)
Xanthophthalmum
  segetum

Viola tricolor hybrid

THINNING SEEDLINGS

Individual seedlings
Press on either side of the seedling to be retained (here, larkspur, *Consolida ambigua*) while pulling out the unwanted ones around it. Refirm and water.

Seedling groups
Lift groups of seedlings (here, sweet William, *Dianthus barbatus*) with plenty of soil around the roots if they are to be replanted. Firm in and water the remaining seedlings.

depending on the ultimate size of the plants. Sow seeds thinly and evenly by sprinkling or placing them along each furrow at the appropriate depth for the annuals being sown, then carefully draw back the displaced soil with a rake or hoe to cover them. Label each row and water well with a watering can equipped with a fine nozzle.

Thinning
To prevent overcrowding, the seedlings usually need to be thinned. Do this when the soil is moist and the weather mild, taking care to retain the sturdier seedlings where possible and achieve an even spacing. To minimize disturbance to a seedling being retained, press

the soil around it with your fingers as the surplus seedlings are extracted.

If seedlings are very dense, dig them up in clumps, retaining plenty of soil around the roots; disturb the other seedlings in the ground as little as possible. Some biennials, such as forget-me-nots (*Myosotis*) and honesty (*Lunaria*), germinate readily and if sown where they are to flower should be thinned appropriately—forget-me-nots to 6in (15cm) and honesty to 12in (30cm), for example.

The thinnings may be used to fill sparse areas caused by uneven sowing or irregular germination, or may be transplanted for use elsewhere in the garden. For transplanting, select the strongest

and healthiest of the thinned seedlings, then replant them where needed at the appropriate spacings and water them lightly to settle their roots.

Many annuals and biennials scatter their seeds freely, often producing dense clumps of seedlings; these need to be thinned carefully to the appropriate distances apart, so that the young plants retained may develop without competition.

Sowing in pots or flats

Half-hardy annuals are usually sown in containers so that they may develop under cover and be planted out as young plants when conditions are favorable. Hardy annuals may also be sown in containers left outside, and the seedlings transplanted to their flowering locations when there is sufficient room.

Pots, seed pans, seed flats, and cell packs are all suitable containers, depending on the number of seeds to be sown and the space they require. Biodegradable pots are also useful for seedlings that do not transplant well, because the whole pot may be planted out without disturbing the roots.

Sowing the seeds
Fill the chosen container to its rim with all-purpose potting mix and press in lightly around the edges with the fingertips to make sure that there are no air pockets. To settle the potting mix, tap the container against a hard surface and then gently firm the potting mix level so that the top of the potting mix is just below the rim of the container. Water with a fine nozzle and leave for an hour to drain.

Sow the seeds thinly on the surface of the potting mix, tapping them from the seed pack or from V-shaped paper to achieve an even spread. Large or pelleted seeds may be sown individually in compartmented packs or spaced out in flats or pans. Very small seeds are easier to sow if they are mixed first with the same bulk of fine sand; this produces a more even distribution.

Cover the seeds to about their own depth with sifted potting mix, perlite, or vermiculite; then water lightly, so as not to disturb the seeds or the surface of the potting mix. Dustlike seeds, such as those of begonia, should be left uncovered and watered from below: place each container within 1in (2.5cm) of its rim in water until the surface of the potting mix is moist. Do not leave

PROTECTING AND SUPPORTING SEEDLINGS

Support is required for slender-stemmed or tall annuals. Carefully insert pea sticks or thin twigs into the soil around young plants; the supports should be slightly shorter than the ultimate height of the plants so that they will be concealed when the plants reach their mature size. These supports may also help to protect the seedlings from possible rodent and bird damage.

Alternatively, stretch chicken wire, with a mesh no greater than 1in (2.5cm), over the seedbed, bending it down at the edges so it does not touch the seedlings. Secure firmly in the soil, using sticks or wire pins. The plants grow up through the mesh and cover the chicken wire when fully grown.

Supporting with twigs
Pea sticks or thin twigs may be pushed into the soil among the seedlings. Tall annuals (here, larkspur, *Consolida ambigua*) grow to hide the support.

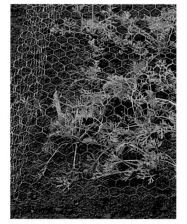

Wire protection and support
Protect seedlings (here, *Eschscholzia*) with chicken wire bent to form a cage. The wire will support the seedlings as they grow through.

SOWING IN A FLAT

1 Fill the seed tray with a standard potting mix and level with a presser board to ½in (1cm) below the rim.

2 Using a V-shaped piece of paper, sprinkle the seeds thinly over the potting mix surface, to achieve an even covering.

3 Cover the seeds with a layer of sifted moist potting mix, perlite, or vermiculite to about the same thickness as the seeds themselves. Water the seeds in lightly.

4 Place a piece of glass or sheet of plastic over the tray to maintain even humidity.

5 Shade the tray with netting if the tray is in direct sunlight. Remove both glass and netting as soon as germination starts.

SEEDS WITH SPECIAL REQUIREMENTS

A few seeds need special conditions to germinate successfully. Coleus (*Solenostemon*), begonia, and *Impatiens* seeds require light and prefer a constant temperature of 70°F (21°C). Primulas prefer light, but need temperatures of no more than 68°F (20°C). Some seeds, including *Phacelia*, pansies (*Viola x wittrockiana*), and other *Viola* should be germinated in the dark. Seeds of *Thunbergia alata* and geraniums require scarifying, sowing, and 70–75°F (21–24°C) to germinate. Seeds of *Moluccella* should be stratified: the seed pan is set in a refrigerator for a couple of weeks before bringing it into a temperature of 64–70°F (18–21°C) for another two or three weeks.

---

them soaking for too long, because waterlogging may cause rotting before germination or encourage seedling diseases (see "Damping off," p.658).

To maintain even humidity, it is advisable to place a piece of glass or sheet of plastic over the container; do not let it touch the potting mix surface, because this may disturb the seeds. Place the container on a heated mat (see Greenhouses and Frames, "Propagation aids," p.580), in a propagator or on a greenhouse bench, and shade with fine netting or newspaper if it receives direct sunlight. As soon as the first seedlings germinate, the cover should be removed. Keep the seedlings in good light and the potting mix moist until they are ready for pricking out.

Pricking out

Seedlings raised in flats or shallow trays need to be transplanted into larger containers before they become overcrowded, because they will quickly become weak and spindly when deprived of sufficient space or light. This is known as pricking off or pricking out seedlings. The process enables the seedlings to continue to develop until they are larger and more robust and therefore ready for planting out in the beds.

Fill the new containers with potting mix and firm gently. Small pots, no more than 3in (7cm) in diameter, or cell packs, are ideal for individual seedlings; larger pots, pans, or flats may be used for several seedlings.

To prick out, first knock the container of seedlings against a tabletop or bench to loosen the potting mix slightly and remove it intact from the container. Then hold each plant gently by the small seed leaves to avoid bruising the stems or growing tips and loosen it with a widger or other small implement. Then carefully lift each plant from the soil, retaining some of the moist

potting mix around the roots to ensure that there will be little or no check to growth when the seedlings are replanted.

Use a dibber to make holes in the potting mix and insert a seedling into each hole. Make sure that all the roots are covered with potting mix, then gently firm in each seedling using fingers or a dibber, and level the mix. As each container is filled, water it from a can equipped with a fine nozzle to settle the potting mix around the roots. Cover the containers with plastic wrap for a few days while the seedlings reestablish,

but make sure that the plastic does not touch the leaves because this may encourage rotting. Then return the seedlings to their previous growing conditions to develop further.

If seedlings are ready for planting out, but this is delayed because of a late frost, pot them on into a larger container and add a liquid fertilizer to ensure that growth is not checked.

Seeds that have been sown singly in packs or space-sown will not need pricking out and may be hardened off before planting out.

PRICKING OUT INTO MODULES

1 When the seedlings (here, *Tagetes*) are large enough to handle, tap the tray on a hard surface to loosen the potting mix.

2 Carefully separate the seedlings, handling them by their seed leaves. Keep plenty of potting mix on the roots.

3 Transplant each seedling into a separate cell of a seed flat. Firm the mix around each one with fingers or a dibber, and water.

ANNUALS IN POTS

Many annuals are excellent potted plants. Prick out young seedlings into divided flats or individual pots and, when the roots have just filled the container, transfer each seedling to a larger pot prepared with soil-based potting mix. The pot size will vary according to the species or cultivar and time of sowing. Put plants sown in late summer into 3in (8cm) pots over the winter when growth is slow, and transfer them later to their final pots—either 5in (13cm), or 7in (19cm), or much larger pots for groups of three or five plants per container. Transplant spring-sown annuals directly into their final pots or containers.

Many annuals (here, *Schizanthus*) provide an early, colorful display in a cool greenhouse or screened porch in spring.

Hardening off

All half-hardy annuals that have been raised either under cover or in any other controlled environment before being planted outdoors need to be acclimatized gradually to the natural conditions outdoors. The goal is to harden the plants, reducing their dependence on artificial heat and protection without exposing them to sudden environmental changes that might cause damage.

Hardening off is most easily done using a greenhouse and a cold frame. Six or seven weeks before planting the seedlings outdoors, move them to a cooler part of the greenhouse for approximately a week. Then transfer them to a closed cold frame; increase the ventilation little by little, eventually dispensing with the frame light (the lid) entirely for the last few days unless frost is forecast.

Keep a close watch on the plants for any indication that the change in temperature is too great or too swift: there may be a check in growth, for example, or the leaves may yellow.

Other equipment that is ideal for hardening off includes glazed frames, the covers of which may be removed completely when conditions are favorable, and row covers, which may be lifted off and replaced as necessary. Alternatively, the young plants may be placed outdoors in sheltered locations and protected (normally only necessary at night) with horticultural fabric, plastic, or other coverings on temporary wood or bamboo frames. Unless weather conditions are poor, the covers should be removed during the day to ensure that the plants always receive sufficient light and ventilation.

Planting out

Plant out half-hardy seedlings once all danger of frost has passed. This is particularly important in the case of the more tender plants, such as begonias and *Salvia splendens*. Provided they have been hardened off, some half-hardy annuals will, however, tolerate cool, but not frosty, conditions for short periods.

Before planting out, prepare the bed (see "Sowing in beds and borders," p.217), water the young plants well, and then leave them to drain for an hour or so. To remove a plant from its pot, invert it, supporting the stem with a finger on either side. Then tap the rim against a hard surface to loosen the root ball from the pot. Break apart packs or divided flats to remove each seedling with its root ball undisturbed.

If plants are in flats without divisions, hold the tray firmly with both hands, and tap one side sharply on the ground to loosen the potting mix. Then gently slide out the contents in one piece. Separate individual plants carefully with the fingers, keeping as much soil as possible around the roots. Alternatively, remove each plant gently using a widger or other small tool, making sure not to damage the young roots.

Make a hole sufficiently large to accommodate the root ball readily. Space the plants so that the leaves will just touch when the plants are fully developed. Normal planting distances range from 6–18in (15–45cm), depending on the habit of the species or cultivar being grown.

Check that the plants are at the same depth as in the container, then firm the soil around the base of the stem, without compacting the soil too much. After planting, gently break up the soil surface between the plants with a hand fork. To settle them in, water the plants thoroughly using a watering can equipped with a fine nozzle so that the soil is not washed off the roots.

Stopping or pinching off

As young annuals develop, some may require stopping or pinching off in order to encourage the plants to produce sideshoots and develop a bushy habit. Stopping is done by nipping the growing tip off a young plant. Even with annuals that branch naturally it may be necessary when a few plants in a bed produce stronger shoots than others. If an even growth habit of plants is required, stop tall plants when they have reached five or six joints by removing the tip of each long shoot back to the required height.

Stopping delays flower production and so should not be carried out if an early display is preferred. Nor should it be done on plants such as antirrhinums or stocks (*Matthiola*) that have strong terminal shoots,

PLANTING OUT INTO OPEN BEDS

1 Break the pack apart and carefully remove each seedling (here, *Tagetes*) with its root ball intact.

2 Place each plant in a hole large enough to take its root ball, ensuring that the plant is at the same level as it was in its container.

3 Return the soil around the roots and gently firm so that there are no air pockets. Water the area.

HARDENING OFF

Row cover
Cover half-hardy annuals (here, *Tagetes*) with row cover. Lift the sides for effective ventilation.

Cold frame
Seedlings may also be placed in a cold frame left open for progressively longer intervals each day.

FIRST-YEAR GROWTH

Biennials such as Canterbury bells have only vegetative (leafy) growth in their first year. Flowers develop the following summer.

HOW TO BUY PLANTS

Bedding plants

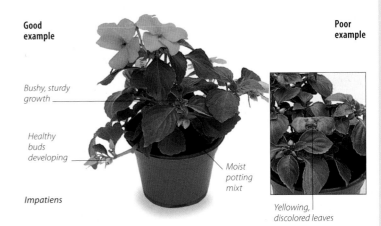

Good example

Compact, vigorous growth

Poor example

Healthy, green foliage

Petunias

Leggy, bare stems

Dead leaves

POT-GROWN ANNUALS

Good example

Poor example

Bushy, sturdy growth

Healthy buds developing

Impatiens

Moist potting mix

Yellowing, discolored leaves

---

since these develop the main flower spikes and will also produce lateral growths naturally during summer to continue the flowering display.

Bedding plants

Buying more mature annuals and biennials to plant out directly into beds, borders, or containers can save time and may be necessary if no greenhouse is available to grow half-hardy annuals from seed. In addition, while seeds of many annuals may be bought only as mixtures, commercial growers are usually able to obtain colors separately, providing gardeners with a much wider range with which to plan their bedding design.

Judging the quality of bedding plants

Sturdy young plants with evenly balanced, short-noded shoots and healthy foliage are most likely to establish well and give the best results. The plants should have well-developed root systems but must not be potbound. Do not buy plants in dry potting mix or with yellowing or diseased foliage because they do not often establish well.

Half-hardy bedding plants are sold at various stages from seedling to flowering plant, frequently well ahead of the date at which it is safe to plant them outdoors. Make sure that you have appropriate conditions under cover to grow them on properly if necessary. Check also that they have been hardened off if they are for immediate planting outside. Acclimatize the seedlings slowly until the danger of frost is past; sudden exposure to frost or even cold wind may kill them, since they may have been produced in heated greenhouses. They may then be planted outdoors.

Annual climbers

Climbing annuals should be planted where they are able to grow naturally through a shrub or tree or be trained against a fence, wall, or some other support. If a twining annual is to climb through a shrub, position the plant on the side where it will receive the most sunlight. Where the climber is intended to be grown up a wall or fence, provide a support that will suit its habit of growth (see CLIMBING PLANTS, "Types of support," p.130); then plant it 12in (30cm) from the base of the wall or fence.

PLANTING BEDDING PLANTS IN A DESIGN

Before planting a bed or border, assemble all the bedding plants to be used and check them off against the plan. Place the plants, still in their containers, roughly in position on top of the prepared soil to ensure that the bed will be neither too crowded nor too sparsely planted. Now is the time to make any final adjustments to the plant positioning—it will be too late once they are in the ground. Keep a few plants in reserve to replace any that may die.

1 Mark the design of the whole bed before planting. Work from the center outward, or from the back of the bed to the front. Use a plank or kneeler so that the soil does not become compacted, making it difficult to work and inhibiting drainage.

2 Plant the seedlings carefully, handling the plants as little as possible. Firm the soil around each. Complete one section of planting before moving on to the next.

3 As each section of planting is completed, trim off any damaged, uneven, or straggly shoots to make the patches of plants more compact. Water thoroughly, section by section, so that the seedlings planted first do not dry out while the others are being planted.

PLANTER'S GUIDE TO BEDDING PLANTS

Ageratum
Antirrhinums
Argyranthemum
Begonias
Bidens
Calendula
Callistephus
Coreopsis
Cosmos
Dahlias (single)
Erysimum x marshallii and other wallflowers
Eschscholzias
Fuchsias
Impatiens
Nicotiana
Pelargoniums
Petunias
Ricinus communis
Rudbeckia hirta
Salvia farinacea, S.splendens
Senecio cineraria
Solenostemon (Coleus)
Tagetes
Verbena
Viola

Petunia
Resisto Series

Annual geraniums

Annual geraniums (*Pelargonium*) are almost all tender, evergreen, perennial plants of South African origin. When introduced to Britain, they were given the common name "geranium" because of their botanical similarity to the hardy, herbaceous species of the genus *Geranium*, which was commonly cultivated at that time. This common name still remains in widespread use today, although most of the plants usually referred to as geraniums belong to the genus *Pelargonium*.

Types of annual geraniums

Annual geraniums may broadly be divided into five groups, according to the main characteristics of the plants. The groups are: zonal, dwarf and miniature zonal, regal, ivy-leaved, and scented-leaved.

Zonal

These geraniums have rounded leaves, usually marked with a distinct dark zone, and single, semidouble, or double flowers. Some cultivars, however, do not have a zone and others have gold- or silver-variegated, or tricolored leaves.

In warmer regions, they grow well in the open garden and are ideal for summer bedding; they bloom continuously from early summer until late fall. They also thrive in window boxes, hanging baskets, and containers. Zonals will happily adapt to the growing conditions in a greenhouse or conservatory.

Dwarf and miniature zonal

Dwarf zonal geraniums should be 5–8in (13–20cm) tall, measured from soil level to the top of the plant, not including stem length and flower. They make excellent window-box plants and container plants for display in greenhouses and conservatories. Miniature zonals should be 3–5in (7–13cm) tall, measured in the same way as dwarfs. These very floriferous plants bear double and single blooms in a wide range of colors, and have green to greenish-black leaves.

In recent years, F1 and F2 hybrid zonal geraniums have been developed. These are grown from seed and are used mainly for bedding. They are single-flowered and are available in the same range of colors as the cultivars that have been propagated vegetatively.

Regal

These geraniums (also known as Martha Washington geraniums) are small, shrubby plants with rounded, deeply serrated leaves and wide, trumpet-shaped flowers.

They may be grown in the open garden, but in colder climates they are usually grown indoors or in a greenhouse or conservatory, because rainfall easily spoils the flowers. In warmer climates, where they may be planted out permanently, they make splendid flowering shrubs, almost continuously in bloom year-round.

Ivy-leaved

These trailing geraniums have rounded, lobed, ivy-like leaves, and flowers similar to those of zonals, available in a rich assortment of colors. They are used mainly in hanging baskets and other containers, where their flowers on trailing stems can be displayed to best advantage. They may also be planted so that they spill over the edge of a raised bed or a wall.

Scented-leaved

Scented-leaved geraniums have small, delicate flowers with five petals, and fragrant foliage (for which they are chiefly grown). They make excellent houseplants and greenhouse plants and, in colder climates, may be grown outside during the summer and fall, in containers or as bedding plants.

Watering and fertilizing

Geraniums in containers should be watered as soon as the top of the soil mix dries out. All geraniums, especially those grown in containers, need weekly fertilizing throughout summer with a high-potassium fertilizer such as tomato fertilizer. This helps the plants continue to produce a mass of good-quality blooms without becoming too leafy. Nitrogen-rich fertilizers are not a good choice because they will stimulate too much leaf growth at the expense of flower production. Start fertilizing three weeks after potting and continue through the summer.

Overwintering

Geraniums must be kept frost-free, except for *Pelargonium endlicherianum*, a rare, hardier species from Turkey. In cold-winter areas, plants grown outside may be saved for the next season by moving them under cover before the first frost. Lift the plants before frost is expected, shake as much soil as possible off the roots, trim back the roots and stems, and remove any remaining leaves.

For storage, use a wooden or strong cardboard box with deep sides, and make a few small drainage holes in the bottom. Half-fill the box with soilless potting mix, which should keep the plants alive but contains insufficient food for them to grow vigorously during storage. Place the prepared stock plants in the box, so that they are close together but not touching. Fill in with more soil mix around each plant and firm it in stages until

TYPES OF GERANIUMS

Zonal
Pelargonium **'Dolly Varden'**
Rounded leaves, with a darker zone, and single to double flowers.

Regal
P. **'Purple Emperor'**
Deeply serrated leaves and broadly trumpet-shaped flowers.

Ivy-leaved
P. AMETHYST ('Fisdel')
Trailing plants with lobed leaves and single to double flowers.

Scented-leaved
P. **'Royal Oak'**
Plants with small, often irregularly star-shaped flowers, grown for their fragrant leaves.

Dwarf zonal
P. **'Timothy Clifford'**
Bushy, free-flowering plants, similar to zonals, 5–8in (13–20cm) tall.

P. 'Dolly Varden'

P. 'Frank Headley'

P. 'Mrs. Quilter'

P. 'Lady Plymouth'

Geraniums in containers
Planting a combination of zonal and scented-leaved types provides attractive foliage as well as a long-lasting display of decorative blooms.

Contrasting habits
Use trailing, ivy-leaved geraniums to spill over the edge of a container. These will make an attractive contrast with upright forms in the center.

the soil is level with the top of the box. Water the soil mix thoroughly and leave the box outside for a day to drain. The plants should be watered again during the winter only if they become very dry. Store the box where it will receive plenty of light and remain frost-free; if the temperature remains just above freezing, the plants will not grow much but should survive.

By midwinter, new shoots will begin to appear on the stock plants; these may be used as cuttings in early spring. Alternatively, the stock plants may be potted up separately and grown on for planting out in the early part of the summer.

Propagation from cuttings

Geraniums are easily propagated from cuttings, and the method used is the same for all types. Taking cuttings is an inexpensive way of producing new plants and allows the old plant to remain flowering outside in the garden until the first frost, thus prolonging the display.

Selecting the cuttings

Although it is possible to take cuttings from spring onward, the best time is in late summer, when light conditions are good and the weather is still warm. Select strong, healthy shoots (nonflowering

ones if from a regal or scented-leaved geranium), cutting just above the third joint below the growing tip. Trim each cutting just below the lowest joint and carefully remove the lower leaves.

Inserting the cuttings

Choose the pot size according to the number of cuttings: a 5in (13cm) pot will take up to five cuttings. Fill the pot with standard rooting medium, press down firmly, and place the pot in a container of water until the soil surface becomes moist. Remove the pot and allow it to drain. Insert the cuttings, pressing them down gently to eliminate any air pockets beneath the bases of the cuttings. Do not water them yet.

Aftercare

Place the pot in a light, warm position, but not in full sun. One week after insertion, water the cuttings from below (as above). Water again a week or ten days later, by which time the cuttings should be rooting. If watered from above, the cuttings may suffer from gray mold/*Botrytis* (p.661)or other damping off diseases. For the same reason, do not use a propagator or cover the cuttings with clear plastic. Always allow free circulation of air around them. As soon as the cuttings have rooted (when fresh leaves appear), pot them singly into 3in (7cm) pots.

Growing F1 and F2 hybrids from seed

Seed-sown F1 and F2 hybrids are quite easy to grow, and given good light, the plants will flower in as little as three months from sowing. Start the seeds in late winter. Sow them on a moistened piece of coffee filter or paper towel in a covered glass dish. They often germinate erratically. After germination, transfer the sprouted seeds to individual cell packs or to 2in (5cm) pots. Be careful not to overwater the seedlings; a slightly dry soil mix is best to promote healthy growth.

When the seedlings are 6in (15cm) tall, pinch out the growing tips to encourage bushy growth. Grow the seedlings in a cool greenhouse during the winter and spring; the plants should then flower throughout the summer and fall. Particularly good-quality plants may be overwintered as for other geraniums (see left).

TAKING CUTTINGS

1 Choose a healthy shoot and cut straight across the stem just above the third joint below the growing tip.

2 Using a sharp knife, remove leaves from each cutting, leaving two at the top. Pinch out any flowers or buds.

3 Carefully trim the base of each cutting to just below the lowest joint with a straight cut.

4 Make holes 1in (2.5cm) deep in pots of moist, firmed sowing or propagation mix. Insert the cuttings and firm the soil.

OVERWINTERING

1 Lift the plants before the first frost and shake off any loose soil. Cut down the stems to about 4in (10cm) and remove the leaves. Trim back roots to about 2in (5cm).

2 Half-fill a box at least 6in (15cm) deep with fresh potting mix. Put in the plants so that they do not touch one another. Fill around them with more potting mix, then water and drain.

3 Store in a frost-free place until new shoots start to appear, then pot up the plants. Use the new shoots to take cuttings from, as necessary, later in spring.

Routine care

Because they have a relatively short life, annuals generally require little maintenance unless they are grown in a container (see CONTAINER GARDENING, "Routine care," p.332). They do need to be watered regularly during drought, however, especially if they are grown in containers, and deadheaded to prolong flowering. Continue to pinch out the growing tips (see p.218). Tall annuals may require staking at or soon after planting to prevent them from blowing over or toppling under their own weight. When the foliage starts to die down after flowering or at the end of the season, the plants should be cleared away.

Watering, fertilizing, and weeding

Young annuals and biennials that are planted in open ground should be watered on a regular basis with a sprinkler or watering can, soaking the bed thoroughly. Once the plants have become established, water only during prolonged dry weather. Those planted against a wall or fence may need extra attention when watering, because they may naturally receive less water (see *Rain Shadow*, p.608).

Annuals rarely need extra fertilizer if the soil has been well prepared. A liquid fertilizer may be applied on very poor soils as flower buds develop. Biennials may benefit from a little extra compost, but keep in mind that rich soil conditions produce vigorous vegetative growth at the expense of flowers. Container plants may benefit from the addition of slow-release fertilizers and the application of foliar feeds (see CONTAINER GARDENING, "Fertilizing," p.332).

Keep annuals and biennials nearly free from weeds because these compete for light, water, and soil nutrients. Pull out any weeds by hand while they are still small and remove self-sown seedlings in the same way if they are not required or are too numerous.

Providing supports

Many annuals and biennials have rather slender stems, which benefit from some support. Use small, bushy branches (peasticks) gathered from trees or shrubs, such as hazel and willow, for plants with a mature height of up to 3ft (1m). When the plants are only a few inches tall, insert the sticks in the soil around them so that they can grow up through the sticks, which

Pot-grown annuals
Push stakes into the potting mix, and tie string around them, to support tall annuals like *Salpiglossis*.

will quickly be covered and hidden. Take care not to damage the plants, especially their young roots, when pushing in the sticks.

Taller annuals will flourish and flower more freely if supported by a tepee, tripod, obelisk, arbor, trellis,

fence, wall, or strong tree or shrub, or on wires or trellises between pillars. Supports should be positioned before the annuals are planted. Tall annuals in containers may be supported by inserting a few stakes around the edge of the pot and tying soft string around the stakes—as they grow, the plants will hide the stakes.

Very tall plants, like hollyhocks (*Alcea*) or sunflowers (*Helianthus*), may need to be individually staked. Push the stake into the soil where it will be least visible and, as the plant develops, tie stems to the stake as needed.

Many twining annuals and those that have tendrils, such as sweet peas, reach 6–10ft (2–3m) during their short life, and these are best guided to their support with plastic ties or soft twine until they take hold. The twine should be tied loosely around the leading shoot and support using a figure-eight knot, to prevent chafing against any hard surfaces and to allow for stem expansion. Some scrambling annuals that do not twine or have tendrils will also need to be tied to their support.

CONTROLLING ANNUAL AND BIENNIAL "VOLUNTEERS"

Discovering self-sown seedlings (often called "volunteers") is one of the great pleasures of gardening—especially if they are growing in the right place. Annuals and biennials such as marigolds, honesty, and foxgloves are particularly eager self-sowers, but a range of other plants also oblige. With meadow gardening and naturalistic styles on the increase, gardeners can exploit this volunteer force to produce colorful, long-lasting, informal displays in sunny, open areas, particularly in sandy soil.

To achieve similar results on heavier but well-drained soil, cover the area with a layer of gritty sand, 10cm (4in) deep, and sow seed (or use plugs) of suitable annuals and biennials that will flower, self-seed, and continue the display in the following and subsequent years. Once established, many should self-seed naturally, although there will always be some that fade away.

Such designs are not entirely self-sufficient, as inevitably species of some genera, like *Eschscholzia*,

Limnanthes, and *Myosotis*, can become dominant and may need thinning out in spring if too dense. Others may fail and leave gaps that need seeding with different species to provide further variety.

The aim is not to exactly replicate a natural wildflower garden, but to create a kaleidoscopic mix of plants from different countries with similar habitats. Try blending common annual cornflowers, poppies, forget-me-nots, and campions with California natives like *Collinsia*, *Ipomopsis*, *Gilia*, and *Leptosiphon* species, as well as *Osteospermum*, *Gazania*, *Heliophila*, and *Nemesia* species from South Africa. You may want to do a little research to discover annual flowers and grasses native to your area to add to the mix.

By their nature, such plantings are experimental and need amending as some species die out and local weeds creep in; when successful, they provide great satisfaction throughout summer and fall.

ANNUALS AS DRIED OR CUT FLOWERS

Dried or fresh flowers of many annuals and biennials are decorative indoors. Harvest everlasting flowers, such as *Xeranthemum*, *Helipterum*, and *Limonium*, when they are about half open, then hang them upside-down in a warm, well-ventilated area. Cut strawflower

Xerochrysum flower heads before they show color to help keep their shape when dried. Cut fresh flowers as the buds show color. Dip Iceland poppy (*Papaver nudicaule*) stems into boiling water for a few seconds, to seal them and avoid air locks that prevent water uptake.

1 Cut flowers for drying (here, statice, *Limonium sinuatum*) as the heads start to open. The best time of day to do this is when the weather is cool, in early morning, or in the evening.

2 Many everlasting flowers may be dried upside-down in bunches fastened with soft string or raffia. Once they have dried, any excess stem may be cut off to suit the flower arrangement.

DEADHEADING

To prolong flowering, remove flower heads as they fade, cutting near the base of the stalk. The plants (here, pansies) will produce new blooms for some time.

Deadheading

In many cases, the flowering season of plants may be extended and their appearance improved by promptly removing any flower heads that are fading or dead; this prevents a plant from setting seed, and its energy is used to produce additional flowers. Snap off any faded flowers between the fingers and thumb, breaking the stems cleanly; use a pair of sharp scissors or pruners for tougher stems or where there is a danger of disturbing the plant as the dead flower heads are removed.

Do not deadhead if the seeds or fruits form part of the ornamental characteristic of the plant—as they do with honesty (*Lunaria*), *Hibiscus trionum*, and ornamental corn (*Zea mays*). Nor should plants be deadheaded if their seeds are required for growing the plant again during the following season.

A few annuals and biennials, such as poppies (*Papaver*), do not produce any more flowers after deadheading.

SAVING SEEDS

1 Seeds may be collected when the capsules or seed heads (here, *Nigella*) have been dried on newspaper and release their seeds.

2 Once the seed head has dried, shake seeds out, and separate from any other debris. Store in a labeled envelope in a dry place at a cool temperature.

Saving seeds

Seeds are easy to collect from many annuals for sowing the following year. However, the seeds saved from most garden-grown cultivars will not produce plants that possess flowers or habit characteristics similar to those of their parents. It is usually worth saving seeds only from those annuals and biennials.

Deadhead any plants with poor flowers so seeds are not formed and later collected for sowing the next year. Such seeds are unlikely to produce plants with good-quality flowers.

Self-sown seedlings are likely to vary to some extent in character and quality but may nevertheless produce quite acceptable plants. Distinct cultivars of *Eschscholzia*, Excelsior Series foxgloves (*Digitalis*), sweet alyssum (*Lobularia maritima*), pot marigolds (*Calendula*), forget-me-nots (*Myosotis*), and many other annuals and biennials usually vary in flower color and other characteristics from the original plant.

When seed capsules turn brown and begin to split, cut them off and spread them on paper-lined flats in a warm, sunny place until they are fully dry. Extract the seeds and separate out any debris. Package, label, and store them in dry, cool conditions until they are required for sowing.

Clearing the bed

In fall, once the flower display is over, lift and compost all dying plants after any seeds required have been gathered. Trash diseased plants so that they do not spread infection elsewhere in the garden. Perennials grown as annuals or biennials, such as pansies

FALL CLEARANCE

When annuals have finished flowering, carefully loosen the soil around their roots with a fork, then rake up and compost the old plants.

(*Viola* x *wittrockiana*) and primroses, may be lifted and replanted elsewhere, where they may grow and flower satisfactorily for several years. Others, such as wallflowers (*Erysimum*) and snapdragons, seldom grow as well after their first year and are generally not worth retaining for future use.

Tender perennials like begonias and impatiens may be lifted and potted in late summer to continue flowering indoors or in a conservatory or greenhouse. Hollyhocks (*Alcea*) and other short-lived perennials may be cut down in fall and retained. They sometimes survive for several seasons, although the quality and vigor of the plants will deteriorate. It is not worth keeping plants of the new F1 strains of tender geraniums because they are quite easy to raise from seed, and you eliminate the risk of overwintering diseases. Where hardy, *Eccremocarpus scaber*, too, will survive for years in protected locations outside.

Pests and diseases

The pests most likely to be troublesome to annuals and biennials when they are seedlings, as well as when they are more mature, are slugs and snails (p.669), cutworms (p.658), fungus gnats (p.661), aphids (p.654), and caterpillars (p.657); plants may also be attacked by gray mold/ *Botrytis* (p.661) and other fungal problems (see "Fungal leaf spots," p.660). Fungicides may prevent or slow these diseases, but often little can be done beyond pulling out and discarding badly infected plants. Young seedlings growing under cover may suffer from damping off (p.659)—a group of soilborne diseases that causes the plants to rot and collapse.

CUTTING DOWN SHORT-LIVED PERENNIALS

1 Not all seed heads ripen at the same time. To prevent self-seeding, remove flowered stems before any seed heads ripen fully.

2 Short-lived perennials such as hollyhocks may flower for several seasons if cut down immediately after flowering.

3 Carefully cut each stem at its base, ensuring that the new growth that has been produced during the growing season is not damaged in the process.

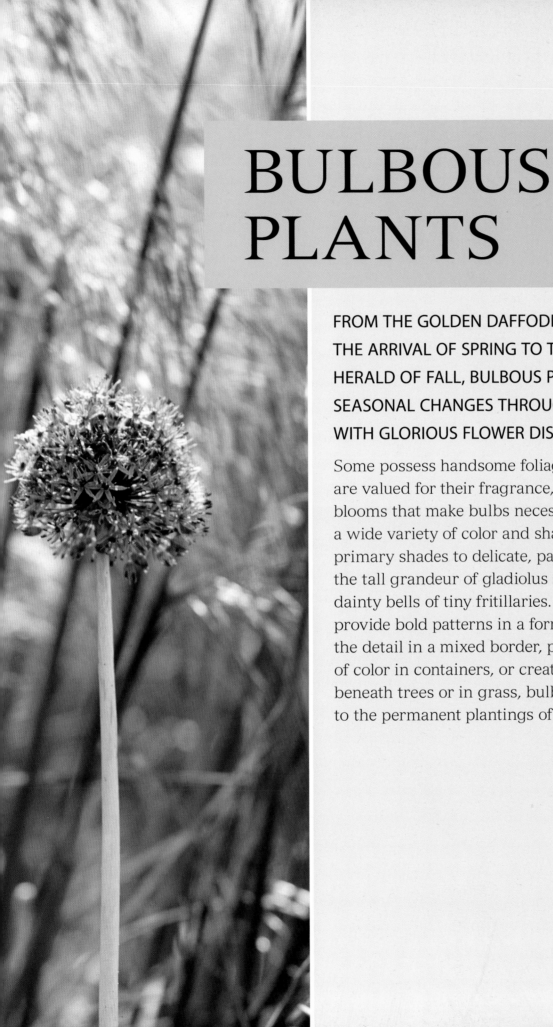

BULBOUS PLANTS

FROM THE GOLDEN DAFFODIL TRUMPETING THE ARRIVAL OF SPRING TO THE COLCHICUM, HERALD OF FALL, BULBOUS PLANTS RING THE SEASONAL CHANGES THROUGHOUT THE YEAR WITH GLORIOUS FLOWER DISPLAYS.

Some possess handsome foliage, and others are valued for their fragrance, but it is their blooms that make bulbs necessary. They offer a wide variety of color and shapes, from bright, primary shades to delicate, pastel hues, and the tall grandeur of gladiolus spikes to the dainty bells of tiny fritillaries. Whether they provide bold patterns in a formal bed, fill in the detail in a mixed border, provide a splash of color in containers, or create highlights beneath trees or in grass, bulbs bring vitality to the permanent plantings of the garden.

Bulbs for the garden

Growing bulbs is an easy way of brightening up the garden with decorative, often flamboyant, and sometimes fragrant displays. The bulbs that are grown in the garden are dominated by hardy favorites, for example, crocuses, cyclamen, daffodils, hyacinths, and tulips, of which there is an immense variety of both species and cultivars. Many tender bulbs also deserve a place in the garden, including the starry *Ixia*, *Sparaxis* with its loose, gaudy spikes, and the fiery *Tigridia*. Also popular are the alliums, which flower from spring to midsummer and provide both vivid color and architectural form.

Frosted beauty Leave seed heads on for winter interest.

Using bulbs

The key characteristic of bulbs is that they provide visual interest for only one season, remaining dormant and unnoticed for the remainder of the year. This can be an asset with careful planning, making bulbs invaluable as border plants as well as ideal for naturalizing in grass or growing in containers.

In many gardens, bulbs may be left to increase naturally from year to year while their dying foliage is hidden by the developing growth of herbaceous plants or shrubs that provide a succession of interest. Many bulbs, including the popular crocuses, daffodils (*Narcissus*), and snowdrops (*Galanthus*), increase very rapidly in most sites. Bulbs may

also be lifted after flowering and replanted each year to provide room for other seasonal plants, making them especially convenient for small gardens or restricted areas.

Seasons of interest

The main bulb season is from early spring to early summer, but many other bulbs flower outdoors or under cover at other times of the year. For color in winter when most of the garden is dormant, early bulbs such as the pink *Cyclamen coum*, the tiny, deep blue *Iris histrioides* 'Major', and snowdrops may be grown outdoors, and other bulbs forced indoors. Bulbs that flower in summer or fall are often larger, and of more exotic shapes and hues, than spring bulbs.

Where to grow bulbs

If given the well-drained soil that they need to grow and flower well, bulbs are among the easiest of all garden plants to cultivate. There are numerous cultivars and species now available that thrive in all sun exposures except deep shade.

Many bulbs in cultivation come from areas with a Mediterranean climate, so need to be grown in sunny sites and prefer hot, dry summers—although a huge range of bulbs flourishes in the home landscapes in regions with summer rainfall.

Bulbs that would normally grow in woodland thrive in moist, light shade. Many others, including some bulbs described as "sun-loving," are happy in light shade cast by nearby shrubs, walls, or trellises. Even dry shade is tolerated by most hardy cyclamen. Bulbs with white or pale flowers appear

Hot bed A mix of bulbs can provide fiery red and yellow displays like this with *Crocosmia* 'Lucifer', *Canna* 'Wyoming', and *Coreopsis* 'Schnittgold'. The *Pleioblastus* to the right provides a cool green foil.

almost luminous in dusky light, so look very attractive when planted in a shaded site. Whatever the setting, bulbs look best planted in groups of the same species or cultivar, whether jostling shoulders with other plants or forming a single, swaying sea of color in a formal bed or in grass.

Formal beds

Bulbs make a valuable contribution to formal bedding displays. Spring-flowering bulbs are excellent for planting *en masse* in a bed that is to be occupied by bedding annuals at a later point in summer, because they may be lifted and stored during their dormant season. Classic bedding bulbs are hyacinths and tulips because of their strong, sculptural forms; in general, the larger, showy flowers of hybrid bulbs are best grown in a formal location in the garden. Plant in blocks of color, each block one type of bulb, or in mixed groups that flower at different times throughout the season in order to provide a prolonged display of color during the spring. Bulbs may either completely fill the bed, or could be combined with companion plants with flowers in complementary or contrasting colors, such as deep blue forget-me-nots (*Myosotis*) or fiery wallflowers (*Erysimum*).

There is also scope for effective formal planting with summer- or fall-flowering bulbs: *Galtonia*, with its elegant, white or green spikes, or the more compact cultivars of gladioli, especially the Primulinus or Butterfly groups, look impressive when planted in large blocks bordered by purple-blue violas, or any similar, low-growing groundcover. *Agapanthus* Headbourne Hybrids, with their large, rounded flower heads of blue or white, combine well with the graceful, pink blooms of *Nerine bowdenii*.

Mixed herbaceous and shrub borders

Bulbs fill in the permanent planting of a border with a lively variety of seasonal color. Loose drifts may blend in with the general design or draw the eye with splashes of color. Architectural bulbs, such as *Crinum x powellii*, with its huge, pink or white trumpets, punctuate the flow of a border with an arresting contrast of height and form. Grow some bulbs through low groundcover plants so that their blooms appear to float above the mat of foliage. For a more informal English border, choose species bulbs because florid hybrids may sometimes look out of place.

Mixed plantings for spring flowering

Planting bulbs in a mixed border extends the flowering season, and provides an array of fresh, bright color from late winter through to early summer. Before the herbaceous perennials and deciduous shrubs in the border begin to grow and spread, bring the

THE DIFFERENT TYPES OF BULBOUS PLANT

In this book, the term "bulb" refers to all bulbous plants, including corms, tubers, and rhizomes as well as true bulbs. The terms "corm," "tuber," and "rhizome" are used only in their specific sense throughout. With all bulbous plants, a portion is swollen into a food storage organ that enables the plant to survive when dormant or when conditions are unsuitable for growth.

Bulb (*Tulipa* 'Giuseppe Verdi')

Bulbs

True bulbs are formed from fleshy leaves or leaf bases, and frequently consist of concentric rings of scales attached to a basal plate. The outer scales often form a dry, protective skin or tunic, as found in daffodils, Reticulata irises, and tulips. With some lilies (*Lilium*) and *Fritillaria* species, the scales are separate and no tunic is formed. Juno irises are unusual in having swollen storage roots beneath the bulbs.

Corm (*Gladiolus murielae*)

Corms

Corms are formed from the swollen bases of stems and are replaced by new corms every year. They are common in the family Iridaceae, which includes crocuses, gladioli, *Romulea*, and *Watsonia*; usually they have a tunic that has been formed from the previous year's leaf bases. In the Liliaceae and related families, they are found in such genera as *Brodiaea* and *Colchicum*.

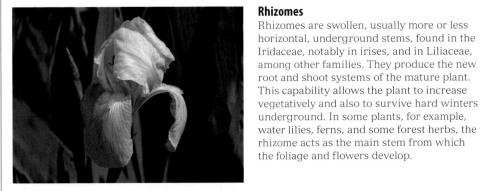

Rhizome (*Iris germanica*)

Rhizomes

Rhizomes are swollen, usually more or less horizontal, underground stems, found in the Iridaceae, notably in irises, and in Liliaceae, among other families. They produce the new root and shoot systems of the mature plant. This capability allows the plant to increase vegetatively and also to survive hard winters underground. In some plants, for example, water lilies, ferns, and some forest herbs, the rhizome acts as the main stem from which the foliage and flowers develop.

Tuber (*Dahlia* 'Harvest Inflammation')

Tubers

Tuberous is a term applied to many plants with swollen, often irregularly shaped stems or roots used for food storage. It is often misapplied, for example, to the tuberlike roots—actually rhizomes—of *Anemone blanda* and the long, thin rhizomes of *A. nemorosa* (for convenience, both are included here as "bulbous plants"). True tubers of various kinds are found in *Dahlia*, *Corydalis*, some orchids, such as *Dactylorhiza*, cyclamen species (although these are often called "corms"), and in plants such as *Ranunculus asiaticus*, where they are lobed or clustered together.

front of the border to life with the smaller daffodil species, pale or dark blue Reticulata irises, snowdrops, and the golden cups of winter aconites (*Eranthis hyemalis*).

Plant starry carpets of pink and blue *Anemone blanda*, *Chionodoxa*, and *Scilla bifolia*, or pale yellow drifts of the more freely increasing dwarf daffodil species and hybrids beneath such early-flowering shrubs as *Corylopsis*, forsythia, and witch hazel (*Hamamelis*) to complement their display.

For later in spring, a much wider range of bulbs is available and larger plants, such as the tall daffodils, *Fritillaria* species (for example the purple-black *F. persica* and the regal *F. imperialis*) or tulips, may be used in casual groups to give height among the shrubs and perennials.

Mixed plantings for summer and fall flowering

A number of bulbs add greatly to the beauty of the garden in summer. Although they are often regarded as only of secondary importance, in fact many summer- and fall-flowering bulbs are tall and robust enough to hold their own among surrounding flowering perennials and they offer a dazzling range of colors and flower forms.

Early in the season, try *Camassia leichtlinii* with its creamy-white flower plumes, vivid gladioli, *Triteleia laxa* (syn. *Brodiaea laxa*) for its loose, purple-blue clusters of bloom, and the bold, scarlet goblets of *Tulipa sprengeri*.

Follow them in mid- to late summer with the imposing Indian shot (*Canna*), arching sprays of blazing red or yellow *Crocosmia*, sun-loving lilies (*Lilium*), and later, slim pink, red, or white spires of *Schizostylis*. In warmer gardens, greenish-white *Eucomis* with its pineapplelike flower heads brings an exotic touch to the border planting.

In fall, continue the display with the fragrant, pink trumpets of *Amaryllis belladonna*, the brilliant yellow funnels of *Sternbergia lutea* or *S. sicula*, and blue to white forms of fall-flowering crocuses.

Work of nature The delicate beauty of *Fritillaria meleagris*, the snake's-head fritillary, is a common sight in spring gardens. This bulb naturalizes well in grass or borders.

Naturalizing bulbs

When left undisturbed, many bulbs will readily increase to form flowing drifts of color. Allowing them to naturalize in this way gives interest to areas of the garden that otherwise might not be given over to flowering plants. Species, which are more delicate in hue and form than the majority of cultivars, create a natural effect when planted in large, informal groups.

Planting bulbs with specimen trees

Bulbs make perfect partners for specimen trees that have deep roots and light, deciduous canopies. Select bulbs that will flower predominantly in spring or fall to form a decorative groundcover when the tree has few leaves to deepen the shade. In spring, the soil beneath the tree tends to be moist and sunlit, creating an ideal environment for anemones, crocuses, daffodils, or *Scilla*. Hardy, fall-flowering cyclamen, with mottled, silvery foliage and softly folded petals, tolerate the dry summer conditions, and enjoy partial shade.

The flowers of bulbs can effectively complement a tree's habit. White-flowered bulbs, for example, mirror the white blossoms of ornamental cherries (*Prunus*); the crisp shape of crocuses echo the chalice form of magnolia blooms; and bulbs with pendent flowers imitate the habit of a weeping tree.

Use dwarf cultivars to naturalize the area around a newly planted tree or shrub, because rapidly increasing bulbs, such as daffodils, reduce the available food.

Woodland settings

Bulbs are invaluable when planted in large, informal pools of color, because they enhance the natural beauty of deciduous woodland and any mossy groundcover. Many bulbs relish these woodland conditions, and will blend well with other woodland plants, such as ferns, hellebores (*Helleborus*), and primulas.

Plant bulbs for a succession of flowers, as well as for contrast of form and height; subtle variations on a color theme will reflect the tranquil mood of woodland. Snowdrops (*Galanthus*) and cyclamen species in pinks and purples make a striking combination, while drifts of *Scilla* and *Chionodoxa* add shades of blue. Spanish bluebells (*Hyacinthoides* x *massartiana*, syn. *H. hispanica* of gardens) or many of the more rampant grape hyacinths (*Muscari*) provide swathes of blue, pink, and white, together with tiny, white sprays of lily-of-the-valley (*Convallaria majalis*). These can colonize considerable areas once established. English bluebells (*Hyacinthoides non-scripta*) should only be planted on their own because they will rapidly invade other plantings.

Planting in grass

Bulbs can transform grass, whether they are planted on a bank, a section of a lawn, or an entire meadow; they will create a cheerful

carpet of spring or fall color that spreads more thickly year after year. The bulbs must be robust species that can withstand competition from grass roots. Many larger bulbs look best in grass in which their fading foliage is less obtrusive once they have finished flowering.

Plant earlier-flowering bulbs in grass that is to be mown from spring onward so that their leaves have sufficient time to die down before the grass is cut. Later-flowering bulbs, such as terrestrial orchids (*Dactylorhiza*), may be grown with grass and wildflowers in "meadows" that are not cut until mid- or late summer. Bulbs that bloom in fall start into growth and flower before the end of the usual mowing season so the grass must be left unmown until after late summer. Alternatively, plant bulbs in irregular but defined areas so that it is possible to mow around them.

Daffodils are the classic choice for grass and a remarkable range—especially the more robust species and hybrids—may be grown in this way. In addition to this, many crocuses will grow well in grass. Alternatively, a more delicate effect may be achieved by coupling the pendent bells of the summer snowflake (*Leucojum aestivum*) with the snake's-head fritillary (*Fritillaria meleagris*) which will shiver softly in the breeze.

Where the grass is less vigorous, particularly in partly shaded areas, some of the dwarf bulbs do extremely well: the purple flowered *Crocus tommasinianus*, *Chionodoxa*, some daffodils (for example, *Narcissus cyclamineus*), *Scilla*, and snowdrops all flourish in these conditions.

An area on the outskirts of a garden that is naturalized with bulbs provides a harmonious transition between the flowerbeds of a formal garden and the grassy fields of the surrounding countryside by combining elements of both.

Bulbs with alpines

Using bulbs in the rock garden, trough, or raised bed prolongs the season because most alpines flower in late spring. The erect habit, upright flowers, and spearlike leaves of bulbs contrast well with the low, mounded, or spreading habit of most alpine plants, as well as introducing a greater variety of form. Choose dwarf bulbs with dainty blooms to complement the character of the alpines, and plant some bulbs to grow through and lift the alpine planting. Avoid mat-forming alpines that exhaust the soil around the bulbs and so deprive them of food.

In the rock garden

Many smaller bulbs, especially the more temperamental species for which sharp drainage is essential, thrive in rock gardens, in sun or partial shade. Dwarf bulbs look attractive when planted in pockets of rock or offset against the grit topdressing of the bed, which also keeps their delicate flowers from being muddied during wet weather.

If planting very small alpines in the bed, do not use the taller bulb species, which would appear out of proportion to their neighbors.

Bulbs in troughs

Old stone troughs make an attractive setting for a collection of dwarf bulbs and smaller alpine plants where their tiny charms may be appreciated close at hand. The bulbs benefit from the gritty, well-drained soil, and may easily be given the careful watering that they need.

To keep the display in proportion, grow the smallest species and their less robust hybrids; rapidly increasing bulbs may swamp neighboring alpines. Grow the smaller *Fritillaria* species for their intriguing flowers, whether the purplish-brown and yellow *F. michailovskyi* or the checkered green *F. whittallii*.

Rhodohypoxis are excellent for growing in troughs, producing pink, red, or white starry flowers throughout most of the summer. Keep the bulbs moist during the growing season, and give them an occasional liquid fertilizer. The genus *Cyclamen* includes species that are suitable for troughs in spring and fall, and they range in hue from pure white to deepest purple-pink.

Planting bulbs in a leaf mold bed

A shady raised bed filled with leaf mold and well-rotted garden compost provides a perfect environment for the dwarfer "woodland" bulbs, whether they are planted on their own or along with lime-hating shrubs or alpines. Try erythroniums, with their dainty, reflexed flowers in shades of

pink, white, or yellow, which you can then view from underneath, or plant any of the trilliums in a leaf mold bed.

Bulbs to associate with water gardens

A few bulbs flourish in damp, poorly drained conditions and provide some of the most striking flowering plants to grow around water. Their strong shapes and colors create pleasing reflections; plant them in clumps to contrast with the flat, open surface of the water. Several handsome rhizomatous irises as well as the arum lily (*Zantedeschia aethiopica*), with large, white spathes above broad, arrow-shaped leaves, thrive in pond margins. Both the snake's-head fritillary and summer snowflake (*Leucojum aestivum*) grow naturally in water meadows, and therefore enjoy a moist site or damp beds around ponds.

Other bulbs that will enhance water gardens include the magnificent, purple-red *Iris ensata* (syn. *I. kaempferi*), the white-flowered *I.* 'Geisha Gown', with its deep pinkish-purple veins, and *Dierama pendulum*, with its wandlike flower sprays. However, all of these prefer a soil that is not only moist but is well drained, too.

Growing bulbs in containers

Growing bulbs in ornamental pots, window boxes, and other containers provides a varied and spectacular display, which can be extended throughout the season by moving containers into view as they come into flower (see also "Changes in focus," p.306). Careful choice of bulbs may lengthen the season to include late winter as well as spring and

Woodland glory In late April and early May many woodland areas in dappled shade are carpeted with a magnificent display of bluebells, *Hyacinthoides non-scripta*, which can be used to great effect in a shady part of the garden.

summer. Plant a single species or cultivar in each container to provide a uniform, even effect and then group the containers together for a mass of color.

Place pots of bulbs with fragrant flowers (for example, hyacinths or Tazetta daffodils) close to the entrance of the house where they may be fully appreciated. Pots used for spring bulbs may be used for summer-flowering plants later: when the bulbs die down, lift and replant them in the garden (or store them) and replace them with annuals or tender perennials.

Some larger bulbs are sufficiently striking to be planted on their own in containers. Tall lilies (*Lilium*) or *Crinum x powellii*, in pink or white forms, are particularly effective. Any *Agapanthus* species or hybrid will provide a long season of showy flowers. Alternatively, group several types of bulb of varying heights and colors in a large container such as a half-barrel to provide a feature on a patio.

Window boxes

When planting in window boxes, choose smaller bulbs that are in proportion to the size of the container. They are excellent for planting in layers below other plants to make the best use of limited space; in time, the bulbs will thrust through the surface planting to create a pleasing contrast of height and form. Combining the plants with winter-flowering pansies (*Viola x wittrockiana*) and ivy (*Hedera*), followed by trailing tender perennials and annuals, gives the window boxes a prolonged display of color.

Bulbs under cover

Growing bulbs under cover extends the range that may be cultivated to include many rare species that need particular care. In temperate or cold regions, tender bulbs may be grown that would not survive unprotected in the flower beds. In regions with summer rainfall, it is the most practical way of growing many of the species bulbs currently in cultivation because they need a dry, summer resting period in order to flourish and flower well. Bulbs may be planted in pots or in a greenhouse bed or bulb frame. This allows easier control of the local environment to accommodate the individual needs of a wide range of bulbs, be it a summer drying-off period or protection from excessive winter wet, cold, or frost.

Bulbs in pots

Growing bulbs in pots allows each plant to be grown in conditions that best suit its individual requirements, especially when cultivating small stocks of uncommon bulbs. The pots are easily transferred from outdoors to the shelter of cold frames or greenhouses when required, or from the greenhouse to the conservatory to enjoy them when in full bloom.

Pot cultivation in an unheated greenhouse enables many bulb species that are otherwise of borderline hardiness in temperate climates to be grown. Many are South African and South American bulbs with an exciting diversity of richly colored blooms, such as *Watsonia* with its dense spikes of deep pink, white, and red. To enjoy tender bulbs, such as *Gloriosa*, and winter-flowering *Veltheimia*, a frost-free greenhouse is needed. Overwinter other tender species or cultivars of such genera as begonias, *Canna*, or *Crinum* in a cool greenhouse and bring them out when in bloom to enhance the summer display in the garden.

Bulbs may be grown in shade and the potting mix adjusted accordingly in order to grow small "woodland" bulbs, including *Trillium rivale*, which has finely spotted petals in pink or white, or tender, terrestrial orchids, such as the free-flowering *Calanthe* species. Gardeners with an alpine house may add a little height and splashes of color to displays by mixing plants with pots of dwarf spring bulbs. The alpine house is suitable for rare or tender bulbs such as ice-white *Narcissus cantabricus* or bright blue *Tecophilaea cyanocrocus*.

Greenhouse beds

Tender bulbs may be planted out directly in prepared greenhouse beds, rather than in pots, for a more natural and vigorous display. The bulbs may be combined in a mixed bed with other plants that flower in summer when the bulbs are dormant. Choose companion plants that tolerate a dry period coinciding

BULBS FOR CUT FLOWERS

Many bulbs have flowers that can be cut for the house since their shapely, often solitary, flowers on long stems make them especially suitable for floral arrangements. A few have powerful scents that can fill a room and most are long-lasting if they are picked before the blooms reach maturity. Some, such as daffodils, are so vigorous and prolific that they may be cut without leaving a gap in the garden display. Alternatively, set aside a separate area to grow bulbs especially for cutting.

Gladioli make fine cut flowers and are often used in this way, because the taller cultivars are difficult to place satisfactorily in an open border.

The pretty, wonderfully fragrant freesias are the only tender or half-hardy bulbs that are commonly grown under cover to provide cut flowers. They have a long flowering season during the winter but make somewhat straggly pot plants that need staking, so they are best cut for display indoors where they will last well.

Schizostylis coccinea 'Sunrise'

Crocosmia 'Lucifer'

Narcissus 'Cheerfulness'

Dahlia 'Zorro'

Freesia 'Everett'

Gladiolus 'Tesoro'

Zantedeschia aethiopica 'Crowborough'

Nerine bowdenii

***Alstroemeria* Ligtu Group**

Tulipa 'Clara Butt'

Allium giganteum

Lilium 'Enchantment'

with that needed by the bulbs, or that can be plunged in plastic pots and watered without the moisture reaching the bulbs around them.

Spreading, heat-loving plants, such as *Osteospermum* or gazanias, and many silver-foliaged plants could be used in this way, and then removed or cut back hard at the end of summer when the bulbs start into growth. Late-flowering *Brodiaea*, *Calochortus*, and *Triteleia* prolong the flowering season still further: group them together and water them separately. Summer-growing bulbs, such as *Eucomis*, some *Gladiolus* species, and the tender *Nerine* species do not need interplanting.

Bulb frames and raised beds

The term "bulb frame" usually refers to a raised bed devoted solely to bulbs; it is covered with a cold frame or plant lights during the natural resting period of the bulbs in summer, and also in winter to protect them from excessive rainfall, which could cause them to rot. Alternatively, a frame may simply cover bulbs in pots plunged in a sand bed. Such frames may be made more attractive by using stone for the sides.

Bulb frames are the best alternative to the alpine house as a place to grow tender or demanding bulb species without the root restriction of pots, and are used mainly by enthusiasts or collectors. This method of cultivation is suitable for most bulbs, other than those used to some summer rainfall, such as "woodland" and high mountain species. Some crocus, daffodil, *Fritillaria*, and tulip species, Juno and Reticulata irises, and the more difficult *Brodiaea* and *Zigadenus* species tend to be less successful in temperate climates as bedding plants; they may not survive unless they are protected from excess moisture in bulb frames or seasonally covered raised beds throughout the dormant season.

Forcing bulbs

Bring color and fragrance indoors during winter and early spring by forcing bulbs in pots. Keep in a cool, dark place for a few months before bringing them into the light to encourage them to flower earlier than they do naturally. *Hippeastrum* with its giant, exotic blooms, scented hyacinths, and daffodils, especially *Narcissus papyraceus*, or paperwhites, are all suitable and often seen for sale as "prepared" bulbs. These have had an artificial cold period in imitation of winter cold to speed up the natural flowering cycle. Many hardy spring bulbs, such as tulips, can be forced, but some, such as crocuses, may abort their flowers if forced too quickly. A gentler method is to grow bulbs under cover in pots and bring them indoors when the flowers begin to show color, a week or two before they would normally bloom, so that the warmth stimulates flowering.

PLANTER'S GUIDE TO BULBOUS PLANTS

EXPOSED SITES
Bulbs that tolerate exposed or windy sites
Anemone
Chionodoxa
Colchicum
Crocus
Cyclamen
Fritillaria (dwarf spp.)
Galanthus
Ipheion
Iris reticulata (cvs)
Muscari
Narcissus (dwarf spp. and cvs)
Ornithogalum
Oxalis
Scilla
Sternbergia lutea
Triteleia
Tulipa (dwarf spp.)

WALL PROTECTION
Bulbs that prefer the protection of a wall
Agapanthus (most spp.)
Alstroemeria (except Ligtu Group)
Amaryllis belladonna
Anomatheca laxa
Belamcanda chinensis
Bloomeria crocea
Eucomis
Fritillaria persica
Gladiolus (tender spp.)
Gynandriris sisyrinchium
Habranthus (some spp.)
Ixia
Lycoris squamigera
Moraea spathulata
Nerine bowdenii
Rhodophiala advena
Scilla peruviana
Sparaxis
Sternbergia lutea, S. sicula
Tulbaghia
Watsonia
Zephyranthes candida

DRY SHADE
Bulbs that tolerate dry shade
Anemone nemorosa
Arum italicum 'Marmoratum'
Cyclamen coum, C. hederifolium, C. repandum
Galanthus nivalis (forms)
Hyacinthoides non-scripta
Ranunculus ficaria (cvs)

MOIST SHADE
Bulbs that prefer moist shade
Anemone apennina, A. blanda, A. ranunculoides
Arisaema (most spp.)
Arum italicum
Cardiocrinum
Corydalis (some spp.)
Eranthis
Erythronium
Fritillaria camschatcensis, F. cirrhosa
Galanthus
Ipheion uniflorum
Leucojum aestivum, L. vernum
Lilium (some spp.)
Narcissus cyclamineus, N. triandrus
Nomocharis
Notholirion
Scilla bifolia
Trillium
Tulipa sylvestris

FLOWERS FOR CUTTING
Agapanthus
Allium (some spp.)
Alstroemeria (taller spp. and cvs)
Amaryllis belladonna
Anemone coronaria St. Bridgid Group, A. coronaria De Caen Group
Camassia
Clivia
Crinum

Crocosmia
Dierama
Freesia
Galtonia
Gladiolus
Iris Dutch Hybrids, I. latifolia, I. xiphium
Ixia
Lilium
Narcissus
Nerine
Ornithogalum (tall spp.)
Ranunculus asiaticus (forms)
Sparaxis
Tulipa
Watsonia
Zantedeschia

ARCHITECTURAL PLANTS
Allium cristophii, A. giganteum
Canna
Cardiocrinum giganteum
Crinum x powellii
Fritillaria imperialis
Lilium (most spp. and cvs)

BULBS FOR ROCK GARDENS AND ALPINE HOUSES
Albuca
Allium (dwarf spp.)
Anemone (some spp.)
Anomatheca
Arum (some spp.)
Babiana
Bellevalia
Biarum
Bongardia chrysogonum
Bulbocodium vernum
Calochortus
Colchicum (small spp.)
Corydalis (some spp.)
Crocus
Cyclamen
Fritillaria (most spp.)
Gagea
Galanthus
Habranthus

Hippeastrum (dwarf spp.)
Iris (dwarf spp.)
Leontice
Leucocoryne
Leucojum (some spp.)
Merendera
Moraea (some spp.)
Muscari, (some spp.)
Narcissus (dwarf spp.)
Ornithogalum, (dwarf spp.)
Oxalis (some spp.)
Pancratium (some)
Pinellia
Puschkinia
Rhodohypoxis
Romulea
Scilla
Sternbergia
Tecophilaea
Tulipa (dwarf spp.)
Zephyranthes
Zigadenus

Tulipa 'Showwinner'

Tulips and daffodils

Tulips (*Tulipa*) and daffodils (*Narcissus*) are highly valued for the bold splashes of color they bring in spring. Grow them together to extend the flowering season in a mixed border: some daffodils bloom very early in the year, while many tulips last into late spring. Tulips are excellent for beds or borders, while many daffodils are especially suitable for naturalizing in the lawn. Dwarf forms are ideal for rock gardens or containers, where they may be seen at close range.

Tulips

This diverse, versatile genus is horticulturally classified in 15 divisions based on flower form, but may conveniently be grouped by flowering season and garden use.

Early tulips

Early single tulips have classic, goblet-shaped blooms, some with striped, flushed, or margined petals. Early double tulips have long-lasting, open bowl-shaped flowers, often flecked or margined in contrasting colors. Traditionally used for cutting, in formal bedding, or as border edging, many can also be grown in containers indoors. In informal designs, their elegant outlines contrast well with spreading or prostrate plants.

Midseason tulips

This grouping includes Triumph tulips, with their simple, conical blooms, and the Darwin hybrids, with rich and intensely colored flowers, often with a satiny basal blotch and dark, velvety anthers. Both types are sturdy, robust, and noted for their weather resistance.

Late tulips

Some of the most vibrant colors and intricate forms are seen in late-flowering tulips. They include the graceful lily-flowered types, vivid and extravagant Parrot tulips, green-tinged Viridifloras, and the exuberantly striped and feathered Rembrandts. Peony-flowered forms are well suited to informal cottage gardens. All are effective used informally with dark green or gray groundcover plants or in formal bedding designs.

Dwarf species and hybrids

The compact Kaufmanniana hybrids produce their brightly colored blooms very early in the spring, while the slightly taller Fosteriana and Greigii tulips usually flower a little later. Many have very attractively marked foliage. The dwarf species are ideal for containers, raised beds, or rock gardens. *Tulipa sprengeri* and *T. sylvestris* tolerate light shade and will naturalize in fine grass.

Cultivation and propagation

Most tulips thrive in fertile, fast-draining, humus-rich soil, in sun and with shelter. In ideal conditions, some robust cultivars persist from year to year. Many, however, are best regarded as short-lived perennials, to be lifted after a few years and discarded. Where soils warm up rapidly,

Tulips in a spring border
The strong, vertical stems and distinctive cups of tulips provide height and structure, as well as vivid color, in an informal spring border.

Growing in containers
The lily-flowered tulip 'West Point' here displays its ornate blooms.

TYPES OF TULIPS

Tulips include an impressive range of flower forms, from the simple, upright goblets of single-flowered tulips to the frilled and twisted petals of Parrot tulips and the open, double blooms of peony-flowered forms. They are available in most colors, except blue, from the purest white to the deepest purple, with many glorious shades of yellow, red, and crimson in between. Many of the dwarf tulips also have attractively marked leaves.

Single

***Tulipa* 'Dawnglow'**
Darwin hybrid

T. 'Queen of Night'
Single, late

T. 'Spring Green'
Viridiflora

Double and Parrot

T. 'Peach Blossom'
Double, early

T. 'Estella Rijnveld'
Parrot

Dwarf Species and Hybrids

T. tarda
Dwarf species

T. 'Dreamboat'
Greigii hybrid

T. 'Giuseppe Verdi'
Kaufmanniana hybrid

T. 'Greuze'
Single, late

Daffodils

Grown for their cheerful spring blooms, daffodils (*Narcissus*) are among the easiest and most rewarding of bulbs to grow. They are horticulturally divided into 13 groups, based on the form of the flowers.

Daffodils in containers

Most daffodils can be grown in pots, if they are deep enough to allow at least 2in (5cm) of potting mix beneath the bottom of the bulbs. Tazettas, with clusters of up to 12 scented blooms, are often grown in containers to bloom from late fall to spring. The richly fragrant jonquil hybrids make cheerful household decorations. Small species, such as *N. cantabricus* and *N. romieuxii*, produce blooms early in the year in an alpine house; they may also then be brought indoors.

Extending the flowering season
Growing tulips and daffodils together provides a continuous display of color from early to late spring.

Daffodils in the garden

Valuable for formal spring bedding and to give early color in the mixed border, daffodils are among the most reliable of bulbs for naturalizing: they rarely need lifting in borders or the lawn. Even tiny species, such as *N. cyclamineus* and *N. minor*, will thrive in fine grass. Dwarf daffodils are ideal for rock gardens and raised beds; some, such as *N.* 'Little Gem', *N.* 'Tête-à-tête', and *N. asturiensis*, flower early in the year.

Cultivation and propagation

Daffodils will grow in almost any soil type, but prefer well-drained, moist, slightly alkaline conditions.

Naturalizing daffodils in grass
In an informal or wild garden, daffodils may be planted through grass, bringing welcome color to a dark corner or the ground beneath a tree.

They thrive in sun or light, dappled shade. Plant the bulbs 5–6in (12–15cm) deep in late summer or early fall. When bulbs are naturalized in a lawn, do not cut the old foliage until at least six weeks after flowering. Bulbs in containers must be grown in cool conditions, with plenty of fresh air. Temperatures above 45°F (7°C) while rooting is taking place may cause flowers to fail. Place the pots in a cold frame after planting, and bring them into a cool room about 12–16 weeks later. Once flower buds have formed, blooming can be advanced by raising the temperature gently, although not exceeding 55°F (13°C).

Propagate by offsets (see p.245), or by chipping (see p.249); new hybrids and species may also be raised from seed (see p.246). Daffodils may be affected by both narcissus nematodes (see "Stem and bulb nematode," p.671) and bulb flies (p.656).

TYPES OF DAFFODILS

Daffodils provide a wide variety of shapes and forms, ranging from the tiny, exquisite Cyclamineus hybrids, with their swept-back petals, to the tall, trumpet daffodils and the showy double forms. Modern developments include the split corona and collarette types. In addition to the characteristic bright yellow flowers, cultivars include those with pale butter-yellow blooms or brilliant white petals and fiery orange cups.

Dwarf Species and Hybrids

Narcissus triandrus
Dwarf species

N. romieuxii
Dwarf species

N. 'Jumblie'
Cyclamineus hybrid

N. 'Pride of Cornwall'
Tazetta

Single

N. 'Passionale'
Large-cupped

N. 'Fortune'
Large-cupped

N. 'Ambergate'
Large-cupped

Double

N. 'Irene Copeland'
Double

N. 'Tahiti'
Double

in the original soil mix are exhausted. Use a granular fertilizer sprinkled on the potting mix surface as the bulbs come into growth, or apply a liquid feed every two or three weeks. In the latter part of the season, use a high-potash, low-nitrogen feed to produce a good display of blooms.

Bulbs in pots under cover

Bulbs that need a warm, dry summer, and a winter and spring growing period, grow well in an unheated or cool greenhouse, where the bulbs' feeding, watering, and drying off may be controlled to satisfy their needs. Keep such bulbs dry from the time their leaves die down until their natural growing period starts in late summer or early fall.

During the growing season, soak the pots thoroughly when they are nearly dry, but make sure not to overwater them, especially in winter. Give them extra water in the growing season up to flowering time, after which gradually reduce watering until the leaves die down. Do not allow some hardy bulbs, such as crocuses from mountainous areas and "woodland" bulbs, to dry out completely; keep the potting mix slightly moist during the summer.

Bulbs such as *Galtonia* from areas with summer rainfall, for example, parts of South Africa and South America, must be watered regularly so that they keep growing during the summer; they should then be allowed to dry out during their natural dormancy in winter.

Renewing soil mix

Changing the top layer of potting mix in a pot of bulbs supplies them with enough nutrients for another year. Before they start to grow, gently scrape away the old potting mix to expose the tops of the bulbs. If they are healthy and not overcrowded, cover them with fresh, moist potting mix of the same type that is in the pot. Separate and repot overcrowded bulbs or, if they are hardy, plant them out.

Repotting

Bulbs may sometimes be kept in the same pot for several years but they eventually become overcrowded and need to be repotted—usually indicated by a failure to flower well and by undersized or unhealthy foliage. At the end of dormancy, repot the bulbs to encourage them to start into growth. Pot up larger bulbs singly, as for the initial potting, and in a similar potting mix (see "Planting in pots and under cover," p.237). Plant

small bulbs or bulblets between the adult ones or pot them up separately (see "Care of seedlings," p.245).

In early spring, repot tender bulbs that are dormant in winter when the new growth is about to begin.

Fertilizing

If the bulbs are kept in the same pot for several years, feed them regularly throughout the growing season at alternate waterings with a liquid feed containing a high-potash, low-nitrogen fertilizer. Extra feeding is unnecessary if the bulbs are repotted, or the top layer of potting mix in the pot is replaced each year.

Care of forced bulbs

When they are ready to be brought into the light, place forced bulbs (see p.238), according to their needs, on a shady windowsill or in a cool, bright room. The bulbs tolerate slightly warmer conditions when their flower buds are well formed. Rotate the bowl periodically if the shoots turn to the light and keep the potting mix moist. Forced bulbs are generally in a poor condition after flowering.

Discard them or plant them out in the garden where they will eventually, perhaps after two years or more, flower again in their normal season.

Hippeastrum hybrids that have been forced may be kept in a good condition each year by replanting them after flowering in a humus-rich, well-drained potting mix in the same pot. Do not water them from early fall until midwinter, and repot them if they are overcrowded.

Bulb problems

Bulbs occasionally fail to flower, and are then known as "blind" bulbs. Within a long-established clump, this problem is often due to overcrowding, so bulbs should be lifted and replanted separately in fresh soil (see "Overcrowded bulbs," p.241). Shortage of water during the growing season is another possible cause of "blind" bulbs.

Newly planted bulbs that are blind may not have been stored correctly, or they may not yet be fully mature. *Iris danfordiae*, *Fritillaria* species, such as

F. recurva and *F. thunbergii*, and some other bulbs, do not flower regularly even in nature and so are described as "shy-flowering." Do not dig up such bulbs unless they look unhealthy or seem crowded, because they may eventually flower if left undisturbed. It may be helpful to plant the bulbs especially deeply because this discourages them from dividing into bulblets.

Pests and diseases

During the growing season, keep a careful watch for the symptoms of pests and diseases and control any problems as soon as they arise. When planting, repotting, or propagating dormant bulbs, inspect them and destroy any badly afflicted bulbs.

Bulbs may suffer especially from rot or fungal diseases, which severely affects Reticulata irises. Daffodils may fall prey to narcissus bulb fly (see "Bulb flies," p.656). Aphids (p.654) sometimes infest bulbs and can cause the spread of viruses (p.672). Spider mite (p.670) occasionally affects bulbs grown under cover.

REPOTTING OVERCROWDED BULBS

1 Remove some potting mix from the pot to inspect the bulbs (here daffodils). If they have become overcrowded in the pot, they should be repotted.

2 Carefully pour out the contents of the pot and remove the bulbs from the potting mix. Discard any dead material or any bulbs that show signs of pests or diseases.

3 Separate any pairs or clumps of bulbs with large offsets into individual bulbs by gently pulling them apart.

4 Select only healthy bulbs and clean them, rubbing with finger and thumb to remove any loose, outer tunics.

5 Replant the bulbs in a pot of fresh, moist, bulb-potting mix. Insert them at twice their own depth and space them at least their own width apart.

be propagated by cutting them up, as long as each section has a growing point. Prepare 2–3in (5–8cm) pots with several holes in the bottom for good drainage and almost fill them with well-drained potting mix. Then insert the sections one at a time, growing points uppermost, in the potting mix. Cover the tubers with more potting mix. Topdress the pots with grit, label, and leave in a cold greenhouse until they begin to grow. Keep the potting mix moist enough to sustain the sections until growth starts.

Grow them on in well-lit conditions in a cold frame, and shade them from the hot summer sun. Water with care; do not let the young plants dry out when in growth. Plant them out the following fall.

Simple cutting

Make cuts ¼in (5mm) deep with a sharp knife through a bulb's basal plate; the number of cuts depends on the bulb's size. Keep the bulb in a plastic bag of damp perlite or vermiculite, in a warm place.

The damage to the basal plate induces bulblets to form along the cuts. When these have formed, insert the bulb upside down in a gritty potting mix made of 1 part peat substitute to 1 part perlite or coarse sand. Bulblets will develop

HOW TO PROPAGATE HYACINTHS BY SCOOPING

1 Use a clean, sharpened teaspoon, or a knife, to scoop out the inner part of the bulb's basal plate, leaving the outer rim intact. Discard the basal plate.

2 Lay the bulbs with their scooped areas uppermost, on a tray of sand. Place the tray in a warm, dark spot.

3 Water the sand lightly to keep it moist. When bulblets form around the edge of the scooped base, separate them from the parent and pot them up.

above the old bulb. A year later, carefully separate the bulblets, and plant them in flats in a cool greenhouse to continue growing.

Scooping hyacinths

Scooping is a technique used for the commercial propagation of hyacinths. The center of the basal plate of the bulb is scooped out and discarded, and the bulb kept upside down in warm, dark

conditions. Numerous bulblets form on and around the cut surface. They may then be separated from the parent bulb and grown on in the same way as bulblets (see "Propagation from bulblets and bulbils," p.244) in individual pots.

Basal cuttings

The sprouting tubers of a few bulbs may be used in late winter for basal cuttings—young shoots

that retain a piece of the parent tuber from which new roots develop. Cuttings are placed in moist potting mix until they root and are then potted up. For details of the technique, see DAHLIAS, *How to Propagate by Basal Cuttings*, p.251. Grow on rooted cuttings in a warm greenhouse until danger of frost is past. Harden off in a cold frame and plant out in early summer. Propagate tuberous begonias and gloxinias (*Sinningia speciosa*) in this way in spring.

SCOOPING AND SCORING TRILLIUMS

Various cutting techniques may be used to propagate *Trillium* rhizomes in late summer, after the leaves have died down.

One method that avoids lifting the parent plant is to remove sufficient soil to expose the tops of the rhizomes and to score lightly a shallow cut around the growing point of each rhizome. Cover the rhizomes with a

topdressing of equal parts peat substitute and coarse sand, or cover them with light, well draining soil. Small rhizomes should form along the cut surfaces and in time become large enough to propagate.

Alternatively, lift rhizomes and scoop out their growing points. Make concave "scoops," rather than cutting across the base of

the growing points, to ensure that no soft tissue remains that could rot. Then replant the rhizomes. Small rhizomes should then form around the excised growing tip.

One year later, expose the rhizomes, remove the young ones, and grow them on in pots as described for young seedlings (see "Care of seedlings," p.245).

CUTTING OUT GROWING POINTS

1 Remove the growing point of the rhizome entirely by making a cut in the form of a concave "scoop" with the tip of a clean, sharp knife.

2 Cover them up again with soil and firm the soil down lightly.

HOW TO PROPAGATE TRILLIUMS BY SCORING

1 Carefully scrape away the topsoil to expose the rhizome. Score a shallow incision around it with a sharp, clean knife, just below the growing point (see inset).

2 Carefully cover the scored rhizome with a mix of peat substitute and coarse sand in equal parts to the same level as before. Gently firm it with your fingers.

3 A year later, remove the topsoil to expose the rhizomes and remove any young ones that have formed. Pot them up individually and grow them on.

Dahlias

Dahlias flower from the middle of summer through to the first frost in fall, providing bright color in the garden for several months. The top growth is very frost tender, but the tubers may survive outdoors in warmer regions if planted deeply and given a thick but loose winter mulch. Otherwise, they are treated as annuals or lifted and stored over winter. They are excellent sunny border plants and can be grown in nearly any fertile, well-drained soil.

If grown for exhibition or for cut flowers, they are best planted in rows in specially prepared beds. Dwarf bedding dahlias are grown by vegetative propagation—that is by cutting or division of tubers of named cultivars, or by growing annually from seed (see ANNUALS AND BIENNIALS, "Sowing in pots or flats," p.216). Dwarf dahlias are suitable for planting in containers. Dahlia flower heads have a diversity of petal forms in a wide color range, from white to rich yellow, through pinks and reds to purples.

Dahlias are divided into ten groups: single-flowered; anemone-flowered; collarette; waterlily; decorative; ball; pompon; cactus; semicactus; and miscellaneous. Four of these groups have been subdivided by the size of their blooms. For waterlily dahlias, there are miniature, usually under 4in (102mm) in diameter; small-flowered, usually 4–6in (102–152mm) in diameter; and medium-flowered ones, usually 6–8in (152–203mm) in diameter. Decorative, cactus, and semicactus dahlias have two additional subdivisions: large-flowered, usually 8–10in (203–254mm) in diameter; and giant-flowered ones, usually over 10in (254mm) in diameter. Ball dahlias are subdivided into: miniature ball, usually with flowers 2–4in (52–102mm) in diameter; and small ball, usually 4–6in (102–152mm) in diameter. Pompon dahlia flowers will be under 2in (52mm).

DAHLIA FLOWER GROUPS

(1) Single
Dahlia **'Yellow Hammer'**
Flower heads with 8–10 broad florets surrounding an open, central disk.

(2) Anemone
D. **'Comet'**
Fully double flower heads with one or more rings of flattened ray florets surrounding a group of shorter, tubular florets.

(3) Collarette
D. **'Easter Sunday'**
A single yellow disk of stamens in the center, with a collar of small florets lying between the stamens and the large, outer florets.

(4) Waterlily
D. **'Vicky Crutchfield'**
As their name implies, these flower heads look like water lilies, and have broad, flat florets.

(5) Decorative
D. **'Frank Hornsey'**
Fully double. Florets have broad petals rounded at the ends, usually curling gently inward along their length, flat, and slightly twisted.

(6) Ball
D. **'Wootton Cupid'**
Rounded flower heads that have spirally arranged florets. The petals are rolled for over half their length.

(7) Pompon
D. **'Small World'**
Similar to ball dahlias but smaller, to a maximum diameter of 2in (52mm), and more globular; the petals are rolled for their length.

(8) Cactus
D. **'Lavender Athalie'**
Fully double, with narrow, pointed petals curled backward or quilled, which are either straight or incurving.

(9) Semicactus
D. **'So Dainty'**
Fully double. The ray florets have pointed, straight or incurving, broad-based petals that curve backward.

Cultivation

Dahlias thrive in well-drained, fertile soils of about pH 7. Prepare the soil early in the year. They are gross feeders, so dig in plenty of manure or garden compost; then add bone meal at 4 oz/sq yd (125 g/sq m), allowing the soil to settle for a few weeks before planting.

Where and when to plant

Dahlias may be planted as pot-grown plants, as dormant tubers, or as rooted cuttings taken from tubers. Plants in leaf may be preferable to tubers—they are often more vigorous. Dormant tubers, however, may be planted directly, about three weeks before the last frost, while plants in leaf should not be planted until after the final frost.

Choose an open, sheltered site in full sun. Immediately before planting, topdress with a balanced fertilizer at normal rates worked well into the soil. Tie young plants into stakes for support as they develop.

Planting pot-grown dahlias

When planting pot-grown dahlias, stakes should be positioned at appropriate spacings. Dahlias that will grow 4–5ft (120–50cm) tall are planted 2–3ft (60–90cm) apart, and

PLANTING TUBERS

Insert a 3ft (1m) stake in a planting hole. Place soil around the clump of tubers so that the base of the new shoots is 1–2in (2.5–5cm) below soil level.

those that will grow 2½–3½ft (75cm–1.1m) tall, 2ft (60cm) apart. Shorter bedding dahlias are planted 18in (45cm) apart. Water the plants in their pots and leave to drain. Plant with care, to avoid disturbing the root ball, and firm gently, leaving a slight depression at the stem base. Water thoroughly. The plant will make a clump by late fall; this may be lifted and stored for replanting in spring.

Planting tubers

Dormant tubers can be planted directly in the border about three weeks before the last frost is expected. The ground is prepared as for pot-grown plants. Prepare a planting hole about 9in (22cm) across and about 6in (15cm) deep, place the clump or tuber in the hole, and cover over. Mark the position of the tuber with a labeled thin stake placed just to the side; this will indicate the exact position of the tuber when inserting its support stake. The plant takes about six weeks to develop a shoot above ground. If the shoot emerges above ground level while there is still a risk of frost, cover the shoot with fabric for protection.

Planting rooted cuttings

Established tubers can be grown in the cold frame or greenhouse to provide cuttings (see "Propagation," opposite). Plant out rooted cuttings after all risk of frost has passed. Water the plants moderately as growth develops; to retain moisture, mulch when the plants reach a height of 12–15in (30–38cm) with well-rotted compost or manure. Be careful not to allow the mulch to touch the base of the plants because this may encourage stem rot. Untreated composted grass clippings can also be used as mulch for dahlias.

PINCHING

1 When the plant is about 15in (38cm) tall, pinch out the central shoot to encourage the development of sideshoots.

2 When the plant has 6–8 sideshoots, pinch off the top pair of buds. Tie the stems to stakes.

Pinching and disbudding

When the dahlias have grown to about 15in (38cm), remove the growing points to encourage the sideshoots to develop. Insert two more stakes and tie the shoots in.

The number of shoots allowed to develop should depend on the size of the blooms desired. For giant or large blooms, restrict each plant to 4–6 shoots; for medium and small blooms, allow 7–10 shoots. To produce high-quality blooms, disbud some from each shoot (see below).

DISBUDDING

To encourage show-quality flowers, pinch out the side (wing) bud and 1 or 2 pairs of sideshoots below the terminal bud.

Summer feeding

Six weeks after planting, feed with a high nitrogen and potasssium fertilizer, either in granular form, or by weekly applications of liquid fertilizer to the roots or leaves. As flower buds develop, extra potassium in the liquid fertilizer gives strong stems and good flower color, especially in pinks and lilacs; this is important when growing for exhibition.

The tuber's development during late summer and early fall is stimulated by the shortening day length. During this period, apply a split application of tomato fertilizer and superphosphates at the manufacturer's recommended rate. Avoid contact with leaves or stems since this may cause scorch.

Pests and diseases

Dahlias are attacked particularly by aphids (p.654), thrips (p.671), spider mites (p.670), and earwigs (p.659). Use appropriate controls on a regular basis. Immediately discard any plants infected with viruses (p.672).

Lifting and storing tubers

When the foliage has been blackened by the first frost in the fall, trim back the stems to about 6in (15cm). Carefully lift and clean the soil from the tubers and trim off any fine roots. Place them upside down for a few weeks to ensure that no moisture remains in the stems and leaves.

Label the tubers and pack them in wooden boxes in vermiculite, peat, or a similar medium. Store in a dry, cool, frost-proof place. Inspect the tubers regularly in winter; if any mildew or rot has developed, cut it out with a clean, sharp knife.

LIFTING AND STORING

1 Cut the stems to about 6in (15cm) above ground level. Loosen the soil and ease the tubers out. Remove excess soil.

2 Store the tubers upside down for about 3 weeks in a frost-free place so that the stems dry out thoroughly.

3 When the stems have dried out, place the tubers in a wooden box and cover them with coir, vermiculite, or a similar medium. Set the box in a cool, frost-free place. Keep them almost dry until spring.

Propagation

Divide established tubers in spring. First, establish them in a cold frame or greenhouse. Press the tubers gently onto the top of a flat of propagation mix, spray with water, and keep warm and damp. As shoots develop, divide the tuber into sections with a sharp knife, ensuring that each piece has at least one growing shoot. Pot each section separately using planting mix.

Alternatively, in late winter, force tubers at 59–64°F (15–18°C). When each shoot has a growing point and two or three pairs of leaves, take basal cuttings, trim at a node, and root in a propagating case with bottom heat. Grow on under cover and harden off before planting out.

Showing dahlias

Cut blooms with a sharp knife in the morning or evening, making sure that the stem length is in proportion to the bloom. When exhibiting, blooms should always be well developed with undamaged petals. Read the schedule and present the correct number of stems staged in the vase, with the blooms facing forward.

HOW TO PROPAGATE BY BASAL CUTTINGS

1 In late winter, force the tubers under cover. Take cuttings when the young shoots are 3in (7.5cm) long.

2 With a knife, remove each shoot with a thin segment, or heel, from the parent tuber. Trim at a node. Remove bottom pair of leaves.

3 Insert the cuttings in a pot of moist potting mix. Place in a propagator or plastic bag to root. Then pot up singly to continue growing.

ROCK, SCREE, AND GRAVEL GARDENING

ALPINE PLANTS GROW IN SOME OF THE MOST REMOTE REGIONS OF THE WORLD, YET MANY WILL THRIVE IN ROCK OR GRAVEL GARDENS IN A WELL-DRAINED SITE WITH A SUNNY EXPOSURE.

Gardeners who want to grow a wide variety of plants in a limited space, or who live in an area prone to drought, could consider creating a feature with rock or stone products. Many such gardens emulate high alpine sites, or the sun-baked, stony soil of Mediterranean and desert environments. The increased interest in these extreme growing conditions has generated an appreciation of the often diminutive beauty of plants adapted to prosper in such regions. Whether a traditional rock garden, or a simple gravel bed or paved area studded with aromatic creeping plants and succulents, such features bring many rewards to the plant enthusiast.

Alpine and rock gardening

The restricted size of alpine and rock garden plants fits particularly well into the confines of the small, modern garden. Few other types of plants are so characteristically neat and compact and this allows a substantial collection of species and hybrids to be grown in a relatively small space. Alpines are plants that grow at high altitudes above the tree line, although the term is often loosely used to include a vast range of low-growing rock garden plants, including many bulbs, that may be grown successfully at relatively low altitudes.

Mat-forming rosettes *Sempervivum* thrives in a bed of moss.

Alpine and rock plants

The diminutive form and graceful habit of alpine plants make them suitable for grouping together in fascinating, brilliantly colored collections. Rock plants are simply slow-growing plants of relatively small stature that are suitable in scale for growing in rock gardens.

True alpines

Alpines may be deciduous or evergreen woody plants, or they may be herbaceous, or grow from bulbs, corms, or tubers; few are annuals. They are characteristically hardy, adapted to survive in extremes of climate, and compact, with few more than 6in (15cm) tall. In their native mountains, the dwarf or creeping habit of alpines reduces their wind resistance and helps them resist the crushing weight of heavy snow in winter.

Plants in alpine regions experience very high sunshine and fresh, constantly moving air. Their cushion- or mat-forming habit and their small, fleshy, hairy, or leathery leaves protect them from water loss in high winds and hot sun. For example, edelweiss (*Leontopodium alpinum*) has its entire surface covered in wooly hair, which helps conserve moisture, while the leaves of hens-and-chicks (*Sempervivum*) have fleshy, water-retaining tissue.

Alpines are adapted to extremes of temperature, but few withstand constant wetness at the roots in winter or warm, humid, summer conditions. In their native habitats, they often grow in thin, poor soil that lacks nutrients and has a low organic content but allows rapid drainage. Most develop extensive, spreading root systems to seek out nutrients and moisture.

Easily grown alpines

Many alpine species, and their more showy cultivars, are undemanding in their cultural requirements and easy to grow in the open garden. They present a wealth of habits and forms, from tiny, cushion-forming plants to spreading mound- and mat-formers; some of the easier alpines bloom well into summer, almost invariably producing a profusion of flowers. The low-growing cultivars of *Aubrieta*, *Dianthus*, *Phlox*, and *Veronica* form mats of clear, bright color, and may be used to edge beds, their informal, spreading habit gently softening straight lines.

Specialist alpines

Other alpine genera, like the Aretian *Androsace* and the tight cushion-forming saxifrages, have special requirements, in particular a need for very free-draining soil and protection from excessive winter moisture. Most also require plenty of sun but their roots must be cool; lower-altitude, woodland species often prefer dappled shade and may need moist, acidic soil.

The rich and varied colors and diverse forms of many specialized plants may still be enjoyed, however, as long as they have well-drained conditions and a suitable exposure. The best way to fulfill these needs is to raise the plants above the underlying soil, planting them in specially constructed or carefully controlled environments and using prepared, gritty, free-draining soil or planting mixes.

Some alpine plants need to have cool roots and shelter; rock gardens and pockets within stone or brick walls are ideal for such plants and display them to their best advantage in natural-looking surroundings. In more formal settings or if space is limited, raised beds or troughs and sinks are attractive alternatives, especially when they are constructed from materials that complement any existing hard landscape features. Freestanding troughs and sinks also allow color to be introduced at a variety of heights and on hard surfaces, such as patios and paths.

Rock plants

They include dwarf trees and shrubs, which are useful for framework (background) plantings, architectural plants, which give focus to a planting layout, and many other plants that are not necessarily from alpine regions. Some, like *Armeria maritima*, occur in coastal habitats, while many miniature bulbs are native to sunny, Mediterranean hillsides. In common with true alpines, they share the need for free-draining soil and so are suitable for planting among alpines. Small perennials and dwarf drought-tolerant plants can be used to set the framework in a rock garden; they are also useful in a low-maintenance, gravel or scree garden.

Diverse planting Many rock plants retain the charm of wildflowers but selected forms and hybrids often display greater numbers of attractive, sometimes larger flowers in a range of bright colors.

Since many true alpines bloom in the spring and early summer, late-blooming rock garden plants are especially valuable because they may extend the season of interest.

The rock garden

A sunny, south- or southwest-facing slope makes an ideal site for the stony outcrops of a rock garden. Well-constructed gardens emulate natural rock formations and create striking features. They replicate, as closely as possible, the natural habitat of alpine plants, creating the conditions in which they thrive—the soil beneath the rocks provides the cool, moist, but freely draining root space that they particularly enjoy.

Planning a rock garden

For the greatest visual impact, a rock garden should be constructed on as generous a scale as the site allows. Where possible, choose a naturally sloping, open site that provides good drainage. A series of rocky outcrops with gullies running between them is highly effective, especially if streams and pools are included in the design.

A sunny exposure will suit most rock plants, although those that prefer shade may be grown in cooler, shady pockets on the north side of large rocks. Careful placement of the rocks at the construction stage (see p.263) will provide a wide range of planting areas and rock niches to meet the needs of many different alpines.

Choosing plants

Several alpine species, such as *Gentiana verna*, with its flowers of intense blue in spring, prefer deep pockets of well-drained, gritty soil, while the mat-forming *Persicaria affinis* 'Donald Lowndes', for example, thrives in broader terraces between rock strata. Both *Lewisia* cotyledon hybrids and *Saxifraga* 'Tumbling Waters', which have cascades of white flowers over rosettes of lime-encrusted foliage, are most at home in the narrow crevices between vertical stone faces. Alpine or dwarf pinks, such as *Dianthus alpinus* and *D.* 'Mars', provide evergreen, gray or green mats or cushions of neat foliage and masses of often clove-scented, single to double, red, pink, or white blooms throughout the summer and into fall; they are at home in any well-drained site.

Plan the layout to include as much seasonal variation as possible. Alpine bulbs such as *Crocus laevigatus* and *Iris histrioides* 'Major' help bring the garden to life in late winter or early spring, and *Cyclamen hederifolium* and *Sternbergia lutea* add interest in fall. For year-round color, include a few evergreens, such as the dwarf *Chamaecyparis obtusa* 'Nana Pyramidalis' and *Juniperus communis* 'Compressa', and dwarf shrubs, such as *Hebe buchananii* 'Minor'.

Dotted color A minimalist mix of slate and stepping stones is brightened and punctuated by a mix of green, yellow, and pink alpines.

Add texture and structure to the planting by using species with unusual leaves or stems and variation in height and form. Contrasting leaf texture can be particularly striking: bold, fleshy, rosette-forming plants may be used to offset the delicate, feathery leaves and flowers of *Pulsatilla* species, for instance, and a combination of spreading, cushion-forming, and trailing alpines with several dwarf shrubs or trees provides great visual interest. The sword-shaped, silver leaves of *Celmisia coriacea* contrast well with mat-forming plants such as *Polygala calcarea* 'Bulley's Form', with deep blue flowers in late spring and early summer, and *Campanula cochleariifolia*, with clusters of pale blue or white bells in summer.

Scree formations

On mountains, natural weathering produces a mass of small, broken rocks and stones. These loose stony slopes, known as screes, are home to plants that need plenty of moisture at their roots during the growing season, but grow best through an apparently dry 6in (15cm) surface layer of stones. Scree dwellers are among the most beautiful and jewel-like of alpine plants and well worth the extra care needed to grow them.

The scree bed

Scree beds attempt to recreate the specialized habitat of natural scree dwellers. Screes are deep, preferably gently sloping beds of loose rock fragments of varying size, into which is mixed a suitable soil mix (see p.262). Screes may be constructed on flat sites, raised from ground level to assist drainage, becoming, in effect, a form of raised bed (see p.257). Scree dwellers usually form low mats or cushions of dense foliage, and many bear small brilliant

blooms in such profusion that flowers almost completely obscure the leaves. The neutral background of small stones offers an ideal foil for rich textures and colors of this type of planting.

Specialized plants such as *Vitaliana primuliflora*, *Anchusa cespitosa*, and *Myosotis alpestris*, thrive in screes. Other rock garden plants that are easier to grow also appreciate these conditions. Some, such as *Achillea clavennae* and *Artemisia glacialis*, are grown primarily for their silver foliage, which provides a cool contrast for stronger colors. A number of species, including pink *Androsace carnea* subsp. *laggeri*, naturally self-seed. Tiny, blue, bell-shaped flowers of *Campanula cochleariifolia* can also spring up around the garden but may become a nuisance if they begin to compete with less robust species.

Integrating the scree bed

If space is available, scree beds may be integrated with a rock garden to form a bold, unified design and provide a range of habitats. A backing of large rocks skirted by scree beds is particularly effective. Alternatively, add pockets of scree mixture to a rock garden to accommodate scree dwellers needing good drainage around their necks. *Dianthus haematocalyx*, for example, is a tightly tufted pink that benefits from a soil surface of loose, dry stones.

The visual effect of a scree bed is enhanced by incorporating just a few larger rocks. Plants may then be allowed to skirt their base or to grow over them to soften their outlines.

Gravel beds and paving

Areas of gravel and paving stones are alternatives to traditional, labor-intensive and water-hungry features, such as herbaceous borders and lawns. Environmental concerns about the use of hard materials have been partially allayed by the increasing range of manufactured stone products, many utilizing by-products of the quarrying industry. In appearance these are far more natural looking than previous offerings, and much more attractive and easy to blend into the garden.

These hard landscaping features must be planted if they are not to appear harsh and sterile. However, in order to use successfully the rock garden and drought-tolerant plants that complement such materials, it is esssential that the underlying soil has the free drainage that they need. It may be necessary to improve the drainage by adding grit to the soil or even installing a rubble sub-base to act as a soakaway for excess water (see p.623). Incorporating a slope will also assist drainage.

A gently sloping site facing the sun, with free-draining soil topdressed with gravel or pebbles, is an ideal environment for a Mediterranean-style mixed planting. Coastal plants such as sea pinks (*Armeria*), sea lavender (*Limonium*), and horned poppies (*Glaucium flavum*) will also thrive. Instead of dwarf conifers as accent plants, try small gray-leaved shrubs, such as *Convolvulus cneorum* and spiky perennials such as *Phormium*.

On a sunny patio, crevices and planting spaces between paving stones filled with free-draining soil provide ideal conditions

Dramatic contrast The jewel-like colors of *Dianthus alpinus* 'Joan's Blood' can provide a very effective contrast to the rocks on which it grows.

Scree bed Mimicking a natural scree area can be an effective way of displaying plants of differing forms, as well as being a low maintenance way to garden.

Rock and water Combining gravel and stone areas around the edges of a raised bed water garden is a good way of increasing the scope of planting niches and therefore the variety of plants that can be grown.

for low-growing, sun-loving plants. Patios also make attractive settings for containers of rock plants (see also "Troughs, sinks, and other containers," p.258).

Ericaceous plants

Alpine plants that require an acidic soil or a woodland environment are not always easily accommodated in a rock garden. Acid-loving plants such as *Arctostaphylos*, *Cassiope*, gentians, and most *Vaccinium* species will only thrive in soil with a low pH, and woodland plants prefer moist, shady conditions and leafy, humus-rich soil. Specially constructed beds containing acidic soil mix provide a moist, acidic growing medium and, when sited in dappled shade, closely imitate woodland conditions.

Site and materials
Such acidic-humus beds may be constructed either as individual garden features or as extensions to a rock garden. The shady, north-facing side of a rock garden provides ideal conditions. Do not place an acidic-humus bed directly beneath trees because the drip from the leaves after rain may damage plants. For best results, the site should be in sun for part of the day. Traditionally, such beds are filled with sphagnum peat moss, which is generally acidic. However, depending on the source of the peat, it may be slightly alkaline. Before purchasing large quantities,

determine the pH of a single bale by using a pH meter to ensure it is acidic enough. Always moisten the peat moss in its bag by adding water and leaving overnight. Dry peat added to a bed is very difficult to moisten.

In regions where sphagnum peat is not harvested locally, gardeners may prefer to use bark or coconut fiber, although both may have been transported a considerable distance as well.

Raised beds

In small gardens, raised beds make highly economical use of limited space. In larger gardens, narrow raised beds may make a useful and attractive boundary feature. The formal appearance of raised beds blends in well with the design and layout of many modern gardens and, in areas where suitable rock is not easily available, or is prohibitively expensive, a raised bed provides a good substitute for a rock garden.

Because drainage is independent of the underlying soil, raised beds are especially useful in gardens with poorly drained soils (such as wet, heavy clay) that are otherwise unsuitable for the cultivation of alpines. In addition, the dimensions of a raised bed may be planned so that the bed will easily accommodate a frame light to allow cultivation of choice species that require protection from too much winter moisture, without restricting airflow around the plants. Various materials may be used for

constructing a raised bed, including traditional bricks or dry stones and weathered railroad ties. For further information, see STRUCTURES AND SURFACES, "Raised beds," p.599.

Planting in raised beds
Large raised beds may be divided into separate compartments, and different soil mediums used in each to suit the specific requirements of different plant groups. Rocks may be added to the surface of the soil and bedded in to provide textural contrast and vertical niches for plants that require them.

Rectangular raised beds have several exposures so that plants with different requirements may be planted in niches on their sunny or shady side. As well as growing plants in the bed itself, the walls may be designed to incorporate planting niches, in the same way as walls used for trailing species.

Choose plants that will give successional interest as the seasons progress. Dense, evergreen rosettes of *Haberlea rhodopensis* send up sprays of funnel-shaped flowers in spring, and may be succeeded in summer by *Aquilegia flabellata* 'Nana', a clump-forming alpine that produces bell-shaped, soft blue flowers, each with fluted petals and a short spur. Both these plants prefer semishade and are small enough to be planted in a raised bed without overcrowding it.

For a sunnier exposure, choose compact species of *Dianthus*, such as *D. alpinus* and *D.* 'Bombardier', with *Erinus alpinus* 'Dr. Hähnle' trailing from the retaining wall.

Walls

Garden walls may be modified to provide excellent sites for alpines and rock garden plants. The walls of raised beds and those used to retain banks of earth on a terraced slope may be modified in the same way. If possible, leave spaces, crevices, or cracks between the stones or brickwork during the construction of such walls so that these may be planted up when building is complete.

Choosing plants

Mat-forming plants are very suitable, like *Acantholimon glumaceum*, which forms evergreen cushions that are clothed in pink flowers during summer, or *Dianthus deltoides* and other alpine pinks. Plants prone to rotting at the collar, such as *Lewisia* and *Ramonda* species, are well suited to being grown in walls, because the roots enjoy the cool conditions and extra drainage provided by the crevices. Trailing, semievergreen *Asarina procumbens*, with creamy-white, snapdragonlike flowers, and shrubby *Penstemon newberryi* f. *humilior*, with a profusion of flowers on arching branches, are also ideal.

Dry-stone walls

These provide ample room for the root systems of many rock garden plants to penetrate, and also allow sharp drainage. Freestanding, single or double dry-stone walls with carefully chosen plants are extremely attractive features. The well-drained tops provide an ideal home for mat-forming plants, such as *Gypsophila repens* or *Saponaria ocymoides*; both will cascade attractively over the edge of the wall. The neat, spreading rosettes of lime-encrusted saxifrages and hens-and-chicks (*Sempervivum*) may be dotted at intervals across the surface, and using both vertical faces of a wall will allow both sun and shade-loving plants to be grown.

Troughs, sinks, and other containers

Containers provide an opportunity to grow alpines in a small garden, and may also be used to flank pathways or steps. Old stone sinks and troughs make handsome containers for rock plants, although both are scarce and expensive. However, troughs made of reconstituted stone or hypertufa, and glazed sinks coated with this material (see p.266) are inexpensive alternatives. Troughs and sinks can be used as features for patios and courtyards, or on terraces and graveled areas in larger gardens (see also CONTAINER GARDENING, "Using containers," pp.306–317).

Planting in troughs

The smallest alpine species are often the most intricate. *Antennaria dioica* 'Minima' and other compact alpines and rock plants should be used for such displays. By careful selection, a plant community of dwarf and slow-growing species can be planted to make up a rock garden in miniature.

Try to introduce some variation in height. Use small conifers, such as *Chamaecyparis obtusa* 'Nana Pyramidalis' or *Juniperus communis* 'Compressa', and dwarf trees, such as *Ulmus parvifolia* 'Geisha', as framework plants, choosing others such as *Campanula zoysii*, *Dianthus alpinus*, or *D. microlepis* for the middle and foreground. Miniature shrubs may be added to provide contrasting form and color throughout the year.

Other containers

If an appropriate soil mix is used and plants are well maintained, almost any container may be used to good effect, provided that it has adequate drainage. Large pots and tubs are suitable for small collections of the tiniest alpines, especially those that trail over edges, such as *Silene schafta*. Small containers suit compact, slow-growers, such as *Androsace*

chamaejasme and *Sempervivum arachnoideum*. Old urns or pots make attractive features planted with *Sedum* or *Sempervivum* species. Containers are especially suitable for cultivating miniature species, and allow plants, such as the tiny *Primula scotica*, with its golden-eyed purple flowers, to be appreciated in a situation where they will not be swamped by more vigorous neighbors. Grouping several containers together provides an opportunity to build up collections devoted to plants of one genus that flourish under similar conditions.

The alpine house

In the wild, many alpines spend their winter dormancy insulated by a deep snow blanket that shields them from excess water, cold drying winds, and severe cold; temperatures under the snow cover hover at, or just below, freezing point. In yards at lower altitudes, where conditions are very different, the more exacting alpines need to be covered.

A simple row cover may be sufficient protection for some plants but a specially designed greenhouse, or alpine house (see GREENHOUSES AND FRAMES, "Alpine house," p.569), extends the range that may be grown, and allows the gardener to try growing some of the most challenging plants.

Using an alpine house

An alpine house will keep a huge range of alpines in carefully controlled conditions. The season of interest may be maintained through the early winter months, when color in the garden is scarce. Interest increases rapidly in early spring, when the majority of true alpines flower. Where dwarf shrubs, bulbs, conifers, and ferns are also included in the collection, there will be something to attract attention throughout the year (see also ALPINE HOUSES AND FRAMES, pp.277–279).

Dry habitat *Lewisia* 'George Henley', with its small pink flowers, grows well in a dry stone wall.

Vertical home Alpines are often found wedged between rocks in natural settings, and this crevice garden showing a mix of alpines growing in slate in a stone trough recreates this look.

PLANTER'S GUIDE TO ROCK PLANTS

EXPOSED SITES
Rock plants that tolerate exposed or windy sites
Antennaria dioica
Campanula portenschlagiana
Carlina acaulis
Chiastophyllum oppositifolium
Crepis incana
Dryas octopetala
Erigeron karvinskianus
Eryngium
Euphorbia myrsinites
Hebe
Helianthemum
Limonium bellidifolium
Pterocephalus perennis
Sedum
Sempervivum
Silene uniflora
Veronica spicata

AIR POLLUTION
Rock plants that tolerate polluted air
Aubrieta
Aurinia saxatilis
Campanula garganica,
   C. poscharskyana
Erinus alpinus
Euphorbia
Sedum
Sempervivum

DRY SHADE
Rock plants that tolerate dry shade
Ajuga pyramidalis,
   A. reptans
Dianthus carthusianorum,
   D. deltoides
Diascia barberae 'Fisher's Flora',
   D. barberae 'Ruby Field'
Erodium guttatum
Genista sagittalis
Gypsophila repens
Helleborus
Lamium maculatum
Saponaria ocymoides
Waldsteinia ternata

MOIST SHADE
Rock plants that prefer moist shade
Adonis amurensis
Cassiope
Cyclamen hederifolium,
   C. purpurascens
Daphne blagayana
Galax urceolata
Hepatica nobilis,
   H. transsilvanica
Hylomecon japonica
Iris cristata
Meconopsis cambrica
Primula
   (many spp. and cvs)
Sanguinaria canadensis
Shortia uniflora
Stylophorum diphyllum
Trillium

SCREE GARDENS
Acantholimon glumaceum
Aethionema grandiflorum,
   A. 'Warley Rose'
Alyssum montanum
Androsace lanuginosa,
   A. sarmentosa,
   A. sempervivoides
Dianthus alpinus,
   D. anatolicus,
   D. erinaceus
Erinus alpinus
Gypsophila aretioides
Linaria alpina
Papaver burseri,
   P. fauriei,
   P. rhaeticum
Pritzelago alpina
Sempervivum
Silene acaulis
Viola cornuta 'Minor',
   V. jooi

CREVICES AND PAVING
Aubrieta deltoidea
   (many cvs)
Aurinia saxatilis
Campanula cochleariifolia,
   C. portenschlagiana
Erinus alpinus
Erodium reichardii
Geranium sanguineum var. striatum
Globularia cordifolia
Mentha requienii
Onosma alborosea,
   O. echioides
Pratia pedunculata
Scabiosa graminifolia
Thymus

WALL CREVICES
Antirrhinum hispanicum,
   A. molle
Aurinia saxatilis 'Citrina'
Campanula portenschlagiana
Erinus alpinus
Globularia cordifolia
Haberlea rhodopensis (shade)
Lewisia cotyledon hybrids
Onosma taurica
Polemonium pulcherrimum
Ramonda myconi (shade)
Saxifraga callosa,
   S. cochlearis,
   S. longifolia,
   S. paniculata
Silene uniflora
   'Robin Whitebreast'

PLANTING IN TROUGHS
Anchusa cespitosa
Androsace (small spp. and cvs)
Antennaria dioica 'Minima'
Arenaria purpurascens
Asperula suberosa
Daphne (some)
Dianthus alpinus,
   D. freynii
Dryas octopetala 'Minor'
Edraianthus pumilio
Gentiana saxosa,
   G. verna subsp. angulosa

Helianthemum oelandicum
Linum suffruticosum subsp.
   salsoloides 'Nanum'
Myosotis alpestris
Omphalodes luciliae
Oxalis enneaphylla
Paraquilegia anemonoides
Petrophytum hendersonii
Phlox subulata
Primula farinosa,
   P. marginata
Saxifraga
   (many spp. and cvs)
Sedum cauticola
Soldanella alpina,
   S. montana
Thymus serpyllum
   'Minus'
Vitaliana primuliflora

PLANTING IN TUFA
Androsace (small spp. and cvs)
Campanula piperi,
   C. zoysii
Draba mollissima,
   D. polytricha
Edraianthus pumilio
Paraquilegia anemonoides
Physoplexis comosa
Potentilla nitida
Saxifraga (many types,
   especially the Kabschias)
Viola cazorlensis,
   V. delphinantha

RAISED BEDS
Aethionema 'Warley Rose'
Androsace
Antirrhinum molle,
   A. sempervirens
Aquilegia discolor,
   A. flabellata 'Nana'
Armeria juniperifolia
Bolax gummifera
Callianthemum anemonoides
Campanula raineri,
   C. zoysii
Daphne arbuscula,
   D. cneorum,
   D. petraea 'Grandiflora',
   D. x susannae 'Cheriton'
   D. x whiteorum 'Beauworth'
Dianthus
Draba rigida var. bryoides
Edraianthus dinaricus,
   E. graminifolius
Erinacea anthyllis
Gentiana acaulis,
   G. verna subsp. angulosa
Globularia meridionalis,
   G. repens
Haberlea rhodopensis
Leontopodium alpinum,
   L. alpinum subsp. nivale
Lewisia (some spp. and hybrids)
Origanum (some spp. and hybrids)
Oxalis adenophylla,
   O. enneaphylla,
   O. 'Ione Hecker'
Papaver burseri,
   P. fauriei
Paraquilegia anemonoides

Primula auricula,
   P. marginata
Ramonda myconi
Saxifraga cotyledon,
   S. longifolia,
   S. 'Tumbling Waters'
Sempervivum
Silene acaulis
Verbascum 'Letitia'

DWARF SHRUBS
Berberis x stenophylla
   'Corallina Compacta'
Betula nana
Chamaecyparis obtusa
   'Intermedia'
Cryptomeria japonica
   'Vilmoriniana'
Daphne cneorum,
   D. retusa,
   D. sericea
Erinacea anthyllis
Euryops acraeus
Genista sagittalis
   subsp. delphinensis
Hebe buchananii 'Minor'
Ilex crenata 'Mariesii'
Juniperus communis
   'Compressa'
Lotus hirsutus
Ozothamnus coralloides.
Picea abies 'Clanbrassiliana',
   P. abies 'Gregoryana',
   P. glauca var.
   albertiana 'Conica'
Potentilla fruticosa 'Beesii'
Salix x boydii
Sorbus reducta

Key
 Rock garden species only

Erinus alpinus

Construction, soil preparation, and planting

Various methods may be used to grow alpine plants in gardens. Planting them in a rock garden is perhaps the best-known method, although this can take up a great deal of space. For a smaller display, screes, raised and peat beds, and the crevices of walls can be very attractive features. Where space is more limited, troughs, sinks, and other containers may also be used for a fine alpine display.

Buying plants

The rock garden, with careful choice of plants, should be regarded as a feature that will provide interest all year round.

ROCK PLANTS FOR ACID SOIL

Arctostaphylos alpina
Cassiope
Corydalis cashmeriana,
   C. flexuosa
Cyananthus
Epigaea gaultherioides,
   E. repens
Galax urceolata
Gaultheria
Gentiana sino-ornata
Glaucidium palmatum
Haberlea rhodopensis
Kalmia angustifolia, K. microphylla
Leiophyllum buxifolium
Leucopogon fraseri
Leucothöe keiskei
Linnaea borealis
Lithodora diffusa
Menziesia ciliicalyx
Mitchella repens
Ourisia caespitosa, O. coccinea,
   O. 'Loch Ewe'
Paris polyphylla
Phyllodoce caerulea, P. nipponica
Pieris nana
Polygala chamaebuxus, P. vayredae
Primula boothii alba, P. gracilipes,
   P. nana, P. sonchifolia
Pyrola rotundifolia
Rhododendron (dwarf spp.)
Sanguinaria canadensis f. *multiplex*
Shortia soldanelloides
Soldanella villosa
Tanakaea radicans
Vaccinium delavayi,
   V. myrtillus, V. uliginosum

Phyllodoce caerula

Before buying any plants, refer to reference guides to find out the likely range of plants that is suitable for a particular type of locality in terms of climate, soil, and other site factors. Visit established rock gardens in parks and botanical gardens, as well as specialty nurseries, to assess the relative merits of various plants for your own requirements. The shape, form, and color of foliage, fruit, stems, and the overall growth habit are often as important as flowers.

Where to buy plants

Plants are available from a wide range of sources, including garden centers and specialty nurseries. Nonspecialty outlets often sell a limited range of colorful cultivars and easily grown species; these may form large, spreading clumps that quickly overwhelm more delicate plants in the rock garden.

The experienced horticulturalist is able to advise on the most suitable choice of plants for a particular site, and often has display beds of mature plants. These give a good indication of the ultimate size, spread, and habit of different plants, and are invaluable at the planning stage. Such specialty growers may also be consulted for information on soil mixes and suppliers of rock.

A much wider range of plants will be offered by the specialty grower, who is also able to provide detailed advice on cultivation—this is particularly useful for the beginner. Demand for rare or unfamiliar plants sometimes means that general suppliers may carry plants that are best left to the specialty nurseries, because they are often unsuitable for the average rock garden. Such plants may be attractive but are often expensive and may be difficult to cultivate. They offer a rewarding challenge, but only purchase them after obtaining advice on growing them.

Selecting alpine plants

Choose plants that have healthy, compact foliage, and no sign of pests and diseases or water deprivation. Do not buy plants with yellowing or weak growth: this indicates that they have been kept in poor light. Labels should bear the name of the plant as well as details of flowering times and brief cultivation requirements. Plants should not be potbound, and the roots should either not be visible, or only just, through the hole in the base of the pot. Do not purchase any plants that have rooted into the

HOW TO SELECT ALPINE PLANTS

Good example

Saxifraga

Healthy looking, compact growth

Weed-free soil mix

Poor examples

Unbalanced, weak growth

Weeds in soil mix

Roots curled around inside of pot

material on the surface of the display area—these are almost certain to be potbound.

The topgrowth of a plant may remain healthy for some time after the root system has been damaged or has actually died, so check that the plant has a healthy root system by sliding it out of its pot and inspecting the root ball carefully.

Large specimens are sometimes available but unless they have been grown correctly, with careful attention to watering, they may take much longer to become established than smaller, vigorous ones.

Select plants that are as weed-free as possible. Before planting, scrape off grit or surface soil mix to remove weed seeds. Introducing weeds, such as pearlwort (*Sagina procumbens*), as well as several kinds of oxalis, causes problems that, once established, are difficult to eradicate.

A number of plants that are sold for growing in the rock garden, such as some of the ornamental onions (*Allium*), are overly prolific seeders. Choose plants carefully to avoid introducing such problem plants.

Siting a rock garden or scree bed

Good siting is critical for a rock garden or scree bed, because alpine plants require good light and well-drained conditions in order to thrive. The rock garden or scree should also blend in well with the rest of the garden. Before beginning construction, sketch a rough plan on paper showing the rock garden or scree bed in relation to other garden features. A scree can be integrated into a rock garden or, alternatively, built as a separate feature.

Choosing the site

Choose an open, sunny site away from overhanging trees; trees drip water onto plants beneath, and

SITING A ROCK GARDEN

Limit of afternoon shade from nearby plants

Sloping ground

Limit of morning shade from hedge

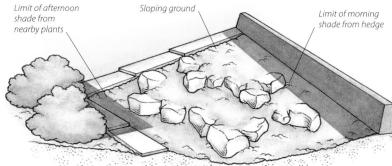

Build a rock garden on sloping ground, if possible, to ensure good drainage. Choose an open site that receives full sun, away from the roots and overhanging branches of trees and large shrubs.

leaves shed in the fall may also smother plants or create a damp atmosphere that rots them. Tree roots may also compete with the plants for moisture and nutrients. Do not site a rock garden or scree in a frost pocket or on a site exposed to cold, drying winds. A sloping site is ideal for a rock garden; it will have excellent drainage, and artificial outcrops of rock may be made to look more natural, and provide different pockets and exposures to suit a variety of plants. Scree beds (see p.264) or raised beds (see p.269) are usually better for level sites.

A rock garden or scree is best sited where it will blend into an informally planted area of the garden, on a slope, by a patio, or as a natural-looking outcrop from an area of shrubs. Plan any water features, such as a pond or stream, into the design from an early stage. If the rock garden or scree is to be next to a lawn, ensure that it does not interfere with cutting and edging. It is unlikely to look natural next to herbaceous borders, bedding displays, or any other formally planted areas, such as the vegetable or fruit garden. If the main garden is formal, it may be better to grow alpines in a rectangular raised bed (see p.269) rather than trying to integrate the informality of a rock garden into the design.

Choosing stone

Use locally available stone for rock garden construction wherever possible to harmonize with the local landscape and reduce transportation costs. Visit local quarries to inspect the rock and choose suitable pieces

NATURAL STRATA

Sedimentary rock, such as limestone, occurs naturally in distinct layers, or stratum lines, that are clearly visible to the eye. Rocks of this type may easily be split along the stratum lines for use in rock gardens.

Sedimentary rocks that occur in nature always have stratum lines following the same direction; it is important to place the stones in a rock garden to create the same kind of effect, otherwise they will look too obviously artificial.

Natural stratum lines

that are not too large to handle after being delivered. Choose rocks in a range of different sizes to construct a natural-looking outcrop. Garden centers may offer a range of rocks, although there is sometimes a limited choice of size and shape, especially in regions where supplies of natural rock are limited.

Natural stone

Limestone is useful for creating gardens for plants that prefer alkaline soil. Where it occurs locally, try to get weathered rock from fields or woods. These will be slightly rounded and will have a patina of moss or lichens. New rock, for example, from building sites or road cuts, takes several years to mellow.

Do not use soft, quick-weathering rock, such as shale, or hard, featureless, igneous rocks without strata, such as granite and basalt. Hard stone with no clear strata may be cheap but is difficult to use, takes several years to acquire a

weathered appearance, and seldom looks natural. Other materials, such as slate, are also used but are sometimes difficult to blend in.

The most suitable rocks are the various sandstones, in which the natural strata or layers are clearly visible. One great advantage of using rocks with stratum lines is that they may split easily, making it relatively easy to create planting pockets and natural-looking fissures in the rock. Alternatively, you may be lucky enough to find a source of tufa, a porous, limy rock filled with air pockets. Its light weight makes it easy to transport and handle. Cavities for plants may be dug or drilled out of its relatively soft surface. It provides ideal conditions for plants that require free drainage, but it is scarce and expensive.

Artificial rocks

Reconstituted rocks made from quarry waste and even fiberglass "rocks" can also be obtained; they may be more or less convincing in appearance and need careful blending in with suitable topdressings (see pp.264–265) and planting to appear natural. It is possible to produce artificial rocks on a garden scale from a mix of 2 parts sharp sand, 2 parts coir, and 1 part Portland cement, to which coloring may be added. The mix is worked into molds formed from plastic-lined holes excavated in the soil.

Soils and soil mixes

In nature, many alpines and rock garden plants grow in "soil" that is largely made up of rock fragments and gravel, usually with some accumulations of humus-rich detritus, which retains moisture. Such a growing medium is extremely well drained, and it is important to simulate this as closely as possible in a rock garden or scree

TYPES OF STONE

Tufa is an excellent choice for the rock garden because its soft, porous nature means that plants may be grown in cavities on its surface as well as in crevices between the stones. Natural-looking, weather-worn sandstone is also a good choice, as is limestone (if available secondhand).

Sandstone

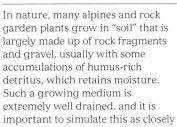

Tufa

Limestone

ROCK PLANTS FOR SANDY SOIL

Acaena caesiiglauca,
  A. microphylla
Achillea × kellereri
Aethionema 'Warley Rose'
Arabis procurrens 'Variegata'
Arenaria montana
Armeria juniperifolia
Artemisia schmidtiana 'Nana'
Ballota pseudodictamnus
Cytisus × beanii
Dianthus carthusianorum,
  D. deltoides
Erodium guttatum
Gypsophila repens
Helianthemum
Iberis saxatilis
Lewisia cotyledon hybrids
Linum suffruticosum
Onosma echioides,
  O. taurica
Phlox bifida
Saponaria ocymoides
Sedum
Sempervivum

ROCK PLANTS FOR VERY ALKALINE SOIL

Achillea
Aethionema
Alyssum
Anemone multifida
Aubrieta
Campanula
Dianthus
Draba
Erysimum helveticum
Geranium farreri
Gypsophila repens
Helianthemum
Leontopodium alpinum
Linaria alpina
Origanum
Papaver burseri,
  P. nudicaule
Pulsatilla
Rhodanthemum hosmariense
Saponaria ocymoides
Saxifraga
Sedum
Sempervivum
Silene schafta
Thymus caespititius

Helianthemum
'Fire Dragon'

bed. Ordinary garden soils may be adapted, to some extent, for cultivating most rock garden plants and alpines by adding peat substitute (or peat) and/or grit, but large quantities of grit are required to provide the rapid drainage needed for the more moisture-sensitive species, such as those grown in scree beds.

Standard mix

A mix of 1 part clean garden soil, 1 part compost or peat, and 1 part sharp sand or coarse grit is suitable for most rock garden plants. The humus-rich materials ensure moisture retention, while the sand or grit maintains good drainage.

Scree mixture

Scree plants will require a very freely draining soil mix. Make a soil mixture using the same ingredients as for the standard mix, but in different proportions: 3 parts coarse grit or stone chips (not sand) instead of 1 part. In order to produce an even freer-draining soil mix, increase the proportion of stony material included in the mix. In dry areas, this proportion of stone chips may have to be reduced to 2 parts; alternatively, use a more water-retentive mix consisting of 2 parts soil, 2 parts leaf mold, 1 part sharp sand, and 4 parts stone chips.

Special mixes

Some choice alpines, such as the tiny, cushion-forming *Androsace* species and saxifrages, need very freely draining soil mixes. These plants usually come from high altitudes where soil nutrient levels are low. Use a mix of 2 or 3 parts chips or gravel, to 1 part compost or leaf mold (or peat).

For acid-loving plants use a mix of 4 parts nonalkaline leaf mold, peat, composted bark, or compost with 1 part coarse sand. On an alkaline soil, however, growing plants in pockets of acidic mixture is only effective in the short term, due to the inevitable percolation of lime, which soon kills them. A better solution is to grow these plants in peat beds (see p.269).

Constructing a rock garden

Never attempt to construct rock gardens when the soil is wet, because heavy rocks may compact the soil and severely damage its structure; this interferes with drainage and causes problems with the establishment and growth of the plants. If the area is grassed, cut the sod carefully and remove it for later use when constructing the rock garden.

Clearing weeds

Remove all perennial weeds from the site and, if positioning the rock garden near trees or shrubs, remove any suckers that these may have produced. Perennial weeds are very difficult to eradicate from an established rock garden, so it is important to dig them out or kill them (see PLANT PROBLEMS, "Weeds," pp.645–649).

Drainage

Make sure that the site, especially if level, is well drained, and if necessary install a French drain or other drainage system (see SOILS AND FERTILIZERS, "Improving drainage," p.623). This is important on heavy clay soils. Do not simply dig deep holes—these act as sumps in which the water remains, unless they are connected to a drainage ditch. Raising the rock garden above the level of the surrounding ground is advisable because it helps improve drainage. On naturally sloping sites drainage is not usually a problem, although a drainage ditch may be needed at the lowest point.

If the underlying drainage is good, just dig the soil over and remove any perennial weeds. Then settle the soil by compacting it gently to avoid subsequent sinking; fork over the surface of the soil to maintain good soil structure.

PLANTING AND TOPDRESSING

1 Before starting to plant, water all the plants and allow them to drain. To check the planting arrangement, arrange the pots on the surface of the bed, taking account of the eventual height and spread of the plants.

2 Carefully remove each plant from its pot and loosen the root ball a little to encourage the roots to spread. Remove any moss and weeds before planting.

3 Using a trowel, dig a hole large enough to accommodate the root ball. Ease the plant into the hole, and label.

4 Fill in around the plant with soil mix and firm gently, making sure that there are no air pockets between the root ball and the soil mix.

5 Topdress the soil mix with a layer of grit or gravel, easing a little around the collars of each of the plants.

6 Continue to plant in the same way until the rock garden is complete. Check that the whole area is properly topdressed, and water in the plants well.

The finished rock garden
The plants will soon grow to produce an attractive and mature-looking rock garden.

PLANTS FOR CREVICES

Aethionema 'Warley Rose'
Antennaria dioica cvs
Androsace chamaejasme
   A. sarmentosa,
   A.sempervivoides
Aquilegia alpina
Arenaria purpurascens
Campanula cochleariifolia,
   C. garganica, C. raineri
Daphne x hendersonii cvs
Dianthus alpinus, D.x arvernensis,
   D.erinaceus, D. 'La Bourboule'
Draba acaulis, D. mollissima
Edraianthus pumilio
Erinus alpinus
Haberlea rhodopensis
Lewisia cotyledon hybrids,
   L. 'Little Plum', *L. rediviva,*
   L. tweedyi
Primula allionii, P. clusiana,
   P. hirsuta and many others
Ramonda myconi
Saxifraga cochlearis, S. cotyledon,
   S. longifolia, S. paniculata,
   S. 'Tumbling Waters',
   S. 'Whitehill'
All silver *Saxifrages* plus spp.
   such as *S. oppositifolia;*
   numerous other cushion cvs
   such as 'Peach Melba'
Sempervivum spp. and cvs
Thymus serpyllum cvs

Lewisia trevosia

Building the base

Put down a 6in (15cm) layer of coarse rock, broken bricks, stones, ballast, angular gravel, or pea gravel. Spread over this pieces of inverted sod, if available; these prevent soil mix from the rock garden from clogging the free-draining layer at the base, without inhibiting normal drainage. If sod is not available, use either landscape fabric or a few layers of burlap. Purchase topsoil or bring in good soil from elsewhere in the garden, ensuring that it is as weed-free as possible; use this for the top layer of the rock garden. Specially prepared, well-drained soil mix (see p.262) should be used for filling in between rocks where plants are to be grown.

Placing the stone

Rock is heavy and rough on the hands, so always wear gloves and protective footwear when you are working with it. Use rollers to move large rocks, and arrange for the product to be delivered as close to the site of the rock garden as possible. To maneuver large rocks into their final positions, it may be necessary to use a block and tackle, with a steel crowbar as a lever for final adjustments. Mark the approximate positions of larger rocks first, to avoid unnecessary labor.

Select first the large rocks that will act as "keystones." These are the dominant rocks from which each outcrop is developed. Position the largest of the keystones first, and then arrange the remaining ones so that the strata flow naturally from them to form outcrops. Additional large stones acting as subsidiary keystones may then be used to extend the outcrops. Use enough rock to make the outcrops realistic, while leaving sufficient room for planting. Check progress visually as construction proceeds. If the rocks that are being used have stratum lines, ensure that these all run in the same direction and at the same angle.

The rocks should be placed to provide the widest range of opportunities for planting. For example, butting rocks together serves to create the narrow crevices in which a variety of plants may thrive. Where space allows, a carefully planned, tiered rock garden may produce a number of useful, broad planting pockets between the rocks.

Bury the rocks to a third of their height and tip them backward slightly. This ensures stability and allows water to drain back off the rock into the soil of the bed rather than onto the plants beneath. Stand on the rocks to make sure that they are completely stable.

As rocks are positioned, fill in all planting spaces with prepared soil mix and firm it in. Any obvious unconformities in the rocks may then be masked by careful planting.

To provide a cool, well-drained cavity for alpines and rock plants, plant them between two layers of stone as the rock garden is constructed. Position the plants in the soil close to a stone that has already been firmed in and add a little soil mix around the roots, firming gently. Use small rocks to protect the plants as the next rock is positioned against the first to form a planting pocket. The small rocks can then be removed, and the second large rock firmed into place. Add more soil mix around the plants and fill in with soil between the rocks before topdressing.

CREVICE GARDENING

Creating special crevice gardens, either as part of a rock garden or as a separate feature, is a creative way to grow a large number of alpines and rock plants in a relatively limited area. Crevices are ideal for growing alpines that enjoy cool, well-drained sites that allow their extensive root systems to spread widely into the soil below.

Plants in crevices may be hard to establish and need extra care when planting. To avoid the risk of a rock slipping when planting horizontal crevices, support the upper rock with small stones and plant between them. When planting in vertical crevices, small stones can also be used to retain the soil mix (see "Planting in vertical crevices," p.268). If planting in the crevices of an established rock garden, use a small tool, such as a widger, to make a planting hole.

Use young, rooted cuttings with vigorous root systems. If only pot-grown plants are available, trim the root balls and top growth to the appropriate size. Put a small stone in the crevice, place a little soil mix on top, then ease in the roots with a widger so that the plant faces outward. Add more mix and firm in, placing a small stone on top of the root ball for extra support.

Crevice garden construction

Layers of narrow stone or slate may be placed almost vertically to mimic rock strata; fill between rocks with a free-draining soil mixture: 2 parts soil, 2 parts leaf mold, 1 part sharp sand, and 4 parts stone chips.

Using color and texture

This crevice garden is dominated by stone and punctuated by plants. Here, contrast is achieved and interest is added by using a seam of broken slate among the larger, more structurally important stone. The red foliage of the *Sempervivum* complements both types of stones.

Planting a rock garden

Alpines and rock garden plants are almost always purchased as pot plants and may be planted at any time of the year, although it is better not to plant them when the ground is either wet or frozen, or during very warm or dry periods.

Water all the plants thoroughly before planting and allow them to drain. Set the plants out in the planned positions while still in their pots to get an idea of the finished planting. Rearrange as needed at this stage and adjust planting distances, allowing for the vigorous and rapid growth of some types. Slide each plant carefully out of its pot and remove any weeds from the soil mix. Inspect the roots and top growth for pests and diseases and treat, as necessary, before planting (see PLANT PROBLEMS, pp.639–673).

Make a planting hole with a trowel or hand fork, ensuring that the hole is big enough to handle the roots. Loosen the root ball

gently, position the plant in the hole, and firm in the compost. The plant should sit with the collar slightly above the surface of the soil to leave room for a topdressing of gravel or rock chips.

When all the plants are in place, water them in thoroughly. Keep them moist, watering at intervals until they are established and starting to add new growth. If planting is followed by a dry period, water the plants at

approximately weekly intervals until the roots have penetrated the surrounding soil mix. After that, there should be no need to water except during a drought.

Aftercare

Use netting or other deterrents to protect newly planted alpines from birds. Periodically refirm any plants that may have worked loose, adding new soil mix if necessary. Label the plants or

WILDLIFE IN THE ROCK GARDEN

Although rock gardens are not garden features that are obviously likely to benefit wildlife, there are many rock garden species and cultivars that bees and butterflies, as well as other beneficial insects, visit to obtain nectar and pollen.

Among rock-garden plants that will attract insects are *Aubrieta*, *Arabis*, and *Iberis* species and cultivars, as well as dwarf marjorams, like *Origanum*

amanum and sedums, pinks, bellflowers, and some *Crocus* and *Muscari* species.

Similarly, dwarf shrubs like *Daphne cneorum*, *D. collina*, and *D. x hendersonii* cultivars, rock roses (*Helianthemum* species and cultivars), and lavenders, which are all rich in nectar or pollen, provide food for a multitude of butterflies, moths, beetles, bees, and many other insects.

maintain a planting plan to record their names at the time of planting; update the planting plans and labeling as plants are added, replaced, or relocated.

Constructing a scree bed

Prepare the site in a similar way to a rock garden, installing artificial drainage, if necessary (see SOILS AND FERTILIZERS, "Improving drainage," p.623). Sloping sites have naturally good drainage but on flat ground screes are best raised slightly above the ground to assist drainage, and retained within low walls, logs, or old railroad ties in the same way as raised beds (see p.269).

Scree beds should be 12–16in (30–40cm) deep; about half the depth should be composed of coarse stones, as for rock gardens, and the upper layer of scree mixture (see p.262). Mark out the site with a rope or hose and remove the sod from grassy areas. Lay the stone foundation, then line the entire planting area with thinly cut, inverted pieces of sod or landscape fabric cut roughly to shape.

Finish off the bed with a 6–8in (15–20cm) layer of scree mixture, and firm by gently walking over the whole area. Water the bed and allow it to settle, then top off with scree mixture any areas that may have sunk before loosening the surface with a hand fork.

Planting in a scree bed

It may be more difficult to establish plants in a scree bed than in a rock garden, because the freely draining soil mix tends to dry out before the plants are established. Care during planting and conscientious watering are the keys to success. The well-developed root systems of pot-grown alpines do not readily penetrate the gritty scree soil mix, so gently shake off most of the soil mix (especially if peat-based) from the roots. Keep the bare roots moist. Place the plant in a planting hole with its roots spread out, and fill in carefully with scree mixture. Topdress around the plant with stone chips, and water immediately and thoroughly.

Scree mixes are fast-draining, so water young plants regularly until they are established. Try to minimize wetting the foliage. In their natural habitats, scree dwellers have deep and extensive root systems to seek out water

MEDITERRANEAN-STYLE PLANTING ON AN INCLINE

1 If necessary, work sharp sand or grit into the soil to improve drainage. Dig and firm in larger stones. Arrange the plants in their pots (here, a selection of herbs).

2 Plant the large and then the small plants at the same depth as they were in their containers, and water well. Let the soil surface dry a little before adding topdressing.

3 Add smaller rocks and then a thick layer of stone chips or pea gravel. Use a trowel or your hands to spread it carefully between and around the plants.

The finished "Mediterranean" bank

Such a drought-tolerant garden provides an attractive low-maintenance area that should need little watering once the plants are established. The surface layer of chips or pea gravel will help conserve moisture in the soil, reflect heat onto the sun-loving plants, and keep down weeds. Remove by hand any weeds that do appear as soon as you spot them.

PLANTING A GRAVEL GARDEN

1 Cut landscape fabric to fit the bed or border. For a large area, cut several pieces, leaving a generous overlap, and pin securely in place.

2 Place the plants on top of the fabric, moving them around until you are happy with the overall arrangement. Keep in mind their eventual height and spread.

3 Cut a cross in the fabric directly under each plant and fold back the flaps. Ensure there is a large enough space to dig a good-sized planting hole.

4 Using a trowel, dig a planting hole a little larger than the plant's root ball. Remove the plant from its pot, placing it into the hole at the same level as in its pot.

5 Fill around the root ball with soil and firm in. Tuck the flaps back around the plant stem, pinning the fabric in place if there are any gaps. Water well.

6 Spread a thick layer of gravel or another topdressing over the fabric. Be generous in order to prevent the fabric from showing through. Level with a rake.

The finished gravel garden
Water regularly until the plants are established, using a watering can fitted with a fine rose or a hose set to a fine spray to avoid dislodging the gravel. If necessary, gently level the gravel occasionally, and pull out any weeds that may appear.

and nutrients, so when established they will survive for long periods without watering.

Topdressings, gravels, and pebbles

After planting, a rock garden or scree bed may be topdressed with stone chips, grit, or gravel. If possible, this should match the rock used at the construction stage.

Topdressing has a number of advantages: it provides an attractive and natural setting for plants and blends in better with rocks than bare soil, creates especially good drainage around the collars of the plants, inhibits weed growth,

conserves moisture, and protects the soil surface from compaction during heavy rain or watering. The layer of topdressing on a rock garden should be at least 1in (2.5cm) deep; on a scree bed it can be ¾–6in (2–15cm) deep, depending on the plants grown; for most screes, a ¾–1¼in (2–3cm) layer is sufficient.

On gravel beds and gardens, a water-permeable geotextile fabric used beneath the gravel will assist in weed suppression and extend the life of the topdressing by preventing it from gradually working into the soil. These fabrics also help retain more moisture than a surface layer of gravel or pebbles alone. They are ideal where a low-maintenance feature is needed. However, because they

stop ornamental plants from self-seeding, they do prevent plants from spreading in a natural way.

Stone chips and gravels needed to dress areas of planting in gravel are offered by garden centers and hardware stores in a variety of grades and colors. If the surface will be walked on regularly, or used as a patio area on which to set garden furniture and containers, a fine grade of gravel (pea gravel) is recommended because it gives a smooth, more easily negotiable surface. Small paving stones may be set unobtrusively in the gravel layer to provide strategic support points where stability is important.

Choose a color for the topdressing that blends in with local rock for a natural look. Striking, modern effects

may be created by using contrasting tones—for example, "rivers" of dark slate chips between outcrops of paler rock—although such features need to be skillfully designed to avoid looking clumsy.

Cobblestones and pebbles
Never collect any quantity of stones or gravel from natural areas, such as beaches or rivers. Doing so would probably damage the area and contribute to erosion, and in many places it is illegal as well.

Good garden centers should offer responsibly sourced, washed gravel. You may also be able to find them at water garden suppliers now that they have become popular decorative items to use in enhancing small fountain features.

Troughs, sinks, and other containers

Alpines and rock plants look particularly attractive grown in troughs and sinks, although most frost-proof containers with good drainage are suitable. Choose the correct site at the outset because, once filled, they are difficult to move. Rocks may be placed in the containers to create the effect of a miniature rock garden; do this before planting.

Types of containers

Old stone animal troughs and sinks, traditionally used to grow alpines, are now scarce and expensive. Glazed sinks coated in hypertufa, or troughs made entirely of hypertufa or reconstituted stone, are now often used, as are large pottery and terra-cotta pots and tubs. All should have drainage holes to ensure that there is a free flow of water through the soil mix. If extra drainage holes are needed, they should be at least 1in (2.5cm) in diameter; if the base of the container is not flat, make the drainage holes at the lowest point. Plants in glazed sinks do not need nearly as much water as those in stone or hypertufa troughs, so, to prevent waterlogging in all but dry areas, an extra drainage layer should be added under the soil mix.

Covering glazed sinks

Deep, glazed, flat-bottomed sinks may easily be made to resemble stone containers by coating them with hypertufa. Ensure that the sink is clean and dry, then score the surface with a tile- or glass-cutter to form a rough surface to help the hypertufa adhere to the sink. To aid adhesion further, paint the surface with a bonding agent before applying the hypertufa.

Make hypertufa from 1–2 parts sifted sphagnum peat moss, 1 part coarse sand or fine grit, and 1 part cement. Add sufficient water to form a thick paste. Apply this to the outside of the sink and also inside, down to well below the final level of the soil mix. Put the hypertufa on by hand (wear gloves); it should be ½–¾in (1–2cm) thick. Roughen the surface so that it resembles stone.

GLAZED SINK WITH HYPERTUFA COATING

Glazed sinks covered with hypertufa make fine containers for alpines.

When the hypertufa is fully dry, after about a week, scrub the surface with a wire brush and coat with liquid manure, buttermilk, or mossy soil to discourage algae and encourage the growth of mosses and lichens to achieve a more natural look.

Hypertufa troughs

Troughs may be made entirely from hypertufa, if desired. Prepare the mixture as for coating but increase the proportion of sand and grit to three parts in order to make a stiffer mix.

Use two wooden boxes that fit inside one another, with a space of 2–3in (5–7cm) between them. Stand the larger box on blocks so that it may be lifted out once finished. Pour a thin layer of the hypertufa mix into the base. Cover the mix and the sides of the box with wire netting (such as chicken wire), then pour in another layer of hypertufa mix. Press thick dowels or pegs through the hypertufa to make drainage holes. Fit the smaller box inside the larger, and fill the space with the mix, tamping it down to remove air pockets.

When the cavity is full, cover the trough with a sheet of plastic for at least a week while the mix sets and protect the trough from frost, if necessary. When the mix has set hard, remove the boxes and dowels. If the boxes do not slide off easily, ease them off carefully with a fine chisel and a small hammer. Roughen the surface of the trough with a wire brush, and paint on a coat of liquid manure to encourage algal growth.

HOW TO MAKE A HYPERTUFA TROUGH

1 You will need two boxes to make the trough, one slightly larger than the other. Coat the surfaces of the boxes with oil to prevent the hypertufa from sticking.

2 Place a 1in (2.5cm) layer of hypertufa mix in the base of the larger box and put wire netting on top of this layer and around the sides to reinforce the trough. Then add another layer of hypertufa.

3 Press several thick, wooden dowels into the wire and hypertufa base to make the drainage holes for the bottom of the trough.

4 Center the smaller box on top of the hypertufa base, making sure the vertical netting is between the two boxes. Fill the cavity with the hypertufa mix, tamping down well as you fill.

5 Cover the top of the hypertufa with plastic sheeting until the mix has set (which usually takes about a week). Secure the sheeting in place with a weight and protect the trough from cold.

6 When the hypertufa has set, remove the wooden form from the outside of the trough. If the hypertufa has stuck to the box, carefully dismantle the box with a hammer and chisel.

7 The surface of the hypertufa will be smooth and straight; for a more natural-looking appearance, scrub the outside of the trough with a wire brush or coarse-grained sandpaper to roughen the surface.

8 Remove the smaller box, using a hammer and chisel if necessary. To encourage moss and lichen growth, paint the outside surface of the trough with liquid manure.

Positioning containers

An open location, with sun for at least part of the day, is ideal for most plants. Do not place containers in windy sites, unless tough plants are being grown, or on lawns—it will be difficult to maintain the surrounding grass. Avoid slopes, which cause instability, and put containers as close as possible to a spigot or hose.

Raise troughs and sinks off the ground, up to a height of about 18in (45cm); the plants may then be viewed comfortably and water will drain away readily. Stone or brick pillars at the corners of a container provide sturdy, stable supports. These must bear the weight of the container without danger of tipping and should not block the drainage holes. Sinks with single drainage holes should be tilted so excess water drains off.

Placing rocks and tufa

Virtually any type of rock may be used in troughs and sinks. Rocks give height, and allow a greater depth of soil mix. A few large rocks are better than many small ones. Niches and crevices in the rocks may also be used to support plants, especially if hard tufa is used. Tufa's light weight and the ease with which planting holes can be excavated in it make it ideal. Roots spread into the porous rock, which is well aerated but also retains water.

Whatever type of rock is used, bury from one-third to one-half of each stone in the soil mix to ensure that it is firmly seated.

Filling the container

Rock garden plants need a soil-based potting mix, with some additional drainage material, in order to extract the nutrients they need to thrive. Add about one-third by volume of perlite or ¼–⅜in (6–9mm) stone chips, and mix in some slow-release fertilizer to the soil mix. Acid-loving plants need an acidic soil mix, with added granite or sandstone chips.

Cover the drainage holes with screening or wire gauze and fill the bottom quarter to one-third of the container with coarse aggregate, gravel, or stone chips. Fill up with slightly moist soil mix, and firm it gently.

Position pieces of rock or tufa on the soil mix, and bed them in as the container is filled. Place rocks to form crevices and niches, providing both shaded and sunny faces to suit different plants, and add randomly placed smaller pieces of stone to simulate a small-scale rock garden. Water thoroughly and leave to drain completely before planting.

Planting

Choose slow-growing plants that will not overwhelm their neighbors and quickly exhaust the available nutrients. Do not overplant the container, and replant when it is overcrowded (see *Replanting an Alpine Trough*, p.271).

Position container-grown plants, still in their pots, on the soil mix or make a plan on paper of the planting design. Make planting holes, carefully slide the plants out of their pots, and loosen the root balls. Place the plants in the holes, fill in with soil mix, and firm. When complete, water thoroughly. Then add a topdressing of chips or gravel to help ensure good drainage.

Planting in tufa

If plants are to be grown in tufa rock, use a drill or a hammer and chisel, and make holes 4–5in (10–12cm) apart. They should be about 1in (2.5cm) in diameter and 2–3in (5–7cm) deep, angled at 30–45° on vertical or sloping surfaces, or straight down on horizontal planes. Soak the tufa, then put a little sharp sand in each hole with some soil mix. Use young, rooted cuttings or small plants, which establish easily. Wash the roots before planting; ease them into the holes with a dibber or pencil and sprinkle in soil mix to fill the hole. Ensure that the neck of the plant is bedded in and not standing above the hole. Firm the soil mix, and wedge small pieces of tufa around plants to hold them in place. Water thoroughly and keep the tufa moist until plants are established. In hot, dry weather, soak the tufa regularly.

HOW TO PLANT AN ALPINE TROUGH

1 If planting in tufa, first drill holes in it about 1in (2.5cm) wide, 3in (7cm) deep, and no less than 4in (10cm) apart. Immerse tufa in water overnight.

2 Lay fine-mesh netting over the trough base or cover the holes with pot shards; add 3–4in (7–10cm) of coarse grit.

3 Partly fill the trough with a gritty, moist soil mix, firming it in stages. Set the tufa in place so that at least ⅓–½ of it is buried to keep it stable.

4 Continue to fill with soil mix and firm well to allow about 2in (5cm) for topdressing and watering. Insert a little soil mix into the tufa holes for planting.

5 Wash the roots of the plants to go in the tufa, and ease them into the planting holes. Trickle soil mix into the holes, firm, and put small rock pieces around the plants.

6 Set the plants, still in their pots, on the soil mix to check that the arrangement and spacing are satisfactory, then plant and firm them in.

7 Water the soil mix thoroughly, then topdress the trough with a 1–2in (2.5–5cm) deep layer of coarse gravel or stone chips.

The finished trough

Helianthemum oelandicum subsp. alpestre

Androsace pubescens

Sisyrinchium 'E.K. Balls'

Penstemon pinifolius

Saxifraga cotyledon

Sempervivum arachnoideum

Oxalis 'Ione Hecker'

Draba aizoides

Saxifraga cochlearis 'Minor'

Talinum okanoganense

Phlox douglasii cv.

Saxifraga paniculata

Oxalis enneaphylla 'Minutifolia'

Rhodohypoxis baurii

Dianthus 'La Bourboule'

Walls

Alpines and rock garden plants may be grown in the crevices of dry-stone walls, including the retaining walls of raised beds and sloping banks. Trailing plants are especially attractive when grown in this way. For details on constructing a wall, see "Dry-stone walls," p.598.

If possible, plan for any planting in walls before construction work starts. The most practical approach is to leave planting niches in the wall at intervals and plant them up when the building work is finished.

It is also possible to position the plants as construction proceeds. This produces excellent results—the plants may be placed at the desired level, ensuring good contact between the roots of the plants and any soil behind the wall. Planting during construction also makes it easier to eliminate air pockets in the compost and firm around the roots.

Planting in existing walls is another option, but some of the soil will need to be removed first with a widger or teaspoon before planting. Use young plants or rooted cuttings that fit easily in the crevices.

HOW TO BUILD A DRY-STONE RETAINING WALL

Making the footings
Dig a trench 15in (38cm) deep; fill it with 10in (25cm) of crushed stone with a large, sturdy rock on top.

Placing the rocks
Slope the rocks backward and downward for stability and so that water is carried into the soil mix.

Filling between rocks
As you build, fill crevices between the rocks with a mix of soil, leaf mold, and sand or grit.

Planting

Use the following soil mix for filling the planting crevices in walls: 3 parts good clean garden soil, 2 parts coarse peat, and 1–2 parts sharp sand or grit. Use extra grit, sand, or stone chips for plants that are to be grown in the wall itself, because this will help to ensure good drainage. Choose plants that grow well in the exposure and conditions available in the wall. Carefully remove old soil mix from the roots and ease them into the hole, using a widger, small dibber, or pencil. Do not try to cram roots into too small a space because this damages the plants. Holding the plant in position with one hand, trickle in fresh, moist soil mix, then firm it with the widger to remove any air pockets. It may also be helpful to wedge small stones around the collars of the plants to hold them in place and prevent the soil mix from becoming dislodged.

Water thoroughly from the top of the wall and spray the plants regularly until established. After several days, top off any sunken areas with spare soil mix. Periodically check the plants and firm any that have worked loose.

HOW TO PLANT IN A DRY-STONE WALL

1 If planting in an existing wall, check that there is an adequate amount of soil mix in the crevices to support the plants.

2 Use seedlings or small rooted cuttings. Place them on the flat of a stone and, using a widger, ease the roots into the crevices. The plant shown here is a *Sempervivum*.

3 Bed the plants down into the soil mix and pack more compost into the crevices to hold the mix in position. Firm the plants in with your fingers.

4 For larger plants, scoop out some soil mix from the crevices. Ease the roots into the holes, and add more soil mix while holding plants in position.

5 When all the plants are in position, water them from the top of the wall or with a spray mist. Keep the plants moist until established and refirm any that work loose. Planted with the *Sempervivum* are two saxifrages.

PLANTING IN VERTICAL CREVICES

1 Fill the crevice with a gritty soil mix. Carefully ease in the roots of the plant (here, *Campanula*).

2 Cover the roots with soil mix, then wedge in a small rock, sloping it down the larger rock-face. Firm more mix into the crevice.

Softening surfaces
Soften the edges of steps, retaining walls and paving by inserting low, spreading plants in gaps and crevices. Fill in any gaps around them with gritty soil mix. Be careful that growth does not obscure steps and render them hazardous.

Raised beds

A wide range of alpine plants may be grown in raised beds, both in the beds themselves and in crevices in the supporting walls. The bed's design should harmonize with the house and yard. Depending on the needs of the chosen plants, a raised bed may be positioned in either sun or shade. Fill the bed with well-drained soil mix to suit the plants (see "Soil for raised beds," below). If necessary, plants may be protected in winter with glass or plastic covers placed over the bed.

Siting

For most alpines and rock garden plants, raised beds should be placed in an open, sunny location away from the shade cast by overhanging trees or nearby buildings and fences. Place a raised bed in shade only if woodland or other plants requiring cooler, shadier conditions are to be grown.

To aid mowing, a raised bed that is positioned on a lawn should be surrounded by paving slabs or bricks set just below the level of the grass. Raised beds that are constructed for elderly or disabled gardeners may need to be built with wheelchair access, and the beds should be of a height and width to allow plants to be tended easily from a seated position. On sites where the construction of a ground-based scree bed is not possible because of poor drainage, a scree may be placed on the surface of a raised bed instead (see p.264).

Materials and design

Raised beds may be made from stone, brick, old wooden railroad ties, or any other suitable and attractive material. Stone is the most expensive; new or secondhand bricks and railroad ties are cheaper.

The bed can be almost any shape, but it should harmonize with the general design of the garden.

Rectangular beds are the most common. The ideal height is 24–30in (60–75cm), although a tiered bed is also attractive and may be more appropriate where space is limited. The bed should be no more than 5ft (1.5m) wide to allow access—the center of the bed should be within arm's reach to allow weeding from all sides.

Large beds may need an irrigation system; install water pipes and inlets before filling the beds with soil mix.

Construction

Brick retaining walls for raised beds should be vertical; the thickness of one brick is usually adequate. They are built in the same way as a conventional wall and can be mortared, but leave small gaps between bricks at intervals for plants. There should also be gaps at the base for drainage. For further information, see STRUCTURES AND SURFACES, "Raised beds," p.599.

Raised beds may also have stone retaining walls. If they are built without mortar, they need a slight inward slope for stability (see "Dry-stone walls," p.598). Dry-stone walls are time-consuming to build, because each stone needs to be chosen and positioned carefully. Large crevices may be left between the stones to be planted up with alpines. If railroad ties are used, crevice-planting is not possible.

Soil for raised beds

Use a mix of 3 parts good clean garden soil, 2 parts coarse fibrous peat substitute (such as acidic leaf mold or garden compost) or peat, and 1–2 parts grit or sharp sand. For plants that require acid conditions, use acidic soil and grit. To grow plants that need different soil types in a large bed, divide the bed into sections with plastic sheeting to keep the sections apart, and fill each with appropriate soil mix (see p.322).

Preparing the raised bed

Fill the bottom third of the bed with coarse gravel or crushed stone, then place a layer of inverted sod or fibrous peat substitute (or peat) over the top to prevent the drainage material from becoming clogged. Fill the bed with prepared soil mix, which should be well worked into all the corners and firmed as filling proceeds. Incorporate a slow-release fertilizer. Some settling always occurs, so water the bed thoroughly and leave it for two or three weeks. Top off any sunken areas with spare soil mix before planting.

Adding rocks gives the effect of a rock garden in miniature and enhances the appearance of raised beds. Set pieces of rock of varying sizes into the compost to provide suitable sites for a range of different plants. Several large pieces of rock arranged together as outcrops are more effective than scattered rocks.

Planting and topdressing

Make a planting plan or set out the plants on the surface of the bed to see how they will look. Dwarf conifers and small shrubs, tufted and cushion-forming alpines, trailing alpines at the edges of the bed, and smaller bulbs are ideal.

Select plants for year-round interest. Plant as for rock gardens (see p.264); crevices in the retaining walls may also be planted as for dry-stone walls (see p.268).

After planting, topdress the bed with stone chips or coarse grit, to match any rocks. Work a ½in (1cm) deep layer of the topdressing carefully around the plants and beneath their collars. This looks attractive, suppresses weeds, and reduces evaporation. Water the bed regularly until the plants are established.

Winter protection

Many alpines dislike excessive winter moisture, even in the well-drained conditions of a raised bed. The alpine beds can be protected with cloches or sheets of glass or plastic, supported with bricks or a wire frame. Fasten down the covering, so that it does not blow away. Such protection should be put in place in the late fall and removed the following spring. If the whole bed needs protection, build a wooden framework for a glass or plastic roof. Plenty of air must circulate around the plants so that they remain as dry as possible, so do not cover the sides of the frame.

BEDS FOR ACIDIC SOIL-LOVING PLANTS

Acidic-humus or peat beds provide ideal conditions for a wide range of acidic soil-loving and woodland plants. In gardens with alkaline soil, such beds should always be isolated from the ground with a plastic or synthetic rubber liner so that alkalinity cannot enter. Surround each bed with logs or old railroad ties.

Consider the needs of the plants when deciding where to place a peat bed, and construct the bed so that it blends in well with the rest of the garden. It is not necessary to use pure peat in the bed, because acidic peat substitutes are widely available. A wide range of acidic soil-loving plants may be grown both in the bed and in wall crevices to create an attractive display.

Siting

Choose a site that receives sun and dappled shade, ideally facing away from direct sun. An area next to a rock garden, on a slope, or by the side of a building is appropriate. Acidic-humus beds on exposed sites in full sun lose moisture rapidly and need frequent watering. Dense shade of trees is unsuitable, and the tree roots nearby soon exhaust the moisture and nutrients. Waterlogged sites and frost pockets are not suitable either.

A finished bed
Plant acidic-humus beds with acidic soil-loving rock garden plants for a fine display. Water often to keep the soil moist, especially in the first year. Topdress the bed with bark mulch to conserve moisture and suppress weeds. Feed the plants regularly with a balanced fertilizer.

Routine care of rock plants

Even when alpines and rock plants are established in the garden, it is essential to care for them regularly. Beds, troughs, and sinks must be kept clean and free of weeds. Although the plants do not usually need nutrient-rich soil, they should be fertilized at intervals and watered whenever the soil becomes dry. Topdressings, which improve drainage around the collars of the plants, suppress weed growth, and reduce evaporation of water from the soil, should be replenished occasionally.

Alpines and rock garden plants benefit from periodic removal of dead wood, leaves, and flowers, and should be kept trimmed. Troughs, sinks, and other containers should be replanted as soon as they become overcrowded. Check plants routinely for signs of pest infestation and disease, and treat them as necessary. In cold or wet weather, some plants may need winter protection.

Weeding

The use of clean soil mix when planting should minimize problems with weeds, at least for the first few years. Always try to remove all weeds as soon as they appear, certainly before they flower and set seed. If established perennial weeds are difficult to remove, as a last resort, paint the foliage carefully with a translocated weedkiller, which is transmitted to the roots and kills them. For further information, see PLANT PROBLEMS, "Controlling weeds," p.646.

When weeding, use a three-pronged hand cultivator to loosen and aerate compacted soil around young plants, if necessary, taking care not to disturb the plant roots.

Fertilizing

Newly planted areas should not normally need fertilizer for some years if the original soil mix is correctly prepared and includes slow-release fertilizer. After some time, however, the growth of the plants may begin to slow down and flowering become sparser. To remedy this, apply a dressing of bone meal and balanced organic fertilizer around the plants each spring.

Alternatively, carefully remove any topdressing and a layer of about ½in (1cm) of soil from the surface of the bed and replace it with fresh soil mix and a further topdressing of grit.

Topdressing

The type of topdressing used for alpines and rock garden plants depends on the plants that are grown, although it should match any of the rocks and stones that feature in beds and rock gardens as closely as possible. Topdressings used in troughs, sinks, or raised beds should also harmonize with the pot or retaining walls.

Coarse grit or stone chips are suitable for most situations, but limestone chips should never be used around lime-hating plants. For plants grown in peat beds, a topdressing of bark chips will complement the plantings.

Renewing topdressings

Topdressings may need to be renewed from time to time. Grit or stone chips gradually wash away, especially on slopes, and bark tends to decompose and mix in with the underlying soil. Watch for bare patches throughout the season and top off as necessary. Pay close attention to topdressings in the fall, to ensure good soil coverage in winter and avoid compaction by heavy rain. Check again in spring and top off, as necessary. A slow-release fertilizer may be applied at the same time.

Watering

Established plants growing in rock gardens and screes root deeply into the soil and do not usually need more water than is supplied by rainfall. In droughts, however, the area should be

WEEDING

Weed around young plants with a hand fork or similar tool, which also loosens and aerates the soil. Remove any topdressing first and replace it after weeding.

RENEWING TOPDRESSING

1 Remove the old topdressing and some soil (see inset). Fill in around the plants with fresh soil mix (see p.262).

2 Topdress the bed with a fresh layer of coarse grit or gravel, adding some around and beneath the collars of the plants.

thoroughly soaked. Do not water in very frosty conditions or during the heat of the day—early mornings or late evenings are the best times. Soak occasionally rather than giving small amounts of water frequently. If the soil is dry at a depth of 1¼–2in (3–5cm), water thoroughly until the water has penetrated to the full depth of the roots. During an average summer this should only be needed two or three times, but in very dry summers it may be required more frequently.

Watering in containers, raised beds, and under cover

Alpines and rock garden plants that are grown in raised beds, sinks, and troughs, under frames, and in the alpine house will need more regular watering, since the soil dries out more quickly than in rock gardens and scree beds.

It is preferable to hand-water troughs and sinks if specialty collections of plants are being grown, so that each plant may be provided with the correct amount of water. This is time-consuming, however, particularly where there are several containers to be watered.

Plants grown in pots in alpine houses and frames should be watered individually. If the pots are plunged in gravel or stone chips, water both the pots and the surrounding material. Some alpine plants have water-sensitive foliage and therefore dislike overhead watering; if this is the case, regularly soaking only the plunge material should provide sufficient moisture.

Trimming and pruning

Alpines and rock garden plants need to be cut back periodically to maintain a natural, compact shape and healthy growth, and to restrict them within their allotted space.

Pruning woody plants

To keep rock garden shrubs and woody perennials healthy, any dead, diseased, or damaged wood should be removed. Check the plants on a regular basis and prune them as cleanly as possible, using pruners or sharp scissors.

Severe pruning is unnecessary because most dwarf shrubs are slow-growing and do not outgrow their positions for many years. When pruning, aim to

REMOVING DEAD GROWTH

In spring, after all danger of frost has passed, cut out any dieback from plants, trimming carefully to healthy growth with sharp scissors or pruners.

REMOVING DEAD ROSETTES

1 To remove dead rosettes from plants such as saxifrages, cut out the rosettes with a sharp knife without disturbing the rest of the plant.

2 Topdress the exposed soil to prevent weeds growing from through the gaps until the plant produces fresh growth.

CUTTING BACK AFTER FLOWERING

1 After flowering, cut back stems (here, *Helianthemum*) to half their length to encourage healthy new growth.

2 The plants will remain compact and produce a good crop of flowers the following year.

RENOVATING AN ALPINE BED

1 Plants that spread rapidly (here, *Paronychia kapela*) may eventually smother less vigorous plants nearby. Cut them back in spring.

2 Dig up or pull out clumps of encroaching plants. Straggly plants should be cut back severely. Make sure that plants nearby have plenty of room to grow.

3 Add a dressing of balanced fertilizer to the bed, before placing a fresh layer of topdressing on the surface of the soil around the plants.

maintain the natural shape of the plant, especially in the case of dwarf conifers.

Removing dead flowers and foliage

Regularly remove all dead flowers and leaves, and any unwanted seed heads, with a sharp knife, pruners, or scissors. Pick over small alpine plants by hand, using tweezers, if necessary, to remove dead leaves and flowers. Cut out dead rosettes from plants such as saxifrages; do not pull them off by hand—this may loosen healthy rosettes.

Helianthemum species and cultivars, in particular, need clipping with shears annually after flowering, cutting back the stems by about half their length to encourage growth for flowering the following year. Genera such as *Arabis*, *Aubrieta*, and *Aurinia* also benefit from hard annual pruning (after flowering), which helps to keep them compact and free-flowering. Plants may produce a second flush of flowers if cut back before they set seed.

Encroaching plants

Overly vigorous plants as well as old, straggly plants that start to encroach on their neighbors should be cut back in early spring. Mat-forming plants may simply be pulled out by hand; others may need to be lifted with a hand fork. Support nearby plants and replace any that are accidentally lifted. Remove or cut back plants to allow a clear area of bed around all the remaining plants so that they can grow unimpeded. Hard-pruned plants should be topdressed with a balanced fertilizer in order to promote strong, new growth.

Winter protection

Plants in troughs, sinks, or raised beds, and some alpine bulbs, may need protection from winter rain. Use a single, propped pane of glass, an open cloche, or, for large areas, a cold frame sash, which will give overhead protection without inhibiting air circulation. Ensure that covers are firmly secured. To increase snow retention (which has an insulating effect) place a layer of evergreen branches loosely over the plants.

Controlling pests and diseases

Few serious problems affect alpines and rock garden plants, but some of the more common pests and diseases may need to be controlled. Regular, basic garden hygiene is often sufficient to control most problems encountered. Aphids (p.654) are likely to be troublesome if alpines are grown in too rich a soil, which induces soft, lank growth.

Coarse topdressings around plants tend to deter slugs and snails, but some control is still necessary, particularly for choice alpines, such as *Campanula zoysii*, which are susceptible to attack from these pests. Control insects such as ants (p.654), which will excavate under cushion-forming plants. Prevent birds from disturbing newly planted specimens by covering them with tepees of sticks or wire pushed into the soil.

Fungal diseases may quickly become established in alpine houses and frames (see pp.277–279).

REPLANTING AN ALPINE TROUGH

Plants in containers eventually need replanting when nutrients in the soil are exhausted. Water thoroughly before carefully removing the plants. Discard the soil and replace it with a fresh, suitable mix (see p.262), containing a slow-release fertilizer. Trim roots and topgrowth before returning plants to the container; allow for their eventual spread and topdress with gravel.

Helianthemum sp.

Iris cristata

Ramonda myconi

Helianthemum sp.

Propagation

Many alpines and rock garden plants may be propagated from seed, although some plants are sterile and do not produce seed. In addition, cultivars seldom come true from seed and must be increased in other ways. Alternative methods include cuttings (of various types) and division.

Seed

Propagation from seed is the best way to produce large numbers of plants. Since many alpines flower in early spring, ripe seed is often available from midsummer, and may be sown right away. Germination will usually occur rapidly and strong seedlings will be produced before winter. Fall-sown seeds may remain dormant until spring; if germination occurs, overwinter the seedlings in cold frames. It may sometimes be better to store seed over winter and sow in early spring, although short-lived seed should be sown as soon as it is ripe.

Seed collection and storage

Collect seed as the seed heads become ripe. Remove them while still attached to the stems and place them in paper (not plastic) bags to dry out. Enclose in envelopes any that might split open on drying. Store seeds in a cool, dry, well-ventilated place. Most alpines have seed capsules from which seed may be extracted by rubbing between the fingers. Fleshy fruits may need to be squashed and left on paper to dry.

Separate the seed from the debris by sifting or hand-picking when dry. Put it in sealed, labeled envelopes, and place these in an airtight container in a cool place.

Presowing treatment

Seeds with hard coats need special treatment to allow them to absorb water. Scarify by chipping the seed coat with a sharp knife or rubbing with a file or fine abrasive paper. In some cases, soaking the seed for 12–24 hours will accelerate the takeup of water.

Hard-cased seeds of woody rock garden plants do not respond to scarification alone; they also need exposure to cold, or stratification. Store the seeds in boxes of moist sand outdoors for two or three months during winter, and sow in spring; alternatively, sow the seed in pots of seed-sowing mix and keep in the freezer or refrigerator,

sealed in plastic bags, for several weeks before plunging the pots in the ground outside until the seed germinates. Some seeds, such as *Trillium* and peonies (*Paeonia*), need alternating periods of cold and warmth to germinate successfully.

Sowing the seed

Use clean clay or plastic pots, and place a piece of screen over the drainage holes. A mix of equal parts sifted peat substitute or peat and perlite is suitable, or use soil-based seed-sowing mix blended with an equal amount of perlite or sharp sand. Fill the pots and firm the soil. Tap out small seeds thinly and evenly and space large seeds by hand, covering them with their own depth of soil. Mix fine seeds with fine, dry silver sand before sowing but do not cover them with more seed-starting mix.

After sowing, cover all but fine seeds with a ¼–½in (5–10mm) layer of ¼in- (5mm-) diameter grit or pea gravel, to deter mosses and liverworts and protect the seed from heavy rain or watering. Label the pots and stand them in water to half their depth, removing them when the soil surface becomes moist. Keep the soil moist at all times.

Germination

Speed of germination depends on the type and age of the seed and when it is sown. Some seed takes months or even years to germinate.

A cool, sheltered site outdoors is ideal for the seeds of most alpines. Plunge pots in moist sand to maintain an even temperature and reduce the need for watering. When seedlings appear, move the pots to a cold frame. Germination may be speeded up by placing the pots in gentle heat in early spring, but do not expose the seeds to high temperatures.

Pricking out and potting up

Prick out seedlings when they are ¼–½in (5–10mm) tall and when two true leaves have formed. Tap out the soil and separate the seedlings. Handle only by the leaves or cotyledons to avoid damage to stems and roots. Pot up seedlings individually in small clay pots or plastic pots, or in cell packs using low-fertility soil-based potting mix blended with an equal amount of grit. Fill the container, settle the soil, and make a hole for the roots. Put the seedling in the hole, fill with potting mix, and firm lightly.

Topdress seedlings in individual pots with a ¼–½in (5–10mm) layer of grit. Water the pots thoroughly with a fine spray of water and place the containers in a lightly shaded position until the seedlings are established. Water as required. When the roots are visible through the drainage holes, pot them on.

Seeds that are slow to germinate often do so erratically, and if only a few seedlings appear, prick them out as soon as they are large enough to handle. Disturb the rest of the soil as little as possible, and cover it with fresh topdressing. Put the pot back into the frame in case more seeds germinate.

ROCK PLANT SEED TO SOW FRESH

Anemone
Codonopsis
Corydalis
Cyclamen
  (alpine spp.)
Dodecatheon
Hepatica
Meconopsis
Primula
  (alpine spp.)
Pulsatilla
Ranunculus
  (alpine spp.)

Anemone coronaria
De Caen Group

SOWING SEEDS

1 Prepare a pot by filling it with equal parts of seed-sowing mix and horticultural sand. Firm the mix gently to level the surface and eliminate air pockets.

2 Small seeds (here, *Lewisia*) should be tapped out evenly over the surface of the soil. Space larger seeds by hand.

3 Cover the seeds with a fine layer of seed-starting mix, then topdress with grit to prevent the growth of mosses. Water in and label.

4 Prick out seedlings when they have two true leaves (see inset). Lift the seedlings carefully, handling them by the leaves only.

5 Fill pots with equal parts of soil-based potting mix and grit. Pot up the seedlings singly, firming with a dibber.

6 Topdress with grit, water, and place the seedlings in light shade. Repot the seedlings when the roots fill the pot.

Softwood and greenwood cuttings

Softwood cuttings are taken from the nonflowering, leafy shoots of a plant during periods of active growth, usually in spring.

Greenwood cuttings are taken in early summer when growth has slowed down; although slightly riper than softwood cuttings, they require the same treatment.

Taking the cuttings

Take the cuttings early in the morning, when the shoots are fully turgid. For softwood cuttings select strong, young shoots that are soft and pliable, with no trace of woodiness or hardening; greenwood cuttings may be just beginning to harden at the base. Take cuttings about 1–3in (2.5–7cm) in length, using a sharp knife. Place them immediately in a plastic bag to conserve moisture and prevent them from wilting.

Inserting the cuttings

Trim the base of each cutting cleanly with a sharp knife just below a node (leaf joint) and remove the lower leaves. Pinch off any shoot tips that are soft, particularly if these are showing signs of wilting.

Fill pots with standard propagation mix and make holes with a small dibber. Insert each cutting into a hole by up to half its length so the lowest leaf is just above the surface.

Label the cuttings and water them, using a fungicide solution if you've had past disease problems. Place them in a closed propagator with gentle bottom heat, or in a mist propagation unit. Alternatively, seal the pots in plastic bags. Keep the cuttings in good light but out of direct sun, as otherwise the air and soil temperature may become too hot and wilt the cuttings.

Use tweezers to remove dead and diseased cuttings, which can infect their healthy neighbors. Watering is seldom required until after rooting. Look for signs of new growth, and check for rooting by gently pulling at the cuttings. Once they are well rooted, pot them up.

Potting up

Water the rooted cuttings well, and gently slide them out of the pot. Carefully separate the cuttings before potting them up individually, in a blend of equal parts potting mix and grit.

Topdress with a ½in (1cm) layer of sharp grit. Water the cuttings thoroughly and return them to the

propagator, keeping them out of direct sun. Keep the cuttings well watered. Once fresh growth appears, place the cuttings in a cold frame and harden them off carefully before planting them out.

Semiripe and ripewood cuttings

Semiripe cuttings are taken in mid- to late summer from nonflowering shoots of the current season's growth; the shoots offer distinct resistance to pressure when bent gently and should be beginning to harden at the base. Ripewood cuttings are taken from evergreen plants during late summer and fall when the wood has fully ripened.

Taking the cuttings

The cuttings will vary in length with the plant concerned, from ½–1½in (1–4cm) or more. Cut them from the parent plant using a sharp knife or pruners. Make a clean cut below a node and remove soft tissue at the tips. Trim off the lower leaves and dip the ends of the cuttings into hormone rooting powder. Alternatively, take cuttings with a "heel" and trim the heel with a sharp knife to remove any snags.

Potting up

Small cuttings root best in pots of propagation mix topped with a ½in (1cm) layer of fine sand. Make holes in the sand and insert the cuttings by one-third to one-half of their length. Label and water the cuttings, using a fungicide solution if needed. Place in a propagator in a cool greenhouse. Check regularly for disease. Water sparingly and, as growth begins, apply a diluted liquid fertilizer.

If you take a large number of cuttings, insert them in a cold frame, with drainage at the base. Fork over the soil in the frame and then add a mixture of 1 part peat substitute (or peat) and 1 part grit; top with a 1in (2.5cm) layer of sand. After inserting the cuttings, water them and close the frame. Open the frame in mild weather. If there is a danger of frost, insulate the frame.

The following spring, repot or pot up those in frames in equal parts potting mix and grit, or plant out in a nursery bed, but only after the last frost. Water well.

Grow on, keeping the rooted cuttings moist and sheltered from direct sun. Give a liquid fertilizer in the growing season. Transplant into their permanent positions in fall.

SOFTWOOD CUTTINGS

1 In spring, choose young, nonflowering shoots (here, from *Gypsophila repens*) and take cuttings 1–3in (2.5–7cm) long. Put the cuttings in a plastic bag.

2 Trim off the base of the cuttings, and the lower leaves and soft tips (see inset). Fill a pot with moist potting mix, inserting the cuttings by up to half their length.

3 Water and label the cuttings. Place the pot in a sealed plastic bag, keeping it in good light but out of direct sun.

4 When rooted, pot up the cuttings singly, holding them by the leaves only. Topdress the pots, water well, and label.

ROCK PLANTS FROM CUTTINGS

Softwood

Adenophora
Anchusa caespitosa
Anthemis
Asyneuma
Aubrieta (spp. and cvs)
Campanula (spp. and cvs)
Cassiope
Daphne jasminea
Dianthus
Dionysia
Draba
Eriogonum ovalifolium
Eriophyllum lanatum
Gypsophila aretioides, G. repens
Penstemon
Phlox (spp. and cvs)
Polygala
Primula (alpine spp.)
Silene acaulis
Viola (spp. and cvs)

Greenwood

Aubrieta (spp. and cvs)
Aurinia
Cassiope
Erodium
Geranium

Semiripe

Cassiope
Claytonia
Clematis alpina, C. ×cartmanii 'Joe'
Convolvulus boissieri, C. sabatius
Daphne
Diascia
Erica
Erinacea anthyllis
Hebe (spp. and cvs)
Helianthemum
Helichrysum selago
Lepidium nanum
Lewisia
Linum arboreum
Lithodora diffusa
Origanum amanum,
  O. rotundifolium
Ozothamnus selago
Parahebe catarractae
Phlox 'Chattahoochee',
  P. subulata (and cvs)
Polygala
Rhododendron (spp. and cvs)
Veronica

Phlox paniculata 'Graf Zeppelin'

ROCK PLANTS FROM CUTTINGS (CONT.)

Ripewood

Dryas
Eriogonum
Juniperus communis
  'Compressa'
Rosa
Salix

Rosette

Androsace
Armeria juniperifolia
Azorella trifurcata
Bolax gummifera
Draba
Helichrysum milfordiae
Jovibarba
Saxifraga
  (spp. and cvs)
Sempervivum
  (spp. and cvs)

Leaf

Haberlea
Jancaea (spp. and hybrids)
Primula gracilipes
Ramonda
Sedum
Sempervivum

ROCK PLANTS FROM "IRISHMAN'S" CUTTINGS

Achillea ageratifolia
Arenaria montana
Aurinia
Gentiana acaulis,
  G. verna
Primula auricula
  (and cvs),
  P. marginata (and cvs)
Silene
Veronica peduncularis

Sempervivum tectorum

Leaf cuttings

This method is suitable for plants with fleshy leaves, such as *Haberlea*, *Ramonda*, and *Sedum*.

Using a sharp knife, cut healthy, strong, and relatively young leaves from the stem at their base. Prepare pots with a mixture of equal parts of standard propagation mix and sand; insert each cutting at a 45° angle, so that it is just held in place by the soil. Enclose each pot in a plastic bag and, when the plantlets appear, pot them up individually.

Basal cuttings

Some plants, such as *Primula marginata* and its cultivars, may be propagated from basal cuttings. These are taken from young shoots at the base of the plant at, or just above, soil level. Basal cuttings are usually taken in spring, but may also be taken in summer or fall.

Use a fast-draining propagation mix, or a blend of equal parts of soil and peat or compost with 2 parts grit. Fill pots with the mix and firm.

Trim the base of each cutting cleanly just below a node. Make sure that the cutting is not hollow at the base. Remove the lower leaves and dip the base in hormone powder.

Insert one-third to one-half of each stem into the soil, keeping the leaves clear of the soil surface. Water well and place the pots in a shaded, closed propagator or cold frame. Rooting takes three to six weeks, after which the cuttings may be potted up individually or lined out in nursery beds or a cold frame to grow on.

BASAL CUTTINGS

Primula marginata

In spring, take cuttings 2–3in (5–7cm) long with new leaves and a short stem. Trim the base and remove the lower leaves, inserting the cuttings to the depth indicated.

SELECTING CUTTING MATERIAL

For all types of cuttings, always choose strong, healthy stems or leaves that show no sign of pests or diseases. Nonflowering shoots that are in active growth should be used. Except for basal cuttings, do not take the cuttings from the base of any plant because this part may be weaker than elsewhere. Do not take all the cuttings from the same area on the parent plant because this may make it look lopsided.

After taking the cuttings, immediately place them in a clean plastic bag to prevent any moisture loss. Many cuttings will root readily if they are inserted into pots of potting mix with added grit. Alternatively, simply use horticultural sand. Insert the cuttings at the depths indicated.

Semiripe
(*Phlox*)
In mid- to late summer, select shoots that are just hardening but not woody. Remove 1¼in (3cm) lengths, trimming to about ½in (1cm).

Greenwood
(*Erodium*)
Take cuttings from the soft tips of new shoots in early summer. Remove 1–3in (2.5–7cm) lengths and trim them to about ½in (1cm).

Rosette
(*Saxifraga*)
In early to mid-summer, select new rosettes. Cut them about ½in (1cm) below the leaves. Trim each cleanly across the base.

Ripewood
(*Dryas*)
In late summer and fall, select new shoots and take cuttings about 1in (2.5cm) long. Trim to about ½in (1cm) below the base of the leaves.

Leaf
(*Sedum*)
Throughout the growing season, select mature leaves that are undamaged, cutting off selected leaves. Trim each cleanly across the base.

"IRISHMAN'S" CUTTINGS

1 Lift the rooted shoots close to the base of the plant (here, *Veronica*) and remove them with a sharp knife. Trim off sideshoots and straggly roots (see inset).

2 Pot up the cuttings individually. Place a little gritty potting mix in a pot, insert the cutting, then add more mix. Firm gently, water, and topdress.

Division

Many alpines and rock garden plants may be successfully propagated by division, and in some cases division is the only practical method of increasing the stock if seed is rarely produced or the plant is sterile.

Plants that are particularly suitable for division include mat-forming species, which produce a mass of fibrous roots, and clump-forming plants that produce clusters of shoots that are readily separated.

A number of clump-forming plants have a tendency to die out at the center. These may be divided to rejuvenate them by replanting only the youngest, most vigorous pieces.

When to divide

Most plants are best divided in early spring, when new growth is just beginning; do not divide plants in cold and frosty weather, or when the ground is frozen or waterlogged.

Plants can also be divided in early fall, which allows new roots to be produced while the soil is still warm. Where hard winters are expected, spring division may be safer, because this allows a full growing season for establishment. Some plants—for example, primulas and *Meconopsis*—should be divided immediately after flowering, when they enter a period of strong vegetative growth. They must be well watered after replanting until they are fully reestablished.

How to divide

Lift plants and shake off the soil. For large clumps, insert the tines of two garden forks back-to-back into the center of the clump and pry the plant apart in two halves. Tease these smaller clumps apart by hand or cut them with a sharp knife to produce a number of small pieces with healthy roots and growth buds. The older, woody, central part of the plant should be discarded.

If not replanting or potting up the divisions immediately, wrap them in plastic bags or moist burlap and store them out of direct sun. Divisions of most hardy plants may be replanted immediately into their permanent positions. If, however, plants are particularly precious, or the divisions are quite small, it may be safer to pot them up and place them in a cold frame until they are established before planting them out. Use 1 part low-fertility, soil-based potting mix and 1 part grit or a lime-free mix for acid-lovers. If replanting in the open ground, make holes large enough to allow the roots to be spread out fully. Firm in and water well. Keep the soil moist until the plants are established.

"Irishman's" cuttings

These are essentially sideshoots that have already rooted. Thymes and other creeping rock plants produce this type of cutting. The technique is particularly useful for plants with woody rootstocks that are not easily divided, or for those that naturally produce offsets or runners.

Before taking the cuttings, brush away surface soil from the base of the parent plant. Cut rooted pieces from the plant with a sharp knife and pot them up in equal parts of low-fertility, soil-based potting mix and grit. Alternatively, plant them out in a cool, sheltered spot in the garden until well established.

HOW TO PROPAGATE BY DIVISION

1 Plants with fibrous roots (here, *Gentiana acaulis*) may be divided and replanted to provide new plants. Lift a clump of the parent plant and shake off the soil.

2 Using hand forks back-to-back, loosen the root mass and divide the clump into pieces. If necessary, cut away sections from the clump with a knife.

3 The plants should have a good root system. Replant them outdoors into their permanent positions, firming around the roots. Add topdressing around the plants and water thoroughly with a fine spray of water.

ROCK PLANTS TO DIVIDE

Achillea ageratifolia
Alchemilla alpina,
  A. ellenbeckii
Allium sikkimense
Antennaria dioica
Arenaria montana
Artemisia schmidtiana
  'Nana'
Campanula carpatica,
  C. cochleariifolia
Chiastophyllum
  oppositifolium
Gentiana acaulis,
  G. sino-ornata
Meconopsis
Primula allionii
Sagina subulata
  'Aurea'

ROCK PLANTS FROM ROOT CUTTINGS

Anacyclus pyrethrum
  var. *depressus*
Carduncellus rhaponticoides
Centaurea pindicola
Geranium
Meconopsis delavayi
Morisia monanthos
Papaver lateritium
Phlox
Primula denticulata
Pulsatilla
Roscoea cautleyoides

Pulsatilla
vulgaris

Root cuttings

A limited number of alpines and rock garden plants, such as *Geranium sanguineum* and *Primula denticulata*, may be propagated from root cuttings. Take root cuttings from the healthiest-looking roots in either late fall or early winter, when the plants are dormant.

Selecting material

Choose a strong, healthy plant and lift it from the soil. Select young, vigorous roots and cut them from the parent plant. The cuttings should be about 2in (5cm) long. Cut the roots straight across at the top end (nearest the plant's stem) and use sloping cuts at the lower end (nearest the root tips). Wash the cuttings in tepid water and replant the parent stock immediately or, if old and straggly and no longer required, discard it.

Inserting the cuttings

Use pots at least 4in (10cm) deep. Put screening over the drainage holes and place over these a 1in (2.5cm) layer of low-fertility soil-based potting mix. Fill the pots with washed sand, then firm. Make several planting holes in each pot around the edges.

Insert the cuttings into the holes, with the straight ends uppermost and the tops level with the surface of the sand. Cuttings of plants with thin, wiry roots may be laid flat on the surface of the soil. Topdress with fine grit. Label the pots, water thoroughly, and place them in a cold frame on a layer of grit or gravel, or in a propagator. Close the frames in cold weather; otherwise they should be ventilated freely.

Water the pots when new growth appears. When the new shoots are growing strongly, check that the cuttings have rooted before potting them up: gently tap them out of their pots to inspect their roots.

Potting up rooted cuttings

Slide the cuttings out of their pots and separate them carefully. Pot them up singly, using low-fertility, soil-based potting mix blended with an equal amount of sand. Instead of

HOW TO PROPAGATE BY ROOT CUTTINGS

1 In late fall or early winter, using a hand fork, carefully lift a healthy plant (here, *Primula denticulata*) with a well-developed root system.

2 Wash the roots clean of soil, then select thick, healthy roots for the cuttings. Using a sharp knife, cut off selected roots close to the crown of the plant.

3 Prepare 2in (5cm) lengths of root, cutting each one straight at the thicker end (closest to the parent plant) and angled at the lower end.

4 Place a layer of potting mix in the base of a pot, then fill almost to the brim with sharp sand. Insert the cuttings so that straight ends are just level with the sand surface.

5 Cover the sand with a ½in (1cm) layer of grit. Water and label the cuttings, then place the pot in a propagator or on the greenhouse bench.

sand, a mix of peat and sand may be used. Topdress the pots with ½in (1cm) of sharp sand or grit. Water and then place outside, out of direct sun. Leave until the new plants are established, watering as required.

Scooping rosettes

Plants that grow quickly or form rosettes, such as *Primula denticulata*, may be propagated

in situ in early spring from root cuttings by scooping out the rosettes with a sharp knife to expose the top of the rootstock. Select strong-growing rosettes. If gray mold (see p.661) has been a problem previously, brush the tops of the roots with fungicidal powder. Cover the pots with a thin layer of horticultural sharp sand.

Shoots should soon appear on each root apex. When the shoots are about 1–2in (2.5–5cm) tall, lift the clump carefully with

a hand fork. Separate the clump into individual, small plants that have healthy-looking, vigorous shoots and roots, pulling them apart by hand or dividing them with a sharp knife.

Pot up the young plants to grow on, using equal parts of potting mix and horticultural sand. Water thoroughly, and place outside in a shady site. Keep moist and plant out the young plants when their roots have filled the pots.

HOW TO SCOOP ROSETTES

1 Scoop out the live crowns of rosette-forming plants (here, *Primula denticulata*) with a sharp knife, so that the tops of the roots are visible (see inset).

2 Dust the exposed roots with fungicidal powder (see inset) to protect them from molds and fungi. Lightly cover with sharp horticultural sand.

3 When new shoots appear from the roots, lift the whole clump, using a hand fork or trowel. Take care not to damage the new roots.

4 Divide the clump into individual plants, each with one shoot and well-developed roots. Pot them up using equal parts potting mix and sand.

Alpine houses and frames

Although some high-altitude alpines grow well in the open garden in temperate climates, provided that their specific requirements of situation and soil are satisfied, most will perform considerably better if they are grown under cover. Many alpines bloom in late winter and very early spring when, if left in the open, their delicate flowers may be damaged by inclement weather, or eaten by slugs or snails.

In an alpine house, plants are protected from winter rain, cold, drying winds, and sudden sharp frosts, as well as from the attentions of most pests. This enables a far wider range of alpines and rock plants to be grown, either in pots or in ground-level or raised beds, to provide an eye-catching and lasting display.

Using an alpine house

An alpine house is a cold or cool/frost-free greenhouse, designed for growing and displaying alpines

Using an alpine house
Part of the house may be used to grow young plants (foreground) in beds supported by brick pillars.

and rock plants under controlled conditions. Often, half of the house is used for growing the plants, and the other half for displaying them. Alternatively, the plants may be grown in cold frames and brought temporarily into the house for display. Alpine houses are not practical in areas with very cold winters or long, very hot summers.

Displaying the plants

Alpines can be displayed in pots simply placed on the benches or, more commonly, plunged up to their rims in a layer of sand. Plunging keeps roots cool and moist and reduces temperature fluctuations, while allowing easy irrigation of plants that dislike overhead watering. Specially built display beds are an attractive option. Create miniature rock gardens in the alpine house, either waist-high where benches are strong enough to support the weight, or at ground level. These may have some permanent planting as well as areas of sand or sandy soil into which different plants may be plunged, according to season. Lightweight tufa rocks may be incorporated and planted to enhance this type of display.

Siting the alpine house

Choose a firm, level site away from the shade of trees, fences, walls,

An alpine house display
A wide range of rock plants may be grown in pots and attractively displayed in raised sand beds in an alpine house.

and tall buildings if possible. Siting the alpine house on a north–south axis is ideal, but any open, sunny location is acceptable. Always avoid hollows where cold air forms frost pockets and do not site it in exposed, windy situations. Try to position the alpine house where it will harmonize with other landscape features, perhaps even using it as a focal point. For further information on greenhouses, benches, shading, and ventilation, see GREENHOUSES AND FRAMES, pp.575, 576, and 579.

Using cold frames

Cold frames should be sited near the alpine house, where they may be used to protect a range of choice plants from climatic extremes, as an overflow area, or for storage when

plants are not in flower. They are very useful for bulbs that need to be kept dry when dormant, or for plants that will not tolerate the very hot conditions that may arise in summer. Frames incorporate a top sash that must be opened as required to provide good ventilation; a standard sash frame is suitable but other types are available. The sashes may be removed in summer if necessary, but they should be kept on if the frame contains dormant bulbs. Those plants that do not tolerate direct summer sun can be protected by covering the frame with mesh shading (see GREENHOUSES AND FRAMES, "Meshes and fabrics," p.576). Pots in a frame are usually plunged in a material such as washed builder's sand over a layer of gravel to give them good drainage.

CARE OF ALPINES AND DWARF BULBS AFTER FLOWERING

Alpines indoors
After flowering, pots of alpines (here, *Dionysia* spp.) needing careful watering should be plunged in sand under cover.

Alpines outdoors
Alpines that tolerate variable summer weather conditions, such as saxifrages, may be plunged in open cold frames after flowering.

Bulbs indoors
Pots of dwarf bulbs (here, irises) that have finished flowering may be kept dry by plunging in sand or gravel under benches.

Protecting flowering alpines
Alpines coming into flower may be grown in outdoor frames before bringing them into the alpine house for display.

Alpines in pots

Growing alpines in pots ensures that special watering, soil, or fertilizer requirements can be provided for individual plants.

Plastic and clay pots

Although plastic pots are suitable for growing alpines and retain moisture well, clay pots are more attractive—important if the plants are to be exhibited. The soil in plastic pots dries out more slowly than in clay pots, so take care not to overwater the plants. Clean and sterilize all pots before use: sterilants based on household bleach are suitable, mixing 10 parts water to 1 part bleach.

Potting medium

All alpines need a freely draining soil mix and benefit from the presence of grit, perlite, or coarse vermiculite in the mix. Even moisture-loving plants will not tolerate stagnant conditions.

Most species grow well in soil-based potting medium, mixed with an equal amount of grit. Those from high, alpine habitats of scree and rock-face crevices, such as the Aretian *Androsace* species and other cushion-forming plants, need a less fertile and more freely draining mix if they are to retain their neat, natural habit. In rich soil, they quickly become soft and lush and are then more prone to attack by pests and diseases. For these plants, use a mix of up to 3 parts grit to 1 part soil-based potting mix. Introduce plants to these "lean mixes" when they are young, since they may not adapt easily if they have been repotted from a more fertile medium.

A number of species, usually ones from woodland habitats, or those that occur in humus-rich pockets in rocky habitats, such as *Haberlea* and *Ramonda*, prefer well-drained potting medium that is rich in organic matter. For these, a mix of 1 part each of soil-based mix and grit, with 2 parts leaf mold, peat, or compost will be suitable. Take care to check on the individual needs of each plant in order to select an appropriate soil mix, and ensure that mixes for acidic-soil-loving plants are free of alkalinity.

Topdressings

After planting the pots (see right), topdress them with a layer of grit or stone chips to enhance the plant's appearance, to keep the neck of the plant well drained, and to prevent the growth of mosses and liverworts. Use a topdressing that is appropriate to the pH requirements of the plant—for example, limestone chips for alkalinity-loving species or granitic grit for acid-loving plants.

Some small, cushion-forming alpines are sensitive to the presence of water around their necks, so, as well as topdressing with grit, prop small wedges of rock beneath their cushions in order to keep them clear of the surface.

Repotting

When a plant has outgrown its pot, transfer it carefully into a slightly larger pot, disturbing the root ball as little as possible. Repot herbaceous and shrubby plants in spring and summer, when they are growing strongly; bulbs should be repotted when they are dormant. Plant to the same level as in the previous pot, firm in fresh potting mix, and then add a new layer of topdressing.

Water well after potting by standing the pot in at least 1–2in (2.5–5cm) of water until the surface of the soil becomes moist. Then remove the pot to avoid the risk of root rot.

Planting in beds

The beds may be at ground level or raised about 3ft (1m) high. A raised bed allows plants to be tended and viewed more easily and is especially useful for elderly or disabled gardeners. The benches must drain well and be solidly constructed to bear the weight of the bed (see also GREENHOUSES AND FRAMES, "Raised beds," p.578).

REPOTTING A SAXIFRAGE

1 The roots of this saxifrage can be seen growing through the drainage hole at the bottom of the pot. The plant is potbound and should be repotted.

2 Choose a pot that is one size bigger than the one that the plant is growing in. Use pot shards and gravel to provide drainage at the base of the pot.

3 Arrange the pot shards curved-side up over the drainage hole, then cover with a layer of gravel.

4 Remove the plant from its pot by tapping gently on the base to loosen the root ball; tease out the roots to encourage fresh roots to penetrate the new potting medium.

5 Add some soil mix to the correct level (so that the neck of the plant is at the same level as in the original pot), then fill in with more potting mix.

6 Spread the gravel topdressing over the surface of the potting mix, taking care to tuck it under the collar of the plant to keep it sharply drained.

7 Place the pot in a bowl of water and leave it until the soil mix and gravel topdressing appear damp.

8 Then remove the pot and place it on a layer of sand in a cold frame, where any excess moisture can easily drain off. This will prevent any risk of root rot.

9 The repotted plant may then be plunged in sand in a cold frame or bed to grow on.

REMOVING DEAD LEAVES

Tweezers should be used regularly to remove any brown or withered leaves from alpine plants such as this *Campanula dasyantha* subsp. *chamissonis*.

Use a mix of 3 parts loam (or good sterilized garden soil), 2 parts coarse fibrous peat, and 2 parts sharp sand or grit. Add rocks to the bed to create a miniature rock garden. Tufa is particularly useful because it is lightweight and moisture-retentive, and plants can be grown in the rock itself. Plant out alpines in the bed, avoiding species that are invasive and free-seeding, but leave some gaps for plunging a succession of seasonal, pot-grown specimens. Grow ferns and other shade-loving species under a raised bed.

Routine maintenance

Since alpines have specialized growing requirements, they need considerable attention through the growing season. Plants that are regularly repotted rarely need additional feeding, but when fertilizers are used be sure that they are low in nitrogen—high-nitrogen fertilizer will lead to soft, lush growth that is uncharacteristic of alpines and more prone to pests and diseases.

Ventilation

Ventilating surfaces must occupy at least 25 percent of the glass area because the aim is to provide the maximum possible air circulation at all times. In spring and summer, the vents and the greenhouse door can remain open permanently, unless there is strong wind or heavy rain. Use a screen of small-diameter mesh over vents and doors to keep out animals and birds. During heavy rain and windy weather, close the vents on the windward side to avoid water drops on the foliage and reduce strong drafts that may damage foliage and flowers. In severe winds, it is safest to close all vents and doors.

In winter, open the vents fully (unless it is windy, raining, or snowing) but close them before nightfall to retain any residual warmth. In very cold weather, allow temperatures in the alpine house to rise gradually before ventilating; on bright, sunny days, however, open the vents as soon as possible |to prevent the temperature from rising too rapidly. In damp, foggy weather, especially in areas with high levels of atmospheric pollution, close down the house completely to keep out cold, damp air, and use a cool air fan to maintain air circulation.

Temperature

Shading will be necessary during sunny weather, from late spring to fall, to avoid scorching tender new growth, and to help reduce temperatures. Do not use heavy shading—this might cause etiolation or lop-sided leaning of plants toward the light source. In hot weather, thoroughly wet down the house floor to reduce temperatures and maintain atmospheric humidity; plants may be lightly misted with cool water during sultry evenings.

Heating must be used to prevent pots from freezing in severe weather, and a method of heating that does not produce excessive fumes or moisture is best (see Greenhouses and Frames, "Heating," p.574).

Hygiene

Remove dead foliage and faded flowers regularly to reduce the risk of fungal attack. Check the plants for pests and diseases and treat any outbreaks promptly (see Plant Problems, pp.639–673). Always keep the floor of the house clean to minimize the risk of diseases, and make sure that the glass is clean so that plants receive maximum light.

Watering

Water regularly throughout the season, especially on sunny spring and summer days, when water loss is rapid. If plants are allowed to dry out between waterings, growth may be severely checked, and flower buds may shrivel. For pots standing on benches, water from above but avoid splashing the foliage. Plunged pots derive moisture from the surrounding material but may need additional watering in warm periods. For plants that are sensitive to moisture on their foliage, water the plunge medium around the pots. As fall approaches, reduce watering as plants prepare for dormancy. During winter, alpines need to be kept dry but not dust-dry (for plunged pots, the plunge medium should be just damp to the touch).

Winter maintenance

A spell of clear, dry weather during late winter is a good time to store the plants in a frame and clean the alpine house (see Greenhouses and Frames, "Routine maintenance," p.583). Clean and top off the sand or grit on beds and renew labels. Then transfer pots back from the frame.

Exhibiting

Alpines for showing should be in the best possible condition on exhibition day. No matter how perfect the plant, it will lose marks if poorly presented in a less than scrupulously clean pot, or if topdressings are thin or show evidence of algal growth. Remove all evidence of weeds, pests, and diseases. Check plants for dead, discolored,

TRANSPORTING PLANTS

When transporting fragile plants (here, *Fritillaria uva-vulpis*) make a tripod from split stakes bound at the top with twine, and tie in stems.

or misshapen leaves and faded flowers, and remove these carefully with tweezers.

Clay pots should be scrubbed clean with a wire brush or scourer. Alternatively, they may be double-potted: insert the specimen in its pot into a larger, new pot, covering the inner rim with topdressing. Renew all topdressings with materials appropriate to the plant's natural habitat, then relabel. Support tall, fragile plants during transportation with tripods of split stakes. Water plants thoroughly the day before the show and allow to drain before packing to transport. Carry spare topdressing to renew any lost in transit.

PREPARING PLANTS FOR EXHIBITION

1 Use fine sand together with a wire brush or scouring pad to clean the outside of clay pots. This will remove any algae or fertilizer salts that may be present.

2 Replenish the topdressing. For this *Dionysia aretioides* the medium is coarse gravel; but stone chips, grit, or pine needles may be used, depending on the plant.

3 Add new, clearly written labels. Pack the pots carefully in a tray using newspaper to hold them steady, and carry extra topdressing for last-minute renewal.

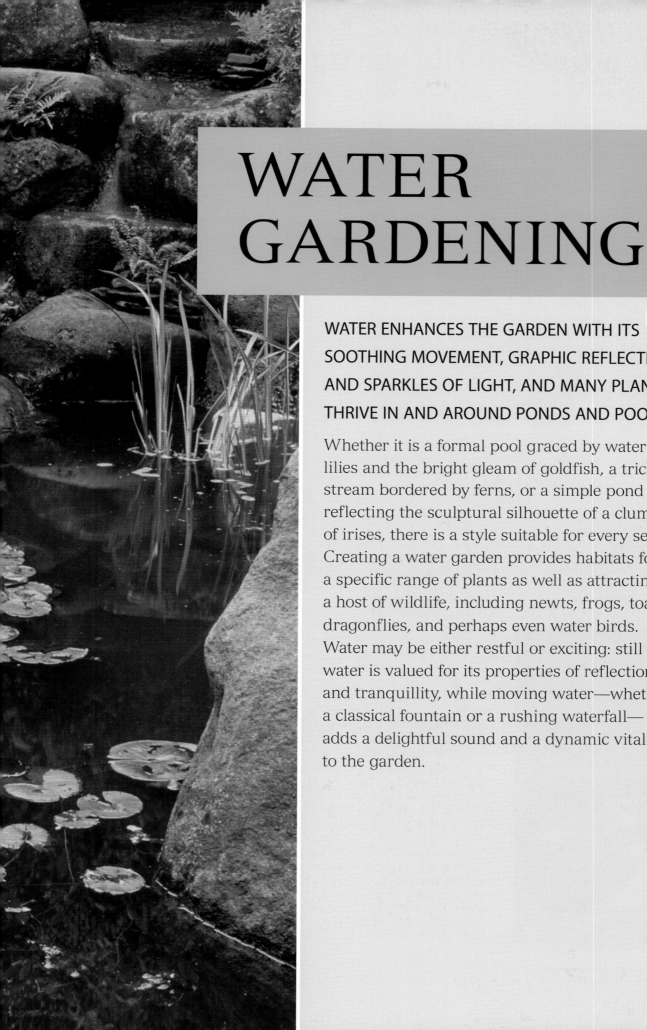

WATER GARDENING

WATER ENHANCES THE GARDEN WITH ITS
SOOTHING MOVEMENT, GRAPHIC REFLECTIONS,
AND SPARKLES OF LIGHT, AND MANY PLANTS
THRIVE IN AND AROUND PONDS AND POOLS.

Whether it is a formal pool graced by water
lilies and the bright gleam of goldfish, a trickling
stream bordered by ferns, or a simple pond
reflecting the sculptural silhouette of a clump
of irises, there is a style suitable for every setting.
Creating a water garden provides habitats for
a specific range of plants as well as attracting
a host of wildlife, including newts, frogs, toads,
dragonflies, and perhaps even water birds.
Water may be either restful or exciting: still
water is valued for its properties of reflection
and tranquillity, while moving water—whether
a classical fountain or a rushing waterfall—
adds a delightful sound and a dynamic vitality
to the garden.

Water features in the garden

Unlike any other element in the garden, water brings an ever-changing pattern of reflections, sound, and movement that is particularly appealing. Even when frozen, its surface provides contrasts of color and texture. A pond is a popular form of water feature but there are others: a waterfall, fountain, or watercourse, for instance. Even small gardens can accommodate a water feature in the form of a waterproof container or pot filled with a few appropriate plants. Water is a beneficial addition that attracts wildlife and adds another dimension to the garden.

Pond favorite Water lily *Nymphaea* 'Froebelii' carpets a pond.

Ways with water

A home water feature allows you to grow many plants that do not thrive in any other conditions, from the floating frogbit (*Hydrocharis morsus-ranae*) and water hyacinth (*Eichhornia crassipes*) to the bog garden candelabra primulas.

When deciding which type of water feature to create, bear in mind the size and style of the garden. If large and informal, a meandering stream may be effective, while in an enclosed city garden, a raised formal pool might be appropriate. Water may even be included in a garden for children in the form of an attractive bubble fountain—in which the water splashes over stones and is recirculated without forming an area of any depth.

Informal ponds

In an informal yard, a natural, sunken pond may look most attractive. Usually, this is in an irregular, curved shape with natural materials, such as sod or stones, used to link it with the garden. The water surface is, however, only part of the total design: the inclusion of marginal and moisture-loving plants around the pond, to soften or hide its outline completely, helps to create a lush and refreshing effect.

As when planting in a raised bed, consider how the plants will combine to create complementary and contrasting associations of color, texture, and form.

Formal ponds

In contrast to the natural effect of an informal pond, a formal pond is a much bolder feature. It may be raised or sunken and is usually of a regular, geometric design. As a rule, less space is devoted to planting than in an informal pond, although plants with floating leaves and flowers (e.g, water lilies) are often included; sculptural plants, such as certain ferns, grown next to the pond, provide attractive reflections. A fountain or water spout to complement the style of the pond can be an ornamental and dramatic addition.

Far from being disguised, the edge of the pond may form an important feature, perhaps made of attractive paving stone or, if the pond is raised, wide enough to form a seat; this type of design is particularly suitable for elderly or disabled people.

In many cases formal ponds are sited so that they form a striking focal point in the yard, at the main axis of paths, for example, or where they may be conveniently viewed and enjoyed from the windows or patio of the house.

Fountains

The style and size of a fountain should be considered in the context of the surrounding pond and the overall design of the landscape. Often used in a formal garden as a focal point, a fountain is also invaluable for adding height to a design, and for its dynamic contribution of sound and movement and the scattering of light. In addition, a fountain is particularly effective if lit at night.

A stone or bubble fountain, in which water bubbles over stones into a small underground reservoir, looks more informal than a standard fountain and is ideal in a garden that is used by children.In addition to being ornamental, fountains also provide a practical function: the splashing action introduces oxygen into the water and this is beneficial to fish. Most aquatic plants do not flourish in disturbed water, however, so they should not be grown close to a fountain.

Water spouts

While a fountain or waterfall might be too large in an average garden, a water spout provides all the pleasure of running water scaled down for the smallest garden or even a sunroom. There are many styles, from the classical lion's head or gargoyle above a pond to the simplicity of an Asian bamboo pipe trickling water over stones. A water spout is usually attached to a wall, with a pump and pipe similar to those used for a watercourse; the pump moves water from a pond or reservoir to the rear of the spout and out of the "mouth."

Streams, waterfalls, and watercourses

Few yards have a natural stream or waterfall, but it is possible to create a circulating watercourse spilling out into a pond or underground reservoir. Making a watercourse or waterfall is an attractive way of exploiting a change of level in the yard. It may be used to link parts of the yard as well as providing points of interest between levels.

In an informal garden, a watercourse may be made to look more natural by being edged with rocks or stones and moisture-loving plants, such as ferns and irises. Ornamentals that have large leaves, for example, *Rheum palmatum*, are particularly valuable for watercourses made from liners or preformed units because they help to disguise the edges.

Water in small gardens

In a small yard, or where major construction work is impractical, it is still possible to have a water feature. The most suitable one might be a small quantity of water being continually recirculated by a small pump, which fills a basin or other container, or a "bubble" fountain, which conceals a reservoir. Such "covered" features are particularly suitable in family settings, where safety is a concern.

Wall fountains are available in many styles, both formal and informal, in a range of materials such as stonework, pottery, or metal. A miniature pond could also be introduced by using an appropriate ornamental container, such as a sealed and lined half-barrel or terra-cotta pot (see also WATER GARDENS IN CONTAINERS, p.296). Larger containers could also include a simple fountain or Japanese water feature.

Underlit pond Underwater lights can highlight a water feature such as a fountain, surrounded by lush leafy plants, here, including *Fatsia japonica*.

WATER CONSERVATION VERSUS WATER FEATURE

As changes in weather patterns become more frequent and global warming increases, it is important to take into account the adverse environmental impact of using an outdoor spigot to supply water in a garden. This is particularly the case when water features need to be refilled.

During periods of hot, dry weather when evaporation from the surface is high, it is important to raise water levels to maintain the pond's ecological balance. As the water level drops, the water quality in the pond deteriorates as the oxygen level decreases and the water temperature rises. This adversely affects the health of water plants, fish, and other wildlife in the pond. It is possible to alleviate this, to some extent, by adding to the number of oxygenating plants in the pond and spraying the water surface from a hose, which increases the oxygen content of the water, but these measures are only palliative.

Adding water to the pond from an outdoor water spigot is the easy solution, but, in times of severe drought and water shortages, there is inevitably an environmental cost. It is better to plan ahead and collect rainwater in water barrels for this purpose. Never be tempted to use "gray" water (see p.615) in ponds.

Plants are generally incidental within a small feature, but if it includes any moving water, it is important that the surrounding plants are able to tolerate the high humidity caused by the fine spray.

Bog and wildlife areas

In an informal or natural-looking design, a bog garden makes an attractive and unconventional feature. Usually most appropriate next to ponds, bog gardens provide a gradual and natural transition from aquatic to moisture-loving plants and ideal conditions for wildlife.

Bog gardens

Creating a bog garden is a far better way of using waterlogged land than struggling against nature by trying to drain it. Although the ground next to a man-made pond is unlikely to be wet enough to provide suitable conditions for growing bog plants, using a liner under the soil will help to retain sufficient moisture.

Bog gardens bring a freshness of growth in late summer when many other plants are showing the effects of drought; most bog plants, however, die back naturally in the fall, so they do not provide great interest in winter months.

Linking levels Creating a waterfall or series of stepped stone levels is a good way of introducing sound and movement to a landscape and will also encourage a wide range of wildlife by providing a damp and shady habitat.

Wildlife ponds

Simply adding a water feature will increase diversity in the wildlife garden, as such features provide ideal habitats for ducks, geese, frogs, and an enormous range of insects. Limiting the planting to native species only will attract more wildlife, although many native plants can prove to be invasive; the inclusion of some exotic ornamentals creates a greater opportunity to make the pond a highly decorative feature as well. Informal ponds with muddy bottoms and shallowly sloping edges interspersed with large, flat stones are particularly suitable, providing ideal conditions for amphibians, which can easily enter and leave the pond.

Situating a pond

Exploit the reflective quality of water by situating a pond where it mirrors an eye-catching feature—a specimen plant or statue, perhaps. It may help to lay a reflective sheet on the proposed site to give an idea of reflections to be seen during the day and evening; check it from major viewpoints, such as the house and patio. An open,

sunny location, away from overhanging trees, provides the best conditions in which to grow most water-loving plants.

If planning to create a pond on wet land that is prone to flooding, check that there is no danger of fertilizer or pesticide residues leaching into the water from an adjacent vegetable garden or farmland. These substances invariably affect pond life adversely. Direct potential overflows to a suitable drainage system. Land with a high water table may cause problems because, in very wet periods, water pressure from below may push a pond liner out of shape.

Do not site a pond in a frost pocket or in a very exposed site, because this restricts the range of plants that may be grown and protection may have to be provided in winter.

Water garden plants

In any water garden, plants are vital to the design. Lush foliage and flowers enhance the pool and link it with the rest of the garden, while certain plants help to maintain clear water and, in the case of oxygenators,

good conditions for fish. Plants suitable for a water garden range from those that thrive in deep water to those requiring moist soil only around their root tips. They are usually grouped into six categories: oxygenators, deep-water plants, surface floaters, marginals, bog plants, and moisture-loving plants.

Oxygenators

Lagarosiphon major (syn. *Elodea crispa*) and *Myriophyllum* are typical oxygenators: submerged, rapidly growing plants that help to clean and oxygenate the water. During sunny weather, submerged algae may turn a new pond completely green within a week or two; oxygenators compete for the dissolved mineral salts on which algae thrive and starve them out so the water eventually becomes clear once more. Oxygenators are essential if fish are kept in the pool.

Deep-water plants

These flourish in a depth range of 12–36in (30–90cm). This category includes plants such as *Aponogeton* and *Orontium*, with water lilies (*Nymphaea*) forming the largest group (see pp.286–287). Aside from their ornamental value, their floating leaves also help to reduce algae by cutting down the amount of light allowed to reach the water.

Surface floaters

Floating plants, such as *Trapa natans* and *Azolla filiculoides*, perform a similar function to deep-water plants, especially in the establishment phase. It is vital not to let them cover too much water because oxygenators suffer if there is not enough light.

Marginals

Marginal plants grow in shallow water usually about 3–6in (7–15cm) deep. Many of these plants are extremely attractive, such as *Iris laevigata* 'Variegata' with fans of green- and cream-striped leaves and lavender-blue flowers, and they are valuable in an informal pond for breaking up the outline. In a wildlife pool, marginal plants provide cover for wildfowl and other small creatures. Some species such as *Mentha aquatica* and *Veronica beccabunga* also help to oxygenate the water.

Bog plants

Bog-loving plants such as *Lysichiton* or some *Caltha* species thrive in waterlogged soil and can withstand occasional flooding. Under a bog plant heading, nursery catalogs may include plants that grow in moist or even wet soil but do not tolerate a waterlogged soil; when ordering, ensure that any plants chosen tolerate high water levels around the roots.

Moisture-loving plants

These thrive in soils that contain extra moisture without being waterlogged. Moisture-lovers include many herbaceous perennials, such as *Astilbe*, *Ligularia*, and *Primula florindae*. They all associate well

Pebble pool This pump-operated bubble fountain makes a minimalist but attractive feature in a paved area of the garden and will support irises and other plants while being safe and quite shallow.

with marginal plants in the areas surrounding natural, informal ponds where growing conditions are ideal.

Planting associations

Create a varied and attractive display by mixing plants with different heights and growth habits around the pond. Similar design principles should be applied as for planting in the rest of the landscape to develop a successful design with a diversity of shapes and forms (see also "Principles of planting," pp.42–49). Site *Gunnera manicata*, for example, so that its immense, platterlike leaves tower over the jutting swords of *Acorus calamus*.

Use plants at the edge of the pond to act as a foil for floating plants or deep marginals—an island of water lilies, such as *Nymphaea alba* with its pure white blooms, would be beautifully offset by a drift of ostrich-feather ferns (*Matteuccia struthiopteris*). Plants with contrasting colors and textures can also provide some spectacular combinations. For example, the upright, scarlet flower spikes of *Lobelia cardinalis* would form a fine contrast with the heart-shaped, blue-gray leaves of *Hosta sieboldiana*.

Plan the planting to supply interest throughout the seasons. Including evergreen foliage plants, such as *Bergenia* (species and hybrids), at the pond margins provides continuity of form and color, while other types of plant—ranging from the deep golden flowers of the marsh marigold (*Caltha palustris*) in spring to the summer-long display of the water forget-me-not (*Myosotis scorpioides*) with its delicate, blue flowers—may be used to create a changing seasonal display.

Fish

While most ornamental fish live in harmony with aquatic plant life and will be happy in all but the smallest ponds, the inclusion of larger specimen fish necessitates certain precautions in pond design. Depending on what kind of fish you have, it is important to check the depth if they are to be left over winter safely in the pond.

Ponds for koi, for example, should be large and at least 3ft (1m) deep, with vertical sides projecting above the surface so that the carp cannot leap out. Goldfish and mosquito fish, which are voracious eaters of insect larvae and algae, and are able to survive cold winters in a sufficiently deep pond.

In the wildlife garden, be certain to research appropriate species for your area to choose fish that are non-invasive and beneficial.

PLANTER'S GUIDE TO WATER PLANTS

DEEP-WATER PLANTS

Aponogeton distachyos
Euryale ferox
Nuphar advena, N. lutea
Nymphaea, some
Nymphoides indica, N. peltata
Orontium aquaticum
Victoria amazonica

DEEP MARGINALS

(12in/30cm depth of water)

Acorus calamus,
  A. calamus 'Variegatus'
Alisma lanceolatum,
  A. plantago-aquatica
Butomus umbellatus
Cyperus papyrus
Glyceria maxima 'Variegata'
Hottonia palustris
Iris pseudacorus
Nelumbo lutea,
  N. nucifera 'Alba Grandiflora',
  N. nucifera 'Alba Striata',
  N. nucifera 'Rosea Plena'
Phragmites australis,
  P. australis 'Variegatus'
Pontederia cordata,
  P. cordata var. lancifolia
Ranunculus lingua 'Grandiflorus'
Saururus cernuus
Schoenoplectus lacustris,
  S. lacustris subsp. tabernaemontani
  'Albescens', S. lacustris subsp.
  tabernaemontani 'Zebrinus'
Sparganium erectum
Thalia dealbata,
  T. geniculata
Typha angustifolia, T. latifolia
  'Variegata', T. laxmannii
Zantedeschia aethiopica
  'Crowborough'

SHALLOW MARGINALS

(6in/15cm depth of water)

Acorus gramineus,
  A. gramineus 'Variegatus'
Alisma plantago-aquatica
  var. parviflorum
Calla palustris
Caltha leptosepala, C. palustris,
  C. palustris var. alba,
  C. palustris 'Flore Pleno'
Carex elata 'Aurea', C. pendula,
  C. riparia
Colocasia esculenta
Cotula coronopifolia
Cyperus involucratus,
  C. longus,
  C. papyrus 'Nanus'
Decodon verticillatus
Eriophorum angustifolium,
  E. latifolium
Houttuynia cordata,
  H. cordata 'Chameleon',
  H. cordata 'Flore Pleno'
Hydrocleys nymphoides
Iris laevigata, I. versicolor
Juncus effusus, J. effusus f. spiralis,
  J. effusus 'Vittatus', J. ensifolius
Lobelia paludosa
Lysichiton americanus,
  L. camtschatcensis
Mentha aquatica
Mimulus cardinalis, M. cupreus,
  M. guttatus, M. ringens
Myosotis scorpioides,
  M. scorpioides 'Mermaid'
Peltandra sagittifolia
Persicaria amphibia
Sagittaria latifolia, S. sagittifolia,
  S. sagittifolia 'Flore Pleno'
Sparganium natans
Typha minima
Zizania aquatica

SUBMERGED OXYGENATORS

Callitriche hermaphroditica
Ceratophyllum demersum
Ceratopteris thalictroides
Crassula helmsii
Egeria densa
Fontinalis antipyretica
Hydrocleys parviflora
Lagarosiphon major

Mentha cervina
Myriophyllum aquaticum
Potamogeton crispus

SURFACE FLOATERS

Azolla filiculoides
Ceratopteris pteridioides
Eichhornia azurea, E. crassipes
Hydrocharis morsus-ranae
Lemna trisulca
Limnobium spongia, L. stoloniferum
Nymphaea
Nymphoides aquatica
Pistia stratiotes
Salvinia auriculata, S. natans
Stratiotes aloides
Trapa natans
Utricularia minor, U. vulgaris
Wolffia arrhiza

BOG AND MOISTURE-LOVING PLANTS

Alnus glutinosa, A. incana
Anemone rivularis
Aruncus dioicus 'Kneiffii'
Arundo donax var. versicolor
Astilbe × arendsii, A. chinensis,
  A. simplicifolia
Astilboides tabularis
Cardamine pratensis
Carex elata 'Aurea', C. pendula
Cornus alba
Darmera peltata
Eupatorium purpureum
Euphorbia palustris
Filipendula rubra, F. ulmaria
Gunnera manicata, G. tinctoria
Hemerocallis (most spp.)
Hosta (most spp.)
Iris ensata, I. sibirica
Leucojum aestivum
Ligularia dentata, L. przewalskii
Lobelia cardinalis
Lysimachia punctata
Lythrum salicaria
Mimulus cardinalis, M. luteus
Osmunda regalis

Parnassia palustris
Persicaria amplexicaulis,
  P. bistorta, P. campanulata
Phalaris arundinacea
Phragmites australis
Primula alpicola, P. denticulata,
  P. florindae, P. japonica, P. prolifera,
  P. pulverulenta, P. rosea,
  P. secundiflora, P. sikkimensis
Rheum alexandrae, R. palmatum,
  R. palmatum 'Atrosanguineum'
Rodgersia aesculifolia, R. pinnata,
  R. podophylla
Salix alba, S. babylonica,
  S. babylonica var. pekinensis
  'Tortuosa', S. daphnoides
Scrophularia auriculata 'Variegata'
Senecio smithii
Taxodium distichum
Trollius chinensis, T. × cultorum,
  T. europaeus

Zantedeschia aethiopica 'Crowborough'

Water lilies

The elegant, floating cups and lush foliage of water lilies such as *Nymphaea* are a graceful addition to any water garden, whether it is in a natural rural setting or a formal city courtyard. The flower forms vary from open and starlike to goblet-shaped peonylike blooms, with colors ranging from the simple purity of white or cream to striking shades of red, yellow, or even blue. Some are offset by dark purplish-green leaves, while others have foliage that is attractively mottled. Certain species have richly perfumed flowers; these are best grown in a raised pool where their scent may be easily enjoyed.

HARDY (H) AND TROPICAL (T) WATER LILIES

Nymphaea 'Attraction' (H)

N. 'Pygmaea Helvola' (H)

N. 'Fire Crest' (H)

N. 'Marliacea Chromatella' (H)

N. 'American Star' (T)

N. 'Blue Beauty' (T)

N. 'Escarboucle' (H)

N. 'Virginia' (H)

N. 'Marliacea Carnea' (H)

While most water lilies bloom in the daytime, some tropical cultivars such as 'Missouri' and 'Red Flare' open at dusk—these are best enhanced by complementary lighting to create a bold display after dark. Native to tropical and subtropical zones, these lilies may be grown in cold-winter regions in a conservatory pool or outdoors in hot summers.

Water lilies need several hours of full sun each day, otherwise they develop a mass of leaves but few blooms, so they should be grown in the open, sunny part of a pond. They also prefer calm water; if there is a fountain or waterfall, grow the lilies well away from it so that they are not disturbed by the movement. Tropical species usually grow more quickly than hardy ones and require high light intensity, an ample food supply, and warm water at a minimum of 68°F (20°C).

As well as being decorative, water lilies help to keep the water clear because their large, spreading leaves create shade, thereby helping to control the growth of algae.

Care and cultivation

Most water lilies have thick tubers that grow roughly vertically, with fibrous roots beneath; cultivars of *N. odorata* and *N. tuberosa* have longer, fleshy rhizomes that grow horizontally near the soil surface.

Planting
Plant hardy water lilies between late spring and late summer so that the plants will be well established before winter; do not plant out tropical water lilies until the risk of frost has passed.

For planting, use containers that are 12–14in (30–35cm) across and 6–7½in (15–19cm) deep, depending on the size and vigor of the cultivar. Alternatively, plant in submerged beds 12–18in (30–45cm) deep and 18–24in (45–60cm) square.

Prepare the plant by trimming back long roots and cutting off old or damaged leaves and flower buds. The older leaves make the plant more buoyant and difficult to anchor under water and they produce little food for the plant. New leaves will quickly replace them. When planting tropical water lilies, insert a tablet of slow-release fertilizer.

If the planted container is not too heavy, water well before placing it in the pond so that any soil shrinkage can be corrected. Lower the basket into place with strings as for planting deep-water plants (see p.299).

In a new pond, the containers may be positioned on the bottom before the pond is filled. Cover them with only 3–6in (8–15cm) of water initially; raise the containers on blocks if necessary, so that they have the correct depth of water above them. As the plants grow, gradually lower the containers in stages until they finally rest on the bottom. Tropical water lilies may be planted at their permanent depth immediately, however, since they grow quickly and prefer shallower water than most hardy cultivars.

Feeding
Water lilies usually benefit from limited additional feeding; insert a tablet of special slow-release water lily fertilizer into the soil approximately every six weeks during the growing season. This

PLANTING A TUBEROUS WATER LILY

1 Using pruners or a sharp knife, trim back to within 2in (5cm) of the tuber any roots that are damaged or excessively long.

2 Cut off any dead or damaged leaves, or those with broken stalks. Retain new, young leaves and flower buds.

3 Line the basket and partly fill it with dampened soil. Position the tuber so that the crown is within 1½in (4cm) of the rim.

4 Pack soil firmly around the tuber, ensuring that the crown remains 1½in (4cm) above the level of the soil.

A floating garden
The strong, straight lines of a wooden deck bridge offset the platelike leaves and colorful blooms of an island of water lilies.

gradually releases small quantities of plant food without discoloring the water or encouraging algae.

Other maintenance tasks
Water lily flowers last only three to four days and should be removed before they sink and rot, as should the leaves. These can turn yellow or brown quite quickly, depending on conditions; regularly cut their stems below the water line and discard.

During hot weather, spray leaf surfaces with a garden hose to dislodge insects such as leafhoppers and aphids. In areas subject to winter freezes, take in tropical water lilies and store the tubers at 41–45°F (5–7°C) in moist sand, and protect them from rodents.

Division
To maintain healthy growth, divide water lilies when the foliage is crowding the water surface, or when the roots have outgrown the container. Cut off pieces from the crown, each with a young, strong shoot and about 6in (15cm) of attached tuber, and replant these in fresh soil. The old crown may be discarded.

Propagation

Most tuberous water lilies may be propagated by means of bud cuttings; rhizomatous types may have their rootstocks divided (see p.302). Some water lilies may be raised from seed, or by separating plantlets.

Bud cuttings
Some tuberous water lilies produce sideshoots or "eyes" that may be used to propagate new plants. Cut the eyes from the roots and dust them with charcoal or sulfur. Press each cutting into a prepared pot, topdress, and immerse in water; leave the pots in a greenhouse or cold frame at 59–64°F (15–18°C). As the plants develop, repot them and gradually increase the water depth until fall. Overwinter in a cool place and plant out the following spring.

Seed
With the exception of *N. odorata* and *N. tetragona*, hardy water lilies do not readily set seed, but tender or tropical water lilies set large quantities. Before collecting seeds, enclose the ripening capsules in muslin bags to prevent them from floating away. Sow hardy seed at once, before it dries out; tropical water lily seed should be washed and allowed to dry, then stored in bags at room temperature. Tropical water lily seed is best sown in spring.

Sow the seed evenly, still attached to its jellylike bladders, in pans of seed-starting mix. Sprinkle with more seed mix, water, then place the pans in a container and cover with 1–2in (2.5–5cm) of water. Hardy water lily seed requires a minimum temperature of 55°F (13°C) to germinate, tropical seed 73–81°F (23–27°C).

When the seedlings are large enough to handle, carefully lift, rinse, and plant them in pans submerged in 2–3in (5–7.5cm) of water. Repot later into 2½in (6cm) pots in 3–4in (8–10cm) of water.

After overwintering, the tubers produce young plants that may be detached and potted.

Plantlets
Certain day-blooming, tropical water lilies produce plantlets that may form and bloom while still attached to the parent leaf. Alternatively, the plantlets may be transplanted into shallow pans in water and then grown on at a temperature of 59–64°F (15–18°C); gradually increase the water level, then repot them into aquatic containers.

PROPAGATION BY BUD CUTTINGS

1 Remove the plant from its container and wash it. Using a sharp knife, remove strong-growing buds from the root by cutting flush with the tuber.

2 Fill 4in (10cm) pots with soil or aquatic potting mix, firm, and press a single cutting into the surface. Topdress with grit.

3 Immerse the pots in water and keep them in a greenhouse or cold frame, partially shaded; plant out the following spring.

PROPAGATION BY DIVISION

1 In late spring, lift a mature clump when the leaves begin to appear. Dip the rhizome in water and wash the soil from the roots.

2 Cut the rhizome into sections, each with 2 or 3 growth buds. Remove any damaged or overlong roots. Pot each section and keep in shallow water until it shows signs of growth.

Constructing ponds and pools

For many years, garden ponds were generally constructed from heavy materials such as stone, concrete, or brick. Since the advent of plastics and fiberglass, however, it has become easier to install your own pond and also to create a more naturalistic design, if desired.

The best shape, size, and material for the pond depends to a large extent on the size and style of your garden, the preferred method of construction, and cost. Flexible liners allow you maximum freedom of shape and size, and are ideal where a natural look is required because the edge may be easily concealed and the lining material itself is relatively unobtrusive; they are the best choice for large ponds. Rigid, preformed ponds are easier to install, but there is only a limited range of shapes and sizes. While they are excellent for small ponds, larger units are difficult to maneuver and very large sizes are not available. Hard materials such as concrete provide the strongest and most long-lasting ponds but these are also the most difficult and slowest to construct.

Ponds built by any method can accommodate a simple fountain, or a pump that drives a recirculating water feature (see p.292). Pumps may be powered by a suitable, safe, external electricity supply; solar-powered pumps are also available.

Flexible liners

Most new garden ponds are constructed using a flexible lining sheet of synthetic rubber or plastic, which provides a waterproof barrier between the soil and the water. These flexible liners are available in a wide range of sizes and can be cut to fit any shape of pond. Before buying a liner, decide on the site and size of the pond: marking out the desired shape with sand or string and stakes makes it easier to check the placement.

Butyl rubber (or EPDM) is arguably the best pond-lining material. Butyl rubber is a natural rubber; EPDM is synthetic. Rubber liners are much stronger than PVC (polyvinyl chloride) liners, with a life expectancy of about 20 years for EPDM and 40 to 50 years for butyl rubber. Rubber is very pliable, and is tough enough to resist tearing or deterioration caused by ultraviolet light, bacterial growth, and temperature extremes. To line an informal pond, particularly if part of the material may be exposed to sunlight, it is best to use a topquality butyl liner that is ¼in (7mm) thick.

PVC liners are reasonably strong and tear-resistant, and some are guaranteed for ten years. They are resistant to both cold and fungal attack, but after several years of exposure to sunlight they may harden and crack. These liners are usually blue or black, or black on one side and beige on the other. It is usual to place them with the dark side on top because darker colors absorb light and heat and look more natural than lighter colors.

Measuring for the liner

To calculate the size of the liner required, first determine the maximum length, width, and depth of the pond. The liner should measure the maximum width of the pond plus twice its depth, by the maximum length plus twice its depth. Add 1ft (30cm) to both width and length measurements to allow for a flap at the edge of the pond, to prevent leakage. A pond measuring 6 x 8ft (2 x 2.5m) and 2ft (60cm) deep would require an 11 x 13ft (3.4 x 4m) liner.

Installation

First spread out the liner away from the site, in the sun if possible: the warmth will make it more flexible and easier to handle. Mark the required shape of the pond on the site with string and pegs, a hose, or a length of rope, then mark the soil just inside this line.

Dig to a depth of about 9in (23cm), making the pond sides slope outward at an angle of 20° from the vertical; this slope prevents the

MAKING A POND WITH FLEXIBLE LINER

1 Mark the proposed shape of the pond using sand or string. Then position marker stakes at equal intervals around it, setting the first stake at the ideal level for the pond edge.

2 Use a straightedge and level to align the remaining pegs with the first one. Then excavate the hole until it is 9in (23cm) deep all around. Slope the sides slightly outward.

3 Rake the base of the hole so that it is flat. If a marginal planting shelf is desired, make a line, 9–12in (23–30cm) wide, with sand all around the hole, for the shelf.

4 Dig within the marked central area to a further 20–24in (50–60cm) deep. Remove any roots and sharp stones, then rake over the base until it is level.

5 Press a layer of sand or sifted soil, 1in (2.5cm) deep, over the base and sides of the hole. If using a fabric underlayment, drape it over the hole's contours and press it down.

6 Carefully unroll the flexible liner over the sand or fabric until it is draped over the entire hole and there is generous overlap at the sides. Fold in the creases evenly.

7 Fill the pond with water, using bricks to hold the liner in position. Move the bricks as the liner settles. Trim its edges, leaving a 1ft (30cm) overlap.

sides from caving in, makes it easier to install the liner, and ensures that if the pond freezes the ice can expand upward without causing damage. Reserve the excess—such topsoil could prove invaluable elsewhere in the garden.

If planning to grow marginal plants, cut a shelf about 9–12in (23–30cm) wide to provide adequate planting positions, and then continue digging at a slight angle until the desired depth—normally 20–24in (50–60cm)—is reached. Check that the rim of the pond is level all around by using a straightedge and level across both the length and the width of the hole. This is extremely important, because if the pond is not level, water may spill over the edge. If including edging stones, remove 2in (5cm) depth of soil to a width of 12in (30cm) all around the pond, so the stones can be bedded in later.

Once the hole is excavated, remove any roots and sharp stones that could puncture the liner, and tamp the soil firmly. To protect and cushion the liner, spread an underlayer of fiberglass insulation or heavy-duty landscape cloth, or a 1in (2.5cm) layer of damp sand in the hole. Insulation or fabric are preferable because they are both stable and durable; sand may shift, leaving part of the liner exposed to damage from stones.

Drape the liner over the hole, so that the center touches the base, leaving an overlap on all sides. Anchor it all the way around before starting to fill the pond. Weighed down by the water, the liner will sink to mold itself into the contours of the pond. As more liner is required, remove some anchoring stones, tug the edges of the liner to make it straight, and form neat folds at the sides if it starts to crease.

When the pond is filled, remove the remaining stone weights and check again that the rim is level all around; add or take away soil if necessary until it is level. Cut off any excess liner, leaving a 6in (15cm) flap all around the edge; this surplus may be hidden beneath rocks, sod, or paving stones bedded on mortar (see also "Edging a pond," p.291). Take care not to let any mortar slip into the water; if this happens you should empty the pond and refill it.

Preformed ponds

The simplest ponds to install are those preformed from fiberglass or plastic. These are available in a variety of shapes and are often

PREFORMED MOLDS

Preformed fiberglass or plastic ponds are available in a wide range of sizes and shapes. Most designs include planting shelves for marginal plants.

contoured to provide ledges on which to grow marginal plants. Fibreglass ponds are more expensive than those made of plastic, but they are tough and weather resistant, with a life expectancy of at least ten years.

Installation

Level the site as much as possible and clear away any debris. If the mold is symmetrical in shape, invert it and mark its outline using pegs and string. For asymmetrical shapes, stand the mold the right way up, supporting it on bricks to prevent it from flexing and

cracking; mark the contours with long stakes, pushed vertically into the ground, and string or rope.

To dig a hole that matches the mold, first remove soil down to the level of the marginal shelf. The topsoil may be reserved for use in the garden, while the subsoil should be set aside for backfilling around the pond later. Place the pond in the prepared hole, and press it down firmly onto the earth to leave a clear impression of the shape of the base. Lift out the mold, then dig out the central, deeper area that has been marked out by the pond base, allowing

approximately 2in (5cm) extra depth all over the entire hole for the cushioning material.

Clear the hole of any sharp stones, tree roots, or debris, tamp the soil firmly, and line the excavation with pond underlay or a 2-in (5-cm) layer of damp sand, heavy-duty landscape cloth, or fiberglass insulating material. Put the mold in place and check that it is level, otherwise the water will run to one end when the pond is filled.

Ensure that the pond sits firmly on the bedding layer, then add about 4in (10cm) of water. With sand or sifted soil, backfill around the sides to the same depth as the water, ramming the soil firmly under the shelf; ensure that there are no gaps and that the pond remains absolutely level. Continue this process of adding water, backfilling, and checking the level until the pond is full. Finally, firm the soil around the pond and mask the edges with paving stones bedded on mortar or sod (see also "Edging a pond," p.291).

INSTALLING A PREFORMED POND

1 Firmly support the fiberglass or plastic mold with bricks to keep it level and upright, and then mark its shape by pushing a series of stakes into the ground all around the edges. Lay a length of rope around the canes to mark the precise outline that will need to be excavated.

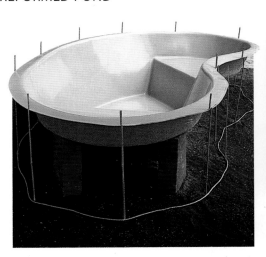

2 Excavate the hole 2in (5cm) deeper than the mold, following its profile of shelves and base as accurately as possible.

3 Use a plank of wood, laid across the width of the pond, and a measuring tape to check that the depth of the hole is correct, and use a level to check that the base is flat.

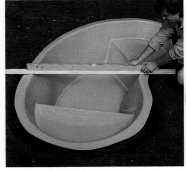

4 Remove any tree roots and sharp stones, and then line the hole with a 2in (5cm) layer of sand. Lower the mold into place and check with a level and plank that the mold is set level.

5 Fill with water (here pond water) to a depth of 4in (10cm). Backfill around it to the same depth with sifted soil or sand. Tamp firmly. Continue to add water, backfill, and tamp.

MAKING A CONCRETE POOL

1 Excavate a hole to the desired size. Dig a trench, 8in (20cm) wide, around the perimeter of the base. Presoak the trench, pour in concrete, tamp, and level with the hole base. Allow to dry.

2 Add a layer of sand to the soil base and firm it level with the concrete foundation trench. Skim the sand with a ½in (1cm) layer of fiber-reinforced cement, overlapping the concrete by 2in (5cm).

3 After 24 hours, build walling block walls onto the foundations. Fill the voids with a fairly stiff concrete mix. Once dry, fill the gap between the block and soil walls with the same mix.

4 To achieve a smooth, level top to the walls, mortar one or two courses of house bricks onto the walling blocks. Scoop up any excess mortar carefully, so that a smooth finish is achieved.

5 After 48 hours, first dampen then render the walls with a ½-in (1-cm) layer of fiber-reinforced cement. Build up a furrow where the base and side walls meet for additional corner strength.

6 Mortar coping stones (such as the paver bricks used here) onto the wall sides so there is a 2-in (5-cm) overlap on the inside of the pond.

7 After 48 hours, brush the interior walls of the pool to remove any debris. Then paint the whole inner surface with a commercial waterproof sealant.

Concrete ponds

Concrete is durable and suitable for ponds and pools of almost any size. It is often used for formal pools, where its rigidity is an advantage. Construction does, however, require more skill and expertise than is needed for installing a liner or preformed mold.

In areas prone to long periods of severe cold, concrete pools should be constructed with walls that slope outward at an angle of 30 to 45 degrees; this minimizes the risk of cracking, because it allows ice in the pool to expand upward and outward as it forms. Ponds of the same size that have vertical walls provide a larger area of deep water, which may be important if you plan to keep fish. Construction is more laborious than for a pool with sloping sides because the wet concrete has to be supported with a wooden form until it hardens (see below).

Construction

When digging the hole for a concrete pool, add an extra 8in (20cm) to all dimensions to allow for the volume occupied by the concrete; if there is to be a shelf for marginal plants, see "Flexible liners: Installation, " p. 288. Line the hole with 500-gauge plastic sheeting, then spread 2in (5cm) of concrete over the base. For added strength, place a sheet of galvanized wire reinforcing mesh over this and cover with a second 2in (5cm) layer of concrete. When the concrete has slightly hardened, roughen the surface around the edge to a width of 6in (15cm) to form a firm grip for the side walls.

After about 48 hours, or when the base is dry, install a vertical wooden form 4in (10cm) in from the sides, bracing it at the corners. Thoroughly soak the form with water, slide a piece of galvanized wire mesh between the form and the sides of the hole, then pour in the concrete. If a walled, marginal shelf is required, this form will need to be higher (see below). Leave the form for about two days to allow the

concrete to set completely. For a marginal shelf, repeat the procedure with another two stages as for the main body of the pond. Remove a band of soil around the pond edge to a depth of 3in (8cm); lay crushed stone in this area as a base for the edging stones.

A few days later, apply a sealant that prevents lime in the concrete from leaching out into the water and harming the plants and fish. Finally, fill the pond and check the alkalinity of the water with a pH test kit. If close to neutral (pH 7) it is safe to introduce plants, and, after a further two weeks, fish. If alkaline, this may be due to hard water or ineffective sealant. In either case, delay planting water lilies and marginals for a few weeks; the pH will gradually become more neutral. Oxygenators and surface-floaters generally tolerate alkaline water, and may therefore be introduced sooner.

Raised pools

The walls of raised pools must be strong enough to resist the pressure of the water; if necessary, seek professional help. Raised pools are far more vulnerable to frost damage than sunken ponds, and a minimum depth of 24in (60cm) is needed for fish in areas where the water is likely to freeze for even a short period of time. For more advice on the depth of water needed for keeping fish in your area of the country, consult a local expert or enthusiast; there are many businesses and amateur organizations interested in keeping fish in ponds.

Construction

The best way to construct a raised pond is with double walls, similar to house cavity walls. The exterior wall can be made from walling stones or bricks. The interior wall, which will be hidden, can be constructed with a cheaper brick or walling stone. The walls need to be close enough together to be

Raised pool
Wide slabs have been used for this contemporary raised pool so that the edge also forms a seat. The adjacent patio is also made from the same slabs in order to create a harmonious design.

CONSTRUCTING A CONCRETE POOL WITH A FORM

Making the pool
Line the pool area with plastic sheeting. Build the pool in stages, allowing the concrete to set at each stage. Lay the base first, using reinforcing wire mesh between 2 layers of concrete. Once set, install a vertical form braced at the corners, insert mesh between the pool wall and form, and pour in concrete. Repeat the process for a marginal shelf.

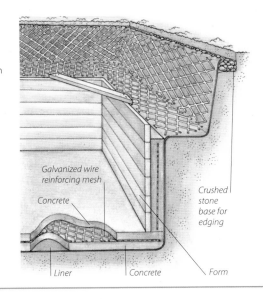

Galvanized wire reinforcing mesh

Concrete

Liner

Concrete

Form

Crushed stone base for edging

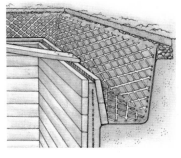

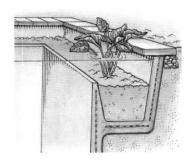

Making a walled marginal shelf
A walled marginal shelf allows direct planting. Proceed as before, making the vertical form higher to retain at least 9in (23cm) of soil (left). Once set, concrete the base of the shelf as before and then the outer shelf wall. After the concrete has set, lay the edging stones so that they will overlap the water by about 2in (5cm). Apply sealant and fill the marginal shelf with soil. Add the plants, then fill the pool with water (right).

linked with commercial, wire wall ties. A flexible liner is used inside the interior wall.

Mark the shape with string and pegs, then construct concrete foundations for the walls (see *Making a Concrete Pool*, opposite), 4–6in (10–15cm) deep and 15in (38cm) wide. Rake over the base, remove sharp stones, and cover with a layer of sand or polyester matting. Then construct the double side walls, incorporating wire ties at intervals to link the walls.

Lining a raised pool
The liner may be fitted so that an attractive stone or brick surface is exposed above the water on the inner wall: before laying the top two courses, fit the liner in the pool over the inner wall and into the cavity of the double wall. The top two courses

of the walls should then be mortared in place, securing the liner; the surplus liner is tucked underneath the coping. This prevents the appearance of conspicuous white "tide lines" on black liners when the water level drops in summer due to evaporation; it also ensures that no leakage occurs through the stone. Finally, mortar the coping stones on top of the double wall and cut off any surplus liner to create a neat edge to be covered by the coping.

Making planting beds

It may be desirable to plant vigorous water plants in permanent beds or containers such as large concrete pipes or trash cans rather than in planting baskets. These larger beds allow a greater root run and tall

plants are less likely to be displaced by wind. Beds may be sited on the marginal shelves or on the pond base for growing deep-water aquatics.

To build retaining walls on the shelves of a pond liner, first install the pond and fill it with water to stretch the liner into its ultimate shape, then lower the water level to expose the shelves. Protect the surrounding liner with a cushion of surplus liner scraps, then build the walls. The bed should be a minimum of 9in (23cm) deep and wide. Apply pond sealant to the bed (and allow it to set) before planting.

Edging a pond

While informal ponds can be edged in a naturalistic fashion with soil, sod, or rocks and pebbles, paving

may be desired to enhance the clean lines of a formal pool, or to create a small viewing area at one side of a pond. Safety must be the paramount consideration; slabs must be securely mortared down, on solid foundations if your soil is light. If slabs are to overlap the water, they must be mortared down; consult or hire a local contractor for information on how to do this properly and for maximum safety.

The choice of materials is also important for safety around water. Traditional, natural stone surfaces, such as old, reclaimed, sandstone paving, are likely to be extremely slippery in wet weather. By contrast, many precast concrete paving slabs have roughened or riven surfaces, making them more resistant to algae growth and less slippery.

STYLES OF EDGING

Formal pools require a crisp outline so straight- or curved-edged, precast concrete paving is ideal. For circular pools or ponds, small units such as waterproof bricks and granite or sandstone setts work well because they need no cutting. Similarly, irregularly shaped pavers can be used, with the shortest edges laid along the side to create the curve. Wooden decking is appropriate to both formal and informal ponds and pools because it is easy to cut and shape. For an informal pond, stone products such as washed cobblestones and small boulders make a gradual transition to surrounding plants, and are easy to lay.

Simple and easy edging
Conceal a flexible liner with rocks and stones that gradually decrease in size as they get closer to the water, creating a beachlike effect.

Informal but mortared
Align irregularly shaped slabs so that one side follows around the shape of the pond's rim. Always secure them with cement for safety.

Geometric formality
Manufactured paving blocks give a uniform and clean appearance to the edge of a pond. They must be mortared into position.

Constructing moving-water features

The principle behind all features in which water travels along any type of watercourse is that the water moves naturally from a higher to a lower point, where a powered pump drives it back through a delivery pipe to the top, or "head," of the feature. The gradient may only need to be very slight—in, for example, a formal canal—to achieve the desired effect. Steeper gradients may be used to create faster-moving streamlike features, perhaps with intermediate pools and waterfalls.

Pumps and filtration

Two types of pumps are available for landscape use: surface-mounted and submersible models. The power of pump required will depend on the volume of water to be moved and the gradient of the feature. A submersible pump is quite adequate for most small water features. Larger installations may need a surface-mounted pump housed in a separate, ventilated chamber.

If using a submersible pump, place it in the base or reservoir pool, raised on bricks or blocks to help prevent debris from being sucked into the inlet strainer. Link the reservoir and header pools with flexible pipe attached to the pump.

The pipe may be pushed down into the header pool to hide it; in this case, a check valve should be added. Alternatively, keep the end of the pipe above the water surface and disguise it at the pool edge with an overlapping stone or slab. Sink the pipe in a trench alongside the watercourse to conceal it.

Seek the advice of a professional electrician, if necessary, to install a safe external power supply. Only use approved waterproof connectors with pumps and other electrical fixtures. Protect outdoor cables with armored sleeving and always include a ground fault circuit interrupter.

In most circumstances, there should be no need for filtration. If there are large numbers of fish or if it is difficult to maintain submerged plants, physical or biological filtration may be needed. Filter kits that fit onto the suction inlet of submersible pumps are available, but larger installations may need a biological filter.

Using flexible liner

Flexible liners (see also p.288) are ideal for informal and meandering watercourses. They can be used to give a natural appearance, and the material easily enables changes of direction and width. The edges can also readily be disguised.

If the water movement is powered by a pump, the outlet for the proposed watercourse, usually a header pool, must contain enough water not to show major variations in level when the pump is turned on and off. One unobtrusive way of creating an outlet is with an underground header pool with a flexible liner. Cover the pool with heavy hardware cloth and place a layer of rocks and stones on top of it; the water pours out between the rocks into the watercourse. As well as the flexible liner, nonporous

rocks are needed to disguise the watercourse edges and to create waterfalls, while small pebbles or stones are attractive on the bottom of the watercourse.

Calculating liner size

The path, dimensions, and changes of level in the watercourse are the factors that determine how much lining material will be required.

If the route is fairly straight, one piece of liner may be used. This should be the maximum width plus twice the depth by the length of the watercourse, allowing for changes in height between the top and bottom, plus at least

---

CIRCULATING STREAM WITH WATERFALLS

Moving from the reservoir to the header pool, each pool should be raised higher to allow water to fall naturally, but must be deep enough to allow some water to be retained should the pump be switched off.

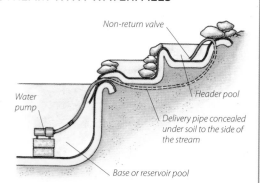

Non-return valve
Header pool
Delivery pipe concealed under soil to the side of the stream
Water pump
Base or reservoir pool

MAKING A WATERCOURSE WITH FLEXIBLE LINER

1 Build a soil bank to the required height, if necessary, and mark the watercourse, with the position and depth of any height changes. Working from the bottom, shape the steps and header pool.

2 When complete, compact the soil with the back of a spade. Remove sharp stones and line the course with a cushioning underlay of sand or a polyester mat, cut to fit.

3 Lay the liner in place, ensuring that the bottom edge generously overlaps the base pool. Cut to fit, leaving 12in (30cm) on each side. Smooth the liner into the contours of the channel.

4 Starting at the base, set rocks in place to form the steps. Tuck the edges of the liner behind the rocks. Backfill firmly with soil. Work upward, arranging rocks and pebbles so the water spills as desired (see right).

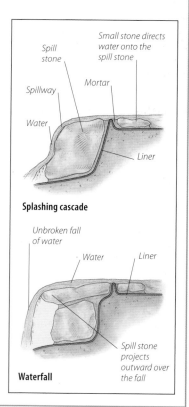

Splashing cascade

Spill stone
Small stone directs water onto the spill stone
Spillway
Mortar
Water
Liner

Waterfall

Unbroken fall of water
Water
Liner
Spill stone projects outward over the fall

MAKING A WATERCOURSE WITH RIGID UNITS

1 Mark the watercourse. Working from the bottom up, dig a shallow trench with a slight backward slope. Bed the first unit on soft sand, its lip slightly overlapping the edge of the pond.

2 Repeat the process up to and including the header pool. The lip of each unit should overhang the unit below it. Hide the delivery pipe in a 6in (15cm) trench dug alongside the stream.

12in (30cm) so that it can overlap into the base pools. A twisting watercourse is best made from a succession of liner pieces, each overlapping the one below it by at least 6in (15cm) to prevent leaks and avoid awkward folds. Allow for these overlaps when calculating the amount of liner needed.

Construction

If necessary, make a bank of soil slightly larger than the dimensions of the watercourse. Then mark the outline on the soil. Starting from the lowest point, cut steps into the bank to form the falls and cascades; the flatter sections— the "treads" of the steps—should be made with a slight fall in the opposite direction to the water flow so that they are covered by water even when the water supply is turned off. For the header pool,

dig a hole at the uppermost point at least 24in (60cm) square and 16in (40cm) deep. Rake the base and remove any sharp stones, then compact the soil with the back of a spade. Spread heavy-duty polyester matting or similar material over the course. The flexible liner may then be laid in the channel, allowing approximately 12in (30cm) of liner on either side, which will later form the side walls.

If using more than one piece of liner to form the length of the watercourse, overlap the pieces by 6in (15cm). Place the higher "piece so that it overlaps the lower one where there is a fall or downward slope so that water flows away from the seam. Dig a channel next to the watercourse for the pipe that will circulate water from the base to the header pool.

Set rocks in place to form the steps and sides of the watercourse, arranging them until the grouping is satisfactory. Use a hose or watering can to check that water spills over falls in the desired way. Then lift the liner at the sides behind the rocks and pack soil in to just above the waterline. For stability, mortar rocks into position with waterproof cement.

Using rigid units

Preformed modular units may be combined in several ways and installed to incorporate falls of different heights. Strong, interlocking units are unlikely to move should any future subsidence of the underlying soil or sand occur. Installation by two people is recommended, because final adjustments in levels may require lifting one side of a unit while backfilling with sand.

Mark the proposed area with string and dig out the watercourse to accommodate the units. Allow extra depth for a level layer of sand, 2in (5cm) deep, beneath them. Work from the bottom upward, positioning the lowest unit so that the lip overlaps the base pool and ensuring that it is level. Remove it and bolt on a vertical plate that determines the height of the waterfall. To ensure watertight seams, use a silicone sealant around each bolt. Install the linked units, making final adjustments by backfilling or removing excess sand so that they are level. Once the first unit is level, a small amount of water may be added to increase stability.

Additional units, and the final header pool, are then bolted on in the same way. Once each is

attached and the levels checked, partially fill the watercourse with water and backfill with sand around the outside edges as before. Install the pump, and conceal and soften the edges of the watercourse with rocks and plants.

Canals and formal rills

Canals and rills are a feature sometimes used in formal gardens to link raised pools or fountains or for adding emphasis to sculptures and urns. A canal only 12in (30cm) wide can have a dramatic impact. Because garden canals are shallow, they are best made of concrete. Bricks or glazed tiles used along the edge in a contrasting color to the surrounding paving will add emphasis. If pipes and cables will run beneath any surrounding paving, install conduit pipes accordingly.

After marking out the canal's width and length on a level site, excavate the area to a depth of 8in (20cm) and add a layer of sand 2in (5cm) deep. Check that the sides are level, then drape heavy plastic into the excavation and pour in concrete. Tamp it with a flat-sided piece of wood. Once the concrete has hardened, after 48 hours, construct the side walls using bricks mortared onto the base. If decorative brick pavers or tiles are to form the surrounding edges, mortar these at right angles to the wall bricks with a slight overlap on the inside edge of the canal. Once the mortar has hardened, skim the inside of the canal as shown below. In areas with severe winters, canals may need to be drained for the winter.

MAKING A CANAL OR FORMAL RILL WITH CONCRETE

1 Excavate the canal site to a depth of 8in (20cm). Cover the base and sides with soft sand, 2in (5cm) deep. Check the site for level, then line the canal with heavy-duty plastic.

2 Pour a 2-in (5-cm) layer of concrete onto the plastic, then tamp down and level it with a thin, straight plank. Check that the sides of the canal are at exactly the same height.

3 After 48 hours, mortar a course of bricks onto the foundations to make the canal walls. Mortar decorative pavers at right angles on top of the bricks, overlapping the inside edge of the canal by 2in (5cm).

4 After 48 hours, dampen and skim the floor and insides of the canal walls with a 1/2-in (1-cm) layer of fiber-reinforced cement. When dry, paint on a coat of waterproofing sealant.

Small water features

To look at their best, water features should be in scale with their surroundings. Fortunately, for small gardens, there are suitably diminutive features, including ones that recirculate water, which will fit into a variety of nooks and crannies. They can be used to provide an endless trickle of water over a brimming pot, a gurgling bubble fountain over pebbles, or a stylish fountain on a wall. Such moving-water features bring small spaces to life by introducing a mixture of sound and movement, adding an element of surprise, and providing a theme for interesting plant selections in the vicinity.

Small water features are much safer for small children than an open pond because there is little or no exposed water. They are also generally quick and easy to construct and there are no large volumes of soil to be disposed of. Those features that do not include aquatic plants, like the pebble fountain here, can also be sited in shade, whereas a planted pond could not. Maintenance is much easier, too, the main job being regular replenishment of water to compensate for losses by evaporation.

Wall fountains

Small, enclosed town gardens, courtyards, patios, and conservatories, where there is often insufficient space for a freestanding feature, make ideal situations for a wall fountain. These range from antique stone masks (or less costly plaster or fiberglass copies) to modern metal designs. A wall trellis can be used to hide the water delivery pipe between the reservoir pool and the fountain's spout. The reservoir must have enough capacity for prolonged running of the submersible pump: a minimum of 5–6 gallons (22–27 liters) is required for even a small wall fountain. The reservoir can be open and attractively planted (see below), or concealed below ground.

Cobblestone fountains

Another successful and popular small water feature is the cobblestone fountain, which has several variations on a theme—all basically relying on water being pumped up through cobblestones or pebbles, which are supported on a piece of galvanized-steel mesh, and falling back into a reservoir pool below ground.

Cobblestone fountains are available in kit form and provide a cheap, simple, and creative opportunity to enjoy moving water within the garden. One of their greatest fascinations can be the top of the water spout, which can be adjusted either to gush or bubble gently. The source of the water spout need be no more than a rigid tube from the pump—the wider the pipe, the more restful the

fountain becomes. The sound of the fountain changes as the height of the spout increases above the reservoir. A further refinement is possible by altering the water level: if the reservoir is full, splashing dominates the sound; if only half full the sound takes on an echoing dimension, emphasizing the cascading rivulets of water falling down beneath the stones.

INSTALLING A COBBLESTONE FOUNTAIN KIT

1 Dig a hole that is wider and slightly deeper than the tub reservoir. Insert the tub, using a level to ensure that it is level. Backfill around the sides, and firm the soil with a stick.

2 Lay a plastic sheet over the tub; cut out a circle 2in (5cm) smaller than the tub width. Connect the delivery pipe to the pump outlet. Put the pump on a brick at the bottom of the tub.

3 Center the galvanized-steel mesh over the hole in the plastic. Make a small hole in the mesh and feed the delivery pipe through it. Fill the bin with water to 6in (15cm) from the top.

4 Arrange a few cobblestones around the pipe and cut it to length. Then turn on the pump. Lift the mesh and experiment with the pump's flow adjuster until you achieve the desired fountain effect.

5 Add more cobblestones as required. Once the area onto which the water falls is established, trim the surplus plastic sheet, burying the edges, 4in (10cm) wide, under the soil. Alternatively, to allow for possible future enlargement, fold or roll up the surplus before burying it.

MOUNTING A SIMPLE WALL FOUNTAIN

1 Screw a trellis panel to battens on the wall. Thread the delivery pipe up behind the struts and connect to the mask's mouth. Screw the mask in place.

2 Connect the delivery pipe to the pump outlet. Stand the pump on a brick in the reservoir. Fill the reservoir with water, turn on the pump, and adjust the flow.

Finished feature
Planting in and around the reservoir conceals the pump, while climbers hide the trellis and vertical delivery pipe.

Natural and wildlife ponds

Most garden ponds attract some wildlife, but the more informal and natural they are, the more inviting they become to a wide range of creatures. You could be lucky and have a natural pond in your garden, but if not, it is possible to construct one that will have a naturalistic look and great appeal to wildlife.

A wildlife pond should be positioned where it can be viewed from a house window, yet not so close that shy creatures might be deterred from visiting. Ideally some vegetation should be planted on the far side of the pond, to give cover. A wildlife pond should also have a shallow beach at one edge, and a layer of soil over the bottom. The beach allows easy access for birds, amphibians, and small mammals, and the mud layer provides a home for many tiny creatures in summer and a hibernation spot in winter.

Lining a natural pond

Traditionally, natural ponds were lined with compacted or "puddled" clay to make them watertight, but the cost of importing clay has made this practice prohibitively expensive in all but heavy clay areas.

A more economical way to clay-line ponds is to use sodium bentonite. This powdered mineral clay swells to 10–15 times its volume when mixed with water, forming a waterproof gel. It is also available sandwiched in a tough, woven geotextile mat (see right), which, for ponds of more

than 50 sq m (60 sq yd), can be moved only with the use of heavy-lifting equipment.

Flexible, low-density polythene or PVC liners can be used, too. Such liners will be covered by a generous layer of soil, so they need not be resistant to ultraviolet deterioration.

Bog gardens make ideal companions for ponds and should be made independently with a separate lining, pierced in a number of places on the bottom to allow slow drainage.

Planting the pond

To encourage the maximum variety of wildlife, the planting in a natural pond should contain a high proportion of native species. Many of these are rampant and quickly smother smaller species, so it is a good idea to create pockets of different sizes and depths for different species (see also below).

The soil layer will encourage plants to spread. Tempting though it is to plant thickly for a natural effect, avoid really rampant growers in small ponds. Many of these have vicious root systems that can penetrate flexible liners. Eventually, even deeper zones may become choked by native marginals forming rafts with their thick, spongy roots, and periodic cutting back will be required. If not thinned, some native submerged species, such as water fringe (*Nymphoides peltata*) also tend to spread uncontrollably to cover the water surface, excluding sunlight. It may take some experimentation before a stable balance of planting is achieved.

Quick to establish
Native plants will rapidly cover a pond surface and must be chosen carefully if a clear area of water is required. Similarly, vigorous marginals will soon surround the pond, but keep open a small area for access.

WOVEN GEOTEXTILE MATTING

One option for lining a pond is bentonite in the form of a saturated, geotextile quilt, which can be draped over the pond excavation in overlapping strips. The matting is thick enough that it is not vulnerable to tunneling animals or most plant roots. It should be covered with a soil layer, 12in (30cm) thick, to prevent chemicals from leaching into the water.

Waterproofing
Line the hole with textile matting, and then conceal it with topsoil.

CREATING A VARIETY OF HABITATS

A great advantage of using a flexible liner in a water garden is the wide range of planting opportunities and levels you can provide, increasing the feature's attractiveness and usefulness to aquatic wildlife and other garden creatures. Varied environments maximize the range of sheltering, feeding, and breeding sites.

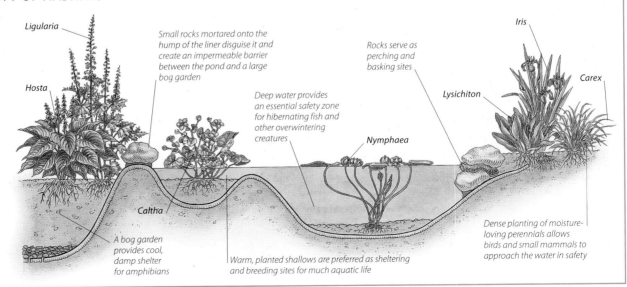

Ligularia

Hosta

Small rocks mortared onto the hump of the liner disguise it and create an impermeable barrier between the pond and a large bog garden

Deep water provides an essential safety zone for hibernating fish and other overwintering creatures

Rocks serve as perching and basking sites

Iris

Carex

Lysichiton

Nymphaea

Caltha

A bog garden provides cool, damp shelter for amphibians

Warm, planted shallows are preferred as sheltering and breeding sites for much aquatic life

Dense planting of moisture-loving perennials allows birds and small mammals to approach the water in safety

Water gardens in containers

Several factors determine the success of a container water garden. The plants must be carefully selected and then placed in appropriate light conditions if they are to achieve their potential. The pot should blend with its surroundings and provide an adequate depth and surface area of water to suit the chosen plants. Vigorous plants can quickly take over if the gardener fails to exercise proper control. The surface should also be partly covered with foliage, so the water does not become fouled by algal growth.

Choosing plants

There are one or two plants, notably the deep marginal lotus (*Nelumbo*), that are very effective used on their own in a small water garden. However, the more usual approach is to use a scaled-down mixture of conventional pond plants. Keep in mind that if you use any invasive plant species in your container water garden, never dispose of them in or near a natural water body.

The number that can be accommodated depends largely on the volume and surface area of the water. In a standard half-barrel, which holds about 12 gallons (50 liters), there is room for one dwarf or pygmy water lily, three or four shallow marginals, one or two plants of a noninvasive oxygenator, and a surface floater.

Siting the container

Be sure the container is correctly positioned before you fill it. Once full of water and plants, it will be heavy and difficult to maneuver. It must be on a firm, level surface and close to a water supply so that it can

Miniature pond

Surface floaters, including the tender water lettuce (*Pistia stratiotes*) and compact shallow marginals, such as a variegated Japanese rush (*Acorus gramineus*), crowd the surface of this pond made from a half-barrel. Marginals are planted in special aquatic baskets and placed on bricks so that they stand just above the water surface.

be topped off as necessary. The ideal site is sheltered, but well away from trees, and in sun but shaded during the hottest parts of the day.

Planting

Cover the base of the container with 2in (5cm) of washed gravel, then fill two-thirds full of water. Plant aquatics individually in ordinary garden soil in plastic-mesh baskets lined with burlap to keep the soil from washing out. Place the plants deep in the baskets, work the soil

around the roots, and firm in gently so that the finished surface is 1in (2.5cm) below the rim. Topdress with washed gravel. Stand containers of marginals on bricks so that the plants reach the water surface (see *Planting depths*, p.298). Finish filling the pool slowly to within 2in (5cm) of the rim to avoid disturbing the soil in the planting baskets. If you are including surface floaters in the planting design, add them after the container has been filled.

AQUATIC PLANTS FOR CONTAINERS

Shallow marginals (6in/15cm depth of water)
Acorus gramineus 'Ogon',
 A. gramineus 'Variegatus'
Caltha palustris
Iris laevigata
Juncus effusus f. *spiralis*
Myosotis scorpioides

Deep marginals (12in/30cm depth of water)
Cyperus papyrus 'Nanus'
Nelumbo 'Pygmaea Alba'

Deep-water plants
Nuphar pumila
Nymphaea 'Aurora', *N. candida*,
 N. 'Ellisiana',
 N. 'Laydekeri Liliacea',
 N. 'Laydekeri Purpurata',
 N. 'Laydekeri Rosea Prolifera',
 N. odorata var. *minor*,
 N. 'Helvola', *N. tetragona*

Submerged oxygenators
Eleocharis acicularis
Fontinalis antipyretica

Surface floaters
Azolla filiculoides
Pistia stratiotes
Wolffia arrhiza

PLANTING A CONTAINERIZED WATER GARDEN

1 Presoak the barrel to swell the wood and make it watertight, then set it on a level base. Cover the bottom with gravel. Fill two-thirds full with water.

2 Line a plastic-mesh basket with burlap, fill it with garden soil, and place plant in soil. Topdress with gravel or coarse grit.

3 Lower oxygenators, water lilies, and other deep-water plants carefully onto the bottom of the barrel so as not to disturb the soil in each basket.

4 Place bricks or half-bricks on the bottom of the barrel to raise the height of any container holding marginal plants.

5 Adjust the bricks until the plant is slightly exposed above the water's surface. Top off the barrel to within 2in (5cm) of the barrel's rim, if needed.

Planting and stocking

While most plants are grown for their ornamental features, some also help to maintain the quality and appearance of water by keeping down algae (see "Water garden plants," p.284). There is a wide range of planting containers available, allowing flexibility when planting and making routine maintenance relatively simple.

SELECTING PLANTS FOR THE WATER GARDEN

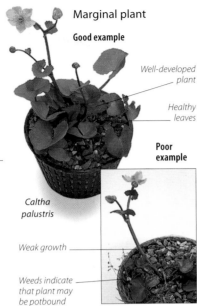

Marginal plant

Good example

Well-developed plant

Healthy leaves

Poor example

Caltha palustris

Weak growth

Weeds indicate that plant may be potbound

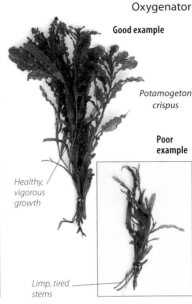

Oxygenator

Good example

Potamogeton crispus

Poor example

Healthy, vigorous growth

Limp, tired stems

Surface floater

Good example

Young, fresh growth

Poor example

Stratiotes aloides

Damaged growth

Old, rotting foliage

Selecting water plants

When selecting plants, look for clean, fresh-looking, and vigorous specimens, growing in tanks that are free from algae and duckweed (*Lemna*). Check that the undersides of the leaves are free from jellylike deposits of snail or whelk eggs, and that there are no strands of blanketweed in the foliage. Mail-order plants should appear plump and green; if they look weak and limp, they are unlikely to grow well.

A good nursery or other supplier will be able to advise on the quantities of plants to buy, so that you obtain the required delicate balance between submerged, oxygenating plants (such as *Ceratophyllum demersum*) and floating-leaved plants (such as water lilies). The latter should cover one-third to half of the water surface to provide some shelter from the sun. If buying plants by mail order, use a specialty supplier. It is worth paying a slightly higher price because the plants are more likely to be disease-free, and to have been propagated in the nursery. Reputable suppliers should pack the plants with care, and dispatch them on the same day they are lifted.

When buying oxygenators for a new pool, you should allow at least five bunches for every square yard or meter of water surface. They are often sold as bunches of unrooted cuttings about 9in (23cm) long. They should be weighted at the

bottom with a stone or other object to keep the plants anchored, in case they become loosened after planting.

Oxygenators are extremely susceptible to drying out, so they should be kept moistened in a plastic bag or submerged in water until they are ready for planting.

Containers and planting beds

The most convenient way of growing aquatics is in specially-made baskets or crates. This makes it easy to lift and divide or replace the plants when necessary, and it is also a relatively simple matter to alter the planting arrangement when desired. Plastic pots and flexible pots made of tightly woven fabric are also available especially for use with aquatic plants.

Commercial containers

Aquatic containers have wide, flat bases to provide stability in the water, which is important for tall marginals on narrow shelves. Containers have open lattice walls, allowing water and gases to circulate through the soil. Most should be lined with close-weave landscape fabric or burlap to prevent soil from seeping out, although very fine-mesh containers eliminate the need for a liner.

Containers range in size from 16 x 16in (40 x 40cm) square with a 6½ gallon (30 liter) capacity, suitable for medium-sized water lilies, down to 1½in (4cm) in diameter with a 2 fl oz (50ml) capacity, for aquarium planting. Larger, circular tubs without lattice walls are also available for vigorous water lilies.

Planting directly in soil beds

In wildlife ponds, aquatics can be planted directly into soil on the bottom and on marginal shelves. In most ponds, however, this is inadvisable since the vigorous species spread rapidly, swamping their slower-growing neighbors. In addition, subsequent removal or thinning of plants can be difficult.

Permanent beds

A good compromise is to build permanent planting beds on the pool base and around the edges during construction, which are easily planted before the pool is filled (see also "Making planting beds," p.291). This maintains a natural appearance while controlling the plants' spread.

Planting

The pond should be filled with water a few days before planting to allow the water temperature to reach that of the surrounding air, and to mature. During this period the pool may become populated with micro-organisms that disperse impurities in the water and create an environment beneficial to plants, fish, and other pond life.

Unlike the majority of terrestrial plants, aquatics should be planted while in active growth, preferably between late spring and midsummer. If planted in late summer and early fall, the plants have little time to become established before they die back. Water lilies need time to build up food reserves before winter if they are to survive and grow satisfactorily the following season.

The planting medium

Aquatic plants grow well in good garden soil, preferably a clay soil; if possible, use soil that has not been fertilized or manured recently. Sift out any loose organic matter. This will rot or float when the planting crate is submerged. Old sod that has rotted down thoroughly for a few months makes ideal aquatic compost. If the suitability of the garden soil is in doubt, buy aquatic compost from a specialty supplier.

Commercial potting mixes made for terrestrial plants should not be used for aquatics; as well as peat or peat substitute, which tends to float, they contain added fertilizers, which will encourage the growth of algae (see p.300).

PLANTING BASKETS

Planting baskets are available in various sizes to suit different plants. All except those with a very close-weave mesh should be lined.

Standard mesh

Close-weave mesh

Planting depths

The ideal planting depth varies, depending on the plant type, and can differ even within a group of plants. Measure planting depths from the top of the soil in the crate to the water surface (see right).

It is important not to plant too deeply: without adequate sunlight for photosynthesis, plants will die. When planting young specimens, it may be necessary to stand the containers on bricks or blocks at first so that the plants are not submerged. As the plants grow, gradually lower the crates until they reach the appropriate depth.

Bog and moisture-loving plants

The area bordering a natural pond is ideal for bog and moisture-loving plants, but correct growing

conditions can be supplied next to a man-made pond by creating special beds.

Mark the planting beds, then dig out at least 18in (45cm) depth of soil, removing any roots of perennial weeds, such as couch grass. Form sloping sides at the edges. Drape a flexible liner (thick-gauge plastic is suitable for this purpose) into the hole, ensuring that the top edge of the liner finishes just below the existing soil level.

Although a number of vigorous, moisture-loving plants tolerate saturated soil, most of them will grow better if the liner is pierced to allow some slow seepage of water from the bed. This slight movement of water through the soil also helps to prevent stagnant conditions from developing. Cover the drainage holes with gravel so that they do not become clogged up with soil.

Simplify watering in summer by sinking a perforated, rigid pipe into the bed. The pipe should be blocked at the far end and covered with a layer of gravel or stones to prevent the holes from becoming blocked with soil. Fit the end of the pipe to a hose connector, which should remain above the soil surface.

Refill the bed with soil, and then mulch with a deep layer of coarsely sifted organic matter to prevent moisture loss. Do not incorporate bulky additives throughout the whole bed since sufficient moisture is retained by the liner.

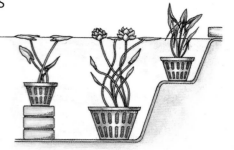

PLANTING DEPTHS

Place plants at the appropriate depth for the species, measured from the top of the soil to the water's surface. When planting young water lilies (*Nymphaea*), raise the crates on bricks. Lower the crates as the plants grow.

Planting, which is best done in spring, is carried out in the same way as in ordinary soil, although the whole bed should be thoroughly soaked afterward. Plants should be placed in the hole at the same depth as they were in the container. Plants that enjoy moist conditions will grow vigorously, so very invasive species are best confined to sunken containers to prevent them from crowding out other plants.

Marginal plants

Primarily included for their ornamental flowers or foliage, marginal plants are grown at the pond edges with their roots in shallow water. Ornamental ponds usually include a shelf to accommodate marginal plants, which may be grown either in baskets or in pockets built directly onto the shelf (see also "Making planting beds," p.291).

Most marginals require about 3–6in (8–15cm) of water above their crowns; it may be necessary to raise the baskets to ensure that plants are at the correct depth until they are established. The more vigorous species, known as deep marginals, should be planted in 12in (30cm) or more of water, either on a deeper shelf or on the bottom, away from the margin.

When planting marginals, note their height, spread, and vigor. Plant rampant growers singly in containers to keep them from smothering slower-growing plants. If planting in containers, make sure that there is sufficient room for root development; for most marginals, a container at least 9in (23cm) in diameter is needed. Plant marginals in prepared containers or planting beds of soil and topdress with pea gravel; if using containers, place them on the marginal shelf or the bottom of the pond, as appropriate, so plants are at the correct depth.

CHOOSING OXYGENATING PLANTS WITH CARE

When planting a pond in temperate regions, surface-floating plants can discourage algal growth. Many plants sold for this purpose are from tropical areas, so must be used with caution anywhere other than very small ponds and aquaria.

The floating species to avoid are water hyacinth (*Eichhornia crassipes*), water lettuce (*Pistia stratiotes*), water clover (*Marsilea quadrifolia*), water chestnut (*Trapa natans*), butterfly fern (*Salvinia auriculata*), and fairy moss (*Azolla filiculoides*). Although many of these would be killed by frost in temperate ponds and waterways, there is a greater risk of some surviving as global temperatures rise. These gradually choke waterways—as has already occurred in some warmer regions.

Be very careful not to introduce certain species, sometimes sold as oxygenators, that spread fast

and are difficult to eradicate. Two highly invasive species in most of North America are Eurasian milfoil (*Myriophyllum spicatum*) and parrotweed (*M. aquaticum*). Some other species of *Myriophyllum* are not as rampant. Swamp stonecrop (*Crassula helmsii*) is another invasive to use with caution, especially in areas where water never freezes.

Curly water thyme (*Lagarosiphon major*) is a submerged oxygenator from Africa. Cut back regularly to keep in check; remove dead stems to keep them from decomposing in the water.

Water crowfoot (*Ranunculus aquatilis*) is from temperate parts but still spreads fast. Its stems are submerged, but the floating leaves and flowers will give some shade.

PLANTING OXYGENATORS

Incorporating oxygenating plants is one of the first priorities when planting in a new pond. This is because their cleaning and oxygenating properties are vital to the health of the fish population and the oxygen content of the water.

Keep plants wet after buying them and until you are ready to plant them. Even during the planting process, they should not be left exposed to the air longer than is absolutely necessary.

Species vary in the rate with which they oxygenate the water, depending on the time of year and the pH of the water, so plant a selection of four or five species to ensure that enough plants thrive to maintain correct oxygen levels throughout the year. Keep a single species in each container to prevent stronger-growing plants from crowding out less vigorous species.

Prepare a planting crate and make planting holes in the soil, then insert a group of cuttings into each hole and firm them in. Cover the soil with grit or ½–1in (1–2.5cm) gravel, water thoroughly, and place the crate on the bottom of the pond at a depth of 18–24in (45–60cm).

Almost fill a lined crate with damp potting mix. Plant bunches of cuttings (here, *Lagarosiphon major*). Trim off excess liner, then topdress the soil.

Deep-water plants

As with marginals, these plants are usually grown in aquatic containers or planting beds. Most of them are best planted fairly shallowly at first so that their leaves are able to float and photosynthesize in the sun.

Whether planting in beds or freestanding containers, settle the plants firmly in the soil because they are very buoyant and may be dislodged. Always plant in moist soil, and soak containers well before immersing them in the pool. A topdressing of small gravel or pebbles to a depth of 1in (2.5cm) prevents soil from floating out and clouding the water and discourages fish from disturbing the plant roots.

When submerging the containers in deep water, thread string through the sides to form handles; this makes it much easier to position the crate, because it may then be gradually lowered onto the bottom.

Stocking with fish

Fish are best introduced to the pool during the warmer months. In cooler temperatures, fish become semidormant and are more prone to stress when moved. Allow at least two weeks after planting before stocking the pool with fish to allow plant roots to establish.

Unless there is supplementary filtration, overstocking with fish may encourage algae, which feed on excess waste. As a guide, calculate a maximum of 20in (50cm) of fish body length (when fully grown) per square yard or meter of water surface or 2in (5cm) per 1 sq ft (1,000 sq cm). It is advisable to stock the pool in two stages, introducing half the fish eight to ten weeks before the rest. This allows the bacteria that feed on the fish waste products to multiply to a sufficient level to deal with the waste. If too many are introduced at once, the water may become polluted and the fish starved of oxygen. Leaving a fountain or waterfall on overnight, to agitate the water will provide temporary relief.

Fish are usually supplied in a large, clear plastic bag containing a small amount of water and inflated with oxygen. On arrival, do not release the fish right into the pond: they are very sensitive to sudden changes in temperature, and the water in the pond is likely to be colder than that in the bag. Float the bag unopened on the water until the water temperature in the bag is the same as in the pond. In hot, sunny weather, shade the bag with a cloth. A small amount of pond water may be gradually introduced into the bag before the fish are released. Do not lift the bag to examine the fish closely—this causes them extreme stress.

Other water creatures

As well as fish, a number of other aquatic life forms can be introduced to the pond as scavengers. Trapdoor snails are often sold specifically for this purpose. Ordinary pond snails are likely to be a nuisance, because they eat water lily leaves.

For larger ponds, mussels and freshwater clams are excellent scavengers, cleaning up where ornamental fish have been overfed. Mussels require a pan of coarse sand 2–3in (5–8cm) deep in which to burrow.

DEEP-WATER AND MARGINAL PLANTS

1 Choose a planting crate to accommodate the plant roots and line it with burlap or close-weave polypropylene.

2 Fill the crate with heavy, moist soil mix to a depth of at least 2in (5cm). Set the plant (here, *Aponogeton distachyos*) in the center of the crate.

3 Fill with more potting mix to within ½in (1cm) of the rim of the crate, firming the plant in well to give it good anchorage.

4 Topdress the container with washed grit or pea gravel to a depth of 1in (2.5cm).

5 Trim away any surplus liner with scissors. Tie string handles to the rim of the crate on opposite sides.

6 Hold the crate by the string handles and gently lower it onto blocks or the marginal shelf. Release the handles.

ADDING FISH TO A POND

Float the unopened bag until the water temperature in the bag matches that of the pond. Slowly introduce some pond water to the bag before gently releasing the fish.

Routine care

Good construction and siting and ensuring the right balance of water, plants, and fish should help keep a pond relatively trouble-free, but occasionally structural repairs may be necessary, if the pond is damaged or leaks, for example. Algae and weeds must also be kept in check, while many plants will benefit from periodic division.

Structural repairs

Any sudden or persistent loss of water is likely to indicate a leak. If a pond is leaking, it will be necessary to drain and inspect it. The fish and plants can be accommodated in a suitable container, such as a wading pool. Most ponds can be drained either with an electric pump or by siphoning off the water. Check first that the pond's edges are level; water may be overflowing at the lowest point. With a watercourse, switch off the pump and check the level in the base pool: if constant, the leak is in the watercourse.

Flexible liners
If the water level in a lined pond drops or the flow of water in a watercourse decreases, check that no part of the edge of the liner has slipped below water level. Leaks may also be caused by punctures. The simplest way to repair a rubber liner is with double-sided adhesive tape obtainable from water garden suppliers. This is used to secure a patch of rubber liner over the hole. The pool may be refilled after one hour.

Preformed ponds and units
If a pond or watercourse unit is inadequately supported or the ground underneath it is not properly compacted, it may eventually crack under the weight of the water. Repair cracks with a fiberglass repair kit as used for car bodies and boat hulls. Position any patch on the underside of the unit so that it is hidden from view in clear water. Allow the compound to harden thoroughly because it may be toxic when liquid. Before

REPAIRING A FLEXIBLE POND LINER

1 Dry the area of damaged liner and then clean it carefully with denatured alcohol and a soft cloth.

2 Apply special double-sided adhesive sealing tape over the tear and allow it to become tacky.

3 Cut out a patch from spare liner and press it firmly onto the adhesive, ensuring that the edges are stuck down flat.

refilling with water, ensure that the base is firmly bedded down and that soil is compacted around the sides to support the water pressure.

Concrete ponds
The most common cause of leaking is through cracks created by frost damage or subsidence. Inspect the pool carefully because water can escape through even a hairline crack. If the crack is very fine, it is usually necessary to widen it slightly and brush clean any loose debris before sealing it with mortar. Leave the mortar to dry, then paint it with sealant.

Water quality

Once a good balance of plants and animal life is established, the water should remain clear without needing further attention. If there are marked changes in the number of fish or plants, or if there is a sudden introduction of tap or flood water, however, the water balance may be upset and a surge of unsightly, algal growth may result.

Algae
Algae depend on sunlight, carbon dioxide, and dissolved mineral salts for their survival. Reduce the amount of light that they receive by growing sufficient plants (water lilies, deep-water aquatics, and floaters) so that their floating leaves cover between 50 and 70 percent of the water surface. The introduction of oxygenating plants, which absorb minerals and carbon dioxide, helps starve the algae. In addition, regularly remove dead and decaying leaves and flowers.

Green water due to algal growth may occur in a newly planted pond, or one that has recently been cleaned. Normally this problem

clears itself. If not, control the algae by anchoring a fine-net bag filled with barley straw under the water or by using a commercial pad of barley straw. You should replace these every four to six months.

If the water is persistently cloudy, it may be necessary to check it with a simple pond test kit. If this shows the water is very acidic or alkaline, there are commercial pH adjusters in simple-to-use, granular form, which should be applied according to the manufacturer's instructions.

Blanketweed
A filamentous form of algae called blanketweed (*Spirogyra*) is sometimes found in ponds with otherwise clear water; if left unchecked, it chokes the plants and restricts the free movement of fish. Remove periodically by winding it onto a stick or lifting it out with a garden rake; in severe cases use an algicide. Clear out the dead material quickly, since decaying matter will reduce the water's oxygen content.

REPAIRING A CRACK IN A CONCRETE POND

1 If a crack is very fine, use a club hammer and chisel to widen it slightly.

2 Clean off any algae and debris from the surrounding area with a wire brush.

3 With a trowel, fill the crack with mortar or a commercial sealing compound. Allow it to dry.

4 Brush with a pool sealing compound to prevent any toxins from leaching into the water.

REMOVING BLANKETWEED

Insert a stick into the mass of blanketweed (*Spirogyra*) and twist it. The weed wraps around the stick and may then be pulled free.

THINNING OUT AN OVERGROWN OXYGENATOR

1 In spring or fall, thin out overgrown submerged plants, either by combing them off the water's surface with a rake, or by lifting out the basket and trimming back with a sharp knife.

2 Thinning out oxygenating plants prevents them from becoming congested. Do not remove too much growth, however, or this may leave the pond's surface area too exposed to sunlight, and allow algae to proliferate. Oxygenators are best thinned little and often.

FLOATING LOG

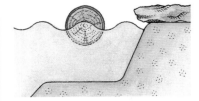

In freezing conditions, floating a log or ball on the water will absorb the pressure of the ice and help prevent cracks in pond walls. Break up the ice occasionally, to oxygenate the water (*very gently*, to avoid harming fish).

Pond cleaning

If the water is kept clear of fallen leaves and the plants are regularly trimmed, it should only be necessary to clean the pond every few years to remove decaying organic matter from the base (see also *Weed-infested Ponds*, p.649). After cleaning, the water chemistry must again be carefully balanced.

Plant care and control

Water plants do not require much attention, but periodic division and repotting helps to keep them healthy and attractive. Their overall vigor normally makes it necessary for them to be kept in check rather than encouraged, although certain water lily cultivars will require some feeding (see p.286).

Thinning out and division

In late spring or early fall, thin out or divide plants that are overgrown or crowding their neighbors. Lift container-grown plants and check whether they have become root-bound. If so, remove the plants from their containers and divide them with back-to-back forks or by hand. Tight and thick roots may need to be split with a spade or a knife. Replant the divided clumps singly.

After the first growing season, submerged oxygenating plants may become overgrown and entangled with weeds. In small ponds, the oxygenators are easily thinned by pulling out a few handfuls; in larger ponds, use a garden rake to comb out excess growth.

Alternatively, lift the container from the pond and cut back the plants by a third to a half. Do not thin out all the plants drastically at any one time because this causes a sudden change in the water balance and encourages algal growth.

Fall maintenance

The most important task in the fall is to keep the water free from decaying vegetation. When the waterside plants begin to die down, remove dead and dying foliage regularly and prune back the excess growth of submerged plants. If there are deciduous trees and shrubs nearby, cover the pond surface with a fine-mesh plastic net to catch leaves, and keep it in place until the trees are bare of foliage.

In cold areas, protect tender plants by removing them from the pond and placing them in a bucket of water to overwinter in temperatures that remain above freezing. Cut off the ripe seed pods of invasive plants to prevent them from setting seed. Before they go into hibernation for the winter, feed the fish with floating wheat-germ pellets.

If a pump is fitted, remove it from the pool and clean it thoroughly. Replace any parts that may be worn, and store it in a dry place until spring.

Winter care

In winter, ice may form, trapping methane gas released by submerged, decaying vegetation, with potentially lethal effects on the fish. Ice also exerts pressure on the sides of concrete ponds as it expands and may cause them to crack. Ensuring that a small area of the pond remains ice-free prevents this and allows methane to escape into the air. Either float a log on the surface or use a floating electric pond heater. This gives out just enough heat to maintain a small area of open water.

Pests and diseases

Pests are less of a problem in ponds stocked with fish, because fish eat the insect larvae. Infestations can be cleared by hand or washed off plants with a hose; insecticide sprays are unsuitable for water gardens and are highly toxic to fish. In late summer aphids (p.654) often attack water lilies and other aquatics, causing decay and discoloration. Dislodge them with a jet of water or submerge the leaves for 24 hours, weighting down affected parts with burlap.

Diseases affecting aquatic plants are relatively few, and mostly concern water lilies. Fungal disease is indicated by the premature yellowing or spotting of the leaves. If the symptoms persist, treat the plant with copper fungicide in a separate tank.

REPOTTING A MARGINAL

1 Plants that are growing in containers will eventually become root-bound and need thinning out. Roots protruding through the container wall indicate that a plant should be divided and repotted into a larger basket.

2 Remove the plant from its container and divide it into smaller clumps, teasing the roots out by hand. Very tightly packed roots may be pried apart with hand forks used back-to-back.

3 Repot each clump in a separate container filled with damp soil. Water well and topdress with grit or pebbles before placing in the pool. Trim off surplus burlap with scissors.

Propagation

Most water plants, especially marginals, can be propagated by division. Other methods are also used, depending on the type of plant: many submerged oxygenators and some creeping marginals, for example, are propagated by cuttings, while a number of floating plants naturally produce runners, plantlets, or turions, which grow into new plants. Moisture-loving species that grow around the pond edge, as well as some aquatics, can be raised from seed or increased by division.

Cuttings are best taken and plants divided in spring or early summer, when high temperatures and long daylight hours provide excellent conditions for new plant growth.

WATER PLANTS FROM CUTTINGS

Bacopa monnieri
Cabomba caroliniana
Callitriche hermaphroditica
Ceratophyllum demersum
Decodon verticillatus
Egeria densa
Elodea canadensis
Hydrilla verticillata
Hydrocleys parviflora
Hygrophila polysperma
Lagarosiphon major
Limnophila heterophylla
Ludwigia arcuata
Myriophyllum
Potamogeton crispus
Trapa natans

WATER PLANTS TO DIVIDE

Tubers

Aponogeton distachyos
Colocasia esculenta
Nelumbo nucifera
Zantedeschia

Rootstock

Acorus calamus
Butomus umbellatus
Calla palustris
Caltha palustris
Cryptocoryne ciliata
Damasonium alisma
Darmera peltata
Decodon verticillatus

Nelumbo nucifera

Division

A large number of marginal plants may be readily propagated by division. The exact technique that should be used depends on both the plant's root system and its pattern of growth. For further information, see "Dividing perennials," p.198.

Plants with fibrous or creeping roots

Plants that have extensive fibrous or creeping roots, such as *Colocasia esculenta*, can be divided by pulling apart the rootstocks. Simply pull the rootstocks apart with your hands; if the roots are tightly compacted, use two garden forks positioned back-to-back and pry them apart.

Each divided portion should include a growing point (a horizontally placed, terminal shoot). Cut off the old, brown roots and remove any dead leaves. Trim the new roots before replanting the divided portions in individual containers. Level the soil with the base of the shoots. Firm them in, then topdress lightly with a layer of gravel. Cover the container with approximately 2–3in (5–8cm) of water.

Butomus umbellatus may be divided, but may also be propagated from bulbils that form in the axils of the leaves. These are separated and then grown on individually (see LILIES, *Propagating from Stem Bulbils*, p.239).

Rhizomatous plants

For plants with strong, rhizomatous roots, such as irises, pull apart the root mass and divide it into sections with a sharp knife, each containing at least one bud and preferably some young roots. Cut off any long roots and trim back the foliage,

if needed. Do not trim the foliage back to below the water line, because the newly cut surface tissue may begin to rot.

Plant the division in a suitable container, firming the soil around the roots but leaving the rhizome itself almost exposed. Cover the soil with a layer of gravel and immerse

---

PROPAGATING BY CUTTINGS

1 In spring and summer, cut off healthy young shoots. Tie with wire into small bunches of three to six cuttings 4–6in (10–15cm) long.

2 Using a dibber, make holes in damp soil in a prepared planting crate lined with burlap. Insert the bunches of cuttings to a depth of about 2in (5cm).

the crate in the pond so that the roots are covered by about 2–3in (5–8cm) of water. Rhizomatous plants with creeping, surface stems, such as *Calla palustris*, can be lifted and divided into sections, each containing a bud. Replant them individually in the same way as other rhizomatous plants.

DIVIDING FIBROUS ROOTSTOCKS

Remove the plant from the container or lift it from the soil with a fork. Insert two forks, placed back-to-back, into the root mass and lever them apart, dividing the plant. Repeat to divide further, then trim and replant the divisions. The plant shown here is *Acorus calamus*.

DIVIDING RHIZOMATOUS PLANTS

1 Lift the plant (here, *Acorus calamus*). Split the root mass into sections with your hands. Each part should have a good root system and several healthy shoots.

2 Use a sharp knife to trim back long roots and foliage by approximately a third to a half of their original length.

3 Line a container with burlap and partially fill with damp soil. Plant each division so that the rhizome is just covered with a thin layer of soil.

Cuttings

Most submerged oxygenating plants can be very easily propagated by softwood cuttings taken in spring or summer; this process also helps to keep plants in check. Fast-growing oxygenators, for example *Elodea canadensis* and *Potamogeton crispus*, should be regularly replaced by young stock.

Prepare the cuttings by pinching or cutting off healthy, young shoots, inserting them into pots or trays of soil, and submerging them. The cuttings can be inserted individually or tied into small bunches of six. Cuttings of some creeping marginal plants, for example *Mentha aquatica* and water forget-me-nots (*Myosotis scorpioides*), should be inserted singly rather than in bunches. The cuttings establish quickly and may be potted and planted in position after two to three weeks.

Some tuberous water lilies may also be propagated by cuttings, although a different method is used (see "Bud Cuttings," p.287).

Runners and plantlets

Many of the floating plants that are found in tropical lakes and rivers propagate themselves by means of runners or plantlets produced on long, adventitious shoots. The water hyacinth (*Eichhornia crassipes*) and *Pistia stratiotes* can populate vast areas of warm water in this way. In shallow water, the young plantlets quickly root into the rich mud at the bottom, drawing up fresh nutrients and sending out yet more runners. The plantlets may simply be snapped off and placed on the water surface to grow separately.

A dwarf form of the Egyptian paper reed, *Cyperus papyrus* 'Nanus' (syn. *C. papyrus* 'Viviparus'), forms young plantlets in the flower head. If the head is bent over and immersed in a container of soil and water, the plantlets root and develop; these can be divided and potted up separately.

Turions

Some water plants, for example *Hydrocharis morsus-ranae*, produce swollen buds known as turions that become detached from the parent and survive the winter at the bottom of the pool. In spring, these turions rise to the surface of the water again and develop into new plants.

The turions of *Hottonia palustris* develop from the mud in spring without floating to the surface.

PROPAGATION OF RUNNERS OR PLANTLETS

1 Some floating plants (here, water hyacinths, *Eichhornia crassipes*) form offsets. Propagating these is not recommended in North America.

2 Please note that offsets of water hyacinth spread rampantly, and it can be very invasive. Some regions may have laws that forbid planting it.

These are difficult to collect, so wait for them to develop into young plants before lifting and replanting them in their new positions.

The turions may also be collected in the fall and stored in soil in a submerged seed flat covered with 6in (15cm) of water throughout the winter. In spring, when the emerging buds float to the surface, they can be collected and potted up into prepared containers of soil.

Seed

Most moisture-loving plants, and certain aquatics, including *Aponogeton distachyos, Euryale ferox, Orontium aquaticum, Trapa natans*, and tropical water lilies (see *Hardy and Tropical Water Lilies*, p.286) can be grown from ripe seed collected in summer or fall.

Keep the seeds cool and moist until ready to sow. If using dried seeds, germination will be delayed or the seeds may lose viability. Aquatic plant seeds should be grown in submerged or partially submerged conditions, similar to their natural habitat. When sowing seed, first prepare containers such as seed flats by filling them with an appropriate aquatic planting mix or garden soil passed through a ¼in (7mm) sieve. The growing medium should not include any fertilizers. They encourage algae, which could smother germinating seedlings.

Sow the seeds on the surface of the growing medium, and then cover them with a shallow layer of fine grit before placing the flat in a large watertight container, such as a plastic bowl or an aquarium. Fill the container with water until the pan is just covered, and leave it on a greenhouse bench in partial shade, or on a well-lit windowsill, at a minimum temperature of 64°F (18°C). The following spring, the seeds should start to germinate.

When the first pair of true leaves appears, carefully prick out the seedlings into individual pots and leave them immersed in water in the greenhouse for another year. Transfer the plants to the pond when the water warms up in spring.

WATER PLANTS TO DIVIDE (CONT.)

Rootstock (cont.)

Eriophorum angustifolium
Lysichiton
Mentha aquatica
Menyanthes trifoliata
Myosotis scorpioides
Nuphar lutea
Pontederia cordata
Ranunculus lingua
Sagittaria sagittifolia
Saururus cernuus
Thalia dealbata
Typha latifolia

Offsets

Eichhornia crassipes
Hydrocharis morsus-ranae
Limnobium stoloniferum
Marsilea quadrifolia
Nymphoides aquatica
Pistia stratiotes
Sagittaria graminea,
  S. sagittifolia 'Flore Pleno'
Salvinia auriculata,
  S. natans
Stratiotes aloides

Plantlets

Aponogeton undulatus
Azolla filiculoides
Baldellia ranunculoides
Ceratopteris cornuta
Eichhornia crassipes
Hottonia palustris
Nuphar advena
Nymphaea
Utricularia gibba

Lysichiton americanus

SOWING SEED

1 Sow the seeds evenly by tapping them from paper onto a pan of firmed aquatic potting mix or sifted garden soil.

2 Cover the seeds with a shallow layer of fine grit. Then place the pan in a large plastic bowl.

3 Gradually add water to the bowl so that the pan is just covered. Place in a well-lit location at about 64°F (18°C) until germinated.

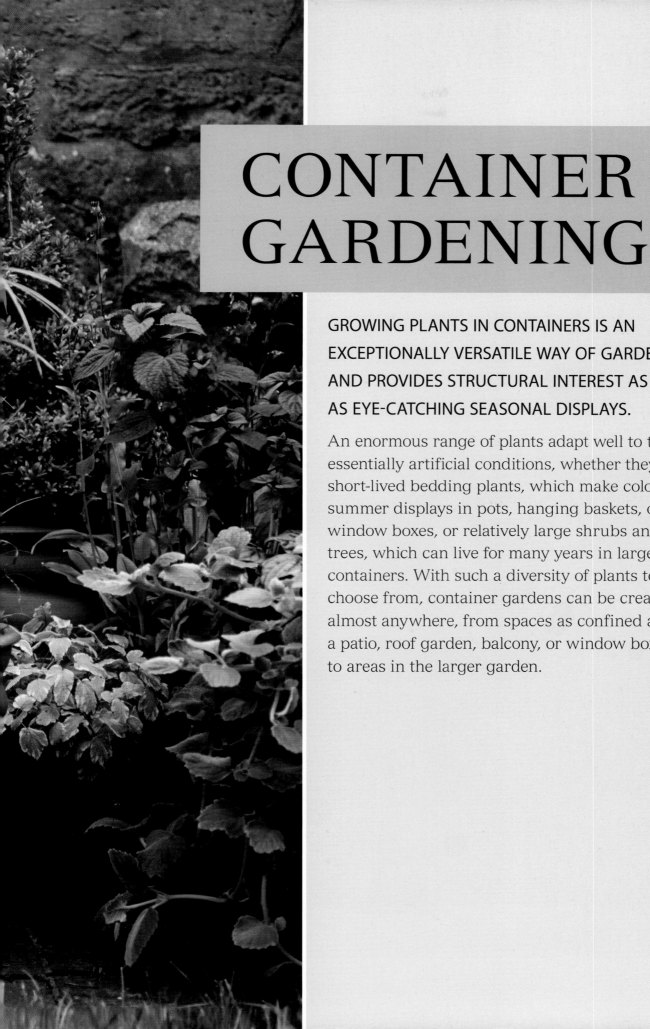

CONTAINER GARDENING

GROWING PLANTS IN CONTAINERS IS AN EXCEPTIONALLY VERSATILE WAY OF GARDENING AND PROVIDES STRUCTURAL INTEREST AS WELL AS EYE-CATCHING SEASONAL DISPLAYS.

An enormous range of plants adapt well to these essentially artificial conditions, whether they be short-lived bedding plants, which make colorful summer displays in pots, hanging baskets, or window boxes, or relatively large shrubs and trees, which can live for many years in large containers. With such a diversity of plants to choose from, container gardens can be created almost anywhere, from spaces as confined as a patio, roof garden, balcony, or window box to areas in the larger garden.

Container gardening

Growing plants in containers is one of the most flexible of gardening techniques. For many modern gardeners, who are aiming to create a pleasing environment in a limited space, container gardening is practical and appealing. For centuries plants have been grown in containers to allow them to be placed where there is no garden soil. Plants are also pot-grown to give them prominence in a display—their unique qualities being easier to appreciate when they are placed in an inconspicuous pot—or to enhance them in a container that is attractive in its own right.

Wall flowers Herbs, flowers, and fruit blend well in pots.

Using containers

Growing plants in containers also allows the cultivation of types that may not thrive in a particular garden's soil, by using tailored formulations of growing mixes. These include lime-free (acidic) mixes for lime-hating plants, such as rhododendrons and azaleas, or very gritty mixes for alpine plants or succulents, which need freer drainage.

Pots can be very useful in places where there is no garden soil, for example in a paved courtyard, on a balcony (see p.316), or under cover in the home (see INDOOR GARDENING, pp.352–383), greenhouse, or conservatory (see CONSERVATORY GARDENING, p.356).

Changes in focus

In a conventional home landscapes, plants are grown in open beds and displays are relatively static because the components cannot easily be moved around. In those yards, containers can play a role as focal points, for specimen planting, and for filling gaps in beds and borders. In the container garden, pot-grown plants are easily regrouped: with subtractions and additions, a planting design can be quickly rejuvenated or even completely transformed. Container gardening, therefore, is ideal for the experimental gardener wishing to create stimulating arrangements that can be changed when they have outlived their initial appeal.

Formal and informal styles

These two broad approaches to garden design are as relevant to container gardening as they are to gardening in open beds. The formal style is based on geometric order, with a division of space into balanced, often symmetrical units, and the repetition of elements at regular intervals. The informal approach has little or no geometry and the elements are arranged without obvious symmetry. At their most effective, informal arrangements take their cue from the irregularity of natural landscapes, although there is usually a carefully thought out, underlying balance of mass, form, and space.

Many popular manufactured containers are of a regular outline that is perfectly suitable for formal arrangements. Most plants, however, naturally grow in an informal way and so can be used to obscure the lines of the container. When arranging container-grown plants, it is just as easy to create an informal style— with soft, freestyle planting—as it is to ensure formality by planting to emphasize and echo the regularity of the container's shape.

An alternative approach to the informal style is to use "found" or recycled containers, such as ceramic mixing bowls, old sinks, or drinking troughs, whose original purpose was quite different than for growing plants.

Selecting a container

The choice of container is a matter of personal taste and aesthetics. Whether the container is manufactured or improvised, however, it must

Striking display This *Cordyline australis* 'Torbay Red' makes a bold statement in combination with *Osteospermum jucundum* and *Helichrysum petiolare* 'Limelight', in a striking gray ceramic container.

Pot of herbs A mixture of herbs is both useful and looks attractive in a pot that can be kept near the kitchen door.

satisfy key practical requirements to make it suitable for the cultivation of plants. The most fundamental elements are that a container holds sufficient growing mix to sustain the plants and has provision for excess water to drain away.

The materials of which containers are made will also affect the final choice. These include unglazed and glazed terra-cotta, natural or reconstituted rock, concrete, metal, wood, fiberglass, and plastic. No material has a longer history of use than unglazed terra-cotta and its warm, earthy color and matte-textured surface provide one of the most favorable foils for foliage and flowers. Terra-cotta lends itself to decoration with etched or relief patterns that are pleasing, but not distracting. It also blends in well with most architectural features, whether they are of stone, wood, or metal.

More opulent effects can be achieved with containers of marble, or more austere ones in other types of stone. The severity of concrete containers, or the strong lines of light-reflecting, galvanized zinc ones, make them particularly suitable for an ultra-modern style, while wooden ones can be used to create more rustic atmosphere. Containers in fiberglass and plastic can look inconspicuous, but both materials have practical virtues, in terms of moisture retention, for example; and the best successfully imitate much more expensive materials.

Plants and their containers should complement rather than compete with each other, and the texture, color, and surface finish of a container are considerations as important as the material itself. To a large extent, this is a matter of individual preference, but it is worth bearing in mind that containers of a bright color, a bold, high-gloss finish, or with conspicuous decoration will demand an equally strong planting design.

Size, shape, and scale

The size and shape of a container are governed by practical considerations as well as visual appeal. The container must be large enough to accommodate the plant or plants to be grown. It is equally important to match the size of the pot to the visual mass of the planting it will hold. A small stone trough, for example, would be in scale with diminutive alpines; a large urn would suit a vigorous trailing specimen, and a French box planter is ideal in both style and capacity for a topiary specimen. For a packed and colorful display of upright and trailing summer plants, a generously proportioned copper tub (used long ago for boiling or washing) might be appropriate.

As a general rule, the larger the pot the better, and larger pots need less frequent watering. One advantage of smaller pots, however, is that they can be placed into arrangements as plants reach their prime, and removed when past their best. This technique works best in conjunction with a holding area, such as a cold frame, in which plants are brought to near perfection, and to which they are returned to recover and grow on afterward, as required.

Pot mobility Plants in containers, such as this standard bay tree with an attractively twisted trunk, can be moved to fill a gap in the border, or simply to add height and interest.

Recycled cans Improvised pots are most attractive when displayed in a group, here using *Festuca glauca* (Blue fescue), *Aster*, and a grass (above).

Focal point A simple large pot in a prominent location overflowing with plants makes a very striking display. In this terra-cotta pot, purple *Heuchera* 'Can Can' is set against the fresh green *Teucrium scorodonia* 'Crispum' and the corkscrew stems of the *Juncus effusus* f. *spiralis* (left).

Single specimens in containers

Growing single plants in individual containers is very practical: the growing mix, watering, and feeding regime can be geared to the plant, which is also freed of competition for moisture and nutrients. It can also work well in design terms, particularly if the plant has a strong architectural shape. The spiky New Zealand cabbage palm (*Cordyline australis*) and yuccas make fine specimens, as do plants of softer, weeping shapes, such as cultivars of the Japanese maple (*Acer palmatum*). Arching and mound-forming grasses, such as the green-and-gold variegated *Hakonechloa macra* 'Aureola', also look good alone in containers, as do species that are formally trained, such as a frame-grown English ivy (*Hedera helix*) or a clipped topiary specimen, such as boxwood (*Buxus sempervirens*). Clematis and other moderately vigorous climbers can be allowed to trail from tall containers, or be trained upward on a simple obelisk. Trailing shrubs, such as groundcover roses, look perfect when trailing their stems over the container's edge, and many other modest plants—heathers, primulas, and pansies—have a special charm when given the luxury of their own pot.

Mixed planting

Individual plants in their own containers can be grouped to give the impression of a mixed planting. But a greater challenge is to bring together a number of plants that complement one another and give a sustained display for several weeks or even months. The keys to success are to select plants that share the same or similar cultural needs, and to create arrangements of compatible colors and contrasting forms and textures in foliage and flowers. Mixed displays are most effective with a strong structure, for example where a vertical or domed centerpiece is surrounded by lesser "uprights," with trailing plants breaking over the edge of the container to form an irregular "skirt."

A spring mixture, for example, might contrast upright dwarf irises and crocuses with a mat of small-leaved thyme (*Thymus serpyllum*); richly colored polyanthus among mounds of sky-blue forget-me-nots (*Myosotis sylvatica*); or daisies (*Bellis perennis*) with tulips as strong verticals. In summer, the choice is almost endless—by selecting long-flowering bedding and foliage plants, it is possible to assemble rich and varied arrangements that provide many months of color.

Color themes

When packing several plants close together, color clashes become much more conspicuous than in the less condensed conditions of the open garden. In containers, it is perhaps more important to devise combinations of plants based on color harmonies or contrasts. The harmonies of closely related colors can be quiet and subtle, as in a warm plan based on cream, soft yellow, and pale apricot, while more heavily saturated colors—rich purples with violets and blues—create more vibrant harmonies. Contrasts are based on complementary colors: red with green, blue with orange, or yellow with violet. The eye is comfortable with these opposites, which look good with each other.

Alternatively, more shocking combinations can be tried, for example, orange with magenta-pink. Color clashes can be stimulating, but, in a small space, it is often helpful to ease the tension by using pale flower colors—creams or near-whites—or foliage as a buffer. Gray-leaved plants, such as *Helichrysum petiolare*, are invaluable in this respect, as are white- or cream-variegated plants, such as small-leaved cultivars of English ivy (*Hedera helix*).

Siting containers

Planted containers can be used simply as isolated features, but are often most attractive in the garden when used as an integral part of a wider design. In the formal garden, for example, containers can provide accents that reinforce a sense of geometry. Similarly, looser arrangements can underline the more subtle rhythms of a more natural-looking theme.

The position of containers should be based on practical as well as aesthetic considerations. Container-grown plants need frequent watering in summer, so easy access to a water supply is vital, especially in sunny sites where plants may need attention at least once daily during spells of hot, dry weather.

It is worth remembering, too, that theft can happen in gardens as well as houses, and a valuable urn or antique jar is safer placed in full view of the house, rather than in a more secluded location, and may even be best fixed or bolted to the ground.

Defining accents

Placing containers to create accents is a useful technique for delineating areas of the garden, or marking boundaries. At its simplest, a row of containers may mark a boundary, perhaps in conjunction with a wall or fence. Try lining pots along the base of a fence or along the top of a wall, provided they are secure and will not topple, or even suspend them from it. The effect can be achieved for little cost—perhaps with brightly painted, recycled cans planted with long-flowering and colorful geraniums. Containers can also be used to define compartments within a garden, for example, when set singly or in clusters at the corners of a rectangular paved area.

Container accents are invaluable for enhancing other features. A square arrangement around a circular pool, for example, forms a very attractive contrast; alternatively place pots in the curved quadrants to emphasize the line of the pool's edge. Accents such as this can fulfill a dual role by defining a shape while also softening a hard outline. This is especially useful in integrating the severe geometry of a rectangular pool into the wider garden: containers arranged around the pool echo its shape, yet, if filled with loose arrangements of plants, they soften the effect. It is best to set containers back from the water's edge so that they are not a hazard, and to reduce the risk of dead leaves and flowers dirtying the water.

Containers as focal points

The main lines of a small, modern landscape in a formal style rarely terminate in a natural view of a landscape or an architectural landmark, but, even on a small scale, a vista that does not lead to a natural conclusion can seem unsatisfying. Features that are traditionally introduced to terminate vistas include trees and statues, but on a smaller scale an urn, or large pot or tub, can fulfill the role equally well. Such focal points give an almost instant effect and, in comparison with statues, are generally much less costly. Even an empty container can make an attractive eye-catcher, provided that the scale is right; but when planted with an upright plant or group of plants, surrounded by a fringe of trailers, the design is far more lovely.

There is no simple rule of thumb for ensuring the correct scale; it is often most satisfactory to do it by eye. Do a preliminary test by positioning a stake where the container is to stand, and then check its position from various points along the vista. In some cases, it may be necessary to raise the container on a platform to achieve the desired effect. This can be a ready-made, architectural platform or can be improvised, for example, with a stack of unmortared bricks, or wooden blocks, depending on the desired style.

In garden compartments, a central focal point is usually a good idea. A planted container is often a much simpler and cheaper option than a statue, sundial, or fountain. A formal herb garden divided into quarters, for example, may include a central paved or graveled area—an ideal spot for a large pot planted with an architectural specimen, such as angelica (*Angelica archangelica*). Alternatively, to maximize the growing area, the

container could stand on a platform in the middle of the bed, but ensure that access for watering and maintenance is provided for, perhaps by means of stepping stones.

Containers may also be used as focal points to direct the eye through the beds, for example by placing a large pot at a turning point on a path, or to act as a distant feature that leads the observer on to another view or vista. In landscapes where one mass of planting deliberately masks another, the unexpected has special value. A carefully placed container can introduce such an element of surprise, and an empty container of architectural quality—erect or on its side—can be just as dramatic as one full of plants.

Emphatic arrangements

Containers, especially if arranged in pairs, are an ideal way of marking a transition in the landscape. This can be as simple and low-key as a one-step change of level, for example by using clipped balls of boxwood (*Buxus sempervirens*) in terra-cotta pots to flank the step, emphasize the change, and warn people of the step. Flights of steps can be treated with more flair, with paired containers at the top and base and others at different landings, to create a dramatic setting. But when using containers on steps in this way, they must be carefully placed so they do not become a hazard.

Paired containers can also play a supporting role to another feature, such as a garden bench, that may not have sufficient impact by itself. Setting matched containers on either side of a bench strengthens the central feature, which assumes greater visual weight. For strictly formal, long-term designs, pots could be planted

Old A romantic effect can be obtained by combining a traditional urn with bedding plants, such as trailing and upright geraniums, petunias, and fuchsias.

Modern Boldness of form and color provided by the dark, strappy leaves of the *Cordyline* and the orange *Agastache* suits the shape and color of this container and its background.

Traditional This classic look is achieved by using ivy topiary, which grows much faster than boxwood, in a terra-cotta pot, underplanted to soften the ball shape formed by the ivy.

Statement pot An unusual woven-effect metal container enhances a border with its varied display of plants using complementary forms and colors.

Twin pots Using a single type of plant in a pot or container (here, a pale pink and maroon iris) can be very effective, and doubling that up in identical pots, which echo the color of the paved surface, helps to emphasize the strong architectural elements in this contemporary garden.

with a topiary or, to announce the seasonal changes, a spring display of tulips could be followed with summer bedding plants that will bloom continuously for several months.

Paired containers can give particular emphasis when positioned to form an "avenue." This formal pattern can work well on a relatively small scale: even in confined spaces, the effect can be monumental, for example, when citrus trees in large terra-cotta pots or urns are placed in bays along a broad walk. On a more modest scale, pots of evergreens or seasonal flowers can be introduced to mark the main axis of a tiny garden.

Containers in borders

Plants in containers, when placed above plantings in open ground, can be used to create contrast or to reinforce a color theme in beds and borders: for example, violet-purple flowers like heliotrope (*Heliotropium arborescens*) or petunias could oppose a border theme of oranges, creams, and yellows. Alternatively, subtle harmonies can be created, like the pale pink of the double tulip 'Angélique' in pots beside beds of wallflowers, such as *Erysimum cheiri* Fair Lady Series, in shades of pink, yellow, and cream.

Container-grown plants are particularly valuable when the garden is relatively empty. Winter-flowering pansies, such as *Viola* x *wittrockiana* Universal Series, brighten dull days for many weeks in winter and early spring and can gradually be supplemented with a succession of bulbs, such as daffodils and tulips. In the fall garden, container-grown shrublike plants, such as *Argyranthemum*, fuchsias, and *Phygelius* will perform well until the first frost.

Another approach is to boost beds and borders with pot-grown plants plunged into the ground. This is a particularly useful way to fill gaps in a border when the foliage of summer perennials, such as the Oriental poppies (*Papaver orientale* cultivars), has died back. It can also be used to supplement the display when newly planted perennials and shrubs have yet to attain their full size in a bed.

Containers in paved gardens

The pleasures of gardening, and the contribution that plants make in enhancing the living environment, are being appreciated by more and more people. At the same time, gardens are increasingly being thought of as outdoor rooms, to be used for relaxing and entertaining, dining, and cooking. In the summer months, an outdoor room may even be much busier than the living room indoors.

For many people, particularly in urban areas, the "yard" is a small paved space bounded by walls or fences: a courtyard, patio, or terrace. There are also other areas of hard landscaping in gardens, such as paths, and while the range of surfaces includes a huge variety of stone, tile, gravel, concrete, or a wooden deck, open soil is often at a premium. The only way to include plants in such sites, where soil and space are so limited, is to grow them in containers.

Plants for paved areas

A large number of plants are suitable for containers in paved areas. In enclosed yards, especially near sunny walls, there is often a very favorable, warm, and sheltered microclimate (see p.609). Tender plants, such as the fragrant-leaved lemon verbena (*Aloysia citrodara*) or myrtle (*Myrtus communis*), often succeed here when they may not thrive in a more open site. In some cases, the proximity

of buildings and walls means that a paved area receives little or no direct sun for all or part of the day. While painting walls white helps to make such shady areas brighter, the plants that really thrive in these conditions are committed shade-lovers, such as hostas and ferns. These plants grow more lush and look beautiful for much longer periods in cool shade, providing the possibilities of sumptuous arrangements of foliage color and texture.

Where direct light penetrates for several hours a day, many more plants will thrive, especially those that occur naturally in the dappled shade of a woodland setting, such as camellias and rhododendrons. When light levels are low, try moving the plants around from time to time, so that they have more exposure to sunlight; it helps promote balanced growth and encourages them to flower more freely.

Two other features of a paved environment affect the choice of plants: the weight of a pot and the watering regime. Solid walls often create turbulence because they deflect wind, and unstable pots may be toppled by sudden downdrafts; the growing mix also dries out more rapidly in windy conditions. Containers close to walls may also stand in a rain shadow, where natural rainfall does not penetrate (see *Rain Shadow*, p.608). Even after heavy rain, plants may not receive sufficient water, so provision must be made for adequate watering.

Choosing containers

There are no hard-and-fast aesthetic rules when choosing containers for paved areas. They can be matched closely in texture and material to architecture and hard surfaces—terra-cotta pots are ideal against brick, for example. An equally valid approach is to use containers that stand out in a paved setting. Glazed jars, painted wooden tubs, and galvanized metal cubes and containers are just some of the choices that can help to define a distinctive style.

Arranging containers

Any arrangement of containers must take practicality into account. For example, it is important to leave some clear space for access and to allow enough room for the unrestricted use of furniture. But from fall to spring, when many paved areas are less heavily used, containers can be rearranged to provide displays that are visible from indoors. Stacked arrangements of pots loaded with bulbs, evergreens, or winter-flowering pansies (*Viola* x *wittrockiana* cultivars), placed in view of French windows, allow the display to be enjoyed in warmth and comfort.

The most difficult aspect of managing changing displays is finding a place for plants before and after their most decorative season— only a limited number of those past their best can be hidden among plants in their prime. In the absence of a holding area, one solution is to rely heavily on annuals and biennials that are discarded when their season is over, leaving containers available for a succession of seasonal displays. Another option is to use containers that are ornamental in their own right; if carefully selected, they can be attractive even when empty. And if more permanent plantings of bulbs, perennials, and shrubs should outlive their usefulness, they are often gratefully received by friends with more space in their yards.

Formal arrangements

The most usual formal arrangements in paved areas are paired containers flanking doors, benches, or other furniture set against walls. Where there is room, the symmetry can be expanded to include matching clusters of containers, with additions and subtractions as the seasons advance. At times of the year when the paved area is used frequently, arrangements —formal or otherwise—are best kept to the perimeter, but this does not preclude using them as a focal point, perhaps where they can be viewed from a door or window.

Although space may be limited, there is no need to restrict containers to small pots with flowers just above ground level. Arrangements such as this may not be to scale; fewer but larger plants will have much more impact. If there is no room for loose, rounded shapes, such as those of *Fatsia japonica* or the mophead *Hydrangea macrophylla* cultivars, consider naturally narrow, upright plants, such as a slow-growing conifer like *Juniperus communis* 'Sentinel', or plants such as yew (*Taxus baccata*) and boxwood (*Buxus sempervirens*), which can be clipped to form a narrow cone or column.

To bring color to the plan, use flowering plants, such as clematis and miniature climbing roses, or variegated foliage plants, such as

Paved gardens The straight edges of hard landscaping can be softened considerably by the judicious placing of densely planted containers of annuals, such as petunias.

cultivars of English ivy (*Hedera helix*), and train them onto upright obelisks or narrow, pyramids of willow branches.

Many urban gardens have a paved path between a wall or fence and the house. Without plants, these passageways can appear bleak, but there is seldom enough room at ground level for pots or tubs. One solution is to place deep, narrow troughs at the foot of the wall. They can be filled with freestanding arrangements, or even with climbing plants that will cover the wall if given support. Another option is to fix containers securely to the wall top, so that plants can cascade down the wall's face. There is also a wide range of flat-backed, half-round containers available that are specifically designed to be mounted on the vertical surface of a wall or stout fence.

Stands for containers

A plant stand with shelves at different heights provides a support for a neat and attractive display of container-grown plants and has the advantage that a diverse display can be created within a relatively small area. The best choice and most durable are usually made of aluminum and are of simple design with stairstepped and slatted shelves. The slats allow water to drain away freely and the angle of the shelves means that plants on the top shelf do not overshadow those lower down. Most stands can be fixed against a wall or placed in a more open position, but some are specifically designed to fill corners, and these make good use of a potentially awkward space. An alternative to commercial stands are those made from stacked bricks, clay drainpipes, or overturned flowerpots as uprights, and plain wooden planks as a standing surface. Such improvised structures have the advantage of being easily dismantled and reassembled as the need arises.

The location of a stand is frequently a matter of compromise, especially in the summer when the area is most heavily used. A good location for viewing from the house is against a wall opposite a door or window overlooking a courtyard or patio. In winter, when the patio is less often used, a staged display can be placed more centrally. Wherever the stand is put, the best results are usually achieved with a balanced combination of flowering and foliage plants.

Informal clusters

Stray containers, unless carefully placed, can be both a nuisance and a hazard in paved areas, but informal clusters can be an effective way of displaying plants and their pots. An interesting range of plants in containers of different heights and sizes can, to some extent, mimic the layered effect of plants in the open garden. This can be enhanced by standing some containers on bricks to give additional prominence and by varying the height of their contents.

Any irregularly shaped cluster is a useful way of filling a corner, and informally planted containers along the borders of a patio or terrace can help mitigate the formal severity of paving. Very pleasing, unifying effects can be achieved by using differently shaped containers in the same material—unglazed terra-cotta pots, for example, are available in a wide range of shapes and sizes.

Keep it clean

The main disadvantage of clustered containers is that, inevitably, dust, dead leaves, and other debris accumulate around their bases, which can be difficult to sweep away. A power hose is useful for keeping the surfaces clean, but it is also worth considering investing in wheeled bases for pots. These not only make it easier to sweep debris away but are also an invaluable aid when moving heavy pots to recreate displays as plants fade at the end of their season.

Hanging containers

A variety of manufactured and improvised containers can be suspended or mounted to create a planted environment above ground level. They are particularly useful where space is limited, but even in conventional gardens there are many opportunities to use aerial displays of plants. They are invaluable for softening architectural environments—helping to lift the eye above other planting—and can be integrated into ambitious plans where plants are arranged on several levels.

Hanging baskets

The traditional hanging basket is a simple suspended container consisting of a wire frame where a liner holds sufficient growing mix to sustain one or, more likely, several plants. A number of other suspended containers— either ready-made or improvised—serve the same purpose and are planted and displayed in a similar way as hanging baskets.

Wire-framed baskets and other suspended containers are best planted so that the container itself is concealed by full and trailing growth. This may be achieved with a single vigorous trailer, such as *Tradescantia zebrina*, a popular house- or conservatory plant that can also be moved outdoors in summer.

In general, however, it is easier to create a floating cloud of foliage and flowers with a mixture of several different, less tender plants. The aim is to achieve a loosely rounded shape, using plants of different habits, so that growth hides the container. One approach is to use upright and rounded plants to form a crown above an irregular, hanging fringe of trailing or spreading plants. This could be achieved by including erect cultivars of geraniums and *Verbena x hybrida*, flanked by trailing fuchsias, lobelias, and petunias. Another option is to use containers that are in themselves ornamental, so that, even when the display is at its peak, some of the container is visible.

Hanging baskets are often hung as isolated features, perhaps to take advantage of an existing support. This might be an arch or the crosspiece of a pergola, for example. Another approach is to fit specially made supports for single or multiple hanging baskets. Brackets can be simple and inconspicuous, or ornamental and in a style that suits the surroundings. A hanging basket can make a dramatic focal point to enliven a blank wall, especially if it can be seen from a window or door. They can also be eye-catching when suspended from the corner of a building, but for safety they must be well above the height of passersby.

The most obvious of the multiple arrangements are pairs of baskets, mounted, for example, on either side of a door or combined with other containers. An attractive design can be created by using a large container, such as an urn, at ground level against a wall, with hanging baskets mounted above it and on either side. The plants in the hanging baskets may match or contrast with those in the large container. For a more ambitious plan, hanging baskets can be hung in rows, for example, on a series of arches, or on brackets along a wall. Carefully coordinated or contrasting plantings can be dramatically staged by using smaller baskets

All-around display
A traditional mix of summer bedding plants— petunias, lobelia, geraniums, and verbena—is displayed here in a hanging basket, which has been completely covered by the plants (above).

Elevated eye-catcher
A group of nasturtiums (*Tropaeolum majus*) planted in an old straw basket (left) and hung from a garden post can be an unusual and charming display in the summer garden.

on either side of a large one, or by introducing variations in the height at which the containers are suspended. Using the crosspieces of a pergola, a series of paired hanging baskets on either side of a path makes an impressive walkway, although it is worth remembering that such features will be time-consuming to water.

Window boxes

These containers are available in a wide range of materials, including wood, terra-cotta, concrete, and plastic. They are sometimes designed to be ornamental on their own account, with painted or relief decoration. Plain wooden window boxes can be painted to match other architectural details, but for more adventurous effects consider painting window boxes on the front of a building in a bold color to make them stand out. The planting style and content of a window box

depends to some extent on the position from which it is viewed. For some apartment-dwellers, for example, their whole garden may amount to one or two window boxes, so the view from inside matters more than that from ground level. The greatest pleasure may be in choosing plants of refined beauty, good scent, or aromatic foliage. If window boxes form an integral part of the decoration of a house front, on the other hand, the view from outside is what really counts. The most valuable plants in this sort of display will be those that perform reliably over a long season, and might include evergreens such as boxwood (*Buxus sempervirens*) or hebes.

If window boxes are in windy, exposed positions, they will not work well for tall plants, which will be battered by wind; they may also block out the light. But to avoid a dull, uniformly low display, position compact but rounded plants, such as geraniums, in the center, with lower plants on either side and trailing plants cascading from the front. There are many variations on this theme, using a wide range of plants, including evergreens for winter or year-round effect.

Wall-mounted containers

The types of containers that can be wall-mounted include semicircular wire or strip-metal baskets, metal-frame troughs, and plastic or terra-cotta half-pots. Brackets can also be fixed to walls to hold standard pots of small or medium size, and more solid brackets can be used to support large troughs—but be sure that they are attached securely. Wall-mounted containers filled with plants are invaluable in breaking up the blankness of bare walls, whether used on their own or in conjunction with other planting. They are also useful where windows open outward or lack a sill. The best alternative to a window box can be a trough mounted on brackets below the window. Wall-mounted containers are perhaps of greatest value in narrow spaces, or where a courtyard or passage is partly shaded. In a raised position, plants have greater access to light, and will often thrive better when elevated than they would at ground level.

In general, stone or brick walls make a beautiful backdrop for plantings, but, to take full advantage of their possibilities, it is important to choose containers that blend or contrast with the background color. Full planting and generous use of trailing plants is generally the best option but, if the container itself is decorative, it should obviously be visible. The siting of wall-mounted containers is also important. Too many, indiscriminately arranged, will create a messy and overly busy effect. A few large containers create more impact than many small ones, and in addition will be easier to maintain, especially when watering. Nevertheless, with careful placement, either in a symmetrical or asymmetrical pattern, pretty displays can be made with individual pots of flowers. For winter and spring color, try double primroses, such as the rich violet *Primula vulgaris* 'Miss Indigo' or soft yellow 'Double Sulphur', or English daisies, such as *Bellis perennis* Pomponette Series. For summer, there is a huge range of vibrant geraniums that flower for several months, and often into the fall.

Plants for container gardening

All categories of plants—annuals, biennials, perennials, shrubs, and trees—are available for the container gardener. The traditional approach focuses on compact, long-flowering summer annuals, which are undeniably valuable for creating colorful displays; but container gardening becomes much more interesting and challenging if the repertoire of plants is extended. Using all types of plants allows for arrangements of different scale, and exploits the range of habits. Foliage, for example, is often neglected in favor of flowers, yet it has special value in the container garden. Evergreens provide year-round pleasure, and even deciduous foliage is longer lasting than most floral displays. It can create rich but calming textures that are a welcome alternative to riotous, colorful flowers. Good foliage plants, such as ferns and hostas, are often the best choice for shady corners. In areas with cold winters, where the soil in containers will freeze solid, plants that are normally hardy may not survive. It is safer to use plants that are at least one or preferably two zones hardier than your region.

Annuals and biennials

Summer-flowering annuals, including a number of tender perennials that are usually grown as annuals, are popular plants for container gardening. As a result of breeding programs, many plants are available of more compact habit, with single, semidouble, or double flowers in many colors or shades, sometimes with even more dramatic differences of flower or petal form. It is now possible to put together a varied mixture, even with a limited number of plants.

Although the range is much smaller, another important group is that comprising annuals and biennials that flower in winter and early spring. The winter-flowering pansies (*Viola* x *wittrockiana*) create colorful displays before the main bulb season and then often carry on for many weeks more. Other plants that help to give continuity through spring are English daisies (*Bellis perennis*), primroses of the Primrose and Polyanthus groups, and wallflowers (*Erysimum cheiri*).

Most annuals and biennials are relatively easy to raise from seed; the F1 and F2 hybrids, although more expensive, provide more vigorous and uniform plants. If space does not permit raising plants from seed, there is usually a good selection of very young plants at garden centers in late spring and early summer, and these can be a convenient way of acquiring a good range of plants in small numbers. Choose plants that are just about to come into flower, so the container garden is almost instantly colorful and remains so for months.

Perennials

The perennials that are traditionally used in container gardening are tender ones that are raised annually from seed, or overwintered under glass. Geraniums are tender, shrublike perennials that make excellent container specimens. Some are F1 or F2 hybrids raised annually from seed, while others can be overwintered to provide material for cuttings that are brought on for the new season; the parent plant can then be discarded. The zonal and trailing ivy-leaved geraniums flower prolifically over a long season and are the most widely used in outdoor container gardening—

Wall-mounted container
A bare expanse of wall can be enhanced by a brightly planted container placed at a convenient height to allow easy access for watering and maintaining.

Flowers and foliage
Fences can be brightened up by the use of well-placed containers. Here, yellow *Osteospermum*, pink geraniums, ivy, and variegated *Tradescantia* planted in a white wooden window box look lovely on a sunny site on a gravel path.

Strong shapes

Square pots are the perfect foil for boxwood balls (above), here combined with African marigolds (*Tagetes*). These containers are cement boards bracketed together and sprayed with a metallic bronze paint and waterproof sealant.

Spring display

Two large pots filled with pink flowering cherry trees and grape hyacinths make a perfect seasonal backdrop for the smaller, bulb-filled pots in the foreground (left).

the trailing ivy-leaved kinds being particularly useful in hanging baskets and window boxes or on balconies.

Scented-leaved geraniums are an interesting and underused group. The silver-margined, eucalyptus-scented leaves of *Pelargonium* 'Lady Plymouth', for example, are excellent for breaking up large blocks of flower color, and the leaves release their evocative fragrance when handled. The flowers tend to be small, but the spice-scented *P.* 'Copthorne' is one of several with large, attractively marked blooms.

Border perennials are not widely used in container gardening, but there is no reason not to experiment. Those with evergreen foliage help fill the gap between fall and spring; many bergenias, for example, have large spoon-shaped leaves that take on rich copper-red tones in cold weather, and the sprays of pink, magenta, or white flowers in spring are long-lasting. *Heuchera* is another useful genus: *Heuchera villosa* 'Palace Purple' has large, glossy, jagged leaves that are deep bronze-red, topped in summer by showers of tiny white flowers and pink seed heads.

The length of their flowering season makes some hardy herbaceous perennials potentially useful plants for containers. Although individual flowers are short-lived, the low-growing daylilies bloom over many weeks in mid- to late summer—those of *Hemerocallis* 'Stella de Oro' being pale orange—and many produce sheaves of attractive foliage. Other herbaceous perennials with distinguished foliage include hostas, in an enormous range of sizes, colors, and textures. A clump of the blue-gray, corrugated leaves of *Hosta sieboldiana* var. *elegans* fully justifies a container for itself.

Bulbs

In this context, the term "bulbs" also includes plants with corms, tubers, and rhizomes. It is a group that is very important in container gardening; their value lies in their remarkably reliable flowering, even though few have foliage of any great ornamental value and individual plants rarely flower for more than a few weeks. By planting a range of spring bulbs, however, a succession of colorful explosions can be enjoyed from late winter through to early summer.

This long season begins with snowdrops, dwarf irises, and early crocuses, overlaps with the earliest daffodils, which are followed by the later daffodil varieties, hyacinths, and tulips. There are many other small bulbs, such as *Scilla*, *Muscari*, and *Puschkinia*, that fit into this flowering program.

The most useful summer and fall bulbs include lilies, dahlias, and cannas with their huge variety in flower color and shape as well as in height.

Match bulbs and containers for size and take account of the location the containers will occupy. Tall-growing tulips, for example, are likely to suffer wind damage when planted in window boxes. There are excellent dwarf tulips, as well as other low-growing bulbs that are better for exposed locations.

The flowers of bulbs generally last longer if the containers are in light or partial shade, but the flowers of some, including crocuses and tulips, open fully only in sun. For densely packed containers, two or even three layers of bulbs can be planted at different depths (see p.327).

With bulbs, there is inevitably a gap between planting and flowering. One way to overcome this is to keep containers in a cold frame until bulbs begin to flower. The containers can then

be brought into view and then removed once flowering is over. Another option is to plant bulbs of different kinds in the same container to give a successional display, or to create mixed plantings. Many dwarf bulbs combine well with winter-flowering pansies (*Viola* x *wittrockiana*) and low evergreens, such as thyme (*Thymus*) or small-leaved cultivars of English ivy (*Hedera helix*). Bulbs can also be used as an underplanting to spring flowering shrubs such as *Skimmia*.

Although some container-grown bulbs flower well for several years if the growing mix is renewed annually, the performance of most bulbs deteriorates after the first season. For high-quality displays, it is best to plant new stock each year. Otherwise, allow bulbs to die back in their containers, then lift and store for replanting later in the growing season, or replant directly in the garden for reduced displays in subsequent years.

Trees

Many evergreen and deciduous trees can adapt to life in containers and, if well cared for, will flourish for many years, although they seldom reach the size they would attain in the open landscape. Those that feature foliage, flowers, and fruit among their ornamental virtues include small rowans, such as *Sorbus cashmiriana*, and flowering crabapples, for example *Malus* 'Red Jade'; both have spring flowers and long-lasting fruit, borne amid a blaze of fall foliage color. The height and architectural presence of container-grown trees, such as hornbeam (*Carpinus betulus*) or colored-bark birches, such as *Betula albosinensis* var. *septentrionalis*, lend a strong structural element to a design. They are particularly useful for screening and help create privacy and areas of cool shade.

When choosing trees for patios, courtyards, and roof gardens, scale is important. Compact conifers, like conical *Chamaecyparis lawsoniana* 'Ellwoodii', are among the most useful. Deciduous small trees include the Kilmarnock willow (*Salix caprea* 'Kilmarnock') with pendulous branches loaded with white, then yellow, catkins in spring. Trees that respond well to clipping are of particular value where space is limited. One of the most useful evergreens for container gardening is the sweet bay (*Laurus nobilis*), which can be trimmed in a variety of shapes.

Shrubs

Shrubs, which are much more widely used in container gardening than trees, span a range from large spreading specimens, which require heavy, broad-based containers, to dwarf bushes, for example many dwarf conifers, which are suitable for window boxes. When choosing a shrub, consider its scale within the setting, the plant's shape, and the qualities of foliage, flowers, and fruit that will keep the plants interesting over a long period.

Compact evergreens with good foliage and a pleasing shape include a large number of dwarf conifers. Some broadleaved evergreens, such as boxwood (*Buxus sempervirens*) or *Osmanthus* x *burkwoodii*, that tolerate clipping, can be trimmed to formal or more whimsical shapes.

In some cases, it is foliage color that gives a plant a special value, as with variegated plants, such as *Euonymus fortunei* 'Emerald Gaiety'. Many low-growing cultivars of heather (*Calluna vulgaris*) provide colored winter foliage as well as flowers. With camellias, dark, glossy foliage is matched by single to fully double flowers of great beauty. Some rhododendrons also combine highly ornamental foliage and exquisite flowers; *Rhododendron yakushimanum* hybrids have a pleasingly dense habit and densely furry undersides to the new leaves that follow the flowers.

For delicate summer foliage textures and brilliant fall colors, the Japanese maples (*Acer palmatum* cultivars) are hard to beat. Other deciduous shrubs grown mainly for their flowers include *Hydrangea macrophylla* cultivars, with flower heads that last for months, often with pleasing color changes as they age. Fuchsias produce new flowers without interruption throughout summer until checked by cold. The trailing kinds are useful for spilling over the rim of hanging baskets and tall containers, while some of the upright ones, such as *Fuchsia* 'Lady Thumb', make compact bushes that are ideal centerpieces in any container.

Roses

The best roses for container gardening are miniature roses, patio roses, and some of the groundcover roses. Miniatures, such as POUR TOI ('Para Ti') and LITTLE BO-PEEP ('Poullen'), are small twiggy bushes, to 1ft (30cm) high, with a myriad of tiny leaflets; they are perfect for window boxes, needing only 8–10in (20–25cm) depth of soil. Patio roses are slightly larger bushes covered with clustered flowers from summer to fall; reliable performers include the brilliant orange TOP MARKS ('Fryministar'), the soft apricot-peach SWEET DREAM ('Fryminicot'), and the pale pink PRETTY POLLY ('Meitonje'). They look especially good in a stone trough or an unglazed terra-cotta pot.

Groundcover roses spread as they grow and are ideal for hanging baskets and tall pots, where the sinuous stems can trail over the pot rim or basket's edge. Try PINK BELLS ('Poulbells') with its bright pink, pompon blooms, or MAGIC CARPET ('Jaclover') with its semidouble, magenta flowers.

Climbers

The versatility of climbers in containers can hardly be overstated. They can be as effective trained upward on obelisks or other frames as they can be when used in less conventional ways. Some can simply be allowed to trail. A small-flowered clematis, such as *Clematis* 'Frances Rivis', looks particularly elegant when spilling from tall pots or jars. Some of the more compact, large-flowered clematis, like the white-flowered *C.* 'Miss Bateman', are also successful if grown this way. Other more unusual, trailing plants include the tender perennial *Rhodochiton atrosanguineus* with its pendent, red-purple, tubular flowers.

Cultivars of English ivy (*Hedera helix*) can look just as good as trailers or climbers. The small-leaved kinds are among the best trailing evergreens for hanging baskets, and for softening the hard edges of window boxes and other containers. These adaptable plants also lend themselves to more elaborate training. Try growing them on wire frames—they can be a good imitator of clipped topiary (see TOPIARY, p.108).

Strict training is usually the best way to manage vigorous climbers, including wisterias and vines (*Vitis*). With rigorous summer and winter pruning, they can be grown as standards. But among the easiest are annuals, such as the sweetly scented sweet peas (*Lathyrus odoratus*) or those like *Ipomoea tricolor*, that are treated as annuals. Grow them on tepees of bamboo stakes laced together with string, on rustic pyramids made of branches of brushwood, or on custom-made trellis panels.

Container supports
Compact climbers, such as *Jasminum officinale*, (above) can be used to increase height in a display, but may need a support on which to climb.

Patio fragrance
Miniature or patio roses bloom for many months and do well in pots, giving those with limited space a chance to enjoy their beauty and scent (left).

Balconies and roof gardens

Balconies and areas of flat roof can be converted to architecturally pleasing spaces in which container-grown plants can be used with extraordinary effect to create gardens in the air. Large-scale roof gardens can incorporate many of the features of a garden at ground level, including seating for relaxing and entertaining, barbecues, ornamental pools, and trees and climbers on supports. But even the smallest balcony can be transformed into a green and flower-filled outdoor room—a valuable extension of the living space indoors and a beautiful frame for the world beyond.

Partial screening
A see-through screen helps to create an intimate, sheltered atmosphere in this roof garden. New Zealand flax (*Phormium*) stands up well to windy conditions, and is used here to make an impressive focal feature in a large but lightweight urn.

Special challenges

Almost any balcony or flat roof area has planting potential, but such spaces do present special challenges, and safety is a major consideration. Plants, moist growing mix, containers, and all the other features that make up a garden weigh a considerable amount, which must be within the structure's load-bearing capacity. In addition, flooring must be waterproof and adequately drained. It is always advisable to consult an architect or structural engineer

before planning a roof or balcony garden, and check that local laws permit such structures. Expert advice should include suggestions for fortifying structural support, or on how to place heavy elements to use the existing load-bearing capacity of walls or joists. With careful choice of materials, the accumulated weight of garden components can be minimized. For example, consider wooden decking rather than tiling as a flooring material. Select plastic or fiberglass containers rather than those made

of very heavy materials, such as stone and concrete; and use soilless rather than soil-based growing mix to reduce the load further.

Balconies and roof gardens need barriers to protect those using the space: consult relevant building regulations governing minimum standards and heights for railings and walls. Balconies and roof gardens are much more likely to be affected by turbulence and strong winds than gardens at ground level, so all containers must be firmly secured. It is important, too, that none of the contents of a balcony or roof garden fall off, putting at risk people and property below. Even within a roof garden or balcony, falling pots and large plants can cause damage, for instance, to windows. To prevent them from being blown over, lightweight containers may need ballast or

anchoring in position. Remember that pots with tall, narrow bases are much less stable than those with squat, broad bases.

The blustery winds that are a typical feature of balconies and roof gardens may damage fragile growth and wither tender foliage on plants such as Japanese maples (*Acer palmatum* cultivars). Drying winds combined with full sun create challenging growing conditions. The most successful plants are tough and drought-tolerant; however, a wide range of plants will grow well provided they receive an adequate and regular water supply. On a large roof garden, an automated irrigation system can be the most efficient way to maintain satisfactory moisture levels, provided that provision is made for dealing with excess water. It is important that the structure

Shade in summer
This lightweight bamboo screen provides invaluable shade from fierce overhead summer sun on a roof or balcony garden.

Well-managed space
On this wooden, first-floor deck, container-grown plants are carefully grouped so that they do not impede access to the steps.

Planting for an exposed location
Flowers and foliage plants, including gray-leaved *Senecio cineraria* and spreading *Scaevola* with fan-shaped flowers, make a wind-tolerant mixture.

incorporates drainage channels so that water does not form puddles after rain or snowfall. Wooden decking can be laid to disguise any drainage systems required.

Planting on balconies

Plants for balconies can be grown in pots and troughs that stand on the balcony floor, in wall-mounted containers, or in those that are securely fixed to railings. When a balcony forms a garden extension to a room, the appearance of the containers and plants is most often judged from inside. Use planting to frame rather than obscure a good view, perhaps by grouping containers at either side of a clear central area. If, on the other hand, the view is dull or mediocre, use container-grown plants to block it out. In a similar way, trailing plants, spilling from pots or troughs mounted at the top of railings, can ensure privacy by screening the room within from view.

Balcony plantings can be just as attractive from within as from outside a building. Balconies, like window boxes, can be planted to complement the architecture, perhaps with plans that coordinate with plantings at ground level and on the floors above. Good trailing plants for sunny balconies include ivy-leaved geraniums; these are reasonably drought-tolerant and flower freely through summer and into fall. Many bushy and upright plants also adapt well to life on sunny balconies, including aromatic herbs, such as hyssop (*Hyssopus officinalis*) and long-flowering annuals, such as the kingfisher daisy (*Felicia bergeriana*).

While the choice for shady balconies is more limited, elegant designs can be created using cultivars of English ivy (*Hedera helix*) and evergreens, such as boxwood (*Buxus sempervirens*), which provide year-round interest. Add extra color with compact, shade-tolerant annuals and biennials, such as winter- and summer-flowering pansies (*Viola x wittrockiana*) or impatiens (*Impatiens walleriana*), which bloom for several months during summer.

Planting in roof gardens

Large balconies and roof gardens often provide views of dramatic cityscapes. If this is the case,

Carefully placed containers
These colorful hanging baskets of petunias, placed near pillars so they do not obscure the lush garden beyond, provide a jewel-like contrast to the predominantly green foliage. The surrounding plants have been encouraged to grow through the railings to soften the lines, creating a relaxed and exotic effect.

Minimalist formality
Strip decking, squared-up layout, and rounded topiary all contribute to the formality of a roof garden that includes planted and empty containers.

capitalize on the view and use planting to frame it. Whether the design is formal or informal, try to group containers so that the revelation of a view is gradual. Alternatively, create frames for a series of different vistas, which will ensure that the greatest one of all does not lose its novelty.

Perhaps more common than a beautiful vista is a dreary view from a drafty and overlooked space. In this case, the best option is to create a more inward-looking garden. A climbing plant, barrier, or trellis not only helps to block out ugly views but also establishes an intimate atmosphere and helps reduce wind turbulence. Within the defined space, the design could be formal, using relatively few shrubs trimmed to simple geometric shapes, or plants could be assembled to suggest the whimsy of a traditional English cottage garden. For colorful, long-lasting displays, massed bedding plants are a good option, but there is also a chance to experiment with vegetables and herbs, or subtropical and tropical plants. By creating compartments with screens, or even a pergola, variety is increased and intimacy enhanced.

Whatever the chosen style, arrange containers so they do not clutter areas used for seating or entertaining. For the most wind-resistant results, choose bushy and compact plants; they are less likely to be damaged or desiccated by strong winds. Compact cultivars of most popular bedding plants are readily available, and there are many bushy shrubs to choose in preference to those that are tall and topheavy.

Patio fruit

A considerable number of different fruit crops may be grown successfully in large containers on decks, patios, or porches where there is adequate room for them to develop. As well as providing seasonally attractive blooms and edible crops, some tree and bush fruits may be used as feature plants to provide contrast in flower beds or borders, or used as focal points of a vista.

Choosing container fruit crops

Several of the tree fruits suitable for container culture are grown on dwarfing rootstocks that curb their natural vigor without affecting their capacity to produce flowers and fruit. Apple container crops are best grown using the dwarfing rootstocks 'M27' or 'EMLA 27' to produce bush or pyramid forms. Similarly, pear cultivars grafted on the semidwarfing 'Quince A' rootstock. There are several choices of dwarfing rootstocks for plums, peaches, and nectarines that can be very successful in containers. If you are growing apples and pears, remember that it is important to choose compatible cultivars to ensure fertilization occurs (see pp.435–437 and 444–445). Figs and various citrus fruit are also highly suitable as container plants. Cherries are sometimes grown in bush form on a semidwarfing rootstock; however they are usually better grown as fan-trained plants rather than in pots.

Several kinds of berry crops including black currants, red currants, gooseberries, raspberries, and strawberries will crop successfully in containers.

Blueberry cultivars, which are mainly derived from *Vaccinium corymbosum* and related species, also grow well as container plants, provided an acidic soil mix is used.

Preparing and positioning the container

Choose stable clay containers or strong plastic pots with a diameter of at least 12–18in (30–45cm) and room for drainage materials at the base (see also CONTAINER VEGETABLES, p.331). Use a fairly rich multipurpose soil mix to which extra garden compost has been added. been added. Young, vigorous plants may need repotting annually after leaf fall to prevent them from becoming potbound, which may restrict their growth and reduce flowering.

Hardy fruit in containers should generally be placed in a sunny site, and ideally protected from strong winds. Early flowering tender crops such as peaches, nectarines, and citrus fruit are best brought into a conservatory or greenhouse to flower unless the site is frost-free. Stand containers on bricks or pot feet to allow free water flow from the drainage holes.

FRUIT CROPS TO TRY IN CONTAINERS

Apples

Blueberries

Raspberries

Cherries

Peaches

Pears

Figs

Red currants

Plums

Watering and feeding

When grown in containers, fruit crops generally require more attention to feeding and watering than they do in the open garden. The soil mix in the containers should never be allowed to dry out because this will slow the growth of young trees and bushes. Container fruit tend to be thirsty, and the plants need plenty of water to crop well. Give them plenty of fertilizer: provide a potassium-rich liquid fertilizer every two weeks through the growing season to encourage flower and fruit production, which otherwise may be sparse.

Tender container crops
In most areas citrus and early flowering fruit like peaches, nectarines, and apricots will require winter protection.

Fruit baskets
Strawberries generally bear well in pots. They are a good choice for hanging baskets, provided they are fed and watered regularly.

CULTIVARS FOR CONTAINERS

Apples
A wide range of choices do well in containers; stick with moderately vigorous cultivars on dwarfing rootstocks.

Apricots 'Garden Annie', 'Moor Park'

Blueberries 'Bluecrop', 'Sunshine Blue', 'Tophat', 'Northsky'

Cherries
  Sweet: 'Stark Crimson', 'Glacier', 'Stella'
  Tart: 'Morello', 'North Star'

Citrus fruits Calamondins; Kumquat 'Nagami'; Lemon 'Improved Meyer'; Satsuma 'Owari', 'Okitsu', 'Miyagawa'; Clementine 'Nules'

Figs 'Brown Turkey', 'Celeste', 'Green Ischia'

Nectarines 'Panamint', 'Harflame', 'Crimson Snow'

Peaches 'Harrow Beauty', 'Honeybabe', 'Madison','Midpride', 'Reliance', 'Pixzee'

Pears 'Beurre Hardy', 'Conference', 'Rochester'

Raspberries 'Autumn Bliss', 'Glen Ample', 'Glen Magna', 'Glen May', 'Glen Prosen', 'Malling Admiral', 'Malling Jewel', 'Polka', 'Tulameen'

Red currants 'Red Lake'

Strawberries Nearly all varieties do well, including 'All Star', 'Tristar', 'Hood', 'Albion', 'Seascape', 'Yellow Wonder'

PLANTER'S GUIDE TO CONTAINER PLANTS

TREES AND SHRUBS

See also p.59 for larger trees. For dwarf conifers, see p.62

Abutilon
Acer japonicum,
  A. palmatum
Anisodontea capensis
Argyranthemum
  (subshrub)
Brugmansia
Buxus balearica,
  B. microphylla,
  B. sempervirens
Calluna vulgaris
Camellia
x Citrofortunella microcarpa
Codiaeum variegatum
  var. pictum
Cuphea
Dracaena, some
Erica
Euonymus fortunei
x Fatshedera lizei
Fatsia japonica
Fuchsia
Gardenia
Hebe
Hibiscus rosa-sinensis
Hydrangea macrophylla (and cvs),
  H. paniculata,
  H. quercifolia 'Snowflake'
Lantana
Lavandula
Nerium oleander
Prunus laurocerasus
Rhododendron
Rosa (Groundcover, Miniature,
  and Patio hybrids)
Santolina
Senecio cineraria (as an annual)
Skimmia japonica
Solanum rantonnetii
Tibouchina
Viburnum davidii,
  V. tinus
Yucca, some

PALMS AND CYCADS

Chamaedorea
Chamaerops
Cocos
Cycas revoluta
Howea
Jubaea
Phoenix
Rhapis
Sabal
Trachycarpus fortunei
Washingtonia

BAMBOOS, GRASSES, AND GRASSLIKE PLANTS

Carex
Deschampsia cespitosa (cvs)
Fargesia murielae,
  F. nitida
Hakonechloa macra (cvs)
Himalayacalamus falconeri
Imperata cylindrica 'Rubra'
Indocalamus tessellatus

Pennisetum alopecuroides
Phalaris arundinacea
  var. picta
Phyllostachys aurea,
  P. flexuosa,
  P. nigra
Pleioblastus variegatus,
  P. viridistriatus
Shibataea kumasasa

PERENNIALS

See also Planter's guide to rock plants, Planting in troughs, p.259

Achimenes
Agapanthus
Alchemilla
Astilbe
Begonia Rex Group
Bergenia
Calceolaria integrifolia (cvs)
Campanula (dwarf)
Canna
Catharanthus roseus
Chrysanthemum
Convolvulus sabatius
Dianthus
Diascia
Ensete ventricosum
Fittonia
Glechoma hederacea
  'Variegata'
Heuchera
Hosta
Houttuynia cordata
  'Chameleon'
Lamium maculatum
Lysimachia nummularia
  'Aurea'
Musa basjoo
Nepeta
Osteospermum
Pelargonium
Peperomia
Phlox (dwarf)
Phormium
Plectranthus
Primula Polyanthus Group
Salvia discolor,
  S. uliginosa
Tiarella
Tolmiea menziesii
Tradescantia fluminensis (cvs),
  T. zebrina

CLIMBERS

☆ Annual, or commonly grown as one

Bougainvillea
Clematis, many
Clerodendrum
  thomsoniae
Cobaea scandens ☆
Eccremocarpus scaber ☆
Hedera helix
Jasminum
Lathyrus odoratus ☆
Passiflora
Rhodochiton atrosanguineus ☆
Stephanotis
Thunbergia alata ☆
Trachelospermum

CACTI AND SUCCULENTS
See p.342

FERNS

Adiantum
Asplenium
  scolopendrium
Athyrium
Blechnum
Davallia
Dicksonia antarctica
Nephrolepis
Platycerium
Polypodium
Polystichum

BULBS

Amaryllis belladonna
Anemone blanda,
  A. coronaria (cvs),
  A. x fulgens
Begonia (tuberous)
Canna
Chionodoxa
Clivia
Crocus
Cyclamen
Dahlia
Freesia
Galanthus
Hippeastrum
Hyacinthus (cvs)
Iris (bulbous)
Ixia
Lachenalia
Lilium, some
Muscari
Narcissus
Nerine
Scilla (some spp.)
Tulipa

ANNUALS AND BIENNIALS
§ Perennial or subshrub commonly grown as an annual or biennial

Ageratum
Antirrhinum
  (dwarf cvs)
Bellis perennis (cvs)
Bidens §
Brachyscome
Brassica oleracea
  (ornamental cvs)
Calendula officinalis
Celosia §
Dianthus barbatus,
  D. chinensis § (cvs)
Erysimum
Exacum affine §
Gazania §
Helichrysum petiolare §
Heliotropium §
Impatiens §
Iresine §
Lobelia erinus § (cvs)
Lotus berthelotii §,
  L. maculatus §
Matthiola Brompton Series,
  M. East Lothian Series
Mimulus hybrids

Nicotiana §
Pericallis §
Petunia §
Primula Polyanthus
  Group §
Ricinus communis § (cvs)
Salvia coccinea §,
  S. farinacea §,
  S. patens §,
  S. splendens §,
  S. viridis §
Scaevola §
Schizanthus pinnatus (cvs)
Solanum capsicastrum §,
  S. pseudocapsicum §
Solenostemon §
Tagetes
Tropaeolum majus
  (cvs and hybrids)
Verbena hybrids §
Viola x wittrockiana §
Zinnia

FRUIT

Apples (on dwarfing rootstocks)
Blueberries
Citrus (most)
Figs
Grapes
Peaches (dwarf)
Pears
Plums
Raspberries
Red currants
Strawberries

HERBS

Most herbs described on pp.407–410 can be grown in containers

Hydrangea macrophylla 'Blue Bonnet'

Choosing containers

A suitable container in which to grow plants must satisfy many criteria. It should hold sufficient potting mix to give plants adequate space for root development and to supply the moisture and nutrients necessary for growth. A container must also allow excess water to drain away, usually by means of one or more drainage holes in the base. Stability is also important; if a container is easily knocked or blown over, it may create a safety hazard and both the container and the plants in it may suffer damage.

Many commercially available containers satisfy these requirements and, being mass-produced, are relatively inexpensive. Other, more expensive ones are made individually or in small quantities, but these, along with homemade or improvised containers, often have more character and make an eye-catching statement of individual taste.

Assorted containers
Plants can be successfully grown in a wide variety of specially made and improvised containers—in many shapes and sizes—provided they have at least one drainage hole.

Materials and finishes

Containers are available in a range of materials and finishes, each having practical and aesthetic advantages that should be taken into account before making a choice. Bear in mind where a container is to stand; its weight, for example, can be an important factor. Decide whether the style of container is to complement that of the landscape or whether the container will play a functional but subordinate role to the plants it contains. Consider also matching accessories, such as trays or saucers, which are useful for

Change of use
A galvanized tub makes an eye-catching container for a clump of mixed tulips and grape hyacinths (*Muscari*). With adequate capacity for potting mix, and holes drilled in the base for drainage, this old-fashioned tub has been cleverly transformed into an unusual and attractive container for plants.

watering from below and help to keep the surfaces the pots stand on free of stains. Detached clay pot feet are particularly useful for lifting flat-bottomed containers above smooth surfaces so that excess water can drain freely.

Clay
Traditional unglazed pots of fired clay (terra-cotta) have been valued for centuries for their beauty as plant containers—large jars and urns can be very handsome features in a yard, even when left unplanted. Clay is readily molded to many

sizes and shapes, and can be either plain or have a molded decoration. Small to medium-sized plain pots are generally inexpensive, although costs rise as sizes increase. The most expensive are cold-resistant ones, which will not flake or crack if exposed to low temperatures during winter. Before the winter cold sets in, clay containers that are not frost-proof should be protected with an insulating material, such as bubble plastic, or be moved under cover. All clay pots must be handled carefully; any kind of shock is likely to cause chipping, cracking, or breakage.

Clay is a porous material, so a pot should be soaked in clean water before being filled with potting mix. Evaporation from planted clay pots helps keep plant roots cooler in summer than in nonporous ones and, while more frequent watering is necessary, there is less risk of waterlogging. This makes clay ideal for alpines and other plants that demand good drainage. The porosity also gives acceptable results with capillary watering systems (see p.577).

In most circumstances, the weight of terra-cotta pots filled with moist potting mix is an advantage because it produces stability. Once planted, however, they are hard to move and the weight can be a serious drawback if they are to be placed on balconies and roof gardens (see pp.316–317).

Clay's warm, earthy color, in shades of orange- or red-brown, can at first seem rather brash but, once weathered with algae, terra-cotta blends unobtrusively into many settings and complements a wide range of plants. If necessary, algal growth can be scrubbed off between plantings, using warm soapy water and a stiff-bristled brush.

Glazed ceramics
Whether glossy or matte, the variously colored, shaped, and textured finishes on glazed pots can make them distinctive ornamental features in the landscape. In addition to brightly colored and vividly patterned glazes, those imitating the subdued green of celadon ware may also be worth considering for a more subdued design. Unless specifically labeled as cold resistant, glazed containers should not be left outdoors during winter. Their surface is not porous, so there is less water loss than from unglazed pots and they are also easier to wipe clean.

Plastic
Plastics are versatile materials that can be molded into many different shapes and are now widely used in the manufacture of inexpensive containers. The most durable pots are made of a polyethythene and polypropylene mix, which does not

Container accessories
A saucer will protect a surface from staining, but it must not store excess water. Raise flat-bottomed pots up on pot feet, so they drain freely.

become brittle in low temperatures— unlike polypropylene when used on its own.

Plastic containers are made in almost any color; they can be plain, textured, or with a relief design, and can be glossy or matte. Plastic is often used to simulate other materials and perhaps this is why it is sometimes viewed as second-rate, but it does have many virtues. It is lightweight, for example, and, therefore, useful on indoor shelves, balconies, and roof gardens that are not strong enough for heavier materials. Plastic is not porous, so water is not lost through the sides of containers, and frequency of watering is less than with clay pots. Plastic pots are also

more effective with capillary watering systems than clay ones (see p.577).

Grow bags are specialized plastic containers made from flexible sheet plastic and filled with a lightweight soilless potting mix. The potting mix will sustain a main crop, such as tomatoes and usually also a secondary crop, after which the potting mix can be spread in the garden and the container disposed of. Grow bags are functional containers are not particularly good looking, but can be masked by plants in full growth.

Wood

Wood is a particularly useful material forcustom-fitted containers such as window boxes. It is also the material of first choice for a number of other traditional containers, including French box tubs and half-barrels, in which the staves are held together by metal bands. Hardwoods, which should come from a renewable source, last longer than softwoods, but are more expensive. Preservative treatments will extend the life of softwoods but check before using that the preservative is labeled as being harmless to plants.

Stone and concrete

Natural stone, available in many different textures and colors, is a desirable container material that

ADAPTING CONTAINERS

Plants can be grown in almost any container that holds potting mix and permits free drainage of water. Drill drainage holes in the base of galvanized metal containers, old buckets, and cans to transform them. Potential containers that are already

pierced, such as kitchen colanders, should be lined so that the potting mix does not fall out. Use dark-colored, flexible plastic sheeting or a plastic bag of an appropriate size. Prick the bottom of the liner so that excess water can drain away freely.

Colander basket
To convert a colander into a hanging container, attach chains and line it with pierced sheeting.

Drilling drainage holes
Masking tape placed over the position of the drainage hole provides a secure grip for the drill bit.

is expensive and heavy. Marble, which is often used in classical urns, can be intricately carved and given a high polish, while sandstone containers are frequently left with a rough finish. Various kinds of reconstituted stone are also used in the manufacture of containers. These too are heavy and expensive, but generally cheaper than natural stone. Concrete containers may be cheaper still.

All heavy containers should be placed in their final location in the garden or sunroom before being filled with potting mix. The algal growth that develops on such materials helps to soften the initial raw appearance. Concrete and rough stone are difficult to clean.

Metal

Lead is a traditional material for cisterns, garden ornaments, and containers, and can be introduced to reinforce a period style in a garden. Whether antique or modern, lead containers are expensive, heavy, and easily dented or distorted, because of the softness of this metal.

Cast iron was in vogue in the 19th century and the numerous vase and urn shapes popular then are available again now. Cast iron, however, is expensive and will rust unless powder-coated or painted.

Galvanized metal containers are both lightweight and available in a wide range of attractive shapes and sizes. Now often used to lend a modern flavor, especially in urban gardens, most are inexpensive enough to discard as tastes and fashions change.

Many hanging baskets and brackets are made of wire, which is usually covered with plastic to provide a suitable background color to plants and to prolong the life of the container.

Fiberglass

Fiberglass is a lightweight material that is easily molded into many different shapes. It is frost-proof, strong, and long-lasting; although rather brittle, it can be repaired. Because of its relative cheapness and versatility, it is often used to simulate other materials, including stone, metal, and wood.

Unusual container materials

A number of domestic, agricultural, architectural, and industrial items can be transformed into highly individual containers (see *Adapting Containers*, above). Salvaged and recycled items, such as wooden boxes or old paint cans, can also make unorthodox plant containers.

Most such containers can be decorated with paints, stains, or other materials, which are available for use on a variety of surfaces.

Size and proportion
When planning the scale and proportion of a display, it is important to consider the growth habit of the species you have chosen. Here, plants have been carefully selected to complement the size of container.

Potting mixes for containers

The growing medium used in containers should give plants the best chance of maximizing their ornamental or productive potential. It must be well aerated and moisture-retentive, with a resilient structure that can withstand heavy watering. Ordinary garden soil should not be used; its structure, chemical balance, and nutrient levels are variable, and it will almost certainly contain weed seeds, pests, and disease organisms. The best results are achieved with precisely formulated potting mixes that are produced commercially or prepared or modified at home.

Potting mixes

There are two main types of potting mix: soil-based ones, which should have sterilized, high-quality soil as their main ingredient; and loamless potting mixes, which contain no soil and are usually based on a peat substitute or peat.

Soil-based potting mixes

These potting mixes are free-draining and have good aeration and structure, which encourages root development. They provide a steady supply of nutrients to sustain the long-term growth of plants and are less prone to waterlogging than other potting mixes. They also dry out more slowly, making them easier to manage in containers. Being heavier than soilless potting mixes, soil-based ones are especially useful in counterbalancing topgrowth. Plants that are cultivated in soil-based potting mix and then transplanted into garden soil are likely to become established quickly and develop well. The structure and nutrient content of soil-based potting mixes do, however, deteriorate in storage. Buy a recognized brand name from a reputable supplier and use the potting mix as soon as possible.

The soil used in these potting mixes should have a high organic content. Good-quality soil is developed commercially by stacking sod for at least six months. It is then sterilized by heat or chemical treatment to kill pests, diseases, and weed seeds.

You can make your own soil-based or soilless potting mix, and vary the ingredients for the particular purpose you have in mind. Soils for potting mixes should have a high organic content. One way to produce such a soil is by stacking up sod and allowing it to break down for at least six months.

A basic recipe for a soil-based potting mix is one-third garden soil, one-third garden compost, and one-third sand. It helps to screen the soil and compost first. If the only soil available to you is low in organic matter, then reduce the proportion of soil and increase the proportion of compost in the mix overall. Compost supplies a broad range of nutrients, and many plants will grow well in this basic mix. An advantage of using compost as an ingredient in potting mixes is that the beneficial microorganisms in compost generally outcompete any pathogenic microbes in the soil, so there's no need to sterilize the soil.

If you don't have a supply of compost, you can substitute peat, coir, or leaf mold in its place. Since these materials are lower in nutrients than compost, you'll need to bolster the mix by adding bonemeal (to supply phosphorus), dried blood (a nitrogen source), and possibly ground limestone (to balance soil pH).

Potting mixes for plants with special needs
Azaleas and other rhododendrons are intolerant of alkaline soils. In a container they are best grown in an acidic potting mix, which is soil-based but lime-free.

COMMON INGREDIENTS FOR POTTING MIXES

Sterile soil
Sterilized garden soil, with good nutrient supply, drainage, aeration, and moisture retention.

Grit
Various grades of grit are added to potting mix to improve drainage and aeration.

Peat
Well-aerated and moisture-retentive but low in nutrients. Hard to rewet.

Vermiculite
Expanded, air-blown mica acts like perlite, but holds more water and less air.

Fine bark
Used as a peat substitute, especially in potting mixes formulated for acid-loving plants.

Perlite
Expanded, volcanic rock granules retain moisture but drain freely. Aids aeration.

Coir
This peat substitute dries less rapidly than peat but needs more frequent feeding.

Sand
Coarse and fine (silver) sands aid the creation of more open-textured potting mixes.

Leaf mold
Used as a peat substitute and potting mix additive, especially for woodland plants.

Acidic potting mixes

Most commercial potting mixes cover the needs of large numbers of plants, but you'll need to seek out a special mix for rhododendrons and other plants that thrive only on neutral to acidic soils. These require special soil-based mixes that do not contain limestone. Such low-pH mixes are usually labeled "acidic" or "rhododendron mix." Rarely, the label may describe them as "ericaceous," referring to the acidic soil-favoring Ericaceae (azalea family).

Soilless potting mixes

Soilless potting mixes are widely used in container gardening. They are usually based on 3 parts (by volume) of peat or peat substitute and 1 part sand. The fertilizer content varies. Some also contain perlite or vermiculite to aid aeration and drainage.

All soilless potting mixes are relatively clean to use as well as lightweight, and are generally less expensive than soil-based ones. North America has huge reserves of peat and less than one percent has been harvested to date. Conservation practices used by the major peat companies ensure the harvested areas will regenerate. The European practice of using other materials is unnecessary here. However, if you choose to avoid peat, suitable peat substitutes for use in potting mixes are fine bark, coir (coconut fiber and bark), and leaf mold.

Many potting mixes based on peat require careful watering; although the surface may be dry, the layers beneath are often adequately moist. Peat combines moisture retentiveness with good aeration, but it does dry out rapidly and, once dry, is difficult to rewet. Conversely, if overwatered, it is prone to waterlogging. In pots, soilless potting mixes based on peat or peat subtitute should be kept evenly moist at all times.

Most soilless potting mixes, including peat-based ones, break down rapidly so that the potting mix shrinks and loses structure. In general, they do not provide as firm of roothold as soil-based potting

MODIFYING POTTING MIX

Most alpines need few nutrients and good drainage, so plant them over a layer of broken crocks in a 50:50 mix of all-purpose potting mix and grit.

mixes. Also, plants moved from them to beds or borders frequently adapt poorly to garden soil.

Soilless potting mixes are suitable for short-term use, such as growing seedlings and annuals and sowing large seeds. Although they provide a suitable medium for many plants in containers, hanging baskets, and on balconies and roof gardens, the shortcomings of soilless potting mixes mean that they are not suitable for long-term plantings, such as of trees and shrubs.

Peat and peat substitutes are naturally low in nutrients, which tend to leach quickly. Regular use of soluble fertilizers can overcome this, but their effect does not last. A more efficient way of maintaining a steady nutrient supply is to incorporate slow-release inorganic fertilizers into the potting mix. These are complete formulations, some slowly degrading in the soil, others absorbing water until they burst open, spreading their fertilizer. Many discharge their nutrients over several months. The expense of slow-release fertilizers is offset by the convenience and the time that is saved in not having

POTTING SOIL ADDITIVES

Water-absorbing polymers
When wetted, these granules expand, providing a reservoir of moisture on which plants can draw.

GOOD DRAINAGE

To ensure good drainage, place terra-cotta pot shards in the bottom of a container; large pebbles and chunks of styrofoam are also effective as drainage material.

to make frequent applications of soluble fertilizers. Yet the nutrient-release pattern of slow-release fertilizers, especially that of long-term formulas, can be very difficult to predict, since it is affected by the pH level, moisture content, and temperature of the potting mix.

To maintain a reservoir of moisture in a container without waterlogging the potting mix, incorporate water-absorbing polymers into the growing mix. When wetted, the granules swell to make a fragmented gel. They may not be effective over very long periods, but the reduction of water loss is particularly useful in soilless potting mixes and in exposed containers, such as hanging baskets, which dry out rapidly.

Special potting mixes
As well as acidic potting mixes, there are other specialized potting mixes produced commercially to

Slow-release fertilizers
These discharge nutrients over an extended period, eliminating the need for frequent fertilization.

ENVIRONMENTALLY FRIENDLY GROWING MIXES

For gardeners preferring to grow plants in containers according to organic principles, it is important to choose a potting mix suitable for the type of plant to be grown in the pot. Long-term container plants, such as shrubs, need a soil-based nutrient-rich medium that is also water-retentive. Use a mix of 1 part soil, 1 part general leaf mold, and 1 part garden compost or well-rotted manure by volume, adding another part of sharp sand if the plants require good drainage. Comfrey leaf mold (see p.625), which is nutrient-rich, may be substituted for general leaf mold, if available.

Short-term, quick-growing container plants as well as hanging basket plants—usually annuals or perennials grown as annuals—are best grown in a soilless potting mix consisting of 3 parts peat or well-rotted leaf mold to 1 part comfrey leaf mold by volume. To improve water retention, an organic moisture retainer based on coarse seaweed meal may be added to the mix.

In both cases, worm compost may be used in place of comfrey leaf mold, because it is both water-retentive and nutrient rich, a bonus for many of the quick-growing plants used.

suit the requirements of particular groups of plants. Orchid potting mixes are free-draining and often contain charcoal and fine bark for good aeration. Cactus potting mixes are even more free-draining, containing a high proportion of grit, and are usually low in nutrients. Aquatic potting mixes, which are heavy for better anchorage, are particularly variable as the major constituent—soil—is not of a consistent standard. Bulb fiber potting mix is made from undecomposed sphagnum moss, which has an open structure and so is suitable for growing bulbs in containers that do not have drainage holes.

Modifying potting mixes
Both commercially produced and homemade potting mixes can be easily adapted for particular plants or groups of plants. Perlite and vermiculite are commonly put in homemade potting mixes to improve both drainage and aeration. The addition of various grades of grit and sharp sand make potting mixes drain more freely. Grit, for example, is often mixed in equal parts by volume to soil mix to make a free-draining potting mix for alpine plants. Leaf mold, which is an excellent peat substitute in homemade potting mixes, can also be added to ready-made potting mixes to produce a moisture-retentive growing mix suitable for woodland plants.

Mulches
Mulches are materials used to cover soils or potting mixes to slow down water loss, to even out soil temperature fluctuations, and to discourage the growth of weeds. The most useful and neatest mulch for most plants in containers is grit spread evenly over the potting mix to a depth of approximately

½in (1cm). A mulch of limestone chips is suitable for alpines that prefer alkaline soils, while granite chips can be used for lime-haters. Coarse gravel used as a topdressing for trees and shrubs can also help to stabilize containers. Organic mulches generally include granulated bark and cocoa shell; some of these tend to be blown around unless they are damp. Composted pine needles can be used for acid-loving plants.

MIXING POTTING MIX

The principal difficulty for amateur gardeners preparing their own sterile potting mix is sterilizing the soil. Special soil-sterilizing units used for large-scale heat treatment are expensive, but smaller-scale units are available from specialty suppliers. To treat small quantities, put the soil through a ¼in (5mm) sieve to remove stones and lumps. Then spread it 3in (8cm) deep on a baking sheet and bake for 30 minutes at 400°F (200°C) in a kitchen oven. Alternatively, put the soil in a roasting bag and heat in a microwave oven on full power for 10 minutes.

Assemble the ingredients on a clean, flat surface. (For exact quantities, see "Soil-based potting mixes," p.322.) Mix the sterilized soil and peat or peat substitute (well moistened if it is dry). Combine the ground limestone and soil mix with some of the sand to ensure even distribution and incorporate this thoroughly into the remaining sand, soil, and peat substitute or peat.

Planting large and long-lived plants

Although many gardeners concentrate on planting annuals to create colorful container displays for late winter, spring, and summer, there are many longer-lived plants that do well in pots. They lend an appearance of maturity and provide a valuable core to a container garden, which can then be supplemented seasonally as other plants reach their peak. Large container-grown, frost-tender plants, such as brugmansias, can be placed outdoors for the summer and moved back under cover between fall and spring.

Plants and materials

For plants to do well for several years in containers, they must have the potential for long life and be given optimal growing conditions to ensure sustained good health.

Selecting plants

Whether buying plants or making a choice from stock raised at home, the best results are achieved by using container-grown, young but well-developed and vigorous plants that are free of pests and diseases. Look for good leaf color and examine the undersides as well as the tops of leaves for signs of disease or pest infestation. Reject any plants with any signs of disease or damage. Slide the plant out of its container and check that the roots are well developed. If the roots are tightly congested, the plant has probably been in its container too long and

may not establish quickly or well. Other signs that indicate that a plant has been overlong in its container include missing or illegible labels, containers covered with algal growth, or potting mix encrusted with moss. If buying a bare-root tree, check that the root system is well developed and has plenty of fibrous roots. Balled-and-burlapped trees and shrubs should have a firm ball of soil and roots encased in an undamaged plastic mesh or burlap cover and should show no signs of having dried out. Before purchasing, check visually from all angles to ensure growth is evenly balanced.

Choosing containers

Containers of many different materials are suitable for growing large and long-lived plants, provided they have adequate drainage. For plants with extensive top growth, it is vital that the container should lend weight and stability; the most suitable include broad-based containers such as large planters and terra-cotta urns (see p.320).

Select a container in proportion with the upper parts of the plant and its root ball. It must be big enough to permit good root development and to hold sufficient soil mix to supply enough moisture and nutrients. A container should be about 2in (5cm) wider and deeper than that from which the plant is being moved. Trees need more room to develop; allow a depth of at least one-and-a-half times that of the root ball and a diameter between a sixth and a quarter of the tree's height.

SELECTING A SHRUB

Good example
Many shrubs are sold container-grown. Choose a plant with a balanced framework of growth and reject specimens showing signs of any pests or disease.

Healthy leaves and vigorous well-balanced growth

Label in good condition indicating that plant is fresh stock

Clean container and weed-free potting mix

Suitable potting mixes

Plants that are to remain in their containers for several years need a growing mix that will provide a steady and continuous supply of nutrients. The most suitable potting mixes are soil-based with compost or slow-release fertilizer added. The nutrients in mixes based on peat or peat substitute are leached relatively quickly, so plants grown in them need feeding at frequent intervals throughout their life. Although a potential disadvantage on balconies and rooftops, the weight of soil-based composts provides stabilizing ballast and

a more secure roothold for plants than soilless mix. The majority of long-term plants thrive in a standard soil-based mix. Use an acidic soil mix for plants such as azaleas, rhododendrons, and camellias.

Planting a container

Before planting, assemble the container, drainage screening, potting mix, and any supports, as well as any pot feet, bricks, or blocks on which the container is to stand. Scrub the inside and outside of containers that are being reused,

PLANTING A SHRUB

1 Place a piece of screening in the base of a container with drainage holes. Partially fill the pot with a suitable soil-based potting mix, breaking it up if it contains lumps.

2 Place the shrub in its container in the center of the pot and fill around it, firming in the soil mix. Lift it out, leaving the hole intact. Water the plant before planting.

3 Remove the shrub from its original container and gently tease out the roots. Lower the shrub into the hole, firm in the soil mix all around, and water in well. Cover with a gravel mulch.

The finished planting

to remove any disease-causing organisms. Soak new terra-cotta pots in clean water. Place the container in its display location before planting; it will be heavy and difficult to move once it has been filled with potting mix.

Place a piece of screening over the drainage holes to prevent the potting mix from being washed out. If pots are to stand directly on the soil, be particularly vigilant for an invasion by earthworms or other creatures. Cover the screening with a layer of gravel for extra drainage, then add soil mix to a depth of 2–4in (5–10cm) to start. If a support is required, place it in position.

Tap the container of the selected plant to loosen the root ball and ease the plant out. It is important to position the plant in the new container at the same depth as it had been growing previously. This level can be detected by the soil mark, indicated by a change of color on the stem. Place the plant in the partially filled container, adjusting its height by adding potting mix if necessary. Top off with more mix, firming gently at intervals, until the finished surface is 2in (5cm) below the container's rim, which will leave room for water. Topdress with an organic

or grit mulch 1–1½in (2.5–4cm) deep. Water thoroughly, using rainwater for pH-sensitive plants.

Stakes and other supports

Many large container-grown plants need some form of permanent support. The most common support is a single stake, inserted at planting before the potting mix is added. This allows roots to spread around the stake and avoids the risk of root damage, which may occur if the stake is pushed in after planting. The stake should reach to just below the head of a standard tree or shrub. To hold the stem firmly, use an adjustable tie with a spacer to prevent the bark from rubbing and adjust it regularly as the stem girth increases.

Other kinds of supports include wooden, metal, and wire frames. Metal frames are available in various shapes, including an umbrellalike support for weeping standards like wisteria. Wire frames are particularly useful for evergreen climbers, such as short-jointed cultivars of English ivy (*Hedera helix*), which can be trained to form topiarylike shapes (see also TOPIARY, pp.108–109).

Container-grown climbers can be trained onto trellis fans (see below). Rustic supports consisting of a wigwam of bamboo

Staking plants
Tall container-grown plants should be staked from an early age so that they develop a straight stem and even growth all around.

poles are effective for slender climbers such as *Rhodochiton atrosanguineus*. Wicker hoops —a traditional support for pinks (*Dianthus*)—can be adapted for use with shrubby perennials such as pineapple sage (*Salvia elegans* 'Scarlet Pineapple').

PLANTING A CLIMBER IN A CONTAINER

Trellis panels, often with "legs" at the base, are specially made for containers and are available in wood or plastic-covered wire. Before using, treat wooden ones with a preservative that is harmless to plants. Match the size of both the container and the trellis panel to the vigor of the selected climber. A heavy container in concrete, stone, or terra-cotta provides the most stable base.

Place the container in position before planting. This should be beside a wall or fence so that the trellis can be attached to it for increased stability—a planted trellis presenting a large surface area to the elements. Fill the pot with an all-purpose soil mix. To avoid damaging the plant's roots, bed the support firmly into the soil mix along one side of the container; then plant the climber. After planting, secure the trellis top.

1 Put screening in the base of the pot. Place the support to one side of the pot and secure it in by working the potting mix around it.

2 Plant the climber at the same level as in the original pot, firming the soil mix so that the surface is 2in (5cm) below the rim.

3 Tie the main shoots to the support, and water the plant to settle the roots. Fix the trellis to a wall or fence for stability.

PLANTS WITH SPECIAL SOIL REQUIREMENTS

Lime-free potting mix

Agapetes
Andromeda
Arctostaphylos
Asteranthera ovata
Beaumontia grandiflora
Berberidopsis corallina
Billardiera
Calluna vulgaris (and cvs)
Camellia
Daboecia
Erica
Gardenia
Gaultheria
Hakea
Kennedia
Lapageria rosea
Lilium (some spp.)
Lithodora
Mitraria coccinea
Mutisia
Pieris
Rhododendron
Vaccinium

Moist, humus-rich potting mix

Acer
Camellia
Clematis
Hibiscus
Hosta
Rhododendron
Rosa
Viola

Free-draining potting mix

Agave
Armeria
Artemisia
Bougainvillea
Calendula
Convolvulus
Dianthus
Dorotheanthus
Erysimum
Eschscholzia
Helianthemum
Juniperus
Lavandula
Rosmarinus
Salvia
Santolina
Sempervivum
Thymus
Yucca

Camellia

Pruning and training

As with the pruning of trees, shrubs, and climbers in the open garden, the aim of pruning plants in containers is to maintain good health and maximize the ornamental display. In the early stages, pruning aims to encourage the development of a well-balanced plant with evenly spaced stems. Many deciduous and evergreen plants need little pruning beyond this. To keep plants healthy, cut out out all dead, damaged, and diseased wood and, on variegated plants, remove shoots with leaves that have reverted to plain green. Such tasks can be done at almost any time of the year, although in spring, check all plants thoroughly and deal with any problems.

Several plant groups, such as hydrangeas, roses, and clematis, however, need annual pruning. For further information, see pruning and training ORNAMENTAL SHRUBS (pp.86–121); ROSES (pp.146–169), CLIMBING PLANTS (pp.122–145), and CLEMATIS (pp.138–140). Topiary specimens require strict formative training and subsequent regular clipping (see TOPIARY, pp.108–109).

Standard specimens

Many trees, shrubs, and climbers can be grown as standards. However standards have a relatively high center of gravity, so choose a container that is heavy and broad-based. Most container-grown trees

are best trained as standards; the simple outline occupies little ground space and allows light to reach the plants grown beneath them. Shrubs or subshrubs that respond well to this treatment include fuchsias (see p.119) and argyranthemums. With strict pruning, even vigorous climbers, including ornamental or fruiting vines and wisterias, can be grown as standards.

During formative training, the stem must be staked until it is sturdy enough to support the head itself, although many standards will require a permanent stake. Ties must be firm; adjust them regularly to avoid constricting the stem as it expands. With trees, retain the lower branches in the initial stages to encourage stem thickening and remove them gradually over two or three years.

With shrubs, shorten the laterals on the main stem, which should also be supported with a stake. Retain laterals for a year to build stem strength, then remove them completely. For fuchsias, pinch out the laterals (see PINCH PRUNING, p.377). On all shrubs, allow the main stem to grow at least 8 in (20cm) beyond the desired head height, then cut it back to a bud or pair of buds to encourage the growth of laterals to form the head. Subsequently, tip prune the laterals to encourage further branching and form a dense crown of foliage.

Standard shrub
When grown as a standard, shrubs such as this *Syringa meyeri* 'Palibin' develop a bouquetlike head, which needs a heavy container to maintain stability.

PLANTS TO GROW AS STANDARDS

Shrubs and subshrubs

Argyranthemum
Brugmansia
Buxus sempervirens
Camellia
Caragana arborescens
x *Citrofortunella microcarpa*
Ficus carica
Fuchsia
Gardenia jasminoides
Heliotropium
Hibiscus rosa-sinensis
Lagerstroemia indica
Laurus nobilis
Leptospermum scoparium
Ligustrum (some spp.)
Myrtus communis
Nerium oleander
Pelargonium
Rosa (many spp.)
Rosmarinus officinalis
Salix caprea 'Kilmarnock'
Solenostemon
Viburnum tinus

Climbers

Bougainvillea
Lonicera (some spp.)
Rosa (some spp.)
Solanum jasminoides
Vitis (some spp.)
Wisteria

Bougainvillea

TRAINING A STANDARD WOODY-STEMMED CLIMBER

Stages of development

In the early stages of training (here, a vine), aim to develop a vigorous main vertical stem. Let sideshoots grow during the growing season so that their leaves can feed the stem, then remove them in the dormant season. Form the head by developing well-spaced laterals at an appropriate height and by pruning annually to maintain a supply of flowering spurs.

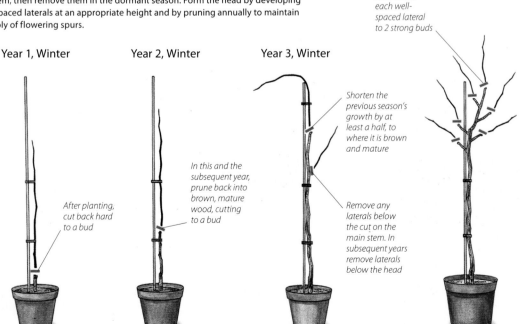

Year 1, Winter

After planting, cut back hard to a bud

Year 2, Winter

In this and the subsequent year, prune back into brown, mature wood, cutting to a bud

Year 3, Winter

Shorten the previous season's growth by at least a half, to where it is brown and mature

Remove any laterals below the cut on the main stem. In subsequent years remove laterals below the head

Year 4, Winter

Prune back each well-spaced lateral to 2 strong buds

Year 5 and onward

Shorten fruiting shoots, when they reach 12–18in (30–45cm) long, in summer

Prune flowered shoots back to two strong buds in winter

Thin spur systems as they build up and become congested

Planting seasonal displays

For many gardeners the essential plants for container gardens are the large number of annuals that give colorful displays over a long period in summer. Other plants to be planted each year include biennials for winter, spring, and summer, and bulbs for spring, summer, and fall. In general, fresh bulbs planted annually give better results than those used for several years.

Annuals and biennials

A wide selection of annuals and biennials is available as bedding plants from garden centers as early as mid-spring. Many are also easily raised from seed in a greenhouse or an enclosed porch. If potting up early under cover, harden plants off by moving containers outside in the day, but return them under cover at night until there is little risk of frost.

Before potting up, always water the chosen plants thoroughly. Then assemble the essential components, such as a clean container, drainage screening, soil-based or soilless potting mix blended with compost or slow-release fertilizer, moisture-holding polymers, and the selected plants. Place the metal or plastic screening over the drainage hole and fill the container three-quarters full with potting mix with added slow-release fertilizer and moisture-absorbing polymers.

With the plants still in their pots, experiment with arrangements that will balance their trailing, bushy, and upright habits. Once the design is satisfactory, begin planting in a systematic way, for example, by working from the center outward or from one side of the container to the other.

CONTAINERS THROUGH THE SEASONS

Spring
A terra-cotta pot planted with spring miniatures, including daffodils, primroses, and irises, provides a welcome splash of early color.

Winter
A harmonious mix of violas, *Choisya*, ivy, *Gaultheria*, and *Lamium* in fresh shades of green, yellow, and red make a charming late-winter feature.

Fall
A blend of purple foliage, shimmering grasses, and variegated ivy creates a dramatic late-season display.

To loosen each plant, tap the container, remove the plant, and place it in its new pot. Add or subtract potting mix as necessary so that each plant is at the same depth as in its original container, there are no air pockets within the mix, and the final level is about 2in (5cm) below the rim. Water the plants to settle them in.

Annuals and biennials for winter and early spring flowering should be potted up in the fall. Garden centers and nurseries, however, sometimes delay making available for sale plants that flower in late

winter and early spring. These can be planted during winter provided the soil mix is not frozen.

Bulbs

Most spring-flowering bulbs are best planted in early fall, as soon as they become available. Tulip bulbs, however, are best planted in late fall or early winter, when they are less susceptible to the fungal disease tulip fire/*Botrytis tulipae* (see p.672). Although bulbs can be mixed satisfactorily in a single container, it is generally better to plant different bulbs in

separate containers because of the difficulties of synchronizing their flowering times.

To extend the flowering display of the same type of bulb, plant more than one layer of bulbs in the container, provided it is deep enough to take several layers as well as soil mix below and above each bulb. For most bulbs, allow a minimum planting depth equal to three times the height of the bulb. To plant two layers of daffodils or tulips, for example, place screening in the base of a container and then cover with a layer of soil-based,

PLANTING A MIXED SUMMER CONTAINER

1 To create an attractive design, arrange your selected plants, still in their pots, to get an idea of how they will fit together. Mix bushy or upright plants with tumblers and trailers.

2 Establish your central feature plant and then work outward. It is possible to position plants closer together in the pot than in the open garden, but there must still be adequate room for growth.

3 Tilt some plants on their side so that they face out toward the rim of the pot. Some of the root ball may be left exposed on the soil surface—if you ensure that it is kept moist, the plant will thrive.

4 Once you are satisfied with the arrangement, add more potting mix to fill the container to about 2in (5cm) below the rim. Water the plants thoroughly to settle them in.

PLANTING A WINDOW BOX

1 If necessary, make drainage holes in the base and cover with screening, then a layer of soil mix. Add fertilizer and moisture-holding polymer.

2 Slide the plants out of their pots, and set them on the soil surface. Ensure that the top of the soil mix is 2in (5cm) below the box rim.

3 Fill around the plants with more soil mix. Put the window box in position, then water well. Continue to water regularly throughout the summer while the plants are in full growth.

4 Deadhead faded blooms regularly to prolong flowering, nip off yellowing leaves to limit disease, and trim excess foliage to keep the display looking well-balanced. Flowers benefit from liquid feeding, especially in later summer.

---

soilless, or bulb compost not less than 2in (5cm) deep. Plant the first layer so they are 1–4in (2.5–10cm) apart, depending on the type. Cover with soil mix so that just the tips are visible. Arrange a second layer of bulbs in the spaces between the first. Top off the container with soil mix until it is within 2in (5cm) of the container rim.

Lilies are among the most important bulbs for summer displays (see LILIES, p.239). They can be planted singly, or in groups of three or more in large containers. In general, lilies look better on their own rather than mixed with other plants in the same container. The best time to plant is in the fall, when bulbs are newly lifted. Select lily bulbs with plump, fleshy scales that are free of disease.

Lilies thrive in a well-drained growing medium, such as four parts soil-based potting mix mixed with one part grit and one part leaf mold, as well as slow-release fertilizer. Stand the container on pot feet, then fill with the potting mix. Plant with the tip of the bulb 4–6in (10–15cm) below the potting mix surface (about two or three times the height of the bulb) and three times the bulb's diameter apart. Stem-rooting lilies, which produce roots on the stem above the bulb as well as from the bulb itself, should be planted more deeply, at about three to four times the bulb's height.

Bulbs with bedding plants

Mixtures of spring bulbs and annuals or biennials make attractive displays in a single pot. Try planting tulips with forget-me-nots (*Myosotis*) or wallflowers (*Erysimum*), and small bulbs, such as scillas, with winter-flowering pansies (*Viola* x *wittrockiana*). Plant bulbs in the fall under a good covering of potting mix and add the annuals or biennials so that, when they are watered in, the surface of the compost is about 2in (5cm) below the container's rim.

Fruit, vegetables, and herbs

Although the yield is less when compared with crops grown in open ground, leafy salad crops and other vegetables, such as zucchini and beans, can be successfully cultivated in soilless potting mix with added compost if watered regularly. Strawberries generally prefer a soil-based potting mix, but tolerate a soilless one, and they must be kept moist at all times. Use special strawberry planters or adapt a wooden barrel by cutting planting holes, 2in (5cm) wide and 10in (25cm) apart at different levels in the sides. Alpine strawberries, such as *Fragaria* 'Baron Solemacher', are a good choice for a partly shaded site.

Herbs are among the most useful culinary plants for containers. Many are easily grown in pots of soilless mix with added grit (one-fifth by volume) to ensure good drainage.

SECURING WINDOW BOXES

A fully planted window box may appear to be stable, but when placed at a height on a wall or against a building, it is often subject to wind turbulence. If dislodged, such a heavy container poses a serious threat to the safety of people passing below and may cause considerable damage. All window boxes must therefore be secured firmly with heavy-duty metal brackets or wedges. The latter are ideal for sloping windowsills with a depth of at least 8in (20cm); they can be further secured in position by using mirror plates and hooks.

Mirror plates
These plates are fixed to the back of the window box, then hooked securely to the window frame.

Inserting wedges on a sloping sill

1 Place a level across a windowsill, then measure the gap between it and the sill to find the height of the wedge needed. Mark this dimension on a wood scrap that is 1¼in (30mm) shorter than the sill depth.

2 Mark a diagonal line to the opposite corner of the wood scrap. Then with another piece, mark out an identical wedge. Cut out both wedges and treat with preservative. Nail or screw to the bottom of the window box.

Planting hanging baskets and mangers

Hanging baskets and wall-mounted containers provide great opportunities to create colorful and imaginative plant displays. Nearly all of them are of open construction and are used with a liner that holds in the soil mix and retains moisture while allowing excess water to drain away. Hanging containers must be fixed to a secure overhead support or attached firmly to a wall well out of the way of pedestrians.

A variety of styles

The standard hanging basket is of lightweight construction in wire, usually plastic-coated, suspended by means of chains. Half-baskets of similar construction are designed to be wall-mounted. More solid baskets and containers, such as hayracks or mangers, are usually made of enameled or plastic-coated strip metal. Alternatives to openwork containers are suspended or wall-mounted pots with solid sides. Many such pots have the advantage of being self-watering, incorporating a reservoir that keeps the soil mix moist.

Types of liner

Many different liners are available, some of which are made to fit specific basket sizes, while others are cut to size. Most are patterned or colored so they are camouflaged within the containers. All can be pierced to allow planting in the sides, although holes are easier to make in some materials than others (see *Planting a hanging basket*, p.330).

Sheet plastic is among the most versatile of basket liners. It can be easily cut to size and slashed to provide drainage or planting holes.

Dark-colored plastic is relatively inconspicuous, particularly as growth develops. If desired, it can, however, readily be disguised with straw or less bulky burlap, for example (see *Planting a basket*, below). In addition to plastic, hanging baskets can be lined with a variety of premade basket liners (see right).

Potting mixes and additives

The most suitable potting mixes for the majority of seasonal displays are soilless formulations, which are light and easy to handle. For longer-lasting displays, for example, of groundcover roses, soil-based potting composts are preferable (see "Potting mixes for containers," p.322).

Fertilizers can be added as slow-release fertilizers or as a liquid such as fish emulsion. The addition of moisture-holding polymers helps to keep moisture levels steady.

Planting seasonal displays

Use trailing plants in tiers to envelop the sides of a hanging basket in flowers and foliage. Position trailing plants around the rim and bushy or upright plants in the center to form a crown. If the basket can be kept frost free, plant a summer basket in mid-spring. Harden off gradually by moving the basket outdoors by day and move to its final display spot only when risk of frost has passed.

Use the same planting technique for spring, fall, and winter displays. Hardy plants do not need hardening off, but should be kept in a sheltered place until well established.

LINING MATERIALS FOR BASKETS

Coir
Natural look; tricky to cut for side planting.

Foam
Absorbent, easily cut; can be conspicuous.

Recycled paper
Cheap, available with push-out planting holes.

Wool
Hard to cut, but good insulation for plant roots.

SECURING BASKETS

When filled, hanging baskets and other wall-mounted containers can be heavy, so they must be securely fastened to strong wall-mounted brackets or overhead supports, such as the crossbeams of a pergola. Wall-mounted containers, which must be hung plumb and level, are usually supplied with brackets; if fixing to masonry, insert wall anchors into the holes before screwing into position.

Bracket for a hanging basket
Holding the bracket plumb and level, mark the position of back plate holes. Insert wall anchors and secure with galvanized screws.

Hayrack fixtures
Mark and drill holes for a hooked bracket. Use a wall anchor and galvanized screw when fixing.

PLANTING A HAYRACK

1 Openwork manger-style baskets must be lined. To camouflage the liner, work in straw against the inner face of the curved front of a hayrack so that, when compressed, it forms a layer 1in (2.5cm) thick.

2 Cut a piece of sheet plastic to make a slightly oversized liner, and fit it inside the basket. Fold the excess toward the straw and tuck it in all around, to make a neat edge. Cut slits in the liner, at the bottom for drainage and at the front, if desired, for planting holes. Fill the hayrack to a third of its depth with potting mix.

3 Remove plants from their pots, tease out the root balls, and insert the plants in the potting mix. Adjust the soil level until the plants are at their original planting depth. Top off and firm the potting mix to within 1in (2.5cm) of the rim. Fix the hayrack in position. Water well.

PLANTING A HANGING BASKET

1 Unhook one of the basket's chains and place the basket on a flat surface, so that it is level. Adjust the liner (here, of coir) to fit the basket. Put a circle of black plastic, with a few slits in the bottom, at the base for water to drain away slowly.

2 Following the package instructions, add slow-release fertilizer granules to the potting mix. Partially fill the basket with the potting mix, then add a moisture-holding polymer and mix well. Use scissors to trim off any liner that extends above the rim.

3 After thoroughly soaking the plants in a bucket, set the specimen plant (in this case, a *Dahlia*) in the middle because this has the largest blooms and will be an eye-catching centerpiece.

4 Carefully position the smaller plants—here, marguerite, *Petunia,* and *Brachyscome*—and set any trailing ones (*Helichrysum*) around the basket rim.

5 Fill around the root balls of each plant with more potting mix to ensure that there are no air pockets, until the basket is filled within 1in (2.5cm) of the rim.

6 Water the basket thoroughly. If desired, cover the surface of the potting mix with an ornamental gravel mulch to minimize any water loss.

7 Taking care not to disturb the plants or potting mix, carefully rehook the chain, making sure that it is securely attached.

8 Allow the plants to establish in a sheltered place before hanging the basket in its final location. Meanwhile, keep the soil mix evenly moist, but do not overwater. In frost-prone areas, keep baskets under cover until the risk of frost has passed. Then choose the side of the basket you would like facing forward before hanging it outside.

Container vegetables

With the advent of compact cultivars bred specifically for their increased yield and ease of cultivation, the range of vegetables that may be grown successfully in pots is expanding rapidly. Container crops are ideal for window boxes, balconies, and small spaces—and for gardens with poor drainage, or where soil-borne pests and diseases are a problem. Position them by paths or on paved areas, and enjoy their productive and decorative qualites.

Choosing vegetables

The best vegetables for containers are compact, quick-maturing plants, such as lettuce, radishes, beets, and stump-rooted or round carrots, as well as robust and undemanding leafy vegetables like chard. Fruiting vegetables—eggplant, cucumbers, peppers, and tomatoes—will also grow well in containers, and dwarf cultivars of snap beans are equally amenable to pot culture. For quick returns, cut-and-come-again mixes of salad leaves or baby-leaf salads (seed mixtures of kale, arugula, radicchio, bok choy, and salad greens), grown in small containers, can be picked six to eight weeks after sowing. Runner beans, peas, and deep-rooted slow-maturing vegetables like cabbage and celery are also practical crops to try in large containers such as half barrels.

Selecting the container

Choose strong, stable containers that are large and deep enough to retain sufficient soil moisture for the crop you want to grow. Plastic, terra-cotta, concrete, or galvanized metal pots are all suitable, as are grow bags, wooden tubs, half barrels, window boxes, hanging baskets, and vertical planters for walls or fences (see p.51). Generally the larger the container and the greater the volume of compost or soil to retain moisture, the better your crops will grow. While salad vegetables and herbs can thrive in pots with depths of 6–8in (15–20cm), deep feeders and stronger-growing crops like tomatoes and potatoes require larger containers between 10–18in (25–45cm) deep.

Position containers with care: avoid windy sites. Very shaded sites are also best avoided to prevent plants from becoming spindly. Warm-season crops like tomatoes need full sun, but will require frequent watering—perhaps even twice daily. Remember that large containers can be very heavy once planted; place them in the chosen location before planting.

Good drainage is essential: crops will not grow well in waterlogged soil mix. Place containers on bricks or "pot feet" to allow water to drain through drainage holes. If there are no holes in the base of the container make several, each one at least ½in (1cm) across. Cover them with screening topped with a thin layer of gravel to prevent blockages. For terra-cotta pots with a single, central hole, use a thicker layer of small stones or gravel to keep plugs from forming. In large containers like half barrels, a layer of packing peanuts at the base may help keep drainage holes clear.

Fill containers to within 1in (2–3cm) of the top with a combination of compost and a good-quality potting mix. For larger containers, a mixture of garden soil with up to 20 percent coarse sand and some well-rotted compost can be used. Covering the surface with stone chips or bark after planting will help reduce water loss.

Watering and feeding

Make sure that container-grown crops never dry out. They must be watered thoroughly—particularly in windy conditions and during hot, dry weather. In many areas natural rainfall is unlikely to be sufficient for plants to thrive in pots outdoors so it is essential to check regularly that they are not too dry. Because plant roots are restricted in a container, the nutrients available from the soil mix are quickly used up, therefore it is very important to provide additional nutrients by regular applications of compost tea or fish/seaweed solution.

CUT-AND-COME-AGAIN SALAD CROPS

 **Red lettuce**
 **Mizuna**
 **Baby lettuce leaves**
 **Arugula**
 **Upland cress**
 **Oriental mustard**

Pots in containers
If you use a cachepot, be sure to check that the drainage of the inner pot not obstucted.

Fiery favorites
Chilies such as 'Numex Twilight' and 'Prairie Fire' are ideal crops for window ledges.

Mediterranean tastes
Tender eggplant started indoors can be moved to a sheltered place in early summer.

PLANTER'S GUIDE TO CONTAINER CROPS

Carrots 'Little Finger', 'Kinko', 'Short and Sweet', 'Thumbelina'
Chard 'Bright Lights'
Cucumbers 'Alibi', 'Miniature White', 'Muncher'
Eggplants 'Bambino', 'Dusky', 'Ophelia', 'White Fingers'
Lettuce 'Red Sails', 'Salad Bowl', 'Tan Tan', 'Tom Thumb'
Peppers 'Apache Chile', 'Cherry Bomb', 'Cubanelle', 'Red Cherry', 'Sweet Banana', 'Sweet Chocolate'
Potatoes 'Epicure', 'Irish Cobbler', 'Kennebec', 'Red Pontiac'
Snap beans 'Bush Blue Lake', 'Contender', 'Green Crop', 'Provider', 'Top Crop'
Summer squash 'Sunburst', 'Spacemiser'
Tomatoes 'Cherry Cascade', 'Garden Pearl', 'Maskatka', 'Vilma'

Routine care

Throughout the growing season, container-grown plants need to be checked regularly. The potting mix must be kept moist, so frequent watering is essential, as is feeding during the growing season to maintain healthy growth and productivity. Deadheading helps to prolong flowering. Plants also require protection from pests and diseases, and, if tender, from cold. Long-term plants need special attention with regard to repotting and topdressing.

Watering

Plants in containers have access to very limited reserves of water when compared to those in open beds and so are dependent to a greater extent on the gardener for their water supply. Even after rainy weather, extra watering may be needed, because the pot plant's foliage may shed the rainwater outside the container. In addition, containers, especially window boxes and those attached to walls, are often in a rain shadow, where the rainfall they receive is much reduced (see *Rain Shadow*, p.608). In hot, dry, or windy weather, plants may need to be watered two to three times a day.

The simplest way to know when a plant should be watered is to push a finger into the potting mix to check if it is moist below the surface. Such a probe is especially useful for plants grown in potting mixes based on peat substitutes; these potting mixes often appear dry on the surface, when they are adequately moist beneath. Do not water if the potting mix is moist; plants are as likely to be killed by overwatering as they are from lack of it.

Watering methods

The most popular method of watering is by hand, using a watering can or a hose. Always water thoroughly with the tip of the spout or hose directed at the potting mix surface rather than the foliage. Maintain the flow until water runs out of the drainage holes. Superficial watering on a regular basis can lead to a buildup of salts in the potting mix that impede drainage and lead to stunted growth or rotting. Tap water is fine for most plants, but if it is hard, it will not suit lime-hating plants, such as rhododendrons. Rainwater from a water barrel can be used for these (see "Collecting water," p.614).

Automated or drip-feed irrigation systems (see TOOLS AND EQUIPMENT, "Watering aids," p.560) can be

WATERING HANGING BASKETS

adapted for use in containers. These systems are excellent, labor-saving ways of watering containers, including window boxes and grow bags. They do, however, need regular maintenance to ensure that lines and drip heads flow freely.

Containers above head height, such as hanging baskets and window boxes, are difficult to reach with conventional hoses and watering cans. A rigid hose lance attachment is invaluable for this, and simple to use. Alternatively, invest in a compression sprayer with a rigid extension and nozzle. Hanging baskets can also be suspended on a locking pulley system. They can be lowered for watering and raised to the required height for display.

Fertilizing

Plants growing in soil-based potting mixes containing slow-release fertilizers will be fed sufficient nutrients for a few seasons, until they are renewed when repotted or topdressed (see p.334). Nutrient levels in soilless potting mixes, however, decline quickly, partly because they are easily leached out by watering. They therefore need a boost from liquid fertilizers. These are quick acting and contain a balanced supply of nitrogen, phosphorus, and potassium,

Watering high-level containers
A lance attachment with a trigger-action is a useful extension to a hose. Alternatively, attach a stake to the hose to gain the necessary rigidity and height when watering.

Adjustable container heights
A rise-and-fall pulley attachment allows a hanging basket to be raised, lowered, and held in a locked position. This simplifies watering and grooming of the plants in the basket.

the major elements needed for plant growth, along with trace elements. Apply liquid fertilizers to moist potting mix two or three times between the start of growth, in early spring, and midsummer, depending on the manufacturer's instructions regarding the strength and frequency of application.

Foliar feeding—the application of diluted liquid fertilizers as a foliar spray—can usefully supplement other kinds of feeding. Although its

effect is not long lasting, it too is a fast-acting treatment for plants that are growing slowly or showing signs of stress. Apply foliar feeds in dull, overcast conditions, but never when plants have sunlight on them.

Grooming

The general appearance of a container garden is greatly improved by regular maintenance.

ORGANIC AND HOMEGROWN LIQUID FEEDS

A number of organic liquid fertilizers are now available in garden centers that maintain plants grown in containers and hanging baskets. These commercial preparations are mainly derived from organic cow, poultry, and other animal manures. Seaweed extracts are also readily available and are particularly valuable as a source of trace elements as well as other nutrients. All may be used as dressings around the plants or as foliar feeds on established plants in containers and hanging baskets to help lengthen the flowering season.

Additionally, organic liquid feeds may be homemade using the foliage of comfrey (*Symphytum*

officinale) or nettles (*Urtica dioica*), both of which are rich in plant foods—and very easy to grow. It is also easy to make: well-developed fresh leaves may be pressed down into a container of water and steeped (soaked) for about a month before draining off the resulting rather strong-smelling liquid and using it either undiluted or diluted with water (see p.625).

Comfrey feed is rich in potash and is best used undiluted for hungry container-grown tomatoes when in fruit; nettle-based mixtures provide a good general liquid feed if used diluted with 5–10 parts of water.

TRIMMING SHOOTS

Vigorous plants, such as this trailing *Helichrysum petiolare*, should be trimmed or pinched back to curb excess growth and encourage good, bushy cover.

By paying close attention to the plants, early infestations of pests and diseases are often identified. These can then be treated in their early stages before they do serious damage to the plants.

In spring, overwintered plants frequently need neatening. Prune out any frost-damaged growth and remove dead and blemished leaves; all are potential sources of infection by fungal diseases. Shorten any weak or straggling stems, such as trailing ivies, cutting back to strong buds to encourage new shoots. Pinching back overlong shoots in spring is also beneficial to most plants, because it will encourage bushy new growth.

During summer, vigorous plants may need to be curbed to prevent overcrowding. Tie climbers to their supports on a regular basis and check that existing ties are not restricting the stems. When grown on upright supports, the stems of vigorous trailing plants, such as *Helichrysum petiolare,* should be tied in frequently, too. The stem tips and sideshoots may also need to be pinched back to ensure the desired dense coverage of their supports.

Deadheading

The removal of dead and fading flowers prevents the formation of fruit and seed, which diverts a plant's energy from the creation of more flowers. Deadheading is a task that few gardeners find enjoyable but it is the most effective way of prolonging the flowering season of a wide range of annuals that are the mainstay of the container garden in summer. Deadheading can be done by pinching between finger and thumb on many soft-stemmed

DEADHEADING

Pinch off dead blooms between thumb and forefinger. Such deadheading encourages flowering and removes a potential source of infection by gray mold/*Botrytis* (see p.661).

annuals, or by using scissors or pruners for firmer flower stems, such as those of roses.

Renewing spent plants

The usual pattern of seasonal designs is to plant up for two or three main displays in a year. But sometimes, part of a display fades prematurely, leaving a conspicuous gap. Rather than starting again with a completely fresh planting, it is often possible to remove faded plants and insert replacements in the gap. This is not invariably successful, especially if pests or diseases have caused early failure of plants, and small new plants can find it difficult to compete with those that are well established.

For the best chance of success, take out as much of the old potting mix as possible, without disturbing the roots of the plants that remain. Partially fill the holes with moist potting mix of the same type that is already in the container. Then plant the replacement

plants, adding more potting mix and working it in firmly around the root balls. Finally, fill the potting mix to its previous level and water well.

Pests and diseases

The range of pests and diseases that attack container-grown plants are much the same as those that are troublesome in the rest of the yard (see PLANT PROBLEMS, pp.639–673). Because of the condensed nature of the container garden, however, damaged plants are more conspicuous. Even if they can be nursed back to health, diseased and damaged plants detract from the overall effect and may form a source of infection for neighboring plants. In many cases, the best policy is to discard plants that are sickly or badly damaged. If replanting whole containers, dispose of the old potting mix, clean the container thoroughly, and begin again with fresh potting mix.

Many problems can be avoided or contained by good hygiene and sound cultivation. Healthy plants show greater resistance to disease and recover more rapidly from pest infestations. Always use sterilized potting mix, clean all containers thoroughly before use, and check new plants to ensure that they are not carriers of pests and diseases.

Prevalent pests

There are several particularly troublesome pests in the container garden. Aphids (see p.654) and other sap-sucking pests cause distorted and stunted growth, and unsightly black sooty mold may infest the honeydew that they excrete. In addition, they often spread virus diseases.

Black vine weevils (see p.655) cause largely cosmetic damage to leaves by cutting irregular holes

GOOD HYGIENE

Inspect plants regularly for signs of pests or diseases, and remove unsightly yellow or decaying leaves promptly to prevent rot.

in leaf margins between spring and fall, but their curved, creamy-white larvae cause far greater damage (see p.672). They feed on plant roots, frequently remaining undetected until the plant wilts. Check the roots of all new plants for signs of infestation before planting.

Slugs and snails (see p.669) eat young growth, frequently causing fatal damage before their silvery slime trails are noted. They may hide beneath pots or their rims, so check such places regularly and dispose of them promptly.

Various fungal diseases, including gray mold/*Botrytis* (see p.661), attack a wide range of plants, but by far the most serious diseases in the container garden are viral. Viruses (see p.672), which are spread by sap-sucking insects, seriously weaken plants and cause stunted, distorted, and often mottled growth. There is no effective way of treating them, and the only practical course is to destroy affected plants.

It is largely a matter of personal choice whether or not to rely on chemical pest and disease control. Frequent checks made on the state of the plant's health allow infestations or infections to be dealt with promptly before they present serious problems (see PLANT PROBLEMS, "Integrated control," p.640). It is preferable to try an organic or biological control initially, and then to resort to chemicals should these fail.

Maintaining shrubs and trees in containers

Container-grown shrubs and trees require more care and attention than those in beds and borders,

RENEWING A CONTAINER DISPLAY

1 Deadhead flowers regularly in order to keep the display attractive. When plants have finished flowering, remove them, taking care not to damage the roots of remaining plants in the pot.

2 Add fresh, moist potting mix and fill the gaps with new plants or bulbs that will continue the floral display. Firm in gently and water thoroughly to help the new plants to establish.

TOPDRESSING

1 To topdress a container-grown plant (here, a rhododendron), remove the top 2–4in (5–10cm) of the old potting mix, making sure not to damage the plant roots.

2 Replace with fresh mix of a similar type and to the same level as before. Water well. Apply a mulch of bark chips or grit if required.

because they have less access to moisture and nutrients. Repotting or topdressing once a year will ensure continued growth and good health.

Repotting woody plants

If grown indefinitely in containers, trees, shrubs, and many long-term shrubby perennials will become potbound and will exhaust the nutrients in the potting mix. A vigorous young tree or shrub is likely to outgrow its pot every one or two years. The roots of mature trees and shrubs, in which growth will naturally have slowed down, will take longer to become congested. As a general guide, mature trees and shrubs need to be repotted every three or four years. Check the state of the roots by laying the container on its side and easing the plant out. Often, however, the plant itself will indicate that it needs to be repotted by exhibiting a lack of vigor and poor color in the leaves. Growth may also appear uneven or unbalanced. If the plant is topheavy, it will almost certainly benefit from being repotted.

Repotting is best done in early to mid-spring, as or just before growth begins for the new season. Mature plants can be returned to their original pots, but vigorous young plants generally need to be moved to pots that are one-and-half times the size of the old one. Expect to continue replanting them in ever-larger containers until they reach maturity and growth slows.

When the tree or shrub has been eased out of its container, remove the surface potting mix and any weeds or moss, and discard all of

this material as well as any loose potting mix. The roots are delicate and should not be handled unnecessarily, although this is a good opportunity to tease out tangled roots and shorten by up to two-thirds a proportion of nonfibrous roots. If there is any delay between removal and repotting, keep the root ball covered with a sheet of plastic or damp burlap to prevent it from being desiccated by the drying effects of sun or wind.

Use an appropriate soil-based potting mix to which slow-release fertilizer has been added, and repot so that the surface of the plant's root ball is at the same level as before when firmed in and watered.

Topdressing long-term plants

In years when shrubs and trees are not being repotted, their potting mix should be refreshed in the spring. Having removed any mulch, the top 2–4in (5–10cm) of potting mix should be loosened and discarded, taking care not to damage the shallow roots of plants such as camellias and rhododendrons. The replacement potting mix must not only be fresh, but also of the same type as the potting mix still in the container. It should also contain a slow-release fertilizer. Use an acidic potting mix and soft water or rainwater when topdressing lime-hating plants.

Surface-rooting plants can be topdressed in a different way, because their fibrous feeding roots are easily damaged when the top layers of potting mix are removed. For surface rooters, discard the potting mix from the bottom of the root ball and replace it with a smaller quantity

of enriched potting mix. The shrub will then sit lower in its pot than previously, leaving room for a smaller amount of topdressing.

Vacation care

The most essential requirement in the gardener's absence is regular watering. An automated irrigation system (see Tools and Equipment, *Hose Timers*, p.561) is an ideal but expensive solution. Failing this, the best option is to ask a friend or neighbor to come in to water on a regular basis. To make the task easier, it is worth grouping the containers together. This massing of the plants together also has the advantage of slowing the rate of water evaporation from each; it will do so to such an extent as to be an adequate solution in itself for an absence of a few days. Place containers in a shaded and sheltered place and water

thoroughly just before going away.

Reduce evaporation even further by packing a number of containers in a crate, tray, or similar container with drainage holes, which is filled with damp sharp sand, potting mix, or peat substitute. For short-term absences, and with relatively small plants, a more involved method is to enclose small potted plants in sealed and inflated plastic bags. If the bagged plants are kept in cool shade, the rate of water loss will be negligible. This is, however, only a short-term fix; fungal diseases proliferate in such conditions and the bags must be removed promptly when the gardener returns.

Capillary matting can be used to supply water to containers (see Indoor Gardening, *Care of Indoor Plants Before Going Away*, p.374). Another way of exploiting capillary action is to use a filled bucket as

REPOTTING A CONTAINER-GROWN SHRUB

1 Carefully lay the shrub on its side; support the main stems with one hand and ease it out of its pot. If necessary, slide a long-bladed knife between soil mix and pot to loosen the root ball.

2 If the roots have become very congested, gently tease them out. Remove the surface mix and any moss or weeds. Prune back about a quarter of the nonfibrous roots by up to two-thirds.

3 Place a piece of screening over the pot's drainage holes, then add the potting mix. Position the plant centrally and vertically in the pot, spreading its roots out evenly within the container.

4 Add more compost around the roots, gently firming until it is at the same level on the plant as it was in its previous pot. Prune out any dead or damaged growth and water in well.

Grouping for effect
Group several containers with different planting designs together to provide a varied and attractive display.

a water reservoir and strips of capillary matting as a wick. The bucket must be raised above the container it is to serve and the wick must be tucked into the potting mix. Commercial wicking systems are also available and these are specially designed for vacation care.

Emergency measures

If plants have wilted when you return from vacation, do not despair immediately. Even when potting mix has become so dry that it has shrunk away from the sides of the pot, plants can sometimes be salvaged by deep immersion. Partially fill a bucket with water, place it in a shady site, and plunge the plant in its container so that the top of the container is just below the surface of the water. Hold the container down until the flow of air bubbles that arises from the potting mix has ceased, then leave the plant to soak for another 30 minutes. When the potting mix is thoroughly wet, remove the container from the bucket and allow to drain well. If woody plants do not revive within two or three hours, there is little point in keeping them. However, it is worth cutting back perennials; they may produce new growth from the base.

Winter protection

In frost-prone areas, container-grown plants that need protection from severe cold include those that are known to be tender, those that are marginally hardy, and

a number of plants that are reasonably hardy, such as rosemary (*Rosmarinus officinalis* cultivars) and lavender (*Lavandula* cultivars) that may suffer frost damage to the roots if the potting mix in the containers becomes frozen.

The most straightforward way of avoiding cold damage is to move plants under cover in fall. Depending on the local climate, even an unheated greenhouse or glassed-in porch can give adequate protection to most plants, especially if they are kept almost dry during the coldest, darkest months.

In some cases, the overwintered plant can be used to provide cuttings in spring and may itself then be discardd. Where space is a problem, it can be much less space-consuming to overwinter plants as cuttings. Overwintered rooted cuttings of plants that make rapid annual growth, such as *Helichrysum petiolare*, will develop in time to use in displays for the following summer. It is always worth overwintering under cover cuttings of marginally hardy plants left outdoors, as an insurance against winter losses. *Pelargonium*, a major genus for container gardening, warrants special attention (see "Overwintering," p.220).

If vulnerable plants are too large to be moved indoors, another way to protect them is to wrap them in insulating material. The plant itself can be protected with garden fabric or bubble plastic. It is important also to insulate the container. A layer of straw

or burlap tied snugly around the container can provide effective insulation for the plant roots and will also help to preserve the pot itself from cold damage. During winter, keep plants in a sheltered site, avoiding frost pockets. The weight of snow can break branches and stems of plants, so do not allow heavy accumulations to build up.

Spring is often a more difficult season than winter. There may be periods without frost and unseasonably warm days in which plants begin to make growth, but the risk of frost remains and its effect on unprotected, soft new growth can be devastating. The same is true of cold, dry spring winds. During a hardening-off period of several weeks, plants that have been overwintered under cover can be gradually acclimatized to outdoor conditions. It is essential, however, to remain vigilant and provide protection at night, when there is greatest risk of temperatures falling below freezing. Keep a sheet of garden fabric handy to cover any vulnerable plant if the forecast is for a cold night.

Security

Although it is far from being a universal problem, gardens are sometimes targeted by thieves, and container-grown plants and the containers themselves are particularly vulnerable. It is difficult to take measures to put off the determined thief, without compromising the relaxed atmosphere of the garden and the quality of its display. There are, however, some sensible precautions that you can take.

Valuable containers in exposed positions close to public access create interest, so reposition these or chain them to the ground, although it is difficult to do this inconspicuously, and the very fact that the container is chained can, in itself, highlight its value. In front gardens, it is generally advisable to use plain but serviceable containers. Plants of great rarity are unlikely to be recognized as such, but they may be difficult to replace, so it is better to grow them in places away from public view.

Lights that are activated automatically by movement provide some measure of security, as do well-maintained walls, gates, and fences. Although these are not impregnable, they do provide the strongest barriers to both thieves and vandals.

PLANTS TO OVERWINTER

As rooted cuttings
Anisodontea
Antirrhinum
Argyranthemum
Convolvulus sabatius
Cuphea
Diascia
Felicia amelloides
Fuchsia
Hedera helix (cvs)
Helichrysum petiolare
Heliotropium
Lantana
Lotus berthelotii,
    L. maculatus
Osteospermum
Pelargonium
Petunia
Plecostachys serpyllifolia
Plectranthus
Salvia
Scaevola
Senecio cineraria
Tropaeolum
Verbena

For cuttings in spring
Fuchsia
Impatiens
Salvia
Solenostemon

Fuschia 'Ballet Girl'

FROST PROTECTION

Wrap topgrowth loosely but securely in horticultural fabric. A double layer of burlap tied firmly around the pot will protect roots from freezing during the winter months.

CACTI AND OTHER SUCCULENTS

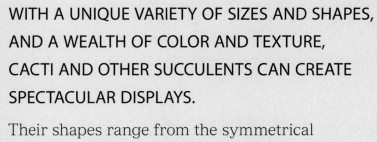

WITH A UNIQUE VARIETY OF SIZES AND SHAPES, AND A WEALTH OF COLOR AND TEXTURE, CACTI AND OTHER SUCCULENTS CAN CREATE SPECTACULAR DISPLAYS.

Their shapes range from the symmetrical rosettes of *Echeveria* to the squat, globular *Echinocactus* and the fluted columns and candelabra of some desert cacti. Many bloom only briefly and have large, brightly colored flowers, while others flower for longer periods, producing a profusion of exquisite blooms. In cool-temperate climates, most cacti and succulents are grown in the greenhouse or as houseplants, but hardier species can also be beautiful garden specimens. In warmer climates, they offer scope to create an outdoor desert garden. Whether grown as focal plants or grouped for contrast of form and texture, cacti and other succulents are ideal for containers, both indoors and out.

Using cacti and other succulents

Many cacti are native to the desert regions of the Southwest, Mexico, and South America, where rainfall is low and intermittent, and there are great extremes of temperature. They owe their success in desert regions to their large water-storage capacity. In contrast, some of the most floriferous cacti originate in the warm, humid rainforests of Central and South America. These are often epiphytic, growing on other plants, either weaving through host trees or lodging in niches in their branches and absorbing moisture and nutrients from the atmosphere.

Bold display *Epiphyllum crenatum* (Orchid cactus).

Other succulents occur in a far greater range of habitats than cacti, and, because they are found in at least 20 different plant families, show a wide diversity of characteristics. Their natural habitats include the semiarid regions of Central America, Africa, and Australasia, as well as the more temperate and cold climates of Asia, and northern parts of Europe and America.

Characteristics of succulents

Cacti and other succulents exhibit a few adaptations, such as reduced leaf size and loss of leaves in very dry weather, designed to conserve water by reducing transpiration. The one distinguishing feature that is common

Natural variety Cacti and succulents show huge variation in size, shape, color, and habit, and have evolved to survive in a variety of naturally challenging growing conditions.

to all, however, is the presence of water-storing, fleshy tissue in the stems, leaves, or roots. It is this tissue that allows succulent plants to withstand long periods of drought.

Cacti are easily distinguished from other succulents by highly evolved structures called areoles—the cushionlike growths on their stems from which the spines, hairs, flowers, and shoots develop.

Succulent plants may be loosely divided into three groups, depending on which part of the plant contains the moisture-retaining tissue. Some genera, for example *Euphorbia*, may be represented in more than one group. Most cacti are stem succulents, as are some succulent plants from the Asclepiadaceae and Euphorbiaceae families. Others, including *Aloe*, *Echeveria*, *Lithops*, and *Sedum*, are leafy succulents. Plants in the third group are known as caudiciform succulents and have the water-storing tissue in a swollen rootstock (the caudex), although

this often extends into the stem, as in *Adenium obesum*. Plants that belong to this group of succulents are mostly found within the families Apocynaceae, Cucurbitaceae, and Convolvulaceae.

Form and habit

The diverse forms and growth habits of cacti and other succulent plants may be used to create a range of effects. Tall columns of *Cleistocactus strausii*, for example, make strong, vertical lines that contrast with foreground plantings of smaller, spherical forms, such as *Echinocactus grusonii*, or the flattened segments of some *Opuntia*.

Several species have a creeping habit that adds a horizontal element to the garden design. *Carpobrotus edulis*, *Lampranthus*, and *Ruschia*, make dense carpets of growth that provide excellent groundcover.

Trailing succulents like *Ceropegia linearis* subsp. *woodii*, *Rhipsalis*, and *Schlumbergera* produce cascades of slender stems or leaves that are seen to best effect in hanging baskets. Several are scrambling climbers: *Selenicereus* and *Aloe ciliaris* add height to mixed plantings if given the support of trellis or the branch of a tree. In frost-free climates, the jointed stems of *Hylocereus*, which climb by means of aerial roots, are most attractive when allowed to spread over walls.

Flowering cacti and other succulents

Cacti and succulents often produce exquisite blooms and flower regularly once they have reached maturity, but this may take from one to forty years. Most are day-blooming, with individual blossoms sometimes lasting several days. Some epiphytic cacti are winter-flowering and have blooms carried in succession over extensive periods.

Others bloom only briefly, the flowers sometimes appearing soon after sunset and fading as evening advances. Many of the large, columnar cacti produce buds that gradually unfold during the evening and then fade in the early morning hours.

The flowers, often of delicate appearance and silken texture, are usually extremely large in comparison with the size of the plant, and their color range is mainly at the warm end of the spectrum with a profusion of rich yellows, hot scarlets, and vivid hot pinks. A few genera, often those of the family Mesembryanthemaceae, and some of the epiphytes, have sweetly scented blooms. Some species, especially members of Agavaceae, are monocarpic, and die after they flower and set seed. A number of small, nonflowering offsets often form around the flowering rosette, however, and these flower in subsequent years.

Outdoor display

With careful selection and skillful arrangement, collections of succulents can be grown outdoors even in relatively cool conditions. But few succulents tolerate excess moisture; even hardy species require good drainage—these grow well in raised beds where water drains away freely. Among the hardiest are prickly pear *Opuntia humifusa*, *Sedum*, and hens-and-chicks (*Sempervivum*), along with some *Crassula* and *Umbilicus*.

A number of desert cacti, particularly some *Opuntia*, and *Echinocereus* tolerate high temperatures in summer and surprisingly low temperatures in winter—although not the combination of cold and wet.

In mild areas with little frost, the range of plants extends to include the spectacular rosettes of *Agave americana* and its cultivars, *A. filifera*, and *Beschorneria yuccoides*. Some

FLOWERING CACTI AND OTHER SUCCULENTS

Aporocactus flagelliformis

Astrophytum myriostigma

Lithops pseudotruncatella subsp dendritica

Oroya peruviana

Parodia chrysacanthion

Rebutia fiebrigii

A SAMPLING OF SUCCULENTS

Agave americana 'Marginata'

Agave filifera

Beschorneria yuccoides

Maihuenia poeppigii

Sedum spectabile 'Brilliant'

Sempervivum arachnoideum

hardy cacti will survive outside over winter in all but the coldest regions given a well-drained soil. For example *Opuntia fragilis*, native to parts of Ontario and Alberta, will survive temperatures down to –40°F (–40°C) at least.

Mixed plantings

When growing nonsucculent and succulent plants together, it is important to choose those that have similar needs for light, soil type, and watering regime. In frost-free gardens, compatible nonsucculents include *Salvia*, *Nerium*, *Gazania*, and *Catharanthus*, all of which provide additional color and variety. Bulbous plants such as *Clivia*, *Cyrtanthus*, and *Sprekelia* are also good choices in mixed planting designs in the appropriate climates.

In cooler regions, slow-growing and compact annual species as well as plants that are grown as annuals, such as the ice plant (*Lampranthus*) and the moss rose

CACTI AND OTHER SUCCULENTS IN A CHANGING CLIMATE

With climate change causing milder winters, warmer summers and falls, and higher mean annual temperatures, many cacti and other succulents once grown only in greenhouses or as houseplants may be successful outside with no, or minimal, winter protection.

Clearly there will be regional differences, and the frequency of snow and frost may vary over the next 50 or more years, but it is forecast that a larger percentage of annual precipitation will occur in winter than at present. This may limit the cultivation of cacti and other succulents that require dry winters; they would need to be grown in very well-drained sites.

Some species of *Agave*, *Aloe*, *Echeveria*, succulent *Euphorbia*, and other genera thrive unprotected in areas of the far West already. Experiment by planting a cactus outdoors that is only marginally hardy for your zone.

(*Portulaca grandiflora*), are suitable for planting outdoors among groups of permanently placed perennial cacti and other succulents.

Desert gardens

While a desert garden with a wide selection of plants is hard to achieve in most of Canada, by using hardy succulents, such as sedums and hens-and-chicks (*Sempervivum*), and potted indoor cacti that are put outside for the summer, the idea of a desert garden can be realized. Providing the drainage is good, the indoor plants will benefit and flower more freely.

Use smaller species at the front of the bed, so that their delicate beauty is not obscured by taller plants. Allow clump-forming plants, such as *Echeveria, Haworthia,* and *Mammillaria,* sufficient space to develop fully. These low-growing species, which have a cluster-forming habit, flower at different periods from spring to fall, to give color during the warmer months.

For background planting, tall, erect, columnar cacti and other succulents are ideal. Choose plants such as the tall, single-stemmed *Cephalocereus senilis,* the branching *Cleistocactus strausii,* or the towering, treelike *Euphorbia candelabrum.*

Containers outdoors

Most cacti and other succulents have shallow roots and respond well to being grown in containers. Select containers that enhance the shape and form of the plants—a wide, shallow bowl, for example, is the natural choice for displaying low-growing and creeping species, while those with stronger form, such as *Agave attenuata,* are much more suitable for large pots or urns.

Troughs are particularly useful for creating imaginative combinations of plants of very different sizes and habits, and hanging baskets are suitable for displaying trailing and pendent species.

Choosing and siting plants

In cool regions, but where temperatures seldom fall below freezing, many species will thrive outdoors in troughs and pots, provided that these are raised above the ground to allow water to drain away freely. A warm, sheltered site such as the corner of a covered patio or balcony, where the plants can more easily be protected from rain, will provide the ideal environment.

The foliage shapes of *Sedum* and neat rosettes of *Sempervivum* may be used to create a contrast with the leafy forms and brilliant blooms of *Lewisia* species and cultivars, or with the green-flowered *Echinocereus viridiflorus* and the scarlet, early summer blooms of *Echinopsis chamaecereus.* Other species, such as *Agave parryi,* with symmetrical rosettes of plump, gray-green leaves, or *Opuntia polyacantha,* which puts on a brilliant

Summering outdoors In areas with less than mild winters, cacti and succulents can be placed outside in a sunny site for the summer but must be moved under cover in the fall.

display of yellow flowers, may make striking focal points if they are planted on their own in large bowls.

In warmer climates, there is much greater scope for growing cacti and other succulents outdoors in containers. In large pots, group plants that flower at different times and have striking foliage forms: the purple-leaved *Aeonium* 'Zwartkop'; *Aloe vera,* which has yellow flowers; and red-flowered *Crassula perfoliata* var. *minor.* These provide structural interest all year, and give a succession of attractive blooms through the warmer months.

Where temperatures do not consistently fall below 55°F (13°C), many dwarf cacti, such as *Gymnocalycium, Mammillaria,* and *Rebutia,* make fascinating displays of shape and texture in outdoor bowls and troughs in the garden. These dwarf, cluster-forming species also give a magnificent display of vibrant color that lasts for many weeks in summer.

Indoor display

The protected environment of the greenhouse or conservatory, which allows almost complete control of light, temperature, humidity, and water, provides ideal conditions for an extensive range of succulents and cacti —most plants recommended for outdoor cultivation in warm climates will thrive under cover in cooler regions. The adaptations these plants have made to help them to survive in harsh, arid environments in the wild also make them very suitable for the warm, dry conditions of a centrally heated home, where many other plants may fail to thrive.

The variation in shape and habit, and their beautiful flowers, ensure that these plants provide interest throughout the year, and because different species are adapted to a variety of environmental conditions, they may be selected for various situations in the home.

Providing the right conditions

Most cacti and other succulents need high light levels, warmth, and good ventilation to thrive, although some, the leafy succulents in particular, may need protection from direct sun in summer to avoid leaf scorch.

There is an important group that requires shady conditions, or at least filtered light: the epiphytes, mainly from humid and shaded rainforests of Central and South America.

Epiphytic plants are among the most floriferous succulents, and they can be used to great effect to add bold splashes of color and interest to shady corners of the home or garden. The best known of this group are the Christmas cactus (*Schlumbergera* x *buckleyi*), *Rhipsalidopsis gaertneri*, and *R. rosea*. Some of the loveliest are the magnificent hybrids created by crossing *Epiphyllum* with species or hybrids of *Echinopsis*, *Heliocereus*, *Hylocereus*, and *Nopalxochia*. They produce extraordinarily beautiful, and sometimes fragrant, flowers in spring and summer, in colors ranging from pure white through cream, yellow, and orange to red and deepest purple.

Plants for the greenhouse and conservatory

Plants in a greenhouse or conservatory can be grown in pots or open beds, either at floor level or raised on benches. Planting in open beds offers potential for growing larger species and even for creating a miniature desert garden.

When in growth, many species from warm habitats need bright light, a fairly dry atmosphere, and a temperature of 64°F (18°C) if they are to develop to their full potential and bear flowers. These conditions are more easily provided under cover than in a home environment, and many cacti grow and flower most successfully in a greenhouse.

Some, notably *Rhipsalis*, require relatively high levels of humidity (80 percent) to thrive, and will nearly always perform best in the humid atmosphere of a conservatory. Other groups that are very suitable for the conservatory and greenhouse are those that need space to flower well. Among them are the clambering *Selenicereus* (the most outstanding species being queen-of-the-night, *S. grandiflorus*) and several species of *Hylocereus*, which all prefer to be sited in indirect, filtered light.

When drawing up planting plans for a greenhouse or conservatory, combine groups of cacti and other succulents that have similar cultural needs, to make maintenance easier.

Container-growing indoors

If provided with warm, bright, and draft-free conditions, many cacti and other succulents will thrive in containers indoors. Use small pots for displaying individual plants, or large bowls for planting a variety of compatible species together.

Make sure that you wear thick, leather gloves when handling spiny plants including *Agave*, *Aloe*, and *Opuntia*, because their sharp spines may easily become embedded in your fingers if you brush against them, causing a painful injury, and are difficult to remove.

Bowl gardens

If planted with different species that have the same cultural requirements, bowl gardens are a particularly attractive way to grow succulent plants indoors. One or two plants with an upright habit, for example, young specimens of *Cephalocereus*, *Cleistocactus*, or other columnar genera, may provide the focal point of the bowl. Alternatively, use a leafy succulent such as *Crassula ovata* as the main plant. Fill the rest of the bowl with smaller plants, such as *Echeveria* and *Haworthia*. Free-flowering cacti such as *Mammillaria*, *Parodia*, and other globular cacti are also good choices for planting in a bowl garden indoors.

Hanging baskets

Cacti and other succulents in hanging baskets make colorful displays in the home or conservatory. Pendent cacti, such as *Aporocactus flagelliformis*, and trailing succulent plants such as *Kalanchoe*, *Hatiora gaertneri*, and *Schlumbergera* are the most suitable plants to choose, because they will trail attractively over the edge of the basket. *Sedum morganianum* and other semitrailing species are also very effective in hanging baskets (see also *Planter's Guide to Cacti and other Succulents*, p.342).

Container displays Small groups of plants can be grown in the same container, although they must be repotted periodically to ensure each has sufficient space. In time, they will need to be separated and grown on individually, especially quicker-growing species and those with a spreading habit.

PLANTER'S GUIDE TO CACTI AND OTHER SUCCULENTS

DAMP CONDITIONS

Succulents that tolerate damp conditions

Crithmum maritimum
Salicornia europaea
Suaeda maritima, S. vera
Umbilicus horizontalis
   var. *intermedius,*
   U. rupestris

SHADE

Succulents that tolerate light shade

Lewisia cotyledon hybrids,
   L. leeana
Orostachys chanetii,
   O. spinosa
Rhodiola wallichiana
Sedum dasyphyllum,
   S. montanum, S. rosulatum,
   S. sediforme, S. spectabile,
   S. ternatum, S. villosum
Sempervivum arachnoideum,
   S. ruthenicum

BOWLS AND TROUGHS

Sun

Adenium obesum
Aeonium arboreum, A. nobile
Agave filifera, A. stricta,
   A. victoriae-reginae
Aloe humilis, A. longistyla,
   A. rauhii
Astrophytum myriostigma,
   A. ornatum
Cephalocereus senilis
Cereus hildmannianus
   subsp. *uruguayanus,*
   C. validus
Cleistocactus straussii
Cotyledon campanulata,
   C. orbiculata var. *orbiculata*
Crassula ovata,
   C. perfoliata var. *minor,*
   C. rupestris, C. socialis
Echeveria agavoides,
   E. derenbergii,
   E. pilosa
Echinocactus grusonii
Echinocereus berlandieri,
   E. pentalophus
Echinopsis
   E. chamaecereus,
   E. oxygona,
Espostoa lanata
Euphorbia flanaganii,
   E. milii, E. obesa
Faucaria felina
Ferocactus cylindraceus,
   F. latispinus
Gasteria batesiana,
   G. bicolor var. *liliputana*
Glottiphyllum linguiforme
Gymnocalycium baldianum,
   G. gibbosum,
   G. mihanovichii
Haworthia cooperi,
   H. limifolia,
   H. reinwardtii
Jatropha podagrica
Kalanchoe blossfeldiana

Lithops dorotheae,
   L. karasmontana subsp. *bella*
Mammillaria bocasana,
   M. compressa,
   M. hahniana,
   M. mystax,
   M. rhodantha,
   M. spinosissima,
   M. vetula subsp. *gracilis,*
   M. zeilmanniana
Opuntia microdasys
Orbea variegata
Pachypodium geayi,
   P. lamerei
Parodia leninghausii,
   P. microsperma
Rebutia arenacea
   R. einsteinni subsp. *aureiflora,*
   R. heliosa,
   R. krugerae,
   R. pulvinosa var. *arbiflora,*
   R. steinbachii subsp. *steinbachii*
Sansevieria trifasciata 'Hahnii',
   S. trifasciata 'Laurentii'
Thelocactus bicolor,
   T. rinconensis

Partial shade

Epiphyllum oxypetalum
   (and hybrids)
Hoya australis,
   H. carnosa
Rhipsalidopsis gaertneri,
   R. rosea
Schlumbergera × *buckleyi,*
   S. truncata (and hybrids)

HANGING BASKETS

Ceropegia haygarthii,
   C. linearis subsp. *woodii*
Disocactus
Epiphyllum oxypetalum
   (and hybrids)
Heliocereus (most spp.)
Hoya lanceolata subsp. *bella,*
   H. linearis,
   H. polyneura
Kalanchoe jongsmanii,
   K. manginii, K. pumila
Rhipsalidopsis gaertneri,
   R. rosea
Rhipsalis cereuscula,
   R. mesembryanthemoides,
   R. pachyptera
Schlumbergera × *buckleyi,*
   S. truncata (and hybrids)
Sedum morganianum
Selenicereus

LOWER TEMPERATURES

Succulents that tolerate temperatures down to 32°F (0°C)

Agave americana,
   A. parryi,
   A. univittata,
   A. utahensis
Echinocereus
   viridiflorus
Echinopsis chamaecereus
Opuntia humifasa,
   O. polyacantha

Sedum anglicum,
   S. cyaneum,
   S. dasyphyllum,
   S. formosanum,
   S. hispanicum,
   S. lanceolatum,
   S. rupestre,
   S. spectabile
Sempervivum (most spp.)
Umbilicus (spp. only)

Succulents that tolerate temperatures down to 45°F (7°C)

Agave attenuata, A. parviflora
Aloe arborescens, A. aristata,
   A. brevifolia, A. distans,
   A. variegata, A. vera
Austrocylindropuntia subulata
Bulbine frutescens,
   B. latifolia,
   B. mesembryanthemoides
Caralluma europaea
Carpobrotus acinaciformis,
   C. edulis
Cereus aethiops,
   C. jamacaru
   (and other columnar spp.)
Crassula sarcocaulis,
   C. sarmentosa
Echeveria coccinea, E. cuspidata,
   E. elegans, E. gibbiflora
Echinocereus enneacanthus,
   E. pentalophus
Echinopsis chamaecereus
Gasteria carinata,
   G. carinata var. *verrucosa,*
   G. disticha
Kalanchoe delagoensis,
   K. marmorata
Lampranthus falcatus,
   L. multifadiatus
Lewisia cotyledon hybrids
Maihuenia poeppigii
Opuntia exaltata,
   O. fragilis,
   O. polyacantha,
   O. rastera
   O. robusta
Orostachys chanetii,
   O. spinosa
Pelargonium acetosum,
   P. echinatum,
   P. tetragonum
Senecio haworthii,
   S. macroglossus

FLOWERING CACTI

Day-flowering

Astrophytum myriostigma
Bergerocactus emoryi
Cleistocactus straussii
Disocactus flagelliformis,
   D. phyllanthoides,
   D. speciosus var. *superbus*
Echinocereus engelmannii,
   E. triglochidiatus
   E. viereckii
Echinopsis aurea, E. famatimensis,
   E. mamillosa, E. oxygona
Epiphyllum anguliger,
   E. crenatum
Gymnocalycium bruchii

Heliocereus speciosus
   var. *superbus*
Mammillaria blossfeldiana,
   M. bocasana,
   M. grahamii,
   M. hahniana,
   M. spinosissima,
   M. zeilmanniana
Matucana aureiflora
Nopalxochia phyllanthoides
Opuntia ficus-indica
Parodia alacriportana,
   P. haselbergii,
   P. leninghausii,
   P. mammulosa,
   P. microsperma
Rebutia arenacea,
   R. einsteinii subsp. *aureiflora,*
   R. krugerae,
   R. neocumingii
Rhipsalidopsis gaertneri,
   R. rosea
Schlumbergera × *buckleyi,*
   S. truncata
Thelocactus bicolor

Night-flowering

Cephalocereus senilis
Echinopsis deserticola,
   E. mirabilis, E. spachiana,
   E. terscheckii
Epiphyllum cartagense
Espostoa lanata, E. melanostele
Haageocereus acranthus,
   H. pseudomelanostele,
   H. versicolor
Harrisia gracilis, H. pomanensis
Hylocereus ocamponis
Pachycereus pringlei
Selenicereus anthonyanus,
   S. grandiflorus, S. pteranthus
Stenocereus (most spp.)

Kalanchoe blossfeldiana

Soil preparation and planting

Many cacti and other succulents grow naturally only in desert or jungle conditions, but they also make striking displays outdoors in cooler climates. Whether they are grown indoors or outside, specially prepared, well-drained soil or potting mix is essential. Most species also require a sunny site with protection from cold.

Buying cacti and other succulents

When buying cacti and other succulents, choose only healthy, unblemished plants that show new growth or have flower buds forming. Do not buy damaged or slightly shriveled specimens, or any with dull, dry, or limp segments. Also reject plants that have outgrown their pots.

Planting in a raised bed or desert garden

Cacti and other succulents require well-drained conditions, so they benefit from being planted in a bed

RAISED BED CONSTRUCTION

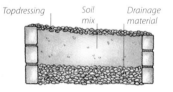

Topdressing   Soil mix   Drainage material

A raised bed has a deep gravel base and fast-draining soil mix.

SELECTING CACTI AND SUCCULENTS

Good example

New buds forming

Healthy growth

Rebutia

Damaged growth

Poor example

Good example

Plump, fleshy leaves

Healthy, new growth

Crassula ovata

Shriveled leaves

Poor example

that is raised at least 10in (25cm) above ground level. To ensure good drainage, make the bed slightly sloping and provide a thick base of gravel or rubble that is at least one-third of the total height of the bed.

Never construct the bed on a concrete or other impermeable base, as this impedes drainage. Choose a bright, sunny site with a minimum temperature of 41°F (5°C). In cooler areas, provide adequate protection for tender species (see FROST AND WIND PROTECTION, pp.612–613).

Preparing the soil mix

Cacti and other succulents do not usually thrive in ordinary garden soil, because it is not sufficiently well drained. It

needs to be replaced by, or supplemented with, a carefully prepared growing medium. Good garden loam that has a pH level of 6–6.5 may be used as the basis of a homemade mix. It must be sterilized first, however, to kill pests or weed seeds that might be present, and to eliminate diseases.

To prepare the soil mix, combine 2 parts sterilized garden soil with 1 part peat or fine shredded sphagnum moss or compost, 1 part sharp sand or washed grit, and a little slow-release, balanced fertilizer.

If the garden soil is alkaline, use a commercial soil-based mix with sharp sand or grit in a ratio of 1 part sand or grit to 3 parts soil mix.

HANDLING CACTI

Most cacti have sharp spines. When moving or planting them, either wear leather gloves or take other protective measures.

When handling spiny cacti, such as this *Ferocactus*, wrap a loop of folded paper around the plant.

Placing the plant in the bed

Remove the plant from its pot. Water the plant, then carefully remove it from its pot. Check the root ball for disease or pest infestation (see also p.345), and treat any infections before planting.

Dig a hole of appropriate size and place the plant so that its base is at the same level in the soil as it was in its container. Fill in around the roots with soil mix, then firm, making sure that the stems and leaves are above soil level. Topdress with grit, to protect the plants from excess moisture and reduce soil-water evaporation. Allow the plants to settle, then water, lightly at first, and gradually increasing the amount until the plants are well established and producing new growth.

PLANTING IN A BED OUTDOORS

Harden off indoor plants for a few days in the shade prior to planting them outdoors. Select a planting site in a prepared, well-drained bed, allowing space for the development of the plant and those around it. Clear the topdressing from the planting area, then dig a hole large enough to accommodate the root ball.

1 Remove the cactus from its pot, wearing gloves if need be. Place the cactus in the hole at the same depth as it was in the pot. Gently spread out the roots in the hole if needed.

2 Firm the soil mix around the root ball. Topdress with a ¼in (5mm) layer of clean ⅛in (3mm) grit. Water after 2–3 days when the plant has settled.

Succulents in containers

A collection of cacti and other succulents grown in pots, bowls, or troughs provides an attractive focal point on a patio or windowsill.

Preparing the soil mix
The soil mix should be well-drained and preferably slightly acidic with a pH of 6–6.5. Use 1 part sand or grit to either 3 parts soil-based potting mix or 2 parts soilless potting mix.

A slightly more acidic potting mix may be needed for epiphytic succulents, such as certain *Hoya*, and cacti—*Rhipsalis* and *Schlumbergera* in particular—native to forest areas. Mix 1 part organic matter (such as compost, sphagnum peat, or leaf mold) with 2 parts standard soil mix; then add sand or grit to ensure adequate drainage.

Choosing the container
Both clay and plastic containers are suitable for growing cacti and other succulents. Potting mix in plastic pots retains moisture longer than that in clay ones, which means that the plants need less frequent watering, but clay pots provide better aeration around the roots. Choose containers that have one or more holes in the base to ensure that water drains away quickly. The size of pot or container should always be proportionate to the size of the plant but never less than 4in (10cm) deep; for tuberous-rooted species such as *Echinocereus*, a pot with a depth of at least 6in (15cm) is preferable.

Planting in containers
Always wash all containers thoroughly before use to remove possible sources of infection.

Put a piece of window screening or similar mesh over the drainage hole(s). If the container is too tall for the root ball, place a layer of gravel or pot shards in the base to approximately one-third of the depth of the container. Fill the container with potting mix to within ½in (1cm) of the rim.

Carefully remove the plant from its pot, discarding any topdressing and loosening the root ball. Insert it into the new container so that the top of the root ball is at the same level in the soil mix as it was in the original pot. Firm the plant into the mix, and topdress with coarse gravel or with grit.

When planting several cacti or other succulents in one container, space the plants so that there is room for them to develop. To create a more natural effect, decorative pieces of rock or pebbles may be added to the composition.

Allow the plants to settle for a few days before watering; water routinely (see p.345) only when the plants are well established.

Hanging baskets
To create an attractive feature, plant trailing succulent species in a hanging basket. Make sure the basket is completely clean. Wire baskets should be lined with a commercial liner or a layer of sphagnum moss. Do not line the basket with plastic, because this will restrict drainage. If using a plastic basket that has a fixed drainage tray, place a layer of small pebbles or gravel in the base instead of sphagnum moss.

Fill the basket with an appropriate potting mix, without disturbing the moss or pebbles, then insert the plants in the same way as for other containers. Do not overcrowd the basket, because most suitable species have a naturally spreading or pendent habit; one plant is often sufficient to fill an average-sized basket. Topdress with gravel or grit if extra drainage is required; allow to settle for a few days before watering. Once the plant is established and showing new growth, routine watering can be started (see p.345).

PLANTING IN A BOWL

Crassula ovata, *Cereus peruvianus*, *Mammillaria muehlenpfordtii*, *Mammillaria polythele*, *Aloe* 'Black Gem'

1 Select a group of plants that have similar cultivation requirements. Plan the group by positioning the pots in the container, placing the taller plants at the back. Moisten the soil mix in the pots.

2 Prepare the container, placing a shallow layer of drainage material—gravel or pot shards—in the base and covering this with a layer of soil mix (1 part sharp sand, 3 parts soil-based potting mix).

3 Remove the plants from their pots, place them in the container, and fill in with soil mix.

4 Topdress the planted container with a ¼in (5mm) layer of ⅛in (3mm) gravel.

PLANTING IN A HANGING BASKET

1 Line a wire hanging basket with a layer of moist sphagnum moss. The layer should be 1¼in (3cm) thick when compressed.

2 Fill the basket almost to the brim with a mix of 1 part sharp sand to 3 parts soil-based potting mix. Prepare a hole for the plant in the center of the basket.

3 Insert the plant (here, a *Schlumbergera*), spreading out the roots. Fill in with potting mix so that there are no air pockets around the roots.

4 Wait for 2–3 days after planting before watering the finished basket.

Routine care

Cacti and other succulents need little maintenance in order to thrive, but they must have adequate light, warmth, and ventilation. Fertilize and water as appropriate for the particular species, and check regularly for signs of diseases or pests. Repot plants in containers as soon as they outgrow them, to prevent them from becoming potbound.

The right environment

Place cacti and other succulents in a position that is appropriate to their cultural needs. Most species need to be in full sun, although some prefer dappled or continuous shade. The ideal maximum daytime temperature in spring and summer should be 86°F (30°C), and the nighttime temperature, 66°F (19°C). During the dormant season, most plants should be kept at a temperature of at least 45°F (7°C), although species originating from the tropics and equatorial regions generally require a warmer environment, with a minimum temperature of 55°F (13°C).

Ventilation

Although good ventilation is essential, cacti and other succulents should not be exposed to drafts. For plants grown in a greenhouse, it may become necessary to use blinds or to apply special shading paint to the outside of the glass, if ventilation is insufficient to keep the temperature below 81°F (27°C) (see "Shading," p.576). If the weather is exceptionally hot, watering the greenhouse floor will help to reduce the temperature. Occasionally, plants grown in the open may need some shade to protect them in conditions of extreme heat.

Watering and fertilizing

Cacti and other succulents require more water when they are growing actively (usually in spring and summer). Take care not to overwater, especially during cool periods, but give them at least a monthly trickle of water to prevent complete dehydration. Succulents from forested areas often bloom between late fall and early spring, and require more water at this time.

Watering

During the growing season, moisten the soil or potting mix thoroughly with water, allowing it almost to dry out before watering again. Provided that the plants are grown in a fast-draining mix, surplus moisture will drain away quickly.

Water early in the day or up through early evening to allow any moisture on the plants to evaporate before nightfall. Alternatively, plants that are grown in pots may be watered by placing the container in a shallow pan of water, so that the water permeates the soil mix but does not touch the stems or leaves. Remove the container from the water to drain as soon as the surface of the soil appears moist; the plants will rot if left standing in water.

Epiphytic plants and those that need shaded conditions should be kept moist but not wet: an occasional, light mist-spray maintains a reasonable level of humidity.

Fertilizing

During the growing season, fertilize cacti and other succulents to help maintain healthy, vigorous growth and to encourage flowering. Several commercial fertilizers are available but a standard, well-balanced liquid fertilizer containing all the major nutrients is also fine. Apply according to manufacturer's instructions. Never apply fertilizer when a plant is dormant or the soil is dry, because this may damage the stems and foliage.

Hygiene

Cacti and other succulents may need occasional cleaning, because dust sometimes accumulates on the leaves or between the spines. During the growing season, houseplants may be sprayed lightly with water; succulents in the greenhouse or garden may be hosed down carefully, as long as they are not in direct sun.

Pests and diseases

Check cacti and other succulents routinely for pests and diseases. The most prevalent pests are mealybugs (p.664), scale insects (p.669), spider mites (p.670), root mealybugs (see "Mealybugs," p.664), and fungus gnats (see "Fungus gnats," p.661).

Diseases of cacti and succulents are rare, although poor cultural conditions or excess nitrogen in the soil may encourage the development of black rot, which principally affects epiphytic cacti and *Stapelia*. The plants become disfigured and may die. There is no treatment, so, if it appears that a plant is likely to die as a result of infection, take healthy shoots or sections as cuttings and root them to replace the diseased plant.

Repotting

Cacti and other succulents should be repotted as soon as the roots begin to show through the drainage holes—usually every two to three years for fast-growing species. Repot slow-growing plants every three to four years. Very lightly water a plant before repotting.

Carefully remove the plant from its current pot. Inspect the roots, looking for signs of pests or disease, and treat if appropriate. Cut out any roots that are dehydrated or dead. Choose a new container one size larger than the currrent one, and repot in fresh soil mix, making sure the planting depth is the same.

REPOTTING SUCCULENTS

1 When a succulent (here *Aloe arborescens*) has outgrown its container, repot it, selecting a container that is at least one size larger than the current one. Carefully slide the plant out of its pot.

2 Gently tease out any roots that have become coiled or compressed.

3 Place some crocks and a little potting mix in the new pot. Position the plant at the same depth as it was in the previous container.

4 Carefully fill in around the root ball with more potting mix. As you add the mix, firm it in stages to eliminate any air pockets between the roots. Wait until the plant is settled in the new pot before watering.

Propagation

Cacti and other succulents may be propagated from seed, from leaf or stem cuttings, by division, or by grafting. Division and cuttings are the easiest methods. Raising plants from seed is slower and more difficult but provides the opportunity to obtain selected variants from within species, and to raise new hybrids by hand-pollination. Grafting is useful for rare species and hybrids, and for slow-growing succulents that are difficult to propagate by other methods.

Propagating plants from seed

Seeds of cacti and other succulents vary widely in shape and size, and some have special requirements. Some fine seeds are slow to germinate, while some of the larger ones have a thick coating (e.g., those of several *Opuntia* species) and seldom germinate unless they have been stratified—they should be placed in a refrigerator for 48 hours.

Sowing

Sow seed under cover between late winter and late spring. Place a layer of coarse gravel, combined with a sprinkling of charcoal chips, in the base of a seed flat or pot. Fill to the top with seed-sowing mix, then level and firm lightly.

Sprinkle fine seeds evenly over the surface, barely cover with sterilized, sharp sand or a sand and grit mix, and then water lightly from above. Larger seeds should be pressed into the soil, allowing ample space between them, and covered with coarse sand or grit. Stand pots or flats of larger seeds in tepid water and leave them until the upper

surface of the soil is moist, then remove the containers and let the surplus moisture drain.

Place the containers in a propagator, maintaining a temperature of 70°F (21°C). If tenting with a plastic bag, make a few small holes in the bag. Keep the seeds in partial shade until they have germinated.

Care of seedlings

When the seedlings appear, remove the pots from the plastic bags or the propagator and provide additional ventilation, which is important to discourage damping off (see p.658). Maintain a temperature of 70°F (21°C), giving more light and air as the seedlings develop.

Pricking out

After 6–12 months (depending on the species), when the seedlings can be handled without damaging them, prick them out singly into 3in (6cm) pots. Prepare the pots with screening over the holes and fill almost to the brim with moist potting mix, then firm gently.

PROPAGATION FROM SEED

1 Cover the base of the pot with screening, then add at least ¹⁄₂in (1cm) of coarse gravel mixed with a little charcoal.

2 Fill the container to the brim with fresh seed-sowing mix, then level with a suitably shaped presser board to ¹⁄₂in (1cm) below the rim.

3 Sprinkle fine seeds evenly over the surface of the potting mix, tapping the seed package with a finger. Mist the surface with water.

4 Cover the seeds with a topdressing of sterilized, fine-grit sand—only a very thin layer is required.

5 Label and place the pot in a pierced plastic bag. Keep in partial shade, at a minimum temperature of 70°F (21°C).

SOWING LARGE SEED

Press each seed into the soil, sowing at twice the seed's own depth. Space seeds about ¹⁄₂in (1cm) apart, so that they have room to develop.

PRICKING OUT SEEDLINGS INTO INDIVIDUAL POTS

1 When the seedlings are large enough to handle, lift a clump from the pot, taking care not to damage the roots.

2 Divide the clump into individual small plants, retaining as much soil as possible around the roots (see inset).

3 Insert each seedling into a tray or pot containing 3 parts cactus mix to 1 part gritty sand. Keep the top growth clear of the surface.

4 Topdress with a ¹⁄₄-in (5-mm) layer of ¹⁄₈-in (3-mm) gravel, and label. Do not water the seedlings for 3 or 4 days.

Remove a group of seedlings and separate them out carefully. Plant out the seedlings singly, topdress them with a thin layer of gravel, and then label each pot. Keep the young plants at a minimum temperature of 59°F (15°C). After a few days, water them, sparingly at first, but then gradually increasing the amount until, after three weeks, the normal watering routine may be followed (see p.345).

Leaf cuttings

Some succulent plants—for example, many species of *Crassula* and *Echeveria*—may be propagated from leaf cuttings. These should be taken from the parent plant in spring or early summer when there is plenty of new growth.

Choose firm, fleshy leaves and remove them carefully from the parent plant. Sever them with a sharp knife or pull them gently downward, ensuring that a small piece of stem remains attached to the base of each. Put the severed cuttings on a clean piece of paper and place them in partial shade at a temperature of at least 50°F (10°C); warmer is better. Leave them for a day or two until the cut end has dried.

PROPAGATION FROM LEAF CUTTINGS

1 Remove a healthy leaf by carefully pulling it away from the parent plant. It should break off at the base, with a small piece of stem attached.

2 Allow 24–48 hours for the wound to callus (see inset). Fill a pot with equal parts fine peat or soil mix and sand. Insert the cutting so that the base is gently but securely held in the mix.

3 Topdress with gravel or grit, and label. After a new plantlet has formed at least a few leaves (see inset), the rooted cutting is ready to pot up into soil-based potting mix.

Fill pots almost to the brim with equal parts of fine peat substitute (or peat) and sharp grit or sand. Each cutting should be inserted in an upright position in a pot so that the stem of the leaf is just held in place in the top of the potting mix. Firm the mix around the cuttings with your fingers.

Cover the surface with a light topdressing of gravel or grit to help keep the cuttings in position. Label the pot, and place it in dappled shade,

making sure that you maintain a regular temperature of 70°F (21°C). Keep the young cuttings moist by watering them every day with tepid water. Use a fine mist-spray to cause least disturbance to the cuttings.

Rooting normally occurs within a few days. Approximately two weeks after new growth appears, pot up the rooted cuttings into suitably sized pots, filling them with standard, soil-based potting mix. Replace the topdressing.

PRODUCING HYBRIDS

When growing cacti and other succulents in a mixed collection, cross-pollination may occur, i.e., pollen from the flowers of one species or cultivar may pollinate those of another to produce hybrid offspring. Sometimes these hybrids are improvements on other types raised and may be worth propagating. More frequently, however, they are not worth keeping.

To be sure of raising plants with the desired characteristics,

it is necessary to control the pollination process. Controlled pollination may be used to produce more plants of the same species, which retain the parental characteristics, or purposely to produce hybrid offspring from different species (which combine the characteristics of the parent plants).

To produce a new hybrid, choose the parent plants (usually species of the same genus) in an attempt to combine the best characteristics (such as leaf shape or flower color)

of both parents. To prevent open pollination by insects, just before the stigma appears receptive or the anthers are ready to dehisce, tie a small paper bag loosely over the flowers that are to be used. Transfer the pollen from the anthers of one parent flower to the stigma of the second parent by hand, using a soft, fine brush. Then re-cover the hand-pollinated flower with a paper bag.

Many cacti and other succulents are not self-fertile, and it is essential to cross-pollinate in order to obtain seed. If a species is self-fertile, however, cover the flowers with a bag, as above, to prevent cross-pollination by insects. A gentle tap on the bag is usually sufficient to spread pollen onto the stigmas within the flower and effect self-pollination.

As the fruits ripen, they become soft and fleshy and may release seed. If not, slice the fruits open and leave them for two or three days in a partially shaded but warm position so that the pulp dries out. Then wash the seed to remove the pulp and dry it on blotting paper before sowing.

To produce a batch of hybrid seed (here, from a *Schlumbergera*), dust pollen from the anthers of one of the selected parent flowers onto the stigmas of the other parent, using a fine-haired brush.

CACTI AND SUCCULENTS FROM LEAF CUTTINGS

Adromischus cooperi
Aeonium arboreum
Begonia peltata ,
  B. venosa
Cotyledon tomentosa
  subsp. *ladismithensis*,
  C. orbiculata var. *oblonga*
Crassula ovata
  C. perfoliata
Dudleya ingens,
  D. rigida
Echeveria
Gasteria batesiana
Glottiphyllum linguiforme
Graptopetalum
Haworthia attenuata,
  H. planifolia
Hoya australis,
  H. carnosa
Kalanchoe beharensis
  K. tomentosa
Lenophyllum pusillum,
  L. texanum
Orostachys chanetii
Othonna dentata
Pachyphytum oviferum
  P. viride
Peperomia dolabriformis
Sedum hintonii,
  S. sempervivoides
Senecio fulgens
Streptocarpus saxorum
Thompsonella platyphylla
Umbilicus chloranthus

Pachyphytum oviferum

SUCCULENTS TO PROPOGATE BY STEM CUTTINGS OR SECTIONS

Adromischus
Aeonium
Bergerocactus
Caralluma
Cephalocereus
Cereus
Ceropegia
Cleistocactus
Cotyledon
Crassula
Disocactus
Echeveria
Epiphyllum
Euphorbia
Gasteria
Greenovia
Haworthia
Heliocereus
Hoya
Huernia
Kalanchoe
Lampranthus
Opuntia
Oreocereus
Oscularia
Pachycereus
Pachyphytum
Pedilanthus
Pelargonium
Pereskia
Rhipsalis
Ruschia
Sarcocaulon
Schlumbergera
Sedum (some spp.)
Selenicereus
Senecio
Stapelia

Kalanchoe
'Wendy'

Stem cuttings and stem sections

Stem cuttings may be used to propagate many species of succulent, including *Euphorbia, Stapelia,* and most columnar cacti.

Take stem cuttings or sections in early to mid-spring. The amount and type of stem material that is removed depends on the plant. Some cacti, such as *Opuntia,* consist of a series of rounded pads or sections that may be severed with a sharp knife at the joint or base for propagation. For plants that have flattened, leaflike stems, such as *Epiphyllum,* make a cut across a stem to remove a short length. To avoid disfiguring the plant, remove a complete "leaf" at the point where it joins the main stem, and treat this as the cutting or cut it into several sections (see below). Most columnar cacti, and some *Euphorbia* species, may have sections of stem removed to provide cuttings (see below).

All *Euphorbia* species and some asclepiads produce a milky latex when cut; to stop the flow, dip the cutting in tepid water for a few seconds. Seal the cut on the parent plant by holding a damp cloth against the wound. Avoid getting the sap on your skin, because it can cause irritation.

Leave stem cuttings in a warm, dry place for approximately 48 hours to allow the ends to dry before potting them up in suitable soil mix.

Inserting the cuttings

Insert one stem cutting centrally into a prepared pot, or place several small ones around the edge of the container. The cuttings should be inserted just deep enough to stay upright but not too deeply, otherwise the base of the cuttings may rot before they have rooted. Stem cuttings from succulents that bear true leaves, such as *Pereskia,* need to have the lower leaves removed before they are inserted, in the same way as nonsucculent plants. Apply a mist-spray of tepid water occasionally, but do not overwater—this may cause the cuttings to rot. Rooting normally takes place after approximately two weeks, although cuttings from some genera such as *Selenicereus* may take a month or more.

STEM CUTTINGS

2 Trim the stem (see inset) below a node. Remove the lowest pair of leaves, if necessary.

1 Choose a healthy, vigorous stem (here, from *Kalanchoe* 'Wendy'). Make a straight cut, severing the stem as close to the base as possible.

3 Insert each cutting into a mix of equal parts fine peat substitute (or peat) and sharp grit or sand. The leaves should be just clear of the soil surface.

PROPOGATION FROM PAD SECTIONS

1 Sever a pad, making a straight cut across the joint. Leave the section in a warm, dry place for about 48 hours to allow the wound to dry (see inset).

2 Insert the cutting into a pot containing equal parts fine peat substitute (or peat) or compost and sharp grit or sand, and label. Once rooted, pot into standard potting mix.

PROPAGATION FROM STEM SECTIONS

Many cacti and other succulents may be propagated from a small section of stem rather than using a complete one. Use lengths of about 2–4in (5–10cm), depending on the species. For columnar cacti, remove a section of stem (below), cutting it off at the appropriate point; for cacti with flattened, leaflike stems, cut the stem laterally into pieces (right). Then treat each section as a stem cutting.

Columnar stem section
Sections of stem taken from some columnar cacti may be treated as cuttings.

Leaflike stem section
Stems (here of *Epiphyllum* 'Oakwood') are cut into sections and inserted with the end nearest the parent stem in the potting mix.

Division of offsets

A large number of clump-forming cacti and other succulents, such as *Conophytum*, *Mammillaria*, and *Sedum*, may be propagated from offsets early in the growing season.

Clump-forming offsets

Scrape away the top layer of soil from around the parent plant to reveal the base of the offsets, and carefully detach one or more from the parent plant, as required, with a sharp knife. Treat any wounds on unrooted offsets with fungicide, allowing the cut end to dry for two to three days. Pot up undamaged offsets immediately.

Rootless offsets should be inserted into a potting mix of equal parts fine peat substitute (or peat) or compost and sand. If the offsets have already developed roots, use a standard potting mix. Use appropriately sized containers with a piece of screening over the drainage holes. Pot offsets separately and water them in lightly.

Keep the potted offsets in semishade for about two weeks at a minimum temperature of 59°F (15°C), and water them again after the first week. Once new growth appears, the plants should be potted on into a standard potting mix and the normal watering routine applied (see p.345).

Offset tubers

Some tuberous-rooted succulents, such as *Ceropegia*, produce small offset tubers around the main tuber of the parent plant. These may be treated as divisions and grown on to produce new plants. During the dormant season, remove some soil to reveal the offsets and separate them from the parent plant using a clean, sharp knife. Treat the cut surfaces of rootless offsets with

fungicide and allow a callus to form. Insert each offset tuber in a clean pot that contains a mix of equal parts peat substitute (or peat) or compost and coarse sand.

If the offsets have roots, place them directly into a standard potting mix. Topdress with a thin layer of washed, sharp grit, and label. Place the pots in semishade and maintain a temperature of 64°F (18°C).

Allow the tubers to settle for three or four days and then water them regularly with a fine mist-spray. As soon as growth starts and some young shoots begin to appear, follow the normal watering routine (see p.345). Pot on into a standard potting mix as soon as the young plants have several shoots and have become well established.

DIVISION OF CLUMP-FORMING OFFSETS

1 Gently scrape away the top surface of soil around an offset. Cut straight across the joint and allow the wound to dry (see inset).

2 Insert the offset just below the surface of a medium composed of equal parts coarse sand and peat substitute (or peat) or compost.

3 Topdress with ¼ in (5 mm) of grit, label, and place in semishade. Water after 3–4 days.

4 When new growth appears, pot on into standard potting mix, topdressing as before.

DIVISION OF OFFSET TUBERS

1 Scrape away some soil from around the main tuber and carefully detach offset tubers. Lift them without damaging the roots, if present (see inset).

2 Treat wounds with fungicide, and allow to dry. If roots are present, insert into potting mix; otherwise use equal parts of fine peat substitute (or peat) and sand.

3 Topdress with a ¼-in (5-mm) layer of ⅛-in (3-mm) sharp grit. Label the pot but do not water for several days.

SUCCULENTS TO PROPAGATE BY DIVISION OF OFFSETS

Agave
Aloe
Aloinopsis
Caralluma
Carruanthus
Conophytum
Copiapoa
Coryphantha
Crassula, many including C. perfoliata, C. socialis
Dactylopsis
Delosperma
Dinteranthus
Dracophilus
Duvalia
Ebracteola
Echidnopsis
Echinocereus
Echinopsis
Epithelantha
Erepsia
Escobaria
Faucaria
Gasteria (most spp.)
Glottiphyllum
Greenovia
Gymnocalycium
Haworthia
Huernia
Juttadinteria
Lithops
Lobivia
Mammillaria
Meyerophytum
Mitrophyllum
Orbea
Orostachys
Parodia
Pleiospilos
Pterocactus
Rebutia
Rhombophyllum
Sedum
Semanthe
Sempervivum
Stapelia
Stomatium
Sulcorebutia
Tephrocactus
Thelocactus
Weingartia
Wigginsia

Rebutia pygmaea

SUCCULENTS TO PROPOGATE BY DIVISION OF ROOTSTOCK

Agave, some
Aloe
Argyroderma
Caralluma
Carpobrotus
Conophytum
Delosperma
Duvalia
Faucaria
Fenestraria
Frithia
Glottiphyllum
Gymnocalycium
Huernia
Mammillaria
Rebutia
Ruschia
Sansevieria
Stapelia
Titanopsis

Aloe
variegata

Division of rootstock

Many species of Aizoaceae such as *Delosperma* and *Frithia*, some clump-forming cacti, and genera such as *Aloe* are readily propagated by division. For some cultivars of *Sansevieria*, division is the most reliable method of retaining the variegation, as leaf cuttings may produce plants that revert. Divide clump-forming cacti and other succulents in the early stages of the growing season.

Lift the whole plant from its pot, and carefully pull apart or cut the rootstock into a number of smaller pieces, each with a healthy bud or shoot and well-formed roots. Treat all cut areas with fungicide and pot up each section separately into standard potting mix. Label, water, and place in a semishaded position until well established.

Alternatively, cut away a piece of the rootstock without lifting the plant, and ease a section out of the soil with a hand fork. Dust the cut surfaces with fungicide and pot up as for offset tubers (see p.349). Fill any gaps that are left around the parent plant, using a standard potting mix, and water lightly.

DIVISION OF ROOTSTOCK

1 Lift the plant (here, *Sansevieria trifasciata*). Divide it into sections by cutting straight through the rootstock.

2 Discard old, woody material and any soft or damaged roots before replanting each new section.

Grafting

Some cacti and other succulents, notably certain members of the Asclepiadaceae, such as *Edithcolea* and *Pseudolithos*, are slow to mature and flower when grown on their own roots. By grafting them onto established specimens of related species that are quicker to mature, they can be induced to flower much faster. During the growing season the topgrowth, or scion, of the required plant is grafted onto the rootstock of one of the more vigorous species. Three grafting methods may be used: apical-wedge grafting, flat grafting, and side grafting.

APICAL-WEDGE GRAFTING

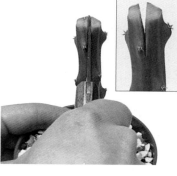

1 Prepare the rootstock by trimming off the tip, making a straight cut through the stem with a clean, sharp knife.

2 Make a slender "V"-shaped cleft (see inset) in the stock, to a depth of about ¾in (2cm).

3 Select the scion material and remove from the parent plant (here, a *Schlumbergera*), cutting straight through at a node with a sharp knife.

4 Trim the lower end of the scion to a narrow wedge shape to match the "V"-shaped cleft in the stock plant.

5 Insert the scion wedge into the cleft in the stock plant (see inset), making sure that they are in close contact.

6 To secure the scion in place in the clefted stock, insert a cactus spine through the grafted area.

Alternative method
Bind the graft firmly, but not tightly, with raffia or a dab of superglue.

Apical-wedge grafting

Epiphytic cacti are often propagated by apical-wedge grafting in order to create an erect "standard" or treelike plant. Use *Pereskiopsis* or *Selenicereus*, which are sturdy but of slender growth, as the rootstock.

To produce the rootstock, take a stem cutting (see p.348) of the selected plant. When this has rooted and shows evidence of new growth, it is ready to be used for grafting. Slice off the tip and then make two slanted, downward cuts into the top of the rootstock stem to produce a narrow, vertical, V-shaped slit approximately ¾in (2cm) long.

Select a healthy shoot from the scion plant and prepare it by trimming the lower end into a wedge shape to match the cleft in the stock. Insert the prepared scion "wedge" into the cleft so that the cut surfaces match as closely as possible. Secure the stock and scion firmly in position either by pushing a cactus spine horizontally through the graft or by binding with raffia or a dab of superglue.

Place the grafted plant in partial shade at a temperature of 70°F (21°C). The stock and scion should unite within a few weeks; once this has happened, remove the spine or raffia; dust fungicide into any holes made by the spine. When fresh growth appears, water and fertilize as for established plants (see p.345).

Flat grafting

This method is used to propagate crested variants (succulents with atypical, often contorted, growth), certain other succulents with tufts of hair, and *Gymnocalycium mihanovichii* and *Echinopsis chamaecereus*, whose seedlings may lack chlorophyll. Genera that can be used as rootstocks include *Echinopsis, Harrisia, Hylocereus,* and *Trichocereus*.

Make a straight, horizontal cut through the stem of the rootstock at the required height. Then remove the rib margins with a sharp knife to form a beveled edge, and trim off any spines near the cut.

Prepare the scion in a similar way, and position its base on the cut surface of the stock plant. Place rubber bands over the top of the scion and under the base of the pot to keep the scion securely in place; make sure that the bands are not too tight.

Leave the grafted plant in a well-lit position, but not in full sun. Keep the potting mix barely moist until the scion and the stock have united (normally in about a month), when the rubber bands may be removed. Thereafter, water and fertilize as for established plants.

When grafting asclepiads, the fleshy tubers of *Ceropegia* or the robust stems of *Stapelia* may be used as rootstocks. The former, in particular, make excellent stock plants for some of the Madagascan and Arabian asclepiads, which may otherwise be difficult to propagate.

Side grafting

This method is useful if the scion is too slender to be grafted onto the top of the stock. It is very similar to spliced side grafting, used for woody plants. Prepare the stock by slicing off the top at an oblique angle, then trim the base of the scion to match the stock as closely as possible. Secure them together with a spine or raffia and treat as for flat grafting.

SUCCULENTS TO PROPAGATE BY GRAFTING

Flat grafting
Alluaudiopsis
Astrophytum
Austrocactus
Aztekium
Blossfeldia
Coleocephalocereus
Discocactus
Duvalia
Echinopsis chamaecereus
Edithcolea
Epithelantha
Frailea
Gymnocalycium mihanovichii (and cvs)
Hoodia
Lophophora
Luckhoffia
Maihuenia
Mammillaria
Mila
Orbea
Parodia
Pediocactus
Pelecyphora
Pseudolithos
Pygmaeocereus
Rebutia
Tavaresia
Turbinicarpus
Uebelmannia

Side grafting
Disocactus
Echinocereus
Haageocereus
Hatiora
Lepismium (flat-stemmed spp.)
Rhipsalidopsis
Rhipsalis (spp. with rounded or angled stems)
Selenicereus
Weberocereus (spp. with rounded stems)

Apical-wedge grafting
Disocactus
Hatiora
Rhipsalidopsis
Schlumbergera
Selenicereus

FLAT GRAFTING

1 Slice off the top of the rootstock with a sharp knife, to produce a flat surface.

2 Trim the cut surface to produce a slightly beveled edge; hold the stem without touching the wounded area.

3 Cut the scion material, slicing through at the base. Bevel the edge of the scion (inset) so that it will fit closely onto the stock.

4 Place the scion on the stock and secure firmly, but not tightly, with rubber bands. Label with the name of the scion plant.

5 Place the pot in good light at a minimum temperature of 61°F (16°C). Remove the rubber bands when new growth appears.

SIDE GRAFTING

If the scion plant is slender, it may be grafted onto the side of the stock. Make a slanted cut in both stock and scion, lace the cut surfaces together, and fasten with a cactus spine and raffia. Leave in good light at 61°F (16°C) until new growth appears.

Gymnocalycium mihanovichii 'Red Head'

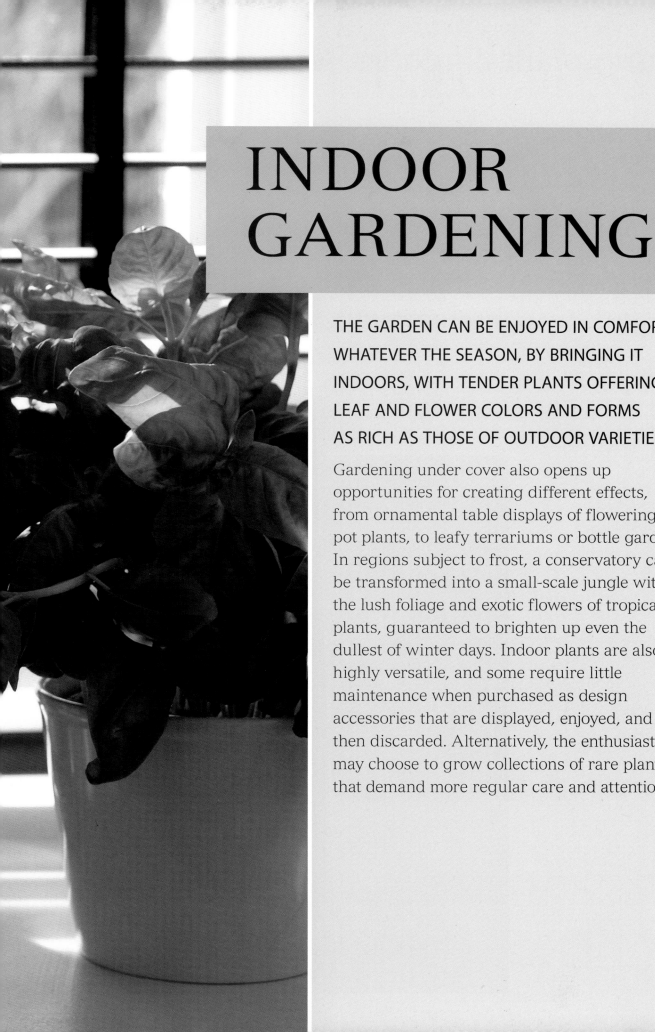

INDOOR GARDENING

THE GARDEN CAN BE ENJOYED IN COMFORT, WHATEVER THE SEASON, BY BRINGING IT INDOORS, WITH TENDER PLANTS OFFERING LEAF AND FLOWER COLORS AND FORMS AS RICH AS THOSE OF OUTDOOR VARIETIES.

Gardening under cover also opens up opportunities for creating different effects, from ornamental table displays of flowering pot plants, to leafy terrariums or bottle gardens. In regions subject to frost, a conservatory can be transformed into a small-scale jungle with the lush foliage and exotic flowers of tropical plants, guaranteed to brighten up even the dullest of winter days. Indoor plants are also highly versatile, and some require little maintenance when purchased as design accessories that are displayed, enjoyed, and then discarded. Alternatively, the enthusiast may choose to grow collections of rare plants that demand more regular care and attention.

Displaying plants indoors

The range of plants that may be grown in a home and a greenhouse offers a wealth of form, color, and texture. Plants may be chosen for their handsome foliage or the beauty of their blooms, from the exuberant hues of bougainvillea to the cool elegance of *Zantedeschia aethiopica*. Others, such as *Solanum pseudocapsicum,* are valued for their brightly colored fruit. Fragrance can also be a reason for choosing a plant for the home; scented-leaved geraniums, for example, blend well with other plants and provide a wonderful scent that adds to the display.

Form and structure Group plants in matching containers.

Choosing indoor plants

The choice of plants depends on whether the display is to be permanent, when plants with interesting form and foliage are the best choice for a year-round display, or temporary, when the seasonal interest of plants, such as *Cyclamen persicum,* may be used to give spots of color.

Plants may reinforce or contrast with the style of the indoor setting, whether it is a rustic country kitchen or a formal and sophisticated urban living room. The plants may dominate the scene and give a room its essential character, create pockets of interest, or simply add to the detail. Whatever effect is desired, select plants that will both thrive in and enhance their intended location.

Foliage and form

Plants that have attractive foliage are invaluable for long-term indoor display. They may have huge leaves, as on the *Fatsia japonica,* or a mass of dainty ones, such as those of *Soleirolia soleirolii,* syn. *Helxine soleirolii.* Leaves may have subtle or striking patterns and colors, as on the *Calathea* species, or interesting shapes, for example, the Swiss-cheese plant (*Monstera deliciosa*).

Foliage also has different textures, from the high gloss of the rubber plant (*Ficus elastica*) to the corrugated surfaces of *Pilea involucrata* and the soft velvet of *Gynura aurantiaca.* Some plants are chosen for their strong shapes, whether they are spiky bromeliads, graceful palms and ferns, or pebblelike *Lithops.*

Grouping plants

When planning an arrangement, choose plants with strongly colored flowers or patterned leaves carefully, so that they do not detract from each other. Experiment with contrasts by arranging plants together in florists, nurseries, and garden centers before making a purchase.

Architectural plants, such as palms, make very fine specimen plants or striking focal points in a group. Smaller plants have impact when arranged together on a tiered stand, but may be used singly as a lovely finishing touch. A tight group of identical plants, for example, a bowl of white hyacinths, makes a strong yet simple statement.

The indoor environment

The specific temperature and light requirements of plants are the most important factors in deciding where to position them indoors (see *Planter's Guide to Indoor Plants,* p.361). If the conditions are incompatible with the plants' needs, they will soon become stressed and unhealthy.

Newly purchased plants that have just come from controlled conditions are especially vulnerable.

Temperature

Although most modern houses are kept warm during the day in winter, the temperature is often allowed to drop markedly at night—a problem for many houseplants of tropical origin. Place these plants where they are protected from drafts and are not subject to wide fluctuations in temperature. Do not leave tender plants on windowsills at night, especially if the drawn curtains close off residual warmth from the room, or place plants directly above radiators or heaters

Plants indoors A sunroom or light, indoor area can house a variety of plants such as *Plumbago*, *Abutilon*, and geraniums, which will coexist happily and enhance their surroundings.

that are in use. To flower, indoor plants need warmth, but if the temperature is too high for the individual species, the blooms quickly fade and die.

Light

Most plants thrive in bright, filtered sunlight or in a well-lit location that is not in direct sun. Plants that have variegated leaves need more light than those with plain green leaves, but overly strong sunlight will damage the foliage. Flowering plants, such as *Hippeastrum,* need good light if they are to flower well, but excessive light can shorten the life of the blooms. In fact, few indoor plants can tolerate direct sunlight.

Insufficient light results in plants with pale, stunted new leaves, and drawn-out, or etiolated, growth with long, thin, weak stems. Some variegated plants may begin to produce plain leaves. In time, the mature leaves will turn yellow and fall. A plant weakened like this is more vulnerable to pests and diseases.

The amount of natural light in a room depends on the number, size, height, and exposure of the windows. Light levels fall quickly as the distance from the window increases. In winter, there is far less

HAZARDS OF A WINDOWSILL

Too much sunlight, excessive heat from radiators, and drafts through the window frame can weaken or kill houseplants that are placed on a windowsill.

natural light than in summer, and some plants may need to be moved in response to the seasonal light variation—a rolling plant trolley is ideal for this purpose.

If plants start to grow lopsidedly toward a source of light, turn them slightly when watering them. If light levels are too low for healthy growth (most plants need 12–14 hours of daylight per day), supplementary growing lights are effective (see *A Growing Light,* p.577). These are particularly valuable when growing African violets (*Saintpaulia*), which need a long day length to flower continuously.

Positioning plants

With a little forethought and planning, it is possible to find striking houseplants that flourish in almost every site indoors, from a brightly lit room to a dim hallway or alcove.

The indoor setting

Give careful consideration to the impact of plants within a room. Are they in proportion to the room? A tiny plant in a pot will appear lost in a large space. Is the background suitable? Plain, pale walls show flowering plants to best advantage. Does the flower or foliage color blend with the decor?

High-level hanging baskets and shelves suit trailing plants best, while eye-level positions are ideal for plants with delicate flowers or foliage. Train climbing plants, such as *Philodendron hederaceum, Cissus antarctica,* and English ivy (*Hedera*), on decorative trellis, a moss pole, or other supports to create a living screen.

Use plants to enliven empty corners or space, such as an unused fireplace, which provides an instant frame for a display. Large plants or groups may play an architectural role as room dividers or as a link between the house and the garden.

LIGHT LEVELS WITHIN A ROOM

The farther away from a window a plant is located, the less natural light it will receive. If the plant is 6ft (2m) away, the light level may be as little as 20 percent of that by the window. Plants that are placed close to a window but to one side of it derive little benefit from the location, especially if the windowsills are very deep.

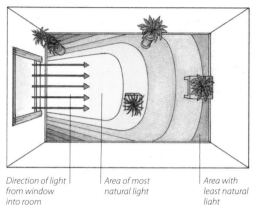

Direction of light from window into room | *Area of most natural light* | *Area with least natural light*

Plants and light levels

Bright, sunny conditions suit succulent plants as well as plants with woolly, waxy, or gray leaves. *Hoya carnosa,* geraniums, and *Ananas comosus* 'Variegatus' will also appreciate direct sunlight. In places with indirect or filtered light, grow foliage begonias, such as *Begonia rex;* epiphytic orchids, such as *Phalaenopsis;* and *Spathiphyllum* with their striking, white spathes.

For corners that are far from a window, choose ferns and tough-leaved plants, such as *Chamaedorea, Fatsia japonica,* and ivy. Expose the plants to slightly brighter light occasionally, if only for a few days.

Kitchens and bathrooms

Temperatures and humidity in kitchens and bathrooms, especially small ones, can fluctuate, so choose plants that can tolerate extremes. Smooth, hard bathroom surfaces contrast well with the soft, feathery forms of ferns and grasses, and some *Cyperus* species. Bathrooms often have low levels of light, ideal for *Episcia, Nephrolepis,* or *Pilea.* Fill high-level bathroom space with trailing plants such as *Philodendron hederaceum.* Do not put trailing plants on top of kitchen cabinets because they may interfere with the cupboard doors; also the light levels high up are likely to be extremely low, so plants will become thin and straggly. In brightly lit locations, use hanging baskets to grow a selection of herbs or tiny tomato cultivars. Herbs are also ideal for growing on a sunny kitchen windowsill.

Tolerant plants

Attractive foliage plants that tolerate a wide range of conditions include *Aspidistra, Chlorophytum, Cissus antarctica,* and *Sansevieria.* Flowering plants are more exacting, but chrysanthemums (see pp.186–187) or forced bulbs (see p.231) may give short-term floral color.

Conservatory gardening

A conservatory is often treated solely as an additional interior living room, comfortably furnished and usually ornamented with potted plants. However, plant enthusiasts may instead want their conservatory to be an enclosed extension of the garden; a protected environment that will meet the needs of more unusual plants. There is no doubt that a conservatory is often chosen in preference to a greenhouse, and when a new conservatory is intended primarily as a place in which plants will thrive, it is worth spending time at the design stage to ensure that the end result is practical and successful in its aim.

Positioning and orientation

With a greenhouse, the orientation and site can usually be chosen for maximum light and best growing conditions, but with a conservatory the priorities are usually where it looks best attached to the house, while at the same time conveniently connecting with a kitchen, hallway, or other living area.

A conservatory in full sun all day needs generous cross ventilation; large roof ventilators, windows that open, and doors that can be folded back in summer, coupled with effective roof shading. One oriented to receive only morning or evening sun, in shade during the hottest parts of the day, will suit plants tolerant of a wide range of conditions. If the best site is relatively sunless, this should not automatically be considered a disadvantage. The shade will encourage foliage growth, and the conservatory will have a relatively even temperature, ideal for shade-tolerant plants.

A conservatory that has warm, humid conditions required by tropical or subtropical plants will quickly rot soft furnishings, books, and magazines—and many gardeners opt for a greenhouse (see GREENHOUSES AND COLD FRAMES, pp.566–583), which can be tailored more exactly to meet the needs of plants.

Basic materials

Most conservatories have brick or wooden base walls supporting a glazed wood or metal framework and a ridged roof. Use shelves or benches to raise small plants to the light. Wide interior windowsills can be useful for pots. Unlike most greenhouses, conservatories are normally double-glazed, to retain heat from within the house. Because of its more robust

structure, a conservatory will never allow in as much light as does a greenhouse, which should be kept in mind when selecting plants, especially if the conservatory receives little sun—tomatoes may perform better in a greenhouse, for example, or an oleander may be more likely to flower on a south-facing terrace.

The most practical flooring materials are slatted and oiled hardwood, tiles, or stone, which are easy to keep clean yet tolerate the humid atmosphere generated by plants, and also repel water when damping down.

Ventilation

Ample roof ventilation is essential for successful conservatory cultivation. There are no precise formulas for calculating the amount of ventilation

A place for plants
A conservatory allows the cultivation of plants that might not thrive in the cooler conditions of the great outdoors; here, peach blossoms, harbingers of fruit to come, can be enjoyed inside.

required, because it depends on exposure and the design of the building. Roof vents allow upward convection of warm air into the roof to escape, and cross ventilation works best when at least a third of the glazed area can be opened. Greenhouse vents, hinged from the

roof ridge, modified to take the weight of double-glazing, and watertight when closed, are effective if large enough. Electric or mechanical openers should be used to operate the vents unless the roof is unusually low, in which case wax-operated greenhouse openers are suitable. See also GREENHOUSES AND COLD FRAMES, "Ventilation," p.575.

Shading

Unless the conservatory receives no direct sunlight, shading will be needed to protect plants from scorching. Roller or pleated blinds are the most common solution, fitted from the roof and supported by fine, taut wires to prevent sagging. Internal roof blinds can be problematic if climbers are being grown, but while external blinds, as used on greenhouses, are practical, they may not look good. Side blinds fitted to windows and doors are used more for privacy than shading. See also GREENHOUSES AND COLD FRAMES, "Shading," p.576.

Heating

Because a conservatory is adjacent to the house, it is relatively easy to keep warm and can often be

Ensuring a through draft
If the building is in full sun, double doors that open out and can be hooked back will considerably aid ventilation. As many windows as possible should be openable.

connected to the house's central heating system. It should ideally have separate ductwork and controls to maintain minimum nighttime temperatures for plants, which may be greater than that desired in the house. If a connection to the heating system is not feasible, use a thermostatic convection heater. All types of heaters are best positioned in a corner on the external, colder sides of the room, as are thermostats.

Underfloor heating, of which there are two types, is another possibility. The first uses electric cables or a small hot-water pipe snaking back and forth over insulation, beneath the subflooring. These heat up the floor to provide even, continuous heat and are best used in a north-facing conservatory where there will be little direct sunshine. The second type of underfloor heating is trench heating, which consists of central heating pipes, usually branching to give greater output, set in a channel 12in (30cm) wide, placed around the perimeter of the conservatory and covered with a grille of plain or decorative cast-metal. Trench heating is more expensive to install than electric cables but is more quickly adjusted; it is also easier to raise humidity simply by pouring water through the grille to create steam.

Humidity

Conservatories can become very dry, which will not suit many plants and will also encourage pests and diseases. Grouping plants together will help, because transpiration from their leaves will produce a miniature, moist climate. Trays of gravel or shallow pans kept filled with water will increase humidity. On hot days, damping down—splashing water on the floor—will be necessary, especially because doors and windows will need to be open simultaneously to provide ventilation. Another reliable source of humidity is a wall fountain or, if there is sufficient space, an indoor pool. See also GREENHOUSES AND COLD FRAMES, "Humidity," p.576.

Watering

Irrigation systems, although effective, are often difficult to disguise in a conservatory. Most

gardeners rely on hand watering. The water used should be at the same temperature as the plants and their potting mix. Traditional conservatories often had storage tanks inside, set in the floor. Water drawn from a faucet or from an outdoor barrel or tank should be left in watering cans or buckets for a couple of hours before use.

In a hard water area, watering will leave deposits of lime and gradually increase the alkalinity of the soil, which for many conservatory plants, such as citrus, camellias, and gardenias, will cause chlorosis and poor growth. This can be overcome by installing a water softener or by using rainwater collected from the conservatory's guttering diverted into a rain barrel (see also p.614). Ideally a pipe should be fitted just above its base leading to a spigot in the conservatory, and the barrel raised high enough for the spigot to be fed by gravity, or use an electric pressure-release pump.

Displaying plants

Some plants are better grown in soil beds than in pots. Beds in the floor are rarely practical because they will interfere with damp-proof courses, are difficult to keep clean (especially if pets have access to the room), and are permanent, making it inconvenient to alter the layout. Raised brick or block beds are preferable, and make gardening

particularly convenient for the elderly or less able. Raised beds should be as deep as practical to allow ample root growth and have a waterproof lining, with a gravel base layer for drainage (see also "Raised beds," p.269).

Climbers can be grown on wall trellis or wires fixed to the wall and roof. Container-grown plants may be also trained on freestanding supports, such as tapering wire frames (see also CONTAINER GARDENING, p.325). In a wooden roof, fit long-stemmed screw eyes to keep training wires 6in (15cm) or more away from the glass. With a metal or plastic roof, self-tapping screws and specially made brackets are generally available. Make sure that climbers are kept well clear of light fixtures.

Roof and side blinds
The traditional fabric, pinoleum, is made from woven pine "twigs" and provides 70–75 percent shading. Satisfactory alternatives are stiffened cotton, foil-backed plastic to reflect the sun, and fiberglass mesh.

Plant health

Conservatories have the same range of problems as a greenhouse (see p.375), but, because of the close proximity to the house and the fact that a conservatory is used by people, the methods of control will vary. Biological control is effective for many pests if used at the right time (see PLANT PROBLEMS, "Biological control," p.643). Routine fumigation will be out of the question in most cases, as will the regular use of sprays. If these are needed, it is best to take the plants outside on a mild day, cleaning them thoroughly before treating. Allow the spray to dry before bringing plants indoors again.

Planting beds
This raised planting bed sits on a watertight, edged gravel base that can be topped off with water, increasing the humidity levels for plants, such as bromeliads (here, *Neoregelia*), that enjoy such conditions.

Containers

Choose a container whose material, color, and shape blends with the decor and shows the individual plant or group to its best advantage. The choice is enormous, both in style and materials, presenting a range of effects from rustic to ultramodern. The most unlikely household objects—birdcages, cooking utensils, urns—can be used to provide unusual and striking plant holders.

Hanging baskets

Hanging baskets are popular features on porches, balconies, patios, and terraces, but are also attractive ways to grow indoor plants. Hang them in stairwells, from rafters, by windows, or from freestanding supports for an economical and colorful use of space (see CONTAINER GARDENING, "Hanging baskets," p.312).

Arching fern fronds, the rosettes of epiphytes, and the cascading habit of many foliage plants lend themselves perfectly to hanging baskets. Vary the planting during the year to make seasonal displays. Christmas cactus (*Schlumbergera buckleyi*) provides a mass of bright color for winter, as do fuchsias in summer. Temporary arrangements may be created by planting a basket with potted plants, but they will need replanting each year. Permanently planted baskets are easier to manage, especially if they contain a single, large plant.

Choosing hanging containers

Hanging baskets are available in various materials and designs. When choosing and positioning them, take into account the fact that most plants require frequent watering. Plastic-coated wire hanging baskets are practical indoors only in rooms that have water-resistant floors; some rigid, plastic baskets have built-in drip saucers that provide a practical solution. Also available are attractive, although heavy, pottery and terra-cotta hanging pots, and wrought iron, wooden, or wicker baskets. A planted basket is heavy, especially when just watered, so it must be supported by strong rope or chain from a hook or bracket fixed securely to a ceiling joist or a solid wall.

Terrariums and bottle gardens

Terrariums are enclosed glass containers, often very decorative in their own right, used to display small plants in the home. They were extremely popular in the 19th century as a way of providing a suitable microclimate for ferns, but any slow-growing ornamental plants that need a humid atmosphere thrive in a terrarium. A selection of plants with contrasting leaf textures and colors is the most effective—it is best to avoid flowering plants because the dead blooms rot in the moist conditions. Terrariums may be built permanently into a window to house a lush arrangement of larger plants.

Bottles may also be used to create a diminutive landscape of foliage plants. As long as the neck is sufficiently wide to allow the insertion of the plants and routine aftercare, any shape or color of bottle may be used, but remember that tinted glass cuts out some of the light.

Indoor lighting

Flood- and spotlights may enhance displays; up- or downlighting make dramatic contrasts of light and shade. Do not place plants too close to light sources, because heat may damage them. Ordinary incandescent bulbs do not significantly improve growth or food production (photosynthesis).

Plants for the office

Introducing plants into an office not only brightens it up, but deadens noise, refreshes the air, and creates a less stressful atmosphere. In a modern, open-office plan that is totally enclosed and air-conditioned, temperatures are constant, air pollution is minimized, and light is plentiful: ideal growing conditions. Old buildings with small windows and little climatic control present more of a challenge.

Use self-watering pots, especially if they are near electrical equipment, or plunge several plants into a large container. Be sure someone is responsible for their care.

Suitable plants

Evergreen, shiny-leaved plants are as tough and tolerant in an office as they are at home. The popular genus *Ficus* includes plants of every shape and size, from lustrous, huge-leaved *F. lyrata* (give it solitary splendor in a large space) to *F. deltoidea* with its small, leathery-textured leaves.

Complementary groupings
Plants grouped together, such as orchids and maidenhair ferns, will create a humid microclimate around their leaves. Mist plants daily to maintain a humid atmosphere, or place on a tray of damp gravel or clay pellets.

COOL CONSERVATORY

The foliage and flowering plants shown here are among the many that thrive in the cool, but frost-free, conditions of a lean-to conservatory to create a fine display.

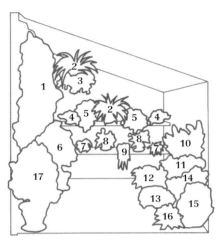

1 *Plumbago auriculata*
(syn. *P. capensis*)
2 *Chlorophytum comosum*
(syn. *C. capense* of gardens)
3 *Campanula isophylla*
4 *Saxifraga stolonifera* 'Tricolor'
(syn. *S. stolonifera* 'Magic Carpet')
5 *Pelargonium* 'Mini Cascade'
6 *Camellia japonica*
7 *Sedum morganianum*
8 *Streptocarpus* 'Heidi'
9 *Ceropegia linearis* subsp. *woodii*
10 *Callistemon citrinus*
'Splendens'
11 *Correa pulchella*
12 *Calceolaria* 'Sunshine'
13 *Nierembergia scoparia*
'Purple Robe'
14 *Prostanthera rotundifolia*
15 *Polygala* x *dalmaisiana* (syn.
P. myrtifolia 'Grandiflora')
16 *Rehmannia elata*
17 x *Citrofortunella microcarpa*
(syn. *Citrus mitis*)

Philodendron is another large and impressive genus, including climbers and trailers, with handsome leaves. The tenacious, long-lived Swiss-cheese plant (*Monstera deliciosa*) climbs slowly but eventually reaches a dozen or more feet in height and spread.

Sunrooms and conservatories

The garden may be brought indoors, either into a sunroom, a living space furnished with container plants, or a conservatory, often devoted to plants. In temperate climates, both may be used to give winter shelter to pot-grown plants that spend the summer months outdoors; a conservatory may also provide the warm, humid environment needed by tropical and subtropical plants (see also CONSERVATORY GARDENING, pp.356–357).

High light levels in conservatories encourage colored leaves to assume intense hues, and plants flower well. Fragrant plants such as *Jasminum polyanthum* are welcome in confined spaces where scent lingers in the air.

Select plants to suit the conservatory exposure and temperature. Bear in mind glass structures can be costly to heat in winter and very hot in summer.

Create a profusion of planting by making full use of the space: grow plants at different levels in raised and ground-level soil beds, in pots on the floor, on windowsills, shelves, and in hanging baskets. Large tropical or subtropical plants and freestanding climbers may be trained on trellis or wires attached to the walls or roof. Use plants that complement those in the yard; this visually links the two, and creates a sense of space.

Indoor water features

A sunken or raised pool or a half-barrel may accommodate tropical water lilies or other tender aquatic and marginal plants. A simple and elegant water spout will provide the restful murmur of falling water and help to maintain high humidity (see also WATER GARDENING, pp.280–303).

Growing plants in a greenhouse

The control of light, temperature, and humidity in a greenhouse will allow a much more extensive range of plants to be grown than in a yard that is subject to cold. Using a greenhouse also extends the season of display and cropping from early spring until late fall, or even all year round if desired.

Uses for greenhouses

Greenhouses are useful in cool temperate climates, where there is frost, strong winds, or excessive rain: they may be used for propagation; raising and growing tender plants or flowers for cutting; or for crops like salads, early vegetables, or even fruit. Many plants grow faster under cover and fruit or flower more profusely than they do outdoors. Half-hardy plants may be grown in containers outdoors and transferred to temporary shelter in the greenhouse as needed.

Some gardeners use greenhouses to grow specific plants like auriculas or fuchsias (see p.119); others may house collections of carnivorous plants, alpines (see pp.277–279), orchids (see pp.368–371), cacti (see pp.338–351), or ferns (see pp.202–203).

The greenhouse layout

The traditional, freestanding greenhouse interior comprises a central path with waist-high benches on the sides and far end; wider greenhouses may also have benches in the center. Benches (see also p.579) are needed; even if they are removed in summer for border crops, they may be used at other times of year for raising seedlings, propagating cuttings, and displaying pot plants. Slatted or meshed benches are best for pot plants to avoid puddles of standing water and ensure air circulates freely, especially in winter.

For extra display space, use tiered benches, bench beds, or soil borders. If the glass begins at ground level, ferns and other shade-loving plants, and dormant plants, may be grown or rested under the benches. Raised beds are useful to display small plants, such as alpines and cacti, that are planted directly in the beds or in pots plunged into gravel or sand.

The ornamental greenhouse

Although a greenhouse is often used more for practical purposes than a conservatory, part or all of it may be devoted to ornamental displays. Groups are usually more attractive than widely spaced plants. Feature a single genus such as *Streptocarpus*, or mixed plants

An interior garden
Where space allows, a natural-looking landscape may be created within a greenhouse. Here, foliage plants provide a lush framework that is offset by the colorful blooms of flowering plants.

displayed in random patterns or as a miniature landscape. Include contrasts of leaf form, size, and texture, and control the use of color from flowers and foliage to create a harmonious arrangement.

A lean-to greenhouse against the house wall may double as a conservatory. Make the most of the back wall by growing climbers, which need only a 12in (30cm) wide bed or pot. Paint the wall white to reflect light and provide a contrasting background for the plants.

The greenhouse environment

Essential requirements for success are adequate ventilation and heat, as well as shading in summer. Running water and electricity are also useful. The temperature of a greenhouse depends on its use, but there are four basic conditions: cold or unheated, cool or frost-free, temperate, and warm. For further information, see GREENHOUSES AND COLD FRAMES, "Creating the right environment," pp.573–577; see also *Planter's Guide to Indoor Plants*, p.361.

The cold greenhouse

An unheated greenhouse protects against extremes of wind and rain and is significantly warmer, even in summer, than outdoors. It extends the growing season by giving plants an artificially early spring and late fall.

Depending on winter severity, many hardy annuals, biennials, and shrubs may be overwintered in an unheated greenhouse, along with half-hardy annuals, bulbous plants, and shrubs being grown to plant out in summer, when the garden soil has warmed

up and danger of frost is past. A cold greenhouse is also useful for raising seed and for getting and early start with fruit or vegetables. As an alpine house, it may be used to provide the specialized conditions needed for growing alpines in pots (see ALPINE HOUSES AND FRAMES, pp.277–279).

An unheated greenhouse does not exclude frost for more than an hour or two, so it is not suitable for overwintering tender plants. Sunlight, or even bright light, raises the daytime temperature, but night temperatures can drop almost as low as those in the rest of the yard. In temperate climates, most greenhouses built against a warm wall have conditions similar to a cool greenhouse (see below), but this will not prevent tender plants from being killed by a few days of hard frost.

The cool greenhouse

Freedom from frost increases the range of plants that may be grown. A frost-free greenhouse is also easier to manage, because protective measures are unnecessary. Day temperatures of 41–50°F (5–10°C) and a nighttime minimum of 36°F (2°C) allow ornamentals to be enjoyed all year.

In a cool greenhouse, hardy bulbous plants, particularly those with delicate blooms that are not noticed in an open garden, flower earlier, providing color in late winter and early spring. Here, tender patio plants may be raised through the winter; houseplants can be revived and propagated in warmer months; and winter-flowering plants, such as the aromatic *Prostanthera*, may be grown in bench beds or in pots. Grown under cover, chrysanthemums and perpetual-flowering

carnations (*Dianthus*) provide a supply of cut flowers, while hardy annuals raised from seed sown in the late summer give early flowers.

The cool greenhouse should be heated enough to exclude frost and maintain a minimum temperature in all weathers (see GREENHOUSES AND COLD FRAMES, "Heating," p.574). Even if the entire greenhouse is not heated, an electrically heated propagator, or a propagating bench, will enable an early start to be made on raising new plants in the spring.

The temperate greenhouse

Raising the temperature to 50–55°F (10–13°C), with a nighttime minimum of 45°F (7°C), widens the scope even further. If they are kept in a temperate greenhouse, plants associated with the essentially frost-free climates of California, the Mediterranean, and South Africa, may be enjoyed in harsher climates than they could normally withstand. These include genera such as *Brunfelsia*, *Jacaranda*, and *Strelitzia*, and orchids such as *Cymbidium* species and hybrids. If zonal geraniums are kept at 48°F (9°C), they will flower all year round.

The warm greenhouse

A minimum temperature of 55°F (13°C) to 64°F (18°C) in a warm greenhouse allows cultivation of subtropical and tropical plants, as well as year-round propagation or flower displays. Frost-tender plants, for example, many bromeliads (see pp.362–363) and a number of orchids (see pp.368–371), may be grown to bring indoors when at their best.

The warm greenhouse needs controllable heating throughout the year, even in summer in cooler climates. This results in high heating costs in temperate zones. Equipment such as thermostats, double glazing, fans, and automatic ventilation, an automated watering and damping-down system, and shading help to control conditions and facilitate routine care. A warm section in a cool greenhouse is a cheaper option; a warm conservatory, or plant room, is another possibility.

Greenhouse protection
Cacti and succulents are some of the plants that benefit from the shelter of a greenhouse over the winter months, and can also be shaded from the heat of the sun during the summer.

PLANTER'S GUIDE TO INDOOR PLANTS

WARM GREENHOUSE
(Minimum 55–64°F/13–18°C)
Flowering plants
Aeschynanthus ☺
Anthurium
Aphelandra ☺
Brunfelsia ☺
Columnea ☺
Euphorbia fulgens,
  E. pulcherrima
Hibiscus rosa-sinensis
Hoya lanceolata
Justicia
Kohleria ☺
Medinilla ☺
Pachystachys
Ruellia ☺
Saintpaulia ☺
Sinningia ☺
Smithiantha ☺
Spathiphyllum ☺

Foliage plants
Aechmea ☺
  (and most bromeliads)
Aglaonema ☺
Begonia rex ☺ (and other spp.)
Calathea ☺
Chamaedorea ☺
  (and most palms)
Codiaeum ☺
Dieffenbachia ☺
Dracaena ☺
Ficus, some
Fittonia ☺
Maranta ☺
Peperomia ☺
Philodendron ☺
Tradescantia, some ☺

TEMPERATE GREENHOUSE
**(Daytime 50–55°F/10–13°C;
night minimum 45°F/7°C)**
Flowering plants
Achimenes
Begonia ☺
Catharanthus
Cyclamen ☺
Exacum ☺
Haemanthus
Impatiens ☺
Schlumbergera ☺
Strelitzia
Streptocarpus ☺

Foliage plants
Asparagus
Jacaranda
Solenostemon ☺

COOL GREENHOUSE
**(Daytime 4–50°F/5–10°C;
night minimum 36°F/2°C)**
Flowering plants
Abutilon
Bougainvillea
Browallia
Brugmansia
Calceolaria ☺
Callistemon
Cestrum

Chrysanthemum, ☺
  x Citrofortunella
Cuphea
Freesia
Fuchsia, some
Gerbera
Hippeastrum
Hoya
Jasminum
Lachenalia
Lantana
Lapageria
Nerium
Passiflora
Pelargonium
Plumbago
Primula
Schizanthus
Senecio
Sprekelia
Streptosolen
Tibouchina ☺
Veltheimia
Zantedeschia
Zephyranthes

Foliage plants
Aspidistra
Chlorophytum
Cissus rhombifolia
Rhoicissus
Ricinus

COLD GREENHOUSE
Flowering plants
Agapanthus (hardy spp.)
Anemone
Antirrhinum (hardy spp.)
Camellia (hardy spp.)
Crocus
Cyclamen (hardy miniature spp.)
Dicentra
Erica
Erysimum (hardy spp.)
Hyacinthus
Jasminum (hardy spp.)
Narcissus
Rhododendron (hardy azaleas
  in shady greenhouse)

Foliage plants
Adiantum ☺ (hardy spp.)
Euonymus
Fatsia ☺
Hedera ☺ (hardy spp.)
Laurus nobilis
Phormium
Tolmiea

DIRECT LIGHT INDOORS
Plants for a warm room
(64°F/18°C and over)
Ananas ☺
Bougainvillea
Euphorbia pulcherrima
Hibiscus rosa-sinensis
Hippeastrum
Justicia
Opuntia
Senecio
Solanum capsicastrum ☺

Plants for a cool room
(40–64°F/5–18°C)
Billbergia
Browallia
Campanula isophylla ☺
Capsicum
Chlorophytum
Clivia
Crassula
Cyclamen ☺
Cyrtanthus
Echeveria
Gerbera
Hyacinthus
Jasminum
Kalanchoe
Nerine
Pelargonium
Solenostemon ☺
Streptocarpus ☺
Veltheimia

INDIRECT LIGHT INDOORS
Plants for a warm room—medium light
(64°F/18°C and over)
Adiantum ☺
Aechmea ☺
  (and all bromeliads)
Caladium
Codiaeum ☺
Cryptanthus ☺
Dieffenbachia ☺
Exacum ☺
Howea
Hypoestes
Kohleria ☺
Mandevilla ☺
Maranta ☺
Neoregelia ☺
Peperomia ☺
Pilea ☺
Saintpaulia ☺
  (needs direct light in winter)
Sansevieria
Schefflera
Sinningia ☺
Spathiphyllum ☺
Stephanotis ☺
Streptocarpus ☺
Syngonium ☺
Thunbergia
Tradescantia ☺

Plants for a warm room—poor light
(64°F/18°C and over)
Asplenium
Calathea ☺
Chamaedorea ☺
Cissus
Dracaena ☺
Episcia ☺
Fittonia ☺
Philodendron

Plants for a cool room—medium light
(40–64°F/5–18°C)
Epiphyllum
Epipremnum
Fatsia ☺

Grevillea
Monstera
Platycerium ☺
Primula malacoides,
  P. obconica
Schefflera ☺
Sparrmannia ☺

Plants for a cool room—poor light
(40–64°F/5–18°C)
Aspidistra
x Fatshedera ☺
Hedera ☺
Pteris ☺
Rhoicissus

HYDROCULTURE
Anthurium
Chamaedorea ☺
Cissus
Codiaeum ☺
Dieffenbachia ☺
Dracaena ☺
Euphorbia milii
Ficus benjamina
Hedera ☺
Monstera
Nephrolepis ☺
Saintpaulia ☺
Schefflera
Spathiphyllum ☺
Streptocarpus ☺

Key
☺ Requires high humidity

Schizanthus pinnatus

Bromeliads

Bromeliads, the 2,000 or so members of one of the most diverse and exotic families, the Bromeliaceae, are a fascinating group of plants that can make curiously beautiful specimens for the home, the warm greenhouse, or conservatory. Most are tropical epiphytes growing naturally on tree branches and rock faces, clinging by means of anchorage roots. These plants obtain moisture and nutrients via their leaves directly from the atmosphere, often from mists and low, moisture-laden clouds. Others are terrestrial, growing in the soil.

Almost all bromeliads are rosette-forming, frequently with strikingly colored or variegated foliage, and many produce flamboyant blooms. Their forms range from the long and graceful, silvery strands of Spanish moss (*Tillandsia usneoides*) to the imposing *Puya alpestris*, which holds its massive spike of tubular, metallic-blue flowers above a rosette of arching, spiny foliage.

Displaying epiphytes

Most epiphytes are displayed to their best advantage if attached to a section of tree or branch, simulating the way that they grow in nature. This method also avoids the risk of root and basal rot, which may occur if plants are grown in soil mix. Old, branched sections of trees cut to size are ideal. Attractive pieces of driftwood can also be used.

When attaching the plant to its display mount, it is usually easiest to start working from the bottom of the root ball. Move upward, gradually firming moss around the roots and keeping it in position with wire, string, or raffia.

Bromeliad trees

If using an upright branch, secure it firmly in a deep container with cement or, if small, a strong adhesive. Alternatively, it is possible to construct an artificial tree or branch from a metal or wire framework covered in bark. There is a wide range of epiphytes suitable for displaying in this way, including many species from the genera *Aechmea*, *Cryptanthus*, *Guzmania*, *Neoregelia*, *Nidularium*, *Tillandsia*, and *Vriesea*. Use young plants if possible—they are easier to mount and tend to become established more quickly.

Prepare the plants by removing any loose soil mix from around the roots, then wrap the roots in moistened sphagnum moss and bind them to the support. Before long the plants will root onto their support, after which the binding may be removed. Some small plants may be lodged

WRAPPING WITH MOSS

Wrap moistened sphagnum moss around the roots of a plant *(here, a cultivar of Tillandsia latifolia)* and attach it to the mount by binding the root ball to it with wire, string, or raffia. The moss must be kept moist at all times.

securely in crevices without the need for binding, as described for *Tillandsia*, below.

Displaying *Tillandsia*

Tillandsia species are often known as air plants: almost all lack roots and obtain their nutrients mainly from air-borne moisture. They occur naturally in a range of forest, mountain, and desert habitats (in North, Central, and South America), lodged among tree branches and

rocky outcrops. In cultivation, *Tillandsia* species may be mounted individually or in groups on cork bark or driftwood, on rocks, or even on natural crystal. Lodge the plant in a crevice or press it onto the mount and secure with twine. Air plants should never be glued.

Epiphytes as potted plants

A number of naturally epiphytic genera, particularly those with colored foliage and the usually epiphytic species and cultivars of *Aechmea*, *Billbergia*, *Neoregelia*, *Nidularium*, and *Vriesea*, may also be grown as potted plants, provided that an appropriate potting mix is used. It must be an extremely light, porous mixture, high in organic matter. For this, use half coarse sand or perlite, and half peat substitute (or peat) or leaf mold. To ensure that extra moisture drains away swiftly, add pieces of partly composted tree bark to the potting mix.

Growing terrestrials

There are several hundred terrestrial bromeliads belonging to the genera *Ananas*, *Deuterocohnia*, *Dyckia*, *Hechtia*, *Portea*, and *Puya*, but one of the best known is pineapple (*Ananas comosus*). In regions where temperatures never fall below 45–50°F (7–10°C), many terrestrials can be grown outdoors. *Fascicularia bicolor* may even be grown without protection in

BROMELIADS SUITABLE FOR GROWING INDOORS

Tillandsia stricta

Tillandsia caput-medusae

Neoregelia carolinae 'Tricolor'

Bromelia balansae

Ananas bracteatus 'Tricolor'

Aechmea fasciata

Cryptanthus bivittatus

Guzmania lingulata

Guzmania lingulata var. minor

Vriesea splendens

temperatures as low as 32°F (0°C). Terrestrial bromeliads often have stiff, spiny leaves and a spreading habit. While they may be grown in pots as houseplants, they perform much better if given more space in a greenhouse or conservatory border or, where conditions permit, outdoors. With their eye-catching foliage and strong outlines, they make a distinctive addition to the garden, particularly if combined in designs either with cacti and other succulents or with subtropical plants.

Bright filtered light is preferred by epiphytic bromeliads during the summer, while bright light with several hours of direct sunlight will keep leaf color high and encourage flowering in winter and spring. Terrestrials prefer bright light throughout the year. Low levels of light and short day-lengths will usually induce a period of rest.

Routine care

Because most bromeliads originate from tropical rainforests, they need warm, humid conditions in order to thrive; most need a minimum temperature of 50°F (10°C). In the right conditions they require very little maintenance but indoors, special attention is needed to maintain the necessary humidity.

Watering

Epiphytes draw moisture from the air, so they should be mist-sprayed once a day rather than watered conventionally; use soft water or rainwater when possible, particularly for genera that do not tolerate alkalinity, such as *Aechmea*, *Neoregelia*, *Nidularium*, *Tillandsia*, and *Vriesea*. In spring and summer, add diluted quarter-strength liquid orchid fertilizer to the spray every 4–5 weeks to keep the plants healthy and vigorous (see ORCHIDS, "Feeding," p.370). Provided they have adequate humidity, plants grown in cool temperatures can be encouraged to take a winter rest by reducing the frequency of watering.

Where plants are growing with sphagnum moss around their roots, the moss must be kept constantly moist by regularly spraying it with tepid water and also mist-spraying the foliage occasionally.

Bromeliads whose rosettes form a natural well or "urn" in the center should be kept filled with water, particularly in hot, dry conditions. Change the water and apply diluted foliar feed to the leaves occasionally. Stop watering the "urn" as soon as

DIVIDING ROOTSTOCKS

Gently tease or cut the offset away from the parent plant (here, *Billbergia nutans*) so that the root system remains undamaged.

a developing flower spike becomes obvious; this prevents detritus in the "urn" from causing blemishes on the developing flower head.

Propagation

Bromeliads may be propagated by vegetative methods or by seed. Most epiphytic plants produce offsets that may be removed and grown on separately, while stoloniferous terrestrial kinds may be divided at the start of the growing season.

Offsets of epiphytes

Many epiphytic bromeliads are monocarpic, meaning that the rosettes flower only once and then die. Before they flower, however, they form offsets around the base of the mature rosette. The offsets should be left in place until they are about one-third the size of the parent plant. (If they are removed

earlier than this, the offsets will take longer to become established on their own.) In many cases, the offsets may be removed by hand, but some will have to be cut off with a sharp knife, as close to the parent plant as possible. If the offsets have already developed any roots, these should be carefully retained. Replant the parent plant, so that it can produce more offsets.

Once removed, the offsets should be transferred immediately into prepared pots of free-draining potting mix, comprising equal parts peat, well-rotted leaf mold, and sharp, gritty sand, with their bases just held firm in the soil (see "Epiphytes as potted plants," opposite). Keep the young plants slightly shaded at about 70°F (21°C), and lightly mist-spray them with tepid water daily.

Offsets of the nonmonocarpic species may be detached from the parent plant and then attached to mounts in the same way as for adult plants. The offsets may have no roots, but these will soon develop if the plants are regularly mist-sprayed and if a few strands of moist sphagnum moss are attached at the base of the rosettes in order to retain moisture.

Offsets of terrestrials

Some terrestrial bromeliads, including some *Ananas* and *Hechtia*, have stoloniferous root stocks that also produce offsets. At the start of the growing season, lift the parent plant from the ground, or remove it from its container, so that the offsets may be cut off without injuring the parent plant. Very often the offsets will have some roots growing from them, and as many of these should be retained as possible. Replant the

parent and pot the young offsets in a potting mix of 1 part shredded peat, 1 part leaf mold, and 3 parts coarse sand.

Raising plants from seed

Most bromeliad seeds are sown like other seeds, although it is important to sow them when they are fresh because, with a few exceptions, they do not remain viable for long.

A less conventional method is used for *Tillandsia* seeds, which are generally "winged" for easy dispersal—much like dandelion seeds. Sow the seeds on bundles of conifer twigs, such as *Thuja*, that are packed with well-moistened sphagnum moss and then bound together. Hang the bundles in a slightly shaded position, mist-spray them regularly, and ensure that there is free air circulation but no drafts. If kept at a temperature of about 81°F (27°C), seeds will germinate in around 3–4 weeks. Young plants may then be transferred to branches or other types of support and grown on.

PROPAGATING TILLANDSIA BY SEED

1 Make a bundle of conifer twigs interspersed with moist sphagnum moss, binding it with string, raffia, or wire. Sprinkle seed evenly over the prepared bundle; it will adhere readily to the moss.

2 Water the seeds with a light mist-spray and then hang up the bundle in position (see inset). Continue to mist-spray regularly.

PROPAGATING BY DIVISION OF OFFSETS

1 When the offsets are about one-third of the size of the parent plant (here, *Aechmea*), sever them at the base with a knife. Retain any roots that they may have.

2 Pot each offset into a mix of equal parts shredded peat or peat substitute, decomposed leaf mold, and sharp, gritty sand, inserting it so that the base stays on the surface.

Soil preparation and planting

Strong, healthy plants suitable for an indoor environment are vital for success. Potted plants grow in a limited amount of soil, so it is important to use appropriate potting mixes and to maintain nutrient levels in the potting mix with correct feeding.

Choosing plants

Most indoor plants are container-grown. If possible, check their date of delivery at the point of sale and buy those that have recently arrived. Each plant should be labeled with its full name and cultivation details.

Look for sturdy plants with strong stems, healthy foliage, and vigorous growing points; reject any that have weak growth, dieback, or discolored, wilting, or brown-edged leaves. Choose younger plants, which should adapt more easily than larger specimens to new conditions. Do not buy potbound plants or those with dry, weedy, or moss-covered potting mix—they have been starved of nutrients and seldom recover fully. Make sure that the growing tips and leaves are free of pests and diseases.

Flowering plants should have plenty of buds that are just starting to color. Climbing plants should

be correctly pruned and trained. Do not buy tropical plants in winter, because sudden fluctuations in temperature may have damaged them. If transporting plants in cold weather, wrap them in plastic and newspaper for insulation.

Positioning a plant

Place each plant in a room that provides the levels of temperature, humidity, and light that it requires. Flowering houseplants that are of subtropical or tropical origin flower poorly or not at all if kept too cool or in poor light, while many foliage plants tolerate cool and shady areas. Cacti and other dry-atmosphere plants need light, airy, and dry conditions; plants such as *Begonia rex* require more humidity. If conditions in your home are not ideal for a particular plant, a different cultivar of the same genus may be more suitable.

Potting mixtures

Always use good-quality, prepared potting mixes for indoor plants. Soil-based mixes are generally most suitable, because they contain and retain more nutrients, dry out less

quickly, and are easier to rewet than peat-based mixes. They are also heavier, providing stability for big pot plants.

Potting mixes based on peat or peat substitute are often used for short-lived plants, for example, *Primula malacoides*. They have little inherent fertility compared with soil-based mixes, and plants grown in them require careful, regular feeding. These mixes tend to lose their structure in time, causing poor aeration and watering difficulties.

Lime-haters, such as camellias need special acidic potting mixes. Other groups of plants such as orchids (see pp.368–371) need special potting mixes. For more information, see "Potting mixes for containers," pp.322–323.

Grouping plants

For ease of management, group together plants with similar needs for water, humidity, temperature,

SELECTING A HOUSE PLANT

Good example

Vigorous, healthy topgrowth

Strong stems

Leaves of good color

Moist, weed-free potting mix

Solenostemon (Coleus)

Poor example

Spindly, unbalanced topgrowth

Pallid leaves

Dry or weed-infested potting mix

PLANT SUPPORTS

Various supports are available for houseplants. Choose one that is suitable for the growth habit of the plant, taking into account its speed of growth and eventual size.

Plants with aerial roots grow well up a moss pillar; tie in the shoots until the roots penetrate it; keep the pillar damp by misting. Trailing or climbing plants with several stems may be trained onto wire hoops. Use a single hoop or several, depending on the plant's vigor. A balloon shape of up to eight wires is attractive, allowing good air circulation and access to light for plants with many stems.

Many climbers support themselves by means of twining stems, leaf stalks, or tendrils, and grow readily up bamboo tripods; they may need to be tied in at first. Single-stemmed plants require only a bamboo stake for support; insert the stake before planting to keep from damaging the roots. For details of support aids, see TOOLS AND EQUIPMENT, "Ties and supports," p.564.

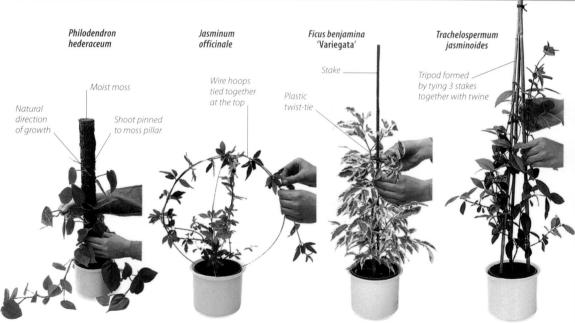

Philodendron hederaceum

Moist moss

Natural direction of growth

Shoot pinned to moss pillar

Jasminum officinale

Wire hoops tied together at the top

Ficus benjamina 'Variegata'

Stake

Plastic twist-tie

Trachelospermum jasminoides

Tripod formed by tying 3 stakes together with twine

Moss pillar
Twine stems with aerial roots around a pillar, tying them in so that they are in contact with the moss.

Wire hoop
Train trailing plants around wire hoops inserted into the potting mix. Tie them in regularly as they grow, adding extra hoops if necessary.

Stake
Insert a stake into the potting mix before planting. Tie in the stem of the young plant.

Bamboo tripod
Encourage stems or tendrils of climbing plants to twine around the stakes by tying them in.

and light. If planting into the same container, ensure that the potting mix is suitable for all the plants. In permanent arrangements, use plants with similar growth rates, otherwise vigorous specimens may swamp their more delicate neighbors.

To increase the humidity level in a dry, centrally heated building, group individually potted plants on wet gravel in shallow bowls or trays. Alternatively, place plants on upturned pots in a tray of water, with their roots above water level.

Plunging pot plants

Plants arranged in large containers may be plunged in their individual pots in water-retentive material, such as clay pellets, to reduce water loss and improve the local humidity. Clay can absorb up to 40 percent of its own weight in water, so use a watertight outer container. Any plant that is past its best or too big may then be easily removed. Alternatively, divide (see "Propagation by division," p.378) and replant it.

Coconut fiber, bark, and peat are used as plunge materials, but plants may root into the medium, making them difficult to remove. Overwatering peat may result in waterlogging, which can rot the roots. Moisture indicators are useful in gauging when the plants need water.

GROUPING PLANTS

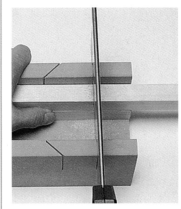

Dracaena fragrans
Demerensis Group
'Lemon and Lime'

Calathea
zebrina

Calathea
louisae

Calathea
picturata

This arrangement of complementary foliage plants is easy to manage, because they require similar levels of light, temperature, and water. The grouped plants work together to create the slightly higher humidity calatheas prefer.

Planting a hanging basket or box

Conventional wire baskets, with a 2in (5cm) mesh, make versatile hanging containers for a balcony, sunroom, or greenhouse (see CONTAINER GARDENING, "Hanging containers," p.312). A traditional, slatted, wooden orchid box is an attractive alternative; this can be purchased or easily built (see right). Where dripping water would cause damage, use solid or plastic-lined baskets or boxes, with integral drip trays or an outer container that has no drainage holes. Water these with care to prevent waterlogging.

While planting a hanging container, place it on a bucket or large pot to keep it stable and clear of the ground. Line an open-sided container with green florist's foam or plastic sheeting, to reduce moisture loss. Alternatively, use sphagnum moss; a plant saucer placed between the moss and the potting mix forms a small reservoir of moisture. All-purpose potting mixes based on soil or peat are suitable, although soil-based potting mixes are easier to rewet.

Plant the container in stages from the base. If necessary, cut the plastic to insert plants through the sides of the hanging basket or box.

HOW TO MAKE A SLATTED WOODEN BOX

1 Measure and mark ³/₄ x ³/₄in (20 x 20mm) lumber into 14 side pieces, each 10in (25cm) long. To ensure a straight edge, use a panel saw and miter box to cut the lengths. Place one of the side pieces over an offcut of wood and secure to the workbench.

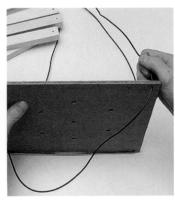

2 Mark drilling holes on one face of the side piece, centered on the width and ⁵/₈in (1.5cm) in from each end. Drill the holes using a ¹/₈in (3mm) wood bit. Mark and drill similarly placed holes on the other side pieces, always drilling with the offcut underneath.

3 Cut out a 10in (25cm) square of plywood board. Mark and drill holes ⁵/₈in (1.5cm) in from each side at the corners of the square, using the ¹/₈in (3mm) wood bit. Mark and drill 7–9 evenly spaced holes for drainage, using a ³/₈in (8mm) wood bit.

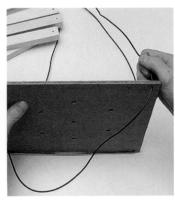

4 Use pliers to cut 2 pieces of strong, plastic-coated wire, at least 12in (30cm) long. Working from the same side, thread each piece of wire through 2 corner holes in the plywood board, then pull flush with the board.

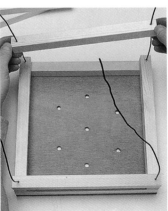

5 Make sure that there are 4 equal pieces of wire above the board, then build up the sides of the box. After threading the final side piece, twist each wire end around a pencil to make a secure loop. Cut off excess wire. Finish with a nontoxic paint.

Creeping fig
(Ficus pumila
'Variegata')

Blechnum
chilense

RECOMMENDED PLANTS FOR TERRARIUMS

Acorus gramineus var. *pusillus*
Adiantum raddianum
Asparagus densiflorus 'Sprengeri'
Asplenium nidus
Begonia 'Tiger Paws'
Callisia
Ctenanthe amabilis
Chamaedorea elegans
Cissus discolor
Codiaeum
   Cryptanthus acaulis
   C. bivittatus
   C. bromelioides
   C. zonatus
Dracaena sanderiana
Elatostema repens
Episcia
Ficus pumila
Fittonia albivenis
  Verschaffeltii Group
Hedera (miniatures)
Hypoestes phyllostachya
Nertera granadensis
Pellaea rotundifolia
Peperomia caperata

Pilea cadierei
Plectranthus oertendahlii
Pteris cretica
Saintpaulia (miniatures)
Sansevieria trifasciata 'Hahnii'
Schefflera elegantissima
  (seedlings)
Selaginella
Soleirolia soleirolii
Strobilanthes dyeriana
Syngonium hoffmannii
Tradescantia cerinthoides
  T. fluminensis
  T. spathacea

Fittonia albivenis
Verschaffeltii Group

Planted hanging baskets and boxes are heavy, so ensure that supporting chains and fixings are sound. A universal hook fixture allows the container to be rotated to receive an even amount of light.

Planting in a terrarium

Before planting, clean the terrarium thoroughly to avoid contamination with algae and fungal diseases, which thrive in enclosed and humid environments. Choose a mixture of tall, upright plants and smaller, creeping ones and decide how to arrange them before starting to plant.

A terrarium is self-contained, so it must have a layer of drainage material, such as clay pellets, gravel, or pebbles, as well as some horticultural charcoal, which absorbs gaseous by-products and helps keep the potting mix fresh. A lightweight, free-draining, but moisture-retentive potting mix is

the most suitable planting medium. Extra peat or perlite may be added to keep the soil well aerated.

Use young plants with root systems that are sufficiently small to establish easily in shallow potting mix. Soak them thoroughly before planting, and remove dead foliage. Insert the plants into the potting mix, allowing space for them to spread. If the terrarium is too small to accommodate a hand easily, attach a split stake to a widger to assist planting, and a cork or thread spool to another stake to make a firming implement. Cover bare areas with moss or pebbles to stop the potting mix from drying out, and water lightly before replacing the lid.

Once established, terrariums require very little or even no watering (see "Terrariums and bottle gardens," p.374). If excess condensation appears on the glass, ventilate it a little until only a slight misting of the glass is discernible in the morning.

PLANTING A TERRARIUM

1 Plan the arrangement with taller plants either at the back (as here) or in the center, depending on whether the terrarium will be viewed from the front only or from all sides. The plants used here are:

Asparagus densiflorus 'Sprengeri'

Ctenanthe amabilis

Ficus pumila 'Variegata'

Selaginella martensii

Soleirolia soleirolii

Selaginella kraussiana 'Aurea'

2 Cover the terrarium base with a 1–2in (2.5–5cm) deep layer of pebbles and a few pieces of horticultural charcoal. Add 1in (2.5cm) of moist potting mix.

3 Remove each plant from its pot and shake off any loose potting mix. Gently tease out the roots, reducing the size of the root ball, to help the plant establish.

4 Use a widger or other small implement to make hollows for the plants and insert them carefully, allowing space between them for further growth.

5 Fill in around the plants with more moist potting mix and firm the surface. A cork attached to the end of a split stake provides a tamper of suitable size.

6 Using tweezers, place a layer of moss (or pebbles) over any bare areas of potting mix between the plants. This will prevent the potting mix from drying out.

7 Spray the plants and the moss lightly with a fine mist of water and replace the lid. The terrarium is now ready for display.

GROWING PLANTS IN A SOIL BENCH

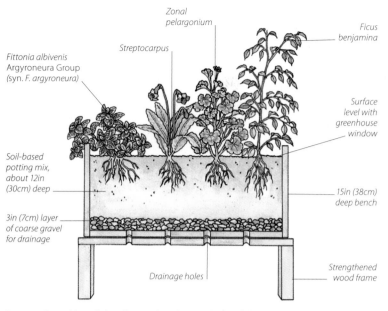

Zonal pelargonium

Streptocarpus

Ficus benjamina

Fittonia albivenis Argyroneura Group (syn. *F. argyroneura*)

Surface level with greenhouse window

Soil-based potting mix, about 12in (30cm) deep

15in (38cm) deep bench

3in (7cm) layer of coarse gravel for drainage

Drainage holes

Strengthened wood frame

Prepare the soil bench for planting by placing a layer of drainage material in the bottom and then filling the bench with soil-based potting mix. Plant a selection of ornamentals for a fine display in the greenhouse.

Soil preparation and planting under cover

Conservatories and greenhouses allow control of the environment, and extend the range of plants that can be grown in temperate or cool climates.

Soil beds and bed benches

Although conservatory and greenhouse ornamentals may be grown in pots, a large number, particularly climbers and woody shrubs, may be planted permanently in raised soil beds. For a new conservatory, consider at the planning stage if raised soil beds are needed. Raised and well-drained soil beds provide a good method of display. Prepare soil beds well, because ornamentals will be in place for some years. Make the beds about four weeks before planting to allow the soil to settle, and at least 12–18in (30–45cm) deep, with 3–6in (7–15cm) of drainage material at the base.

A bench bed is useful for propagating and raising different plants, and for specialized plant collections. Bench beds are shallow raised beds, usually at waist height, on supporting frames or pillars. They are ideal for small plants and for use with soil-warming cables (see p.580), mist units (see p.580), and automated watering systems (see p.577). Site the bench to make maximum use of available light.

Bench beds are usually built from aluminum or wood, lined with wire mesh or perforated plastic. They should be at least 6–9in (15–22cm) deep and no more than 3ft (1m) wide for easy access. A 3in (7cm) layer of drainage material is sufficient.

Potting mix under cover

For soil beds, use a well-drained, soil-based potting mix enriched with organic matter at a rate of 2¼ gallons/10 sq ft (10 liters/sq m). Do not use unsterilized garden soil, because it can harbor pests, diseases, and weeds. No safe chemical soil sterilization methods are readily available for domestic use, and heat-sterilizing units, although effective, are expensive.

In general, use soil-based potting mixes under cover. They contain their own nutrients and trace elements that do not leach out as readily as in less rich peat-based potting mixes; soil-based mixes are also easier to rewet.

It is important to select the appropriate potting mix for specific purposes and for groups of plants with special needs. Most container-grown plants require a good-quality, soil-based potting mix that is free-draining and of pproximately neutral pH. Tropical plants prefer more humus-rich, leafy soils, so incorporate additional leaf mold in the potting mix before filling containers or soil beds. Most ferns, heathers, and many lilies (*Lilium*) need an acidic potting mix, as do hydrangeas, in order to produce blue flowers rather than pink ones.

Ornamental plants grown in raised beds need a dressing every year of 2–3oz/sq yd (50–85g/sq m) of a balanced fertilizer with a mulch

PLANTING A BOTTLE GARDEN

Bottle gardens provide an attractive way of growing very small, slow-growing plants in an enclosed microclimate. Many of the smaller plants grown in terrariums are suitable (see *Recommended Plants for Terrariums*, opposite).

Use any clean, plain, or slightly colored, glass bottle, as long as the neck is wide enough to allow plants to be inserted easily. If the neck is too narrow for a hand, make special tools, from split stakes, loops of wire, and common household utensils such as a dessert fork and teaspoon, to help with planting and routine care.

Using a funnel or cardboard tube, pour clay pellets into the bottle to make a 1¼in (3cm) layer of drainage material, and add a handful of horticultural charcoal to keep the potting mix sweet. Cover it with a 2–3in (5–7cm) layer of dampened, peat substitute-based potting mix. If the bottle

is to be viewed from the front, use a widger to bank up the potting mix at the back. Level the mix if the bottle is to be viewed from all sides.

Begin planting at the sides of the bottle and work in toward the center. Remove the plants from their pots, and shake off any excess potting mix. Carefully lower each plant into a planting hole, using tweezers, tongs, or a length of wire twisted into a noose. Space the plants at least 1¼in (3cm) apart to allow room for growth. Cover the roots with potting mix, and use a cork tamper to firm it gently.

Trickle a cupful of water down the sides of the bottle interior to dampen the potting mix; cover bare areas with sphagnum moss to keep it moist. Clean the inside of the glass with a sponge fixed to a length of stake or stiff wire. If the bottle garden is not sealed after planting, water occasionally.

Hypoestes phyllostachya 'Purpuriana'

Dracaena sanderiana

Hedera helix 'Eva'

Hypoestes phyllostachya 'Splash'

Asplenium nidus

Saintpaulia cv

Selaginella kraussiana

Sphagnum moss

of well-rotted compost in spring. If the planting needs renewal after several years, remove and dispose of the plants, having propagated them first. Then dig in some well-rotted compost or manure and incorporate a slow-release fertilizer or base dressing prior to replanting.

In beds of ornamental plants, there is seldom such a buildup of pests and diseases that it is necessary to change or sterilize the soil. With crop plants grown in raised beds where pests and diseases may increase rapidly, the soil usually has to be replaced annually or sterilized if a suitable method is available. Crop plants are better cultivated in grow bags or containers, where the potting mix can be disposed of if problems occur. Always ensure that the bases

of containers with drainage holes do not come into contact with the raised bed soil. This avoids cross-contamination by pests and diseases.

Planting

Always select plants that grow well in the range of temperatures provided (see *Planter's guide to indoor plants*, p.361). Make sure that ornamentals or crop plants are planted at spacings that allow free air circulation and so inhibit the spread of pests and diseases. Position the plants to receive optimal light and ventilation for their growing requirements. Make full use of temperature, light intensity, humidity, and air-circulation controls that are provided in a well-built and equipped greenhouse.

Orchids

Included in the orchid family are some 750 genera, nearly 25,000 species, and more than 100,000 hybrids. Their exotic blooms and intriguing habit make them very desirable ornamental plants, mostly for indoor display, although some terrestrial species are hardy.

Terrestrial orchids

As the name suggests, these orchids grow in the ground, in widely varying habitats. Most of those that inhabit temperate to cold regions die down after flowering and exist in a resting state as tubers or similar underground storage organs during the winter. These hardy terrestrials often have flowers that, although individually small, are borne in dense spikes. Many are attractive plants for the rock garden or alpine house (see pp.277–279).

Some terrestrials, such as the slipper orchids (*Paphiopedilum*), come from warmer regions, where they inhabit sheltered sites. These remain evergreen throughout the year, but because they do not tolerate frost, they need to be cultivated in a greenhouse.

Epiphytic orchids

Epiphytic orchids, which form a very large proportion of those grown by enthusiasts, are fundamentally different in their structure and habit of growth. As implied by their name (derived from the Greek *epi*, upon, and *phyton*, plant), they make their homes in the branches of trees.

They are not parasites, since they do not feed off the tree; instead, they derive nourishment from substances dissolved in rainwater and from debris accumulated around their roots. A few orchids, known as litho-phytes, live in a similar manner on rocks. In cool climates, epiphytes need to be grown under cover.

Sympodial and monopodial
Epiphytes have two methods of growth: sympodial and monopodial. Sympodial orchids, such as *Cattleya* and *Odontoglossum* species and hybrids, have creeping rhizomes. Each season new growths arise from growing points on the rhizomes, and these develop into swollen stem structures known botanically as pseudobulbs. Flowers of the different sympodial species vary greatly, and may appear from the top, base, or side of the pseudobulbs.

Monopodial orchids grow in an indeterminate manner. The stem elongates indefinitely, growing taller as new leaves are produced at the apex. Monopodials include many of the most spectacular orchid genera, such as *Phalaenopsis* and *Vanda*. These are native to warmer regions of the world, climbing toward the light through dense, jungle foliage. Most monopodials bear their flowers in branched, often gracefully arching, sprays from axillary points along their stems; aerial roots are also often produced from these points.

Where to grow orchids

Some orchids demand fairly rigorous growing conditions, but many hybrids are bred for ease of cultivation and can be successfully grown in the home. Before choosing which to grow from the vast range of types available, consider the conditions and care that you are able to provide. Many indoor plants need a slightly humid environment away from drafts.

While the hardy terrestrials (notably *Cypripedium*) do well in a rock garden or alpine house, others (usually described as half-hardy) may also be grown in unheated conditions in mild areas. They include the cool-growing genera *Pleione* and *Bletilla*, which need only enough heat to ensure frost-free conditions.

A cool greenhouse, with a minimum night temperature in winter of 50°F (10°C), is suitable for a large number of different orchids, including some *Brassia*, *Coelogyne*, *Cymbidium*, *Dendrobium*, *Laelia*, *Odontoglossum*, *Oncidium*, and *Paphiopedilum* species and hybrids.

An intermediate house, with a minimum winter night temperature of 55–59°F (13–15°C) will greatly extend the range of possibilities, to include species and hybrids of *Cattleya* and its relatives, and a wider selection of the *Odontoglossum* group and of *Paphiopedilum* and *Phragmipedium* species and hybrids.

A warm house, with a minimum night temperature of at least 64°F (18°C), provides the necessary conditions for species and hybrids of *Phalaenopsis* and *Vanda* and their many relatives, as well as the heat-loving species and hybrids of *Dendrobium*, and many orchids from the hot and humid lowlands of the tropics and subtropics.

Choosing plants

If you are a beginner, it is best to obtain plants from a specialty orchid nursery. Nursery staff can also provide valuable advice on suitable species for the conditions you have at home. Hybrid orchids are generally the easiest to grow, having been bred partly for vigor and ease of care. The species thrive best in environments similar to those in which they grow naturally, which are not always easy to recreate.

Thanks to commercial techniques of mass production, many orchids are no longer prohibitively expensive. For a modest price, plants that are attractive but have not yet won a special award from the American Orchid Society or other national societies may be bought when you visit specialty nurseries and see them in flower. Least expensive of all are the unflowered seedlings that may take several years to come into bloom; the result is uncertain, but there is always the exciting possibility that one of the seedlings may be a future award-winner.

Cultivation

The unusual structure and growth habit of epiphytic orchids give them a reputation for being delicate and

---

RECOMMENDED ORCHIDS

Dendrobium nobile

Cymbidium Strath Kanaid gx

Vanda Rothschildiana gx

Paphiopedilum callosum

Guarianthe bowringiana

Miltonia candida

POTTING MATERIALS FOR EPIPHYTIC ORCHIDS

Fibrous peat

Crushed charcoal

Coarse grit

Medium bark

Orchid mix

The different components combine to provide the perfect growing medium: bark and peat retain moisture, grit aids drainage, and charcoal prevents the mix from becoming too acidic.

difficult to grow. With a little knowledge, however, most of the difficulties are easily remedied or avoided.

Potting mix

Although most epiphytes can be grown in pots, their roots are specially adapted to open conditions on trees or rocks (lithophytes), so they cannot endure the close-textured potting mix suitable for most other plants. Orchid mixes must drain quickly after watering; if they remain wet for long, the roots are likely to rot.

Chopped pine or fir bark makes an excellent potting mix, with some additions to keep the mixture loose and prevent it from becoming sour. A suitable mix is as follows: 3 parts medium-grade bark (dust-free), 1 part coarse grit or perlite, 1 part charcoal pieces, and 1 part crumbled dry leaves or shredded coconut fiber (coir) or peat. Specialized mixes can usually be obtained from orchid nurseries.

Terrestrial orchids also require a much more free-draining potting mixture than most plants. A suitable mix can be made of 3 parts coir or peat, 3 parts coarse grit, and 1 part perlite, with the addition of 1 part charcoal.

Potting

When a plant has filled its container, it should be transferred to a new pot a size or two larger to provide space for further growth. Choose a pot that will accommodate the roots and allow for one or two years' growth but no more; a pot that is too large for the root system is likely to lead to stagnant conditions in the growing mix. To fill space, many growers fill the bottom quarter of the pot with pot shards, pieces of plastic foam, or very coarse grit. Shards and grit add extra weight to plastic pots, making them less likely to be knocked over.

Hold the plant with one hand so that the crown is just below the rim of the pot and place the potting mix around the roots, tapping the pot sharply in order to settle it. Use relatively dry mix, which should be thoroughly watered after repotting. The plant, especially the roots, should be disturbed as little as possible.

Some epiphytes do well in containers that allow more air to reach the roots, such as hanging baskets made of wire or wooden slats. Such containers are essential for species of

Stanhopea, because their flowers grow down through the basket to emerge on the underside.

When potting on sympodials, old pseudobulbs of two to three seasons' growth that have lost their leaves (usually called "backbulbs") may be removed and used for propagating (see p.371). Place the rear of the plant against one side of the pot, leaving space for the new growth to develop.

Support

Many flower spikes are sturdy enough not to need support. Others, however, require careful staking to look their best, particularly long flowering stems that carry many heavy blooms. Use upright stakes or sturdy wires, to which the stems may be tied as unobtrusively as possible. Do this as the stems are growing and before the flower buds open. Avoid changing the position of the plants or the effect will be spoiled because the flowers will face in different directions.

Growing on bark

Some orchids that do not grow successfully in containers will thrive if mounted on pieces of either bark or tree fern with moss at their

roots, although they do then require a constantly humid atmosphere. Initially they must be tied to the slab; nylon thread is recommended. New roots will gradually appear, which will adhere to the slab and secure the plant.

Routine care

For successful cultivation, it is vital to provide orchids with their particular care requirements.

Watering and humidity

These are perhaps the most important factors in orchid cultivation. Watering should be frequent enough to avoid drying, but not so frequent that the mix becomes soggy—once or twice a week for most of the year is usually sufficient. Remember that pot type, temperature, and amount of sunlight also affect how quickly mix will dry out. In the summer, plants may need watering every day, while during short winter days they may require water only once every two or three weeks.

Rainwater is usually recommended, but drinkable tap water is safe. Water the plants in the early morning. Do

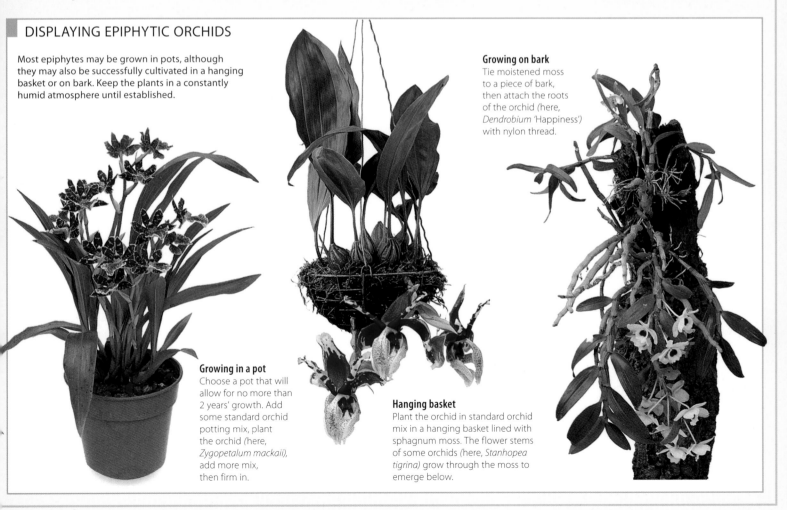

DISPLAYING EPIPHYTIC ORCHIDS

Most epiphytes may be grown in pots, although they may also be successfully cultivated in a hanging basket or on bark. Keep the plants in a constantly humid atmosphere until established.

Growing in a pot
Choose a pot that will allow for no more than 2 years' growth. Add some standard orchid potting mix, plant the orchid (here, *Zygopetalum mackaii*), add more mix, then firm in.

Hanging basket
Plant the orchid in standard orchid mix in a hanging basket lined with sphagnum moss. The flower stems of some orchids (here, *Stanhopea tigrina*) grow through the moss to emerge below.

Growing on bark
Tie moistened moss to a piece of bark, then attach the roots of the orchid (here, *Dendrobium* 'Happiness') with nylon thread.

not let any water remain too long on the foliage, or it may cause leaf spotting.Overwatering must be avoided, but water thoroughly, so that the mix is evenly moist. Allow it to become nearly—but not quite—dry before watering again; if in doubt, delay watering.

During the growing season, orchids need a high level of humidity. This may be achieved by dampening down the orchid house by spraying water over the paths and ground and on the benches between plants. Do this early in the morning; as the day progresses, the water will be drawn up as vapor. This daily spraying may be discontinued when natural conditions are cold and damp. Be careful, however, because in extremely cold weather the heating system may make the air very dry, and the greenhouse may need to be dampened more often.

Orchids grown in the home as windowsill plants must be chosen from those species that do not demand very high humidity. Even these relatively tolerant plants may benefit from additional humidity provided by standing them on a layer of moist gravel or expanded clay aggregate in a tray or deep saucer.

Fertilizing

Modern orchid potting mixes contain little nourishment, so orchids will need feeding during their growing period. Liquid fertilizers are the most convenient and these can be added during watering. Any general-purpose brands sold for houseplants may be used. Orchids are not heavy feeders, so it will be necessary to dilute the fertilizer to half the strength recommended for other house-plants. Feed the orchids

once every three weeks from spring to fall, and only every six weeks (if at all) during the winter.

Ventilation

Most orchids, especially the popular cool-greenhouse kinds, require free-moving air conditions. They dislike cold drafts, however, which can cause flower buds to drop and slow down growth. Vents should be only partially opened in spring, when sunny days may be accompanied by chilly winds, and closed well before the temperature starts to drop in the late afternoon. As days become warm, vents may be opened wider and for a longer time. Remember, however, that water vapor is quickly lost through open vents and humidity is reduced, so that extra dampening down is needed. A small electric fan, inexpensive both to buy and run, will keep the air moving without letting out humidity or letting in drafts.

Shading

Although different orchids may have different light requirements, from the shade-loving *Paphiopedilum* orchids to the sun-loving *Laelia* species and hybrids, some form of shading is needed to protect new growth from being scorched by the sun and to prevent the greenhouse from overheating. The cheapest method is to use a greenhouse shading compound. White is more efficient than green in reflecting back the sun's rays, and it becomes almost transparent in rain, letting in more light on rainy days. More effective, but more expensive, are manual or automatic roller blinds, made either of wood slats or plastic mesh.

Dormancy

An important and integral part of an orchid's life cycle is the dormant

period, when growth is halted. During this time, which in the case of some orchids may last only a few weeks and in others several months, they need very little water, if any, in order to survive.

Although plants' requirements vary, the general rule is that those orchids that lose their leaves while dormant should not be watered until new growth begins. Water sparingly at first, then normally (taking care not to overwater). Plants that keep

their leaves will need to be given only a little water during the dormant period to avoid dehydration.

Propagation

Vegetative propagation methods are the easiest for the amateur to learn. They also have the advantage of producing offspring that are identical to the parent plant, so that the results are predictable.

PROPAGATING BY KEIKIS

1 When a new plantlet with aerial roots has formed from a leaf node, cut it away carefully from the parent plant with a sharp, clean knife.

2 The selected cutting should have healthy leaves and an evenly developed root system.

3 Holding the plantlet by its stem at planting level, pot the young plant in a 3in (7cm) pot with the roots just below the surface.

PROPAGATING BY STEM CUTTINGS

1 Using a sharp knife , cut off a section of stem at least 10in (25cm) long, just above a leaf node or at the base of the plant (here, *Dendrobium*).

2 Divide this into lengths of about 3in (7cm), cutting midway between leaf nodes. Each cutting should have at least 1 node.

3 Lay the cuttings in a tray on a layer of moist sphagnum moss and store in a humid place out of direct sunlight.

4 After several weeks, the dormant buds will have developed into plantlets, which will then be ready for potting.

Keikis

The simplest cuttings, which are known as keikis, are small plantlets that appear adventitiously (that is, atypically) from the nodes on stems of monopodial orchids, such as some *Dendrobium* and reed-type *Epidendrum*, and occasionally *Phalaenopsis*. As soon as these plantlets have

developed a few vigorous roots, they should be severed from the parent plant with a sharp knife, and then potted into a standard orchid mix. Water them sparingly at first, but remember to spray the leaves with a fine mist until the roots have established and the plants have had a chance to become accustomed to their new environment.

Stem cuttings

Cuttings may also be made from the stems (often called canes) of many *Dendrobium* orchids. With a sharp knife, cut off sections up to 12in (30cm) in length. Divide these into cuttings 3–4in (7–10cm) long, each with at least one dormant bud. Lay the cuttings on damp sphagnum moss or a

similar moist material, and keep them in a humid, shaded place. When the buds have produced plantlets, detach these and pot them separately.

Division

The usual method of propagating sympodial orchids such as *Cattleya*, *Cymbidium*, and *Odontoglossum* is by division. Simply cut through the rhizome between pseudobulbs and pot the pieces separately. Each piece should have at least three healthy pseudobulbs and a healthy dormant bud to produce new growth.

Backbulbs offer another way of propagating sympodials such as *Cymbidium*. Remove a backbulb, preferably one with roots, by pulling or cutting the rhizome just beyond it. Insert the backbulb at one side of a pot of grit, sharp sand, or standard orchid mix, with the cut side of the bulb nearest the edge to allow space in the center for new growth. Place in a cool, shady spot, and keep moist. Shoots should appear in two or three months. When the bulbs have developed roots, pot them.

Commercial techniques

Growing orchids from seed is difficult and requires specialized knowledge and skills. Orchids raised commercially from seed are germinated in flasks of nutrient jelly in a controlled laboratory environment. They are sometimes also propagated by meristem culture, a laboratory technique in which microscopic pieces of plant tissue are used to mass-produce replicas of the original plant. As a result, first-class cultivars may be purchased at a reasonable price. Both of these techniques are highly specialized and seldom practiced by amateurs.

PROPAGATING BY DIVISION

1 When the orchid has grown too large for its pot and has several leafless bulbs, it may be divided. The plant shown here is a *Cymbidium*.

2 Remove the orchid from its pot, then divide the plant by separating or cutting it into 2 sections; each section should have at least 3 healthy pseudobulbs.

3 When dividing the orchid, any leafless backbulbs may be pulled away. Discard shriveled ones, and retain those that are firm for potting separately.

4 Trim each section of the divided plant by removing surplus potting mix and cutting off dead roots with pruners.

5 To replant each section, hold the plant with the oldest pseudobulbs at the back of the pot and at planting level, and place the potting mix around it. New growth will develop in front of the plant.

PROPAGATING BY BACKBULBS

1 Plant selected backbulbs singly in 3in (7cm) pots. Insert each bulb with the cut side nearest to the edge of the pot.

2 Within 2 or 3 months the backbulb will produce a healthy new shoot.

PROPAGATING IN FLASKS

Meristem culture takes place under sterile conditions. Microscopic pieces of plant tissue are placed in a flask on a special nutrient medium such as agar jelly; they then develop into young orchid plants.

Routine care

Unlike plants grown outdoors, indoor plants are not subject to the extremes of the seasonal cycle so need relatively little attention. They require only watering and fertilizing, and an annual repotting, to perform at their best.

Watering and humidity

A common problem in the care of indoor plants is overwatering. In general, water when the potting mix is nearly dry. Take special care with coconut fiber mixes, because the surface is inclined to dry out while the rest stays moist.

Water plants frequently while they are in active growth, less in winter when they are dormant—twice a month or even less may be enough. Wet the potting mix thoroughly, but do not leave the pot standing in water. Some plants, such as cyclamen, are susceptible to root rot; to water them, stand the pots in a little water until the potting mix is dark and damp. If tap water is hard, use distilled water or rainwater for lime-hating plants.

Buildings are often poorly ventilated and the atmosphere dry and unsuitable for many indoor plants. Maintain humidity by grouping potted plants on wet gravel in trays or in containers (see "Grouping plants," pp.364–365), or on capillary matting (see *Care of HousePlants Before Going Away*, p.374).

Electric and ceramic humidifiers are readily available; bowls containing water placed in a room so that the water evaporates are also effective. Plants that need high humidity benefit from being mist sprayed with soft water. Use sprays sparingly on plants with hairy leaves, and avoid sunlight—spots of water on the leaves can cause scorch.

Cleanliness

Always remove dead leaves and flowers promptly, because they may harbor diseases or pests. Do not allow dust or grime to build up and block the leaf pores; dust the foliage with a soft brush. Thoroughly spray the plants occasionally to keep them clean and fresh, but do not spray cacti or plants with hairy leaves unless it is warm enough for any excess moisture to evaporate rapidly or the leaves may rot. Only use leaf-shine on glossy-leaved plants and check that it is compatible with individual species.

Fertilizing

Potted plants grow in relatively small volumes of potting mix and soon use up the available nutrients. Frequent watering also leaches out nutrients and the plants could starve without regular feeding throughout the growing season.

Balanced fertilizers are available in various forms: water-soluble or liquid (most convenient for indoor plants), granular, and solid. Always be careful to follow the manufacturers' instructions and never apply fertilizer to dry potting mix because it will not soak through evenly and may damage the roots.

Stopping

The appearance of many potted plants, especially trailing plants, may be improved by pinching off growing tips on young plants to encourage production of more sideshoots. This keeps the foliage bushy and increases the number of flower buds. Only stop plants that are in active growth.

MAINTAINING PLANT HYGIENE

Cleaning smooth-leaved plants
Gently wipe each leaf (here, variegated *Ficus elastica*) with a clean, moist, soft, and lint-free cloth.

Removing dead leaves
Pinch off dead leaves and stems at the base of the plant (here, *Nephrolepis exaltata*) or cut them out.

Neglected plants

With the exception of orchids and palms, most plants that have weak, leggy, or damaged growth produce new, vigorous growth if cut back hard to a healthy bud or joint. This is best done in early spring. Cut back a neglected fern to the crown; keep the root ball moist and in medium light to induce growth.

Plants that root readily are best renewed from cuttings, while some plants are rejuvenated by air layering (see p.383). Revive exhausted plants by repotting or by resting in a shaded greenhouse. To rescue overwatered plants, remove drenched potting mix from the root ball, trim off rotting foliage and roots, and repot in fresh mix. Refresh an underwatered

CARING FOR HOUSE-PLANTS ORGANICALLY

House plants often spend years in pots, so it is important to grow them in a fertile medium, such as one containing equal amounts of soil, manure, and leaf mold, which is both nutrient- and humus-rich.

Plants in the same pot for more than a year will need feeding: liquid fertilizers based on seaweed extracts are ideal; homemade comfrey or nettle feeds are also suitable (see p.332). Topdressing with worm or garden compost is another way to provide nutrients (see pp.627–628).

Regular hygiene is vital for good health: remove dead or damaged foliage, and keep ahead of pests and diseases using biological controls. If possible, water with filtered or "gray" water that is not contaminated with detergents, soap, or grease. Remove dust, grime, and watermarks from glossy-leaved plants like *Ficus elastica* by sponging or spraying the foliage with filtered water. Avoid using leaf-shines that are not organically approved.

RENEWING TOPDRESSING

Hippeastrum

1 Use a widger to remove the top 1–2in (2½–5cm) of the old potting mix, taking care not to damage the plant's roots.

2 Replace it with fresh, moist potting mix including a small amount of fertilizer. Firm in around the crown and water.

PRESERVING HUMIDITY AROUND POTTED PLANTS

Create suitably humid conditions for indoor plants by providing them with their own microclimate. Loosely pack a shallow tray with clay pellets or gravel and fill it with water. Group several potted plants on the tray. Keep the water level high enough that the gravel or pellets remain wet.

Pilea cadierei

African violet (*Saintpaulia*)

Begonia

Streptocarpus

plant by immersing the pot in water until the bubbles stop, and then allowing it to drain well.

Repotting and topdressing

Indoor plants also need periodic repotting to accommodate their growth and to replenish the potting mix. A potbound plant has retarded growth, fails to thrive, and water runs right through its pot. Repot before this stage so that the plant's development is unimpeded. A few plants, such as *Hippeastrum*, enjoy confined roots, so topdress instead of repotting them.

The best time to repot is at the start of the growing season, although fast-growing plants may need repotting several times in one season. This may delay flowering because the plant initially puts its energy into new root growth. Never repot a dormant plant.

Repotting

Ensure that the root ball is completely moist so that it comes easily out of its pot without damaging the roots. Turn the pot upside down and slide the plant out into your hand. If the pot is too big to lift easily, run a knife around the inside; then lay the pot on its side. Support the plant with one hand and rotate the pot, gently tapping the sides with a wooden block to loosen the potting mix fully before removing the plant.

Put fresh potting mix in the new pot until the plant is positioned at the same depth as before, with space allowed for watering. Check that the roots are spread out and the plant centered, fill in with more potting mix, and firm gently. Water, but do not feed the plant for four to six weeks so that it will send out new roots into the potting mix in search of food. Keep the plant out of direct sun for a few days.

Renewing

If a plant is in the largest available container, has grown to its full size, or is very slow-growing, repot it into the same-sized pot to renew the potting mix. Take the plant out of its pot, removing as much of the old potting mix as possible. Prune out damaged or diseased roots before repotting the plant in fresh mix.

Topdressing

With plants that react badly to root disturbance, or enjoy confined roots, do not repot, but at the start of each growing season replace the old, surface potting mix with fresh potting mix of the same type and enrich it with balanced fertilizer.

REPOTTING AN INDOOR PLANT

1 Before repotting a plant (here, *Dracaena fragrans* 'Warneckei'), make sure that its root ball is moist by watering it thoroughly an hour beforehand. Select a pot that is one or two sizes larger than the old one. Make sure the pot is clean (whether washed, disinfected, or new) to keep from spreading diseases. The fresh potting mix should be of the same type as that in the old pot.

2 Remove the plant by inverting the pot and sharply tapping the rim on a hard surface to loosen the root ball. Support the plant as it slides out of the pot.

3 Gently tease out the root ball with a hand fork or fingers. Put some moist potting mix in the base of the new pot.

4 Insert the plant so that its soil mark is level with the rim base. Fill in with potting mix to within ¹/₂in (1.5cm) of the rim, firm, water, and place in position (right).

KEEPING PLANTS FROM YEAR TO YEAR

When all danger of frost is past, flowering plants grown for their winter color should be plunged in outdoor beds in their pots to rest during the warmer months of the year. Choose a cool place, with indirect light, and keep them watered with soft (lime-free) water. At the end of summer, repot or topdress them, then bring them indoors, and feed them regularly once flower buds have appeared. To keep a cyclamen after it has flowered, do not water it until new growth starts, then remove old roots, and repot the plant in soil-based potting mix so that the corm is level with the surface of the soil. Put it in a cool, well-lit place, and water it regularly.

Winter-flowering potted plants
In late spring, transfer the plants, here, azaleas (*Rhododendron*), to a plunge bed in semishade outdoors. Sink each pot up to its rim in weed-free soil or another suitable plunge material, allowing space for the plants to grow. Bring them in before frost threatens, and keep them cool until the buds open.

Cyclamen
Let the leaves die down naturally after flowering. Place the plant on its side, in its pot, under a greenhouse bench or in a cold frame.

REPLANTING A TERRARIUM

Asparagus densiflorus 'Sprengeri'

Ficus pumila 'Variegata'

Hypoestes phyllostachya 'Splash'

Dracaena

Selaginella kraussiana 'Aurea'

Fittonia albivenis Verschaffeltii Group

Selaginella martensii

1 When a terrarium becomes overgrown, carefully remove any plants that have grown too large. Divide them or select new, small plants. Try to leave the surrounding potting mix undisturbed.

2 If needed, trim the remaining plants with scissors. Thin out the surface moss where necessary by removing some with tweezers, keeping adjacent plants firmly in place with a cork and stake tamper.

3 Divide low-growing plants that have outgrown their allotted space. Use a widger to replant the divisions and the new plants (see inset). Firm with a little fresh potting mix, using the tamper.

4 Trickle water down the inside of the glass until the potting mix is just damp. Then replace the lid.

Hanging baskets

Hanging baskets require regular care. Never allow the potting mix in a basket to dry out. Water it well; in very warm weather, this will need to be done both morning and evening. If the plants wilt, soak the basket in a bowl filled with water.

Feed plants in a basket regularly with a balanced liquid fertilizer, and control any pests. Deadhead flowering plants, clip back over-long trailers, and thin messy or tangled growth. Remove and replace dead plants.

Terrariums and bottle gardens

A closed container rarely needs water; but if required, use a long-necked watering can to trickle water against the glass inside to keep from disturbing the potting mix. Use just enough water to clean the glass and moisten the surface. If the glass is continuously obscured by mist, the potting mix is too wet—remove the cover or cork until it clears. To get rid of condensation or algae inside the glass, use a small sponge attached to a length of stake. Keep the container out of direct sunlight and move it occasionally, especially if it is in a shaded place in winter. Remove dead leaves and control pests and diseases.

Trim the plants from time to time so that each has enough light and space. A razor blade inserted into the end of a stake is useful for pruning plants in small-necked bottle gardens. If any plants encroach on others, either replace them with smaller plants or replant the entire container (see above).

Greenhouse plants

These need regular, sometimes daily, attention, even if the greenhouse is equipped with automatic systems. Watering, ventilation, misting, and feeding are especially important in summer, as is heating in winter and proper hygiene at all times. Routine care of potted plants, including feeding and potting (see pp.372–373), is similar to that of indoor plants.

Watering

In the enclosed greenhouse environment, correct watering is crucial. The amount needed varies with the season and the weather. In summer, water more on sunny than on cloudy days. Use a hose in a big greenhouse, with a low water pressure to keep from washing surface potting mix away from the roots. A watering can is best in a small or mixed greenhouse, where plants have differing water needs: some potted plants may need watering several times on a hot day. Stand the can in the greenhouse until the water temperature is the same as that of the plants. Do not overwater, especially in winter, because wet soil leads to rotting.

CARE OF INDOOR PLANTS BEFORE GOING AWAY

When going away, it is possible to ensure that indoor plants do not dry out. To keep water loss to a minimum, move plants into the shade and use one of the following watering methods. To use a capillary mat, group potted plants on an upturned tray, drain board, or shelf. Let the mat trail into another tray, the sink, or bath that is filled with water to supply the plants. Holes in plastic pots allow water through, and clay pots are as good if saturated beforehand. Stand large or single pots on wick waterers, which draw water into the potting mix from a reservoir by means of a wick. Alternatively, water the plant well, allow it to drain, and place it in a sealed, plastic bag to prevent moisture loss. Check for and control any pests or diseases before going away.

Guzmania lingulata

Syngonium podophyllum 'Albolineatum'

Aglaonema

Adiantum capillus-veneris

Capillary matting

Place potted plants on one end of a piece of wet matting. Leave the other end submerged in a water reservoir. The plants must be above the water so that they can draw it up as they need it.

Ficus pumila 'Variegata'

Plastic bag

Hold a clear, plastic bag away from the foliage with thin stakes. Seal with a twist-tie or fold the neck of the bag under the pot.

For full instructions on watering (e.g., by capillary matting, drip feeds, or trickle systems), see p.577. Self-watering pots are also useful; an outer pot holds water that is borne by capillary action along a wick to the potting mix in an inner pot.

Humidity

Plants need moist, but not stagnant, air. In hot, sunny weather, damp down by splashing the floor, particularly hard surfaces, with water each morning and evening, or more often in very hot weather. This keeps the greenhouse humid and temporarily cools the air. Soil floors hold more moisture, while tiled or concrete floors dry more quickly. If the air is too humid, water vapor cannot transpire from the leaves to keep them cool, and they may overheat and wilt, so ventilate the greenhouse to dry out the air. In very hot climates or for plants with particular needs, automated damping-down systems and special humidifiers may be necessary (see GREENHOUSES AND FRAMES, "Humidity," p.576).

Dank, cold air encourages fungal diseases to attack plants. In winter, keep the air dry by ventilating when weather permits or install a fan or a dehumidifier.

Temperature regulation

Use ventilation to control greenhouse temperatures and avoid fluctuations that can harm plants. Too much ventilation slows growth, and too little leads to high temperatures. On windy days, ventilate the greenhouse on the leeward side to avoid harmful drafts. For more information, see GREENHOUSES AND FRAMES, "Ventilation" (p.575) and "Shading" (p.576).

Hygiene

Keep the greenhouse clear of debris that may harbor pests, and remove dead leaves and flowers before they rot. Wash or renew the aggregates on benches if they are infested with tiny snails or clogged with soil. Each fall, take the plants outside and clean the greenhouse. Choose a still, warm day when the change in their environment is least likely to affect the plants. A thorough scrub down is preferable, otherwise give the greenhouse a good sweeping and hosing down (see GREENHOUSES AND FRAMES, "Routine maintenance," p.583).

Cold protection

In unheated greenhouses, stop plant roots from freezing in cold weather by keeping them nearly dry. Cover plants with a layer of plastic sheeting,

HYDROCULTURE

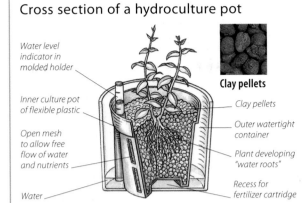

Cross section of a hydroculture pot

Water level indicator in molded holder

Inner culture pot of flexible plastic

Open mesh to allow free flow of water and nutrients

Water

Clay pellets

Clay pellets

Outer watertight container

Plant developing "water roots"

Recess for fertilizer cartridge

A tabletop display

Chamaedorea elegans

Euphorbia milii

Syngonium podophyllum

Aucuba japonica 'Variegata'

Pilea 'Norfolk'

This system has developed from hydroponics, a method of growing plants in water with added nutrients. In hydroculture, water roots, which differ from roots growing in soil, are supported by inert growing media, with water and nutrients added as required. Plant roots need oxygen to thrive and this method allows more air to the roots than potting mixes.

Hydroculture has advantages: it is easy to provide precise amounts of water and nutrients; the growing medium is clean, well drained, not too acidic, odorless, and free from clogging, discouraging diseases, pests, and weeds; growth is often faster and stronger than in soil. Bulbs, cacti, bonsai, orchids, and many popular indoor plants flourish under hydroculture.

The porous clay pellets used as the growing medium absorb more than their own weight in water and nutrients; these are taken up by the plant as required, which means less frequent watering. The terra-cotta pellets do not shrink or compact, and are clean, easy to use, and attractive. Water indicators change color when the root ball is dry, and nutrients are added at every watering, so plants are kept well nourished. Different types of liquid fertilizer have been formulated for foliage and flowering plants.Other methods of hydroculture need a two-part

container—an aggregate one and a watertight one—but the clay medium is suitable for any pot.

Setting up the system

Choose a watertight container twice the size of the current pot. Measure how much water it holds: waterings need a quarter of that volume to prevent waterlogging. Fill a third of the pot with pellets. If the plant was previously in potting mix, gently wash soil or debris off the roots. Place the root ball on the pellets and infill with more. Push the tip of the watering indicator into the center of the root ball, so the gauge window is visible. Pour a measured amount of water (a quarter of the pot capacity) containing a liquid fertilizer over the pellets. The gauge window will turn from red (dry) to blue (wet). Set the plant in a well-lit location.

Routine maintenance

Wait until the gauge turns red before watering with the same volume of water and liquid fertilizer, and replace water indicator yearly.

Houseplants need watering and fertilizing all year. Plants in active growth use more water than those resting (semidormant) so the red-window signal appears more often.

In active growth, feed succulents, cacti, and orchids at half strength. During winter dormancy, keep cacti and succulents in a brightly lit place; do not fertilize succulents,

but water at half the normal volume. Cacti should be drier—water sparingly but do not add fertilizer. Give orchids a quarter-strength feed every four to six weeks if growth or flower spikes appear in a rest period. Repot plants into larger containers if needed. Clay pellets can be washed, dried, and reused.

Propagation from cuttings

With good aeration, cuttings root quickly in moist pellets. Prepare as normal (see p.380), and insert cuttings to a third of their length in a watertight pot filled with pellets. Treat as for rooted plants, but fertilize at half the usual rate. Use free-draining pots in greenhouses, but increase humidity by covering with a plastic bottle or bag to prevent water loss. Keep cuttings in bright, indirect light until rooted. Remove covers when new growth appears. Repot plants and start normal watering and feeding.

Seeds will germinate and grow on in clay pellets in watertight or free-draining pots. After sowing, add a quarter water and half-strength fertilizer, then cover with plastic film or a bag. Place in shade until new growth appears; take off the cover and move the pot into indirect light. If the pot is watertight, start normal watering and fertilizer, but let pellets in free-draining pots dry out between applications.

or newspaper, and beds with mulch or straw. Surround the base of shrubs and climbers with insulating material, secured with netting or twine. Plunge small pots in sand.

Pests and diseases

Regularly check buds, growing points, and the backs of leaves, and take early remedial action. Destroy

badly infested plants, and isolate less affected specimens until they are clear of trouble. Isolate newly purchased plants for two weeks and control pests and diseases before placing them with other plants. Particular problems may be caused by black vine weevil grubs (p.655) and spider mite (p.670), especially in dry, centrally heated air in winter.

In warm, moist, greenhouse conditions, pests and diseases,

such as gray mold/Botrytis (p.661) and powdery mildew (p.667), aphids (p.654) and hence viruses (p.672), and whiteflies (p.673), can spread rapidly. During the annual cleanup, (see "Routine maintenance," p.583) remove plants likely to be harmed by chemicals; fumigate the greenhouse and control any pests or diseases before replacing the plants. See also PLANT PROBLEMS (pp.639–673).

Training and pruning plants grown under cover

The basic principles of training and pruning under cover are much the same as for outdoors, although it may be necessary to adapt these to accommodate extended flowering periods and limited space. Climbing plants that are too tender to be grown outdoors may be readily cultivated under cover. If properly trained and pruned, they make efficient use of confined space and provide shade for other plants.

Plant supports

Plants that need support when grown under cover include ornamental climbers, some shrubs, annuals, fruiting vegetables, fruit trees, and vines (*Vitis*). True climbers find their own way up supports (see "Climbing methods and supports," p.124), while shrubs grown as climbers against a wall need tying in.

Some climbers need a permanent rigid support securely attached to the framework of a wooden greenhouse or to the bars of a metal-framed one. Wires, stretched horizontally along the walls of the greenhouse, are useful for training all climbers. In lean-to greenhouses,

stretch the wires between eye hooks attached to the rear wall to avoid blocking out light. Alternatively, attach the wire to drilled and bolted, vertical wall battens. Keep the wires taut by using a straining bolt at the end of each wire. Space the wires at equal intervals: vines require 10in (25cm) spacing; fruit trees 15–18in (38–45cm). Tie in the stems of climbers with soft string to horizontal or vertical support wires.

Netting may be attached to the framework of the greenhouse and used to support plants. Plastic netting breaks down and needs replacing after one or two seasons, so it is not suitable for perennials. Instead, use plastic-coated wire net.

There are also some useful wire-mesh frameworks and various forms of wooden trellises available: attach them securely to battens attached to the greenhouse wall. Train the plants gently along netting or mesh as they grow, and tie them in with soft string.

Annual ornamental climbers, or fruiting vegetables, such as tomatoes, may be tied with soft string to bamboo stakes placed vertically at 6–12in (15–30cm) intervals. Alternatively, drop lengths of strong string from secure anchors in the roof to the base of the plants. Tie the string loosely below the plant's first true leaf, then wind it around the stems and run it back to the frame. Never let the string become too tight around the stem of the plant. For details of the treatment you should give to particular plants, see the pruning and training sections in the relevant chapters.

Pruning plants grown indoors

Like plants that are grown outdoors, many indoor plants require regular pruning to maintain their vigor and encourage flowering. Others simply become too big for the available space, or need cutting back to maintain an attractive and balanced framework. With pruning, cutting back, or pinching off, most plants can be trained and shaped. Drastic pruning is required only to remove old, weakened sections or to renovate a neglected plant.

Pinching off

To improve the shape and increase the number of flowering shoots that are produced on young, scandent,

or trained shrubs, pinch off the tips of new shoots during the growing season. Shrubs that respond well include fuchsias, *Abutilon*, *Brunfelsia*, *Centradenia*, *Hibiscus*, *Reinwardtia*, and *Tibouchina*. Repeated pinch pruning (see opposite) can also be used to form certain plants into novel shapes for display.

When and what to prune

The best time for pruning depends on the flowering season of the plant and on the age of wood on which plants bloom. Some plants flower only on the new season's growth, and on these the old growth may be safely cut back in the spring without harming production of the next season's flowers. Others flower on older wood and should be cut back only after flowering. See pruning guides for shrubs (pp.100–107), climbers (pp.134–137), and on pruning to produce fruit on vines (pp.461–466) and tree fruits (pp.435–460).

Pruning to restrict growth

Under cover, space for shrubs and climbers is always limited. Although major problems may be avoided by choosing the most suitable plant for the size of the greenhouse, it may be necessary to restrict growth to

stop plants from blocking the light. Climbers growing in the ground have a freer root run and must be rigorously controlled when they have filled their allotted space, or they may overwhelm other plants.

Few shrubs and ornamental climbers grown under cover flower on old wood (but check first), so pruning back fairly hard after flowering is generally advisable and safe. Cut back overly long stems in fall; remove unwanted shoots whenever they appear.

Some plants flower for much of the year under cover, yet must be pruned to control them. In early spring, cut out the previous season's growth on mature *Abutilon* hybrids, and cut back *Coronilla* and *Hibiscus*. The flowers of *Hoya* are produced on short, woody spurs on both new and old growth; retain as many of these spurs as possible. Each can produce flowers over several years. *Agapetes* also flowers on old wood, but may need cutting back to induce bushiness.

The stems of some plants— particularly figs, like the rubber plant (*Ficus elastica*), and euphorbias, such as poinsettia (*Euphorbia pulcherrima*)—bleed sap profusely when cut. The flow can be staunched by wetting the wound.

ESTABLISHING THE SUPPORT FRAMEWORK

Stretch wires tightly between eye hooks (see inset). Tie in the stronger shoots and prune them to downward-growing buds to encourage horizontal growth.

CLIMBING PLANTS TO GROW UNDER COVER

Prune after flowering

Allamanda cathartica 'Hendersonii' ◉
Bougainvillea
Clerodendrum thomsoniae ◉
Distictis buccinatoria
Jasminum, some
Kennedia rubicunda
Mandevilla splendens ◉
Pandorea jasminoides
Passiflora, most
Senecio, some
Solanum wendlandii ◉
Stephanotis floribunda ◉
Thunbergia

Prune as required

Agapetes macrantha
Cissus
Cobaea scandens
Gynura aurantiaca ◉
Hoya
Ipomoea horsfalliae
Lophospermum erubescens

Key

◉ Requires high humidity

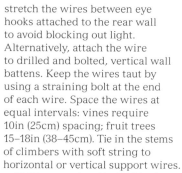

Mandevilla splendens

CUTTING BACK AFTER FLOWERING

Cut back the flowered shoots to leave two or three buds. This encourages the production of next season's flowering shoots, which should be tied horizontally onto the wires.

FALL PRUNING TO RESTRICT GROWTH

In the fall, cut out the weaker shoots and reduce dense growth; this allows plenty of light to penetrate the foliage and encourages the development of strong shoots to form a sturdy framework.

Pinch pruning

Also known as finger-and-thumb pruning, the technique of repeated pinch pruning as a plant develops can be used to produce decorative shapes in a range of tender subshrubby plants, such as coleus (*Solenostemon*), fuchsias, *Helichrysum*, and tender geraniums. Simple shapes such as fans and cones are well within the grasp of a novice gardener, and with experience, all manner of forms are possible—favorites being a ball, pillar, and pinch-pruned standard. Pinching, though in itself a simple technique, must be repeated at frequent, regular intervals during the growing season. No tools are generally required.

Finished coleus fan

Shaping the plant

Plants must be healthy in order to respond well to this technique. Site plants growing under cover in a well-lit, well-ventilated location. Always pinch-prune young plants right from the start, encouraging them to form bushy mounds before beginning to form a more specific shape.

With finger and thumb, pinch out the tip of the shoot just above an opened leaf. Remove only the very tip to stimulate the maximum number of buds into producing sideshoots. Side buds will then break and develop into shoots. When these have developed two to four leaves (or two pairs), repeat the process.

Repot young plants regularly while they are maturing. For some shapes, such as a fan, two or more specimens should be planted in the same pot. Do not pinch-prune a week or so before or after potting to enable root systems to reestablish well. After that, start pinching the growing tips off of young plants regularly once again, to encourage dense growth and a compact form.

Training frames and supports

Once plants are in their final pot, a supporting framework may be erected around them to assist training to the desired shape. Bamboo stakes, wire and wire netting, both large- and small-gauge, can be used to create a variety of interesting shapes, such as cones, pillars, and fans. If a large framework is needed, ensure that the pot is also sufficiently large to give the trained plant stability. The head of a pinch-pruned standard needs no frame, but is formed entirely by bushy growth, pinch-pruned to create and maintain an even shape (see also *How to Train a Standard Fuchsia*, p.119). However, no subshrub can, in one season, produce a stem sturdy enough to support the head, so staking with a stake is required initially.

Routine care

Pick off discolored leaves as soon as you see them. Feed young plants with a fertilizer high in nitrogen in order to stimulate growth, then, when pinching stops, switch to a high-potassium fertilizer to stimulate flower development or, in coleus, to allow the leaf color to develop fully.

With flowering plants, such as fuchsias, once the shape is formed to your satisfaction, stop pinching about two months before flowers are desired, to give the terminal flower bud time to develop. Flowering should be simultaneous—and dramatic. With foliage plants, where flowers are not wanted (such as coleus and *Helichrysum*), continued pinching will prevent the formation of flower buds.

In cool climates, plants can be moved outdoors after the danger of frost has passed, either onto a patio or planted out as summer bedding, then, if desired, brought back under cover for the winter. In spring, trimming and pinching are resumed as new growth begins.

Do not fertilize flowering plants while they are dormant.

PINCH-PRUNING A COLEUS FAN

1 Pinch out all shoots as they develop until the plants are 10in (25cm) tall. Then pinch only on two opposite sides, giving a flattened shape to the plants.

Supporting framework
When the plants are 20in (50cm) tall, they will need the support of a framework, made from bamboo stakes tied as a fan.

2 Carefully insert the stakes that form the fan's ribs into the pot, along the flattened outline of the plants, and tie in crossbars to brace them.

3 Using figure-eight knots and soft twine, tie in stems to the stakes wherever possible, gently drawing some growth down to the horizontal.

4 Allow all shoots that extend toward the perimeter of the fan to grow on, tying them in at regular intervals to the stake framework. Continue pinching all shoots on the flat faces of the fan.

Side view of fan
Once the frame is covered, the fan shape can be maintained by pinching all growth. This will also stimulate fresh, bright young leaves.

Propagation

Propagating indoor plants is an economical way to increase your stock and to replace old plants with younger, more vigorous specimens. Successful propagation requires clean conditions, warmth, light, and sufficient humidity.

The easiest method of propagation is by division, which produces only a few plants at one time. The majority of new plants for growing indoors or under cover are grown from seed or cuttings, however, since these methods usually yield a greater number of new plants. Some plants may be increased by layering.

Propagation by division

Division is a quick and easy way of propagating plants. Many plants produce plantlets, runners, offsets, or bulbils, which root themselves and may be severed from the parent and potted.

Dividing the rootstock

Before dividing a pot plant, water the root ball thoroughly and allow it to drain. Herbaceous and clump-forming plants may be gently pulled apart or cut into pieces, each with its own root system, and repotted. Use a sharp knife to separate the fleshy roots of rhizomatous plants; retain vigorous sections with young growth and fibrous, feeding roots. Prune any long, thick roots, and any that are damaged. Replant each division in a clean pot using a soil mix similar to that used for the parent plant. Water the plants and keep them in bright light, but out of direct sun, until they are established. See also "Repotting and topdressing," p.373.

Dividing plantlets

Plantlets are small versions of the parent plant that grow on its leaves, stolons, stems, or inflorescences. Once they are large enough to handle, detach them with about

1¼in (3cm) of the leaf stalk or stolon, where appropriate. Insert the plantlet stalk in a pot of peat substitute- or peat-based potting mix so that the plantlet rests on the surface. Water the pot and cover it with a clear plastic bag to preserve the humidity. Roots should form in about three weeks. After this, the plantlet takes up to five weeks to resume growth, at which point it is ready to repot.

Dividing rooting runners

Some plants, such as *Saxifraga stolonifera* (syn. *S. sarmentosa*) and *Episcia*, spread by runners. If these are rooted individually in pots of soil mix, they may then be severed from the parent to make new plants.

Dividing offsets and bulbils

Offsets are small plants that develop around the base of plants. Choose a well-developed one with some roots; cut or break it off cleanly from the main stem and insert it in

PROPAGATING POT PLANTS BY DIVISION

1 Thoroughly water the plant (here, *Calathea*) an hour before dividing it. Support the plant, then invert the pot and tap its rim on a hard surface. Slide out the plant.

2 Remove surplus soil mix, either by gently shaking the plant or by teasing some of the soil away with your fingers, so that the roots are accessible.

3 Use hands or a hand fork to pry the root ball into sections, each with a portion of roots. Take care not to damage the stems or fibrous roots.

4 Using a clean, sharp knife, trim back any thick roots so that the divisions will fit into their new pots, but be careful to leave the delicate, fibrous roots intact.

5 Select sections with healthy, young shoots (see inset) for replanting. Insert each section in a pot of moist, soil-based potting mix. Gently firm the potting mix and water well to encourage the roots to establish. Label the pot.

PROPAGATING BY ROOTING RUNNERS

1 Peg down runners (here *Saxifraga stolonifera*) in individual 3in (7cm) pots of moist propagation mix. Keep them well watered.

2 After a few weeks, separate each rooted plantlet, in its pot, from the parent by cutting the runner close to the young plant. Label the pot.

a pot of moist potting mix. Cover the pot with a clear plastic bag until new growth is produced.

Some plants produce bulbils on the fronds or in the leaf axils. Detach these and root them in moist, soil-based potting mix. For further information, see LILIES, *Propagating from Stem Bulbils*, p.239.

Growing indoor plants from seed

The seed of pure species breeds true, but that of many hybrid indoor plants does not. Uniform results may be obtained, however, from selections, or first generation (F1) hybrids, of biennials, annuals, and a small number of perennials, such as cyclamen and geraniums.

Seed mixes and containers
Use a soil mix prepared specifically for seed (see TOOLS AND EQUIPMENT, "Standard seed compost," p.565). It should be a free-draining and open-textured mix, which holds moisture without becoming soaked or forming a hard crust on the top. A variety of containers can be used, such as half-pots, pans, and half or quarter seed flats. Always use a size of container that is appropriate to the number of plants required. Special cell flats that allow each seed to grow in its own individual plug of soil are also readily available.

When to sow
Most seeds are spring-sown, but seeds of early spring-flowering species are usually sown in the fall. Annuals may be sown in several batches from spring to early summer for a succession of blooms. Seeds of many exotic species are spring-sown but often germinate freely if sown as soon as they are ripe. It may be difficult, however, to keep the young seedlings alive in winter.

Preparing the seed
Some seeds need special treatment to help them germinate. Seeds with hard coats often need presowing treatment, such as soaking in warm water; the time required varies from about 10 minutes for *Cordyline australis* to about 72 hours for banana seed. Other hard-coated seeds, such as *Caesalpinia pulcherrima*, will not germinate unless the seed coat is chipped with a knife or file. If the seed is too small to handle, gently abrade it between two sheets of fine sandpaper. Follow the supplier's instructions on the seed package to ensure success.

Sowing the seed
Overfill the container with standard seed-starting mix and tap it on the bench; scrape off the surplus so that the mix is level with the container rim. Firm the mix to within ½in (1cm) of the rim.

Water the seed mix before sowing the seed, and allow the container to drain well. Watering with a watering can after sowing may "bunch" the seed or wash it together, leading to problems with overcrowding and damping off later.

Sow all seed thinly and evenly. Tiny seed is easier to sow if it is first mixed with horticultural sand. Place large seeds far enough apart to allow the seedlings to grow without being thinned later on. Alternatively, sow the seeds singly into small pots, cell flats, or soil blocks.

As a general rule, cover seeds with soil to the depth of their smallest diameter. Very tiny seeds, however, or seeds that require light to germinate, should be left uncovered on the surface of the growing medium. Then cover the container with a sheet of glass, a clear plastic bag, or a propagator lid to maintain humidity and stop the soil from drying out. Place the container in the correct temperature, in bright light but out of direct sunlight, and leave the seed to germinate.

Germination temperatures
Seeds usually germinate at 10°F (5°C) higher than the minimum needed by the same plant in growth. As a general rule, a temperature of 59–64°F (15–18°C) is suitable. The correct temperature varies for different seed, so follow the instructions given on the seed packets. Plants that are raised under cover for growing outside germinate at 50°F (10°C) or less. Many tropical or subtropical plants need 75–79°F (24–26°C) to germinate. If it is hard to maintain such temperatures indoors, consider using a heated propagator. There are many different types and sizes, and most have thermostats that allow a specific temperature to be maintained.

Aftercare of sown seed
Wipe any condensation off covers to discourage fungal diseases. After seven to ten days, check the containers daily for signs of germination and remove the covers as soon as the seedlings appear. Germination times vary greatly, however, so some larger seeds may take several months to germinate. Keep the soil mix moist; use either a watering can or, for very delicate seedlings, a mist-sprayer.

Feeding should not be necessary if seed was sown in mix containing a small amount of nutrients, but seedlings that are to stay in their container for some time may benefit from a liquid feed as they grow. If the seedlings start to bend toward light, turn them daily and shade with cardboard or shade netting if there is danger of sun scorch.

Pricking out the seedlings
When the seedlings are ½in (1cm) high, they may be pricked out into larger pots or packs. Water them first, allow them to drain for an hour, then loosen them by tapping the side of the container. Lift the seedlings out of the container using a small, flat implement. If the seedlings are clumped together, use a dibber or pencil to tease them apart. Handle the seedlings carefully by the leaves since the stems are easily damaged.

Use a dibber to make holes in some fresh potting mix in a container. Lower each seedling into place so that it is at the same depth as before. Place more mix around the roots and lightly firm in each

RAISING INDOOR PLANTS FROM SEED

1 Mix very fine, dustlike seed (here, *Campanula*) with dry, fine sand in a bag; this makes it possible to sow the seed more evenly. Sow larger seed by hand.

2 Sow the mixture thinly onto a pot of moist, seed-starting mix, using a small funnel of paper held close to the surface. Label, and place in a propagator.

3 When the seedlings are large enough to handle by their leaves, use a dibber to prick them out into a container of moist potting mix.

4 Once the seedlings have become established, pot them on singly into individual pots or cell packs. Water, and label each pot.

INDOOR FLOWERING PLANTS FROM SEED

Alonsoa
Begonia (fibrous-rooted and tuberous kinds) ⊛
Browallia
Caesalpinia pulcherrima
Campanula ⊛
Clitoria
Cobaea
Cordyline australis
Cuphea
Cyclamen, some ⊛
Exacum affine ⊛
Impatiens ⊛
Jacaranda mimosifolia
Pelargonium (modern zonal hybrids)
Primula kewensis ⊛,
　P. malacoides ⊛,
　P. obconica ⊛,
　P. sinensis ⊛
Salpiglossis
Schizanthus
Sinningia ⊛
Thunbergia
Torenia

Key
⊛ Requires high humidity

Campanula 'Burghaltii'

INDOOR PLANTS FROM SOFTWOOD CUTTINGS

Abutilon
Acalypha ☉
Aeschynanthus ☉
Alloplectus ☉
Bougainvillea
Brunfelsia pauciflora ☉
Callisia
Catharanthus
Cissus
Codiaeum ☉
Columnea ☉
Crassula, some ☉
Crossandra ☉
Elatostema ☉
Epiphyllum ☉
Epipremnum
Euphorbia pulcherrima
Ficus benjamina
Fittonia ☉
Gardenia ☉
Gynura ☉
Hibiscus
Hoya
Impatiens ☉
Iresine ☉
Ixora coccinea ☉
Jasminum mesnyi
Justicia
Kalanchoe
Mandevilla splendens ☉
Pachystachys
Passiflora
Pelargonium
Pellionia
Pentas lanceolata
Peperomia ☉
Pilea ☉
Plumbago auriculata
Polyscias ☉
Rhipsalidopsis gaertneri,
   R. rosea
Rhipsalis ☉
Rhoicissus tomentosa
Ruellia ☉
Schlumbergera ☉
Solenostemon ☉
Sonerila ☉
Sparrmannia ☉
Stephanotis ☉
Streptosolen
Syngonium ☉
Tibouchina ☉
Tradescantia ☉

Key

☉ Requires high humidity

*Tibouchina
urvilleana*

seedling. Small seedlings should be set about 1in (2.5cm) apart, and larger ones about 2in (5cm). Water the seedlings with a fine-rosed watering can. For seedlings sown individually in a cell flat, lift the seedling with its plug of soil, and pot it up.

Repotting

Once the roots of plants have filled the containers, they need repotting (see p.373). The new pot should be large enough to allow for a 1in (2.5cm) gap all around the root ball. Insert the plant so that the base of its stem is level with the surface of the potting soil. To settle the mix, tap the pot on a bench, firm it lightly, and water, using a fine spray.

Once repotted in regular potting mix, the new plants can be treated as mature specimens. Ensure that the correct conditions are maintained; different indoor plants have widely varying requirements.

Propagation from cuttings

Most tender indoor plants may be readily propagated from softwood (tip) cuttings (rooted in potting mix or in water), leaf-bud or leaf cuttings. Semiripe or woody cuttings may be taken from indoor shrubs. The chief factors for success are timing, hygiene, warmth, and humidity.

Semiripe cuttings

Take cuttings of semiripe wood from the current season's growth, in summer after the main flush of fast, spring growth but before the wood is fully ripe; suitable material is firm, but flexible, and offers some resistance if bent. Plants grown under cover may reach maturity before midsummer, so check any new shoots carefully from early summer on. For details of the technique, see ORNAMENTAL SHRUBS, "Semiripe cuttings," p.111.

Leaf-bud cuttings

Genera such as *Ficus* and *Hoya* may be increased by leaf-bud cuttings, a type of semiripe cutting. Cut stems into 1–2in (2.5–5cm) lengths, each with a single leaf and leaf axil bud. Then insert them into pots of propagation mix and place the pots in a propagator at a temperature of 59–64°F (15–18°C). For further details, see ORNAMENTAL SHRUBS, *Leaf-bud Cuttings*, p.112.

Softwood cuttings

These are taken in early spring. Select new, short-noded sideshoots and remove them with a clean, sharp knife. When preparing cuttings, make clean, precise cuts so that no snags are left on the stems. Dip the base of each stem in hormone rooting powder, and, using a dibber or pencil, insert several cuttings into a pot of standard propagation mix. The cuttings may be close together in a pot or placed around the edges as long as their leaves do not touch.

Place the pot in a propagator or cover it with a plastic bag to reduce water loss—make sure that the bag does not touch the cuttings, however. Leave the pot in a warm, light location but out of direct sunlight. Check the cuttings each day or two and, if necessary, clear any condensation by opening the propagator or bag for a while.

It should take about four to six weeks for new roots to form. At this stage, when young growth may be seen, transfer the cuttings to individual pots of peat- or soil-based potting mix to grow on. Keep the young plants in a warm, lightly shaded place until they are well established.

PROPAGATING FROM SOFTWOOD CUTTINGS

1 Fill a 5in (13cm) pot with moist propagation mix and tamp it down until it is level.

2 Using pruners or a clean, sharp knife, cut off, just above a node, some new, short-noded shoots 4–6in (10–15cm) long. The plant shown here is *Gynura urantiaca*.

3 Trim each cutting just below a node, removing the lower leaves to create a length of clean stem at the base (see inset). Do not leave snags, which might rot.

4 Dip the base of the cuttings into hormone rooting powder. Insert them in the pot so that the leaves are just above the soil mix.

5 Water and label the cuttings. Place the pot in a propagator in a warm, light place and maintain a soil temperature of 64–70°F (18–21°C) until the cuttings are rooted and ready to repot.

Rooting softwood cuttings in water

The simplest method of rooting softwood cuttings is to place them in a glass or jar of water in a bright, warm site. Prepare each cutting as for a normal softwood cutting, ensuring that the lower leaves are cleanly removed. Support the cutting on chicken wire placed over the glass so that the stem is suspended in the water. When the roots develop and there is fresh growth, pot up the cuttings. Prepare pots with drainage material and 1in (2.5cm) of potting mix. Hold each cutting in a pot with its roots spread and fill in with mix until the roots are covered. Firm and water the cuttings thoroughly.

Propagating from leaves

Some plants may be propagated easily from whole leaves or leaf sections. In some cases, the leaves are inserted in potting mix (or water), while in others they are scored or cut up before being inserted in or secured flat onto the potting mix. Each leaf should produce a number of small plantlets where the leaf veins have been cut.

Whole leaves

Certain plants, often those with fleshy leaves growing in rosettes such as African violets (*Saintpaulia*) and gloxinias (*Sinningia speciosa*), as well as Rex and rhizomatous begonias, and some succulents (see p.347) may be increased from leaf cuttings.

For the cuttings, choose healthy, undamaged, fully grown leaves and cut them off close to the base of the leaf stalks. Trim each stalk with a straight cut 1¼in (3cm) below the leaf blade; insert the cuttings individually into prepared pots of propagation mix (1 part sand and 1 part peat),

label, and water. Place the pots in a propagator or cover each one with a clear plastic bag or improvised cloche (see below). As soon as each cutting produces plantlets, remove its cover. Grow the cuttings on until the plantlets are large enough to be teased apart and potted individually. Alternatively, leaves with long stalks

(especially African violets) can be rooted in water, although rooting tends to take longer than in potting mix.

Scored or cut leaves

The leaves of plants with prominent veins, such as Rex begonias and various members of the family

PROPAGATING SOFTWOOD CUTTINGS IN WATER

1 Using a sharp, clean knife, remove healthy, short-noded cuttings, 4–6in (10–15cm) long, from a healthy, vigorous plant (here, *Solenostemon*). Cut each stem carefully just above a node.

2 Trim each cutting below a node and remove the lower leaves to create a length of clean stem at the base (see inset).

3 Insert the stems through a piece of chicken wire over the top of a jar of water. Ensure that the stems are in the water.

4 Keep the water topped off so that the lower end of each cutting is always below the surface. A network of roots should develop.

5 When the cuttings are well rooted, carefully plant each one into a 3in (7cm) pot of sandy potting mix.

HALF-LEAF SECTIONS

1 Divide the leaf by cutting out the midrib and exposing the veins (here, *Streptocarpus*).

2 Insert the sections, cut edges down, in shallow trenches. Gently firm them in.

PROPAGATING INDOOR PLANTS FROM LEAF CUTTINGS

1 Cut healthy leaves from the parent plant (here, *Saintpaulia*). Insert each stalk in a small pot of propagation mix so that the leaf blade is just clear of the soil surface.

2 Water, label, and cover the pots. Small cloches made from the bases of plastic drink bottles work well. Leave them in a warm, light place out of direct sunlight.

3 Each leaf should produce several plantlets. When these develop, remove the covers, and grow them until they are large enough to pot individually.

Gesneriaceae, for example *Streptocarpus*, will produce small plantlets if they are scored or cut up and the cut veins are then kept in contact with moist propagation mix; the leaves may be divided either in half or into small sections, or they may be scored through.

Whichever method is used, keep the container in a propagator or in a clear plastic bag in a light place but out of direct sunlight; inflate the bag so that it does not touch the leaf sections, and seal it. The leaves being propagated should be kept at 64–75°F (18–24°C).

When clumps of plantlets develop from the cut veins, carefully lift and separate them, retaining a little soil around the roots of each plantlet, and pot them individually into 3in (7cm) pots containing potting mix.

Some succulent plants, including *Sansevieria* and those that have flattened, leaflike stems such as *Epiphyllum*, may also be propagated from "leaf" sections although these are treated slightly differently. For details, see CACTI AND OTHER SUCCULENTS, *Propagation from Stem Sections*, p.348.

PROPAGATING FROM CUT LEAVES

1 Select a young, healthy leaf (here *Begonia rex*) and make a ½in (1cm) long incision with a sharp knife straight across each of the strongest veins on the underside of the leaf (see inset).

2 Place the leaf, cut-side downward, on a flat of cutting mix. Pin its veins to the surface. Label, and place the flat in a propagator or a clear plastic bag.

3 Leave the flat in a warm place out of direct sunlight. When the plantlets have developed, carefully separate them from the leaf (see inset) and pot them on singly.

LEAF SQUARES

1 Cut 4 or 5 square sections the size of a postage stamp from a healthy leaf. Each piece should include a strong vein.

2 Place the sections, veins down, on moist cutting mix. Pin with wire hoops, then treat as other leaf sections.

PROPAGATION OF TUBEROUS BEGONIAS

When begonia tubers die back naturally in the fall, store them in their pots at 41–50°F (5–10°C) in a dry place over winter. Alternatively, lift and clean the tubers, and store them in boxes of dry sand vermiculite, peat substitute, or peat.

At the beginning of the growing season, place the tubers in a flat of moist, sandy potting mix (1 part sharp sand, 1 part peat substitute or peat-based potting mix). Store them at a minimum temperature of 55–61°F (13–16°C). When new buds are visible, cut the tubers into sections, making sure that each has at least one bud and some roots. Leave the sections to dry for a few hours in a warm place. When the cut surfaces have formed calluses, pot the sections in soil-based potting mix. Do not firm the mix heavily or water it, because this will encourage fungal attack.

Alternatively, allow new shoots to develop on the tubers, and use these as basal cuttings. Take the cuttings so that each retains an eye. Dip the base of each cutting in hormone rooting powder and insert them, ¾in (2cm) deep, around the edge of a pot or pan of soil-based potting mix.

1 In the fall, lift the dormant tubers and clean them. Dust the crowns with fungicide (optional) and overwinter them in a dry place.

2 In the spring, place the tubers, concave side up, 2in (5cm) apart and 1in (2.5cm) deep, in a flat of moist, sandy potting mix.

3 When shoots appear, cut tubers into sections, each with a bud and some roots. Allow the cut surfaces to dry.

4 Pot up the sections singly in 5in (13cm) pots, with the top of each level with the mix surface. Label each container.

5 Keep the pots in a propagator in a warm, frost-free place until the sections are established, then pot them on singly.

Basal cuttings

Remove 2in (5cm) shoots from the tuber, each with an eye of the tuber at the base. Pot them up and treat them as divided tubers.

Propagation by layering

Layering involves wounding the stem of a plant, inducing it to produce roots, and then separating the rooted stem. This method has a high success rate since the layered stem receives nutrients from the parent plant while it is developing.

Some indoor plants may be propagated by layering—either in air or in the soil. Air layering produces a fairly large new plant from an older specimen, but it may take considerable time. Simple layering in soil mix provides new stock quickly.

Air layering

This is a good method for replacing old or damaged houseplants, for example the rubber plant (*Ficus elastica*) and its relatives. The top of the plant, or tip of a branch, may be encouraged to form new roots, and is then severed from the parent.

Choose a section of stem of new growth that is straight, about 4in (10cm) long, and of at least pencil thickness. Cut the bottom off a clear plastic bag to create a transparent sleeve and slip it over the stem or, if the leaves are too large, fold a clear plastic sheet around the stem and tape up the seam. Secure the sleeve below the selected area of the stem.

Using a sharp knife, make a shallow, upward-slanting cut in the side of the stem, then wedge this tongue open with moist sphagnum moss. Alternatively, on woody plants, score two rings ½–¾in (1–2cm) apart below a healthy leaf joint on the selected area of the stem; the scores should be just deep enough to penetrate the bark without harming the wood. Peel off the bark between the rings, leaving the cambium undisturbed.

In both cases, dust the cut area with rooting powder. Pack the sleeve with damp moss, and seal it so that the area is tightly enclosed to prevent it from drying out. If the stem is heavy, provide support.

It may be many months before the roots show. water, and reseal. When roots appear, sever the layered stem from the parent and pot it with a soil-based potting mix. Water the young plant sparingly until it is established.

Simple layering

Climbing or trailing shoots may be layered into soil while they are still attached to the parent plant.

Choose a long, vigorous shoot and pin it down into a small pot of moist propagation mix. After three to four weeks, roots should start to grow and new shoots begin to form; the rooted layer may then be detached from the parent plant. If required, several shoots may be layered at the same time, each in its own pot.

When severing the new plants, take care not to spoil the shape of the parent plant. For further information, see CLIMBING PLANTS, p.145.

SIMPLE LAYERING

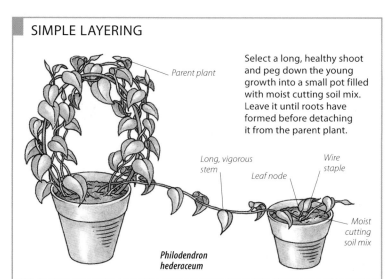

Select a long, healthy shoot and peg down the young growth into a small pot filled with moist cutting soil mix. Leave it until roots have formed before detaching it from the parent plant.

Parent plant · *Long, vigorous stem* · *Leaf node* · *Wire staple* · *Moist cutting soil mix*

Philodendron hederaceum

PROPAGATING BY AIR LAYERING

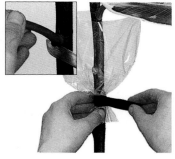

1 Trim the leaves (here, *Ficus elastica*) from a straight length of stem (see inset). Slide a plastic sleeve over the stem and fix the lower end with adhesive tape.

2 Fold down the sleeve. Hold the stem firmly and cut a "tongue" in it, making a slanted, upward incision ¼in (5mm) deep and 1in (2.5cm) long.

3 Apply hormone rooting powder to the wound and push moist sphagnum moss into the incision, using a split stake or the back of a knife blade.

4 Roll the sleeve back into position around the packed incision. Fill the sleeve with more moist sphagnum moss.

5 When the sleeve is tightly packed with moss, secure the upper end to the stem with adhesive tape.

6 When the new roots are visible through the sleeve, cut through the stem just below the root ball with pruners. Remove the plastic sleeve.

7 Gently loosen the moss ball and tease out the roots. Pot the rooted layer into a container that allows a 2in (5cm) space around the root ball. Fill this with soil-based potting mix and firm it very gently, making sure that the new roots are not damaged. Water, label, and place the pot in a shaded location until the young plant is established.

THE LAWN

FROM THE STRIPED GREEN EXPANSE IN A
FORMAL GARDEN TO THE CLOSELY MOWN
TURF OF A SPORTS AREA OR ROUGH
GRASSLAND UNDER A GROVE OF TREES,
THERE IS A LAWN TO SUIT ALL SITUATIONS.

Whether it is a showpiece in its own right, a
foil for colorful borders, a playing surface for
children, or simply a relaxing haven, the lawn
can be both functional and a design feature.
Frequently undervalued as merely a flat surface
underfoot, the lawn can make a much more
important contribution to the garden, softening
hard surfaces, helping to define distinctive
features, and unifying the garden as a whole.
For centuries, grass has been used to create lawns
because it is visually appealing, tolerates wear,
and may be cut very low without being damaged,
although chamomile and other low-growing
herbs make wonderful scented alternatives
for ornamental use.

Creating lawns

A well-maintained lawn is an attractive feature that provides a clear area in which to walk, play, and relax. Grass also serves well as a surface for wide paths and on gently sloping banks. Some dense, low-growing plants, such as chamomile (*Chamaemelum nobile*), may also be used for lawns, although they are much less hard-wearing. When choosing the type and shape of the lawn, consider how it will link with the rest of your yard so that it forms a compatible, unifying part of the landscape.

Formal lawns A well-kept formal lawn is an elegant feature.

Grass

Grass is the plant most commonly chosen for a lawn because it is durable and attractive. It may also be repeatedly cut without damage, because the growing points are at the base of the plants.

Mown lawns

A primarily ornamental, high-quality lawn used to be the ideal, but the concept of lawns is changing as we better understand the environmental costs of the perfect lawn. If your lawn is likely to be subject to heavier wear—by being used as a play area, for example—set your sights on a utility lawn; it will still be attractive but may contain minor imperfections and requires less frequent routine maintenance.

If you want to maintain a lawn area with a particularly hard-wearing surface for sports such as soccer, site it separately from your main lawn so you can provide the proper care for it.

Long grass and meadows

As part of a wild garden or orchard, unmown grass or a flower-rich meadow can be a very attractive choice. It needs very little maintenance, so it also may be suitable for an area such as a slope or a stream bank where mowing is difficult. Meadows often thrive on less than fertile soils, so this may be a good way of using a part of the yard where little else grows.

Mixing long and short grass

Using different grasses in various parts of the landscape, or varying the height of cut, helps define separate areas and adds textural contrast. A closely mown path running through a long, flower-rich meadow provides an eye-catching shift in height, color, and texture, and also encourages people to walk only on the intended path.

In large yards, consider having a low-cut lawn area near the house where its fine appearance will be most appreciated; a path or steps could then lead to a grassy play area farther away; while an area of meadow with long grass and wildflowers could be included at the far end of the yard. Mixing grasses in this way provides contrasting but complementary play and wildlife-attracting areas. Mowing time is also reduced since part of the area requires cutting only infrequently.

Designing a lawn

Because lawn is an important part of the landscape, plan its position and shape carefully within the overall design. Take into account practical and aesthetic considerations so that the lawn will be pleasurable to use, convenient to maintain, and an enhancing part of the overall landscape plan.

Siting a lawn

Lawn grass grows best in an open, sunny area, because many types of lawn grass require good light, well-drained, nutrient-rich soil, and regular moisture to thrive. A partially shaded spot can be used, provided it is laid with shade-tolerant sod or sown with a seed mixture that is suitable for shade (see "Choosing the right mixtures," p.389). Alternatively, it might be better to introduce a nongrass lawn of shade-tolerant plants that tolerate some wear (see "Nongrass lawns," p.389). A chamomile or other herb lawn can be a good choice for people who don't like to mow grass, because these plants do not need mowing to keep them looking neat.

If the proposed lawn is to surround a tree, leave an area at least the width of the tree's canopy bare (covered with wood mulch), because the tree may outcompete the grass for nutrients and moisture. Alternatively, plant difficult areas with shade-tolerant grass (see "Problem areas," p.389) or groundcover.

Shape

The shape of the lawn should harmonize with the landscape style. A symmetrical layout of geometrically shaped lawns bordered by paths would be appropriate in a highly stylized, formal yard. In a small garden, a simple shape such as a circle could be visually striking and might be echoed imaginatively by the introduction of a circular pond or patio and containers packed with ornamental plants.

A curved, irregular design lends fluidity, linking different landscape elements with a sweeping plane of even color. Broad, flowing curves can be created to set off the planting in a nearby border, and to lead the eye toward an attractive focal point. Avoid busy, scalloped edges or awkward angles, however, because they may detract from the impact of other plantings and make mowing difficult.

Design functions

As well as being attractive in its own right, the lawn may fulfill different design criteria for both plants and hard features. Uniform areas of grass create a natural bond between otherwise disparate elements, leading the eye from one part of the landscape to another. A statue or specimen tree sited in a lawn has maximum impact since the surrounding sea of plain color separates it from other, more distracting elements. One or two flower beds in an expanse of lawn can also create a very pleasing composition. Avoid overdoing this, because dotting a lawn with too many beds or trees makes maintenance more time-consuming, and can create an overall effect that is cluttered and disjointed.

The uniform texture and color of grass forms a neutral backdrop that enhances other plantings particularly well. The level surface acts as a foil for more sculptural plants—the strong silhouette of a columnar tree or the jutting spread of a prostrate shrub—as well as the variety of shapes, colors, and textures found in a mixed or herbaceous border.

Paths and access

Narrow areas of grass are usually subject to heavy wear and are difficult to mow; for these reasons, paths narrower than about 3ft (1m) may be impractical. For a frequently used route across a lawn, such as from the house to the garden shed, consider laying stepping-stones or a hard path to prevent uneven wear. If possible, leave at least one side of the lawn open for access; if there are only one or two narrow openings, the grass is likely to become damaged at these points.

Edging

Edging the lawn with paving stones or bricks helps to define its shape and that of the borders, and also has practical advantages. It makes it easier to cut the lawn right to its edge while avoiding the isk of damaging other plants. Trailing plants may be allowed to overhang the edge, breaking up any awkward rigidity, but without depriving the grass beneath of light. In addition, ornamental containers may be set on the hard edging as focal points or to provide an interesting change of level. Alternatively, a narrow mowing strip of mulched soil may be created at the edge of a lawn.

A formal lawn Here, the pristine expanse of a high-quality, formal lawn provides a uniform, fine-textured foil for an elegant seat and the surrounding planting.

Climatic considerations

Lawn grasses are commonly divided into two main groups depending on their temperature tolerance. Those that grow mainly in a temperate climate, preferring temperatures of 59–75°F (15–24°C) are known as cool-season grasses; those that grow best in subtropical or tropical climates, thriving in temperatures of 79–95°F (26–35°C), are known as warm-season grasses. The latter are not normally used for lawns in temperate regions because they turn brown during the winter as they become dormant. They will not survive the low temperatures found in much of Canada and are not covered here.

Cool-season grasses

Temperate or cool-season grasses are widely used for lawns throughout North America. The grasses that are most commonly found in cool-season lawns are bents (*Agrostis*), tall and fineleaf fescues (*Festuca*), bluegrasses (also know as meadow grasses, *Poa*), and perennial ryegrass (*Lolium perenne*).

Bents are low-growing and, of all the grasses, are the most tolerant of close mowing. They are widely used on high maintenance areas such as lawn bowling greens, which are mowed almost daily. In the home lawn their presence should be discouraged because, if allowed to grow to the height of an average lawn, they leave brown, dead-looking patches when mowed. They also require large amounts of fertilizer and water and are drought intolerant.

Fescues are fine leaved and may be cut low; they are quite hard wearing, and some species grow in poor soils. They also tolerate dry conditions, the competition from tree roots, and shade, making them the best choice for growing under trees. Their fertilizer requirements are moderate, but they grow poorly in high temperatures and should never be closely mowed then. Red fescue (*Festuca rubra*) is tolerant of acidic soils but does poorly in areas with hot and humid summers. Tall fescue (*F. arundinacea*) is more hardwearing than the other species and is a good choice for areas that receive heavy foot traffic. It will take more heat and sun than the other species but must not be cut too short or it will quickly begin to die out.

Decorative edges Brick edging makes an attractive divider between hard surfaces and the lawn. Such edging should be installed below the height of mower blades.

LAWNS AND BIODIVERISTY

The traditional grass lawn supports relatively little biodiversity because it is essentially a monoculture, a mix of only two or three grass species, blended to provide a dense green carpet in which other plant species are discouraged. This goes against the natural tendency toward diversity, so maintaining a grass lawn requires a great deal of care and attention.

A better and more sustainable approach is to adopt a "greener" approach to lawn care. This involves mowing less frequently using a higher mower setting, 3–4in (8–10cm) tall. Give up the use of herbicides and allow low-growing plants like clover to establish. Keep in mind that even plants we regard as "weeds" have benefits for beneficial insects and wildlife. Dandelions, for example, are one of the best sources of pollen for beneficial insects in early spring. Another helpful change you can make is to stop collecting your grass clippings. Instead, use the mulching setting your mower and leave the clippings on the lawn as natural fertilizer. The clippings can also be used occasionally as mulch for vegetable garden beds too.

HIGH-QUALITY OR UTILITY

Grass varies in appearance, growth rate, and wear resistance: high-quality grass (right) has a fine texture; utility grass (far right) is better for a family lawn.

High-quality

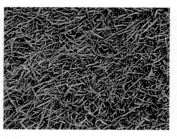

Utility

Selecting the right grass

Before selecting seed or sod, assess the relative importance of the lawn's appearance, wearability, and maintenance needs. Of the many different grass mixtures available, some are particularly good for areas of heavy use, while others give attractive color and texture. The grass should also be suited to the growing conditions, such as soil type and drainage, and the degree of shade.

High-quality lawns

To create formal, high-quality lawns, select grass species that create an attractive, uniform texture and color. For the highest-quality lawns, a mixture of Kentucky bluegrass, perennial ryegrass, and red fescue is the best choice for most soils in eastern Canada and on the west coast. On the prairies, where additional water can be given, use a mix of equal parts Kentucky bluegrass and red fescue. A high-quality lawn can only be achieved by growing the right grasses for your region, fertilizing at the correct time, mowing frequently to the correct height, and giving supplementary water during periods of drought. For special areas, such as home putting greens, bents may be used, but they require close, frequent mowing to remain green.

Utility lawns

Lawns that are primarily functional, perhaps providing a play area for children or a space for outdoor entertaining, need to be relatively durable, but they must still provide an attractive, even surface. Grasses for this purpose do not usually create the impression of perfectly uniform texture and color of a high-quality lawn, since this is inevitably of secondary importance.

For hard-wearing lawns, the major grass is perennial ryegrass; it is usually mixed with red fescue, Kentucky bluegrass, and chewings fescue (*Festuca rubra* var. *commutata*). Turf-type varieties of tall fescue (*F. arundinacea*) are very hard-wearing and hardy to at least -20°F (-30°C), but they must not be mowed lower than 2½in (6cm). On the prairies, use a 50/50 mix of Kentucky bluegrass and red fescue where additional water can be given,

or one of the native grasses that can withstand drought conditions where it cannot.

The more desirable grass varieties have the smallest seeds. The price of commercial lawn seed mixes reflects this; an inexpensive grass seed mix contains a higher percentage of poor, large-seeded species and therefore far fewer seeds. Read the label carefully before buying a grass seed mixture to be sure it contains the best species for the location and purpose you have in mind.

Games and sports areas

Areas of grass used for ball games or sports need particularly wear-tolerant species and selected cultivars. Some sports lawns must also tolerate a very low cut and have a fine finish in order to minimize the effect of the grass on the run of the ball.

A mixture of bluegrass, ryegrass, and fescues as for high-quality lawns (see left) tolerates some wear and is suitable for areas such as croquet lawns. Bowling greens and putting greens need the very fine-leaved grasses such as bentgrass. These are very high maintenance species that will not stand up to heavy use and need specialized care to keep them in top shape. If a more hard-wearing surface is needed, such as for football or soccer, it is better to opt for a mixture containing ryegrass or tall fescue (see "Utility lawns," left).

Meadows

For meadows, whenever possible use grass species that are native to the area. They are more likely to flourish, and they do not look incongruous or artificial (see also MEADOW AND PRAIRIE PLANTING, p.401). Usually a meadow-seed mixture consists of slow-growing grasses and various native, broad-leaved flowering species. In addition to climate, factors such as soil type, soil moisture, and sun exposure may influence the choice of species; some prefer extremely dry, well-drained conditions, while others grow well on marshy ground.

Bents and fescues are usually included, while a short-lived grass, such as Italian ryegrass (*Lolium multiflorum*), may be added for initial, quick groundcover. If mown, Italian ryegrass will die out within two years, leaving

Bluegrasses are more resistant to wear but cannot be mowed very low, and some have quite coarse leaves. They are the grass of choice for most of Canada, and are at their best in spring, when they recover from the winter and start into growth sooner than most other species. They spread by stolons (underground shoots) and can rapidly fill in any bare patches, but perform poorly unless grown in sunlight. Bluegrasses need at least six hours of full sun each day to thrive and are able to withstand high summer temperatures, although they grow best in cooler weather. Do not cut lower than 2in (5cm) during the growing season, although this height can be reduced in late fall to lessen the risk of diseases such as snow mold during winter.

Ryegrass is extremely hard wearing and tolerates most soils, including heavy clay, but is coarse textured and does not like to be closely mowed. It is short lived but germinates rapidly and is frequently included in seed mixes to act as a nurse for other, more desirable species, giving them shelter until they become established.

Annual bluegrass (*Poa annua*) is also found in many lawns, but is often considered a weed by gardeners since it quickly runs to seed, forming coarse patches among fine-leaved grasses.

Cool-season grasses are often sown as mixtures of more than one species, although in some areas Kentucky bluegrass, which is also known as smooth-stalked meadow grass (*Poa pratensis*), and tall fescue are grown on their own. If sowing a single-species lawn, however, it is common to mix several cultivars together, because this improves the lawn's disease resistance and overall color (see "Choosing the right cultivars," opposite).

behind the fine-leaved grasses and broad-leaved flowering plants. Some species need an overwintering or cold period before they will germinate, and so may not appear during the first year after sowing.

Meadows should be mowed at least once each year unless you want them to revert to nature. Mowing will kill off most tree and shrub seedlings that may have germinated, although some aggressive species such as poplar (*Populus*) may survive and require removal by hand.

Problem areas

For lawns in difficult sites, such as shady, wet, or dry areas, choose a grass mixture that is specially designed for such conditions. In extreme cases, it may be better to grow groundcover shrubs or perennials instead (see pp.101 and 180).

In wet, shady areas, grass does not readily grow into a dense, vigorous turf. There are some species, however, that are more tolerant than others: rough-stalked bluegrass (*Poa trivialis*), with Kentucky bluegrass, and red fescue will form a lawn that will stand up to both wear and close mowing. In dry shade, use mostly red fescue, with some Kentucky bluegrass added for a better appearance. For areas where maintaining a lawn permanently is not possible because of dense shade or excessive wear, for example, sow perennial ryegrass seed in spring and fall. It will provide adequate coverage during the growing season.

In very dry regions, use grasses native to such areas, such as western wheatgrass (*Pascopyrum smithii*) or buffalograss (*Buchloe dactyloidesa*), both of which grow naturally on the great plains of North America, or fairway crested wheatgrass (*A. cristatum*), native to the dry, cold plains of Russia and Siberia. The wheatgrasses generally produce medium- to low-quality lawns; cut to a height of 2in (5cm) or taller to prevent weeds from encroaching.

Choosing the right cultivars

Many modern grass cultivars have been specially bred to provide qualities particularly valued in lawns, such as even color, disease resistance, wear and shade tolerance, and compact growth. When selecting grass seed or the type of sod best suited to your site, make sure that the mixture includes not only the correct species but also a modern cultivar of that species. New cultivars are introduced annually, so check with the retailer to determine which cultivars are the best ones available for your particular lawn needs.

Flower meadow The grass in this informal area is dotted with a colorful mixture of wild and cultivated flowers, and provides a perfect habitat for wildlife.

The grass mixture should not contain agricultural cultivars; these are bred to produce vigorous, vertical leaf growth for grazing and need frequent mowing. They also tend to spread less, and so do not always produce a dense, uniform cover.

Nongrass lawns

Other evergreen plants can create a pleasing lawnlike appearance. These include chamomile (*Chamaemelum nobile*), *Cotula* species, *Dichondra micrantha*, and even various species of moss. Unlike many grasses, these groundcover plants do not stand up to heavy, continual wear, so they are rarely the best choice for a main lawn; they may, however, be used for primarily ornamental areas. Grow them in a patio or courtyard garden to provide a welcome patch of green; as a living "skirt" at the base of a fountain, raised pond, pedestal urn, or statue; or next to a patio or path to creep over the edges and relieve the rigidity of the hard surface.

Chamomile leaves release a sweet, apple-like fragrance when crushed underfoot, but they do not tolerate heavy wear; the non-flowering clone 'Treneague' is naturally low-growing and especially suitable for lawns.

Cotula, which has fernlike leaves, is considerably more durable because it forms a thick carpet of creeping stems; it also flourishes in moist conditions. *Dichondra*, a ground-hugging plant, has small, round leaves that look like waterlily pads. Prepare soil as for a lawn, and plant small rooted cuttings spaced about 12in (30cm) apart. In shade, plants may grow up to 6in (15cm) tall and will need regular mowing; in sun, they remain short. Dichondra grows best in warm areas; it does not survive temperatures lower than 25°F (-4°C).

A few of the tough perennial ground cover plants can be used as a grass substitute. For example, bugleweed (*Ajuga reptans*) forms a thick carpet andthrives in sun or shade; if mown immediately after flowering, it will not spread by seed into nearby flower beds.

Another option is to create a "tapestry lawn" with a patchwork effect by growing a number of low, mat-forming plants together. It is best to use plants that grow at a similar rate, like the various creeping thymes, for example *Thymus praecox* var. *arcticus* 'Coccineus' and 'Doone Valley', and *T. caespititius*; otherwise, one species may gradually predominate and so upset the balance of the original design. As for other nongrass lawns, mixed tapestry lawns should not be heavily used.

Soil and site preparation

Thorough site preparation is the key to establishing a successful new lawn. Although this may be time-consuming and expensive, in the long run it is easier and cheaper to prepare the site properly at the outset than to try to alleviate problems later. The general principles of preparation apply to all sites, but decisions on drainage, soil improvement, and irrigation will depend on the individual site and the climate.

Clearing the site

It is important to clear the site completely, removing any large stones and rubble, and all plant growth, including any tree stumps or roots. If the site is already a lawn but is in too poor a condition to be worth renovating, then remove all the turf (see also "Renovating a neglected lawn," p.399).

Eradicating weeds

Take particular care to eliminate any perennial weeds with underground rhizomes or deep taproots, such as quackgrass (*Elymus repens*), dandelion (*Taraxacum officinale*), bindweed (*Convolulus arvensis*), and Canada thistle (*Cirsium arvense*), because they regenerate rapidly from small pieces of root or rhizome (see PLANT PROBLEMS, "Perennial weeds," pp.646–647).

Once the lawn grass is established, broad-leaved weeds can still be controlled using selective weedkillers, but weed grasses will be more difficult to eliminate, so it is vital to remove them completely when clearing the ground initially.

Annual weeds, for example lamb's quarters (*Chenopodium album*) and shepherd's purse (*Capsella bursa-pastoris*), may be controlled by mowing after the grass has germinated. Weeds will continue to germinate until the lawn gets thick enough to exclude light.

Preparing the soil

The ideal topsoil for a lawn is a well-drained, sandy soil at least 8in (20cm) and preferably 12in (30cm) in depth, overlying a well-structured and free-draining subsoil. In these conditions the grass becomes deep-rooted and obtains ample water and nutrients from the soil. If the soil depth varies, during dry weather brown patches will rapidly appear where the soil is shallow.

Other soils may also be suitable, but if the soil does not drain freely and the lawn is likely to be heavily used, even in wet conditions, the drainage should be improved. If the topsoil is very shallow or poor, it may be necessary to add new topsoil; this can be moved from other parts of the lawn or bought, although for large areas the latter is very expensive.

If the soil has a naturally high sand content, and is, therefore, too fast-draining, incorporate some well-rotted, organic matter to help retain nutrients and water (see "Soil structure and water content," p.620). Be careful, however, not to add too much because organic matter quickly rots down, and this may result in soil sinkage and an uneven surface.

After clearing the site, plow, rototill, or dig over the whole area, removing any large stones that are brought to the surface, then rake the ground to produce a fine tilth. Breaking up the soil in this way makes subsequent leveling easier, as well as relieving compaction and improving the soil structure. On heavy, clay soils, however, rototilling or plowing may create a compacted layer below the soil surface, which could impede drainage: if necessary, break it up using a subsoiling machine or by double digging. For further information, see "Soil cultivation," pp.618–621.

Drainage

Lawns on free-draining soils, and those in regions with low rainfall, are unlikely to require draining. In heavy, clay soils, drainage may be improved by digging washed and sieved river sand into the soil. Up to 6in (15cm) can be added, but this is expensive and laborious. In any soil that is not free-draining, it is preferable to install a drainage system during the preparation stage to avoid continual and expensive attempts to alleviate the problem after the lawn has been established.

The best type of drain for lawns consists of a row of pipes laid in a trench, which is backfilled with gravel. The ideal depth of the drain, and the distance between drains, will vary from site to site depending on the type of soil and the rainfall. For most loamy soils receiving moderate rainfall, one drain every 15–25ft (5–8m) is needed. Heavier, clay soils or sites with a high rainfall will need drains laid at closer intervals (see also SOILS AND FERTILIZERS, "Improving drainage," p.623).

Adjusting the soil pH

For new lawns, the pH is unlikely to need adjusting, unless previous use has left the site in poor condition. Most grasses grow well at pH levels of 5.5–7. Fineleaf and tall fescues grow best at pH 5.5–6.5, while perennial ryegrass (*Lolium perenne*) and Kentucky bluegrass (*Poa partensis*) grow better at pH 6–7. Soil-testing kits for measuring pH are available from most garden centers.

If the soil is very acidic (below pH 5), dig or till lime into the soil, the exact amount depending on the degree of acidity (see "Liming," p.625). Then leave the site for about a week before applying fertilizer. Lime may be added once the lawn is established but, because large amounts spread on grass may encourage certain diseases, only use a small quantity and repeat the following year if necessary. If uncertain about what to do, seek advice from a college, a reputable garden center, or a horticultural consultant.

Leveling the site

In yards that have only minor undulations and deep topsoil, the site may be roughly leveled by raking soil from the high spots to fill the hollows, firming at intervals to settle the soil. Although it is not essential for the ground to be precisely level, awkward bumps and hollows may cause problems when mowing. In some instances—for example, for an orchard or an

HOW TO LEVEL THE GROUND

1 Firm the site well, especially at the edges, by tamping with the back of a rake or by treading on it. Mark some stakes at the same distance from the top of each. Insert a row of stakes at the site edge. If next to paving, the marks should be level with its surface.

2 Add a second, parallel row of stakes about 3ft (1m) from the first row. Place a level on top of these to check that they are level with the previous row. Adjust the stakes as necessary.

3 Repeat the process to create a grid of stakes all at the same level. Rake up the soil to the top of the marks on the stakes, adding topsoil to fill any hollows. Once the ground is level, the stakes can be removed.

ACCURATE LEVELING

To level the ground, first create a grid of premarked stakes and sink them into the soil at the same depth. Add or remove soil until it is level with the marks on the stakes.

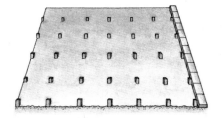

area of rough sports grass—leveling by eye is sufficient. But if a perfectly level surface is desired, such as for a formal lawn, a more accurate method should be used.

Achieving an accurate level

After leveling the ground roughly, an exact level may be achieved by knocking stakes into the ground all at the same depth to form a grid.

Start from a straight edge such as a path or patio, or create a taut line with string. Then take a number of identical stakes and make a mark on each one at the same distance from the top. Starting from the straight edge, knock them into the ground at equal intervals so that the marks are at the required level of the lawn or approximately ¾in (2cm) below this if sodding. Add a second row of stakes and then further rows until the site is covered by a grid of stakes.

Use a level—placed on a straight plank of wood if necessary to span across the rows—to check that the stakes within the rows are all at the same height. Then adjust the level of the soil so that it is aligned with the mark on each peg.

Substantial leveling

If the site needs more substantial leveling or the topsoil is very shallow, the subsoil must be leveled first. To do this, remove the topsoil, rototill or dig over the subsoil, then rake, level, and firm it roughly before replacing the topsoil in an even layer at least 8–12in (20–30cm) deep. To prevent the filled areas from sinking later, firm them thoroughly at intervals, adding more topsoil if necessary, and allow the site to settle before preparing the surface.

Creating a slope

Making the lawn slope gently away from the house or patio improves drainage and ensures that water does not drain into the foundation. A method similar to leveling is used, but each successive row of stakes is marked farther up or down

to form a sloping grid. For example, to create a gradient of 1:100, make the marks on each row of stakes successively lower by ¾in (2cm) and space stakes 6ft (2m) apart. A lawn angled toward a house must have its drainage system sloping in the opposite direction, that is, away from the house, to prevent water from reaching the building.

Final site preparations

Once the soil has been drained and leveled, the final surface can be prepared so that the site is ready for establishing a lawn.

Firming and raking

Use a lawn roller or tread evenly to firm the soil and to ensure there are no soft spots which might later sink, making the lawn vulnerable to being scalped during mowing. It may be necessary to tread the area about three times before the soil is settled enough, but take care not to compress the soil too much, and do not firm wet soil or it will become compacted. Even after firming, the soil may settle further over the course of a year or two, leaving small hollows. These should be leveled by applying a sifted, sandy topdressing (see p.398).

After firming, thoroughly rake the surface to produce a fine tilth and a level surface. If sowing seed, remove any stones larger than about ½in (1cm) across during raking; if turfing, it is only necessary to remove stones over 1in (2.5cm).

Leave the prepared site for about 3–4 weeks to allow any weed seeds to germinate; any emerging weeds should then be either hoed off carefully or treated with a contact weedkiller and gently raked off two or three days later once they have died, taking care not to disrupt the leveled soil unduly.

Fertilizing

A few days before establishing the lawn, and once the surface has been prepared, apply fertilizer to the site. This should contain the three major nutrients to ensure good growth: nitrogen (N), phosphorus (P), and potassium (K). Sites that have not been fertilized for many years may be deficient in all three. Phosphorus is especially important during the early stages of growth. Use a balanced organic fertilizer, such as pelleted chicken manure, compost, or a compound granular or microgranular fertilizer that contains all three of the nutrients; apply it according to the manufacturer's instructions.

CREATING A SLOPE

Decide how many rows of stakes will be used and mark them for each row at different heights in order to achieve the desired gradient (see above). Using a level, create a grid of stakes as for leveling, and rake soil up to the marks.

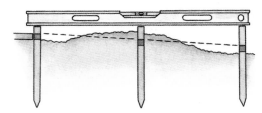

INSTALLING A DRAIN

Position the drain at the lowest point, sloping the ground away from the house. Dig a trench, lay pipes at the base, and cover with crushed stone. Add topsoil, then sod or seed.

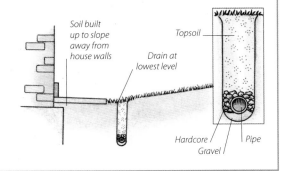

Soil built up to slope away from house walls

Topsoil

Drain at lowest level

Drain at lowest level

Hardcore

Gravel

Pipe

PREPARING THE SOIL SURFACE

1 Firm the surface by walking on it evenly, or by tamping it with the back of a rake. Repeat, if necessary, until the entire site is well firmed.

2 Rake the soil to a fine tilth and leave it to allow any weeds to germinate. When they appear, apply a contact weedkiller and, after about 2–3 days, rake off the weeds.

3 Apply a base dressing of a balanced granular organic fertilizer and lightly rake it into the surface. Leave the site for a few days before sodding or seeding.

Establishing a lawn

There are various methods of establishing a lawn. For cool-season grasses in temperate areas, the gardener may choose between seed or sod. Most often, seed is used for small areas and sod for larger ones, but new developments are almost always sodded.

Seeding a lawn is usually the cheapest method, but it takes up to a year before the lawn can be subjected to heavy wear. Establishing a lawn by vegetative means takes longer and is more costly than seeding. Sodding, although more expensive, gives an immediate visual effect, and the lawn may be used within two to three months; it is advisable to use sod if you have pets that may disturb grass seedlings before they are established.

Sod

There is a range of sod types available, including specially and commercially grown sod, meadow and treated meadow sod, and fine-grass sod; the type chosen largely depends on considerations of site and expense. Always buy sod from a reputable garden center or sod farm.

If possible, inspect the sod before buying it to make sure that it is in good condition, of the right quality (see "Selecting the right grass," p.388), and that the soil is a free-draining loam rather than a heavy clay. Check that there are no weeds, pests, or diseases, nor an excessive amount of thatch (the organic matter consisting of decaying grass, stolons, and rhizomes that accumulates on the soil surface); there should, however, be enough organic matter to hold the sod together. If possible, purchase only sod that is certified free of weeds and other crop grasses.

Commercially grown sod

Commercially grown sod is widely available and contains different grasses for various uses. It is raised from the newest grass cultivars and treated to make it free from weeds and disease. Sod that is certified free of troublesome weeds is also available from better producers at a slightly higher price.

If you need a very large quantity of special sod and are prepared to wait 18 months for it to be grown and harvested, it may also be grown to order, but this is costly.

HOW TO ESTABLISH A LAWN USING SOD

1 Lay the first row of sod alongside a straight edge such as a patio or path. Place each new piece or roll exactly flush with its neighbor.

2 Place a plank on the first row of sod. Use this to kneel on. Then lay the next row with the sod joints staggered, as in a brick wall. Proceed in exactly the same way for the rest of the lawn.

3 Tamp down each sod with the back of a rake to make sure that there are no air pockets. Alternatively, roll the lawn with a light roller.

4 Apply a light topdressing of sieved, sandy soil and brush this in well, filling any gaps between the rows.

5 If no rain is forecast, water the sod well. Take care to keep it moist until it has rooted into the topsoil, or the pieces may shrink and gaps will appear.

Meadow sod

This is usually grown for agricultural purposes and therefore is less fine in texture; it may have been either sown recently or grown in a long-established field. It is usually the cheapest sod, because it may contain coarse, vigorous, agricultural grasses and broad-leaved weeds. The quality varies greatly, however, so it is especially important to buy meadow sod from a reputable supplier to ensure that it is of reasonable quality. If the weeds are eliminated by the use of selective weedkillers, the improved sod is described as treated meadow sod. Lawns established with meadow sod may have a coarse appearance and need more frequent mowing. Meadow sod is appropriate for use only where low quality is acceptable and minimal traffic is expected.

Fine-grass sod

Considered by many to be the finest sod available, fine-grass sod contains fine fescues (*Festuca*) and bents (*Agrostis*). It is used mainly for croquet lawns and golf putting greens and requires high maintenance. In the home landscape, it should be mowed frequently, or the lawn will turn brown upon mowing. Commercially grown sod with new cultivars is sold at larger sod farms.

Sod sizes

Sod is available in a range of sizes and shapes. High-quality sod is often sold in 1ft (30cm) squares and lower quality sod in lengths of 3 x 1ft (90 x 30cm).

Major producers also usually supply turf of all qualities in units of 1sq yd (1sq m).

Storing sod

Sod is best lifted and relaid in its new site within the same day. If there is an unavoidable, long delay, lay the sod flat on pavement or plastic sheeting, preferably in a slightly shaded area, and keep it watered; in hot weather, it may dry out very quickly, so check it regularly. If sod is left rolled up,

STORING SOD

Lay the sod as soon as possible; if it is essential to store it, spread the sections out flat—grass-side up—so that they receive enough light, and keep them watered.

it will not receive enough light, so the grass will turn yellow and eventually die.

Laying sod

Sod may be laid at almost any time of the year except during prolonged spells of extreme temperatures or when the ground is frozen. If possible, choose a time when rain is expected in the next day or two. Sod should be laid on moist, but not wet, soil to encourage rapid rooting. Provided the site is correctly prepared, sod is easy to lay. Expert contractors can do the job for you, if required.

Starting at the edge of the site, lay the first row of sod in a straight line. Standing on planks placed on the sod, rake the soil on which the next row is to be laid. Lay this next row so that the end of each sod piece or roll is staggered with adjacent pieces or rolls.

Do not finish a row with a small segment of sod beside the edge—it will be vulnerable to damage and drying out. If necessary, lay the last complete piece of sod at the edge, and fill the gap with the trimmed

segment. Lay further rows until the site is covered.

When all the sod has been laid, cut the edges to shape. For a curved edge, lay a hose or rope along the curve required, and cut just inside it. For a straight edge, mark the proposed lawn edge with taut string. Align a plank with this guideline and cut along it using a half-moon or powered edger. Move the plank along the guideline and repeat the procedure until the entire edge has been cut.

Aftercare

Either tamp down the sod with the back of a rake or roll the lawn with a light roller to ensure that there are no air pockets. In wet conditions, however, do not roll until the pieces have rooted and knitted together. Brush a light topdressing (see p.398) between the pieces to encourage the roots to spread.

Do not allow the sod to dry out before the grass has rooted through. It is essential to water the sod thoroughly so that it reaches the soil below, otherwise the pieces may shrink in dry or hot weather.

Moving sod

Sometimes it may be necessary to lift and re-lay an area of sod. It should be cut and lifted in uniformly sized pieces so that they fit together easily when they are re-laid.

Cutting

First, divide the sod to be lifted into lengths 12in (30cm) wide by cutting along the edge of a plank with a half-moon edger. Move the plank 12in (30cm) in from the previous cut to form each new length. Then cut each length at right angles to form pieces about 18in (45cm) long. Alternatively, a mechanical sod lifter may be rented; this cuts the sod to the size and depth required and also lifts it.

Lifting

Once cut, lift the sod with a flat spade, carefully severing them from the underlying soil and roots. As work begins, remove a wedge of sod next to the first piece to be

TRIMMING THE LAWN EDGE

Curved edge
Lay a hose or rope in the required shape and secure with wire. Standing on a board, cut just inside the hose.

Straight edge
Stretch a taut string along the required line and align a plank with this. Then, standing on the plank, cut along its edge.

LIFTING SOD FOR RELAYING

1 Cut the sod to be lifted into strips: insert 2 short stakes a little way apart, 12in (30cm) in from the sod edge, and lay a plank flush against them. Stand on the plank and cut along its edge.

2 Cut each strip into pieces about 18in (45cm) long, then undercut the sod to a depth of at least 1in (2.5cm). To stack them, lay grass to grass, soil to soil, on a path or piece of plastic sheeting.

lifted, then insert the spade under the sod without damaging the edge. Undercut each sod to a uniform depth of at least 1in (2.5cm). Stack the lifted sod grass to grass, soil to soil, on a hard surface, such as pavement or concrete.

Trimming

After the sod has been lifted, trim each piece to the same depth using a specially constructed shallow box the same size as the cut sod. Leave one of the shorter sides open and, if possible, cover the remaining top edges with a smooth metal strip. Place each piece of sod upside down in the box and, using a sharp blade, remove the excess soil by slicing along the top of the box.

ESTABLISHING A NONGRASS LAWN

To create a new lawn from broad-leaved species, such as chamomile (*Chamaemelum nobile*), prepare the site as for a grass lawn, including adding fertilizer to the soil. Plant pot-grown specimens, rooted cuttings, divisions, or seedlings at 6–12in (15–30cm) intervals.

They may be planted closer together or farther apart—the closer they are, the faster they will form a lawn and, of course, the greater the expense. Keep the site well watered during dry periods. Once the plants have covered the site, trim the lawn with a rotary mower, string

trimmer, or hand shears when necessary. If growing chamomile, it is best to use the nonflowering cultivar 'Treneague', which is naturally very low-growing. Flowering types may be grown from seed, but they require more frequent trimming and the dead flower heads may look unsightly.

1 Prepare the ground, adding grit or sharp sand, and clear all weeds. Divide chamomile plants into segments, ensuring that each has plenty of roots.

2 Chamomile has a fast-growing, creeping habit, so give plants space to spread. Lay them out about 4–6in (8–15cm) apart, plant, then firm in well.

3 Give plants a good watering, and water them regularly through the summer to keep them from drying out. Avoid walking on them for three months.

Seeding

Grass seed is best sown in warm, moist conditions so that it will germinate and establish quickly: early fall is usually the best time. Spring-sown grass can also be successful, but the soil is colder than in the fall and there is more competition from weeds. Seed may be sown in summer if irrigation is available, but in hot conditions young grass seedlings may suffer heat stress and wilt or even die.

Sowing rates

Grass sowing rates vary, depending on the mixture or species (see chart, below). Although there is some leeway to allow for factors, such as depletion caused by birds eating the seeds, it is important not to sow seed in much greater or smaller quantities than the recommended rate. Sowing too little seed may give weed seedlings space to compete with the grass, and the lawn will take slightly longer to establish. Sowing too much seed may cause more problems by producing humid conditions among the seedlings. This encourages damping off (see p.658), which can damage the young lawn in a very short time, particularly in warm, humid weather.

Sowing seed

Seed may be sown either by hand or, faster and more evenly, by a spreader. First calculate the amount of seed needed by multiplying the size of the area to be sown (in square yards or meters) by the recommended sowing rate (the amount of seed per square yard or meter). Before sowing the seed, shake the container to mix the seeds thoroughly and ensure that small seeds do not settle to the bottom, resulting in an uneven distribution of grass types.

Sowing with a spreader

This is the best way to sow grass seed over a large area. Measure out the correct amount of seed for the lawn and divide it in half. For even coverage, sow half of the seed in one direction and half at right angles to this. A well-defined lawn edge may be achieved by laying plastic sheeting or burlap at the site edge and running the spreader just over it; this also prevents the uneven distribution that may occur when stopping the spreader at the end of a strip.

Sowing by hand

If sowing by hand, first divide the area into small, equal-sized sections, using string and stakes or pegs; this makes it easier to sow the seed evenly. Then measure out the correct amount of seed for one section and accurately divide the batch of seed in half. Transfer one half-batch into a measuring cup, to make it easier and faster to measure out each subsequent amount. Work on one section at a time, scattering half of the seed of a batch in one direction, then sowing the other half at right angles to this before moving on to the next section.

Aftercare

After sowing, lightly rake over the surface. Rolling is recommended because it aids good seed-to-soil contact. Spread a natural product (such as grain straw) to help prevent

ESTABLISHING A LAWN BY SOWING SEED

1 If using a spreader, sow half the seed in one direction and half at right angles to this. For a defined edge, lay down plastic sheeting and push the spreader just over it at the end of each row.

Alternative step
If sowing by hand, mark the site into equal areas. Weigh out enough seed for a single area, then scatter it evenly, half in one direction and half at right angles to this.

2 After sowing, lightly rake over the surface. In dry conditions, water the site regularly to encourage the seeds to germinate.

3 The grass seedlings should take 7–14 days to emerge. Once it is about 3in (7.5cm) high, cut it to a height of 2in (5cm) with a rotary mower.

soil erosion and to keep soil from drying out. Unless rain is forecast, water the site with a sprinkler. Germination will occur in one to two weeks, depending on which grass species have been used, the soil and air temperature, and moisture. Protect the site from birds by covering it with netting or brushwood until the seedlings are established.

Water the site regularly in dry weather because young grasses are very susceptible to drought. Once the seedlings have emerged, the surface may be gently firmed with a light-weight roller (220lb/100kg), although this is not essential.

Cutting

When the grass has reached approximately 3in (7.5cm), cut it to a height of 2in (5cm). For the first two or three cuts, use a rotary mower, because a reel mower with a roller may tear the vulnerable young leaves. Then carefully rake up and remove all excess clippings. If the lawn was sown in late summer or early fall, continue to mow when necessary through late fall in order to maintain it at about 2in (5cm) tall. Young grasses are particularly vulnerable to damage by wear,

so try to use the lawn as little as possible during its first full growing season.

Hydromulching

Hydromulching may be considered as a method for establishing very large utility lawns. Grass seed is mixed with water, fertilizer, and fiber mulch, and then sprayed directly onto the seedbed. The mixture holds the seeds in place and helps retain moisture while protecting the seed from birds and other pests.

Hydromulching generally costs more than seeding, but less than sodding. Unlike seeding, however, the procedure can be used successfully during the summer. Apply hydromulch only on dry days and do not let the slurry come into contact with lawn furniture, bicycles, grills, and other objects that may be harmed by the chemicals it contains.

Because of the equipment involved, hydromulching is usually done by lawn care companies who will need easy access for machinery to the area involved. Kentucky bluegrass and perennial ryegrass are most frequently used but other species could be applied equally easily.

SOWING RATES

Mixtures	oz/sq yd	g/sq m
Fineleaf fescues and bents	$^5/_{16}$–$^1/_8$	10–15
Perennial ryegrass and other species	$^5/_8$–$^3/_4$	20–25
Tall fescue and Kentucky bluegrass	$^3/_4$–$^7/_8$	25–30
Single species		
Bents (*Agrostis*)	$^1/_{16}$–$^1/_8$	3–5
Bermudagrass (*Cynodon dactylon*)	$^1/_8$–$^1/_4$	5–8
Fineleaf fescues (*Festuca* spp.)	$^1/_2$–$^5/_8$	15–20
Perennial ryegrass (*Lolium perenne*)	$^3/_4$–1	25–35
Kentucky bluegrass (*Poa pratensis*)	$^1/_4$–$^1/_2$	8–15

Routine care

Once the lawn is well established, regular maintenance is needed to ensure its health and attractive appearance. The attention required depends on the lawn's size and type as well as the site and climate. In general, the most frequent tasks are mowing and watering, but annual maintenance may include fertilizing, topdressing, aerating, and, where necessary, controlling moss, weeds, pests, and diseases. For large lawns, using mechanical or powered tools, which may be rented, often makes maintenance tasks faster and easier (see "Lawncare tools," pp.558–559).

Mowing

In addition to making the lawn a pleasure to walk on, regularly cutting the grass helps create a dense, healthy lawn with an even, attractive finish. Mowing is needed in mid- to late spring and early fall for cool-season grasses, and late spring and summer for warm-season grasses. During drought conditions, however, it is best either not to mow at all or to set the mower to a higher cut. Delay mowing during very wet or frosty weather: wet grass can clog the mower or the mower may slip, and mowing in frost damages the grass. When using a power mower, always wear sturdy or steel-toe shoes with nonslip soles and heels, especially when mowing a slope. Use eye protection if mowing stony areas or near gravel driveways or paths.

Mowers
For most lawns, either a reel or a rotary mower will provide a suitable finish. A mower with a roller provides the finest finish for a formal lawn, but a rotary

Formal lawn
Cutting a lawn in overlapping runs produces a fine, finished effect.

mower alone perfectly acceptable surface for a utility lawn. A mulching mower leaves clippings on the lawn to nourish the grass, which promotes soil health and reduces the need to fertilize. The type of mower selected should depend on the size of the lawn and the finish required (see also "Lawnmowers," p.557).

Frequency and height of cut
The frequency of mowing and the height of cut depends on a number of factors, including the type of grasses grown, how the lawn is used, and the time of year, but little and often is a good general rule to follow. Try to remove no more than a third of the leaf growth at any one time. If the grass is cut sporadically and drastically, it will struggle to recover after each mowing and there will be a noticeable decline in the lawn's quality. For cool-season grasses, frequent mowing is necessary during the spring flush of growth. This tapers off with the arrival of summer, and it may not be necessary to mow at all for part of the summer. Growth begins again with cooler weather. In mild areas, an occasional mowing may be required in winter.

Formal lawns may be cut as low as ½in (1cm) but they should be mown frequently—every two or three days in active growth—to maintain their appearance. This practice is not recommended for home lawns, because the grass does not tolerate such a low cut; taller grass also stands up better to heavy wear and tear.

You can experiment with mowing some areas to different heights. Try two or three heights of cut for different grass areas to add texture and interest to the lawn. For practical reasons, cut the main area to be used for walking or playing to a height of about 2–3in (5–8cm). Keeping the grass at this length protects the surface against drying. Mow the areas under trees less

MOWING STRIPS

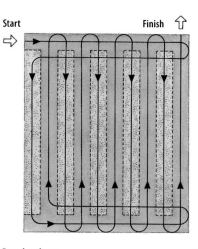

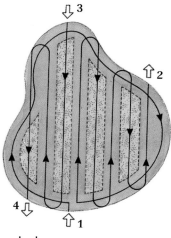

Regular shape
First mow a wide strip at each end of the lawn for turning space, then mow up and down the lawn in slightly overlapping runs.

Irregular shape
Mow a strip around the lawn edge, then mow a straight strip up the center. Mow up and down one half of the lawn, then the other half.

frequently—every two to three weeks in the summer—especially fineleaf fescues. Leave any areas of meadow at 6in (15cm) or more; they will need no more than three cuts per year and should not be cut until the flowering species have shed their seed in midsummer (see MEADOW AND PRAIRIE PLANTING, p.401). These areas are mown infrequently, so they produce much more growth and debris, which should be raked up and removed after mowing.

Mowing efficiently
Efficient mowing, especially with a riding mower, can save a great deal of time. If the lawn is square or rectangular, first mow a wide strip at either end of the lawn to provide turning space. Then mow up and down in straight strips, slightly overlapping the previous run to make sure that all the grass is mown.

If the lawn is of an irregular shape, first mow all around its edge. Then, starting at the center

of one end, mow a straight line down the middle by picking out an object or tree beyond the end of the lawn and pointing the mower directly toward it. Mow straight strips up and down one half of the lawn, then return to the center and mow the other half in a similar fashion.

Mowing sports fields
On areas that will be used for ball games, such as baseball, croquet, or for putting, vary the direction each time you mow to prevent a "grain" from developing. Grain is produced by grass growing in one direction and affects the run of the ball.

Grass clippings
On fine lawns where a high-quality finish is required, use a mower that collects grass clippings as it cuts or rake them up afterward and add them in layers to the compost heap. On most lawns, it's best to use a modern mulching mower, which cuts the clippings into small

FREQUENCY AND HEIGHT OF CUT

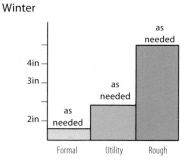

Winter

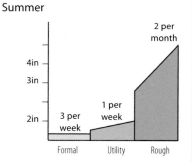

Spring/Fall — Summer

pieces and drops them in place. The clippings act as free fertilizer, benefiting the lawn. It also reduces the time spent on mowing chores. Grass clippings quickly break down, and they encourage the activity of earthworms, which returns plant nutrients to the soil. Another related way to recycle nutrients is by composting lawn clippings. Leaving clippings on the lawn or composting them is preferable to sending them to landfills, where their valuable organic matter is lost to the ecosystem for all practical purposes.

Removing fallen leaves

In fall and winter, clear away any fallen leaves from the lawn by raking them up, and save them for mulch or to compost. A layer of leaves on the lawn reduces evaporation, and the resulting humidity can encourage lawn diseases.

Trimming edges

After mowing, create a neat finish by trimming the lawn edges with long-handled edging shears, a mechanical edger, or a nylon-line trimmer with an adjustable head for edging (see "Lawn-care tools," pp.558–559). If the lawn edges become irregular, recut them once or twice a year with a half-moon edger, cutting against a plank for

a straight line; for very large lawns, it is faster and less laborious to use a power edger for this task.

Fertilizing

As with all plants, grasses require nutrients to grow; regular applications of fertilizer help ensure a vigorous, healthy lawn. Most of the nutrients that are essential for growth are plentiful within the soil, but four—nitrogen (N), phosphorus (P), potassium (K), and iron (Fe)— are often applied as a supplement. Nitrogen is the nutrient most commonly added, especially when grass clippings have been removed: it is needed for producing further growth that is stimulated by mowing. Nitrogen-deficient grass is generally yellow-green in appearance and lacking in vigor.

Applying screened compost or fertilizer is the easiest way to add nutrients to a lawn; both organic and synthetic fertilizers are available (see also "Soil nutrients and fertilizers," pp.624–625). The exact amount of fertilizer that is required depends on how quickly water drains from the soil, how much rainfall or irrigation is received, whether or not the grass clippings are removed, and on the types of grasses being grown. On

CLEARING LEAVES

Rake up
Remove any fallen leaves and debris by raking the lawn briskly with a spring-tined rake. For large lawns, use a leaf blower to help speed up the task.

heavy, clay soils that are rich in nutrients, and where rainfall or irrigation rates are low, only light fertilizing is necessary. Light, sandy soils that are well watered, however, need greater amounts of fertilizing because they lose nutrients quickly by leaching.

Types and constituents of fertilizer

Seek local recommendations, but in general for cool areas, apply a spring fertilizer as soon as the grass begins to green up. Fertilize again in late summer/early fall. Use screened compost or a packaged blended fertilizer recommended for lawns. Potassium should be applied in amounts equal to

50–100% of the nitrogen applied. Corn gluten meal is a natural nitrogen fertilizer that also suppresses weed seed germination; it's useful for fertilizing established lawns, but not new lawns.

In most of Canada, the late fall fertilizer should be one of the winterizing type. There are two forms of this, one low in nitrogen but high in potassium and phosphorous to help the lawn survive the winter. It is applied in late fall. The other is high in nitrogen and is applied just before freeze up to give the lawn a quick boost in early spring.

Where their use is not prohibited, weed-and-feed products are

CUTTING THE EDGE OF THE LAWN

Edging by machine
Periodically recut the lawn edge to retain the lawn's shape and create a well-defined finish. For large lawns, use a power edger: align the cutting blade along the desired new edge, and guide the machine forward.

Trimming the edge
After mowing, trim the grass overhanging the lawn edge with long-handled edging shears; or use a nylon-line trimmer that is adapted to work vertically.

Edging by hand
If recutting the edge manually, use a sharp half-moon edger, cutting along the line of a plank to achieve a straight edge.

LAWNS AND WATERING

As a consequence of changing climatic conditions, and the hotter summers and falls of recent years, acute water shortages and periods of drought are now commonplace. While gardeners value the esthetic appeal of a well-kept swath of lush lawn, it is important to use little or no water during drought periods simply to maintain green lawns.

During prolonged dry spells, grass will turn brown and appear to be dead. Most lawn grasses, however, simply become dormant under such conditions, and experience in recent years has shown that once some rain does fall, they quickly recover and become green again.

Thorough initial preparation of the lawn pays off during drought; it establishes strong-growing, deeply rooted sod. Annual maintenance is equally important: the grasses will withstand water shortages better than those on untended lawns.

It is, however, necessary to water newly planted lawns thoroughly in dry periods to maintain growth and color—provided there are no

watering restrictions in place. Start to water as soon as you notice that the grass does not spring back up after the lawn has been walked on—a state known as "footprinting."

The best time to water is either early morning or in the evening, to minimize evaporation. It is vital to give the lawn enough water; the soil should be moistened to a depth of 4–6in (10–15cm). Shallow watering encourages plant roots to remain near the surface, making the lawn more susceptible to drought. Dig a small hole to see if the soil is damp to the required depth, and note how long it took to water sufficiently. Alternatively, use a battery-powered moisture meter to register soil moisture levels.

On heavy soils where drainage is poor, do not apply too much water because this inhibits oxygen and mineral intake by the grass roots. If pools remain on the lawn for some time after heavy rain or watering, the lawn may need additional drainage (see "Improving drainage," p.623).

HOW TO APPLY FERTILIZER

Measure the correct amount of fertilizer for the area and divide it in half. Apply the first half in one direction, working up and down the lawn in adjoining but not overlapping runs. Apply the second half at right angles to this. Close off the supply when you turn the spreader at the end of each run.

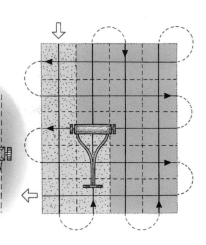

designed to help control broad-leaved weeds and fertilize the lawn all with one application. However, a weed-and-feed product will not eliminate all lawn weeds. You may find better success with long-term weed control by overseeding with desirable grasses, increasing mowing height, and watering deeply and infrequently to encourage strong, deep root growth.

How to apply fertilizer

It is important to apply fertilizer evenly to avoid variations in growth and the risk of damaging or even killing the grass. Any variation in the rate of application will generally be more than obvious within a week, and excessive applications may leave a bare patch behind. Although fertilizer may be spread manually, it is both easier and more accurate to apply it with a spreader.

Probably the simplest method of spreading fertilizer is to use a drop-type spreader. This is pushed up and down the lawn, as if mowing, but so that each pass is next to the previous one, without overlapping it. To ensure that coverage is even, it is best to divide the fertilizer into two batches and apply half in one direction; the rest is distributed at right angles to it.

UNEVEN DISTRIBUTION

Be careful to apply fertilizer evenly because uneven distribution may make the lawn patchy; it may damage or even kill areas of grass.

Alternatively, a cyclone or broadcast spreader may be used to apply the fertilizer over a larger area; the spread may be uneven, however. To reduce the risk of fertilizer being distributed unevenly, set the spreader to half the application rate and make adjacent runs at half the distance apart of its spread. For example, if the extent of spread is 6ft (2m), make the runs 3ft (1m) apart. After using either type of spreader, be certain to wash it out thoroughly because some fertilizers are corrosive and may, therefore, damage any metal parts.

Before applying fertilizer, calibrate the spreader to obtain the correct distribution rate. To calibrate a spreader, first find a dry, flat area of concrete or asphalt, and mark out a measured area of 4sq yd (4sq m), for example. Set the spreader to medium and fill it one-quarter full. Spread the fertilizer as evenly as possible over the marked area, as if over the lawn, then brush up all the fertilizer within the area and weigh it. Divide this weight by the area, in this case 4sq yd (4sq m), to give the application rate in ounces per square yard (grams per square meter). Adjust the spreader setting accordingly, and then check the application rate again over the same measured area. Continue this process until the rate is correct.

Annual maintenance

In addition to routine tasks such as mowing and watering, regular maintenance is required to keep a lawn healthy and to reduce the risk of serious pest or disease problems (see chart, below). A maintenance program should involve aeration (including thatch removal, or scarifying), fertilizing, and the control of weeds, moss, pests, and diseases (see "Lawn weeds," p.400, and "Pests and diseases," p.400).

It is also important for the continued good health of the lawn to topdress the grass as well as to rake it regularly to clear away leaves and other debris (see "Removing fallen leaves," opposite). Tasks that may be necessary at least once a year include recutting any edges that have become uneven or jagged and repairing any damaged or worn patches of grass by resodding or reseeding (see "Repairing lawn damage," p.399).

Winter, when the lawn is no longer in need of such regular attention, is the most convenient time to check all equipment carefully. Sharpen all cutting edges, oil tools where necessary, and send the mower for servicing, so that it will be in peak condition for the first cut of the new season.

Aerating and dethatching the sod

Aeration is key because it allows deep root growth and helps the sod become established as well as reducing soil compaction. It is also important to reduce excessive thatch, the organic matter consisting of decaying blades of grass, rhizomes, and stolons that accumulates on the soil surface. A certain amount of thatch—up to about ½in (1cm) deep—is beneficial; it reduces evaporation and helps protect the lawn from wear. In excess, however, it prevents water from reaching the soil beneath and may itself become saturated, interfering with drainage. The removal of thatch also encourages new grass growth and so promotes a healthy, vigorous lawn.

There are several ways to aerate the soil and remove thatch. These include scarifying, slitting, hollow tining (also known as coring), and spiking. It is preferable not to undertake these tasks in dry conditions, however, because they make the lawn more vulnerable to drought. Early spring is often the best time because the grass is

ANNUAL MAINTENANCE PROGRAM

Maintenance procedure	Early/ mid-spring	Mid-/late spring	Early/ midsummer	Mid-/late summer	Early/ mid-fall	Mid-/ late fall	Winter
Mowing	Roll before mowing if sod is lifted by frost	Mow weekly. Adjust mower to summer cut height	Mow 1–3 times a week as required	Mow 1–3 times a week (set mower higher in dry periods)	Raise height of cut as growth rate slows	Set mower to winter cut height	Lightly mow if there is new growth
Watering			May be needed in dry regions	Water as necessary	Water well in dry periods	Occasionally water if dry	
Fertilizing		Apply spring fertilizer			Apply fall/winter fertilizer		
Aerating and scarifying	Dethatch if necessary when dry enough	Lightly scarify			Spike or slice areas subject to heavy wear	Aerate lawn if not done in early fall	
Weed and moss control	Apply corn gluten to established lawns	Apply weedkiller if necessary		Apply weedkiller if not applied in early summer	Apply weedkiller if necessary		
Pest and disease control		Check for insects/ diseases, and treat as needed				Look for chinch bug; treat if found	
Other procedures	Recut edges if required. Carry out any restoration work	Reseed or re-sod any bare areas if necessary			Reseed or renovate cool-season grasses, if needed	Remove fallen leaves	Remove leaves. Service tools.

AERATING

Slicing
Slicing, which must be done with a special machine, allows air into the soil; push the machine back and forth across the lawn.

Hollow tining
Use a specially-designed tool, working methodically across the lawn to lift out cores of grass and soil ¼–¾ in (0.5–2cm) wide.

Spiking
For small lawns, spiking using a garden fork is adequate; insert the fork straight, then lean it back slightly to create a larger hole.

RENTING TOOLS

Good aeration is vital for the health of any lawn, and if your lawn has been neglected, it may be necessary to rent a large, powered lawn aerator. These can usually be fitted with either hollow corers or solid spikes and can complete the job efficiently in a fraction of the time it takes to do it manually.

It is also possible to rent a heavy-duty powered or riding mower if the grass is too long for your mower to cut well.

When renting any equipment, always check that it has been maintained properly before use.

growing rapidly and will recover quickly from these renovation procedures. Whichever the aeration technique, first mow the lawn to its normal topdressing height. After maintenance work, apply a low nitrogen fertilizer and avoid using the lawn for one to two weeks to encourage recovery.

SCARIFYING

By hand
Pull a spring-tined rake vigorously across the lawn to remove thatch and dead moss. Ensure that the tines of the rake reach well down into the soil surface.

Scarifying

This technique helps to remove thatch and permits air to enter the surface of the lawn. These processes are important because the soil organisms that naturally break down thatch require air to live. For small areas, scarifying may be done manually by vigorously raking the lawn with a wire or spring-tined rake. This is hard work, however, so it may be worth renting a mechanical or powered scarifier instead. To remove the maximum amount of thatch, scarify the lawn in two directions, one at 90° to the other. Do not scarify areas of moss because that may simply spread it to other parts of the lawn (see "Moss," p.400).

Slitting

For slitting, a special machine is used that penetrates the soil with flat, knifelike blades to a depth of 3–4in (8–10cm). The blades cut slits through the thatch, which allow air into the soil thereby encouraging a dense, healthy lawn.

Hollow tining or coring

This removes thatch, aerates the soil, and relieves soil compaction, all in one operation. A mechanical or hand tiner removes a core of grass, thatch, and soil, making a series of holes across the lawn, about 4in (10cm) apart. Leave the cores in place on the lawn surface. Once they have dried, they can be crushed by being raked or walked on, becoming a topdressing. Hollow tining may take longer to do than spiking and slitting because soil is removed rather than simply pushed sideways.

Spiking

This allows air into the soil, encouraging root growth; it can also relieve soil compaction. Use a mechanical or hand spiker, or, for small areas, a garden fork. Angle the spikes back slightly to raise the sod gently without breaking it up. This encourages deep root growth by creating fissures in the soil.

Topdressing

Where soils are shallow and the lawn is poor, it will be beneficial to topdress the lawn with sifted compost. Topdressing also helps break down thatch by keeping the lawn open and aerated, fills core holes, and helps level the surface. For most lawns, a ½in (1cm) layer of sifted compost is a valuable amendment that will go far in revitalizing the soil and grass. You may also need to apply specific soil amendments if the soil if low in nitrogen, potassium, calcium, or other nutrients.

Ensure that the topdressing does not smother the grass by pressing or brushing it into the surface and any core holes. This also helps level any slight surface irregularities of the lawn.

Rolling

Rolling is not essential, but if done in spring it may help resettle the surface after any maintenance work carried out the previous fall and correcting any possible disruption caused by frost. A roller should not be filled more than about a quarter full with water and should not be used at all on clay soils. The

TOPDRESSING

Medium-fine sand

Sieved soil

Peat-substitute

1 Prepare the topdressing by mixing medium-fine sand with topsoil and peat, or leaf mold. Pass the mixture through a ¼in (5mm) mesh sieve.

2 Measure the correct amount of topdressing for the lawn area and apply it on a dry day. For a large lawn, it is best to use a spreader.

Alternative step
For small areas, the topdressing may be applied by hand; spread it evenly over the lawn with a shovel or spade.

3 Use the back of a rake to work in the dressing. Keep a steady pressure to distribute it evenly, then water the lawn well.

traditional practice of rolling lawns frequently is unnecessary and could cause problems of compaction, particularly on heavy soils.

Renovating a neglected lawn

In some cases, a neglected, patchy lawn may be improved by renovation; if, however, it is dominated by weeds and moss, it may be preferable to remove the old grass and establish a new lawn. The best time to start renovation work is either early spring or late summer. Avoid midsummer, when the lawn is under heat stress.

A renovation program involves a series of procedures that restore the lawn to a good condition. First, in early spring, cut the grass to about 2in (5cm) with a rotary mower, and remove any clippings. Apply a high-nitrogen fertilizer such as 10–6–4 at about a quarter of the recommended rate. Repeat the fertilizer application every three to four weeks, except when the lawn is experiencing heat stress. Water thoroughly during drought. Once the daytime temperature is above 70°F (21°C) but below 86°F (30°C), apply a selective weedkiller. Reseed any remaining bare patches at least eight weeks before freeze up to give the new grass time to become established before winter arrives. At the beginning of fall, aerate the lawn (except any newly seeded areas) and apply a fall/winter fertilizer. A regular maintenance program should then be followed to keep the lawn in optimum condition (see *Annual maintenance program*, p.397).

Repairing lawn damage

If an area of the lawn becomes damaged or patchy, it may usually be repaired by removing the affected part, then sodding or seeding. It is important to use sod or seed that is the same type as the rest of the lawn so that it blends in well; if this is unknown, use a piece of sod from a less prominent part of the lawn to replace the damaged area. If the problem of lawn damage occurs repeatedly, it may be necessary to consider introducing a completely different and more durable surface, such as gravel or paving (see STRUCTURES AND SURFACES, pp.584–605).

Repairing a damaged edge
Edges that have been damaged in only one or two small areas may be repaired very simply. Using a half-

moon edger and a straight edge, such as a short plank of wood, mark a small section of sod that contains the damaged part. Slice under the section of sod with a sod float or spade, and push it toward the lawn edge until the damaged area is outside the lawn. Then trim off the damaged part to align the sod with the existing lawn edge. This leaves a gap within the lawn, which should be gently forked over and a granular or liquid fertilizer added. Then resod or add a little soil and reseed with an appropriate grass mixture. Ensure that the

repair will be flush with the rest of the lawn. Alternatively, lift the sod, then turn it around and replace it so that the damaged area is within the lawn. Repair the damage by sodding or seeding, taking care to ensure that any new sod is laid level with the surrounding lawn.

Repairing a damaged patch
If there is a damaged patch within the lawn, first carefully cut out and lift a piece of sod containing the damaged area. Fork over the soil underneath, then fertilize it, if

required, and lightly firm the soil. Lay a new piece of sod to fit the exposed space, raising or lowering the soil level beneath, if necessary, so that the new sod is level with the rest of the lawn, and tamp it down in position with the back of a rake or your hands. Topdress and water the repaired surface well.

Leveling a hump or hollow
Small humps or hollows within the lawn may be leveled easily. First, cut a cross through the sod that is growing over the

---

HOW TO REPAIR A DAMAGED EDGE

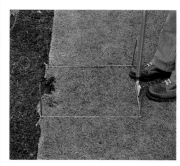

1 Using stakes and string, mark a small, straight-sided section of sod containing the damaged part; cut out the area with a half-moon edger.

2 Carefully undercut the sod with a spade, then slide it forward until the damaged part is beyond the lawn edge.

3 Align a plank with the lawn edge, then cut along it to trim off the damaged section so that the sod is level with the rest of the lawn edge.

4 Cut a new piece of sod to fit the resulting gap and ease it into the hole; if it is too large, trim it so that it is an exact fit.

5 Adjust the soil level beneath the new sod, if necessary, by adding or removing soil until the new piece sits level with the rest of the lawn.

ALTERNATIVE METHOD

1 Cut out a section containing the damaged part. Turn it so that the damaged piece faces the lawn and firm it into place.

6 Once the level is correct, tamp the new piece firmly into place with the back of a rake or a medium-weight roller.

7 Sprinkle some sandy topdressing over the repaired area, particularly into the cuts, and water thoroughly.

2 Add a little sandy soil, if necessary, so that the damaged part is level with the rest of the lawn, then sow grass seed over the damaged section, and water well.

HOW TO REPAIR A DAMAGED PATCH

1 Using a half-moon edger and the edge of a plank, cut around the damaged area, then undercut the sod with a spade and remove it.

2 Lightly fork or rake over the area of exposed soil to loosen it, and then apply sifted compost or a liquid or granular fertilizer if required.

3 Carefully tread over the soil to settle it and firm the surface before resodding.

4 Place a new piece of sod in the hole, cutting it to fit with a half-moon edger.

5 Check that the new sod is level with the rest of the lawn; if necessary adjust the soil level beneath the sod. Then firm in the sod and water well.

ALTERNATIVE METHOD

Reseed bare patches of lawn by forking over the area, raking in grass seed, and watering it in.

affected area and peel back the cut sod. To fill a hollow, fork over the soil beneath and fill in with topsoil, then lightly firm the ground. To level a hump, gradually remove the excess soil until the ground is level, and firm. Fold back the cut sod and tamp it down with the back of a rake before topdressing and watering the area.

On larger uneven areas, it may be necessary to remove complete sections of sod entirely, level the soil beneath (see "Leveling the site," pp.390–391), and then carefully re-lay the sod over the original but newly leveled area.

Lawn weeds

Although some weeds, such as slender speedwell (*Veronica filiformis*) and white clover (*Trifolium repens*), may look attractive in utility lawns, they are generally considered undesirable in formal, closely mown lawns, because they can be quite conspicuous.

Many broadleaved weeds can survive in grass that is mown, but excessive numbers can make the grass suffer so, even in a utility lawn, control may be needed. Unless the lawn clippings are collected, mowing may even spread weeds that can root from small pieces of stem.

On small lawns, dandelions and plantains (*Plantago*) may be cut out singly by hand, but for a large lawn, hand-weeding can be quite time-consuming. If you are permitted to use a weed and feed product, follow the manufacturer's instructions on the package.

Moss

Moss may be found in lawns for many reasons, including soil compaction, poor drainage, low fertility, insufficient light, mowing too closely, and extremes of soil pH. One simple option is simply to allow the moss to spread—it creates a soft, green surface that is a fine lawn alternative. If you wish to get rid of moss, try to identify and correct the possible causes; this may involve improving soil aeration, drainage, and fertility and, on light soils, topdressing to assist water retention. Adopting an annual maintenance program should help control the problem. For further details see PLANT PROBLEMS, "Lawn weeds," pp.648–649.

Pests and diseases

Several sod diseases, including brown patch (see "Drought," p.659), dollar spot, fairy rings, snow mold, and red thread attack lawns, particularly in hot, humid areas; snow mold is a problem in cold regions too and may even occur under snow. Preventive sprays may help, but in cooler temperate and maritime climates it is usual to spray only in serious cases.

There are several species of insects that live in the soil and feed on grass roots. These include white grubs (the larvae of June bugs and Japanese beetles), chinch bugs, and sod webworms. Moles and ants can also cause problems by excavating soil and forming hills.

LEVELING A HOLLOW OR HUMP

1 Cut a cross right through the hump or hollow in the sod, using a half-moon edger; the cross should reach just beyond the affected area.

2 Fold back the cut sections of sod, being careful not to pull them too harshly or they may crack.

3 For a hollow, fill in the ground beneath with a good, sandy topsoil; for a hump, remove some of the soil until the entire surface is level.

4 Replace the folded back sod and lightly firm to check that the level is correct. Adjust the soil level beneath, if necessary, firm, topdress, and water well.

Meadow and prairie planting

A wildflower meadow is an attractive and colorful feature that brings a breath of the country into the city or suburbs. It can be the ideal way of using a part of the garden that is difficult to cultivate conventionally, perhaps because it is too dry, slopes steeply, or has poor soil, and can play a part in the conservation of species that are threatened by the destruction of their natural habitats. A meadow also attracts seed-eating birds, mammals, and insects into the garden—many butterflies and beneficial insects rely on long grasses as food for their larval stages.

Types of meadow

Grassland plants occur in habitats ranging from cornfields and dry downlands to wetlands and woodland margins. When planning a meadow, consider soil type, moisture levels, light conditions, and shelter to determine the plants that will both thrive and look natural.

An open, sunny site with well-drained soil is ideal for ox-eye daisies (*Leucanthemum vulgare*), field scabiosa (*Knautia arvensis*), and lady's bedstraw (*Galium verum*). It also suits a cornfield area with annual poppies (*Papaver rhoeas*) and cornflowers (*Centaurea cyanus*), for which the soil must be cultivated each spring. In damp ground, plants such as meadow-sweet (*Filipendula ulmaria*), ragged robin (*Lychnis flos-cuculi*), and common spotted orchid (*Dactylorhiza fuchsii*) will flourish. Shady areas under trees are perfect for dog's tooth violets (*Erythronium dens-canis*) and Jack-in-the-pulpit (*Arisaema triphyllum*). A look at the local wild flora will show which species to grow, but never take plants or seeds from the wild. A huge range of wildflowers is offered by many nurseries as plugs and young plants.

Extending the season

Meadows generally peak in summer, but can be given a longer span of interest. Try introducing spring bulbs, such as crocus (especially *C. tommasinianus*, *C. vernus*, and *C. chrysanthus* cultivars), wild daffodils (*Narcissus pseudonarcissus* and *N. poeticus*), snake's-head fritillaries (*Fritillaria meleagris*), and tulips. Early summer bulbs include starry-flowered quamash (*Camassia quamash* and *C. leichtlinii*) and for fall, *Colchicum autumnale* and *Crocus speciosus* cultivars (see "Naturalizing bulbs," p.228).

Establishing meadows

Meadow flowers are adapted to soils of low fertility and thrive best among fine sod grasses, such as bents (*Agrostis*) and fescues (*Festuca*), that will not swamp them. Many ordinary grass seed mixes contain vigorous rye grass (*Lolium perenne*) that out-competes wild flowers, so choose a mix without it. Various meadow mixes are available for different sites and soils. Reduce soil fertility by avoiding fertilizers, mow regularly, and remove clippings. Stripping existing sod helps, but it is

Haven for insects
Many wild species bloom more profusely in the garden than in the wild, providing a rich food source for bees, butterflies, and larvae.

not advisable to remove topsoil unless it is very deep and fertile, because this may damage soil structure.

Sowing and planting

Sow a meadow in early fall, or in spring in cold areas or wet soils. Dig out all perennial weeds or smother them with a black plastic sheet mulch before sowing. Cultivate the soil to a fine tilth and water. Allow a flush of annual weeds to germinate and hoe them off, then firm the soil by treading or rolling. Sow seed at a rate of $^{1}/_{8}$oz/sq yd (4g/sq m) or as advised by the supplier.

If starting a meadow in existing grassland or orchard, reduce fertility over one or two years by mowing and removing the clippings weekly. Introduce pot- or plug-grown wildflowers in spring or fall.

Maintenance

During the first summer after seeding, spot-treat any undesirable plants, such as thistles or plantains, as they appear. If annuals were

included in the seed mix, they will bloom the first year, but the perennials will not bloom until the second summer. Mow the meadow in the fall, after plants have seeded, cutting to 3–4in (7–10cm). Rake up and remove the clippings so that soil fertility remains low. If permitted, you may decide to adopt a burnoff program to remove plant debris, but do this with great care.

PLANTS FOR MEADOWS

Asclepias tuberosa (butterfly weed)
Aster novae-angliae (New England aster)
Carex divulsa (Berkeley sedge)
Chelone glabra (turtlehead)
Daucus carota (Queen Anne's lace)
Echinacea purpurea (purple coneflower)
Eryngium spp. (sea hollies)
Eschscholzia californica (California poppy)
Eupatorium purpureum (Joe-Pye weed)
Gaillardia aristata (indian blanket)
Helianthus spp. (sunflowers)
Helictotrichon sempervirens (blue oatgrass)
Iris douglasiana (Douglas iris)
Liatris spp. (blazing star)
Lupinus texensis (bluebonnets)
Mondarda didyma (bee balm)
Nassella tenuissima (Mexican feather grass)
Papaver spp. (poppies)
Pennisetum spp. (fountain grass)
Penstemon spp. (penstemons)
Ratibida columnifera (prairie coneflower)
Rudbeckia varieties (coneflowers)
Salvia spp. (sages)
Schizachyrium scoparium (little bluestem)
Solidago spp. (goldenrod)

The wildflower meadow
At the height of summer a wildflower meadow has a profusion of blooming flowers, such as camomile, cornflowers, corncockles, and field poppies.

The wild prairie
A sweep of wildflowers, grasses, and herbaceous flowering plants light up prairie plantings with color and provide food and shelter for insects and other wildlife.

GROWING HERBS

WHETHER GROWN ON THEIR OWN AS AN ORNAMENTAL FEATURE, WITH OTHER PLANTS IN A BORDER, OR AMONG THE ORDERED RANKS OF A VEGETABLE PATCH, HERBS ARE AN INVALUABLE ADDITION TO ANY GARDEN.

They have always been prized for their culinary, cosmetic, or curative uses, but they also make decorative garden plants. Although few have spectacular flowers, many are graced by attractive foliage and almost all are worth growing for their scent alone—ranging from the citrus tang of lemon balm to the aniseed aroma of fennel and the sweet apple perfume of chamomile. Their fragrance is hard to resist and their nectar-filled flowers tempt bees and butterflies, so adding the drowsy hum of insects to complete the restfulness of an herb garden.

Designing with herbs

Herb growing combines the delights of the flower garden with the productivity of the vegetable plot. The results are decorative, excellent in aroma and flavor, and inexpensive to produce. By definition, an herb is any plant that has culinary or curative uses, and the range is surprisingly wide—including annuals, perennials, shrubs, and trees. Historically, herbs have been used for flavoring and preserving food, as well as for making medicines and toiletries. Their aesthetic appeal has always been important, and their ornamental qualities, as well as their practical uses, are of equal value today.

Mixed planting Herbs combine well with many other plants.

Herbs in the home

Although fresh and dried herbs are widely available in stores and supermarkets, they rarely have as fine an aroma or flavor as those harvested directly from your own garden. Enjoy their scents indoors as well as outside by using them fresh in flower arrangements or dried to make potpourri, or to fill herb pillows. All over the world, herbs are considered invaluable in cooking to enhance and enliven other foods, elevating even the simplest meal to the level of *haute cuisine*. The curative and cosmetic properties of herbs are also renowned: for thousands of years, they have been used in many natural medicines and beauty products.

Culinary uses

Freshly harvested herbs are an important ingredient in many classic combinations, such as tomato and basil salad, potato salad with chives, and May wine with sweet woodruff. In some cases, the flowers may be used as an edible decoration: borage, chives, elder, and pot marigold are all easy to grow, and produce attractive flowers. Stalks, such as angelica for crystallizing, or branches of rosemary or bay for barbecues, are also easily grown but are rarely available otherwise. Aromatic seeds and spices are easier to obtain but are simple, and mostly cheap, to produce.

Certain herbs, such as aromatic lemon balm, chamomile, and peppermint, may be infused in boiling water to make herbal teas,

which may be preferable to ordinary tea and coffee because they do not contain tannin or caffeine. Most herbal teas are made using dried leaves, flowers, or seeds, although they may also be made from fresh herbs.

Medicinal herbs

In many parts of the world herbal medicine is commonplace and the herb garden is a source of home-grown treatments for all sorts of ailments; mint, for example, is a mild local anesthetic, a powerful antiseptic, and a remedy for digestive problems. Herbal essential oils are used by aromatherapists in massage. Herbs are also processed into drugs by the pharmaceutical industry. In general, it is inadvisable to use herbs for medicinal purposes without expert knowledge.

Cosmetic and scented preparations

A number of herbs have beneficial effects on the condition of skin or hair, and are included in beauty products: rosemary, chamomile, and mint are used in shampoos and conditioners, thyme as an antiseptic for mouthwashes, and pot marigold and elderflower in skin lotions.

Aromatic herbs may be enjoyed all year round if they are made into scented household articles such as pomanders and linen sachets.

Herbs in the garden

The majority of herbs grown today are still the wild species, but many cultivars are also now available, differing in habit or in the color of their foliage or flowers. This diversity makes them more valuable as decorative garden plants, while their scent and other properties are usually similar to, if not identical with, that of the species.

The appeal of herbs lies largely in their fragrance, which in contrast to other plants usually derives from the foliage, rather than the flowers. Essential oils are released when the leaves are warmed or crushed, and on a sunny day, an herb garden can fill the air with pungent, sweet-smelling scents.

A few herbs have brightly colored flowers that may be used in garden planting plans to great advantage: the orange of pot marigolds (*Calendula officinalis*) offset by bronze fennel (*Foeniculum vulgare* 'Purpureum'), or the brilliant blue of borage (*Borago officinalis*) with silver-gray wormwood (*Artemisia absinthium*), for example.

Certain herbs are reputed to benefit other plants: some pungent plants, such as southernwood (*Artemisia abrotanum*), repel insects if crushed or infused, while growing chamomile (*Chamaemelum nobile*) in the garden reputedly increases the health and vigor of other plants nearby.

Where to grow herbs

As for other plants, herbs should be grown in conditions that are similar to their natural habitat to ensure that they are healthy and vigorous. Many herbs are

HERBS THAT TOLERATE MOIST SHADE

Angelica (*Angelica archangelica*)
Chervil (*Anthriscus cerefolium*)
Chives (*Allium schoenoprasum*)
Elder (*Sambucus nigra*,
  S. nigra 'Aurea',
  S. nigra 'Marginata')
Feverfew (*Tanacetum parthenium*,
  T. parthenium 'Aureum')
Lemon balm (*Melissa officinalis*,
  M. officinalis 'All Gold',
  M. officinalis 'Aurea')
Lovage (*Levisticum officinale*)
Mint (*Mentha*)
Parsley (*Petroselinum crispum*)
Sorrel (*Rumex acetosa*)
Sweet cicely (*Myrrhis odorata*)
Woodruff (*Galium odoratum*)

Mediterranean in origin, and these usually prefer plenty of sunshine and a free-draining soil.

Several herbs tolerate a damp, partially shaded site, provided they are not waterlogged or in dense or permanent shade. Most variegated and golden cultivars thrive in light shade. As a rule, gray-foliaged herbs do not tolerate high humidity. Pineapple mint (*Mentha suaveolens* 'Variegata') and golden forms of lemon balm (*Melissa officinalis*) and feverfew (*Tanacetum parthenium*) retain their color best when they are lit by morning or evening sun but shaded at midday.

Herbs can be grown in a wide variety of different situations. A separate herb garden in an attractive design provides an appealing feature and need not take up much space, but it may be preferable to have a culinary herb patch, or herbs in containers, within easy picking distance of the kitchen. Some herbs are decorative enough to be grown with other plants in a bed or border, while others may be better sited in the vegetable garden. Herbs intended for culinary or medicinal use should always be sited away from possible contamination by pets or roadside pollution.

Herb gardens

If there is space, it is worth creating a separate herb garden and growing a wide variety of different herbs together for a stronger impact and to enjoy their combined scents in one place. Making a special feature of the plants provides the opportunity to create a number of interesting patterns or designs using blocks of complementary or contrasting colors.

As well as being a more ornamental way of displaying the herbs, it also makes harvesting them easier. Traditionally, herb gardens have been bordered by low, clipped hedges of boxwood (*Buxus sempervirens*), but a less formal, equally attractive edging could be created by using hyssop (*Hyssopus officinalis*) or lavender (*Lavandula*).

Beds and borders

Herbs may also be grown with other ornamental garden plants. This is useful where there is no space for a separate herb garden, or for herbs that are border plants in their own right, such as bee balm (*Monarda didyma*) and rue (*Ruta graveolens*). Gray-leaved species are especially fine in a silver border or as a contrast to plants with blue, purple, or pink coloring, such as purple sage (*Salvia officinalis* 'Purpurascens').

Stately, architectural plants are valuable as focal points on their own or at the back of a border. Fill gaps in borders with colorful annuals, such as poppies (*Papaver*), blue borage, and dark opal-leaved sweet basil (*Ocimum basilicum* var. *purpurascens*).

Planting aromatic herbs next to doors, paths, and seats makes it easy to enjoy their scents. Low-growing, spreading herbs, such as wild thyme (*Thymus serpyllum*), lawn chamomile (*Chamaemelum nobile* 'Treneague'), and creeping savory (*Satureja spicigera*), are suitable for rock gardens or *en masse* to form a fragrant carpet. These and more upright herbs such as chives (*Allium schoenoprasum*) make an attractive edging to a border or path.

Dedicated herb garden Growing herbs together makes them easier to maintain and harvest, and can make an attractive feature in the yard if colorful cultivars are chosen. The pale lilac of the oregano flowers contrasts well against the acid yellow-green of the marjoram leaves and the darker green of the lavender leaves.

Herbs in vegetable gardens

For culinary herbs that are used in large quantities, such as parsley (*Petroselinum crispum*), the vegetable plot may be the best site. This may also be the most convenient place for fast-growing herbs, such as cilantro (*Coriandrum sativum*) and dill (*Anethum graveolens*), that are sown in succession and do not transplant successfully.

Growing herbs in containers

Many herbs thrive in containers. From a hanging basket to a strawberry jar, almost any container is suitable, provided that it has drainage holes. If not, add a layer of drainage material before planting in it.

In small gardens or on balconies, the entire herb garden may consist of containers, imaginatively positioned on walls, steps, shelves, windowsills, and at ground level. If space is at a premium, using a strawberry jar (a pot with small planting pockets in the sides) offers an attractive way of growing different plants together. Even if you have a separate herb area, it is convenient to have some commonly used herbs near the door.

Some of the best herbs to grow in containers are cilantro, parsley, chives, compact marjoram (*Origanum vulgare* 'Compactum'), rock hyssop (*Hyssopus officinalis* subsp. *aristatus*), and thyme (*Thymus*). Large plants, such as rosemary (*Rosmarinus officinalis*) and bay (*Laurus nobilis*), look best grown as single specimens in pots or tubs. Growing slightly tender herbs, such as myrtle (*Myrtus communis*), lemon verbena (*Aloysia citrodora*), and rose-scented geranium (*Pelargonium* 'Graveolens'), in containers is convenient because they may simply be brought inside during winter; they also make good conservatory plants.

Paving and patios

Planting herbs in the gaps between paving stones is an attractive option for those herbs that prefer well-drained conditions, such as

Patio containers Herbs that prefer well-drained soil grow well in containers, but should be watered regularly during summer to encourage new growth for frequent picking.

Planting in crevices Many creeping herbs release their scent when stepped upon, and they are robust enough to withstand the traffic. Plant them between paving stones.

thyme and creeping savory. Allow the plants to spread onto the paving stones, where an occasional light tread will crush the leaves and release the fragrant essential oils.

Patios are often ideal areas to display a variety of tender or Mediterranean herbs that enjoy warmth and shelter, while an exotic touch can be added by including tender plants, such as lemon trees (*Citrus limon*), cardamom (*Elettaria cardamomum*), or ginger (*Zingiber officinale*), grown in ornamental containers, and given winter protection.

Raised beds

Growing herbs in raised beds makes it easier to enjoy their fragrance at close quarters as well as being practical for the disabled or elderly, providing easy access for planting, maintenance, and harvesting. Raised beds must have strong retaining walls and should be no more than approximately 30in (75cm) wide and at a comfortable height for working (see also "Raised beds," p.599).

Raised beds are also a good option for growing herbs on paved areas against a wall and in any site where the soil is not free-draining. Choose small, compact herbs and control their spread by pruning and dividing.

Herb garden design

Whether informal or formal, an herb garden should be designed so that it is congruous with the style of the rest of the yard and the house. Take into account maintenance resources when planning: in general, informal herb gardens need less initial structural work than formal ones, and routine care may be less time-consuming. It is also possible to combine elements of both formal and informal designs; for example, a well-defined, symmetrical pattern of paths could form a framework for a free planting of herbs of different heights, habits, colors, and sizes.

Informal designs

An informal design depends upon the complementary habits and colors of the herbs for its success. Variegated and colored-leaved forms, such as golden marjoram (*Origanum vulgare* 'Aureum') and purple sage, are very attractive in such a plan. Try planting green- and gold-leaved plants together, or those that have purple and silver foliage.

There is greater freedom to use plants of different heights and habits than in a formal design: tall ones may be introduced to create a striking effect without upsetting the balance and impact of the design, and the overall impression of colorful harmony and rich abundance allows greater flexibility for experimenting with bold combinations.

Formal designs

These designs are usually based on geometric patterns and framed by low hedges or paths. Each small bed created by the pattern is then planted with one kind of herb, giving bold blocks of color and texture. At its simplest, the design may take the form of a cartwheel bedded into the soil with a different herb planted in each segment. These designs often look particularly impressive when viewed from above, so consider siting the herb garden where it may be overlooked from an upstairs window or a slope. When choosing plants, do not include tall, invasive, or sprawling herbs that may spoil the rest of the design when fully grown.

A formal garden with paths is labor-intensive at first but soon looks mature and needs little structural maintenance. Including dwarf hedges that require regular clipping may be much more demanding. The hedging may outline the design or form a more complex knot garden (see also "Formal Gardens," p.18). Good plants for dwarf hedges include boxwood, hyssop, lavenders, germander (*Teucrium*), and winter savory (*Satureja montana*) planted 9–12in (22–30cm) apart.

Making a plan

To draw up a plan, first measure the site and surrounding features accurately, taking any changes in grade into account. Also note where shadows fall in different seasons as well as at different times of day.

Whether the garden is to be formal or informal, remember that herbs should be within arm's reach for convenient harvesting; for beds or borders in open ground, provide access by paths or stepping stones so that the soil is not walked on, to prevent compaction.

Transfer the measurements to graph paper, working to scale; in order to compare a number of different designs more easily, draw each variation on a sheet of tracing paper laid over the master plan.

Finally, decide which herbs to grow, taking into account their cultivation requirements, habit, color, height, and spread, then mark them on the plan. Include herbs in attractive containers to provide focal points.

Directory of common herbs

Chives
(Allium schoenoprasum)

Herbaceous, clump-forming
perennial needing sun or semishade
and moist but well-drained, rich
soil. Good as a low edging for borders.
May be forced for winter use (see
p.411). Use the leaves, which have a mild
onion flavor, as a garnish and flavoring
in salads, dips, soft cheeses, and soups;
the edible flowers make a decorative
addition to salads.
Harvesting and storing Cut leaves
and flowers as available to use fresh.
For freezing and drying, cut leaves
before flowering occurs and chop finely.
Propagation By seed sown in spring (see p.196)
or by division in fall or spring (p.198).
Related species and variants Variations in
height, flower color, and flavor are available;
Chinese or garlic chives (A. tuberosum) have
a mild garlic flavor and white flowers.

Lemon verbena
(Aloysia citrodara)

Upright, deciduous shrub requiring
a sunny, well-drained soil. Plants
may be cut back by frost but grow
again from the base outdoors in
mild areas. The leaves have a
strong, lemon scent and
are used in herbal teas, desserts,
and potpourri.
Harvesting and storing Pick
leaves during the growing season
for using fresh or for drying.
Propagation By softwood cuttings
(see p.110).

Dill (Anethum graveolens)

Upright annual with feathery, blue-
green leaves. Grow in sunny, well-
drained, rich soil but not near
fennel—cross-pollination may result
in the loss of its distinctive flavor.
Runs to seed quickly. Use the leaves
or, for a stronger flavor, the aromatic
seeds in soups, sauces, potato salad,
pickles, and fish dishes.
Harvesting and storing Pick leaves in
spring and summer before flowering occurs.
Cut seed heads as they ripen in summer.
Propagation By seed sown in spring and early
summer (see p.214); may not transplant well.

Angelica (Angelica archangelica)

Biennial with large, divided leaves and large
flower heads. Grow this bold, architectural plant
in sun or shade and moist, rich soil. Unless seeds

are needed, remove seed
heads before ripening to
prevent self-sowing.
The young stalks may be
candied; the leaves are
used, especially in fruit
desserts and fish dishes.
Harvesting and storing Gather
fresh leaves in spring and summer.
Cut young stalks for crystallizing
either in spring or early summer. Cut
seed heads as they ripen in summer.
Propagation By seed sown in fall or
spring (see p.214).

Chervil (Anthriscus cerefolium)

Annual needing semishade and
moist, rich soil. Runs to seed quickly
in hot, dry conditions. The leaves
have a fine, subtle flavor that is
reminiscent of parsley and anise.
Use the leaves in egg dishes, salads,
soups, and sauces.
Harvesting and storing Gather
leaves before flowering occurs. Freeze or
dry them gently to preserve their delicate flavor.
Propagation By seed sown at monthly intervals
from spring to early fall (see p.214); do not
transplant. May also be sown in flats under
cover in early fall for winter use.

Horseradish
(Armoracia rusticana)

Perennial with persistent, stout,
white-fleshed roots, which have
a pungent flavor and are grated into
coleslaw, dips, and sauces, especially
in horseradish sauce. Young leaves are
used in salads or sandwiches. Needs
sun and moist but well-drained, rich soil.
Harvesting and storing Pick the young
leaves in spring. Harvest the roots in fall
when the flavor is best, or as required.
Propagation By 6in (15cm) root cuttings in winter
(see p.201) or by seed sown in spring (p.196).

Southernwood (Artemisia abrotanum)

Semievergreen subshrub with finely
divided, gray-green foliage. Good
for a low hedge or in mixed
borders. Grow in sunny, well-
drained, rich soil. Use the
aromatic leaves in potpourri
and as an insect repellent.
Harvesting and storing
During summer, pick leaves
as required for using fresh
or for drying.
Propagation By softwood
cuttings in summer, semiripe heel
cuttings in late summer (see p.112).

Wormwood (Artemisia absinthium)

Deciduous subshrub with deeply
divided, grayish-green leaves.
Good as a border plant or
informal hedge. Requires
sun and well-drained, neutral
to alkaline, rich soil. Prune to
within 6in (15cm) of the ground
in spring. The aromatic leaves are
intensely bitter; they were formerly
used to flavor alcoholic drinks
but are now regarded as toxic.
The foliage is attractive in herbal
decorations and bouquets.
Harvesting and storing Pick foliage
in the summer for use fresh or dried in
decorative arrangements.
Propagation By softwood cuttings in
summer (see p.110) or semiripe heel
cuttings in late summer (see p.112).
Variants 'Lambrook Silver' is a cultivar
with deeply divided, silver-gray foliage.

French tarragon
(Artemisia dracunculus)

Perennial with upright stems and
glossy, narrow leaves. Grow in
sun and well-drained, neutral to
alkaline, rich soil. In cold areas,
may need winter protection, but
may be forced for winter use. The
leaves are commonly used in
béarnaise sauce, tartar sauce, *fines
herbes*, in egg and chicken dishes,
and to flavor vinegar.
Harvesting and storing Cut sprigs of foliage
throughout the growing season, leaving two-
thirds of the stem to regrow. The leaves are
best frozen but may also be dried satisfactorily.
Propagation By division of rhizomes in spring
(see p.199). Seed is not available: that sold as
tarragon is the Russian subspecies.
Related species Russian tarragon
(A. dracunculus subsp. dracunculoides)
is hardier, but it has an inferior flavor.

Borage (Borago officinalis)

Upright annual that needs sunny,
reasonably drained soil. Add the
cucumber-flavored leaves, and
the flowers, to cold drinks
(such as lemonade) and
salads. Flowers can
be crystallized for use
in cake decoration.
Harvesting and storing Pick
young leaves and use fresh. Gather
the flowers (without calyces) during
summer to use fresh, freeze in
ice cubes, or crystallize.
Propagation By seed sown in spring
(see p.214). Self-sows in light soils.
Variants There is also a form with
white flowers, B. officinalis 'Alba'.

Pot marigold (Calendula officinalis)

Bushy annual with bright orange flowers. Grows in sun and well-drained, even poor soil. Deadhead to prolong flowering. Use the petals to flavor and color rice, soft cheese, and soups, and to garnish salads. Chop the young leaves into salads. Dried petals may be used to add color to potpourri.

Harvesting and storing Pick open flowers in summer and remove petals for drying. Gather leaves when young.

Propagation By seed sown in fall or spring (see p.214). Self-sows freely.

Variants Double-flowered forms in cream, yellow, orange, and bronze are widely available.

Caraway (Carum carvi)

Biennial needing sunny, well-drained, rich soil. Aromatic seeds are used in baking, cheeses, confectionery, and meat stews like goulash. Add the leaves to soups and salads.

Harvesting and storing Gather leaves when young. Collect the ripe seed heads in summer.

Propagation By seed sown in fall (see p.214).

Chamomile (Chamaemelum nobile)

Dense, creeping, evergreen perennial needing sunny, light, well-drained, sandy soil. Good at the edge of paths and borders, or between paving stones. May be planted as an ornamental lawn (see p.393). Use the apple-scented leaves in potpourri; the aromatic flowers are used in potpourri and herbal teas.

Harvesting and storing Pick leaves at any time as required. Gather flowers when fully open in summer and dry whole.

Propagation By division in spring or fall (see p.198), or by stem-tip cuttings of sideshoots in summer (p.200).

Variants 'Treneague' is a dwarf, nonflowering form that is particularly suitable for lawns and gaps in paving. *C. nobile* 'Flore Pleno' has attractive double flowers.

Cilantro (Coriandrum sativum)

Annual with divided foliage and small, white or pale mauve flowers. Grow in sun or semishade and well-drained, rich soil. The plants have a distinctive smell

and are not commonly grown indoors. The lobed, lower leaves (cilantro) are used in curries, chutneys, sauces, and salads. The seeds (coriander) are used in curry powder, baking, and sausages.

Harvesting and storing Pick young leaves for using fresh or for freezing. Gather seed heads as they ripen and use whole or ground.

Propagation By seed sown in spring or fall (see p.214).

Cumin (Cuminum cyminum)

Annual with white or pale pink flowers. Needs sunny, well-drained, rich soil, and heat for the seeds to ripen. The aromatic seeds are used in curries, pickles, yogurt, and Middle Eastern dishes.

Harvesting and storing Gather seed heads as they ripen.

Propagation By seed sown in late spring in a warm location or under cover (see p.215).

Fennel (Foeniculum vulgare)

Perennial with fine, filigree leaves and clusters of yellow flowers. Grow in sun and well-drained, rich soil. Use the leaves and leaf sheaths for their anise flavor in salads, and meat and fish dishes. Seeds are used in baking, fish dishes, and herbal teas.

Harvesting and storing Cut leaves and leaf sheaths when still young. Gather seed heads as they ripen.

Propagation By seed sown in spring (see p.196) or by division in fall (p.198).

Variants 'Purpureum' is an attractive bronze cultivar; Florence fennel (*F. vulgare* var. *dulce*) is grown as an annual for use as a vegetable (see p.540).

Woodruff (Galium odoratum)

Creeping perennial that has star-shaped, white flowers above whorls of narrow leaves in spring and early summer. An excellent groundcover plant in damp shade. The dried leaves are used in potpourri and herbal tea.

Harvesting and storing Gather the leaves for drying just before the flowers open in spring.

Propagation By division in fall or spring (see p.198) or by seed sown in early fall (p.196).

Hyssop (Hyssopus officinalis)

Semievergreen subshrub with spikes of small, dark purple-blue flowers. Needs sunny, well-drained to dry, neutral to alkaline soil. The aromatic leaves are used in soups, bean dishes, stews, game, and pâté.

Harvesting and storing Gather leaves any time for fresh use; pick young leaves in early summer to dry.

Propagation By seed (see pp.113–114), by division (see p.198) or by softwood cuttings in spring (p.110).

Orris (Iris germanica 'Florentina')

Perennial with off-white flowers and sword-shaped leaves that needs sunny, well-drained soil. Plant so that the rhizomes are partially exposed. The thick rhizome develops a violet scent after drying and prolonged storage. It is ground for using as a perfume fixative in potpourri and linen sachets.

Harvesting and storing In fall, dig up rhizomes at least three years old. Peel, split, and dry, leaving for up to two years before grinding.

Propagation By division of rhizomes in late spring or early fall (see p.199).

Bay (Laurus nobilis)

Evergreen tree or shrub needing sun or semishade and moist but well-drained soil. Makes an excellent topiary or container plant. Use the leaves for flavoring stock, and meat and fish dishes.

Harvesting and storing Pick leaves any time for using fresh. Dry mature leaves in summer.

Propagation By semiripe heel cuttings of sideshoots in late summer (see p.112) or by layering in summer (p.115).

Variants 'Aurea' has yellow-flushed leaves.

Lavender (Lavandula angustifolia)

Evergreen, bushy shrub with upright, mauve flower spikes. Grow in sunny, well-drained soil. Good for low hedging. The flowers are used in potpourri, linen sachets, herb pillows, and tea. They may also be crystallized or used to flavor oil or vinegar.

Harvesting and storing Gather flowering stems in summer, and air-dry.

Propagation By cuttings of semiripe nonflowering shoots in summer (p.111).

Related species There are several other species and many cultivars, varying in habit, foliage, flowering time, and flower color. They include dwarf cultivars, such as 'Hidcote', and white-flowered forms, for example 'Nana Alba'; French lavender (*L. stoechas*) has dark purple flowers crowned by conspicuous purple bracts.

Lovage (*Levisticum officinale*)

Perennial needing sun or semishade and deep, moist but well-drained soil. A tall plant, suitable for the back of a border. The leaves have a strong flavor, resembling celery and yeast, and are used in soups, stocks, and stews; add the fresh, young leaves to salads. The aromatic seeds are used in baking and vegetable dishes, and the young stalks can be crystallized. Blanch plants under pots in spring for use as a vegetable.
Harvesting and storing Pick young leaves in spring and freeze or dry. In spring, gather young stalks for crystallizing. Cut stalks after two to three weeks of blanching in spring, leaving central shoots to grow.
Propagation By seed sown as soon as ripe in late summer or fall (see p.196) or by division in spring or fall (p.198).

Lemon balm (*Melissa officinalis*)

Clump-forming perennial that needs sunny, moist but well-drained, poor soil. Add the lemon-scented leaves to cold drinks, sweet and savory dishes, or infuse them.
Harvesting and storing Pick leaves before flowering for using fresh or for drying.
Propagation By seed sown in spring (see p.196) or division in spring or fall (p.198). Self-seeds.
Variants Yellow-variegated cultivars, such as 'Aurea', are available; grow them in partial shade to avoid leaf scorch.

Mint (*Mentha spicata*)

Herbaceous perennial that may be invasive (see p.411). Grow in sun and poor, moist soil. Use the leaves to make mint sauce, in salads, drinks, and with potatoes or peas.
Harvesting and storing Pick leaves before flowering and dry or freeze, or chop and infuse in vinegar.
Propagation By stem tip cuttings in spring or summer (see p.200), by division in spring or fall (p.198), or by seed sown in spring (p.196).
Related species There are numerous species and cultivars with slightly differing foliage and scents. Some, such as pineapple mint (*M. suaveolens* 'Variegata'), have variegated leaves. Peppermint (*M.* x *piperita*) has purplish-green leaves used in peppermint tea and in syrups and desserts, while eau-de-cologne mint (*M.* x *piperita* f. *citrata*) has a fine

perfume. Bowles' mint (*M.* x *villosa* var. *alopecuroides*) has rounded leaves with a fresh, spearmint aroma and purplish-pink flowers.

Bee balm (*Monarda didyma*)

Herbaceous perennial with heads of red, claw-shaped florets in summer. An excellent border plant for sunny, rich, moist soil. Infuse the aromatic leaves in tea for an "Earl Gray" flavor, and add them to summer drinks, salads, pork dishes, or potpourri. Use the attractive florets to add color to salads and potpourri.
Harvesting and storing Pick leaves in spring or just before flowering occurs in summer for using fresh or drying. Gather flowers in summer, to dry.
Propagation By seed in spring (see p.196), by stem cuttings in summer (p.200), or by division in early spring (p.198).
Related species and variants Hybrids with red, pink, white, or purple flowers are available. *M. fistulosa* has lavender flowers and tolerates drier soil.

Sweet cicely (*Myrrhis odorata*)

Herbaceous perennial needing semishade and moist, rich soil. The fernlike leaves, which have an anise flavor, are used in fruit dishes or are added to salads. The thick taproot can be eaten raw or cooked as a vegetable. The large seeds are added to fruit dishes.
Harvesting and storing Pick leaves in spring and early summer for drying. Collect unripe seeds in summer and dry or pickle them. Dig up roots in fall for using fresh.
Propagation By seed sown outdoors in fall (see p.197) or by division in spring or fall (p.198). Self-sows readily.

Basil (*Ocimum basilicum*)

Annual with toothed, pointed oval leaves. In colder regions, basil must be grown under cover or in a sheltered, sunny site in light, well-drained to dry, rich soil. Grows well in pots on a sunny windowsill. The highly aromatic leaves are used in salads, vinegars, pesto, and tomato pasta dishes.
Harvesting and storing Pick leaves when young in summer and freeze, dry, or use to flavor herb oil or vinegar; or pack leaves in jars of oil.
Propagation By seed sown in spring (see p.215).
Related species and variants Var. *purpurascens* is an attractive, purple-leaved variety with pink flowers. The compact bush basil (*O. minimum*) is hardier but has less flavor. *O. basilicum* 'Green Ruffles' has crinkled, toothed, pale green foliage.

Marjoram (*Origanum vulgare*)

Herbaceous perennial that has tiny, white, pink, or mauve flowers in summer. Needs warmth an full sun for its flavor to develop. The aromatic leaves are used widely in cooking, especially in pasta sauces.
Harvesting and storing Pick leaves during the growing season; for drying or freezing, pick just before flowers open.
Propagation By seed in spring (see p.196), by division in spring or fall (p.198), or by basal stem cuttings in spring (p.200).
Variants There are various species and hybrids, differing in hardiness, flavor, and flower and foliage color, for example golden marjoram (*O. vulgare* 'Aureum'). The low-growing 'Compactum' is ideal for containers and edging.

Parsley (*Petroselinum crispum*)

Biennial with bright green, crinkled leaves. Grow in sun or semishade and well-drained, rich soil. Good for growing in pots. Use the leaves whole or chopped as a garnish and in *bouquet garni*, sauces, and egg and fish dishes.
Harvesting and storing Pick leaves from plants in their first year and use fresh or freeze.
Propagation By seed sown at intervals from early spring to late summer (see p.214).
Variants Italian parsley (*P. crispum* var. *neapolitanum*) is flat leaved, with a stronger flavor.

Anise (*Pimpinella anisum*)

Annual with deeply divided leaves and, in late summer, heads of tiny, white flowers. In colder regions, it must have a sunny, sheltered site in well-drained, sandy soil for the seed to ripen. Add the leaves to fruit salads. The aromatic seeds are used in baking, confectionery, and both sweet and savory dishes.
Harvesting and storing Pick lower leaves in spring for immediate use. Collect seed heads as they ripen in fall.
Propagation By seed sown in late spring in its final location, because it is difficult to transplant successfully (see p.215).

Rosemary (*Rosmarinus officinalis*)

Evergreen shrub with dense, needlelike leaves and pale blue flowers in spring and summer or, in mild regions, all year round. Grow in sunny, well-drained soil. May be grown as an informal hedge. The leaves, which have a strong,

resinous aroma, are used in meat dishes, especially with lamb, and to make potpourri and hair rinses. The flowers may be added to salads.
Harvesting and storing Pick leaves and flowers as required for immediate use. Gather sprigs for drying during the growing season.
Propagation By seed sown in spring (see pp.113–114) or by semiripe cuttings in summer (p.111).
Variants Cultivars with flowers in various shades of blue, pink, and white are available. The vigorous, erect cultivar 'Miss Jessopp's Upright' is suitable for hedging; 'Severn Sea' has bright blue flowers and a dwarf, arching habit that is ideal for containers.

Sorrel (*Rumex acetosa*)

Upright perennial that needs sun or semishade and moist soil. Prolong leaf production by removing flower spikes. Protect with cloches for a winter supply. The sour-tasting, young leaves are used in salads, soups, and sauces.
Harvesting and storing Pick young leaves before flowering occurs, for using fresh or freezing. May be frozen.
Propagation By division in either spring or fall (see p.198), or by seed sown in spring (p.196).
Related species The low-growing species, French, shield, or buckler-leaf sorrel (*R. scutatus*), has small, fine-flavored leaves.

Rue (*Ruta graveolens*)

Evergreen subshrub with divided, gray-green foliage and greenish-yellow flowers in summer. Thrives in a hot dry location. An excellent plant for borders or low hedges. Handling rue on sunny days may cause a skin rash. Use the pungent leaves with discretion in salads, sauces, and to flavor cream cheese.
Harvesting and storing Pick leaves as needed for immediate use, protecting hands with rubber gloves on sunny days.
Propagation By seed sown in spring (see pp.113–114), or by semiripe cuttings in summer (p.111).
Variants Some cultivars have cream-variegated and blue leaves, for example, 'Variegata' and the compact 'Jackman's Blue'.

Sage (*Salvia officinalis*)

Evergreen subshrub with gray-green foliage. Grow in sunny, well-drained, rich soil. An excellent plant for shrub borders and rose gardens. The aromatic leaves are used in stuffings, meat dishes, to flavor cheese, and in herbal teas.
Harvesting and storing Pick leaves as needed to use fresh. Gather leaves before the flowers open for drying.

Propagation By seed sown in spring (see pp.113–114), softwood cuttings in summer (p.110), or semiripe heel cuttings in early fall (p.111).
Variants Cultivars include purple sage (*S. officinalis* 'Purpurascens') with strongly flavored, purple leaves, and the less hardy 'Tricolor', with white-margined, pink-flushed leaves.

Lavender cotton (*Santolina chamaecyparissus*)

Evergreen subshrub with silver-gray leaves and, in summer, masses of yellow, button flower heads. Grow in sun and well-drained, poor to moderately fertile soil. Good as a low hedge, it also provides a contrasting color in knot gardens (see "Formal garden styles," p.18). Add the scented leaves to potpourri, and dry the flowers for decorative purposes.
Harvesting and storing Pick leaves for drying in spring and summer. In summer, gather flowers as they open for drying.
Propagation By cuttings of semiripe sideshoots in late summer (see p.111).

Winter savory (*Satureja montana*)

Evergreen subshrub with tiny, white to pink flowers in summer. Grow in sunny, well-drained soil. Use the aromatic leaves in bean and cheese dishes.
Harvesting and storing Pick any time for using fresh. Gather leaves to dry or freeze as flower buds form.
Propagation By seed sown in spring (see pp.113–114), by division in spring or fall (p.117), by softwood cuttings taken between late spring and early summer (p.110).
Related species Creeping savory (*S. spicigera*) is a low species ideal for containers, edging, and rock gardens. The annual summer savory (*S. hortensis*) has lilac flowers and a fine flavor.

Costmary (*Tanacetum balsamita*)

Perennial that requires semishade and well-drained soil. The leaves have a citrus-mint fragrance; they should be used sparingly in cooking, and may be added to potpourri.
Harvesting and storing Gather fresh leaves in spring and summer for using fresh or for drying.
Propagation By division (see p.198), seed (p.196), or basal cuttings (pp.200–201) in spring.
Variants Subsp. *balsametoides* is camphoraceous.

Feverfew (*Tanacetum parthenium*)

Semievergreen perennial with long-lasting, daisylike flowers in summer and fall. Grow in a sunny, well-drained soil in borders and containers. Use the pungent leaves in sachets to deter clothes moths. The aromatic flowers can be added to potpourri.
Harvesting and storing Pick leaves and flowers in summer for drying.
Propagation By seed sown in fall (see p.196), by division in spring or fall (p.198), or by basal stem cuttings in summer (pp.200–201). Self-sows freely.
Variants There are cultivars varying in height and foliage, with single or double flowers. Highly recommended is the golden-leaved 'Aureum'.

Thyme (*Thymus vulgaris*)

Evergreen, low-growing subshrub with tiny leaves and, in summer, pale lilac flowers. Grow in sunny, well-drained soil. May be grown as an edging for borders, between paving stones, and in containers. Add the aromatic leaves to *bouquet garni*, stuffings, sauces, soups, stocks, and meat dishes.
Harvesting and storing Pick leaves at any time to use fresh. Gather flowering tops for drying, stripping leaves and flowers from the stalks when very dry. Fresh sprigs may also be infused in oil or vinegar.
Propagation By seed (see pp.113–114) or division (p.117) in spring, by layering in spring or fall (p.115), or by semiripe heel cuttings in late spring or early summer (pp.110–111).
Related species and variants There are many species and cultivars, varying in height, foliage, and flower color. Wild thyme (*T. serpyllum*) is a low, mat-forming plant with mauve flowers; *T. serpyllum* 'Snowdrift' and *T. Coccineus* Group have, respectively, white and magenta flowers; and *T.* 'Doone Valley' has scented foliage with gold markings. *T. x citriodorus* has lemon-scented leaves and lilac flowers; *T. vulgaris* 'Silver Posie' produces silver-margined leaves.

Ginger (*Zingiber officinale*)

Deciduous perennial needing sun or semishade and well-drained soil. The thick, tuberous rhizome is highly aromatic and is used in baking, preserves, confectionery, chutneys, sauces, and many Asian dishes.
Harvesting and storing Dig up young rhizomes and peel them for using fresh or preserving in syrup. For drying, dig up the rhizomes as the leaves turn yellow.
Propagation By division of rhizomes as they start to sprout (see p.199).

Soil preparation and planting

The ideal site for an herb garden is sunny, open but sheltered, with neutral to alkaline soil, and good drainage. These conditions suit the majority of common herbs such as lavender (*Lavandula angustifolia*), winter savory (*Satureja montana*), sage (*Salvia officinalis*), marjoram (*Origanum vulgare*), rosemary (*Rosmarinus officinalis*), and thyme (*Thymus vulgaris*), most of which are Mediterranean in origin.

Preparing the site

If possible, prepare the ground well in advance, preferably in fall. First, remove all weeds, taking care to eliminate any persistent, perennial weeds such as couch grass (see PLANT PROBLEMS, "Perennial weeds," p.646). Then dig over the soil, leaving it in a rough state, to be broken down by frost.

In early spring, remove any weeds that have appeared subsequently, fork in well-rotted organic matter (such as garden or mushroom compost), and rake the soil to a fine, level tilth. The aim is to provide a free-draining and reasonably fertile soil. Feeding with manure or synthetic fertilizers is not recommended, especially for Mediterranean herbs, because it produces soft growth with little aroma or resistance to cold.

On heavy, clay soil, you may need to improve the drainage (see SOILS AND FERTILIZERS, "Improving drainage," p.623); alternatively, grow the herbs in raised beds or in containers. Most herbs tolerate a slightly acid soil; if the pH is below 6.5, however, add a dressing of lime when preparing the soil (see SOILS AND FERTILIZERS, "Liming," p.625).

PLANTING INVASIVE HERBS

If planting invasive herbs, such as mint (*Mentha*), tansy (*Tanacetum vulgare*), or woodruff (*Galium odoratum*, syn. *Asperula odorata*) in open ground, restrict their spread by growing them in sunken containers. Old buckets, large pots, or even heavy-duty plastic bags are suitable, although you must make drainage holes at the base. For best results, lift and divide the plants each spring and replant young, vigorous pieces in the containers using fresh potting soil; if not replenished, nutrients are quickly depleted and the herbs may deteriorate and become more prone to disease, such as rusts (see p.662).

1 Dig a hole large enough to accommodate a large pot or an old bucket. Make drainage holes in the pot base, then place it in the hole and fill with a soil and potting mix combination.

2 Plant the herb (here mint), firming in well; add enough potting mix to conceal the pot's rim, and water thoroughly. Each spring, replant and replace the potting mix in the container.

Herbs in winter

Although herbs are harvested mainly during spring and summer, the availability of many can be extended almost all year round.

Sown in late summer or early fall, a number of herbs such as chervil (*Anthriscus cerefolium*), cilantro (*Coriandrum sativum*), and parsley (*Petroselinum crispum*) continue to grow throughout the winter if they are protected from severe cold by a cold frame or cloches. They also grow well in pots placed on a sunny windowsill.

Herbaceous perennials that die down in winter, such as chives (*Allium schoenoprasum*), French tarragon (*Artemisia dracunculus*), and mint, can be forced for winter use. In early fall, dig up mature plants, divide them, and replant in containers of soil-based potting mix. If kept in a bright place that

is free from frost and drafts, they produce fresh shoots throughout the winter that may be harvested regularly. Discard forced plants in spring or plant them outside; if planted outside, do not pick their leaves for at least a season to allow them time to recover vigor.

Evergreen herbs, such as winter savory, thyme, and rosemary, may be gathered throughout the year, but limit winter harvesting to reduce stress on the plants.

Planting container-grown herbs

Container-grown herbs can be planted throughout the year, but the best time is in spring when they establish rapidly. If they have been kept in a heated greenhouse during the winter,

gradually harden them off (see p.218) in a cold frame before planting them.

Soak well before planting, because dry root balls are difficult to wet once below ground. To avoid trampling and compacting the soil in a bed while planting, it is best to stand on a plank while planting in order to work comfortably. Set out the herbs while still in their pots, according to your planting plan, and check that each has sufficient room to develop, depending on its growth rate and spread.

Whatever the weather, water thoroughly after planting in order to settle the soil around the plants and provide even moisture for new root growth. After planting, pinch out the tips of clump-forming herbs and trim back shrubby herbs to encourage new sideshoots and to develop a bushy habit.

HOW TO GROW HERBS FOR FRESH WINTER USE

1 Choose a dry day in early fall to lift a clump of herbs (here, chives) from the garden using a fork.

2 Divide the clump into smaller pieces with your hands or a hand fork. Shake loose as much of the soil from the roots as possible.

3 Plant up the divided pieces into pots or flats of potting mix; water well and cut back the top growth.

4 Place the plants in a light, frost-free place. Once they are about 4in (10cm) tall, harvest the leaves regularly to stimulate new growth.

PLANTING AN HERB GARDEN IN A DESIGN

Whether creating an intricate, formal design or a simple, informal one, careful planning, both on paper and on site, is essential for success. Make plans well in advance: start in the winter for planting in the spring, or as early as the preceding summer if you are raising the plants yourself.

As for all planting, thoroughly prepare the ground, clearing any weeds and raking the surface of the soil to a fine tilth (see "Preparing the site," p.411).

Once you have determined the design and the planting plan on paper, mark the basic outline of the herb garden, including any paths, on the prepared site. Make any adjustments to the layout at this stage, if required. It is most convenient to use container-grown herbs—they can easily be set out according to the plan and the arrangement checked before planting begins.

If using sod or heavy materials such as paving, bricks, or stone, lay them before planting, while paths made of lighter, loose materials, such as grit, gravel, or bark chips, may be laid before or after planting. When making paths of grit or gravel, provide retaining boards or edging tiles to prevent the material from spreading onto plants in the beds.

1 First prepare the soil for planting. Then, using string and stakes, or grit, mark the planned design for the herb garden, including any paths or paved areas, on the site.

2 Lay out the plants, still in their pots, to check the overall effect and spacing. If using grit or gravel for the paths, sink boards at the edges to keep the material in place.

3 Once the design is finalized, plant the herbs and water them; you may prefer to plant them densely to achieve the desired effect quickly.

4 Lay the paths, adding grit or gravel evenly in between the boards; level the surface.

5 Keep the herb garden watered and weeded. Pinch out growing tips to promote bushy growth and prune as necessary.

DESIGN FOR A HERB GARDEN

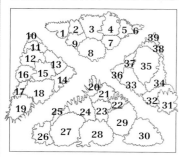

1 Chives (*Allium schoenoprasum*)
2 Compact marjoram (*Origanum vulgare* 'Compactum')
3 Bee balm (*Monarda didyma*)
4 Wormwood (*Artemisia absinthium*)
5 Hyssop (*Hyssopus officinalis*)
6 Wild thyme (*Thymus serpyllum*)
7 Silver-variegated thyme (*Thymus vulgaris* 'Silver Posie')
8 Marjoram (*Origanum vulgare*)
9 Pineapple mint (*Mentha suaveolens* 'Variegata')
10 Chamomile (*Chamaemelum nobile*)
11 French sorrel (*Rumex scutatus*)
12 French tarragon (*Artemisia dracunculus*)
13 Variegated sage (*Salvia officinalis* 'Icterina')
14 Parsley (*Petroselinum crispum*)
15 Sweet cicely (*Myrrhis odorata*)

16 Lavender cotton (*Santolina chamaecyparissus*)
17 Creeping savory (*Satureja spicigera*)
18 Golden lemon balm (*Melissa officinalis* 'Aurea')
19 Chinese chives (*Allium tuberosum*)
20 Orris (*Iris germanica* 'Florentina')
21 Borage (*Borago officinalis*)
22 Pink hyssop (*Hyssopus officinalis* f. *roseus*)
23 Purple sage (*Salvia officinalis* 'Purpurascens')
24 Pink lavender (*Lavandula angustifolia* 'Loddon Pink')
25 Thyme (*Thymus vulgaris*)
26 Opal basil (*Ocimum basilicum* var. *purpurascens*)
27 Rosemary (*Rosmarinus officinalis*)
28 Summer savory (*Satureja hortensis*)
29 Southernwood (*Artemisia abrotanum*)
30 Sweet marjoram (*Origanum majorana*)
31 Costmary (*Tanacetum balsamita*)
32 Golden feverfew (*Tanacetum parthenium* 'Aureum')
33 Chervil (*Anthriscus cerefolium*)
34 Pot marigold (*Calendula officinalis*)
35 Bronze fennel (*Foeniculum vulgare* 'Purpureum')
36 Woodruff (*Galium odoratum*)
37 Lavender cotton (*Santolina chamaecyparissus* 'Lemon Queen')
38 Sorrel (*Rumex acetosa*)
39 Lemon thyme (*Thymus.* 'Culinary Lemon')

This small garden includes a wide range of aromatic and culinary herbs; they have been grouped in beds by flower and foliage and divided by symmetrical paths for a traditional, formal effect, softened by the informal plant groupings within the beds.

Routine care

Most herbs flourish and require little attention once they are established. Maintenance largely consists of cutting back plants in spring and summer to encourage healthy growth, and tidying up dormant plants in winter. Herbs in containers usually need routine watering and feeding during the growing season, while periodic repotting or topdressing is also necessary. Growing herbs in the right conditions should minimize any pest or disease problems; take action as necessary (see PLANT PROBLEMS, pp.639–673) but you must wait one or two weeks after any chemical treatment before using the herbs.

Cutting back

Herbs that are valued for their fresh, young foliage can be cut back to produce a regular supply of leaves. Remove the flowering stems of sorrel (*Rumex acetosa*) as they appear; chives (*Allium schoenoprasum*) and marjoram (*Origanum vulgare*) can be left

until after flowering because the flowers are useful as flavorings; variegated forms of marjoram, mint (*Mentha*), and lemon balm (*Melissa officinalis*) fade, but produce bright new foliage if the plant is cut back hard shortly before flowering as its colors fade.

The growth of invasive herbs should be checked regularly: even when planted in sunken containers, they produce surface runners which must be removed before they spread too far. Remove any reverted, plain shoots from variegated herbs as soon as they appear.

Deadheading and pruning

Unless planning to save the seed, remove the dead flower heads from most herbs so that energy is channeled into growth. Deadheading annuals such as borage (*Borago officinalis*) lengthens the flowering season. Certain herbs such as angelica (*Angelica archangelica*) self-sow prolifically; these may become a nuisance if they are left to set seed.

Deadhead and prune shrubby herbs, such as lavender (*Lavandula*) and thyme (*Thymus*), by trimming lightly with shears after flowering. Hard pruning in spring encourages sideshoots and new growth from the base; thyme, however, is best pruned little and often during the growing season.

Mulching

Mulch only established herbs that thrive in moist soil, such as mint and bee balm (*Monarda didyma*). In summer, mulch after rain to retain moisture and to improve the soil as it breaks down. Use an inorganic mulch, such as grit, around Mediterranean or gray-leaved plants in heavy soil to reduce the risk of rotting.

Fall clearance

The extent to which herbs are cut back in fall partly depends on personal preference. In cold areas, leaving the dead foliage of herbaceous perennials until spring helps protect them against cold and wind. Remove any dead leaves that have fallen on thyme and other low-growing, evergreen herbs because they may encourage fungal attack.

Winter protection

In cold weather, tender herbs should either be brought under cover or otherwise protected (see FROST AND WIND PROTECTION, pp.612–613). In spring, cut them

PRUNING LAVENDER

1 In late summer or early fall, cut off all the dry flower stalks with pruners and lightly clip the shrubs to maintain a neat finish.

2 Early the following spring, cut back shoots by 1in (2.5cm) or more of the previous year's growth, making sure that some green growth remains.

PLANTING AN HERB POT

1 Choose a large pot with holes in the sides. Place screening over the holes in the base and fill the pot with soil-based or multipurpose potting mix and some grit to just below the holes.

2 Use compact herbs in the side holes; make sure the growth is protected, as shown, as they are inserted into the side holes.

3 Add potting mix to cover the roots and firm well. Level the surface and try different arrangements of herbs on top while still in their pots. Consider final heights and spreads before planting.

4 Water the herbs still in pots, and then plant in their final locations. Fill around the root balls with mix, ensuring stems and leaves are not buried, and firm in. Water the pot well.

back and plant them outside again, or propagate new plants from cuttings. The hardiness of a number of herbs, such as sage (*Salvia officinalis*) and lavender, depends on the species or variety; check this when buying.

Herbs in containers

Most herbs are easy to grow in containers and need little maintenance (see also CONTAINER GARDENING, p.328). In hot weather, check soil moisture daily and water thoroughly when dry. During the growing season, feed the herbs every two weeks with a weak liquid fertilizer.

In cold periods, bring herbs in containers under cover in good light. Frost-proof pots may be left outdoors, but bury them or insulate them well.

Repotting

Inspect herbs periodically to check that they are not becoming pot-bound. Also look out for such signs as rapid drying out, pale foliage, and weak new growth. Repot in the growing season to encourage new root growth.

If repotting is impractical, renew the top 1–2in (2.5–5cm) of potting mix, incorporating well-rotted organic matter or a slow-release fertilizer. It will not be necessary to feed the herbs for about a month.

Propagation

Herbs can be propagated by a wide variety of methods, depending on the type of plant and the quantity of new plants required. Sowing seed is a simple, inexpensive way to raise a large number of plants and is necessary for annuals and biennials, although it can also be used for other plant groups. Cuttings may be used to propagate various perennials as well as shrubs and trees, while division is suitable for a number of perennials, and layering is a good method for some shrubby herbs. For further information on propagating individual species and cultivars, see "Directory of common herbs," pp.407–410.

Raising new plants from seed

It is easy to collect seed from most herbs and to grow them from your own seed (see PRINCIPLES OF PROPAGATION, "Seeds," p.629); they can be sown in containers or, where large quantities are required, in drills in the open ground. Seed can also be sown direct into the cracks between paving stones where it would be difficult to insert plants. Prepare a fine seedbed for any seedlings that you intend to transplant outside from containers. Spring is generally the best time for sowing seed, although some annual herbs may also be sown in early fall.

Annuals and biennials

Hardy annuals such as borage (*Borago officinalis*) and pot marigolds (*Calendula officinalis*) can be sown in the spring or—to provide flowers late in the next spring—in fall. Sow biennial herbs, for example caraway (*Carum carvi*) and angelica (*Angelica archangelica*), outdoors in late summer or early fall for flowering the following summer. Thin out the seedlings twice: once after germination so that two or three remain at each location, and again after a few weeks so that only the strongest is left in place.

Short-lived herbs that are used regularly in large quantities, such as parsley (*Petroselinum crispum*), cilantro (*Coriandrum sativum*), and chervil (*Anthriscus cerefolium*), may be sown at intervals of three to four weeks from early spring to early fall. This provides a succession of foliage for harvesting throughout the year, although in some areas it may be necessary to provide protection from cold with cloches. Annual herbs of the Umbelliferae family—chervil and dill (*Anethum graveolens*) for example—are difficult to transplant successfully and are best sown directly in their final locations.

Basil (*Ocimum basilicum*) is one of the more difficult herbs to grow from seed unless kept warm and moist. In colder areas, sow basil seed very thinly indoors in flats in late spring, and keep at a minimum temperature of 70°F (21°C). Prick out seedlings once they are large enough to handle and keep them in a sunny, well-ventilated place. In cold, damp conditions, basil seedlings are prone to damping off (p.659) and gray mold/*Botrytis* (p.661). Plant out the seedlings once all danger of frost is past or grow them in containers under cover. In warm climates, basil may be sown outdoors (see ANNUALS AND BIENNIALS, "Sowing in open ground," p.215).

Perennials

If raising perennial herbs from seed, sow the seed in warmth in spring and grow the seedlings in pots until they are large enough to be hardened off and planted out. Plant and care for them as for container-grown herbs (see p.411).

Most cultivars of perennial herbs do not come true from seed and must be propagated by cuttings or layering; an exception to this is variegated rue (*Ruta graveolens* 'Variegata'). Nonflowering forms, such as lawn chamomile (*Chamaemelum nobile* 'Treneague'), cannot be raised from seed; propagate by cuttings or division to obtain new plants.

Mound layering

This method is particularly useful for propagating shrubs such as sage (*Salvia officinalis*), rosemary (*Rosmarinus officinalis*), lavender (*Lavandula*), and thyme (*Thymus*) that tend to become woody at the base or center with little or no new growth. In spring, mound free-draining soil over the base of the plant, leaving the top exposed. This stimulates new shoots to develop roots in a manner similar to stooling (see ORNAMENTAL SHRUBS, p.116). Leave the soil in place, replenishing it if it is washed away, until new roots have grown in late summer or fall. Then cut the shoots off from the parent plant and treat them as rooted cuttings.

SOWING BASIL SEED IN CONTAINERS

1 Tap seeds from a piece of paper onto firmed seed-starting mix. Just cover with more mix, and keep moist at a minimum temperature of 70°F (21°C).

2 Once the seedlings are large enough to handle, carefully lift them with a widger, holding them by the leaves not the stems.

3 Prick out the seedlings individually into cell packs or flats of firmed potting mix. Plant them out after danger of frost has passed, or grow them in pots under cover.

MOUND LAYERING SHRUBBY HERBS

1 To stimulate rooting, mound 3–5in (7–12cm) of sandy soil over the crown of the plant (here, thyme) so that just the tips of the shoots are visible.

2 Once the layered stems have established new roots, remove them with a knife or pruners. Pot the rooted layers individually or plant them out.

HERBS TO PROPAGATE BY MOUND LAYERING

Hyssop (*Hyssopus officinalis*)
Lavender (*Lavandula angustifolia*, *L. stoechas*)
Lavender cotton (*Santolina chamaecyparissus*, *S. pinnata*, *S. rosmarinifolia*)
Rosemary (*Rosmarinus officinalis* 'Prostratus')
Sage (*Salvia lavandulifolia*, *S. officinalis*)
Southernwood (*Artemisia abrotanum*)
Thyme (*Thymus cilicicus*, *T. x citriodorus* and cvs, *T. vulgaris* and woody cvs)
Winter savory (*Satureja montana*)
Wormwood (*Artemisia absinthium*)

Thymus vulgaris

Harvesting and preserving

The flavor of herbs can vary according to the growing conditions, the season, and the time of day. As the level of essential oils fluctuates with light and temperature, it is important to harvest herbs at the right time to ensure that the oil levels are at their peak. There are various methods of preserving herbs so that their scents and flavors may be enjoyed all year round. For advice on specific herbs, see the "Directory of common herbs," pp.407–410.

Harvesting

Herbs should be harvested on a warm, dry day after the dew has dried but before the plants are exposed to hot sunshine, which evaporates the essential oils. Always try to harvest herbs in a way that helps to maintain the plant's shape and vigor: choose straggly or invasive shoots, and with clump-forming herbs, such as chives (*Allium schoenoprasum*) and parsley (*Petroselinum crispum*), pick outer leaves to encourage new growth in the center. Only use foliage free from damage and insects.

Leaves and shoots may be picked at any time during the growing season but are at their best before the herb develops flowers. Evergreen herbs may be harvested lightly in winter. Always handle aromatic leaves gently as bruising releases the essential oils. Use or preserve herbs as soon as possible after harvesting.

Collecting flowers, seed, and roots

When harvesting flowers, pick them on a warm, dry day, when they are fully opened. Collect seed by cutting off whole seed heads in summer or early fall as they turn brown but before they are completely ripe and starting to shed. Lift roots at any time of year, but the flavor is best in fall.

Preserving

The main methods of preserving herbs are drying and freezing. In addition, a number are suitable for flavoring vinegars, oils, or jellies, while a few may be crystallized (candied) for decorating cakes and desserts. Store dried herbs in dark glass or ceramic containers—exposure to light will speed the deterioration of their aromas.

Air-drying

Do not wash herbs because this may encourage molds to develop. Dry herbs by hanging them upside down in a warm, dry place, away from direct light. Alternatively, place leaves, flower heads, or petals in a single layer on a rack covered with cheesecloth, netting, or paper towels. Leave them in a warm, dark, and well-ventilated place until crisp.

Microwave drying

Wash the herbs and pat them dry, then place them in a single layer on paper towels. Microwave them for two to three minutes, checking every 30 seconds and rearranging them if necessary to ensure even drying. Cool, then crumble and store as for air-dried herbs.

Drying seed heads

Cut seed heads in summer or early fall as they turn brown, then place them in a paper bag or hang them upside down and cover them with cheesecloth to hold the seeds as they fall. Keep them in a warm, dry place to ripen; when dry, remove the seeds and store them. Seed for sowing should be kept in a cool, dry, frost-free place.

Drying roots

Most roots are best used fresh, but some can be dried and ground. First wash them thoroughly, then peel, chop, or slice them, before spreading them out on absorbent paper. Dry them in a low oven at 122–40°F (50–60°C) until brittle, then crush or grind before storing.

Freeze-drying

Many soft-leaved herbs, such as parsley and basil, retain their color and flavor better when frozen than when dried. Simply pack whole sprigs into labeled plastic bags, and freeze them; they crumble easily for use once frozen.

For long-term storage, blanch them before freezing by dipping them first in boiling water, then in iced water. Pat dry and freeze.

Freezing in ice

Herbs may be frozen in water to form ice cubes; this is a good way of preserving borage flowers and mint leaves to use as a decorative addition to drinks, and the ice also protects the herbs from damage during storage. Herbs for cooking should be chopped before freezing—this is difficult to do once thawed. Place the ice cubes in a sieve and drain the water before use.

Making herb vinegars

Many herbs, such as thyme, French tarragon, oregano, and lavender, may have their flavors preserved by being steeped in vinegar.

To make flavored herb vinegars, lightly crush some fresh herbs and then loosely fill a clear glass jar with the crushed herbs. Do not use metal-lidded containers, because the acid vinegar will corrode the lid and taint the contents. Warm either wine or cider vinegar, pour it over the herbs, and seal the jar. Leave the jar in a sunny spot for two weeks, shaking or stirring daily. Strain and bottle, adding a fresh sprig of the herb for identification. For a stronger flavor, replace the herbs and leave the herb vinegar for a further two weeks.

Basil leaves can be preserved by packing in jars of oil; the leaves themselves may then be used in cooked dishes. For herb-flavored oils, follow instructions from a reputable source and store them properly for short periods only to avoid risk of botulism.

PRESERVING HERBS BY AIR-DRYING

1 Pick healthy, unblemished shoots or leaves (here, sage) on a dry morning, before the heat of the day releases the herb's essential oils.

2 Tie the shoots into bundles, then hang them upside down in a warm place; once dry, strip the leaves from the stalks and store them in dark glass jars.

FREEZING HERBS IN ICE CUBES

Freeze borage flowers and mint leaves singly in ice cube trays for adding to drinks. Chop fresh herbs such as parsley or chives and place in ice cube trays, adding about 1 tbsp of water to each 1 tbsp of herb.

DRYING SEED HEADS

Cover the seed heads with cheesecloth or a paper bag, secured in place with string or a rubber band, then hang them upside down in a warm place until dry.

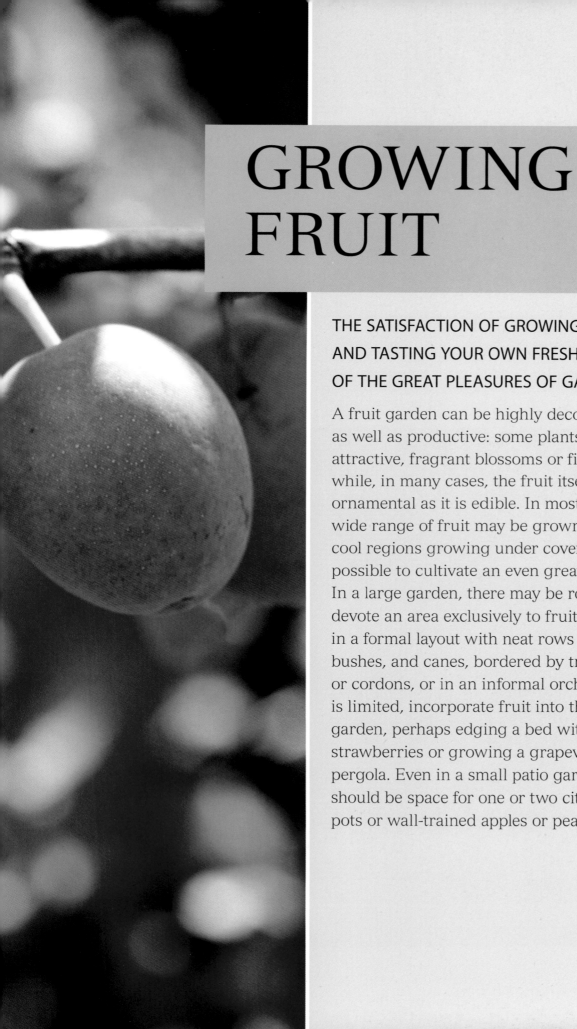

GROWING FRUIT

THE SATISFACTION OF GROWING, HARVESTING, AND TASTING YOUR OWN FRESH FRUIT IS ONE OF THE GREAT PLEASURES OF GARDENING.

A fruit garden can be highly decorative as well as productive: some plants have attractive, fragrant blossoms or fine foliage while, in many cases, the fruit itself is as ornamental as it is edible. In most areas, a wide range of fruit may be grown, while in cool regions growing under cover makes it possible to cultivate an even greater variety. In a large garden, there may be room to devote an area exclusively to fruit—whether in a formal layout with neat rows of trees, bushes, and canes, bordered by trained fans or cordons, or in an informal orchard. If space is limited, incorporate fruit into the rest of the garden, perhaps edging a bed with alpine strawberries or growing a grapevine over a pergola. Even in a small patio garden, there should be space for one or two citrus trees in pots or wall-trained apples or pears.

Planning the fruit garden

Fruit has traditionally held a prominent place in the garden, and today, with a wide range of cultivars and many dwarf fruit trees available ideal for the average garden, fruit growing is increasing in popularity. There are always some fruits that will thrive in the given climatic and growing conditions, although the majority prefer a good soil and a sunny situation. In hot-summer areas, a wide range of fruit may be cultivated outdoors. In mild-winter regions, seeking low-chill varieties of fruit that require a period of cold dormancy before flowering is important.

Common fig These trees thrive in dry, sunny sites.

Choosing fruit trees

Where only a few fruit plants are desired, the gardener may prefer to grow them within the ornamental garden rather than in a specialized home orchard; many fruit trees are suitable for growing as specimens in a lawn. Alternatively, if space is very limited, most fruits may be cultivated in containers, either freestanding or trained against a support such as a garden fence, or grown on a "family" tree (see p.420).

If planning to grow plants in large numbers, however, it is best to create a separate home orchard in the landscape; this makes it possible to grow fruit with similar requirements together, and to protect them against birds and frost damage. This is possible even in a small yard, as long as suitable rootstocks are chosen, and trees are carefully trained. If grown as espaliers, fans, or cordons around the edges of a yard, fruit trees may be both ornamental and a source of fresh-picked fruit.

Another consideration may be the type of blossoms you wish your trees to bear: some cultivars of many types of fruit produce flowers in particularly attractive colors and/or larger than usual sizes.

Thoughtful planning as well as careful selection of cultivars and methods of training make it possible to provide fresh fruit supplies over several months, and if there is some storage and freezing space available, the produce from a home orchard may be enjoyed all year round.

In cool areas, the range of fruits that may be grown is even wider if some protection under cover is available. Reliable crops of peaches, nectarines, figs, grapes, or more frost-tender fruits may be obtained by growing plants in a greenhouse, although ample room is needed for even a single tree. Careful selection of cold-tolerant varieties and the planting site are required to grow these crops outdoors in short-season areas.

The range of fruits

The different groups of fruit plants may be categorized according to their stature, their growth and fruiting habit, and their frost-hardiness.

Tree fruits include apples, peaches, and figs. The term embraces both pome fruits (those containing a core with small seeds, such as apples and pears) and stone fruits (those containing stones, such as cherries, peaches, and plums), as well as a few other fruits, including mulberries and persimmons. The term "vine" may also be used to describe woody, fruiting climbers, such as kiwi fruit and grapes.

The category soft fruits includes bush fruits, cane fruits, and strawberries, which are herbaceous. Bush fruits are naturally shrublike, forming a compact, bush shape, although they may also be trained into other forms. Black currants, red currants, white currants, gooseberries, and blueberries are the most commonly grown bush fruits. Plants described as cane fruits produce long, canelike shoots that bear the fruits; raspberries, blackberries, and hybrid berries, such as loganberries, are in this group. Most cane fruits develop their canes in one season and bear fruit on these the next, while producing new canes that will fruit in the following year.

Certain fruit-bearing plants cannot withstand frost and require warm, subtropical temperatures in which to develop and ripen fully; these may be categorized as tender fruits. Tender fruits include pomegranates, pineapples, tree tomatoes, prickly pears, and all kinds of citrus.

Apple espalier
Apples are ideal as espaliers, and this one, *Malus* 'Lord Lambourne', is trained by means of strong horizontal wires that are attached to sturdy upright supports.

TREE SHAPES

When selecting a tree shape, there are three main factors to consider: growth habit, space, and maintenance. An espalier, for example, is ideal for growing against a wall, particularly for apples, which develop naturally on short spur shoots. Several cordons will occupy the same space as a fan, and so might be better in a small garden. Multiple cordons may be grafted with more than one cultivar, giving you the opportunity to have one "arm" as a pollinator for the main cultivar. Free-growing forms, like open center or spindle, need pruning only once a year; more elaborate shapes, such as cordons and espaliers, require training and pruning more often.

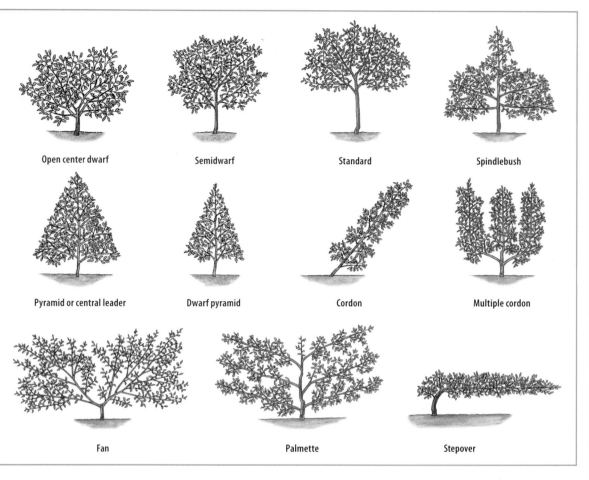

Open center dwarf   Semidwarf   Standard   Spindlebush

Pyramid or central leader   Dwarf pyramid   Cordon   Multiple cordon

Espalier   Fan   Palmette   Stepover

Some of these are also tree fruits, but have been grouped here with tender fruits because of their need for consistently warm temperatures.

Nuts include all plants that produce fruits with a hard outer shell around an edible kernel, for example, hazelnuts, almonds, and pecans.

Unrestricted and trained forms

Many fruit crops, particularly tree fruits, and to a lesser extent vines and some soft fruits, may be trained into a wide variety of shapes. When deciding which forms to grow, keep in mind the space available for the mature tree or bush, the relative ease of harvesting, and the degree of pruning and training needed to produce a plant that bears well. The choice of rootstock also determines their ultimate size (see "Rootstocks and tree size," p.423).

With the correct technique, trees and bush fruits may be trained almost as desired. The principle is to train young shoots into the required shape while they are still pliable; the branches then retain this form with regular, basic pruning.

Unrestricted tree forms

These forms develop, with limited pruning, in much the same way as a natural tree; they include the open center tree, standard, semidwarf, and spindlebush. The open

center and spindlebush are more compact than the standard and semidwarf, and are suitable for small yards.

An open center dwarf tree has a trunk up to 3ft (90cm) tall, with branches radiating out from the top third. It has an open center, allowing branches maximum light and space. Dwarf trees are small to medium-sized, that is, 5–12ft (1.5–4m).

The semidwarf is similar to the dwarf but the trunk measures 3–5ft (1–1.5m) and the overall height is 12–15ft (4–5m). The standard is similar in form, but with a trunk measuring 5–7ft (1.5–2.2m) and an overall height of 15ft (5m) or more.

The spindlebush is a small tree growing up to 7ft (2.2m) tall with branches that are trained to radiate out from the central leader at a wide angle. It has fewer branches than other lightly pruned forms, but each branch is pruned to be as productive as possible. The lowest branch is usually about 18in (45cm) from ground level.

Trained forms

Some fruit trees and bushes are suitable for growing in trained (or restricted) forms. These include cordons, fans, and espaliers. They need careful training initially, and are then maintained by regular summer pruning, to restrict vegetative growth, with a minimum of winter pruning. Most require support wires, either secured to freestanding posts or against a wall or fence. Wall-trained forms

are often favored in cool climates for fruit, such as peaches, because the fruit receive maximum sun and also benefit from the reflected heat of the wall. All the trained tree forms are ideal for small yards because they make it possible to cultivate a variety of fruits in a restricted space. Maiden trees that have been grafted onto dwarfing rootstocks are usually used for training restricted forms.

A cordon is restricted to a single stem, 5–6ft (1.5–2m) long, covered with fruiting spurs to produce a high yield in a small area. It is usually grown against a wall, or on posts and wires, and is planted at an angle of about 45°. It may also be grown vertically or horizontally. Most commonly

Training cherries
Cherry trees can be successfully trained, despite being very vigorous. Fix supports and wires in place before planting.

Family trees
In small gardens, a convenient way to grow a variety of fruit is to plant a family tree, in which two or more cultivars are grafted onto the same rootstock so the tree bears different fruit on different branches.

Home orchard
Growing fruit trees together can help with pollination and maintenance. Use the correct pruning techniques to keep them within bounds and with a good branching structure.

used for apples and pears, it is useful for red and white currants and gooseberries, too. Double (sometimes known as "U"), triple, or multiple cordons may be formed by pruning a maiden plant so that it becomes two or more parallel stems. Cordons that have more than a single stem are usually trained vertically. A variation on this is a stepover cordon, with the main stem trained horizontally. It is usually freestanding, supported on strong wires, and can be used to create an attractive, low edging to a bed.

A fan is trained with the main branches radiating in a fan shape from a short 10in (24cm) trunk and is suitable for tree fruits that are grown against walls and fences, especially peaches and cherries.

An espalier is trained with pairs of horizontal branches extending at regular intervals from a central stem. Each branch is covered with short, fruiting spurs. The number of pairs of branches depends on space and tree vigor. This method is particularly suitable for apples and pears grown against walls or fences. It is not suitable for stone fruits. A less rigid variation on the espalier is the palmette shape, in which staggered tiers of branches are angled slightly upward rather than horizontally.

Unlike the other trained forms, the pyramid is freestanding; its branches radiate from a central trunk, with an overall pyramidal form that is maintained by regular summer pruning to produce small to medium-sized trees. Dwarf pyramids are grown on a more dwarfing rootstock. Adventurous gardeners might want to try training apple and pear trees into forms such as arcure and goblet.

These shapes, among others such as espalier, are of French origin. For the arcure, leading shoots are trained left then right in alternate years, curving downward in an arc. The goblet has shoots trained horizontally from a predetermined height on the trunk. From these, further shoots are trained upward, to form the goblet. For all such shapes, wires and bamboo stakes are used to train the shoots into the desired shape. All surplus shoots should be removed in summer, once those needed are in place (see p.438).

"Family" trees

"Family" trees carry several cultivars—usually three—of the same fruit on a single tree. Such trees provide for a succession of fruit and are a very useful space-saving measure. Used originally by the Greeks and Romans, they were reintroduced during the 1950s and have remained a popular way to grow apples and pears.

When young, a tree is grafted with two other cultivars suitable for cross-pollination and of similar vigor. Good apple combinations include: 'Yellow Delicious', 'Early Summer Red', and 'Granny Smith'; 'McIntosh', 'Rome', and 'Lodi' or 'Red Delicious'; 'Dorset Golden', 'Anna', and 'Fuji'. For Asian pears try 'Shinseiki', 'Chojuro', and 'Hosui'. For peaches try 'Redhaven', 'Gleason Early Elberta', and 'Cresthaven'.

Trees are available on a variety of rootstocks, and it is important to select one that will suit your soil and grow to the tree size required (see pp.435 and 444).

Be aware that there are some family trees grafted with as many as five different cultivars onto the rootstock. You must pay close attention to the condition of all of the cultivars to make sure one does not overgrow and outcompete the others.

Integrating fruit into the garden plan

Fruits may be grown either in a separate area on their own or intermingled with other, ornamental plants; the choice depends on space, personal preference, and the range of fruit to be included. In either case, assess the impact that the fully grown fruit plants will have on the adjacent or surrounding plants. Planning and siting are particularly important because most fruit cultivars are long-term plants that require consistently good conditions to flourish and bear well over many years; in addition, with the exception of a few kinds, such as strawberries, it is seldom practical or worthwhile transplanting them to other locations.

The planned home orchard
Where a range of different fruits is required, it is well worth growing the plants together in a single area. When planning a home orchard, take into account the preferred growing conditions of each type of plant and recommended planting distances; for example, site tall fruit trees where they will cast the least shade on smaller bushes nearby. Also make sure that the space allocated for each plant is sufficient for it to develop to its mature size.

Plants that have similar cultivation requirements may be grouped together in order to simplify practical operations, such as applying fertilizer: for example, red currants and gooseberries need more potassium than other fruits. Grouping plants also makes it easier to protect them from birds (with a fruit cage) or wind damage (with a windbreak).

For an ornamental border, edge the orchard with a row of trained trees; cordons or dwarf pyramids are particularly suitable because they need a minimum of support and occupy comparatively little space.

In planning the location of fruit trees (particularly apples, pears, sweet cherries, and some plums), remember that a self-sterile cultivar should be sited near a cultivar with which it will cross-pollinate (see "Pollination requirements," p.424), or it will produce few, if any, fruit.

For many fruit plants there is a wide choice of cultivars that ripen at different times in the season; this makes it possible to plan for a succession of fruit that may be regularly harvested rather than a single glut. Some fruit, late-ripening apples and pears for example, may be stored for long periods of time, so if a steady supply is required, more space should be devoted to growing these than to earlier-ripening cultivars.

Fruit in the small yard

There are various ways to make the most of a limited area for fruit growing so that it provides a high yield and is an attractive feature. Whenever possible, choose trees that have been grafted on dwarfing rootstocks (see p.423) and use training methods that make the best use of the available space. For example, plant "family" trees (see opposite) or Ballerina cultivars (see p.435). Train trees and soft fruits such as red currants and gooseberries as cordons against the house or a boundary fence or wall, rather than as bushes, because cordons require less room for a comparable fruit yield than fans or espaliers. Grow grapevines over a sturdy pergola or ornamental arch. Cane fruit may also be trained in a variety of ways depending on the space available. Strawberries may be grown in vertical grow bags attached to a stake, fence, or other similar structure, or in a classic strawberry jar on the patio.

If there is room for only a single tree, then it is essential to choose a self-pollinating cultivar (see "Pollination compatibility," p.423). Select plants with a prolonged bearing season, unless there is ample storage and freezer space.

Berry fruits
Blueberries are a good crop for a small yard: they do not require much space. They grow best in acidic, humus-rich soil, fruiting freely on sideshoots produced the previous year.

Mixed planting

In a home landscape that is mainly ornamental or where there is insufficient space for a dedicated orchard, fruits may be planted among other plants. One or more fruit trees can make attractive specimens in the lawn, or grown in containers on a

PLAN FOR A LARGE HOME ORCHARD

A large plot, 35 x 56ft (11 x 17m), provides space for a range of fruit. Here, the chosen apple and pear cultivars will bear over a long period, and the soft fruit has been grouped for easier maintenance. The more tender peaches and grapes thrive in a lean-to greenhouse.

1 Apple 'Discovery' (on 'M26'/'Ottawa 3')
2 Apple 'Lodi' (on 'M26'/'Ottawa 3')
3 Apple 'Red Delicious' (on 'M26'/'Ottawa 3')
4 Apple 'Sunset' (on 'M26'/'Ottawa 3')
5 Apple 'Cox's Orange Pippin' (on 'M26'/'Ottawa 3')
6 Apple 'Golden Delicious' (on 'M26'/'Ottawa 3')
7 Plum 'Redcoat' (on 'Pixy')

8 Plum 'Victoria' (on 'Pixy')
9 Damson 'Prune' (on 'Pixy')
10 Pear 'Rescue' (on 'Quince A')
11 Pear 'Bartlett' (on 'Quince A')
12 Pear 'Doyenné du Comice' (on 'Quince C')
13 Pear 'Golden Spice' (on 'Quince A')
14 Black currant 'Boskoop Giant'
15 Black currant 'Ben Lomond'
16 Black currant 'Ben Sarek'
17 Red currant 'Red Lake'
18 Gooseberry 'Careless'

19 Gooseberry 'Leveller'
20 Raspberry 'Autumn Bliss'
21 Sour cherry 'Meteor'
22 Raspberry 'Royalty'
23 Loganberry (thornless)
24 Tayberry
25 Blackberry 'Lucretia'
26 Grape 'Black Hamburgh'
27 Peach 'Harbrite' (on 'St. Julien A')
28 Strawberry 'Tristar'
29 Sweet cherry 'Stella' (on 'Colt')
30 Fig 'Brown Turkey'

SMALL FRUIT GARDEN

This small, fenced area supports no fewer than 17 fruit cultivars, providing abundant crops from early summer to fall. The plot measures 12 x 28ft (4 x 9m) with a 6ft (2m) fence surrounding it; careful choice of cultivars and rootstocks coupled with correct training of the trees allows a wide range of fruit to be accommodated.

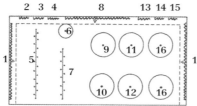

1 Sweet cherry 'Stella' (on 'Colt')
2 Pear 'Earlibrite' (on 'Quince C')
3 Pear 'Concorde' (on 'Quince C')
4 Pear 'Doyenné du Comice' (on 'Quince C')
5 Raspberry 'Marcy' (summer-fruiting)
6 Plum 'Victoria' (on 'Pixy')
7 Raspberry 'Autumn Bliss' (fall-fruiting)
8 Peach 'Redhaven' (on 'St. Julien A')
9 Gooseberry 'Careless'
10 Gooseberry 'Leveller'
11 White currant 'White Grape'
12 Red currant 'Red Lake'
13 Apple 'Lodi' (on 'M9')
14 Apple 'McIntosh' (on 'M9')
15 Apple 'Sunset' (on 'M9')
16 Black currant 'Ben Sarek'
17 Sour cherry 'Meteor' (on 'Colt')

sunny patio or deck. Fruit cordons or dwarf pyramids look nice when used as an ornamental divider, providing an unusual and productive screen, with attractive blooms in spring and ripening fruits from late summer to fall. Trained forms of bushes or trees may be grown on almost any type of garden structure such as a pergola, fence, or shed, provided that the exposure is suitable.

When fruits are planted along with ornamentals, make sure that all the plants' needs are compatible. If, for example, the fruits need protection from birds with netting, this may impede the growth of surrounding plants and look out of place.

Late summer bounty
Blackberries are extremely tolerant of most site and soil conditions, but thrive in full sun and enriched soil.

Particular care is also needed to ensure that any spreading crops such as blackberries don't overwhelm neighboring ornamental plantings.

Strawberries are often grown among other plants either in the vegetable garden or—a popular use for alpine strawberries—along the edge of a border or raised bed.

Choosing a site

A sunny, sheltered location, where the plants will produce fruit of good quality and flavor, is ideal. Sites with some light shade are also acceptable but provide fewer ripening hours, so are best used for soft fruit or early-ripening cultivars of apples, pears, and plums. Plants on a south-facing slope can produce crops earlier but, because they also flower earlier, they are more likely to suffer frost damage.

Growing against supports

Walls, fences, pergolas, and arches all provide ideal sites for growing trained trees, especially if they are exposed to maximum sun. These structures make good use of space in the garden and allow the fruit to develop and ripen well; fruit trained on supports is also easier to protect from birds and frost than fruit in the open yard.

The wall or fence must be high enough to accommodate the chosen fruit: 4ft (1.2m) would be enough for soft fruit, or apples or pears trained as cordons or espaliers, but a height and spread of 6ft (2m) or more are required for a fan-trained apple, pear, cherry, plum, or peach. Pergolas and arches are

likely to provide sufficient height, but ensure that there is enough space for the plants to spread as they mature. The structure must be sufficiently sturdy to be able to support heavy crops, even in strong winds.

Frost and wind

Avoid planting in frost-prone sites because flowers, unopened buds, and fruitlets are all susceptible to frost damage. The coldest air collects where the ground is lowest, and a frost pocket will form in a valley floor or at the foot of a slope, behind walls, hedges, or buildings.

Exposure to wind discourages pollinating insects and therefore greatly reduces the regularity of fruit production. Strong winds also cause considerable crop damage. Drafty sites, such as between two buildings, are not recommended, but a suitable, well-placed windbreak may be very effective in diverting or filtering wind to improve the conditions. Trees or large shrubs are preferable to solid barriers because they filter wind that would otherwise swirl over the barrier and damage plants on the other side (see also CLIMATE AND THE GARDEN, "How a windbreak works," p.609).

Growing fruit under cover

Crops native to warm climates, such as peaches, nectarines, and grapes, are ideal for greenhouse cultivation in cooler climates, but skill and attention to detail are required to maintain them in good condition and to obtain satisfactory yields. Greenhouse or cold frame protection can also be a very satisfactory means of growing temperate fruit, such as strawberries, because, with careful selection of early-fruiting cultivars, the season can be lengthened by several weeks in early summer. In areas with a short growing season that experience early fall frost, it also improves cropping of everbearing or late-fruiting cultivars.

If fruit is to be grown with other plants in the same greenhouse, ensure that the temperature, humidity, and ventilation requirements are compatible. It is important that the greenhouse has the maximum possible number of bottom and top vents to provide a free flow of air. As for planting in open ground, the soil needs to be fertile and well-drained for the plants to thrive.

A number of tender fruits, such as tamarillos (tree tomatoes) and pomegranates and even olives, may be grown successfully under cover; in temperate climates, they are often grown as ornamentals because they seldom bear heavily, even under cover.

Trained fruit

Compatible tree fruit and soft fruit that are suitable for training may also be grown in a greenhouse. Check that there is sufficient space for the chosen cultivar to develop and grow to its mature size, and ensure that suitable fittings for training the plant in the chosen form are in position before it is planted.

Fruit in pots

Strawberry plants that are grown in individual pots in a greenhouse or hoop house will produce ripe fruit earlier than those in the open, thereby prolonging the fruiting season if both cultivation methods are used. Tender fruit trees, such as citrus, may be grown in pots that are placed outdoors during summer and returned under cover for winter.

Deciding which plants to grow

Whether planning an entire fruit garden or choosing just two or three trees, it is vital to select plants that will thrive in the given soil and climatic conditions without growing too large for their allotted space.

It also makes sense to choose good-flavored, less commercial cultivars that are seldom readily available in the stores. More unusual fruits, such as red or white currants, are also worth considering, because they are often expensive to buy. If freezing soft fruit, such as strawberries or raspberries, is a priority, seek out cultivars that are suitable for the purpose.

Check the compatibility of different cultivars for pollination purposes before deciding which to grow (see "Pollination requirements," p.424). The final choice should also depend on the size of the crop required and the harvesting time.

Sheltered pear trees
Pears need more warmth and sunshine than apples to grow and bear fruit. They also flower earlier so are more susceptible to frost damage. Plant pears in a warm, sheltered location that is protected from frost.

Rootstocks and tree size

Tree size is determined largely by the rootstock onto which the tree has been grafted. Choose rootstocks that are of appropriate vigor for the planting area or training space available. Apple trees grown on dwarfing rootstock, such as 'M27', for example, are likely to suit most yards; their relatively small size makes picking, pruning, and spraying easier. If a large tree is required, select one that is grown on a more vigorous rootstock. For further details, see pp.424 and 435.

Pollination compatibility

Most cultivars of apples, pears, sweet cherries, and some plums are not satisfactorily self-pollinating, and therefore need to be planted close to one or more suitable cultivars of the same fruit that are in flower at about the same time, so that insects are able to cross-pollinate all the trees. For example, the apple cultivars 'State Fair', 'Delicious', and 'Wolf River' need to be planted together for all to be successfully cross-pollinated. (See under individual fruits for further details.) When planning a home orchard, be sure of the minimum number of trees required for pollination to occur and position compatible cultivars adjacent to each other to ensure satisfactory bearing.

Crop size and timing

Within the limits of space available, the amount of fruit that is required will determine the number of plants that should be obtained, remembering that crop levels inevitably vary from year to year. The amount of storage or freezer space available may govern the size of crop that can be handled. Try to balance the numbers of early-, mid-, and late-ripening cultivars

of each fruit cultivar grown in order to provide a consistent supply of fruit over a long period rather than a brief glut.

Early-ripening apples and pears do not keep well for more than a day or two, so do not grow more than can be consumed quickly: one or two cordons yielding 5–11lb (2–5kg) per tree should suffice. If you have plenty of storage space, plant several late-ripening cultivars, the fruit of which can be stored for several months. Plums are also liable to produce gluts and the fruit must be used quickly unless they are frozen or otherwise preserved.

When deciding whether to plant early- or late-ripening cultivars, remember to take climatic factors into account: for example, late-ripening apples or pears are not a good choice for a region with a short summer or if the proposed site is shady, because there will not be enough time or sun for the fruit to ripen fully.

Grape canopy
Taking care to promote healthy grape foliage is important to prevent ripening fruit from being scorched by the sun.

Site, soil preparation, and planting

Fruit-bearing plants require soil that is well-structured, adequately drained, and fertile. Before planting fruit, therefore, choose and prepare a suitable site so that it provides the necessary conditions.

Preparing the site

Prepare the site at least two months before planting. Remove all weeds, especially perennial ones, before any soil preparation takes place (see PLANT PROBLEMS, "Weeds and lawn weeds," pp.645–649).

Soil types

A loam soil is ideal and produces high yields of good-quality fruit. Clay soils may produce very good crops if drainage is good but are slow to warm up in spring; growth and therefore cropping may be later. On sandy soils, plants come into growth earlier because the soil warms up quickly in spring. Heat is lost equally rapidly, however, which creates a greater risk from frost and cold; sandy soil is also prone to drought. Sandy soils are usually less fertile than others, so the quality and flavor of fruit grown on these may be inferior to those produced on more fertile soil.

On alkaline soils, lime-induced chlorosis caused by manganese and iron deficiencies (see p.664) may be severe, causing the leaves of plants to turn yellow and adversely affecting the quality and yield of fruit. In extreme cases, it will prove impossible to grow certain fruits satisfactorily; pears and raspberries, in particular, suffer badly. The use of chelated iron alleviates the problem, but regular treatment may be necessary and is expensive. Annual mulches of manure and compost help by providing some of the trace elements required.

Improving the soil

For soft fruit, dig in generous amounts of well-rotted manure or garden compost and fertilizer to improve water retention and fertility. In preparation for planting tree fruits, fertilizers should not be used unless the soil is very poor and infertile, or else it may produce excessive soft growth rather than fruiting wood.

Drainage problems

Although poor drainage is more likely on heavy, clay soils, it may occur in many types of soil. Improve the soil structure where possible (see SOILS AND FERTILIZERS, "Soil structure and water content," p.620), and install a drainage system if necessary (see Installing Drains, p.623). Where drains cannot be installed, plant fruits in raised beds (see STRUCTURES AND SURFACES, "Raised beds," p.599).

Adjusting the pH level

Soil with a pH level of 6–6.5 is ideal for all fruits except blueberries, which need an acid soil of pH 4–5.5. Soils below about pH 5.8 will need liming (see p.625). If soil pH is more than 7, add composted sawdust or pine bark or powdered sulfur to reduce the pH in the short term.

Preparing the support for a trained fruit tree or bush

If a fruit tree or bush is to be trained against a solid support, such as a wall or fence, fix horizontal, parallel wires to the support with vine eyes and a tightener to keep the wires taut as the fruits develop. The vine eyes should hold the wires 4–6in (10–15cm) from the support to allow air to circulate around the branches and leaves of the plant. The spacing of the wires will vary, depending on the type of fruits grown. If using a freestanding post-and-wire support, secure the wires firmly to the posts. Just before planting, attach bamboo stakes to the wires at the appropriate angles, and tie in the young plants to begin the training process.

Buying plants

Always choose fruits that will thrive in the conditions in your garden. Check that the ultimate size of the plant or tree will fit the available space and that there is room to train it into the desired form. Pollination needs must also be considered before deciding which cultivars to buy.

Specialty fruit nurseries are often the best and most reliable source of supply. They offer a wide range of old and new cultivars and will also advise about suitable rootstocks. Wherever possible, buy fruits that are certified free from disease.

It is best to buy young plants, because they these become established quickly and may be shaped and trained to your own requirements. Plants are available bare-root or in containers. Container-grown plants are available all year round, but bare-root plants only in late fall and winter when the plants are dormant and may safely be lifted. Reject plants with a potbound root system—they seldom develop well.

BUYING FRUIT TREES

Bare-root tree

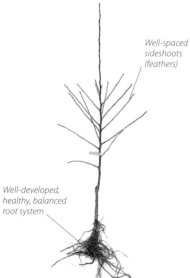

Well-spaced sideshoots (feathers)

Well-developed, healthy, balanced root system

Container-grown tree

Moist, weed-free soil mix

Vigorous, healthy roots that have not become congested and potbound

When buying bare-root plants, make sure the roots have not dried out and select plants with balanced main and fibrous roots.

Choose fruit trees that are healthy with sturdy growth and, if two or three years old, with well-spaced laterals. Inspect plants carefully and do not buy any with signs of pest infestation, damage, disease, or those that are lacking in vigor.

Pollination requirements

Most soft fruits and some tree fruits are self-pollinating, that is, they produce a crop without needing a pollinating cultivar nearby, and may therefore be grown singly. Apples, pears, most sweet cherries, and some plums are not reliably self-pollinating, however. To produce a successful crop, self-sterile cultivars need to be cross-pollinated by another cultivar of the same fruit. Usually, one pollinating cultivar is sufficient but some apples and pears must be grown close to two other

ROOTSTOCK

A graft union between rootstock and scion is identifiable by a noticeable kink in the stem 4–12in (10–30cm) above the soil mark, especially on young fruit trees that have only recently been propagated. When planting, make sure that the graft union is not below soil level.

cultivars for all trees to produce good crops. For cross-pollination to occur, the flowering periods must overlap. In most of North America, the blooming seasons are so short that all flowering periods overlap. In areas with longer seasons, cultivars are divided into several flowering groups, from early to late. Cultivars for cross-pollination should be in the same, preceding, or following group. Nursery staff, catalogs, and websites can provide information.

Certain cultivars of some fruits, however, will not cross-pollinate, although they may flower at the same time. Sweet cherry and pear cultivars are classified in incompatiblity groups, which are indicated in the plant lists. Seek advice, if in doubt. A few sweet cherry cultivars, known as universal pollinators, will pollinate all other cultivars in flower at the same time.

Selecting rootstocks

Many tree fruit cultivars offered for sale will have been grafted onto a compatible rootstock, because cultivars do not breed true from seed and cannot be raised consistently from cuttings. The rootstock controls the growth rate and size of the mature tree, while the scion determines the fruits produced. Some rootstocks have a dwarfing effect (useful for a small garden) and induce early fruiting. A few rootstocks are resistant to certain pests and diseases.

Selecting fruit trees

Young fruit trees may be purchased at several stages of growth—choose the one most appropriate for the form that the tree is to take. Maiden whip trees (with no sideshoots) take at least one year longer than others to train and fruit. One-year-old feathered maidens are popular with experienced growers because their sideshoots enable the earliest possible training. Two-year-old trees fruit more quickly, and good specimens are easily trained. Three-year-old, trained trees are more expensive and can be harder to reestablish.

Planting in open ground

Container-grown plants can be planted at any time except when the ground is frozen or waterlogged, or during drought. Plant bare-root plants in late fall (in mild-winter areas) or early spring, while they are dormant; soak the roots well before planting. In frosty periods, heel them in temporarily in moist, frost-free soil until conditions are suitable for planting.

Planting fruit trees

If planting a number of trees, measure the site and mark the planting locations with stakes. Dig a hole for each tree at least a third wider than the tree's root system; firm the base of the hole and slightly mound it.

Insert a stake into the hole about 3in (7cm) away from the center to allow for the tree's growth in girth as it matures. The height of the stake depends on the form into which the tree is to be trained (for details, see under individual fruit). Fruit trees on dwarfing rootstocks need permanent staking; remove the stake of those on other rootstocks after three years.

Place the tree in the hole, making sure that the soil mark on the stem is at ground level, and spread out

the roots. Do not cover the union between rootstock and scion: this encourages scion-rooting and the rootstock's influence will be lost.

Backfill in stages with soil, while another person holds the tree upright, shaking it gently from time to time so that the soil settles in between the roots. Firm the soil; when the hole is nearly full, break up the soil around the edges to obtain a uniform soil firmness over a greater area. Firm and level the area, and attach the tree to the stake using a soft, pliable, plastic tie with a firm cushion between tree and stake to prevent chafing. Protect the tree from rabbits and other animals with a sleeve of wire fencing.

Fruit trees to be planted against a wall or fence should be positioned 6–9in (15–22cm) away from the support, with the branches sloping gently inward. This ensures that the roots are in good soil and allows for future expansion of the trunk.

Planting soft fruits and vines

Bush and cane fruits are planted as for fruit trees, but no staking is needed. Plant only up to the soil mark: planting too deeply will inhibit the plants' growth. For vines, make the planting holes or trench wide enough for the roots to be fully extended, and train the vines against a support.

Planting in containers

Water the young plant thoroughly before planting. Use a moist, soil-based potting mix, leaving 1in (2.5cm) between the soil mix surface and the rim of the pot for watering. Water again after planting and keep the soil mix moist until growth begins, then water regularly.

PLANTING CORDONS

In the open ground
Space trees 2½ft (75cm) apart (top). Attach a stake at an angle of 45° to horizontal wires (bottom left) stretched between sturdy posts. Tie each tree securely to a stake (bottom right).

Against a fence
Fix wires 4–6in (10–15cm) away from the fence to allow trees to grow and to promote good air circulation. Plant the trees 6–9in (15–22cm) from the fence.

PLANTING A FRUIT BUSH

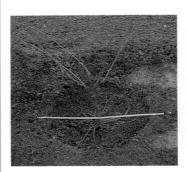 

1 Dig a hole large enough to accommodate the roots of the bush when spread out. Place a stake across the hole to check that the level of the surrounding soil is the same as the soil mark on the main stem.

2 Backfill the hole with soil; step on the soil gently to ensure that no air pockets remain between the roots. Rake over the soil lightly to level the surface.

PLANTING A FRUIT TREE

1 Dig a hole a third wider than the tree's root system. Drive in a stake to a depth of 18in (45cm) about 3in (7cm) from the center of the hole.

2 Slightly mound the soil at the base of the hole and place the tree in the center. Use a stake to check that the soil mark on the stem is level with the soil surface.

3 Spread out the tree's roots, then gradually fill the hole with soil. Firm to ensure that the tree is well anchored and that there are no air pockets between the roots.

4 Attach a buckle-and-spacer to the top of the stake and then to the tree so that the cushion is between the stem and the stake (see inset). Adjust as necessary.

Routine care

Most fruit plants need regular maintenance to ensure that they are healthy and produce high-quality crops. Routine operations vary, depending on the type of fruit, growing conditions, and season.

Fruit thinning

Fruit thinning is necessary for a number of tree fruits, particularly apples, pears, and plums, in order to provide good-sized, high-quality fruit. It also prevents branch breakages by ensuring balanced crop distribution. In addition, thinning helps to prevent biennial bearing (to which some fruit cultivars are prone), that is, bearing a heavy crop one year and little or none the next.

Thin by hand or with scissors, leaving the fruit room to develop fully and receive enough sun and air to ripen. Details of how and when to thin are given under each fruit.

Fertilizing, mulching, and watering

Apply manures and fertilizers when needed, observing performance of crops and checking for leaf discoloration that may denote nutrient deficiencies. In hot, dry summers, watering will usually be necessary; a drip hose (see p.561) uses water most efficiently, and a soil auger is vital for ascertaining the level of soil moisture at depth.

Care of tree fruit
In early spring, mulch newly planted trees and any that are not

FERTILIZING FRUIT TREES

Using string and a stake, mark a circular area around the tree, slightly beyond the spread of the branches. This indicates where fertilizer should be applied, that is, over the whole span of the tree's root system.

HOW TO THIN FRUIT

1 Thinning of some fruit is required to obtain fruit of a good size and quality; if it is left unthinned, the fruit is usually small and of poor flavor.

2 Remove unhealthy or disfigured fruit first, then reduce the remainder to at least 2–3in (5–8cm) apart, depending on the type of fruit.

thriving with manure or compost. At the same time check that any problem is not caused by a pest or disease; if it is, treat as recommended in PLANT PROBLEMS, pp.639–673. Once the trees reach flowering size, apply a balanced fertilizer at a rate of 3–4 oz/sq yd (105–140 g/sq m) in early spring. Do not overfeed, particularly with nitrogen, because this may produce soft, disease-prone growth.

If a particular nutrient is required, use a specific fertilizer that will supply the nutrient needed, whether it is nitrogen, potassium, or phosphorus. Apply these in spring at the rate recommended on the package directions, or according to soil test recommendations. Correct magnesium deficiency (p.663) by spraying the foliage, after flowering, with a solution of Epsom salts. In severe cases, repeat the treatment after three weeks. Other deficiencies, especially of manganese/iron (p.664), may also arise. If, more rarely, deficiencies of zinc, copper, or other elements are suspected, seek expert advice.

Apply fertilizers evenly over an area just beyond the branch spread. Where trees are grown in grass, mow regularly and leave the cuttings *in situ*; they rot down and return nutrients to the soil, helping to avert potassium deficiency.

Care of soft fruit
Mulch soft fruit regularly in spring with well-rotted manure. Use fertilizers as indicated for tree fruit; nitrogen and potassium are the most essential nutrients. Apply fertilizer over the whole area; in the case of raspberries, spread the dressing at least 2ft (60cm) on either side of the row; be careful to avoid the foliage. For strawberries, dig manure into the soil prior to planting.

Fruit in containers
Although potting mixes contain nutrients, plants should be fed in the growing season in order to replace the nutrients as they are used; nitrogen and potassium in particular are often needed. Fruit plants in containers require watering more frequently than those planted in open ground. Check regularly, at least once a day in hot, dry weather, and keep moist. Each winter, fruit trees and bushes

ORGANIC FERTILIZERS FOR FRUIT TREES

Fruit trees that are in good health and fruiting freely seldom need additional fertilizers. If growth is weak, apply topdressings of well-rotted organic manure or garden compost in spring. However, if these topdressings are not available, a number of organic fertilizers may be applied in spring or early summer.
- Blood meal and bone meal are good general fertilizers that will encourage growth.
- Alfalfa meal provides a steady source of nitrogen.
- Kelp meal—worked into the soil at planting—and diluted kelp extract, which is applied as a foliar spray, are both good sources of micronutrients.
- Pelleted chicken manure also has a high NPK content and is a useful amendment for poor soils.
- Organic garden wood ash will provide fruits with potassium (potash), which is important for fruit production.

Other useful fertilizers for fruit trees include:
- Bone meal and rock phosphate as amendments before planting.
- Ground or dolomitic limestone to raise soil pH if required.

in pots should be topdressed or repotted. To topdress, replace the top 1in (2.5cm) of soil mix with fresh mix. In alternate winters, where possible, repot the plant. Remove the plant from its container, and gently comb away some of the old soil mix from the root ball, using a hand fork or wooden stick. Cut out any coarse roots, being careful not to damage the fibrous roots, and repot into a larger, clean container (see also "Planting in containers," p.425).

Stakes and ties

The stakes and ties of both trained and freestanding fruit trees should be checked regularly. When the cushioning or ties are weak or worn out, the tree may rub against the stake, and *Nectria* canker (p.664) on apples, or bacterial canker (p.655) on stone fruits, may develop. Check the base of the stake: this can rot and then topple with the tree in high winds, particularly just before a heavy crop is to be gathered. On trained trees, ensure that all branches are not tied too tightly to stakes or wires because this will restrict growth. Loosen any ties if necessary.

Supporting branches
Tree fruits grown in unrestricted shapes may need to have their branches supported when the tree is heavily laden with fruit, even if the fruits have been correctly thinned. If only one or two branches are affected, support them on forked stakes or rope them to stronger branches. If several branches are overloaded, secure a sturdy stake either to the trunk or to the main stake and tie a rope

to each branch and to the top of the stake; this technique is known as "maypoling."

Protecting plants

Fruit trees and bushes may need to be protected from bad weather or frost with windbreaks or insulation. Protection against birds and animals may also be required.

Wind protection

Maintain windbreaks (see p.609) so that they remain effective, and prune natural barriers, such as trees or shrubs, if they become thin to encourage bushier growth. Check that posts supporting windbreak netting or fences are secure and repair them as necessary.

Frost protection

Most frost damage is caused by spring frost that kills or injures buds, flowers, or fruitlets overnight. Severe winter frost can cause bark splitting and dieback, but in areas where low temperatures are common, select cultivars that are bred to withstand the conditions. In subtropical regions, there should be few problems; if necessary, cover small trees and bushes with old bedsheets or large sheets of row cover.

A very slight frost seldom causes any serious damage: 28°F (-2°C) is frequently the danger point. The duration of the frost is usually more important than the temperature alone: 27°F (-3°C) for a quarter of an hour would cause little or no damage while, sustained over three hours, it could cause substantial losses.

If frost is forecast, protect strawberries, bushes, and even small trees by using fabric, burlap, or layers of newspaper to cover the plant completely and trap warm air around it. Remove the covers each day once the temperature has risen above freezing point, and replace when frost is again forecast. For further information, see FROST AND WIND PROTECTION, pp.612–613.

Protection from birds and squirrels

In winter, squirrels may damage fruit buds by feeding on the nutritious center of the buds. This damage is more serious than the loss of ripe fruit as it ruins whole branches, making it necessary to prune them back to obtain new shoots, which will not fruit for two or more seasons. The best protection from bird damage is to place nets over the trees or bushes. If snow is forecast, support the net

or remove it temporarily because the weight of the snow on the net may damage branches underneath. In rural and semi-rural areas, browsing deer may cause severe winter damage.

Ripening fruit should also be protected against birds; small areas may be temporarily covered with netting, but for large areas it is preferable to erect a fruit cage instead. It is impractical to protect large fruit trees, although those trained against supports may be enclosed by attaching netting to

the support. The mesh of any net used must be small enough to exclude tiny birds. Protect strawberries with a low, temporary cage.

Pest, disease, and weed control

It is advisable to check plants once a week for signs of pest and disease problems; they may then be treated at an early stage before extensive

damage has been caused (see PLANT PROBLEMS, pp.639–673). If virus diseases (p.672) are suspected, seek professional advice to ensure that this is the problem; strawberries, raspberries, loganberries, blackberries, and black currants are especially vulnerable. The only practical solution is to dig up infected specimens with their roots and discard them, otherwise the virus can spread to adjacent plants.

Weed control is also essential to produce the best fruit yields. Remove seedling weeds and mulch to inhibit germination of weed seeds. Perennial weeds should be dug out or spot-treated as soon as they are noticed. For further details, see "Weeds and lawn," pp.645–649.

Plants under cover

In much of Canada, some fruits may need to be grown under cover. These include all the tender fruits, and a number of other fruits that either have flowers that are vulnerable to damage by spring frost or requires a long ripening period, for example, peaches and many late-ripening grapes.

In mild winter areas, fruit trees are rarely grown under cover, because the only climatic problems encountered are exceptionally cool periods and heavy rainfall, which most are able to tolerate.

Plants that need to be under cover all year are best grown in greenhouses; walk-in polytunnels are of limited use because temperature levels and adequate ventilation are difficult to maintain (see also GREENHOUSES AND FRAMES, "Choosing a greenhouse," pp.568–571).

Particular care is needed in order to maintain free air circulation around plants that are grown in greenhouses to discourage diseases that may be caused by the increased heat and humidity. Support wires for trained fruit cultivars should be secured at least 12in (30cm) away from the glass or plastic of the greenhouse. Control any pests and diseases and apply fertilizer as recommended under individual tree fruit entries. For details of pruning fruit grown in a greenhouse, see "Pruning under cover," p.430.

Growing tender fruit (for example, citrus, papaya, guava, pomegranate, and olive) in containers makes it possible to bring them under cover when necessary. In cool areas, place tender plants grown in pots outside in a sunny location in spring and bring them under cover again in fall. Overwinter the plants in the greenhouse at a temperature of at least 50–59°F (10–15°C).

PROTECTING AGAINST BIRD AND ANIMAL DAMAGE

Bud-stripping
Animals or birds stripping buds from branches over winter cause permanent damage, leading to unproductive, bare wood.

Netting strawberries
Protect fruit by erecting a frame 4ft (1.2m) tall and draping and tying ¾in (2cm) mesh netting over it. Secure the base so that birds and squirrels cannot get underneath.

Fruit cage
Fruit bushes or small fruit trees may be protected by a cage constructed from metal supports covered with wire or plastic netting.

Protecting trained trees
Fruit trees trained against supporting wires may be protected with a ¾in (2cm) mesh net fixed at the top and secured firmly to the support.

Pruning and training

Fruit trees and bushes need correct, regular pruning and, in many cases, training to yield a good crop. The degree and method required depend on the desired shape and the fruiting time and habit as well as on the individual type of fruit. Relatively limited pruning is needed to produce an open-center bush tree, for example, while extensive, formative pruning and training are required for a fan or espalier to produce a symmetrical network of well-trained branches.

Aims of pruning and training

Initially, young trees and bushes should receive formative pruning and training to produce the desired shape (such as an open center) and to develop a strong, balanced framework. With established plants, the aim of subsequent pruning is to maintain the health and shape of the plant and ensure a good yield of fruit.

Pruning

This is the cutting out of unwanted shoots and branches, either because they spoil the plant's framework or because they are unproductive. Correct pruning maintains an open, uncrowded structure to allow the maximum amount of sun to reach the ripening fruits and to simplify spraying and harvesting. It also includes the removal of dead, diseased, damaged, or old, unfruitful wood.

On young plants, pruning may be combined with training to form a particular shape; unwanted shoots are removed completely, while those retained may be cut back to stimulate the growth of sideshoots. The established, bearing tree, bush, or plant is pruned to encourage optimal growth and fruit production.

Training

The selection and tying in of shoots to create a specific shape is called training. Forms close to the natural shape, such as the open center, require much less training than, for example, a fan, which is produced by precise selection, spacing, and tying in of individual shoots onto a supporting framework.

Over- and underpruning

Take care not to over- or underprune because this restricts fruitfulness and may encourage disease. Repeated, severe pruning results in increased, vigorous, vegetative growth, and little or no fruit, because few fruit buds are able to develop. This is especially damaging on a plant that is already vigorous. Underpruning leads to overcrowded branches that will receive less sun, which is essential to ripen the fruit; the branches may also rub together, exposing the tree to the risk of diseases, such as *Nectria* canker (p.664). Pruning a young tree too lightly may also cause early excessive fruit production that could stunt the tree and even break branches by overloading them.

When to prune

The time of pruning depends on the specific treatment and on the kind of fruit. In the pruning procedures described here and under the individual fruit, "year one" refers to the first 12 months after planting, "year two" to the following 12 months, and so on.

Winter pruning is standard practice on all untrained apple, pear, quince, and medlar trees, on grapevines, and on black, red, and white currants, gooseberries, and blueberries. Watersprouts, which take much energy from the tree and spoil its shape, should be cut flush to the branch from which they arise. Any diseased wood and borer-infested branches (see "Stem borers," p.671) should also be removed. Summer pruning is essential on trained types of tree fruits, grapevines, currants, and gooseberries. This reduces their vigor and contains them within the restricted space that they occupy; it also concentrates the plants' energies on fruit production. Many of the tender fruits need to be pruned directly after fruiting.

How to prune

When deciding on the extent of pruning, always take into account the vigor both of the individual shoot and of the whole tree. Vigorous growth should be pruned lightly; this usually involves thinning out a percentage of shoots completely and leaving the remainder unpruned. Prune weak growth more severely, but check first that no disease, such as canker, is causing the weakness.

Where to cut

It is important always to prune to just above a healthy bud and to make a clean cut; cutting midway between buds or leaving a ragged

INCORRECT PRUNING

Underpruning
A tree that is pruned irregularly or very lightly will develop overcrowded shoots that will not receive enough light to ripen the fruits, which may be small. The branches may also rub together, increasing the risk of certain diseases.

Overpruning
If a fruit tree is pruned excessively, this will stimulate a mass of vigorous, vegetative shoots. These shoots will produce few, if any, fruit buds, so the crop will be poor.

WHERE TO MAKE A PRUNING CUT

Cutting to a bud
Cut just above a bud at a 45° angle, sloping the cut away from the bud. Do not cut too close or the bud may be damaged, nor too far away, or the stem may die back.

Cutting to a replacement shoot
As when cutting to a bud, make an angled cut sloping away from the replacement shoot.

Cutting back to a main branch
Make a clean cut, leaving the branch collar intact (inset, top). The tree is then less susceptible to disease, and the wound heals faster (inset, bottom).

end may cause dieback and increase the shoot's vulnerability to disease. If removing a shoot or branch completely, cut it back to the point of origin but leave the bark ridge and branch collar intact rather than cutting flush with the parent stem.

To prevent the branch or bark from tearing before cutting is completed, undercut first before finishing the cut from above. Cut back to the point of origin or to a well-placed, healthy branch as a suitable replacement. Do not leave a stub or the cut end will die instead of healing. Pare away any rough edges with a sharp knife (see *Removing a branch*, p.71).

Fruiting habits

How a plant is pruned depends on its fruiting habit. For example, sweet cherries form fruit mainly on spurs of two-year-old and older wood, so many of the older shoots must be retained. Tart cherries, however, fruit on one-year-old shoots; when pruning, leave most of the young shoots but remove some of the old, unproductive wood.

Training for shape and fruit

A young tree is usually bought as a feathered maiden (a one-year-old tree with sideshoots). Initial pruning consists of selecting shoots to be retained, shortening them as desired, and removing unwanted shoots. If a young tree is bought as a maiden whip (a one-year-old tree without sideshoots), it should be cut down to a bud after planting, the height depending on how the tree is to be trained. This encourages the growth of sideshoots. When these develop, the tree, now two years old, is the equivalent of a feathered maiden. Formative

PRUNING A MAIDEN WHIP TO FORM A FEATHERED TREE

Winter, Year 1
To produce vigorous feathers (sideshoots) on a maiden whip tree, cut it back with an angled cut just above a bud at the required height.

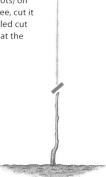

Winter, Year 2
By the following winter, a number of new sideshoots should have been produced below the pruning cut.

pruning continues for the first two or three years until the desired shape has been obtained.

The vigor and fruitfulness of shoots can be adjusted by raising or lowering selected laterals or, with oblique cordons, the whole tree. Horizontal growth is more fruitful than vertical, so tying a lateral closer to the horizontal makes it produce more fruit. If one lateral is less vigorous than another and more sideshoots are needed, raising it will stimulate vegetative growth. For an established, bearing tree or bush, pruning is more important than training; even on an untrained tree, less fruitful or unbalanced shoots can be tied down in summer to increase their yield.

Curbing excessive vigor

Extremely vigorous trees that produce rapid vegetative growth at the expense of bearing may benefit from root pruning. On apples and pears only, bark-ringing (see p.437) may also be used as a last resort to curb vigor; it should not be used on stone fruits because

it may kill them. Both methods will induce the formation of fruit buds, so the beneficial effects will be seen in increased blooming and fruiting one or possibly two years later.

Root pruning

Trees may be root pruned at any age, but only when they are dormant. When pruning the roots of a young tree, first lift it by digging around it, then remove soil carefully from around the fibrous roots, being careful not to damage them. Cut back a few of the thick roots in the process. Then replant the tree firmly and stake it.

Larger trees need to be root pruned *in situ*, pruning one side of the root system one winter, and completing the other side a year or two later. To do this effectively, make a trench 18in–4ft (45cm–1.2m) wide, depending on the size of the tree, to expose the main roots. These should be severed and a section of each root removed. Then fill in the trench, firm, and mulch; in some cases, staking may be required to provide support until the tree is stable.

ROOT PRUNING TO IMPROVE FRUITING

1 Mark the position for a trench around the tree using string and a stake. It should be an even semicircle just below the outermost spread of the branches.

2 At the base of the trench, use a fork to remove soil from around the thick roots without damaging the fibrous roots.

3 Sever each woody root on either side of the trench with a pruning saw, discarding the central section. Leave the fibrous roots unpruned.

TRAINING ON STAKES

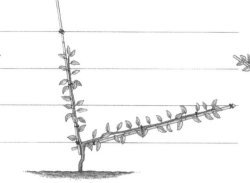

1 The vigor of laterals of trained trees may be altered by adjusting the angle at which they are trained. This technique corrects uneven growth on either side of the same tree.

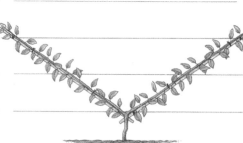

2 Lower a young, strong-growing lateral, with its stake, at the start of or during the summer to reduce its vigor; raise a lateral to encourage it to grow more quickly. Retie the stakes to the wires.

3 By the end of the summer, the branches can be returned to their original positions; they should be more even in length.

Pruning under cover

Prune back branches and shoots of plants grown in a greenhouse so that they do not touch the glass or plastic surfaces, otherwise they may suffer sun scorch and growth will be constricted or damaged. Regular pruning also allows more light to reach the developing fruit and helps them to ripen.

Renovation

If a tree is too old to bear well, and has split, rotten, or severely diseased branches or trunk, it should be removed. If the trunk and the main branches are sound, however, and the tree is merely overcrowded, it can be rejuvenated by means of renovative pruning followed by correct, routine care.

Renovation work should be carried out in spring or summer on stone fruit and in winter on apples, pears, and other pome fruit. Cut out any branches that are dead, damaged, or diseased, or so low that they may trail on the ground when laden with fruit. Also remove crowded or crossing branches, because these will shade the developing fruit, and, if they rub together, may become prone to diseases, such as canker. On a vigorous tree, it is advisable to stagger this pruning over more than one year; pruning too severely on a single occasion may only induce more vigorous, vegetative growth.

Once this initial thinning has been achieved, more precise pruning, such as spur thinning, may be carried out (as described for routine pruning under individual fruit entries). Chemical inhibitors are available to curb the regrowth of watersprouts around the cuts, but wound paints are not recommended because they may seal in any infection.

RENOVATING A NEGLECTED TREE

1 Remove overcrowded, rubbing, or crossing branches to let in light and air by cutting them back to their point of origin, or to a vigorous sublateral facing the desired direction.

2 Any branches that are damaged or affected by a disease, such as canker (shown above), should be removed completely, or cut back to a healthy shoot.

RENOVATING A NEGLECTED APPLE TREE OVER TWO YEARS

Growth has been allowed to cross, rubbing and chafing bark.

Trunk and lower parts of framework branches are clear of growth.

1 In the first year, remove dead, diseased, and damaged wood. Remove or shorten crowded and crossing branches. In the second year, improve fruiting potential; shorten overlong and unproductive growth to a replacement shoot, and thin regrowth from the sites of previous cuts. On apples and pears, reduce congested spur systems (see p.105).

2 Two years later, the tree has a crown of well-spaced strong branches on which fruiting growth has room to develop. Now introduce routine pruning; shorten long, young shoots to start the formation of fresh spur systems. To keep new growth balanced, prune weak shoots hard and vigorous shoots lightly.

RENOVATING AN OVERPRUNED TREE (PEAR) OVER THREE YEARS

Remove completely shoots on the trunk and the lower portions of main branches.

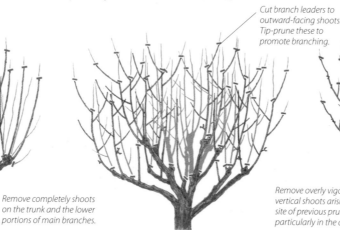

Cut branch leaders to outward-facing shoots. Tip-prune these to promote branching.

Remove overly vigorous vertical shoots arising from the site of previous pruning cuts, particularly in the center.

1 Hard pruning has stimulated overly vigorous shoots, growing vertically without branching as they compete for light. In Year 1, remove approximately one in two, leaving the remainder evenly spaced. Tip-prune the longest remaining shoots to induce branching.

2 Remove half of the upright growth again, leaving, as in Year 1, well-spaced, well-positioned young branches. Prune these to encourage further outward-facing growth. If it still seems overcrowded, remove larger sections of wood from the center, being careful not to damage branch collars.

3 In Year 3, continue to make pruning cuts to correct and balance new growth. Some flower buds should be forming; from this stage on, introduce routine pruning in the correct season to suit the fruit in question. This pear is being winter-pruned to start fresh spur formation.

Harvesting and storing

Many homegrown fruits may be enjoyed long after their normal harvesting time if correctly harvested and stored. While most are at their best eaten fresh, some keep their flavor well, even after prolonged storage. For details on harvesting and storing specific fruits, see the individual fruit entries.

Harvesting

Most fruit is best picked when fully ripe for using fresh. Fruit for storing is harvested slightly earlier, however, when it is mature but not yet completely ripe and still firm. Not all of the fruits on a single plant ripen at the same time, so it is usually necessary to harvest over a period of time, and this provides an extended period of fresh fruit.

For tree fruit such as apples and pears, test for ripeness by holding a fruit in the palm of the hand, then gently lift and twist. If ripe, the fruit will come away easily, complete with its stalk, otherwise it should be left for a day or two.

When harvesting, discard any damaged, diseased, or bruised fruit because it will quickly become infected with rot, which then spreads rapidly to adjacent fruits when in storage.

Soft fruit must be picked completely dry otherwise many may be affected by rot unless the fruit is used immediately. Regular picking, at least every other day, is advisable for strawberries, raspberries, blackberries, and hybrid berries.

Always be careful not to damage the plant when harvesting—by pulling fruit off hard, for example. Some types of fruit, such as cherries, grapes, and mangos, should be cut off the plant to avoid the risk of accidental damage.

Storing

There are various ways of keeping fruit for later use, including cool storage, freezing, and preserving; the most suitable method depends on the type of fruit. Some fruit, especially those such as apples, apricots, and figs, which have a high acid and sugar content, may also be oven-dried at 120–140°F (49–60°C). Fruit also dries well in a food dehydrator.

When preparing fruits for storage, handle them carefully to avoid bruising. Always store different cultivars in separate containers that are free from any residues or aromas that can taint the fruit.

Cool storage

Apples and pears in particular can be kept for several weeks, or even months in the right conditions—consistently cool, dark, and slightly damp. Various other tree fruits, such as lemons, may also be stored this way although they do not usually keep for such a long period, while most nuts keep well for up to a few months. Soft fruit cannot be stored in this way. The required temperature and degree of humidity vary for different fruit, but most should be stored in slatted trays and boxes to allow free air circulation. Some apple and pear cultivars, however, tend to shrivel and are better kept in clear plastic bags. Check unwrapped fruit regularly and remove any that show signs of disease or rotting.

Freezing

This is ideal for most soft fruit, except strawberries, and for a number of tree fruit. Small fruit, such as raspberries, are usually frozen whole, while large fruit, such as apples, are best chopped or sliced beforehand to ensure even and thorough freezing. Remove any stalks (and fruit stems of currants) then open-freeze whole fruits spread out on trays. Once they are frozen—after two to four hours—transfer the fruit to plastic boxes or bags, excluding as much air as possible, and keep them frozen until needed. Strawberries and some soft-fleshed tree fruit, such as plums, are often puréed before being frozen.

Preserving and bottling

All soft fruit and a number of tree fruit, such as apricots and plums, can be made into preserves. In most cases, the entire fruit is used, while some, such as grapes and blackberries, are better strained and only the juice used to make a sweet jelly.

Citrus fruit, pineapple, and most stone fruit, such as cherries, may be bottled in sugar syrup with alcohol (such as rum, brandy, or cognac) if desired to preserve them. Citrus peel may also be candied or dried for use in baking.

FREEZING SOFT FRUITS

Spread out soft fruit, such as raspberries, on trays so that they are not in contact with one another, then freeze them. Once they are frozen, they can be packed into suitable containers and kept in the freezer until they are needed.

STORING APPLES

1 Wrap each fruit individually in tissue paper to keep it in good condition and prevent it from rotting.

2 Carefully fold the tissue paper around the fruit, holding it lightly so that you do not bruise it.

3 Place each wrapped fruit on its folded end in a wooden slatted box, or other well-ventilated container, and store in a cool place.

ALTERNATIVE METHOD

Store fruits of cultivars that tend to shrivel quickly in a plastic bag. Make several holes in the bag before filling it with no more than 6lb 8oz (3kg) of fruit. Seal the bag loosely.

FRUIT THAT FREEZES WELL

Apples **P**
Apricots **P**
Black currants **Sk**
Blackberries and all hybrid berries **Sk**
Blueberries **Sk**
Cherries (sweet) **Sk**
Cherries (tart) **Sk**
Damsons **Sk** (with or without stones)
Gages **Sk**
Gooseberries **Sk**
Grapes **Sk**
Nectarines **P**
Peaches **P**
Plums **Sk**
Raspberries **Sk**
Red currants **Sk**
White currants **Sk**

Key
P Remove cores or stones and slice and peel if required
Sk Remove stalks (and stones where applicable)

Propagation

Tree fruit (except figs) are usually propagated by grafting; figs, vines, and many soft fruit by cuttings, although if *Phylloxera* (see p.461) is a problem, grapevines should be grafted. Some fruit produce runners, layers, or suckers; all may be used to produce new plants. Several tender fruit and some nuts may be grown from seed but hardy fruits seldom grow true to type from seed.

Bud-grafting

Both chip-budding and T-budding are used to increase the stock of fruit trees. They are economical methods of propagation, because a new tree is produced from a single bud. Grafting should be carried out in midsummer, using as the rootstock an established plant with a stem that is at least ½in (1cm) thick. A bud from the scion plant is cut from a ripe shoot (the budstick) of the current season's growth, and grafted onto an incision in the rootstock.

Propagating by chip-budding

Select a healthy budstick and carefully remove a bud (the bud chip), taking care not to damage the cambium layer. Remove a sliver of rind from the rootstock and place the bud chip onto the exposed wood of the rootstock so that the cambium layers are in close contact. Bind the bud chip tightly onto the rootstock to hold it in place. When the bud and rootstock have united the bud will start to swell and the binding can be removed. The following winter, trim the rootstock just above the grafted bud to encourage a strong shoot to develop from the graft in spring.

CHIP-BUDDING

1 Choose a vigorous shoot of the current season's ripened wood as the budstick. The shoot should be approximately pencil thick and have well-developed buds.

2 Hold the budstick firmly and, using a clean, sharp knife, slice off the soft tip and remove all the leaves to produce a clear length of stem.

3 To remove a bud chip, first slice into the budstick about ¾in (2cm) below a bud. Cut down to a depth of about ¼in (5mm), slanting the blade at an angle of 45°.

4 Make another incision about 1½in (4cm) above the first. Slice downward behind the bud toward the first incision, being careful not to damage the bud.

5 Remove the bud chip, holding it by the bud to keep the cambium layer clean. Place the bud chip in a plastic bag to keep it from drying out.

6 To prepare the rootstock, stand astride the plant and, using a sharp knife, remove all the shoots and leaves from the bottom 12in (30cm) of stem.

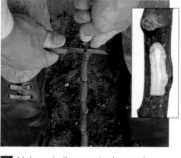

7 Make a shallow cut in the stock. Remove a sliver of rind to reveal the cambium layer (see inset), leaving a "lip" at the base. Do not touch the exposed wood.

Bud chip in position on rootstock

8 Place the bud chip onto the prepared lip of rind, offset if necessary, so that the exposed cambium layers of bud chip and rootstock match and touch.

9 Bind the bud chip to the root stock with plastic tape. Carefully remove the tape after a few weeks when the bud chip has united with the rootstock.

10 The following late winter, remove the top of the rootstock. Cut cleanly with pruners just above the grafted bud, using an angled cut.

11 During the summer, a shoot from the grafted bud will develop. The new tree is then at the maiden whip stage (see "Selecting fruit trees," pp.424–425).

Propagating by T-budding

In this technique the rootstock and scion bud are prepared in a similar way to chip-budding, except that two slits are made in the rootstock, to form the shape of a "T." This allows the bark of the rootstock to be lifted slightly so that the scion bud may be tucked behind it. Removing the scion bud with a leaf stalk attached makes it easier to handle; the stalk is removed before the bud is bound to the rootstock. The rootstock should be cut back the next winter.

For this technique to be successful, the bark of the rootstock must lift smoothly: in dry weather, rootstocks need to be watered for up to two weeks before T-budding takes place.

Whip-and-tongue grafting

This is a common method of grafting for tree fruit. It may be used as an alternative to budding but it is usually more successful with pome than with stone fruit. Use well-established rootstocks that have been planted either the previous winter or, preferably, two winters before grafting takes place.

The scion material should have at least three buds and should be taken in midwinter from a healthy shoot of the previous season's growth. Heel it in until ready for grafting. In late winter or early spring, prepare the stock by cutting off the top of the stem and removing any sideshoots. Using a sloping cut, slice off a small piece of bark from the top of the remaining stem; make a

further shallow incision in the exposed cambium layer, to create a tongue.

Trim the scion to a length of three or four buds then, using a sloping cut, slice off a small piece of bark close to a bud but on the opposite side from it. Make a further, shallow incision, to match that in the stock, and hook the resulting tongue onto the one on the rootstock. Make sure that the cambium layers of both stock and scion are in close contact, then bind the graft firmly. Remove the binding carefully when a callus

T-BUDDING

1 Select a ripened shoot as the scion from the current season's growth and remove the leaves. Remove a bud by slicing underneath it (see inset).

2 Make a "T"-shaped cut in the stock about 9in (22cm) above ground level and pry open the flaps of bark.

3 Place the bud behind the flaps of bark, trimming the top level with the horizontal cut on the stock. Bind the bud as for chip-budding.

WHIP-AND-TONGUE GRAFTING

1 In midwinter, remove healthy, vigorous hardwood shoots from the scion tree. Cut lengths of about 9in (22cm), cutting obliquely just above a bud.

2 Make bundles of 5 or 6 scions. Choose a well-drained, sheltered site and heel them in to keep them moist but dormant, leaving 2–3in (5–8cm) above the soil surface.

3 In late winter or early spring, prepare the rootstocks just before bud break. Cut off the top of each rootstock about 8–10in (20–25cm) from ground level.

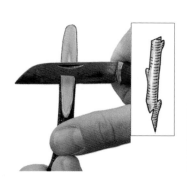

4 Trim off any shoots from the rootstock with a sharp knife, then make a 1½in (3.5cm) upward-sloping cut on one side to receive the scion.

5 Make a slit ½in (1cm) deep about one-third of the way down the exposed cambium layer, to form a tongue into which the scion may be inserted (see inset).

6 Lift the scions, cut off any soft growth at the tips, and trim to 3 or 4 buds. For each, cut off a piece of bark behind a bud that is about 2in (5cm) from the base.

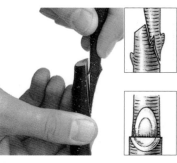

7 Without touching the cut surface with your hand, cut the cambium layer (see inset) to match the tongue in the rootstock.

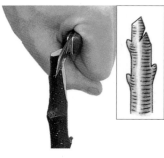

8 Place the scion into the tongue on the stock (inset, top). Use the arches of the cambium layers as a guide (inset, bottom) to ensure the exposed surfaces fit together well.

9 Bind together stock and scion with clear plastic tape. When the cut surfaces start to callus, remove the tape by carefully scoring it downward.

has formed around the graft union. By spring, buds on the scion will have started to grow. Select the best shoot that develops (keeping others pinched back) to form a maiden whip tree (see "Selecting fruit trees," pp.424–425).

Cuttings

Hardwood, softwood, and leaf-bud cuttings may be used to propagate certain fruit. Cutting material should always be selected from a healthy parent plant that bears regularly.

Hardwood cuttings

Figs, grapevines, currants (white, red, and black), and gooseberries may be propagated from hardwood cuttings, usually taken in the fall.

Select a well-ripened shoot of the current season's growth and trim off the leaves and soft tip. Remove some or most of the buds, depending on the fruit being propagated, and trim off the top and base. The exact preparation and length of the cuttings varies slightly; details are given under individual fruit entries.

If the soil is well cultivated and not too heavy, the cuttings may be inserted into a narrow trench in the open ground. If the soil is heavy, however, place the cuttings in a pot of moist, sandy soil mix. The cuttings should be ready for transplanting one or two years later.

Softwood cuttings

Guavas, pomegranates, tree tomatoes, and blueberries are propagated from softwood cuttings (where the climate is warm enough for the wood to ripen sufficiently, blueberries may also be propagated from hardwood cuttings). Take the cuttings in midsummer and place them in pots of propagation mix (see p.478). Harden off the young plants before they are transplanted to their permanent locations.

Leaf-bud cuttings

Stocks of blackberries and hybrid berries may be increased quickly by leaf-bud cuttings (see p.472). Take the cuttings in late summer: remove short lengths of stem, each with a bud and leaf attached; insert them in soilless mix with the buds just above the surface. Once rooted, cuttings may be potted or planted outdoors.

Runners, layers, and suckers

Some fruit sends out runners, layers, or suckers, which root naturally at stem nodes while still attached to the parent plant. This process may be exploited to increase fruit stocks.

Runners

Strawberries (but not all alpine strawberries) produce creeping horizontal stems, or runners, which root where they come into contact with the ground and may be used for propagation. As the runners are produced, spread them out evenly. Allow them to root, and then lift and sever them (see p.470).

Layers

Blackberries and hybrid berries may be propagated by layering, although some hybrids are slow to root. The tip of a shoot is induced to root by carefully pegging it down in the soil or in a pot of moist soil mix (see "Tip layering," p.471). A year later, when the tip has rooted and produced new growth, it may be severed from the parent plant and transplanted to its permanent location.

Suckers

Established cane fruit, such as raspberries, produces suckers that are usually hoed off. If retained, rooted suckers may be lifted and severed in the fall, when the plants are dormant but the soil is still warm. Transplant the rooted suckers directly to their permanent locations (see *Propagating by Suckers*, p.474). Figs, hazelnuts, and filberts also produce suckers: if they have good root systems, sever them with a spade and replant in the same way.

Seed

Propagation from seed is the usual method of increasing stock of many tender fruit, including avocado (see p.486), guava, and papaya.

The alpine strawberry is one of the few hardy fruits that may be raised successfully from seed (see p.470). Hazelnuts, filberts, walnuts, and chestnuts may also be raised from seed with a good chance of success, although cultivars selected for the quality of their fruit need to be propagated vegetatively. For details, see ORNAMENTAL TREES, "Raising trees from seed," p.80.

HARDWOOD CUTTINGS

1 Dig a narrow trench 6in (15cm) deep. If the soil has a high clay content, sprinkle a little sand into the base of the trench to improve drainage.

2 Choose a ripened stem from the current season's growth (here, from a fig tree). Remove lengths of at least 12in (30cm), cutting flush with the main stem.

3 Cut off all the leaves and the soft growth at the tip of each cutting, then trim to about 9in (23cm): make an angled cut above the top bud and a straight cut at the base.

4 Place the cuttings in the prepared trench, spacing them 4–6in (10–15cm) apart and burying two-thirds of the stems. Firm the soil, and label.

5 The cuttings will take several months to root. Toward the end of the following growing season, they should have developed sturdy new growth.

6 After leaves drop in fall, carefully lift the rooted cuttings, wrapping the roots in plastic to stop them from drying out. Transplant the cuttings to their permanent positions to continue growing.

Tree fruit

The fruit in this group are the largest-growing forms in the nontropical fruit garden. They may be divided into two main categories: pome fruits, such as apples and pears, have a seed-containing core; and stone fruits, such as cherries, peaches, and apricots, have a hard central stone. There are also certain other fruits within this group that fit into neither of the above categories, such as figs, mulberries, and persimmons.

Cultivating tree fruits is a long-term undertaking that requires careful planning. The size and shape or form of the trees are important considerations. Left to grow naturally, many fruit trees would become much too large for the average-sized yard. Smaller forms grown on dwarfing rootstocks have been developed, however; fruit trees may also be trained and pruned as fans, espaliers, or cordons and grown flat against walls or fences, making it feasible to grow them successfully in even the smallest of spaces.

Pears

Apples

Apples

Quinces

Another factor to consider is the number of trees required. Many fruit trees are self-sterile and, to produce crops, need at least one other suitable cultivar of the same fruit to act as a pollinator. Even self-fertile trees bear more heavily if pollinators are present.

Some tree fruit, such as figs, prefer a long, hot growing season and are difficult to cultivate in cooler climates; growing them under cover provides protection and improves fruit and crop size, as well as flavor.

Once a tree fruit has been selected and planted, it is important to follow the correct pruning methods. Good pruning not only builds a strong framework of branches, but also encourages and maintains maximum bearing for many years.

STRATEGIC DEFENSES

The young shoots of many fruit trees can provide a tasty meal for rabbits and deer. These unwelcome visitors are liable to vandalize tree bark by rubbing it off, or gnawing it away. (Voles gnaw bark near soil level, too.) Rabbits are particularly partial to bark at the base of young apple trees; if bark is lost from most, or all, of the trunk's circumference, the tree will die.

The most environmentally friendly solution is to protect the trees with wire fencing. To keep out rabbits this should be 3ft (90cm) tall and extend 12in (30cm) below ground and angling out. A deer-proof fence should be a minimum of 6ft (2m) tall. Alternatively, you can protect individual plants with tree guards and netting (see pp.67 and 427).

Apples (*Malus domestica*)

Apples are one of the most widely grown hardy fruits, and both dessert and culinary cultivars offer a great variety of flavors and textures. Tree size may also be varied—dwarfing rootstocks and "family" trees (see p.420) allowing a number of different apples to be grown in a small garden on a single tree. Apple trees may readily be trained into almost any shape. Cordon-, espalier-, and fan-shaped forms require more work, but grow well against walls and fences. Columnar trees are dwarf, single-stemmed, compact apple trees with short fruiting spurs. Several cultivars are available in this form.

The extensive choice of cultivars covers a period of ripening from midsummer to late winter, and fruit may be stored until mid-spring, given suitable conditions. There are cultivars and rootstocks suitable for most climates, including those with severe winter temperatures. For flowering to occur, the trees must be subjected to at least 900 hours below 45°F (7°C): the chilling requirement. Apples are not grown successfully in tropical or subtropical regions.

Site and planting

When planting, ensure that each tree has sufficient space to develop to its full size. Select the most appropriate size of tree (largely determined by the rootstock) for your yard. In most cases, more than one apple tree will be required for pollination.

Site

A sunny, sheltered site is essential for consistently good crops. Walls for trained fruit should preferably be in full sun. For shaded areas or those in a region with short summers and cool temperatures, choose cultivars that ripen early. Where late frosts occur, select late-flowering cultivars so that the blossom will not be damaged.

Apples will grow in most well-drained soils, if it is given adequate preparation (see p.424). The more dwarfing the rootstock, however, the more fertile the soil should be.

Rootstocks

Choice of rootstock depends on the tree size required and the soil type. Traditional apple rootstocks are prefixed by M or MM, which stand for Malling and Malling Merton respectively, the research stations in the UK where the rootstocks were developed. Other rootstocks are also available, including 'Ottawa 3', developed at the Central Experimental Farm in Ottawa, Ontario. The BUD rootstocks originated in the former Soviet Union but may be a good choice as well. Check with your supplier to decide which rootstock will be best for your region and conditions. Where the soil is poor, use a more vigorous rootstock to compensate. For example, for a dwarf tree use 'Ottawa 3' instead of 'M9' or 'M26'. The vigor of the chosen cultivar also determines the size of the mature tree. Triploid cultivars grow larger than diploids (see below); use a more dwarfing rootstock for a triploid than for a diploid cultivar to attain a tree of similar size.

Pollination

No apples are reliably or consistently self-fertile: diploids must be planted near a second, compatible cultivar; triploid apples, which will not pollinate other cultivars, require two compatible cultivars nearby to pollinate them. Cultivars are divided into flowering groups according to their time of flowering; a cultivar from one group may be cross-pollinated by another from the same group or one in the group before or after it if flowering times overlap However, short North American blooming seasons make flowering group designations less meaningful. Some cultivars are incompatible: of those listed on pp.436 and 437, 'Cox's Orange Pippin' will not pollinate 'Kidd's Orange Red' or 'Suntan' and vice versa. If in doubt about compatibility, ask a fruit nursery for advice.

Planting

Bare-root trees are best planted when dormant in spring or fall. Fall is the better choice in Zones 6 and warmer. Container-grown trees may be planted at any time, unless the ground is frozen or very wet; water before planting so that the roots are moist. Using the soil mark as a guide, plant each tree at its original planting depth (see also *Planting a Fruit Tree*, p.425).

If the tree is to be trained, fit the supports and wires before planting (see under individual tree forms). For untrained trees, staking at planting is vital and should be permanent for

ROOTSTOCKS

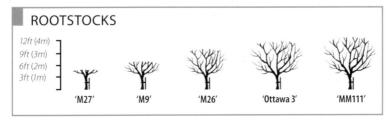

12ft (4m)
9ft (3m)
6ft (2m)
3ft (1m)

'M27'   'M9'   'M26'   'Ottawa 3'   'MM111'

DESSERT APPLES TO TRY

Early

'Akane'
'Discovery'
'Empress'
'George Cave'
'Ginger Gold'
'Gravenstein' **P**
'Jerseymac'
'Pristine' **D**
'Red Astrachan'
'Transparent'
'William's Pride' **D**
'Zestar!'

Mid-season

'Arlet'
'Blushing Golden'
'Corail'
'Cox's Orange Pippin'
'Delicious'
'Empire'
'Fameuse'
'Freedom' **D**
'Gala'
'Golden Delicious'
'Golden Supreme'
'Honeycrisp'
'Jonafree' **D**
'Jonagold' **P**
'Idared'
'Liberty' **D**
'Macoun'
'McIntosh'
'Ribston Pippin'
'SirPrize' **D**
'Spartan'
'Spitzenburg'
'Wealthy'
'Winter Banana'
'Worcester Pearmain'

Late

'Ashmead's Kernel'
'Calville Blanche d'Hiver'
'Cameo'
'Enterprise' **D**
'Fuji'
'Golden Russet' **D**
'Goldrush' **D**
'Granny Smith'
'Idared'
'Lady'
'Mutsu' **P**
'Northern Spy'
'Orleans Reinette'
'Pink Lady'
'Ruxbury Russet'
'Stayman'
'Winesap' **P**
'Winter Banana'
'Wolf River'

Key

D   Disease resistant
P   Poor pollen source

those on dwarfing rootstocks. Planting distances (see right) depend on how the trees are to be trained, as well as on the vigor of the chosen rootstocks and cultivars.

Routine care

Establish a regular maintenance program to ensure that trees stay healthy and bear well. Feed and mulch periodically as required. Pruning and fruit thinning are annual tasks that are required to ensure satisfactory yields. Check trees regularly for signs of pests and diseases and damage from rubbing stakes and ties.

Blossom-thinning and biennial bearing

Certain apple cultivars, such as 'Northern Spy', tend to produce heavy crops in alternate years, and bear little or no blooms or fruit in intervening years. This is known as biennial bearing.

Blossom-thinning can largely correct this; it involves removing nine of every ten blossom clusters by pinching them out, leaving the rosette of young leaves around each intact. The tree then produces a moderate, rather than heavy, crop and its resources are channeled into producing fruit buds for the following year, which would otherwise have been fruitless. On large trees, where it would be impractical to thin blossoms over the entire tree, biennial bearing can be corrected by blossom-thinning a few branches.

If trees that normally produce regularly start to bear biennially, this may be due to the loss of blossoms from frost and hence the crop; this may then induce a tree to overbear the following year. The tree may not have sufficient resources to develop adequate fruit buds for the third year and a biennial tendency is set in motion. Disease or pest infestation causing a setback in one year may produce a similar effect.

Fruit thinning

Thinning is essential where heavy crops have set to improve fruit size, quality, and flavor and to help prevent branches from breaking. On young trees, overly heavy fruit load strains the tree's resources and slows the growth of new buds. Some thinning is useful on the young fruitlets, but it is simpler to carry out the main task in early summer, after the "June drop," when the tree naturally sheds imperfect and infertile fruit.

PLANTING DISTANCES

Tree form	Rootstock	Distance between trees	Distance between rows
Open center	'M27'	4–6ft (1.2–2m)	6ft (2m)
	'M9'	8–10ft (2.5–3m)	10ft (3m)
	'M26'	10–14ft (3–4.25m)	15ft (5m)
	'Ottawa 3'	11–18ft (3.5–5.5m)	18ft (5.5m)
Semidwarf	'MM111'	24–28ft (7.5–9m)	24–28ft (7.5–9m)
Standard	'MM111', 'M25' (or seedling crab)	24–32ft (7.5–10.5m)	24–32ft (7.5–10.5m)
Spindlebush	'M9' or 'M26' (and triploids on 'M27')	6–7ft (2–2.2m)	8–10ft (2.5–3m)
	'MM106'	6–7ft (2–2.2m)	12ft (4m)
Cordon	as open center	30in (75cm)	6ft (2m)
Fan/espalier	'M9'	10ft (3m)	
	'Ottawa 3'	14ft (4.25m)	
	'MM111'	18ft (5.5m)	
Dwarf pyramid	'M27'	4ft (1.2m)	6ft (2m)
	'M9' or 'M26'	5ft (1.5m)	6–7ft (2–2.2m)
	'MM106'	6ft (2m)	7ft (2.2m)

Use scissors to remove the center (or "king") fruit of each cluster, which is sometimes abnormally shaped; then cut out any fruit that is damaged. In about midsummer, thin the clusters again so that there is one good fruit per cluster. Fruit of dessert cultivars should be spaced 4–6in (10–15cm) apart, and that of culinary cultivars 6–9in (15–22cm) apart.

Fertilizing, watering, and mulching

Water trees in periods of hot, dry weather, apply fertilizer annually, and mulch as necessary (see "Care of tree fruits," p.426). If growth is poor, apply ammonium sulfate in spring at a rate of 1oz/sq yd (35g/sq m) on the area under the canopy.

Stakes and ties

Inspect stakes and ties regularly to check that they are not rubbing against the bark of trees and that ties are effective; adjust them as necessary. Trees grown on dwarfing rootstocks, such as 'M9' and 'M26', produce few taproots and therefore need permanent staking to provide support and compensate for their lack of anchorage.

Pests and diseases

Common pests that may be troublesome include codling moths (p.657), European apple sawflies (p.659), apple maggots (p.654), tent caterpillars (p.671), apple psyllids, plum curculios (p.666), roundheaded apple tree borer, spider mites (p.670), and wasps (p.672). Diseases that can affect apples include scab (p.668), powdery mildew (p.667), brown rot (p.656), fire blight (p.660), rusts (p.668), and *Nectria* canker (p.664).

APPLE THINNING

1 Thinning is essential if the tree is carrying a heavy crop. After the "June drop," which is a normal occurrence, the remaining fruit will need further thinning if the crop is still heavy.

2 Remove sufficient small fruitlets (especially any that are malformed or very small) to leave about 4–6in (10–15cm) between each and only one fruitlet per cluster.

Pruning and training techniques

Apple trees produce flowers and fruit mainly on shoots that are two years old and older, and on short spurs that are produced on the older wood. Two-year-old shoots carry both large fruit buds and smaller, pointed growth buds. Fruit buds produce flower clusters and then fruit, while growth buds form into fruit buds for the following year or into sideshoots or fruiting spurs. One-year-old shoots may also carry fruit buds but these flower later than those that occur on older wood. Tip-bearing cultivars produce markedly fewer spurs (see below).

Once their branch framework is established, trained apple trees need to be pruned (mainly during the summer) in order to maintain the desired shape, curb vegetative growth, and stimulate the production of fruit buds. Untrained trees require moderate pruning during the winter to stimulate growth for the next season's fruit and to maintain an open and well-balanced structure so that they bear well and the fruit is of good quality.

FRUIT BUDS AND GROWTH BUDS

Fruit bud

Growth bud

Large fruit buds develop on two-year-old and older wood. The smaller buds are growth buds, and are found mainly on one-year-old wood.

NICKING AND NOTCHING

Nicking
To weaken bud growth, make a nick in the bark just below the bud and into the cambium layer.

Notching
To stimulate bud growth, make a notch through the bark into the cambium layer just above the bud.

Tip bearers and spur bearers

Cultivars differ in the way they bear most of their fruit. Tip bearers carry much of the crop at, or near, the shoot tips, whereas spur bearers carry it along the whole shoot on short-jointed spurs from which further growth develops each year.

Some well-known cultivar names such as 'Delicious' encompass many different varieties. When buying new trees, determine whether they are spur or tip bearers. Spur bearers, easily trained as cordons, espaliers, and fans, are preferable for small yards. Tip bearers work best when grown in an upright form; once established, they need renewal pruning only (see p.438).

Nicking and notching

Sometimes it may be necessary to correct the balance of the branch framework of a trained tree; this may be achieved by nicking, which weakens the growth of a particular bud, or notching, which strengthens it. Notching may also be used to stimulate the production of sideshoots on bare lengths of stem. Nicking and notching are most effective in spring when the sap is rising. Make a nick or a small incision with a sharp knife just below a bud to inhibit its growth; make a notch just above it to increase its vigor and stimulate new growth.

Bark-ringing

On excessively vigorous apple and pear trees (but not on stone fruits) that produce unsatisfactory crops, bark-ringing may be used as a last resort to curb vegetative growth and induce a greater fruit set. In late spring, remove a narrow band of bark from around the trunk through to the cambium layer at a height of about 3ft (1m). This reduces the flow of nutrients and hormones back to the roots, so that they are concentrated in the upper part of the tree.

Bark-ringing must be carried out carefully or the tree may die. First, measure out the width of the band, which must be only 1/8in (3mm) on a small tree, graduating to no more than 1/2in (1cm) on a large tree, then score the band with a knife. Cut through the bark and the cambium layer and remove the bark down to the hardwood all the way around. Seal the wound with several layers of waterproof adhesive tape, covering the wound without touching the cambium layer.

BARK-RINGING

1 Stick tape around the trunk as a guide for two parallel cuts. The ring may be 1/8–1/2in (3mm–1cm) wide, depending on the age and size of the tree.

2 The parallel cuts should be made through both the bark and the cambium layer. Carefully remove the ring of bark with the blunt side of the knife blade.

3 Wind waterproof tape around the ring so it covers the wound without touching the cambium layer. Remove the tape when the wound has healed.

CULINARY APPLES TO TRY

Early
'Chenango Strawberry' **De**
'Earligold'
'Jerseymac'
'Melba' **De**
'Parkland'
'Red Astrachan'
'Redfree' **D**
'Twenty Ounce'
'William's Pride'
'Yellow Transparent'

Mid-season
'Blenheim Orange' **P**
'Collet' **De**
'Cortland' **De**
'Cox's Orange Pippin'
'Elstar'
'Empire'
'Enterprise' **D**
'Freedom' **D**
'Golden Delicious' **De**
'Golden Nobel'
'Gravenstein' **P, B**
'Jonagold'
'Liberty'
'McIntosh' **De**
'Macoun' **De**
'Sweet Sixteen'

Late
'Braeburn'
'Calville Blanche d'Hiver'
'Edward VII'
'Idared'
'Golden Russet' **De**
'Granny Smith' **De**
'Haralson'
'Melrose' **De**
'Mutsu' **De, P**
'Newton Pippin' **De**
'Northern Spy' **B**
'Novaspy' **De**
'Rhode Island Greening' **B, P**
'Rome'
'Stayman'
'Winesap' **De**
'York Imperial'

Key
B Biennial bearing
D Disease resistant
De Dessert use also
P Poor pollen source

The wound should heal over by the fall, when the waterproof tape may be removed. The following year, the tree should produce many more blossoms and, consequently, a much heavier crop of fruit because the reaction of any wounded plant is to reproduce.

Winter pruning

There are three main techniques for winter pruning, all of which stimulate new growth. Spur pruning and thinning should be carried out only on cultivars that produce plenty of spurs, not on tip bearers. Renewal pruning is appropriate for spindlebushes and all tip bearers, as well as for vigorous cultivars that would be overstimulated by hard pruning. Regulated pruning is suited to cultivars that are naturally very vigorous, particularly triploids, such as 'Gravenstein', 'Mutsu', 'Spigold', 'Winesap', and 'Jonagold'.

It may be necessary to vary the degree and type of pruning from year to year depending on the extent of growth, the quantity of fruit produced, and the age of the tree.

Spur pruning involves cutting back branch leaders and young laterals to stimulate the growth of sublaterals and fruiting spurs. The extent of pruning required depends on the tree's vigor—the greater the vigor, the lighter the pruning, because pruning stimulates growth.

Shorten branch leaders on vigorous trees by no more than a few buds but on weaker ones by up to one-third to stimulate new sublaterals to form. Shorten young laterals to three or six buds where growth is good but to three or four buds on weaker trees so that spurs form. On a stronger tree, shoots up to 6in (15cm) long may be left unpruned.

Spur thinning is necessary as a tree ages to prevent fruit from becoming overcrowded. If left unthinned, the spurs become entangled and carry inferior fruit. When spur systems become congested, remove the older wood in favor of the younger. In time, it may be necessary to saw off whole spur systems.

Renewal pruning involves the annual cutting back of a proportion of older, fruited shoots to their base to stimulate the growth of new, young wood. Prune an open-center tree by cutting out any vigorous growth that is crossing or shading other laterals so that all the branches are well spaced. Remove a little, if any, of the tip from branch leaders and none at all on vigorous trees.

Regulated pruning consists of removing shoots and sometimes long sections of large branches that are crowded or crossing, particularly in the center of the tree, to keep the branch framework open. Remove old wood to make room for young shoots. Do not tip prune the branch leaders.

Summer pruning

This is carried out to keep trained trees within their allotted space. It involves removing a large proportion of the new growth each summer to slow down vegetative growth.

The Modified Lorette System is the standard method of summer pruning in temperate climates with cool, unpredictable summers. It is carried out once the young shoots have become woody at the base. Maiden (new) laterals more than 9in (22cm) long that grow directly from the main stem or a main branch should be reduced to three leaves above the basal cluster. Prune back sideshoots arising from spurs and existing laterals to one leaf above the basal cluster. Continue to prune in this way as shoots mature. To help prevent sideshoots, or secondary growths, from developing behind

WINTER PRUNING

Spur pruning

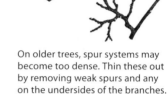

Spur thinning

1 Cut back young laterals to between three and six buds of the current growth, depending on the vigor of the shoot.

2 Prune back the current season's growth on branch leaders by one-quarter to one-third of their length.

On older trees, spur systems may become too dense. Thin these out by removing weak spurs and any on the undersides of the branches.

Renewal pruning

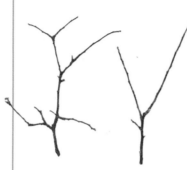

Prune out a good proportion of the older shoots that have already borne fruit (left). This will encourage new shoots to develop (right).

Regulated pruning

On this tree there is congested growth; correct this by removing any branches that are crossing or touching each other, and thinning out any sublaterals or laterals that are overcrowded.

SUMMER PRUNING (MODIFIED LORETTE SYSTEM)

Prune trees when the lowest third of all new growth has become woody.

Cut back laterals on the main stems to 3 leaves above the basal cluster.

Basal cluster

Before pruning

Trim any sideshoots to 1 leaf.

After pruning

the pruning cut, leave a small number of the longer shoots unpruned; tie these shoots securely to other branches so that they are roughly horizontal and draw the sap down. Do not shorten any of them until after fruiting. Then, in mid-fall, cut back any secondary growth shoots to one bud.

The Full Lorette System should be used in warmer climates. Prune back new laterals to about 2in (5cm), repeating at intervals throughout the summer. Shorten the laterals to ¾in (2cm) once they are woody at the base. Prune any secondary growths in late summer in the same way.

Open center

The open-center or goblet-shaped tree is comparatively simple to maintain; it is ideal for larger yards where there is plenty of space.

Formative pruning

Start with a well-feathered maiden tree; the laterals will form the first branches. After planting, while the tree is dormant, cut back the leader to a strong lateral 24–30in (60–75cm) above ground level, leaving at least two or three well-spaced laterals below it radiating out like the spokes of a wheel. These form the basis of the branch system; shorten them by two-thirds, cutting to an upward-pointing bud. Remove all other laterals.

If a maiden whip is used, or a feathered maiden tree that has few or no suitable laterals, cut back the leader in winter to a strong bud 24–30in (60–75cm) from the base, then make a small nick under the top two buds; this depresses their growth and encourages shoots from the lower buds to grow at wider angles. Remove any unwanted laterals completely.

By the end of the following summer, three or four strong, healthy laterals should have developed to produce a plant equivalent to a pruned, feathered maiden.

Strong growth should develop the following summer. If one lateral grows faster than the others, tie it down nearly horizontally to slow its growth. Remove weak, inward-, and downward-growing shoots.

In the second winter, select several well-spaced growths arising from the original laterals to build up the branch framework, and shorten them by half, cutting to outward-facing buds. If any are not needed for the framework, shorten them to four or five buds, and remove altogether any shoots crossing the open center. As growth continues in the second summer, remove any

vigorous, upright shoots that unbalance the shape of the tree. By the third winter, the final branch formation should be established, with eight to ten main branches as well as several subsidiary ones.

Routine pruning

Only winter pruning (see opposite) is necessary for open-center trees once the framework is established; the pruning required will depend on the amount of growth made by the tree and on whether it is a tip or spur bearer. A tip bearer requires renewal pruning, while spur bearers require spur pruning and thinning.

Standard and semidwarf

If your yard is large enough to accommodate a standard or semidwarf tree, they make fine specimen trees.

Two or three years' training and pruning is needed to produce a clear stem of 4–4½ft (1.2–1.3m) for a semidwarf, or 6–6½ft (2–2.1m) for a standard. After planting a feathered maiden or maiden whip, tie in the leading shoot to a stake and cut any laterals hard back to

OPEN CENTER APPLE
Year 1, Winter pruning

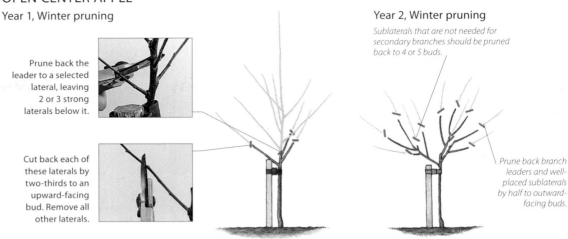

Prune back the leader to a selected lateral, leaving 2 or 3 strong laterals below it.

Cut back each of these laterals by two-thirds to an upward-facing bud. Remove all other laterals.

Year 2, Winter pruning

Sublaterals that are not needed for secondary branches should be pruned back to 4 or 5 buds.

Prune back branch leaders and well-placed sublaterals by half to outward-facing buds.

Established open center, spur pruning in winter

Prune vigorous branch leaders, leaving two-thirds of the previous season's growth. Weaker branch leaders should be cut back by two-thirds.

Cut back to 5 or 6 buds any young sideshoots growing from permanent branches to form spurs.

Established open center, renewal pruning in winter

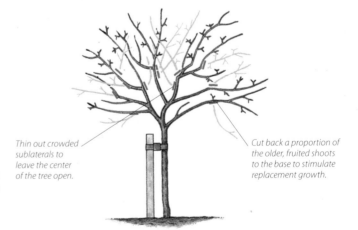

Thin out crowded sublaterals to leave the center of the tree open.

Cut back a proportion of the older, fruited shoots to the base to stimulate replacement growth.

1in (2.5cm) in winter. In spring and summer, periodically pinch or cut back any feathers to a few leaves; this helps thicken the main stem. Repeat this in the second year.

In the following winter, remove most of the laterals and cut back the leader to the desired height, either for a half-standard or standard; if the tree is not of the required height, grow it on for a third year. Several laterals should then develop below the cut; select

and retain three or four well-spaced laterals to form the basic branch framework. Then train as for an open-center tree (above).

Subsequent pruning of the tree is also the same, but growth will be much stronger because the tree is grafted on a vigorous or extremely vigorous rootstock. Carry out regulated pruning on the established tree; it is only necessary to prune hard if the tree is not growing satisfactorily.

Spindlebush

A spindlebush is trained into the shape of a pyramid or cone, to a height of 7ft (2.2m). Once it is established, only renewal pruning is required to keep the shape.

The basic aim of the spindlebush pruning method is to keep the three or four lowest branches dominant by removing shoots that would otherwise develop in the center of the tree. Any shoots that do develop higher in the tree are allowed to fruit and are then pruned back hard, to be replaced by fresh growth.

Formative pruning

Plant a strong feathered maiden of a spur-bearing cultivar, supporting it with a 6ft (2m) stake. Cut back the leader in the winter to about 3ft (1m), or to just above the topmost lateral if this is higher. Select three or four vigorous and evenly spaced laterals that are about 2–3ft (60–90cm) from the base. Prune back each lateral by half to a downward-pointing, healthy bud and remove all other laterals.

If growth is strong, tie down any upright laterals toward the end of the first summer, in order to suppress growth and encourage the tree to fruit. If growth is weak, the upright laterals do not need to be tied down until the next summer.

Tie down the laterals with strong string secured to wooden or hooked metal stakes driven into the ground at an angle around the tree. If using wooden stakes, hammer a large U staple into the top of each one so that a string may be secured to it. Tie each string loosely so that it pulls down the branch to a 30° angle. Long branches may need to be tied in two places.

Remove any excessively vigorous shoots growing upward from the main stem or laterals; do not try to tie them down because they may break. Train the central stem vertically by tying it to the stake.

The second winter after planting, shorten the central leader by one-third of the new growth, cutting to a bud on the opposite side of the pruning cut made the previous winter. This helps maintain a straight stem. Make sure that the strings are not constricting the tied-down shoots; once the growths have hardened and will remain in a more or less horizontal position, remove the strings. The following summer, tie down some of the vertical shoots and remove completely any that are exceptionally vigorous or too close to the main stem, or that unbalance the branch framework. By the third winter, laterals higher in the tree should have developed and been tied down to form further tiers of branches. They should be nearly horizontal because this encourages early fruiting, and should not overshadow the lower framework branches if possible.

In the third summer, when the tree should produce fruit for the first time, tie down selected new sideshoots in late summer and remove any excessively strong shoots.

Routine pruning

From the fourth or fifth year onward, renewal pruning (see p.438) is necessary in winter: shorten some of the old, fruited wood. Some of the shoots, particularly those that are higher in the tree, should be pruned back hard close to the trunk to encourage the development of replacement growth.

If the central leader is too vigorous, it may be cut back a little to a weaker lateral that will replace it. This concentrates vigor in the lower branches and helps retain the pyramid shape, allowing maximum light to reach the fruits. In summer, continue cutting out completely any excessively vigorous and strongly upright-growing shoots.

Cordon

A spur-bearing feathered maiden may be trained as an oblique cordon on wires that are secured to posts or to a wall or fence. Tip bearers are not suitable as cordons (see "Tip bearers and spur bearers," p.437). Space three horizontal wires about 24in (60cm) apart; the lowest wire should be 30in (75cm) from the ground. Fix the wires about 4–6in (10–15cm) clear of the supporting wall or fence to allow free air circulation and thereby prevent the buildup of pests and diseases. Attach a stake to the wires at an angle of 45°, then plant a feathered maiden by it (see p.425) and tie in the main stem to the stake, using a figure-eight knot.

Formative pruning

In the winter after planting, shorten to four buds all lateral shoots that are over 4in (10cm) in length. For tip-bearing cultivars, shorten the leader by about a third; do not attempt to prune it further.

APPLE SPINDLEBUSH

Year 1, Winter pruning

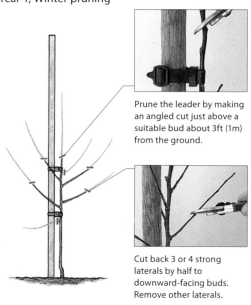

Prune the leader by making an angled cut just above a suitable bud about 3ft (1m) from the ground.

Cut back 3 or 4 strong laterals by half to downward-facing buds. Remove other laterals.

Year 1, Summer pruning

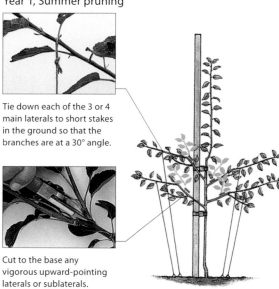

Tie down each of the 3 or 4 main laterals to short stakes in the ground so that the branches are at a 30° angle.

Cut to the base any vigorous upward-pointing laterals or sublaterals.

Year 2, Summer pruning

Repeat summer pruning as for Year 1, concentrating on removing any upright growths.

Established spindlebush, Winter pruning

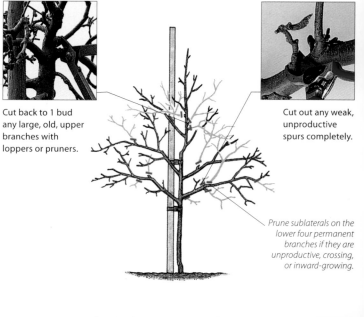

Cut back to 1 bud any large, old, upper branches with loppers or pruners.

Cut out any weak, unproductive spurs completely.

Prune sublaterals on the lower four permanent branches if they are unproductive, crossing, or inward-growing.

From the first summer on, prune the new shoots in mid- to late summer, once they have become woody at the base. Not all shoots ripen together, so pruning should continue over several weeks. Use the Modified or Full Lorette System (see "Summer pruning," pp.438–439).

Routine pruning

Winter pruning is essential to prevent congestion: reduce overgrown spur systems and remove those that are overcrowded. If the cordon is not producing enough well-spaced laterals, shorten the leader by about one-quarter of its length to encourage strong growth.

Once a cordon has extended beyond the top wire, lower its angle of growth slightly to provide space for the leader to extend. When it reaches the top wire, trim it back to one leaf of new growth in late spring. Alternatively, if the leader is vigorous, cut it back in late spring to a sideshoot near the top wire.

Continue pruning on the Modified or Full Lorette System; this involves cutting sideshoots to one leaf on an established cordon.

Double cordon

A double cordon is usually grown vertically. Feathered maidens and maiden whips may be trained as double cordons. The process is similar in each case, except that maiden whips must be pruned to stimulate low sideshoots before training can begin (see "Forming a double cordon," right). Alternatively, cut back a feathered maiden to two suitable and oppositely placed laterals. Tie them at about 30° to support stakes and shorten by half. In summer, once a spacing of 18in (45cm) between the young leaders is attainable, turn and tie them to an upright position.

Fan

A wall or fence is an ideal support against which to grow a fan-trained apple tree; select a spur-bearing cultivar on a dwarfing rootstock so it may be comfortably accommodated in the available space. Tip bearers are not suitable to grow as fans (see "Tip bearers and spur bearers," p.437). Fix horizontal support wires about 6in (15cm) apart, starting at 15in (38cm) from soil level. The initial development of the framework is as for peaches (see p.453); once established, it should be pruned on the Modified Lorette System (see pp.438–439), with each stem being treated like a single cordon.

APPLE CORDON
Year 1, Winter pruning

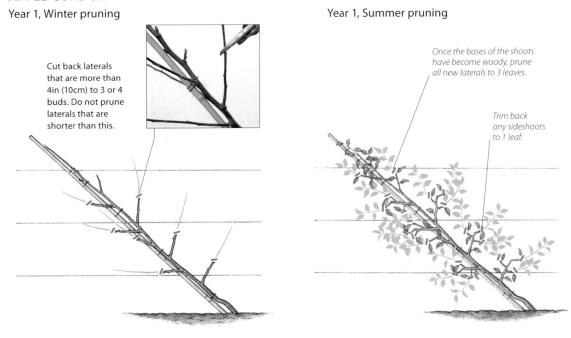

Cut back laterals that are more than 4in (10cm) to 3 or 4 buds. Do not prune laterals that are shorter than this.

Year 1, Summer pruning

Once the bases of the shoots have become woody, prune all new laterals to 3 leaves.

Trim back any sideshoots to 1 leaf.

Established cordon, winter pruning

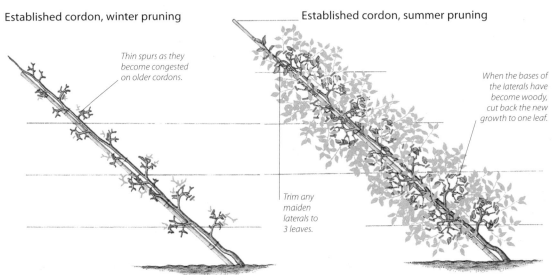

Thin spurs as they become congested on older cordons.

Established cordon, summer pruning

When the bases of the laterals have become woody, cut back the new growth to one leaf.

Trim any maiden laterals to 3 leaves.

FORMING A DOUBLE CORDON FROM A MAIDEN WHIP

To train a maiden whip as a double cordon, cut back the newly planted tree to about 10in (24cm) from soil level during the first winter, leaving a strong bud on either side below the cut. The following summer, when new shoots have been produced, tie the two uppermost shoots to stakes at an angle of 45°, lowering them to 30° later in the season. When the tips of these shoots are more than 18in (45cm) apart, train them upward by tying them to vertical stakes.

Once the basic U-shape of the double cordon has been formed, the two vertical arms should each be pruned in the same way as a single cordon.

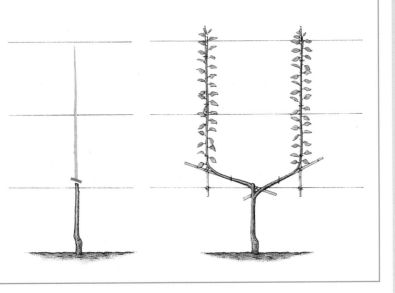

Espalier

For this tree form, one or more pairs of opposite shoots are trained at right angles to the main stem onto support wires that are placed at intervals at 15in (38cm) apart. An espalier usually has two or three tiers but more are possible with trees of sufficient vigor. If a maiden whip is used, the first tier may then be trained more readily at the required height. Only spur bearers are suitable to grow as espaliers (see "Tip bearers and spur bearers," p.437).

Formative pruning

After planting a maiden whip, prune back the leader to a bud just above the lowest wire. The following summer, train the uppermost shoot vertically to form a new leader; as the two strongest laterals below this develop, tie each to a stake at an angle of 45° to form the first branch tier. Cut or pinch back all other, lower shoots to two or three leaves. Tie down the laterals of the first tier into their horizontal position toward the end of the first growing season. If the two main arms develop unevenly, lower the more vigorous shoot to check growth and raise the weaker shoot to induce vigor. Once the two are balanced, tie them into their horizontal positions (see also *Training on Stakes*, p.429).

The following winter, remove any laterals that have developed other than the main arms. To create the second tier, first look for two strong buds about 15in (38cm) above the first tier, then cut back the central leader to the bud above these. Shorten each first tier arm by a third to a downward-facing bud; where growth is vigorous, leave the arm unpruned.

The bud to which each arm is cut back will produce a shoot that should be trained horizontally during the second summer after planting. Cut back other sublaterals according to the Modified Lorette System (see pp.438–439). The second pair of arms will form and these should be trained in the same way as the first pair. Repeat this process as necessary to obtain the required number of tiers.

Routine pruning

Once the arms of the topmost tier are well established, prune back the central leader in winter to just

APPLE ESPALIER

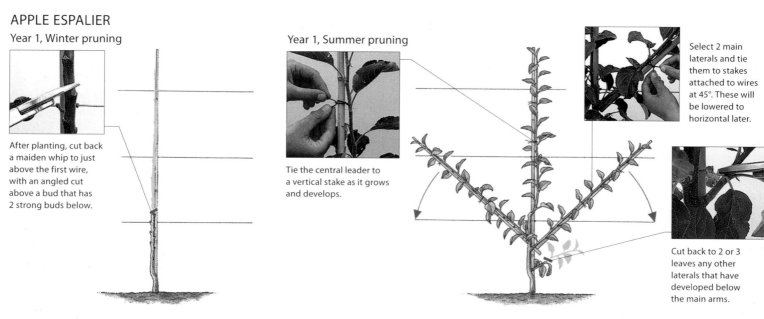

Year 1, Winter pruning

After planting, cut back a maiden whip to just above the first wire, with an angled cut above a bud that has 2 strong buds below.

Year 1, Summer pruning

Tie the central leader to a vertical stake as it grows and develops.

Select 2 main laterals and tie them to stakes attached to wires at 45°. These will be lowered to horizontal later.

Cut back to 2 or 3 leaves any other laterals that have developed below the main arms.

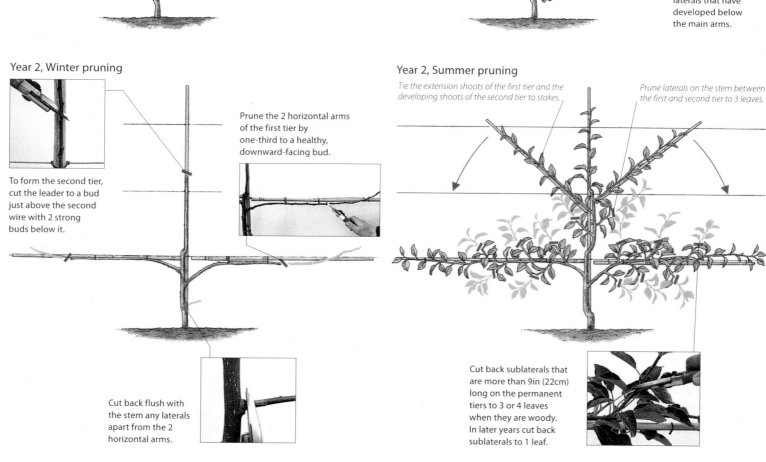

Year 2, Winter pruning

To form the second tier, cut the leader to a bud just above the second wire with 2 strong buds below it.

Prune the 2 horizontal arms of the first tier by one-third to a healthy, downward-facing bud.

Cut back flush with the stem any laterals apart from the 2 horizontal arms.

Year 2, Summer pruning

Tie the extension shoots of the first tier and the developing shoots of the second tier to stakes.

Prune laterals on the stem between the first and second tier to 3 leaves.

Cut back sublaterals that are more than 9in (22cm) long on the permanent tiers to 3 or 4 leaves when they are woody. In later years cut back sublaterals to 1 leaf.

PICKING

Support the apple in the palm of your hand and twist it slightly. If the apple comes away easily from the spur, it is ready for picking.

above this tier. The espalier should thereafter be pruned in summer following the Full or Modified Lorette System (see pp.438–439).

Dwarf pyramid

The dwarf pyramid is a compact tree form that is suitable for a small yard or container. Such a shape is suitable for spur-bearing cultivars (see "Tip bearers and spur bearers," p.437). It needs permanent staking if grown on an 'M27' or 'M9' rootstock; cultivars on other rootstocks need staking for four or five years. For pruning, see "Pear: Dwarf pyramid," p.445.

Secondary growth often develops after summer pruning. These unwanted shoots inhibit the formation of fruit buds, so prune them at least two or three weeks later than usual to help retard their growth if this is a problem. If secondary growth continues to appear, leave one or two shoots unpruned to act as sap-drawers (see "Summer pruning," p.438).

Harvesting and storing

Early-ripening apples should be gathered just before they are fully ripe or they soon become mealy. Late-maturing cultivars must not be picked too soon, however, or the fruits will shrivel while they are in storage.

Wrap fruits individually in wax paper or tissue paper and store them in slatted boxes or crates in a cool place (see p.431), such as a basement. Fruits from young or overvigorous trees store less well than those from more mature trees and should therefore be used first. For further information on harvesting and storing, see p.431.

Propagation

Apple trees may be propagated by chip-budding or T-budding in summer (see pp.432 and 433) or whip-and-tongue grafting in early spring (see p.433). If possible, use certified scions and rootstocks.

Grafting over

Grafting over is a technique used to graft scions of a selected cultivar onto an established apple or pear tree to replace the original cultivar or to create a "family" tree (see p.420). This is usually done to introduce a new pollinator for adjacent trees or to try a new cultivar; because the roots and main branch system are already established, the new cultivar should bear fruit quickly. There are two methods: topworking and frame-working.

Topworking

Initially, this entails heading (cutting) back most of the main branches to within 24–30in (60–75cm) of the main branch fork in spring. Leave one or two smaller branches unpruned to act as sap-drawers to reduce the number of new shoots that may form around the pruning cuts. Trim the cuts where branches have been sawn off. Two or three scions are used per branch but only the most vigorous one is grown on; the presence of the others may initially help to stop canker developing. These may be either rind- or cleft-grafted (the latter is rarely used by amateurs).

For rind grafting, take dormant scions from the previous season's growth of the desired cultivar and prepare them with angled top cuts and tapering basal cuts. Cut away a sliver of bark on the other side of the tapering cut to prevent the bark from being damaged when inserted into the branch. When rind grafting branches of about 1in (2.5cm) in diameter, place two scions opposite each other. Larger branches can accommodate three evenly spaced scions. Make a vertical cut for each scion in the

bark of the prepared branch. Carefully lift the bark and slide the scion into position underneath. Bind the graft firmly into position and seal the cut surfaces with grafting wax. Scion growth is rapid and ties must be released.

Retain the most vigorous scion and remove the others. Frequently, more than one shoot will develop from the selected scion; allow the best one to grow unchecked as the basis for the new branch. Shorten any others if they are less vigorous, but remove them completely if they are of equal vigor. After three or four years the new cultivar should start to bear regularly. From then on, prune the new branch according to the tree requirements.

Frame-working

In this method, most of the branch framework is retained and many scions are grafted onto different parts of the tree. Frame-working is preferred by commercial growers because trees bear more quickly than if topworked.

HOW TO RIND GRAFT

1 In early spring, cut off most of the main branches to within 24–30in (60–75cm) of the trunk. Leave one or two branches uncut to draw the sap.

2 Make a vertical cut 1in (2.5cm) long through the bark of one of the trimmed branches. If it is 1in (2.5cm) in diameter, make two evenly spaced cuts; if larger, make three cuts.

3 Use the blunt side of the knife blade to ease the bark away from the cambium layer.

4 Prepare scions three buds long, each with an angled cut at the top and a 1in (2.5cm) tapering cut at the base. Insert them with the tapering cut facing in.

5 When two or three scions have been inserted, bind the grafts tightly with strong string or grafting tape, winding it around the whole branch to hold the scions in place.

6 Apply grafting wax to the exposed areas. When the scions have united with the branch, retain the most vigorous and remove the others.

Pears (*Pyrus communis*)

Pears need more consistently warm conditions than apples to bear reliably. Late-ripening cultivars require dry and warm conditions throughout late summer and early fall. They have a winter chilling requirement of 600–900 hours below 45°F (7°C).

Pears can be trained in a similar way to apples; open center, dwarf pyramid, cordon, and espalier forms are the most suitable for small gardens. Pears can be grown on quince rootstocks, but disease resistant OHxF series pear rootstock may be a better choice.

DESSERT PEARS TO TRY

Early
'Ayres' **R**
'Bartlett'
'Clapp's Favorite' **H**
'Chapin'
'Gifford'
'Harrow Delight' **R**
'Hosui' **A**
'Marguerite Marillat'
'Mericourt'
'Moonglow' **R**
'Shinesekei' **A**
'Summercrisp'

Mid-season
'Aurora'
'Beurré d'Anjou'
'Beurré Superfin'
'Bosc'
'Bristol Cross'
'Chojuro' **A**
'Concord'
'Conference'
'Devoe'
'Douglas'
'Doyenné du Comice'
'Fondante d'Automne'
'Highland'
'John'
'Lincoln' **R, H**
'Magness' **R, H**
'Maxine'
'Max-Red Bartlett'
'Merton Pride' (triploid)
'Morgan' **R**
'Orcas'
'Packham's Triumph'
'Potomac'
'Rescue'
'Sekel' **R**
'Shinsui' **A**
'Spartlett'

Key
A Asian
H Notably hardy
R Resistant to fire blight

Site and planting

Pears flower earlier than apples, in mid- to late spring, and may be damaged by frost. Pears are not fully self-fertile; cross-pollination is needed for a good crop.

Site

Pears require a warm, sheltered, and sunny site. The soil should retain moisture—particularly for trees on quince rootstocks (see below)—but must also be well drained; pears tolerate wetter conditions than apples. Trees on poor or sandy soils produce fruits of inferior flavor, while those on shallow alkaline soils may suffer from lime-induced chlorosis, a nutritional problem caused by deficiencies of manganese/iron (see p.664). Such sites can be improved by regularly mulching with large amounts of organic matter and occasionally applying chelated iron and manganese.

Rootstocks

As well as producing relatively small trees, growing pears on quince rootstocks induces early fruiting. 'Quince A' is dwarfing. The OHxF 333 pear rootstock is also semidwarfing, resulting in trees that reach 12–20 ft (3.5–6 m) at maturity.

Pollination

Provision for cross-pollination should always be made by planting two compatible cultivars. Some cultivars are triploid, and a very few are male sterile: these require two pollinators nearby. This is only likely to be a problem if you are growing some of the more obscure varieties. Most commercially available young trees will cross-pollinate readily.

Planting

Plant bare-root pears in spring, or in the fall when the soil is still warm. This allows trees to establish

ROOTSTOCKS

12ft (4m)
9ft (3m)
6ft (2m)
3ft (1m)

'Quince C'   'Quince A'

before coming into growth, which may occur very early in a mild spring. Planting distances (see below) depend on the choice of rootstock and the form in which the trees are grown (see "Pruning and training," right).

Routine care

Regular maintenance including fruit thinning, feeding and watering, and checking for pest and disease problems, is similar to that required for apples (see p.436). For general information, see pp.426–427.

Fruit thinning

After the natural shedding of fruitlets at or soon after midsummer, thin out to leave one fruit per cluster if the crop is heavy, but two if it is bearing is lighter.

Feeding, watering, and mulching

Water and fertilize trees as needed (see p.426). It is important to supply sufficient nitrogen but not to overfeed because the resulting flush of growth could readily by infected by fire blight. Mulch around newly planted trees in spring.

Pests and diseases

Pears may be affected by birds (p.655), rabbits (p.669), wasps (p.672), aphids (p.654), caterpillars (p.657), fire blight (p.660), pear thrips (p.671), scab (p.668), and brown rot (p.656). Pear leaf blister mites produce pustules in the leaves. Destroy infected leaves throughout the summer.

Some pears, especially 'Conference', may develop parthenocarpic fruits. These have a cylindrical shape and may be produced when partial fertilization has occurred; the fruit grows but is misshapen. Treat by providing a suitable pollinator and giving shelter to encourage more pollinating insects.

Pruning and training

Pruning requirements and techniques are similar to those for apples, but pears tolerate harder pruning once they have started to bear. Fruiting occurs predominantly on two-year-old and older wood. Spur production on pears is usually more prolific than on apples, and spurs should be thinned regularly on established trees. Very few pear cultivars are tip bearers.

To formally train and prune to develop a cordon or an espalier, follow the steps as for apples. Both are pruned by the Modified Lorette System in temperate areas or, in warmer climates, by the Full Lorette System (see "Apples: Summer pruning," pp.438–439). A fan is formed in the same way as for peaches (see p.453) but, once established, prune as for an apple fan (see p.441). Pears should be pruned two or three weeks earlier than apples, once shoots mature at the base.

Where excessive vigor occurs at the expense of bearing fruit, root pruning (see p.429), if applicable, or, as a last resort, bark-ringing (see p.437) can be utilized.

Open center

Initial training and pruning of an open-center tree are the same as for apples (see p.439). Several pear cultivars (for example 'Doyenné du Comice') have an upright growth habit; when pruning branch leaders of these cultivars, cut to an outward-pointing bud. Shoots that are upright should be tied down before they ripen fully at the base, as part of the initial training process, to encourage a wider angle of growth. Pruning on very vigorous trees should be much lighter after the second year. Where vigor is lacking, shorten new laterals to five or six buds or fewer.

The few tip bearers (for example, 'Merton Pride') need to be renewal pruned as described for tip-bearing apples (see p.437). Established spur-bearing trees need

PLANTING DISTANCES

Tree form	Rootstock	Distance between trees	Distance between rows
Open center	'Quince C'	11ft (3.5m)	18ft (5.5m)
	'Quince A'	14ft (4.75m)	18ft (5.5m)
Cordon	'Quince A' or 'C'	30in (75cm)	6ft (2m)
Espalier	'Quince C'	11ft (3.5m)	
	'Quince A'	14ft (4.75m)	
Fan	As espalier	As espalier	
Dwarf pyramid	'Quince C'	4ft (1.2m)	6ft (2m)
	'Quince A'	5ft (1.5m)	6ft (2m)

considerable spur shortening and thinning, and occasional branch thinning, in winter.

Dwarf pyramid

Prune back the leading shoot of a feathered maiden after planting to 20–30in (50–75cm) from the ground, and reduce any laterals to 6in (15cm); remove weak or low laterals. In the first summer, prune extension growth on the laterals, and any new laterals, to five or six leaves to downward-facing buds. This encourages horizontal growth and induces early fruiting. Cut back sublaterals to three leaves. The following winter, prune the leading shoot to leave 10in (25cm) of the new growth, cutting to a bud on the opposite side to that of the previous year's pruning. In each subsequent year, prune the leader to buds on alternate sides. When the leader reaches the required height, prune back in late spring to leave one bud of the new growth.

PEAR, DWARF PYRAMID

Year 1, Winter pruning

Cut back the leader with an angled cut just above a bud, 50–75cm (20–30in) from the ground.

Prune back each lateral to a downward-facing bud about 15cm (6in) from the main stem.

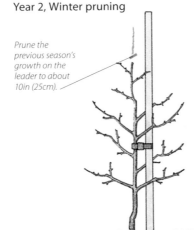

Cut back entirely any low laterals on the main stem.

Year 1, Summer pruning

Cut back new growth at the tips of the main laterals to 5 or 6 leaves on the extension growth.

Prune new laterals growing directly from the main stem to 5 or 6 leaves.

Cut back any sublaterals growing from the main laterals to 3 leaves. These will start to form spurs for the following summer.

Year 2, Winter pruning

Prune the previous season's growth on the leader to about 10in (25cm).

Year 2 and routine summer pruning

Trim sublaterals from existing laterals or spurs to 1 leaf beyond the basal cluster.

Cut back new growth at the ends of the permanent branches to 5 or 6 leaves.

Cut back laterals growing from the main branches to 3 leaves.

Established dwarf pyramid, winter pruning

When the leader reaches the required height, prune it to one bud of the previous season's growth.

Before
The spurs on the darker wood at the base of this shoot are congested and require thinning.

After
Thin by removing any unproductive or overlapping spurs. Trim out excess fruit buds to leave 2 or 3 evenly spaced buds per spur.

DESSERT PEARS TO TRY (CONT.)

Mid-season (cont.)
'Starkcrimson'
'Twentieth Century' **A**

Late
'Atago'
'Beurré Bosc'
'Comice'
'Duchess' **R**
'Dumont'
'Golden Russet Bosc'
'Golden Spice' **R**
'Gorham'
'Highland'
'Joséphine de Malines'
'Kieffer' **R**
'Luscious'
'Niitaka' **A**
'Olympic'
'Shinko' **A**
'Thomas' **H**
'Warren' **R**
'Winter Nelis'
'Ya Li' **A**
'Yoinashi' **A**

CULINARY PEARS TO TRY

Mid-season
'Bartlett'
'Catillac'

Late
'Seckel'
'Vicar of Winkfield' (triploid)

Key
A Asian
H Notably hardy
R Resistant to fire blight

Once the initial framework has been formed, nearly all pruning is carried out in mid- to late summer, depending on season and location. It is important that shoots have grown woody at their base before they are pruned; the operation is therefore spread over three or four weeks and a few shoots may not be ready to prune until early fall. Do not shorten shoots that are 6in (15cm) or less in length. Cut back branch leaders to six leaves of new growth and prune any sublaterals to one leaf above the basal cluster. Any shoots arising directly from the main branches should be shortened to three leaves. If secondary growth develops, leave a few shoots unpruned as for apples (see "Summer pruning," p.438) to draw the sap.

The only major operation for winter pruning is the shortening of the central leader already described, plus, in later years, some spur thinning and shortening. If the spur systems are allowed to become congested, the tree loses vigor and small, overcrowded fruit are produced.

Harvesting and storing

Time of picking is most important, especially for cultivars that ripen in late summer and early fall. If left on the tree too long, the fruit will have turned "sleepy" and brown at the center. Gather them at the first sign of a change of ground color on the skin from dark to slightly lighter green. If in doubt, gently lift and twist a fruit: if it comes away easily, it is almost ripe and will be at peak flavor in a few days. If the stalk breaks, wait for a few days longer. Several harvests need to be made because all fruit do not ripen simultaneously. Fruits of late-ripening cultivars and those grown in cool climates must be left on the tree until mature to develop their full flavor.

Store pears in cool conditions, laying them in slatted boxes. Do not wrap them—this makes the flesh discolor. The fruits of later-ripening cultivars should be conditioned before eating: keep them at room temperature for a day or two and eat when the flesh gives under gentle pressure by the thumb near the stem. The flavor should then be at its fullest.

Propagation

For most pear cultivars, whip-and-tongue grafting or chip- or T-budding (see "Propagation," p.432) onto a quince or OHxF series rootstock is usually successful.

■ DOUBLE-WORKING PEAR CULTIVARS

The few pear cultivars that are incompatible with quince rootstocks need to be double-worked: a cultivar that is compatible with both the quince rootstock and the selected scion cultivar is used as an "interstock" between the two. The cultivar 'Beurré Hardy' is the most widely used interstock; 'Vicar of Winkfield' can also be used for all pear cultivars that require double-working. These include 'Dr. Jules Guyot', 'Marguerite Marillat', and 'Packham's Triumph'. Two methods of double-working may be used: double chip-budding and double grafting.

Double chip-budding entails carrying out chip-budding two years in succession: in the first year, a scion of the interstock is budded onto a suitable quince rootstock; in the second year,

Double budding
Insert the bud chip 2in (5cm) above the first graft and on the opposite side, so that the resulting stem will grow out straighter when the bud develops. Cut off the interstock above the new bud once the scion shoot has developed. Remove any shoots on the interstock.

a scion of the selected cultivar is budded onto the interstock on the opposite side. The method is as for chip-budding (see p.432).

For double grafting the same principle should be followed. Graft the interstock onto the quince rootstock in early spring using the whip-and-tongue method (see p.433). In late winter or early spring, cut back the

Double grafting
This follows the same principle as double budding: cut back the interstock a year after it is grafted, once the sap starts to rise, and graft on the required scion. Leave 2in (5cm) between grafts; position the scion graft on the opposite side from the previous one.

grafted interstock and graft the incompatible cultivar scion onto the interstock. Alternatively, the incompatible cultivar scion may be budded onto the interstock in summer, following the grafting of the interstock in spring. Remove shoots from the interstock, but retain those from the cultivar scion for strong growth in future seasons.

Quinces (*Cydonia oblonga*)

Quinces are fruit grown mainly in temperate regions. As bushy trees, they reach 10–15ft (3.4–5m); they may also be trained as fans. The apple- or pear-shaped fruit are covered with grayish-white down. The most widely grown cultivars are 'Champion', 'Orange', 'Portugal', and 'Smyrna'. Quinces have a cold-weather requirement of 100–450 hours below 45°F (7°C) in order to flower.

Site and planting

Quinces require a reasonably sunny site. The protection provided by a nearby wall may be beneficial in cold areas. Moisture-retentive, slightly acidic soils are preferred; marked alkalinity usually causes lime-induced chlorosis.

'Quince A' is normally used as a rootstock. Where trees are grown on their own roots, suckering may be difficult to control. Quinces are generally self-pollinating but the provision of pollinators is claimed to improve crop levels.

Plant quinces in spring if bare-root, or throughout the year if container-grown, spacing them about 12–15ft (4–4.5m) apart.

Routine care

Cultivation requirements are as described under "Care of tree fruits," p.426. Once established, quinces need little attention. Occasional fertilizing at the recommended rate may be necessary, particularly on poor soils, while watering and mulching may also be required. Quinces are comparatively easy to grow but fungal leaf spots (p.660) may be a problem.

Pruning and training

Quinces fruit on spurs and on the tips of the previous summer's growth. Bushes may be left to grow into multistemmed trees or pruned in the early stages as for apple bushes (see p.439) with an open-centered, well-spaced branch framework. Pruning of established trees is minimal, with occasional thinning in winter of old, overcrowded growth. Not every lateral should be pruned, however, because this removes too many fruit buds.

Harvesting and storing

Pick the fruit when the skins have turned from green to gold, usually in late fall. Store in boxes in a cool, well-ventilated, dark place. Do not wrap the fruit: quinces stored in plastic bags will discolor internally. Store quinces separately. Otherwise, their strong aroma may contaminate the flavor of other stored fruit. They are often used in preserves.

Propagation

Quince trees may be propagated either by chip-budding onto 'Quince A' rootstocks in summer (see p.432) or by taking hardwood cuttings in fall (see p.434).

Quince tree
Leave a generous grass-free area around young quinces, so that all the nutrients are absorbed by the trees and not shared with the grass.

Medlars (*Mespilus germanica*)

Medlars are decorative, spreading trees with golden fall color and large, white or pinkish-white flowers in mid- to late spring. They are most commonly grown as dwarfs or semidwarfs. Recommened cultivars are "Blue Damson', 'French Damson', and 'Farleigh'. Medlars are self-fertile and have a chilling requirement of 100–450 hours below 45°F (7°C). The fruits are apple-shaped and somewhat flattened with prominent, horny calyces. Their flavor is an acquired taste. The fruit is often used for preserves.

Medlars

Site and planting

A sunny, sheltered site is preferable, although medlars tolerate partial shade. They may be grown in a wide range of soils, with the exception of those that are highly alkaline or poorly drained. Adequate moisture is essential to obtain strong growth and a good crop of fruits.

Trees grown for the quality of their fruits are usually grafted on 'Quince A' rootstocks, although semidwarf trees are sometimes available on seedling pear rootstocks.

Medlar trees are best planted in spring or fall. Semidwarf trees should be spaced at a distance of 25ft (8m), and bushes at 14ft (4.25m).

Routine care

Cultivation requirements are generally as for apples (see p.436). Medlars may sometimes be affected by leaf-eating caterpillars (p.657) and fungal leaf spots (p.660).

Pruning and training

Train a dwarf tree as for apples (see p.439). For semidwarfs, pruning is initially as for apples. Once the main framework is established, occasionally thin branches in winter to maintain an open framework, removing overcrowded, diseased, or dead growth.

Harvesting and storing

Leave fruit on the tree for as long as possible so that they develop their full flavor. Pick them in late fall when the stalk parts easily

Ripening medlars
The small, brown fruits ripen in fall and measure 1–2in (2.5–5cm) across.

from the tree, preferably in dry weather. The fruit is unpalatable immediately after picking, and must be stored before use. Dip the stalks in a strong salt solution to prevent rotting, then store the fruits, calyces downward, on slatted trays, so that the fruits do not touch. Use when the flesh has become soft and brown.

Propagation

Propagate by chip- or T-budding (see pp.432 and 433), or whip-and-tongue grafting (see p.433).

Plums, gages, damsons, and bullaces (*Prunus x domestica*)

Various kinds of plum are grown for their fine fruit. These include: European plums (selections of *Prunus x domestica*); damsons, Mirabelles, and bullaces (*P. insititia*); gages (*P. x domestica* and *P. insititia*); and the Japanese plums (*P. salicina*). Crosses of Japanese plums with native American plums (such as *P. americana*) have produced hybrids that combine the sweetness of Japanese plums with the hardiness of American plums.

Regions with cool-temperate climates are ideal for European plums, damsons, and bullaces; in warmer areas with earlier springs, Japanese plums and Mirabelles are more widely grown. All types of plum prefer areas that have plenty of sun and relatively low rainfall. Myrobalan plums often used as vigorous rootstocks.

There is a wide range of cultivars adapted to different climates and, with more dwarfing rootstocks now available, plums are ideal for even small yards; damsons are usually smaller than plums. The compact pyramid tree and open-center forms are particularly suitable for small yards; for the choicest fruit in cool climates, grow fan-trained trees on warm, sunny walls. European plums and damsons have a chilling requirement of 700–1,000 hours below 45°F (7°C), and the Japanese plum, 500–900 hours.

Site and planting

Plums need a warm, sheltered site to ensure that the flowers are pollinated successfully. Their pollination requirements are complex—some cultivars are self-fertile while others require suitable pollinators planted nearby. Make sure that there is enough room on the proposed site for the required number of trees, allowing for their mature height.

Site

All plums flower early in spring, Japanese plums markedly so and cherry plums earlier still, so that spring frosts are always a hazard. They are, therefore, best planted in a relatively frost-free site. Plums need to be sheltered from wind to avoid damage to the trees and also to encourage pollinating insects.

Most soils are suitable, but avoid those that are highly alkaline and poorly drained. Plums on poor, sandy soils need extra feeding and watering to maintain good growth and cropping, and to improve flavor (see "Feeding, watering, and mulching," p.448).

Rootstocks

'Pixy' (semidwarfing) and 'St. Julien A' (moderately vigorous) are best for small- to medium-sized plum trees, 7–12ft (2.2–4m). For

ROOTSTOCKS

12ft (4m)
9ft (3m)
6ft (2m)
3ft (1m)

'Pixy'　　'St. Julien A'　　'Brompton'　　'Myrobalan B'

trees up to 14ft (4.25m), choose 'Myrobalan B' (incompatible with some cultivars) or 'Brompton' (universally compatible). 'Marianna' is excellent for Japanese plums, but is incompatible with some European plums. Plums tend to produce suckers, but this is less common with modern rootstocks.

Pollination

European plums and damsons may be self-fertile, partially self-fertile, or self-sterile. Fortunately, some very popular cultivars, such as 'Stanley', are self-fertile, but planting suitable

pollinators nearby will ensure more consistent bearing. Cultivars that are not self-fertile must always be planted with compatible pollinators nearby. Cherry plums are self-fertile. Some Japanese plums are self-fertile, but most give better results when planted near a suitable pollinator. Plum cultivars that will not pollinate certain others are indicated in the lists of recommended cultivars on pp.448 and 449, which also give details of flowering times. Seek advice about pollination of individual trees when buying.

PLANTING DISTANCES

Tree form	Rootstock	Distance between trees	Distance between rows
Open-center dwarf	'St. Julien A'	12–15ft (4–5m)	18ft (5.5m)
Semidwarf	'Brompton' or 'Myrobalan B'	18–22ft (5.5–7m)	22ft (7m) minimum
Fan	'St. Julien A'	15–18ft (5–5.5m)	
Pyramid	'St. Julien A' or 'Pixy'	8–12ft (2.5–4m)	12–20ft (4–6m)

Planting
This should be completed as early as possible in late fall or early winter because growth starts early in spring. In cold areas, plant in spring only. All trees are best staked for two years; stake those on 'Pixy' rootstocks permanently. Planting distances (see p.447) are determined by the chosen tree form and by the vigor of the rootstock.

Routine care
Feed and water trees regularly, and check for pests and diseases. Thin fruit as necessary. If spring frosts are likely, protect wall-trained trees in bloom with a cover (see FROST AND WIND PROTECTION, pp.612–613).

Fruit thinning
Thinning gives larger, better-flavored fruits and reduces the risk of branches breaking from the weight of too many fruits. Fruitlets may be thinned early if the set is heavy. After the stones have formed and natural fruit drop has occurred, thin the remaining fruit to about 2–3in (5–8cm) apart for small fruits and 3–4in (8–10cm) for larger cultivars (such as 'Victoria'). Scissors are best for this job because they are quicker to use than pruners.

Feeding, watering, and mulching
Plums need plenty of nitrogen; apply a spring dressing at the rate recommended under "Care of tree fruits," p.426. Mulch annually with well-rotted manure or compost, and water as required, particularly in prolonged hot weather. Plums planted against walls or fences will need more regular watering than those in the open.

Pests and diseases
Plums may be attacked by deer (p.659), rabbits (p.669), wasps (p.672), aphids (p.654), and plum curculio (p.666). Diseases that may affect plums include black-knot gall (p.655), bacterial canker (p.655), and brown rot (p.656). Any trees that are badly infected with black knot, bacterial canker, or (less commonly) with viruses (p.672) should be dug up and discarded without delay. Untreated diseases and viruses can reduce yields and eventually kill the trees.

All stone fruit trees may be affected by the physiological disorder known as gummosis. Trees that have this problem exude a translucent, amber-colored, gumlike substance from the trunk and branches, while plums may also form gum around the stone within the fruit. The gum is produced by the trees as a result of stress that is caused by disease, adverse soil conditions, or physical damage caused by, for example, strong winds or a heavy crop. If gummosis is noticed, try to identify the cause and alleviate the problem if possible. Birds may also be troublesome; if they attack the fruit buds, it may be necessary to place fine mesh nets over the trees during the winter to prevent damage (see also p.655).

Pruning and training
Plum trees produce fruit at the base of one-year-old shoots, as well as on two-year-old wood and spurs. Once initially trained, they require less pruning on unrestricted forms than apples or pears. In cool-temperate climates it is essential to prune in summer (after training) to minimize the risk of black knot (p.655). Trained trees require routine summer pruning to maintain their restricted shape. Remove any damaged or diseased branches immediately, cutting back to healthy wood.

Dwarf
In early spring when the buds are breaking, start training a newly planted feathered maiden. Select

PLUM BUSH
Year 1, Early spring pruning

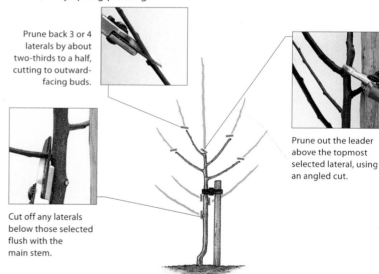

Prune back 3 or 4 laterals by about two-thirds to a half, cutting to outward-facing buds.

Cut off any laterals below those selected flush with the main stem.

Prune out the leader above the topmost selected lateral, using an angled cut.

Year 2, Early spring pruning

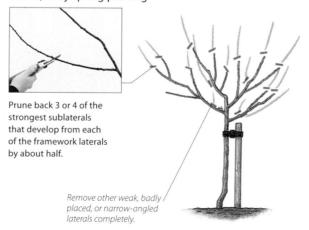

Prune back 3 or 4 of the strongest sublaterals that develop from each of the framework laterals by about half.

Remove other weak, badly placed, or narrow-angled laterals completely.

FRUITING HABIT

Plum trees develop fruit at the base of one-year-old shoots and then along the stems on two-year-old wood and spurs.

three or four strong, evenly spaced laterals, the highest at about 3ft (90cm) from ground level, and prune them by about two-thirds or a half, to healthy, outward-facing buds. These laterals will form the basic framework of branches. Then prune out the leader, making an angled cut above the highest of the selected laterals. Cut back to the main stem unwanted laterals below those selected.

The following early spring, choose three or four of the strongest sublaterals that have developed on each of the pruned laterals and shorten them by half. To achieve a balanced framework, trim off weak or badly placed laterals and pinch out any shoots growing from the main stem.

Subsequently, restrict pruning of young trees to the removal, in summer, of excessively vigorous or awkwardly placed growths. With older trees, thin some branches in summer to avoid overcrowding.

If using a maiden whip, prune it to about 3ft (90cm). The following spring, laterals should have developed, and it may then be trained as a feathered maiden.

Semidwarf
Choose three or four well-spaced laterals on a feathered maiden; cut back the leader just above the uppermost lateral at 4½ft (1.3m), then prune each of the chosen laterals by one-third to a half. Remove any lower laterals.

Subsequent pruning of the sublaterals and training to form an open-center head is the same as for a dwarf. Semidwarf trees are less easy to manage than pyramid or dwarf plums when mature because of their greater size.

Spindlebush
Similar in shape to a plum pyramid (see p.450), the spindlebush requires a little more space but does not need the same annual summer pruning. Pruning and training are as for apple spindlebushes (see p.440) but prune in early spring when the buds break.

Tie down upright shoots and keep the top of the tree in check by removing the more vigorous

JAPANESE-AMERICAN HYBRID PLUMS TO TRY

'Alderman'
'AU Producer'
'AU Roadside'
'Elite' **H**
'Ember'
'Kahinta'
'La Crescent'
'Pembina'
'Perfection'
'Pipestone'
'Redcoat'
'South Dakota'
'Superior'
'Toka'
'Underwood' **H**
'Waneta'

CHERRY PLUMS TO TRY

'Beta'
'Compass'
'Deep Purple'

DAMSONS TO TRY

'Blue Damson'
'Farleigh' **Psf**
'French Damson'
'Prune', syn. 'Shropshire' **Sf**

Key
H Notably hardy
Sf Self-fertile
Psf Partly self-fertile

ESTABLISHED PLUM FAN
Spring pruning

Thin new sideshoots to about 4in (10cm) apart.

Cut out any sideshoots that are growing toward the center of the fan or are badly placed.

Summer pruning

Tie in any ribs needed to extend the framework or replace older wood.

Cut back sideshoots that are not needed for the permanent rib framework to 5 or 6 leaves.

Cut back wrong-pointing or awkward shoots to shoots facing in the required direction or flush with the stem.

AFTER FRUITING

In the fall, after the fruit has been harvested, prune back to three leaves all the sideshoots that were shortened to five or six leaves earlier in the summer.

shoots and retaining the less vigorous ones to produce fruit. In this way the conical shape of the spindlebush is maintained.

Fan

Train a plum fan initially as for a peach fan (see p.453) to produce main branches or ribs to train against horizontal support wires. When training the young fan, retain some sideshoots to fill in gaps and pinch back others to one bud. Remove any very vigorous sideshoots or those growing at an awkward angle.

On an established fan, in spring or as soon as they appear, remove sideshoots growing inward toward the wall or fence, or the center of the fan. Thin the remainder to 4in (10cm) apart and pinch or cut them back to six leaves during the summer unless they are required to fill

spaces in the fan framework. After the crop has been picked, shorten these shoots to three leaves.

Pyramid

Plant a feathered maiden against a strong stake and, in early spring, cut back the central leader to a healthy bud at a height of about 5ft (1.5m). Remove any laterals growing below 18in (45cm) from the ground. Shorten the remaining laterals more than 9in (22cm) long by half their length. When the bases of the young shoots are turning woody later in the summer, cut back extension growth on the main branches and new (maiden) laterals, to about 8in (20cm); at the same time, reduce sublaterals to about 6in (15cm). To start forming the pyramid shape, cut main branches and sublaterals back to downward-facing buds so that growth is more or less horizontal. Remove any

laterals that are very vigorous or upward-pointing. Tie in the central leader to the stake, but do not prune it until the following spring, then shorten it by two-thirds of its new growth. Once the tree has reached a height of about 6ft (2m) on 'Pixy' or 8ft (2.5m) on 'St. Julien A', cut back the central leader. This should be delayed until late spring, however, because this reduces its subsequent growth; cut it back to a bud about 1in (2.5cm) from the old wood. Continue annual summer pruning as previously described, cutting branch leaders to downward-pointing buds and removing any excessively vigorous, upright shoots, especially those growing in the upper parts of the tree, to maintain the pyramid shape.

On mature pyramids, overcrowding will develop; in summer, trim off any badly placed, old wood as necessary. Maintain

the pyramid shape by keeping any vigorous or dominant upper branches in check.

Harvesting and storing

For the best flavor, allow fruits to ripen fully; for freezing or preserving, pick them when ripe but still firm. In wet weather, gather the ripening crop before brown rot or wasps spoil it. Split skins may occur with some cultivars in moist conditions. Keep the fresh fruits in a cool, dark place and use within a few days.

Propagation

Chip- or T-budding is most usual (see pp.432 and 433); whip-and-tongue grafting (see p.433) is less reliable for plums than for apples and pears.

PLUM PYRAMID

Year 1, Early spring pruning

Cut back the leader with an angled cut above a strong bud about 5ft (1.5m) from soil level.

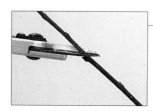

Prune the remaining laterals by half to downward-facing buds.

Remove completely any laterals less than 18in (45cm) from soil level.

Year 1, Summer pruning

Any new laterals forming too narrow an angle with the main stem should be removed. Do not prune the central leader.

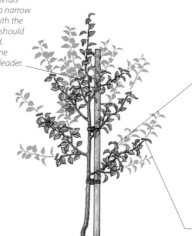

Cut back any sublaterals to 6in (15cm) with an angled cut just above a leaf.

Cut back new growth at the tips of the main branches to about 8in (20cm) and to a downward-pointing bud.

Year 2, Early spring pruning

Just before bud burst, shorten the central leader by two-thirds of its new growth.

Established pyramid, summer pruning

Remove any laterals that are crossing or overcrowded.

Repeat the routine summer pruning of main branches and sublaterals.

Cut back any dead or unproductive wood to a healthy shoot or to the point of origin.

Peaches and nectarines (*Prunus persica* and *P. persica* var. *nectarina*)

Peaches and nectarines are challenging to grow in some regions. They have a chilling requirement of 600–900 hours below 45°F (7°C). Sunny, reasonably dry summers are essential to produce good crops; in cooler climates, peaches may be grown under cover. A range of cultivars is available for different climates (see *Peaches to Try*, right, and *Nectarines to Try*, p.452); they are yellow-, pink-, or white-fleshed. On cling peaches the flesh tends to cling to the stone; other peaches are known as freestone. The nectarine is a smooth-skinned form of the peach and requires very similar treatment, although it prefers slightly warmer growing conditions.

Open center pruning is common for peaches and nectarines, but fan pruning can work well because it allows the fruit to receive the maximum sunlight needed for ripening. Some naturally compact (genetic dwarf) cultivars are ideal for growing in pots.

Site and planting

Peaches flower early in the year and so should be protected from frost; a south-facing wall is an ideal site.

Site
Maximum sun is important, in a sheltered site that is not susceptible to spring frost. In cooler climates, a sunny wall or a greenhouse is the best or only option. Peach trees in areas with high rainfall may be badly affected by peach leaf curl (p.665) unless given some protection.

Deep, fertile, slightly acidic soils (pH 6.5–7) are ideal for growing peaches. If they are grown on sandy soils, peaches need extra feeding and watering; shallow, alkaline soils often give rise to lime-induced chlorosis.

Rootstocks
There are many choices of peach rootstock. Some have a dwarfing effect while others do not. Some are

HAND-POLLINATION

Peaches may be hand-pollinated once the blooms are fully out. On a warm, dry day, use a small, soft brush to transfer the pollen from the anthers of one flower to the stigmas of another.

resistant to root-knot nematodes. Consult with the staff at your nursery supplier or online sources for recommendations.

Pollination
Nearly all cultivars are self-fertile. An exception is 'J.H. Hale', which requires a nearby pollinator that flowers at the same time (seek advice when buying). In areas with wet or uncertain weather, pollination may be erratic but can be improved by hand-pollination.

Planting
Plant bare-root trees in the early spring and container trees in the spring. Planting distances vary depending on the tree form and choice of rootstock.

Routine care

For details of cultivation, see "Care of tree fruit," p.426. Lime-induced chlorosis may lead to manganese/

PROTECTING PEACH FANS

In the fall, as the leaves drop, cover the tree with a plastic shelter open at both ends for ventilation. This keeps the leaf buds dry and inhibits peach leaf curl spores from germinating.

iron deficiency (p.663), which must be treated as soon as possible. It may be possible to protect fan-trained peaches from disease and frost to some extent, with a plastic lean-to in the winter and early spring.

Fruit thinning
To produce large fruit, thinning will be needed. When the fruitlets are the size of hazelnuts, thin them to one fruit per cluster. Later, when they are walnut-sized and some fruitlets have been shed naturally, thin to a spacing of 6–9in (15–22cm); in warm climates closer spacing may be used.

Feeding, watering, and mulching
In dry areas, watering is necessary to support growth and fruiting. Mulching in spring once the soil

PEACHES TO TRY

Early
'Candor' **W, S, Y**
'Dixired' **Y**
'J.H. Hale' **Y, Wh, H**
'Redhaven' **Y**
'Rising Star' **Y**
'Tejon' **Y, Lc**

Mid-season
'Avalon Pride' **Y,S**
'Bonanza' **Gd, Y**
'Bonita' **Lc**
'Belle of Georgia' **Wh, H**
'Harrow Beauty' **Y**
'Loring' **Y**
'Reliance' **Y**
'White Lady' **Wh**

Late
'Babygold No. 5' **Gd, Y, C**
'Canadian Harmony' **Y**
'Fayette' **W, Y**
'Redskin' **Y**
'Zachary Taylor' **C, Y**

Key
W	Warm climate needed
Gd	Genetic dwarf (good for pot culture)
C	Cling
S	Semifreestone
Y	Yellow flesh
Wh	White flesh
Lc	Low chilling requirement
H	Notably hardy

ROOTSTOCKS

12ft (4m)
9ft (3m)
6ft (2m)
3ft (1m)

'St. Julien A'   'Citation'

THINNING

1 As they form, thin peaches to one fruit per cluster, removing first any fruits growing toward the wall or fence.

2 The remaining fruit will need thinning again later, in order to leave one fruit every 6–9in (15–22cm).

PLANTING DISTANCES

Tree Form	Rootstock	Distance between trees	Distance between rows
Open center	Dwarfing	15–18ft (5–5.5m)	18ft (5.5m)
	Nondwarfing	18–24ft (5.5–7.5m)	24ft (7.5m)
Fan	Dwarfing	11–15ft (3.5–5m)	

Year 3, Early spring pruning

Cut back each of the main ribs by one quarter to stimulate further growth and extend the framework.

Year 3, Early summer pruning

Thin young sideshoots to 4–6in (10–15cm) apart by pinching out unwanted shoots. Pinch out any shoots that are growing toward the wall or fence or in the wrong direction.

Year 3, Summer pruning

Pinch back any shoots that overlap the ribs to 4–6 leaves as they develop.

As the remaining sideshoots develop, tie them to stakes to fill in the framework. These shoots should fruit the following year.

ESTABLISHED FAN, PRUNING AFTER FRUITING

Cut back each fruited shoot to a suitable replacement near its base.

Tie in the replacement shoot to fill the gap. These shoots should be evenly distributed over the whole fan.

Harvesting and storing

Harvest the fruit when they are fully ripe. Rest them in the palm of the hand and apply gentle pressure with your thumb on the part of the fruit nearest to the stalk. If the flesh "gives" slightly, the fruit is ready for picking. For the finest flavor, peaches and nectarines are best eaten as soon as possible after picking. If necessary, they can be stored for a few days by placing the fruits in a container lined with soft material and keeping it in a cool place.

Propagation

Peaches and nectarines are usually propagated by chip- or T-budding (see pp.432 and 433) in summer. Seedling peaches are variable in quality, but are often vigorous and may produce excellent crops.

Apricots (*Prunus armeniaca*)

Apricots are more difficult to grow than many other fruit. Not all cultivars thrive in certain areas, so always seek advice when selecting trees. The chilling requirement for apricots is 350–900 hours below 45°F (7°C), most cultivars being at the lower end of this range. They flower extremely early in the year.

Although dry, sunny summers are needed for successful bearing, drought conditions may cause serious bud drop late in the season. In cool climates, apricots can be grown under cover or fan-trained against a warm wall. Open center trees grow well in warm regions.

Site and planting

Apricot trees should be planted in a sunny, sheltered, and frost-free site to produce good crops of fruit. In cool areas, it is essential to grow them against a sunny wall or in a greenhouse to protect the flowers, or try planting varieties especially bred for cool climates.

A deep, slightly alkaline loam is the most suitable soil. Apricots are least likely to thrive on sandy and alkaline soils. It is also best to avoid planting them on heavy soils, particularly in areas that have cool, wet winters, because this may make them prone to dieback.

For rootstocks, seedling apricots, plums, and peaches are widely used. A seedling peach tolerates wetter conditions than a seedling apricot and produces a smaller tree. Seek advice from your local supplier. The plum rootstock 'St. Julien A' is often used. Apricots are self-fertile; in cool areas, however, flowers should be pollinated by hand.

Plant in late fall or very early winter (see *Planting Distances*, p.455) before bud break. Stake bush trees securely for the first two years.

Tree	Rootstock	Distance between trees	Distance between rows
Open center	'St. Julien A'	15–18ft (4.5–5.5m)	18ft (5.5m)
	Seedling peach or apricot	18–22ft (5.5–7m)	22ft (7m)
Fan	'St. Julien A'	15–18ft (4.5–5.5m)	

Routine care

In general, maintenance and cultivation requirements are as for other tree fruits (see "Care of tree fruits," p.426).

In warm regions where heavy bearing is common, blossoms may need thinning to counteract biennial bearing (see p.436). Remove badly placed fruitlets and carry out the main thinning after any fruit have dropped naturally and the stones have started forming. Thin so that there is a single fruit on each truss, to leave about 3in (7cm) between fruit.

In cool areas, branch dieback occurs quite frequently; cut back affected branches to clean wood as soon as possible. Birds (p.655), earwigs (p.659), bacterial canker (p.655), brown rot (p.656), and gummosis (see "Plums: Pests and diseases," p.448) cause problems.

Pruning and training

Fruit are borne both on one-year-old shoots and on older spurs. Pruning is aimed at maintaining the shape of the tree and removing old, unproductive wood. If young trees are too vigorous, they may be root-pruned (see p.429). Prune and train an open center tree as for plums (see p.448).

The initial training of a fan is as for peaches (see p.453). On an established fan, thin young shoots to 4–6in (10–15cm) apart as they develop in the spring, and remove any shoots that are pointing downward, toward the center of the fan, or inward to the wall. Retain growths that are needed to fill gaps in the framework. Pinch back sublaterals to six leaves if they are not needed to fill gaps and any sideshoots to one leaf later in the season. After fruiting, prune sublaterals to three leaves.

Harvesting

Pick the fruit when it is fully ripe and comes away easily from its stalk. Use immediately because fresh apricots do not store well; alternatively they may be frozen, used in preserves, or dried (see p.431).

Propagation

Apricots may be propagated by chip- or T-budding (see pp.432 and 433), using seedling peach or 'St. Julien A' rootstocks.

APRICOTS TO TRY

Early
'Goldbar'
'Goldrich'
'Goldstrike'
'Sundrop' W
'Tomcot'
'Veecot'

Mid-season
'Goldcot' W
'Harglow'
'Hargrand' W
'Perfection'
'Rival'
'Sun-Glo'
'Westcot' H

Late
'Blenheim'
'Farmingdale' H
'Harlayne' W
'Harogem' W

Key
W   Warm climate needed
H   Notably hardy

ESTABLISHED APRICOT FAN, EARLY SUMMER PRUNING

To fill gaps in the framework, tie in young sideshoots once they have hardened at the base.

Cut or pinch off altogether any shoots pointing downward or toward the wall or fence.

Cut or pinch back to five or six leaves any sublaterals not needed as replacement shoots.

THINNING

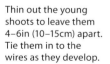

Thin out the young shoots to leave them 4–6in (10–15cm) apart. Tie them in to the wires as they develop.

AFTER FRUITING

Using pruners, cut back to three leaves the shoots that were reduced to six leaves earlier in the summer.

Sweet cherries (*Prunus avium*)

Sweet cherry trees may grow to a height and spread of 25ft (7.5m). Because most cultivars are self-sterile, two trees are often needed to produce a crop. Choose a self-fertile cultivar where just one tree is required or space is limited. New dwarfing rootstocks (see p.456) allow sweet cherries to be trained and pruned as an open center tree. Fan training a sweet cherry on a wall or fence also restricts its growth and makes it easier to protect the tree from attack by birds and from rain just before picking, which may cause the fruit to split. Sweet cherries have a chilling requirement of 800–1,200 hours below 45°F (7°C).

Duke cherries are thought to be hybrids between the sweet cherry and the sour cherry. They are not very widely grown but where chosen require similar treatment and spacing to sweet cherries. Some Duke cherry cultivars are self-fertile and combinations of sour cherries and Duke cherries are compatible.

Site and planting

Sweet cherries need a warm, sheltered site to produce a good crop. It is important to choose cultivars carefully to make sure that they will pollinate each other; this should be checked before buying trees (see "Pollination requirements," p.424).

ROOTSTOCKS

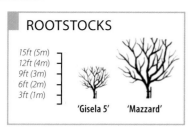

15ft (5m)
12ft (4m)
9ft (3m)
6ft (2m)
3ft (1m)

'Gisela 5'   'Mazzard'

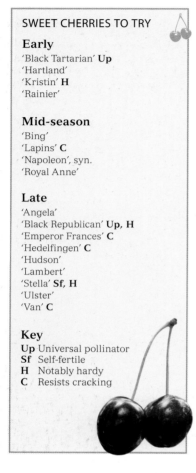

SWEET CHERRIES TO TRY

Early
'Black Tartarian' **Up**
'Hartland'
'Kristin' **H**
'Rainier'

Mid-season
'Bing'
'Lapins' **C**
'Napoleon', syn.
'Royal Anne'

Late
'Angela'
'Black Republican' **Up, H**
'Emperor Frances' **C**
'Hedelfingen' **C**
'Hudson'
'Lambert'
'Stella' **Sf, H**
'Ulster'
'Van' **C**

Key
Up Universal pollinator
Sf Self-fertile
H Notably hardy
C Resists cracking

Site

Choose an open, sunny, and sheltered site. If the cherry is to be grown as a fan, the support must be at least 8ft (2.5m) high and 15ft (5m) wide for 'Colt' or 6ft (1.8m) high and 12ft (4m) wide, with a reasonably sunny exposure; a tree grown on a cold wall will produce fruit of poor quality and flavor. Deep, well-drained soil is essential, because trees grown on shallow, poor soils produce small fruit and are less long-lived.

Rootstocks

'Mazzard' is one of the most popular rootstocks for sweet cherries, good for wet and heavy soils. 'Colt', a semidwarfing rootstock, and 'Gisela 5', a dwarfing rootstock, are suitable for open center or fan-trained trees in small gardens. Check with suppliers for new rootstock options.

Pollination

The pollination needs of sweet cherries are complex. The majority are self-sterile and they fall into distinct groups within which any combination is incompatible. Unless a self-fertile cultivar is obtained, it is vital to choose a pair of trees that are from different groups and that flower at the same time. A few sweet cherries are universal pollinators, that is, they will pollinate any cherries that flower at about the same time (see *Sweet Cherries to Try*, left).

Planting

Sweet cherries should be planted in early spring if bare-root, or throughout spring if container-grown. Construct the necessary supports and wires before planting fan-trained plants. Allow about 15–18ft (5–5.5m) between trees that are to be fan-trained and between semidwarf trees.

Routine care

Fruit thinning is unnecessary. Little or no feeding should be needed, apart from mulching as described under "Care of tree fruits," p.426. If growth is poor, apply compost or a blended fertilizer. Sweet cherries need thorough watering in dry conditions, but sudden watering on dry soils may cause the fruit to split.

As the fruit begins to color, protect it from birds by draping netting over fan-trained trees. Open center and semidwarf trees are difficult to net, however, so pick fruit as soon as they ripen.

The most likely pests and diseases to afflict sweet cherries are birds (p.655), cherry aphids (see "Aphids," p.654), tent caterpillars (p.671), brown rot (p.656), black knot (p.655), and bacterial canker (p.655); cut out any branches with signs of black knot or bacterial canker as soon as they are noticed.

Pruning and training

Sweet cherries fruit on spurs on two-year-old and older wood. Mature trees should be pruned in summer to restrict vegetative growth and induce the formation of fruit buds. Train and prune semidwarf and open-center trees as for plums (see p.448).

Fan

Sweet cherry fans are established as for peaches (see p.453). If there are conveniently placed laterals on a feathered maiden, however, it may be possible to select four rather than two arms to speed up the development of the fan. Tie these arms to stakes (attached to wires), which radiate out at 35–45 degrees from the stem. In the spring following planting, prune back the arms to 18–24in (45–60cm) and remove all other laterals that have developed.

During the summer, select two or three well-placed shoots, or "ribs," from each arm and tie them in to fill the available space; remove the remainder. All ribs on the young tree may be tip pruned at bud break (but never earlier) to reduce the risk of black knot and bacterial canker.

On older fans, spurs may be thinned or shortened in spring (see "Winter pruning," p.438) and ribs pruned to shorter replacement shoots to reduce height. In summer, pinch back all shoots not needed for the framework to six leaves, then to three after fruiting. Upright or very vigorous growths should be removed or tied horizontally to prevent the fan from becoming unbalanced.

Harvesting and storing

Pick fruit when fully ripe, complete with stalks, and eat or cook the cherries immediately. If the fruit is to be frozen (see p.431), pick when firm.

Propagation

Chip- or T-budding are the usual methods of propagation (see pp.432 and 433). 'Gisela 5' and 'Mazzard' rootstocks are compatible with most varieties; ask your supplier to confirm.

ESTABLISHED SWEET CHERRY FAN, SUMMER PRUNING

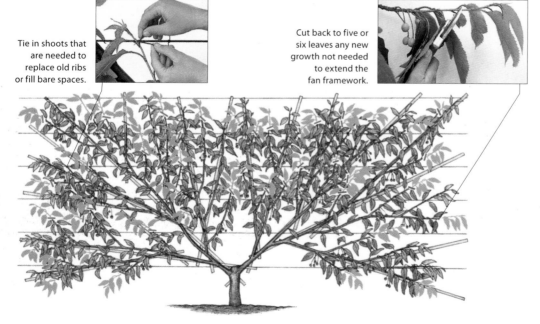

Tie in shoots that are needed to replace old ribs or fill bare spaces.

Cut back to five or six leaves any new growth not needed to extend the fan framework.

AFTER FRUITING

After the crop has been harvested, cut back all the side shoots that were pruned to six leaves in early summer to three leaves.

Sour cherries *(Prunus cerasus)*

Sour or acid cherry trees are much smaller than sweet cherries and most cultivars are self-fertile, so they are more suitable for the average garden. The fruiting habit also differs in that the crop is mostly borne on one-year-old shoots produced the previous summer. The fruit is not usually eaten raw but is prized for preserves and other culinary uses. Sour cherries have a chilling requirement of 800–1,200 hours below 45°F (7°C).

ROOTSTOCK

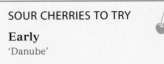

12ft (4m)
9ft (3m)
6ft (2m)
3ft (1m)

'Gisela 5'   'Mazzard'

Plant trees to be trained as open center or fans 12–15ft (4–5m) apart and for fans provide a minimum support height of 6½ft (2.1m).

Site and planting

Site and soil requirements are generally as for sweet cherries (see p.455) but sour cherries are hardier and may also be grown against a north- or east-facing wall or fence.

Good rootstock choices, as for sweet and Duke cherries, are 'Mazzard' and 'Gisela 5'. It is best to obtain cultivars such as 'Meteor' from a specialty fruit nursery to avoid inferior, less fertile selections.

Routine care

Sour cherries have the same cultivation requirements as sweet cherries (see p.455). Greater attention to feeding, particularly with nitrogen, may be necessary to encourage young, replacement shoots, but do not overfeed. Irrigation is important in dry areas. Netting is essential to protect the fruit from birds (see p.427); sour cherries may be trained into dwarf tree forms,

such as the dwarf pyramid, so they may be grown in a fruit cage. Sour cherries are affected by the same pests and diseases as sweet cherries (see "Routine care," p.456).

Pruning and training

Sour cherries are pruned on a renewal system to produce a constant supply of one-year-old wood on which fruit is produced. A proportion of the older wood should be removed each year. Prune trees in spring and summer because this reduces the risk of disease.

Fan

This is trained as for a peach fan (see p.453). Renewal pruning to encourage young growth once bearing starts is important because of the restricted space. In spring, on an established fan, pinch out badly placed or overcrowded new shoots and thin the rest to leave them 4in (10cm) apart. Tie these in to support

wires as they develop. Retain one or, where space permits, two developing shoots low down on each fruiting shoot. Tie in one of these to replace each fruiting shoot that is cut out after harvesting. The second shoot may be used as a reserve in case the first is damaged, or to fill a gap in the fan. To rejuvenate older fans, prune back to young shoots on older wood in spring and fall.

SOUR CHERRIES TO TRY

Early
'Danube'

Midseason
'Montmorency' **Sf**

Late
'North Star' **H**

Key
H   Notably hardy
Sf   Self-fertile

ESTABLISHED SOUR CHERRY FAN

Spring pruning

Remove any wrong-pointing, young shoots, cutting them back flush with the stem.

Thin the young, developing shoots to about 4in (10cm) apart, if necessary.

Summer pruning, after fruiting

Cut back each fruited shoot to a suitable replacement near its base.

Tie in the replacement shoots to maintain even spacing. These should fruit the following year.

Remove any wrong-pointing shoots that have developed and were not removed in the spring, cutting them back flush with the stem.

ESTABLISHED SOUR CHERRY TREE, PRUNING AFTER FRUITING

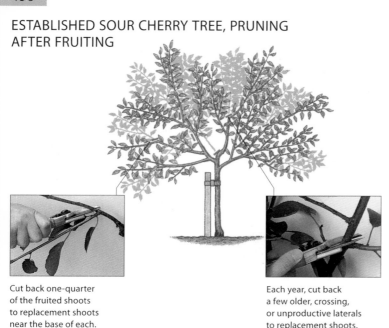

Cut back one-quarter of the fruited shoots to replacement shoots near the base of each.

Each year, cut back a few older, crossing, or unproductive laterals to replacement shoots.

Open center
The open center is built up as for peach (see p.453). After the third or fourth year, once it is established, renewal pruning is essential. In early fall, after fruiting, cut out one-quarter of the fruited shoots, preferably to replacement shoots, to maintain even spacing and leave room for the young growth that will carry the next year's crop. Remove old or unproductive wood at the same time. If pruning is neglected, fruiting will decrease and be restricted to the tree's outer edge.

Harvesting
Cut the stalks with scissors because picking may injure the shoots and encourage infection. Cook, freeze, or preserve soon after picking (see "Harvesting and storing," p.431).

Propagation
The usual methods are chip- or T-budding (see pp.432 and 433). 'Colt' rootstock is compatible with all cultivars; 'Gisela 5' is widely compatible.

PICKING SOUR CHERRIES

Harvest by cutting each stalk close to the lateral, not by pulling—this may damage the bark and increase the risk of bacterial canker.

Persimmons (*Diospyros kaki* and *D. virginiana*)

Asian persimmons (*Diospyros kaki*) are deciduous, slow-growing trees that will eventually reach a height of 30–50ft (10–15m) and a spread of about 30ft (10m). The fruit are globular, and they may be yellow, orange, or red when ripe. The hardier American persimmon (*D. virginiana*) attains similar dimensions; the fruit is typically smaller than those of Asians.

Outdoor cultivation in areas with a minimum temperature of 50°F (10°C) is possible, but a range of 61–72°F (16–22°C) during fall is preferable. Most Asian cultivars have a low chilling requirement of 100–200 hours below 45°F (7°C). During the active growing season they need at least 1,400 hours of sunshine to fruit successfully. American persimmons are hardier, with a greater chilling requirement.

Site and planting
A sheltered and sunny site is preferable. A well-drained and fertile soil is essential, with a pH of 6–7; mature trees are relatively

Persimmon

drought-resistant, but they require irrigation if there is inadequate rain in the growing season. Vigorous seedlings of *Diospyros kaki* are suitable as rootstocks, but *D. virginiana* is most frequently used for this purpose.

Although some persimmon cultivars have both male and female flowers on the same tree, a number have only one or the other. The most widely grown cultivars have only female flowers; these will produce fruit without pollination although the fruits are small and astringent. A pollinator cultivar, with male flowers, must therefore be grown nearby. A ratio of one pollinator plant to eight or ten female-flowering plants is usually adequate.

Prepare planting holes; add organic material and balanced fertilizer. Space trees about 15ft (5m) apart.

Routine care
Apply a balanced fertilizer around the trees every three to four months, using a general-purpose mixture with medium nitrogen levels. Conserve moisture in the soil by mulching with organic matter, and water the tree regularly in the dry season. Keep the ground around the trees weed-free.

The major pests that affect persimmons grown in the open are thrips (p.671), mealybugs (p.664), scale insects (p.669), and fruit flies. Common diseases that may cause problems include crown gall (p.658), anthracnose (p.654), and other fungal leaf spots (p.660).

Growing under cover
If you are growing persimmons in a greenhouse, plant them in prepared beds or in large containers with a minimum diameter of 14in (35cm); use a very fertile soil mix incorporating a general-purpose fertilizer with medium nitrogen levels. Maintain a temperature of at least 61°F (16°C) and a humidity of 60–70 percent. Water regularly during the growing season and apply a general-purpose fertilizer every three to four weeks.

It is necessary to pollinate the flowers by hand for a successful fruit set (see *Hand-pollination*, p.451). During the summer, move plants in containers into the open; leave them until the fall until their chilling requirement has been met.

Pruning and training
Cultivars vary greatly in vigor. Dwarf and semidwarf cultivars are usually trained in a similar way to an apple spindlebush (see p.440). Prune trees for the first three years during the dormant season to form a framework. Subsequent pruning should be relatively light: restrict it to the removal of crowded, crossing, or unproductive branches, and to cutting back branch leaders annually by about one-third of their new growth.

Harvesting and storing
Pick fruit when it is fully ripe. Cut fruit from the tree, leaving the calyx and a short fruit stalk attached. Seal the fruit in clear

PERSIMMONS TO TRY

American
'Early Golden'
'Garretson'
'Meader'

Asian
'Chocolate'
'Hanafuyu'
'Hayakume'
'Izu'
'Jiro'

plastic bags and store it at 32°F (0°C); it should remain in good condition for up to two months.

Propagation
Persimmon trees may be propagated by seed, by grafting, from cuttings, or from rooted suckers.

Sow seed taken from mature fruit immediately in containers; kept at 82°F (28°C), it usually germinates in two to three weeks. In 12 months, the seedlings provide stocks suitable for grafting. Handle seedlings carefully when transplanting.

Cultivars may be propagated by chip- or T-budding (see pp.432 and 433), or by whip-and-tongue grafting (see p.433). Softwood cuttings (see p.77) taken in summer and treated with hormone rooting powder should root in a mist unit with basal heat.

Rooted suckers may be detached from the base of the parent tree (if it has not been budded or grafted). Establish them in containers before planting in their final location.

Figs (*Ficus carica*)

Figs are among the oldest fruit in cultivation, and belong to the family Moraceae. They have a low chilling requirement of 100–300 hours below 82°F (7°C) and thrive in regions with a long, hot growing season.

Site and planting

Figs require a sunny location and in cool areas need a wall or fence for more warmth and protection from frost; this should be at least 10–11ft (3–3.5m) wide by 7ft (2.2m) high.

Figs prefer slightly alkaline, deep, rich, moisture-retentive soils, and a warm, dry climate. Cooler, wetter conditions induce too much growth, with poorer crops. When the pH is less than 6, lime the soil (see p.625).

Where space is limited, a concrete or brick "pit," or box, may be built below soil level to restrict the root system and produce a smaller tree. The pit should be 2ft (60cm) square and have a base that is not solid but filled with rubble or stones to a depth of 10–12in (25–30cm); this will provide drainage and restrict root growth downward.

In cool climates, figs may also be grown in pots placed in a sunny, sheltered site and transferred to cold but frost-free conditions in winter. Use a container 12–15in (30–38cm) in diameter, with several large drainage holes, and filled with a soil-based potting mix.

No rootstocks have yet been introduced, and trees are grown on their own roots. Modern cultivars are self-fertile.

Select two-year-old, pot-grown specimens and plant these in winter, teasing the roots gently loose from the soil ball before planting. Unrestricted trees need to be spaced 20–25ft (6–8m) apart; those planted in a pit need only half this spacing.

Routine care

To protect branches carrying the embryo figs from frost, tie a dense layer of leaves or straw around them

FRUIT PLACEMENT

Ripening fruits

Embryo fruits

(see also Frost and Wind Protection, *Burlap and Straw Cover*, p.612). At the same time, remove any unripe figs from the previous summer. It may be necessary to protect the ripening fruit against birds and wasps.

Feeding, watering, and mulching

A spring mulch of well-rotted manure is all that is normally required, but trees with restricted roots need extra nutrients. This may be in the form of a balanced fertilizer applied at a rate of 2oz/sq yd (70g/sq m), and supplemented during the summer with occasional liquid feeds. Avoid overfeeding fig trees.

Watering is essential in hot, dry weather, especially where the roots are restricted. Pot-grown figs need regular watering throughout the growing season. Repot and root-prune them every two years.

Pests and diseases

Figs in the open are usually problem-free, but wasps (p.672) and birds (p.655) may attack fruits. Under cover, spider mites (p.670), mealybugs (p.664), whiteflies (p.673), mice (rodents, p.668), and *Nectria* canker (p.664) may be troublesome.

Growing under cover

In cool areas, fan-trained figs may be grown under cover and will crop more regularly than in the open. The roots must be contained to restrict growth. Once growth starts, water regularly but reduce watering as the fruit ripen to prevent the skins from splitting. Prune as for figs grown outdoors but leave a more open tree to allow as much light as possible to reach the leaves and fruit.

Pruning and training

In warm climates, figs need only light pruning and are usually grown in open-center form. Two crops per season are normally produced, an early one from embryo figs (about the size of small peas) formed late in the previous season, followed by the main crop, which is both formed and ripened during the same summer. Meanwhile, further embryo fruits develop to repeat the process.

In cool climates, figs are trained either as open-center bushes or fans. Only the first crop from embryo figs will have time to ripen.

ESTABLISHED FIG TREE
Spring pruning

Cut back frost-damaged shoots to healthy wood and thin out wrong-pointing shoots and any that are overcrowded.

Cut out some of the remaining shoots or, on older trees, branches to one bud to promote new growth.

Summer pruning

Pinch out the tip of each new shoot when it has developed 5 or 6 leaves.

Remove those that do not ripen to concentrate the tree's energies into producing new embryo fruit.

Bush

Purchase a tree with three or four branches arising about 2ft (60cm) above ground. Prune these back by half their length in the first winter to encourage further branches to form and establish a basic framework. Pot-grown trees should branch at 15in (38cm) from the base so that they are compact and not top heavy.

Pruning of established trees differs with the climate. In warm climates in spring, shorten spreading branches to more vertical shoots and leave some growth in the tree's center to protect the bark from sun scorch. In cooler climates, remove crowded, crossing, or frost-damaged branches; keep the center open by taking out all upright shoots and pruning to buds on the lower sides of branches.

Lengths of bare wood should be cut back to one bud to promote new growth. In the summer, pinch out new shoots or sideshoots to five or six leaves to encourage fruit to form.

Fan

Plant a two-year-old tree with two or three strong shoots. Tie

FIGS TO TRY

Early
'Calimyrna'
'Celeste'
'Osborne Prolific'
'White Marseilles'

Mid-season
'Alma'
'Brown Turkey'
'Kadota'
'King'
'Mission'

Late
'Conadria'

down the two best placed as for peach fans (see p.453) and tip prune lightly. Prune back trees without suitable sideshoots to about 16in (40cm) to encourage lateral growth. The fan is then developed as for peaches but with greater space between branches to allow for the fig's larger foliage.

Prune the established fan in early spring to remove old, fruited wood and any that is frost-damaged or badly placed, and leave the younger wood. Also prune back a proportion of younger shoots to one bud to induce fresh growth close to the main branches. Wherever possible, tie in the unpruned shoots to fill any spaces and remove all others. Pinch out the tips of new growth to five leaves in midsummer. The resulting new shoots should then develop embryo fruit for overwintering.

Harvesting and storing

Pick the fruit when fully ripe. Ripe fruit tends to hang down, is very soft to the touch, and may have slight splits in the skin. Figs are best eaten fresh, but may also be dried.

Propagation

Seed-raised plants vary in fruit quality. Hardwood cuttings of one-year-old wood from selected cultivars should be used. Take cuttings (see p.434) 12in (30cm) long and insert them in well-prepared, well-drained ground. Protect them from frost with cloches. Figs may also be propagated by rooted suckers, severed from the parent tree and transplanted.

Summer pruning

Pinch back new shoots to 5 leaves to encourage embryo fruits to form in the leaf axils.

ESTABLISHED FIG FAN
Spring pruning

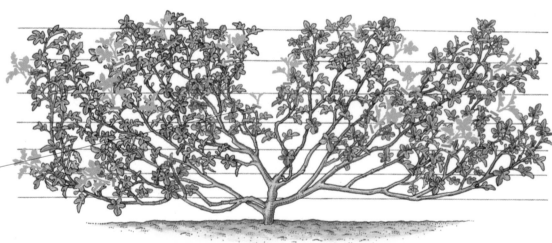

Once all risk of frost has passed, cut all cold-damaged shoots back to their point of origin.

Cut back a proportion of young shoots to one bud to encourage replacement growth that will produce embryo fruit.

Tie in the shoots so that they are evenly spaced over the fan.

Cut off wrong-pointing shoots to the point of origin or to a well-placed sublateral.

Cut back a proportion of old, bare wood to 1 bud or node to promote new growth.

Mulberries (*Morus nigra*)

Mulberries belong to the Moraceae family. Black mulberries reach a height of 20–30ft (6–10m), and are grown for their fruit. White mulberries (*M. alba*) are not usually grown for their fruit. They grow up to 20ft (6m) tall. The chilling requirement is high, and the trees begin growth late in the season.

Site and planting

Moist, slightly acidic soil is preferable. Mulberries are usually grown on their own roots, and are self-fertile. Plant in late fall to winter, 25–30ft (8–10m) apart; in cold areas, plant in spring.

Routine care

Cultivation requirements are similar to those of apples (see p.436). Mulch and water as needed in dry weather. Mulberries are mainly untroubled by pests and diseases.

Pruning and training

Mulberries are grown as either semidwarfs or standards. Prune them only to establish a strong framework of four to five branches, and thereafter only remove branches if they are badly placed or crowded. The trees should be pruned when fully dormant in winter because

shoots and roots bleed profusely if they are cut or otherwise damaged between early spring and fall.

Harvesting and storing

Pick the fruit when it is fully ripe in late summer, or allow it to drop onto a suitable temporary surface (such as a sheet of plastic) to keep it clean. Eat mulberries fresh, or freeze them (see p.431).

Propagation

Mulberries may be propagated by simple or air layering (see pp.115–116) or by hardwood cuttings about 7in (18cm) long, taken with a heel (see pp.112–113), known as "truncheons."

Black mulberry

Vines

Vines require full sun and good air circulation for healthy growth and to ripen their fruits. Grapes, kiwi fruits, and passionfruits all belong to this group. In cool areas, plant them in a sheltered microclimate, or they may be grown under cover. Vines fruit on long, flexible stems of one-year-old wood and need to be pruned after fruiting each year to encourage a supply of new shoots; these grow rapidly and need to be carefully trained into their supports so that they receive the maximum amount of light and air.

Black table grapes

White table grapes

Kiwi fruits

Grapes (*Vitis vinifera*)

Grapes have traditionally been one of the choicest fruits for eating or for wine-making. The European grape (*Vitis vinifera*) and its cultivars are often considered to be of the highest quality. American grapes (*V. labrusca*) have been hybridized with *V. vinifera* to widen the choice of cultivars for table and wine grapes in cooler climates. Many cultivars are suitable for both table and wine use.

The fruits need a hot, dry summer to ripen. Warm-temperate regions suit a wide range of cultivars; many may be grown successfully in cooler climates, however, in protected sites or in greenhouses. Decorative pergolas, arches, or other suitable structures may support vines. Pruning methods vary: vines grown for table grapes are pruned to produce fewer, higher-quality fruits; vines grown for wine grapes are pruned to obtain the greatest quantity of fruits.

Table grapes

It is comparatively easy to produce high-quality table grapes in warm areas. In cooler climates, they may be grown against a sunny, warm wall or, preferably, in a greenhouse. Grapevines are usually self-fertile and wind-pollinated, but hand-pollination is advised when growing them under glass (see right).

Site

A warm, south-facing slope free from frosts at flowering time is ideal. Vines need a reasonably fertile, well-drained soil, with a pH of 6–7.5. Planting them on very rich soil, will encourage excess growth at the expense of fruits. Sharp drainage is essential— they do not tolerate wet soils. Improve the soil or install a drainage system if necessary (for details, see SOILS AND FERTILIZERS, "Improving drainage," p.623).

The intensity of flavor in table grapes roughly corresponds to the season of fruiting. Grapes that ripen early in the season tend to be the sweetest; muscats, ripening midseason, are said to have the best flavor; and those that bear late in the season are typically strong-growing and vinous but less flavorful.

In cool climates, vines grown on a warm, sunny wall give reasonably good results but will not match the quality of vines grown under cover. Early-ripening cultivars should be used for wall cultivation to obtain table fruits by late summer. Support vines with horizontal wires, held in place by eye bolts, 1–2in (2.5–5cm) from the wall.

Grapes are usually grown on their own roots, except in areas where *Phylloxera* is a hazard (see "Pests and diseases," right); in this case, seek local advice on which rootstock to use. The use of a rootstock may have other advantages, too, such as greater tolerance of a high pH or wet soil conditions, and control of overly vigorous growth.

Planting

Cultivate the soil thoroughly before planting. In poor or sandy soils, add ample, well-rotted manure or compost, then firm the area and water well. Plant bare-root vines in early spring but containerized specimens may be planted during any season. Space single cordons at least 4ft (1.2m) apart, double or U cordons at twice that spacing; the arms of multiple cordons should be 24in (60cm) apart.

Routine care

Water thoroughly during the growing season whenever conditions are dry, reducing watering as the fruit ripens. Particular care is needed with grapes grown on a wall, because they may be in a rain shadow. Mulch to retain moisture. Once vigorous young shoots develop, feed with a high-potassium fertilizer every two or three weeks; if growth is poor, give high nitrogen instead. Stop feeding when fruits start to ripen.

If using the cordon system, retain only one bunch per 12in (30cm) of vertical stem, or rod, for best-quality grapes; remove intermediate bunches at an early stage. Thin the fruits to obtain both well-shaped bunches and large, evenly sized grapes (and to discourage mildew). Use grape-thinning scissors and a small forked stick to expose portions of the bunch so small fruits in the center may be removed. Some cultivars need a second thinning as the fruits develop further.

Pests and diseases

Grapevines are affected by problems such as scale insects (p.669), black vine weevil (p.655), spider mite (p.670), whiteflies (p.673), wasps (p.672), downy mildew (p.659), and gray mold/*Botrytis* (p.661). Under cover, mealybugs (p.664) and powdery mildew (p.667) may also be troublesome.

Grape *Phylloxera* is a serious pest in warmer climates, where this aphidlike insect attacks the roots of European grapes; galls may also form on the leaves. The attack causes severe stunting and is often fatal. Little treatment is available, although the use of resistant rootstocks and resistant hybrids of American grape cultivars has greatly reduced its incidence. This pest badly affected French wine grapes until it was discovered that grafting French grapes onto American rootstocks could save the vines.

Growing under cover

In cool climates, grow grapes in a greenhouse, preferably with heating. Other crops with compatible temperature and humidity requirements may also be grown in the greenhouse. In a lean-to greenhouse, the warmth from the back wall is particularly beneficial, especially if there is little or no direct heating. Greenhouses with both top- and side-ventilation give the best results.

The soil must be fairly fertile, weed-free, and well drained, with a pH of 6–7.5. Any drainage must be 2½ft (75cm) deep because vines are deep-rooted. Plant as for vines grown outdoors. Either train vines directly onto the back wall or plant them at the foot of the glass wall, training them on support wires that are 9in (22cm) or more from the glass. In freestanding houses, plant vines at one end, then train up and along the roof on wires. For details of cultivation, see "Routine care," left. A soil auger may be used to gauge levels of moisture in the soil; use tepid water for the first waterings of the season.

THINNING GRAPES

1 Once the bunches have been thinned to 12in (30cm) apart, the fruits will need thinning as they swell to increase the size of individual grapes and allow air circulation between them.

2 Use a forked stick and grape-thinning scissors to expose portions of the bunch and snip off unwanted grapes. The thinned bunch should be wide at the top and tapering toward the base.

TABLE GRAPES TO TRY

Early

'Beta' Bl
'Buffalo' Bl
'Edelweiss' Wh
'Einset' R, H
'Ontario' Bl
'Reliance' R, H
'Seneca' Wh
'Swenson Red' R
'Van Buren' Bl
'Vanessa' R

Midseason

'Alwood' Bl
'Canadice' R, S, H
'Cimarron' Bl
'Concord' Bl, H
'Himrod' R, S
'Lakemont' Wh
'Mars' Bl, S
'New York Muscat' Bf
'Remaily' G, S
'Saturn' R, S
'Venus' Bl, S
'Vinered' R

Late
Late-ripening cultivars ripen outside only in areas with reliably warm summers

'Blackrose' Bl
'Cardinal' R
'Dawn Seedless' S
'Golden Muscat' G
'Jumbo' Bf, M
'Orlando Seedless' Wh, S
'Ribier', syn. 'Alphonse Lavalee' Bf
'Sheridan' Bf
'Sultanina', syn. 'Thompson Seedless' G, S

Key

Bf   Black fruit
Bl   Blue fruit
G   Gold fruit
R   Red fruit
Wh White fruit
M   Muscadine fruit
S   Seedless available
H   Notably hardy

Control ventilation carefully; keep it at a maximum in winter to ensure adequate winter chilling of the vines. Reduce ventilation to a minimum in late winter to induce growth. Vary the amount according to the weather to maintain even temperatures. Slight ventilation is always advisable and adequate warmth is needed at flowering to aid pollination. Pollination requires extra care for grapes grown under cover.

Hand-pollinate by gently but firmly tapping the stems or supports around midday or by drawing your hand gently down the flower cluster. This will release pollen onto the flowers below. After fruit set, good air circulation is needed to control gray mold/ *Botrytis* and mildew.

Damping down and mist-spraying help control spider mite. Do not, however, damp down either on overcast days or during flowering or ripening periods.

Fork over the bed carefully in late winter, avoiding the root area; remove ½in (1cm) of soil from the surface and replace it with soil-based mix. After the first watering, mulch with well-rotted manure or compost around the base of the vines.

Once the fruits ripen, they need a finishing period during which they remain on the vine to attain maximum color and flavor: allow two to three weeks for early cultivars, and longer for late-ripening ones. Provide good ventilation, netting ventilators to exclude birds if these are a problem.

Pruning and training

The usual method for table grapes is to develop single or double (U) cordons or rods on which permanent fruiting spurs are formed. These produce high-quality fruits.

Grapes fruit on the current season's growth. Spring and summer pruning, therefore, is aimed at restricting new growth from the rods so that one bunch of grapes develops from each spur. It also restricts the growth of foliage sufficiently to expose the developing fruit to sun, particularly in cool climates. In hot climates, take particular care that sun scorch does not occur on the vine. Carry out winter pruning before midwinter to restrict bleeding.

Single cordon After planting, while the vine is dormant, shorten the stem to a strong bud a few inches above the ground. In summer, train one leading shoot onto a vertical bamboo stake and pinch or cut back any laterals to

GRAPE, SINGLE CORDON

Year 1, Winter pruning

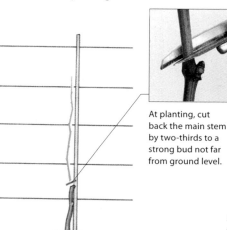

At planting, cut back the main stem by two-thirds to a strong bud not far from ground level.

Year 1, Summer pruning

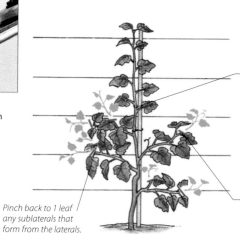

As the main leader develops, tie it in to the vertical stake.

Cut back each of the main laterals to 5 or 6 leaves.

Pinch back to 1 leaf any sublaterals that form from the laterals.

Year 2, Winter pruning

Cut back the leader by about two-thirds of the new growth.

Prune back the laterals that have formed to 1 strong bud.

Year 2, Summer pruning

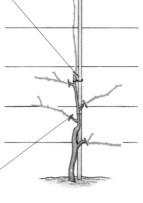

Pinch back to 1 leaf any sublaterals that form from the laterals.

Pinch out any flower clusters that form on the laterals.

Cut back each lateral when it has reached 5 or 6 leaves.

five or six leaves. Shorten all the sublaterals (shoots that are growing from the laterals) back to one leaf. Remove any shoots that develop from the base.

During the second winter, reduce the leader by two-thirds of the new growth to well-ripened wood and prune laterals back to one bud. In the second summer, tie in the leading shoot as it extends. Pinch or cut sideshoots back to five or six leaves and sublaterals to one leaf, as for the first summer. Remove any flower clusters; do not allow the vine to fruit until the third year.

In the third winter, shorten the leading shoot by two-thirds of its new growth and cut back all the laterals to one strong bud to create spurs that will bear fruiting shoots.
Routine pruning Carry out routine pruning from the third year onward. In spring, let two shoots

grow at each spur and pinch out others. Retain the stronger of the two for fruiting, and pinch back the weaker to two leaves, keeping it as a replacement in case the fruiting shoot breaks. In summer, as flower clusters develop, retain the best, pruning out the others to leave one per lateral. Stop laterals at two leaves beyond the chosen flower clusters. Pinch out laterals not carrying flowers at about five leaves and any sublaterals at one leaf.

Each winter continue to remove two-thirds of the new growth from the leader, but when it has reached the top of its support cut it back annually to two buds. Cut laterals to one strong bud. If spur systems become congested in later years, either remove part of the system with a pruning saw or, if there are too many spurs on the rod, remove some of them completely. The spurs

should be 9–12in (22–30cm) apart. The rod should be untied from its wires to about halfway down its length and bent over until nearly horizontal for a few weeks during winter to encourage the even development of shoots the following spring; then retie the rod vertically.
Double cordon This may be formed by training in two shoots horizontally in the first summer. Prune each back to 2ft (60cm) the following winter. The next year, train the extension growths vertically. These form two vertical arms; prune each arm as a single cordon.
Multiple cordon Train in two shoots in the first summer and in winter prune each back to 2ft (60cm). Train the extension growths horizontally, and choose a strong shoot every 2ft (60cm) to train vertically in order to form

HARVESTING TABLE GRAPES

Avoid touching the fruits, which could spoil any powdery bloom. Cut each bunch complete with a handle consisting of 2in (5cm) of woody stem from either side of the bunch.

Year 3, Winter pruning

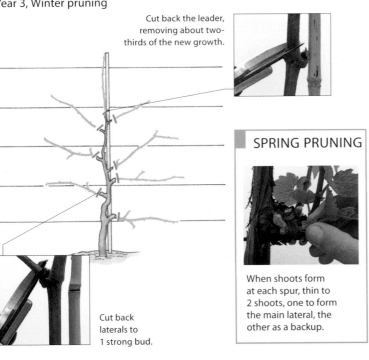

Cut back the leader, removing about two-thirds of the new growth.

Cut back laterals to 1 strong bud.

SPRING PRUNING

When shoots form at each spur, thin to 2 shoots, one to form the main lateral, the other as a backup.

Established single cordon, summer pruning

If any lateral is not fruiting, cut back the tip to 5 or 6 leaves.

Cut all fruiting laterals back to 2 leaves beyond the flower cluster.

Pinch back any sublaterals that form on the laterals to 1 leaf.

Pinch out any weak flower clusters to leave no more than 1 per lateral.

Established single cordon, winter pruning

When the leader reaches the top of the support, cut the new growth back to 2 buds.

Cut the vine loose, and tie the upper half in a nearly horizontal position.

Cut back all lateral shoots to the first strong bud.

If spurs become congested, saw off any surplus wood with a pruning saw.

MULTIPLE CORDON

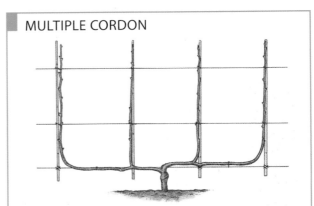

A multiple cordon may be trained with as many vertical rods as space allows. Once established, each arm is pruned in the same way as a single cordon.

Early
'Aurora' **Wh, H**
'Delaware' **Wh, Tu, H**
'Muscat Ottanel' **G**
'St. Croix' **Wh**

Mid-season
'Baco Noir' **Bf**
'Cabernet Franc' **R**
'Cayuga White' **Wh**
'Chambourcin' **R**
'Chardonnay', syn. 'Pinot
    Chardonnay' **Wh**
'Dechaunoc', syn 'Seibel 9549' **Bl**
'Duchess' **Wh**
'Geneva White 5' **Wh**
'Gewurztraminer' **Wh**
'Marechal Foch' **Bl**
'Niagara' **Wh, Tu, H**
'Pinot Noir', syn.'Spätburgunder' **Bl**
'Seyval' **Wh**
'Sovereign Rose' **P**
'Sovereign Tiara' **G**
'Traminette' **Wh**
'White Riesling' **Wh**
'Zinfandel' **R**

Late
Late-ripening cultivars ripen
outside only in areas with
reliably warm summers.
'Blanc du Bois' **Wh**
'Cabernet Sauvignon' **R**
'Catawba' **R**
'Chenin Blanc' **Wh**
'Doreen', **Br, M**
'Hunt' **Bf, M**
'Pinot Gris' **R**
'Sauvignon Blanc' **Wh**
'Seyval Blanc' **Wh**
'Steuben' **R**
'Vidal 256' **Wh**
'White Riesling' **Wh**

Key
Bf	Black fruit
Bl	Blue fruit
Br	Bronze fruit
G	Gold fruit
P	Pink fruit
R	Red fruit
Wh	White fruit
M	Muscadine fruit
Tu	Table use also
H	Notably hardy

the number of arms required. Once established, prune each arm as a single cordon.

Alternative pruning methods
Some cultivars will not produce adequate fruit-bearing shoots from the basal buds left by spur pruning. In such cases, longer lengths of ripened wood, or stakes, are retained when winter pruning the buds from which fruit-bearing shoots will be produced. Other stakes are cut back to three or four buds to produce strong new growths to replace the old fruiting canes the following winter. This process is repeated annually. Many other renewal systems may also be used to train table grapes (for details on the double Guyot system, see "Pruning and training: Guyot system," opposite).

Harvesting and storing
Tie back or remove some of the foliage to allow more sun to reach the ripening fruits. Cut ripe bunches from the vine with a short piece of woody stem—the handle—and place in a container with a soft lining so that the fruits are not damaged and the bloom not spoiled.

Bunches may be stored for a week or two at room temperature by cutting a longer handle and placing this in a narrow-necked container of water, with the fruit hanging down on the outside of the container.

Propagation
Vines may be propagated by hardwood cuttings or grafting (for details, see "Wine grapes: Propagation," p.466, and "Bud-grafting," p.432).

Wine grapes

Grapes may be grown for wine in areas with average to long, dry, sunny summers and adequate soil moisture. In cooler climates, early- and mid-season cultivars grown on warm walls or under cover give good results.

Site and planting
Most well-drained soils with a pH of 6–7.5 are suitable. Clear weeds before planting. Rootstocks are as for table grapes (see "Table grapes: Site," p.461). The flowers are usually self-fertile, and are wind-pollinated. Before planting, erect a row of support posts. Attach a single wire 15in (38cm) above the ground and double wires at 30in and 4ft (75cm and 1.2m). Each of the double wires is looped

GRAPE, DOUBLE GUYOT

Year 1, Winter pruning
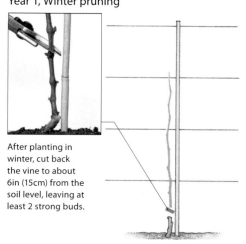
After planting in winter, cut back the vine to about 6in (15cm) from the soil level, leaving at least 2 strong buds.

Year 1, Summer pruning

As it develops, tie in the leader to a vertical stake with a loose figure-eight knot.

Prune any laterals that develop back to 5 leaves.

Remove any competing shoots developing below the main leader.

Year 2, Winter pruning
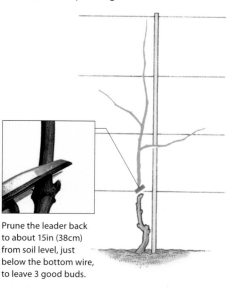
Prune the leader back to about 15in (38cm) from soil level, just below the bottom wire, to leave 3 good buds.

Year 2, Summer pruning
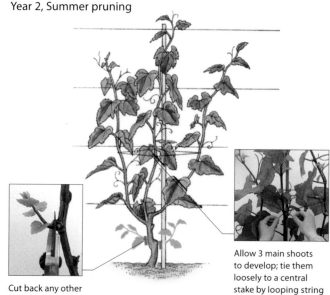
Cut back any other shoots flush with the stem.

Allow 3 main shoots to develop; tie them loosely to a central stake by looping string around all 3 shoots and the stake.

around the posts to form a figure-eight. Plant one- or two-year-old vines in winter, 5–6ft (1.5–2m) apart, in rows 6ft (2m) apart.

Routine care

Remove weeds, and water to establish young vines in dry conditions; water fruiting vines only in drought; too much water reduces grape quality. Give a light, annual, early spring application of a balanced fertilizer, and apply potassium sulfate in alternate years. Use a foliar spray of magnesium sulfate to correct deficiencies of magnesium (see p.664). Mulch every other year with plenty of well-rotted compost, or annually if the soil quality is poor. Fruit size is not important for wine quality so thinning is only necessary in cold areas, to improve sugar levels.

Pruning and training

Some cultivars need spur pruning (see "Table grapes: Pruning and training," p.462); many, however, require annual replacement of old canes to fruit regularly.

Guyot system This is widely used for wine grapes, because it produces a prolific crop in a limited space. It involves annual training of horizontal rods from which fruiting shoots are trained vertically. In the double Guyot two rods on each plant are trained in this way, in the single Guyot system only one.

To train a vine by the double Guyot system, cut it back during the first winter to two strong buds above ground level. In the first summer, let one shoot develop and tie it to a vertical stake or wires.

Year 3, Winter pruning

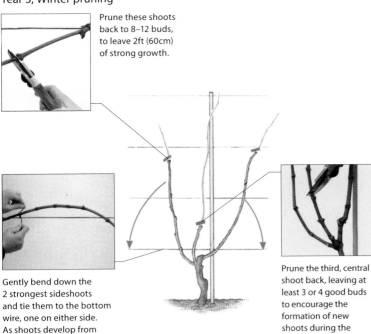

Prune these shoots back to 8–12 buds, to leave 2ft (60cm) of strong growth.

Gently bend down the 2 strongest sideshoots and tie them to the bottom wire, one on either side. As shoots develop from these, train them vertically.

Prune the third, central shoot back, leaving at least 3 or 4 good buds to encourage the formation of new shoots during the following season.

Year 3, Summer pruning

Trim any sideshoots on the three vertical replacement shoots back to 1 leaf.

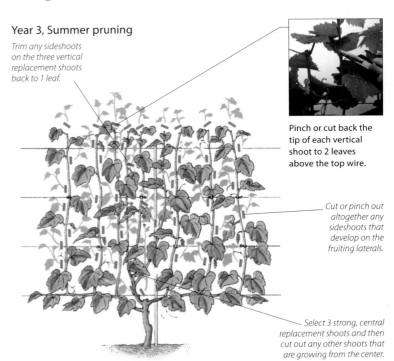

Pinch or cut back the tip of each vertical shoot to 2 leaves above the top wire.

Cut or pinch out altogether any sideshoots that develop on the fruiting laterals.

Select 3 strong, central replacement shoots and then cut out any other shoots that are growing from the center.

Established double Guyot, winter pruning

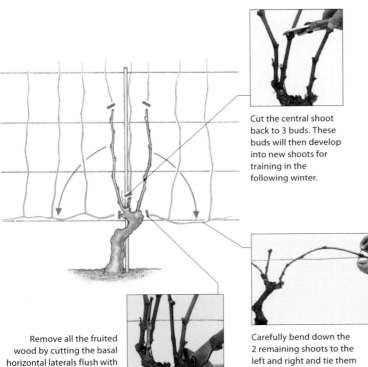

Cut the central shoot back to 3 buds. These buds will then develop into new shoots for training in the following winter.

Remove all the fruited wood by cutting the basal horizontal laterals flush with the main stem, leaving the 3 replacement shoots.

Carefully bend down the 2 remaining shoots to the left and right and tie them to the first or second wires. Tip prune to 8–12 buds.

Established double Guyot, summer pruning

Pinch out the tips of the vertical fruiting shoots, two leaves above the top wire.

Pinch or cut back to 1 leaf any sideshoots that have been produced on the three vertical replacement shoots.

Cut out overcrowded shoots that are either likely to obscure the developing fruits or are surplus to requirements.

Pinch out completely any sideshoots on fruiting shoots.

Remove other low shoots and cut any laterals to five leaves. In the second winter, cut back to just under the lowest wire, making sure that there are at least three strong buds remaining.

The next summer, let three strong shoots develop and tie them in vertically. Remove low shoots.

REMOVING FOLIAGE

When the grapes are developing, cut off any leaves that shade the ripening fruit directly. Do not remove too many as this may cause scorch from excess sunlight.

HARVESTING WINE GRAPES

Bunches of wine grapes may be harvested simply by cutting the stalk with pruners.

In the third winter, tie down two of the shoots to the bottom wire, one on either side. Tip prune these to 8–12 buds; they will produce fruiting shoots the following summer. Cut the third shoot back to three or four buds to produce replacement shoots, so that the whole process may be repeated. (For the single Guyot system allow two shoots to develop; tie down one and cut back the other.)

During the third summer, select three of the best central shoots growing from the rod and tie loosely to a central post or stake; cut out other, weaker, central shoots. Pinch back to one leaf any sideshoots that form on the three replacements. Train the shoots from the two arms vertically through the parallel wires. If growth is strong, allow a few bunches of grapes to develop on them. Pinch or cut out shoot tips at two leaves above the top wire; remove any sideshoots on the fruiting shoots.

Routine pruning For winter pruning, cut out all old, fruited wood leaving only three replacement shoots. Tie two of these down, one on either side, and tip prune as for the third winter. Prune the third shoot to three strong buds. Routine summer pruning and training of replacement shoots is as for the third summer. Cut out any overcrowded shoots obscuring the fruits. Remove any leaves shading the grapes six weeks before they are expected to ripen.

Harvesting

Cut the bunches from the vines with pruners; the grapes should be fully ripe and completely dry.

Propagation

Propagate from hardwood cuttings prepared in winter when pruning,

using wood from the hardened base of one-year-old shoots. To plant outdoors, take sections about 8in (20cm) long, trim above and below a bud, and insert the cuttings 6in (15cm) deep in sandy soil.

Under cover it is possible to use shorter one- or two-bud cuttings. Grow these singly in 3½in (9cm) pots or insert five cuttings in an 8in (21cm) pot. Place the pots in a cold frame. Pot on each young rooted plant the following summer.

HARDWOOD CUTTINGS

Trim the stems into lengths of about 8in (20cm), making an angled cut above a bud at the top and a flat cut below a bud at the base. Insert the cuttings to two-thirds their length into a trench in sandy soil.

TWO-BUD CUTTINGS

1 While pruning at leaf drop, trim off a long section of ripened wood from the current season's growth. Then remove any remaining leaves or tendrils.

2 Divide the stem into cuttings with 2 buds, with an angled cut above the top bud and a horizontal cut between two nodes below the lower bud. Remove a ½in (1cm) length of rind above the lower cut.

3 Insert cuttings in a rooting mix of 2 parts peat or peat substitute, 1 part loam, and 1 part sand, with the lower bud just below the surface. Label, water, and place in a protected spot.

4 When the cuttings have rooted, they should be potted individually in 4in (10cm) pots to grow on.

Kiwi fruits (*Actinidia deliciosa*)

Kiwi vines will grow up to 28ft (9m) in length. The berries have a hairy, brown skin and green pulp, with small, black seeds.

Warm, moist conditions are preferable during the growing season, the optimum temperature range being 41–77°F (5–25°C). Dormant plants will, however, tolerate several degrees of frost and require chilling for a period of at least 400 hours below 45°F (7°C) to encourage good flower production. Hardy kiwi (*A. arguta*) is hardy to Zone 4.

Site and planting

A. deliciosa can only be grown in the open in sunny, sheltered areas, because plants in growth are

sensitive to adverse weather conditions. The soil should be well-aerated, deep, and rich in organic matter, with a pH of 6–7. Incorporate a general-purpose fertilizer into the site at a rate of 2–4oz (50–110g) per plant.

Kiwi fruits are mostly dioecious, with plants bearing either male or female flowers. One male is needed for every eight or nine female plants to ensure adequate fertilization.

Erect a post and wire support, with wires at 12in (30cm) intervals. Plant either rooted cuttings or grafted plants 12–15ft (4–5m) apart in rows 12–18ft (4–6m) apart, staking the vines until they are tall enough to reach the supporting wires.

Routine care

Mulch the plants heavily and apply a general-purpose fertilizer rich in phosphate and potassium. Water regularly, particularly in prolonged dry periods. Keep rows weed-free. Fruit thinning is rarely necessary.

Plants grown outdoors may be liable to root rot (see *Phytophthora* root rots, p.666). Under cover they may be infested with thrips (p.671), scale insects (p.669), and root-knot nematodes (p.668). Fruit rots may also occur as a result of infection of the petals. Infection spreads to the fruits, which then drop early. The spread of the disease is promoted by

KIWI FRUITS TO TRY

'Abbot' **F**
'Blake' **F**
'Chico No. 3' **M**
'Hayward' **F**
'Issai' (*A. arguta*) **F**
'Ken's Red' (*A. arguta*) **F**
'Monty' **F**

Key

F Female
M Male

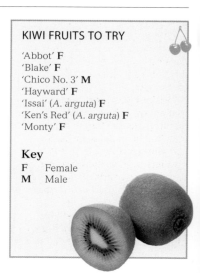

HOW TO SUPPORT KIWI FRUIT

A common method is to train the plants as espaliers on horizontal wires with two main laterals per plant arising from the main stem, with fruiting laterals (see inset) at intervals of about 20in (50cm).

high humidity. Spraying flowers at petal fall with thiram or a similar fungicide gives reasonable control.

Growing under cover

This is rarely practicable due to the long, trailing growth of the plants; in exposed conditions, however, plants grown in the open may be protected from excessive wind and hail by a light plastic screening material.

Kiwi fruits may be grown in walk-in polytunnels if the appropriate environmental conditions can be provided.

Soil preparation and cultivation details are the same as for plants grown outdoors.

Pruning and training

Commercial crops are often grown on a "T" bar or overhead pergola structure. Another commonly used system is to train plants as espaliers on horizontal wires: each plant then has two main laterals arising from the main stem, and fruiting branches at intervals of 20in (50cm). For details, see "Apple: Espalier," p.442.

The fruits are produced on one-year-old wood only, so all fruited sideshoots should be cut back to two to four buds in the dormant season.

Harvesting and storing

Kiwi fruits start to bear fruit three to four years after planting.

Harvest them as they soften. Snap or cut them from the branch, with the calyx attached; keep them cool. If wrapped in plastic film, fruits store for several months at 32°F (0°C).

Propagation

Both soft- and hardwood cuttings may be rooted successfully. Softwood cuttings should be taken in spring; trim to 4–6in (10–15cm) and insert in cutting compost (see p.434). Hardwood cuttings are taken in late summer; these should be 8–12in (20–30cm) long and inserted in sandy soil (see p.434).

Selected cultivars may also be grafted onto vigorous seedling stocks; the most common methods are T-budding and whip-and-tongue grafting (see p.433).

Passionfruits (*Passiflora* spp.)

Passionfruits are climbing plants, with individual stems reaching many yards in length. The globular fruits are either purple or yellow when ripe, and may be up to 3in (7cm) in diameter. Two recommeded selections are the yellow-fruited *P. edulis* f. *flavicarpa* 'Brazilian Golden' and the purple *P. edulis* 'Black Knight'.

The optimum temperature range for the purple passionfruit is about 68–82°F (20–28°C). The yellow passionfruit prefers temperatures over 75°F (24°C) and does not tolerate frost; purple types may withstand frost for short periods. Moderate to high humidity is required for satisfactory growth.

Site and planting

Select a sunny site, protected by windbreaks, if necessary. Soils may vary in type but must be well drained, with a pH of about 6.

Cross-pollination by insects, normally bees, is usual, but hand-pollination may be necessary in wet weather; hand-pollination has been found to increase the yield of plants that are grown in the open.

Passionfruits require support, in the form of a wire trellis. Before planting, insert stout uprights, 10ft (3m) long, at intervals of 12ft (4m) each way. Link adjoining uprights in rows by tying with one or two strands of wire.

Take care to prepare the planting holes thoroughly, adding both organic material and a general-purpose fertilizer with medium to high levels of nitrogen. Establish the plants at about 10–12ft (3–4m) apart each way, or less if only a few plants are grown. The yellow form is usually planted 10ft (3m) apart each way.

Routine care

Apply a general-purpose fertilizer that has a medium to high nitrogen content at a rate of 1–2lb (0.5–1kg) per plant per year, preferably in equal dressings at intervals of three to four months. Apply an organic mulch in spring, and weed and water regularly during the dry season.

Pests affecting plants in the open as well as under cover include fruit flies, aphids (p.654), spider mites (p.670), and various scale insects (p.669). Root-knot nematodes (p.668) and *snow mold* (p.670) may also be serious in some subtropical areas.

"Woodiness" is caused by cucumber mosaic virus (see "Viruses," p.672), which is transmitted by aphids. Because passionfruit vines are susceptible to nematodes and various wilt diseases, replace the plants every five or six years with healthy seedlings, or rooted cuttings, or grafted plants.

Growing under cover

This is possible in temperate areas, but fruits may not be produced unless the optimum temperatures and conditions are provided; hand-pollination is generally necessary. Provide wire supports as for outdoor plants. Grow plants either in prepared beds or in large containers at least 14in (35cm) in diameter. Use a well-drained, fertile soil mix with a high organic content, incorporating a general-purpose fertilizer into the compost before planting. Maintain a minimum temperature of 68°F (20°C) and humidity of 60–70 percent. Apply a liquid feeding or a general-purpose fertilizer at monthly intervals, and water regularly.

Pruning and training

Train two main growing stems along the wires to form a permanent framework. If these have not produced laterals by the time they are 2–3ft (60–90cm) long, pinch out their tips. Allow the lateral shoots, on which the fruits will be produced, to hang down as they develop each spring. Prune these laterals so that they are never less than 6in (15cm) from the soil. Once the plant is established, each winter cut back the current season's fruited shoots— these will not bear fruit again.

Harvesting and storing

Pick fruits when they begin to change color, from green to either purple or yellow. The fruits should be ripe 8–12 weeks after fruit set depending on the cultivar. Fruits may be stored for up to 21 days if maintained at an even temperature of at least 43–45°F (6–7°C) and at a constant humidity level of 85–90 percent.

Propagation

This is usually by sowing seed or raising cuttings; passionfruits may also be propagated by bud-grafting.

Seed may be extracted from the fully ripe fruits, and should be fermented for three to four days, then washed and dried. Sow the seed under cover in trays or 3–3½in (7–9cm) pots of seed compost, and keep at a temperature of at least 68°F (20°C). When the germinated seedlings are 8–14in (20–35cm) tall, transplant them to open ground, after hardening off, or grow them on under cover.

Cuttings 6–8in (15–20cm) long should be prepared and inserted into a tray or pot filled with rooting medium. Apply bottom heat and mist-spray to encourage rooting.

For details of bud-grafting, see p.432. Healthy bud-grafted plants should be transplanted into their permanent positions to grow on when approximately 6in (15cm) tall.

If nematodes or wilt diseases are a serious problem, the purple cultivars may be grafted onto resistant rootstocks. Vigorous seedlings of the yellow-fruited type are normally used for this purpose.

Passionfruits

Soft fruits

All the usually cultivated soft fruits are bush or cane fruits, except for strawberries, which are herbaceous perennials. Bush fruits include blueberries, gooseberries, and black, red, and white currants. Cane fruits include blackberries, hybrid berries, and raspberries. All produce succulent fruits that are eaten fresh, or preserved, canned, or frozen. Most soft fruits grow best in cool climates. They prefer a well-drained, moisture-retentive, and fertile soil. A sunny site is best and gives fine-quality fruit, but in most cases a little shade is tolerated. Almost all cultivars are self-fertile. Pruning methods depend on whether fruit is produced on one-year-old wood, on older wood and spurs, or on both.

Blackberries

Yellow raspberries

Blueberries

Strawberries

Boysenberries

Red currants

Raspberries

Strawberries (*Fragaria* x *ananassa*)

Strawberries are low-growing, herbaceous plants that may be grown in most gardens, either in the open ground or in containers. There are three distinct types of strawberry plant: summer-fruiting, everbearing, and alpine.

Summer-fruiting strawberries produce nearly all their fruit in an intensive two- to three-week period in midsummer. Some cultivars also give a smaller crop in fall.

Everbearing strawberries produce berries briefly in summer, cease for about two months, and then produce a succession of fruit in fall. They grow best in regions that have mild, frost-free fall weather.

Alpine strawberries produce small, delicately flavored fruit from midsummer to fall.

Variations in day length (see GROWING VEGETABLES, pp.494–495) affect the formation of flowers in some cultivars. It is therefore important to choose those appropriate for the latitude of the particular garden: nearer the Tropics, for example, the cooler temperatures that are essential for growth and berry production may be found only at high altitudes so choose berry cultivars wisely.

Site and planting

Strawberries are best grown where new plantings may be made regularly on fresh ground, because yield, fruit size, and plant health deteriorate if the same ground and plants are used after the third year. If you have room, grow one-, two-,

and three-year-old plants in succession, discarding the oldest plants and planting new runners in fresh ground each year.

Site

Sunny, warm sites give the best-flavored fruit. Sandy soils produce the earliest crops; loams and well-drained clays, the heaviest and most flavorful; alkaline soils do not produce good results. Slightly acidic conditions with a pH of 6–6.5 are ideal. Good drainage is vital to avoid soil-borne diseases. It can be risky planting strawberries after potatoes, because the ground may be infected with *Verticillium* wilt (p.672).

To prolong the fruiting season, plantings may be split among several locations—choose a warm, sheltered spot for the earliest crops;

sunny, open ground for the main crop; and a site that is less sunny for late-ripening fruit.

Pollination

Most cultivars are self-fertile. However, some cultivars fruit only if several plants of a different cultivar that flowers at the same time grow nearby.

Planting

The planting time for strawberries depends on geographical location. In cold-winter areas, spring planting is best and ensures the heaviest crops during the following summer. For late summer and fall plantings, remove flowers the following spring in order to allow the plants to become well established before they begin to bear fruit.

PLANTING STRAWBERRIES THROUGH A PLASTIC MULCH

1 In moist soil, mark a 3ft (90cm) wide bed with string. Mound the soil in the center, and cover the bed with a length of black plastic 4ft (1.2m) wide.

2 Dig a narrow trench on either side of the bed and, using a spade, anchor the edges of the plastic sheet firmly in the trenches to keep it from blowing away.

3 Make cross-shaped cuts in the plastic (see inset) at 18in (45cm) intervals. Plant the strawberries through the slits and firm the soil around their crowns.

4 Tuck in the cut plastic around the crowns of the plants. The finished row of strawberries should be slightly raised so that rain drains away from the plants.

Use plants of certified stock, if possible, and plant them in fresh ground, where strawberries have not been grown for at least three years. Replace plants every two or three years and uproot and discard any old plants that remain nearby to prevent the spread of viral diseases. Clear all weeds and apply generous amounts of well-rotted manure over the area, unless plenty remains in the soil from the preceding crop. On hungrier sandy or alkaline soils, enrich the soil by raking in a balanced fertilizer as well, at a rate of 3oz/sq yd (105g/sq m), just before planting. Space strawberries at 18in (45cm) intervals in slightly raised rows, 2½ft (75cm) apart, so that rainwater runs off. Plant with the base of the central crown at soil level, firm in the plants, and water well. On wet sites, plant in raised beds (see STRUCTURES AND SURFACES, "Raised beds," p.599).

Strawberries may also be planted through black plastic mulch, which smother weeds, retain soil

HOW TO KEEP STRAWBERRIES CLEAN

When the strawberries are in flower or the fruits are forming, put a thick layer of straw underneath and between the plants to prevent the ripening fruits from touching the soil.

ALTERNATIVE METHOD

Alternatively, strawberry mats may be laid carefully around the crowns to protect the developing fruits.

REMOVING RUNNERS

Remove excess runners as they develop. Pinch them out close to the parent plant, taking care not to damage other foliage.

moisture, and encourage early bearing by warming the soil. Anchor the plastic firmly before planting, then make planting slits by cutting the plastic at the required intervals.

Routine care

Strawberries need regular watering. Ripening fruits should be netted against pests, and kept off the soil to keep them clean. Remove surplus runners, weed, and regularly check for pests and diseases. Flowers may need protection from frost in spring: double-thickness sheets of newspaper are very effective.

Before the fruit clusters develop fully, lay clean, dry straw or commercial mats beneath them to prevent soil splash; this is not needed for plants grown through plastic. Protect the fruits from birds before they redden, using fruit nets (see p.427).

Train runners if desired to produce matted rows. Otherwise, pinch them out as they appear (see "Growing under cover," below).

Watering and weeding
Water when newly planted, then regularly in the growing season, especially after flowering to promote the development of high-quality fruit. Water plants under plastic only in very dry weather, watering through the planting slits. Keep beds free of weeds.

Pests and diseases
Strawberries may be eaten by birds (p.655), small animals (p.669), and slugs (p.669), and are vulnerable to aphids (p.654), strawberry root weevils, viruses (see p.672), gray mold/*Botrytis* (p.661), fungal leaf spots (p.660), and spider mites (p.670). Dig up and discard diseased or stunted plants. Red stele disease can be serious where it occurs.

PICKING FRUIT

Pick dessert strawberries by the stalk to avoid bruising the fruit. Strawberries for jam may be picked without the stalk.

Red stele is a fungal disease, more prevalent in heavy soils, causing the foliage to collapse and die. The only remedy is to change the site. Tarnished plant bug feeding causes "catfacing" of fruits. Cover plants with row cover to keep the bugs away.

Growing under cover

Strawberries grown in a heated greenhouse fruit up to one month earlier than those grown outdoors, but have less flavor. Establish runners in 2½in (6cm) pots of sowing medium as early as possible (see p.470). Before the roots fill the pots, transplant into 6in (15cm) pots of potting mix; keep the plants outside until midwinter, protected from heavy rain, then place them in the greenhouse in maximum light. When new leaves form, maintain minimum temperatures of 45°F (7°C) at night and 50°F (10°C) during the day.

Adjust the ventilation to maintain these temperatures. Water and damp down frequently to keep a moist atmosphere and reduce the risk of spider mite infestation. Increase the temperature by about 5°F (3°C) when flower clusters start to develop; during flowering, raise the temperature again by the same amount and stop damping down. Pollinate flowers by hand with a soft brush; do this around midday on a bright day. Remove late-forming flowers to improve the size of the ripening fruits. To enhance their flavor, lower the temperature as they begin to ripen.

For plants grown in the garden, cloches placed over plants in late winter advance ripening by about three weeks (see p.582), and low tunnels by one to two weeks. Both should be well ventilated on warm days. Covered plants may perform well in matted rows, in

STRAWBERRIES TO TRY

Summer-fruiting
Early
'Annapolis'
'Cornwallis'
'Earliglow'
'Honeoye'
'Mohawk'
'Northeaster'
'Veestar'

Mid-season
'Cardinal'
'Catskills'
'Cavendish'
'Guardian'
'Jewel'
'Kent'
'Lester'
'Raritan'
'Redchief'
'Scott'
'Secord'
'Tennessee Beauty'

Late
'Allstar'
'Lateglo'
'Sparkle'

Perpetual-fruiting
'Autumn Beauty'
'Gem'
'Ogallala'
'Puget Beauty'
'Rockhill'
'Tribute'
'Tristar'

Alpine
'Alexandria'
'Baron Solemacher'
'Mignonette'

which the planting distance is halved to give maximum yield. Runners may be retained to increase the density of the planting. Revert to the usual spacing after the first year by removing every other plant, otherwise fruit quality will deteriorate and routine care will become difficult.

Harvesting and storing

Harvest dessert strawberries when fully ripe, complete with stalks, and use them at once for the best flavor. Pick strawberries for jam when ripe but still firm. Pick the fruit every other day and remove and burn diseased or damaged fruit. Strawberries may also be canned or preserved. If frozen, the fruits, except those of the cultivar 'Veestar', lose their firmness.

After harvesting, clear away surplus runners, weeds, and mulch. Cut off the old foliage from plants, taking care not to damage the young leaves. Apply a balanced fertilizer and water it in if the soil is dry. Where plants are growing through a plastic mulch, make a fresh planting unless they are thriving.

Propagation

Each year plant one or two certified virus-free young plants away from established fruiting beds. Control aphids and remove flowers as they develop. The plants will produce a healthy supply of runners for transplanting for up to two years; then start again with new, certified stock. Some everbearing cultivars produce few runners.

CLEARING THE FOLIAGE AFTER HARVESTING

As soon as the crop has been picked, remove the old foliage to leave 4in (10cm) of stem above the young leaves and crown. Clear away and burn straw, foliage, and other debris from around the plants to minimize the risk of pests and diseases.

HOW TO PROPAGATE BY RUNNERS

1 Plant certified virus-free plants especially to produce runners. As they form, spread them out evenly around the parent plant.

2 Once a runner has rooted and is making vigorous new growth, lift it carefully, using a hand fork, without damaging the roots.

3 Sever the rooted runner from the parent plant. Transplant it to well-prepared soil or pot it up singly for planting out later.

ALPINE STRAWBERRIES

Alpine strawberries (*Fragaria vesca*) have small, fragrant, sweetly flavored fruits and make a neat and attractive edging for flower borders or vegetable plots. They tolerate cooler conditions than most other strawberries and prefer partial shade in the summer in warm areas. Their fruiting season lasts from midsummer through to late fall.

Plants deteriorate after about two years, so should be propagated regularly from either runners or seed. To separate seed from the fruits, leave the strawberries to dry and squash them between finger and thumb. Sow the seed in pots of standard sowing medium and maintain them at 64–75°F (18–24°C). Prick out seedlings when they have two true leaves. Plant out young strawberries in early summer.

Alpine strawberry

How to propagate from seed

1 Use dried fruits, squashing them gently between finger and thumb so that the seeds fall off. Hold the fruits over a clean container to collect the seeds.

2 Fill a 3in (6cm) pot with sowing medium. Sprinkle the seeds thinly on the surface, then cover them with a thin layer of medium and a layer of fine grit.

Blackberries and hybrid berries (*Rubus fruticosus* and *Rubus hybrids*)

The fruits of cultivated blackberries and hybrid berries, such as loganberries and boysenberries, are borne on canes in late summer. The hybrids have arisen from crosses between different *Rubus* species or cultivars.

Site
Before planting, the ground should be well prepared and fertilized, as for raspberries (see p.472). Buy blackberries and hybrid berries from specialty nurseries and, if possible, choose plants that are included in a certification program to ensure healthy, virus-free stock. Thornless cultivars are usually less vigorous than prickly ones. Blackberries and hybrid berries are all self-fertile and consequently may be grown singly. Blackberries and hybrid berries need a sunny or partially shaded spot. Do not plant them in exposed sites.

Provide support for the canes: walls and fences, with horizontal wires set up at 12in (30cm) intervals, are ideal.

A post 10ft (3m) long sunk 2ft (60cm) into the ground may also be used as a basic support, but for vigorous cultivars erect a post-and-wire fence. Position the posts at 12–15ft (4–5m) intervals with four horizontal wires running between them, the lowest at 3ft (90cm) from the ground, the highest at 6ft (2m). On light, sandy soils, you should provide extra support for the end posts by bracing them with diagonal wooden props. This will help prevent the wires from sagging under the weight of the canes.

Planting
Plant during late fall; if the weather is severe, delay until late winter or early spring. Some hybrids may be killed in very cold areas so seek local advice. Plant shallowly, spreading out the roots well and firming the soil at the base of the plants. Space more vigorous cultivars 12–15ft (4–5m) apart, less vigorous ones 8–10ft (2.5–3m) apart. After planting, shorten the canes to 9in (22cm).

BUYING HEALTHY BLACKBERRY PLANTS

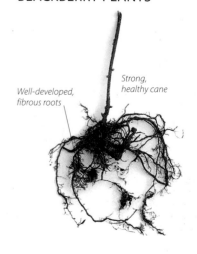

Strong, healthy cane

Well-developed, fibrous roots

METHODS OF TRAINING

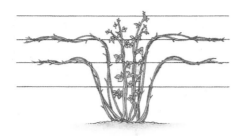

Alternate bay
Train new canes to one side of the plant, while the older ones fruit on the other side.

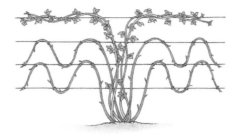

Rope
Train fruiting canes in groups along wires, leaving new canes to grow centrally.

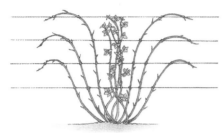

Fan
Fan-train fruiting canes individually to the left and right, and train new canes centrally.

Weaving
Weave fruiting canes through the lower wires. Train new canes centrally and along the top wire.

BLACKBERRIES TO TRY

Early
'Brazos'
'Cherokee'
'Cheyenne'
'Comanche'

Late
'Chester'
'Darrow'
'Dirksen'
'Hull'
'Olallie'

HYBRID BERRIES TO TRY

Boysenberry
Loganberry
Marionberry
Salmonberry
Sylvanberry
Thimbleberry
Tayberry

ESTABLISHED BLACKBERRIES AND HYBRID BERRIES

Pruning after fruiting

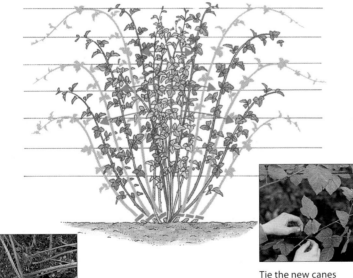

Cut down all the fruited canes to ground level near the base of the stem.

Tie the new canes securely to the horizontal wires according to the training system used.

Tip pruning cold-damaged stems

Inspect the canes for signs of cold damage in early spring and, if necessary, cut back the tips of affected canes to healthy wood.

Routine care
Maintenance requirements are as for raspberries (see p.473).

Pests and diseases
Problems may be caused by raspberry borers, fruitworms (p.667), gray mold/*Botrytis* (p.661), and viruses (p.672), although resistance varies among the various hybrids.

Pruning and training
The plants fruit on one-year-old wood, so training needs to separate fruiting canes from the newly developing ones. Canes can be tied informally to a trellis, or by formal methods as shown above. For small plantings, the rope and fan methods (see above) serve well. The alternate bay and weaving systems use much more space, but weaving works best for more vigorous plants.

After harvest, cut out the fruited canes at ground level. Retain and tie in those canes that have grown during the current season but remove any that are weak or damaged. In early spring, cut back the tip of each cane if it shows any signs of dieback resulting from cold.

Harvesting and storing
Pick the fruits regularly; unlike raspberries, the central plug stays within the picked fruit. They may be stored by canning, preserving, or freezing.

Propagation
To provide a few new plants, use tip layering (see below). In summer, bend a shoot to ground level and

TIP LAYERING

1 Bend over the tip of a healthy, vigorous shoot and place it in a hole 4in (10cm) deep. Fill the hole with soil and firm down well.

2 Once the tip has rooted in late fall or winter, cut the old stem close to the young, rooted plant to sever it from the parent. Pot it up, if required, or transplant in spring.

place the tip in a hole dug in the soil. Cover it with soil and firm. Once the tip has rooted in winter, sever it from the parent plant. Transfer the young plant to its final growing location in spring.

To produce a larger number of young plants, remove shoots, 12in (30cm) long, of the current season's growth in late summer; take leaf-bud cuttings from them, with a leaf and a piece of stem. Place several cuttings in one 5½in (14cm) pot in a moist atmosphere or cold frame; they should root in six to eight weeks. Harden them off and plant them out in late fall or, where winters are harsh, in early spring. Transplant the young canes to their final locations a year later.

HOW TO PROPAGATE BY LEAF-BUD CUTTINGS

1 Select a strong, healthy shoot from the current season's growth, taking at least 12in (30cm) of stem with plenty of well-developed leaf buds.

2 Make a cut ½in (1cm) above a bud: slice downward to remove the bud and a portion of stem about 1in (2.5cm) long, with a leaf attached.

3 Place 3 cuttings in a 5½in (14cm) pot, with stem portions at an angle and growth buds just above the soil. Water, label, and place in a cold frame.

Raspberries (*Rubus idaeus*)

A number of raspberry cultivars have been produced by crossing the European wild red raspberry (*Rubus idaeus*) with the American raspberry (*R. idaeus* var. *strigosus*) and the North American black raspberry (*R. occidentalis*).

Raspberries are a cool-season crop, growing best where there is plenty of moisture. Fruits vary in color from dark red through to yellow. There are two main types of raspberries: summer-fruiting, which has a short season of heavy production in high summer, and fall-fruiting, which has a protracted fruiting period beginning in late summer and continuing until the start of winter frosts.

Site and planting

The site needs thorough preparation before planting because raspberries do not bear well on poor soils, particularly if in competition with weeds. Raspberries are self-fertile.

Site

Raspberries should be planted in a sheltered, sunny site. They tolerate partial shade, and in hotter regions some shade may be a positive advantage.

The soil should not only be rich in humus and moisture-retentive but also well drained, because raspberries do not tolerate poor drainage. Sandy, alkaline, and poor, stony soils need an annual, heavy dressing with humus-rich material, and regular watering. In addition, if raspberries are grown on alkaline soil they may suffer from chlorosis (see "Manganese/iron deficiency," p.664).

Preparation

Clear all perennial weeds before planting because they are extremely difficult to deal with later. Prepare an area at least 3ft (90cm) wide and dig in plenty of well-rotted manure.

Construct permanent supports. A simple T-bar trellis with one wire extending along each side of the row is sufficient. Other, more involved, training method, are possible too. For a post-and-wire support, set a single row of stout posts 10ft (3m) apart. Run three lengths of wire between the posts at heights of 30in (75cm), 3½ft (1.1m), and 5ft (1.5m). Keep the wires or strings taut and tie in the canes with twine by weaving between the canes and wires.

The parallel wires method requires two rows of posts, with posts at the above spacing and rows 30in (75cm) apart. Run two pairs of parallel wires along the posts, one pair at 30in (75cm), the other at 5ft (1.5m), then crisscross between them with wire or strong string. The canes are supported by the cross-wires and do not need to be tied in.

For the Scandinavian system, erect two rows of posts, as above, but with 3ft (90cm) between rows, then run a single wire along each row at a height of 3ft (90cm). Twist fruiting canes along the wires, allowing new canes to grow in the open, central space.

Obtain certified virus-free canes; otherwise use suckers taken from established plants of known good health and yield performance.

Planting

Plant dormant canes in well-manured ground at 15–18in (38–45cm) intervals, in rows 6ft

SUPPORTING AND TRAINING METHODS

The post-and-wire method is useful if space is limited. The parallel wires method gives the canes more room, but is not suitable in windy conditions. The Scandinavian system bends young canes around each other and the wire; the canes are not tied in or tip pruned. This method needs more space than the others.

Scandinavian system

Post and wires

Parallel wires

HOW TO PLANT RASPBERRIES

1 Prepare a trench 2–3in (5–8cm) deep in well-manured ground. Plant the canes 15–18in (38–45cm) apart. Spread out the roots carefully and backfill the trench with soil.

2 Firm the soil around the bases of the canes, ensuring that they remain vertical. Prune canes back to a bud, about 10in (25cm) from the ground. Rake the soil lightly.

(2m) apart. Plant in spring in most areas; fall in warm-winter areas. Spread out the roots evenly at a depth of 2–3in (5–8cm), and gently firm them in. Prune the canes to 10in (25cm) from the ground.

Routine care

In spring, mulch with well-rotted manure. Apply on either side of the row, taking care not to bury canes. If manure is unavailable, apply regular dressings of a balanced fertilizer (see "Care of soft fruits," p.426). Avoid excess mulch after the first year of growth.

Flowers usually appear too late to be damaged by frost so do not need protection. Remove weeds and water the plants regularly and thoroughly. Remove any suckers more than 9in (22cm) from the main row.

Pests and diseases

Raspberry borers and fruitworms (p.667) are the main pests. Gray mold/*Botrytis* (p.661), spur blight/cane blight (p.670), and viruses (p.672) may also be a problem.

Pruning and training

As soon as new canes are established, by about midsummer, cut out any of the canes that were shortened at planting time.

Summer-fruiting raspberries should have all fruited canes removed at ground level after harvest. Tie in the new canes (see *Supporting and Training Methods*, p.472), spacing them evenly 3–4in (8–10cm) apart. Cut out damaged and weak canes so that those remaining receive as much light and air as possible. Loop over and tie in tall canes to prevent wind damage. The following spring, trim canes to 6in (15cm) above the topmost wire, cutting back any tips with frost damage. Remove dead, diseased, or crowded canes or any more than 9in (22cm) from the row.

Fall-fruiting raspberries (see p.474) should have all canes cut to ground level in late winter. The new canes grow, then fruit in the fall.

Harvesting and storing

Pick the fruit when it is firm to ripe for preserves and freezing, and when it is fully ripe for eating fresh,

HOW TO REMOVE UNWANTED SUCKERS

If suckers become overcrowded or are growing too far outside the row, as here, lift them and sever from the parent plant.

PRUNING AT THE END OF THE FIRST SEASON

1 By about midsummer, cut down to ground level the old canes that were shortened when planting was carried out.

2 Tie the current season's strongest canes to the support wires (see inset) when they reach about 3ft (90cm). Remove weak shoots and those growing more than 9in (22cm) from the row.

SUMMER-FRUITING RASPBERRIES TO TRY

Early
'Boyne' **R**, **H**
'Canby' **R**
'Prelude' **R**
'Reveille' **R**
'Southland' **R**
'Trent' **H**

Mid-season
'Bristol' **R**
'Dundee' **Bf**
'Jewel' **R**
'Latham' **R**
'Royalty' **Pu**

Late
'Cumberland' **Bf**

FALL-FRUITING RASPBERRIES TO TRY
'Anne' **Y**
'Autumn Britten' **R**
'Golden Harvest' **Y**, **H**
'Heritage' **R**

Key
Bf Black fruit
R   Red fruit
Pu Purple fruit
Y   Yellow fruit
H   Notably hardy

ESTABLISHED RASPBERRIES, PRUNING AFTER FRUITING

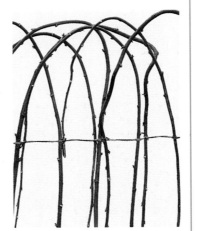

1 When all the fruit has been picked, cut back all the fruited canes to ground level.

2 Tie the current season's strongest canes to the support wires when about 3ft (90cm) tall, spacing them 4in (10cm) apart: here the continuous lacing method is used.

3 At the end of the growing season, loop any tall canes over the top wire and tie them in, if desired.

SPRING PRUNING

Before the growing season begins, tip prune all the canes to a healthy bud. Wherever possible, the cut should be made about 6in (15cm) above the top supporting wire.

harvesting every other day, if possible. Detach fruit from the central plug and stalk; pick fruit for exhibiting complete with stalk, however. Remove and burn diseased or damaged fruits promptly to prevent the spread of infection to healthy fruit.

Propagation

In late fall, pick strong suckers that are growing away from the main fruiting row, and lift and replant them while they are dormant. Ensure that they are from plants that are healthy and high-yielding; if in doubt, use certified virus-free canes from fruit nurseries.

PROPAGATING BY SUCKERS

Lift suckers carefully in fall and sever them from the parent plant. Remove any remaining foliage. Ensure that the suckers are healthy and replant where new stock is required. Water in thoroughly.

FALL-FRUITING RASPBERRIES

These should be sited in a sunny, sheltered location where the plants will quickly become established and the fruits should ripen in as short a time as possible. The fruits are borne freely on the upper part of the current season's canes. Planting and cultivation requirements are as for summer-fruiting raspberries.

Pruning of fall-fruiting raspberries is carried out in late winter before growth starts; the fruited canes are all cut down to the ground to stimulate new canes, which will fruit in the fall.

Late winter pruning
Before new growth starts, cut down all the canes to ground level. Fruit will be produced in fall on the new season's canes.

Black currants (*Ribes nigrum*)

Black currants thrive only in cool-temperate regions. The bushes flower early, so are prone to frost damage on exposed sites. They fruit in midsummer. In some areas their cultivation is prohibited because they are hosts for white pine blister rust. Rust-resistant cultivars are available. Jostaberries, a hybrid between black currants and gooseberries, are cultivated in the same way.

Site and planting

The ground should be well prepared before planting to provide the best conditions for the continual production of new fruiting shoots. Remove all weeds from the site before planting and dig in plenty of well-rotted manure or compost.

Site

Choose a sunny, sheltered site; some shade is tolerated. Protect from spring frosts if necessary (see FROST AND WIND PROTECTION, pp.612–613). Black currants grow in a range of soils but deep, moisture-retentive soil is most suitable; avoid wet, poorly drained ground. A pH of 6.5–7 is preferable; lime very acidic soils (see p.625). Black currants are self-fertile.

Planting

Plant disease-free bushes from certified stock. Bushes that are sold under certification plans are normally two years old, but one-year-old plants from disease-free stock are also ideal. Planting in late fall is preferable but black currants may be planted throughout the winter. Handle the plants carefully to avoid

damaging the basal buds. Space the bushes 4–5ft (1.2–1.5m) apart, with the same distance between the rows. After planting, cut down all the shoots to one bud to encourage strong, new growth.

Routine care

In spring, apply a mulch of well-rotted manure as well as potassium fertilizer. If manure is not available, use nitrogen fertilizer and mulch around the base of bushes with compost or leaf mold to conserve soil moisture.

Water in dry weather, but not as the fruits ripen, because this may cause the skins to split. Net bushes to protect ripening fruits from birds.

Pests and diseases

Sawfly larvae (p.668), aphids (p.654), and gall mites (p.661) may affect black currants. Gray mold/*Botrytis* (p.661), powdery mildew (p.667), and fungal leaf spots (p.660) may also be troublesome.

Pruning and training

Black currants are grown with as many young shoots as possible originating at or near ground level. Most of the fruits are borne on shoots produced the previous season, and regular pruning is essential to maintain high yields. Pruning, together with adequate feeding, encourages strong, new shoots to develop.

Cut all stems to one bud above ground level after planting. The following year, remove any very weak, downward-pointing, or horizontal shoots. Thereafter, prune established bushes as buds begin to burst, before late winter, by cutting to the base one-quarter to one-third of two-year-old wood, and any older, weak wood. No tip pruning is required. New shoots are a pale tea color, two-year-old wood is gray, and older wood black.

If a bush needs rejuvenating, cut out a greater proportion of the old wood, retaining only those branches from which strong, young shoots have developed.

NEW AND FRUITED SHOOTS

Pale, new shoot

Dark, fruited wood

If few shoots develop yet the bush is healthy, cut down the whole plant to just above ground level in winter. Most bushes then rejuvenate well if fed and mulched, but one year's crop is sacrificed. The new shoots that develop may need thinning, retaining the strongest. After ten years or so it is better to replace a bush than to try to rejuvenate it.

BLACK CURRANT BUSH
Year 1, Winter pruning

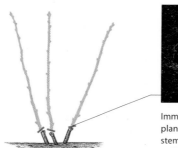

Immediately after planting, cut back all stems to 1 bud above soil level.

Year 2, Winter pruning

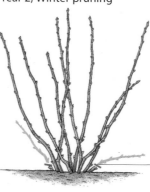

The bush should develop 7 or 8 strong, new shoots. Cut back any weak or low-growing shoots to about 1in (2.5cm) above soil level, to encourage new growth from the base.

ESTABLISHED BUSH, PRUNING AFTER FRUITING

Cut out the old wood and one-quarter to one-third of two-year-old stems to stimulate new growth.

Remove any weak, damaged, or low-growing shoots, cutting close to the main stem.

Harvesting and storing

Black currants are borne on "fruit stems" in bunches. Harvest the fruits when dry and ripe but still firm. Remove the whole bunch, not the individual fruit, which may otherwise be damaged. Early-ripening cultivars soon shed their fruit but late-ripening cultivars retain their fruit much longer. Fruit may either be eaten fresh or stored by canning, preserving, or freezing.

Propagation

Black currants are propagated from hardwood cuttings (see p.434) taken from healthy bushes in fall. Retain all buds on the cuttings to encourage basal shoots to grow. Hardwood cuttings are an excellent way of creating more bushes because they are quick and easy to take, and have a very high success rate. In addition, the cuttings do not require any protection or warmth.

HARDWOOD CUTTINGS

Insert 8–10in (20–25cm) cuttings in a trench, leaving two buds exposed.

Red and white currants (*Ribes rubrum*)

Red and white currants need a cool climate. White currants are simply a color variant of red currants; both fruit in midsummer and need the same growing conditions.

Site and planting

Red and white currants need a sunny site but tolerate some shade; in hot climates some shade may be necessary. Protect plants from winds to prevent their stems from breaking, and in high temperatures to prevent scorching.

Prepare the soil well before planting, as for black currants. Heavier, moisture-retentive, but well-drained soils are ideal. Potassium deficiency may occur on sandy soil. All cultivars are self-fertile.

When buying young bushes, ensure the plants are from healthy stock that bears well. There is no certification plan, however. Plant in spring or fall: space bushes 4–5ft (1.2–1.5m) apart, cordons at 12in (30cm), and fans at 6ft (1.8m).

Routine care

For details of maintenance, see black currants (p.474). Maintain high potasssium levels by applying

potassium sulfate if necessary (muriate of potassium may scorch the foliage).

Pests and diseases

Keep the plants covered with netting throughout the winter to prevent birds from damaging the buds. If the buds are damaged, delay winter pruning until just before bud-burst and then prune to healthy buds. Aphids (p.654), sawfly larvae (p.668), gray mold/ *Botrytis* (p.661), and spider mites (p.670) may affect plants.

Pruning and training

Red and white currants are normally grown as open-center bushes but may be trained on supporting wires as cordons, double cordons, or fans. Fruits develop on spurs produced by pruning back the sideshoots.

Bush

A one-year-old bush should have two or three strong, young shoots; shorten these by half in late winter. Remove any that are less than 4in (10cm) from the ground to produce a short leg.

The following winter, shorten new growth by half to form the main branches, pruning to an

RED CURRANT BUSH
Year 1, Winter pruning

Remove any sideshoots growing within 4in (10cm) of soil level by cutting flush with the stem. This will form a short leg at the base.

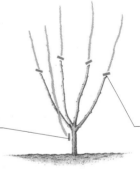

Prune each stem to an outward-facing bud (or to an upright shoot) about halfway along its length.

Year 2, Winter pruning

To form the permanent branches, shorten leaders and sideshoots by half of the new growth, cutting to outward-facing buds.

Cut back to 1 bud any sideshoots crowding the center or growing downward.

ESTABLISHED BUSH, WINTER PRUNING

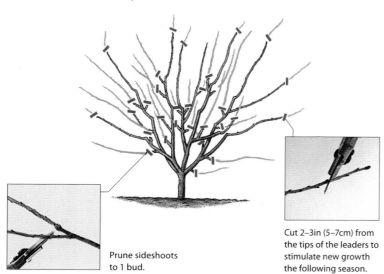

Prune sideshoots to 1 bud.

Cut 2–3in (5–7cm) from the tips of the leaders to stimulate new growth the following season.

outward-pointing bud. Prune sideshoots growing in- or downward to one bud. Prune established bushes by cutting back sideshoots to one bud and tip pruning main branches.

Cordon

Single cordons are usually trained vertically. In order to do this, set up wires at 24in (60cm) and 4ft (1.2m) from the ground. Select a main shoot on a one-year-old plant and train it against a cane; prune back the shoot by half, then cut back all the other shoots to just one bud.

In summer, prune sideshoots to five leaves of new growth. Shorten these sideshoots to one or two buds in winter, and prune the leader by one-quarter of the new growth. When the leader reaches the top of its support, trim it to one bud. A double cordon is developed by training two shoots at about 30°

to the ground as for apples (see *Forming a Double Cordon*, p.441); they are subsequently trained vertically when 12in (30cm) apart. Each branch is then pruned as for a single cordon.

Fan

Fan-trained red and white currants are established as for a peach fan (see p.453). Each branch should then be pruned as a cordon.

Harvesting and storing

Harvest red and white currants as for black currants. The plants tend to retain their ripe fruits a little longer than most black currants. They may be canned or frozen.

Propagation

Take hardwood cuttings in early fall. Use young shoots 12–15in (30–38cm) long, and remove all but the top three or four buds, to produce a plant with a short stem.

Insert the cuttings in moist, fertile soil, burying them by about half their length, and firm well. Once rooted, transplant to their final locations.

Hardwood cuttings may take a few months to root and this is best done in early fall when the soil is still warm.

RED CURRANT CORDON

Year 1, Winter pruning

Cut back the leader by half of its new growth to stimulate new sideshoots.

If there are any sideshoots at planting, cut them back to 1 bud.

Year 1, Summer pruning

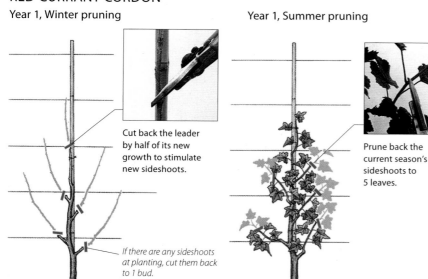

Prune back the current season's sideshoots to 5 leaves.

Established cordon, winter pruning

If the leader has reached the top wire, prune to 1 bud, or prune it back by one-quarter of the summer's growth.

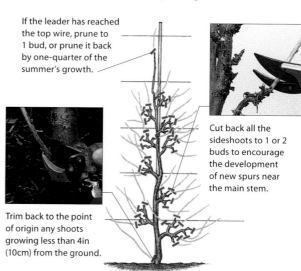

Trim back to the point of origin any shoots growing less than 4in (10cm) from the ground.

Cut back all the sideshoots to 1 or 2 buds to encourage the development of new spurs near the main stem.

Goji berries (*Lycium barbarum* and *L. chinense*)

Several Chinese species of *Lycium*, deciduous shrubs with arching growth, have become naturalized in many countries. They are now much cultivated for the plentiful, bright red or orange, succulent, often egg-shaped, nutritious fruit. They produce trumpet-shaped, purple and white flowers from spring into fall, often fruiting well 2–3 years after planting.

Site and planting

Goji berries are hardy to zone 6 and prefer well-drained soil in a sunny spot. Well-rotted organic matter should be incorporated when planting, and they should be well watered for the first year, after which they are reasonably drought-tolerant.

Routine care

Goji berries benefit from regular mulching, either with leaf mold or well-rotted manure. Light pruning is recommended for better production of fruit and feeding with specially formulated fruit-bush feed in spring will help to increase the yield.

Pests and diseases

The bushes are usually free from insect attack if they are healthy. In some areas you may need to protect the berries from birds, and the leaves from rabbits and deer.

Gooseberries (*Ribes uva-crispa*)

Gooseberries are easy to grow. Gooseberry fruits ripen yellow, red, white, or green, depending on the cultivar. The Worcesterberry (*Ribes divaricatum*) resembles an overvigorous, very thorny gooseberry bush, with small, red-purple fruit that make excellent jam, and has similar needs to a gooseberry bush.

Site and planting

Like currants (*Ribes*), gooseberries need cool conditions and, if summer temperatures are high, adequate shade. Growing conditions and restrictions as well as planting distances are the same as for red currants (see pp.474–475). All cultivars are self-fertile.

Routine care

General maintenance is largely as for black currants (see p.474). Gooseberries require high potassium levels and regular mulching, ideally with well-rotted manure. New shoots on young bushes are vulnerable to breakage and need protection from strong winds. If the crop is heavy, thin the fruits in late spring.

Pests and diseases

Deer (p.659) may cause severe bud loss, so cover plants with netting.

If the buds have been attacked, delay winter pruning until bud-burst, then prune to live buds. Gooseberry plants may be affected by powdery mildew (p.667), sawfly larvae (p.668), and bacterial or fungal leaf spots (pp.665 and 660).

Pruning and training

Young plants may be trained as bushes, cordons, or fans as for red currants. A number of gooseberry cultivars have a natural drooping habit, however; to prevent stems from trailing to the ground, prune to upward-pointing buds, especially when training young bushes.

Bush For initial pruning, see red currants (p.475); aim to create an open-center bush on a stem 4–6in (10–15cm) long. Established bushes may be pruned by regulated or spur pruning in winter, to give big fruit.

Regulated pruning is the simpler method: remove low, crowded, and crossing shoots to maintain well-spaced growth at the center of the bush; also remove any old, unproductive branches and select new, young shoots to replace them.

Spur pruning is more labor-intensive: all sideshoots are shortened to a suitable bud 3in (8cm) from the main branches. The branch leaders also need to be tip pruned.

Standard Cultivars to be trained as standards are grafted onto *Ribes odoratum* or *R. divaricatum* stock. Select one shoot of the rootstock and train it vertically, keeping any sideshoots short. It will take about three years to grow to a suitable height. When the stem has thickened and reached about 3½–4ft (1.1–1.2m), trim off the sideshoots and graft on the selected cultivar using whip-and-tongue grafting (see p.433). Use a strong stake to support the stem. The scion will develop and branch naturally the following summer. The next winter establish the framework as for a bush and then prune and train in the same way.

Cordon and fan These are trained as for red currants (see p.476). Once established, prune in summer, reducing new sideshoots to five leaves. In winter, shorten shoots to 3in (8cm) and tip prune leaders.

Harvesting and storing

Fruits should ripen by midsummer. Gooseberries for cooking should be picked while still green, but allow dessert-quality cultivars to ripen fully on the bush for the best flavor, ensuring that they are protected from birds. Yellow-, white-, and red-berried cultivars should be left to ripen

to their full color before they are picked. Gooseberries freeze well.

Propagation

Layering is the easiest method. Gooseberries are easy to root from hardwood cuttings. When the rooted cutting is lifted, rub off all low buds and sideshoots; otherwise, troublesome suckers may develop.

HARDWOOD CUTTINGS

1 In early fall, trim young shoots to 12–15in (30–38cm), with an angled cut above a bud at the top and a straight cut at the base. Dip in rooting hormone and insert in a trench to half their length.

2 The following fall, carefully lift the rooted cuttings. Remove basal buds or shoots less than 4in (10cm) from the base (see inset), before transplanting the young plants.

GOOSEBERRIES TO TRY

Early
'Golden Drop' (yellow)
'May Duke' (red)
'Rokula' (red) **Rm**

Mid-season
'Careless' (white)
'Greenfinch' (green) **Rm**
'Invicta' (green) **Rm**
'Keepsake' (green)
'Lancashire Lad' (red)
'Langley Gage' (white)
'Leveller' (yellow)
'Pax' (red) **Th, Rm**
'Whinham's Industry' (red)
'Whitesmith' (white)

Late
'Captivator' (red) **Th**
'Hinonmäki Röd' (red) **Rm**
'Lancer' (green)
'London' (red)
'White Lion' (white)

Key
Rm Some resistance to mildew
Th Nearly thornless

GOOSEBERRY BUSH

Year 1, Winter pruning

Prune back all the shoots by a half to three quarters to an outward-facing bud.

Established bush, regulated pruning, winter

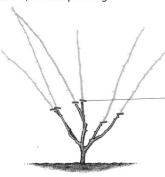

Cut out older branches to prevent overcrowding and to maintain an open center.

The bush should have mainly young shoots, evenly spaced, pointing up- or outward.

Established bush, spur pruning, winter

Prune all new sideshoots to a bud about 3in (8cm) from their base.

Tip prune the branch leaders to 3 or 4 buds of the new growth. This encourages the formation of spurs.

Blueberries (*Vaccinium corymbosum* and *V. ashei*)

Highbush blueberries (*V. corymbosum*) are derived from the American wild blueberry. They produce clusters of fruits that are a dark, hazy purple-blue with a gray bloom; their flavor is enriched by cooking or preserving. They require a cool, moist climate, needing 700–1,200 hours below 45°F (7°C) and very acidic soil (pH 4–5.5). Highbush blueberries grow to a height of 4½–6ft (1.3–2m) and are deciduous, with white flowers in spring, and striking gold and scarlet fall color.

Rabbit-eye blueberries (*Vaccinium ashei*) are grown in the same way as the highbush group, but tolerate less acidic soils and drier conditions. The fruit are smaller and more gritty than highbush blueberries.

Fruit production, in mid- to late summer, is light at first but after five or six years yields of 5lb (2.25kg) of fruit per bush may be obtained, and on older bushes considerably more. Blueberries are self-fertile, but yield better when two or more cultivars are planted close together.

Site and planting
Blueberries need a sunny location, although they tolerate some shade. The soil must be well drained. Clear all perennial weeds from the site before planting and, if the soil is alkaline, correct this by mixing a 6in (15cm) layer of acidic compost with the existing soil to a depth of at least 2ft (60cm). Alternatively, apply elemental sulfur according to soil-test recommendations.

Blueberries may also be grown in large pots or tubs with a diameter of 12–15in (30–38cm), filled with acidic soil mix. Plant in

Highbush blueberry bush

late fall or early spring, spacing bushes 5ft (1.5m) apart. Cover the roots with 1–2in (2.5–5cm) of soil, and mulch with acidic compost or leaf mold. Growing a mixture of cultivars results in better fertilization and heavier crops.

Routine care
To promote growth and fruiting and to maintain acidity, apply a topdressing each spring of an acidic fertilizer as recommended by your nursery supplier.

Keep plants mulched with wood chips or an acidic compost, and water as needed with rainwater. Avoid root disturbance when weeding.

Pests and diseases
The fruits may be eaten by birds, so provide protection by netting the bushes (see "Protection from birds," p.427). Other pests and diseases rarely cause any trouble.

ESTABLISHED BLUEBERRY BUSH, WINTER PRUNING

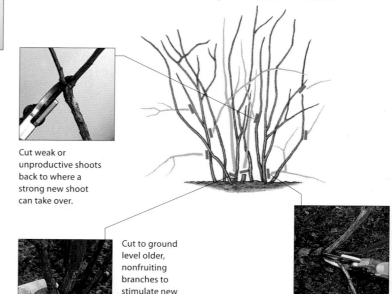

Cut weak or unproductive shoots back to where a strong new shoot can take over.

Cut to ground level older, nonfruiting branches to stimulate new basal shoots.

Cut back any low or downward-pointing branches to their point of origin or to a branch growing in the required direction.

Pruning and training
Blueberries fruit on two- or three-year-old wood. New bushes need little pruning for two or three years, but cut out weak shoots to provide a strong basic framework.

Thereafter, prune to ensure regular production of new shoots from the base, as for black currants (see pp.474–475), by cutting out some of the oldest wood each year.

Harvesting and storing
The fruits ripen over a period of several weeks. Pick over the bushes carefully, harvesting only the ripe fruit, which should part easily

from the cluster. Blueberries may be successfully stored for later use by means of preserving, canning, or freezing.

Propagation
Take 4–6in (10–15cm) softwood cuttings in midsummer, dip them in hormone rooting powder, and then insert them in an acidic, peat/sand rooting mix. Place the cuttings in a propagator until rooted, then transplant them to a larger pot. Harden them off thoroughly using a greenhouse, cold frame or cloche, before planting them out.

HIGHBUSH BLUEBERRIES TO TRY

Early
'Bluehaven'
'Ivanhoe'
'Patriot'
'Reka'

Mid-season
'Bluecrop'
'Blueray'
'Chandler'
'Herbert'
'Ivanhoe'

Late
'Jersey'
'Nelson'

BLUEBERRY SOFTWOOD CUTTINGS

1 Select suitable softwood material and take cuttings at least 4in (10cm) long. Cut just above a leaf joint.

2 Trim the base of each cutting just below a node with a sharp knife, and remove the leaves from the lower third of the cuttings. Dip the ends of the cuttings in hormone rooting powder.

3 Prepare a pot of acidic propagation mix. Make holes with a dibber and insert each cutting so that the basal leaves are just above the medium. Water, label, and place the pot in a propagator.

Tender fruits

Most tender fruits originate from tropical and subtropical regions, where they thrive in the warm, dry conditions. Apart from olives, many may be eaten straight from the tree, or stored for a short period of time in suitable conditions. Most of the tender fruits covered in this section will not tolerate frost and therefore can be grown outdoors only in the summer.

Members of the citrus family that are too acidic for eating, such as lemons and limes, are grown for either for their juice or for use in preserves and marmalades.

Tender fruits are generally grown in hot climates, where the soil may be lacking in nutrients, so it is important to prepare the site adequately when planting: an extra 4–6oz (110–180g) of slow-release fertilizer forked into the base of the planting hole will help the plants establish quickly.

Many tender fruits grow well in containers or under cover if the correct temperature and humidity levels are provided. Although many do not consistently ripen their fruits indoors or under cover, nevertheless they make attractive ornamentals.

Pineapple
Limes
Mango
Sweet oranges
Avocado
Lemons

Pineapples (*Ananas comosus*)

Pineapples are tropical perennials that produce terminal fruits, each composed of up to 200 seedless fruitlets. For best results they need full sun and temperatures of 64–86°F (18–30°C) with humidity of 70–80 percent. Cultivar groups include the Cayenne Group, the Queen Group, and the Spanish Group, of which the Spanish has the sweetest flavor.

Site and planting
Select a sunny site that is sheltered from strong winds. Pineapples tolerate a wide range of soils, but prefer a sandy, medium loam with a pH of 4.5–5.5. Plant suckers about 12in (30cm) apart, with 24in (60cm) between rows, or at a spacing of 20in (50cm) each way.

Routine care
Use a general-purpose fertilizer with medium potassium and high nitrogen levels at intervals of two to three months, at a rate of 2oz

(50g) per plant. Correct for iron and zinc deficiencies by spraying with a 2 percent solution of ferrous or zinc sulfate. Water pineapples regularly in dry weather and apply an organic mulch to conserve soil moisture.

Pests and diseases
Pests that may affect pineapples include mealybugs (p.664), root-knot nematodes (p.668), scale insects (p.669), spider mite (p.670), and thrips (p.671).

The most serious disease affecting pineapple plants in the open is heart rot, caused by *Phytophthora cinnamoni* and *P. parasitica*, fungi that often affect pineapples grown in wet conditions. This is difficult to treat, so it is advisable to guard against infection by planting resistant cultivars where these are available; all suckers that are required for propagation should be dipped in a fungicide, because the fungus enters through wounds.

Growing under cover
Plant rooted pineapple cuttings in well-prepared beds with good drainage, or use pots at least 12in (30cm) in diameter. Use a soil mix with a high organic content and apply a liquid feed every three to four weeks. Maintain a temperature of at least 68°F (20°C) and humidity of about 70 percent. Water regularly and thoroughly, particularly while young plants are establishing.

Harvesting and storing
Harvest the fruits when they begin to turn yellow by cutting the stem 1–2in (2.5–5cm) below each fruit. Pineapples may be stored for up to three weeks at 46°F (8°C) and at 90 percent humidity.

Propagation
The terminal crown shoot may be used as a cutting; remove it with about ½in (1cm) of the fruit attached. Pineapples may also be propagated by the suckers that

PROPAGATING PINEAPPLES FROM SUCKERS

Sever basal shoots or suckers and leave to dry before inserting in a sandy rooting medium (see inset).

develop from below the fruit or at the base of the stem, as well as those that are produced in the leaf axils; these may be detached with a sharp knife. Dip the cut surfaces of suckers in a fungicide, then leave them to dry for several days. Remove the lower leaves and insert the cuttings in pots of sandy rooting medium. Pot them on into 6in (15cm) pots when rooted.

Pineapple

PROPAGATING PINEAPPLES FROM THE CROWN SHOOT

1 Scoop out the crown shoot of a ripe pineapple with a sharp knife, ensuring that you do not cut through the base of the shoot. Dip the wound in fungicide and leave for several days to dry.

2 Insert the prepared cutting into a pot of sandy rooting medium and maintain at a temperature of at least 64°F (18°C). The cutting should be rooted and ready to pot on within a few weeks.

PINEAPPLES TO TRY

Cayenne Group
'Hilo'
'Smooth Cayenne'
'Sugar Baby'

Queen Group
'Natal Queen'
'Ripley Queen'

Spanish Group
'Red Spanish'
'Singapore Spanish'

Avocado tree

cinnamoni) are preferable. Avocados may be self-pollinated, but the best crops are produced if at least two cultivars are planted near each other. Choose cultivars whose flowering periods coincide or overlap. When planting, allow 20ft (6m) each way between the trees.

Routine care

Apply a general-purpose fertilizer with a medium potassium and nitrogen content, when the trees are in active growth. The recommended rate is 3½–4½lb (1.5–2kg) per tree every year, preferably in two or three doses. Use an organic mulch around the base of each tree, leaving 10in (25cm) clear around the stems.

Water avocado trees during dry periods, particularly during the first three years when they are becoming established. Keep the area around the base of the trees free from all weeds. It is not normally necessary to thin the fruits on avocado trees.

Pests and diseases

Avocados may be affected by avocado root rot (see "*Phytophthora* root rots" p.666), anthracnose

(p.654), and *Cercospora* spot or blotch (see "Fungal leaf spots," p.660), as well as by such pests as whiteflies (p.673), thrips (p.671), spider mite (p.670), and mealybugs (p.664).

Growing under cover

Establish young plants either in well-prepared beds or in containers with a minimum diameter of 8in (21cm). Maintain temperatures of 68–82°F (20–28°C) and humidity of 70 percent. For container-grown plants, pot on into containers at least 12in (30cm) in diameter, taking care not to disturb the plants' root systems.

Water containerized avocados regularly, and apply either a general-purpose fertilizer with a medium level of both potassium and nitrogen at intervals of two to three weeks, or a liquid feed. In temperate climates, flowering and fruiting are rare under cover, due to the trees' daylength and light-intensity demands.

Pruning and training

Avocado trees need little pruning beyond shaping the tree during its early growth to ensure that

an evenly spaced, rounded canopy develops. Once the tree is established, remove any diseased, damaged, or crossing branches after fruiting.

Harvesting and storing

Seed-raised trees start to bear fruit when they are between five and seven years old; budded or grafted plants are productive at three to five years after planting. The fruits may remain on the tree for up to 18 months without maturing, but they usually ripen rapidly after harvesting.

Cut the fruits from the tree using pruners. Handle them carefully to avoid bruising. Store them at temperatures above 50°F (10°C) and at 60 percent humidity. Any damaged fruits should be discarded.

Propagation

Avocado trees are easily grown from seed and reproduce virtually true to type. Select undamaged, healthy seeds and soak them in hot water for 30 minutes at 104–125°F (40–52°C) to inhibit infection from avocado root rot. Cut a thin slice from the pointed end, then dip the wound in a

Ripe avocados

fungicide. Sow the seed in sandy rooting medium with the cut end slightly above the soil surface; germination usually takes about four weeks. The seedlings may be grown on in containers until they are about 12–16in (30–40cm) tall. They should then be ready for transferring to their final positions.

To propagate named cultivars onto disease-resistant rootstocks, side-wedge grafting (see PRINCIPLES OF PROPAGATION, p.636) or saddle grafting (see ORNAMENTAL SHRUBS, pp.110–118) may be used. Propagation through grafting helps to maintain a predictable quality and quantity of fruit produced.

GROWING AVOCADOS FROM SEED

1 Soak the seed in hot water and then prepare it by cutting about ½in (1cm) off the pointed end with a sharp knife. Dip the wound in fungicide.

2 Place the seed in a 6in (15cm) pot of moist sandy sowing medium so that the cut top of the seed is just above the soil surface.

3 Several weeks later the seed will have germinated to produce a shoot and roots.

Guavas (*Psidium guajava*)

Guava trees grow to a height of about 25ft (8m) and have a spread of 22ft (7m). They are widely grown in both tropical and subtropical regions and thrive in temperatures ranging from 72–82°F (22–28°C). The preferred humidity level is 70 percent or less: a higher level may affect the quality of the fruits produced.

Guava fruits are 1–4in (2.5–10cm) in diameter, with either white or pink flesh. The flowers are normally pollinated by insects, particularly bees.

Site and planting

A sheltered site is preferable, protected by a system of windbreaks if necessary. Guavas will tolerate a wide range of soils, but a well-drained loam is the ideal type. The pH may range from 5 to 7, but a pH of approximately 6 is most desirable.

When planting, allow a spacing of 15ft (5m) in each direction between the trees. The young trees should be securely staked in areas that are exposed to strong winds.

Routine care

Guavas respond well to applications of a general-purpose fertilizer with a medium potassium and nitrogen content. It is beneficial to use this at a rate of 2–4½lb (1–2kg) of fertilizer for each tree per year, divided into two or three topdressings during the growing season.

Weed the area around the bases of the trees, keep them well watered, and apply a mulch of organic matter, which will help retain soil moisture.

Guavas

Guava tree

a minimum temperature of 72°F (22°C) with humidity of 70 percent. Water plants regularly, and apply a liquid feed every three to four weeks. To improve the chances of fruiting, cross-pollination by hand may be necessary. A relatively dry atmosphere should be maintained during the flowering period.

Pests and diseases

Pests are rarely a serious problem, but in the open, aphids (p.654), fruit flies, and scale insects (p.669) may require control. Anthracnose (p.654) occurs in many areas. Plants under cover may also be infested by whiteflies (p.673), and thrips (p.671). Guava seedlings are sensitive to damping off (p.659).

Growing under cover

Guavas may be grown in well-prepared beds or containers at least 12–14in (30–35cm) in diameter, using a fairly rich soil mix with a slow-release fertilizer. Maintain

Pruning and training

When the young trees are about 3ft (1m) tall, cut back the leading shoot by about two thirds, to encourage branching. Subsequent pruning can be limited to the removal of any dead, crossing, or diseased branches, and any low branches that droop down and touch the soil.

Harvesting and storing

Guavas cultivated in the open generally fruit after one to three years, depending on cultivar and environmental conditions. The fruits ripen about five months after fertilization and may be picked when they begin to turn yellow. Handle them carefully—they bruise easily. Guava fruits may be stored for up to three or four

weeks at a temperature of 45–50°F (7–10°C), with relative humidity of 75 percent.

Propagation

Guavas are usually propagated from seed; for the increase of specific cultivars, however, air layering, cuttings, or grafting may be used.

Sow seed in a fertile, sterile sowing medium in flats or 3in (7cm) containers; germination normally occurs in two to three weeks. The seedlings may vary in quality: pot the strongest ones on into 6in (15cm) pots when they are 8in (20cm) tall. Harden the young plants off and transplant them when they are 12in (30cm) tall.

Selected guava cultivars may be side-wedge grafted (see p.636) onto vigorous seedling guava rootstocks, the stems of which should have a diameter of at least ¼in (5mm). No specific rootstocks are recommended; select strong, healthy plants, preferably self-pollinated, as parents for rootstock seeds.

Guavas may also be increased by softwood cuttings 5–6in (12–16cm) long (see p.632). Plants produced by

these graftings or cuttings may be planted out when they are about 12in (30cm) tall. In the open, guavas may be increased by simple layering (see ORNAMENTAL TREES, p.81) or by air layering (see INDOOR GARDENING, p.383). With the latter, hormone rooting powder applied to the girdled sections increases the success rate.

Pomegranates (*Punica granatum*)

Pomegranates form small, ornamental trees or bushes 6–10ft (2–3m) tall with a spread of 3–5ft (1–1.5m). They are evergreen in the subtropics but deciduous in cooler climates. The globular fruits are up to 4in (10cm) in diameter with leathery, yellow or red skins.

The optimum temperature range is 64–77°F (18–25°C), but temperatures just below freezing are tolerated for short periods. Dry weather and a high temperature, ideally 96°F (35°C), are required for fruiting. Pomegranates will fruit well outdoors in some parts of California and Arizona; a dwarf variant of the species, *Punica granatum* var. *nana*, fruits freely under cover or indoors in temperate areas.

Site and planting

Select a sunny site, sheltered by windbreaks in exposed conditions. Heavy loam soils with a pH level of about 7 are generally suitable, if they are well drained. Most cultivars are self-fertile. Plant seedlings, rooted cuttings, or suckers 12–20ft (4–6m) apart each way.

Routine care

Once plants are established, apply a general-purpose fertilizer every two to three months at a rate of 4oz (110g) for each tree per year. Mulch the site and keep it free of weeds; water the trees regularly during dry weather. Cut out all suckers.

Pests and diseases

Pomegranates grown in the open are generally trouble-free; under cover, they may be affected by whiteflies (p.673), aphids (p.654), spider mite (p.670), and thrips (p.671).

Growing under cover

Plant pomegranates in well-prepared beds or containers with a minimum diameter of 14in (35cm), using a fertile soil mix with slow-release fertilizer added. Maintain a temperature range of 64–77°F (18–25°C) and humidity of 60–70 percent. Apply a liquid fertilizer every three to four weeks, and

water the plants regularly. Plants in containers may be moved into the open in summer.

Pruning and training

Select three or four main branches to form a framework and remove any crowded, crossing, or diseased branches. Cut out any suckers not required for propagation.

Harvesting and storing

Fruiting should start about two to three years after planting. Harvest the pomegranates when they turn yellow or red; they may then be stored for several weeks at 39–43°F (4–6°C).

Propagation

Pomegranates are usually propagated from cuttings or root suckers. Insert hardwood cuttings (see p.434) in sandy soil mix, and give bottom heat until they have rooted. Softwood cuttings (see *Blueberry Softwood Cuttings*, p.478) require bottom heat and mist (use a medium with neutral pH). Pot on both types into 4–6in (10–15cm) pots when they have rooted. Root suckers may be carefully separated from the parent plant and replanted. Alternatively, dry off the seed; sow it in pots or flats of seed soil mix, and maintain a temperature of 72°F (22°C).

Pomegranate tree

Pomegranate flower and fruit

Nuts

Several nut-bearing trees and bushes are suitable for home landscapes; they prefer a sunny, open site. Some, such as chestnuts, walnuts, and pecans, eventually form large trees and make handsome specimens. In small yards, an almond tree may make a fine feature, although it may produce nuts only in warm climates. Hazelnuts and filberts may be pruned as compact bushes in a home orchard or planted in informal groups in a wild garden. Most nuts (but not almonds) are monoecious, having separate male and female flowers on the same plant.

Pecans — Walnuts — Hazelnuts — Chestnuts — Almonds

Pecans (*Carya illinoinensis*)

Pecans are deciduous and may grow to 100ft (30m) high with a spread of 50–70ft (15–20m), so they are suitable for large yards. They grow best in warm-temperate climates: temperatures over 100°F (38°C) may lead to bark damage and low-quality nuts; flowers may be damaged if the temperature drops below 34°F (1°C). Pecan trees must be chilled for 150–250 hours below 45°F (7°C) in order for flowering to occur.

Pecans are monoecious but male flowers are often open before the females on the same tree, so grow two or more cultivars near each other to ensure fertilization. Pecans are wind-pollinated, so heavy rainfall during flowering may affect pollination, after which crops may be poor. The nuts are ovoid, ¾–1in (2–2.5cm) long, and have a thin shell.

Site and planting
Choose selected cultivars that have been grafted onto pecan seedling stock because trees raised from seed may not produce fruit of good quality. Pecans quickly develop a long taproot, so plant young trees: older, pot-grown plants with congested roots are seldom successful. Pecans need a site that is sheltered from strong winds and thrive on deep, fertile soils with a pH of 6–6.5.

Plant the trees when dormant (see *Planting a Fruit Tree*, p.425), spacing them 25ft (8m) apart.

Routine care
Apply a topdressing of a balanced fertilizer at a rate of 2–4oz/sq yd (70–140g/sq m) annually. Keep the planting site weed-free, and water the trees during dry periods until they are established. Pecans are moderately resistant to drought but require plenty of water during the summer months. Pecan trees are seldom affected by pests and diseases; *Phytophthora* root rots (p.666) and aphids (p.654) may sometimes be a problem.

Pruning and training
Train pecans with a central leader initially (see "Central-leader standards," p.72). Once the trees are established, pruning is restricted to removing crossing and congested branches and any dead wood.

Harvesting and storing
The first crop may be produced after five years; full production is reached after 15–20 years. The nuts are usually harvested by hand. They may be stored, in cool, dry, airy conditions for several months.

Propagation
Whip-and-tongue grafting of selected cultivars onto vigorous pecan seedling rootstocks is the most usual method of propagation (see p.433). The seedlings to be used as stock plants should be raised in deep pots or plastic sleeves, because their long taproots are sensitive to damage during transplanting.

Pecans

PECANS TO TRY

'Desirable'
'Elisabeth'
'Elliot'
'Mohawk'
'Moore'
'Moreland'

Walnuts (*Juglans regia*)

English walnuts (strictly speaking, Persian) are deciduous trees that may reach a height of 60ft (18m) with a similar spread; they are suitable only for large yards. Named cultivars should always be planted for fruit because seedlings may produce poor-quality nuts. Walnuts are monoecious and wind-pollinated. Most are self-fertile but some cultivars produce male catkins and pollen before the female flowers are receptive. To overcome this problem, plant nearby a reliable pollinator such as the old French cultivar 'Franquette'. Walnuts have a chilling requirement of 500–1,000 hours below 45°F (7°C). The gnarled nuts develop within a pitted shell.

Site, planting, and routine care
A well-drained, moisture-retentive soil is best. Walnuts prefer a pH of 6.5–7 but tolerate some alkalinity. Since flowers and young shoots are susceptible to frost damage, avoid cold sites. Walnuts have a long taproot, so select young plants rather than older, pot-grown ones whose roots may be congested. Plant in spring or fall (see *Planting a Fruit Tree*, p.425), with 40–60ft (12–18m) between trees.

Walnuts may be slow to establish, but after two or three years, once the root system is well developed, stronger growth occurs. Bacterial leaf blotch and blight may be a problem (see "Bacterial leaf spots and blotches," p.655).

Pruning and training
Walnuts should be trained as central-leader standards (see p.72). Prune in midwinter because the trees do not bleed when they are dormant. Remove any strong shoots that make a narrow angle with the stem, to leave a well-balanced framework of evenly spaced branches. Thereafter, little pruning is required apart from cutting out overcrowded, crossing, or congested branches in winter and removing dead wood as required.

Harvesting and storing
Walnut trees may not bear fruit for many years. Pick walnuts for pickling in summer before the hulls and shells harden. In early fall, the hull cracks to release the nut. Gather the crop before the shells become discolored. Clean, then gently dry the nuts. Store them in cool, airy, slightly humid conditions.

Propagation
The usual methods are whip- and-tongue grafting (see p.433) or chip-budding (see p.432) cultivars onto seedlings of the American black walnut (*Juglans nigra*). In cool climates keep a grafted tree under glass until the graft has taken, then move the pot to a protected site in the open. Plant young trees in their final positions in fall or winter.

Walnuts

WALNUTS TO TRY

All cultivars listed are self-fertile.

'Colby'
'Hansen'
'Lake'
'Metcalfe'
'Somers'
'Young's B1'

Hazelnuts and filberts (*Corylus avellana* and *C. maxima*)

Hazelnuts and filberts are valued for their winter catkins and their nuts. Unpruned, they reach a height and spread of 12–15ft (4–5m). They are deciduous and monoecious, and crop best in cool, moist summers. The chilling requirement is 800–1,200 hours below 45°F (7°C). Winter temperatures below 14°F (-10°C) may damage male flowers (catkins), although female flowers are usually less vulnerable. The nuts are brown and egg-shaped. The outer husk of the hazelnut does not completely envelop the nut. The filbert has a husk that is longer than the nut and often completely encloses it; a subgroup of filberts has frilled

husks and is known as frizzled filberts. Hazelnuts and filberts are wind-pollinated; many are self-fertile. Recommended cultivars include 'Barcelona', 'Daviana', 'Du Chilly', 'Ennis', 'Royale', 'Rush', and 'Winkler'; 'Rush' and 'Winkler' are the hardiest.

Site and planting
A partly shaded, sheltered position is preferable. A soil pH of 6 is best; very rich soil may cause excessive soft growth at the expense of cropping. Adequate moisture with good drainage is important. Plant in spring or fall, 15ft (5m) apart (see *Planting a Fruit Tree*, p.425).

Hazelnuts

Filberts

Routine care
Weed and mulch regularly; water in dry spells. On poor soils apply a balanced fertilizer in spring at a rate of 3oz/sq yd (100g/sq m). Trees are usually trouble-free, but may be attacked by nut weevils; squirrels (p.661) can strip the tree of nuts.

Pruning and training
Hazelnuts and filberts are grown as open-center bushes, each with a 18in (45cm) stem and eight to twelve main branches. On young plants, prune the leaders in winter to 22in (55cm); good laterals should then develop. Remove shoots growing low down on the main stem and all but the best-placed, strongest shoots needed to develop the framework. Shorten these by one third in winter. The following winter remove any very strong, upright growth and tip prune sideshoots to form a good framework. Older bushes bear heavier crops if pruned in late summer using the "brutting" method. Break longer sideshoots halfway along their length, and let them hang. This opens up the bush

BRUTTING HAZELNUTS

In late summer, strong shoots of the current season's growth that are about 12in (30cm) long are broken and left hanging. This helps form flower buds.

and encourages female flowers to form. In winter, shorten the brutted shoots to three or four buds.

Harvesting and storing
Nuts are borne after three or four years. Gather them when the husks begin to yellow. Dry, then store.

Propagation
Use suckers for propagation. In winter, remove them, each with a root ball, and grow on. Otherwise, use layering (see p.115) in fall.

Almonds (*Prunus dulcis*)

Unpruned, sweet almonds grow about 15–20ft (5–6m) tall, with a similar spread. They bear regularly only in areas with warm, dry summers and frost-

Almonds

free winters. The chilling requirement is 300–500 hours below 45°F (7°C). Almonds are insect-pollinated. Most cultivars are partly self-fertile, but crops will be better if a pollinator is planted nearby. The nuts are flattened and pointed, with a pitted shell.

Site, planting, and routine care
Almonds require a sheltered, frost-free site and a well-drained soil, preferably with a pH of 6.5. Plant almond trees 20–22ft (6–7m) apart (see *Planting a Fruit Tree*, p.425). Cultivation of almonds is the same as for peaches (see p.451).

Diseases such as peach leaf curl (p.665) and bacterial canker (p.655) may affect almond trees.

Pruning and training
Almonds are often pruned and trained as open-center trees, as for peaches (see p.452). Nuts are borne on one-year-old wood. In summer, on older trees, remove one-quarter of old shoots that have borne in previous seasons to encourage fresh growth.

Harvesting and storing
The nuts are borne after three to four years. Gather them as their hulls start to crack. Clean and dry the almonds before storing them.

Propagation
Almonds are usually propagated by chip-budding (see p.432). Root stocks vary according to soil type: almond seedlings are often used in dry regions while peach seedlings are more suitable for heavier soils.

ALMONDS TO TRY

'Ayles'
'Ferraduel'
'Ferragnes'
'Guara'
'Steliette'

Chestnuts (*Castanea* spp.)

A fungal diseas has made the native American chestnut (*Castanea dentata*) all but extinct. Better results can be obtained from the Chinese chestnut (*C. molissima*) and Spanish chestnut (*C. sativa*). Both of these trees produce excellent fruit; however, their malodorous flowers are a liability. Choose modern Chinese-American hybrids or hybrid of Chinese, Japanese, and European chestnuts, such as 'Colossal'. Chestnuts are monoecious and wind-pollinated.

Site, planting, and routine care
A fertile, moisture-retentive soil of pH 6 is best; allow 30–40ft (10–12m) between trees (see *Planting a Fruit Tree*, p.425). Water young trees and keep the site weed-free. On well-prepared sites, fertilizer is unnecessary. Trees may be affected by *Armillaria* root rots (p.654).

Pruning and training
Train as central-leader standards (see p.72). Remove congested, crossing, or dead branches on older trees.

Harvesting and storing
Nuts are borne after about four years. Harvest them in the fall. Cook nuts fresh, or hull the nuts, soak them for 48 hours, discarding any that darken, then dry and store them in a cool, airy place.

Propagation
Chestnuts can be propagated from selected cultivars either by bud-grafting or whip-and-tongue grafting onto seedling stock of chestnut (see pp.432 and 433).

Sweet chestnuts

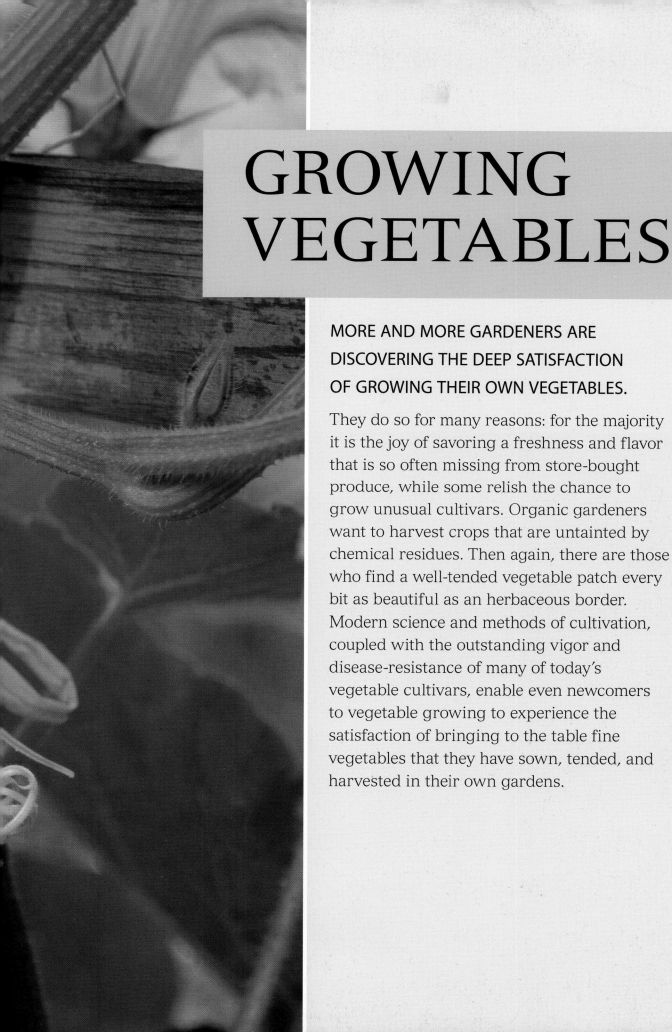

GROWING VEGETABLES

MORE AND MORE GARDENERS ARE DISCOVERING THE DEEP SATISFACTION OF GROWING THEIR OWN VEGETABLES.

They do so for many reasons: for the majority it is the joy of savoring a freshness and flavor that is so often missing from store-bought produce, while some relish the chance to grow unusual cultivars. Organic gardeners want to harvest crops that are untainted by chemical residues. Then again, there are those who find a well-tended vegetable patch every bit as beautiful as an herbaceous border. Modern science and methods of cultivation, coupled with the outstanding vigor and disease-resistance of many of today's vegetable cultivars, enable even newcomers to vegetable growing to experience the satisfaction of bringing to the table fine vegetables that they have sown, tended, and harvested in their own gardens.

Designing a vegetable garden

A healthy, productive area for growing vegetables may be created in a yard of any size, from a large, sunny in-ground garden to a few containers on a patio. The vegetables may be grown in a separate kitchen garden or integrated with flower beds. Good growing conditions are essential for an abundant, high-quality harvest. However, virtually any site can be made suitable, perhaps by setting up a windbreak for an exposed site, or taking steps to improve soil fertility and drainage. This cannot be done overnight, but within a year or two, very satisfactory results may be obtained.

Crop protection A greenhouse extends the growing season.

Choosing the site

Most vegetables lead short but very pampered lives, and the ideal situation for a vegetable garden provides warmth, sunlight, shelter, and fertile, fast-draining, loamy soil with an adequate water supply. The chosen site should be open, with good airflow, but not exposed, and not too overshadowed: nearby trees shade and drip on plants, and they also remove

Growing in beds A system of beds makes it easier to maintain crops without walking on and compacting the soil. The beds can be temporary or permanent.

significant quantities of nutrients and moisture from the soil, while buildings may create deep shade and funnel damaging winds through the garden.

Shelter and windbreaks
Providing shelter from wind is an important factor in vegetable growing. Wherever possible, avoid windy sites: even light winds may decrease vegetable yields by 20–30 percent, while strong winds are often devastating. Vegetables in coastal gardens may be damaged or killed by desiccating windborne salt spray.

In gardens exposed to wind, windbreaks should be erected; they should be about 50 percent permeable, allowing the wind to filter through, rather than solid structures, which force the wind over them, creating an area of turbulence on the other side (see also FROST AND WIND PROTECTION, pp.612–613, and CLIMATE AND THE GARDEN, "Wind," p.608).

An effective windbreak may be a living barrier, such as a hedge, or a structure like a slatted fence or latticework. Hedges are attractive but take time to become established, require maintenance, take up space, and compete for soil, water, and plant

nutrients; they are therefore only appropriate in very large gardens. For more information, see HEDGES AND SCREENS, pp.82–85. A windbreak of trees could be used at the boundaries of a very large garden. In smaller yards, surrounding the vegetable garden with a fence or latticework supported by sturdy stakes is a more practical choice.

A windbreak provides maximum shelter over a distance roughly five times its height. For a very exposed garden you may need a windbreak at least 6ft (2m) tall. In this case, barriers and posts must be strong, because they will be subjected to great strain in high winds. Alternatively, erect lower, short-term windbreaks between rows of plants or beds; for example, set up netting barriers no more than 18in (45cm) tall and 10–12ft (3–4m) apart, attached to stakes.

If gaps in buildings or trees create a wind funnel across the garden, erect a barrier extending 3ft (1m) across the gap in each direction. Plant deciduous shrubs or a hedge in the gap, using an artificial windbreak to provide shelter until they are established.

Orienting the beds

A sloping site is less easy to work than a flat one and soil erosion after heavy rain may be a problem on steep slopes; setting beds across the slope may help. A site on a south-facing slope is an advantage in cold-winter regions because it warms up rapidly in spring. In hot climates, site beds on a north-facing slope, which provides relief from intense sun.

The orientation of vegetable beds makes little difference to open-ground crops, but greenhouses and cold frames should be oriented so that their sloping surfaces face the sun to maximize efficiency. Position tall crops, such as pole beans, carefully: in cooler climates, put them where they will not shade short crops from the sun, but in hotter climates use them to provide such shade.

In cold-winter regions, the ground at the foot of a south-facing wall is a warm, sheltered place that is useful for growing early spring and late fall crops and, in summer, tender, sun-loving crops, such as, tomatoes and peppers. Keep the beds well watered so that the soil does not dry out. North-facing walls can provide some shade for plants, such as lettuces and peas, that suffer in high temperatures.

Maintaining soil fertility

A friable loam (the "ideal" soil, made up of a balance of sand, silt, and clay particles) is best for growing vegetables: it is rich in plant nutrients, and supports the earthworms and microorganisms that break down organic matter. It has a good structure, and remains workable even in adverse conditions: it does not become sticky in wet weather or dusty in dry periods, but almost always retains a crumbly texture, so that the soil is well

Protective measures In raised beds, not only does the soil drain freely, making them ideal for root crops, but it also warms up more quickly in spring, allowing you to sow and plant earlier. The wooden planks provide a neat edge and a solid structure to which protective nets or covers may be attached as desired.

aerated; this is important both for the living organisms in the soil and for root crops. Most vegetables will grow quite well in a soil that is both well drained and moisture-retentive, with a slightly acidic pH (6.0-6.5).

Soil types

Vegetables may be grown successfully in a range of different soil types. At one extreme is porous, sandy soil, which warms up quickly in spring and is ideal for early crops. Nutrients are rapidly washed out of these soils, though, and crops planted in them often need extra fertilizing. At the other extreme are heavy clays. Naturally sticky and cold (and sometimes waterlogged), clay soils warm up slowly in spring but are rich in nutrients. Once their structure has been improved by incorporating organic matter, they are fertile and retain moisture well. Heavy feeders such as the cabbage family grow well on clay soils.

In practice, most soils are a mixture of types. Although few of us start with perfect soil, it can usually be improved by working in organic matter regularly.

Crops continuously remove nutrients from the soil and from naturally decomposing organic matter. In almost all soils, fertility must be maintained by replenishing organic matter regularly. The main forms available to gardeners are compost, rotted leaves, animal manures (preferably with a high straw content), and seaweed.

A layer of organic matter 1–2in (2.5–5cm) deep, applied over most of the ground each year, will maintain structure and fertility. Gardens in hot, humid climates may need as much as double this amount. It may be spread on the surface or dug into the soil. Spreading organic matter over the surface in the fall is particularly beneficial for light soil, where heavy winter rainfall can cause leaching of nutrients. Any organic matter remaining on the surface in spring should be forked in as soon as the soil can be worked. Well-rotted organic matter is a useful mulch and can be used throughout the growing season (see also "Mulching," p.502).

Green manures

This is the practice of growing crops specifically to dig into the soil to improve its fertility. In the vegetable garden, green manures may be grown and then dug in between crops, or grown over winter in order to augment soil nutrients and avoid leaving the soil bare (see SOILS AND FERTILIZERS, "Green manures," p.625).

Drainage

Good drainage is absolutely essential; where there is a serious problem, it may be necessary to lay tile drains (see SOILS AND FERTILIZERS, "Improving drainage," p.623). In most cases, working in large quantities of organic matter improves drainage markedly, because it encourages earthworm activity, which improves the soil structure by creating an extensive network of small drainage channels.

Preserving soil structure

Good soil structure is easily destroyed by physically damaging it—for example, by walking on it or cultivating it when it is either too wet or too dry, or from heavy rain beating on the surface. Laying out the garden in beds (see THE BED SYSTEM, p.496) to minimize the need to step on the soil, and keeping the surface mulched (see "Mulching," p.502) will help to preserve soil structure.

Planning the vegetable garden

The layout of a vegetable garden will depend on its overall size and shape and the choice of crops you want to grow. Every gardener's choice of crops is unique to their goals. These may be to attain self-sufficiency, to grow gourmet vegetables or unusual heirloom cultivars, to grow all your family's favorites, or to save money. The following are a few guidelines to help you balance various important factors as you plan your garden.

A place for perennials

Most vegetables are grown as annuals on a different piece of ground each year. The few common perennial vegetables, such as rhubarb, asparagus, and globe artichokes, should be grouped together, at one side or end of the garden. If there is space, you can grow quick crops of fast-growing vegetables such as lettuce among the perennial crops.

Vegetables in containers

Gardeners who are limited to patios, roofs, or balconies often grow vegetables in containers to provide a productive display that can also be very attractive (see CONTAINER GARDENING, p.331). Although vegetables are more difficult than flowers to grow well in containers, they are worth the effort. Place containers on paths and low walls to make the best use of available space, and plant them with dwarf and decorative cultivars. Plant in terra-cotta pots and wooden half-barrels, or in container systems designed especially for vegetables.

Maximizing space

To maximize yields in a given area, crops may be combined in a single bed. Seeds of a fast-growing crop, such as radishes, can be intersown simultaneously and in the same row as slower-growing parsnips. Garlic, shallots, onion sets, and bunching onions are also suitable for intercropping. Likewise, a rapidly maturing "catch crop," such as lettuce, can be grown among slow-maturing brassicas. A checkerboard pattern will give maximum efficiency, but alternate rows also work well.

Alternatively, catch crops can be sown before or between rows of slower crops—for example, spinach with tomatoes or winter brassicas. The fast growers make immediate use of the available space, but mature before the slower-growing crops need the room. Ensure that the short-term crop is not shaded by the slower-growing one. Careful timing is essential and, in dry summers, lack of water can be a problem.

Vegetables in flower beds

If you don't have space for a separate vegetable garden, or if you just enjoy garden experiments, try edible landscaping: integrating vegetables into flower beds, or planting them in groups of beds to create an attractive pattern. Wherever possible, select cultivars for their decorative qualities, and group them using the same design principles you would for a flower bed. The only important requirement for growing vegetables in flower beds is to ensure soil fertility is maintained at the level necessary for the chosen vegetables.

Climatic factors

Most vegetables grow only when the average daytime temperature rises above about 43°F (6°C) between spring and fall. The number of growing days with suitable daytime temperatures that occur between these seasons is governed by factors such as latitude, altitude, and degree of exposure, and largely determines sowing dates and the type of crops that may be grown outdoors in any given locality.

Temperature requirements

Vegetables are sometimes classified as warm- or cool-season crops, depending on their physiological needs, particularly those relating to temperature. Most brassicas and several bulb and stem vegetables cannot withstand intense heat, whereas more tender vegetables, such as tomatoes, are damaged or killed by freezing temperatures. Cultivars of some vegetables have been bred to resist cold, and the growing season of many vegetables may be extended at either end of the season by growing them under cover (see p.505). Refer to detailed information on individual vegetables for their specific temperature requirements, pp.507–548.

Day length

The number of daylight hours, or day length, differs according to the latitude and season, and vegetable cultivars have a varying response to day length at different stages of their growth. Short-day plants develop seed only if the day length is less than 12 hours; long-day plants only if it is longer. This affects the sowing time, particularly of crops that are grown for their seeds, such as beans; others must be harvested before flowering. Onions are also influenced by day length. When the critical day length for a given variety

---

GROWING VEGETABLES THE ORGANIC WAY

You can grow your own organic vegetables simply by following the basic principles that generally apply to organic gardening.

- Maintain fertile soil that is fast-draining and humus-rich. This is perhaps the single most important factor to ensure that you are growing healthy crops.
- Ensure that only organic soil amendments and mulches are used; check the bag to be sure.
- Where possible, choose reliable, pest- and disease-resistant cultivars.
- Practice good hygiene: remove decaying foliage and plant debris regularly to help maintain a good airflow around the plants and lessen the likelihood of disease spreading throughout the crop.

- Use approved organic sprays—which do not harm beneficial predators—only if you need to treat a very severe pest or disease problem.

Crop rotation—the practice of growing related types of vegetables in different sections of the vegetable garden in consecutive years—can be helpful to avoid a buildup of pests and diseases in the soil. For example, if brassicas, which are susceptible to attacks from cabbage maggot and clubroot, are planted year after year in the same site, it is possible that the plants may become stunted and deformed by these and other pests and diseases, and the crop yield will be very poor. Avoid growing crops belonging to the same botanical family on a site for at least 3–4 years in order to minimize such problems.

Container crops Large containers work well for growing climbing crops, such as runner beans, in a small space. Pay careful attention to watering and feeding container crops.

Smaller plots Growing crops among ornamentals makes best use of limited space and also attracts beneficial wildlife that will help control vegetable pests, such as greenfly.

is reached, it stops producing leafy growth and starts developing a bulb. The more leafy growth that has been made up to this point, the larger the bulb that forms; so timing is important to allow onions to develop as much leafy growth as possible before the day length increases.

Cultivars are available that have been specially bred and adapted to long or short days, or that are day-length neutral. Examples are mentioned throughout the chapter; the safest course is to choose cultivars recommended for your area.

Rainfall
The average annual rainfall of a region has a significant influence on the growth of vegetable crops planted there. In areas of low precipitation, there is a real risk of drought at the important stages of crop development, such as flowering, the swelling of peas and beans, or leaf growth in lettuces. In low-rainfall areas, regular watering and surface mulching to conserve soil moisture become critical considerations.

In high-rainfall areas, it is essential to maintain or create good soil drainage to avoid the problems associated with waterlogging, and more vigilance is called for in order to recognize and deal with the effects of slugs, snails, and fungal leaf diseases, all of which proliferate in damp conditions. With high rainfall, nutrients are also more likely to be leached from the soil and lost, especially in gardens where the soil is light and sandy, and supplementary fertilizer may be necessary.

Making the most of your site
Although the climatic factors of a locality cannot be altered, their worst effects can be alleviated by good soil management and by taking steps to improve the microclimate (the environmental conditions within a garden). Consequently, it is important to develop and take advantage of the physical aspects of your chosen garden site. Providing wind shelter through the use of fences, screens, or hedges reduces water loss from vegetables and soil, and promotes higher average soil temperatures, which in turn aids growth. Walls or fences facing the sun form warm niches that are particularly beneficial to crops such as tomatoes, peppers, and eggplant, which do best at higher temperatures. Ground that slopes toward the sun warms soonest in spring and is therefore ideal for early crops. Conversely, be alert to the disadvantages of tall walls in blocking sunlight and rain, and avoid planting in frost pockets.

The bed system

Fruit and vegetables are best grown in full sun, either in a standard open garden or in raised beds. In these situations the soil benefits from rainfall and weathering, and the plants have a free root run. Most home gardeners set aside a particular area of the yard specifically for fruit and vegetables. This area can be a wide, open plot, but an excellent, more sustainable alternative is to set out the vegetable garden as a series of narrow raised beds divided by pathways.

Close cropping
The high soil fertility in this raised bed permits close and equidistant plant spacing in staggered rows. Narrow beds like these are also particularly convenient when using a standard width of row cover to protect crops.

Traditional vegetable gardens

In the traditional kitchen garden, long rows of vegetables usually run across the plot. This is the most efficient way to grow produce; it allows large areas of ground to be cultivated and used with maximum flexibility, but it also creates more growing space within a small area.

Growing crops, however, requires constant access for sowing, thinning, planting, watering, topdressing, pest and disease control, weeding, harvesting, and clearing. Each task involves walking through the garden, which compresses the soil. This reduces the air in the soil, impedes drainage, and results in poor growth. Compaction can be reduced by taking care not to tread on wet soil and by walking on planks to spread the weight, but the use of narrow beds totally removes the need to walk on planted areas.

Using beds

In a bed system, the garden is divided into semipermanent or fixed beds. The beds should be narrow enough to bring their central areas within arm's reach, so that cultivation tasks can be carried out from the dividing pathways, without stepping onto the soil in the beds. This avoids soil compaction and has the additional advantage that harvesting and other tasks can be done soon after rain without the usual risk of damaging soil structure. There is also less need to dig beds once they are established and fertile, and the need to cultivate is reduced because the soil stays loose and is usually covered with crops or mulch. The regular addition of organic matter is concentrated on a smaller area, so it is easier to build up high levels of fertility, and to improve soil aeration and drainage, which in turn leads to stronger root growth.

The concentration of crops into relatively confined spaces makes the bed system an ideal solution for worthwhile vegetable production in small gardens. The increase in soil fertility allows plants to be grown at closer spacings. Romaine and crisphead lettuces, for example,

may be grown 8in (20cm) apart each way in staggered rows, as opposed to rows 12in (30cm) apart in more traditional layouts. Each plant gains the maximum root space in the smallest possible area, making the best use of the soil available and increasing the total yield.

The close spacing of plants has further indirect benefits. Irrigation using low-level distribution systems, such as soaker hoses (see p.561), becomes more manageable, because smaller areas are served; water can also be used less wastefully using more conventional watering techniques. Close spacing results in more effective smothering of annual weed growth, so weeding is also reduced.

Using a bed system can make crop rotation (see p.498) much easier because each crop group can be allocated to a bed and moved on to a different one the following year according to the rotation requirements.

MAKING A RAISED BED

1 Measure and mark beds. Edge with 6 x 1in (15 x 2.5cm) boards sunk into a 2in (5cm) slit trench and supported by wooden stakes driven into the ground every 3–4ft (1–1.2m).

2 Fill the bed with good-quality topsoil that has been enriched with organic matter such as well-rotted manure or garden compost. Take care to avoid creating air pockets at the edges and corners.

3 Spread out the soil evenly using a rake. Break up any lumps, aiming to achieve an even, firm texture. Make the finished soil surface roughly level with the top of the boards, filling as necessary.

4 Level the soil with the back of the rake to leave a smooth finish. Top up with more soil as necessary in later weeks when the filled bed settles and the level of the soil falls.

PLANTING IN A BED

The bed should be no more than 5ft (1.5m) wide, so that the center is within easy arm's reach from either side. All work can then be carried out from the surrounding paths without any need to tread on the soil, thus avoiding damage to the soil structure.

Planning bed layouts

Beds may be rectangular, square, or even curved; the prime consideration is that they must allow the whole bed to be cultivated from the paths.

The ideal width is 4ft (1.2m); this can be increased to 5ft (1.5m) if it makes better use of available space, or reduced to 3ft (1m) for areas that are to be protected with glass or plastic cloches. Narrow strips are particularly suitable for strawberries, for ease of mulching and harvesting.

The bed length can be adjusted to suit the site; while their orientation is not of vital importance, running them from north to south generally ensures the most even distribution of sunlight.

The width of the paths between beds needs to be at least 18in (45cm) to allow for easy access, both on foot and with wheelbarrows.

Types of beds

Many terms are used to describe beds: they include flat or semiflat beds, deep beds, and raised beds. A flat or semiflat bed is simply marked out from the surrounding garden and cultivated. With yearly additions of bulky organic dressings, soil depth is increased as the bed surface is gradually raised above path level.

Deep beds

Organic growers often aim to minimize soil cultivation to preserve its natural structure and fertility and reduce the growth of weeds. Deep beds are an ideal way of achieving this. In deep beds, soil is improved to the required depth with one thorough cultivation that incorporates large amounts of organic matter (see *Double Digging*, p.620). After this, further digging is avoided so that a natural soil structure develops, encouraged by the organic matter and a high worm population. Further organic matter is added only as mulches and topdressings. The only disturbance to the soil surface occurs when planting, so weed seeds below germination level remain dormant and only weed seedlings from wind-blown seeds need to be removed.

Raised beds

Raised beds are constructed by marking beds and then building the sides up to 12in (30cm) high, by using lumber, bricks, or cement blocks. Walls can be dispensed with, but in that case, the base of the bed should be about 12in (30cm) wider than the finished top to ensure stability.

Raised beds have all the advantages of flat beds, but they have improved drainage and warm up faster in spring. Making a raised bed higher along one side than the other, so the sloping surface faces the sun, has the added advantage of warming the bed even more effectively and promoting early plant growth.

Raised beds provide a means of gardening successfully on the most unpromising ground, such as where a site is naturally very badly drained or perhaps even concreted over.

Higher beds can also extend the pleasure of gardening to people who have limited mobility. Walls can be built up to 24–36in (60–90cm) high and the base filled with rubble (for good drainage). The bed is then topped with 12–18in (30–45cm) of fertile soil.

Making paths

Paths between beds can be maintained as soil areas from which any weed growth is regularly skimmed off. A mulched path requires more initial effort, but reduces maintenance in the long term, especially if it is laid over a weed-suppressing landscape fabric. When topped with bark or gravel, this creates a firm, hard-wearing surface.

Grass pathways are most successful when a durable edging, such as rigid plastic or concrete blocks, is laid around the beds; the grass surface must stand above the edging to allow for unobstructed mowing.

THE "NO-DIG" SYSTEM

Paradoxically, cultivating the soil creates conditions in which weeds flourish; it exposes weed seeds to the light needed for germination. Digging may also cause a natural soil structure to deteriorate as air incorporated by digging causes rapid breakdown of organic matter. The "no-dig" system is a method of cultivation that is used by organic gardeners to preserve soil structure and reduce loss of nutrients. It exploits minimal soil disturbance, and regular surface applications of organic matter (applied well in advance of cropping so that earthworms can incorporate it) will help suppress weeds, conserve moisture, and maintain soil fertility and structure. The success of the technique demands thorough initial weed clearance, especially of perennial weeds, by means of sheet mulches (or chemicals for nonorganic gardeners). The no-dig technique is well suited to bed systems, and can be useful in reducing the labor of trenching and earthing up potatoes.

NO-DIG POTATOES

To grow potatoes, lay the tubers on the surface of the soil, then cover them with a 6–8in (15–20cm) layer of mulch, making a mound shape. Cover the mounded mulch with black plastic, tying it down securely. Make slits in the black plastic for the potato shoots to grow through.

MAKING A PATH BETWEEN BEDS

1 Mark, level, and firm the path. Cut a 1in (2.5cm) slit along each edge. Cut landscape fabric to length, and 8in (20cm) wider than the path.

2 Fold the fabric edge into the slit on one side. Secure with 4 x 1in (10 x 2.5cm) wood edging and hammer level. Pull fabric taut and repeat on opposite side.

3 Cut crosses in opposite pairs in the fabric close to each plank, 6ft (2m) apart. Knock a wooden peg through each cross, to 1in (2.5cm) below the plank top.

4 Apply the mulch (here, of bark chips). Rake and tamp down, so that the mulch is level with the plank tops and the support pegs are concealed.

Crop rotation

Crop rotation is a system in which vegetable crops are grown in different areas of the garden in succession over consecutive years.

Advantages of rotation

The principal reason for rotating crops is to prevent a buildup of soilborne pests and diseases specific to one group of crops. If the same type of host crop is grown every year in the same soil, its pests and diseases increase rapidly and often become a serious problem, whereas in the absence of their host they gradually die out. Various types of potato and tomato nematodes; clubroot, which attacks most brassicas (crucifers); and onion white rot are some of the common garden problems that may be alleviated by rotation.

Other benefits also stem from rotating vegetables. Some crops, such as potatoes, blanket the soil so well that they smother most weeds, so it is useful to follow them with crops that are difficult to weed, such as onions. In addition, most root vegetables, and especially potatoes, help break up the ground and keep the soil structure open and well aerated.

Most vegetables in the legume family, such as peas and beans, fix nitrogen in the soil and make it available for the next crop. Therefore nitrogen-hungry brassica crops and potatoes should follow legumes. Conversely, root crops, which have a relatively low nitrogen requirement, can follow brassicas.

Several vegetables, including perennial types and many salad plants, do not fall into a main rotation group. Salad plants stay in the soil for a short time and are therefore useful for intercropping or filling gaps in vegetable beds. As with the other crops, they should not be grown in the same soil year after year. Perennial vegetables are best grown in a permanent bed of their own and so are not rotated.

Drawbacks of rotation

A weakness in the rotation theory is that to be completely effective, rotation should take place over a much longer time scale than the usual three or four years: clubroot and white rot infections can stay in the soil for up to 20 years. Rotations on that scale are unrealistic in most gardens. Another shortcoming is that, in practice, the distance between beds in a home garden is often so small that soilborne pests and diseases can easily spread from one to the next.

Some gardeners with small areas prefer to grow a crop repeatedly in the same bed, then avoid it selectively when infestations occur. It is, however, better to regard rotation as an aid to suppressing of pests and diseases, rather than as a means of total prevention or cure. It may not create dramatic results, but overall it can contribute to the health and productivity of your garden.

ROTATION OF VEGETABLE CROPS

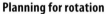

LEGUMES AND POD CROPS
Snap beans, fava beans, hyacinth beans, lima beans, okra, peas, runner beans

ALLIUMS (ONION FAMILY)
Asian bunching onions, bulb onions, Welsh onions, garlic, scallions, leeks, pickling onions, shallots

BRASSICAS (CABBAGE FAMILY)
Asian mustards, broccoli, Brussels sprouts, cabbage, sprouting broccoli, cauliflower, Chinese broccoli, Chinese cabbage, kale, kohlrabi, komatsuna, mizuna, bok choy, radishes, rutabagas, turnips

SOLANACEOUS, ROOT, AND TUBEROUS CROPS
Beets, carrots, celeriac, celery, taro, eggplant, parsnips, potatoes, salsify, scorzonera, peppers, sweet potatoes, tomatoes, wonderberries

Planning for rotation

Despite the disadvantages, rotation is a long-standing practice that you may want to try. The most crucial aspect is to have at least one, preferably two, complete cropping seasons without repeating a vegetable group in a given site if at all possible.

Draw up a list of the main vegetables that you want to grow, with a rough indication of quantities. Avoid growing crops that are climatically unsuited to the locality, especially in small gardens, and concentrate on premium crops that are expensive to buy.

List the various beds in the vegetable garden. Group the selected vegetables in their rotation groups (for example, all legumes and pod crops, or all brassicas), with a miscellaneous category for vegetables not in the main groups (see *Rotation of Vegetable Crops*, above). Members of the miscellaneous group may be placed in one main group or another, depending on available space and quantities required.

Month-by-month planning

Make a chart with a column for each month of the year, and for every vegetable on your list fill in the months during which it will be in the ground. Remember that this period may be shortened by raising plants in containers (see "Sowing indoors," p.501) for transplanting later, and lengthened by the use of some form of cover early and late in the season (see "Growing under cover," p.505). Some crops are sown once a year (parsnips and winter cabbages, for example), but with others, such as lettuces and radishes, repeat sowings may be made to provide a continuous supply throughout the growing season.

Planning a layout

Allocate each bed (or several beds if needed) to a different rotation group of vegetables, and write in the most important crop that each bed will grow. Refer to your month-by-month chart, and indicate a suitable crop to precede or follow it. For example, if the spring spinach crop is finished producing by early summer, you can follow it with tomatoes or beans. Assume that most pieces of ground will bear only two crops a year. Use this basic plan in subsequent years and move the crops to different beds.

Consider the overall plan as a rough guide only. Many factors—not least the unpredictability of the weather and seasons—have a bearing on the success and failure of crops. The key to success lies as much in flexibility as in strict adherence to the plan.

Keeping records

Recording your activities in the vegetable garden is time well spent, especially a planting diary to help plan crop rotations. Notes on weather conditions, particularly the dates of the first and last frost, can be an invaluable guide to improving future yields. Records of cultivars grown, sowing and planting dates, quantities harvested—and those particularly enjoyed—are also useful for future reference. They can help identify gluts and shortcomings, so as to avoid them in following years. It is also useful to record problems faced and remedies used, whether caused by pests, diseases, or disorders.

Plan the space Decide how much of a given crop you hope to harvest and allocate the space accordingly. Some quick-growing crops will give more than one harvest a season.

Sowing and planting

The most common method of raising vegetables is from seed. There are several methods for sowing outdoors or under cover; use the most suitable for the chosen cultivar and the space available. Care in the early stages ensures healthier, more productive crops. Thin or transplant seedlings to their final location in a bed, greenhouse, or container before they become overcrowded.

Choosing seed

In the past, seed was sold only as ordinary, "naked" seed, but it is now also available prepared in a variety of ways to make both sowing and germination easier.

Purchasing seed

Always buy good-quality seed, preferably vacuum-packed to preserve viability. Many popular cultivars are F1 hybrids, but there are seed companies that specialize in heirloom open-pollinated varieties as well. Hybrids are usually very vigorous and productive; heirlooms may offer superior flavor and texture. Vegetable seeds differ widely in their viability: to be safe, use seed under three years old, or test a sample before sowing. Store seed in cool and dry conditions; lettuce seeds are best kept in a refrigerator.

Prepared seed

Pelleted seeds are individually coated with clay to form tiny balls and are easier to sow evenly than naked seed. This is particularly useful for handling small seeds, such as those of carrots. Pelleted seeds should be carefully placed in a furrow one by one, which saves transplanting later. They are sown in the normal way, but it is important that the clay coating is kept moist until after germination.

Seed is also available embedded, evenly spaced, in paper sheets or tapes, which disintegrate in the soil after sowing. The tapes are laid in a furrow and covered with soil, as for ordinary seed. The backing gives protection in the early stages of germination and reduces thinning later.

Pregerminating seed

To start ordinary seed early, it may be pregerminated indoors. This is useful for seed that germinates slowly in cold soil and may rot before germination. Space seeds on damp paper towels and put them in a warm place. Keep them moist until germination, then sow them carefully in containers or in open ground. This method may also be used to test a sample of old seed for viability before sowing.

Storing seed

Packs often contain more seed than is required for the current season. If stored incorrectly, seed will lose its viability quite quickly. To save seed with the least loss of germination potential, fold over the pack and seal it with tape. Put all the packs in a food-storage container with a tight-fitting lid. Before sealing the container, add a stay-dry sachet (such as those that come with electronic equipment) to absorb moisture. Store the container in the coldest part of the refrigerator. Most vegetable seeds can be frozen without any harm.

Sowing outdoors

Vegetables are either sown *in situ*, where they grow to maturity, or in a seedbed and then transplanted to their permanent position. *In situ* sowing is used for crops that are harvested young, such as green onions and radishes, or vegetables that do not transplant well, such as carrots and parsnips. Most others may be sown in a seedbed, in rows up to 6in (15cm) apart.

Successful sowing outdoors requires warm and well-prepared soil. Germination occurs for most vegetables once temperatures are over 45°F (7°C), so do not sow seed in cold soil. In several cases, such as lettuce, germination is poor at high temperatures. Temperature requirements for germination are given in individual vegetable entries. Soil temperature may be measured with a soil thermometer, but most gardeners use their own knowledge of soil conditions to assess if it is warm enough for germination to occur.

Preparing the ground

Before sowing, dig the soil, then rake the surface until it has a fine texture or tilth, removing stones and large clods of earth. Rake when it is neither very wet and heavy nor very dry. If soil sticks to your shoes, delay until it has dried out a little, but not so much that it is dusty. If sowing in wet soil, standing on a board avoids damaging the

---

SOWING IN A FURROW

1 Make the furrow using stakes and string. Use the corner of a hoe or a trowel to ensure that it is the depth required for the seed.

2 Stand on a plank placed parallel to the furrow to prevent compaction of the soil. Sprinkle the seeds thinly and evenly along the furrow, then cover and firm carefully.

ALTERNATIVE METHODS

Wet conditions
If the soil drains slowly or is very heavy, sprinkle a layer of sand at the base of the furrow, sow the seed, then cover it.

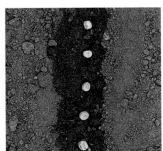

Dry conditions
When the soil is very dry, water the base of the furrow, then sow the seeds and lightly press them in before covering with dry soil.

---

structure of adjacent soil. This is not necessary with the bed system (see p.496) because the seed may be sown from the surrounding path.

Guidelines for sowing

Seeds are sown at different depths according to their size. Unless otherwise directed, sow small seed, such as onions, about ½in (1cm) deep, peas and sweet corn about 1in (2.5cm) deep, and beans up to 2in (5cm) deep. The most important requirement is to sow thinly so that seedlings are not crowded in the early stages. Whichever method is used, it is vital to conserve surface moisture. In cold weather, cover the soil after sowing with newspaper or row cover. Remove any covering when the seedlings appear.

Sowing in a furrow

This is the most common method of sowing vegetables. Mark a row with a string line and make a small, even channel (a "furrow") in the soil to the required depth. There are several methods of sowing: sprinkle a pinch of seed from between thumb and fingers, or gently tap seed out from your palm or the pack. Small handheld devices are available, designed to gradually release differently sized seeds; or sow in groups of up to three seeds at the final planting distance, then thin to one seedling per grouping. If seed is sown directly into a furrow, place each seed at half the required distance between the mature plants, for example at 1in (2.5cm) intervals to thin to 2in (5cm). After sowing, cover the seed with soil, drawing it back lightly with a rake, firm the area gently, and water with a fine spray from a hose or watering can.

If sowing in unavoidably wet conditions, line the furrow before sowing with dry, sharp sand or vermiculite. If conditions are dry,

SOWING IN A WIDE FURROW

1 Use a draw hoe to create parallel furrows 6–9in (15–23cm) wide and flat at the base.

2 Sow seeds the required distance apart in the furrow.

3 Cover the seeds with soil using the hoe. Take care not to dislodge them.

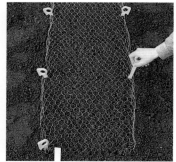

4 Protect them from birds or animals by putting wire netting over the furrow.

water the furrow before lightly pressing each seed into the soil; then cover them with dry soil. This slows down the evaporation rate and helps keep seeds moist until germination.

Wide rows

Use wide planting rows for plants that are grown closely together, such as peas, early carrots, and crops grown for harvesting at the seedling stage (see "Successional crops," right). Make each furrow up to 9in (23cm) wide and to the proper depth. Space the seeds evenly in the furrow, and cover with soil.

Large seed

The seed of beans and squash may be sown individually. Place a seed in a hole made by a dibber or a finger, ensuring that each seed is at the base of the hole and in contact with the soil. Cover sowings of tender plants, such as melons, with glass jars or cut-off plastic bottles and remove once the seedlings emerge.

Broadcasting seed

In this method, the soil is first raked to produce a fine tilth; the seed is then scattered as evenly as possible either by hand or from a pack. Rake the soil lightly again afterward to cover the seed.

Successional crops

Vegetables that grow fast, but quickly pass their prime or go to seed, such as lettuce, should be sown little and often. To avoid gluts or gaps in harvesting, wait until one sowing emerges before making the next. Many leafy or salad vegetables may be sown for harvesting at the seedling stage and, once cut, often regrow to produce successional flushes of cut-and-come-again vegetables. This is a very productive way to make use of a small area, and such crops are ideal for sowing under

or between other, slower-maturing vegetables. To obtain seedling crops, sow seed in wide furrows and cover with row cover. Seedlings do not need thinning and will be ready for the first cut in a few weeks.

Using row cover for protection

Row cover tucked into the soil or held down with stones helps warm the soil before sowing. It encourages early establishment and keeps off birds, animals, and some insect pests. Remove it before the seedlings' growth is restricted.

Thinning

Young seedlings must be thinned to prevent overcrowding. Thin to the final spacing in stages, to allow for losses from pests and diseases; at each stage, aim to leave a seedling just clear of its neighbors. If seeds have been sown *in situ*, continue to thin until they are at the spacing required for mature plants. Discard thinnings or their scent may attract pests. Lift seedlings of plants such as lettuce, cabbage, and onions for transplanting when conditions are suitably moist, and refirm the soil around the remaining ones. Lettuce is liable to bolt if it is too warm.

Planting

Plant vegetables into their final location when they are as young as possible so they can grow without further check. Exceptions to this are plants that have been raised in containers or cell packs (see p.501). Do not transplant root vegetables once the taproot has started to form because this may distort its shape.

Before taking plants from a seedbed, water around their roots; if the ground into which they are being planted is dry, water the furrow. Pick up a plant by a leaf,

THINNING SEEDLINGS

To thin small seedlings, nip them out at ground level so that the roots of the remaining seedlings are not disturbed.

not the stem or roots, which are easily damaged. Make a hole slightly bigger than the roots. Position the plant in this hole, replacing the soil so that the lower leaves are just above soil level. Firm around the stem to anchor the plant. In hot weather, water seedlings, then shade them with fine-mesh netting or newspaper cones until established. Keep soil moist for a few days after planting (see "Critical watering periods," p.502).

TRANSPLANTING SEEDLINGS

Using a plant label or a dibber, lift the seedlings gently, keeping as much soil around the roots as possible. Replant quickly to avoid moisture loss.

PLANTING DEPTH

Plant vegetable seedlings so that their lowest leaves are just above soil level. Planting too high exposes the stalk, which may not support the weight of the mature vegetable.

BROADCASTING

1 Prepare the area to be sown by raking carefully in one direction to produce a fine tilth. Sprinkle the seed thinly and evenly over the surface.

2 Rake lightly at a right angle to the original direction to cover the seed, then water thoroughly with a fine spray from a hose or can.

Spacing

Different vegetables have individual spacing requirements, which sometimes determine their final size. Traditionally, vegetables are grown in rows with a recommended spacing between the plants, and between the rows. Alternatively they may be grown with equidistant spacing between the plants—the average of the recommended spacing between plants and rows; so plants 6in (15cm) apart, in rows 12in (30cm) apart, may alternatively be grown 9in (23cm) apart each way. This method gives good results: plants have an equal share of light, air, moisture, and nutrients, and as they mature they form a canopy over the soil that suppresses weeds (see also The Bed System, pp.496–497). Vegetables may also be grown close together within widely spaced rows.

Sowing indoors

Vegetable seed may be sown indoors, in a cool greenhouse, or on a windowsill. This is helpful in climates with cool or short summers for tender vegetables, and for those needing a long growing season. It also helps to produce healthy seedlings and overcomes germination problems, because temperature is more easily controlled. After germination, keep most seedlings at a lower temperature in a spacious, light, protected environment until they are planted out. Where this is impossible, it may be practical to buy more mature plants.

Sowing in containers

Cell packs are individual units in which seeds are sown and plants grown on for planting out directly. This produces high-quality plants that grow well: seedlings have no competition and develop a healthy root ball that is hardly disturbed when planted out in their final position. They do, however, need more space and soil mix in the early stages than those planted in trays.

Many types of cell packs are available, the cheapest being plastic or styrofoam cellular trays. Small containers include clay or plastic pots, degradable pots, and blocks made of compressed mix. This mix may be enclosed in netting, which roots can penetrate.

Sow into cell packs of 24 or 40 cells—these fit neatly into a standard seed tray. Sow two or three seeds per unit; then thin the seedlings to leave the strongest. In some cases, such as leeks, onions, turnips, and beets, several seeds are sown together, planted

---

SOWING AND TRANSPLANTING

1 Fill the cell pack with seed-starting mix. Make a hole ¼in (5mm) deep in each. Sow one or two seeds per section. Cover with more mix, then water.

2 Remove each plant from the cell pack. Make a hole for its root ball. Put the plant in the hole with its lower leaves just above the surface; firm, and water.

---

out as a unit at a wider spacing than usual, and grown on to maturity.

Alternatively, sow seed in a small pot or seed flat, in seed-starting mix (see "Sowing in pots or trays," p.216). When the seedlings have two or three small leaves, prick them out into a larger flat with soil mix, spaced 1–2in (2.5–5cm) apart, or into cell packs. Seedlings usually need to be kept slightly warm. Put them in a well-lit, draft-free place to grow strongly and evenly. You may want to transplant tomatoes and peppers to individual pots to gain more size before planting out in garden beds.

Hardening off

Plants raised indoors need to be acclimatized to wind and lower temperatures before being planted out, by placing them outdoors for increasing lengths of time over a period of 10 to 14 days. Eventually leave them out overnight in a protected place, and then plant them out in garden beds.

Vegetative propagation

A few vegetables are usually raised vegetatively, from offsets, tubers, corms, bulbs, or cuttings. This may be because they rarely set seed or, if raised from seed, are not consistent, or because vegetative propagation is faster. Details are given under individual vegetables (pp.507–548).

Growing vegetables in containers

Containers are useful for growing vegetables where space is limited, or to extend the vegetable garden into a paved area. They are also used in the greenhouse, especially if soil is infected with diseases and it is impractical to sterilize or replace it. Vegetables need a richer growing

---

medium and a more consistent and thorough watering than flowers and so must be carefully maintained; see Container Vegetables, p.331.

Grafting vegetables

Grafting has been used for many years as a method of propagating woody plants, such as roses and rhododendrons, but this method has only been practiced commercially for vegetables in relatively recent years. The rootstocks used are variants, usually of the same species, which are selected for their vigor and resistance to diseases, qualities passed on to the popular cultivars grafted onto them. Grafted vegetables grown commercially include eggplant, squash, melons, cucumbers, tomatoes, and peppers.

Some grafted vegetables are also sold by mail-order companies for home gardeners to grow. While they are more expensive to buy than seed-grown cultivars, they are usually more vigorous and may be more disease-resistant or higher yielding than vegetables grown on their own roots. Grow in pots at least 12in (30cm) deep; ensure that they are planted with the graft about 2in (5cm) above the soil level to discourage rooting from the scions. Use a high potassium fertilizer once or twice a week once the fruits begin to set. Most grafted vegetables require staking with strong stakes whether pot grown or planted out (see also "Grafting tomatoes," p.528). Trailing vegetables, such as squash, may also benefit from a strong support.

APPROACH GRAFTING TOMATO CULTIVARS

Cut down stock above leaf node

Lowest leaf

Scion

Tongues fit together snugly

1 Sow the rootstock 4–5 days before the scion. Remove it from the pot when it is 6in (15cm) tall. Make a ¾in (2cm) downward cut, 3in (8cm) from the stem base. Make an upward cut of the same length on the scion (see inset).

2 Fit the tongues of the scion and stock plant together. Bind the graft firmly with grafting or transparent adhesive tape, so that the cuts are completely covered. Cut down the stock, making an angled cut just above the lowest leaf.

Scion

Rootstock — *Graft*

Cut roots off scion

3 Pot the grafted plant in a 4in (10cm) pot in soilless potting mix. Grow in high humidity at 59–64°F (15–18°C). After 2–3 weeks, the graft should take, or callus over. Remove the tape carefully.

4 Knock the plant out of its pot. Cut through the base of the scion, making an angled cut just below the graft union. Pull away severed roots; replant the grafted plant into its final location.

Routine cultivation

The best vegetables are produced when plants are maintained in the optimal conditions for growth. Keep free from weeds, and water thoroughly as required. Mulches may be used to retain moisture and to suppress weeds. The level of nutrients must be maintained as crops grow.

Watering

Most crops need fairly moist soil, but vary in the amount of water required, and in when they need it most (see "Critical watering periods," below). Overwatering can lead to loss of flavor in tomatoes and carrots, and, in root crops, to the development of leaves at the expense of root.

How to water

It is more effective to water heavily and occasionally rather than frequently and lightly; very young plants, however, should be watered lightly and frequently to ensure that they never dry out. Light watering evaporates rapidly without reaching the plants' roots, and encourages shallow surface rooting rather than the deep rooting that enables plants to withstand drought. Direct the water at the base of each plant. Water in the evening when less moisture will evaporate, and allow enough time for the plants to dry before nightfall.

Watering equipment

Water young plants with a fine spray from a can. For general watering in small gardens, a can may be adequate; in larger gardens, use a handheld hose, regulating the flow with a nozzle attached to the end.

A practical choice for use in vegetable gardens is either a drip hose or a soaker hose laid among the plants (see also TOOLS AND EQUIPMENT, "Drip hoses," p.561). Water seeps through the holes or pores, usually watering a strip about 12in (30cm) wide. The hose can be easily moved from area to area, and some porous types may be buried shallowly in the soil.

Critical watering periods

The most critical time to water varies according to the individual vegetable. During prolonged dry weather confine watering to these periods.

Germinating seeds, seedlings, and newly transplanted plants should never be allowed to dry

out, so water frequently and lightly and ensure that water reaches the roots.

Leafy and salad vegetables, such as spinach, Swiss chard, broccoli, and lettuce, require a thorough watering once a week to help them grow lushly. The most critical watering period for these vegetables is between ten days and three weeks before maturity; during this period, but only in very dry conditions, apply a single, heavy watering of 5 gallons/sq yd (22 liters/sq m)—adjust the total quantity if you have very heavy or very light soil. Outside this period, give half of this amount weekly during dry weather.

The critical point for fruiting crops like tomatoes, peppers, zucchini, beans, cucumbers, and peas is when flowers form and fruits or pods develop. If it is dry at this time, water weekly at the rate for leafy crops (above). Do not water heavily before the critical period; this produces leafy growth at the expense of fruit.

Root crops such as carrots, radishes, and beets need moderate watering in the growing period. In the early stages, water at a rate of 1 gallon/sq yd (5 liters/sq m) if the soil is dry (adjust the total to suit your soil). Increase this rate fourfold when the roots start to swell, watering every two weeks if dry conditions persist.

Minimizing the need to water

To conserve soil moisture, particularly in dry areas, dig the soil deeply, working in plenty of organic matter to improve soil structure and moisture retention and thereby encourage deep rooting. Keep the soil surface mulched (see "Mulching," right), and keep down weeds, which compete for moisture. Do not hoe in dry weather because this allows moisture to evaporate from the soil. Erect windbreaks to protect the plants from desiccating winds (see "Shelter and windbreaks," pp.492–493). In areas prone to drought, adopt slightly wider spacing so that t he roots can spread farther to take moisture from a larger area.

Controlling weeds

A vegetable garden should be largely free of weeds. They compete for water, nutrients, and light; can crowd out crops; and may harbor

WATERING VEGETABLES WITH A DRIP HOSE

A drip hose laid between rows of vegetables ensures that the water reaches the roots of the plants and penetrates deeply into the soil.

pests and diseases (see PLANT PROBLEMS, "Weeds and lawn weeds," pp.645–649).

Minimizing weed growth

During the growing season weed growth may be reduced by mulching or planting through a plastic or paper mulch and by planting crops at equidistant spacing (see "Spacing," p.501). Once they have reached a reasonable size, most form a weed-suppressing canopy over the ground.

Stale seedbeds

Spring sowings or plantings are the most vulnerable to annual weeds. If soil has not been cultivated recently and may be full of weed seeds, prepare the seedbed in advance: allow the first flush of weeds to germinate, then hoe them off before sowing or planting (see also SOILS AND FERTILIZERS, *The Stale Seedbed Technique*, p.620).

CONSERVING SOIL MOISTURE

Many vegetables, such as beans, drop their flowers if the soil around their roots dries out. Water the plants well, then apply a mulch by carefully forking it onto the bed. A mulch prevents soil-moisture evaporation, and also insulates the soil, suppresses weeds, and protects the surface from heavy rain and erosion.

Mulching

A mulch is a layer of organic or inorganic material laid on the soil around plants. Where the surface is kept mulched, the need to cultivate is lessened or even eliminated.

Organic mulches

Bulky organic mulches add nutrients to the soil and improve the structure. They may be well-rotted animal manures, garden compost, spent mushroom compost, dried lawn clippings, kelp, or straw. Do not use any materials derived from wood, such as sawdust and shredded bark, unless they are at least two years old, because they use up soil nitrogen during decomposition. Organic mulches are best applied to growing crops in spring and early summer when the soil is moist. They maintain the temperature and moisture levels of the soil once they are applied so, if possible, mulch after the soil has warmed up in spring but before it starts to dry out. Never mulch cold, wet, or very dry soil. In areas with high rainfall and on heavy soil, however, an organic mulch is best spread on the ground in the fall to prevent soil damage.

In practice it is often easiest to apply organic mulches when planting, watering plants first if necessary. Alternatively, mulch young seedlings that are already planted and growing strongly and are at least 2in (5cm) high. A mulch may be 1–3in (2.5–7cm) deep; aim for a deep mulch if the purpose is to keep down weeds.

Plastic mulches

These are sheets of plastic that may be black or transparent. Depending on which kind is used, they raise soil temperatures to bring on crops early, suppress weeds, reflect heat up to ripening fruit, and keep fruiting vegetables clean and free from soil splash. Reflective mulches help deter flying pests.

Black plastic is mainly used to suppress weeds, although it also raises soil temperature if it is spread tightly over the soil surface. Early potatoes may be grown under black films instead of being earthed up (see "Potatoes," p.547).

White mulches are mainly used to reflect light and warmth onto ripening fruit, such as tomatoes and melons. Some films are made with the lower side black to suppress weeds, and the upper side white to reflect light. These mulches raise soil temperatures up to 12°F (7°C) more than black plastic. Clear plastic mulch is used mainly to warm up the soil in spring, or to prevent soil splash.

It is simpler to lay plastic before planting or sowing crops. If desired, lay drip or porous hoses in position first, then lay plastic on the ground or over the bed to be covered. Make slits 3–4in (7–10cm) deep in the soil around the bed, and anchor the mulch by tucking the edges into the soil, using a spade (see *Anchoring Plastic Sheeting*, p.626). This is easier on slightly mounded beds. To plant, cut cross-shaped slits in the plastic with a knife, make a hole in the soil beneath, then carefully ease the plants through into the soil, and firm. Sow large seeds, such as sweet corn, by making holes in the

PLANTING THROUGH A BLACK-AND-WHITE PLASTIC MULCH

1 Dig a trench around the area to be planted, lay down the mulch with the white side upward, and secure its edges firmly into the earth.

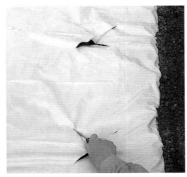
2 Make cross-shaped slits in the plastic the required distance apart and dig a hole in the soil large enough to accommodate the plant's root ball.

3 Remove the plant (here a tomato) from its pot, and place it in the hole. Firm the soil around the root ball and water. Stake if necessary.

plastic and pushing the seeds through. When seedlings appear, guide them through the holes so that they are not trapped.

When necessary, water carefully through the planting holes. Slugs may be attracted to plastic mulch: lift the film edges carefully and remove them or otherwise use a commercial slug killer.

Alternatives to conventional plastic mulch are planting paper or biodegradable plastic mulch.

Feeding

In fertile garden soils, into which plenty of organic matter is regularly worked, most plants grow satisfactorily without additional fertilizers. It takes a few years to build up soil fertility, however, so supplementary feeding will be necessary on poor soils or to correct deficiencies and, in some cases, to obtain higher yields.

Soil nutrients

Plants need a range of nutrients; the three most important for vegetables, and those most often in short supply in the soil, are nitrogen (N), phosphorus (P), and potassium (K). For further information, see "Soil nutrients and fertilizers," pp.624–625.

Maintain adequate levels of phosphorus and potassium with annual applications of garden compost at 5–11lb/sq yd (2–5kg/sq m), or well-rotted manure at 12lb/sq yd (5.5kg/sq m). Alternatively, use packaged organic or synthetic fertilizer products at recommended levels. Potassium is washed out of the soil only slowly, so reserves last into the following season. Phosphorus is not lost through leaching, but may be "locked up" in insoluble forms and not available to plants; reserves may

need replenishing if soil analysis indicates that they are low. Nitrogen is constantly leached out and reserves need to be replenished continually by adding either organic matter (which releases nitrogen as it breaks down) or artificial fertilizers.

Vegetables vary in their need for nitrogen. For further information, see *Nitrogen Requirements*, p.504. This indicates the broad requirements of different groups using a fertilizer with 21 percent nitrogen content. Rates therefore vary according to the fertilizer used; nitrogenous fertilizers include alfalfa meal, blood meal, ammonium nitrate and potassium nitrate.

Applying fertilizers

Fertilizers are sold in dry forms (dusts, granules, and pellets) and as concentrated liquids (see "Types of fertilizers," p.624). Apply either as a soil amendment before sowing or planting, or as a topdressing to give a boost during growth (see "Applying fertilizers," p.625).

Apply nitrogenous fertilizers as close to sowing as possible to avoid leaching; additional applications may be made later in the growing season. In most areas, do not apply nitrogen in the fall, because it will be washed out of the soil before most vegetables are planted. An exception is beds where fall crops will be grown under cover, and mild-winter areas where crops are grown throughout fall and into the winter. Organic fertilizers that supply phosphate and potassium, such as bone meal, can be applied at any time.

Feeding in organic systems

Organic fertilizers may provide nutrients more slowly than synthetic ones, over a longer period of time. Organic fertilizers include

fish, blood, and bone meal, and dried blood (relatively fast-acting). Various commercial and general-purpose liquid fertilizers are available, some based on animal manures and others on kelp extracts. The latter claim to be rich in trace elements as well as plant hormones that promote healthy, vigorous plant growth, even though their nutrient levels are not very high. They are either watered in or applied as a foliar feed.

Container-grown vegetables

The soil mix in containers can dry out very rapidly in hot weather. To conserve moisture, keep the upper surface mulched with up to 2in (5cm) of organic material, pebbles, or a sheet mulch. Be prepared to water containers thoroughly twice a day and, in very hot weather, water grow bags three times a day.

Use an organic or synthetic fertilizer at diluted strength, according to the manufacturer's instructions. Topdress the soil mix in the container in spring, or for best results, start with fresh mix every year to avoid compaction and loss of productivity.

Pests and diseases

Healthy plants can resist most pest and disease attacks. Therefore, good basic care of plants will keep problems caused by pests and diseases to a minimum. Learn to recognize the most common pests and diseases in your garden, and take the appropriate preventive measures wherever feasible. Avoid using sprays in the vegetable garden as far as possible. Apart from their inherent danger and the risk of residues in the soil, as well as on the plants, sprays can kill the natural enemies of many pests and diseases. If using pest control products seems unavoidable, make an effort to choose organically approved products at least. For general information and details about specific pests and diseases, see PLANT PROBLEMS, pp.639–673.

Common pests

Animals that may attack vegetables include deer, rabbits, woodchucks, raccoons, mice, voles, and birds. In cases of persistent attack, erect wire fences or nets around the garden or over crops, use humane animal traps, and deter large birds with humming wire and small ones with strands of black thread. In damp climates slugs and snails may be the most serious pests. They are mainly night-feeders; collect them after dark by flashlight and destroy them.

Soil pests, such as slugs and cutworms, commonly attack young plants, sometimes biting through the stems of plants at ground level. They tend to be worse in newly cultivated ground. Thorough digging exposes them to the birds. Many soil pests are night-feeders and may be easily caught by using a flashlight.

Nematodes are microscopic soil-dwelling pests that attack certain plant groups. Rotate crops to

HEALTHY PRACTICES

To reduce pests and diseases, keep soil fertile and well drained, work in organic matter, and rotate crops (see p.498). Grow crops that suit the climate, and if possible, choose pest- or disease-resistant cultivars. Always purchase disease-free plants. Start your own seedlings in cell flats if feasible or buy locally raised transplants. Harden off plants raised indoors. Use clean seed flats and pots and a high-quality seed-starting mix. To avoid problems like mildew, give plants enough space to ensure good air circulation.

prevent pests from becoming established, and grow resistant cultivars where they are available.

Sucking insects, which include aphids, carrot rust flies, cabbage root maggots, and thrips, damage a range of plants by sucking their sap, and may spread virus diseases in the process. Knowledge of the pests' habits may help prevent attacks—by earlier or later sowings, for example. Use water sprays to wash off aphids, collars (see *Collaring Seedlings*, p.507) to deter cabbage root maggots, and netting barriers to protect carrots from carrot rust flies (see p.544).

Various caterpillars attack a range of plants; pick them off by

CREATING HEALTHY GROWING CONDITIONS

Keep vegetable beds (here of ornamental cabbage and carrots) and paths free of weeds and debris; remove and burn diseased plant material. Water and feed carefully —too much can be as damaging as too little. Thin seedlings early to avoid overcrowding, and remove the thinnings. Encourage rapid germination of homegrown plants by sowing indoors if conditions are adverse outside.

hand frequently. Row covers can be placed over vegetables to prevent adult butterflies or moths from laying eggs on the plants. Small beetles, for example, flea beetles, nibble seedling leaves of cabbage; row cover or insect-proof mesh also protects crops from these beetles. Other beetle pests include Colorado potato beetles and cucumber beetles.

Pests may multiply rapidly in high temperatures. The most serious are whiteflies and spider mites, both of which attack a wide range of crops, and have become resistant to most synthetic chemical sprays. As soon as these pests are noticed, some form of biological

control should be introduced to restrict their numbers (see "Biological control," p.643).

Common diseases

Diseases are caused mainly by fungi, bacteria, and viruses. Infected plants develop a range of symptoms, which in some cases disfigure them, but in others will kill them. Damping off diseases, for example, infect and kill young seedlings; dig up and dispose of affected plants.

Diseases spread rapidly in conditions that favor their development and once established, they are difficult to control. Preventive measures and good garden hygiene are vitally important to keep diseases from spreading and establishing. A few sprays, such as potassium bicarbonate spray, may be used in anticipation of an attack. Choose disease-resistant cultivars.

Clubroot, a soil infection, is a serious problem affecting plants in the cabbage family. Raise soil pH by applying lime (see "Liming," p.625), and grow crops in cell flats in sterile soil, making them vigorous and helping control it.

Physiological disorders

Some problems with vegetables are due to incorrect cultural conditions. Most common is premature bolting (flowering and setting seed), caused by sudden low or high temperatures, drought, or sowing at the wrong time. Fruit failing to set may be due to lack of pollination, erratic watering, drought, high night temperatures, and windy, cold conditions. If there are mineral deficiencies in the soil, cauliflower curds may fail to grow. For more details, and advice on how to create healthy growing conditions, see individual crops, pp.507–548.

NITROGEN REQUIREMENTS (USING FERTILIZER WITH 21 PERCENT N CONTENT)

Very low 1/2oz/sq yd (12g/sq m)	Low 1–1 1/3 oz/sq yd (25–35g/sq m)	Medium 1 1/2–2oz/sq yd (45–55g/sq m)	High 2 1/2–3 1/2oz/sq yd (70–100g/sq m)	Very high 4oz/sq yd (110g/sq m)
Carrots	Asparagus	Amaranths	Beets	Asian mustards
Garlic	Beans (all)	Bell peppers	Brussels sprouts	Bok choy
Radishes	Celery root	Broccoli	Celery	Cabbage (spring,
	Chicory (all)	Broccoli raab	Leeks	summer, winter)
	Cucumbers	Cabbage (for storage)	Malabar spinach	Chinese broccoli
	Endive	Cauliflower	Melons	Chinese cabbage
	Florence fennel	Eggplant	Potatoes (main crop)	Komatsuna
	Gherkins	Hot peppers	Swiss chard	Mizuna greens
	Globe artichokes	Jerusalem artichokes		Rhubarb (cutting years)
	Kohlrabi	Kale		
	New Zealand spinach	Lettuce		
	Okra	Potatoes (early)		
	Onions (all)	Rhubarb (young)		
	Parsnips	Spinach		
	Peanuts	Sprouting broccoli		
	Rutabaga	Sweet corn		
	Salsify	Sweet potatoes		
	Scorzonera	Taro		
	Tomatoes	Watermelon		
(Peas do not require any	Turnips (and turnip greens)	Winter squash		
extra nitrogen)	Zucchini	Wonderberries		

Growing under cover

The productivity of a vegetable garden may be increased greatly in climates with a short growing season by growing plants under cover in a protected environment for some or all of their life cycle. The shorter the growing season, the more effective the cover will be.

Under cover, air and soil temperatures are increased, and crops are sheltered from cold winds. This lengthens the growing season by up to two months. The quality and yields of many crops are improved by higher temperatures and shelter.

Cover may be used to start crops early in spring for planting outside when temperatures rise. Half-hardy summer vegetables that would not mature outdoors during the growing season may ripen under cover; in cool climates, okra and eggplant, for example, only ripen fully under cover. The winter cropping period of many vegetables may be extended; for example, lettuce, Asian cabbage, peas, and spinach all stop growing in the open but continue under cover.

Make the most of cover by ensuring that the soil underneath is fertile and weed-free. Vegetables require extra watering under cover —mulch them where practical to cut down on watering. Plants started under cover may struggle if abruptly exposed to the elements. Harden off gradually where appropriate.

Greenhouses and frames

Cover may be provided by anything from a greenhouse to a cold frame or a plastic tunnel cloche. For full details, see GREENHOUSES AND COLD FRAMES, pp.566–583.

Greenhouses
A permanent, glazed greenhouse provides an excellent growing environment. It is easily ventilated and retains heat at night better than plastic film. Diseases may build up in soil if crops such as tomatoes are grown for several consecutive years, and the soil must then be changed or sterilized, or crops grown in containers. Supports may be required for tender, climbing vegetables.

Hoop houses
These are made of heavy-duty, clear plastic sheeting on metal or other supports. They are cheaper and easier to erect than greenhouses, and may be moved to a different site if required. Ventilation is hard to control, however, increasing the risk of pests and diseases if temperatures rise rapidly; some designs allow for the sidewalls to be rolled up to ventilate the house. The sheeting needs to be renewed every three to five years.

Low tunnels
These are cheap, mobile, and flexible; the lightweight plastic film may be rolled back for ventilation and watering. They provide shelter from wind and are useful in most gardens, especially for the final stages of hardening off seedlings and protecting vegetables in unsettled spring and fall weather. However, low tunnels are limited by their height and flimsiness, and give little protection against low temperatures. They also need to be well anchored in especially windy situations.

Cold frames
Being relatively small, cold frames are most beneficial in gardens lacking the space for a greenhouse or tunnel. Some types are portable. They are easily ventilated, and may be heated by electric soil-warming cables. They are useful for raising and hardening off seedlings; their

Plastic bottle cloches
Simple cloches made from plastic bottles will protect individual young plants; in exposed conditions, traditional glass cloches offer better protection against frost and wind.

low height limits the range of crops grown, although the lids may be removed to allow crops to grow to maturity. Garden frames may be blacked out for forcing crops, such as Belgian endive and endive.

Cloches
Although individual cloches only cover a small area of the garden, when placed end to end they can be used to cover an entire row. To make maximum use of cloches, move them from one crop to another during a season; for example, first protect overwintering salad greens, then start early potatoes or dwarf beans in spring, then ripen early melons in midsummer.

Row covers

There are various types of row covers, including perforated plastic sheeting, netting films, and nonwoven row covers, as well as improvised materials, such as old bedsheets. All may be laid over wire hoops or directly over crops after sowing or planting, and anchored shallowly in the soil or weighted down. The row covers are lifted by the crops as they grow.

Floating row covers promote earlier crops and higher yields by raising temperatures and protecting plants from wind as well as, in certain cases, insect pests. All types give better ventilation than unperforated plastic films.

Weed beds carefully before laying row covers, because they are awkward to lift for weeding later.

Netting films
Fine netting films are strong and last for several seasons. They are well ventilated so may usually be kept on until plants mature. They have little effect on temperature, but protect against wind and therefore tend to produce larger, and sometimes more leggy, plants. Provided that they are well anchored at the edges, they protect against many insect pests.

Non woven row covers
These light, soft materials usually last one season only; they are more permeable to light and air than plastics. Depending on the film's weight, it may protect against frost and flying insect pests; be careful with cucumbers and melons, however. They need to be uncovered to allow bees to pollinate the flowers. Many vegetables may be grown under row covers until they are mature, especially if using one of the thinner textured types.

USING LIGHTWEIGHT ROW COVERS

Lightweight row covers can be spread over a bed of seedlings and buried at the edges so that they are loose enough to allow for growth. Netting film is used to protect plants against insect pests and wind damage, while nonwoven row cover is effective against frost as well as deterring insect pests.

Netting film

Nonwoven row cover

LOW TUNNEL

Use wire hoops pushed into the ground 3ft (90cm) apart to support plastic film, which is tied at each end to a stake. Tie strings over the plastic and secure them at the base of each hoop.

Harvesting and storing

How and when vegetables are harvested, and whether they are used fresh, stored, or both, depends on the nature of the vegetable and the climate. The shorter the growing season and the more severe the winter, the greater the incentive to store vegetables, either naturally or by freezing. For details, see individual vegetables (pp.507–548) and *Vegetables that Freeze Well*, below.

Harvesting

Follow the guidelines under individual vegetables for how to harvest. Most vegetables are harvested at maturity, but some, notably leafy plants and cabbage-family crops, may be cut at various stages, and will often resprout for a second and third crop.

Cut-and-come-again harvesting

This method of harvesting is suited to vegetables that resprout after an initial cut has been made, enabling them to be used fresh over a fairly long period. Crops may be harvested at the seedling stage, or later when they are semimature or mature.

Harvest seedling crops when they are 2–4in (5–10cm) high, cutting about ¾in (2cm) above soil level. Some, for example, arugula and cress, may be cut and left to resprout several times in succession. See also "Successional crops," p.500.

Some semimature or mature crops, if harvested by cutting 1–2in (2.5–5cm) above soil level, will resprout and after a few weeks produce more leaves and, in some cases, edible flowering shoots (see "Cultivating Chinese cabbages," p.513).

The technique is suited to certain types of lettuce, endive, sugarloaf chicory, Asian greens, and Swiss chard. It is useful in cool climates in the fall and early winter—plants treated this way survive lower temperatures than they would otherwise and may be very productive, especially under cover.

Storing

The length of time that vegetables may be stored depends on the storage conditions and on the vegetable or cultivar. For details, see individual vegetables. The main cause of deterioration after harvesting is water loss, so aim to keep this to a minimum. Do not store damaged or diseased specimens because they may rot.

Vegetables often freeze well; almost all need to be blanched either in steam or boiling water and cooled quickly before freezing. The only exception to this is sweet peppers, which may be frozen without any initial preparation.

Leafy vegetables and brassicas

Leafy vegetables and various types of brassicas, such as broccoli and cauliflower, have such a high water content that few of them store well. An exception is the winter-storage cabbage, which may be stored either hanging in nets or on a bed of straw in a frost-free shed or cold frame. Several brassicas freeze well: some cultivars are bred for the purpose. Freeze only topquality produce.

Fruiting vegetables

Vegetables such as eggplant, tomatoes, and cucumbers usually have an optimal time for harvesting, although fruit may also be harvested immature. If they are to be stored for winter use, they are best made into preserves or deep frozen.

Some types of peppers keep in good condition for months if whole plants are pulled up and hung in a dry, frost-free place. Some cultivars of squash may be stored for several months. Leave them to mature on the plant, then pick and "cure" it in the sun to harden the skin, forming an excellent barrier to water loss, and store it in a dry, frost-free environment (see also "Pumpkins and winter squash," p.525).

Bulbs

Certain cultivars of onions, shallots, and garlic will keep for many months. Lift the crop when mature or nearing maturity, and dry it in the sun (or under cover in wet climates), until the outer skins are papery. Handle the bulbs carefully to avoid bruising. Hang them as braided strings, in nets, or spaced out on trays, in well-ventilated, frost-free conditions (see also *Storing Onions in a Box*, p.535).

Root vegetables

Some root vegetables, such as carrots and potatoes, may be either harvested young and eaten while small or left to mature and lifted and stored at the end of the season. A few, such as parsnips, are extremely hardy and, except in severe winters, can be left in the ground until needed.

Prepare vegetables carefully for storing, removing any foliage because this will rot. Store only healthy, unbruised specimens. Potatoes are susceptible to freezing; store them packed in light-proof sacks in a frost-free place.

Root vegetables, such as beets and carrots, easily lose moisture, so store them in layers in boxes of moist sand in a cool shed or cellar (see *Storing Carrots*, p.544). They may also be stored in outdoor piles: store them on straw and cover with more straw, and, in cold areas, a layer of soil to give protection against freezing (see *Making a Rutabaga Pile*, p.543).

VEGETABLES THAT FREEZE WELL

Asian cabbage **1 2**
Asparagus **1**
Beets **1 3**
Lima beans **1**
Broccoli **1**
Broccoli raab **1**
Brussels sprouts **1**
Carrots **1 3**
Cauliflower **1 2**
Celery **2**
Chinese broccoli **1**
Chinese cabbage **1 2**
Eggplant **1 2**
Hot peppers **1 2**
Hyacinth beans **1**
Kale **1**
Kohlrabi **1 2**
Lima beans **1**
New Zealand spinach **1**
Okra **1**
Parsnips **1 3**
Peas **1**
Potatoes (small and new potatoes only) **1**
Rhubarb **2**
Rutabaga **1 2**
Scallions **2**
Scarlet runner beans **1**
Snap beans **1**
Spinach **1**
Sprouting broccoli **1**
Summer squash **1 2**
Sweet corn **1**
Sweet peppers **2**
Swiss chard **1**
Tomatoes **1**
Turnips **1 2 3**
Winter squash **2**
Wonderberries **1**
Zucchini **1**

Key

1 Blanch
2 Dice, slice, purée, or shred
3 Freeze only when young

STORING STRINGS OF ONIONS

Braid the dried onion leaves to form strings of bulbs. These may be hung outside in warm weather to dry further, and then brought indoors to be stored in frost-free conditions.

STORING RED CABBAGES

Lay the cabbage on slats covered with straw in a cool, well-ventilated, frost-free place. Leave gaps between them to allow free air circulation and discourage rotting.

Cabbage-family crops

Cabbage-family crops (also called brassicas) include kale, cauliflower, cabbage, Brussels sprouts, broccoli, sprouting broccoli, turnip greens, kohlrabi, rutabagas, and turnips. For kohlrabi, rutabagas, and turnips, see pp.540, 542, and 543.

Cabbage-family crops are naturally biennial but are cultivated as annuals for their leaves and roots, and as biennials for flower heads and shoots. Each type displays considerable variation, and there is often a range of cultivars for different seasons. They are usually cooked, but some are used raw. Crops in the cabbage family are cool-season crops with varying degrees of frost tolerance; most perform poorly at high temperatures, so in hot-summer areas grow them in winter. In most other regions, they are spring and fall crops.

Siting cabbage-family crops
A sunny site with fertile, well-drained, moisture-retentive soil is required. Rotate brassicas (see p.498) to avoid a buildup of clubroot. If this is a problem, lime the soil (see p.625) to bring the pH to 6.5–7 and discourage the disease. Most need high levels of nitrogen (see p.504), but they should not be planted on freshly manured ground because this causes overlush, leafy growth that is prone to pests. A preplanting application is a good option. (see "Applying fertilizers," p.503).

Sowing and planting
Brassicas prefer firm soil; they may be planted after a previous vegetable crop without forking the soil. Many types of brassicas, including cabbage, broccoli, and Brussels sprouts, do best as transplants rather than direct-sown. If sowing indoors, sow in flats and prick out into modules, transferring to 3½in (9cm) pots. If clubroot is a problem, then transplant so that the plants have a healthy start and are more likely to mature without infection. Tall, topheavy brassicas, such as Brussels sprouts or sprouting broccoli, should be planted 4in (10cm) deep. Hill up the stem as it grows by building a small mound of soil around it to a depth of about 4in (10cm); in windy sites, support the stem with a stake 3ft (1m) high. Plant brassicas firmly, with the lower leaves just above soil level. In some cases, spacing may be varied to determine the size of the brassica. If plants are widely spaced, they may be intercropped with salad crops or radishes.

Cultivation
If you direct-sow brassicas, be sure to cover the seedbed with row cover to prevent insect damage to seedlings. Seedlings need protection even if grown in a greenhouse or frame. Mulch after planting to suppress weeds. In dry weather, water as for leafy vegetables (see "Critical watering periods," p.502). Apply a nitrogenous fertilizer during growth.

Pests and diseases
Flea beetles (p.660), slugs and snails (p.669), damping off (p.658), cabbage root maggots (p.656), whiptail (p.673), and cutworms (p.658) all affect young plants. Caterpillars (p.657), whiteflies (p.673), mealy aphids (see "Aphids," p.654), clubroot (p.657), and birds (p.655) attack plants at all stages.

COLLARING SEEDLINGS

Where cabbage root maggots are a problem, place a collar around the stem of each seedling. Make sure that it is flat on the ground to prevent the adult fly from laying its eggs at the base of the stem.

Broccoli
Cauliflower
Winter cabbage
Curly kale
Brussels sprouts
Savoy cabbage

Kale (*Brassica oleracea* Acephala Group)

Grown as annuals or biennials, depending on the type, dwarf kale is 12–16in (30–40cm) tall, with a 12in (30cm) spread; tall types grow to 36in (90cm) and spread up to 24in (60cm). Collards are a close relative of kale. Most kale produces leaves from a central stem; the leaves may be plain or curly (see below) or curly-broad hybrids. Good cultivars include 'Champion' (collards), 'Redbor', 'Red Russian', 'Toscano', and 'Winter Red'. The leaves of all kale, and the spring-flowering shoots and young leaves of broad-leaved types, are used cooked or raw. Kale is the hardiest brassica, some surviving at 5°F (-15°C); many also tolerate high temperatures. All prefer fertile, well-drained soils that will not become waterlogged, and require medium nitrogen levels (see p.504).

Sowing, planting, and routine cultivation
Sow seed in early spring for summer crops, and in late spring for fall and winter crops. Sow *in situ* or in seedbeds or seed flats for transplanting; dwarf forms should be spaced 12–18in (30–45cm) apart, tall forms 30in (75cm) apart. Give overwintering types a nitrogenous topdressing in spring to encourage growth. In severe winters, grow dwarf cultivars under cloches or low polytunnels. Kale is usually unaffected by pests and diseases.

Growing under cover
For very early, tender kale, sow seed in early spring in rows 6in (15cm) apart, or in wide furrows. Either harvest them as large seedlings, or thin the seedlings to 3in (7cm) apart and cut when they form plants 6in (15cm) tall, leaving the stumps to resprout for a second harvest. Alternatively, pick individual leaves.

Harvesting and storing
Some cultivars mature seven weeks after sowing, but plants can stand a long time in the ground. Snap off the leaves as required in fall and winter to encourage new growth. Pick the shoots in spring when they are about 4in (10cm) long, before flowers open. Kale freezes well.

Curly kale

Ornamental kale
Ornamental kale is grown mainly for winter decoration in the garden or for garnishing salads. Leaves are variegated green, red, white, or purple.

Cauliflower (*Brassica oleracea* Botrytis Group)

Grown as annuals or biennials, cauliflower forms a head (or curd) of about 8in (20cm) in diameter; plants are 18–24in (45–60cm) tall, with a spread of up to 36in (90cm). They are classified by the main season of use, usually winter (with a distinction between those for frost-prone and frost-free areas), summer, and fall, although these groups overlap (see *Cauliflower Types*, below right). Most types of cauliflower have creamy or white curds, but there are attractive, distinctively flavored types with green or purple curds. The curds, and in some cases the young green leaves surrounding them, are cooked or used raw in salads. Smaller curds, or mini-cauliflower, about 2in (5cm) in diameter, may be specially grown from early summer cultivars.

Cauliflower is a cool-season crop and do not usually grow well in areas with high summer temperatures. Several cultivars are frost hardy, but cauliflower may only be harvested all year round in areas with frost-free winters. For details on soil and site see "Siting cabbage-family crops," p.507; overwintering cauliflower need protection from winter wind

CAULIFLOWER TO TRY

Winter
'Glacier'

Early summer
'Early Dawn'
'Early Snow Ball'
'Milkyway'
'Minuteman'
'Pathfinder'
'Quasar'
'Snow Crown'

Late summer/fall
'Amazing'
'Cumberland'
'Fremont'
'Serrano'
'White Rock'
'White Sails'

Colored cultivars
'Burgundy Queen' (purple)
'Cheddar' (orange)
'Graffiti' (purple)
'Panther' (green)

and can be protected in a low plastic tunnel. All cauliflower varieties need a moisture-retentive soil, with medium nitrogen levels (see p.504), and a pH of 6.5–7.5.

Sowing and planting
Success with cauliflower depends on sowing the correct cultivar at the appropriate time, and allowing plants to develop with as few checks to growth (from transplanting or dry soil, for example) as possible. Where drought is likely in summer, grow spring-heading types, which will benefit from fall rainfall, or fast-maturing mini-cauliflower.

The main sowing times and spacings are given in the chart below. Cauliflower is usually sown in seed flats, cell packs, or a seedbed for transplanting. Growing cauliflower from seed sown directly in the garden is difficult. Generally, the later the planting, the larger the cauliflower will grow and the wider the spacing required. Seed germinates best at a temperature of about 70°F (21°C).

In mild-winter areas, try sowing seed in fall, in cell packs or flats, then pot up seedlings. Put the pots into a well-ventilated cold frame or under a plastic low tunnel for the winter. Alternatively, sow *in situ* in cold frames, thinning to 2in (5cm) apart. Harden off seedlings before planting them out in spring. For a later crop, sow indoors in gentle heat in early spring, and prick out into small pots or modules. For summer/fall and

Mini-cauliflower

winter groups, sow the first batch indoors in seed flats or modules, or *in situ* in cold frames or under cloches. Starting plants in succession over time offers insurance that at least some of the plants will produce a good harvest.

To obtain mini-cauliflower heads, select an early summer cultivar to be sown in spring or early summer; although these can be direct-sown, for best results, raise plants in modules and plant them out 6in (15cm) apart. For a continuous supply, make successive sowings.

Routine cultivation
Cauliflower needs regular water throughout the growing period. In dry conditions, water heavily every two weeks. Overwintering types require low nitrogen levels when planted or they will be too soft to survive the colder conditions, so do not apply too much fertilizer. However, a fertilizer that supplies nitrogen, such as fish emulsion, must be applied in spring about six to eight weeks before the expected harvest, or poor-sized cauliflower will be produced.

To prevent white curds from discoloring in the sun, tie the leaves over them. This may also be done in winter to protect curds from the elements; most modern cultivars, however, have leaves that naturally tend to cover the curds.

PROTECTING CAULIFLOWER CURDS

1 In winter and early spring, protect mature curds of overwintering types from severe cold.

2 Wrap the leaves up around the central curd, securing them with soft string.

Pests and diseases
For cauliflower pests and diseases, see "Cultivation," p.507.

Harvesting and storing
The time from sowing to maturity varies from approximately 16 weeks for summer/fall cauliflower to about 40 weeks for winter ones. Cut the curds while they are still firm and tight, especially when maturing in cold weather. Mini-cauliflower matures about 15 weeks after sowing and should be picked immediately since they deteriorate quickly. If heads are tied closed, check them every few days to be sure the heads are not becoming overly mature. All cauliflower, and in particular the mini-cauliflower, freezes well.

Purple-headed cauliflower

CAULIFLOWER TYPES

Group	When to sow	When to plant	Spacing in rows	When to harvest
Winter (frost-free areas)	Late spring	Summer	28in (70cm)	Winter/very early spring
Winter	Late spring	Summer	28in (70cm)	Early spring
Early summer	Fall/early spring (sow under cover)	Spring	24in (60cm)	Early to midsummer
Summer/fall	Mid- to late spring	Early summer	24in (60cm)	Late summer to late fall

Cabbage (*Brassica oleracea* Capitata Group)

Most cabbage is grown as an annual. Plants are generally 8–10in (20–25cm) tall, with a spread of up to 28in (70cm). The average head is about 6in (15cm) in diameter.

They are grouped according to their season of maturity, although there is some overlap between the groups. Leaves are dark or light green, blue-green, white, or red, and smooth or crinkled (savoy). Cabbage heads are pointed or round, and vary in their density. Spring greens are either loose-leaved cultivars or standard spring cabbage harvested before the head forms. Cabbage leaves are eaten either cooked or raw and sliced in salads. They may also be pickled. If they are tender enough, stems and stalks may be sliced finely and cooked. Some types of winter cabbage may be stored.

Cabbages grow best at 59–68°F (15–20°C). Do not plant in temperatures over 77°F (25°C) or they are liable to go to seed. The hardiest cultivars may survive temperatures as low as 14°F (-10°C) for short periods. Cabbages are not usually grown under cover.

To grow well, cabbages need soil that is fertile, moisture-retentive, and humus-rich with a pH level above 6. Spring, summer, and fresh winter cabbage require very high nitrogen levels, and winter storage

Mature spring cabbages

cabbage needs medium nitrogen (see p.504). Do not give spring cabbage extra nitrogen at planting, because the nitrogen will probably be washed from the soil over the winter or produce soft growth that is liable to frosting; topdress in spring instead.

Sowing and planting

Sow the chosen cultivars at the correct time for their group (see below). Sow seeds in seedbeds or modules and transplant seedlings to beds in the garden about five weeks later. Appropriate spacing varies according to type

(see chart below), and it may be modified to vary the size of the head. Adopt closer spacing for smaller heads, and wide spacing to produce larger heads. A collar may be placed around each seedling stem when transplanting to protect against cabbage root maggots (see *Collaring Seedlings*, p.507). Ensure that young seedlings have sufficient moisture to become well established.

In most regions, cabbage is spring-planted for harvest from summer on. In mild-winter areas, cabbage can be planted in fall and overwintered for spring harvest.

CABBAGE TO TRY

Spring
'Earliana'
'Early Jersey Wakefield'
'Early Marvel'
'Emerald Acre'
'Golden Cross'
'Greensleeves' (greens only)
'Primax'
'Savoy Express'
'Stonehead'

Early summer
'Cheers'
'Dynamo' F1
'Golden Acre'
'Gonzales' F1
'Primero' F1 (red)
'Spivoy' F1
'Tastie' F1

Summer
'Blue Vantage'
'Cheers'
'Gourmet'
'Red Dynasty'
'Savoy Ace'
'Savoy Queen'
'Super Red'
'Taler' (savoy)

Fall
'Emblem'
'Grand Prize'
'Megaton' F1
'Primavoy' (savoy)
'Vantage Point'

Winter (for storage)
'Danish Ballhead'
'Hilton'
'Multikeeper'
'Ruby Perfection' (red)
'Sanibel'

Winter (to use fresh)
'Aquarius'
'Celtic' F1
'Ice Queen' F1 (savoy)
'January King 327'
'Julius' F1 (savoy)

Fall cabbage

Red summer cabbage

Savoy cabbage

CABBAGE TYPES

Group (time of maturity)	Description	Main sowing period	Average spacing
Spring	Small, pointed or round	End of summer	12in (30cm)
	Loose-leaf greens	End of summer	10in (25cm)
Early summer	Large, mainly round heads	Very early spring (sow under glass)	15in (38cm)
Summer	Large, round heads	Early spring	18in (45cm)
Fall	Large, round heads	Late spring	18in (45cm)
Winter (for storage)	Smooth, white-leaved, winter white types	Spring	18in (45cm)
Winter (to use fresh)	Blue, green, and savoy leaf types	Late spring	18in (45cm)

HARVESTING SPRING GREENS

Plant spring cabbages 6in (15cm) apart. When they have grown, but before they start to form a compact head, harvest every other plant, cutting them at the base. Use these as spring greens.

HOW TO OBTAIN A SECOND CROP

1 To produce a second crop of greens, make a cross-shaped cut in the stalk after harvesting the cabbage head.

2 A few weeks later, several miniature heads should have sprouted, ready for a second harvest.

Cut spring cabbage young as loose greens; every second or third plant can be left to head up if a heading cultivar is used.

Routine cultivation

To increase their stability, hill up winter cabbage as they grow. Protect spring cabbage under row cover or a low tunnel, and apply a liquid fertilizer such as fish emulsion in spring; feed others in the growing season. Keep cabbage moist throughout their growth (see "Critical watering periods," p.502).

Pests and diseases

For pests and diseases that may affect cabbages, see "Cultivation," p.507. Southern blight (p.670) may also occur.

Harvesting and storing

Spring and summer cultivars vary in their ability to last in good condition once the head has matured; modern cultivars often last longer than traditional ones. Normally the plant is dug up once the head has been cut, but spring and early summer cultivars may produce a second crop if the head is cut to leave a 4in (10cm) stalk in the ground. Using a sharp knife, make a shallow cross on the top of the stem to encourage new growth. Provided that the soil is fertile and moist, three or four more heads may develop together on the stalk.

Storage cabbage (winter white cultivars and appropriate red cabbage) should be lifted before heavy frost. Dig them up and

PREPARING CABBAGE FOR STORING

Before storing cabbage, carefully remove any loose or discolored, outer leaves without damaging the head (see inset). Inspect the cabbage regularly while it is in storage, and remove leaves that are rotting.

carefully remove any loose, outer leaves. Refrigerate them or place them on slatted supports or straw on the floor of a shed, or suspend them in nets. Store the heads at just above freezing, with relatively high

humidity. They may also be stored in a cold frame, provided that it is ventilated on warm days to discourage rotting (see also *Storing Red Cabbage*, p.506). Cabbage may keep for four or five months.

Brussels sprouts (*Brassica oleracea* Gemmifera Group)

These are biennials grown as annuals, and vary in height from about 14in (35cm) for the dwarf forms to 30in (75cm) for the tall forms, with a spread of up to 20in (50cm) in both cases. Brussels sprouts are loosely divided by their time of maturity into early, mid-season, and late groups. The earlier types tend to be dwarfed and less hardy. The modern F1

Dwarf Brussels sprout plant

cultivars are an improvement over older, open-pollinated ones; they perform better on fertile soils, are less prone to lean (because they have a stronger root system), and have more compact, uniform sprouts. The tight sprouts that develop on the stem are delicious when oven-roasted, but may also be shredded raw into salads. The mature leaves of the plants may also be eaten. 'Rubine' has purplish-red sprouts.

Brussels sprouts are typical cool-season brassicas; the hardiest cultivars survive temperatures of 14°F (-10°C). Plant them in succession from early to late spring for a long harvest from early fall well into winter. A general fertilizer may be applied shortly before planting; high nitrogen levels are needed (see p.504). Avoid using freshly manured ground because this encourages loose, rather than firm, sprouts. For soil and site requirements, see "Siting cabbage-family crops," p.507.

HILLING UP BRUSSELS SPROUTS

About a month after planting out, hill up Brussels sprouts by drawing the soil around the base of the stem to increase stability; this is usually difficult to do using collars (see below). At this stage they may also be staked if they are in an exposed area.

Sowing and planting

Sow in succession from early to mid-spring starting with the early-maturing cultivars. For a very early crop, sow in heat under cover in early spring. Sow 2in (5cm) apart either in

seed trays or in a seedbed to produce good sturdy plants for transplanting. Plant firmly in good soil. Use collars to protect against cabbage root maggots or cover with row cover for the first month.

Thin out or transplant to the required spacing in early summer, generally four to five weeks after sowing. Plant tall cultivars about 24in (60cm) apart. Use closer spacing to produce smaller sprouts of a more uniform size, and wider spacing for large sprouts that mature in succession and so may be picked over a longer period. Wide spacing also encourages good air circulation, which keeps plants healthy and disease-free. Plant tall cultivars deeply and hill up the stems as they grow to provide extra stability. Keep young plants moist until they are well established.

REMOVING LEAVES

Snap off any yellowing or diseased leaves that develop. These may carry fungal diseases that could spread to the whole crop. This also improves air circulation.

Brussels sprouts, with their slow rate of growth, can be intercropped in the first few months with fast-maturing vegetables.

Routine cultivation
Keep beds weed-free. Plants are widely spaced, so extra watering is required only in very dry conditions, when they should be watered at the rate for leafy crops (see "Critical watering periods," p.502). A topdressing of a balanced fertilizer or a drench with liquid fertilizer may be applied in late summer if the plants are not growing vigorously.

If sprouts are required for freezing, grow an early cultivar that matures in fall, and nip off the sprout top or growing point in late summer, when the lower sprouts are roughly ½in (1cm) in diameter. All the sprouts will then mature for picking together, rather than in succession.

Pests and diseases
Mealy aphids (p.654) can colonize individual sprouts; use an appropriate control if needed. Choose cultivars resistant to fungal leaf spots. Downy mildew is also a problem (p.659). For other diseases likely to affect Brussels sprouts, see "Cultivation," p.507.

Harvesting and storing
Brussels sprouts are ready to harvest about 20 weeks after sowing. Their flavor is improved after exposure to frost. Pick the lowest sprouts first by snapping them off at the base; the upper sprouts will continue to develop. If sprouts are intended for freezing, pick them before the outer leaves are damaged by winter weather; freeze only topquality sprouts. Sprout tops can be harvested by cutting them off at the end of the season.

After harvesting, dig up the plants and break up the stems with a hammer. This deters the buildup and spread of brassica diseases, and enables the stems to rot down more quickly when composted.

Where winters are very severe, uproot whole plants before the ground freezes and hang them in a cool, frost-free place; the sprouts will remain fresh for several weeks.

F1 AND OPEN-POLLINATED SPROUTS

Modern F1 hybrids produce sprouts that are compact, evenly spaced, and of uniform size. Traditional, open-pollinated cultivars are more likely to produce loose sprouts widely varying in size.

F1 hybrid

Traditional cultivar

BRUSSELS SPROUTS TO TRY

Early
'Churchill'
'Franklin'
'Jade Cross E'

Mid-season
'Bubbles'
'Nautic' F1
'Vancouver'

Late
'Diablo' F1
'Rubine'
'Trafalgar' F1

Sprouting broccoli (*Brassica oleracea* Italica Group)

These large, biennial plants may reach a height of 2–3ft (60–90cm) and a spread of 2ft (60cm). There are purple and white types; the purple is more prolific and hardier. The flowering shoots that develop in spring are eaten cooked. Sprouting broccoli is considered one of the hardiest winter vegetables, surviving temperatures of about 10°F (-12°C). Because it is a slow-maturing vegetable that occupies the ground for up to a year, this type of broccoli requires a fertile soil and medium nitrogen levels (see p.504). Avoid shallow and sandy soils and sites exposed to strong winter winds.

Sowing, planting, and routine cultivation
Sow from spring to midsummer, either in a seedbed or in modules. Transplant from early to midsummer, spacing plants at least 2ft (60cm) apart and planting them deeply for stability.

Plants may need staking in the fall. Protect plants with row cover to avoid insect or bird damage in the winter. For further cultivation requirements, see "Cultivation," p.507.

Pests and diseases
Sprouting broccoli is prone to the common brassica pests (see "Cultivation," p.507); in mild winter areas it may be host to infestations of whiteflies. Birds can also be attracted in the winter.

SPROUTING BROCCOLI TO TRY

'Italian Sprouting'
'Purple Sprouting'
'Santee'

Harvesting and storing
Depending on the cultivar and region, pick shoots from fall into winter, when they are about 6in (15cm) long, while the flowers are in bud. Pick regularly to encourage more shoots; plants may produce for up to two months. Sprouting broccoli freezes well.

Purple sprouting broccoli

Broccoli (*Brassica oleracea* Italica Group)

Regular broccoli (nonsprouting) is grown as an annual or biennial, and produces compact plants about 18in (45cm) tall, with a spread rarely more than 15in (38cm). Cultivars are classified as early, mid-season, and late, with the earliest maturing the fastest. F1 hybrids are generally more productive than the heirloom varieties. The compact, terminal head and the young sideshoots are best when eaten lightly cooked.

Broccoli is a cool-season crop and may not do well in the summer heat. Young plants tolerate some frost, but frost may damage embryonic and young heads once they start to develop. Broccoli needs a sunny site in moisture-retentive, fairly fertile soil with medium nitrogen levels (see p.504).

Sowing and planting

For the best success with broccoli, start seeds indoors or buy transplants. Harden off transplants carefully before setting out in the garden, and protect young plants from exposure to excessive cold, which can lead to premature head formation. Sow seeds again in early summer to produce plants for a fall harvest. Broccoli seedlings do not transplant well, so sow two or three seeds per station *in situ*. First sowings made indoors are especially prone to bolting

HARVESTING BROCCOLI

1 Just before the flower buds open, harvest the first central head by cutting through the stalk.

2 This encourages sideshoots to develop; these can also be harvested and more sideshoots will be produced.

when transplanted. Broccoli plants grow well at various spacings. For the highest overall yield, space plants 9in (22cm) apart each way, or 12in (30cm) apart in rows spaced at 18in (45cm). Closer spacing produces smaller terminal shoots, which mature together and are suitable for freezing.

Routine cultivation

Keep the bed weed-free. Broccoli plants need plenty of water to

yield well— 2 gallons/sq yd (11 liters/sq m) every two weeks. In very dry conditions, water as for leafy crops (see "Critical watering periods," p.502). A granular or liquid nitrogen-rich fertilizer may be applied once the terminal heads have been cut in order to encourage additional sideshoots to develop.

Pests and diseases

For pests and diseases that may affect broccoli, see "Cultivation,"

BROCCOLI TO TRY

Early
'Blue Wind' F1
'Packman' F1
'Windsor' F1

Mid-season
'Belstar' F1
'Gypsy' F1
'Premium Crop' F1

Late
'Arcadia' F1
'Marathon' F1
'Veronica' F1

p.507. Problems may also be caused by nutrient deficiencies and downy mildew (p.659).

Harvesting and storing

Broccoli is a fast-maturing brassica, ready 11–14 weeks after sowing. The main head should be cut when it is 3–4in (7–10cm) in diameter, while still firm and before the flower buds open. Sideshoots will subsequently develop; cut these when they are about 4in (10cm) long. Broccoli freezes well.

Turnip greens and broccoli raab (*Brassica rapa*)

Over the centuries different brassicas have been grown for cutting in the immature stages for use as quick-maturing greens. The two types commonly used for this purpose today are turnip greens (*Brassica rapa* Rapifera Group) and broccoli raab (*Brassica rapa* Utilis Group), which is also

known by a number of Italian names such as *cime di rapa*, *rapini*, and *broccoletti*.

They are grown as annuals or biennials, generally with single stems that reach a maximum height of about 12in (30cm). The leaves, young stems, and sweetly flavored young flower heads

are eaten cooked as spring greens, or raw in salads.

Turnip greens and broccoli raab are cool-season brassicas. Grow them in spring and fall in hot climates, or all season where summers are cool. All turnip cultivars are suitable; broccoli raab has few named cultivars. Both grow best in fertile, moisture-retentive soil and require low to medium nitrogen levels (see p.504).

Sowing, planting, and routine cultivation

Sow thinly broadcast or in rows about 4in (10cm) apart. For larger plants only, thin to 6in (15cm). For an early crop in cold areas, make the first sowing indoors in early spring. Plants need little attention subsequently.

Harvesting and storing

Harvest plants within seven to eight weeks of sowing. Make the first cut when they are leafy and 4in (10cm) tall, or wait until the immature

Turnip greens

flowering shoots appear and the plant is 8–10in (20–25cm) tall. Cut about 1in (2.5cm) above ground level. In cool weather, the plants resprout to give two or three further cuttings over a period of four or five weeks. Cut as long as the stems are tender. Use turnip greens and broccoli raab fresh because they do not store well.

Broccoli raab

Asian greens

Several types of Asian greens have become very popular for home vegetable gardens. They have many features in common with other cabbage-family crops but tend to be faster growing and have a wider range of uses than Western brassicas. If they are given the right conditions, they are highly productive. They are grown as annuals or biennials.

Asian greens are cultivated mainly for the leaves and leafy stems, but also for their young, sweetly flavored flowering shoots. Leaf shape and color vary from the glossy, white-ribbed leaves of some bok choy cultivars, and the feathery green leaves of mizuna greens, to the purplish green of Oriental mustards. Asian greens are crisp, nutritious, and succulent, and mild to peppery in flavor. Cook by stir-frying or steaming, or use young leaves and shoots raw in salads.

Asian greens are best suited to climates with cool summers and mild winters, although many cultivars are available that are adapted for hotter climates. The majority will withstand light frost, especially if harvested when they are semimature as a cut-and-come-again crop (see p.506). A few of them, such as komatsuna and some of the mustards, are extremely hardy.

In temperate climates, Asian greens grow best in late summer and fall. Where winter temperatures fall only a few degrees below freezing, they may be grown as a winter crop under cover in unheated hoop houses or cold frames; if planted late in the summer, they may produce from fall to spring, although they will stop growing at low temperatures.

Asian greens require similar conditions to other types of brassicas but, because they are fast growing, hungry, and thirsty plants, the soil must be rich in organic matter, moisture-retentive, and fertile. They never develop well in poor, dry soil. Most have very high nitrogen requirements (see p.504).

Sowing and planting Asian greens

All standard methods of sowing may be used; where there is a risk of plants going to seed prematurely (bolting), sow seed in cell packs or *in situ*. Many have a tendency to bolt when days are lengthening, particularly when this is combined with low spring temperatures. In these cases, in northern latitudes, delay sowing until midsummer, unless plants are started off in heat or cultivars with bolting resistance are used. If bolting continues to be a problem, grow Asian greens as seedling crops, and harvest the leaves before the plants start to bolt.

Their rapid rate of growth makes Asian greens ideal for intercropping among slower-maturing vegetables, especially for cutting as a cut-and-come-again seedling crop, when their flavor is superb.

Loose-leaved Chinese cabbage

Tight-headed Chinese cabbage

Bok choy

Bok choy

Cultivating Asian greens

Asian greens are generally shallow rooting so they need regular watering. In very dry conditions, water at the rate for leafy crops (see "Critical watering periods," p.502). They should also be kept mulched.

Asian greens are susceptible to the same pests and diseases as other cabbage-family crops (see "Cultivation" p.507). Those with tender leaves are very prone to slugs (p.669), caterpillars (p.657), and flea beetles (p.660). They may be grown under row covers to provide some protection.

Harvesting and storing

Most Asian greens mature within two to three months after being sown. They may be harvested at four different stages, from seedling to mature plant. At the seedling stage they may be harvested using cut-and-come-again techniques (see "Cut-and-come-again harvesting," p.506), or left a few weeks longer and cut as semimature plants. When the plants are fully mature they may be either harvested all at once or alternatively cut about 1in (2.5cm) above ground level so that they sprout again for a second crop. The flowering shoots that develop naturally from mature plants may also be harvested before the flowers open.

Asian greens are mainly used fresh, although most will keep for a few days if refrigerated. In the Far East, leaves of Asian greens are either pickled or dried, and Chinese cabbages are stored for off-season supplies.

Oriental mustards (*Brassica juncea*)

The mustards are a varied group of annuals and biennials, forming large, often coarse-leaved plants. Leaf texture may be smooth, blistered, or deeply curled. Some cultivars are purple-leaved. The mustards are naturally very robust and less prone to pests and diseases than most Asian greens. Several, including the purplish green 'Miike Giant' and 'Xue Li Hong', survive at least 14°F (-10°C). The distinctive flavor may be piquant in certain cultivars, becoming stronger as they go to seed. The leaves are used cooked but may also be eaten raw in salads when young or if sliced.

Sow in late spring in cold regions for summer harvest; from mid- to late summer in temperate climates, and until early fall in warm climates, for harvesting from fall to spring. The seed is small and is sown in shallow soil *in situ* or in cell packs. Thin or plant out seedlings 6in (15cm) apart for harvesting young, and 14in (35cm) apart for larger plants. If they are planted under cover in fall, plants are more tender, but will go to seed earlier the following spring.

Oriental mustards mature in 6–13 weeks, depending on the cultivar. Cut single leaves as required.

Purple-leaved Oriental mustard

Chinese broccoli (*Brassica rapa* var. *alboglabra*)

This annual crop, also know as Chinese kale, forms stout plants with thick, blue-green leaves, growing up to 18in (45cm) tall. The succulent, fine-flavored, chunky flower stems, which may be ¾in (2cm) thick, are generally cooked.

Chinese broccoli tolerates higher summer temperatures than many other brassicas, and withstands light frost. In warm and temperate climates, sow from late spring to late summer. For a very early crop, make the first sowings under cover in spring to transplant outside. For a protected early winter crop, plant under cover in fall. In cool climates, delay sowing until midsummer because sowings earlier than this may bolt.

Sow seed *in situ* or in cell packs. For small plants, to be harvested whole as soon as the flowering

Chinese broccoli

shoots appear, grow them 5in (12cm) apart with 4in (10cm) between rows. For large plants, to be cropped over a longer period, space them 12in (30cm) apart each way. Cut the main shoot first, as for broccoli (see p.512); further sideshoots will continue to develop for harvesting later. Large plants take nine to ten weeks to mature.

Bok choy (*Brassica rapa* var. *alboglabra*)

Bok choy is a biennial usually grown as an annual, forming a loose head of fairly stiff leaves with wide midribs that broaden out markedly and overlap at the base. There are many types, the most common being white-ribbed or green-ribbed, available as F1 cultivars 'Joi Choi' (white) and 'Mei Qing Choi' (green). They vary in size from squat forms about 4in (10cm) tall to large plants about 18in (45cm) tall. Bok choy is succulent and mild in flavor, and may be eaten either cooked or raw.

Bok choy grows best at cool temperatures of 59–68°F (15–20°C). Most cultivars will tolerate some frost in the open but survive lower temperatures under cover grown as winter cut-and-come-again crops. A few are suited to hotter climates.

In temperate climates, sow seed throughout the growing season. There is some risk of premature bolting with spring sowings, so confine these to cut-and-come-again seedling crops. Sow seed *in situ* or in cell packs. Spacing depends on the cultivar and size of plant required, ranging from 4in (10cm) apart for small cultivars to about 18in (45cm) apart for the largest ones. In late summer, transplant bok choy under cover for an fall crop.

Bok choy may be harvested at any stage from seedlings to the young flower shoots of mature

Bok choy

HARVESTING SEEDLINGS

Bok choy may be harvested at the seedling stage. If they are cut about 1in (2.5cm) from the ground, new leaves will sprout.

plants. Seedling leaves will be ready for harvesting in three weeks. They may be cut 1in (2.5cm) above ground level and will resprout. Mature plants may be cut higher and will also resprout for a second harvest.

Mizuna greens (*Brassica rapa* var. *nipposinica*)

Annuals or biennials, depending on climatic conditions, mizuna greens have dark green, glossy, deeply serrated, almost feathery leaves and slender, white, juicy stems forming a rosette up to 18in (45cm) in diameter and about 9in (23cm) tall. They are highly decorative, especially when grown as an edging or in blocks. Mizuna greens are eaten cooked, or raw when leaves are harvested young and tender.

They are very adaptable, capable of tolerating both high summer temperatures (provided that they are in moisture-retentive soil) and winter temperatures down to 14°F (-10°C).

They may be sown throughout the growing season. Bolting resistance is good and seed may therefore be sown in seed flats or cell packs, in a seedbed for transplanting, or *in situ*. For an extra, tender, winter crop, sow in late summer to transplant under cover. Space plants 4in (10cm) apart for small plants harvested young, up to 18in (45cm) apart to obtain large plants. Mizuna greens are useful for intercropping if cut at the seedling stage.

Mizuna greens mature eight to ten weeks after sowing and may be harvested at all stages; seedling leaves may be ready within two or three weeks (see "Harvesting and storing Asian greens," p.513). The plants are vigorous, and are capable of resprouting several times after they have been cut initially.

Mizuna greens

Chinese cabbages (*Brassica rapa* var. *pekinensis*)

These are annuals or biennials usually grown as annuals. Chinese cabbages have dense, upright heads. The leaves are marked by prominent white veins, the broadened midribs overlap at the base rather like bok choy. The barrel type forms a stout head about 10in (25cm) high, the cylindrical type a longer, less compact head up to 18in (45cm) high. Leaf color ranges from dark green to almost creamy-white, especially in the center. There are also some very attractive, loose-headed types. Mild-flavored with a crisp texture, Chinese cabbages are excellent in salads and lightly cooked.

For preferred climatic conditions, see "Bok choy" (left). Most headed types are likely to bolt if they are sown in spring, unless a temperature of 68–77°F (20–25°C) is maintained during the first three weeks of growth. It is best to delay sowing until early summer. Some loose-headed types may be sown in spring. If they start to bolt, treat them as cut-and-come-again crops, although the leaves of some cultivars may be rough-textured and hairy when young. Sow seed in cell packs or *in situ*; thin or transplant seedlings to 12in (30cm) apart. Plenty of moisture throughout growth is vital. Chinese cabbages have soft leaves that are susceptible to pests (see "Cultivating Asian greens," p.513).

Chinese cabbages mature eight to ten weeks after sowing, and can be harvested at any stage

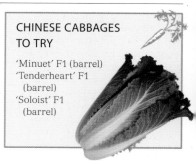

CHINESE CABBAGES TO TRY

'Minuet' F1 (barrel)
'Tenderheart' F1 (barrel)
'Soloist' F1 (barrel)

HARVESTING CHINESE CABBAGES

1 Harvest Chinese cabbage (here a loose-leaved cultivar) by cutting about 1in (2.5cm) above soil level.

2 After a few weeks, new leaves will have formed and may be cut. Stumps may resprout several times.

because they respond well to cut-and-come-again treatment both after the main heads have been cut, and during growth, as semimature plants.

Komatsuna (*Brassica rapa* var. *perviridis*)

The komatsuna group, also known as mustard spinach, is extremely diverse; its members form large, productive, robust, healthy plants, often with glossy leaves that may be up to 12in (30cm) long and 7in (18cm) wide. The flavor of the leaves resembles cabbage, with a touch of spinach, and they are eaten cooked, or raw, finely sliced in salads.

Komatsuna plants tolerate a wide range of temperatures and will survive 10°F (-12°C). Some cultivars are suitable for tropical climates.

Plants are less likely to bolt from early spring sowings than most Asian greens and are more drought-tolerant. For sowing and spacing, see "Mizuna greens" (left). Komatsuna makes a useful and successful winter crop under cover.

Komatsuna

Leaves may be harvested at all stages (see "Harvesting and storing Asian greens," p.513). Mature plants are usually ready to be harvested eight weeks after sowing.

Leafy and salad vegetables

This group of vegetables is grown for the great variety of leaves that it produces, which may be eaten raw in salads, or cooked. The freshly picked leaves are delicious and highly nutritious. The range of leaf color also gives them decorative value. Careful choice of cultivar and the right growing conditions ensure an year-round supply. If seeds are sown in succession, gluts of crops maturing together may be avoided. Due to the high moisture content of the leaves, many store for only two or three days; a few are suitable for freezing, however.

Butterhead lettuce

Loose-leaf lettuce

Spinach

Cos lettuce

Witloof chicory

Amaranths (*Amaranthus* spp.)

These rapidly growing annuals reach a height of about 24in (60cm) and a spread of 12–15in (30–38cm). *Amaranthus cruentus*, the most commonly grown as an edible crop, has oval, light green leaves. Named varieties are not always easy to find. *A. tricolor*, called Chinese spinach or Joseph's coat, has red, yellow, or green leaves and greenish white flowers; cultivars include 'Red Calaloo' and 'Wario'. *A. caudatus* has pale green leaves and is often grown as an ornamental plant for its vivid red, tassel-like flowers. Amaranth species are also known as African or Indian spinach. The leaves of the plants and immature flower buds are cooked and eaten in the same way as spinach.

Amaranths are tropical and subtropical plants that require temperatures of 72–86°F (22–30°C) with a humidity of above 70 percent to crop well. In cooler areas, they may be grown in greenhouses. Moderately deep, well-drained, fertile soil with a pH of 5.5–7 and medium to high nitrogen levels are required (see p.504).

Amaranthus cruentus

Sowing and planting
Sow amaranths outdoors in spring, once the temperature is high enough, in rows 8–12in (20–30cm) apart. Thin seedlings to 4–6in (10–15cm) apart when they are about 2–3in (5–7cm) high. Protect them either with plastic covers or under cloches until the young plants have become established.

In cool areas, or to obtain an earlier crop, seed may be sown in flats in a greenhouse; prick out seedlings into 3 or 3½in (7 or 9cm) pots when they are large enough to handle. Transplant the seedlings outdoors when they are 3–3½in (7–9cm) tall, spacing them about 4–6in (10–15cm) apart.

Routine cultivation
Keep amaranth beds weed-free, and water regularly. Apply a balanced fertilizer or organic liquid feed every two to three weeks. Give additional dressings of nitrogen and potassium every three weeks on less fertile soils. Apply an organic mulch around the base of the plants to retain moisture and warmth. When the plants are 8in (20cm) tall, pinch out the growing point to encourage lateral shoots and to produce a heavier crop.

Pests and diseases
Downy mildew (p.659), powdery mildew (p.667), caterpillars (p.657), and aphids (p.654) may affect amaranths outside, and thrips (p.671) and damping off (p.658) under cover.

Growing under cover
When seedlings are 3–3½in (7–9cm) tall, transplant them to 8in (21cm) pots, grow bags, or beds, spacing them 15–20in (38–50cm) apart each way. Keep them at a minimum temperature of 72°F (22°C). Water, and maintain 70 percent humidity by damping down in hot weather. Avoid allowing plants to go to seed or they may become weedy.

Harvesting and storing
Amaranths are ready to harvest eight to ten weeks after sowing. Using a sharp knife, cut young shoots up to 4in (10cm) long when the plants are about 10in (25cm) tall; they will produce further shoots over several months. Continue picking them as required. Amaranths are best eaten fresh; alternatively, they may be stored for up to one week at 32°F (0°C) and 95 percent humidity.

Amaranthus tricolor

Malabar spinach (*Basella alba*)

Also known as Indian or Ceylon spinach, these short-lived, twining perennials may grow to 12ft (4m) tall if supported. Var. *alba* has dark green leaves; var. *rubra* has red leaves and stems. The oval or round leaves are eaten cooked; the purple berries are not normally eaten.

Malabar spinach is a tropical and subtropical plant that requires a temperature of 77–86°F (25–30°C). Lower temperatures reduce the growth rate, resulting in smaller leaves. Larger leaves are, however, produced in light shade. Well-drained and highly fertile soil with a pH of 6–7.5 and high nitrogen levels (see p.504) are required for good growth.

Sowing and planting
Sow in seed flats or in 3 or 3½in (7 or 9cm) pots, maintaining the required temperature range. When seedlings are 4–6in (10–15cm) tall, transplant them to well-prepared beds, spacing the plants 16–20in (40–50cm) apart each way.

Routine cultivation
Support plants by staking or by fastening stems to a vertical or horizontal trellis. Keep plants weed-free and water as necessary. Mulch with organic material. Apply a balanced fertilizer or liquid feed every two to three weeks during the growing period. When the seedlings reach a height

SUPPORTING MALABAR SPINACH

Malabar spinach may be supported on a trellis parallel to the ground, raised about 12in (30cm) above soil level. The stems should be evenly spaced on the trellis so that they do not become overcrowded.

of approximately 18in (45cm), pinch the growing tip to encourage branching. Remove flowering shoots to encourage leaf production.

Propagate plants by taking cuttings 4–6in (10–15cm) long; insert these in small pots until rooted and then transplant as described for seedlings.

Pests and diseases

Malabar spinach is generally free of pests and diseases. Root-knot nematodes (p.668) may, however, affect plants, and aphids (p.654), whiteflies (p.673), leafhoppers (p.663), and spider mite (p.670) may also be troublesome.

Growing under cover

Transplant seedlings to grow bags or to 8–10in (20–25cm) pots. Remove the growing tips when the seedlings are about 12in (30cm) tall to encourage branching, and damp down regularly to maintain high humidity. Tie in developing shoots.

Harvesting and storing

Harvest 10–12 weeks after transplanting by cutting young terminal shoots that are 6–8in (15–20cm) long; this encourages further shoots to develop over several months. Eat leaves within two days of picking, or refrigerate for a few days.

Swiss chard and spinach beet (Beta vulgaris subsp. cicla var. flavescens)

These spinachlike biennials belong to the beet family. Swiss chard, also known as seakale beet, forms large, glossy-leaved plants. Individual leaves may be up to 18in (45cm) long and 6in (15cm) wide. The midribs widen into broad leaf stalks up to 2in (5cm) in diameter that may be white, red, creamy-yellow, or pink. Leaf color varies with the cultivar, from deep green ('Fordhook Giant') to greenish yellow ('Lucullus') and reddish green ('Rhubarb Chard'). 'Bright Lights' has multicolored stems and bright green leaves. The leaves and midribs are normally

White-stemmed Swiss chard

cooked; the latter require longer cooking. Spinach beet, or perpetual spinach, forms smaller-leaved plants, with narrow, green-leaved stalks. It is eaten either lightly cooked or raw.

Although chard and spinach beet are essentially cool-season crops, growing best at 61–64°F (16–18C°), they tolerate higher summer temperatures than spinach (see p.519) without bolting, and survive winter temperatures of 7°F (-14°C). They may be grown in a wide range of soils other than acidic ones, provided that the soil is moisture-retentive and fertile, containing plenty of organic matter. Plants may remain in the ground for up to 12 months, so they need high nitrogen levels (see p.504).

Sowing and planting

For a continuous supply, sow seed in spring (plants may crop until late spring the following year), and again in mid- to late summer (for plants cropping until the following summer). Sow *in situ* in rows 15in (38cm) apart for spinach beet or, for Swiss chard, 18in (45cm) apart; thin seedlings early to 12in (30cm)

Red-stemmed Swiss chard

apart. Plants may be grown closer together in more widely spaced rows, but avoid overcrowding.

Alternatively, seed may be sown in seed flats or cell packs for transplanting. Germination is usually rapid. Spinach beet may be sown closely for use as a cut-and-come-again seedling crop (see "Successional crops," p.500).

Routine cultivation

Chard and spinach beet are naturally healthy and vigorous and usually require little attention. Apply an organic mulch to keep down weeds and preserve

moisture; apply a nitrogenous fertilizer or organic liquid feed during the growing season if plants are not developing well.

Pests and diseases

Earwigs (p.659) may attack seedlings. Bacterial leaf spots (p.655) or fungal leaf spots (p.660) and downy mildew (p.659) may also be problems.

Growing under cover

In mild climates, chard and spinach beet are excellent winter crops under cover. Sow seed in cell packs during late summer and transplant under cover in early fall or broadcast spinach beet for cut-and-come-again seedling crops. They often last through winter and early spring.

Harvesting and storing

Leaves are ready to be harvested 8–12 weeks after sowing. Cut the outer leaves first and continue picking as required; alternatively, harvest the whole plant by cutting the leaves about 1in (2.5cm) above ground level. Further leaves are then produced from the base over many months. Both Swiss chard and spinach beet may be frozen.

Endive (Cichorium endivia)

ENDIVE TO TRY

Curled (early and summer)
'Bianca Riccia'
'Rhodos'
'Green Curled'
'Tosca'

Escarole (all sowings)
'Full Heart Batavian'

Endive is an annual or biennial plant that forms a flat or semiupright rosette of leaves 8–15in (20–38cm) in diameter. The two most distinct types of endive are the serrated- or curled-leaved endive, and the broad-leaved escarole, but there are also intermediate types. Outer leaves are dark to light green and the more tender, inner leaves creamy-yellow. Endive is slightly bitter and is blanched to make it sweeter. Used mainly in salads, it is shredded to reduce bitterness, or may be cooked.

Endive is a cool-season crop that grows best at 50–68°F (10–20°C), but withstands light frost in the open; the hardier cultivars survive 16°F (-9°C). Bitterness generally increases at high temperatures. Some curled types are quite heat-tolerant, while escarole types tend to withstand

greater cold. There is a risk of premature bolting from spring sowings if temperatures fall below 41°F (5°C) for an extended period. Endive performs much better than lettuce in the low light levels of northern winters and therefore makes a useful winter greenhouse crop.

For soil and site requirements, see "Lettuces," p.518. Summer crops may be grown in light shade; always grow fall crops on well-drained soil to avoid the risk of rotting. Endive has a low nitrogen requirement (see p.504).

Sowing and planting

Choose appropriate cultivars for each season. Sow in late spring for a summer crop or in summer for an fall crop, either *in situ* or in cell packs or seed flats. Thin or plant out the seedlings 10–15in (25–38cm) apart, using the wider

spacing for spreading cultivars. Curled types may be sown as cut-and-come-again crops (see "Successional crops," p.500), most usefully in late spring and late summer.

Routine cultivation

To blanch leaves, choose nearly mature plants with dry leaves and blanch a few at a time because they deteriorate rapidly after blanching.

For complete blanching *in situ*, cover each plant with a bucket. For partial blanching, lay a large plate or piece of cardboard over the center. With escarole types bunch up the leaves and tie them together. Protect the plants against slugs until they are ready for harvesting, which is after about ten days. In fall, plants for blanching should be lifted before severe weather disfigures them;

BLANCHING ENDIVE

1 Ensure that the endive is dry, then lay a plate over the center to blanch the leaves partially.

2 The center should have turned white and be ready for harvesting after about ten days.

transplant them into a darkened frame or dark area under greenhouse benches, then blanch as for Belgian endive (see below).

Pests and diseases
Slugs (p.669) and aphids (p.654) are the most common problems. For other pests and diseases that affect endive, see "Lettuces," p.518.

Growing under cover
Protecting plants under cover provides a year-round supply. For use in winter and early spring, transplant seedlings in early fall from seed flats or cell packs under cover. Sow as a cut-and-come-again seedling crop under cover in spring for harvesting early, and in early fall for a late crop.

Harvesting and storing
Harvest endive between 7 and 13 weeks after sowing, depending on the cultivar and season. Pick individual leaves as needed, or cut across the crown, leaving the plant to resprout. Mature plants respond well to cut-and-come-again treatment (see "Cut-and-come-again harvesting," p.506). Endive leaves do not store well, so they should be eaten fresh.

Chicory (*Cichorium intybus*)

There are many types of chicory, all with a distinctive, slightly bitter taste. Nearly all are very hardy and are useful crops for growing in cooler months. Their diverse colors make them attractive in salads, and some types may also be cooked. All types have low nitrogen requirements (see p.504).

Belgian endive

Similar in appearance to dandelions, these biennials have pointed leaves about 8in (20cm) long, with a spread of about 6in (15cm). Their "chicons" (the whitened, compact, leafy shoots obtained from lifting the roots and forcing and blanching them to make them sweeter) are eaten raw or cooked. The green leaves may also be used, but taste more bitter.

Belgian endive grows best at temperatures around 59–66°F (15–19°C). It is generally forced for

winter use. Grow plants in an open site in reasonably fertile—but not freshly manured—soil.

The plants require a fairly long growing season. Sow seed outdoors *in situ* in spring or early summer, in rows 12in (30cm) apart. Thin the seedlings to about 8in (20cm) apart. Keep plants weed-free. Water the plants whenever necessary to prevent the soil from drying out.

Belgian endive may be forced *in situ* in light soils and areas with mild winters. In early winter, cut the green leaves about 1in (2.5cm) above ground level. Cover the stumps with soil, making a ridge about 6in (15cm) high; the chicons will grow and force their way through.

Force indoors if the garden soil is heavy or winters are severe, or if an earlier crop is required. Dig up the plants in late fall or early winter. Cut the leaves to 1in (2.5cm) and trim the roots to about 8in (20cm); reject any that are very thin. The roots may be forced immediately or stored for forcing a few at a time in succession during the winter and early spring. To store the roots, lay them flat in boxes with moist sand between each of the layers and keep them in a frost-free shed or cellar until they are required.

To force indoors, plant several of the prepared roots in a large pot or box filled with soil mix or garden soil, and cover with an inverted pot or box of the same size. Block any drainage holes to keep out light. Keep the soil moist, and maintain a temperature of 50–64°F (10–18°C).

Roots may also be planted under greenhouse benches or in a coldframe. Make a light-proof area by stretching black plastic sheeting over wire hoops or attaching it

to a wooden support. Do not use plastic sheeting in spring if temperatures soar, because aphid damage and rotting may occur. Belgian endive is normally free of pests and diseases.

Harvest chicons forced outside after 8–12 weeks when about 4in (10cm) high by moving the soil and cutting the heads 1in (2.5cm) above the neck. Plants forced indoors should be ready after three to four weeks. Stumps may resprout to give a second small crop. Keep chicons wrapped or refrigerated after cutting because they become green and bitter on exposure to light.

FORCING AND BLANCHING CHICORY

1 In late fall or early winter, lift the mature plant carefully. The central leaves may be tender enough to eat.

2 Using a sharp knife, trim the leaves to 1in (2.5cm) from the crown and slice off the base of the root and any side roots, leaving a 8in (20cm) length.

3 Put a layer of moist soil mix or garden soil into a 9in (24cm) pot. Place three trimmed roots in the mixture and firm so that they stand upright, then fill the pot to within 1in (2.5cm) of the rim and firm, leaving the crowns exposed.

4 Line another pot with aluminum foil or black plastic to cover the drainage holes and place it over the roots to block the light. Keep at 50–64°F (10–18°C). Harvest the chicons three to four weeks later by cutting just above soil level.

Radicchio

This is a varied group of perennials usually grown as annuals. The typical radicchio, also known as red chicory, is a low-growing plant with bitter, reddish green outer leaves and a compact heart. It is eaten raw in salads, shredded to reduce bitterness, or may be cooked.

Radicchio tolerates a wide range of temperatures and soil conditions, but is mainly grown for use in the cooler months. Cultivars vary in their frost tolerance. 'Fiero' is exceptionally hardy; it may be forced in the same way as Belgian endive (see p.517). The new F1 hybrids produce more solid heads than traditional cultivars. Sow in early and midsummer, *in situ* or in seed flats for transplanting. Plant 10–14in (24–35cm) apart depending on the cultivar. Transplant summer-sown crops under cover in fall.

Eight to ten weeks after sowing, pick single leaves or harvest the whole head. Radicchio stands a long time after maturing; in cold climates, protect with low tunnels in late fall so that the plants develop more solid heads.

Sugarloaf chicory

Sugarloaf chicory is green leaved, forming a conical head not unlike romaine lettuce in both shape and size. Its inner leaves are naturally blanched and slightly sweetened. For use, and for climate, soil, and cultivation requirements, see "Radicchio" (left).

Sugarloaf chicory may be sown in spring as a cut-and-come-again seedling crop (see p.500); harvest the seedlings before temperatures rise, causing leaves to coarsen. For mature plants, thin seedlings to 10in (25cm) apart, and harvest during late summer or fall. The plants tolerate light frost, and provide winter crops if grown under cover.

Harvest leaves as needed, or cut the heads when mature. The heads keep for a few weeks in cool, dry, frost-free conditions. They may also be piled up, turned inward, and covered with straw to form clamps (see *Making a Rutabaga Pile*, p.543).

Sugarloaf chicory

Lettuces (*Lactuca sativa*)

Lettuces are annual, low-growing plants; although green leaves are standard, new varieties with red or reddish green leaves are very popular.

Romaine (cos) lettuces have long, substantial, well-flavored leaves with fairly loose hearts; semicos are shorter with very sweet, crunchy leaves. Butterhead, or Boston, lettuces have smooth, soft leaves, forming a rounded, compact heart; crispheads (known as icebergs when sold with the outer leaves removed) have crispy leaves forming a heart.

Loose-leaf lettuces, typified by the "Salad Bowl" types, do not form hearts so are slow to bolt and may be cut over a long period; their leaves are often indented and are very decorative. They are the most nutritious form of lettuce and may also be used for cut-and-come-again seedling crops (see p.500).

Lettuces vary from 4in (10cm) to over 12in (30cm) in spread. The romaine types are about 10in (25cm) tall, others about 6in (15cm) high. Lettuces are primarily used as salad vegetables, but outer and older leaves may also be cooked or used in soups.

Lettuces are cool-season crops, growing best at 50–68°F (10–20°C). Cool nights are essential for good results. Some cultivars are tolerant of heat or frost. Germination is poor above 77°F (25°C); at these temperatures, plants tend to bolt rapidly and may become bitter, although loose-leaf lettuces are slower to bolt than other types.

Grow in an open site, or in light shade in very hot weather. Lettuces need fertile, moisture-retentive soil and, although they fall into none of the rotation groups, should not be grown

Loose-leaf lettuces ('Lollo Rossa')

in the same patch of soil for two years in a row to prevent the build-up of fungal disease. They require medium nitrogen (see p.504).

Sowing and planting

Cultivars appropriate for the season must be sown. For a year-round supply in cool climates, sow from early spring to late summer at two- to three-week intervals. At the end of summer or in early fall, sow hardy cultivars that overwinter outdoors or under cover for a spring crop. In warm climates, only heat-tolerant cultivars should be sown during the summer; many types will grow well in fall and winter.

In cool climates, sow seed *in situ*, in a seedbed, or in flats or cell packs for transplanting. Sowings in summer are best made *in situ*, because seedlings wilt when transplanted unless they have been raised in cell packs. Seed may become dormant in high temperatures; this is most likely to occur several hours after sowing and may be overcome by watering after sowing to cool the soil, by putting seed flats or cell packs in a cool place to germinate, or by sowing seed in the afternoon so that the critical period occurs at night when temperatures

HARVESTING LOOSE-LEAF LETTUCES

Loose-leaf lettuces may be harvested by cutting across the leaves 1in 2.5cm) above ground level. Leave the stump to resprout.

LETTUCES TO TRY

Romaine
'Devil's Tongue'
'Green Forest'
'Flashy Trout's Back' (baby leaf)
'Jericho'
'Outredgeous' (baby leaf)

Semicos
'Winter Density'

Butterhead
'Burpee Bibb'
'Buttercrunch'
'Tom Thumb'

Loose-leaf
'Black-seeded Simpson'
'Grand Rapids'
'Green Deer Tongue'
'Lollo Rossa'
'Midnight Ruffles'
'New Red Fire'
'Oakleaf'
'Red Sails'
'Salad Bowl'

Crisphead/Summer Crisp
'Cherokee'
'Crispino'
'Mottisone'
'Saladin'
'Nevada'
'Red Iceberg'
'Summertime'

are lower. Transplant lettuces in moist conditions when they have five or six leaves, with the base of the leaves positioned just above soil level. In hot weather, shade young plants until they are established. Space small cultivars 6in (15cm) apart, and larger ones about 12in (30cm) apart.

Sow hardy cultivars for overwintering outdoors *in situ* or under cloches or in coldframes; thin to 3in (7cm) apart in fall and to the full distance apart in spring. Row covers or cloches put over the plants in spring improve their quality, and help them mature earlier.

Most types of lettuce may be grown as cut-and-come-again seedling crops, especially the loose-leaf lettuces, such as the traditional European "cutting" cultivars, and some romaine varieties (see "Successional crops," p.500).

Routine cultivation
Keep lettuce beds weed-free. Apply a nitrogenous fertilizer or organic liquid feed if growth is slow. In dry conditions, water the plants at a rate of 5 gallons/sq yd (22 liters/sq m) per week; adjust this rate if you have either very light or very heavy soil. The most critical watering period is about seven to ten days before maturity (see also p.502).

Pests and diseases
Problems that affect lettuces include aphids and root aphid (see "Aphids," p.654), cutworms (p.658), slugs (p.669), mosaic virus (see "Viruses," p.672), downy mildew (p.659), boron deficiency (p.656), and gray mold/ *Botrytis* (p.661); birds may attack seedlings (p.655). Some cultivars show aphid resistance and others show some tolerance to mosaic virus and downy mildew.

PROTECTING SEEDLINGS

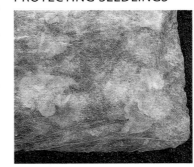

Protecting seedlings with row cover helps them mature more quickly early in the season.

Growing under cover
In cool climates, earlier lettuce crops may be obtained by sowing or planting in early spring in an unheated greenhouse, beneath cloches or perforated row covers, or in cold frames. Some cultivars may also be grown under cover in winter for early spring cropping; for midwinter crops, gentle heat is usually required.

Harvesting and storing
Loose-leaf lettuces should be ready about seven weeks after sowing, butterheads after 10 or 11 weeks, and romaine and crispheads after 11 or 12 weeks. Cut romaine, butterhead, and crisphead types soon after maturing to prevent bolting. They may be stored for a few days in a refrigerator. Pick the leaves of loose-leaf types a few at a time, as required, since they do not store well, or cut across the plants 1in (2.5cm) above soil level; the stumps will resprout within a few weeks.

Spinach (*Spinacia oleracea*)

Spinach is a fast-growing annual that reaches a height of 6–8in (15–20cm), with a spread of about 6in (15cm). The highly nutritious leaves are smooth or crinkled, and round or pointed, depending on the cultivar. They are eaten lightly cooked or, when young, raw in salads.

A cool-season plant, spinach grows best at 61–64°F (16–18°C), although it will grow well at lower temperatures. Small plants and seedlings may survive 16°F (-9°C). Grow cultivars recommended for the area; for example, many are prone to bolt in long days (see "Daylength," pp.494–495), especially after a cold period or in hot, dry conditions. Recommended spinach cultivars that may be used as seedling crops or mature plants include 'Melody', 'Space', and 'Tyee'. Spinach plants tolerate light shade during summer, and need a soil with medium nitrogen levels (see *Nitrogen Requirements*, p.504). For other soil requirements, see "Swiss chard and spinach beet," p.516.

Sowing and planting
Spinach will not germinate in temperatures above 86°F (30°C). Sow *in situ* in cool seasons, spacing seeds 1in (2.5cm) apart in rows spaced about 12in (30cm) apart. For a continuous crop, sow in succession, after seedlings of the previous sowings have appeared. Thin early as for Swiss chard (see p.516), to about 3in (7cm) for young plants, or to 6in (15cm) apart for large plants.

Spinach may also be grown as a cut-and-come-again seedling crop for use in salads (see p.500). For this, sow in early spring and early fall under cover, and also in late summer for an overwintering crop in the open. For routine cultivation, pests and diseases, and growing under cover, see "Swiss chard and spinach beet," p.516.

Harvesting and storing
Cut leaves between five and ten weeks after sowing at any stage once the plants are about 2in (5cm) tall. Either cut individual leaves, or cut the heads about 1in (2.5cm) above the ground and leave them to resprout; alternatively, pull up whole plants. In warm areas, harvest plants young, before they start to run to seed. Use the leaves fresh soon after picking, or store by freezing.

Spinach

New Zealand spinach (*Tetragonia tetragonioides*, syn. *T. expansa*)

A creeping perennial, New Zealand spinach is also grown as an annual. The plants have thick, triangular leaves about 2in (5cm) long with a spread of 3–4ft (90–120cm). The leaves taste similar to and are used in the same way as spinach (see above).

New Zealand spinach tolerates high, even tropical, temperatures, and drought, but cannot withstand frost. It grows best in an open site on reasonably fertile and moisture-retentive soil, and needs low nitrogen (see p.504). It is generally less prone to bolting than spinach.

Seeds may be slow to germinate, so to aid germination soak them in water for 24 hours before sowing.

In cool climates, sow seed indoors and plant out at 18in (45cm) each way after all risk of frost has passed. Otherwise sow seed *in situ* outdoors after the last frost, thinning in stages to the final spacing. Keep seedlings weed-free (mature plants cover the soil, suppressing weeds). Pest or disease problems are rare.

Start picking the young leaves and the tips of the stems six or seven weeks after sowing. Pick frequently to encourage further young growth for three or four months. New Zealand spinach should be used fresh immediately after cutting, or frozen.

PICKING NEW ZEALAND SPINACH

Pick the young leaves and tips of stems of New Zealand spinach before seed heads start to form. Plants will continue to make new growth that may be harvested until the first frosts.

Minor salad vegetables

There are many lesser-known vegetables worth cultivating to use raw in salads, either on their own or mixed with other vegetables. They are suitable for growing in small gardens and containers. The leaves are distinctly flavored and nutritious, especially if used young. Apart from summer purslane and iceplants, all tolerate a few degrees of frost, or even lower temperatures on well-drained soil with wind protection. In cool climates, most may be grown under cover in winter for higher yields. Most salad plants are fast-maturing but make lusher growth in nitrogen-rich soil. Many are best sown as cut-and-come-again crops (see p.500). They are usually free of pests and diseases.

Upland cress (*Barbarea verna*)

This biennial, low-growing plant has a spread of 6–8in (15–20cm). Upland cress is also known as American land cress. The glossy, deep green leaves have a strong flavor similar to watercress, and are used as a watercress substitute, either raw or cooked. Upland cress is very hardy, often remaining green in winter. It grows best in the shade; in heat it runs to seed rapidly, becoming coarse and very hot-tasting. It may be intercropped between taller vegetables or used to make a neat edging for beds.

Grow upland cress in fertile and moisture-retentive soils. Sow seed in spring for an early summer crop, or in late summer for a fall and overwintering crop. It may be grown in unheated greenhouses in winter. Sow *in situ*, thinning to 6in (15cm) apart, or in seed flats to transplant. Pick leaves seven weeks after sowing when they are

Upland cress

3–4in (7–10cm) long. If a few plants are left to go to seed in spring they seed freely, and the seedlings may be transplanted where they are needed. Flea beetles (p.660) may attack young plants.

Mustard (*Sinapis alba*)

Mustard is similar to cress in its habit and is often partnered with it. It is grown for the sharply flavored seedling leaves, which may be used raw in salads. It is a cool-season crop that runs to seed very rapidly in hot weather; its leaves tend to become coarse if it is grown in areas with heavy rainfall.

In temperate climates, outdoor sowings are most successful in spring and fall *in situ*, using any of the methods suggested for cut-and-come-again seedlings (see p.500).

Mustard, like cress, is a useful crop for growing under cover from fall to spring. It may be sown without soil either on moist paper towels in a saucer placed on a windowsill, or in a sprouter; alternatively it may be sown in a seed flat of potting soil mix or soil. These methods may be used all year round. Mustard germinates faster than cress, so if the two are

Mustard

required together, sow the mustard two or three days later than the cress. A sowing every seven to ten days ensures a continuous supply.

Harvest mustard by cutting as required when the seedlings are about 1½–2in (3.5–5cm) tall. It runs to seed much more rapidly than cress, and will normally provide no more than two or three cuts.

Salad rapini (*Brassica napus*)

This annual plant has light green, mild-flavored leaves and is often used as a substitute for mustard in mustard and cress salads. It is fast-growing but slower to go to seed than mustard or cress. The leaves are used raw as seedlings; larger leaves may be cooked as greens.

Salad rapini survives temperatures of 14°F (-10°C) and tolerates moderate heat. The plants grow in a wide range of soils. In temperate climates, sow under cover in early spring and late fall; sow in succession outdoors until early fall. Indoors, grow on a windowsill as for mustard (left). Outdoors, sow broadcast, or in narrow or wide rows. Make the first cut after ten days; when plants reach 24in (60cm), harvest small leaves over several months.

HARVESTING SALAD RAPINI

Cut leaves of salad ripini at any stage, from seedling to 3in (7cm) long. In good conditions, three cuts of seedling leaves may be possible.

Arugula (*Eruca vesicaria* subsp. *sativa*)

This spicy-leaved Mediterranean plant is used in salads; older plants may be cooked. Arugula is also known as rucola, salad rocket, Mediterranean rocket, or roquette. It grows best in cool weather in moisture-retentive soil; in cool climates, it is excellent under cover in winter, and as a cut-and-come-again crop. Sow broadcast or in rows to cut as seedlings, or thin to 6in (15cm) to cut when larger. Seedlings are ready in three weeks. Flea beetles (p.660) may attack arugula.

Arugula

Cress (*Lepidium sativum*)

This fast-growing plant is grown for its seedling leaves, which are used raw. Cress is also known as garden cress, curly cress, or peppercress. There is a fine-leaved and a broad-leaved form. It is a moderately hardy, cool-season crop, running to seed rapidly in hot weather, unless sown in light shade. In cool climates, cress grows well under cover in the winter months. It may stop growing at very low temperatures, but starts again when temperatures rise. It is useful for inter- and undercropping.

Except in very cool areas, cress is best sown in spring and late summer or early fall; avoid sowing in hot weather. Either sow on moist paper in a saucer and place on a windowsill or sow in a sprouter; this will give one cut. To obtain several consecutive cuts, sow in a seed flat of light soil, or in the

Broad-leaved cress

ground, broadcast, in single rows, or in wide rows. Cut ten days after sowing when seedlings are up to 2in (5cm) high. If sown in the ground, up to four successive cuts may be made.

Iceplants (*Mesembryanthemum crystallinum*)

Grown as perennials in warm climates and as tender annuals elsewhere, iceplants have a sprawling habit, succulent stems, and thick, fleshy leaves covered with sparkling bladders. The leaves and young stems taste refreshing and slightly salty. They are used raw in salads or cooked like spinach.

Iceplants need a sunny position in light, well-drained soil. In warm climates, sow *in situ* outdoors; in cool climates, sow indoors in the spring, transplanting to 12in (30cm) apart after all risk of frost has passed. Slugs (p.669) may attack seedlings. Plants may be propagated by means of cuttings (see PERENNIALS, "Stem tip cuttings," p.200). The first picking of the young leaves and tender pieces of stem may be made about four

Iceplants

weeks after planting. Harvest plants regularly to encourage further growth, and remove any flowers that appear. Leaves and stems keep fresh for several days.

Miner's lettuce (*Claytonia perfoliata*)

This annual has heart-shaped leaves and dainty flowering shoots. The mildly flavored, slightly succulent leaves, stems, and flowering shoots are used raw in salads. Also known as winter purslane or claytonia, it thrives in cool weather. It prefers well-drained conditions but grows well even in poor, light soil. Once established, it self-seeds rapidly; invasive seedlings are shallow-rooted and easily pulled up.

Make the main sowing in late summer for a fall to early winter crop outdoors. Sow in spring for a summer crop. Grow either broadcast as a cut-and-come-again seedling crop, or in narrow rows, or 4in (10cm) wide rows; seed may

Miner's lettuce

be sown *in situ* or in seed flats. Transplant or thin seedlings to 6–9in (15–23cm) apart. Start cutting 12 weeks after sowing, leaving the plants to resprout.

Summer purslane (*Portulaca oleracea*)

This low-growing plant has slightly succulent leaves and stems that are used raw or cooked. There are green- and yellow-leaved forms; the green type has thinner leaves, is more vigorous, and possibly better flavored, but the yellow or golden form is attractive in salads. The plants need a warm, sheltered site with light, well-drained soil.

Grow summer purslane either as a cut-and-come-again seedling crop or as single plants. In cool climates, sow in a seed flat in late spring, planting out 6in (15cm) apart, after all risk of frost. Make earlier and late summer sowings under cover as a cut-and-come-again seedling crop. In warm climates, sow *in situ* outside throughout the summer.

Golden summer purslane

Cut the seedlings, or young shoots of single plants, from about four to eight weeks after sowing. Cut regularly, always leaving two basal leaves, and remove any flowers that develop. Slugs (p.669) may attack plants.

Watercress (*Rorippa nasturtium-aquaticum*)

An aquatic perennial, watercress (also known as *Nasturtium officinale*) has nutritious, sharply flavored leaves, which are used in salads and soups. Its natural habitat is fresh-running streams, with slightly alkaline water at about 50°F (10°C).

Root cuttings by placing stems in fresh water; they will soon root and may be planted at the edge of a stream in spring, spaced 6in (15cm) apart. Watercress may be grown in moist garden soil, but is easier to grow in 6–8in (15–21cm) pots. Put a layer of gravel or moss in each pot, fill with rich soil, and stand

Watercress grown in a pot

it in a dish of cool, clean water. Plant three or four rooted cuttings in each pot, and place the pots in a sheltered position in good light. Change the water at least daily in hot weather. Cut leaves as needed.

Dandelions (*Taraxacum officinale*)

Vigorous perennial weeds, dandelions spread up to 12in (30cm). Wild and cultivated forms are grown for the young leaves, which are used raw. The cultivated forms are larger and slower to go to seed. Dandelion leaves are slightly bitter but blanching sweetens them. The flowers and roots are also edible. Dandelions tolerate a range of well-drained soils.

Sow in spring, in seed flats for transplanting, or *in situ*, spacing 14in (35cm) apart. Blanch in succession from late summer, covering dry plants with a large, light-proof bucket. Harvest the leaves when they are elongated and creamy-yellow. Dandelions die back in winter, but reappear in spring; the plants will continue to grow for several years.

BLANCHING DANDELION

When the plant has several leaves, cover it with a bucket 12in (30cm) tall. Harvest the creamy-yellow, elongated leaves after several weeks.

Corn salad (*Valerianella locusta*)

Grown for fall and winter salads in cool climates, this annual forms small, mild-flavored plants. Corn salad is also known as lamb's lettuce or mache. There are two types: the floppy, large-leaved type, and the hardier smaller, upright type with darker green leaves. They tolerate a wide range of soils. In cold climates, grow them under cover in winter to obtain more prolific and tender-leaved plants. Corn salad is a useful crop for inter- or undercropping vegetables, such as winter brassicas.

Corn salad may be grown as a cut-and-come-again seedling crop, or as individual plants. Sow from midsummer onward *in situ*, broadcast, or in narrow or wide rows. Keep the seeds moist until they have germinated. Thin seedlings to 4in (10cm) apart.

Large-leaved corn salad

Corn salad is slow-growing and may take 12 weeks to mature. Harvest leaves individually or cut across the plants, leaving them to resprout for a second cut.

Fruiting and flowering vegetables

Some of the most popular and succulent vegetables fall into the fruiting and flowering group of vegetables. Many—tomatoes, peppers, eggplants, and melons, for example—are tropical or subtropical in origin; in cooler areas these may need to be grown using heat-promoting covers or mulches. In many areas, starting seeds of crops, such as squash, pumpkins, and sweet corn, early indoors ensures the crop will reach maturity. In hot-summer areas these crops will produce well. Where garden space is limited, many of these vegetables may also be grown successfully in pots or other containers on a patio or paved area. Use compact, fast-maturing cultivars for the best results. (See also p.331.) All need a warm, sheltered situation for their fruit to ripen and for successful pollination.

Honeydew melon — Eggplant — Summer squash — Sweet peppers — Zucchini — Cherry tomatoes — Muskmelon — Plum tomatoes — Cucumbers — Sweet peppers — Sweet corn

Sweet peppers (*Capsicum annuum* Grossum Group)

Also called bell peppers, these annuals have a bushy habit and may grow up to 30in (75cm) tall with a spread of 18–24in (45–60cm). The fruits are usually oblong, ranging in size from 1¼–6in (3–15cm) long and 1¼–3in (3–7cm) in diameter, and may be green, cream, yellow, orange, red, or dark purple. The mature fruit is eaten cooked or raw, whole or sliced.

Sweet peppers are tropical and subtropical plants needing a minimum temperature of 70°F (21°C) with a humidity of 70–75 percent for best growth. Temperatures over 86°F (30°C) may reduce fruit set and cause buds and flowers to drop. Select a sunny, sheltered site for peppers. Moderately deep, fertile, well-drained soil with medium nitrogen levels (see p.504) is required.

Sowing and planting
Sow seed in spring indoors in flats or cell packs of soil mix with a pH of 5.5–7. Move the seedlings into 3–4in (6–10cm) pots and plant out 10–12 weeks after sowing in well-prepared beds, spacing the plants 18–20in (45–50cm) apart each way.

Sweet peppers

Harden off plants for several days, and do not plant outdoors until all danger of frost has passed and nights are warm or flowers will drop off.

Routine cultivation
Pinch out the terminal growing point of established plants to encourage a bushy habit, and stake cultivars more than 24in (60cm) tall. Water regularly to prevent leaf and bud drop, and mulch with organic material. Apply a balanced fertilizer or liquid feed every two weeks during the growing season, then stop feeding to encourage ripening. Protect plants outdoors with row covers, if necessary.

Pests and diseases
Plants may be attacked by aphids (p.654); they may also be affected by spider mites (p.670), thrips (p.671), caterpillars (p.657), and blossom end rot (see "Calcium deficiency," p.656).

Growing under cover
Sow as above in early spring. When seedlings are 3–4in (8–10cm) tall, pot them into 8in (21cm) pots or transplant into grow bags or beds. Space plants 20in (50cm) apart and stake taller cultivars. Maintain a humidity of 70–75 percent by regularly damping down.

SWEET PEPPERS TO TRY
'Ace' F1 (red)
'Aconcagua' (yellow)
'Big Bertha' F1 (red)
'California Wonder' (red or orange)
'Flavorburst' F1 (yellow/orange)
'Lipstick' (red)
'Nardello' (red)
'Purple Beauty' (purple)
'Red Knight' F1 (red)
'Sweet Banana' (yellow/red)
'Sweet Chocolate' (brown)
'Yankee Bell' (red)

Ripening Sweet Peppers
As they ripen, the fruits change color from green to red, yellow, or purple, and the flavor becomes sweeter.

Harvesting and storing
Harvest the peppers 12–14 weeks after transplanting and before the first frost if the plants are growing outside. Some cultivars are best used when the peppers are green, but others may be left on the plants for two to three weeks until they change color. A wide variety of colors are available with different cultivars, including red, yellow, creamy white, and purple. Cut off individual peppers; they may be stored in cool, humid conditions for up to 14 days at 54–59°F (12–15°C). Entire plants may also be stored (see "Fruiting vegetables," p.506).

HARVESTING PEPPERS

Some peppers are best harvested when green; others may be left to turn to their mature color. Cut the stalk about 1in (2.5cm) from the fruit.

CHILE PEPPERS (*Capsicum annuum* Longum Group)

This form of *Capsicum annuum* has pointed fruit up to 3½in (9cm) long. Popular chile pepper cultivars include 'Jalapeno', 'Anaheim Chili', 'Serrano', and 'Long Cayenne'.

Cultivated in the same way as sweet peppers, chile peppers are slightly more tolerant of high temperatures. Pick them for use at any stage when the color is green to red. If growing outside, harvest before the first frost. The hot flavor increases with the chile's maturity and comes from the white pith and seeds. If it is too hot, remove and discard them.

Ripening chile peppers

Red chile peppers

Hot peppers (*Capsicum frutescens*)

These plants, also known as cayenne peppers, are branching perennials that grow to 5ft (1.5m) tall and bear small, narrow, orange, yellow, or red fruit that may hang from the branches or be carried upright, depending on the cultivar. Hot peppers are highly spicy and are used in sauces and as a general flavoring.

Hot peppers are tropical and subtropical plants and therefore cannot tolerate frost. Plants should be spaced 24in (60cm) apart in each direction, and cultivated in the same way as sweet peppers (see opposite), although they generally require more water. Staking is not normally necessary.

Hot peppers need a long growing period, and the first fruits are usually produced about 15–18 weeks after planting. They should be allowed to ripen fully before being picked. They may be frozen or dried and stored for several months.

Hot peppers

HOT PEPPERS TO TRY

'Apache'
'Cheyenne'
'Habanero'
'Hungarian Wax'
'Prairie Fire'
'Purple Cayenne'
'Red Hot Cherry'
'Scotch Bonnet Red'
'Super Chili'
'Tabasco'

Watermelons (*Citrullus lanatus*)

Watermelons are annual, tropical, or subtropical plants with spreading stems that grow to 10–12ft (3–4m). Their fruit are rounded or oblong, green or cream, striped or mottled, and may grow to 24in (60cm) in length; they are eaten raw. Plants need a temperature of 77–86°F (25–30°C) and are grown outdoors where the growing season is long; they need at least 70 frost-free days. Well-drained, sandy loam soils with medium levels of nitrogen (see p.504) and a pH of 5.5–7 are needed. Incorporate well-rotted manure and a general-purpose fertilizer into the soil before planting.

Watermelon

frost has passed, spaced at least 3ft (1m) apart. Protect from wind and cold weather with plastic screens.

Sowing and planting
Sow in early spring under cover, in flats or 3–4in (7–10cm) pots, at a temperature of at least 72–77°F (22–25°C). When the seedlings are 4–6in (10–15cm) tall, harden them off. Plant them out after all risk of

Routine cultivation
Mulch to retain moisture and apply a balanced fertilizer or liquid feed every two weeks until the fruit begin to develop. Pinch out the growing points of the main shoots when they are 6ft (2m) long and

train sideshoots between other plants in the row. If you wish, hand-pollinate the flowers (see "Summer squash and zucchini," p.526). Reduce sublateral growths from the sideshoots to two or three leaves after fruits start to develop, and place a pad of dried grass or a block of wood beneath each fruit to protect it from soil-borne pests and diseases.

Pests and diseases
Humidity levels above 75 percent encourage leaf diseases, particularly powdery mildew (p.667) and mosaic virus (see "Viruses," p.672). Other common pests include cucumber beetles (p.658), aphids (p.654), and spider mites (p.670).

Growing under cover
Watermelons are very vigorous and are not normally grown in a greenhouse. They may be grown under row covers, spaced 3ft (1m)

WATERMELONS TO TRY

'Crimson Sweet'
'Moon and Stars'
'Orchid Sweet' F1
'Sangria' F1
'Sugar Baby'

apart; remove covers at flowering time to reduce humidity and to encourage insect-pollination.

Harvesting and storing
Harvest 11–14 weeks after sowing; mature fruits give a hollow sound when tapped. They may be stored for 14–20 days at 50–54°F (10–12°C).

Melons (*Cucumis melo*)

These annuals grow on long, spreading vines, up to 6ft (2m) in length, or as compact bushes. The three major types are cantaloupe, winter or casaba, and muskmelons (including honeydew). Cantaloupe melons

Muskmelon

have gray-green, thick, rough skins with deep grooves and orange flesh; individual fruit weigh up to 1lb 11oz (750g). Winter melons have smooth, yellow, or yellow and green striped skin, and weigh up to 2lb 2oz (1kg). Muskmelons vary in size but are usually smaller than cantaloupe and winter melons and often have fine reticulated markings on smooth skins. Winter melons and some cultivars of cantaloupe melons are suitable for growing in a greenhouse.

Melons are tropical plants requiring a minimum temperature of 64°F (18°C) for germination, rising to 77°F (25°C) during the growing period. They are a favorite home garden crop in the South and other hot summer areas, but farther north, try growing them

under row cover or in a greenhouse. They need a well-drained, fertile soil with a pH of 6.5–7, a high humus content, and high nitrogen levels (see p.504). Add a general-purpose fertilizer and well-rotted compost or manure.

Sowing and planting
Sow seed under cover in early spring in flats or in 3–4in (6–10cm) pots (two seeds per pot), removing the weaker one if both germinate. After about six weeks, and when risk of frost has passed, harden off and plant out the seedlings, spaced 3ft (1m) apart with 3–5ft (1–1.5m) between rows. Plant each seedling on a slight mound and protect young plants until they are established from wind and cold weather with plastic or row cover.

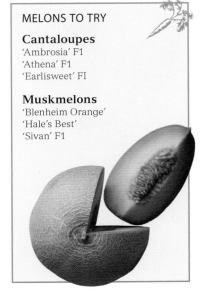

MELONS TO TRY

Cantaloupes
'Ambrosia' F1
'Athena' F1
'Earlisweet' FI

Muskmelons
'Blenheim Orange'
'Hale's Best'
'Sivan' F1

PINCHING MELONS

Allow one flower per lateral to set, and then pinch or cut out the growing tip of each lateral at 2–3 leaves beyond the developing fruit.

Routine cultivation

If you live in a short-season area, pruning vines will encourage better production. After five leaves have developed, pinch out each growing tip to encourage further shoots. When these are well developed, reduce them to about four of the most vigorous shoots. Train two

shoots on either side, between adjacent plants in the row. Remove any protective covering when the plants begin to flower to encourage insect-pollination. Hand-pollinate if required (see "Summer squash and zucchini," p.526).

Thin to one fruit per shoot when the fruits are 1in (2.5cm) in diameter, and stop all sublaterals at two to three leaves beyond the developing fruits. Pinch out the main shoots when they are 3–4ft (1–1.2m) long and remove any further sublaterals that form. Place a pad of dried grass, a tile, or a piece of wood beneath each developing fruit to protect it from soil-borne diseases.

Water regularly and feed every 10–14 days with a liquid feed as the fruit begin to develop; reduce watering and feeding as the fruit ripen.

Pests and diseases

Aphids (p.654), powdery mildew (p.667), spider mites (p.670),

whiteflies (p.673), Verticillium wilt (p.672), and cucumber beetles (p.658) may cause problems.

Growing under cover

To raise melons in a cold frame, plant seedlings singly in the center of the frame. Train the four laterals to grow toward the corners. As the plants develop, increase ventilation and gradually reduce humidity. Once fruit starts forming, remove the sashes, replacing them at night only in cold weather. In hot weather, shade lightly.

Melons may be grown in a greenhouse. Plant seedlings onto well-prepared mounds (see "Cucumbers and gherkins," below). Grow as single or double cordons, training on stakes tied to horizontal wires up to the ridge. Space plants 15in (38cm) apart for single cordons, 24in (60cm) for double cordons. They may also be planted in grow bags.

For a single cordon, pinch out the growing point when the main shoot is 6ft (2m) long to encourage lateral growth. Stop laterals at five leaves and sublaterals at two leaves beyond the flowers. For a double cordon, pinch out the main shoot and let two shoots develop vertically; then train as above. Support developing fruits in 2in (5cm) mesh slings or nets fixed to the ridge. To aid pollination do not damp down during flowering. Maintain a temperature of 75°F (24°C) at night and 86°F (30°C) in the day.

Harvesting and storing

Harvest the fruit 12–20 weeks after sowing. Cantaloupe and muskmelons are sweet-smelling when mature, and the fruit stalks will begin to crack. Separate the fruit gently from the stalks. Fruit can be stored for 14–50 days at 50–59°F (10–15°C), depending on the cultivar.

Cucumbers and gherkins (*Cucumis sativus*)

Cucumbers are annual, trailing vines that grow to 3–10ft (1–3m); there are some compact bush cultivars. The immature fruit are eaten raw, pickled, or served uncooked in cool summer soup.

Cucumbers are characteristically rough-skinned, spiny, and 4–6in (10–15cm) long. Modern cultivars, many of Japanese origin, are smoother and up to 12in (30cm) long, with improved cold tolerance and disease resistance. They are mainly grown outdoors and are insect-pollinated. Gherkins, also called pickling cucumbers, are short, often stumpy fruit up to

3in (7cm) long, harvested young, and used mainly for pickling. Apple and lemon cucumbers are round, yellow-skinned, cucumbers that grow up to 2½in (6cm) in diameter. English or greenhouse fruit are smooth and more than 12in (30cm) long. They do not require pollination to set fruit and, if pollinated, may produce bitter fruit; use the modern all-female cultivars to remove the risk of accidental pollination.

Cucumbers are warm-season vegetables, growing best at a mean temperature of 64–86°F (18–30°C). They have no frost tolerance and

most are damaged at temperatures below 50°F (10°C). In northern latitudes, outdoor types may produce male flowers only early in the season; female flowers, then fruit, occur later. Grow cucumbers in a sheltered site in fertile, humus-rich soil that is well drained but moisture-retentive: the roots must not be allowed to dry out. Lime very acidic soils. The young plants need low nitrogen levels (see p.504) but, after planting, may require higher nitrogen levels.

Greenhouse types must be grown with minimum night temperatures of 68°F (20°C) and in high humidity; shade glass to avoid scorching. Never grow outdoor types in the same greenhouse with all-female cultivars because undesirable cross-pollination will occur.

Sowing and planting

Cucumbers transplant badly, so seed for outdoor varieties should be sown *in situ* after all risk of frost has passed, or in small pots or cell packs. If sowing outside, prepare holes 12in (30cm) wide and deep, working in plenty of well-rotted compost as you backfill. Cover with about 6in (15cm) of manured soil made into a small mound to ensure good drainage. Place seeds on their side about ¾in (2cm) deep, sowing two to three per pot or site.

Seed germinates at a minimum soil temperature of 68°F (20°C). Thin to one seedling after germination. Seed sown in pots needs a minimum

Gherkin

temperature at night of 61°F (16°C) until the seedlings are planted out, about four weeks after sowing. Space climbing types 18in (45cm) apart; bush types, and climbing types if trailing over the ground, should be spaced about 30in (75cm) apart. Protect plants from strong winds.

Routine cultivation

Grow trailing types up supporting fences, nets, or stakes, or allow them to twine up strings. Pinch out the growing tip after five or six leaves have appeared, and train the resulting stronger stems up the support, tying them in if necessary. When these shoots reach the top of the support, pinch them out two leaves beyond a flower; laterals will develop on which more fruit will form. As fruiting continues, feed plants every two weeks with a high-potassium fertilizer or equivalent organic liquid feed. Regular

SOWING AND PLANTING OUT

1 Fill a 2in (5cm) pot with potting mix to within 1in (2.5cm) of the rim. Place 2 or 3 seeds on their sides in the mix, then cover them to a depth of about ¾in (2cm). Water well and label.

2 Prepare a hole 12in (30cm) wide and 12in (30cm) deep, and fill with mature compost. Pile the soil on top to make a mound about 6in (15cm) high. Plant the cucumber on top of this mound. Firm in and water.

Bush cucumbers

watering is essential during the growing period, particularly after transplanting and during flowering and fruiting (see "Critical watering periods," p.502).

Pests and diseases
Snails (p.669), aphids (p.654), powdery mildew (p.667), cutworms (p.658), spider mites (p.670), whiteflies (p.673), squash vine borers (p.671), cucumber mosaic virus (see "Viruses," p.672), cucumber beetles, (p.658), and squash bugs (p.670) may cause problems.

Growing under cover
Grow as in the open using suitable cultivars; the all-female selections are recommended. Pinch the main shoot of each plant at the top of the supports and nip off sideshoots beyond the first leaf. Shoots hang down to crop. Damp down greenhouses to control pests.

Harvesting and storing
Harvest cucumbers regularly from about 12 weeks after sowing when the sides of the fruit are parallel and they are about 6–8in (15–20cm) long. Harvest gherkins when they are 1–3in (2.5–7.5cm) long or when they have reached pickling size.

Climbing cucumbers

CUCUMBERS AND GHERKINS TO TRY

Slicing cucumbers
'Bush Champion' F1
'Diva'
'Garden Sweet Burpless' F1
'Marketmore'
'Olympian' F1
'Spacemaster'
'Sweet Success' F1

Japanese cucumbers
'Tasty Jade' F1

Gherkins
'Adam' F1
'Northern Pickling'
'Salt and Pepper'
'Venlo'

Winter squashes (*Cucurbita maxima, C. moschata, C. pepo*)

This is a very diverse group of annuals, with fruit ranging from 1lb (450g) to more than 65lb (30kg), and includes pumpkins and the inedible ornamental gourds. The skin may be smooth, warty, or ridged, and green, cream, blue-green, yellow, orange, red, or striped—the color often changing with maturity. Their shapes vary considerably and may be round, long, squat, onion-shaped, or a two-layered, turban shape. Most form very large trailing plants with huge leaves; some are compact and bushy. Both young and mature fruit may be eaten cooked, either fresh or after storing. Shoots and young leaves may be cooked and flowers may be eaten raw or cooked. Some cultivars have edible seeds. For climate, site, and soil preparation requirements, see "Cucumbers and gherkins," opposite. Winter squash require medium to high nitrogen levels (see p.504).

Sowing and planting
Seed can be soaked overnight before sowing to hasten germination. Sow as for cucumbers (see opposite). Space plants 6–10ft (2–3m) apart, depending on the cultivar. For large cultivars, prepare holes up to 18in (45cm) deep and 24in (60cm) wide. Insert a marker stake when planting so that the center of the plant can be found if watering is necessary. Protect and mulch after planting.

Routine cultivation
A topdressing of a general fertilizer may be applied soon after planting. Shoots may be trained in circles on the ground using bent wire to hold down the stems, or grown on supports, such as tripods, which, for vigorous cultivars, must be very strong. Where only a few large fruit are needed, remove all but two or three of the fruit while still young.

Winter squash are deep-rooting, so watering should only be needed in very dry weather.

Pests and diseases
Slugs (p.669) may attack in the early stages; later, squash vine borers (p.671) and cucumber mosaic virus (see "Viruses" p.672), cucumber beetles (p.658), and squash bugs (p.670) may cause problems.

Winter squash on a tripod

Harvesting and storing
Cut away any foliage shading the fruit to encourage them to ripen. Harvest winter squash 12–20 weeks after planting. Leave fruit for storing on the plant to mature as long as possible: the stem starts to crack and the skin hardens when the fruit is ripe. Pick before the first frost, cutting each fruit leaving a long stalk attached.

After harvesting, most storage types must be exposed to the sun for ten days to cure (further harden) the skin so that it forms a barrier, slowing the rate of water loss. Cover the fruit at night if frost threatens, or cure indoors at 81–90°F (27–32°C) for four days. Store winter squash in a well-ventilated place at about 50°F (10°C) with a humidity of 95 percent. They may be kept from four to six months or even longer, depending on the conditions and the cultivar grown.

CURING WINTER SQUASH
When ripe, cut the squash off the plant with as long a stalk as possible using pruners or loppers; take care not to pull, because damage may cause rotting. Leave in the sun for about ten days so that the skin hardens. Acorn and 'Delicata' may be stored without curing.

VARIETIES TO TRY

'Blue Hubbard'
'Buttercup'
'Delicata'
'Early Butternut' F1
'Honey Bear' F1 (acorn)
'Peter Pan' F1
'Red Kuri' (hubbard)
'Spaghetti Squash'
'Sunburst' F1
'Sunshine' F1 (kabocha)
'Sweet Dumpling'
'Sweet Mama' F1
'Table Princess' (acorn) F1
'Waltham Butternut'

Summer squash and zucchini (*Cucurbita pepo*)

Summer squash and zucchini are annuals that trail for several yards or form compact plants of 3ft (90cm) spread. They commonly have cylindrical fruit about 9in (23cm) long and 3in (8cm) in diameter. Zucchini are normally harvested young, as are other squash whose fruit are tender-skinned when young. Summer squash may be trailing or bush with green, yellow, white, or striped skin. Patty pan squash have flattish, fluted-edged fruits; crookneck squash have swollen fruits with a bent neck. There are also round-fruited cultivars. Spaghetti squash are squashlike in shape, but with hard skins; when cooked, their flesh resembles spaghetti. Zucchini can be eaten raw or cooked; other types are usually cooked. Squash flowers can also be eaten raw or cooked.

Summer squash and zucchini are warm-season crops, needing temperatures of 64–81°F (18–27°C). Frost tolerance, soil, and soil preparation are as for cucumbers (see p.524). They need low nitrogen levels (see p.504).

Sowing and planting

Sow as for cucumbers (see p.524) when the soil temperature is at least 59°F (15°C). Place each seed about

Bush squash

HAND-POLLINATING

Summer squash and zucchini are generally insect-pollinated but in cold seasons, if fruits are not setting, it may be necessary to hand-pollinate. The female flower has a tiny bump (the embryonic fruit) behind the petals that the male flower lacks (see below); this makes it easy to distinguish between them.

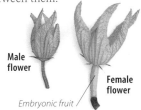

Male flower

Female flower

Embryonic fruit

To hand-pollinate, take a male flower, remove all the petals, and press it against the female flower. Alternatively, use a fine paintbrush to transfer the pollen from the stamens of the male flower to the stigma of the female.

1in (2.5cm) deep or a little deeper in light soils. Sow seed *in situ* once all risk of frost has passed, or germinate in pots indoors. Space bush types 3ft (90cm) apart, and trailing types 4–6ft (1.2–2m) apart. In cool areas, protect young plants with cloches or floating row covers. In hot areas, row covers will also protect young plants against insects. Mulch after planting.

Routine cultivation

Trailing types may be grown up strong supports. The shoots may also be trained in circles, using bent wire to peg down the stems. Toward the end of the season, pinch off the ends of the shoots. Feed and water as for cucumbers (see pp.524–525).

Pests and diseases

Slugs (p.669) may attack in the early stages of growth; cucumber mosaic virus (see "Viruses," p.672), cucumber beetles (p.658), and squash bugs (p.670) may also be a problem.

Growing under cover

This is only appropriate in cool climates when a very early crop is desired. Use bush cultivars.

Harvesting and storing

Harvest summer squash seven to eight weeks after planting. Some types may be stored for a few weeks if they are kept well ventilated at about 50°F (10°C) with a humidity of 95 percent. Spaghetti squash may be stored for several months. Pick zucchini and crookneck squash when they are 4–8in (10–20cm) long. Pick patty pan types when they are from 1–6in (2–15cm) diameter—small squash will be the most tender. If harvesting flowers, pick male ones after the females have set.

HARVESTING ZUCCHINI

Cut zucchini when they are 4–8in (10–20cm) long, with a short stalk. Handle the fruit carefully to avoid bruising them. Regular harvesting will encourage more fruit.

VARIETIES TO TRY

Zucchini
'Black Beauty'
'Black Hawk'F1
'Gold Rush' F1
'Magda' F1
'Raven' F1

Patty pan
'Benning's Green Tint'
'Peter Pan' F1
'Sunburst' F1

Green squash
'Eight Ball' F1
'Geode' F1
'Tromboncino'

Yellow squash
'Horn of Plenty'
'Yellow Crookneck'
'Zephyr' F1

Spaghetti squash
'Vegetable Spaghetti'
'Vermicelli'

Globe artichokes (*Cynara scolymus*)

These perennial plants have blue-gray leaves and thistlelike flowers. Globe artichokes may grow up to 4–5ft (1.2–1.5m) tall with a 3ft (90cm) spread. They are grown for the green and purple flower buds, which have edible, fleshy pads (the hearts) at the base of the outer scales and the top of the flower

stem; the hearts are cooked or pickled. A reliable cultivar is 'Green Globe'.

Globe artichokes grow best in cool climates at 55–64°F (13–18°C) and tolerate light to medium frosts. They need an open but not exposed site, with fertile, well-drained soil into which plenty of compost or

well-rotted manure has been dug, and low levels of nitrogen (see p.504).

Sowing and planting

Globe artichokes are normally increased by division. Using a sharp knife, two hand forks, or a spade, divide healthy, established

plants in the spring; each division should have at least two shoots with a tuft of leaves and a good root system. Plant these divisions 24–30in (60–75cm) apart and trim the tips of the leaves to 5in (13cm). Globe artichokes may be raised from seed either indoors or outdoors in spring, but the results

DIVIDING ARTICHOKES

In spring, lift an established plant and divide it using 2 hand forks, a spade, or a knife. Each division should have at least 2 shoots, and strong roots.

are variable; thin or plant out seedlings at the correct spacing. Replace plants every three years to maintain vigor and cropping levels. For areas where artichokes will not overwinter, grow 'Imperial Star', which will produce flower heads the first year from seed if started indoors early. It needs spring frost to produce well.

Routine cultivation

Keep the planting area free of weeds and well mulched to conserve soil moisture. Do not allow the roots of globe artichokes to dry out in summer or become waterlogged in winter. If severe

cold is expected, hill up the base of each plant, covering with a thick layer of straw; remove in spring.

Pests and diseases

Root aphids (see "Aphids," p.654) may cause problems.

Harvesting and storing

In favorable conditions, some heads may be cut in the late summer of the first season. More flowering stems will be produced in the second season. Pick before the scales open, when the buds feel plump. Remove the hairy choke and stalk before freezing; the hearts may be pickled.

Globe artichoke

Tomatoes (*Lycopersicon esculentum*)

These are annual plants in temperate areas and short-lived perennials in the Tropics. The main trailing stem of the indeterminate (staking) types grows to more than 8ft (2.5m) long in warm climates, with vigorous sideshoots. The shorter (semideterminate) types and the bush (determinate) types stop growing earlier than the indeterminates, with the stems ending in a fruit cluster. Compact dwarf types may grow up to 9in (23cm) across and as tall.

Ripe tomato fruit are red, yellow, orange, pink, or white, and round, flat, plum- or pear-shaped. The tiny currant tomatoes (*Lycopersicon pimpinellifolium*) are ½in (1cm) in diameter, cherry types 1in (2.5cm), the giant beefsteak types up to 4in (10cm). All are eaten raw or cooked.

Tomatoes grow best at 70–75°F (21–24°C), but do not grow well below 61°F (16°C) or above 81°F (27°C) and do not tolerate frost. They need high light intensity. In cool climates, grow them in a sheltered site outdoors or under cover; they are often grown in containers. Tomatoes tolerate a wide range of fertile and well-drained soils, with a pH of 5.5–7; lime very acidic soils (see "Liming," p.625). Crop rotation can be beneficial (see p.498).

Prepare the ground by working in plenty of well-rotted manure or compost at least 12in (30cm) deep, because tomatoes are deep-rooted and heavy feeders. Apply a general fertilizer before planting: tomatoes need high levels of phosphorus (see "Soil nutrients," p.503) but low levels of nitrogen (see p.504).

Sowing and planting

In warm climates, sow seed *in situ* in spring and thin seedlings to the correct spacing. In cool climates, six to eight weeks

Bush tomatoes

before the last expected frost, sow seed ¾in (2cm) deep, at about 59°F (15°C), in seed flats or cell packs. Transplant into 2–3in (5–7.5cm) pots at the two- or three-leaf stage; give the seedlings ample ventilation, space, and light. They can stand short periods of low temperatures if day temperatures rise to compensate. Harden off before planting out when night temperatures are over 45°F (7°C)

or soil temperatures at least 50°F (10°C) and the risk of frost is over.

Staking types Plant indeterminate and semideterminate types on stakes with 15–18in (38–45cm) between plants in single rows 18in (45cm) apart, or in double rows with 3ft (90cm) between the pairs of rows.

Bush and dwarf types Bush types sprawl on the ground; space them 12–36in (30–90cm) apart, depending on the cultivar. Dwarf types may be more closely spaced than this. Cover with cloches or floating mulches in the early stages. Bush types grow well when mulched with black plastic (see "Mulching," p.502).

Routine cultivation

All types of tomato should be watered and mulched heavily once the soil is warm. In dry conditions, water tomatoes weekly at a rate of 2 gallons (11 liters) per plant; adjust the rate if you have very heavy or light soil. Plants in

containers need more frequent watering and supplementary feeding with a tomato fertilizer. Take care not to overwater or overfeed—this may reduce flavor.

Staking types Tie in plants to the support stakes or wires as they grow, and remove all sideshoots when they are about 1in (2.5cm) long. In late summer, remove the terminal shoot two leaves above a cluster to allow the remaining fruits to develop and ripen before the first frost. In cool climates, remove supports at the end of the season, bend over the plants *in situ* on straw, and cover them to encourage the remaining fruit to ripen.

TRAINING STAKED TOMATOES

1 Regularly pinch out sideshoots as they develop to concentrate the plant's energies into swelling the fruits.

2 When the plant has reached the required height in late summer, pinch out the tip of the main shoot two leaves above the top flower cluster.

TOMATOES TO TRY

Staking (indeterminate)
'Better Boy'
'Big Beef'
'Cabernet'
'Early Girl'
'Pink Beauty'
'Roma' (paste)
'San Marzano'
'Stupice'
'Sun Gold'
'Supersteak'
'Sweet 100'
'Yellow Pear'

Determinate
'Balconi Red'
'Balconi Yellow'
'Celebrity'
'Glacier'
'Gold Nugget'
'Oregon Spring'
'Rutgers'
'Taxi'
'Tiny Tim'
'Tumbler'

Pests and diseases

Potential problems for tomatoes include damping off in seedlings (p.658), leafhoppers (p.663), flea beetles (p.660), and late blight (p.663). Tomatoes under cover are affected by whiteflies (p.673), several mosaic viruses (see "Viruses," p.672), gray mold/*Botrytis* (p.661), boron deficiency (p.656), magnesium deficiency (p.664), Southern blight (p.670), foot and root rots (p.660), and blossom end rot (see "Calcium deficiency," p.656). Use disease-resistant cultivars indicated in catalogs and websites by the letters V, F, and N after the cultivar name. Interplanting with marigolds may help deter whiteflies.

Growing under cover

In cool climates, grow tomatoes in greenhouses or hoop houses. Hoop houses, which can be moved, are better than greenhouses, where soil-borne diseases may develop unless the soil is replaced every three years. Alternatively, crops may be grown in containers or by ring culture (plants are grown in "rings" or bottomless pots filled with soil, resting on pea gravel). Cultivars may also be grafted onto disease-resistant rootstocks. After the first cluster has set, feed weekly with a high-potassium fertilizer or an organic liquid feed.

Harvesting and storing

Pick fruits as they ripen. Harvest the earliest bush types seven to eight weeks after planting; before the first frost, these may be pulled up by the roots and hung upside-down indoors to ripen. Harvest staking types after 10–12 weeks. Tomatoes freeze well.

Grafting tomatoes

Grafting tomatoes has been practiced commercially for many years by selecting seed-raised plants that are resistant to soil-borne diseases but produce poor quality fruit, to use as stocks on which to graft high-yielding cultivars that produce high-quality fruit. Seedling tomatoes grafted onto disease-resistant stocks are often more vigorous than those grown on their own roots, as well as giving earlier, larger crops. This allows gardeners to grow some heirloom cultivars that have little disease resistance successfully. Ready-grafted plants are becoming more available and, although they are more expensive than growing from seed, have the advantages, not only of disease resistance but are more vigorous than the same cultivar grown on its own roots.

Approach grafting is the easiest method to use when grafting tomatoes. Seed of tomato grafting rootstocks are now available; sow them 4–5 days before those of the cultivar used for the scion. Once the rootstock is 6in (15cm) high, make a downward-slanted cut 1in (2.5cm) long, 3in (7.5cm) from the base, and an upward cut of the same length on the scion. Fit the tongues of the two together and bind with grafting or transparent adhesive tape. Then cut down the stock just above the leaf node of the lowest leaf (see p.501). Pot up, stake, and grow

GROW BAGS

Tomatoes may be planted in grow bags outdoors or in greenhouses. The bags protect plants from soil-borne diseases.

on with both root systems still intact. Once the graft has taken, cut off the rootstock of the scion just below the graft and pot on or plant out as required.

Wonderberries (*Solanum* x *burbankii*)

These annuals grow to about 30in–3ft (75cm–1m). Several cultivated forms of the wonderberry, or sunberry, are grown; all have oval, light green leaves and round, purple berries up to ½in (1cm) in diameter. The leaves and young shoots are used like spinach. The unripe fruits contain a poisonous alkaloid, so pick only ripe berries and cook them thoroughly.

Wonderberries are tropical and subtropical plants needing temperatures of 64–77°F (18–25°C) with a humidity of at least 70 percent. They may be grown in the open in sites that are both sunny and sheltered, but in most areas, greenhouse cultivation is recommended. A fertile, well-drained soil that has a pH of 5.5–7 is preferable; medium nitrogen levels are required (see p.504).

Sowing and planting

Sow seed in spring in flats in the greenhouse. Prick out the seedlings when they are large enough to handle, into 3–4in (8–10cm) pots. When they are 3–4in (8–10cm) tall, harden them off and transplant them; space plants 16–20in (40–50cm) apart, with about 24in (60cm) between rows.

Routine cultivation

Wonderberries need high levels of soil moisture; mulch well and water regularly. Apply a general-purpose fertilizer or an organic liquid feed every 10–14 days during the growing period. Pinch out the growing point when plants are 12in (30cm) tall to encourage lateral branching, and stake plants that grow higher than 24in (60cm). Keep ground around plants weed-free.

Pests and diseases

Aphids (p.654) are the major pest. Under cover, thrips (p.671) and spider mites (p.670) may also attack plants.

Growing under cover

When seedlings are about 4–6in (10–15cm) tall, transplant into 8in (21cm) pots or growing bags, leaving at least 20in (50cm) between plants, or transplant into well-prepared greenhouse beds, spacing plants 20–24in (50–60cm) apart each way. Reduce the level of humidity during flowering to promote pollination.

Harvesting and storing

Harvest shoots 9–11 weeks after transplanting; continue removing shoots 4–6in (10–15cm) long to encourage lateral growth.

To produce berries, do not remove shoots but allow the plants to become bushy and to flower. Harvest the fruit about 14–17 weeks after sowing, removing bunches with a sharp knife. Ripe berries can be stored for 10–14 days.

Wonderberries

Eggplant (*Solanum melongena*)

Short-lived perennials normally cultivated as annuals, eggplant form small bushes about 24–28in (60–70cm) tall with a spread of about 24in (60cm). Also known as aubergines, cultivars differ mainly in the shape, size, and color of the fruit, which may be oval, pear-shaped, or round, dark purple, yellowish green, or white, and weigh 7–18oz (200–500g). The fruit are usually sliced and cooked.

Eggplant is a tropical and subtropical plant requiring temperatures of 77–86°F (25–30°C), with a minimum humidity of 75 percent. Below 68°F (20°C) growth may be checked. Grow in full sun and protect newly planted plants from cold winds and low temperatures, which may stunt growth and cause bud drop.

Eggplant require a deep, fertile, well-drained soil and medium nitrogen levels (see p.504).

Sowing and planting

In spring, sow seed under cover in flats using a light, slightly acidic (pH 6–6.5) soil mix: soak the seed in warm water for 24 hours first to aid germination. Prick out into 3–4in (8–10cm) pots. In hot summer areas, plant out the seedlings into well-prepared beds when they are 3–4in (8–10cm) tall, spacing them about 24–30in (60–75cm) apart each way. Pinch out their terminal growing points to promote a bushy habit.

EGGPLANT TO TRY

'Black Beauty' F1
'Easter Egg'
'Ichiban'
'Little Fingers'
'Rosa Bianca'

Eggplant

In shorter-season areas, pot up singly into 6in (15cm) pots; plant out after risk of frost has passed. Protect from heavy rain, wind, and cold.

Routine cultivation
Stake cultivars more than 24in (60cm) tall. Keep plants well watered, or the leaves and buds are liable to drop, and mulch to preserve moisture. Apply a balanced fertilizer or liquid feed every two weeks during the growing season. Prune back mature plants in order to stimulate growth. To produce large fruits, restrict the number per plant to five or six.

Pests and diseases
Eggplant may be attacked by aphids (p.654) and flea beetles (p.660). Spider mites (p.670), mealybugs (p.664), caterpillars (p.657), thrips (p.671), and powdery and downy mildew (pp.667, 659) may be troublesome.

Growing under cover
Sow seed in early spring at 68–86°F (20–30°C). When the seedlings are 3–4in (8–10cm) tall, transfer them to 8in (20cm) pots or grow bags, and pinch out the tips. Maintain the temperature above the minimum required during the growing period. Damp down greenhouses to help discourage spider mites.

Harvesting and storing
Harvest 16–24 weeks after sowing, when fruit reach full color and are unwrinkled. Cut the fruit stalks close to the stem. Eggplant may be stored for up to two weeks in humid conditions at 54–59°F (12–15°C).

HARVESTING EGGPLANT

Cut eggplant while their skin is still purple and shiny; once it loses its shine, the flesh will taste bitter. Cut the stalk at least 1in (2.5cm) from the fruit.

Sweet corn (Zea mays)

Sweet corn is an annual that grows to at least 5–8ft (1.5m–2.4m) and has an average spread of 18in (45cm). Male tassels and female ears (cobs) are borne on the same plant. The ears are golden, white, or bicolored white and yellow, and cooked or eaten raw when young. Supersweet (sugar-enhanced) cultivars are available.

Sweet corn needs a long growing season of 70–110 frost-free days after planting. It needs temperatures of 61–95°F (16–35°C), but pollination is poor in hot, dry conditions; in warm climates, grow in an open site. In cool climates, grow early-maturing cultivars in a frost-free, sheltered site. Sweet corn is shallow-rooting and grows on a wide range of fertile, well-drained soils with medium nitrogen (see p.504).

Sowing and planting
Seed does not germinate at soil temperatures below 50°F (10°C). In warm climates, sow seed in spring in situ, 1in (2.5cm) deep and 3in (7cm) apart, thinning to the correct spacing after germination. Seed may be sown through plastic mulches. In cool climates sow indoors in cell packs and plant out seedlings when the soil temperature reaches 55°F (13°C), or sow in situ after all risk of frost has passed; cover with row cover to keep warm and protect from birds. Avoid planting in wet soil or seed may rot.

To ensure good pollination and full ears, plant corn in blocks of at least four plants each way. The average spacing is 12in (30cm) apart; short cultivars may be closer, tall ones farther apart. In cool climates, cover with row cover after sowing or

SWEET CORN PLANTED IN A BLOCK

Male and female flowers are carried on the same plant. The male flowers (inset, top), which release pollen, are produced in tassels up to 16in (40cm) in length at the tip of the plant. The female flowers (inset, bottom) are silky strands under which each ear forms. The strands are sticky to collect pollen. The female flowers are wind-pollinated so plant in a block rather than a row to ensure good pollination.

planting, removing the cover at the five-leaf stage. Supersweet types need higher temperatures to germinate and grow and should not be planted with other types because the sweetness will be lost if they are cross-pollinated. Baby corn is obtained by planting early cultivars about 6in (15cm) apart and harvesting the ears when they are about 3in (7cm) long.

Routine cultivation
Hoe shallowly when weeding to avoid damaging the roots. In exposed areas, hill up the stems to 5in (13cm) to increase stability. Watering is not necessary, except in very dry conditions, until flowering starts and again later when the grains are swelling. Water at a rate

of 5 gallons/sq yd (22 liters/sq m). Mulching with several thin layers of grass clippings helps reduce evaporation.

Pests and diseases
Cucumber beetle larvae (p.658), asparagus beetles (p.654), cutworms (p.658), corn earworms (p.658), smuts (p.670), corn rootworms, armyworms, and raccoons (see "Small animal pests," p.669) may attack.

Harvesting and storing
Plants normally produce one or two cobs. Pick just before cooking, because the sweetness deteriorates within hours; supersweet types retain their flavor for two or three days. Sweet corn freezes well.

SWEET CORN TO TRY

Early
'Earlivee'
'Spring Treat'
'Sugar Pearl'

Late
'Bodacious'
'Peaches 'n Cream'
'Silver Queen'

Supersweet
'Bon Appetit'
'Honey Select'

TESTING SWEET CORN FOR RIPENESS

Once the silk has turned brown, peel back the husk and press into a kernel with a fingernail. If the liquid that appears is milky, the ear is ripe; if watery, it is underripe, and if doughy, overripe.

Legumes and okra

Vegetables in this group produce seed pods. Some are grown for these pods, which may be cooked and eaten whole, while others are grown for the seeds, which are extracted and cooked or eaten raw. The seeds of some may be dried; most may be frozen. Several of the plants are decorative as well as functional and may be used for screening, or trained over arches. Some of these crops need sheltered conditions at specific temperatures for pollination. Beans, peas, and peanuts are legumes and can fix nitrogen with the help of bacteria in the soil.

Green beans
Dried beans
Peas
Navy beans
Fava beans
Kidney beans
Snap peas
Scarlet runner beans
Snow peas
Peanuts
Shelled peanuts

Okra (*Abelmoschus esculentus*)

These tender annual plants are also known as ladies' fingers. The fast-maturing cultivars may grow to 3ft (1m) with a spread of 12–16in (30–40cm); the slow-maturing ones (mainly grown in the South) are up to 6ft (2m) tall. The pods are 4–10in (10–25cm) long and white, green, or red.

Okra

Recommended cultivars include 'Clemson Spineless', 'Green fingers', and 'Silver Queen'. Immature pods are eaten as a cooked vegetable; mature pods may also be dried and powdered for use as a thickener.

Okra requires hot, sunny conditions to thrive, and is difficult to grow in cool-summer areas. Seeds germinate only at soil temperatures of at least 61°F (16°C); after germination a stable temperature in the range of 68–86°F (20–30°C) is needed for optimal growth. Most modern cultivars are day-length-neutral (see "Day length," pp.494–495). Plant in well-drained soil, adding organic material. Okra plants need low to medium nitrogen levels (see p.504).

Sowing and planting
Soak seed for 24 hours before sowing to aid germination. When soil temperatures reach 61–64°F (16–18°C), sow seed *in situ* in rows 24–28in (60–70cm) apart, leaving 8–12in (20–30cm) between plants.

For an earlier start, sow in spring under cover at 68°F (20°C) or above, in trays or 3–3½in (6–9cm) pots. When seedlings are 4–6in (10–15cm) tall, harden off and transplant to well-prepared beds, spacing as above.

Routine cultivation
Stake tall plants and protect from strong winds with plastic covers or screens, if necessary. Remove all weeds, water regularly, and apply an organic mulch to retain soil moisture. Pinch out the growing points when seedlings are about 24in (60cm) tall to promote branching. Apply a balanced fertilizer as needed during the growing season to encourage rapid growth. Do not overfeed with nitrogen because this delays flowering.

Pests and diseases
Plants are likely to be damaged by aphids (p.654), caterpillars (p.657), and powdery mildew (p.667); whiteflies (p.673), spider mites (p.670), root-knot nematodes (p.668), thrips (p.671), and fungal leaf spots (p.660) may also be troublesome.

Growing under cover
Seedlings may be transplanted into well-prepared beds in the greenhouse or in grow bags, spacing the young plants at least 16in (40cm) apart. Maintain a temperature above 68°F (20°C) and a humidity of more than 70 percent. Use appropriate practices to prevent and control pests and diseases, and apply a balanced fertilizer as needed.

Harvesting and storing
Each plant may produce up to a few dozen pods. They can be harvested approximately 8–11 weeks after sowing, depending on the cultivar. Sever the pods from the plant with a sharp knife when they are bright green; overmature pods may become fibrous. Pods may be stored in perforated bags at 45–50°F (7–10°C) for up to ten days.

Peanuts (*Arachis hypogaea*)

These tender annual plants, also known as groundnuts, originate from South America. Plants grow to a height of 24in (60cm) with a spread of 12in (30cm) for the more upright Spanish-Valencia types, or up to 3ft (1m) for the less common, prostrate, Virginia types. The Spanish-Valencia types are often divided into Spanish, with two seeds per pod and light brown seed coats, and Valencia, with up to four seeds per pod and dark red seed coats. The stems of the Valencia types are usually thicker than those of the Spanish. The Virginia forms have two seeds per pod, with dark brown seed coats.

The fertilized flowers produce shootlike structures that penetrate the soil where the immature fruit develop into peanuts. Removed from their pods, the nuts are eaten fresh or roasted, or used in cooking.

Peanuts are tropical plants that need average temperatures of about 68–86°F (20–30°C) and a relative humidity of 80 percent, although some forms will grow well in cooler conditions. Peanuts cannot withstand frost. Rainfall at flowering time may adversely affect pollination.

Peanut cultivars are generally day-length-neutral (see "Day length," pp.494–495). Sandy, well-drained soil with a pH of 5.5–6.5 containing calcium, potassium, and phosphorus are preferable. The plants also need low nitrogen levels (see p.504).

Sowing and planting
Sow seeds *in situ*, removed from their shells, in spring or when soil temperatures exceed 61°F (16°C).

In cooler climates, sow under cover in trays or 3½in (9cm) pots, keeping temperatures over 68°F (20°C).

When the seedlings are 4–6in (10–15cm) tall, harden them off and transplant them to well-prepared beds. Whether directly sown or transplanted, the plants should be spaced 6–12in (15–30cm) apart with about 24–28in (60–70cm) between the rows. Protect them with row cover or plastic low tunnel where necessary.

Routine cultivation
Hill up around the roots when the plants are 6in (15cm) tall, and hoe regularly to encourage the fertilized flowers to penetrate the soil. Remove all weeds, and water well in dry periods. Do not water plants during the flowering period, however, because this may lead to poor pollination.

Spanish-Valencia peanut plant

Pests and diseases
Plants may be affected by aphids (p.654), thrips (p.671), and caterpillars (p.657); spider mites (p.670) and whiteflies (p.673) may also cause problems. Fungal leaf

spots (p.660), root and stem rots (see "Southern blight," p.670), and rosette virus (see "Viruses," p.672) may also be troublesome.

Growing under cover
Sow seed as described above. Transplant the seedlings when they are 4–6in (10–15cm) tall into grow bags or well-prepared greenhouse beds. Maintain a temperature of more than 68°F (20°C), reducing humidity at flowering time to aid pollination.

Harvesting and storing
Harvest the pods 16–20 weeks after sowing for the upright types, and three to four weeks after this for the prostrate types.

Virginia types, which produce two seeds per pod, may require up to 25 weeks from sowing to harvesting. Assess the stage of maturity by uprooting one or two pods; they keep for several months. Dry the pods in the sun, then remove the peanuts for storing in cool, dry conditions.

Peanuts

Peanut pods

Hyacinth beans (*Lablab purpureus*)

These dwarf or climbing, short-lived, tender perennials are also known as dolichos beans and lablab beans. Both long- and short-podded cultivars occur. Climbing forms may grow to 12–20ft (4–6m), while dwarf forms reach a height of 3ft (1m) with a spread of about 2ft (60cm). The pods range in color from green to purple. Young pods and mature seeds are eaten cooked; the latter should be cooked well. Young seedlings, raised in the dark, may be used as bean sprouts.

Hyacinth beans may be grown in hot-summer areas in very favored, sunny sites with protection. The plants require a temperature of 64–86°F (18–30°C) with a minimum humidity of 70 percent; cool weather may adversely affect pollination as it discourages pollinating insects. Day-length-neutral cultivars are available (see "Day length," pp.494–495).

Most soils are suitable for hyacinth beans, particularly those containing plenty of organic matter; good drainage is essential. Some cultivars respond well to added phosphate. Hyacinth beans need low nitrogen levels (see p.504).

Hyacinth beans

Sowing and planting
Sow *in situ*, in spring or at other times of the year if temperatures are high enough. For an early start, sow seeds under cover, in flats, or in 3–3½in (6–9cm) pots at a depth of 1in (2.5cm). When the seedlings are 4–6in (10–15cm) tall, harden them off and transplant into well-prepared beds. Space climbing cultivars

12–18in (30–45cm) apart, allowing 30–36in (75–100cm) between rows; space dwarf cultivars 12–16in (30–40cm) apart with a distance of 18–24in (45–60cm) between rows.

Routine cultivation
Climbing cultivars should be supported by stakes, at least 6ft (2m) tall. Water the plants regularly, and mulch to conserve moisture. Protect as necessary from strong winds and remove all weeds. Apply a balanced organic fertilizer every 10–14 days until flowering. Pinch out the growing points of dwarf cultivars to encourage them to develop a bushy habit; the shoots of climbing cultivars should be trained or tied in to the stakes.

Pests and diseases
Aphids (p.654), thrips (p.671), caterpillars (p.657), root-knot nematodes (p.668), powdery mildew (p.667), fungal leaf spots (p.660), and some viruses (p.672) may be troublesome; whiteflies (p.673) and spider mites (p.670) may also affect plants.

Growing under cover
Transplant seedlings to grow bags or well-prepared beds in the greenhouse, spacing the plants at least 20–24in (50–60cm) apart. Alternatively, seedlings may be grown on in 8–10in (21–25cm) pots (two plants may be grown in the larger pots). Maintain a temperature of at least 68°F (20°C) and reduce humidity by providing adequate ventilation at flowering time to improve pollination. Hyacinth beans may also be propagated from softwood cuttings (see Principles of Propagation, "Stem cuttings," p.632), taken early in the growing season, which root readily in high humidity.

Harvesting and storing
Harvest the young pods six to nine weeks after sowing, when they are fully grown but before the seeds develop; the mature pods containing seeds can be harvested after 10–14 weeks before they become fibrous. If the plants remain healthy after the first crop, cut back the main stems to about half their length to encourage a second crop. Hyacinth beans freeze well.

Scarlet runner beans (*Phaseolus coccineus*)

Scarlet runner beans

These perennial climbers are grown as annuals in most areas. Plants grow to over 10ft (3m) tall, with a spread of about 12in (30cm); some naturally dwarf cultivars form bushes about 15in (38cm) tall. They have pink, red, white, or bicolored flowers.

The flat pods, more than 10in (25cm) long and up to ¾in (2cm) wide, are eaten cooked; immature seeds and mature, dried seeds may also be cooked. With some cultivars, it may be necessary to remove the strings along the pods.

Scarlet runner beans are a temperate or cool-season crop that does not withstand frost. Plants need a growing season of about 100 frost-free days and they grow best at 57–84°F (14–29°C). At higher temperatures,

especially if combined with high humidity, the pods may not set unless the plants are in light shade. In cool climates, choose a sheltered location to encourage pollinating insects. Plants are deep-rooting and need fertile, moisture-retentive soil. Prepare the soil by digging it well and working in some well-rotted straw or compost. Runner bean crops may also benefit from crop rotation (see p.498), and need low nitrogen levels (see p.504).

Sowing and planting
Before planting climbing types, erect a strong support system of poles or stakes over 8ft (2.5m) long, tied to a horizontal pole or to each other to form a tepee. Special supports or towers are

SCARLET RUNNER BEANS TO TRY

Standard
'Apricot Runner'
'Emperor'
'Painted Lady'
'Prize Winner'
'Red Rum'
'Scarlet Runner'
'White Lady'

Stringless
'Desiree'
'Lady Di'
'Red Knight'
'White Knight'

available. Plants may also be trained up nylon netting. Do not use plastic-coated netting because the plants do not cling to it. Sow seed *in situ* 2in (5cm) deep, after all risk of frost has passed, bearing in mind that a

minimum soil temperature of 54°F (12°C) is needed for germination. In cool areas, sow seed indoors in seed flats and harden off seedlings before transplanting outside. Grow climbers in double rows 2ft

(60cm) apart or in circular tepees, spacing the plants 6in (15cm) apart. Bush forms may be grown in groups at the same spacing. Mulch well to retain moisture after germination or planting out.

Routine cultivation

Protect seedlings with cloches or floating mulches. To convert climbing forms into bushes, pinch out the growing shoots when plants are 9in (23cm) tall. Such plants bear earlier but have lower yields.

Watering is especially important when the flower buds appear and pods are setting (see "Critical watering periods," p.502). At these times supply 1–2 gallons/sq yd (5–11 liters/sq m) twice a week depending on your soil type.

Pests and diseases

Slugs (p.669) in the early stages, fungal leaf spots (p.660), anthracnose (p.654), foot and root rots (p.660), halo blight (see "Bacterial leaf spots and blotches," p.655), Southern blight (p.670), and viruses (p.672) may be troublesome.

Harvesting and storing

Harvest after 13–17 weeks. Pick pods when they are at least 7in (17cm) long and tender; continue picking at frequent intervals to prolong the bearing period. Runner beans freeze well.

BEAN SUPPORTS

There are various ways to support climbing beans, depending on the space available. Mature plants will obscure the support structure beneath.

Crossed pole row

Two rows of 8ft (2.5m) poles, crossed and secured to a horizontal bar

Tepee

8ft (2.5m) poles tied near the top

Netting support

4in (10cm) square nylon net fixed to a pole frame

Runner beans on a tepee

Lima beans (*Phaseolus lunatus*)

Dwarf Lima beans

Also known as butter beans, lima beans are tender annuals and short-lived perennials. Some forms of lima beans climb while others are dwarf and branching. Climbing cultivars may grow to a height of 9–12ft (3–4m), dwarf cultivars to 3ft (90cm), spreading to 16–18in (40–45cm). The young pods and mature seeds are eaten cooked; the seeds may also be dried or germinated in the dark for use as bean sprouts.

The lima bean is a tropical plant that needs a minimum temperature of 64°F (18°C) for germination. Temperatures above 86°F (30°C) may adversely affect pollen formation. In subtropical and warm-temperate areas, growing in the open is possible only in full sun, using plastic screens or covers for protection until the plants are fully established.

Small-seeded cultivars flower only in short day lengths of about 12 hours, but the large-seeded cultivars are normally day-length-neutral (see "Day length," pp.494–495). Most cultivars thrive in a wide range of soil types, but a sandy, well-drained soil with a pH of 6–7 is preferable. Lima beans require low to medium nitrogen levels (see p.504). The procedures for sowing, planting, routine cultivation, and growing under cover are the same as for hyacinth beans (p.531).

Pests and diseases

Aphids (p.654), thrips (p.671), caterpillars (p.657), whiteflies (p.673), and spider mites (p.670) may be troublesome. Diseases include powdery mildew (p.667), fungal leaf spots (p.660), and some viruses (p.672).

LIMA BEANS TO TRY

Climbing
'Florida Butter'
'King of Garden'

Dwarf
'Dixie Butterpea'
'Eastland'
'Fordhook 242'

Harvesting and storing

Harvest whole pods young, and mature seeds about 12–16 weeks after sowing. Store both above 39°F (4°C) at 90 percent humidity for up to two weeks. Lima beans may be frozen.

Snap beans (*Phaseolus vulgaris*)

These tender annuals have pole (climbing), bush, and intermediate forms. They are also known as green, French, or string beans. Height and spread are as for scarlet runner beans (see p.531). The pods are 3–8in (7–20cm) long. They may be round, flat, or curved in shape; diameters range from pencil-thickness (for the filet types) to

about ¾in (2cm); they may be green, yellow, purple, red, or green flecked with purple. The yellow, waxpod types have a waxy texture and excellent flavor. Types vary in the stringiness of the pods; stringless cultivars are available. Snap beans may be eaten raw in salads or lightly steamed. Some related beans are grown specifcally for drying the

seeds. These include kidney, pinto, navy, and white beans; all are grown as for snap beans. Dried seeds are used in soups and stews.

Snap beans grow in conditions similar to scarlet runner beans (see p.531) but seeds will only germinate at a minimum temperature of 54°F (12°C). The optimal growing temperature is 61–86°F (16–30°C);

seedlings do not tolerate temperatures below 50°F (10°C). The plants are self-pollinated, and grow best in rich, light soil. Good drainage is essential to prevent root rot. When planting beans in a new location, use bacterial inoculant to stimulate nitrogen-fixing root nodules and improve current and subsequent yields.

Seeds are very sensitive to cold, wet soil and early sowings are risky. Snap beans usually need low nitrogen levels (see p.504).

Sowing and planting

Sowing seeds directly in the garden usually gives best results, but if desired you can

PREGERMINATING SNAP BEANS

1 Spread the beans out on moist tissue paper in a tray without drainage holes. Keep damp, at a minimum of 54°F (12°C).

2 When the delicate shoots begin to appear and before they turn green, carefully pot up the beans or sow them directly in their final location outside.

start seeds in cell packs and transplant. Make successive sowings throughout the summer. If necessary, warm the soil beforehand with cloches or clear plastic sheeting. Space climbing forms as for scarlet runner beans. Bush types may be grown at an equidistant spacing of 9in (22cm) in staggered rows for the highest yields. In cold climates, protect after planting with cloches or floating row cover.

Routine cultivation

Support climbing types as for scarlet runner beans; use twiggy brush to support intermediate types. Stems may also be hilled up to keep plants upright. Mulch and do not allow plants to dry out completely; extra watering may promote better pod set if conditions are dry at flowering time.

Pests and diseases

Slugs (p.669), root aphids and black bean aphid (see "Aphids," p.654), anthracnose (p.654), foot and root rots (p.660), root-knot nematodes, (p.668), halo blight (see "Bacterial leaf spots and blotches", p.655), and viruses (p.672) may affect snap beans.

Growing under cover

In cold climates, bush snap beans may be grown to maturity in a greenhouse or polytunnel, or under row cover. Space plants as in the garden.

HILLING UP

Plant out the beans 6in (15cm) apart, and once they have formed several pairs of leaves, hill them up to support them.

Harvesting and storing

Harvest after 7–13 weeks. Pick young beans regularly to use fresh or freeze. For shelled beans, see below; store in an airtight jar.

DRYING BEANS

In damp climates, pull up plants and hang them by the roots in a dry, frost-free place. Once dried, remove the pods and extract the beans.

SNAP BEANS TO TRY

Pole
'Blue Lake'
'Kentucky Blue'
'Kentucky Wonder'

Bush
'Bush Blue Lake'
'Dorabel' (wax)
'Goldcrop' (wax)
'Provider'
'Rocdor' (wax)
'Roma II'
'Royal Burgundy' (purple podded)
'Tenderlake'

For drying
'Jacob's Cattle'
'Maine Yellow Eye'
'Vermont Cranberry'

Peas (*Pisum sativum*)

Peas are annuals that grow from 18in (45cm) to more than 6ft (2m) tall, with an average spread of 9in (23cm). Plants cling to supports with tendrils; modern semileafless types are almost self-supporting. Peas are grouped according to the time taken to mature. The early groups are shorter and lower yielding than later types. Pods are usually green but there are purple-podded cultivars.

Shelling-pea types are grown for the fresh peas in the pods; some may be dried. Petit pois are small, fine-flavored peas. Wrinkle-seeded cultivars are usually sweeter but less hardy than the smooth-seeded types. Edible-podded types (snow and snap peas) are eaten before the peas mature. Snow peas are flat-podded and eaten young, while the round-podded snap types are used when semimature. Peas and pods are usually cooked, but may be eaten raw.

Semileafless peas

Peas are a cool-season crop, growing best at 55–64°F (13–18°C). The flowers and pods cannot withstand frost. Grow peas on a sunny site, in reasonably fertile, moisture-retentive, well-drained soil; they will not tolerate cold, wet soil, or drought. Work some compost into the soil before

planting. If planting a site with peas for the first time, use the appropriate inoculant to stimulate formation of nitrogen-fixing nodules on the roots. Peas should not require any extra nitrogen during growth.

Sowing and planting

Make the first outdoor sowings as soon as the soil temperature is about 50°F (10°C). Germination is much slower at lower temperatures. The first sowings may be made under row covers using dwarf cultivars. For successive crops, either sow seeds at 14-day intervals or sow cultivars from different groups at the same time so that they mature in succession. Avoid midsummer sowings in warm areas, because high temperatures also impede germination. If sowing an early type late, allow about ten weeks before frost is expected for the pods to ripen. Where winters

are mild, sow hardy, early-maturing cultivars in late fall to overwinter.

Sow the seed 1¼in (3cm) deep in patches so that plants can support one another, spacing individual seeds 2–3in (5–7cm) apart. Alternatively, make a shallow, flat-bottomed planting trench up to 9in (23cm) wide, spacing seeds 2in (5cm) apart each way (see "Wide trenches," p.500). The trenches should be 24–36in (60–90cm) apart, using wider spacing for tall cultivars. Seed may also be sown in double rows 9in (23cm) apart, spacing seeds ½in (1cm) apart.

Routine cultivation

Protect seedlings against birds with horizontal netting as pea guards. Once tendrils have developed, remove the pea guards and erect supports: use wire netting, pea nets, or twiggy brush inserted into the soil on either side of a trench. Semileafless and dwarf types need less support. When the peas have several leaves, mulch them to keep the roots cool.

Once plants are flowering and forming pods, water every week (unless rainfall is high) at a rate of 5 gallons/sq yd (22 liters/sq m).

Pests and diseases

Aphids (p.654) and pea moths (p.665) are the most troublesome pests. Many types of animal pests will eat pea plants and seeds. Damping off (p.658), foot and root rots (p.660), Southern blight (p.670), and *Fusarium* wilt (p.661) are occasional problems.

Growing under cover

Early spring and late fall sowings may be made under cover; grow dwarf peas under row cover for early or overwintering crops.

Harvesting and storing

Harvest early types 11–12 weeks after sowing, and main-season peas after 13–14 weeks. Pick

SUPPORTING PEAS

When seedlings have developed tendrils, push pea sticks into the ground, as upright as possible, all around the outside of the patch (above). As the peas grow, the tendrils wrap around the pea sticks and the peas grow up them (right).

edible-podded types when the immature peas are just forming inside the pods, shelling peas and sugar snap types when the pods

have swollen. Edible-podded types may be left to mature and shelled normally. All may be frozen. For storing pods on plants, see *Drying Beans*, p.533.

Fava beans (*Vicia faba*)

These annual plants are also known as broad beans. They range in height from 12in (30cm) for dwarf cultivars to about 5ft (1.5m), with an average spread of 18in (45cm). Fava beans are grouped according to the time they take to mature. The broad pods are up to 1in (2.5cm) wide and 3–6in (7–15cm) long, with green, white, or pinkish-red seeds ¾–1in (2–2.5cm) long. The immature bean seeds, as well as the young pods and leafy shoot tips, may be cooked. Fava beans can be sauteed or boiled and are a good addition to salads and soups. The shelled beans freeze well.

Fava beans are a cool-season crop, growing satisfactorily only at temperatures below about 59°F (15°C). Some cultivars are very hardy, the immature plants surviving temperatures of 14°F (-10°C) on well-drained soil. Some that are adapted to higher temperatures have recently been bred. Fava beans need full sun, but fall sowings for overwintering benefit from a sheltered site, in reasonably fertile soil. Rotate fava bean crops (see p.498). The plants need low nitrogen levels (see p.504) because their root nodules fix atmospheric nitrogen.

Sowing and planting

Sow seed *in situ* in spring and early summer as soon as the ground is workable. Seed germinates at

Dwarf fava beans

fairly low temperatures. For an early crop, sow seed in late fall to early winter of the previous year—the plants need only be 1in (2.5cm) tall before winter. In very cold areas seed may be sown indoors in winter and transplanted outside in spring after the risk of frost has passed.

Sow seed about 1½in (4cm) deep, spaced about 9in (23cm) apart each way. Grow either in double rows, with 3ft (90cm) between the pairs of rows, or evenly spaced in blocks across a bed. The taller cultivars may be supported with strands of wire attached to strong stakes or poles placed around the rows or blocks of plants. If necessary, dwarf cultivars can be supported with twigs to keep their pods clear of the ground. Overwintering crops and

those sown in early spring may be protected with cloches or floating mulches in the early stages of growth.

Routine cultivation

Water only in dry spells, but water thoroughly every ten days when in flower. Once flowering starts, pinch out the growing tips in order to encourage pods to form and to combat aphids. Hill up plants in the winter to protect them.

Pests and diseases

Rodents (p.668), birds (p.655), aphids, (p.654), and foot and root rots (p.660) may affect fava beans.

PINCHING OUT

When the beans are in full flower, pinch out the growing tip of each plant. This may remove any aphids, and concentrates the plant's energy into producing beans.

Harvesting and storing

Harvest fava beans that were sown in the spring after 12–16 weeks, and those that were sown in the fall after 28–35 weeks. Pick them while the pods are plump with the swelling beans and before they become leathery. The beans may be frozen, or dried at the end of the season for use during the winter months as for snap beans (see pp.532–533).

Bulb and stem vegetables

Vegetables grown for their bulbs or stems include members of the onion family as well as a varied group of other plants that, with the exception of Florence fennel, are mostly hardy and slow-maturing. Celeriac, kohlrabi, and Florence fennel form swollen stems just above ground level,

rather than true bulbs. The onion family should be rotated as one group; for rotation groups for the other vegetables, see p.498. Both asparagus and rhubarb are perennial vegetables that should be planted in permanent beds that have been specially prepared for them.

Garlic
Leeks
Green onions
Celery
Bulb onions
Red bulb onions
Florence fennel
Asparagus
Shallots

Bulb onions (*Allium cepa*)

These are grown as annuals. The bulbs may be rounded, flattened, or have a long, torpedo shape. They normally have brown or yellow skins with white flesh, although some have red skin and pinkish-white flesh; the leaves grow 6–18in (15–45cm) long. Immature and mature bulbs are eaten either raw or cooked. Some cultivars are suitable for storage. The green-leaved thinnings may be used as green onions (see p.536).

Bulb onions are a cool-season, frost-tolerant crop, growing best at 55–75°F (13–24°C). Cool temperatures are required in the early stages of growth. Cultivars need different day lengths in order for the bulbs to swell; long-day types should be chosen for northern latitudes, and short-day types for southern latitudes (see also "Day length," pp.494–495).

Grow them in a sunny site, on fertile, medium to light soil that is well drained. Prepare the soil by digging in a good deal of well-rotted manure, preferably the fall before planting. Do not plant on newly manured ground. A balanced fertilizer may be worked into the seedbed before sowing. They have low nitrogen requirements (see p.504).

Sowing and planting

Onions may be raised from seed or sets (small bulbs specially grown and harvested immature the previous year). Seed is cheaper but slower to develop; sets are easier to grow but only available for certain cultivars, and more prone to bolting prematurely. Bulb onions require a long growing season, particularly if large bulbs are required or if they are to be stored.

Sow in spring when the soil is workable, on a firm seedbed, sowing seed very thinly ½in (1cm) deep, in rows 9–12in (23–30cm) apart. Thin out the seedlings in stages. For the highest yield of medium-sized onions, space 1½in (4cm) apart; for larger onions, thin seedlings to 2–4in (5–10cm) apart.

To extend the growing season in northern latitudes, start under cover in seed flats or cell packs at temperatures of 50–59°F (10–15°C) from late winter to early spring. Harden off seedlings at the two-leaf stage and plant out at the appropriate spacing. Cell packs may also be multisown with five seeds per cell and each group planted out as a unit, with 10in (25cm) between them (see *Transplanting Leeks*, p.537).

Certain cultivars may be sown in summer or fall to overwinter for earlier crops the following year. This is inadvisable where winters are very severe or very wet because seeds may rot before germination. Traditional, summer-sown cultivars are reasonably hardy and may be sown *in situ* in late summer, thinning to 1in (2.5cm) apart in fall and in stages to the final spacing in spring. Japanese overwintering onions are also suitable for sowing at this time; they are hardier than other bulb onions, but are unsuitable for storage. The precise sowing date for these is critical. Sow during the summer at the recommended date for the area, spacing and thinning as above.

Most sets are planted in the early spring. If using heat-treated sets, consult the suppliers for planting times. Plant at the above spacing in shallow furrows so that the tips protrude just above the soil. Recently introduced sets for planting during the fall may be available.

Routine cultivation

Keep the site weed-free, especially when the onions are young. Onions are fairly shallow-rooted and need little water once established, except in very dry conditions. Overwintering onions may be given a nitrogen-rich organic liquid or dry fertilizer if necessary in spring.

Pests and diseases

Onion maggots (p.665), thrips (p.671), onion white rot (p.665), downy mildew (p.659), and, in storage, onion neck rot (p.665) are common problems that affect onions.

Harvesting and storing

Spring-sown bulb onions will take 12–18 weeks to mature; summer-sown onions up to 42 weeks. Pull or lift them as needed to use fresh.

For storage, wait until the leaves have died back naturally (do not bend them over by hand), and then carefully uproot all the onions. In sunny conditions, leave them in the sun to dry for about ten days, either hung in nets or supported off the

ground on an upturned seed flat to allow maximum ventilation. In wet conditions, hang them in a greenhouse. The outer skins and leaves must all be thoroughly dry before the bulbs are put into storage.

Handle the bulbs gently because any bruises may encourage storage rot. Do not store onions that are bull-necked; these should always be used first. Store onions either hanging in nets or braids (see *Storing Strings of Onions*, p.506) or packed carefully in layers in boxes. They must be kept at 32–45°F (0–7°C) and in low humidity (i.e., below 40 percent). Average storage life is three to six months, depending on the cultivar.

BULB ONIONS TO TRY

Onions for fall harvesting
'Albion' F1
'Carmen' F1 (pink)
'Copra'
'Super Star' F1
'Yellow Granex' F1
'Walla Walla'

Red onions (Use fresh or store)
'Cabernet'
'Ruby Ring'
'Redwing'

Traditional and Japanese overwintering onions
'Beltsville Bunching'
'Candy'
'Evergreen Hardy White'
'Ishikuro'
'Kincho'
'Sierra Blanca'
'Stuttgarter'
'Texas Supersweet'

STORING ONIONS IN A BOX

Prepare onions carefully for storing. Bull-necked onions (those with thick necks above the bulbs, see far right) should be rejected. Be careful not to damage any onions for storing—this encourages rot. Place them in layers in a box and store them in a cold place that is well ventilated and frost-free.

Green onions

Green onions, also called scallions or bunching onions, are cultivars of *Allium cepa* or *A. fistulosum* suitable for using young when leaves are 6in (15cm) tall, with a whitened shank and tiny bulb. 'Guardsman' is a popular early variety. For climate, soil needs, and pests and diseases, see "Bulb onions," p.535. Use lime on acidic soil (see p.625).

In spring, sow thinly *in situ*, in rows 4in (10cm) apart, or bands 3in (7cm) wide and 6in (15cm) apart. For continuous crops, sow every three weeks in summer. Overwintering cultivars (e.g., 'Red Baron' and 'Evergreen Hardy White') may be sown in late summer for an early spring crop; protect in winter with covers. Water the onions in dry conditions.

THINNING GREEN ONIONS

If densely sown, harvest seedling green onions to leave the others spaced 1in (2.5cm) apart. Those remaining will continue to grow and can be harvested as needed.

Pickling onions

These bulb onion cultivars produce small, white bulbs (also known as mini-onions) in northern latitudes, and larger bulbs in southern latitudes. They may be used when they reach about thumbnail size, either fresh or for pickling. Cultivars include 'Purplette' and 'Pearl Drop'. They prefer fertile soil, but tolerate fairly poor soil. For climate, cultivation, and pests and diseases, see "Bulb onions," p.535.

In spring sow seed *in situ*, either broadcast or in bands about 4in (10cm) wide, spacing seeds ½in (1cm) apart. Thin them only if larger onions are required. Harvest them after about eight weeks when the foliage has died back; use them fresh, or dry and store as for bulb onions (see p.535) until required for pickling.

Pickling onions

Shallots (*Allium cepa* Aggregatum Group)

These distinctly flavored onion-shaped bulbs form clumps of about a dozen bulbs. There are yellow- and red-skinned forms; all may be eaten raw or cooked, and used fresh or after storing. The leaves of young shallots may be used as green onions. Suitable cultivars are 'Ambition', 'Saffron', 'Pikant', and 'Santé'.

Climate and soil requirements, routine cultivation, and pests and diseases are as for bulb onions (see p.535). Buy virus-free sets that are ideally about ¾in (2cm) in diameter. Plant in early spring or during winter

in mild areas. Plant as for bulb onion sets (see p.535), spacing the sets about 7in (18cm) apart each way. Each set will develop into a clump, maturing in early summer. For an early crop of green leaves, plant small sets in the fall, spacing them in the ground, or in seed trays under cover about 1in (2.5cm) apart.

Harvest green leaves as needed. For good-sized bulbs, do not pick the leaves; lift the bulbs once the foliage has died down. To store them, dry as for bulb onions (see p.535); good stocks store for up to a year.

PLANTING SHALLOTS

Make a furrow ½in (1cm) deep. Push the sets into the furrow about 7in (18cm) apart so that the tips show above the soil.

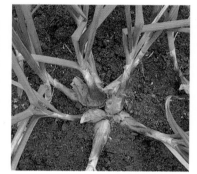

Shallots

Welsh onions (*Allium fistulosum*)

These onions are very hardy perennials. They have hollow leaves up to 18in (45cm) tall and ½in (1cm) in diameter, growing in clumps of 9in (23cm) diameter on average; the bases of the leaves are thickened at and below ground level. The leaves remain green all year, even at temperatures as low as 14°F (-10°C), so they are a useful winter vegetable. The leaves and tiny bulbs may be eaten either raw or cooked.

Climate and soil requirements, cultivation, and pests and diseases are as for bulb onions (see p.535). Sow seed *in situ* in spring or summer in rows about 12in (30cm) apart. Thin the seedlings in stages until they are about 9in (23cm) apart, or propagate by dividing established clumps and carefully replanting the younger, outer sections of the clumps to the above spacing. Leaves may be harvested

Welsh onions

from 24 weeks after sowing; cut individual leaves as required, or pull up part or all of the clump. Established clumps can become very thick and should be divided every two or three years. Welsh onions do not store well.

Asian bunching onions

These have been developed from Welsh onions. They are perennials usually grown as annuals or biennials for harvesting at any stage from seedlings to large plants. Mature plants have thickened, white shafts 1in (2.5cm) in diameter and 6in (15cm) tall. All parts are edible. There are cultivars for planting and harvesting year-round, and for a wide range of climatic conditions.

For soil requirements, see "Bulb onions" (p.535). Sow seed *in situ* in spring and summer, in rows 12in (30cm) apart. Thin out in stages up to 6in (15cm) apart, depending on the size required. Seed may also be sown in trays and planted out. Sow the hardier cultivars, such as 'Heshiko' or 'Ishikura',

in fall and overwinter to use in early spring. Some cultivars, such as 'Ishikura', may be hilled up several times during growth to obtain long, white shafts. Young leaves may be picked four weeks after sowing.

Asian bunching onions

Leeks (*Allium porrum*)

These are biennials grown as annuals, reaching up to 18in (45cm) tall and 6in (15cm) across. The edible part is the sweetly flavored, thick, white shank that forms below long, blue-green leaves. This may be blanched by hilling it up or by deep planting. Leeks with short, thick shanks are called pot leeks. All types are used cooked, as a vegetable or in soups.

Leeks are a cool-season crop, and grow best below 75°F (24°C), but will tolerate higher temperatures if kept moist. Cultivars range from early and moderately hardy to late and very hardy. Grow in sunny sites on fertile, moisture-retentive soil, working in plenty of manure or compost and a nitrogen-rich fertilizer if the soil is low in nitrogen (high levels are needed; see p.504). Do not plant on compacted soils. Rotate leeks if possible (see p.498).

Sowing and planting

Leeks need a long growing season; start them as early in the year as possible, sowing in succession. Sow ½in (1cm) deep in an outdoor seedbed for transplanting when 8in (20cm) tall. Alternatively, sow *in situ* in rows 12in (30cm) apart.

Leek plants

SOWING IN A CELL FLAT

Fill a cell flat with seed-starting mix to within ½in (1cm) of the top. Sow 4 leek seeds in each cell on the surface of the soil. Cover with a thin layer of soil mix, and water lightly.

Thin or transplant seedlings at the three-leaf stage to 6in (15cm) apart. Use closer spacing if smaller leeks are preferred. For well-blanched stems, make holes 6–8in (15–20cm) deep with a dibber and drop a seedling in each, making sure that the roots reach the soil at the base. Water gently, then allow soil to fall in around the plants as they grow. Leeks may also be planted on flat ground and blanched by hoeing up soil around the stems, 2in (5cm) at a time, as they grow.

To extend the growing season, sow under cover as for bulb onions (see p.535). Leeks respond well to being multisown in modules with up to four seeds per cell. Plant out the groups of seedlings at an even spacing of 9in (23cm).

Routine cultivation

Water thoroughly until the leeks are well established, and thereafter only in exceptionally dry conditions. Keep beds weed-free. Mulch to retain soil moisture if necessary.

Pests and diseases

Stem and bulb nematodes (see "Nematodes," p.664), thrips (p.671), onion maggots (p.665), and onion white rot (p.665) are likely problems.

TRANSPLANTING LEEKS

Each section of a cell pack may be planted out as a whole; plant the clumps 9in (23cm) apart.

SINGLE SEEDLINGS

Leeks sown outdoors can be transplanted to their final site in holes 6–8in (15–20cm) deep and 4–6in (10–15cm) apart.

Harvesting and storing

Leeks may be harvested 16–20 weeks after sowing but can stand for many months. Lift them as required starting from summer onward; the hardy cultivars may be lifted throughout winter into spring, except in very severe climates. Leeks do not store well out of the ground. If the site they occupy is required, prolong the season by digging them up and heeling them in elsewhere.

HEELING IN LEEKS

To store outdoors, lift the leeks and lean them against one side of a "V"-shaped trench. Cover the roots and white stems with soil and firm lightly. Lift and use as required.

LEEKS TO TRY

'Arkansas' l
'Bandit' l
'Blue Solaise' l
'Giant Musselburgh' m
'King Richard' e
'Lancelot' e
'Lexton' l
'Lincoln' (all season)
'Megaton' e
'Roxton' e
'Tadorna' l

Key
e early
m mid-season
l late

Garlic (*Allium sativum*)

Biennials grown as annuals, garlic plants grow up to 2ft (60cm) tall with a spread of about 6in (15cm). Each produces an underground bulb up to 2in (5cm) in diameter. There are pink- and white-skinned forms, and many selections are available that are adapted to different climatic zones. Garlic is grown mainly for the strongly flavored cloves, used for seasoning, may be eaten both cooked and raw, and are either used fresh or may be stored for a year-round supply. Garlic greens can also be cut and used fresh in salads or pesto or sauteed and added to soups.

Garlic tolerates a wide range of climates, but needs a period of one to two months at about 32–50°F (0–10°C) in winter. Use those recommended for your area. Garlic grows best in an open, sunny spot on light soil that does not have to be very fertile, so do not grow it on freshly manured ground. Good drainage is vital. Garlic needs low levels of nitrogen (see p.504).

Sowing and planting

For planting, split off individual cloves at least ½in (1cm) in diameter from a mature bulb. Always use healthy, virus-free stock. To produce large bulbs, garlic needs a long growing season, so wherever possible plant cloves in the fall. In very cold areas and on heavy soils, delay planting until the early spring, or plant the cloves in cell packs in winter, one per section. Then place the cell packs in a sheltered site outdoors to provide them with the necessary cold period. Plant them out in the garden after they have started to sprout in spring.

Plant the cloves upright with the flat base-plates downward, at about twice their own depth. Space them about 7in (18cm) apart each way or 4in (10cm) apart in rows

PLANTING GARLIC CLOVES

Garlic cloves can be planted directly into the ground between fall and spring, with their tips pointing up.

12in (30cm) apart. The bulbs tend to push themselves upward as they grow.

Routine cultivation

Little attention is required during growth other than keeping the beds free of weeds. For pests and diseases that may affect garlic, see "Bulb onions," p.535.

Harvesting and storing

Garlic takes between 16 and 36 weeks to mature, depending on the strain and when it has been planted. Uproot the plants as soon as the leaves have started to fade

so that the bulbs do not resprout; if they are allowed to resprout they are much more likely to rot when stored.

Dry them thoroughly after lifting as for bulb onions (see p.535). Handle the bulbs very carefully when preparing them for storage to avoid bruising. Store the bulbs hanging in bunches or braids made with the dried leaves or place them loose on trays kept in dry conditions at 41–50°F (5–10°C). Garlic may be stored for up to 10 months, depending on the strain and storage conditions.

STORING GARLIC

After harvesting the garlic, tie the leaves loosely together with raffia or braid them. Then hang each bunch in a cool, dry place.

Celery (*Apium graveolens*)

A biennial plant, celery grows to 12–24in (30–60cm) tall, with a spread of 12in (30cm). Traditional trench celery has large, white, pink, or red stems that are blanched before use. Self-blanching types have creamy-yellow stems that may be partially blanched. There are green-stemmed types, and intermediates are also available. Celery stalks are eaten raw or cooked, and the leaves used as a seasoning or garnish.

As a temperate-climate crop, celery grows best at 59–70°F (15–21°C). Depending on the cultivar and conditions, it tolerates light or moderate frost; trench cultivars with red stems are hardiest. Some have improved resistance to bolting. Grow celery in a sunny site in fertile, moisture-retentive, but well-drained soil; lime acidic soil (see p.625). Rotate celery if possible (see p.498); avoid planting it near parsnips or carrots, which have similar pest problems. Dig plenty of well-rotted

Celery seedlings in a block

organic matter into the soil before planting. For trench celery, prepare a trench 15in (38cm) wide and 12in (30cm) deep in the fall before planting; work in manure or compost, and replace the soil to ground level. Celery needs high nitrogen levels (see p.504).

Sowing and planting

It is possible to sow celery in spring *in situ* after all risk of frost is past, but for best results, start seeds

indoors in flats or cell packs at 59°F (15°C) no more than 10 weeks before the last expected frost. Sprinkle it onto the sowing mix or cover it shallowly; the seeds need light for germination. Do not sow too early; plants may bolt if the temperature falls below 50°F (10°C).

Thin out seedlings with four to six true leaves; plant out indoor-sown seedlings after all risk of frost is past. Reject any with blistered leaves. Plant self-blanching types 9in (23cm) apart in blocks to increase natural blanching. Young plants may be covered with floating row cover, which should be removed after a month. Plant trench celery seedlings 15in (38cm) apart in single rows. They may be planted in trenches, or on flat ground.

Routine cultivation

Celery requires steady growth, with no checks from water shortage or sudden drops in temperature. Apply a nitrogen-rich granular or liquid fertilizer about one month after planting. Once the plants are established, water them weekly at a rate of 5 gallons/sq yd (22 liters/sq m).

To sweeten self-blanching types, tuck a thick layer of loose straw around the plants when they are 8in (20cm) tall. To blanch celery in a trench, tie the stems loosely together with soft string and fill in the trench gradually, hilling up the stems as they grow. If planted on flat ground, wrap specially made collars or 9in (23cm) strips of heavy, lightproof paper around the stems when the plants are 12in (30cm) tall. To extend the blanched area, add a second collar three weeks later. In winter, cover trench celery with straw to protect against cold.

Pests and diseases

Slugs (p.669), leafminers (p.663), cabbage root maggots (p.656),

CELERY TO TRY

Self-blanching
'Galaxy'
'Golden Self Blanching'

Trench
'Ideal'
'Matador'
'Picaor'
'Ventura'

Green
'Tango'
'Utah 52-70'

LIFTING CELERY

Lift self-blanching celery plants before the first frost. Clear the straw from around the stem and use a fork to uproot the whole plant.

boron deficiency (p.656), and fungal leaf spots (p.660), are the most common pests and diseases.

Harvesting and storing

Harvest self-blanching and green celery 11–16 weeks after planting and trench celery in late fall. Cut the stalks before they become pithy. Before frost threatens, lift and store the remaining plants in high humidity in a cool, frost-free place. They will keep for several weeks.

BLANCHING CELERY

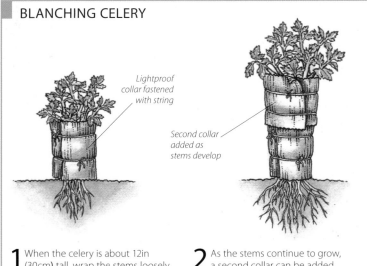

Lightproof collar fastened with string

Second collar added as stems develop

1 When the celery is about 12in (30cm) tall, wrap the stems loosely with lightproof paper so that the leaves are still exposed to the light.

2 As the stems continue to grow, a second collar can be added to blanch the new growth.

Celeriac (*Apium graveolens* var. *rapaceum*)

This is a biennial plant that grows about 12in (30cm) tall with a spread of 15in (38cm). The swollen "bulb" at the stem base can be cooked or grated raw in salads. The leaves are used for seasoning and garnishing.

Celeriac is a cool-temperate crop, withstanding temperatures of 14°F (-10°C) if the crowns are protected with straw. Plants tolerate light shade if the soil is moist. For soil requirements, see "Celery,"

opposite; celeriac needs low nitrogen levels (see p.504).

Sowing and planting

Celeriac needs a six-month growing season for the bulb to develop. Germination may be erratic. Sow seed indoors in early spring, preferably in cell packs. If using trays, prick out the seedlings to 2–3in (5–7cm) apart or pot them singly into small pots or modules. Harden off the young plants before planting out when they are about 3in (7cm) tall. Space them 12–15in (30–38cm) apart with their crowns at soil level, not buried.

Routine cultivation

Mulch after planting, and water well, especially in dry conditions. Plants may be fertilized during the growing season (see "Celery," see opposite). Toward the end of the summer, remove some of the coarse, outer leaves to expose the crowns; this encourages the bulbs to develop. To protect from cold, tuck a loose layer of straw 4–6in (10–15cm) thick around the crowns.

Pests and diseases

Celeriac may be affected by the same pests and diseases as celery (see opposite), but is normally healthy.

PLANTING OUT CELERIAC FROM A CELL PACK

Plant out celeriac from a module when it is 3–4in (8–10cm) high with 6 or 7 leaves. Space the young plants 12–15in (30–38cm) apart; take care not to bury the crowns.

CULTIVATING AND PROTECTING CELERIAC

1 Toward the end of the summer, as the swollen stem bases develop, remove a few of the outer leaves to expose the crowns.

2 Before the first frost, mulch around the base of the plants with a 6in (15cm) layer of straw to protect the crowns.

Harvesting and storing

Celeriac may be harvested from late summer until the following spring. The bulbs are ready for use when they are 3–5in (7–13cm) in diameter.

The flavor is best and the bulbs will keep longer if the roots are left in the ground for the winter. Where winters are very severe, dig up the plants in early winter without damaging the bulbs; trim off the outer leaves, leaving a central tuft, and store the plants in boxes of damp soil in a cool, frost-free place.

CELERIAC TO TRY

'Brilliant'
'Diamant'
'Mars'
'President'
'Prague'

Asparagus (*Asparagus officinalis*)

Asparagus is perennial and may be productive for up to 20 years. Its light, fernlike foliage grows more than 7ft (2.1m) tall, with a spread of about 2ft (60cm). It is cultivated for the delicious young shoots or spears that push through the ground in spring. Male and female plants are available; the females produce berries. Male plants are higher yielding; choose all-male, F1 hybrid cultivars for the best yield and results. Asparagus is normally eaten cooked.

Asparagus is a cool-season crop, growing best at 61–75°F (16–24°C) in regions with cool winters that provide the necessary dormant period. Choose a sunny site, but avoid exposed locations and frost pockets. Asparagus tolerates a wide range of moderately fertile soils although acidic soils should be limed (see p.625). Good drainage is essential. Do not make a new asparagus bed where asparagus has been grown before, because soilborne diseases may persist.

Remove all perennial weeds from the site and prepare the ground by digging it over and working in manure or compost. Asparagus may also be grown in raised beds to improve drainage. It has low nitrogen requirements (see p.504).

Sowing and planting

Asparagus is traditionally grown by planting one-year-old purchased plants or "crowns" in spring. The crowns are fleshy and must never be allowed to dry out before planting.

Grow them about 15in (38cm) apart, either in single or double rows, with the rows spaced 12in (30cm) apart. Plant the crowns about 4in (10cm) deep by first making a small trench with a central, mounded ridge along the flat base. Spread out the roots evenly over the ridge and cover them with soil to the level of the crowns. Fill in the rest of the trench with soil gradually as the stems grow, always leaving 3–4in (8–10cm) of the stems exposed.

ASPARAGUS TO TRY

Traditional
'Martha Washington'
'Mary Washington'
'Purple Passion'
'Viking'

All-male cultivars
'Jersey Giant'
'Jersey King'
'Jersey Knight'
'Jersey Supreme'

Raising asparagus from seed is cheaper, but the results are more variable. Sow seed 1in (2.5cm) deep *in situ* in spring, and thin out to about 3in (7cm) apart. Plant out the largest the following spring; alternatively, sow indoors in modules in early spring at

PLANTING ASPARAGUS CROWNS

Dig a trench about 12in (30cm) wide and 8in (20cm) deep with a central, mounded ridge that is 4in (10cm) high. Place the asparagus crowns on the ridge about 15in (38cm) apart. Spread the roots out evenly and cover them with about 2in (5cm) of soil to the level of the crowns.

CUTTING BACK ASPARAGUS STEMS

Using pruners, cut back the stems in the fall to within about 1in (2.5cm) of ground level.

55–61°F (13–16°C). The seedlings grow rapidly, and may be planted out in a permanent bed in early summer.

Routine cultivation
Asparagus requires little attention other than keeping the beds free of weeds. Hoe shallowly to avoid damaging the roots. When the foliage turns yellow in the fall, cut the stems back to about 1in (2.5cm) above the soil.

Pests and diseases
Slugs (p.669) at an early stage and asparagus beetle (p.654) on more mature plants are the most serious pests. The soilborne

fungal disease crown rot (p.658) may destroy plants in long-established beds.

Harvesting and storing
Asparagus must be allowed to build into a strong plant before it is harvested in mid-spring. Good, modern cultivars may be cut lightly in the second season. The following year, limit cutting to a six-week period; subsequently, cutting may continue over eight weeks if the plants are growing well. Harvest the spears when they are about 6in (15cm) tall and fairly thick. Cut each one at an angle, taking care not to damage nearby spears. Remaining spears will continue to grow. Asparagus freezes well.

HARVESTING ASPARAGUS

When the spears are 5–6in (12–15cm) high, cut each stalk 1–2in (2.5–5cm) below soil level.

Kohlrabi (*Brassica oleracea* Gongylodes Group)

These annual plants from the brassica family are grown for the white-fleshed, turniplike, swollen stem or "bulb" that forms just above the ground. Kohlrabi reaches a height of 12in (30cm) and has an average spread of 12in (30cm). The outer skin is green (sometimes described as "white") or purple. The bulbs are nutritious, well flavored, and used cooked or raw.

Kohlrabi is a cool-season crop, growing best at 64–77°F (18–25°C). Young plants tend to bolt prematurely in temperatures below about 50°F (10°C). For soil requirements, see "Siting cabbage-family crops," p.507. Kohlrabi grows well in light soils and withstands drought better than most brassicas. It has low nitrogen requirements (see p.504).

Sowing and planting
In mild climates, sow seed outdoors in succession from spring through

to late summer, using the hardier purple forms for late sowings. In hot climates, sow in spring and fall. Sow *in situ* either in rows about 12in (30cm) apart, thinning seedlings to about 7in (18cm) apart, or space the seeds about

Green kohlrabi

10in (25cm) apart in each direction. Under cover, sow earlier in gentle heat in flats or cell packs. Plant out seedlings when they are no more than 2in (5cm) tall. Protect early outdoor crops with cloches or floating mulches.

Routine cultivation
Kohlrabi is fast-maturing; little attention is required during growth other than keeping beds weed-free.

Pests and diseases
Flea beetles (p.660), cabbage root maggots (p.656), and clubroot (p.657) may affect kohlrabi. See also "Cultivation," p.507.

Harvesting and storing
Depending on the cultivar and season, kohlrabi may be ready for cutting 5–9 weeks after sowing. Traditional cultivars should be eaten when they are no larger than

KOHLRABI TO TRY

Traditional
'Purple Vienna'
'White Vienna'

Modern
'Grand Duke'
'Kolibri' F1
  (purple)
'Winner' F1

tennis balls or they will become woody; improved, modern cultivars are still tender at a diameter of about 4in (10cm).

Leave later crops in the ground until heavy frost threatens, the flavor deteriorates once lifted. In cold areas, harvest in fall. Leave a central tuft of leaves on each bulb to help keep them fresh; store them for up to two months in boxes of moist sand.

Florence fennel (*Foeniculum vulgare* var. *dulce*)

Grown as an annual, Florence, or sweet, fennel is distinct from the perennial herb fennel. The plants grow up to about 2ft (60cm) tall and have a spread of about 18in (45cm). The anise-flavored, flattened "bulb" of overlapping scales that develops at the base of the leaf stalks is eaten cooked or raw. The highly decorative fernlike foliage may be used as a flavoring or garnish.

Florence fennel tolerates a wide range of climates, from temperate to subtropical. It thrives at a warm, even temperature, but mature plants can withstand a light frost. Grow it in a sunny site, in very fertile, moisture-retentive,

but well-drained soil into which plenty of humus has been worked. Florence fennel grows well in light soils but must not be allowed to dry out. It has low nitrogen requirements (see p.504).

Sowing and planting
In cool, northern latitudes, sow seed from early to midsummer; traditional cultivars are likely to bolt if sown in spring, so use modern, bolt-resistant cultivars for earlier sowings. In warmer climates, sow in spring for a summer crop and again in late summer for a fall crop. Florence fennel does not transplant well and may bolt

prematurely if checked, so either sow seed *in situ* or in modules for transplanting when the seedlings have no more than four leaves. Space the young seedlings about 12in (30cm) apart each way. Early and late crops may be protected from the frost by covering with cloches or floating row cover.

Routine cultivation
Little attention is required; keep beds weed-free. Florence fennel needs to be kept moist, so water thoroughly and mulch. When bulbs start to swell, mound them up to half their height to make them whiter and sweeter.

Florence fennel

HARVESTING FLORENCE FENNEL

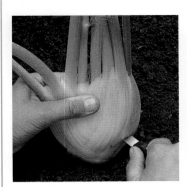

1 Cut the fennel bulb about 1in (2.5cm) above soil level. Leave the base in position.

2 Feathery leaves will usually sprout from the base of the stem within a few weeks.

Pests and diseases
Florence fennel rarely suffers from any pests or diseases. Most problems stem from lack of water, fluctuating temperatures, or from transplanting, all of which may cause bolting.

Harvesting and storing
Harvest the bulbs when they are well rounded, about 15 weeks after sowing, or two to three weeks after hilling up. Pull them up whole, or cut across the bulbs about 1in (2.5cm) above ground level. The stump will normally resprout to produce sprigs of ferny foliage that may be used for flavoring or as a garnish. Florence fennel does not store well; eat it as fresh as possible.

FLORENCE FENNEL TO TRY

'Finale' **Br**
'Orion'
'Perfection' **Br**
'Romanesco'
'Sweet Florence'
'Wadenromen'

Key
Br Bolt-resistant

Rhubarb (*Rheum* x *cultorum*)

This perennial lasts more than 20 years in good conditions. Rhubarb grows about 24in (60cm) tall or more and up to 6ft (2m) across. The leaves may be 18in (45cm) wide. The pale-green or pinkish-red leaf stalks, which may be 2ft (60cm) long, are harvested young and used cooked.

Rhubarb is a temperate-climate crop and does not thrive in high temperatures; the roots survive lows down to -20°F (-30°C). Recommended cultivars include 'Valentine', 'Crimson Red', 'Glaskins Perpetual', and 'Victoria'. It grows on a range of soils, as long as they are rich and well drained. Before planting, dig in plenty of rotted manure or compost. Rhubarb needs medium nitrogen levels when young and very high levels once mature (see p.504).

Sowing and planting
Rhubarb is normally propagated by planting "sets," each consisting of a fleshy rootstock with at least one bud. Sets are about 4in (10cm) in diameter. Plant in the dormant season from fall to spring, preferably fall. Buy virus-free sets, or separate a set from a healthy, two- or three-year-old plant, once leaves have died back, by lifting the plant and slicing through the crown; then replant the parent. On light soils, plant so that 1in (2.5cm) of soil covers the buds; on heavy or wet soils, plant with buds just above ground level. Space 3ft (90cm) apart.

Rhubarb may also be raised from seed, although the results are variable. Sow seed in spring, 1in (2.5cm) deep in rows 12in (30cm) apart, in a seedbed outdoors. Thin the seedlings to 6in (15cm) apart, and plant out the strongest ones in their permanent positions in fall, or in spring the following year.

Routine cultivation
Mulch the plants heavily, and water them in dry weather. Apply a heavy dressing of compost every fall or spring. If plants lack vigor, apply fish

DIVIDING RHUBARB

1 Lift or expose the crown. Cut through it carefully using a spade, ensuring there is at least 1 main bud on each section. Prepare the soil by digging in compost.

2 Replant the sections (sets) 2½–3ft (75–90cm) apart. Fill in around each root so that the bud is just above the surface. Firm, and rake around the bud.

emulsion or another nitrogen fertilizer in spring as well. Remove any flowering stems.

For extra-tender stems, try forcing rhubarb. Cover the dormant crowns in late winter with a 4in (10cm) layer of straw or leaves, then a large clay pot or a large bucket, at least 18in (45cm) tall; leave this on for about four weeks until stems are large enough to harvest.

Pests and diseases
Crown rot (p.658) and viruses (p.672) may attack mature plants.

Harvesting and storing
Harvest in spring and early summer. With plants raised from sets, starting pulling lightly the year after planting; with seed-raised plants, wait until the second year. In subsequent years, pull heavily until quality starts to deteriorate in summer. Forced stems are ready about three weeks earlier than unforced ones.

HARVESTING RHUBARB

When the rhubarb stems are ready, they can be harvested by gripping each stem at the base and twisting it while pulling it upward and outward.

FORCING RHUBARB

For an earlier, tender crop, cover the dormant buds (see upper inset) in winter with straw or leaves inside a forcing pot or any large container that excludes the light. The plant will produce tender, pink stems a few weeks later (see lower inset).

Root and tuberous vegetables

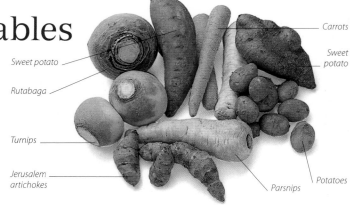

Root vegetables are the mainstay of many kitchen gardens. As the name suggests, most are grown for their swollen roots or tubers. A few, such as turnips, beets, and taro, are also used for their young, leafy growth; some radish cultivars also produce edible seed pods. A variety of root vegetables can be grown and harvested in succession for a steady supply; many store very easily, sometimes still in the ground, for use throughout the winter. Salsify and scorzonera may both be overwintered in milder areas for their flowering shoots produced in the spring.

Carrots

Sweet potato

Sweet potato

Rutabaga

Turnips

Jerusalem artichokes

Parsnips

Potatoes

Beets (*Beta vulgaris* subsp. *vulgaris*)

Beets are a biennial plant grown as an annual. They grows to about 6in (15cm) tall and about 5in (12cm) across. The swollen root forms at ground level and may be round, flat, or cylindrical. It is on average 2in (5cm) in diameter, and about 4in (10cm) or more deep in the long forms. The flesh is normally red but may be yellow, white, or even have pink and white concentric rings. The skin is similarly red, yellow, or off-white. The sweetly flavored roots are mainly used cooked, either fresh or stored, but may also be pickled. The fresh, young leaves (tops) may be used as greens.

Beets grow best and develop the deepest colors in cool, even temperatures, ideally of 61°F (16°C). Grow them in a sunny site on rich, light soil with high nitrogen levels (see p.504). Apply half the nitrogen before sowing. Lime very acid soils.

THINNING SEEDLINGS

When the beet seedlings have produced 3 or 4 leaves, thin clumps growing close together to the required spacing by pinching off the top green leaves at soil level without disturbing the remaining seedlings.

Sowing and planting

Beet "seeds" each contain a cluster of two or three seeds, the seedlings of which must be thinned out early. Some cultivars, such as 'Mobile' and 'Monopoly' have been bred to produce single, or monogerm, seed, which needs little or no thinning.

Soak seed in warm water for 30 minutes before sowing to overcome slow germination. Some cultivars may bolt if sown early or in unfavorable conditions so choose bolt-resistant cultivars for early sowings.

In spring, sow seed *in situ* outdoors when the soil is workable and has warmed up to at least 45°F (7°C). Sow seed ½–¾in (1–2cm) deep, with the spacing determined by the type of beets and the size required. Grow beets in rows 12in (30cm) apart, thinning to 3–4in (7–10cm) apart. For pickling beets about 1in (2.5cm) in diameter, space rows 3in (7cm) apart, thinning seedlings to 2½in (6cm).

For earlier crops, sow in early spring under covers, in cold frames, or indoors in seed trays or modules, transplanting outside when seedlings are 2in (5cm) tall. Sow three monogerm or ordinary seeds per cell (see "Sowing in containers," p.501), thinning as necessary. Early beets needs plenty of space, so plant indoor-sown seedlings in rows 9in (23cm) apart, then thin them to 3½in (9cm) apart. For continuous supplies of young beets and beet tops, sow seeds every two to three weeks until hot summer weather begins. Sow cultivars intended for storage in late summer, at least ten weeks before the first heavy frost is expected. In the deep South, beets may be grown through the winter.

Routine cultivation

Beets need little extra care, so water infrequently, only to prevent the soil from drying out, every two weeks. Apply the remaining nitrogenous fertilizer during active growth.

Pests and diseases

Beets may be affected by cutworms (p.658), aphids (p.654), damping off (p.658), fungal leaf spots (p.660), and boron deficiency (p.656).

HARVESTING BEETS

Grip the stems and pull the beet from the soil; it should lift easily because it is shallow-rooted. Avoid damaging the roots, which will bleed if they are cut.

Harvesting and storing

Harvest beets at any stage from small, immature roots 1in (2.5cm) in diameter to fully mature roots; this will be from 7–13 weeks after sowing, depending on the cultivar, the season, and the size required. In mild areas, beets may be left in well-drained soil in winter, protected with a layer of straw up to 6in (15cm) deep, but they eventually become rather woody. Otherwise lift them before severe frost. Twist off the leaves (cutting causes bleeding) and store the roots in moist sand in a frost-free place. Beets normally keep until mid-spring.

BEETS TO TRY

'Bull's Blood'
'Burpee's Golden' (stores well) **Br**
'Chioggia Striped' **Br**
'Cylindra'
'Detroit Dark Red'
'Early Wonder'
'Formanova'
'Lutz Green Leaf'
'Merlin' F1
'Pacemaker III'
'Red Ace' F1 **Br**
'Touchstone Gold'

Key
Br Bolt resistant

Rutabagas (*Brassica napus* Napobrassica Group)

Biennials from the brassica family, rutabagas are grown as annuals and reach a height of 10in (25cm) with a spread of 15in (38cm). The root flesh is usually yellow, but sometimes white, and the skin generally purple, buff, or a combination of both. The large, often irregularly shaped, underground roots, which may be 4in (10cm) in diameter and as long, are sweetly flavored and used cooked. This hardy, cool-season crop grows best on light, fertile soil with low nitrogen levels (see p.504). For climate and soil requirements, see "Siting cabbage-family crops," p.507.

Sowing and planting

Rutabagas need a growing season of up to 26 weeks to mature fully. Sow seed from early to late spring *in situ*, ¾in (2cm) deep, in rows 15in (38cm) apart, thinning early and in stages until the seedlings are about 9in (23cm) apart.

RUTABAGAS TO TRY

'Laurentian'
'Purple Yellow Top'
'Wilhelms-burger'

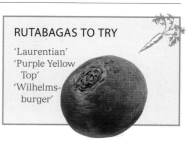

Routine cultivation
Keep beds weed-free; if conditions are very dry, water thoroughly to moisten the soil fully.

Pests and diseases
Downy mildew (p.659), powdery mildew (p.667), boron deficiency (p. 656), and flea beetles (p.660), unless grown under row cover, may affect rutabagas. Some cultivars are resistant to mildew. For other pests and diseases, see "Cultivation," p.507.

Harvesting and storing
Rutabagas generally mature in the fall and, being hardy, may be left in the soil until the end of the season, when they should be lifted carefully to prevent them from becoming woody; except in very cold climates, covering with a thick layer of straw provides sufficient protection until the rutabagas are lifted. Store rutabagas in piles outdoors or in wooden boxes under cover (see *Storing Carrots*, p.544) for up to four months.

MAKING A RUTABAGA PILE
Choose a sheltered, well-drained site and stack the roots on an 8in (20cm) layer of straw in a pyramid, with their necks facing out. Cover with a layer of longer straw. In very cold climates, protect further with a 4in (10cm) layer of soil.

Turnips (*Brassica rapa* Rapifera Group)

These are biennials from the brassica family grown as annuals. The plants are about 9in (23cm) tall with a spread of about 10in (25cm). The underground roots swell to 1–3in (2.5–7cm) in diameter and are round, fairly flat, or long. The flesh may be either white or yellow and the skin white, pink, red, or yellow. Young turnip leaves can be eaten as greens (see "Turnip tops and broccoli raab," p.512). Turnip greens are used either fresh or stored and are normally cooked.

Turnips are a temperate-climate crop, growing best at about 68°F (20°C). They are reasonably hardy, tolerating light frost. For general climate and soil requirements, see "Siting cabbage-family crops," p.507. Grow turnips in moist soil because they bolt prematurely in dry conditions. Early types, many of which are small and white, are fast-growing and excellent for early spring and summer crops; hardier types are used fresh during summer and winter and

for storage. They require low to medium nitrogen levels (see p.504).

Sowing and planting
Start sowing seed of early turnips in spring as soon as the ground is workable, or sow under cover. Make successive sowings at three-

HARVESTING TURNIPS

Harvest turnips by pulling them from the soil by their leaves. Do not leave them in the ground too long or they may become woody.

week intervals until early summer. Sow storage types from mid- to late summer *in situ*, ¾in (2cm) deep. Space early types in rows that are 9in (23cm) apart, thinning seedlings to 4in (10cm); space main-season types in rows 12in (30cm) apart, thinning to 6in (15cm).

Routine cultivation
Keep beds free from weeds. During dry conditions water thoroughly to moisten the soil completely.

Pests and diseases
Flea beetles (p.660) may seriously damage seedlings; other problems include cabbage root maggots (p.656), unless grown under insect-proof mesh, and boron deficiency (p.656). Wireworms will also bore into the roots, leaving behind brownish tunnels as they feed; this is rarely a serious condition, but discard all affected crops. For other pests and diseases, see "Cultivation," p.507.

Harvesting and storing
Harvest early turnips after about five weeks, storage types after six to ten weeks. Pull them before they become woody. Lift turnips for storage before the first frost, then store them for up to three or four months in outdoor piles covered with straw.

TURNIPS TO TRY
'Golden Ball'
'Hakurei' F1
'Purple Top White Globe'
'Royal Crown' F1
'Tokyo Cross' F1
'Topper'
'White Lady' F1

Taro (*Colocasia esculenta*)

These herbaceous, frost-tender perennials grow to about 3ft (1m) tall, with a spread of 24–28in (60–70cm). The plants have large, long-stalked leaves, which may either be green or greenish-purple. Taro, sometimes known as cocoyam, is grown for its large, swollen tubers, which are eaten

Taro plant

cooked. The young leaves and shoots are also edible, and may be cooked and used as greens.

Taro is a tropical and subtropical plant requiring temperatures of 70–81°F (21–27°C), with humidity levels over 75 percent. In temperate areas it needs a very sheltered, sunny site, or it may be grown under cover. Taro is adapted to short day lengths of about 12 hours (see "Day length," pp.494–495); it rarely produces flowers. Some forms are tolerant of light shade. Moisture-retentive soil is essential because many forms of taro are sensitive to dry soil conditions.

Fertile soil that has a high organic content and a slightly acid pH level of 5.5–6.5 is recommended. Taro requires medium to high levels of nitrogen (see p.504).

Sowing and planting
Seeds are rarely available, therefore propagation is usually from existing tubers. Plant mature tubers or portions of tubers with dormant buds *in situ* in well-prepared beds. Space the tubers about 18in (45cm) apart with 3ft (90cm) between rows.

Taro may also be propagated by cuttings. Sever the tops of tubers with a horizontal cut; each cutting should consist of several leaves 4–5in (10–12cm) long, a central growing point, and a small portion of the tuber. Plant the cuttings in their final locations at the above spacing; if the temperature is below the optimal 70°F (21°C), plant them in 8–10in (21–25cm) pots of potting mix to grow on under cover until the temperature is high enough for transplanting outside.

Routine cultivation
Taro needs a constant supply of water for the highest yields, so water regularly. Apply an organic mulch to conserve moisture, and feed with a balanced fertilizer at two- to three-week intervals. Keep beds free of weeds. The plants should be hilled up around the stems once they are established to encourage the tubers to develop.

Pests and diseases
These are rarely serious for taro that are grown in the open, but aphids (p.654), thrips (p.671), spider mites (p.670), and fungal leaf spots (p.660) may reduce tuber yields. Under cover, taro is vulnerable to the same pests and diseases as those grown outside; whiteflies (p.673) may also be troublesome.

Growing under cover

Propagate from tubers (see p.543). When these have rooted, transfer them to well-prepared greenhouse beds, 8–12in (21–30cm) pots, or grow bags, ensuring that the roots are disturbed as little as possible.

Water and feed the plants regularly, maintaining a temperature of 70–81°F (21–27°C)

and a humidity of more than 75 percent by damping down. Tubers that are cultivated under cover tend to be smaller than those grown outdoors.

Harvesting and storing

Taro is slow to develop and reach maturity. Harvest the tubers 16–24 weeks after planting when the leaves start to turn yellow

and plants die down. Lift taro grown in the open carefully using a fork; plants under cover may be lifted gently out of their pots or grow bags. Try not to damage the tubers because this can cause rotting.

Healthy tubers may be stored for about 8–12 weeks at a temperature of 52–55°F (11–13°C), with humidity of 85–90 percent.

Taro tuber

Carrots (*Daucus carota*)

These are biennials grown as annuals. Their swollen, orange taproots may be up to 3in (7.5cm) in diameter at the neck and up to about 12in (30cm) in length. The feathery, green foliage grows to about 24in (60cm), with a 12in (30cm) spread. Carrots are normally long and tapered but may be rounded. There are many types: small, slender early carrots; thick, heavy storage types, and colored varieties with purple, yellow, or cream-colored roots. All are eaten either cooked or raw.

Carrots are a cool-season crop, and tolerate the same temperatures as beets (see p.542). Grow in a sunny site on light, fertile soil. Deep-rooted types require

reasonably deep, stone-free soil. Work in plenty of organic matter, preferably in the fall before sowing. The fertile, loose soil of established raised beds is particularly suitable for growing carrots. Rake the soil into a fine tilth before sowing. Rotate carrots if possible (see p.498). They need very low nitrogen levels (see p.504).

Sowing and planting

Sow early types in spring *in situ* as soon as the soil is workable and has warmed up to 45°F (7°C). Earlier sowings may be made under cloches, in cold frames, or under floating mulches; remove these after a few weeks. Sow main season types from late spring until early summer. A second sowing of early types may be made in late summer and protected with cloches.

Sow seed sparingly about ½–¾in (1–2cm) deep, either broadcast or in rows 6in (15cm) apart. Thin early carrots to 3in (7cm) apart; main season carrots should be thinned to 1½in (4cm) to obtain medium-sized carrots or farther apart if large carrots are needed. Carrots do not transplant well unless sown in cell packs: sow seed of deep-rooted cultivars singly, those of round-rooted ones, several together. Round-rooted carrots sown in cells do not need thinning and should be planted out as a group at slightly wider spacing than for main crop carrots.

PROTECTION AGAINST CARROT RUST FLIES

Protect young carrots from carrot rust flies and other pests by growing them underneath insect-proof mesh. Secure it around the base to deter any intruders. This is most easily achieved by burying the edges of the mesh under 2in (5cm) of soil. Do not stretch the mesh too taut—this may open the weave and allow pests access.

Routine cultivation

Remove weeds diligently once the carrots have germinated, because the seedlings cannot compete with weeds. Continue until the carrot foliage hinders further weed growth. Water the soil deeply every two or three weeks.

Pests and diseases

Carrot rust flies (p.657) may be a serious problem; avoid by growing under insect-proof mesh or row cover. The egg-laying, adult fly is attracted by the smell of carrot foliage; thin in the evening, snipping off the seedlings at ground level and removing the tops from the site. Root

and leaf aphids (see "Aphids," p.654), viruses (see "Viruses," p.656), boron deficiency (p.655), and sclerotinia disease (p.669) may be troublesome.

Harvesting and storing

Harvest early cultivars about seven to nine weeks after sowing, main season cultivars after 10–11 weeks. Loosen the soil with a fork before pulling them out. On well-drained soils in areas with mild winters, carrots may be left in the soil in winter (see *Protecting Parsnips*, p.546). Otherwise lift them before heavy frost, cut or twist off the foliage, and store healthy roots in boxes in a cool, dry place for up to five months.

CARROTS TO TRY

Early
'Earlibird Nantes' F1
'Little Finger' (baby)
'Mokum' F1
'Nantes Half Long'
'Nelson' F1
'Parano' F1
'Sweetness'
'Thumbelina'
'Touchon'
'Yaya'

Maincrop
'Imperator'
'Danver's Half Long'
'Deep Purple' F1
'Eagle'
'Red Cored Chantenay'
'Royal Chantenay'
'Sugarsnax' F1

Storage and winter
'Bolero' F1
'Merida' F1

THIN SOWING

Sow carrot seeds about 1in (2.5cm) apart so that the seedlings will need little thinning later. The seed should be ½–¾in (1–2cm) deep.

HARVESTING YOUNG

Early cultivars can be harvested when they are very young. Pull them up in a bunch when they are 3–4in (8–10cm) long.

STORING CARROTS

Twist the foliage off the carrots; place them on a layer of sand in a box. Cover them with more sand and continue in layers.

Jerusalem artichokes (Helianthus tuberosus)

These are perennial plants, also known as sunchokes or girasoles. The distinctively flavored tubers are 2–4in (5–10cm) long, about 1½in (4cm) in diameter and, in most cultivars, very knobbly. 'Stampede' produces very large tubers. The plants may grow up to 10ft (3m) tall. The tubers are normally cooked but may be eaten raw. Jerusalem artichokes grow best in temperate climates and are very hardy. They tolerate a wide range of soils and require medium nitrogen levels (see p.504). They may be planted as a windbreak screen.

Smooth tubers

Knobbly Jerusalem artichoke tubers

Sowing and planting

Plant tubers as soon as the ground is workable in spring. Those the size of a hen's egg may be planted whole; cut large ones into pieces, each with several buds. Make a furrow, planting about 5in (12.5cm) deep and 12in (30cm) apart. Cover with soil.

Routine cultivation

When the plants are about 12in (30cm) tall, hill up the stems to half their height for stability. In late summer, cut the stems back to 5ft (1.5m), removing any flower heads at the same time. In very exposed sites, stake or support the stems. Water in very dry conditions. When the leaves start to yellow, cut the stems back to just above ground level.

Harvesting and storing

Harvest the tubers 16–20 weeks after planting. Lift them only when

PLANTING

Make a furrow 4–6in (10–15cm) deep. Place the tubers in the furrow 12in (30cm) apart with the main bud facing up. Cover carefully so the tubers are not dislodged.

CUTTING DOWN

Toward the end of the summer, cut down the stems to about 5ft (1.5m), so that the plants will not suffer wind damage. The tubers will continue to develop unchecked.

required, because they keep best in the ground, and take care not to damage the roots. Save a few tubers to replant or leave some in the soil for the following year. Otherwise, remove even small tubers because

they rapidly become invasive. In severe climates or on heavy ground, lift in early winter and store in a cellar or in piles outdoors (see *Making a Rutabaga Pile*, p.543) for up to five months.

Sweet potatoes (Ipomoea batatas)

These tender perennials are grown as annuals. They have trailing stems that grow to 10ft (3m) or more if unpruned. Cultivars vary considerably in leaf shape and tuber size, shape, and color. Tubers are eaten cooked; the leaves may be used in the same way as spinach (see p.519).

Sweet potatoes are tropical and subtropical plants that need a temperature of 75–79°F (24–26°C). They grow well in areas with long, hot summers. In cooler or short-summer areas, use black plastic mulch and row covers to stimulate better growth and yield. Most cultivars are short-day plants (see "Day length," pp.494–495).

Highly fertile, well-drained, sandy soil with a pH of 5.5–6.5 and medium to high nitrogen levels (see p.504) is ideal for this crop.

Sowing and planting

Wait until the soil has warmed before planting sweet potatoes. Most suppliers offer them as "slips," which are rooted shoots. You can also start your own slips from tubers, but some suppliers offer certified disease-free slips. Starting sweet potatoes from seed is not advisable because it takes up to a month longer for plants to produce tubers. Make raised ridges about 30in (75cm) apart, then plant the tubers 2–3in (5–7cm) deep in the ridge, spacing them 10–12in (25–30cm) apart. Optionally, take 8–10in (20–25cm) long stem cuttings

from mature plants and insert them to half their length just below the top of the ridge.

Routine cultivation

Water and weed regularly, and mulch to conserve moisture. Train shoots to spread around the plant. Apply a balanced fertilizer at two- to three-week intervals until the tubers have formed. Protect from winds.

Pests and diseases

Aphids (p.654), caterpillars (p.657), root-knot nematodes (p.668), fungal leaf spots (p.660), *Fusarium* wilt (p.661), southern blight (p.670), and various viruses (p.672) affect sweet potatoes growing outdoors. Under cover, whiteflies (p.673), thrips (p.671), and spider mites (p. 670) may be troublesome.

Growing under cover

If you want to grow sweet potatoes in the greenhouse, you can do so in grow bags or in beds in the ground. Take cuttings and insert three or four into 6in (15cm) pots. Maintain a minimum temperature of 77°F (25°C) and a humidity of more than 70 percent by damping down regularly. When roots develop, transfer plants to greenhouse beds or grow bags. Water regularly and remove the growing points of shoots longer than 2ft (60cm) to encourage lateral shoots. Keep the temperature below 82°F (28°C), and the growing area well ventilated.

Harvesting and storing

Harvest 12–16 weeks after planting, when the stems and leaves turn yellow. Lift the tubers with a fork,

Sweet potato plant

without damaging them and, for better flavor, leave in the sun to cure. In order to store sweet potatoes, they must first be cured for four to seven days at temperatures of 82–86°F (28–30°C) and humidity of 85–90 percent (see "Pumpkins and winter squashes," p.525). They may be stored in shallow trays at 50–59°F (10–15°C) for several months.

STEM CUTTINGS FOR GROWING UNDER COVER

1 Select healthy, vigorous shoots and cut them off the parent plant with pruners.

2 Remove the lower leaves and trim each shoot below a node to 8–10in (20–25cm). Insert in pots and continue growing under cover.

SWEET POTATOES TO TRY

'Beauregard'
  (orange-fleshed)
'Centennial' (orange-fleshed)
'Georgia Jet' (orange-fleshed)
'Jewel' (white-fleshed)
'Vardaman'
  (orange-fleshed)
'White Yam' (white-fleshed)

Parsnips (*Pastinaca sativa*)

Parsnips are biennials grown as annuals. The taproot grows to 2in (5cm) across at the neck and about 4in (10cm) long in short forms and up to 9in (23cm) in long types. The leaves are about 15in (38cm) long and 12in (30cm) wide. The roots are eaten cooked.

Parsnips are a hardy, cool-season crop, and prefer light, deeply cultivated, stone-free soils. On shallow soils, grow the shorter forms. Lime very acid soils and, if possible, rotate crops (see p.498). Parsnips have low nitrogen requirements (see p.504).

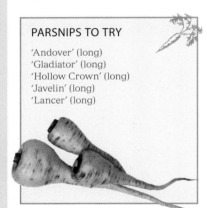

PARSNIPS TO TRY

'Andover' (long)
'Gladiator' (long)
'Hollow Crown' (long)
'Javelin' (long)
'Lancer' (long)

Sowing and planting

Always sow fresh seed. Parsnips need a long growing season and so should be sown as soon as the soil is workable in spring, but not in cold or wet soil. Sow seed *in situ* ¾in (2cm) deep, in rows 12in (30cm) apart. Thin the seedlings to 4in (10cm) apart to produce large roots, or 3in (7cm) for smaller roots. A faster-germinating crop such as radishes may be intersown; to allow for this, sow several parsnip seeds at intervals of 4in (10cm), and thin to one seedling per station. To start parsnips earlier, sow seed in cell packs with gentle heat under cover and transplant seedlings before the taproots develop.

Routine cultivation

Always keep beds free of weeds. In very dry conditions water the plants as for carrots (see p.544).

Pests and diseases

Parsnips may be attacked by celery flies (see "Leafminers," p.663), root aphids (see "Aphids," p.654), and carrot rust flies (p.657). Use cultivars that are resistant to parsnip canker (p.665) whenever possible; 'Andover', 'Javelin', and 'Cobham Improved Marrow' are resistant. Boron deficiency (p.656) may occasionally be troublesome.

Harvesting and storing

Parsnips mature in about 16 weeks. Their flavor is improved by frost and, except in very severe climates, they may be left in the soil during winter and lifted as required. The leaves die back in winter, so mark the ends of the rows with stakes so that the plants are easily found to harvest. Where winters are very severe, cover the rows with 6in (15cm) of straw to keep the soil from freezing and to make lifting easier. Young parsnips may be lifted and frozen.

INTERSOWING

In a prepared furrow, sow 3 parsnip seeds every 4in (10cm) and then sow radish seeds between them, about 1in (2.5cm) apart.

PROTECTING PARSNIPS

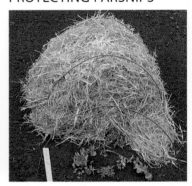

In severe climates, cover the plants with layers of straw or leaves, to a depth of 6in (15cm). Hold in place with wire hoops and mark each row.

Radishes (*Raphanus sativus* and *Raphanus sativus* Longipinnatus Group)

There are several types of radishes, some biennial and others annual; all are grown for the swollen roots. Small, round types have roots up to 1in (2.5cm) in diameter; small, long types up to 3in (7cm) long. The leaves of both may grow to about 5in (13cm) tall. Large forms include Asian radishes (Longipinnatus Group), known as daikon or mooli, and the large, overwintering, winter radishes. Roots of large, round cultivars may be over 9in (23cm) in diameter; those of large, long cultivars up to 24in (60cm) long, while the plants grow 24in (60cm) tall with a spread of 18in (45cm).

Radish skin color is red, pink, white, purple, black, yellow, or green; the flesh is normally white. Small roots are used raw when fresh, and large roots are used raw or cooked, fresh or stored. Immature seed pods from cultivars such as 'Münchner Bier' and young seedling leaves from most cultivars are edible raw.

Radishes are mainly a cool-season crop, but there are cultivars suited to a wide range of growing conditions. Some daikon and all overwintering types are frost-tolerant. Grow radishes in a sunny site, although midsummer crops tolerate light shade. Radishes prefer light, rich, well-drained soil, preferably manured for the previous crop, and very low nitrogen levels (see p.504). Rotate radishes if possible (see p.498).

Sowing and planting

Once the soil is workable, sow standard, small types outdoors throughout the growing season. Sow at 15-day intervals for a continuous crop. Very early and late sowings can be made under cover, using small-leaved cultivars bred for growing under cover. Delay sowing most Asian daikon until summer to prevent bolting. Some bolt-resistant cultivars may be sown earlier. Sow overwintering radishes in summer.

Radishes are normally sown *in situ*. Small types grow very fast and may be used for intercropping (see "Parsnips," above). Broadcast seed very thinly, or sow ½in (1cm) deep in furrows 6in (15cm) apart. Thin the seedlings to at least 1in (2.5cm) apart, never allowing them to become overcrowded. Alternatively, seeds may be spaced 1in (2.5cm) apart so that no thinning is needed. Sow large types about ¾in (2cm) deep, in rows about 9in (23cm) apart, thinning to 6–9in (15–23cm), depending on the cultivar. Small types may be used for cut-and-come-again seedling radish leaves (see "Successional crops," p.500).

Routine cultivation

Radishes should never be allowed to dry out. In periods of dry weather, water the

HARVESTING

Radishes are ready to harvest 3–4 weeks after sowing. If the radishes are being used for intercropping, pull them up carefully without disturbing the roots of the other seedlings in the row.

RADISHES TO TRY

Small
'Champion'
'Cherry Belle'
'D'Avignon'
'Easter Egg'
'French Breakfast'
'Long White Icicle'
'Snow Belle'
'Sparkler'
'Valentine'

Daikon
'April Cross' F1 (slow bolting)
'Miyashige'
'Summer Cross' F1

Overwintering
'Black Spanish Round'
'China Rose'
'China White'
'Watermelon'

crop every week or more often if needed. Overwatering, however, encourages leaf rather than root development.

Pests and diseases
Radishes may be attacked by flea beetles (p.660), cabbage root maggots (p.656), and slugs (p.669).

Harvesting and storing
Small radishes mature three to four weeks after sowing, most large types after eight to ten weeks. Pull small types soon after they mature, because most will become woody if they remain in the ground for long. Large types, however, may be left in the ground for several weeks with no risk of deterioration. Overwintering radishes may be left in the soil for lifting when required, except in severe winter weather or if they have been grown in heavy soil. In these cases, lift the roots and store them in boxes of moist sand in a frost-free place, or outside in piles for three or four months (see *Making a Rutabaga Pile*, p.543). Where radish seed is required for propagation, leave a few plants to produce seed. Harvest the pods while they are still young and green, then dry them, and collect the seeds.

Scorzonera (*Scorzonera hispanica*)

This hardy perennial is normally grown as an annual. Plants grow to about 3ft (90cm) tall and have yellow flower heads. The black-skinned, white-fleshed roots are 8in (20cm) or more long, and about 1½in (4cm) across at the neck They have an unusual flavor and are eaten cooked. The young leaves and shoots (chards) of overwintered plants are edible, and the young flower buds and their flower stalks are also delicious when cooked. For soil, climate, and manuring requirements, see "Carrots," p.544. A fertile, deep, light soil is essential for good roots to develop. Scorzonera has low nitrogen requirements (see p.504).

Sowing and planting
Sow fresh seed *in situ* in spring about ½in (1cm) deep, in rows about 8in (20cm) apart, thinning out seedlings to 4in (10cm) apart. Keep plants well-watered in dry spells. For routine cultivation, see "Carrots," p.544. Pests and diseases rarely affect scorzonera.

Harvesting and storing
The roots need at least four months to develop. They may be left in the soil throughout the winter (see *Protecting Parsnips*, p.546), or lifted and stored in boxes in cool conditions. Start lifting the roots for use in the fall and continue into spring. If they are only pencil-thin, leave the remaining plant roots to thicken for harvesting the following fall.

For chards, cover the plants with about 5in (13cm) of straw or leaves in early spring. The young, blanched leaves will push through this layer. Cut them when about 4in (10cm) tall.

For flower buds, leave a few roots in the soil during winter with no covering; these will flower the following spring or early summer. Pick the unopened buds with about 3in (8cm) of stem.

Scorzonera roots

Scorzonera plants

Salsify (*Tragopogon porrifolius*)

A hardy biennial with purple flowers, salsify is known as vegetable oyster or oyster plant, due to its taste. Similar to scorzonera in appearance and use, it has the same climate, soil, cultivation, harvesting, and storage requirements. Salsify roots need to be eaten in their first winter.

Salsify roots

If the roots are overwintered, the flower buds can be eaten the following spring. Pick the buds with short stalks, preferably in the morning before they open.

Potatoes (*Solanum tuberosum*)

Potatoes are tender perennials that grow to an average height of 2ft (60cm), with a similar spread. There are numerous potato cultivars, displaying enormous variation in their underground tubers.

A typical mature tuber is about 3in (7cm) long and 1½in (4cm) wide with white or pinkish-red skin and white flesh, but there are yellow- and blue-fleshed cultivars, often used in salads. Potatoes are eaten cooked, fresh or after storing.

Potatoes are a cool-season crop, growing best at 61–64°F (16–18°C). Neither plants nor tubers tolerate frost. Depending on the cultivar, they require a growing season of 90–140 frost-free days. They are divided into early, mid-season, and late groups, depending on the number of days required to mature.

The early potatoes grow fastest but are generally lower-yielding. Potatoes need at least 20in (500mm) of rainfall or irrigation during the season.

Grow potatoes in a sunny, frost-free site; they need well-drained, fertile soil at least 2ft (60cm) deep that is rich in organic matter. Although tolerant of a wide range of soils, acid soils (pH 5–6) are preferred.

Potatoes are subject to several soil-borne pests and diseases, and rotation is encouraged (see p.498). Prepare the ground well by digging in plenty of organic matter. A balanced fertilizer may be worked in just before planting. Early potatoes need medium nitrogen; high nitrogen is required for late potatoes (see p.504).

Planting
Grow cultivars recommended for the area. Plant small tubers (known as "seed potatoes") that have been specially raised and are certified disease-free. In northern areas with a short growing season, potatoes (especially the earlies) can be sprouted, or chitted, indoors to start them into growth about six weeks before planting. Place the tubers in a shallow flat, with the eyes or buds facing up, in even light in a cool but frost-free room. Planting is easiest when the sprouts are about ¾in (2cm) long, but they may be planted with sprouts of any length. For large, early potatoes, leave only three sprouts per plant, rubbing off the others. Otherwise, the more sprouts per tuber, the higher the yield.

SPROUTING SEED POTATOES FOR PLANTING

To sprout seed potatoes, place them in a box or flat in a single layer with the end of the potato containing the most "eyes" facing up. Store in a light, frost-free, but well-ventilated place until the sprouts have grown to about ¾in (2cm) in length.

Plant outside when there is no longer risk of heavy frost and once the soil temperature has reached 45°F (7°C). Make furrows 3–6in (7–15cm) deep or make individual holes, and place tubers upright with the eyes or sprouts at the top, covering them with at least a 1in (2.5cm) layer of soil. Plant early potatoes 14in (35cm) apart in rows 17in (43cm) apart, mid-season and late potatoes 15in (38cm) apart in rows 27in (68cm) and 30in (75cm) apart respectively.

In cool areas, cover early potatoes with medium or lightweight row covers, supported on wire hoops (see p.505). Monitor conditions and remove the covers if there is any danger of the foliage underneath overheating. Lightweight row covers can be left in place to protect against pest damage if the covers are sealed with soil at the edges.

POTATOES TO TRY

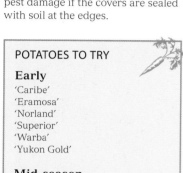

Early
'Caribe'
'Eramosa'
'Norland'
'Superior'
'Warba'
'Yukon Gold'

Mid-season
'All Blue'
'All Red'
'Carola'
'Kennebec'
'Red Cloud'
'Rose Gold'
'Ruby Gold'
'Viking'

Late season
'Butte'
'Canela Russet'
'Cherokee'
'Chieftain'
'Desiree'
'German Butterball'
'Green Mountain'
'Katahdin'
'Pink Pearl'
'Russet Burbank'

For salads
'German Yellow'
'Lady Fingers'
'Rose Finn Apple'
'Ruby Crescent'
'Russian Banana'

Potatoes can also be surface-planted, with the seed potatoes laid directly on the surface of a prepared planting bed. Heap up several inches of straw or shredded leaves over the potatoes and continue layering on the mulch as the plants grow, until it is at least one foot deep. This method makes the tubers very easy to harvest, but the plants may be more prone to drying out. Potatoes are sometimes grown from seedlings, plantlets, or eyes. These are planted in flats and transferred outside, after hardening off, once all risk of frost has passed.

Routine cultivation
If frost threatens after the leaves have appeared, cover them at night with a light layer of straw or newspaper. Plants normally recover from light frost damage. Unless grown under black plastic, potatoes need to be hilled to prevent tubers near the surface from becoming green and unpalatable and sometimes toxic. When the plants are about 9in (23cm) tall, hoe up soil around the stems to a depth of about 5in (13cm). This may be done in stages.

In dry conditions, water early potatoes every week to 10 days, depending on your soil type. Delay watering late potatoes until the young potatoes are the size of marbles (check the size of the tubers by scraping back the soil beneath one plant) then give one generous watering. Potatoes may be given a liquid feed or a topdressing of granular nitrogen fertilizer during growth.

Pests and diseases
Cutworms (p.658), slugs (p.669), golden nematodes (p.661), millipedes (p.664), blackleg on potatoes (p.655), and common scab (p.668) may be troublesome. For full details of late blight (including resistant cultivars) and other pests and diseases affecting potatoes, see PLANT PROBLEMS, pp.650–673.

Harvesting and storing
Harvest early potatoes when, or just before, the flowers open. Potatoes under black plastic may be harvested by lifting the sheeting—they should be on the surface. Leave healthy late potatoes in the soil for as long as possible; in fall, cut the haulm (the stems) of each plant to about 2in (5cm) above ground level, and leave the potatoes for another

two weeks, to harden the skins, before lifting. In areas with warm, wet summers where late blight is prevalent, cut the haulm in late summer and trash the foliage; lift the potatoes two weeks later.

Lift potatoes for storage on a dry, sunny day and leave them in the sun for two hours, then store them in the dark in paper sacks in a cool, frost-proof place. Give extra protection if frost threatens. Potatoes may also be stored for up to six months outdoors in well-insulated piles (see p.543) or in a root cellar. Young or new potatoes may be frozen. For new potatoes to be eaten during winter, plant a few tubers in the middle of summer and then cover them in fall.

PLANTING POTATOES

1 Make a furrow 3–6in (7–15cm) deep, using a draw hoe. If planting late potatoes, place them in the furrow 15in (38cm) apart with the sprouts up. Cover carefully once planted.

2 Draw up the soil around the stems when the foliage is about 9in (23cm) tall. Hilling up prevents tubers that form near the surface from turning green and being unfit to eat.

GROWING POTATOES IN BAGS

1 To grow potatoes in a bag or sack, first ensure that it has adequate drainage holes. Fill with 8in (20cm) of compost or potting mix and place one or two seed potatoes inside. Cover with 4in (10cm) of potting mix and water.

2 Mound up your potatoes as they grow, making sure that none of the tubers are exposed to the light. Keep the plants well watered. Once the foliage begins to die back, check that the tubers are ready to harvest, then dig them out and store them.

HARVESTING POTATOES

In the fall, cut the haulm (stems) cleanly with a knife just above ground level. Leave the potatoes in the ground for another 2 weeks before lifting.

Salsify (*Tragopogon porrifolius*), see Scorzonera, p.547

PART TWO

MAINTAINING THE GARDEN

PRACTICAL ADVICE ON TOOLS AND EQUIPMENT, GREENHOUSES, AND BUILDING MATERIALS AND TECHNIQUES; UNDERSTANDING SOIL TYPE AND CLIMATE, HOW PLANTS GROW AND REPRODUCE, AND HOW BEST TO DEAL WITH PROBLEMS

TOOLS AND EQUIPMENT

Keeping your yard looking its best throughout the year involves a certain amount of maintenance, from routine tasks, such as mowing the lawn to hedge trimming and seed sowing. While it is unnecessary and expensive to invest in an entire catalog's worth of garden equipment, having the correct tool for the job makes the work easier and produces a more professional result. Besides basic tools that will be in almost constant use, for example a spade, fork, or pair of pruners, there will be other items that you cannot do without—a wheelbarrow for moving garden materials, or a sprinkler system for watering. Assessing the type of work you do in your yard makes it easier to decide which tools you need; choosing them with care ensures that they will be comfortable to use as well as durable and functional.

Buying and using tools

The majority of modern gardening tools are based on traditional designs, although some may be improvements or variations on old concepts. A few completely new tools, however, have been successfully introduced. For example, until the 1980s, shredders and nylon-line trimmers were hardly known; yet they are now firmly established because they fulfill a demand not met by traditional tools.

Before buying a tool, the most important point to bear in mind is its function—it must perform correctly the task it is meant to do. Consider exactly what you need a particular tool for and how frequently you will use it. A simple, inexpensive pair of pruners, for example, will be adequate if wanted only for pruning a few rose bushes once a year; if they are required for intensive use, however, it is much better to invest in a high-quality pair. Before purchasing a tool, wherever possible always try to check that it is:
■ the best type of tool for the task;
■ the right size and model to suit your needs;
■ comfortable to use.

In large yards, or for laborious or time-consuming tasks, consider the possibility of using power tools. However, because they are expensive and require careful handling and safety precautions, as well as regular maintenance, you must be sure that they are really needed.

To ensure that tools perform well and last a long time, it is important that they are properly maintained. Immediately after use, always clean off any soil, grass clippings, or other plant material and wipe metal parts with an oily rag; all pruning and cutting tools will also need regular sharpening. Tools that are not needed over the winter months should be cleaned and well oiled, then stored in a dry place.

In addition, it is necessary to take factors such as expense and storage space into account: if a tool is needed only infrequently, renting may be a more sensible option than buying, especially for tools that are relatively expensive, heavy, and bulky.

Renting tools

If you decide to rent tools, it is a sensible idea to reserve equipment in advance, especially tools that are likely to be in seasonal demand, such as power aerators and rototillers, and check whether the rental company will deliver and collect the tools.

The condition of rented tools varies considerably. Some, especially power tools, may even be potentially dangerous to operate. For this reason, you should always:
■ Check for missing or loose parts. These may not be obvious, but if in doubt do not accept the tool.
■ Look for loose bolts and fittings on tools, such as power rototillers, which are subject to a certain amount of vibration.
■ Ask for power tools to be started, and check carefully for excessive vibration and noise.
■ On electrical tools, take a careful look for frayed, cut, or exposed wires. Do not assume that the wiring is fine just because the tool works.
■ On four-cycle engines, check the oil in the engine and transmission.
■ Ask either for a demonstration or instructions if you have never operated the tool before. This is particularly important with power tools, such as chainsaws, which can be dangerous to use for those without experience.
■ Buy or rent any recommended protective clothing (for example, goggles, gloves, and ear protectors).
■ Before signing the delivery slip, comment on the contract or delivery slip if you have noticed any issues with the equipment.

SAFE USE OF TOOLS

If you are not sure how to use a tool, ask for advice when buying or renting, or contact the manufacturer. Correct use gives good results and helps prevent accidents. Make sure that the weight and length of the tool are suitable: a tool that is too heavy will be difficult to handle; one that is too short may cause back strain. Keep all power tools in good repair and follow any safety recommendations. To minimize risks, make sure that each electrical tool is fitted with a residual current device— sometimes called an earth leakage circuit breaker— which severs the supply in microseconds if the circuit leaks power (see also *Electrical Safety*, p.556).

Digging correctly
Keeping your back straight, not curved, when digging, hoeing, or raking helps prevent backache.

Using powered tools
Take particular care when using power tools, and always wear appropriate protective clothing.

Cultivation tools

The type of cultivation tools required depends on the nature of your yard. If you grow mainly vegetables or are installing new beds, tools for digging will be a priority. If, however, the garden is well established, with lawns and perennial borders, surface cultivation tools, such as hoes will be more important.

Spades

A spade is an essential tool, excellent for general cultivation, lifting soil, and digging holes for planting. There are two major types: standard digging spades, and the smaller and lighter border (also called ladies') spades. Some manufacturers also produce an intermediate-sized or medium spade that is suitable for general digging but lighter than a standard spade.

Some spades have a tread, which makes it easier to push the blade into the soil and helps prevent damage to footwear; these spades are, however, heavier and more expensive. For extensive digging, a larger spade (known as a "heavy"), which has a 12 x 8in (30 x 20cm) blade, may prove quicker to use.

If you find digging difficult or have a large area to dig, it may be worth buying an automatic spade to make the task less of a strain.

Forks

Garden forks are used for general cultivation, lifting root crops (which are more likely to be damaged with a spade), and shifting bulky material, such as manure and garden compost. They are also ideal for relieving soil compaction, and for lightly forking in topdressings of organic matter. Two forks back-to-back can be used to divide thick clumps of perennials with little effort.

Most garden forks have four square metal prongs, and are generally available in two sizes: standard and border (or ladies'). Less common are medium, or "youth", forks, an intermediate size between standard and border forks. Other variations are also sometimes found. For example, a potato fork has broad, flat prongs and, generally, a larger head than a standard fork; it may be easier to use than a spade when digging heavy ground.

The head and neck of a fork should be forged in a single piece, the shaft fitting into a long socket in the neck.

Standard digging spade
This is useful for shifting large amounts of soil, but it is heavy and therefore may be unsuitable or uncomfortable for some gardeners. It has a rectangular blade of about 11 x 7in (28 x 19cm).

D-type molded hilt gives a good grip

Plastic hilt is comfortable even in cold weather

Tread makes digging easier

Coated blade may be easily cleaned

Stainless steel blade
This is useful for a spade because it makes light work of digging and never rusts.

Automatic spade

Operating on a spring-lever system, the spade throws the soil forward without the need to bend. It may be worthwhile for the disabled or for those with back trouble or with a large area to dig.

Border spade
With a blade only 9 x 5in (23 x 13cm), this is designed for digging in confined spaces, for example a planting hole in a border, but it is also good for any general light work.

Standard fork
This fork is useful for cultivating heavy soil, lifting vegetables, and shifting large loads, but some people may find it heavy to maneuver. Its head is about 12 x 8in (30 x 20cm).

Wooden shaft fitting into long socket in neck

Neck and head formed from one piece of metal for strength

Head

Potato fork
Primarily for lifting potatoes, this flat-tined fork may also be used for digging and moving compost or garden refuse.

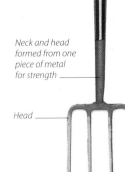

Border fork
This is best for light work in borders and similar restricted areas. The size of the head—9 x 5½in (23 x 14cm)—makes it suitable for anyone needing a small, lightweight fork.

WHICH METAL?

Carbon steel is used for most garden tools. If cleaned and oiled after use, it should not rust, and it can be sharpened. Although stainless steel is more expensive and cannot be sharpened, it does make digging easier because the soil falls away from the blade more readily. Tools that have a nonstick coating may make working the soil and cleaning easier but the coating may wear off after long use.

HANDLES AND HILTS

A spade or fork shaft should be the correct length for the user's height to minimize back strain. The standard shaft length is 28–29in (70–73cm); a longer shaft, available up to 39in (98cm) long, will almost certainly be more comfortable for people more than 5ft 6in (1.7m) tall.

Shafts are made from wood or metal, the latter sometimes covered with plastic or nylon. Both are generally strong, but even metal shafts may break if put under too much stress, and, unlike wooden ones, they cannot be replaced. Metal shafts, even plastic-coated, are colder than wood to hold in winter. Handle the tool, as if using it, to assess which type feels best.

D-type hilts
These are the most common type, but they may be uncomfortable for those with large hands, particularly when wearing gloves.

Y-type hilts
Similar to D-type hilts, but they may be weaker because they are formed by splitting the shaft wood.

T-type hilts
These have a cross-piece joined to the shaft end. Some gardeners find them comfortable, but they are not commonly available and may have to be ordered.

Hoes

Hoes are used for weeding and aerating soil; some types may be used to form seed furrows. The Dutch hoe is probably the most versatile and is ideal for weeding between rows of plants and for creating furrows. Apart from draw, digging, and onion hoes, there are other hoes available for specific uses.

Using a Dutch hoe
Hold the hoe so that the blade is parallel to the soil surface.

Dutch hoe
This traditional hoe is excellent for weeding around plants. It cuts through surface weeds without damaging the plant roots.

Combination hoe
This is suitable for chopping off weeds, making furrows, and hilling. Use the prongs to break up soil and make furrows.

Triangular hoe
Use the point for drawing a V-shaped furrow; the flat side is for weeding narrow spaces in between plants.

Digging hoe
This has one or two chisel-like blades. It is used with a swinging motion to break up small areas of hard ground.

Short-handled hoe for use in confined areas

Molded handle ensures a secure grip

Onion hoe
This small hoe (above), also called a hand, or rock garden, hoe, is for weeding between onions and other closely grown plants where a normal hoe might cause damage. It is like a short-handled version of a draw hoe, and is used while squatting or kneeling.

Draw hoe
This hoe (right) is good for chopping weeds, hilling up earth around plants, making flat-bottomed furrows, and, with the blade corner, making V-shaped furrows.

Curved neck makes the hoe easier to use in between plants without damaging them

Rakes

Rakes are excellent for leveling and breaking up the soil surface before planting and for gathering garden debris. There are two main types: general garden rakes and lawn rakes (see "Rakes and aerators," p.559).

A flathead rake is stronger than a bowhead rake. The more teeth a rake has, the faster an area is covered; 12 teeth are adequate, 16 or more are preferable for large areas. A 3ft (1m) wide wooden rake is useful in a large yard.

HEADS AND SHAFTS

Most rake and hoe heads are made from solid carbon steel; stainless steel ones are more expensive and do not work any better, although they are easier to clean and do not rust. Some rakes have a nonstick coating.

Shafts may be made from wood, aluminum, or plastic-covered metal. Shaft length is important: you should be able to stand upright while hoeing or raking to reduce strain on the back. Most people find a 5ft (1.5m) shaft comfortable, but a longer handle may be preferred.

Garden rake
This has short, wide, rounded teeth and is valuable for leveling soil, clearing the ground, and general garden cleanup.

Using a garden rake
A rake is useful for creating a fine tilth in which to sow seeds.

Trowels and hand forks

A trowel is useful for digging holes for small plants and bulbs, and for working in containers and raised beds. A hand, or weed, fork may be used for weeding, lifting small plants, and for planting.

Most trowel blades and hand fork prongs are made from stainless steel, coated steel (e.g., chrome-plated), or ordinary carbon steel. Unlike carbon steel, stainless steel does not rust and is easy to keep clean but it is expensive. Coatings gradually tend to wear off in time. Some trowels have extra-long handles—up to 12in (30cm)—for more leverage.

Hand forks with handles 4ft (1.2m) long reduce the need to bend when weeding the back of a border. Wooden, plastic, and plastic-coated handles are all generally comfortable to hold; metal ones tend to be cold.

Hand fork
Often used for lifting small plants or loosening the soil when weeding. Unlike a trowel, it does not compact the soil, so it may be preferable to use when planting in heavy soil.

Narrow-bladed trowel
Sometimes known as a rock garden or transplanting trowel, this is ideal for working in very confined areas such as rock gardens as well as for general transplanting tasks.

Wide-bladed trowel
This is useful for planting bulbs and bedding or other small plants, especially in confined areas such as containers and window boxes.

HAND-WEEDING TOOLS

For weeding between paving, bricks, or rocks, a patio weeder, which has a narrow, hooked blade, is ideal. A daisy grubber has a pronged blade suitable for prying out lawn weeds.

Specialized weeders

A Cape Cod weeder (right) can be used in narrow crevices. A daisy grubber (middle) may be used to lift lawn weeds without damaging the sod. An asparagus knife (far right) is ideal for prying out deep-rooted weeds.

Manual cultivators

A hand, or pronged, cultivator is used to break up the surface of compacted soil or to loosen weeds. It has a three- or five-pronged, metal head on a long shaft and is pulled through the soil, generally from a standing position. Some adjustable models have removable, central prongs.

Specialized hand cultivators may be useful for certain regular tasks. A star-wheeled cultivator, for example, forms a fine tilth when pushed forward and backward through the soil, so it is good when preparing a seedbed.

Adjustable models

Cultivators with removable central prongs are suitable for tasks such as cultivating each side of a row of seedlings. Some models have a detachable handle that may be fitted to other types of compatible tool head, for example, a rake or hoe.

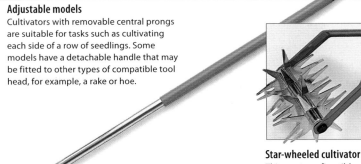

A single detachable handle may be combined with a variety of tool heads

Star-wheeled cultivator
This creates a fine tilth for a seedbed.

Removable prongs

When working in very confined areas, it may be useful to remove some prongs to make the head smaller.

Rototillers

A rototiller is used for tackling laborious tasks like turning the soil when creating new garden beds. It breaks up compacted soil and reduces it to a tilth fine enough for planting. It is impractical for use in heavily planted areas, however, and does not eliminate the need for hand digging. Gasoline-powered rototillers are powerful and usually have a wide range of attachments but need more maintenance than electric ones. Electric cultivators are excellent for small jobs. They are easier to maneuver, less noisy, and cheaper than types with gasoline engines but trailing cords may be a problem.

On most rototillers the handle height is adjustable. Some have handles that pivot and lock sideways, allowing you to walk alongside the machine without trampling the ground already cultivated. There are three types:

Rear-tine rototillers have tines behind the driving wheels. They are easy to steer, but, because of the way the weight is distributed, are best for shallow cultivation.

Mid-engine tillers are propelled by tines rather than wheels. This may make control difficult, but small models are much less expensive than rear-tine tillers and easier to use than with front-engine types.

Front-tine tillers are best for maneuvering in difficult places and for digging deep holes. The tines are mounted in front of the engine. This type of rototiller may be tiring to control.

Versatile tiller
A basic rear-tine tiller for smaller gardens, this model has a fast tine rotation to break up the soil thoroughly, and adjustable handles for better control.

Rear-tine rototiller
This rear-tined gasoline model is stable and easy to control. It is expensive, but does an excellent job of straightforward cultivation over a large area.

Five-tine cultivator attachment
This is used to weed between rows and for general cultivation. The tines can be adjusted for depth and width.

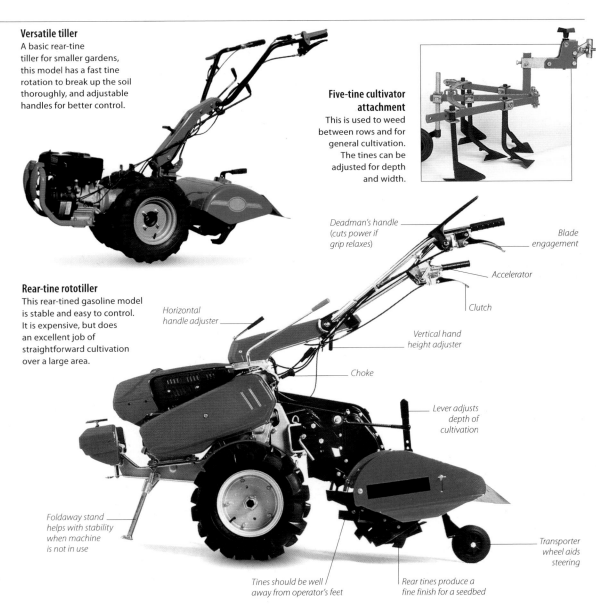

Deadman's handle (cuts power if grip relaxes)

Blade engagement

Accelerator

Clutch

Horizontal handle adjuster

Vertical hand height adjuster

Choke

Lever adjusts depth of cultivation

Foldaway stand helps with stability when machine is not in use

Transporter wheel aids steering

Tines should be well away from operator's feet

Rear tines produce a fine finish for a seedbed

Pruning and cutting tools

When pruning, it is important to use the appropriate tool for the task and to make sure that it is sharp so that it cuts cleanly, easily, and safely. Using a blunt blade can leave a plant with a ragged wound that is prone to infection or that can cause dieback. Take particular care when working with power tools, such as hedge trimmers or brush cutters (see *Electrical Safety, p.556*).

Pruners

Pruners are used for pruning woody stems up to about ½in (1cm) thick and soft shoots of any thickness; they may also be used for taking cuttings for propagation. They can be used single-handed and are more controllable and easier to handle safely than a knife, particularly by inexperienced gardeners.

There are three main types of pruner: bypass, parrot-beak, and anvil. Bypass and parrot-beak pruners have a scissorlike action; anvil pruners have a sharp, straight-edged upper blade that cuts against a square-edged lower anvil. In some designs (swing anvils), the blade is pivoted in such a way that it remains parallel to the anvil as it cuts, slicing rather than crushing the stem.

For cutting soft-stemmed plants, a light, comparatively cheap pair is perfectly adequate. For pruning fruit trees and shrubs with woody shoots up to ½in (1cm) thick, a pair of heavy-duty pruners is well worth the additional expense because the mechanism will not become strained.

If possible, try out the pruners to check that they are comfortable and easy for you to operate; the handle material and shape, how wide they open, and the pressure

Bypass pruners
These use a scissorlike action. They have a sharp, convex, steel upper blade that cuts against a concave or square, steel lower blade to make a clean cut.

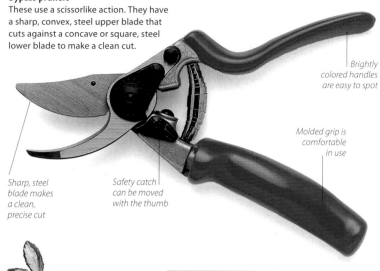

Brightly colored handles are easy to spot

Molded grip is comfortable in use

Sharp, steel blade makes a clean, precise cut

Safety catch can be moved with the thumb

Anvil pruners
These must be kept sharp, otherwise the blade crushes the stem against the anvil instead of cutting it.

Flower gatherers
These are designed to grip the flower stem after cutting.

Safety catch
This catch clips the handles together.

Ratchet system
This makes cutting tough stems easier.

Parrot-beak pruners
These give a clean cut, but may be damaged if used to cut wood more than ½in (1cm) thick.

of the spring keeping them open all vary considerably. Metal handles may be very cold to hold, but most handles are now plastic or plastic-covered metal. All pruners are fitted with a safety catch that locks the blades in the shut position. Check that it is easy to operate with one hand and that it cannot be flicked off accidentally.

Pruner blades may be made from stainless steel, carbon steel, or coated steel. Coated blades are easy to wipe clean, but are unlikely to last as long as high-quality stainless or carbon-steel blades, which keep their sharpness

and cut cleanly and easily. When buying high-quality pruners, ensure that they can be dismantled for sharpening without special tools and that new blades are available. Some models have a ratchet system for cutting through a stem in stages. These require less effort and so are suitable for those who find conventional models a strain.

Flower gathering or picking tools hold the flower stem after cutting. They are invaluable for those who cut flowers regularly; otherwise pruners or scissors will suffice.

MAINTENANCE

Clean the blades of cutting tools after each use with an oily rag or steel wool to remove any sap that has dried on; then lightly oil them. Periodically tighten the blade tension of garden shears; this makes them cut more efficiently and produces a better finish.

Most pruning tools are easy to sharpen. Remove blades that are badly blunted or damaged, and regrind or replace them.

Long-handled pruners or loppers

A pair of long-handled pruners, or loppers, is useful for removing woody stems or branches ½–1in (1–2.5cm) thick, where pruners might be damaged, and for thinner branches that are difficult to reach.

The long handles give additional leverage, making it easier to cut thick stems. They are usually wood or plastic-covered tubular steel or aluminum. Blades are made of stainless steel, carbon steel, or coated steel, as for pruners.

The weight and balance of long-handled pruners are important as you may have to hold them at full

stretch or above your head. Make sure that you will be able to operate them easily and without strain.

Most long-handled pruners have a bypass blade motion, others an anvil action. Both are satisfactory designs, and the choice is a matter of personal preference. Designs with a ratchet are sometimes available and are particularly useful for cutting through thick or tough branches and to reduce the strength needed for cutting.

All long-handled pruners require regular maintenance to keep them in peak working condition.

Long-handled bypass pruners
Using long-handled pruners makes it possible to prune stems that are high up or that are too tough or thick for pruners.

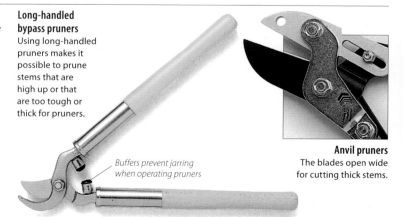

Buffers prevent jarring when operating pruners

Anvil pruners
The blades open wide for cutting thick stems.

Tree pruners

A tree pruner is suitable for cutting branches up to 1in (2.5cm) thick that would otherwise be out of reach. The cutting device is positioned at the end of a pole that is usually 6–10ft (2–3m) long, although some extend to 15ft (5m). The carbon-steel blade is operated by a lever system or a cord; both are efficient, although the lever system is more popular. Some cord models have telescopic poles so that the length may be adjusted; they are also more convenient to store. Tree pruners may have saw or fruit-picker attachments.

Hooked end is lowered over the branch to be cut

Tree pruner

Pruning saws

Use a pruning saw for severing branches more than 1in (2.5cm) thick. Because sawing in a confined space between other branches, and often at an awkward angle, may be difficult, various types of pruning saws have been developed. Those most commonly available are: general-purpose pruning, curved or rigid-handle curved, double-edged or two-edged, folding, and bow saws. If pruning is a major task in your yard, it may be necessary to have more than one saw for different types of work. A curved saw is one of the most useful pruning saws for an amateur gardener.

All pruning saws should have hardpoint, heat-treated teeth, which are harder and stay sharper for longer than ordinary saw teeth. They must be professionally sharpened. Saw handles are plastic or wood; choose whichever feels comfortable and has a secure grip. Score a groove in the branch in which to insert the saw blade to reduce the risk of its slipping during use.

General-purpose pruning saw
Invaluable for most pruning jobs, this saw has a small blade, generally not more than 18in (45cm) long, so that it can be easily used in confined areas and at awkward angles.

Curved saw
This is excellent for confined spaces because it has a curved blade and cuts only on the pull stroke. In restricted areas, it is easier to use pressure on a pull, rather than a push, stroke.

Folding saw
The saw blade folds into the handle, like a knife. Saws based on Japanese bonsai pruners are incredibly sharp and leave a smooth surface on the cut.

Double-edged pruning saw
This is very flexible because it has both coarse and fine teeth but may be difficult to operate in confined spaces without the top teeth damaging a nearby branch.

Bow saw
This is used to cut through thick branches quickly, but is too large to operate in a confined area.

Garden knives

A garden knife may be used for light pruning tasks instead of pruners, and is more versatile. It is also convenient for taking cuttings, harvesting certain vegetables, preparing material for grafting, and cutting string.

There are various types of garden knives available, including general-purpose, grafting, budding, and pruning or peach pruners. Most knives have a carbon-steel blade that is either fixed or folds into the handle. If choosing the folding type, check that it is easy to open, and that the spring holding the blade in position is neither too strong nor too slack. Always dry knife blades after use, and wipe them with an oily rag. Sharpen knives regularly, to the same angle as when new.

A box cutter with disposable blades is a good alternative to a garden knife, or use disposable craft knives for taking cuttings.

General-purpose garden knife
This is useful for all cutting tasks except heavy pruning.

Multipurpose knife
There are various models available. This one has a large blade for general use and pruning, a small one for grafting, and an attachment for budding.

Grafting
This straight-bladed knife is suitable for general tasks and for making accurate cuts when grafting.

Budding
The blade projection is used for prying open the rootstock incision when propagating by bud-grafting.

Pruning
The large blade curves down for a controlled cut when pruning.

Garden shears

Shears are used mainly for trimming hedges, but are also invaluable for cutting small or awkward areas of long grass (see also "Lawncare tools," pp.558–559), clipping topiary, and cutting back herbaceous plants.

For soft-stemmed hedges, a light pair is adequate but for large hedges with tough, woody stems a heavy-duty pair will be needed.

Weight and balance are both important; before buying, check that the shears are centrally balanced and the blades are not too heavy, or they will be tiring to operate.

Most shears have straight blades although a few have wavy-edged blades: these cut through mature wood easily and help trap the shoots so that they are not pushed out with the scissor-action of the blades. They are difficult to sharpen (see also *Maintenance*, opposite).

Standard shears
Shears usually have one notched blade to hold a thick shoot during cutting.

Single-handed shears
These have a spring mechanism similar to pruners that allows them to be operated with one hand. Some types have blades that swivel—useful for cutting at an angle or vertically (as for edging a lawn). They are only suitable for cutting grass or very soft stems.

Hedge trimmers

For gardeners with large hedges to cut, a power hedge trimmer may be worthwhile because it takes less time and effort to use than ordinary manually operated shears.

The longer the blade, the faster the hedge can be cut and the easier it is to reach a tall hedge or across the top of a wide one. Hedge trimmers with very long blades are heavy and often poorly balanced, however. A 16in (40cm) blade is adequate for normal garden use, but if cutting extensive hedges, a 24in (60cm) blade saves considerable time. Blades may be either single- or double-sided; the latter speed up the cutting time but are not as easy to control as single-sided blades, so hedge shaping may be more difficult.

The ease of handling is also affected by the blade action. Models with reciprocating- or double-action blades, which move against each other, are generally preferable for the majority of gardeners. Single-action models, in which one moving blade cuts against a second, stationary blade, cause vibration and can therefore be tiring to operate.

The finish of the cut is largely controlled by the spacing of the teeth along the blade. Narrowly spaced teeth produce a smooth,

Protective clothing
When operating power tools, wear protective clothing, such as goggles, ear protectors, and thick gardening gloves (see also p.563).

Power hedge trimmer
This makes hedge trimming faster and easier than it is when using garden shears. Electric models are light and easy to maneuver, while gasoline versions are powerful and unhampered by trailing cords.

even finish on a hedge that is regularly trimmed, while more widely spaced teeth usually cope better with thicker twigs but leave a rougher cut.

Gasoline or electricity?
Hedge trimmers may be powered by gasoline, electricity, or batteries. Gasoline hedge trimmers may be operated anywhere and are generally powerful and relatively free from vibration. They are, however, noisier, heavier, and more expensive than electric or battery-powered ones and usually require more maintenance.

Electric hedge trimmers are more commonly used by amateurs and are better for small jobs. Being lighter, electric models are easier to handle than gasoline trimmers; they are also cleaner to use and cheaper to buy.

Electric hedge trimmers are the most convenient for hedges within 100ft (30m) of a power supply. As with other electric tools, the trailing cord can be inconvenient and even hazardous, and the machine must not be used in wet conditions. Safety features are very important when handling such a potentially dangerous tool. For example, they

should always be operated with a residual current device, commonly called a ground fault circuit interrupter (see also *Electrical safety*, below).

Battery-powered hedge trimmers are good for hedges in a distant part of a large yard or where there is no convenient power supply. They are usually run from a spare car battery. When fully charged, they are reasonably powerful; however, maintaining a charged battery and moving it around the yard can be time-consuming and laborious. They are more expensive than electric models.

RECHARGEABLE HEDGE TRIMMERS

Hedge trimmers powered by a rechargeable battery are cordless, easy to maneuver, and comparatively cheap. They are excellent for small, regularly trimmed hedges, but lack the power to cut thick shoots and long hedges. Because there are no trailing cords, rechargeable machines present fewer safety hazards than other types of electric trimmer. They can be recharged using the unit provided with the tool.

Brush cutters

A brush cutter is excellent for slashing through tough weeds, undergrowth, and very long grass. The rotating head has a metal cutter or fine-toothed blade. This makes it suitable for far heavier tasks than those that can be tackled with a nylon-line trimmer (see "Lawncare tools," pp.558–559), but it is more tiring to operate. Some models have

plastic blades, but these are not as tough or durable. In addition to their cutting blade, some may be fitted with a nylon line for trimming grass.

Most brush cutters are gasoline-driven because they need powerful engines to work effectively. Electric models are lighter, less noisy, and need less maintenance, but are less efficient for heavy work.

ELECTRICAL SAFETY

■ Keep cords only as long as necessary. Trailing cords are inconvenient and potentially hazardous, because they may be cut by moving blades.
■ Have outside outlets installed by a qualified electrician at suitable points in the yard to keep cords short and safe.
■ If extension cords are needed, ensure that they have the same number of wires as the tool: if the tool is grounded, the extension cable should be too.
■ If the circuit is not already protected, attach a plug fitted with a ground fault circuit interrupter (GFCI) to the tool, or buy an adaptor GFCI to insert between the plug and outlet.
■ Do not use an electric tool during or just after rain because it may cause electrical faults.
■ Always disconnect the power supply before adjusting, inspecting, or cleaning a tool.
■ Never touch a damaged cord before disconnecting the tool from the power supply.

Chain saws

Chain saws are suitable for sawing logs or large branches and for extensive tree surgery and felling. Because they cut with a powered, toothed chain revolving at high speed, they can be dangerous and should be handled with great care; it is advisable to be trained by a professional in their safe use.

Electric chain saws are useful for small jobs and are cheaper than gas types, but strict safety precautions are essential (see right).

Gas-driven chain saws are more powerful and therefore suitable for very large yards or woodlands, but they are noisy, heavy, often difficult to start, and create fumes.

Electric chain saw
An electric chain saw is suitable for most sawing tasks; it is lighter and easier to handle than a gasoline-powered version and generally requires less maintenance.

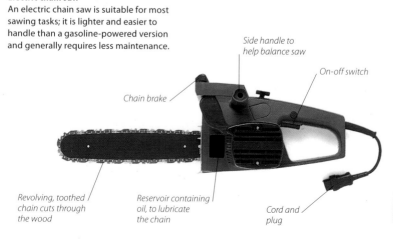

Side handle to help balance saw

On-off switch

Chain brake

Revolving, toothed chain cuts through the wood

Reservoir containing oil, to lubricate the chain

Cord and plug

Lawn mowers

When choosing a lawn mower, take into account the size of your lawn and the type of cut required. If only a small area needs mowing, a manual lawn mower may suffice, but for a larger lawn, buy a power one. There are reel, rotary, and hover mowers available: reel models usually provide the finest cut, while rotary types are better for long, overgrown grass.

Grass should be mown more closely during periods of rapid growth and left longer when less growth occurs, such as late fall, or when hot and dry in summer, so check that the height of cut is easily adjustable (see also The Lawn, "Frequency and height of cut," p.395). A mulching mower chops grass finely and discharges the clippings close to the soil surface, for rapid decomposition and soil nourishment. If you need a fine finish without loose grass, choose a mulching mower with a grass catcher (see also "Grass clippings," p.395).

Manual lawn mowers

Manual mowers are relatively cheap, quiet, and need very little maintenance. There are two types: those that are driven by wheels at the side and those that are operated by a chain drive from a heavy rear roller. A side-wheel mower is easy to push although it is awkward to maneuver at the edge of a lawn.

Power lawn mowers

There are two basic types of power lawn mower: reel and rotary. Most run on either gasoline or electricity. Both types of power mowers are potentially dangerous on steep slopes because they are designed for flat surfaces.

Reel mowers are either self-propelled or they have a power blade; the latter type may be heavy and tiring to operate. Most have a rear roller, which is essential if you want a lawn with a strip pattern; the heavier the roller, the more pronounced the strip.

Gasoline-driven reel mowers often have broader cutting widths than electric ones. This reduces the cutting time; however, it makes these mowers more difficult to maneuver.

Rotary mowers have replaceable metal or plastic blades that cut the grass with a scythelike motion as they rotate horizontally. Rotary mowers have wheels; only a few rotary mowers are fitted with rollers. They work better than reel mowers for sites that are slightly uneven or have long grass, but most models cannot cut the grass very low. Rotary blades can become unbalanced so regular service checks are advisable. Riding mowers are usually rotary models.

Which power source?

Batteries and electricity are more convenient and cleaner than gasoline, but not suitable for powerful engines. For cordless mowers, a handy power outlet is needed for recharging—batteries cannot always be removed from the mower. For an electric mower, access to a power supply is also essential, but the trailing cord may be a hazard. Electric mowers should not be used on wet grass.

Gasoline lawn mowers are also not hampered by cords but are more expensive to buy and maintain. They may not start readily unless they are fitted with an electric ignition.

Safety

■ Blades must be well protected so that they do not come into contact with the operator's feet. However safe the mower appears, the operator should always wear strong, protective shoes.
■ The blade brake must stop the blades rotating within five seconds of being turned off.
■ The mower should have a lock-off switch, which requires two operations to turn on an engine. This reduces the risk of a child accidentally starting the motor.
■ A deadman's handle should be fitted to the mower. This is squeezed to enable the engine to run, and when released, it immediately stops the engine.

MAINTENANCE

A few simple precautions keep a mower working efficiently.
■ After use, disconnect power, then clean engine and blades.
■ Check that the blades are sharp and replace blunt ones.
■ Oil and lubricate regularly.
■ Service the mower yearly.
■ Periodically check that spark plugs are clean and adjusted.
■ Clean filters and air intakes of gasoline mowers regularly.
■ Periodically check the oil level on four-cycle engines.
■ Before you store a gasoline-power model, drain the tank.

SELECTING A LAWN MOWER

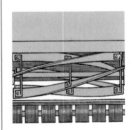

Reel blades
The blades are set along a reel that rotates forward and cuts against a fixed blade.

Reel mowers
A mower of this type provides a fine, close-cut finish. Power models are used more by lawn-care companies than by homeowners. Most models for home lawn use are manual; some electric types are available. The manual varieties add no pollutants to the environment, however they can be tiring to use, since the energy needed to cut the grass comes from the operator.

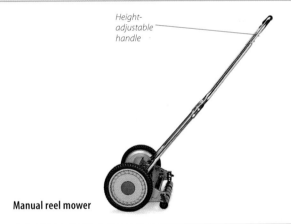

Height-adjustable handle

Manual reel mower

Rotary blades
These blades are fast-moving and act like a scythe, rotating around a vertical axis.

Rotary mowers
Rotary mowers, powered either by gasoline or electricity, are a common choice for homeowners. Some are self-propelled, making them easy to use. A riding mower is useful for extensive grassed areas, including rough and long grass, because it has a powerful engine. The replaceable metal blade cuts horizontally.

Adjustable wheel height

Gasoline, rotary mower

Large volume grass collector

Gasoline, riding rotary mower

Lawn-care tools

In addition to a lawn mower, a number of other tools are useful for maintaining a healthy and attractive lawn. Manual tools are usually adequate for most lawns but, for large areas, power tools are faster and less tiring to use.

Edging tools

A neat, well-defined edge provides the perfect finishing touch to a well-mown lawn and emphasizes the lawn's shape and outline (see also *Cutting the Edge of the Lawn*, p.396). There are two main lawn edging tools: half-moon edgers and long-handled shears, although power edging machines and certain nylon-line trimmers may be used.

Shafts for long-handled shears are wooden, steel, or plastic-coated steel; all of them are strong and the choice is really a matter of personal preference.

Long-handled edging shears
These are useful for trimming overhanging grass around the lawn edge. The handles should be sufficiently long so that there is no need to stoop. If either too short or too heavy, the shears may be tiring to operate.

Half-moon edger
Also known as an edging iron or lawn edger, this is used with a rocking motion to cut away worn or uneven lawn edges and to remove small areas of sod for repair. It has a sharp, curved, metal blade attached to a long wooden or metal handle.

Tang of blade is well secured to shaft neck

Nylon-line trimmers

A nylon-line trimmer is useful for trimming grass in awkward areas that cannot easily be reached by a mower. It may also be used for groundcover plants or soft-stemmed weeds, although a more powerful brush cutter is better for tough undergrowth (see p.556). Because nylon cutting line is flexible and easily replaced, you can work right up to a wall or paving without damaging the tool. It is also safer than a fixed blade if there is an accident. Always wear goggles—flying stones may be hazardous.

Nylon-line trimmers may be driven by electricity or gasoline, and similar issues of safety, convenience, and weight apply. Electric models are light and easy to operate, but their area of use is restricted by cord length. For safety, they must have a deadman's handle and be plugged into a receptacle with a ground fault circuit interrupter. Cordless nylon-line trimmers with rechargeable batteries are suitable for small to medium areas, and where there is no external power supply. They too are lightweight, quiet, and easy to use. Never use electric-powered trimmers while the grass is wet (see also *Electrical Safety*, p.556).

Gasoline-powered trimmers are ideal for larger yards, but are heavier, more expensive, and need more maintenance than others. For safety, they should have a quick, easy way to stop the engine.

Trimmer
This has a flexible nylon cutting line that rotates at high speed to cut through grass and other soft-stemmed plants or weeds. Some models have an adjustable head that may be tilted vertically for trimming lawn edges.

A shaft-handle makes the tool easy to maneuver

Shield protects user from whirling cutting line

Cutting guide
This keeps the nylon line just off the ground to keep it from cutting too low and to produce an even trim.

Rakes and aerators

Tools for clearing up fallen leaves and garden debris and for reducing thatch (a layer of decaying organic matter) and soil compaction help keep a lawn in good condition.

Lawn rakes are primarily used to gather up fallen leaves. Some types may be helpful in removing thatch and dead moss. There are three types of lawn rake: spring-tined, flat-tined, and scarifying, or aerator, rakes (see also "Rakes," p.552). Also available are power lawn rakes, which are suitable for large lawns.

Aerators help reduce thatch and let air into the soil, encouraging good root growth. On small areas, aerating may be done with a garden fork, but for most lawns a more powerful tool such as a hollow-tined aerator or a slitter is better.

Spring-tined lawn rake
This is used for clearing out dead grass and moss, removing small stones and debris, and lightly aerating a lawn. Its light head has long, flexible, rounded wire tines.

Flat-tined lawn rake
Excellent for gathering up leaves and loose material, this has long, flexible, flat tines of plastic or metal, and a light head to minimize damage to new growth.

Scarifying rake
This cuts deeply into thatch and even into the sod. Its rigid metal tines are usually flat, with sharp points. It may be heavy and tiring to use, so a model with wheels on either side of the rake head may be preferable.

Hollow-tined aerator (plugger)
This hollow-tined power aerator penetrates deeply through the sod into the soil. The tines remove cores of sod and soil, opening up compacted soil.

STAR-WHEELED SLITTER ATTACHMENT

This attachment for riding mowers (see p.557) aerates the soil faster than a hollow-tined aerator.

Sweepers and blowers

At its simplest, a leaf sweeper may be an ordinary stiff broom or brush that is used to sweep away small debris. This kind of basic sweeper is ideal for clearing pathways and small areas of the yard. For larger and more efficient garden tools, however, see the rakes (above).

For large leaf-collection jobs, however, using a power leaf blower saves both labor and time. The leaves are quickly blown into rows or piles, which may then be raked up and put out for municipal collection or added to a compost pile. Leaf blowers tend to be overused, however—clearing every leaf off your property is neither necessary or even desirable. Power leaf blowers are also expensive and very noisy to operate. Some power models of leaf collectors and blowers have flexible attachments designed for use among flower beds and other areas of the garden that are particularly hard to reach.

Leaf sweeper
This gathers up garden leaves, using rotating brushes, and collects them in a large bag. It is light, easy to push, and quiet in operation.

Power leaf blower
This type of leaf blower has a knob to switch from a blowing action to a sucking action, as required. It shreds the leaves for easy disposal, mulching, or making leaf mold, and they are collected in the attached bag.

Fertilizer spreaders

A fertilizer spreader is suitable for the accurate distribution of fertilizer, grass seed, and granular weedkillers. It comprises a hopper on wheels with a long handle. Check that the application rate is adjustable and that the flow may be switched off when turning at the lawn edge. After setting the application rate always check that it is correct by fertilizing a test area first (see "Applying fertilizers," p.625). A hose attachment used for applying a fertilizer with water is useful for feeding a lawn (see Sprayers, p.560).

Fertilizer spreader
A spreader applies fertilizer evenly, thus avoiding scorching the grass.

Watering aids

Irrigation makes it possible to grow plants that require more water than is provided by rainfall, and to grow plants both indoors and in the greenhouse. Equipment such as hoses and sprinklers help make routine watering easier and faster.

Watering cans

A watering can is practical in the house, greenhouse, or small areas outside. Choose a lightweight can that will not be too heavy to carry when full. The opening should be wide enough to make filling easy, and the can should feel comfortable and well balanced. A strainer at the base of the spout helps prevent the nozzle from becoming clogged by debris in the water.

Rain barrel

A rain barrel collects rainwater from a house or garage roof, which is invaluable during dry periods and for acid-loving plants. The barrel should have a spigot, and a lid to keep out debris, which pollutes the water and might block the spigot. If necessary, raise the barrel on blocks so a watering can will fit under the spigot. Some barrels divert water to a secondary barrel when they are full; this is often a built-in feature of hose taps (see WATER CONSERVATION AND RECYCLING, pp.614–615).

Garden watering cans
These should have a generous capacity to reduce the need for repeated refilling. For general-purpose use, a 2 gallon (9 liter) can, which holds 18lb (8kg) of water, is a convenient size.

Plastic or metal?
Most watering cans are now made from plastic, but traditional galvanized metal ones, which are heavier and more expensive, are still available; both types are sturdy and durable.

Greenhouse watering can
This has a long spout, so that it is easy to reach plants at the back of a bench, and a reversible nozzle for both fine and coarse sprays for watering seedlings and mature plants.

Indoor watering can
This should have a long spout to reach into plant pots and window boxes, and to help control the flow.

CAUTION WITH WEEDKILLER

Do not use the same watering can or sprayer for watering the garden and for dispensing liquid weedkillers. Keep a dedicated one, clearly marked, for applying chemicals.

WHICH NOZZLE?

Coarse-spray nozzle

Fine-spray brass nozzle

Fine-spray, brass-faced, plastic nozzle

A fine nozzle is best for seeds and seedlings because the spray does not damage them or wash the soil mix or soil away from them. For more established plants, a coarse-spray nozzle, which delivers the water faster, is preferable.

Nozzles are manufactured in a choice of materials: brass, brass-faced plastic, and all-plastic. Plastic is less durable and cheaper than brass but is still satisfactory for most uses. In general, metal nozzles give a finer spray.

Using a dribble bar, which is attached to a watering can, makes it more accurate than a nozzle for applying weedkiller. It also reduces spray drift which can be a problem with a nozzle.

Hoses

A hose is invaluable for irrigating distant parts of the yard and for areas that require copious watering. Most hoses are made from PVC; they vary in the way they are finished or reinforced, which affects their durability, flexibility, and resistance to kinking. Any kinks interrupt water flow and eventually weaken the hose wall. Double-walled and reinforced hoses are resistant to kinking but relatively expensive. Some hoses come on a wall-mounted, retractable reel, for neat storage, while others are on wheels or retract into a plastic box with a carrying handle. These allow water to flow through the hose even when partially wound, so the hose can always be neat yet ready for use.

All types of hose are made in various fixed lengths with connectors and nozzles prefitted or as accessories. Some hoses can be lengthened with one or more extensions. Wherever an external,

cold-water supply is connected to a garden hose, it is advisable to fit the tap or outlet with a double-check, or non-return, valve, to prevent back siphonage of potentially contaminated water into other parts of the system; this is often a built-in feature of hose taps.

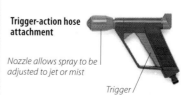

Hose reel
A reel with a handle or wheels is easy to move around the garden. Some reels allow water to flow through the hose even when partially wound.

SPRAYERS

Use sprayers to apply pesticides, herbicides, and fertilizer—either a portable type or an attachment fitted to the end of a hose, and to water or mist-spray plants. Compression types, pumped up before use, are suitable for general use; small trigger-pump sprayers are for misting house plants or applying pesticides to a few plants. For a large area, use a knapsack sprayer.

Trigger-action hose attachment

Nozzle allows spray to be adjusted to jet or mist

Trigger

Compression sprayer
This sprayer is pumped up with the handle and is suitable for treating large areas.

Fertilizer pulse hose attachment

Central chamber for fertilizer

Hose-end attachments
Most attachments simply allow the intensity and range of the water spray to be adjusted. Some have a trigger-action nozzle.

Numerous watering aids are now available, but it is important to accept that it will not be possible to use them in prolonged periods of drought when water use is severely restricted. Watering by hose or using sprinklers will violate regulations, and while watering with watering cans is possible, it would be impractical in many yards, except for short periods.

The practical solution is to store as much rainwater as possible in covered rain barrels or other strong plastic containers that are designed to fit under downspouts. A water pump in the container connected to a hose can then distribute water as required. It is preferable to use a trickle system or a soaker hose so that as little water as possible is lost by evaporation.

Ensure that all watering and spraying equipment, including connectors, is in good condition to avoid losing water through leaks or evaporation.

Drip and soaker hoses

Drip hoses are made of either plastic or rubber and have tiny perforations along their entire length. With the holes facing upward, it produces a fine spray over a rectangular area. When the holes are placed toward or under the soil, water is directed to the base of plants; this is ideal for vegetables and other plants that are grown in rows. Drip hoses should be carefully chosen; some cannot be used as sprinklers because their holes are so small that the water just trickles out even when the holes are facing upward.

Soaker hoses are a variation on drip hoses. A network of soaker

TYPES OF SPRINKLER

Standing sprinkler
Primarily for lawns. Most have a spike to push into the ground. They usually spray in a circle, but a few water in a semicircular, fan, or rectangular, shape. Liable to form puddles, so move around for even distribution of water.

Rotating sprinkler
Good for beds, borders, and lawns. Cover large circular areas and apply water evenly. Spray is delivered from nozzles on the arms attached to a spinning pivot, driven by the force of the water. Long-stemmed types are best for beds or borders.

Pulse-jet sprinkler
Invaluable for large, circular areas of lawn, beds, or borders. A single jet on a central pivot rotates in a series of pulses, ejecting spurts of water. Except on lawns, the delivery head is set on a tall stem for increased coverage.

Oscillating sprinkler
This is best used at ground level; it is not suitable for positions where surrounding foliage will interfere with the range of the spray. Water is sprayed through a series of brass jets in the oscillating arm. This sprinkler delivers water fairly evenly over a rectangular area, the size of which may be easily adjusted.

hoses enables water to seep slowly into the soil. This watering system is particularly suitable for newly planted beds, borders, and vegetable gardens. The water is released directly into the area of the plant's roots; water is therefore distributed economically with no runoff and little evaporation. The low humidity levels reduce the incidence of fungal diseases as well as the spread of pests and diseases that is often triggered by water splash. Weed germination is also discouraged by the dry soil surface.

The connections can be varied, and the system moved around as required on the soil surface, or the hoses may be buried 4–6in (10–15cm) below the surface as a permanent irrigation system.

Garden sprinklers

A garden sprinkler delivers a fine spray of water over a specific area. It works while unattended, saving both time and effort. However, in hot, sunny weather, much water is

lost through evaporation, so sprinklers actually provide less efficient use of water, than either drip or soaker hoses.

A sprinkler is attached to a garden hose. There are various types for different needs: some are best for lawns, while others are preferable for irrigating a flower bed or vegetable garden. The simplest form is a standing sprinkler. Other types, such as rotating, pulse-jet, and oscillating ones, use water pressure to rotate the sprinkler heads, providing better coverage.

A traveling or walking sprinkler is useful for large areas; it is convenient but expensive. It delivers spray over a rectangular area while propelled along a track (usually a hose) by the force of the water.

Underground sprinklers

These are permanent systems, ideal for lawns and rock gardens. They are unobtrusive, simple to operate, and best installed when the area to be irrigated is first constructed. PVC pipes and connecting joints are laid in a grid so they supply various

watering heads, to which hoses or sprinklers are attached. The sprinkler from each head delivers an even supply of water to a circular area. Continue watering until the ground is thoroughly wet, to even out the distribution to any overlapping areas. This type of system requires anti-siphon valves to meet building code regulations, and possibly a water meter.

HOSE TIMERS

Hose timers may be used with ordinary garden sprinklers or more elaborate watering systems. They fit between a spigot and the hose or irrigation pipe. Most such timers turn off the water after a predetermined time. The more sophisticated ones will turn on and off several times a day and can be preprogrammed as well as linked to a moisture detector that prevents watering if the ground is sufficiently wet.

Computerized timer
This allows you to program watering times and duration in advance, to irrigate plants while you are busy or on vacation.

Water timer
This can be set to turn off the water after a preset period, from about 5 minutes to 2 hours.

Trickle, or drip feed, systems

These are used for plants that benefit from individual watering. Water drips gently beside the plant plant, minimizing soil disturbance around the roots. A trickle system works well in a shrub border, along a hedge, or for vegetables; it is also ideal in arid regions where water is scarce or very costly; a trickle system does not give plants more water than they need. Unless fitted with a timer, trickle systems can waste water, and need regular cleaning to prevent tubes and drip heads from getting blocked with algae and debris.

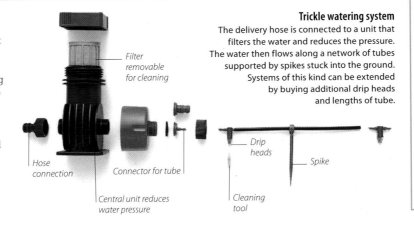

Trickle watering system
The delivery hose is connected to a unit that filters the water and reduces the pressure. The water then flows along a network of tubes supported by spikes stuck into the ground. Systems of this kind can be extended by buying additional drip heads and lengths of tube.

Filter removable for cleaning

Hose connection

Connector for tube

Central unit reduces water pressure

Drip heads

Spike

Cleaning tool

General garden equipment

In addition to tools for cultivating and maintaining the garden, a wide range of other accessories, such as carrying equipment and planting aids, may be useful, depending on your own individual requirements.

Wheelbarrows

Wheelbarrows are useful for transporting plants, soil, and materials, such as compost and garden debris. They may be made of metal or plastic, the former being more durable. Painted metal soon rusts if the paint is chipped; even galvanized metal bins rust eventually. Plastic bins, although lighter, may split.

Most traditional wheelbarrows have an inflatable tire to cushion the load. Check regularly and inflate the tire as needed; an underinflated tire makes pushing the wheelbarrow very difficult, particularly if the tray is heavily loaded. Garden carts, as wheelbarrows with two wheels and a single handle are generally called, are stable and easy to load and unload, but are less maneuverable than standard barrows on uneven ground.

Sheets and bags

A carrying sheet or bag is suitable for transporting light but bulky garden waste, such as hedge

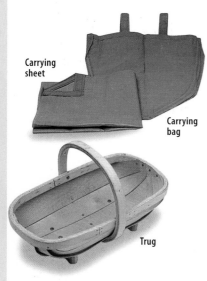

Carrying sheet

Carrying bag

Trug

clippings; when not in use, the carrying bag takes up very little space. It should be lightweight, with strong handles, and made of a tough, tear-proof material, such as woven plastic. Carrying bags have a larger capacity than sheets,

█ TYPES OF WHEELBARROW

Traditional wheelbarrow
Most barrows have a single, solid wheel and a shallow bin, although some models may be fitted with an extension to increase their capacity.

Twin-wheeled wheelbarrow
Barrows with twin wheels are useful for transporting very heavy loads, or for use on rough ground, where the extra stability provided by two wheels is advantageous.

and are easier to use. Trugs and baskets are good for light tasks, such as carrying flowers or fruit.

Plastic bags

Clear plastic bags are excellent for a number of purposes, such as preventing cuttings material from drying out after collecting it, and for covering cuttings in pots to raise humidity around them. Most food and freezer bags are suitable provided that they are made of polyethylene and are not too thin—other materials are less effective at retaining moisture.

Kneelers and knee pads

A cushioned-pad kneeler, covered with a waterproof material, is simply knelt on for extra comfort,

when weeding, for example, whereas knee pads are strapped to the knees and often sold in only one size, so check that they fit before buying. Kneeling stools support the knees on a slightly raised platform and have hand rests to give support when kneeling and

Kneelers
A kneeling stool (top) can be inverted for use as stool; some are heavy to carry. A cushioned pad (bottom) keeps knees clear of damp, hard ground.

█ COMPOST BINS

A compost bin should have a lid to keep warmth in, easy access to the compost by slats or panels, and a capacity of at least 1cu yd (1cu m) to generate sufficient heat to accelerate the rotting process. Avoid wire mesh bins or those with large gaps between the slats, because they allow the heat generated to escape.

Traditional, wooden compost bins are available precut for easy self-assembly. Plastic compost

bins are generally more effective than metal or wooden ones because they conserve moisture and reduce the need to water. There are plastic bins available that may be rotated to turn the compost, but this does not necessarily make good compost more quickly than a well-designed, traditional bin. See also SOILS AND FERTILIZERS, *Making a Compost Bin*, p.627.

standing. They may also be turned upside-down for use as a small stool for working at raised beds or greenhouse benches.

Incinerators

Open burning, once a standard garden practice, is now illegal in many areas. Seek advice from local government officials before you buy an incinerator—you may not be allowed to use one. A better option is to recycle garden waste by shredding and composting it. If you do use any type of incinerator, it must be well ventilated.

Shredders

A compost shredder chops woody or tough garden waste, such as old cornstalks and prunings, until it is fine enough to break down quickly on a compost heap. Most shredders are electrically powered and should not be left outdoors when not in use.

For safety, make sure that the power is disconnected when the hopper is removed (see *Electrical Safety*, p.556). The funnel should be easy to use, but must not be able to touch the blades.

Power should cut out if inlet funnel is removed

Three sturdy legs ensure that shredder is stable in use

Using a shredder
The inlet funnel should not allow direct access to the blades. Wear goggles and gloves to protect against flying debris and thorny stems.

Planting and sowing aids

General garden tools or household items are often used for planting and sowing; for example a stick or pencil, instead of a dibber, will make a planting hole. Specialized tools, however, do make some tedious and repetitive jobs simpler and quicker.

Seed sowers and planters

These facilitate accurate and even sowing of seed. There are four main types: shakers, plungers, wheeled sowers, and seed-tray sowers.
Shakers are hand-held devices that may be used for sowing seed in prepared drills. Skill is required to ensure even seed distribution.
Plungers insert each seed individually to a depth that is predetermined.
Wheeled seed sowers are good for distributing seeds evenly. With a long handle, they can be worked from a standing position.
Dibble boards are thin, plastic or wooden boards with molded protrusions on one side. When pressed onto the seed soil mix they firm the surface and make evenly spaced holes for sowing seed.

Bulb planters

A bulb planter is useful if planting a number of bulbs individually; for planting groups of small bulbs, a trowel or hand fork is better. A bulb planter is usually pushed into the soil with your foot. It removes a plug of soil or sod, which is then replaced on top of the bulb after planting; those with a clawlike action release the plug by pressure on the handle.

GARDENING GLOVES

There is a range of gardening gloves for various purposes: some keep hands clean when working with soil or other media, while others also provide protection against thorns.

Leather and fabric gloves are useful for tasks, such as pruning roses, to guard against thorns. When buying leather ones, check that the leather extends far enough to protect all of the palm. All-leather or suede gloves give very good protection, but may be uncomfortably hot in warm weather. Gauntlet types cover the wrists and lower forearms.

Many gloves are made of fabric and vinyl. Some are impregnated with vinyl, others just have a vinyl grip on the palms. They are good for most jobs and keep hands cleaner than fabric alone. Vinyl-coated gloves are useful for messy jobs, such as mixing concrete, but are too thick for jobs needing a sensitive touch.

Fabric with vinyl grip

Suede gauntlets

Suede and fabric

Cotton fabric

Dibbers and widgers

A dibber is a pencil-shaped tool used for making planting holes. Use a small dibber to transplant seedlings or insert cuttings, a large one for transplanting vegetables such as leeks that require a wide hole to allow space for growth, and for planting through a plastic mulch. A widger, which is like a narrow spatula, is good for lifting seedlings and rooted cuttings with the minimum of root disturbance.

Garden lines

A garden line is mainly used in vegetable plots as a guide for forming straight rows, but is also invaluable for other tasks, such as marking areas when planning or designing, or forming a straight edge when planting up a hedge or constructing a wall or patio.

Garden line
Most garden lines have a pointed stake at either end for inserting into the ground. Grooves allow you to stretch a level line between the stakes.

Sieves

Garden sieves generally have a mesh of ⅛–½in (3–12mm) and are used to separate out coarse material from soil or other medium. Choose a sieve with a large mesh to remove twigs and stones from soil before sowing or planting; use one with a smaller mesh when covering fine seeds after sowing. Those with a wire mesh tend to be more effective and durable than plastic ones.

Thermometers

The best type of thermometer for garden and greenhouse use is a minimum-maximum thermometer, because this records both the lowest and highest temperatures reached. A digital greenhouse thermometer together with a hygrometer, which measures air humidity, are useful to monitor conditions under glass. A soil thermometer outdoors is helpful in deciding when to sow seed.

Minimum-maximum thermometer

Digital Greenhouse thermometer

Rain gauges

A rain gauge is used for measuring amounts of rainfall or irrigation; it is helpful for identifying areas of the garden that are affected by rain shadow. It should have clear markings and a smooth inside surface for easy cleaning. Many gauges have a short spike for inserting into the ground.

Measurements are clear so that water level is easy to read

Spike for stability

Plastic rain gauge

PLANTING AND SOWING TOOLS

Small dibber

Wooden garden dibber for outdoor use

Bulb planter

Widger

Metal garden dibber

Wheeled seed sower

Wire-mesh sieve

Sieve with fine, plastic mesh

Ties and supports

Ties are used for various purposes but in particular to secure climbing, scrambling, or fragile plants; supports are needed to protect some plants from wind or rain. Ties must be secure without constricting the stem, and must be checked annually; use a light material, such as twine or raffia on soft-stemmed plants.

General ties

Garden string or twine in 3-ply is adequate for most tying jobs. Raffia, which is good for binding joins after grafting and as a lightweight tie, and soft strings, such as jute fillis, may disintegrate after a year or so. Clear plastic tape is excellent for use in grafting; special rubber ties are also available. Tar-impregnated string or polypropylene twine is a reliable, weather-resistant tie.

Plastic-coated tying wire is strong and lasts for several years. It is good for fixing labels to training wires or trellis and for joining stakes. It may come on a reel with a built-in cutter.

Plant rings

These are split rings of wire; plastic-covered rings are also available. Plant rings are designed to be opened and closed easily around a plant stem and its support. They are suitable for light jobs, such as attaching a house plant to a stake.

LABELS AND MARKERS

Labels for garden use should be durable, weather-resistant, and large enough to contain all the information you want to note. Plastic labels are cheap and may be reused; if written on with pencil, they should remain legible for a season. Most plastic labels discolor gradually with age and become brittle, but they are ideal for labeling trays of seeds and cuttings. Looped labels and those with ties may be secured around the stem of a plant and are useful if labels at eye level are required.

For more permanent, water-resistant markers, use those coated with a black material; these are written on by scratching through to the white plastic beneath, but they cannot be marked with a new name. Aluminum labels, which are more expensive, will last almost indefinitely, but the lettering may have to be renewed every few years.

Tree ties

Rubber tree ties are strong, durable, and good for securing a young tree to a stake. They should be easily adjustable so that an expanding stem is not constricted. Select one with a buffer so the stake does not chafe the stem, or use a padded tie in a figure-eight form (see also *Tree Ties*, p.65). Nail the ties to stakes.

Wall fixings

Specially designed plant stickers may be used for tasks, such as securing the stem of a climber directly to a wall or other support. Lead-headed nails are stronger; they have a soft spur that may be bent over to fix stems and small branches to a wall. Eye bolts hold stretched wires to which wall plants are then secured. For masonry walls, use a spike-style eye instead.

Stakes

Bamboo stakes are excellent for supporting single-stemmed plants, but will split and rot in time. More permanent and expensive are PVC stakes and plastic-covered steel rods. Support clumps of border plants with metal link or ring stakes (see PERENNIALS, *Staking*, p.193). Support trees and standard roses with sturdy, wooden stakes.

when constructing a pond or trough. For general pest and weather protection, cover plants with polypropylene row covers, which are available commercially in various weights.

Use a plastic snow fence to protect vulnerable plants in exposed sites (see *Windbreaks*, p.609). Knitted plastic netting may deteriorate in about four years, whereas molded plastic should last at least twice as long. Windbreak webbing is even more long-lasting although obtrusive, but it may provide more protection.

PLANT SUPPORTS AND TIES

Stakes and supports

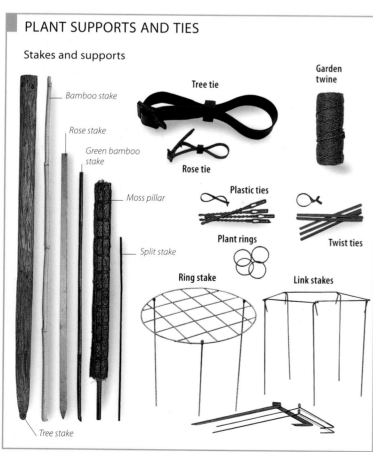

Bamboo stake

Rose stake

Green bamboo stake

Moss pillar

Split stake

Tree stake

Tree tie

Rose tie

Garden twine

Plastic ties

Plant rings

Twist ties

Ring stake

Link stakes

Netting

Netting is available in various materials and mesh sizes for a range of uses, such as supporting plants, protecting fruit from birds, and shading greenhouse plants (see "Shading," p.576). For plant support, choose a mesh of 2in (5cm) or more; it may be hard to disentangle plants from a smaller mesh. For many annual climbers and some clematis, thin, flexible plastic netting is adequate; heavier plants need semirigid plastic nets.

For fruit protection, use commercial plastic netting with a mesh of ½–¾in (1–2cm). Protect seedlings and winter vegetables from birds with 1in (2.5cm) mesh netting. Wire netting may be placed around plants to provide protection from animals, such as rabbits. It is also useful for reinforcing concrete

WALL FIXINGS

Spike-style eye

Eye bolt

Lead-headed nail with spur

NETTING

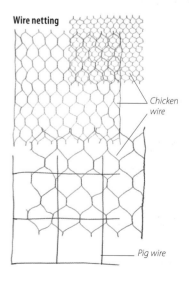

Plastic netting

Shade netting

Plant support netting

Wire netting

Chicken wire

Pig wire

Pots, flats, and growing media

Pots are available in a wide range of sizes but there are two basic shapes: round and square. Although round pots are traditional, square pots hold more medium for the same diameter; to save space use square pots, which pack neatly together. Round pots are classified by the inside diameter at the rim; square ones by the length of the rim along one side. Most pots have slightly sloping sides so that a plant and its root ball may be easily removed intact for repotting or planting out.

Pots are usually made of clay (terra-cotta) or plastic. Clay is traditional; plastic, however, is more common. Most plastic pots are manufactured from polypropylene, which deteriorates in cold weather. Pots made of a polypropylene and polyethylene mix do not become brittle in cold weather.

Standard pots are as deep as they are broad; they are the most common type of pot. Bulb or seed pans are one-half as tall as they are wide at the top, and are useful for germinating seeds. Azalea pots are three-quarters as tall as they are wide at the top. These pots are often used commercially for plants that have relatively small root balls, for example, evergreen azaleas. For very deep-rooted seedlings, sweet pea tubes are used. Long Toms are generally used for plants that will remain in the pot for some time. Tarpaper ring pots, which are bottomless, are sometimes used for

Pots and pans

Pots and pans are used for cultivating plants both indoors and outside. The smaller pots, pans, and azalea pots are suitable for propagating and growing on young plants.

Ornamental terra-cotta pots

Standard pots

Large standard pot

Azalea pot

Seed pan

Pans

Seed, seedling, and cutting pots

greenhouse tomato culture. Other containers designed for specific uses include lattice pots with mesh sides, which can be used for aquatic plants.

Degradable pots and pellets

These are good for plants that are sensitive to root disturbance, because they can be planted out into their final spots in the vegetable garden without being transplanted. The plants' roots grow through the sides and base of the pots into the ground. They are generally made from compressed peat and various other fibers, such as dried cow manure or some kinds of wood fiber. Many gardeners create their own degradable pots from cones of double-thickness newspaper.

Biodegradable pellets are good for seeds and for rooting cuttings; they must be expanded with water before they are used.

Seed flats

Traditional, wooden seed flats have largely been replaced by plastic ones, which are easier to clean but often more fragile. Very thin plastic flats are cheap and flexible but are unlikely to last more than a season. Strong plastics are more rigid and expensive; they may become brittle and split with age but, if stored out of sunlight when not in use, they should last for several years.

Cell packs

Cell packs and modular systems are particularly good for seedlings, such as peas and broad beans, that dislike being pricked out. The tapered sides to each cell allow young plants to be transplanted with only minimal damage to their fragile roots, so they are able to establish quickly in their new surroundings. Modular systems and cell packs are available in plastic, polystyrene, and biodegradable paper, and also in a wide range of cell sizes and numbers, from four to several hundred.

Growing media

When sowing seed and rooting cuttings, a higher success rate is achieved if specialized seed-starting and propagation mixes are used.

Standard seed-starting mix

Fine seed requires good contact with the mix in order to germinate and should be sown in a commercial seed-starting mix, which is fine-textured, moisture-retentive, and low in nutrients, such as salts that may damage seedlings.

Standard seed-starting mix is made using two parts (by volume) sterilized soil, one part peat, and one part sand. Some seed-starting mixes are amended with synthetic fertilizers; others use an all-organic formula.

Standard propagation mixes

Soil mixes for rooting cuttings are free-draining and intended for use in high-humidity environments. They may be based on bark, perlite, or mixes containing a high percentage of coarse sand. Propagation mixes are low in nutrients, so cuttings need feeding once rooted.

A standard propagation mix contains 50:50 sand and peat (or peat substitute). To each cubic yard (meter) is added 7½lb (4.4kg) dolomitic lime; 2½lb (1.5kg) each of gypsum and calcium carbonate; and 4oz (150g) each of potassium nitrate and potassium sulfate. A specialized micronutrient fertilizer should also be added.

Inert growing media

Sterile inert growing materials do not harbor the pest and disease problems associated with soil-based or loamless potting mixes. Some of the most popular are rockwool, perlite, vermiculite, and clay granules (see also *Hydroculture*, p.375).

Flats and cell packs

These are used for sowing seeds, inserting cuttings, or growing on young plants. Use a rigid outer flat to hold flimsy, single-use cell packs. Cells packs are useful for pricking out seedlings and sowing seeds singly.

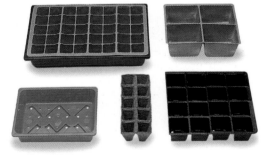

Long Tom
This pot suits deep-rooted plants that would be restricted by a standard pot.

Tarpaper ring pot
This specialized bottomless pot for ring culture holds the medium over the growing aggregate.

Sweet pea tubes
These are excellent for seedlings that quickly develop long root systems.

Bulb basket
Such a basket protects bulbs from animals and is also easy to lift after flowering.

Biodegradable pots
Use for propagating plants that resent root disturbance when transplanted.

Lattice pot
This pot for aquatics lets in water, but should be lined with burlap to retain soil.

GREENHOUSES AND COLD FRAMES

Many people resist the idea of installing a greenhouse in the mistaken belief that it is expensive or requires detailed gardening knowledge to use and maintain properly. This is not the case. The rewards of gardening under cover more than compensate for the initial cost and effort and open up a whole new world of gardening pleasures. As well as being an all-weather space throughout the year, a greenhouse can be a cost-effective investment, allowing you to propagate plants for the garden at relatively little cost. Even if you have a small plot, you will be able to find a compact model to fit; or you could consider installing a cold frame instead—smaller in scale but a great boon to practical gardening.

Gardening under cover

Greenhouses, cold frames, and cloches are useful additions to any garden and are available in an extensive range of sizes to fit whatever space is available. Each type of structure has a distinct function, but they are usually used in conjunction with one another. The most productive gardens use all three.

Unheated structures

Unheated greenhouses are used primarily to advance or extend the growing season of many types of plants. Cold frames fulfill a similar function, although they are also often used for hardening off plants that have been propagated in a greenhouse and for storing dormant plants. Cloches are used *in situ* over plants in the garden itself.

Heated structures

A heated greenhouse is far more versatile than either an unheated greenhouse or a cold frame, and allows a much greater range of plants to be grown. These include many frost-tender species that do not grow satisfactorily in temperate or cold climates without protection. In addition, a heated greenhouse provides a suitable environment in which to propagate plants.

Siting the greenhouse

A home greenhouse is best positioned so that it blends in with the overall garden design. It should also be positioned in a sheltered site but where enough light is available for the plants to grow and thrive: too much shade will limit the range of plants that may be grown easily, while an exposed site will make the greenhouse expensive to heat or may mean that the plants are not adequately protected on cold nights.

Early planning

It is always worth spending the time to make sure that you have chosen the right spot before buying a greenhouse. If possible, make detailed notes in winter or spring of where shadows are cast in the garden by houses and any neighboring garages, trees, or other large, nearby features, so that you do not site a greenhouse where it will be in shade for more than a few hours each day. Orienting the greenhouse north–south by its longer axis makes the best use of light in summer. For raising plants in spring, or overwintering tender specimens, an east–west orientation will provide good light for much of the day.

If there is a possibility that you will want to extend the greenhouse later, or build a second, smaller one, allow enough space on the site.

Freestanding greenhouse

The best place to site a freestanding greenhouse is in a sheltered, bright area away from buildings and large trees. If the site is high or exposed, choose a location that is sheltered by a hedge that acts as a windbreak, or build a

Greenhouse style
This traditional greenhouse is an integral part of the garden. Hedges and trees provide shelter, but are not close enough to significantly reduce light. Maintenance is minimal: treat the wood with preservative regularly.

POSITIONING THE GREENHOUSE

If the greenhouse is used mostly in the summer, its longer axis should run north to south. If good light in spring is a priority, however—when the sun is lower in the sky—orient the greenhouse east to west to make the best use of available light.

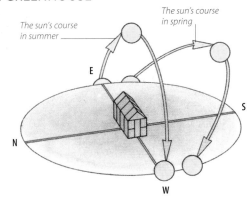

The sun's course in summer

The sun's course in spring

Lean-to greenhouse

Place a lean-to greenhouse against a wall that receives a mix of sun and shade. Do not site it where there is sun for most of the day, otherwise the greenhouse may overheat in summer, even with shading and a good ventilation system.

Access

Remember the need for easy access. A site that is reasonably close to the house is preferable to one at a distance. Also make sure that there is a clear area in front of the greenhouse door for loading and unloading. Any paths leading to the greenhouse need to be level.

Preferably, they should have a hard, resilient surface and be wide enough to accommodate a wheelbarrow.

Utilities

Choose a site that will be convenient for connecting water and electricity, if these services are needed. Although electricity is not essential for heating, it is useful for lighting as well as for some thermostatic controls and timing switches. A water supply makes watering plants more convenient, especially if an automatic system is used, and reduces the need to trail lengths of hose around the garden.

Elegant design
Greenhouses with plastic-covered frames can be extremely attractive, as well as functional. This one is a decorative garden feature in its own right.

fence or other screen. Windbreaks should not cast too much shade onto the greenhouse itself; however, they need not be tall—an 8ft (2.5m) hedge provides shelter for a distance of 40ft (12m) or more.

Do not position a freestanding greenhouse near or between buildings. This could create a wind-funnel effect, which may damage the greenhouse and the plants inside. Sites at the bottom of a slope or near walls, hedges, or fences on the side of a slope should not be used to site a greenhouse because cold air may become trapped there (see CLIMATE AND THE GARDEN, "Frost pockets and frost damage," p.607).

CHOOSING THE SITE

An open but sheltered site is best for a greenhouse—it should not be positioned in the path of a wind funnel. If there is no natural protection from the wind, construct a windbreak.

Poor Positions

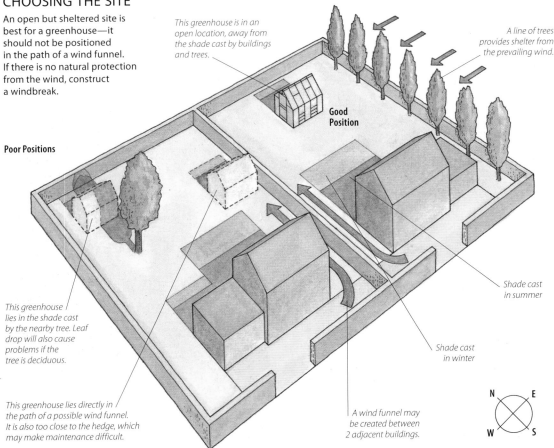

This greenhouse is in an open location, away from the shade cast by buildings and trees.

A line of trees provides shelter from the prevailing wind.

Good Position

This greenhouse lies in the shade cast by the nearby tree. Leaf drop will also cause problems if the tree is deciduous.

This greenhouse lies directly in the path of a possible wind funnel. It is also too close to the hedge, which may make maintenance difficult.

A wind funnel may be created between 2 adjacent buildings.

Shade cast in summer

Shade cast in winter

N E W S

GREENHOUSES, GUTTERING, AND WATER STORAGE

Using water sparingly is as important in greenhouses and cold frames as in the open garden, and it is essential to store water for use during very dry periods to maintain greenhouse plants and propagate material effectively. Capillary systems, seep hoses, and trickle systems can be regulated to deliver water to plants growing in greenhouses or cold frames, but the structures themselves can provide a valuable source of rainwater if guttering, downpipes, and storage tanks are installed. Not all greenhouses are equipped with guttering, so check whether they are included before you buy.

More storage can be provided by sinking galvanized or plastic tanks under greenhouse benches. Fill them with roof water by diverting a downpipe inside the greenhouse above the container.

Check faucets, joints, and containers regularly to ensure water is not lost from leaks.

Choosing a greenhouse

Before purchasing a greenhouse, consider carefully how it will be used to select the most suitable style, size, and materials—a greenhouse that is used as a garden room, for example, will differ significantly from one that is purely functional. If growing tropical and subtropical plants, an attractively shaped greenhouse, perhaps with room for central benches, might enhance the floral display.

Many different styles of greenhouses are available. Some make best use of space or provide optimal ventilation; others conserve heat well or allow better light penetration. When priorities have been decided, the final choice of style will depend on personal preference.

Conventional greenhouses

The more conventional types of greenhouses are suitable for a wide range of plants and include traditional span, Dutch light, three-quarter span, lean-to, and Mansard (or curvilinear) greenhouses. All of these may have an aluminum or wooden framework, and either

TRADITIONAL SPAN

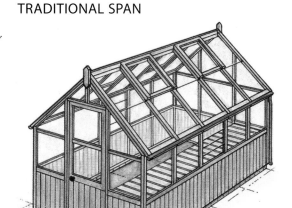

DUTCH LIGHT

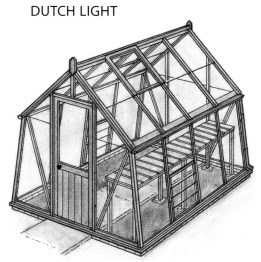

all-glass or part-solid walls (except Dutch light greenhouses). Conventional greenhouses also have a wide range of compatible accessories, including benches and shelves.

Traditional span

The vertical sides and even-span roof of a traditional span greenhouse are extremely practical in terms of growing space and

headroom. For raising seedlings and growing food crops, a traditional span greenhouse is likely to provide the best use of space for the least cost.

Dutch light

The sloping sides of Dutch light greenhouses are designed to allow in maximum light, so these greenhouses are suitable for border crops, especially low-growing ones

such as lettuce. The large sheets of glass are expensive to replace because of the size—the traditional dimensions are 59 x 30¾in (145 x 77cm). The glass panes slide into the frame and are secured using cleats and galvanized nails.

The panes of glass on the roof overlap slightly to keep out rain and increase rigidity. This may cause loss of heat, however, if the panes overlap too loosely.

THREE-QUARTER SPAN   LEAN-TO   MANSARD

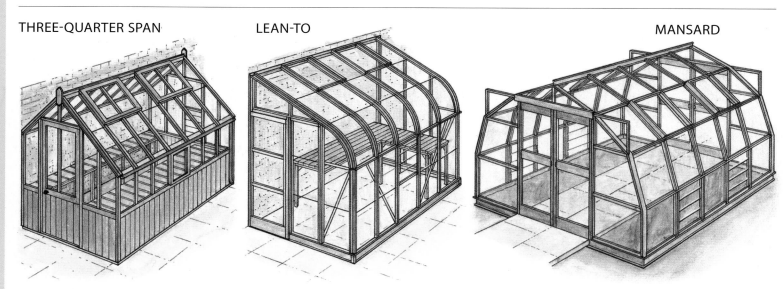

Three-quarter span

A three-quarter span greenhouse is positioned with one of its sides against a wall. Light is a little more restricted than in a freestanding model, so this type of greenhouse is best positioned beside a sunny wall, although this may mean that extra shading is required in summer. The wall provides extra warmth and insulation in the greenhouse, especially if it is a house wall (see also "Lean-to," right).

Lean-to

Where there is insufficient space for a freestanding structure, a lean-to greenhouse is an invaluable choice, particularly if a mainly decorative structure is favored.

Many are similar in appearance to conservatories, and may be used as garden rooms. Installing electricity, natural gas, or a water supply in a lean-to that is adjacent to a house wall is cheaper and generally involves less work than laying cables or pipes to

a greenhouse that is some distance from the house. In addition, the warmth of the house wall may reduce the level of heating required; brick walls store heat, from both the sun (especially if the wall is south-facing) and the indoor heating system, which is then released into the greenhouse.

The brick wall also provides good insulation, so that less heat escapes from a lean-to than from many other types of greenhouse.

Mansard

The Mansard (curvilinear) greenhouse has slanting sides and roof panels, designed to allow maximum entry of available light. The full benefit is gained only in an open location with no shade from surrounding buildings or trees. A Mansard greenhouse is suitable for plants that need maximum light during the winter, when daylight hours are short and light levels are also frequently low.

DOME-SHAPED

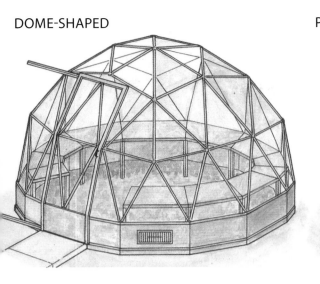

POLYGONAL

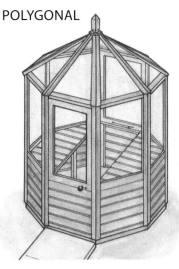

ALPINE HOUSE

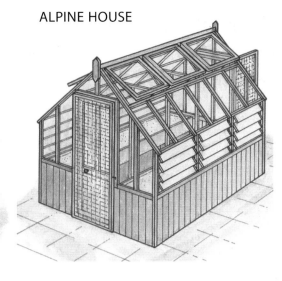

Specialty greenhouses

There are many types of specialty greenhouses, including dome-shaped, polygonal, alpine house, conservation, mini, and polytunnel, all of which differ markedly in appearance from the more conventional types. Some are designed as highly decorative garden features in their own right, while others may be a particularly good buy or be used for specific types of plant.

Dome-shaped

This is an elegant design that is very useful in exposed positions, because it is stable and offers less wind resistance than traditional greenhouses. The multiangled glass panes and aluminum frame allow maximum light transmission. Dome-shaped structures may have limited headroom around the edge, and plants may also be difficult to reach. Extensions are not usually available and fittings may be limited to those produced by the manufacturer.

Polygonal

Octagonal and other polygonal greenhouses are frequently chosen where appearance is important, and may provide a focal point within the garden. They are generally more expensive than traditional greenhouses of similar size and, because they are not very common, there may be a limited choice of accessories. The irregular shape may also restrict growing space. Fitting replacement panes of glass is more difficult than in a conventional structure.

Alpine house

This type of greenhouse is traditionally wood-framed with louver vents extending all along the sides for effective ventilation. Usually, alpine houses are unheated and are closed only in the coldest winter weather, so insulation is not required. Unsuitable for tender plants, they are used for plants that thrive in bright, well-ventilated conditions, yet require some overhead protection from dampness and rain. The shape is similar to that of a traditional span greenhouse.

CONSERVATION

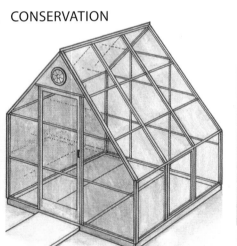

MINI

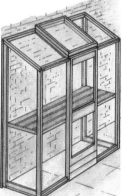

POLYTUNNEL

Conservation greenhouse

This type of greenhouse has many special features that are designed to save as much energy as possible. The roof panels are angled to allow optimal light penetration in winter yet reduce hot summer sun, and mirrored surfaces are also used to reflect light within the greenhouse itself. A solar collector may be used to store heat in winter. Double glazing and insulation are included as standard features.

Mini-greenhouse

These useful, low-cost greenhouses are good for a limited space, and are available in various heights, widths, and depths. There are also freestanding and wheeled versions. A mini-greenhouse is the best choice if only a small number of plants will be grown. It is covered with glass or plastic and is usually framed with aluminum. It should preferably face south–east or south–west so that maximum light penetrates. Adjustable

benches and shelves are available in a range of depths. Access may be an issue—all work has to be done from the outside. Ventilation may be inadequate, and rapid temperature changes often occur. This type of house is normally used only during the spring peak-growing season.

Plastic polytunnel greenhouse

Where visual appearance is not important and low-cost protection is required—such as in the vegetable plot—a polytunnel

greenhouse has many benefits. It comprises a large, tunnel-shaped frame covered with heavy-duty transparent plastic sheets and is widely used for crops that require some protection but not the warm conditions of a traditional greenhouse. Polytunnels keep out the worst of the winter cold and provide useful wind protection throughout the year. They are light and relatively easy to move, so they are often used in plots where crop rotation is carried out.

For a very large growing area, commercial polytunnels are a cost-effective investment, but for a small garden a more traditional shape may be a better choice. A few polytunnels include some benches, although most are intended primarily for growing crops at ground level, planted either directly into the soil, in pots, or in grow bags.

Ventilation can be a problem: the door offers a reasonably efficient method of ventilation—especially in large tunnels with openings at each end—and some have sides that roll up. The plastic sheeting may need to be replaced every few years—it will gradually become opaque, restricting light penetration.

Choosing the size

A greenhouse will almost inevitably seem too small once it is filled with plants so, if possible, buy one that can be extended. Although a large greenhouse costs more to heat than a small one, it is possible to partition off a section in winter, and leave the remainder unheated (see "Thermal screens," p.574).

Space considerations

A greenhouse that is used primarily for ornamentals should have plenty of room inside for benches, which may be tiered, and possibly a central or end display. To provide space for propagation and growing on, it may be necessary to divide up the space with a partition. Alternatively, use a cold frame for propagation.

Length, width, and height

A length of 8ft (2.5m) and a width of 6ft (2m) are the minimum, practical dimensions for a general-purpose, traditional greenhouse. A smaller greenhouse than this limits the range of plants that can be grown, and may make it difficult to control the environment—drafts and rapid heat buildup in summer tend to be more of a problem in small greenhouses, and may lead to sudden fluctuations in temperature. In greenhouses that are more than 6ft (2m) wide, it may also be difficult to reach pots and ventilation toward the back of the benches. Benches of a width of 2ft (60cm) on either side allow a path of the same width down the middle.

If crops will be grown in raised beds, choose a greenhouse that is 8ft (2.5m) wide with beds to a width of 3ft (1m). A width of 8ft (2.5m) is also suitable if a wider path is needed for a wheelchair or to allow room for a wheelbarrow.

Many small greenhouses have low eaves and comparatively low ridges, which make it tiring to work over the beds or benches for long periods. To gain more height, build the greenhouse on a brick base or dig out a sunken path.

Choosing the materials

Greenhouses are made in a range of materials. The most important considerations when choosing both the framework and glazing for the greenhouse are practicality, expense, and the amount of maintenance required. The appearance of the materials may also be important; metal is sturdy, but traditional wood is often preferred.

BUYING A GREENHOUSE

Before buying a greenhouse, use the following as a checklist; it may save disappointment later.

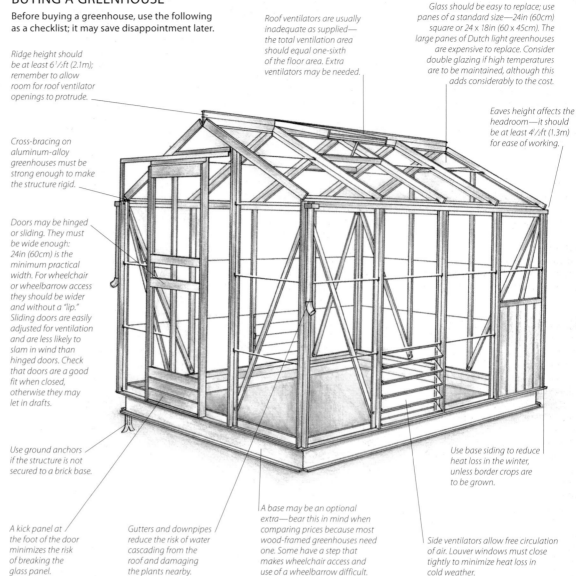

Ridge height should be at least 6¹/₂ft (2.1m); remember to allow room for roof ventilator openings to protrude.

Cross-bracing on aluminum-alloy greenhouses must be strong enough to make the structure rigid.

Doors may be hinged or sliding. They must be wide enough: 24in (60cm) is the minimum practical width. For wheelchair or wheelbarrow access they should be wider and without a "lip." Sliding doors are easily adjusted for ventilation and are less likely to slam in wind than hinged doors. Check that doors are a good fit when closed, otherwise they may let in drafts.

Use ground anchors if the structure is not secured to a brick base.

A kick panel at the foot of the door minimizes the risk of breaking the glass panel.

Gutters and downpipes reduce the risk of water cascading from the roof and damaging the plants nearby.

Roof ventilators are usually inadequate as supplied— the total ventilation area should equal one-sixth of the floor area. Extra ventilators may be needed.

A base may be an optional extra—bear this in mind when comparing prices because most wood-framed greenhouses need one. Some have a step that makes wheelchair access and use of a wheelbarrow difficult.

Glass should be easy to replace; use panes of a standard size—24in (60cm) square or 24 x 18in (60 x 45cm). The large panes of Dutch light greenhouses are expensive to replace. Consider double glazing if high temperatures are to be maintained, although this adds considerably to the cost.

Eaves height affects the headroom—it should be at least 4¹/₂ft (1.3m) for ease of working.

Use base siding to reduce heat loss in the winter, unless border crops are to be grown.

Side ventilators allow free circulation of air. Louver windows must close tightly to minimize heat loss in cold weather.

The framework

Wood frameworks have been the traditional choice and are generally considered to be the most attractive. They may be expensive, however, and are also heavy to construct. If possible, choose a durable wood. Always look for a manufacturer that offers hardwood frames made from renewable sources. A high-quality greenhouse will be rot-resistant, will not warp easily, and, if treated every year or two with a high-grade wood preservative, will retain its color well.

Some woods are regionally abundant or are traditional choices. Check with a local contractor or building supply store to determine which wood is best for your needs and budget (see also "Wooden framework," p.583).

CONSTRUCTION MATERIALS

Wood
A wooden frame is the traditional choice for garden greenhouses. Hardwoods are low maintenance.

Aluminum
Aluminum-alloy frames are light but extremely sturdy and need only minimum maintenance.

Steel
Plastic-coated steel frames are very strong but must be treated regularly to prevent rust.

Greenhouses with aluminum-alloy frames are almost completely maintenance-free. They do not retain heat quite as well as wooden frames, but the difference is minimal.

Galvanized steel is also often used for greenhouse frames. Steel frames are light and easy to construct but extremely strong. They are cheaper than wood or aluminum frames but must be painted regularly (see "Metal framework", p.583).

Aluminum and steel frames are narrower than wooden ones and allow larger panes of glass to be used, resulting in better light penetration.

Glass panes

Ordinary glass is the most satisfactory glazing material for a greenhouse: it allows excellent light penetration, far better than modern high-tech substitutes. It is easy to clean, does not discolor, and retains considerably more heat than plastic glazing materials. Glass is easier to break than plastic glazing, however, so breakages and cracks may be a problem, because the panes must be replaced promptly.

Plastic panes

Plastic panes are generally more expensive than glass; they also discolor more readily than glass and tend to become scratched over time, which is both unsightly and, more importantly, may cut down on the amount of light that is transmitted if the discoloring is severe.

Acrylic sheets are used to glaze the curved eaves of many greenhouses, because the acrylic can be shaped easily to give an elegant outline to the structure. Condensation occurs more readily on its surface than on a conventional glass pane. Rigid polycarbonate sheets are also often used to glaze greenhouses. They are easy to handle, lightweight, virtually unbreakable, and have good insulating properties. They are relatively easily scratched, however, and they tend to discolor.

Twin-walled polycarbonate has particularly good insulating qualities, but its opacity may be a major problem in a greenhouse.

Sizing

Most local glass merchants will cut glass panes to size for little cost. It is important to make sure that any measurements you give are accurate; calculate them carefully, ensuring that there will be

GLAZING MATERIAL

Rigid plastic glazing material is light and easy to fit. This is twin-walled polycarbonate, which provides good insulation.

sufficient clearance for the glass to engage with the mounting system that is to be used. If plastic glazing material is used, it will be supplied in sheets and is not usually difficult to cut to size at home using a sharp utility knife and straightedge.

Building the greenhouse

A greenhouse requires far less maintenance and lasts much longer if it is properly built in the first place. The information listed below is necessarily of a general nature, because it applies to many different greenhouse types and designs: always follow the manufacturer's instructions for specific advice. If in doubt on any point, check the details with either the supplier or the greenhouse manufacturer.

Before beginning to construct a greenhouse, look into the applicable local building codes. Greenhouses often require a building permit, and building inspectors may be involved throughout the process.

Preparing the site

Always erect a greenhouse on firm, level ground, otherwise the frame may warp and become twisted and cause the glass to crack. The chosen site must first be cleared of weeds: persistent weeds are very difficult to eradicate when the greenhouse is assembled and in position. If the site selected for the greenhouse has been recently dug over, allow the soil to settle for a few weeks, and then compact it with a heavy roller.

Foundations

Aluminum greenhouses that are smaller than 6ft wide and 8ft long (2 x 2.5m) do not usually require a thick concrete base. Simply dig a hole at each corner approximately 10–18in (25–45cm) deep, then wedge in the ground anchors (see p.572) with stone chips and pour in a concrete mix to hold them.

If a more substantial foundation is required, dig a trench about 10in (25cm) deep, filling it with 6in (15cm) of packed crushed stone. Mount the anchoring bolts and finish off with poured concrete or paving slabs, making sure that the ground is level.

Brick bases

A brick base must be constructed to the precise measurements provided by the greenhouse manufacturer, on solid concrete footings deep enough to withstand winter conditions. Check with local contractors for the footing depths recommended for the area. For further instructions, see How to Make a Concrete Footing, p.596).

Wooden greenhouses

The sections of a wooden greenhouse are usually supplied in a kit and should only need to be bolted together and then attached to the base.

Base

Interlocking concrete blocks may be used for the base, otherwise a solid concrete foundation or brick base should be built (see "Foundations," left, and "Brick bases," above).

Sides, gable ends, and roof

Before the greenhouse is delivered, check what kind of bolts or hardware are required and whether they will be supplied. First bolt the sides and gable ends together to form the main framework. Follow the manufacturer's advice for the exact method of fixing this to

the base or foundations, because designs vary. The foot of the frame may contain integral anchorage points for securely bolting it down. Bolt any internal partitions to the frame, then add the roof sections and bolt them in place.

Some wooden greenhouses are supplied as sections with unglazed frames, with the glass or plastic glazing supplied separately. Others have preglazed frames but are heavy to move—two or more people may be required to support them.

If the wood has not been treated and is not rot-resistant, it is important to paint the woodwork with a preservative at this stage, before the greenhouse is glazed.

Glazing

If putty is to be used for glazing, it is usually supplied with the greenhouse. Apply it to the glazing bars, and seat the glass carefully. The glass panes are usually secured in place with galvanized steel or brass sprigs; if these are not supplied, they may be purchased from any hardware store.

If a dry glazing system (that is, one that does not require putty) is to be used, simply follow the supplier's instructions.

Whichever method is used, glaze the sides and gable ends first, overlapping the panes by ½in (1cm). Use soft metal overlap clips to hold the glass panes firmly together.

BUILDING A BRICK BASE

If using a brick base for the greenhouse, build it in advance, and lay proper foundation first. Check with the greenhouse manufacturer before building the base to make sure that the dimensions are correct.

CONCRETE FOUNDATIONS

For a solid greenhouse foundation, dig a trench to match the dimensions of the greenhouse, then fill the foundation with crushed stone and a layer of concrete.

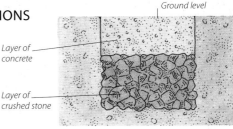

Ground level

Layer of concrete

Layer of crushed stone

GLAZING BARS AND CLIPS FOR METAL GREENHOUSES

Glazing bars
These form the framework of the greenhouse.

"W"-shaped wire clip
Use this type of clip to hold glass and plastic panes firmly in place.

Sprung band clips
An alternative clip, these attach onto the frame.

Ventilators and door

Ventilators are supplied as an integral part of the preassembled sections, so the number you ordered should be in place. Screw on hinged doors and simply insert sliding doors into the runners.

Metal greenhouses

Greenhouses with metal frames are delivered in home-assembly kit form, and the frame is supplied in sections—the base, sides, gable ends, and roof. The sections are in turn divided into separate component pieces that need to be bolted together.

Base

Assemble the base first, ensuring that it is perfectly level and square to prevent any warping and twisting of the frame; measure from each corner to the one diagonally opposite—the measurements must be the same. The base must be securely anchored; this is particularly important in windy or exposed areas.

A GROUND ANCHOR

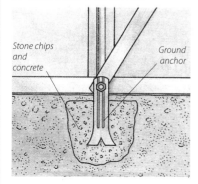

Stone chips and concrete

Ground anchor

Small greenhouses may be secured using ground anchors. Wedge them in place with stone chips first before pouring in a concrete mix.

If attaching ground anchors to a concrete foundation, use the anchoring bolts provided, otherwise set the ground anchors in crushed stone and concrete at each corner of the base.

Sides, gable ends, and roof

Assemble the sides, gable ends, and roof sections in the sequence recommended by the manufacturer on the instruction sheet. The sides are usually put together first.

First make sure that everything has been included, as detailed by the kit contents list. Then, before assembly, lay out on the ground all the pieces for each section, in their correct relative positions. Bolt the pieces for each section (sides and gable ends) together. Decide where the vents are to be positioned and leave suitable gaps for them, as necessary. Do not fully tighten the nuts until all sections are assembled and have been loosely put together.

Bolt the sections to one another, and then to the base, then bolt on the roof bars and ridge bar.

Ventilators

Ventilator frames are assembled separately, then bolted onto the roof and sides before glazing. This gives greater flexibility than with wooden greenhouses when choosing both the number and position of ventilators. The hinges of roof ventilators usually slide in a groove in the molding.

Glazing

Glazing strips are used for metal greenhouses. Cut the strips to length and press them into the grooves in the glazing bars—shaped pieces of metal that form the framework to hold the glass securely in position.

Glaze the sides of the greenhouse first, placing the glass squarely between the glazing bars, leaving about ⅛in (3mm) clearance on each side of the glass panes for the clips to be attached. The upper panes of glass should overlap the lower ones by about ½in (1cm). Secure them with overlap glazing clips—pieces of metal bent into "S" shapes that hook over the lower pane and hold the upper one firmly in position.

Once each pane is in position, use glazing clips, pressing them into place between the glazing bars and panes to hold the glass. A little pressure will be needed to overcome the natural spring in the metal.

Glaze the gable ends of the greenhouse and then the roof, using the same technique.

Installing the door

Metal greenhouses usually have sliding doors. These should be bolted together and slid into the runners provided in the end frame. A stop is supplied for bolting on afterward to prevent the door from coming off the runners if opened too quickly. The door should be glazed once it has been hung.

Installing the benches

The benches supplied by the maker are designed to be bolted or screwed to the frame. This is best done at the same time as the greenhouse is built, especially for octagonal and dome-shaped greenhouses, which have benches specially designed to fit. If solid benches are used, leave a gap several inches wide between the inside of the greenhouse and the benches, to allow air to circulate.

INSTALLING ELECTRICITY, NATURAL GAS, AND WATER

Installing an outdoor power supply is not a job for an amateur. The installation of electricity in a greenhouse must be carried out by a licensed electrician, although considerable savings may be made by digging the trench for the cable yourself and then refilling it later when the job is completed. Alternatively, the cable may be run overhead if your greenhouse is close to the house and it will not be unsightly; your electrician will be able to advise you as to whether or not this is a practical option. Insulated cords and waterproof hardware should always be used for safety.

Electricity has many practical uses in the greenhouse: power for heating, propagators, lighting, timers, heating cables, and electrically powered garden tools of various types.

Natural gas is useful for heating the greenhouse. If the greenhouse is sited close to the house, it may be possible to extend the system; otherwise, use an outside tank. Consult your local utility about the feasibility and cost of installing natural gas lines. You might save money by offering to do the digging yourself.

If you already have an outdoor water faucet, you may be able to add a branch from its pipe and run it to the greenhouse. In regions with cold winters, either the system must be buried below the frost line or, if the greenhouse will not be used during winter, provisions must be made to drain the lines before the onset of severe cold.

REPLACING A PANE IN A METAL GREENHOUSE

Attach overlap glazing clips to the base pane. Wearing gloves, lift the pane into place, gently pressing the top edge into position before hooking the bottom edge onto the lower pane. Secure the pane with glazing clips (see inset), pressing them gently until they slot into position.

Creating the right environment

Creating the right balance of conditions in a greenhouse to suit the plants grown there is the essence of successful greenhouse gardening.

For tender plants, the temperature maintained is vital. In a heated greenhouse, be sure to choose an efficient, reliable, and economical heater. In any greenhouse, good insulation that will retain heat and keep out drafts must be balanced with the need for thorough ventilation. Shading is essential in the majority of greenhouses during the summer to help prevent the plants from overheating; see PRINCIPLES OF PROPAGATION, *Shading Greenhouses (Temperate climates)*, p.636.

Atmospheric humidity should be kept at a level that suits the plants inside. Automatic methods of watering tend to increase humidity so, for most plants, special humidifiers may not be necessary. Special lighting is often useful to increase the growth potential of plants.

Greenhouse temperature

The choice of plants to be grown in a greenhouse is determined largely by the temperature at which it is maintained (see "The greenhouse environment," p.359). There are four categories of greenhouse: cold, cool, temperate, and warm. The environment is controlled slightly differently in each type.

Cold

A cold greenhouse is not heated at all. Insulation (see p.574) is needed to keep out the worst of the winter cold, and some form of shading (see p.576) is needed in summer. Thorough ventilation (see p.575) is important all year round.

A cold greenhouse may be used to grow summer crops, to overwinter slightly tender plants, or to propagate cuttings (although a propagator will increase the success rate, see p.580). An unheated greenhouse can also permit an early display of hardy plants and many types of spring bulbs.

An unheated greenhouse is suitable for alpines—some are specifically designed to provide maximum ventilation for this type of plant (see "Alpine house," p.569), although any greenhouse with louver ventilators along the sides is adequate.

Cool/frost-free

A cool greenhouse is one that is heated just enough to keep out frost. This means that a minimum daytime temperature range between 41°F (5°C) and 50°F (10°C), and a nighttime temperature of no less than 36°F (2°C), is needed.

To ensure that these temperatures are maintained, a heater capable of a substantial temperature shift is a necessity in winter, in case the outside temperature falls many degrees below freezing. A gas heater with a thermostat (see p.574) is most likely to do this efficiently. Insulation, thorough ventilation, and shading control are necessary, as with cold greenhouses.

A frost-free greenhouse may be used to grow all the types of plants mentioned for cold greenhouses. In addition, frost-tender plants can be overwintered, and summer crops or flowering pot plants grown. A propagator will be needed for germinating seeds. Young seedlings will benefit from the extra light provided by a greenhouse light (see p.577).

Temperate

A slightly warmer greenhouse with a minimum daytime temperature range between 50°F (10°C) and 55°F (13°C), and with a minimum nighttime temperature of 45°F (7°C), is suitable for growing a good selection of ornamentals in containers, as well as vegetables and herbs.

Additional warmth is necessary in spring for propagation, supplied by a propagator or by boosting the ordinary heat for the required period. Supplementary lighting provided by a greenhouse light is useful. Shading and good ventilation are required, especially in summer.

Warm

A warm greenhouse has a daytime temperature range between 55°F (13°C) and 64°F (18°C), with a minimum nighttime temperature of 55°F (13°C). Such high temperatures enable an amateur gardener to grow a large range of plants, including tropical and subtropical ornamentals, fruit, and vegetables. A warm greenhouse can also be used to propagate plants and raise seedlings without the aid of propagation equipment, although a greenhouse light would also be useful.

In hot weather, very good ventilation—preferably automatic—cooling pads, an efficient method of shading, and high humidity (see p.576) are essential.

HOW A GREENHOUSE WORKS

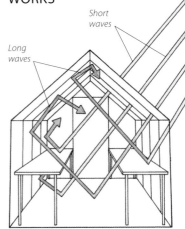

Short waves

Long waves

Light passes through glass as short-wave radiation, warming everything inside, including the floor, benches, soil, and plants. Heat then reradiates from these as long waves, which cannot pass through the glass, leading to a buildup of heat inside the greenhouse.

HOW TO BALANCE THE ENVIRONMENT OF A GREENHOUSE

	Heating (see p.574)	Insulation (see p.574)	Ventilation (see p.575)	Shading (see p.576)	Humidity (see p.576)	Watering (see p.577)	Lighting (see p.577)
Cold No minimum temperature	None.	Insulate against severely cold drafts and damp, foggy weather in winter.	Thorough ventilation is essential to prevent damp, stagnant conditions in winter.	Shade vulnerable plants in summer with a shading wash, blinds, mesh or fabric, or rigid sheets.	Unlikely to be a problem in summer. Maintain a "dry" atmosphere in winter by ventilating.	Water by hand in winter. Use a capillary system, soaker hose, or trickle system in summer.	Greenhouse lights are unlikely to be needed for the type of plants grown.
Cool Minimum temperature 36°F (2°C)	A thermostatically controlled electric heater is preferable, but gas or kerosene heaters may also be used. A cold alarm is useful if tender plants are grown.	In winter, as for a cold greenhouse. In spring, good insulation is extremely important if frost-tender plants are grown.	Ventilate freely, especially if a gas or kerosene heater is used, to disperse water vapor and toxic fumes.	Shade to control the temperature in summer —shading washes or blinds do this most efficiently. Fit automatic blinds, if possible.	Misting is beneficial to increase humidity in summer.	As for a cold greenhouse, except that an overhead system may also be used in summer.	Greenhouse lights may be useful, especially in spring when natural light is poor, for plants at an early stage of development.
Temperate Minimum temperature 45°F (7°C)	A heater (preferably electric) fitted with a thermostat is required. A cold alarm is also essential.	As for cold and cool greenhouses. Thermal screens are useful in spring for propagation.	As for a cool greenhouse. Automatic vent openers are extremely useful in summer.	As for a cool greenhouse.	Maintain high humidity in spring and summer, especially around cuttings and seedlings.	An automatic watering system is useful throughout the year.	Greenhouse lights are useful in winter and spring for extending day length.
Warm Minimum temperature 55°F (13°C)	As for a temperate greenhouse.	Good insulation is essential throughout the year to minimize heating costs.	Automatic vent openers fitted to several vents simplify temperature control enormously.	Automatic blinds are desirable in summer.	High humidity is required throughout the year.	As for a temperate greenhouse.	As for a temperate greenhouse.

Heating

It is important to maintain the correct temperature in the greenhouse for the range of plants you have chosen to grow. Select a heater that is powerful enough to maintain the required minimum temperature efficiently. Other factors to consider when choosing a greenhouse heater include convenience, and the cost of installation and running it.

Electric heaters

These are the most reliable, efficient, and convenient to use in the greenhouse, although an electrical line will be needed to run them (see "Installing electricity, natural gas, and water," p.572). They are usually controlled by a thermostat, which means that no heat is wasted, and they do not require regular refueling or maintenance. Also, electric heaters do not have fumes or water vapor.

A number of different types of electric heaters are available. These include fan heaters and waterproof tubular heaters, both of which heat the greenhouse effectively. Convection heaters can also be used, but these do not distribute heat as efficiently. Tubular heaters need to be fitted to the sides of the greenhouse, just above floor level. Other heaters can be moved around as needed.

Electric fan heaters are particularly useful, because they promote good air circulation, which helps to maintain an even temperature and minimizes the spread of disease. They may also be used to cool the greenhouse in warm weather if the heating element is switched off.

Natural gas or propane heaters

Gas heating systems can be run off your house lines (see "Installing electricity, natural gas, and water," p.572) or from an outside tank. They are not as convenient to use as electric heaters: although they may have thermostats, these are not usually calibrated in degrees, so you will need to experiment to find the correct setting.

If an outside tank is used, most suppliers will routinely check it to keep it filled, depending on the temperature. Propane gas releases fumes and water vapor as it burns, so ventilation is important.

Kerosene heaters

These are not as efficient as electric or gas heaters in their use of fuel because they are not controlled by a thermostat. Kerosene heaters may therefore be expensive to run if a high temperature needs to be maintained, because some energy may be wasted. However, they are inexpensive to buy in the first place and there is no installation cost.

When using kerosene heaters, thorough ventilation is required because some plant-toxic fumes and water vapor are produced as a byproduct of combustion—a humid, stagnant atmosphere may encourage disease if ventilation is poor. Other drawbacks include the need to transport and store fuel, and to check the fuel level and wick every day to ensure that it is burning cleanly.

Circulated hot water

Coal- or wood-based hot water systems are now rarely used in greenhouses. Oil- and gas-fired systems are still sometimes used, but seldom on the small scale of the home greenhouse.

Although the distribution of heat through hot water pipes provides good heat transfer, often only about 50 percent of the energy released is used. Greenhouses attached to a house may be heated by connecting them to the home heating system. Check with local contractors and utilities for details.

Thermometer and cold alarm

If the heater in a greenhouse is not thermostatically controlled, use a maximum/minimum thermometer to check that the correct overnight temperatures are being maintained for the plants grown.

In regions that suffer extremely low temperatures, a cold alarm is a useful safeguard if the greenhouse contains tender plants. If the air temperature unexpectedly drops to near freezing, for example, through a power failure or heater breakdown, an alarm bell will sound remotely (this will usually be somewhere in the home), allowing you time to protect the plants.

A COLD ALARM

Install a cold alarm if growing tender plants that may be damaged or killed if the temperature falls.

INSULATION MATERIAL

Bubble plastic is useful for insulating a greenhouse and reduces heat loss considerably. Cut it to size and attach it securely to the framework.

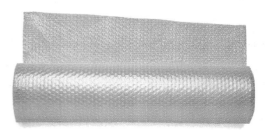

Insulation

Insulation in the greenhouse can reduce heating costs considerably; if a minimum temperature of 45°F (7°C) is required, for example, the cost of insulation may be recovered within just a few seasons—and even in a single winter in very cold areas. The higher the temperature to be maintained, and the colder the region, the more cost-effective insulation is likely to be. Care in choosing the right material is needed, however, because some insulation materials may reduce the amount of light reaching the plants.

Double glazing

The most efficient method of insulating the entire greenhouse is to install double-pane glass. This is best done during construction, if at all possible. Double glazing is expensive, of course, but the long-term money and energy savings can be significant.

Flexible plastic insulation

Bubble plastic, which consists of double or triple skins of transparent plastic with air cells in between, is a very efficient method of insulation. A single layer of plastic sheeting is not as efficient as bubble plastic at reducing heat loss but is less expensive and does not cut out as much light. Plastic sheets can be used in winter as an inexpensive form of double glazing. To attach the insulation material, use suction cups or clips that fit into the greenhouse frame.

Thermal screens

These consist of sheets of clear plastic or translucent material, such as a cross-laminated fabric, that are attached to wires between the eaves and drawn horizontally across the width of the greenhouse in the evening. They are useful for conserving heat at night because they restrict the amount of heat that rises above the eaves, trapping the warmth lower down around the plants.

Vertical screens may also be used to partition off a heated section at one end of the greenhouse with plastic sheeting, leaving the remainder of the area unheated. Plants can be overwintered and early seedlings raised in the heated section.

Special kits for making thermal screens are available, or plastic sheeting and the necessary hardware can be obtained.

Base siding

Base siding on the floor of glass-to-ground greenhouses reduces heat loss significantly. In winter, place polystyrene panels along the foot of the glass panes to provide extra insulation, removing them before raised beds are planted in spring.

THERMAL SCREENS

Horizontal screen between the eaves

Vertical screen that acts as a partition

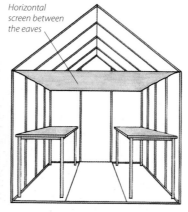
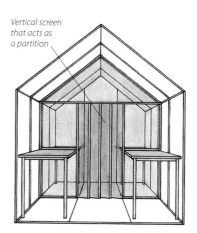

Thermal screens can be drawn horizontally between the eaves. They can also be drawn vertically to partition off a section of the greenhouse that needs to be heated to a high temperature.

Ventilation

Good ventilation is essential in a greenhouse, even in winter, to avoid a buildup of stuffy or damp, stale air, and to control temperature. It is important that the area covered by ventilators should be equal to at least one-sixth of the floor area.

Extra ventilation

Few greenhouses are supplied with enough ventilators as standard, so order additional air vents, hinged louver windows, or extractor fans when buying a greenhouse. This is an especially important consideration with wooden greenhouses, because it is usually difficult to add them later.

Extra ventilation is particularly important if kerosene or propane heating systems are used, to prevent water vapor and fumes from building up to an high level.

Wind-ventilation system

Air exchange in a greenhouse occurs when external movements of air, caused by gusts of wind, replace interior warm, humid air with fresh air. If ventilators are placed on the sides and roof of the greenhouse, and are also staggered, this will ensure that air circulates throughout the entire area—if vents are placed directly opposite each other, air will simply blow straight through the greenhouse.

Doors may also be kept open in summer to increase ventilation. Consider adding a screen door to keep out birds and pets.

Chimney-ventilation system

Chimney-effect ventilation depends on warm, humid air rising out of roof vents and being replaced by fresh air that is drawn in as a result through lower ventilators, which are usually positioned along the sides of the greenhouse either above or below the benches.

Fan-ventilation system

Fan ventilation is a mechanically driven system that works by extracting air from the greenhouse at head height, or slightly higher, and drawing in fresh air through vents lower down and usually at the opposite end of the greenhouse.

Hinged ventilators

These may be fitted to the sides or roof of the greenhouse and should open wide, to an angle of about 45°. This will allow maximum airflow, while at the same time preventing direct gusts of wind from entering the greenhouse and possibly causing damage to the plants or even to the structure itself.

THE PRINCIPLES OF GREENHOUSE VENTILATION

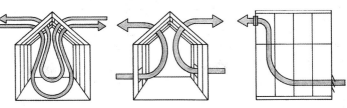

Wind effect
Fresh air blows into the greenhouse, circulates, and then escapes through an open vent on the opposite side.

Chimney effect
Warm air rises and escapes through open vents in the roof, drawing in fresh, cooler air lower down.

Fan ventilation
Air is drawn out by a fan at the top of the greenhouse and drawn in through open vents lower down.

Louver ventilators

Usually positioned below the height of the benches, louver window ventilators are particularly useful for controlling the flow of air throughout the greenhouse in winter, when roof ventilators may allow too much heat to escape. The louver vents must close tightly, however, so that they exclude all drafts.

Automatic vent openers

"Autovent" openers simplify temperature control significantly in the greenhouse—they are designed to open automatically whenever the temperature inside rises above a predetermined level. These devices are essential if a heating system that has no thermostat has been installed in the greenhouse.

With any type of greenhouse, automatic vent openers should be fitted to at least some of the hinged or louver ventilators; this is easily done by closely following the manufacturer's instructions.

They may be set to open at a range of temperatures, but make sure you choose an automatic system that will function within the temperature range required in your greenhouse. Set this to operate at a temperature that is just below the optimum for the plants in order for the vents to open before the temperature inside rises to an unsuitable level.

Many different designs of autovents are available. Some models work by the expansion and contraction of a plug of wax that is contained in a metal or plastic cylinder; the movement of the wax works a piston that opens and closes the ventilator. Other models make use of metal rods that alter their shape as the temperature rises and falls, activating the ventilation mechanism.

Extractor fans

The type of extractor fan that is designed primarily for use in kitchens and bathrooms is also ideally suited for use in the greenhouse. An additional bonus with using these extractor fans is that most of them are fitted with a thermostat, which is an essential requirement for the greenhouse.

Choose a fan that is powerful enough for the particular size of your greenhouse—the extraction feet or meters per hour. As a general guide, a 6 x 8ft (2 x 2.5m) greenhouse requires a fan with a capacity of 10,000cu ft (300cu m) per hour, but a smaller one may be perfectly adequate if other types of ventilation are also used.

A louver window—positioned at the opposite end of the greenhouse to the extractor fan and set lower down—is essential to provide a flow of fresh air to replace the stale air that is drawn out by the fan.

Buy a fan that is fitted with louver flaps that close when the fan is not actually working so that drafts are excluded. To extend the working life of the fan, the motor should not be set to run at maximum capacity; it is much better to choose a model that is slightly more powerful than is strictly necessary for the greenhouse.

Shading

This will help to control the temperature of the greenhouse if the ventilation system is insufficient. It also protects vulnerable plants from too much direct sunlight, reducing the risk

LOUVER VENTS

These are fitted on the side of the greenhouse above ground level to improve the flow of air through the interior. The opening mechanism has a lever and is simple to operate (see insets).

HINGED VENTS

Vents that open by a hinge mechanism are normally fitted to the roof of the greenhouse. Make sure that they open wide and that they are securely fixed when open.

AUTOVENT OPENER

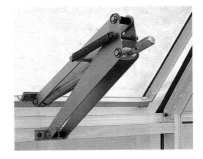

This autovent works by the expansion and contraction of wax in a cylinder as the greenhouse temperature rises and falls.

of leaf scorch, and preventing flower colors from fading in strong sunlight. Shading applied primarily to control heat should be on the outside of the greenhouse; internal shading is unlikely to reduce the temperature significantly.

The amount of shade required in a greenhouse depends on the season and the plants being grown. In the months of strongest sunlight, shading that reduces the light by 40–50 percent is suitable for a typical mixed greenhouse. Ferns generally prefer approximately 75 percent light filtering, while most cacti and other succulents require very little or no shading at all.

Shading washes
These are often the most effective and cheapest method of reducing heat from the sun, while still allowing enough light to penetrate for good plant growth. Paint or spray the wash onto the outside of the glass at the beginning of the sunny season. Reapply if heavy rains prematurely remove the shading before late summer.

Shading washes are inexpensive but they can be messy to apply and remove, and their appearance is sometimes unattractive in a small garden where the greenhouse is a major feature. Some washes become more transparent when wet, so that on rainy days or when the weather is dull they allow more light penetration.

Blinds
These are used mainly on the outside of the greenhouse and control temperature effectively. They are more versatile than shading washes, because they may be rolled up or down, depending on the intensity of light required. They may be used where only a section of the greenhouse needs to be shaded. Manually operated blinds need constant attention, however. Automatic

blinds, which start operating as soon as the temperature rises to a predetermined level, are more convenient to use, but they can be relatively expensive.

Meshes and fabrics
Flexible mesh shading materials are suitable for either interior or exterior use. They are less adaptable than blinds because they usually remain in position for the entire season, and they are less satisfactory than shading washes in helping to control plant growth.

Woven and knitted fabrics are also suitable for both interior and exterior greenhouse use. The amount of light reduction varies considerably, depending on the type of fabric fitted, but the quality of light allowed through to the plants is usually perfectly adequate for good growth, although the temperature is not significantly reduced. Cross-laminated fabric and some plastic meshes are recommended for internal shading only.

Tinted bubble plastic may also be used for shading. It cuts down the light by almost 50 percent, but it reduces temperature only slightly.

FLEXIBLE MESH

Plastic mesh netting may be cut to length and used either internally or externally for shading plants in a greenhouse.

ROLLER BLINDS

Blinds are a versatile method of shading the greenhouse. They should be durable, because they will be in place for long periods of time.

Rigid sheets
Rigid polycarbonate sheets (usually tinted) are sometimes used for shading in greenhouses. The sheets may be fixed either inside or outside, as recommended by the greenhouse manufacturer. They cut down the light effectively, but unless they are white in color the quality of light transmitted may not be sufficient for good plant growth.

Humidity

Humidity is a measure of the quantity of water vapor in the air. The humidity of the air affects the rate at which plants transpire; this is their mechanism for drawing water (along with nutrients) from roots to leaves, where the water then evaporates from leaf pores into the air. As water evaporates, the plant is cooled down.

Establish the preferred humidity levels of the plants in your greenhouse, then control the amount of moisture in the atmosphere to suit them. Humidity may be increased using various techniques (see "Humidifiers," right) and reduced by ventilation (see p.575).

Plant requirements
A very humid atmosphere reduces the rate of transpiration and evaporation to a level that may be harmful to some plants and they may suffer damage from overheating unless cooler, drier air is brought in by ventilation. Many tropical plants from humid climates require high levels of humidity for healthy growth, however, and will not survive in a dry atmosphere.

If the air is dry and the humidity level low, plants transpire more rapidly, often losing a great deal of

moisture. Plants that are not adapted to cope with low humidity will wilt as a result, unless additional water is supplied at the roots. Dry-climate plants often have specific anatomical features that reduce the transpiration rate in drought conditions (see WATER CONSERVATION AND RECYCLING, pp.614–615).

Measuring humidity
The level of humidity in a greenhouse depends to an extent on the temperature of the air— warm air is capable of holding more moisture than cold air before it becomes saturated. Relative humidity is a measure of the amount of water vapor in the air expressed as a percentage of saturation point at the same temperature. A humid atmosphere is defined as having a relative humidity of about 75 percent; a dry atmosphere has a relative humidity of about 35 percent.

Wet and dry bulb thermometers, used in conjunction with hygrometric tables, can be used to measure the relative humidity of the atmosphere. Hygrometers, which have a dial that gives readings for both the temperature and the humidity, are also available. As a general guide, a relative humidity below 75 percent, but above 40 percent, is beneficial for most greenhouse plants during the growing season—at levels above 80 percent, diseases such as gray mold/*Botrytis* and mildew may become a problem.

In winter, humidity should be maintained at a lower level, but the exact level required will depend on the types of plant grown and the temperature of the greenhouse.

Humidifiers
Greenhouses can be humidified during the summer by splashing water—predominantly on the floor and on any benches—from a watering can or hose. This has the effect of increasing the level of atmospheric humidity. An automatic spray system simplifies humidity control, especially for plants that require very high humidity. In a small greenhouse, mist-spraying by hand or providing a tray filled with water that slowly evaporates into the air is usually adequate.

Watering

A traditional watering can is still the best, if perhaps time-consuming, method of watering a mixed collection of plants in a

SHADING THE GREENHOUSE

Shading washes are applied to the outside of a greenhouse to prevent the temperature inside from rising too high, without greatly reducing light. The washes may be left on throughout the season.

small greenhouse. Because you can readily monitor the flow, it ensures that all the plants are watered according to their individual requirements.

An automatic watering system is a useful addition to a greenhouse in summer, however; if the greenhouse is left unattended on a regular basis, an automatic system becomes essential, because some pot plants may need to be watered several times a day in very hot weather.

Capillary systems

Watering systems that rely on capillary action to draw up water are often used in a greenhouse.

Plant pots may be arranged on a ¾–2in (2–5cm) layer of clean sand (which retains moisture well) that is arranged on the greenhouse benches and kept permanently wet. Moist sand adds considerable weight to the benches, however, so make sure that it is sturdy enough to take the extra load. In addition, protect wooden benches from the wet sand by lining them with sheets of heavy-duty plastic, or the wood will rot. Alternatively, the sand can be placed in aluminum or plastic trays.

Add a length of plastic gutter to the edge of the bench and keep it filled with water. This may be done by hand or automatically from an overhead tank connected to the hose bib, in which case the system should be controlled by a ballcock.

Capillary matting, which is widely available in rolls and is simply cut to the required size, is far lighter, easier to keep clean, and just as effective as sand. To keep the capillary matting continuously moist, trail the edge into a water trough or other reservoir of water. The water may be topped off by hand or supplied automatically from the main supply, as above.

For a capillary system to be effective, there must be sufficient contact between the soil mix in the pots and the source of moisture so that water is continuously supplied to the plants' root systems. Plastic plant pots usually allow good contact between the soil and the moist sand or matting. Clay pots, however, may each require a wick. This is cut out of a piece of spare capillary matting or nylon yard and placed in the drainage hole of the pot to bridge any gaps between the soil and the mat.

During the winter months, do not use capillary watering systems in the greenhouse; most plants are dormant or growing only slowly, and therefore require a reduced intake of water. The perpetually damp mat or sand may also increase humidity in the greenhouse to unsatisfactory levels for the plants (see "Humidity," p.576).

Overhead systems

A system of overhead pipes, with nozzles from which water is sprayed onto the plants below, is widely used in commercial greenhouses. This is an ideal system for watering a large number of plants that are all at a similar stage of growth. It is not suitable for the small home greenhouse, however, that contains a wide variety of plants. Overhead watering systems are also expensive to install and create too humid an atmosphere if used in the winter.

Soaker hoses

These are widely used in the garden, and inside the greenhouse to water border crops for fill or to keep capillary matting moist. In very hot weather, however, soaker hoses may not supply a sufficient flow of water to the plants (see also p.561).

Trickle-irrigation systems

This type of irrigation system consists of a series of small-bore tubes, each with an adjustable nozzle. The tubes are placed in the individual pots or grow bags, or near plants growing in greenhouse beds.

Most trickle-irrigation systems are fed with water from a reservoir that is filled in turn from a hose connected to the water supply. It is possible, however, to use water supplied direct from the hose bib.

The rate of water delivery must be monitored very carefully and adjusted according to the needs of the plants; these needs vary depending on time of year and the vagaries of the weather (see also p.561).

Lighting

If an electric power supply is already installed in the greenhouse (see "Installing electricity, natural gas, and water," p.572), lighting units are not expensive to add at any time, and running costs are also low. In addition, the lights produce a little extra heat for the plants. Ordinary fluorescent lamps provide enough illumination to work by comfortably.

Greenhouse lights

The special quality of lighting produced by greenhouse lights is required to increase light intensity and day length (see THE VEGETABLE GARDEN, "Day

WATERING SYSTEMS

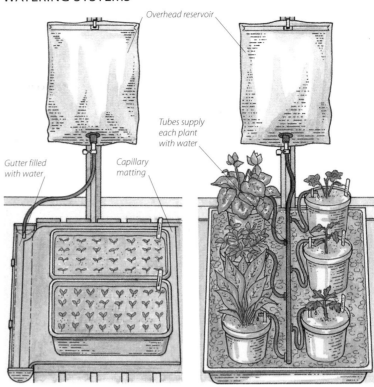

Capillary watering
An overhead reservoir feeds water to a gutter fixed to the benches. The matting soaks up water, which is absorbed by soil mix in the trays.

Trickle irrigation
Trickle systems supply water directly to each pot by means of tubes, which are fed from an overhead reservoir.

length," pp.494–495) for specific purposes during fall and winter when light levels are low.

Fluorescent tubes that produce good light to improve plant growth can be obtained from specialty suppliers and garden centers. They do not produce much heat, and so may be placed close to the plants. The lights are fitted with reflectors that cast the light downward, where it will do the most good. For greatest effectiveness, the tubes should be mounted 10–12in (25–30cm) above the foliage. Mercury fluorescent lamps and mercury vapor lamps also provide a suitable quality of light to encourage good plant growth.

Metal halide lamps are the best, if most expensive, form of greenhouse light, emitting light that is close to the spectrum of natural light. They illuminate a large area but cast light in a circular pattern, which may be inconvenient in a small greenhouse, because the corners may not be strongly lit.

Most greenhouse lights that are suitable for use in the greenhouse need special fittings because of the moist, humid atmosphere. If in any doubt, always ask the advice of a licensed electrician.

Light meters

Where lighting is a very important factor, special plant light meters can be extremely useful in the greenhouse. They measure light levels much more accurately than can be judged by the naked eye.

Light meters are usually supplied with information about the light levels that are preferred by a wide range of commonly cultivated plants, so follow the instructions for the particular plants grown.

A GREENHOUSE LIGHT

This provides additional light to improve plant growth. Secure it directly above the plants, if possible.

Using the space

To make best use of the limited space in a greenhouse, plan the layout carefully. Using raised beds, grow-bags, or containers placed on the ground, benches, or shelves are all good methods; often, a combination may be best.

Raised beds

These are used mainly in alpine houses, where sharp drainage is required. Raised beds can be expensive to construct using new bricks, but old bricks are satisfactory. Leave a large gap between a raised bed and the wall of a greenhouse so that air can circulate and moisture from the soil mix does not penetrate the wall. For details see STRUCTURES AND SURFACES, "Raised beds," p.599.

Beds that are raised to normal bench height are suitable only for lean-to greenhouses or for those with a tall brick base. For small plants that do not require a great depth of soil, a stone trough placed on brick pillars or "legs" can be used. Alternatively, construct a raised container by placing rigid metal sheets or paving slabs on top of brick pillars, making the walls by laying several brick courses around the top, and lining with a sheet of synthetic rubber. The rubber sheet should have several holes pierced in it to ensure that the bed will be adequately drained.

Raised beds for taller plants do not need to be this high and so do not need to stand on brick pillars. They are usually built up from ground level with basal seep holes for drainage and simply filled with potting mix.

Growing in beds and bags

A glass-to-ground greenhouse is required to grow plants directly at ground level, to ensure that plants receive enough light. Beds with a width of 3ft (1m) are acceptable in a greenhouse that is 8ft (2.5m) wide, but make the beds wider if benches are placed above them, so that the benches do not prevent you from reaching the far side easily. Plants in containers can also be placed on top of the border rather than on benches, if required.

The soil in greenhouses may become infected with disease if the same plants are grown repeatedly over many years. If this is the case, or if the greenhouse floor is concrete, grow-bags may be used. Grow-bags provide a convenient method of cultivation, because they retain moisture well and remove the need to dig and fertilize the soil before planting. All the nutrients in the soil mix contained in the

INSIDE THE GREENHOUSE

Organize the elements within the greenhouse sensibly to make the best possible use of the limited space. Here is a well-planned layout for a lean-to greenhouse.

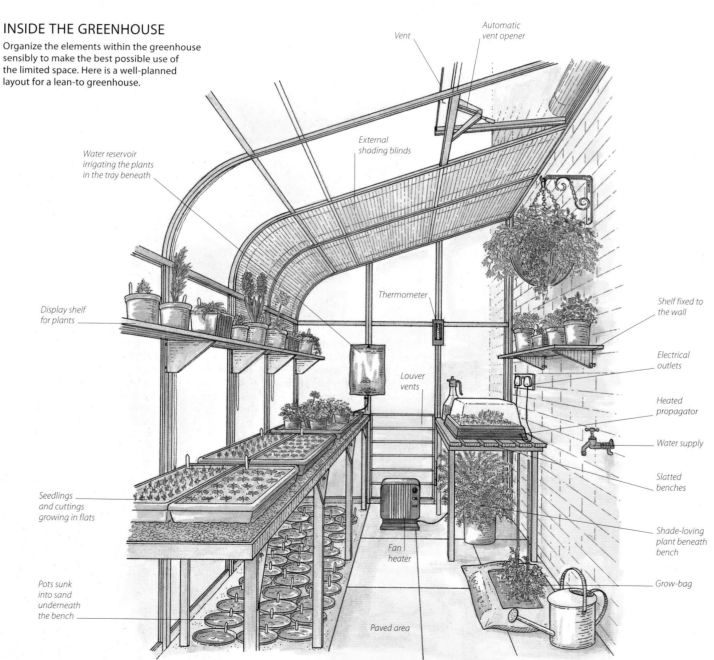

Vent

Automatic vent opener

External shading blinds

Water reservoir irrigating the plants in the tray beneath

Thermometer

Shelf fixed to the wall

Display shelf for plants

Electrical outlets

Heated propagator

Louver vents

Water supply

Seedlings and cuttings growing in flats

Slatted benches

Shade-loving plant beneath bench

Fan heater

Grow-bag

Pots sunk into sand underneath the bench

Paved area

DISPLAYING THE PLANTS

Shelves and benches allow attractive tiered displays of plants of varying heights. If the greenhouse is heated, a wide variety of plants can be grown throughout the year to maintain the display of flowers and foliage. Place dormant or "resting" plants beneath the benches to make more room for other plants in season.

grow-bags are used up during the season, so fresh grow-bags should be used each year.

Benches

Benches are important for any ornamental or mixed greenhouse—they bring plants closer to the light and make watering and care easier. Even if the benches are removed in order to grow border crops in summer, they are necessary for propagating and growing young plants.

Positioning the benches

The most satisfactory arrangement for a small or mixed greenhouse is to have a central path with benches along the sides, and possibly across one end. Remove half of the benches for growing border crops when necessary and retain the permanent benches to display ornamentals. The permanent benches should be positioned on the side where they will cast the least shade on the border crops.

Central benches

Larger ornamental greenhouses that are designed primarily for displaying plants may have benches placed in the center, with a path around the edge. Two benches can be placed back-to-back, preferably with tiered benches in the center to highlight the display of plants.

The right size and height

Most greenhouse benches are 18–24in (45–60cm) wide. Wider benches are useful in a large greenhouse but they may be difficult to reach across. All benches need to be of sturdy construction to support the

considerable weight of plants, containers, and potting mix. Always leave a generous gap between the back of any benches and the sides of the greenhouse to allow air to circulate.

Most home greenhouses also have to serve as a potting shed. A convenient height for benches that are also used as a work surface is approximately 30–36in (75–90cm); it should be lower if a seated working position is needed.

Freestanding benches

It is sometimes useful to have benches that can be dismantled and stored away, then brought into the greenhouse for short periods, for instance, when raising seedlings in spring. Freestanding benches may

FREESTANDING BENCHES

Movable benches allow great flexibility. They can be moved around to accommodate the plants, or removed altogether when appropriate.

FIXED BENCHES

Most greenhouse manufacturers supply permanent, custom-built benches that are made from the same materials as the greenhouse. They are best fitted at the same time that the greenhouse is constructed.

not fit the greenhouse quite as well as benches that are built-in and may not look as attractive but are more flexible in use. They must be easy to assemble and sturdy because they will be in use for many years. If border crops are grown for most of the year, open-mesh benches that fold back neatly against the side of the greenhouse are convenient for short periods.

Freestanding modular systems can be built up in tiers and provide an attractive way of displaying plants. Slatted, mesh, or solid modular systems are available.

Permanent benches

Built-in benches and shelves can put a strain on the framework of a greenhouse, especially light, aluminum alloy structures. Sand or gravel, if used, adds extra weight to the benches, particularly when it is wet. Buy benches that are built to take this additional weight; if in doubt, check with the greenhouse manufacturer before fitting any permanent benches.

Slatted and mesh benches

If you are growing alpines or cacti and succulents in pots, it is preferable to use slatted or mesh benches, which allow a freer flow of air than a solid bench. However, slatted and mesh benches are not suitable for capillary watering systems.

SLATTED BENCHES

Wooden-slatted benches are an attractive choice. The slats allow better air circulation around the plants than solid-surface benches do, but slats are not suitable for a capillary watering system, unless pots are placed in trays on the bench.

For a wooden greenhouse, use wooden slatted benches; for an aluminum alloy or galvanized steel greenhouse, metal or plastic-mesh benches are more appropriate.

Solid surface benches

Solid benches allow more pots to be accommodated than slatted benches (it is difficult to keep pots upright between the slats), but may require more ventilation.

If using a capillary watering system, choose solid aluminum benches that have a level surface for the matting or sand. Some types of benches have reversible sections that produce raised flat surfaces for mats if placed one way, and dishlike sections for sand or gravel if reversed.

Shelves

Shelves in the greenhouse can be used for both storage and display. Permanent shelves often cast shade on the plants below so it is preferable to install foldaway shelves, which can be used in spring when space is short and then put away for the rest of the year.

In a small greenhouse, shelves can be used to display trailing plants where there is not enough headroom for hanging baskets.

Propagation aids

The propagation of many plants requires higher temperatures than may realistically be maintained in the greenhouse. To save on fuel bills, therefore, propagation aids are often used to provide the extra heat required. They may also increase the success rate when sowing seed or rooting leafy cuttings. Choose a propagator for the greenhouse that is large enough to hold at least three standard seed flats.

An electrical power supply in the greenhouse is essential if heated propagators, mist units, or soil-warming cables are to be used. Mist units require a main water supply as well as a power supply.

Unheated propagators are of limited use in the greenhouse but usually provide sufficient humidity for rooting tip, softwood, or semiripe cuttings in summer. On a small scale, a similar effect is created by enclosing a pot of cuttings in a clear plastic bag.

Heated propagators

A heated propagator should have a heating element that is capable of providing a minimum soil temperature of 59°F (15°C) in winter and early spring, when temperatures outside may fall below freezing.

If tropical plants are to be propagated, the unit must have a more powerful heating element that can maintain a temperature of 75°F (24°C). The propagator should preferably be fitted with an adjustable thermostat, which allows greater flexibility of temperature.

Use rigid plastic lids, because these are more likely to retain the heat than thin plastic covers. Adjustable ventilators are useful because they allow moisture to escape and prevent the atmosphere inside the propagator from becoming too humid.

Domestic propagators
Some small heated propagators are designed for windowsill use. Usually holding just two seed flats, they are generally too small to be of practical use in the greenhouse and often do not have a thermostat. They may not generate enough heat in a

cold or cool greenhouse, because the heating element is intended to operate in a room indoors.

Heated bases
These are designed to be used with unheated propagators or ordinary seed flats, either of which may be placed on the heated base. A plastic hood must be placed over seed flats to maintain warmth and humidity. Heated bases do not raise the temperature as efficiently as heated tray propagators (see below).

Heated tray propagators
These have a self-contained heating element in the base, and are best when fitted with an adjustable thermostat.

Mist units

Cuttings may often be rooted more rapidly and in greater numbers in a mist unit than by using other more conventional means. Mist units, which are normally used mainly by horticultural specialists, automatically maintain a high humidity around cuttings and are useful for difficult plants.

The easiest and most convenient mist units to use are self-contained, enclosed ones that include a heating element, thermostat, sensor, transparent cover, and a misting head. The constant humidity in the atmosphere created by the misting head provides suitable conditions in which to root cuttings quickly—by maintaining a constant film of water on the propagating material. Heat loss by evaporation is also reduced, and there is also less risk of the cuttings being affected by fungal diseases because, when the misting head is in operation, most disease spores are washed out of the air and from the leaves before they can infect plant tissues.

For large numbers of plants, a mist propagation unit is more practical. Some units are designed for use without a cover on an open greenhouse propagating bench; they are used in conjunction with soil-warming cables and also require a specially constructed greenhouse

A soil thermostat controls the temperature of the soil mix, which is heated by cables. The misting head is controlled by a sensor (connected to a solenoid) located near the cuttings. When the atmosphere becomes too dry, the misting head is activated.

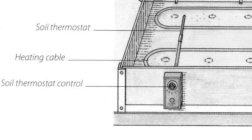

Electrical socket · Shutoff valve · Mist control box · Solenoid · Misting head · Mist control sensor · Sand · Standpipe · Water pipe · Soil thermostat · Heating cable · Soil thermostat control

bench. If sited in a greenhouse where a mixed collection of plants is grown, however, the high humidity created by an open mist unit may prove unsuitable for some plants. In this situation, it would be preferable to install a closed mist unit.

Soil-warming devices

An electric horticultural blanket or a heated flat filled with moisture-retentive matting or sand will also create the basal heat and high humidity needed for successful propagation. More expensive still are soil-warming cables intended primarily for heating the substrate in a conventional propagator or on a mist bench in the greenhouse. Such soil-warming cables may also be used to heat the air in an enclosed space,

such as a cold frame or homemade propagator. The safest system to use is a cable with a wired-in thermostat that is connected to an insulated, fused socket. Buy a screened cable, because it is much less dangerous if the cable is accidentally cut.

Soil-warming cables are sold in lengths designed to heat a given area. A 75-watt cable, for example, measures 20ft (6m) and provides enough heat for a bench area of 7sq ft (0.7sq m) in a greenhouse that has some form of heating. A cable with a higher wattage would, of course, be needed for use in a similar area in an unheated greenhouse or in a cold frame that is outside the greenhouse.

The cable should be laid at a depth of 2–3in (5–8cm) in a series of S bends (with the loops not touching) in a bed of moist sand.

USING SOIL-WARMING CABLES

In this propagating case, cables are used to heat the sand base and the air. Each set of cables has a thermostat, which ensures that the temperature never falls below a preset level.

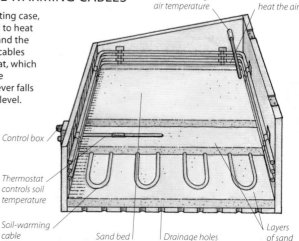

Thermostat regulates air temperature · Cables also heat the air · Control box · Thermostat controls soil temperature · Soil-warming cable · Sand bed · Drainage holes · Layers of sand

A WINDOWSILL PROPAGATOR

Portable propagators should be used indoors, where they will retain the high humidity needed to germinate seeds or root cuttings.

Cold frames and cloches

Cold frames and cloches relieve pressure on greenhouse space, but they are also extremely useful in their own right. They are likely to be used most intensively in spring to harden off plants raised in a greenhouse, but they may also be used throughout the year to grow a wide range of crops. In the colder months, they are useful for protecting winter flowers, overwintering the seeds of hardy annuals sown in the fall, and sheltering vulnerable alpines from the worst of the wet weather.

Cold frames

The most popular type of cold frame has glass (or clear plastic) sides as well as glass "lights" (frame tops that contain the panes of glass), although sometimes wood and brick are used for the construction. Glass-to-ground models usually have a metal framework.

Frame lights

Choose a frame that has removable or sliding lights (tops) for easy access; some also have sliding front panels, which may be useful for extra ventilation. Hinged lights that are wedged open still provide protection from heavy rain but sliding lights are often removed entirely during the day, leaving the plants completely vulnerable to heavy rain. Lightweight aluminum frames with their lights wedged open may be at risk in strong winds, however, so choose a model which has a hinged top and adjustable casement stays to secure the lights safely.

Wooden frames

Traditional wooden frames are now difficult to obtain and are usually expensive, but may be made cheaply at home from wood scraps. The wooden sides retain heat well. It is not very difficult to attach soil-warming cables (see p.580) to the inside of the frame to provide extra warmth. Paint or stain the wood to preserve it.

Aluminum alloy frames

These are widely available and relatively inexpensive. They vary considerably in design but are usually sold packed flat for easy transportation, and assembled on site. Aluminum alloy frames let in more light than either wooden or brick frames, but they do not have very good insulating qualities

and may not be as strong or robust. It may be necessary to use ground anchors for lightweight frames.

Brick frames

These are rarely used any more, but they may still be built at home if a supply of old bricks is available and if the lights can be made. Brick frames are generally warm and draft-proof.

Ideal sizes

The minimum practical size for a cold frame is 4 x 2ft (1.2m x 60cm). Often, however, the frame has to fit into whatever space is available (as near the greenhouse as possible), so choose the largest affordable frame that fits the space.

Height is important if the frame is to be used for plants in pots or for tall vegetable crops. In order to increase the height of a frame temporarily, raise it on loose bricks.

Insulation

The range of plants that may be successfully overwintered in a frame is increased if the frame is well insulated. The frame needs to be draft-proof; there should be no gaps around the framework or glass, and the top and any sliding front panels must fit well.

Glass-to-ground and plastic-sided frames may need insulating in cold weather with sheets of expanded styrofoam or bubble plastic (see "Flexible plastic insulation," p.574). Cut the sheets to size, and place them against the inside of the frame.

On cold nights, particularly when a hard frost is predicted, frames may require additional outer protection: use layers of burlap or old carpet to cover the tops, tied down firmly or held in position with pieces of heavy wood.

This protective covering should always be removed during the day, otherwise plants may suffer from a lack of light. Alternatively, use several layers of thick, clear plastic sheeting or bubble plastic for extra protection—this can be left in place during the day because it does not reduce the light to the same degree.

Ventilation

Good ventilation is important in warm weather. Most frames have lights (lids) that may be wedged open to allow fresh air inside; often, the lights also slide along to allow more ventilation, and are eventually removed completely when young plants need to be hardened off.

Light

Aluminum frames (but not brick or wooden frames) can be moved around the garden to take advantage of the best light at various times of the year. If a frame is permanently sited, it should be positioned where it will receive the maximum amount of light in winter and spring, provided that the site is not too exposed.

Frames need shade in summer but, for year-round use, one that lets in as much light as possible is best.

Glazing materials

Horticultural glass is the best glazing material for cold frames; it transmits light well, allows the frame to warm up quickly, and retains heat better than most plastic materials. Broken or cracked panes should be replaced at once, so a frame that allows the individual panes to be replaced should be chosen. Some are glazed using glazing clips or glass panels that slide into the framework; this makes glass replacement fairly simple.

VENTILATION METHODS OF COLD FRAMES

Hinged lights
Hinged tops can be wedged open on warm days to prevent the plants from overheating.

Sliding lights
Sliding tops are less vulnerable to gusts of wind but plants are not protected from heavy rain.

HOW TO USE COLD FRAMES

Planting in the frame
Plants may be grown directly in the cold frame, if required. Always prepare the base with a thick layer of drainage material, such as broken pot shards or coarse gravel, before adding a 6in (15cm) layer of good garden soil or potting mix.

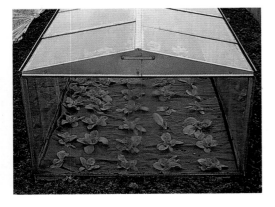

Protecting crops
Here, the cold frame has been placed directly onto the soil in the vegetable garden. Vegetables are growing through slits in a plastic mulch (see "Plastic film mulches," p.503) laid on the surface of the soil.

Where glass may be a potential danger for children or animals, or where the cost of the frame is the main consideration, use plastic glazing material.

Cloches

A wide range of cloche designs and materials is available—choose a cloche that suits the types of plant to be grown. Cloches tend to be used mainly in the vegetable garden but they are equally useful for protecting ornamental plants and seedlings that need a little extra warmth during winter or early in the season (see also "Frost protection," p.613).

Materials
Glass is the best choice of material if cloches are to be used extensively and moved from plant to plant. It has good light transmission and allows the frame to warm up quickly in sunlight. For safety, select ⅛in (4mm) tempered glass, which breaks into little pieces rather than large shards. Clear plastic material is an alternative; plastic cloches are generally less expensive than those made of glass but do not allow as good penetration of light, nor do they retain as much heat or last as long.

Single-thickness plastic is the least satisfactory material for retaining heat, but is cheap and useful where high temperatures are not necessary. Plastic cloches last longer if they have been treated with an ultraviolet inhibitor and are stored out of direct sunlight when not in use.

The minimum thickness that is suitable for cloches is 150 gauge, but 300, 600, or 800 gauge provides much greater protection. PVC is thicker and more rigid, and has similar qualities to polypropylene. Molded PVC and PVC sheeting should last for five years or more if treated with an ultraviolet inhibitor.

Recycled plastic bottles used as cloches

Cloches made from twin-walled polycarbonate offer good insulation and should last for 10 years or more. Polypropylene is used in some injection-molded cloches and in corrugated sheets; it retains heat better than plastic, but not as well as glass or twin-walled polycarbonate. It lasts for five years or more if treated with an ultraviolet inhibitor.

End pieces
These are an important part of most cloches—without them a cloche may become a wind tunnel, damaging the plants inside. The end pieces should fit well to prevent drafts but they should be easy to remove to provide ventilation when required.

Tent cloche
A tent cloche is inexpensive and simple to construct: two sheets of glass are held together by wire or plastic clips, to form a tent shape. It is suitable for germinating seeds, for protecting young seedlings in spring, and for low-growing plants.

Row cover
Row cover can be made from either rigid or flexible plastic. Generally, flexible plastic, continuous row covers are used for crops such as strawberries and early carrots. The plastic must be supported by wire hoops (positioned over the row of plants) and attached with wires. Use heavy-duty plastic that has been treated with an ultraviolet inhibitor.

Rigid models are generally more attractive but more expensive than row covers that are made of flexible plastic. They are also easier to move around, because they do not need to be dismantled first. Some row covers have self-watering features.

Barn cloche
This has almost vertical sides that support a sloping, tent-shaped top. Its extra height makes it useful for relatively tall plants but extra materials and complicated fittings make it more expensive than a tent cloche.

Some glass and rigid plastic barn cloches have lifting or removable tops to provide ventilation in warm weather, while still offering wind protection. This makes weeding, watering, and harvesting easier.

Flexible PVC is sometimes used for barn cloches, but these tend to be lower and therefore less versatile than those using other types of material, unless the top is removable or can be wedged open.

Floating mulch
Floating mulch (also known as a floating cloche) consists of a sheet of perforated plastic sheeting or polypropylene fiber fabric, which is placed over the ground where crops have been sown.

Floating mulch is permeable, allowing rainwater to penetrate to the soil below. This is a great advantage, because it reduces the need to water. The perforations in plastic floating mulch enable the sheet to stretch a little as the crop grows beneath it. Fiber fabric is sufficiently lightweight to grow along with the crop. Both perforated plastic and fiber floating mulch allow air to pass freely through the material and also have useful insulating properties; fiber fabric also protects plants from one or two degrees of frost. For further information, see GROWING VEGETABLES, p.505.

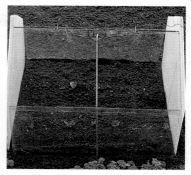

Barn cloche

The sheets or fabric should be anchored firmly into the soil at the edges of the beds with soil, rocks, or pegs. Whole beds may be covered with a floating cloche, if desired, or pieces may be cut to fit smaller areas or even individual plants.

Individual cloche
These are usually used to protect individual plants in the early stages of growth but they may also be placed over any vulnerable, small plants during severe frost, deep snow, heavy rain, and high winds.

Homemade individual cloches, such as wax-paper protectors and cut-off plastic bottles, are easy to make and are much less expensive than commercial models but may not be as attractive as ready-made, rigid plastic or glass, bell, or dome-shaped cloches. These have curved walls, from which condensation trickles to the ground rather than falling on the plants, where it could possibly causing disease or scorching.

Individual cloche

Tent cloche

Row cover

Plastic bell cloche

Routine maintenance

Regular maintenance is necessary to preserve greenhouses, and to keep frames and cloches clean. Fall is usually a convenient time to take care of maintenance: cleaning and disinfecting the structure and equipment at this time of year minimizes number of pests and diseases the next spring.

Do this work on a mild day before very cold weather begins. Tender plants can then be put outside while you prepare for winter.

Exterior maintenance

Choose a dry, still day for routine work on the outside of the greenhouse. Before getting started, gather together all necessary materials for cleaning, repairing, and repainting.

Cleaning glazing panels

Glass can be cleaned with water only, using a hose and long-handled brush, but if it is really dirty, better results are achieved by using diluted dish soap. Protect skin and eyes by wearing gloves and goggles, and rinse off the solution with a solution of water and vinegar.

A commercial window cleaning solution may be used but it will not remove ingrained dirt. Shading products are best removed by rubbing them off with a cloth.

Repairing glass

Slightly cracked panes of glass and plastic may be temporarily repaired with transparent glazing tape. Broken and badly cracked panes, however, should be replaced promptly to prevent harm to plants.

To replace a pane in an aluminum alloy greenhouse, remove the spring glazing clips and adjoining pane, and reglaze with the old clips (see p.572).

If the panes are bedded in glazing putty, remove the glazing tacks and panes of glass. Chip away the putty with a chisel to leave a smooth surface. Clean glazing bars with abrasive paper before reglazing.

Apply priming paint to unpainted or untreated wood on glazing bars. Treat knots in wood where moisture might enter. When paint is dry, replace panes by setting them on a bed of putty or sealant, using glazing tacks to hold them.

Gutters and downspouts

Keep gutters and downspouts in good repair. Clear blockages with a garden hose. Seal small leaks in gutters with sealant, but badly leaking sections of gutter should be replaced completely.

Structural framework

Aluminum greenhouses require only minimal structural attention. Although they lose their bright

CLEANING BETWEEN PANES

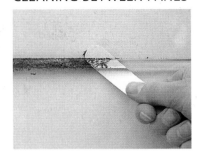

To remove dirt or algae from gaps between overlapping panes in the greenhouse, use a thin, rigid strip of plastic to loosen any deposits before spraying or hosing down with water.

color, the grayish patina that follows protects the metal from the weather.

Check steel frames and fittings for rust and, if necessary, treat with rust remover. Repaint every few years.

Cut out rotting wood and replace it; apply woodworm killer, and renew rusty hinges as necessary. Softwood greenhouses need regular painting: strip off any flaking paint from the wood, wash it down, then apply primer and exterior paint. Hardwood greenhouses are more rot-resistant, only requiring a coat of wood preservative every year or two, which also helps to restore the color.

Ventilators

Check windows and ventilator fans for ease of operation, oil working parts, and clean glass or plastic.

Interior care

Before cleaning and disinfecting the interior, turn off electrical power at the main power box, cover sockets and fittings with plastic, and remove the plants.

Cleaning and disinfecting

Glass and plastic glazing should be cleaned as described above. Scrub glazing bars with disinfectant—fine wire wool can be used (but not on anodized "colored" aluminum).

Scrub brickwork and paths with a garden disinfectant and rinse with clean water. Disinfectant may be used, diluted according to the manufacturer's instructions, to sterilize staging and surfaces. Apply with a paintbrush, or spray, wearing protective gloves, face mask, and goggles.

Although insecticidal and fungicidal smokes are no longer available, sulfur candles can be used to disinfect empty greenhouses before replacing plants. Dormant deciduous plants, such as peaches, are unharmed by sulfur fumes.

MAINTAINING THE GREENHOUSE

An annual check in the fall will be enough to keep your greenhouse in good working order.

Check for rusty hinges and treat with rust remover or replace.

Give panes a thorough cleaning, inside and out.

Strip areas of flaky paint and repaint or treat with preservative.

Replace cracked panes.

Remove rotten wood and replace it.

Clean and disinfect all inside surfaces.

Check all ventilators, ensuring they are watertight.

Repair broken ventilator fittings.

Clear leaves, etc. from gutters.

Cover electrical outlets with plastic before cleaning inside the greenhouse.

Remove weeds from inside the greenhouse.

Check for dirt between overlapping panes. Clean as necessary.

MAINTAINING A PEST-FREE ENVIRONMENT

Many common pests, including aphids, spider mites, mealybugs, scale insects, whiteflies, and black vine weevils, infest plants grown in greenhouses because they enjoy the same humid, warm conditions. Pest populations build up quickly; although chemical controls are available, it is, where practical, better to use natural predators to reduce as rapidly as possible the pests concerned before they cause serious damage.

To succeed with biological controls, wait until the pest has begun to increase before introducing predators—this allows them to feed on the pest and increase their own population. A well-maintained greenhouse with clean glazing panels and no overwintering pests and diseases not only benefits plants, but helps to keep any biological agents under cover if they are needed.

STRUCTURES AND SURFACES

The structures and hard surfaces in a landscape act as the framework around which plants can grow and mature. Well-designed features such as arbors and trellises add welcome height to any planting design as well as providing privacy and shelter. Paths can lead visitors along planned routes; a deck attached to the house makes a perfect setting for a meal. As well as being practical, structures and surfaces can also be attractive design features, providing year-round interest that blends or contrasts with plantings: a circular patio makes a striking contrast with spreading plants, while a large rustic arch forms a complementary support for rambling roses.

Designing with structures and surfaces

Hardscape elements are vital in helping to form the framework of a landscape design and may be as ornamental as they are functional. In a new landscape, features such as a deck or arbor are valuable for providing interest while the plants are growing and becoming established. In a more mature garden, well-designed structures complement softer elements, such as a lawn or the planting in a border, and give the garden solidity and substance all year round.

When planning and designing structures, consider them in the context of their setting and in relation to one another. Materials, style, size, and shape should all be congruous both with the house and the overall design of the garden. A terrace or wall adjacent to the house often looks most effective if built of the same materials, forming a cohesive link between the house and the garden. Local materials are often preferable, because they tend to look appropriate in the setting. The degree of formality is another important consideration to be made; in a formal garden, for example, a mellow brick wall boundary would be ideal, while in an informal cottage garden, a picket fence or wooden pole fence would be more suitable.

Structures may be used to link, define, or separate different elements or parts of the yard. A gently curving path leads the eye through the landscape, providing a unifying line, while a wide, straight path separates the features on either side. Steps create an interesting change of

Designing hardscape features
Here, hard materials have been used to create the main framework of the design, providing contrast to the softer shapes of the plants. The curving design and use of water add a sense of movement, while the innovative use of mixed materials provides satisfying textural combinations.

level and demarcate separate areas as well as joining them visually and providing access from one part to another. If the steps adjoin a patio, they may look best if constructed from the same materials and in a similar style—curved steps would look attractive linked to a circular patio, for example.

The order in which you undertake construction work largely depends on your individual priorities and the requirements of the site. It might, for example, be necessary to build a low wall first to help to retain the soil of a raised bed; in another yard, laying a path might be the first priority to allow easy access with wheelbarrows to the rear of a site where building work is in progress.

This chapter covers most straightforward structural projects that may be undertaken by an amateur, from hard surfaces such as patios, decks, and paths, to boundaries and divisions, including walls and fences, as well as other structures such as raised beds and pergolas. Certain hardscape elements are covered in full in other chapters: see WATER GARDENING, pp.280–303, for details on constructing ponds and watercourses, and ROCK, SCREE, AND GRAVEL GARDENING, pp.252–279, for rock gardens and alpine troughs.

Patios, decks, and terraces

A patio or deck is an ornamental feature as well as a functional one, providing an area for meals and relaxation, with plants in beds or containers, and perhaps a raised pool. An open paved area with a balustrade or low wall is usually called a terrace. Patios and terraces are usually paved; wooden decks (see pp.591–592) are a common alternative.

Choosing a site

Patios and decks are usually sited close to the house, often with French doors or sliding doors for direct access. This provides a convenient power source for lights and other equipment, but if the site is not warm and sheltered, it may be better to find an alternative position. Designing the patio at an angle of 45 degrees to the house, perhaps at a corner, may ensure that it receives sun for most of the day. A patio may also be built away from the house to exploit a fine view across the yard.

Two or more small patios may be more useful than one large one. One may be sited in an open, sunny spot, the other in a cooler place to provide a shady retreat on a summer's day.

Shelter and privacy

A warm, sheltered seating area can be enjoyed for a longer period than one subject to strong winds. If the site is exposed to winds or neighboring properties, create shelter and seclusion with screens or trellises with climbing plants. A pergola (see pp.603–604) roofed with trellises will screen the area from above and provide shade. Avoid siting a patio near large trees: these will cast too much shade, they drip long after rain has stopped, their roots may dislodge the paving, insects could be troublesome, and falling leaves and bird droppings may be a nuisance.

A suitable size

Size is less important for a deck that links house and garden than for a patio that is to serve as an

outdoor room. Keep it in proportion to the garden: too small and it may look trivial; if too large, it may be overpowering. As a guide, allow 4sq yd (3.5sq m) for each person likely to use it. For a family of four, a patio of about 16sq yd (13sq m) is a practical size.

Choosing a surface

Simplicity is the key to good design. If the patio is to have furniture, climbers, and containers, paving should be unobtrusive. Bear in mind that colored paving may look busy and often fades. Create variety by mixing textures: small areas of brick or gravel among paving slabs, timbers intersecting bricks, or cobblestones with stone slabs.

Also consider whether you need a hard-wearing surface, or one that is not slippery when wet: choose from concrete (p.586), paving slabs (p.587), natural stone (p.588), tiles (p.588), bricks and pavers (p.589), or setts and cobblestones (p.591).

Foundations

Patios, paths, and driveways (see p.593) need firm foundations to ensure the paved surface remains stable. Load-bearing requirements must also be considered: few patios have to support very heavy loads, but driveways need more substantial foundations because they may be used by heavy vehicles. Climate is another factor: in areas with prolonged dry periods, for example, concrete foundations may crack if not sufficiently deep; seek professional advice if necessary.

Before undertaking any excavation work, call your local utility companies and wait for them to mark the locations of all underground utilities on your property.

Water runoff

To drain off water, the surface of a patio should slope slightly; a fall of 1in for every 6ft (2.5cm per 2m) is usually sufficient. Calculate the combined depth of the sub-base

STAKING A SLOPE

Mark stakes at the same distance from the top of each, then drive them in, in rows 6ft (2m) apart, the first at the top of the slope. Put a 1in (2.5cm) wood scrap on a stake in the second row. Make the two rows level, remove the wood scrap, and repeat.

1in (2.5cm) piece of wood *Leveling pegs*

Slope of patio

and surface material and mark this as a line at the same distance from the top of each of a number of leveling stakes. Insert one row at the top of the slope so that the mark is at soil level, the top of the stake indicating the desired level of the finished paving. Insert a second row of stakes 6ft (2m) down the slope. On each stake in this row in turn, place a small, 1in- (2.5cm-) thick piece of wood as a spacer, and lay a level on a plank between this stake and one in the first row. Adjust the height of the lower stake until the top of the spacer and the upper stake are level. Remove the spacer and repeat the process down the slope. Then rake the soil so that it is level with the mark on each stake. The base and surface of the finished construction should be parallel.

Basic procedure

Remove plant growth from the area, including tree roots, then dig out topsoil until firm subsoil is reached. Consolidate this using a plate compactor. For most patios and paths, but not those that might bear heavy loads (see p.586), firm subsoil or a 4in (10cm) layer of crushed stone, covered with 2in (5cm) of sand, is an adequate foundation. Use more crushed stone to bring the sub-base up to

PREPARING THE SUB-BASE FOR PATIOS AND PATHS

1 Mark the area with stakes and string, setting the string at the ultimate level of the path or patio. Use a builder's square to check that the corners are set at right angles.

2 Dig down to firm subsoil and tamp with a compactor. Allow for a 4in (10cm) depth of crushed stone, a 2in (5cm) layer of sand, if required, plus the thickness of the surface layer.

3 Drive in a grid of leveling stakes every 6ft (2m). For a patio, create a slight slope so surface water drains away. Use a level and board to ensure that stakes are level with strings.

4 Spread a 4in (10cm) layer of crushed stone over the entire site, and then compact it so that it is level, using the stakes as a guide. Add sand, if needed, and compact the area again.

DIRECTING WATER RUNOFF

Rainwater running off a sloping patio does not have to go to waste. If you install a concrete gutter at the edge of the patio, you can channel the water into a flower bed, onto the lawn, or perhaps into a pond or rain garden. If you have room for one, you could even divert the flow toward a storage tank to be used for gardening purposes; this will allow you to selectively irrigate the garden when and where water is really needed. Also install a grated cover for the gutter so it will not be a tripping hazard.

HOW TO LAY CONCRETE

1 After marking out the site, dig it out to a depth of 8in (20cm). Drive leveling stakes into the ground 3ft (1m) apart along the string lines. Set them horizontal using a plank and a level.

2 Remove the string lines and nail wooden planks to the inner faces of the stakes, butted end-to-face at the corners. This form holds the concrete in place until it sets hard.

3 Divide large sites into sections no more than 12ft (4m) long using forms. Spread crushed stone 4in (10cm) deep and tamp it down with a roller or a landscape timber.

4 Starting with the first section, pour in the concrete and spread it level so that it is slightly higher than the form. Work the concrete into the edges.

5 Using a board that spans the width of the form, compact the concrete with a downward chopping motion. Then slide the beam from side to side to level the surface.

6 Fill any hollows that appear after leveling using fresh concrete, and level it again.

7 Lay a protective, waterproof covering such as plastic sheeting over the concrete until it dries. When the concrete has set hard, remove the form.

---

the required level. On unstable soil, such as muck or heavy clay, or where frost penetrates deeply into the soil, footings should run deeper than normal, as far down as 10in (25cm). Check the footing depths specified by your local building codes.

Load-bearing surfaces

For areas that will support heavy weight, lay a sub-base of at least 4in (10cm) of compacted crushed stone, with 4in (10cm) of concrete on top. This concrete may be the top surface or a base for material like asphalt or pavers bedded in mortar. On clay or unstable soil, or if the surface is to be used by heavy vehicles, lay 6in (15cm) of concrete on top of the crushed stone. If mixing concrete for the foundations, see below. In large areas of concrete, it is essential to leave expansion gaps (see "Expansion joints," p.594).

Concrete

Concrete is quick and easy to lay and is a hard-wearing, durable surface. It may be made more attractive by adding a textured finish (see p.594).

If you intend to lay a large area of concrete and there is access for large vehicles, having ready-mixed concrete delivered will make the job easier and quicker. It requires preparation, though, and usually some helpers, because you will need to tackle the job immediately. Give the supplier the site measurements and information about the intended use of the surface to ensure that the correct amount and mix is delivered, or use a supplier who will mix it for you on site.

Concrete and mortar mixes

The following proportions for concrete and mortar mixes are suitable for most projects. For an explanation of terms, see p.591.

Wall footings, drive foundations, and bases for precast paving
1 part cement
2½ parts sharp sand
3½ parts ¾in (20mm) aggregate (or 5 parts combined aggregate to 1 part cement, omitting the sand)

***In situ* (poured) concrete paving**
1 part cement
1½ parts sharp sand
2½ parts ¾in (20mm) aggregate (or 3½ parts combined aggregate to 1 part cement, omitting the sand)

Bedding mortar (for bedding paving, and jointing paving bricks)
1 part cement
5 parts sharp sand

Masonry mortar (for garden brickwork)
1 part masonry cement
3 parts soft sand

All these proportions are measured by volume and not by weight. The consistency of the mix required for different jobs varies. When mixing concrete or mortar, start by adding about half a part of water to one part cement. This makes a very stiff mix. Continue adding water gradually until you reach the right consistency.

In hot climates, setting retardants may sometimes be necessary in mortar and concrete mixes, while in cold climates, antifreeze products may have to be incorporated: seek local advice. Ideally, avoid laying concrete and mortar at near or below freezing or above 90°F (32°C).

Laying concrete

First mark the area to be concreted with string, then excavate as deeply as needed for local conditions. Drive wooden leveling stakes into the ground at intervals of 3ft (1m) around the edge, using the string as a guide. Nail planks to the inside faces of the leveling stakes to make a form at least 8in (20cm) deep, which will confine the concrete until it sets.

Divide large sites into small sections no more than 12ft (4m) long using more planks. On top of the subsoil, spread a 4in (10cm) layer of compacted crushed stone. Taking one section at a time, pour freshly mixed concrete inside the form to a depth of 4in (10cm) and work it into the edges. Use a board spanning the width of the form to compact the mix, then level it by drawing the board back and forth in long, smooth strokes. Use a trowel or wood float in corners.

UTILITY METERS

Utility meters must always be unobstructed to allow easy access by meter readers. Most meters may be hidden behind a fence or surrounded by shrubs (which should not be thorny, however). When constructing or planting nearby, keep in mind that the utility company may need to destroy plantings or structures in the future in order to service or replace the meter. Pay particular attention to meters when using heavy equipment—even an accidental blow from a shovel may do serious damage.

Paving slabs

Concrete paving slabs are popular for patios, paths, and driveways. They are available in a range of sizes, textures, and colors, and are easy to lay once the base has been prepared. Many home improvement stores stock a range of precast concrete slabs. Some designs may be available only in one area. Large suppliers usually produce catalogs and deliver direct.

Sizes and shapes

Most slabs are either 18 x 18 in (450 x 450mm) or 18 x 24 in (450 x 600mm), with smaller slabs designed to integrate with them. Not all slabs have a shaped edge designed to butt-join; a half-slab may be slightly less than half the size of a full one, to allow for mortar between the joints.

Circular slabs are suitable for stepping stones and small areas of paving with an infill of a loose material, such as gravel. Hexagonal slabs are useful if you prefer a pattern without regular, parallel lines; half-slabs are available for a straight edge. Some slabs are made with a "bite" out of one corner, so that four slabs together form a planting hole.

Quantities

If laying a pattern with slabs of different sizes or colors, draw a plan on graph paper to calculate the number of each required, and allow up to 5 percent extra for breakages (especially if many have to be cut, see p.588). Try to work to dimensions that minimize the need to cut slabs.

Laying paving slabs

If laying a patio, establish a line that you can use as a straightedge and ensure that there is a slight slope for drainage; always slope patio pavement away from an adjoining building. A house wall is a practical baseline to work from, but you may want to leave a small gap between the wall and paving for planting. In that case, start from a level line that is parallel to the house wall. Mark out the area to be paved with stakes and string. Make it a size that requires as few slabs as possible to be cut. If the slabs are not to be butted together, allow about ¼–½in (0.5–1cm) for mortar joints. Seek advice from your supplier if you are in any doubt.

Preparing the site

Clear the site and prepare a sub-base of crushed stone (see p.585). If you intend to cement the stones in place, you will need wooden spacers about ½in (1cm) thick to place between the paving slabs to allow room for filling with mortar.

Positioning the slabs

Work from one corner, placing a row of slabs in each direction with spacers between to make sure that the dimensions are correct. Adjustments are easy to make at this stage. Using a bricklayer's trowel, lay a strip of bedding mortar along each edge where the slab is to be laid, to form an area slightly smaller than the slab. If the slab is 18in (45cm) or more across, lay a cross of mortar within the box. The mortar ridges should be about 1¼–2in (3–5cm) high. This "box and cross" method combines strength with easy adjustment. Lay the slab in position and tamp it down with the handle of a club hammer or mallet. Use a level to check that it is firm and straight. Repeat with successive slabs, using spacers between each one. Check the levels in each direction after every three or four

PAVING SLAB STYLES

Texture
Surface textures range from smooth to stippled, scored, or roughly pebbled.

Hexagonal pavers
These are an attractive alternative to rectangles or squares. Half-blocks are used for straight edges.

Weathered pavers
If a more natural look is desired, "weathered" stone pavers are available.

Pointed slabs
Some slabs are pointed to give special patterns or effects. Those with a "bite" taken out may be fitted together for a planting hole.

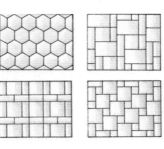

Paving patterns
A variety of pleasing patterns may be created with different shapes and sizes of pavers.

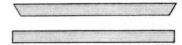

Cast and pressed slabs
Cast slabs (sloping edges) are for light/medium use. Pressed slabs (straight) are lighter but stronger.

HOW TO LAY PAVING SLABS

1 Mark the area and prepare the sub-base (see p.585). Lay strips of mortar to form a square just smaller than the slab. Include a cross strip for large slabs.

2 Position the slab and tamp down. Use a level to check that it is level. Repeat, using spacers for ½in (1cm) mortar gaps between the slabs.

3 Remove the spacers before the mortar sets. After two days, fill the joints with a stiff mortar. Scrape away so they are recessed about ¹/₁₆in (2mm). Brush slabs clean.

Using a jigger
This device has a central slit. After aligning the slit and joint, the gap can be filled without spilling mortar on the slabs.

slabs. Remove the spacers while you can still reach them without walking on the paving, and before the mortar sets. If you have to walk on the paving before the mortar has dried, stand on planks in order to spread your weight.

Finishing

After a couple of days, fill the joints with a very stiff mortar mix (it should almost be "crumbly" to

avoid staining the surface of the paving). Rub a dowel or a rounded piece of wood over the pointing for a crisp finish, leaving it about ¹⁄₁₆in (2mm) below the paving surface. Alternatively, brush a dry mortar of 1 part cement to 3 parts sand into the joints. Brush any surplus off the surface. Spray the joints with a fine mist from a hose-end sprayer or a watering can fitted with a fine nozzle. Sponge excess mortar from the surface immediately, before it stains the slabs.

Cutting paving slabs

If you have many slabs to cut, it is best to rent a power masonry saw. For only a few, use a bolster (a broad-edged cold chisel) and club hammer. Always wear goggles when cutting paving blocks. With a corner of the bolster, score the line where you need to cut all around the slab, then chisel a groove about ¹⁄₈in (3mm) deep along this line; you may have to work around the slab several times, using the bolster to define and deepen the groove. If the slab has to fit into a tight space, cut it about ¹⁄₄in (6 mm) smaller than needed to allow room for any rough edges that may be left when the slab splits.

Place the slab on a firm surface and raise the smaller part of the slab to be cut on a length of wood. Tap it sharply with the handle of a club hammer until a split forms along the line of the groove. Trim any rough pieces carefully with the bolster.

Crazy paving

Crazy (random) paving has an informal appearance. It can be laid on sand, which will allow

plants to be grown between the joints, or on mortar for a firmer finish; if using the latter, fill in the joints with bedding mortar.

Defining the edges

Use string lines to mark out the area to be paved and prepare a sub-base for the paving (see p.585). Allow a slight slope for drainage (see "Water run-off," p.585) if necessary. Define the edges by laying a few yards (meters) of edging material first, working from one corner if laying a patio, the two edges if laying a path. This may simply be large pieces of crazy paving, with at least one straight edge, laid to form the sides of the patio or path, or it could be wood, brick, or concrete. If using paving slabs, mortar these into position, even if bedding the remaining slabs on sand.

Laying the crazy paving

Loosely lay an area about 3ft (1m) square without mortar, fitting the pieces together like a jigsaw puzzle. Keep the gaps small. It may be necessary to trim some pieces to size. Introduce a large piece occasionally, and infill with smaller ones.

Bed the pieces on sand or mortar, using a level on a straightedge to ensure that they are level. Use a mallet or a block of wood and a hammer to bed each piece firmly in position. Lift pieces and add or remove sand or mortar as necessary until they are level.

Filling the joints

If setting crazy paving in sand, finish off by brushing dry sand into the joints. If using mortar, mix a stiff, crumbly, almost dry mortar and use a pointing trowel to fill

the joints (see "Finishing," left). If using a dark-colored stone, such as slate, use a concrete dye (a powder you mix with the sand and cement) to make the joints less conspicuous. The color will look different when dry, so test the dye on a small area and leave it to dry before deciding on the amount of color to add.

Natural stone

Natural stone looks good, but is expensive and difficult to lay. Some types, such as sandstone, may be available cut into regular sizes and with an even edge. Dressed stone looks more natural; it is trimmed to a regular shape and has an attractive, uneven finish. Lay sawn or dressed stone in the same way as paving slabs, adding or removing mortar to produce a level surface.

Fieldstone is irregular in outline and thickness, and has no straight edges. This stone is suitable for laying as crazy paving, and it looks much more appealing than broken concrete paving slabs, but it can form an uneven walkway. Upper and lower faces may differ; try to match them.

Tile surfaces

Quarry tiles, which are made of clay fired at a very high temperature, are useful for linking outdoor and indoor areas— perhaps where the paving inside a conservatory links with that outside. Glazed ceramic tiles may be more ornamental, giving an enclosed patio the impression of a Mediterranean courtyard, for example, but many are not

---

HOW TO CUT SLABS

1 Place the slab on a firm, flat surface and, using the corner of a bolster and a straightedge, score a groove on both faces and edges to mark the cutting line.

2 Using a bolster and club hammer, carefully work along the scored line to deepen the groove on the faces and edges of the paving slab.

3 Raise the slab onto a length of lumber. Align the groove with the edge of the lumber and tap the slab sharply with a hammer handle until it splits.

HOW TO LAY CRAZY PAVING

1 Using string lines and stakes to mark the height of the edges, prepare a sub-base (see p.585). Lay the edging pieces first, placing their straight edges outermost.

2 Fill in the center with large slabs, infilled with smaller ones. Check that central slabs are level with the edging pieces and bed them on sand or mortar. Use a block of wood and a club hammer.

3 Fill the joints with almost dry mortar, or brush in sand. With a mortar finish, use a trowel to bevel the mortar so that surface water will always drain away from the slabs.

frost-proof. When selecting tiles, always check that they are suitable for outdoor use in your area. Tiles are difficult to cut, especially if they are not rectangular, so where possible, design the area to make use of full tiles.

Laying tiles

Tiles are thin and sometimes brittle, so they need to be laid on a level concrete sub-base (see "Load-bearing surfaces," p.586). Quarry tiles may be laid on bedding mortar (see p.591). Soak the tiles for a couple of hours before installations so that they do not absorb too much moisture from the mortar.

Glazed ceramic tiles are best glued to a level concrete base using outdoor tile adhesive (obtainable from a builders' supply store). Spread this on the back of the tiles, following the manufacturer's instructions, then press the tiles into position on the prepared concrete base.

Finish off an area of glazed tiles with grout to fill the gaps, perhaps colored to match or contrast with the tiles.

Bricks and pavers

Bricks and clay or concrete pavers (also called interlock) are most effective when laid in small areas; a large expanse is best broken up with other materials—for example, gravel or landscape timbers. Or lay bricks in two or more complementary patterns or colors.

For a patio situated next to a house built of brick, using bricks

HOW TO LAY BRICK PAVING

1 First, prepare the sub-base (see p.585), allowing space for the edging bricks. Use string lines and stakes to set the edging bricks at the desired height.

2 Mortar in the edging bricks, and bed the others in the required pattern, tamping them level. At intervals, check levels in all directions.

3 Spread a thin layer of dry mortar over the surface and brush it between the joints. Mist with water to set the mortar and clean the surface.

or pavers is an excellent way of linking the house and landscape visually. Bricks and pavers also offer greater design flexibility than large stone or concrete slabs, as they can be laid in a variety of patterns (see *Patterns in Brick*, right).

Choosing bricks

The range of decorative bricks on the market is extensive; you can find a type that suits a patio or terrace designed and constructed in almost any style.

For a large volume of bricks, contact a brick company to see if they will deliver. Building supply stores should be able to deliver bricks in any quantity. Be sure to choose bricks that are appropriate for outdoor paving and resistant to wetting and freezing.

Choosing pavers

Clay pavers are as attractive as bricks and are usually produced in shades of red. They have a thinner profile than concrete pavers or bricks. Concrete pavers may lack the warm colors of bricks but they will make a practical surface. They are generally found in gray, blue-gray, or buff shades and are produced in a range of shapes.

Laying bricks

First make a suitable sub-base (see p.585). Bricks should ideally be bedded on mortar. First lay edging strips (or edging bricks), bedded on a concrete footing and then fixed with mortar between the joints. Prepare the bedding mortar (see p.586) and lay it to a depth

of 1in (2.5cm). Bed the bricks onto this, spacing them evenly to leave joints for mortar; use thin strips of hardboard or wood as spacers between bricks, if desired. Once an area is complete, brush dry mortar over the bricks. To remove air pockets, press this into the gaps with a narrow piece of wood. In damp weather, moisture from the ground and air will set the mortar; in dry weather, speed up setting by spraying with a fine mist of water.

PATTERNS IN BRICK

Bricks may be laid in several different ways to create attractive patterns; three popular examples are shown below.

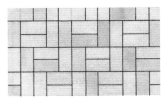

Basketweave

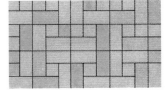

Interlocking boxes

Herringbone

TYPES OF BRICK

Bricks are available in a wide range of styles, textures, and colors, providing an attractive and practical building material; take care to choose the most appropriate type so that they are suitable for the proposed purpose and that they coordinate well with the house, patio, or other hardscape features.

Building bricks
Building bricks are very hard-wearing. If used for paving, make sure they have good wet-weather grip. They may cost more than ordinary bricks.

Cored bricks
Cored bricks have holes. They may be used on edge for paving with a narrower profile, but are not economical for large areas.

Facing or stock bricks
These are used to "face" buildings, providing an attractive finish. They are available in a variety of colors, and may be rough or smooth in texture. They may be unsuitable for paving, because they may not be able to withstand severe weather conditions.

Bricks with "frogs"
A frog is an indentation in one side of a brick. Frogged bricks may be used for paving, if they are laid on edge or the frogs face downward.

Cutting bricks and pavers

Bricks and thick pavers may be difficult to cut. If cutting is necessary, it can be done by the company that supplied the material or by using a rented masonry saw. Whichever you choose, it is possible to cut bricks accurately, and quickly.

Alternatively, bricks and pavers may be cut to the desired shape with a bolster and club hammer (see "Cutting paving slabs," p.588), although the cuts made by these tools may not be as clean.

Laying pavers

Pavers are bedded into sand using a plate compactor; they nest together with small gaps between. The pavers can be lifted and relaid, so this type of paving is sometimes called flexible paving. Blocks 2½–2¾in (60–65mm) thick are adequate for backyard projects.

Preparing the site and laying edge restraints

First, prepare a sub-base of 3in (8cm) compacted crushed stone on firm soil (see p.585). Where there are no existing firm edges (such as walls), lay permanent edging strips. By far the simplest way to do this is to use specially made edge restraints or edging pieces, which are available from paving manufacturers. These must be concreted into position. Alternatively, use 2 x 4in (100 x 35mm) treated lumber held in place with strong stakes at least 2in (50mm) square.

Large areas should be broken up into manageable sizes, such as 3ft (1m) squares, using temporary lumber rails. Spread a layer of sharp sand evenly to a depth of

PAVERS, TILES, SETTS, AND COBBLESTONES

Pavers vary greatly in size, color, and thickness. They are also finished in many different ways, so that their texture and final shape, either formal and geometric or more informal and natural, contribute greatly to the style of the landscape. More distinctive effects may be possible using terra-cotta tiles, granite setts, Belgian blocks, or rounded cobblestones.

Clay pavers
These red pavers may be laid either as stretchers, that is, longitudinally, or as headers, placed end to end.

Wire-cut clay pavers
Wire-cut clay pavers have a dragged finish and a roughened surface on all sides, which serves to provide extra grip in the finished paving.

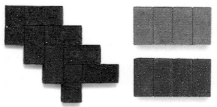

Interlocking pavers
These clay or concrete pavers can be used to create unusual patterns. Pressed pavers in blocks (far right) are produced in a range of colors.

Terra-cotta tiles
Like bricks, terra-cotta tiles are made of clay but allowed to dry in the sun. They are porous and may crack if used in areas prone to frost.

Granite setts
Cut from hard granite, this form of paving is extremely durable. Like cobblestones, the rough surface of the setts creates a natural effect.

Belgian blocks

Cobblestones
Cobblestones (below) are large, rounded stones formed by the action of the sea or glaciers. They can be set in mortar to form an interestingly textured finish, but they are uncomfortable to walk on and should be used only in small areas or in combination with other materials. When laying cobblestones, form firm edges with bricks or lengths of concrete edging, set in concrete.

Imitation granite setts
These reconstituted stone pavers are lighter and cheaper than granite. Belgian blocks have a more weathered look.

HOW TO LAY FLEXIBLE PAVING

1 After preparing the sub-base (see p.585), set edging strips of concrete or landscape timber in position around the edges of the site. Use a level and a club hammer to tap the edges level.

2 Use battens to divide large areas into bays 3ft (1m) square. Add 2in (5cm) of sand. Level the sand to the tops of the battens with a length of wood. Remove the battens and fill the vacated spaces with sand.

3 Lay the pavers to the required pattern, working from one corner of the site. Lay only whole blocks at this stage, leaving until last any cut ones required to fill the gaps in the design.

4 Vibrate the pavers into the sand or tamp down with a club hammer and length of lumber. Brush dry sand over the surface and make 2–3 passes with a plate compactor.

about 2in (5cm). The top surface of the sand should be just high enough that about one-third of the paving block will protrude above the surrounding rails. Adjust the amount of sand as work proceeds.

Positioning and bedding the pavers

Do not walk on the sand while laying the pavers, and keep it dry. Working from one corner of the site, lay the pavers. When some are laid, place a kneeling board over the pavers to continue working. Lay as many whole blocks as possible, then fill in with cut pavers around any obstacles as necessary (see p.588).

When about 6sq yd (5sq m) of paving has been laid, bed the pavers into the sand. The easiest way to do this is with a plate compactor, but do not go too near the incomplete edge. If only laying a small area of paving, the blocks may be tamped down with a heavy club hammer over a block of wood that is large enough to span several pavers at once. Continue to lay pavers and bed or tamp them down.

When the whole area is finished, brush dry sand into the seams between pavers and settle it in position with the plate compactor. Use a mowing edge of bricks, pavers, or concrete slabs where it is difficult to mow right to the lawn edge. Bed the paving material on mortar, with the top just below the grass level, so that the mower is not damaged.

A combination of paving effects
A mixture of different paving materials, including square stone slabs, crazy paving, and brick edging, blends well with informal planting.

Setts and cobblestones

Bed granite or imitation setts on 2in (5cm) of bedding mortar (see p.586) and brush stiff mortar into the joints (see "Finishing off," p.588). Mist the surface with water to clean it and set the mortar mix.

Cobblestones may also be set in mortar. They are uncomfortable to walk on, so use them for small areas or with other materials. When laying, form firm edges with bricks or lengths of concrete edging. Lay 1½in (3.5cm) of bedding mortar over 3in (8cm) of crushed stone.

TERMS EXPLAINED

Aggregate is crushed stone or gravel used in making concrete. Graded ¾in (20mm) aggregate is suitable for most concreting jobs. Combined aggregate contains sand as well as stone.

Bedding mortar is used for laying paving stones. It is made with sharp sand instead of soft (builder's) sand.

Cement is a gray powder containing limestone, the setting agent of concrete and mortar.

Concrete is a hard-setting building material made of a mixture of cement, aggregate, sand, and water.

Crushed stone is used as a sub-base under concrete foundations.

Dry mortar is a stiff mix of sand and cement often used to fill the joints in paving.

Masonry cement has additives that make it unsuitable for concrete. Use only for mortars.

Mortar is a mixture of cement, sand, and water used principally for bricklaying.

Portland cement is not a brand name, but a type of cement. Use ordinary Portland cement for most concreting jobs. It can also be used for mortars.

Sand is graded by particle size. Sharp sand contains no salt. Avoid or wash ocean-beach sand—salt stops cement from hardening.

Decks

Wooden decking is popular as a hard surface in warm, dry climates. Decks may be used anywhere, however, provided that a rot-resistant material, such as plastic lumber, is used.

It is best to build the deck on a level or gently sloping site. For a raised deck on a steep, sloping site and for decking that extends over water, it is advisable to seek professional assistance, because it would need to be well designed and constructed.

In some localities, building regulations state that all exterior areas of decking must be able to support a stipulated minimum weight. It may also be necessary to obtain a building permit and have the work inspected. If in any doubt, check with your municipality. Simple parquet decking (see p.592) laid on a base of gravel and sand should not require a permit.

Wooden deck
A wooden deck or veranda overlooking a garden makes a very imposing feature, especially when crowned with a pergola to provide summer shade. Wooden decks, however, need to be very well constructed, and it is usually best to have the job done by experts. Features such as rails, steps, and supports require regular maintenance (see p.592).

WOODEN DECKING

Western red cedar is a good choice because of its natural rot-resistance, although regularly treating it with a preservative ensures a longer life. Other woods are suitable but must be pressure-treated with a preservative. Lumber suppliers will be able to advise on the most suitable type and grade to use. Short lengths of lumber can be made up into decking panels to produce a variety of attractive patterns.

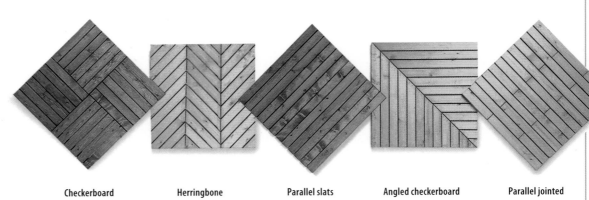

Checkerboard   **Herringbone**   **Parallel slats**   **Angled checkerboard**   **Parallel jointed**

Slatted decking

This type of decking is suitable for level or gently sloping ground. It is simple to construct.

For an area beside a house, construct a concrete foundation (see *How to Lay Concrete*, p.586) with a gentle fall away from the house for water drainage. Onto the concrete base, mortar a row of bricks spaced about one brick apart at right angles to the intended direction of the decking. Add further rows of bricks at intervals of 16in (40cm). Check constantly that all the bricks are level, because they will support the joists.

Lay joists 3 x 2in (75 x 50mm) over the bricks, inserting a sheet of plastic or other vapor-barrier material between the bricks and the joists. If joining lengths of lumber, make sure there is a brick beneath the point where the joists abut and screw a plain bracket across the joint. Check levels between joists accurately with a level and a straightedge. Lay

1 x 10in (250 x 25mm) planks at right angles to the joists. Allow ½in (10mm) gaps for free drainage and a little movement in the lumber. Ensure that joints in the decking are staggered from row to row and that the planks are butt-joined over a supporting joist. Secure the planks with brass or other rustproof screws, counter-sunk beneath the surface. Fill the holes with wood filler that matches the color of the wood.

Finish the deck neatly with a low brick or block edging, cutting the decking so that it overlaps the edging by 2in (5cm). Alternatively, a length of facing lumber can be screwed or nailed along the cut edges.

Parquet decking

It is possible to buy small, parquet-type, wooden squares intended primarily for paths, which can also be used for decking. Alternatively, they can be easily made. About 3ft (1m) square is a practical size. Buy

2x 4in (100 x 50mm) treated lumber, cut into 3ft (1m) lengths, and sand the ends smooth. Two lengths form the supports at opposite sides of the square, while the others are laid across them as slats. Use spacers to ensure that the slats fill the area evenly and secure the slats with two nails at either end. Prepare a base on firmed ground or subsoil with 3in (8cm) of compacted gravel topped with 3in (8cm) of sand. Level and tamp before laying the squares in alternate directions. Nail them together if necessary to stop them from moving, driving the nails in at an angle.

Applying stains

Western red cedar turns a very obvious red color when wet. It may, however, be stained any color to suit the surroundings. It is best to use microporous stains, which allow any moisture in the wood to escape; if trapped beneath an impermeable layer, it would eventually cause the surface color to lift. All wooden surfaces for staining should be dry and free from dirt. Follow instructions regarding stirring or thinning

and apply the stain with a good-quality paintbrush, brushing in the direction of the grain. Do not overload the brush—this will lead to uneven coverage—but work the stain well into the wood. Several applications will be needed, but wait until each coat is completely dry before applying more.

Maintenance

All wooden surfaces need regular maintenance. Once a year, check all surface areas for splits or cracks. Damaged boards will need to be replaced. Check, too, that no bolts, screws, brackets, or nails have rusted. If galvanized hardware is abraded, its protective coating may be damaged and rust will appear. Brass hardware, which does not rust, is preferable in wooden decking. If the stain wears thin in areas of heavy traffic, clean the surface and restain (see above). Algae growths sometimes appear on decking. Algicides are available, but it's better to remove algae by brushing with a stiff broom or scrub brush. In some regions, termites can be a problem; if in doubt, call a pest control firm.

Decking stepping stones
Decking can be used to create an unusual "stepping-stone" path across a pond. When positioned and angled for aesthetic effect, the squares add a stylish, geometric element to informal planting and the soft play of light on the pond surface. Here, parallel slats are laid in alternate directions to add a dynamic sense of movement to the overall design.

SUPPORT FOR WOODEN DECKING

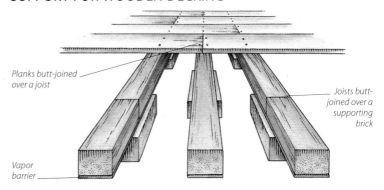

Planks butt-joined over a joist

Joists butt-joined over a supporting brick

Vapor barrier

When joining two lengths of lumber to form a joist, make sure that the joint lies over one of the supporting bricks. Lay the planks at right angles to the joists, positioning all butt-joints directly over a supporting joist.

Paths and steps

Paths and steps play a valuable part in good garden design. They help form the framework of the landscape, link its various elements, and may lead the eye to a focal point. Consider setting a path at an angle, off-center, or following an indirect route. Steps provide interesting changes of level and create very different effects, depending on whether they are straight or curved, wide or narrow, and shallow or steep.

Practical considerations

Paths to a garden shed or compost pile need to be wide enough to accommodate a wheelbarrow and should also provide a dry and solid surface. Those leading to the front door or for strolling through the yard should be wide enough for two people to walk abreast: about 3–4ft (1–1.2m).

Materials and design

The choice of materials and the laying pattern may be used to establish or enhance the landscape style. Combining different materials—for example, pavers with cobblestones, bricks with gravel, or concrete slabs with bricks or clay pavers—often makes a very effective design for a path.

"Stepping-stone" paths may be laid in many parts of the yard. They are a good choice, for example, when you do not want to interrupt the line of a lawn, but they can become muddy in wet weather. Place the paving stones on the surface first to check the spacing; they should be spaced at a natural stride length. On lawns, set them into the grass so that their surface is safely below mowing level.

Where winters are relatively dry, paths may be made of wood, either in the form of log sections used as

stepping stones or to make a series of square, slatted units as described in "Parquet decking," opposite.

On sloping sites, steps may be an essential part of a path. They may also be valuable as a design feature even on a relatively flat site. Steps should harmonize with their setting. For example, in a woodland garden, shallow log risers and gravel treads would be suitable, while in a modern setting, brick risers and concrete slab treads would be more appropriate.

Driveways

A driveway can have a considerable impact on a design, especially in a small yard. There may be little choice where to position a driveway, unless a new garage is to be built at the same time; it is possible to make a driveway look attractive, however, by choosing a suitable surface and positioning attractive plants nearby.

Asphalt

Asphalt is best used for driveways and working paths—the route to a garden shed, for example. It can also be used to cover a damaged concrete path. As well as black, asphalt is available in a range of colors. Stone chips may be rolled into the surface to add texture. Asphalt is best laid in warm weather. Unless well laid, it may break up after a few years; for heavily used areas such as a main driveway, it is worth having it installed by a professional.

Preparations

Asphalt can be laid on any firm surface, such as concrete or gravel. Never lay it on bare soil or crushed stone because it will be difficult

Brick pathways

A brick path can become a design feature in its own right, adding texture and color to an entranceway. Here, the soft pink of the brick harmonizes with the surrounding plants and leads the eye to the rose-covered arch and the informal grass area beyond.

to create a firm and level surface that will last. If necessary, make a stable base by spreading a mixture of gravel and sand 2–3in (5–8cm) thick over firm ground or compacted crushed stone. If an old path or driveway is the base, first paint inside any holes or cracks with asphalt emulsion and leave for about 20 minutes before filling them with asphalt mixture. To ensure good drainage, lay a driveway on a slight slope.

The edges of an asphalt path often weaken and crumble, so use concrete edging blocks, bricks, or lengths of pressure-treated lumber to provide a firm edging.

Application

Apply a layer of asphalt emulsion to bind the surface. Stir it first, then pour it from the container and spread it with a stiff brush. (Wash the brush in hot, soapy water afterward.) When the emulsion has turned black, apply the asphalt mixture and rake it to an even depth of about ¾in (2cm).

Firm the surface by tamping it with the back of a rake to remove large air pockets, then make several passes with a heavy lawn roller. Keep the surface of the roller damp to prevent the tar from sticking to it. Top off any visible depressions and roll the surface again. If using stone chips, sprinkle evenly and roll again to bed them in.

Bricks and pavers

The sympathetic coloring of bricks and clay pavers makes them excellent materials for paths within a garden. Because the individual units are small, it is relatively easy to adjust to changes of level and

even to lay a path on a curve. A variety of effects can be created depending on the laying pattern used (see *Patterns in Brick*, p.589).

Construction

Mark the proposed line of the path with stakes and string, calculating where cut bricks or pavers may be required to create a sharp curve. If the path will be subjected to heavy wear, prepare a concrete foundation (see "Load-bearing surfaces," p.586). For one that will sustain lighter use, a 3in (8cm) sub-base of firmed crushed stone leveled with sand should be sufficient.

First lay a suitable edging (see p.594) along one side of the path, then lay the path itself in sections about 3ft (1m) long. Pavers should be bedded in a 2in (5cm) layer of dry sand (see "Laying pavers," p.590), while bricks will require a 1in (2.5cm) bed of mortar (see "Laying bricks," p.589). As you complete each section, lightly tamp the bricks or pavers into place, checking that they are level with a straight edge and level. Then lay the edging on the other side of the path to complete this section. Repeat the process until the path has been laid.

To finish off a path made of pavers, brush dry sand into the joints. For a brick path, brush a dry mortar mix in between the joints (see "Finishing off," p.588), making sure that there are no large air pockets. If necessary, compact the mortar using a piece of wood slightly thinner than the joints. Finally, sprinkle with water from a watering can or hose with a fine nozzle, or use a hose-end sprayer to moisten the mortar and clean the bricks, if necessary.

Subtlety with stone

Here, the mottled texture of the embedded stones is complemented by *Alchemilla mollis* and defined by seams of moss.

Log sections

Logs sawn into sections make a harmonious series of stepping stones through an area of woodland, blending perfectly with the setting.

Concrete

Concrete cast *in situ* is an economical and hard-wearing surface material that is especially suitable for wide paths and driveways. Its appearance can be made more attractive by adding texture (see below). Concrete can also be colored using special dyes added to the mix. The color often looks different once the concrete has dried, so use dyes with caution. Color a small test piece first and let it dry rather than judge the effect by the wet mix.

Divide a wide concrete path with rows of bricks or lengths of timber that will become part of the finished design. These will avoid the need for laying expansion joints during construction.

Preparing a base

Prepare a suitable foundation (see "Basic procedure," p.585). Next, make the form to hold the concrete until it sets. Use lengths of lumber 1in (2.5cm) thick, and at least the depth of the concrete. Use 2 x 2in (5 x 5cm) stakes, not more than 3ft (1m) apart, to hold the form in place. Lengths of lumber may be joined by nailing a block of wood to the outside of the two pieces to bridge them together.

Making curves

To make gentle curves, mark the shape that you want to create, and hammer stakes into the ground set closely together. Soak lengths of softwood in water to make them pliable and then bend and nail them to the stakes. Sharp curves can be made in a similar way, with the addition of a series of saw cuts on the inside of the curve. The saw cuts should go about halfway through the wood to increase its flexibility. Alternatively, use several thicknesses of thin hardboard, which is easy to bend and shape.

Expansion joints

Concrete will crack if not laid with breaks to allow for expansion and a degree of movement. Divide the area into sections no more than 12ft (4m) long, using lengths of lumber as temporary divisions. If using ready-mixed concrete, where the load has to be used all at once, use hardboard cut into sections and leave these in position until the concrete has set fully.

ADDING TEXTURE

An *in situ* concrete path can be made more attractive by adding texture. Use these techniques on a few sections only, or alternate patterns between sections, to create an interesting overall effect.

Exposed aggregate gives a pleasant, nonslip finish. Spread gravel or crushed stone evenly over the concrete before it sets, then tamp it gently into the surface. When the concrete is nearly hard, brush the surface to expose more of the aggregate, then spray it with water to wash away fine particles.

Brushed finishes are extremely easy to create. After tamping the concrete gently, push the bristles of a soft broom all over the surface to produce a fairly smooth finish; for a ridged effect, use a stiff broom once the concrete has begun to set. You can also brush in a series of swirls, or straight or wavy lines, as desired.

Stamped patterns can be made with special tools, but ordinary objects found in the home or garden may also be used imaginatively—for example, cookie cutters and seashells. This technique is best kept to very small areas. To create attractive leaf impressions, use large leaves, such as maple or horse chestnut. Press the leaves into the surface with a trowel and then brush them out once the concrete has hardened.

Coarse texture

Medium-coarse texture

Fine texture

HOW TO LAY A GRAVEL PATH

1 Dig out the base of the path to a depth of 7in (18cm) and set the edges using pressure-treated or rot-resistant lumber. Compact the base and hammer in stakes at 3ft (1m) intervals to anchor the edge restraints.

2 If the path borders a lawn, dig out an extra 1in (2.5cm) so that the path is below sod level (inset) for easier mowing. Lay successive layers of crushed stone, sand and coarse gravel, and pea gravel. Rake level.

Laying concrete

Mix the concrete (see p.586) and pour it into the form. If mixing in small batches, fill alternate "bays," then remove the dividers once the concrete has set and pour concrete into the remaining bays. Use a board to tamp the concrete level, working from the center toward the joints. If the path or driveway is wide, help from another person will make the job easier. Tamping leaves a slightly ridged surface. If you require a smooth finish, use a wood float in gentle, sweeping motions. A steel float will produce an even smoother surface.

Concrete paving slabs

Paving slabs are available in a wide selection of colors, shapes, sizes, and finishes. They are easier to lay than concrete poured *in situ*, but are more difficult to lay on a curve than bricks or pavers. They combine easily with other materials—for instance, with cobblestones set along the edge, or with small strips of gravel between each slab. This is a useful technique for creating curved paths, because it makes the uneven joints less obtrusive. For details on laying paving slabs, see p.587.

Grass

Grass paths are useful for linking a series of lawns, or for walkways between beds. They should be as wide as possible or they will not stand up to concentrated wear. Wide sod paths also need less water than narrow ones. Put down sod for a grass path in the same way as for a lawn—for full instructions, see THE LAWN, "Laying sod," p.393.

Gravel

Gravel is easy to lay, especially when creating curves, and is not expensive. However, unless well bedded and used with retaining edges, loose gravel can get onto adjoining surfaces and be noisy and uncomfortable to walk on, and it is not an easy surface on which to push a wheelbarrow or a stroller. See also ROCK, SCREE, AND GRAVEL GARDENING, "Gravel beds and paving," p.256.

Construct a base by excavating enough soil to allow for about 4in (10cm) of compacted crushed stone, 2in (5cm) of a sand and coarse gravel mix, and 1in (2.5cm) of gravel. For a fine finish, choose pea gravel. Gravel can also be laid over landscape fabric (see p.256).

In a formal setting with mainly straight edges, concrete edging strips can be used; in other settings, bricks or pressure-treated timbers may be more appropriate. If using timbers, anchor them in place with wooden stakes about 3ft (1m) apart.

Apply gravel in several stages, raking and rolling it to produce a slight camber for better drainage. To help compaction and create a solid path, water occasionally with a fine spray while rolling.

Edging paths

Plastic edging strips, easily cut to size, are available to hold bricks or pavers in place invisibly. Lengths of treated lumber may also be used, held in place with wooden stakes. It is also possible to use lumber pieces temporarily while building the path, then remove them and fill the gaps with concrete. For brick edging, lay the bricks on edge and secure with mortar; this also helps suppress weeds.

Building steps

To calculate the number of steps you need to build, divide the height of the slope by the height of one riser (including the depth of the paving slab and mortar). It may be necessary to adjust the height of the steps to fit the slope. Mark the position of the risers with wooden stakes and then excavate the soil to form a series of steps.

Make a concrete footing (see p.596) for the base riser and leave it to set. Then construct the riser using bricks or blocks set in masonry mortar (see p.586). Check that they are level using a straight-edge and level, and backfill behind the riser with compacted crushed stone or sand and gravel.

Prepare a bed of mortar on top of the riser and lay the first tread; it should slope forward slightly to shed water, and overlap the riser at the front by 1–2in (2.5–5cm). Mark the position of the next riser on the tread and mortar it in place.

TREAD-TO-RISER RATIO

For ease of use, it is important that the width of the tread and the height of the riser are in the correct proportion to each other. As a general rule, the width of the tread and double the height of the riser should total about 26in (65cm). First, choose the height of the riser, double it, and deduct it from 26in (65cm) to give the width of the tread. You may wish to add 1–2in (2.5–5cm) for an overhang.

For the steps to be safe to use, the treads should measure at least 12in (30cm) from front to back. The height of the risers is usually between 4 and 7in (10 and 18cm).

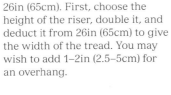

Paving stone treads

Brick risers

Gravel infill

HOW TO BUILD STEPS INTO A BANK

1 Measure the height of the bank to work out how many steps are needed (see left). To do this, drive a stake into the top of the slope and a post at the bottom. Tie string horizontally between the two, then measure the distance between ground level and the string.

2 Use string and stakes to mark the sides, then run strings laterally to mark out the fronts of the treads. Dig out the steps and compact the earth well at each tread position.

3 Construct a footing for the riser, 6in (15cm) deep and twice the width of the bricks. Fill the base of the footing with 3in (7cm) of crushed stone and top with a layer of concrete.

4 When the concrete has fully set, lay the first riser on the footing. Use a horizontal string line stretched between the stakes to ensure that the bricks are laid straight and level.

5 Backfill with crushed stone to the height of the bricks and tamp down firmly. Set the paving slabs on a 1/2in (1cm) layer of mortar, with a small gap between each one.

6 The slabs should have an overhang of 1–2in (2.5–5cm) at the front and a slight forward slope for drainage. Mark the position of the second riser on the slabs and mortar the bricks in place. Fill in and set the treads as before. Continue this for the remaining steps. To finish, mortar the joints between the slabs.

Timber and gravel steps
Here, wooden landscape timber steps are filled with gravel to create a curving flight of gently rising steps, with flanking plants softening the edges.

Walls

Boundary walls have been a feature of landscapes since the early days of enclosures. In the 19th century, walled gardens were a common feature on large estates, providing security, privacy, and ornament. Nowadays, however, large boundary walls are much less common, having given way to less expensive options such as fences or hedges.

Garden walls are often decorative as well as practical. If they have a planting cavity, low walls can be particularly attractive, and, because they require less substantial foundations and supporting piers, they are also easy and relatively inexpensive to build.

Materials

Boundary walls may be constructed from various materials including brick, and, for low walls, water-resistant concrete blocks that are designed for outdoor use. When buying bricks, check with the supplier that they are suitable for garden walls: they should be frost-proof and able to withstand moisture penetration coming from both sides.

Walls may also be constructed from a combination of materials—for example, brick with facing panels of local stone such as schist. Large, plain walls may be painted with a masonry paint (in pale or bright colors) on the garden side. This reflects the light and contrasts well with wall shrubs or other plants growing in front.

How high to build?

There may be restrictions placed on the height of walls by your municipality or homeowners' association. Check this before building. A low, decorative wall is a straightforward DIY job, but for brick and concrete block walls higher than about 3ft (1m), seek advice from a builder or structural engineer. Any wall higher than 3ft (1m) should have a strengthening pier every 8ft (2.5m).

Combined materials
Brick and flint are juxtaposed here to create a striking garden divider. The mixture of straight and curved lines reinforces the blend of styles. When combined in this way, diverse materials can effectively enhance one another.

Concrete footings for walls

The width of the footing for all walls, whether they are built of bricks, blocks, or stone, should be two to three times the width of the wall itself. For walls lower than 3ft (1m) high, deep and substantial foundations are not necessary.

For a half-brick wall (i.e., the width of a single brick), dig a trench the length of the wall and 15in (38cm) deep. Place 5in (13cm) of crushed stone in the bottom and tamp down firmly. Then pour in 4in (10cm) of concrete. Allow this to harden completely for a few days before laying the bricks or concrete blocks.

WALL MATERIALS

Bricks are a very attractive choice of wall material, although concrete blocks manufactured to imitate natural clay bricks may also be used.

If you want to build a wall to match the brickwork of existing buildings, reclaimed bricks may be available from salvage yards or other suppliers.

Smooth-textured bricks
These are most suitable for facing the front of a wall. They come in a range of colors.

Building bricks
These contribute a rough-hewn appearance; they are also the hardest of all the bricks.

Precast concrete blocks
These contain medium-textured aggregate.

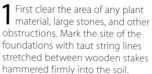

Rock-faced concrete blocks
The brick-red color imitates the look of clay bricks. They are also available colored to look like sandstone.

Smooth blocks
Concrete blocks are suitable for a modern design.

HOW TO MAKE A CONCRETE FOOTING

1 First clear the area of any plant material, large stones, and other obstructions. Mark the site of the foundations with taut string lines stretched between wooden stakes hammered firmly into the soil.

2 Dig a trench of the required depth. Check that the base is level and the sides vertical. Drive in stakes to the level for the concrete. Align with a level and a length of wood spanning the stakes.

3 Soak the trench with water and allow it to drain. Then add 5in (13cm) of crushed stone and tamp it down firmly. Pour in concrete, slicing into the mix with a spade to work it into the crushed stone base and release bubbles.

4 Compact the concrete by tamping it down firmly with a length of lumber and level the surface to the tops of the stakes. Leave the surface slightly rough to provide a key for the mortar for the first course of bricks.

HOW TO BUILD A SIMPLE LOW WALL

1 Once the concrete footing has dried fully—which takes at least 2 days—set out the position of the wall with two string guides, two bricks' width plus ½in (10mm) apart. Dry-position the first course, ½in (10mm) between bricks.

2 Chalk the brick positions on the footing. Throw a mortar bed ½in (10mm) thick along all the first course. As you set each brick on it, use a level to check that it is level both from end to end and from front to back.

3 Before laying, butter an end face of each brick with ½in (10mm) of mortar. Fill the central gap.

4 Throw a mortar bed on top of the first course of lengthwise bricks (the stretcher) and lay the next course (the header) at right angles to the first. Check levels constantly and make any adjustments as required.

5 Raise up both ends of the wall by four courses, alternating stretchers and headers. Scrape off excess mortar as you bed each brick. Neaten joints with a pointing tool. Then complete each course.

6 On the fourth row, insert a half brick after the first header, to maintain staggered joints and avoid having a weak joint running down the wall. As you continue to build, regularly check the levels of each brick as before.

7 Complete the wall with a header course, laying the bricks on their edges. To help deflect rainwater from the surface, point the mortar joints by running a pointing tool against the vertical, then the horizontal joints.

For a full-brick wall, which is two bricks wide, or for a double wall with planting cavities, dig the trench 2in (5cm) deeper and add 2in (5cm) of extra concrete. For a brick or concrete block wall, the top of the footing need only be 6in (15cm) below ground level.

COMBINATION BRICKS

"Combination blocks" that give the appearance of being several individual bricks may look crude close up, but once in a garden setting, and especially when weathered, they are far less noticeable, and they make simple garden-wall construction much quicker and easier. Some are regularly shaped while others interlock, like a jigsaw puzzle, for greater strength and stability.

Combination coping block

For a concrete screen, the top of the footing may be just below ground level, provided reinforcing rebars are used. In heavy clay or in cold areas, increase the depth of the footing so that it is below the frost line. For higher walls, professional advice should be sought.

Bricklaying

To ensure that the first course is straight, stretch two parallel strings along the footing, the space between them equal to the width of the wall plus ½in (10mm). Lay a ½in (10mm) bed of masonry mortar (p.586) along the footing. The first brick of a course is laid unmortared, then the second is "buttered" on one end and laid up against it. As you lay, check frequently with a level that the bricks are level and horizontal. If too high, tap them down gently with the trowel handle. Insert more mortar under any that are too low. Check also that the mortar joints are all ½in (10mm) thick.

Repeat the process for each subsequent course and reset the builder's line for a position guide. For walls with planting cavities, leave weep holes (unmortared gaps between bricks) for drainage in the first course above ground level.

Before the mortar dries, use a pointing trowel to give the joints a neat, beveled finish. The vertical joints should all be beveled in the same direction; the horizontal ones should slope slightly downward to help water runoff.

Brick bonding

There are many brick bonding patterns to use (see right). If you are new to bricklaying, it is best to choose one that does not require many cut bricks. The simplest is a running or stretcher bond, in which all the bricks are laid lengthwise.

Screen block walling

In parts of the yard where a brick wall would form too solid a barrier, a screen wall of specially made pierced concrete blocks may be more appropriate. Such walls are supported at each end and at 8–10ft (2.5–3m) intervals by piers built of hollow pilaster blocks. These are normally reinforced with rebars set in the footing and filled with mortar or concrete. Even so, screen walls are not strong; for walls higher than 6ft (2m), seek professional advice.

POPULAR BONDS

Running bond is commonly used for walls built one brick thick; Flemish and English bonds combine stretchers and headers (bricks that are laid respectively lengthwise and widthwise) in a full-brick wall.

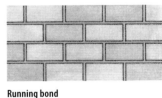

Running bond

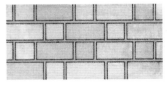

Flemish bond

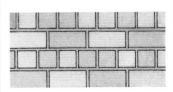

English bond

TYPES OF COPING

A decorative finish
Upright stones have been set in mortar as a coping for a dry limestone wall.

A full-brick wall
This Flemish-bond wall is topped by a course of "headers"—bricks laid across the full width of the wall.

Stone coping
Large stone slabs form a solid coping that complements a wall of flint mortared in courses.

Softening the wall
The hard line of the wall's edge is softened by a colorful display of trailing flowering plants to create a curtain effect. The crevices between the stones provide ideal spaces for many rock-garden plants.

Coping

Coping, which forms the top course of a wall, prevents frost damage by shedding rainwater so that it does not seep into the joints. It also gives the wall a finished appearance.

Specially made, curved coping bricks are available, but these are often only the width of the wall and are strictly caps—they do not throw the drips clear of the wall. Wider concrete slabs are used for copings on brick as well as concrete block walls. If an ordinary brick finish is required, lay a double course of flat roof tiles before the final row to provide a "drip strip." Coping is especially important for pierced screen block walls, because it helps to bond the blocks together.

Dry stone walls

Dry stone walls may be laid on a concrete footing (see p.596) or a foundation of rubble. They may be planted with alpines (see p.268) inserted between stones, and look particularly attractive if a cavity is left in the top for trailing plants.

Dig a trench and make a firm base of compacted crushed stone or rubble. The base of the wall should be one or two courses below ground level. Use a taut line to maintain a level construction, and build up the wall with broad tie-stones and smaller random stones to bond the wall together. The wall should be wider at the bottom than at the top. To achieve a consistent slope or "batter," make a batter board, a wooden frame in the shape of the desired cross-section of the wall. An inward slope of about 1in for every 24in (2.5cm for every 60cm) is usually sufficient. Use a level to keep the batter board

perpendicular. Finish off with large, flat stones or a row of vertical stones laid on edge (and mortared if desired) as a decorative coping.

Retaining walls

Retaining walls may be used to terrace a garden or contain the soil in a raised bed (see opposite). Stones, concrete wall blocks, or bricks may be used. Seek professional advice for any retaining wall more than 30in (75cm) high or one on a steep slope, because it may be necessary to reinforce it to withstand the pressure of soil and water. Rather than building one

large retaining wall, terracing the garden in a series of shallow steps may be easier. In many places, permission is required to build a high retaining wall, and building regulations may demand that contractors be hired to construct it from poured concrete.

Insert a drain (see *Installing Drains*, p.623) running horizontally along the back of the wall, and backfill the lower half of the wall with gravel or rubble. If using bricks or concrete blocks, build the wall on a concrete footing (see p.596) set below the lower soil level, and leave weep holes for drainage between every second or third brick in the lower courses of the wall.

Dry stone walling is a good choice for a low retaining wall, because alpines can be grown in the exposed face. Place large stones on a firm foundation of concrete or compacted crushed stone, and lay subsequent courses of stone with an inward slope (batter) of 1–2in for every 12in (2.5–5cm for every 30cm) of height. The wall should be perpendicular on the retaining side (see *How to Build a Dry Stone Retaining Wall*, p.268). If it is not to be planted with crevice plants, the wall may be mortared to make it stronger (see "Bricklaying," p.597); otherwise, pack garden soil between the stones for additional stability.

CONSTRUCTING RETAINING WALLS

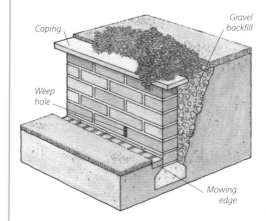

Coping

Weep hole

Gravel backfill

Mowing edge

Any retaining wall used to hold back soil on a slope must be extremely strong. Bear in mind that the higher the wall, the stronger it will need to be. Remember, too, that wet soil is heavier than dry soil, and water must be allowed to drain out through weep holes left at the base of the wall. If the units of construction are large, such as blocks, the retaining wall will be even stronger than if smaller bricks are used.

Construction
On the left is a section of a brick wall with a vertical, unmortared joint acting as a weep hole. On the right is a wall built of hollow concrete blocks (see below). Hollows may be filled with wet concrete, or with soil for plants.

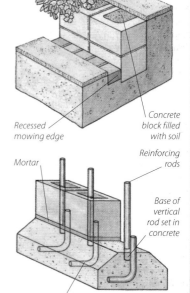

Recessed mowing edge

Concrete block filled with soil

Reinforcing rebars
The strength of a wall built with hollow concrete blocks will be greatly increased if hooked bars are set in the concrete foundation. Further reinforcing bars may be added, passing up through the blocks.

Mortar

Reinforcing rods

Base of vertical rod set in concrete

Hooked rods reinforcing concrete foundation

Raised beds

Raised beds may provide a strong design element in a landscape, perhaps surrounding a sunken garden or providing changes of level. Small groups of raised beds, or a series of linked beds, are ideal for paved areas, while a single raised bed makes a good home for an attractive specimen plant.

Where the soil is poor, or unsuitable for growing certain plants, raised beds can be extremely useful: they allow acidic conditions to be created in a garden with alkaline soil, for instance. Moreover, plants in raised beds have more room to develop and require less attention than those in tubs and other containers, in which the soil dries out quickly.

Raised beds have the great advantage that they can be reached without stooping. Recessed or "kneehole" beds, also known as tabletop beds, provide access for wheelchair users. A well-planned series of raised beds makes gardening easier for elderly or disabled gardeners. The bed height will need to be tailored to the requirements of the individual gardener, and narrow enough for the whole bed to be within easy reach. The beds should be linked together by easily negotiated, wide garden paths (see pp.593–594).

In areas with cold winters, raised beds will freeze more deeply than the open ground. This may limit the range of plants that can be grown.

Materials
Raised beds may be built from a wide range of materials: mortared bricks (see *Types of Bricks*, p.589), concrete blocks (see *Wall Materials*, p.596), unmortared stone (see "Dry-stone walls," p.598), landscape timbers, or sawn logs. If using bricks or concrete blocks, you may wish to finish off the bed with a coping (see p.598) wide enough to sit on.

Bricks

A large, rectangular brick bed is easy to construct, but may appear rather unimaginative. A number of smaller, linked beds at different heights will create a more visually stimulating feature, as would a circular raised bed. Always choose frost-proof bricks. Brick pavers can be used instead of full bricks.

Rectangular beds
Prepare a footing (see *How to Make a Concrete Footing*, p.596) at a depth that allows the first course of bricks

to lie below ground level. When the footing has set, use a masonry mortar mix (see p.586) to lay the courses of bricks (see "Bricklaying," p.597). Lay whole bricks at right angles to form the corners.

Circular beds
For a circular bed, the bricks should ideally be cut to give a smooth curve, but it is possible to use full bricks. First arrange the bricks loosely with a circumference large enough to ensure that there are no wide gaps at the edge. Prepare the footing, and, when this has set, lay the bricks so that they almost touch on the inside edge of the wall. Use wedges of mortar to fill the gaps on the outer face. Stagger the courses as with a conventional bond and use half-bricks for the final course to give a better curve.

Acid-loving plants
If plants that require acidic soil are to be grown in a raised bed, line the inside of the finished walls with rubber pond liner or several coats of a waterproof, bitumen-based paint. This stops lime in the mortar from leaching into the soil and raising its pH.

Concrete blocks

Concrete blocks may be a good choice for raised beds if matching materials have been used for other structures and surfaces. The blocks may be too large for circular beds, but are ideal for rectangular ones. The beds are constructed in much the same way as brick beds.

Natural stone

Raised beds may be built using natural stone without mortar. Use the technique for dry-stone retaining walls (see "Dry stone walls" and "Retaining walls," p.598), but keep the beds low and small.

For a bed higher than about 24in (60cm), it is best to mortar the stones securely in place. Even with a low bed, it may be necessary to mortar the corners for stability.

Landscape timbers

Landscape timbers, which blend unobtrusively with most plants and garden surfaces, are ideal for large, low, raised beds, but they are heavy and difficult to handle: do not make the walls more than

three timbers high. They may be purchased in full or half lengths; try to build walls in multiples of these to eliminate the need for sawing. If sawing is necessary, use a chain saw.

It is not necessary to provide a footing, because the length and weight of the landscape timbers make them extremely stable. Create a level surface to lay them on, using packed gravel, then bond the sleepers like bricks, and, if more than two courses high, use iron rebars driven into the ground to secure them in place: either drill holes for the rebars in the timbers, or position the rebars on the outside of the raised bed as a brace.

If you use treated landscape timbers, line the bed sides with heavy plastic or rubber pond liner before filling the beds with soil.

Sawn logs

Logs make attractive edgings for woodland-style beds, and for very low, informal beds in a natural setting. For higher raised beds,

logs of a uniform size and thickness should be used. These may not be readily available, however, and the corner joints are difficult to construct. If this type of raised bed is to be built, it may be better to buy it in easily assembled kit form.

MATERIALS FOR RAISED BEDS

Brick wall using a running bond

Soil level

Crushed stone base

1in (2.5cm) concrete footing

Bricks
Ideally, brick beds should be built using frost-proof bricks or pavers. After preparing the concrete footing (see p.596), lay the first course of bricks below soil level. Stagger the courses of bricks to strengthen the walls.

Landscape timbers laid like bricks in a running bond

Packed gravel base

Landscape timbers
Landscape timbers are particularly good for low raised beds, but avoid wood that has been treated with toxic preservatives. No footing is needed because the timbers are themselves very stable. Stagger the joints.

RAISED BEDS AND WATERING NEEDS

The growing medium in a raised bed drains more rapidly than the soil in regular garden borders, so it is important to water plants more often. In particular, soil in contact with the retaining walls tends to dry out and shrink. In extreme conditions, this could expose the fibrous feeding roots of plants growing around the edges of the bed, making them vulnerable to frost, heat, or drought. Depending on the plants grown, it may also be necessary to add more organic matter to the soil to help retain moisture (see p.621).

Fences

Fences are often used as boundary markers, but they may also act as windbreaks or as a decorative feature in the landscape. They are quicker and cheaper to erect than walls, and they have the additional advantage of providing almost instant privacy. In general they do, however, require more maintenance than a wall. To make a fence into a decorative element, cover it with climbers or attach trellis panes to the top or sides.

The first step in erecting a fence is to mark the fence line with a string. If it is to be on a boundary between two properties, all the fencing and fence posts must be on your side of the property line.

For other legal requirements regarding fences, see *Laws on Fences,* p.602.

Panel fences

One of the simplest forms of fencing is a panel fence, which can be supported using concrete or wooden posts. With concrete posts, the panels simply slot into grooves on either side; concrete posts also have the advantage that they do not rot. For details, see *How to Erect a Panel Fence*, opposite.

If you prefer wooden posts, the panels have to be screwed or nailed into position. Protect the bases of

wooden fence posts by using either metal post supports or concrete spurs (see opposite). The latter are short posts that are embedded in a concrete foundation. They have predrilled holes through which the wooden posts are bolted to the spur, at just above ground level.

To build a fence with wooden posts, dig a hole for the first post, then stretch string along the run of the fence to ensure it is straight. For a panel 6ft (2m) high, you will need 9ft (2.75m) lengths of lumber for the posts, and the post holes should be 30in (75cm) deep. Fill the bottom with 6in (15cm) of crushed stone, then stand the post in the hole and pack it with more stone to hold it in

POST-HOLE DIGGER

If a number of holes are needed for fence posts, buy, rent, or borrow a manual posthole digger or a posthole digger attachment for a garden tractor outfitted with a hydraulic system.

There are several types of manual digger; each has its merits, so consult a knowledgeable dealer before buying. Using a manually operated posthole digger may be strenuous, depending on the site, type of soil, and amount of moisture in the soil. Power diggers are much easier to use and save time and effort.

FENCE TYPES

Basketweave fencing is usually sold as prefabricated panels, generally in a range of heights. Thin, interwoven slats of pine or larch are held in a light, softwood frame. It provides good privacy, but is not very strong.

Board-on-board fencing consists of overlapping, vertical, feather-edged boards, usually of softwood, nailed to a pair of horizontal rails. The thick edges of the boards are nailed over the thin edges. It may be constructed *in situ*, but is also available (as shown here) in the form of panels. Board-on-board is one of the strongest forms of fencing, offering good security and privacy.

Horizontal-board fencing, made of overlapping horizontal planks, is another fairly sturdy and attractive form of panel fencing (see also p.605). It provides adequate levels of security.

Shingle fences consist of overlapping cedar shingles (wooden "tiles") nailed to a wooden framework to produce a strong, solid fence. They offer good security and privacy, depending on their height.

Picket fences have vertical wooden "pales" spaced about 2in (5cm) apart on horizontal rails, and are more decorative than functional. Vinyl picket fences are available that require far less maintenance than traditional wooden ones. Neither kind offers much security or privacy.

Ranch-style fencing uses thin, planed planks attached horizontally to sturdy posts. The lumber is either painted or treated with preservative. There are vinyl versions of this style of fencing available, which need less maintenance, but neither is secure.

Snow fencing consists of split vertical stakes about 3in (8cm) apart, woven together with strands of galvanized wire. It is suitable only as a temporary fence.

Split-rail fences have two or more horizontal poles or rough-sawn lumber rails between adjacent posts. They form an inexpensive boundary marker.

Shadow-box fencing has horizontal boards on both sides of the posts, with the planks on one side facing the gaps on the other. It makes a better windbreak than a solid fence, and it provides acceptable if not total privacy.

Wattle hurdles are panels of interwoven woody stems and give a rustic effect. Two examples are shown here. They may be made *in situ* or bought as ready-made panels. They are held in place by sturdy stakes and are particularly useful when a new hedge is becoming established, offering interim privacy as well as good protection against both small and large animals. Within a relatively short period of time, however, they can begin to look ragged and unattractive, and they are also troublesome to maintain and repair.

Lattice fences are made from either sawn lumber or rustic wood. They resemble large partitions of diamond-shaped trellis. They can be used as an informal boundary marker, but offer very little privacy.

Chain link consists of a wire mesh, which is usually attached to concrete, lumber, or iron posts. Galvanized wire mesh lasts for 10 years, plastic-coated wire mesh longer. It is a good choice where an animal-proof boundary is required.

Welded wire consists of an open wire mesh stapled to wooden posts and rails. It is used primarily as a barrier to fence off larger animals where appearance is unimportant.

Post-and-chain fences may have chains made of metal or plastic that are attached to wooden, concrete, or plastic posts. They are used to mark boundaries where more substantial fences are not needed.

Concrete fences are made of concrete panels, often pierced, and concrete posts. They are more common around apartment complexes and townhouse developments than single-family homes.

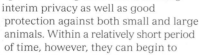

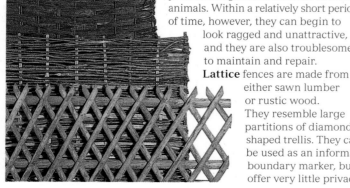

position. Check that it is upright with a level. Using the panel as a width guide, dig a hole for the second post, making sure that it is aligned with the string line. Level the ground between the post and the hole and lay a gravel board—a length of wood (or concrete) fixed between fence posts at ground level

to prevent panels from coming in contact with the soil and rotting. A wooden gravel board should be secured to the first post with galvanized nails. Attach a fence panel to the post using 3in (75mm) galvanized nails driven through predrilled holes, or screw them together with metal brackets.

Place the second post into its hole, ensuring that it is vertical and fits closely against the fence panel; attach the gravel board and panel as before. Repeat with the remaining posts, gravel boards, and panels.

Bed the posts firmly in position with wedges of scrap lumber and crushed stone, checking that they are vertical with a level. Pack a stiff concrete mix (see p.586) around the base of each post, and use a trowel to create a slope away from each side as a runoff for water.

Saw the tops of the posts to an equal height above the panels, if necessary. Treat any sawn surfaces with wood preservative and finish each post with an overhanging wooden cap that deflects rainwater.

Metal post supports

Instead of digging holes for fence posts, metal post supports may be sunk into the ground instead, and wooden posts inserted into them.

This reduces the length of the lumber needed for fence posts and keeps them out of contact with the soil, thus prolonging the life of the wood. Use 24in (60cm) supports for fences that are up to 4ft (1.2m) high and 30in (75cm) supports for fences up to 6ft (2m).

Before driving the support into the ground, put a scrap piece of wood from a post into the socket to protect the support from damage. Manufacturers may also provide a special attachment that fits over the scrap of wood while the support is hammered into place.

Check continually that the spike is entering the ground vertically. Hold a level against each of the four sides of the socket in turn. To secure the post, tighten the clamping bolts in the socket, or if these are not provided, secure it with screws or nails through the slatted holes. For additional strength, metal post supports may also be set in a foundation of crushed stone and concrete.

HOW TO BUILD A PANEL FENCE

1 Dig a hole 30in (75cm) deep and pack a 6in (15cm) layer of crushed stone in the base. Insert the first concrete post and check the height of the post against the fence panel.

2 Pack crushed stone around the post and pour in prepared concrete. Tamp it down to remove air bubbles. Add more concrete and tamp again. Keep checking that the post is vertical.

3 Lay a fence panel on the ground to position the next hole accurately. Use a string line as a guide, then dig the next hole to the required depth.

4 Fit a gravel board between the post holes. Level the ground until the board lies horizontally by packing in or removing soil. Check with a level.

CONCRETE SPURS

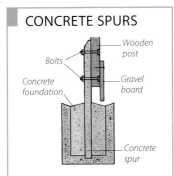

Wooden post, Bolts, Gravel board, Concrete foundation, Concrete spur

To avoid damage through contact with damp soil, bolt wooden fence posts to a concrete spur set in a concrete foundation.

5 Slot the panel into the groove in the first post. Insert the next post and pack into position with crushed stone. Secure molded wooden coping to the top of the panel.

BUILDING A FENCE USING METAL POST SUPPORTS

1 Place a scrap piece of wood and the driving tool, if provided, into the socket of the post support. Use a sledgehammer to drive the support directly into the ground in stages.

2 After every few blows of the hammer, check that the support is being driven in vertically. Hold the level against all four sides in turn and make any necessary adjustments.

3 Insert the fence post into the socket at the top of the support and secure it by nailing through the slatted holes. Some sockets have clamping bolts to tighten up.

4 Using a string guide, hammer in further posts. Nail fencing (here a panel of picket fence, supported on bricks to keep the rails horizontal) to the posts. Repeat until the fence is finished.

CLIMATE AND THE GARDEN

Climate has a major influence on plant growth, and much of the satisfaction in gardening lies in meeting the challenges of the weather, often by exploiting its effects to the gardener's advantage. Choosing plants that thrive in the prevailing climate is fundamental to success, although many plants will adapt to weather conditions alien to their natural habitat. The effects of climate on plants are complex, and responses to the weather are shaped by many factors, including a plant's location within the garden, stage of maturity, and the length and intensity of exposure to inclement conditions. Through an understanding of the effects of climate, a gardener will be better able to grow healthy, productive, and attractive plants.

Climate zones

World climate may be divided into four broad but clearly defined zones; these are tropical, desert, temperate, and polar.

Tropical climates, characterized by high temperatures and heavy, sometimes seasonal, rainfall, support luxuriant, evergreen vegetation. Deserts have average daytime temperatures in excess of 100°F (38°C) but often very cold nights, with annual rainfall of less than 10in (25cm); only plants adapted to these conditions, such as cacti, can survive such extremes. Temperate regions have changeable daily patterns, but rainfall is usually evenly spread throughout the year, and temperatures are less extreme than in the Tropics or deserts; deciduous plants are more common than evergreens because they are better adapted to these conditions. Polar regions experience extreme cold, strong winds and low rainfall, so little plant growth is possible.

In addition to these four broad zones, intermediate zones, such as subtropical and Mediterranean, are also recognized.

Regional climate

Conditions within climate zones are determined by geographical factors such as latitude, altitude, and proximity to the sea, all of which affect both rainfall and temperature.

The North American climate
North America has significant regional variation in climate. The continent can be roughly divided into several climatic regions, but topographical variation and proximity to large bodies of water create differences even within regions. In the US and Canada, coastal climates are influenced by warm air and water currents, and rain from the surrounding oceans.

The great extremes of summer and winter temperatures in central parts of North America are influenced by both latitude and the continental landmass. Because the Atlantic and Pacific oceans and the Gulf of Mexico are too far away to have any moderating effect on temperatures, it is the cold landmass of Canada that has more impact during the winter.

For general purposes, climate regions are defined with respect to temperature range, number of frost-free days, precipitation, humidity, sun, wind, and the plants that may be grown in each region. One of the most useful measures relating climate and plant growth is the Canadian regions and Hardiness Zone map (see pp.610–611 and endpapers).

Within Canada, growing seasons range from the very short Arctic season, with high light intensity, to longer, milder seasons in British Columbia, with lower light intensity. Areas with deep, reliable snow cover can grow a wider range of perennial plants than warmer parts with midwinter thaws.

Friend or foe?
A 2in (5cm) layer of snow on the ground can prevent soil temperatures from falling below 32°F (0°C), protecting plant roots from freezing. Shoots and branches above ground remain vulnerable, particularly if icy conditions follow, so gently remove snow from plant growth.

Elements of climate

The elements of climate that directly affect plants and the techniques used to grow them are temperature, frost, snow, rain, humidity, sun, and wind.

Temperature

Vital processes like photosynthesis, transpiration, respiration, and growth are significantly affected by temperature. Each species has a minimum and a maximum temperature beyond which these processes will not take place. The maximum temperature is about 96°F (35°C) for most plants; the minimum is highly variable. Where extremely low temperatures occur, plant tissue may be physically destroyed (see "Freezing and thawing," below).

Air and soil temperatures are the most important climatic factors influencing the onset and breaking of plant dormancy (see p.610), which determines the length of the growing season and the choice of plants to be grown.

Air temperature
Sunshine produces radiant energy that raises the ambient or air temperature. In temperate and cooler climates, a sheltered site that benefits from the warming effect of full sun may be used for plants from warmer areas that might not otherwise thrive.

Altitude has an important effect on air temperature: given the same latitude, mountainous sites are cooler than low-lying ones—for every 1,000ft (300m) increase in altitude, the temperature drops by 1°F (0.5°C). High-altitude sites have shorter growing seasons, which, together with cooler temperatures affect the range of plants grown.

Soil temperature
The temperature of soil is important for healthy root growth and affects the rate at which plants absorb water and nutrients from the soil. Successful seed germination and shoot development also depend on suitable soil temperatures (see PRINCIPLES OF PROPAGATION, p.630).

The speed at which soil warms up and the temperature maintained during the year depend on soil type and the exposure of the site. Sandy soils warm up faster than clay, and well-drained, fertile soils stay warm longer than those that are compacted or infertile (see also SOILS AND FERTILIZERS, "Soil types," p.616).

Sites with a natural, gentle incline toward the south warm up quickly in spring because they gain more benefit from the sun than level or north-facing ground. They are ideal for early vegetable crops. North-facing slopes stay relatively cool and suit plants that thrive in cooler conditions.

Frost

Frost is a great hazard in gardening and has more impact than the average minimum temperature for the area. An unexpected severe frost has serious implications; even hardy plants can suffer, particularly if they have new growth in spring.

Frost forms on objects when their surface temperature drops below 32°F (0°C). Black frost is likely in a dry atmosphere, and blackens the leaves and stems of plants. In hoar frost, ice crystals form from water condensed from a humid atmosphere. Ground frost results when the soil temperature falls below freezing point; the penetration

FROST POCKETS
Cold air sinks, so it will always collect at the lowest point so it can reach, forming a frost pocket. Valleys and ground hollows are ideal for frost pockets, and any plants in the vicinity will suffer as a result. Cold air also collects behind closely planted hedges and other solid obstructions, such as walls and fences, with the same effect.

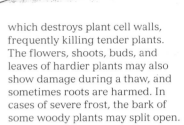

depth depends on its intensity and duration. Still, clear nights when cold air collects just above ground level are particularly dangerous. Most at risk are trees, shrubs, and climbers whose woody tissue has not ripened (hardened) well, usually due to a lack of sun and warmth during the fall.

The risk of spring frost in any area determines the date after which it is safe to sow or plant out tender plants, like runner beans, tomatoes, chrysanthemums, dahlias, and most bedding plants; the onset of fall frost signals the end of their growing season. To keep tender plants from year to year, move them indoors or provide protection (see FROST AND WIND PROTECTION, pp.612–613).

Frost pockets and damage
Pools of frost may collect where dense, cold air flows downward; any valley or hollow is a potential frost pocket. Cold air accumulates in the depression, increasing the area of potential damage as it backs up the sloping sides of the valley.

Thick barriers of trees or hedges along hillsides may obstruct the passage of cold air down a slope, but frost pockets will form in front of them. Thin or remove barriers to allow cold air to flow through.

When the ground is frozen, water is no longer available to plant roots. Deep-rooted trees are not affected by heavy frosts, because their roots penetrate well below the frost line, but plants with shallow roots may not be able to replace the moisture lost by continual transpiration. Severe ground frost often causes newly planted, young, or shallow-rooted plants to rise or "lift" out of the soil; gently refirm when the thaw begins. For preventive measures, see FROST AND WIND PROTECTION, pp.612–613.

Freezing and thawing
Frost itself does not always cause great damage to plants, but alternate freezing and thawing does. Sap expands on thawing,

which destroys plant cell walls, frequently killing tender plants. The flowers, shoots, buds, and leaves of hardier plants may also show damage during a thaw, and sometimes roots are harmed. In cases of severe frost, the bark of some woody plants may split open.

Repeated hard freezes followed by rapid thaws and subsequent soil waterlogging causes most damage to roots. Late spring frosts particularly damage new top growth, causing blackening of the leaves and injury to new buds and flowers.

The duration of frost is also relevant to the amount of damage caused: for example, a temperature of 27°F (-3°C) for 15 minutes might cause no damage, but if the same temperature is sustained over three hours, it could cause substantial plant losses.

Frost and cultivation
Despite the danger to plants, frost can aid cultivation. Soil water expands when it freezes, breaking clods into smaller soil particles; this is particularly useful on clay soils, in encouraging the development of tilth. Low soil temperatures also reduce the numbers of some soil-inhabiting pests.

Snow

When atmospheric temperature falls close to (but not below) freezing, water droplets freeze in clouds or rain and may fall as snow.

Snow provides a useful supply of water as it thaws and often gives plants valuable insulation, especially those recently planted or in heavy soil. Snow also helps reduce frost heaving. However, heavy snow followed by severe frost may damage shoots and branches. Where possible, remove thick layers of snow from vulnerable plants (such as boxwood and many conifers) by sweeping upward with a broom.

RAIN SHADOW

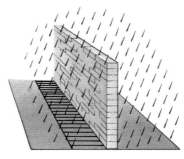

Ground on the leeward side of a wall or solid fence (see shaded area above) receives less rainfall than ground on the windward side, because the wall or fence creates an area of rain shadow.

Rainfall

Water is the main constituent of cell sap and is vital for photosynthesis, the complex means by which carbon dioxide and water are converted into living plant tissue. Photosynthesis is also fundamental to the process of transpiration, which keeps a plant sturdy and transports nutrients to it. Respiration, germination of seeds, and development of roots, shoots, leaves, flowers, and fruit are all dependent on good water supplies.

Rainfall is the principal source of water for plants in the open. Much rain is lost through evaporation and runoff, but moisture that soaks into the soil is absorbed by soil particles or held as a thin film around them. Water and essential nutrients, which are absorbed in solution, are then extracted from soil by plant root hairs.

For optimal growth, plants need a steady supply of water. In practice, rainfall is variable, however, in both regularity and quantity.

Waterlogging

In badly drained soil, a buildup of water leads to waterlogging. Most plants can survive an occasional downpour. If waterlogging is prolonged, roots may die through asphyxiation, except in the case of specially adapted plants, such as marginal aquatics, swamp cypress (*Taxodium distichum*), and willows (*Salix*). On constantly waterlogged sites, most plants fail to establish unless drainage is improved (see SOILS AND FERTILIZERS, p.623).

Drought

Plant development is more often restricted by too little available water rather than by too much. Drought during summer, when temperature and sunlight are at maximum levels, is a common

problem. Wilting is the first outward sign of drought; plant functions slow down until more water is available, and water loss by transpiration is reduced by partial closure of stomata in the leaves (See BASIC BOTANY, "Leaves," p.675).

The soil

In areas of low rainfall, various techniques may be used to increase the amount of water available to plants from soil, such as removing weeds (see pp.645–647), mulching, and increasing humus content by digging in organic matter (see SOILS AND FERTILIZERS, "Mulches," p.626, and "Using soil additives," p.621). Plants benefit more from rainfall if grown in open locations away from buildings, fences, and trees, which often produce rain shadows.

Torrential rain may damage soil structure, but the worst effects can be avoided by gardening on well-drained sites. If this is not possible, drainage may be improved by deep digging or by installing artificial drainage aids (see SOILS AND FERTILIZERS, "Double digging," p.620, and "Installing drains," p.623).

Humidity

Humidity levels are determined by the proportion of water vapor in the atmosphere and the moisture content of the soil. The point at which air becomes saturated varies according to sunlight, temperature, and wind. Atmospheric humidity is referred to as relative humidity: the amount of water vapor in air given as a percentage of saturation point.

In areas of heavy rainfall, atmospheric humidity is high. Some plants, like ferns and mosses, thrive in exceptionally humid conditions. Humidity may be increased by damping down the areas around plants (see "Humidifiers," p.576). This helps in propagating plants to reduce water lost by transpiration.

High relative humidity may have unfavorable effects: fungal diseases like gray mold flourish in the moist conditions created by high humidity.

Sunlight

Sunlight provides radiant energy to raise the temperature and humidity of soil and air, and plays a major role in stimulating plant growth.

For most plants, sunshine and the consequent high temperatures encourage maximum new growth, flowering, and fruiting. A sunny summer also results in greatly enhanced food storage in plants

and helps to firm protective tissue, which means that better propagating material is produced.

Day length

The duration of daylight in a given 24-hour period (day length) is determined by latitude and season, and affects flowering and fruiting in some plants, such as *Kalanchoe*, chrysanthemums, and strawberries. "Short" days have less than 12 hours of daylight; "long" days last more than 12 hours. By using artificial lighting or blacking out natural light, the flowering times of day-length-sensitive plants may be manipulated to advantage. Germination of seeds and seedling development may be advanced by the same method (see GREENHOUSES AND FRAMES, "Growing lamps," p.577).

Plants and sunlight

Plants always grow toward the sun. For example, a shrub positioned close to a wall will develop more shoots and foliage on the side farthest from the wall. In the same way, plants that are subjected to a poor or localized light source become drawn or etiolated as they try to reach more light. The intensity of sunlight dictates flower opening in some plants, for example, *Ornithogalum umbellatum* only opens its flowers in good light conditions.

Most leafy plants require the maximum amount of light to achieve optimum growth. Some garden plants thrive in direct, strong sunshine, but others will not tolerate it. Many annuals, most fruits and vegetables, roses, and plants of Mediterranean origin all thrive best in full sun. On the other hand, many rhododendrons prefer some shade, while ivies (*Hedera*) and some hostas tend to do best in heavily shaded areas.

Strong sunlight may scorch flowers and foliage, especially of houseplants moved outside for summer. It may also cause fruit or bark to split. Avoid by choosing

an appropriate site when planting, and for vulnerable plants provide artificial shade in summer, especially in greenhouses and frames (see GREENHOUSES AND FRAMES, "Shading," p.576).

Wind

Wind often damages plants and adversely affects their environment, but it also has some benefits: it plays an important part in pollen and seed dispersal and may be useful in cooling plants down, provided that they have enough water to prevent desiccation. In addition, gentle winds prevent a stagnant atmosphere from developing, and deter plant diseases that might otherwise thrive.

Conversely, wind may discourage beneficial insects, making it more difficult to control pests, diseases, and weeds. Spraying can be less effective in windy conditions, with nontarget plants damaged by spray drift. Many more serious problems are caused by wind, but there are various ways of protecting plants.

Wind damage

If woody plants are exposed to strong winds continuously, their top growth becomes unbalanced, giving a one-sided appearance. The exposed shoot tips are likely to be damaged or "scorched." Trees that grow on hilltops and on exposed, coastal sites are examples.

The greater the velocity of wind, the more damage it causes. In high winds, shoots and stems of plants break and, in gale force conditions, trees may be uprooted or their root systems seriously weakened. Strong winds may also damage fences, greenhouses, and other garden structures. On sandy or light loam soils, wind may cause soil erosion.

Strong winds in high temperatures increase the rate at which plants lose water, leading to desiccation of leaves and shoots.

SUNSHINE AND SHADE

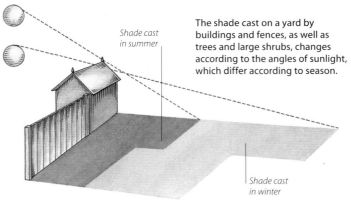

Shade cast in summer

Shade cast in winter

The shade cast on a yard by buildings and fences, as well as trees and large shrubs, changes according to the angles of sunlight, which differ according to season.

WIND TURBULENCE

Exposed areas on rising ground may suffer severe wind damage. Gusts of air meeting resistance from the land are diverted around the sides and over the top of hills, gathering in intensity at the same time.

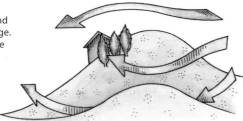

WINDBREAKS

Place windbreaks at a distance of 10 times their height.

A series of windbreaks
Across a large area of flat ground, construct several semipermeable fences or screens to break the force of the wind.

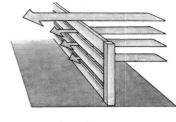

Reducing wind speed
A windbreak should be semipermeable. Gusts of air still pass through, but at reduced speed.

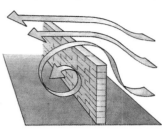

Nonpermeable windbreak
A solid windbreak is ineffective. Air is forced upward, then pulled down to create a downdraft.

WIND FUNNELING

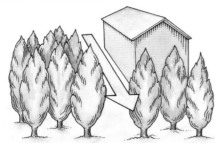

A wind funnel created between buildings and trees may cause a great deal of damage to plants in its path, because air is forced through the narrow channel at great speed. If gardening in such an area is unavoidable, construct a windbreak to protect your plants.

Even moderate winds have a detrimental effect, and may keep plants from reaching their full growth potential. Similar damage occurs if temperatures are very low; plants cannot replace lost moisture if soil water is frozen (see p.607).

Effects of topography
The severity of the wind depends to a large extent on topography. Coastal sites often have no natural protection from salt-laden wind coming in off the water. Hilltop sites may be equally exposed, because the wind gusts around and over the hill. Wind tunnels are created by the channeling of air between hillsides and along valleys, through corridors of established trees, or between adjacent buildings. This intensifies wind speed and strength, so avoid planting in these areas.

Windbreaks are an effective means of providing shelter from wind. They may take the form of fences, screens, or hedges (see HEDGES AND SCREENS, pp.82–85).

How a windbreak works
Whatever the type of windbreak, it should be 50 percent permeable. Solid barriers deflect wind upward, producing an area of low pressure directly behind them, which draws air downward to fill the vacuum, causing further turbulence.

Fences or screens need to be up to 12ft (4m) high for maximum protection as a garden boundary, but may be as low as 20in (50cm) for low-growing plants, such as vegetables and strawberries. For the greatest benefit across a large area, place windbreaks at regular intervals roughly equal to ten times their height.

Microclimate

Topographic differences frequently mean that local microclimates vary from the more generalized pattern within a specific climatic region. A site in a natural dip or hollow may be relatively warm if it is protected from the wind; on the other hand, if the hollow is shaded from sunshine it will be quite cool and may form a frost pocket in winter (see p.607). Rainfall may be significantly less in locations in the lee of high ground than in others in the same locality but on the windward side.

The landscape and its plants further modify local climate and introduce features that give rise to a microclimate specific to the garden; this may differ markedly from that of the surrounding area. To alter the microclimate of a garden, a gardener can readily adapt certain features to provide specific conditions.

Orientation
The soil in raised or sloping beds that face the sun will warm up quickly in spring, producing ideal conditions for growing early crops or flowers. If the soil is free-draining, the same area may be used for plants that prefer dry conditions.

South-facing fences and walls are excellent places to grow tender climbers, wall shrubs, and trained fruit trees, because they are in sun for much of the day, which improves flowering and fruiting. Walls also absorb a great deal of heat, which is then released overnight; this can confer a few degrees of extra frost protection during winter.

Wind shelter
A row of trees or a fence provides a sheltered area for plants that might otherwise suffer wind damage. The growing conditions on each side of the windbreak will be different: the ground close to a hedge or fence on the leeward side will rarely receive rain and may also be sheltered from the warming effect of the sun.

Shaded areas
Areas of shade beneath tree canopies, hedges, or large shrubs receive the same sort of light as in natural woodland and may be suitable for plants that enjoy such an environment. If a greater degree of shade is required, plants may be grown against north-facing walls, although these sites will be colder.

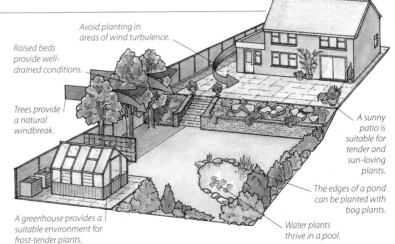

Avoid planting in areas of wind turbulence.

Raised beds provide well-drained conditions.

Trees provide a natural windbreak.

A greenhouse provides a suitable environment for frost-tender plants.

A sunny patio is suitable for tender and sun-loving plants.

The edges of a pond can be planted with bog plants.

Water plants thrive in a pool.

IDENTIFYING MICROCLIMATES

The potential for several different growing environments exists in even the smallest yards. Naturally occurring features create their own areas of microclimate and landscape features may be either exploited or manipulated, as necessary, to provide the conditions that plants from many different regions enjoy.

A bog garden
The edges of a pond or stream, or a low-lying part of the garden where rainwater tends to collect, may be exploited to create the boglike conditions in which moisture-loving plants thrive.

Greenhouses and frames
Using greenhouses, cold frames, and cloches gives complete control over the elements, enabling a gardener to provide a variety of microclimates in a small space (see GREENHOUSES AND FRAMES, pp.566–583).

Gardening in different regions in Canada

Canada has a wide variety of climate, soil, and planting traditions. Differences are significant even within the generally accepted regions: Maritimes, Central Canada, Prairies, and West Coast. The following accounts of these regions describe their climate and soil type and provide general gardening recommendations. The climate zone in which you live is one of the most important factors in determining what will grow well in your garden. The plant hardiness zone map printed on the endpapers is based on data prepared by Natural Resources Canada and Agriculture and Agri-Food Canada. It shows the zones of hardiness for the plants listed on pages 683–690. The US Department of Agriculture publishes a similar map, which also appears in some nursery and seed catalogs. The zone numbering, however, is different for each map, so it is essential to know which map is being used. Many other factors also influence gardening in Canada. Coastal regions and those bordering large lakes, for example, have stronger winds and more rain and snowfall than inland areas. An exposed site is several degrees colder, and accumulates less snow, than a sheltered one. The length of the growing season may be crucial for vegetables and annuals that are started outdoors.

Maritime region

This region of Canada consists of the provinces of Newfoundland and Labrador, New Brunswick, Nova Scotia, and Prince Edward Island, and the eastern seaboard of Quebec.

Environmental diversity in these maritime provinces, caused by size and topographical differences in the area, creates a challenge for the gardener. The sea inevitably has considerable influence on what can be grown, allowing greater scope in coastal areas than in the interior.

Climate

Temperatures range from -30°F (-35°C) to 95°F (35°C) and the growing season ranges from about 130 frost-free days in Kentville, Nova Scotia, down to 95 frost-free days in southern Labrador.

Some areas, such as Fredericton, New Brunswick, experience hot and often dry summers, and soil moisture conservation must be practiced. In coastal areas, rain can be heavy, particularly in spring and fall. The Avalon Peninsula of

Newfoundland receives 60in (150cm) of precipitation a year, roughly one-quarter as snow. Only one-third of the annual precipitation evaporates, leaving a moisture surplus of 40in (100cm) each year. Good drainage is therefore essential when gardening. Inclement winter rains and wet snow in coastal areas can damage woolly-leaved perennials by rotting their leaves and crown.

Humidity is higher on south-facing coastal areas than elsewhere, with day-time relative humidity from midspring to midfall of 75–90 percent; inland levels are 50–80 percent. The average annual hours of sunshine vary from 1,465 in St. John's, Newfoundland, to 1,870 in Fredericton, New Brunswick.

Incessant wind, particularly around coastal areas, can severely hinder plant growth. Winds blowing off a sea studded with icebergs and pack ice are often responsible for a late spring. In such situations, windbreaks are essential.

Soils

Much of this region has shallow, acidic (pH of 5 or lower), and nutrient-poor soils, which need additional organic matter. Most garden soils, except those designated for acid-loving plants, will benefit from an annual application of lime and general-purpose fertilizer. Good soils are often localized and are found in such areas as Prince Edward Island and the Annapolis valley, Nova Scotia.

Soils are usually wet at the start of winter and freeze quickly. Freezing, alternating with frequent midwinter thaws, may heave the plants out of the ground. This problem is particularly prevalent where soils are shallow.

Planting traditions

Trees such as linden (*Tilia*), birch (*Betula*), poplar (*Populus*), oak (*Quercus*), pine (*Pinus*), and spruce (*Picea*) are popular, along with some of the smaller ornamentals such as flowering crabapple (*Malus*) and lilac (*Syringa*). *Magnolia* x *soulangiana, M. stellata*, and *Cercis canadensis* grow in the warmer areas of mainland Maritimes, while St. John's, Newfoundland, is noted for its Scotch laburnums (*Laburnum alpinum*). In the Avalon Peninsula and coastal Nova Scotia a wide range of rhododendrons, azaleas, and heaths flourish, due, in part, to the naturally acidic soil. Primroses such as *Primula juliae, P. sieboldii*, and *P. vialii* also grow well. Many herbaceous perennials are hardy,

and bulbs such as crocuses, snowdrops, and daffodils thrive.

Basic, short-season vegetables are successful, especially cool-season kinds such as lettuce and spinach, but those requiring warm summers—zucchini, sweet peppers, and tomatoes—do well only in the more southerly parts of the region. A wide variety of strawberries, apples, and pears are cultivated, while even grapes, such as 'Valiant' and 'Beta', and the hardiest edible kiwi grow in those areas of New Brunswick and Nova Scotia that have warm springs and summers.

Lawns are popular but need continuous care. Snow mold and chinch bug can be a problem (see p.657 and 670). Grass mixtures containing Kentucky bluegrass (*Poa pratensis*), perennial ryegrass (*Lolium perenne*), and creeping red fescue (*Festuca rubra* var. *rubra*) are favored, while wild white clover is often added to poor sites.

Central Canada region

This region consists of the provinces of Quebec (except the eastern seaboard) and Ontario. It is bounded by permafrost on the north, Prairies on the west, and the US on the south.

Gardening is popular but usually on a limited scale—a lawn, one shade tree, and a few flowers. Most gardens have some display of flowers, but the heat of summer does not encourage the majority of people to work out in the sun.

Climate

There is a wide temperature range between seasons, with those in winter dropping to -10°F (-22°C) even in milder areas. Summer temperatures can reach 95°F (35°C) with high relative humidity (95 percent) in midsummer. Winter has a humidity reading down to 15 percent in cold snaps, when the wind-chill temperature can reach -58°F (-50°C).

Spring is fleeting and is condensed into a few weeks with snowdrops and single late tulips often in flower together. The number of frost-free days ranges from about 110 in the north to 165 in the Niagara peninsula.

Rainfall is generally spread evenly throughout the year, although there is often a summer drought. Annual rainfall is around 26in (60cm) in the populated southern part of this region. Snow may be deep but comparatively short-lived in the south, while it can be very deep and persistent in the north.

Soils

During the Ice Age, glaciers pushed much soil southward through Central Canada so that northern areas have mostly shallow, rocky soils, while in the south soils are deeper and richer. Since the growing season in much of the region is short, the soil has been very slow to build up again.

Much of the region has alkaline soil, the underlying rock being granite or limestone. There are also areas of acidic, peat-based soils, generally the sites of silted-up lakes. These warm soils are used for market gardening and early spring crops. Sphagnum moss is common in Quebec province, on the sites of ancient, large lakes, and harvesting peat moss is a major industry.

Planting traditions

Trees and shrubs are widely available in an increasing range of species and varieties. As winters become colder toward the north of the region, the selection that can be grown gradually narrows. Maple (*Acer*), linden (*Tilia*), and ash (*Fraxinus*), which were extensively planted in the past, are falling out of favor because the mature trees are too large for modern properties. Smaller trees such as crabapples (*Malus*), Japanese tree lilac (*Syringa reticulata*), and honey locust (*Gleditsia*) are more popular. Spiraea, Potentilla, and French hybrid lilacs (*Syringa vulgaris*) are the most widely sold shrubs, whereas arborvitae (*Thuja*)—often known as cedar—and alpine currant (*Ribes alpinum*) are the most favored evergreen and deciduous hedges.

Roses—particularly Hybrid Tea and Floribunda types—are found almost everywhere in the region in spite of the amount of work needed to overwinter them in most parts. Hardy shrub roses, too, are popular, especially the climbing types that do not require winter protection. Tree roses grow successfully only in the Niagara area.

Flower gardening is also becoming more common, with a trend toward perennials, especially peonies (*Paeonia*), irises, and day lilies (*Hemerocallis*). Bulbs are widely planted, although some, especially tulips, divide up in warm soils and become too small to flower after a few years. Annuals give the main color focus for most gardens.

Vegetable production is possible over most of the region, provided that short-season varieties are used. Cool-climate crops such as lettuce do not produce over a long period because the soil warms up so quickly in spring. If started indoors and planted out early, however, they can be successfully grown.

Warm-climate crops such as tomatoes and sweet peppers produce well, providing they are not planted out until the soil is warm. In northern Central Canada, choose cold-tolerant, quick-maturing tomato varieties such as 'Sub-arctic Maxi' to improve the chances of a good crop. All but the long-season, over-wintering varieties of cabbage and their relatives can be grown successfully, especially in the north, where they benefit from the extended daylength.

In the Niagara area, tree fruits such as peaches, nectarines, apricots, sweet cherries, and grapes are widely cultivated. Elsewhere the choice is restricted to pears, plums, sour cherries, and apples. Bush fruits are not as common, and the range of cultivars available to the gardener is more limited.

Lawns are almost all of Kentucky blue-grass (*Poa pratensis*), although tall fescue (*Festuca arundinacea*) is becoming popular because it is hard-wearing. Fine lawns of bentgrass (*Agrostis*) are rarely found in amateur gardens: they require expert care in the humid summers and suffer from many diseases.

Prairie region

The prairies are bounded by permafrost on the north, Ontario on the east, the US on the south, and the Rocky Mountains on the west.

Gardeners in this large territory must choose plants that will survive a dormant season of six months or more, but this challenge does not deter enthusiasm for gardening within this region.

Climate

This region's generally high altitude causes growing seasons that are hot and dry with temperatures up to 110°F (43°C), followed by very cold winters, with temperatures falling as low as -78°F (-61°C).

The short growing season of 60–155 frost-free days (generally 90–120 days in the more populated areas) may be interrupted by frost or snow in early or late summer. Some 54in (135cm) of snow may fall during the year, and total annual precipitation is 18in (45cm). The most humid season is midwinter, with 78 percent relative humidity in the Edmonton area; the lowest (47 percent) is late spring. The average annual hours of sunshine amount to some 2,315.

During the dormant season, areas near the mountains and foothills often experience chinooks —sudden incursions of brisk, warm air from the west. Chinooks encourage plants to start active growth; trees and shrubs may develop leaves and then later suffer die back from cold, desiccating, winter winds through their leaves.

Although severe winters limit the range of plants that may be grown, many borderline plants can survive if protected by windbreaks to create micro-climates around them.

Soils

Heavy clay soils (pH 6.3–7.3), known as chernozemic soils in grassland or grassland-forest communities, are found in much of the prairie region. In most well-populated areas, heavy "gumbo" soils are very fertile, although they severely reduce the time that a garden is workable because the gumbo is sticky in spring and bakes hard in summer. If enough organic material and coarse sand can be added, such soil can become very productive.

In other areas, particularly in the south, soil salinity and alkalinity reduce the number of plant species that may be grown.

Planting traditions

Ornamental trees that are suited to the growing conditions are limited to only some 20 genera, imparting a continuity to the prairie landscape. *Picea pungens* 'Glauca', white birch (*Betula papyrifera*), and mountain ash (*Sorbus aucuparia*) are popular. Trees in this region experience few attacks from insects and disease.

White-flowered Spiraea, a herald of spring, is everywhere in prairie gardens. Other common shrubs include yellowtwig dogwood (*Cornus stolonifera* 'Flaviramea'), redtwig dogwood (*C. alba* 'Sibirica'), lilacs such as French lilac (*Syringa vulgaris*), hardy roses, and Viburnum. Popular hedging plants are *Cotoneaster lucidus*, the native, red-fruited *Crataegus chrysocarpa*, and the black-fruited *C. douglasii*. Nonhardy, broadleaved evergreen shrubs are virtually absent from the prairie landscape, but evergreen shrubs such as *Juniperus horizontalis* are successful. Herbaceous perennials do well in the region, and annuals are popular as bedding plants. The small, spring-flowering bulbs thrive, but larger bulbs, especially daffodils, tend to be short-lived.

In most areas, growing vegetables such as beans, peas, and especially root crops is extremely satisfactory because the long, sunny days bring rapid maturity. Hot spring and early summer conditions, however, do not favor cool-climate crops such as lettuce and spinach. Warm-climate crops, for example tomatoes, sweet peppers, and squash, are best planted only after the soil warms up. Shelter warm-climate crops to make them even more productive.

Tree fruit production is limited to apples, crabapples, a few pears, and plums (mostly Japanese-American hybrids).

Lawns are normally grown using Kentucky bluegrass (*Poa pratensis*) and creeping red fescue (*Festuca rubra* var. *rubra*), but eco-conscious gardeners question the heavy applications of water needed to maintain such quality lawns. Some gardeners are experimenting with "wild meadow" alternatives.

West Coast region

This region is bounded by Alaska to the north, the Rocky Mountains on the east, the US on the south, and the Pacific Ocean on the west.

Proximity to the Pacific Ocean is the most important factor affecting gardens on the West Coast. Air streams from the Pacific, warmed by the Japanese ocean current, cause mild, moist weather, so that the range of plants grown here is different from elsewhere in Canada. Some plants that are common elsewhere, for example hawthorns (*Crataegus*) and crabapples (*Malus*), fail to thrive on the coast, because high rainfall in late winter brings an increase in fungal diseases.

Climate

The influence of the sea results in milder winters and cooler summers than the rest of Canada. On the coast, summer temperatures as high as 91°F (33°C) are common, whereas those in winter may drop to 0°F (-18°C). Winter temperatures are colder in the mainland mountains, and snow is common. The Rocky Mountains greatly affect the local climate; even places only a short distance apart can have widely differing temperatures and rainfall. Occasionally, winters are extremely cold, and commonly grown shrubs may perish in an arctic high sweeping down from the north, or they can be very mild, when there may be virtually no frost all winter and pelargoniums and fuchsias survive. Vancouver averages 216 frost-free days a year; Victoria 280.

The sea also affects the distribution of rainfall. Where the Pacific meets the mountains, rainfall reaches 128in (320cm), whereas the lee of the mountains receives only 25in (63cm). Relative humidity, which is high in the mornings (84–92 percent), drops in the afternoons. During summer, coastal regions experience long spells of dry weather, sometimes even drought. Vancouver, for example, averages 1,920 hours of sunshine per year while Victoria experiences 2,059 hours.

Soils

Coastal soils are acidic, while those in the mountains are often shallow and lacking in nutrients. Both soil types require the addition of large amounts of organic matter. Peaty soils, which produce bountiful gardens and excellent commercial crops of highbush blueberry (*Vaccinium corymbosum*), are common on the Fraser delta. Clay soils occur in the Fraser valley.

Planting traditions

The West Coast features huge native trees and lush native vegetation that will quickly invade if neglected.

Conifers such as *Pseudotsuga menziesii*, *Tsuga heterophylla*, and *Thuja plicata* are established in many gardens. Gardening under these giants is problematic and frequently leads to the consideration of removing these trees altogether.

A wide range of plants can be cultivated along the coast. Mild winters and acid soils enable azaleas, rhododendrons, camellias, *Pieris*, Japanese maples (*Acer* spp.), ferns, and heathers to thrive. Acidic soils also benefits mophead and lacecap hydrangeas (*Hydrangea macrophylla*), which develop blue flowers rather than the usual pink ones associated with alkaline soils. Roses survive most winters but, since springs are damp, are prone to black spot (see "Fungal leaf spots," p.660) and powdery mildew (see p.667). Bold gardeners try tender plants such as *Phormium tenax*, eucalyptus, *Trachy-carpus fortunei*, and *Hebe*.

Tall perennials such as delphiniums, peonies (*Paeonia*), and oriental poppy (*Papaver orientale*) need careful staking to prevent damage in spring downpours. Some annuals may even rot in a wet spring.

The lack of extreme summer heat makes growing warm-climate crops, such as tomatoes, cucumbers, and melons, challenging. Cool-weather crops such as lettuce thrive and can be produced all summer long, especially in the foothills.

On the coast, fruits such as apples, cherries, pears, kiwis, strawberries, raspberries, and blueberries grow well. Diseases can be a problem during a wet spring.

Lawns are mostly of Kentucky bluegrass (*Poa pratensis*), but fine lawn grasses such as the fescues (*Festuca*) thrive.

Cold and wind protection

Select plants that will thrive in a given climate zone rather than attempting to alter the growing conditions. Trying to grow very tender plants in a cold climate will almost always end in disappointment. For species that normally do well in a site but may suffer in harsh winters, providing protection against cold and wind is a sensible precaution. Efficient wind protection enables gardeners to grow a wide range of plants and is particularly useful for large plants, for those in open ground that cannot easily be brought under cover, and for early-flowering plants and trees that are more susceptible to cold than later-flowering species. Protection is also needed from strong winds, which can break the stems of woody plants and damage fragile ones. Winds may also carry salt spray from nearby roads or the ocean, causing browning of foliage.

PROTECTING SMALL TREES AND SHRUBS

Straw insulation
Tie in the branches, then surround the tree with wire netting secured to three stakes in a partial circle 12in (30cm) from the tree. Pack straw into the gap, then secure the netting to a fourth stake. Cover the top with more straw. Wrap and tie plastic sheeting around the netting.

Straw barrier
Pack a thick layer of straw between two layers of wire netting. Surround the plant, filling any gaps with extra straw, and tie in place.

Burlap strips
Tie in the branches or leaves of the crown, then wrap the tree in strips of burlap, winding it around and tying it in place at intervals with string or twine. Protect the base of the trunk with straw.

Burlap and straw cover
Pack straw around the shrub's branches, working from the bottom up. Loosely wrap burlap around, and tie with string.

Netting over a framework
When wall-trained fruit trees blossom, protect them from frost at night with woven nylon netting, rolled down to cover the tree but held away from the blooms by stakes.

Straw and netting for wall-trained plants
Protect a tree or shrub against a fence or wall by packing straw behind the branches. Attach netting at the top and bottom of the fence. Pack more straw between netting and plant, until it is covered.

TRENCHING (TIPPING) ROSES

Mounding up earth
Protect the graft union of bush roses from extreme cold by mounding up earth around the crown, to a depth of 5in (12cm).

1 Loosen the root ball then dig a trench long enough to encompass the branches when the bush is laid on its side, and about 12in (30cm) deeper than the width of the bush.

2 Line the trench with a 4in (10cm) layer of straw and lay the bush down. Pack straw around and above the shoots.

3 Insert stakes and tie strings between them to hold the bush down. Infill with soil, mounding it up to cover the bush to a depth of 12in (30cm).

Preventive measures

Gardeners can take precautions to avoid cold damage: Do not plant in frost pockets and choose sheltered sites (such as in front of a warm wall or on a sunny bank) for susceptible plants. Tender climbers, for example, may be grown against a house wall (which will be warmer than a garden wall) or in containers that can easily be moved to a sheltered location. Seedlings, summer bulbs, and tubers should only be planted outdoors when all danger of spring cold has passed, and roses and other shrubs should not be fed late in the season, because this encourages new, soft growth that may then be damaged by fall cold. Allowing healthy, deadheaded herbaceous plants to dieback naturally means that the foliage and stems will protect the crowns in winter, while a deep mulch of slowly decomposing organic matter provides useful protection for the roots of all plants. Check plants regularly in winter, firming any that have been heaved out of the ground by frost.

Cold protection

The aim of cold protection is to insulate the plants from the extremes of freeze and thaw conditions by maintaining a constant temperature.

Insulation

In milder regions, wrapping plants in burlap, carpet, or several thicknesses of newspaper is effective in protecting the topgrowth from damage. These materials also help moderate soil temperature fluctuations in colder areas, lessening damage to roots. Burlap helps slow the warming process caused by a thaw and keeps the plant dormant through any midwinter mild spells. Straw packed around the plant beneath the burlap provides additional insulation and is suitable for wall-trained trees and shrubs, climbers, root crops, strawberries, and small fruit trees and bushes. Once temperatures rise above freezing, this cover can be removed. Wall-trained plants need to be detached from their support if possible, and the stems gathered together before wrapping.

Small shrubs and trees growing in areas colder than their usual winter hardiness zone can be protected by building a loose wire-netting cage around them and then packing this with dry leaves or straw. Plastic sheeting tied or stapled over the top of the cage will keep the insulating layer dry. Alternatively, pack the straw in between and behind the stems before covering.

Mounding with mulches or soil

For perennial plants that dieback to a dormant crown, place a mulch or a few forkfuls of leaves over the crown and keep it in place with straw or evergreen prunings. Roses and other woody plants can be protected by mounding soil around the base or laying them in a trench. In very cold regions, the soil mound should be covered with a layer of straw. Root vegetables can be protected from cold damage in the same way and can then be harvested even during severe cold spells.

Covers

If only a few individual plants need protection, the best solution is to use a cover, which acts like a miniature greenhouse, warming the soil and maintaining an even temperature. Emerging shoots of cold sensitive plants, such as asparagus, can be protected with almost any household container: a bucket, a large plant pot, or a sturdy cardboard box will all do the job adequately. Plastic foam and clear plastic covers designed for this purpose are available commercially. More permanent protection can be provided by glass row covers, or cold frames (see GREENHOUSES AND FRAMES, pp.566–583).

Wind protection

Wind protection aims to reduce the wind speed before it reaches any plants, thereby reducing physical damage to branches and stems and preventing further water loss. Many tender plants have greatly improved chances of survival if they are planted in the lee of a good hedge. A 5ft (1.5m) hedge will reduce the wind speed by 50 percent for plants within 23ft (7.5m) of the hedge (see HEDGES AND SCREENS, pp.82–85).

Tree and shrub species vary widely in their ability to withstand wind. The most tolerant are those with small, thick, spiny, or waxy leaves, such as x *Cupressocyparis leylandii*, arborvitae *(Thuja)*, *Escallonia*, and hollies *(Ilex)*. Of deciduous trees, alders *(Alnus)*, alpine currant *(Ribes alpinum)*, willows *(Salix)*, and hawthorn *(Crataegus)* are particularly wind hardy. Windbreaks can be used while the hedge grows.

WINDBREAKS

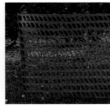

Double netting
Protect plants with fragile stems from wind by using flexible double netting supported by stakes.

Snow fence
Lengths of plastic snow fence, attached to stakes, protect plants from drifting snow and wind.

Commercial windbreaks
Protect plants with commercial windbreaks attached to strong stakes.

Woven hurdles
Place woven hurdles at intervals between the plants, setting them at an angle into the prevailing wind, to deflect any strong gusts.

COVERS FOR FROST AND SNOW PROTECTION

Individual covers
Homemade cloches can be made from clear plastic bottles cut in half and are useful to protect roses and other young tender herbaceous plants.

Low tunnel
Protect low-growing plants, such as strawberries, with clear plastic stretched over wire hoops. Raise the plastic at either side for ventilation during the day.

Newspaper
Protect the new growth of potatoes and other tender crops against frost by covering them with sheets of newspaper, mounded up on either side to keep them in place.

Row cover fabric
This lightweight synthetic fabric warms the soil and gives cold protection while at the same time allowing light and water to pass through to the plants.

Water conservation and recycling

Water conservation in the garden begins with choosing the right plants for the soil and climatic conditions. In dry areas, where the need for water conservation is at its greatest, select species that have fleshy or waxy-surfaced leaves and grasses, which are well adapted to withstand drought, as are a great many plants native to Mediterranean climates. It will be necessary to water plants in containers, which are unable to develop extensive root systems and receive little benefit from natural rainfall. They are also much more susceptible to drying out in windy situations.

Enhancing water retention in soil
Water absorption can be a problem on poorly structured light or neglected soil (left). Such soils should be improved by the addition of bulky organic matter such as well-rotted barnyard manure or garden compost (right).

Improving the soil

Drought-resistant plants must be planted in well-prepared soil (see Soils and Fertilizers, "Soil cultivation," p.618). Improving the soil by incorporating organic matter (see "Soil structure and water content," p.620) and the use of mulches (see "Topdressings and mulches," p.626) can largely eliminate the need for supplementary watering. Where extra watering is needed (see *Reducing High Water Dependency*, right), apply it as efficiently as possible, using the following guidelines.

How to water

To reduce evaporation, water plants early in the morning or in the evening. Refrain from carelessly spraying water or watering lightly Water thoroughly when required, ensuring moisture reaches the plant roots. Do not simply wet the soil surface arbitrarily or at frequent intervals (see Soils and Fertilizers, "Watering techniques," p.622). Inadequate amounts of water encourage surface rooting, which in the long term makes the plant more vulnerable. When symptoms of water stress first occur, apply no more than 5 gallons per sq yd (23 liters of water per sq m) every 7–10 days to maintain plant growth if necessary. Avoid the use of a

sprinkler, which wastefully discharges high volumes of water over a wide area.

Collecting water

In many temperate areas, the water collected from rain falling on the roof of an average house could and should be used to supplement water from the main supply, which should be used as efficiently as possible. As a rough guide to the amount of water that could be saved from a roof, multiply its surface area by the annual rainfall

in the vicinity (all in feet). To convert to gallons, multiply the resulting figure by 6.5. For example, with an annual rainfall of 2ft (0.6m), runoff from a garden shed roof measuring 8 x 11ft (2.5 x 3.5m) would be about 1,100 gallons (5,000 liters). A house

roof measuring 56 x 22ft (17 x 7m) could produce nearly 16,000 gallons (72,000 liters).

Rainwater is readily stored by connecting a rain barrel or tank to a downspout. If the barrel or tank has a lid and is free from algae, the water will remain oxygenated for

Planting through sheet mulch
Cut a slit in a sheet mulch, such as landscape fabric, and plant through the hole. The mulch will reduce evaporation and suppress weeds.

REDUCING HIGH WATER DEPENDENCY

Although some garden features and crops do require supplementary watering, their needs can be reduced in the following ways.

New plantings
- Create a saucer-shaped depression around each stem to hold water and avoid runoff.
- Lay soaker hoses or drip irrigation, which target water to the roots of each plant (see p.561).
- Ensure that the growing mix of container-grown plants is saturated by immersing the plants in a bucket before planting; this ensures that the air is completely expelled. Water again thoroughly immediately after planting.
- Destroy competitive weeds by hoeing the soil shallowly.

Containers and hanging baskets
- Incorporate a water-holding polymer in the growing mix.
- Level the growing mix to within 1–2in (2.5–5cm) of the container rim so there is space for sufficient water to soak the growing mix thoroughly at each watering.
- Place plants in a sheltered spot that is shaded for part of the day. Keep away from drying winds.

- Group containers together rather than placing them individually.

Food crops
- Select crops carefully, especially in dry areas. Several vegetables will fail to develop adequately if short of water at critical periods in their development. Examples are potatoes, which need plenty of water as their tubers are ripening, and tomatoes, zucchini, and runner beans when flowering and fruit is swelling.
- Irrigate with drip or soaker hoses so that supplementary watering is targeted where it is most needed.

Lawns
- Reduce the size of the lawn and create gravel beds or surfaces.
- Select a mixture of lawn grass species that are relatively resistant to drought conditions.
- Raise the mower blade height at which the grass is cut, from ½in (1cm) to 1in (2.5cm).
- Apply an appropriate fertilizer during fall to encourage drought resistance in the lawn.

Patios
- Create partial shade with wooden structures, to reduce the considerable glare from the sun on some patio surfaces. The reflection may affect adjacent plants, increasing their moisture loss. Although trees will provide shade, dry zones occur around the roots, and these can nullify the advantage of shade.
- Angle any slope on a patio so water runs off onto the garden and is not lost in adjacent drains.
- Use the decking, which allows water to percolate through the gaps, rather than concrete or stone slabs.

Water features
- Convert moving water to still-water features. The former inevitably has a higher evaporation rate, particularly when placed in a sunny, exposed location.
- Plant water lilies in order to minimize evaporation from ponds and similar uncovered surfaces.
- Top off any water loss with stored rainwater rather than house water.

Soaker hoses
Hoses with small perforations along their entire length are an excellent way to irrigate strawberries (here) and other plants grown in a row.

Targeted water outlets
Trickle, or drip feed, systems deliver water through individual drippers that are placed permanently near the roots of each plant.

Recycling gray water
Water from showers or baths can be diverted from dedicated downspouts to an adjacent water barrel for immediate distribution and reuse around garden plants. The water barrel must be covered with a lid not only for safety but also to prevent the accumulation of debris and algae.

about six months. (Anaerobic water should not be used on plants.) Such water reservoirs should stand on a firm base and, to facilitate filling a watering can from the bottom spigot, they should be raised on a platform of bricks or wall blocks.

Rainfall occurs irregularly, often in heavy bursts, so a rain barrel will often overflow. Increase the amount stored by joining several barrels together with short pipes inserted into the overflow sockets. Larger water tanks can also be used. Thoroughly clean recycled ones of residues from previous fluids.

By adjusting the downspouts from rainwater gutters, rain barrels can be placed against a wall, which should not be in full sun. If the barrel or a series of barrels are obtrusive, the rainwater downspout can be fitted with a small device that diverts the rainwater through a pipe to a more distant receptacle—for example, one sited behind a garden shed or trellis.

Where there is an insufficient slope for the water to run naturally into these storage tanks, a sump pump should be installed in a small barrel or receptacle at the base of the downspout. Very large storage tanks, even if they are placed low enough to be gravity-fed from the house, will need a pump to redistribute the water around the garden. Sump pumps that have an on/off, cut-out float on the intake are ideal because they prevent damage to the pump if the tank runs dry and the pump has been left on accidentally. The system can be constructed so the pump drives water through a series of small-diameter pipes to the areas of the garden requiring irrigation.

Rainwater diverters fitted on the downspout or the overflow socket on a rain barrel can also channel excess water to a pond. Ponds used for this purpose should be free of blanketweed and should preferably contain oxygenating plants. In a large informal garden, a heavily planted pond can be created with a pebbled edging, for a beachlike effect (see WATER GARDENING, *Styles of Pond Edging*, p.291). This will conceal any large variance in water level from summer to winter. As with other water reservoirs, any pond is likely to require an electric submersible pump to redistribute the water to the rest of the garden.

Gray water
Gray water is the term used for domestic waste water other than sewage. Large volumes of water are available from this source—the average bath using 26 gallons (120 liters)—so in extreme drought conditions it can be a source of water if it is not too heavily contaminated with soaps, detergents, fats, or grease. Buckets of gray water can be taken directly from a bath (or sink) to the garden, or the water could be siphoned from the bath to the garden using a garden hose. Siphoning equipment is available from good hardware stores. Pipe diverters used in the same way as rainwater diverters can be fitted to the waste-water drain from the bathroom and fed into a dedicated gray-water barrel or reservoir, for use soon after it has cooled.

Some types of domestic waste water are better than others. In order of preference they are shower, bath, bathroom sink, and utility sink, provided bleaches or strong detergents have not been used. Water from dishwashers and washing machines is generally unsuitable for garden use, because it contains too much detergent.

Gray water use in gardens is prohibited or regulated in some municipalities, so check local regulations before using it.

Rain barrel
Collect rainwater off greenhouse, shed, and house roofs by attaching pipes between each gutter and water barrel. Always buy a large barrel and position it high enough for a watering can to fit under its spigot.

HOW TO USE GRAY WATER

- Store in a dedicated container and don't mix with other water.
- Use gray water as soon as it has cooled and never keep longer than a few hours. Storing it on summer days can quickly produce a bacterial soup, which can smell unpleasant and breed disease pathogens.
- Apply gray water on soil or compost adjacent to a plant; never water directly on foliage.
- Never use gray water on fruit, vegetables, or herbs or on acid-loving plants—the detergents in the water will be alkaline.
- Never apply gray water with a sprinkler to the lawn or to any area where the water might form puddles; such water is unhygienic. Children may be attracted to play in the puddles, and animals may drink from them.
- Avoid using gray water with "dripper" or fine nozzle irrigation systems, because these will quickly clog up.
- Try to rotate the types of water applied to the garden and avoid the persistent use of gray water in one particular area. Harmful sodium levels may build up if gray water is overused. This can be detected by a soil test. If the pH level is more than 7.5, plant growth may be adversely affected. Very high levels can be remedied with gypsum; apply at a rate of 1lb per 50sq ft (1kg per 10sq m) until the pH level reaches 7 or below.

SOILS AND FERTILIZERS

Soils are highly complex and dynamic materials that are made up of minute particles of weathered rock and organic matter, known as humus, as well as plant and animal life. Healthy soil is essential to successful plant growth: it physically supports plants and supplies them with water, air, and mineral nutrients. If the soil in your garden does not at first appear to be ideal, there are many solutions, and most soils can be improved with a little time and effort. For example, waterlogged soil can be drained and its structure improved, and the water-holding capacity of light soils can be increased by digging in organic matter, such as compost or well-rotted manure. Fertilizers increase nutrients, and lime can be applied to make acidic soils more alkaline, while mulches prevent weed seeds from germinating and reduce water loss from the soil. Finally, nutrients from organic waste can be returned to the soil by making garden compost.

Soil and its structure

Most soil is classified according to its clay, silt, and sand content. The size and proportion of these mineral particles affects the chemical and physical behavior of the soil. Particles of clay are less than $\frac{1}{16000}$in (0.002 mm) in diameter; silt particles are up to 25 times larger than the largest clay particles; and sand particles may be 1,000 times larger—up to $\frac{1}{16}$in (2mm) in diameter.

Soil types

Loam soils have the ideal balance of mineral particle sizes, with between 8 and 25 percent clay, which results in good drainage and water retention, combined with high fertility.

Clay soils are heavy, slow draining, and slow to warm up in spring, but are often highly fertile. They are easily compacted, however, and may bake hard in the summer.

Both sandy and silt soils have a low proportion of clay particles, making them much less water-retentive than clay. Sandy soils are particularly light and free-draining and need frequent irrigation and feeding; however, they warm up quickly in spring and are easily improved with organic matter. Silts are more retentive and fertile than sandy soils but tend to compact more easily. Organic or muck soils are wet and acidic; they support excellent plant growth, however, if drained, fertilized, and limed.

Alkaline soils are generally shallow and free-draining, and have moderate fertility.

The profile of the soil

Soils may be divided into three layers, or horizons: topsoil, subsoil, and a layer derived from the parent rock. Topsoil contains most soil organisms and many of the nutrients. It is generally dark, because it contains organic matter that is added artificially or naturally by leaf fall. Subsoil is usually lighter in color; if it is white, the parent rock is probably chalk or limestone. If there is little or no color change between topsoil and subsoil, the topsoil may be deficient in organic matter.

SOIL CHARACTERISTICS

Clay soils have more than 25 percent clay particles and are characteristically wet and sticky. Soils containing less than 8 percent clay are classified as either silt or sandy soil, depending on whether silt or sand particles predominate. Muck is formed where wet, acidic conditions prevent full decomposition of organic matter, which therefore remains on or near the soil surface. Alkaline soil, however, is alkaline and free-draining, and allows organic matter to decompose rapidly.

Sandy soil
A dry, light, free-draining soil, easy to work but relatively infertile.

Muck
Rich in organic matter, muck is dark and moisture-retentive.

Clay
A heavy, slow-draining soil, usually with a high nutrient value.

Alkaline soil
Pale, shallow, and stony, this soil is free-draining and moderately fertile.

Silt
Silt is reasonably moisture-retentive and fertile but compacts easily.

Weeds and wild plants help to indicate the type of soil in a garden and any characteristics that it may have, although their presence is only a guide. Birch (*Betula*), heathers (*Calluna, Daboecia, Erica*), foxgloves (*Digitalis*), and gorse (*Ulex europaeus*) are all signs of acidic soil, as are many garden plants such as rhododendrons. Beech (*Fagus*) and ash (*Fraxinus*) indicate that the soil is likely to be alkaline. Wild plants may also reveal the chemical profile of the soil: nettle and dock, for example, suggest a rich, fertile soil that is high in phosphorus, while clover indicates a soil that is low in nitrogen.

Acidity and alkalinity

Soil pH is a measurement of acidity or alkalinity—the scale ranges from 1–14. A pH below 7 indicates an acidic soil, while a pH higher than 7 indicates an alkaline soil. Neutral soil has a pH of 7.

The pH of soil is usually controlled by its calcium level. Calcium is an alkaline element that almost all soils tend to lose through leaching (meaning that it is washed through the soil

SOIL PROFILES

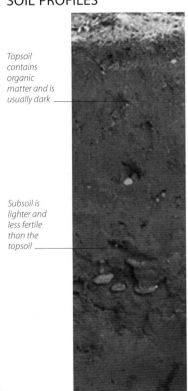

Topsoil contains organic matter and is usually dark

Subsoil is lighter and less fertile than the topsoil

Soil is usually made up of layers of topsoil and subsoil, and a lower layer derived from underlying rock. The depth of each layer can vary.

IDENTIFYING YOUR SOIL

The two main types of soil particles are sand and clay. Sand particles are relatively large and water drains freely through the spaces between them, while clay particles are tiny and trap moisture in the gaps. Rub a small amount of moist soil between your fingers. A sandy soil feels gritty and will not stick together or form a ball, although a sandy soil is slightly more cohesive. A silt soil feels silky or soapy to the touch. A silty soil may show imprints when pressed with a finger. A loamy clay soil holds together well and may be rolled into a cylindrical shape. Heavy clay soil may be rolled even more thinly, and develops a shiny streak when smoothed. All clay soils feel sticky and slightly heavy.

Sandy soil
Sandy soil feels gritty when rubbed between your finger and thumb. The grains do not stick together.

Clay soil
Clay soil feels sticky when wet and may be rolled into a ball that changes shape when pressed.

by water). Soils over limestone, which are rich in calcium, are unaffected; other soils, especially sands, gradually turn more acidic.

Alkalinity may be increased, if necessary, by liming (see p.625), or introducing lime-rich material, such as mushroom compost.

Electronic pH meters and soil test kits may be used to measure soil pH. Make several tests in different parts of the garden; the pH often varies, even within a small area; readings are particularly unreliable after the soil has been limed.

The effect of pH
Above all, pH affects the solubility of soil minerals and their availability to plants. Acidic soils tend to be deficient in phosphorus. Alkaline soils tend to lack boron, manganese, and phosphorus.

Soil pH also affects the number and type of beneficial soil organisms, as well as pests and diseases. For example, earthworms dislike acidic soils, but clubroot and wireworms are common in acidic conditions. On alkaline soils, potato scab occurs more frequently.

TESTING PH LEVEL

Soil test kits use a chemical solution that changes color when mixed with soil in a small test tube. The color is then matched against a chart that indicates the pH level of the soil sample.

A yellow or orange color indicates acidic soil

Bright green indicates neutral soil

Dark green indicates alkaline soil

Optimum pH
The pH range for good plant growth is between 5.5 and 7.5. A pH of 6.5 is usually optimal, depending on the plants to be grown. Muck soils have an optimal pH of 5.8, however. The highest vegetable yields are generally obtained from neutral soils but most ornamentals tolerate a wide pH range. Some are more sensitive; calcicoles (lime lovers) and calcifuges (lime haters) are adapted to extreme pH ranges and their growth suffers if they are planted in soil with the wrong pH level.

Soil organisms

Certain soil organisms are essential to maintain soil fertility. Beneficial bacteria and fungi prefer well-aerated soil and generally tolerate a wide pH, although most fungi prefer acidic soil conditions. Some fungi (mycorrhizae) live in association with plant roots, and improve the take-up of nutrients from the soil.

Small soil animals, such as mites, play a vital part in the breakdown of organic matter. Microscopic worms and nematodes (eelworms) help to control pests—although some are themselves pests.

Larger soil animals, particularly earthworms, improve soil structure when feeding and burrowing; the passage of soil through an earthworm's body binds soil particles into crumbs, increasing aeration and improving drainage.

BENEFICIAL ORGANISMS

Devil's coach-horse beetle

Ground beetles

Earthworm

Centipedes

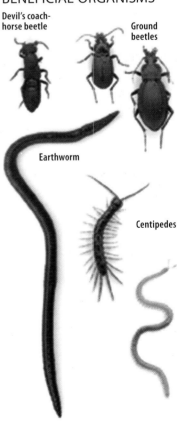

Healthy soil contains a teeming community of earthworms and other organisms, which help to aerate the soil and break down organic matter.

Soil cultivation

Correct methods of soil cultivation, including weeding, digging, and adding soil improvers, are vital to successful long-term plant growth.

Weeds compete with cultivated plants for space, light, nutrients, and water—in fact, all the essentials. They may also harbor diseases of many types, which makes their eradication or control vital.

Several digging techniques are used to cultivate the soil in different ways, depending on the condition of the soil and the plants that are to be grown. If the condition of the soil is poor, it may be improved by the addition of organic material, usually at the same time as digging.

Clearing an overgrown garden

Badly neglected, overgrown plots may be cleared using either tools or chemicals: use whichever method is convenient (see also PLANT PROBLEMS, "Controlling weeds," p.646).

Mechanical clearance

Slash as much top growth as possible using a nylon-line trimmer, brushwood cutter, or scythe, and clear it away from the area. Then, with a rotary mower, cut any remaining growth as low as possible before digging out and removing all the vegetation that is left on the site.

Alternatively, use a rototiller to churn up the soil and chop up the weeds. Make several passes with the tiller to break up the matted vegetation, then rake it up and remove it from the surface. The chopping action of the tines, however, will cut the roots or rhizomes of perennial weeds into pieces that regenerate rapidly. After tilling the soil, therefore, it is essential to rake over the plot and remove by hand all remaining weed fragments. Repeat treatments will be necessary.

Chemical clearance

Following the manufacturer's instructions carefully, spray with a translocated weedkiller, leave it to take effect, and then cut down the top growth. If necessary, respray any vegetation that escaped the first application of weedkiller.

In organic gardens, where it is not desirable to use chemicals, or if the layout of a garden makes it difficult to apply weedkiller evenly, use mechanical or other methods of weed control, such as mulching (see p.626) and organic practices, including the deep-bed system (see pp.496–497). Covering an area of the garden with a black plastic sheet for at least one growing season is also an effective way of clearing ground.

Weed control

In nearly all gardens the soil is full of weed seeds and fragments of perennial weed roots. Weed seeds are brought into the garden from neighboring land by the wind and in the soil or soil mix around bought plants. Cultivation, by its very nature, disturbs the soil, and often brings weed seeds to the surface, where they are able to germinate (see *The Stale Seedbed Technique*, p.620). Soil cultivation also allows small pieces of perennial weed roots to regenerate and start a new growth cycle over again.

CLEARING A SITE OF WEEDS

Clearing coarse weeds
A neglected or weed-infested site must be thoroughly cleared before planting takes place. Smother out coarse weeds if possible, or use a commercial weedkiller.

Forking out weeds
Fork up the roots of large weeds and pull them out, holding the main stem close to the soil so that the whole root system is removed.

It is virtually impossible to clean a soil completely of weeds, but regular weeding, rather than sporadic attempts that are then followed by periods of neglect, is the best method of control. Although tedious, hand-weeding, using a hand fork, is one of the most effective methods of controlling weeds, because you can ensure that the whole plant is removed from the bed. It also causes the least disturbance to existing plants.

Hoeing

Hoes are used to remove annual weeds and also help to aerate the soil (see also p.552). Unless used carefully, however, they may damage the surface roots and top growth of nearby cultivated plants. Hoeing mainly affects the surface soil and seldom goes deep enough to destroy the roots of perennial weeds; dig these out or destroy them with a translocated weedkiller (see PLANT PROBLEMS, p.647).

Soil solarization

Another effective option for combating soil pests and diseases such as root-knot nematodes is soil solarization. This process uses the sun's heat to raise the soil temperature over a period of time to a range that kills many harmful microorganisms and insects as well as weed seeds. Solarization also kills beneficial organisms, but the beneficial organisms rebound more quickly after solarizing than the harmful ones do.

The best time to solarize is during the warmest, sunniest weather in your area. (Solarization works best in hot, dry climates.) To solarize a garden area, first remove all surface plant growth and rake the soil surface as smooth as possible. Wet down the soil thoroughly; the top foot of soil should be moist.

The next step will be to cover the soil with clear plastic. (A plastic paint tarp will work.) Close contact between soil and plastic is important, so begin by digging a trench a few inches deep all around the area to be solarized. Lay out the plastic; bury one edge in a trench, then stretch the plastic tight as you bury the other edges.

Leave the plastic in place for 4 to 6 weeks. Use a soil thermometer to check temperature 110–125°F (43–52°C) is a good goal. After solarizing, remove the plastic. The area can then be planted immediately, disturbing the soil surface as little as possible.

ROTOTILLING THE SOIL

1 For cultivating large areas of soil, it is worth renting a motorized rototiller. Adjust the handlebars to a comfortable position and press down on the handlebars so that the tiller blades penetrate the soil to their full depth.

2 After rototilling, rake up and remove any pieces of perennial weeds from the surface of the soil, otherwise they will reestablish and grow again.

Digging and forking

Cultivating the soil by digging and forking helps to provide suitable conditions for good plant growth by aerating the soil and breaking up any surface crust (cap). Organic matter and fertilizers may be added at the same time, if required. On heavily compacted ground, digging helps to improve soil structure and drainage.

The most common method of cultivation is digging with a spade; single and double digging are in general the most effective and labor-efficient digging methods. Some garden beds, however, may not be suited to such a methodical approach to soil cultivation, especially where there are already many established plants. In these circumstances, forking and simple digging may be useful alternatives.

Disadvantages of digging

Digging increases the rate of breakdown of organic matter, particularly in sandy soils, which in the long term reduces soil fertility. Also, digging heavy, wet soils can cause compaction and make conditions worse. If these soils have a good existing structure, digging can be avoided, particularly for tree and shrub beds.

The "no-dig" and deep-bed techniques, popular with organic gardeners in particular, are cultivation methods that minimize soil disturbance, even in the vegetable garden (see THE BED SYSTEM, pp.496–497). In most cases, initial deep cultivation of the soil, incorporating organic matter to improve its structure, is necessary before these methods can be successfully adopted.

When to dig

It is preferable to dig in the fall, if possible. The soil is then exposed to winter frost and snow, which

help to break down large clods of soil and improve soil structure, especially on heavy ground.

From midwinter until early spring, the ground is often wet or frozen and impossible to work. Heavy soil must never be dug when it is wet.

Using a fork

Much digging work involves lifting and turning the soil. Forks, which are shaped to penetrate the soil easily, are excellent for opening up and loosening soil—but not for lifting it. Forking is less harmful to the soil structure than using a spade, because it tends to break the clods along existing, natural, fracture lines rather than along artificially sliced ones.

Forking works well for rough digging and for turning the soil but not for creating fine tilths (see "Forming a tilth", p.620). It is also useful for clearing weeds from the soil, particularly perennial weeds, such as couch grass (*Elymus repens*), without leaving behind small pieces that will regenerate.

Simple digging

When digging, some gardeners prefer simply to lift out a spadeful of soil, invert it, drop it back in its original position, and chop it up. This method is known as simple digging. It is a quick and relatively easy form of cultivation and is useful for cleaning the soil surface of any debris and nonpersistent weeds, incorporating small amounts of manure and fertilizers, or creating a surface tilth. Simple digging is often the best option when working in irregularly shaped beds or around existing plants.

Single digging

Single digging is the term applied to a methodical and labor-efficient approach to cultivation that ensures an area has been completely dug, to a uniform standard, and to the depth of a spade (known as a "spit").

Mark with lines the area to be cultivated; then, beginning at one end of the plot, dig out trenches to a spade's depth and about 12in (30cm) wide. Place the soil from the first trench in a pile on the ground in front. Work backward along the plot, turning the soil from each subsequent trench into the one in front.

Adopt this method on regularly shaped plots and in situations where soil uniformity is important —in vegetable and community gardens, for example. Single digging is also useful where large quantities of organic matter need to be dug in.

FORKING

Fork over the soil when it is moist but not waterlogged. Work methodically, inserting the fork then turning it over (see inset) to break up the soil and aerate it.

SIMPLE DIGGING

Most spades have a blade 10in (25cm) long. This is the depth of a trench required when digging one "spit" deep.

1 Drive the spade into the soil to its full depth, keeping the blade upright. Press down firmly on the blade with the ball of your foot.

2 Pull back on the handle and lever soil onto the blade. Bend knees and elbows to lift the spade; do not try to lift too much, especially where the soil is heavy.

3 Twist the spade to turn the soil over. This introduces air into the soil and encourages the breakdown of organic matter.

SINGLE DIGGING

Mark the bed area, then dig a series of trenches, working backward so that you do not compact the soil. Turn the soil from each trench into the one in front, using soil from the first trench to fill the last.

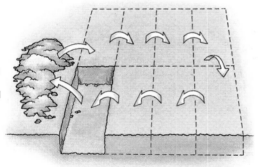

1 Dig out a trench 1 spit deep and about 12in (30cm) wide. Insert the spade vertically and lift the soil onto the ground in front.

2 Dig a second trench, turning the soil into the trench in front. Invert the soil to bury annual weeds and weed seeds.

Take the opportunity to incorporate lime (if needed) and fertilizers, such as bonemeal, into the bottom of each trench before replacing the soil. Weeds, especially deep-rooting perennial ones, should be removed as a matter of course.

Double digging

Double or trench digging, in which the soil is worked to a depth of two spits rather than one, should be carried out if the ground has not been previously cultivated or if drainage needs to be improved. Lime and fertilizers should be incorporated, if required, and perennial weeds removed, as in single digging.

On sites where the topsoil is less than two spits deep, standard double digging should be used—this method ensures that the soil from the upper and lower spits are kept separate. The lower spit containing subsoil should not be brought to the surface—it may be forked or dug over *in situ*, although if more thorough cultivation is required it is also turned.

First, mark the area with lines, as for single digging, then remove the soil from the upper and lower spits of the first trench and from the upper spit of the second, laying it aside on the ground in three separate, clearly marked, piles. Soil may then be transferred from the lower spit of the second trench to the base of the first trench, and from the upper spit of the third trench to the top of the first. In this way, topsoil and subsoil remain completely separate. Continue digging further trenches in the same way and, at the end of the bed, use soil saved from the first two trenches to fill the appropriate spits of the final two.

DOUBLE DIGGING

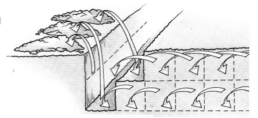
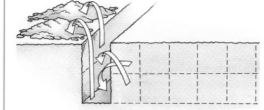

Standard double digging
Dig out trenches two spits deep and turn soil from each trench into the ones in front; do not mix soil from the upper and lower spits.

Double digging for deep topsoils
Where the topsoil is at least two spits deep, soil from the upper and lower spits may be mixed or transferred. Dig out two spits from the first trench, setting the soil aside to fill the final trench, then transfer soil from the upper spit of the second trench to the bottom of the first. Soil from the lower spit of the second trench should be transferred to the top of the first, and so on.

If the topsoil is more than two spits deep, there is no need to keep soil from the upper and lower spits separate, and all the soil from one trench may simply be transferred to the trench in front (see above).

Forming a tilth

A "tilth" is a fine surface soil that is suitable for seed germination. It consists largely of small, even soil particles, and is moisture retentive and level. A surface tilth ensures good contact between seed and soil, so that moisture is absorbed easily.

Prepare seedbeds about one month before sowing by digging the soil and then leaving it to weather. Just before sowing, break up any remaining clods of soil with a rake, level the ground by treading gently, and then rake the surface to provide the fine tilth required for seeds.

IMPROVING STRUCTURE

To improve soil structure, dig in organic material, such as well-rotted manure or compost, according to the soil needs.

Soil structure and water content

For plants to grow and flourish over a period of many years, the soil needs to have a good, inherent structure. On medium and heavy soils, in particular, plant growth depends on good soil structure.

In a well-structured soil, the particles form crumbs that exist as part of an interconnecting network of pores, through which water, nutrients, and air circulate. The structure of the soil therefore affects its ability to hold water, the rate at which it drains, and soil fertility. A poorly structured soil may become too freely drained or waterlogged, and nutrients will be lost by leaching.

Poorly structured soil

A poorly structured soil tends to be too wet in winter and too dry in summer. Water frequently runs off the surface rather than percolating deep down, yet once the soil is wet, it drains slowly. A soil such as this is difficult to work, and in summer it may become hard and like concrete.

SURFACE TILTH

A crumbly, even-textured soil with fine particles makes a good tilth for seed germination. It retains water and nutrients, while providing free drainage needed for good growth.

THE STALE SEEDBED TECHNIQUE

This method of cultivation involves disturbing the soil by shallow digging to bring weed seeds to the surface. Any existing weeds are removed at the same time. The weed seeds are then allowed to germinate and grow, and the seedlings killed with a contact weedkiller or by shallow hoeing—this time disturbing the soil as little as possible. Seed may then be safely sown in the weed-free ground, as required. Further weed seeds inevitably germinate during the season, but because the main weed flush has been destroyed, subsequent weed control will be relatively simple.

1 As an experiment, the soil on the right of this plot has been dug over, while the soil on the left has been left undisturbed.

2 After a few weeks, weed seeds have germinated on the cultivated ground. The undisturbed soil has relatively few weeds.

As a result, plant roots have great difficulty penetrating the soil and plant growth is adversely affected.

Cultivating heavy soil during wet weather may make it compacted. When soil particles are compressed, the amount of air in the soil is reduced and drainage is hindered.

Walking on the soil in wet conditions damages the structure of the surface layer—the soil crumbs break down and fine particles on the surface form a crust, which then effectively prevents oxygen from reaching the plants' roots and also prevents seeds from germinating. This is known as "capping" and may occur on some soils, particularly silts, following heavy rain or if the soil is watered too heavily.

Improving soil structure

To improve poor structure, cultivate the soil to as great a depth as possible by double digging (without mixing subsoil with topsoil), incorporating organic or inorganic additives to help bind the soil particles into crumbs. This will help to improve both aeration and water retention. On severely waterlogged sites, a suitable drainage system may need to be installed (see p.623).

Using soil additives

The choice of additives to use is dependent on the type of soil. Most may either be applied to the surface or incorporated into the soil. Organic material, such as animal manure and garden compost, improves the structure of any type of soil and also provides valuable nutrients. In addition, animal manure encourages earthworms,

which will further benefit soil structure (see "Soil organisms," p.617).

A light, sandy soil may be improved with small amounts of clay (a process known as marling), but enormous quantities of grit or sand would be needed to lighten a very heavy soil.

On compacted soil and clay soil, add manure, compost, and/or lime (but not for acid-loving plants) to improve its structure by encouraging crumb formation.

On silt, add small amounts of clay to improve soil structure, and use manure and compost to encourage crumb formation.

The amount of additive required depends on the soil condition, but a good rule of thumb is to apply about a 2–4in (5–10cm) layer of bulky additives. Some materials, particularly inorganic compounds and moisture-retaining polymers, should be added in much smaller quantities, so it is important to follow the manufacturer's instructions.

Subsidiary benefits of soil additives

Additives also maintain a good balance of air and water in soil. Sand, gravel, and coarse organic matter may be used to improve drainage in silty, compacted, and heavy clay soils. Sand or gravel should be used along channels in the soil, keeping a path open for water, rather than being worked in. Some additives, such as peat (or peat substitute), compost, well-rotted manure, and water-holding gels (which hold many times their weight in water) act as "sponges" and may be used to improve water retention in free-draining, sandy soil.

SOIL ADDITIVES

Adding compost, well-rotted manure, or peat improves the soil structure and helps to hold moisture in the soil. Mushroom compost is alkaline in nature and therefore should not be used with plants requiring acidic conditions. Lime binds clay soil particles together into crumbs by a process known as flocculation.

Mushroom compost   Manure

Lime   Peat

On compacted soil, water-holding gels can be extremely useful for improving water retention without reducing aeration.

Additions of clay will improve the fertility of impoverished soil. Clay, peat, compost, and, to some extent, bark help to retain nutrients that might otherwise be lost by leaching.

Problems with additives

Some additives should not be used in certain soil conditions. Fine sand, for example, added in small amounts to heavy soil may make poor drainage worse by blocking the soil pores. Use a more open material, such as gravel or coarse sand, instead.

Fresh manure gives off ammonia and sometimes other substances that may be toxic to plants. If it is not possible to compost the

manure or mature it until it is well rotted, apply it to the soil surface in the fall and leave the soil uncultivated over winter. Exposure to winter weather will allow the manure to rot down gradually and be incorporated into the soil by earthworms.

Fresh straw, leaves, and bark use up nitrogen during their decomposition process, contributing to a possible deficiency of nitrogen in the soil unless some additional nitrogen fertilizer is applied to the soil at the same time.

For garden compost (see p.627), never use plant remains that are infected with viruses or any material that contains perennial weeds—both are difficult to control or eradicate. This material should be burned or disposed of in some other manner.

COMPARING SOILS

Good soil
A well-structured soil has a crumbly, moist texture, with a network of pores that holds both air and water. The soil crumbs bind together but do not form a hard "cap."

Poor soil
This topsoil is hard and compacted, making it almost impossible to cultivate. Drainage will be poor. Cracks appear where the soil has dried out.

SOIL PROBLEMS

Compaction
In compacted soil, the pores between the soil particles have been badly compressed. This results in slow drainage and poor aeration.

Blue mottling
Blue mottling on the soil surface indicates stagnant, waterlogged soil that needs to be drained. The soil may also have an unpleasant smell.

Hardpan
This is an almost impermeable layer of severely compacted soil. Water will not drain through until the hardpan is broken up and drains are installed.

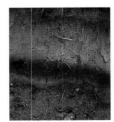

Capping
A crust or "cap" forms on the soil when soil crumbs on the surface are damaged by heavy rain or watering, or by walking on the soil when it is wet.

Water

Adequate water is crucial for good plant growth; the amount available depends to some extent on the plant itself but also on soil type and structure, and the method of watering. Water is often in short supply and should not be wasted, so it is vital to use good watering and water-conserving techniques. It is also useful to know which plants are susceptible to drought (and when) and which are drought resistant.

An excess of water in the soil (waterlogging) can be as damaging to plants as a lack of water. Cultivating the soil and adding organic matter and grit will do much to improve drainage in saturated soil, but on severely waterlogged sites an effective drainage system should be installed.

Soil water

In a well-structured soil, water is held in fine capillary pores, which are usually less than $1/160$ in (0.1 mm) in diameter, with air in the larger pores; it is therefore possible for soil to be described as "both moist and well drained."

Water is most readily available to plants from pores of the largest diameter. As the pores become smaller, it becomes increasingly difficult for the plants to extract moisture, so some soil water always remains unavailable.

Clay soils

Clay soils hold the greatest amount of water, but they have a high percentage of fine capillary pores, so plants are not always able to extract enough water for their needs.

Sandy soils

Sandy soils contain coarse pores; the water held within them is more readily available than in clay. Sandy

HOW NOT TO WATER

Do not water plants at a rate that causes puddling on the soil surface, since this leads to runoff and erodes the soil.

soils, however, drain quickly, and there is little capillary movement of water sideways and upward.

Loamy soil

Loamy soil usually contains a balanced mix of coarse and fine pores—the coarse pores allow rapid drainage while the finer ones retain water, much of which may be extracted by plants in dry conditions.

The water table

Moisture rises toward the soil surface by capillary action from the water table below. Heavy clay soils may be saturated to 6ft (2m) above the water table, with some moisture available to plant roots as much as 11ft (3.5m) above it. Silt and most clay soils are saturated to 5ft (1.5m), with moisture available to roots 8ft (2.5m) above the table. The figures for fine sand are 5ft (1.5m) and 7½ft (2.4m) respectively, and for coarser sand 1ft (30cm) and 3ft (1m). On gravel, there is no water rise at all. In many gardens the water table is too low to have any influence.

Watering techniques

The aim of watering is to recharge the soil so that reserves will be sufficient to last until the next watering or rainfall. Always water thoroughly so that water is available deep in the soil. Frequently applying a little water is of limited value, because much of it evaporates off the soil surface before it has a chance to reach the roots of plants.

Moisture take-up

The water supply to a plant is limited by the size of its root system. When

METHODS OF WATERING

Basin watering
Scoop out soil from around the base of the plant, and fill the resulting basin with water.

Pot watering
Bury a large pot that has a drainage hole close to the plant and fill the pot slowly with water.

planted in soil where the drainage has been improved (see p.623) and any compaction rectified by double digging (see p.620), plants are able to develop deeper root systems, with a comparative increase in growth.

Yet the main limitation when watering is the rate at which the soil takes on moisture. On average, soil absorbs about ⅜in (8mm) depth of water per hour. Water applied to the soil faster than it is absorbed (for example, by a handheld hose or watering can) collects in a puddle on the surface until the area covered is sufficient to take it all in. After watering in dry conditions, it is worth testing the soil with an auger—it may be surprising just how little the water has penetrated. If the soil around the plant roots is still dry, give the area several further applications once the water from the first application has soaked in.

To reduce runoff, the ground can be modified by terracing or digging a basin, creating a hollow trough around each plant (see above), which ensures that water reaches the roots. Pot watering (see above), sprinklers (see p.561), and trickle or drip feed systems (see p.561) are efficient methods of watering, because water is supplied to the roots over several hours.

Water-conserving techniques

Mulching the surface of the soil (see p.626) improves rain penetration and minimizes evaporation. By controlling weeds effectively (see p.618), you will ensure that no soil water is wasted on unwanted plants. See also Water Conservation and Recycling, pp.614–615.

Water deficiency

Once a plant begins to wilt, its growth rate has already begun to slow down. In many areas, water use will exceed water supply during summer, so the soil suffers a net loss of moisture. Digging additives such as manure into the soil improves structure (see p.621) and water retention, which helps to prevent a water deficit from occurring, but unless an existing deficit is made up by irrigation, the soil becomes progressively drier. Regular watering is therefore essential.

The local meteorological office will have figures for the typical monthly water loss from the soil and through leaves by transpiration (known as potential evapotranspiration), and also for the average monthly rainfall. These figures are useful when calculating how often to water but, for greater accuracy, it is better to take your own rainfall measurements each month rather than using the average figures.

Seasonal and establishment needs

The point at which a water deficit begins to affect plant growth depends on the plants themselves. High-yield plants usually need plenty of water, so the soil should be kept moist. Some plants have critical periods of growth, during which time water supplies are vital: the first half of summer, for example, is much more important than the second for young ornamental trees. Fruit trees need ample water as the fruit swell, as do potato tubers.

Watering is especially important for newly planted or transplanted plants, and those in shallow soils and in containers. Seedlings, too, have low drought resistance, and a reliable water supply is essential. Standard trees are likely to require watering throughout their first season, since their top growth is often out of proportion to their roots.

Drought conditions

Even well-established garden plants suffer during prolonged drought, although no perceptible damage may be seen for some time. Moderate drought may, however, improve the flavor of some fruits and vegetables, especially tomatoes.

In areas of low rainfall, there is increasing interest in using plants that are adapted to droughts (xerophytes): lavenders (*Lavandula*) and *Phlomis*, as well as many gray- and silver-leaved plants, are good examples.

Grass tolerates prolonged dry weather well. Lawns may become brown, but quickly recover once rain falls. Watering in summer is not essential, therefore, unless you want to keep your lawn looking green.

Waterlogged soil

Waterlogging occurs when the water entering the soil exceeds the amount draining out. Particularly vulnerable are areas where the water table is high (see p.622) or where the soil is compacted and poorly structured.

Roots (except those of bog plants) are unable to function effectively in waterlogged soil and may eventually die if drainage is not improved. Wet soil is often low in certain nutrients (notably nitrogen) and, as a result, mineral deficiencies may prove a problem. Wet soil tends to be cold, so plant growth may be slow in spring. Diseases, such as clubroot

(see p.657), also flourish in waterlogged soil. Rushes, sedges, and mosses growing on the ground suggest that the soil may be waterlogged, and a sharp division between peaty topsoil and subsoil also indicates poor drainage. On waterlogged clay, the soil may have a stagnant smell and a yellow or blue-gray color, known as gleying.

Poor drainage may be confirmed by pouring water into a hole 12–24in (30–60cm) deep. If the water remains for hours or even days, then the soil needs draining. If digging deeper or trying to push a metal rod into the soil meets with resistance, this indicates that there is a layer of hardpan (see *Soil Problems*, p.621).

Improving drainage

Where waterlogging is not severe and there is excess surface water only, this may be diverted from the site by shaping garden surfaces so

that the water flows into drainage ditches. To improve drainage where there is a high water table, install an underground drainage system, preferably using a specialty contractor. If drains already exist, check for blockages in the drainage ditches, or for damaged pipes. Underground drains will not help if there are drainage barriers, such as a hard pan, above them.

Ditches and French drains
A system of open ditches is the best method of carrying away any excess water from the surface. These should be 3–4ft (1–1.2m) deep, with sloping sides. Just as effective but less obtrusive are French drains, which are gravel-filled drainage ditches topped with upturned sod and topsoil.

Drainage systems and soakaways
A soakaway is a rubble-filled pit into which excess water runs via underground drains or drainage

ditches (see below). This method of drainage is effective on sites where there is surface compaction, because it breaks through any layer of hardpan. To construct a soakaway, dig a hole about 3ft (1m) wide and at least 6ft (2m) deep. Fill it with broken bricks or stones completely surrounded by geotextile fabric. Install perforated plastic pipes or tile drains at least 24in (60cm) below ground level (see below) to lead from the adjacent land to the soakaway.

Water storage areas
Alternatively, create a water storage area where water collects in a pond or large container, or gradually soaks away. A pond is beneficial to wildlife, but its success depends on the degree of sediment in the drainage water—too much will make the pond rich in nutrients, therefore becoming prone to silting up and excessive algal growth. Water collected in containers may be recycled for use in the garden.

HOW TO BUILD A SOAKAWAY

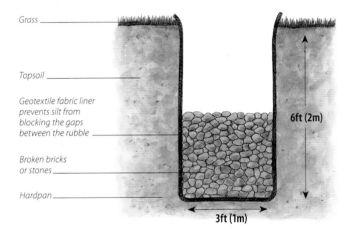

Grass
Topsoil
Geotextile fabric liner prevents silt from blocking the gaps between the rubble
Broken bricks or stones
Hardpan
6ft (2m)
3ft (1m)

1 In a waterlogged part of the garden, dig a hole 6ft (2m) deep with 3 x 3ft (1 x 1m) sides. Line the sides and bottom with a geotextile fabric. Then fill the lined soakaway hole with rubble, such as broken bricks or stones, to a depth of 3ft (1m).

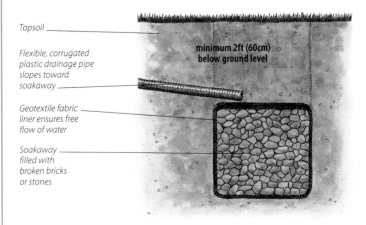

Topsoil
Flexible, corrugated plastic drainage pipe slopes toward soakaway
Geotextile fabric liner ensures free flow of water
Soakaway filled with broken bricks or stones
minimum 2ft (60cm) below ground level

2 Fold the liner over the rubble. Then place the end of a perforated plastic pipe on top of the liner, so that it is ideally 2ft (60cm) below ground level. Fill in the hole with topsoil, and sod the top.

Installing drains
A system of perforated corrugated plastic pipes laid in a herringbone pattern underground provides an effective method of drainage into a rubble-filled ditch or soakaway. Lay the pipes well below ground level, so they do not interfere with future cultivations. Water from the surrounding site can seep into the pipes, which must be angled so they carry the water to the

soakaway. Compared with tile drains (see below), plastic pipes are flexible, easily cut, and absorb the natural movements within the soil. To join two pipes, cut a hole in one pipe to match the diameter of the other pipe; then push it in. Install drains before plants are in place, if possible, because the work causes major upheaval.

A tile drainage system

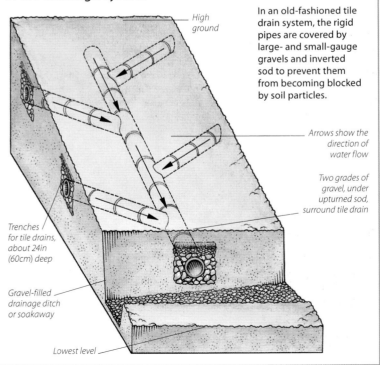

In an old-fashioned tile drain system, the rigid pipes are covered by large- and small-gauge gravels and inverted sod to prevent them from becoming blocked by soil particles.

High ground
Arrows show the direction of water flow
Two grades of gravel, under upturned sod, surround tile drain
Trenches for tile drains, about 24in (60cm) deep
Gravel-filled drainage ditch or soakaway
Lowest level

Soil nutrients and fertilizers

The nutrients utilized by plants are composed of mineral ions, absorbed in solution from the soil through the roots and used with carbon dioxide and water to make food. Macro-nutrients, required in relatively large amounts, include nitrogen (N), phosphorus (P), potassium (K), magnesium (Mg), calcium (Ca), and sulfur (S). Micronutrients, or trace elements, are equally important but required only in small amounts; they include iron (Fe), manganese (Mn), copper (Cu), zinc (Zn), boron (B), molybdenum (Mb).

To ensure healthy plant growth, fertilizers containing nutrients may be added to the soil, but this is only necessary if the soil is unable to provide the nutrients required. On most soils, only nitrogen, which promotes vigorous growth, phosphorus (phosphates), for assisting strong root growth, and potassium, which improves flowering and fruiting, need adding regularly. Nitrogen deficiency (see p.664) causes reduced growth, while potassium deficiency (see p.666) causes leaf discoloration. Phosphate deficiency (see p.666) is less common but is most likely to occur in young plants with poor root systems. Manganese/iron deficiency (see p.664) causes browning of leaves, and may be a problem if acid-loving plants are grown in alkaline soil or watered with hard water.

Types of fertilizer

Deciding the amount and which type of fertilizer to apply can be complex. Understanding how each type works will make gardening more productive and perhaps more environmentally friendly. Note that in this context, the term "organic" may simply mean "of living origin," while "inorganic" refers to artificial, chemical formulations. Gardeners

practicing organic growing, in the environmentally conscious sense, should carefully check the labeling and origin of any fertilizer to ensure that it meets their needs.

Bulky organic fertilizers

Weight for weight, bulky organic fertilizers supply fewer nutrients than inorganic fertilizers. One ton/tonne of manure typically contains 13.2lb (6kg) of nitrogen, 2.2lb (1kg) of phosphorus, and 8.8lb (4kg) of potassium; the equivalent amount of nutrients in a chemical form is provided by 66lb (30kg) of inorganic fertilizer.

Manures are, however, integral to organic growing because the organic matter that makes them so bulky provides greater benefits than a simple nutrient analysis suggests. Manures have high levels of micronutrients, and are a long-term source of nitrogen. They also provide conditions in which worms thrive. Adding manure improves the structure and water content of most soils (see p.620); and since this encourages root growth, it increases plant uptake of nutrients.

Concentrated organic fertilizers

Traditional concentrated organic fertilizers include dried blood, fish, and bone meals, and hoof and horn. Kelp meal and pelleted chicken manure are popular with gardeners using organic methods. Compared with bulky organic materials, they are easy to handle and contain fairly consistent proportions of nutrients but are relatively expensive for each unit of nutrient. Their characteristic slow release of nutrients is partly dependent on breakdown by soil organisms, so they may not be effective when these organisms are inactive, as in cold weather.

Despite some concerns, there are no documented health risks from processed animal-protein fertilizers, such as bone meal, manufactured

for domestic gardens; indeed some argue they are an environmentally sound way of using waste. However, wearing gloves and a dust mask when applying such products, and hand-washing produce (or substituting garden compost where edible crops are being grown) may provide peace of mind. If you prefer not to use animal-derived products, seaweed meal is often a perfectly adequate source of plant nutrition.

Soluble inorganic fertilizers

Concentrated inorganic fertilizers contain high percentages of a given nutrient, weight for weight, and most are easy to transport, handle, and apply, although a few are unpleasant to handle; wearing gloves and a dust-excluding mask is always advisable. They are usually the cheapest source per

unit of nutrient. They give a quick-acting boost to plants deficient in nutrients, and permit precise control over the timing of nutrient release. However, a large proportion of soluble fertilizer may be wasted on sandy soils because of leaching.

When using soluble inorganic fertilizers, be selective about which mineral ions are applied to the soil, because some may damage particular plants. Red currants, for example, are sensitive to chloride salts, such as potassium chloride; sulfates should be used instead. Large applications of some inorganic salts make the soil more saline and may harm beneficial soil organisms. Apply soluble inorganic fertilizers in split applications, sparingly but fairly frequently, rather than in a single, large dose.

NUTRIENT CONTENT OF FERTILIZERS

	% Nitrogen (N)	% Phosphate (P_2O_5)	% Potassium (K_2O)
Organic			
Animal manure	0.6	0.1	0.5
Blood, fish, and bone	5	7	5
Bone meal	3.5	20	–
Cocoa shells	3	1	3.2
Garden compost	0.5	0.3	0.8
Hoof and horn	13	–	–
Mushroom compost	0.7	0.3	0.3
Pelleted chicken manure	4	2	1
Rock phosphate	–	26	12
Kelp meal	2.8	0.2	2.5
Wood ash	0.1	0.3	1
Inorganic			
Ammonium sulfate	21	–	–
Potassium sulfate	–	–	49
Single superphosphate	–	18	–
Slow-release fertilizer	14	13	13

COMPARING FERTILIZERS

Garden compost

Mushroom compost

Cocoa shells

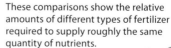

Blood, fish, and bone

Soluble inorganic fertilizer

These comparisons show the relative amounts of different types of fertilizer required to supply roughly the same quantity of nutrients.

SLOW-RELEASE FERTILIZERS

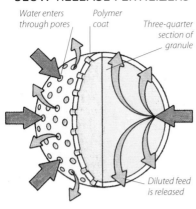

Water enters through pores | *Polymer coat* | *Three-quarter section of granule*

Diluted feed is released

Water enters the fertilizer granules through pores in the polymer coat, which builds up pressure inside, splitting the granules open.

Slow-release fertilizers

These are complex fertilizer formulations that are designed to release nutrients gradually, over many months or even years in some cases. Some slowly degrade in the soil, while others absorb water until they swell and burst open. Many have membranes of varying thickness that gradually release nutrients from an internal storage source. These fertilizers are expensive and are not generally economical to use in the larger garden, but they are especially valuable in the care of container plants (see p.323).

Green manures

These are plants grown purely to be dug back into the soil to improve fertility and add to the organic content. They are planted on land that would otherwise be left fallow and can help to prevent nutrients from being washed away, because fallow land is more prone to leaching. Be careful not to use invasive plants as green manures.
   Borage (*Borago officinalis*), ryegrass (*Lolium perenne*), and comfrey (*Symphytum officinale*)

MAKING COMFREY FERTILIZERS

Comfrey (*Symphytum*) is a coarse, invasive herb, but it is an extremely useful green manure, especially *S. x uplandicum* 'Bocking 14'. The foliage can be used to make organic liquid feed and leaf mold.
   Comfrey liquid fertilizer contains some levels of nitrogen and phosphates, and potassium. A typical recipe is to steep (soak) 7lb (3kg) of cut leaves in 10 gallons (45 liters) of water in a covered container for 4–5 weeks. Strain off the pungent liquid and use frequently; it is relatively weak undiluted as a liquid fertilizer.
   For high-nutrient leaf mold, fill a plastic container or garbage can with chopped comfrey leaves and damp, two-year-old leaf mold in alternating layers, 4in (10cm) thick. As the comfrey decomposes, its nutrients are absorbed by the leaf mold. After three to five months, the enriched leaf mold is ready for use in potting mixtures as a mulch or a soil conditioner.

are excellent perennial green manures. Mixtures of fast-germinating annuals can also be used. Legumes, such as annual lupines, have nitrogen-fixing bacteria in root nodules, which enable them to obtain nitrogen from air in the soil. The organic matter these plants provide may contribute as much nitrogen to the soil as would be added in a standard fertilizing regime; it has a low carbon to nitrogen ratio and so breaks down rapidly, providing easily available nitrogen.

Applying fertilizers

Concentrated fertilizers may be scattered over the surface of the soil or placed around individual plants. Some fertilizers are also available in liquid form for application to the soil surface or as foliar feeds directly onto leaves. All products, organic or inorganic, should be handled with care. Always wear protective clothing where advised. Do not apply on windy days and spread granular or powdered products carefully on the soil—never touching plant stems. Use only the recommended quantities; too much can damage plants.

Broadcast fertilization

Scattering fertilizer over the whole soil surface benefits the greatest area of soil and minimizes the risk of plant injury from overfeeding. In dry weather, the uptake of some nutrients, particularly immobile nutrients like phosphates, may be poor; whenever possible, dig phosphates into the soil.

Fertilizer placement

Fertilizing around the base of a plant is an economical and efficient feeding method, because plant roots quickly spread through the fertilized area.

Liquid fertilizers

An efficient way to apply nutrients, especially during a period when the soil is dry, is to dissolve fertilizer in water before application. Do not use liquid feeds when rain is forecast, because they may be washed away and wasted. Liquid fertilizers sprayed onto leaf surfaces (foliar feeds) can help correct mineral deficiencies caused by some soil conditions, such as high pH. For deep-rooted plants, like fruit trees, foliar feeds may also be used to correct deficiencies in nutrients that are relatively insoluble.

Liming

Liming or adding lime-rich material like mushroom compost increases soil alkalinity. This may be needed to improve yields in vegetable gardens but is rarely worthwhile for ornamentals—it is better to choose plants adapted to existing conditions. Ordinary lime (calcium carbonate) is bulky but easy to handle and safe to use. Quicklime (calcium oxide) is more efficient at raising pH but is caustic and may scorch plants; there is also a risk of over-liming. Slaked or hydrated lime (calcium hydroxide), made by treating quicklime with water, is less efficient than quicklime, but also less caustic.

Applying lime

Lime may be spread on the soil at any time, but apply as far in advance of planting as possible, and dig in thoroughly. Choose a still day and wear goggles. Do not lime every year—over-liming contributes to nutrient deficiencies —and take pH readings in different parts of the garden first, because uneven rates of breakdown cause temporary localized problems. The table below shows average amounts of lime needed for soils to achieve pH 6.5 (see also "Optimal pH", p.617). To raise soil pH quickly, add lime during digging. For established plantings, apply it as a topdressing and water in. Do not apply lime at the same time as manure; they will react and release nitrogen in the form of ammonia. This may damage plants and wastes nitrogen; apply lime and manure in alternate years.

Starting pH	Sand (oz/sq yd)	Loam (oz/sq yd)	Clay (oz/sq yd)
4.5	6.7oz	10oz	14oz
5.0	5.5oz	8.3oz	11.6oz
5.5	4.6oz	6.7oz	9.2oz
6.0	4.2oz	5.5oz	7.6oz

GREEN MANURING

Sow seed for green manures on fallow ground. Cut the plants to the ground when about 8in (20cm) tall, digging them in after a day or two.

HOW TO APPLY FERTILIZER

Broadcasting
To apply fertilizer in accurate amounts over large areas, mark the bed into square yards (or meters), using string or stakes. Fill a pot or bowl with the recommended quantity of fertilizer and sprinkle it evenly over each section of the bed.

Placement
Sprinkle the fertilizer around the base of the plant, making sure that none touches the leaves or stem.

Topdressings and mulches

Topdressings and mulches are materials that are applied to the surface of the soil. They are used to improve plant growth in some way, either by adding nutrients to the soil, by increasing the organic content, or by reducing water loss from the soil. They may also be used in a decorative manner.

Topdressings

The term "topdressing" is used in two ways. First, it describes surface applications of soluble fertilizers around plants. Second, it refers to additives that are applied to the soil surface or to lawns. For example, a lawn may be topdressed with sand or fine organic material, which will eventually be washed in by rain.

Gravel or grit is sometimes used as a topdressing for plants in beds and containers to provide quick drainage away from the "collars" of plants that are sensitive to excess moisture. They also act as a mulch and discourage growth of mosses or lichens on the soil surface.

Plants may also be topdressed with gravel or stone chippings simply to achieve a decorative effect.

Mulches

Mulches are available in organic and inorganic forms and improve plant growth in several ways: they regulate soil temperature, keeping

MATERIALS USED AS TOPDRESSINGS

Topdressings as additives
Some topdressings, such as well-rotted manures and compost, are added to the soil around plants to provide humus and a steady supply of nutrients. Sand, mixed with soil and peat or coir, is used as a topdressing on lawns to improve aeration.

Sand

Decorative topdressings
Materials such as gravel and grit are added to the compost surface in containers or to the soil surface in a border or bed, particularly around low-growing plants such as alpines. These materials improve surface drainage as well as setting off the plants.

Gravel

Compost

Leaf mold

Coarse grit

Cornish grit

roots warm in winter and cool in summer; they reduce water loss from the soil surface; and they keep weed seeds from germinating by stopping light from reaching them.

Always remove all perennial weeds before mulching, otherwise they benefit from the effects of the mulch, to the detriment of your plants. A mulch should not be applied when the soil is cold or frozen, because the insulation effect will be counterproductive and the soil will remain cold—instead, wait until the soil has warmed up in the spring.

Organic mulches

To be effective, an organic mulch should be long-lasting and not easily dislodged by rain. It should also have a loose structure that allows water to pass through it quickly.

Coarse bark is one of the most useful organic mulches because it inhibits weed seeds in the soil from germinating, and weeds that do appear are easily removed. Garden compost, leaf mold, and peat substitutes such as coir are not quite as effective because they provide an ideal medium for the germination of weed seeds and are quickly mixed into the soil, although they do improve the soil's texture as a result.

Inorganic mulches

Inorganic mulches made of biodegradable horticultural paper or thin sheets of woven or bonded, water-permeable fabrics (known as sheet mulches, landscape fabric, or geotextile) are widely available and

simple to lay and secure. They are easy to plant through, and provide good weed suppression while allowing water to penetrate to roots.

A disadvantage of sheet mulches is that, once they are in place, organic matter cannot be incorporated into the soil. However, because they form such a barrier, they are useful laid beneath a layer of loose mulch to extend its life.

Mulches made from impermeable plastic sheet are particularly useful when laid temporarily to warm soil before sowing early crops, or longer-term for weed suppression. However, once in place, almost no water evaporates from the soil, so do not lay over waterlogged soil.

"Floating" mulches are sheets of light perforated plastic or fiber fleece used like cloches—as the crop grows, the floating mulch is raised by the plants. Their main purpose is to increase temperature; they may also act as a barrier against pests.

LOOSE MULCHES

Applying the mulch
A loose mulch regulates soil temperature, retains moisture, and discourages weeds. It should preferably be about 4–6in (10–15cm) deep.

Area to mulch
For small to medium-sized plants, spread a mulch to the full extent of the foliage canopy.

ANCHORING PLASTIC SHEETING

A plastic sheet mulch controls weeds effectively over a large area and raises soil temperature slightly. Using a spade, anchor the sheet by sinking the edges into 2in (5cm) slits dug into the soil.

Landscape fabric controls weeds over a large area and should remain in good condition for several years. Anchor the fabric with pins, then cover it with mulch.

Compost and leaf mold

Garden compost is a good addition to any home landscape. The benefits of the nutrients it provides, as well as the environmental implications of reusing what would otherwise be taken out as garbage, make composting worth the time and effort. Not all materials can be used in the compost heap, however (see *What Not to Compost*, p.628).

Garden compost

The contribution of garden compost to the productivity of the garden can be enormous. As well as supplying nutrients directly, the high levels of humus it contains increase the soil's nutrient-holding capacity and help improve soil drainage and aeration. It also contributes a healthy population of beneficial soil microorganisms. It should be added to the soil when the rate of breakdown of the organic matter has leveled off; by this stage, it should be dark, crumbly, and smell sweet and earthy.

Making garden compost

To make a compost heap, build up a mixture of nitrogen-rich material (such as grass clippings) and carbon-rich material (such as bark and crumpled-up newspaper), preferably in a ratio of 1:2. Almost any vegetable matter, including seaweed, may be composted, but do not use protein and cooked vegetables—these attract vermin.

Do not put grass clippings on the heap for the first few mowings after the application of a weedkiller, and never add thick layers of grass clippings, because they inhibit air movement. If in doubt, avoid vegetation that has been treated with herbicide—the chemicals may persist, making the compost

unsuitable for food crops; it may also damage plants mulched with contaminated compost. There is a health risk, too, especially to children and pregnant women, if cat or dog waste is included, which may contain eggs of the *Toxocara* parasite.

Pruning clippings may be added to a compost heap, although any woody stems should be shredded first. Avoid composting any material that is diseased or infested with pests, because they may survive life in the heap and be spread around the garden in the finished compost. Use only young weeds; those with seed or about to set seed should be put in a garbage can, as should all pernicious, perennial weeds. It is especially important to avoid those with creeping root systems, such as couch grass (*Elymus repens*) and ground elder (*Aegopodium podagraria*).

Compost additives

Many materials will compost satisfactorily, but additional nitrogen speeds up the process. The nitrogen may be provided as an artificial fertilizer, commercial, high-quality, nutrient-rich, starter compost, or as manure, which has the advantage of containing high levels of beneficial microorganisms. Add this to the compost heap as required, so that there are alternate layers of organic material and manure.

If the material in the compost heap is too acidic, microorganisms will not work efficiently—adding lime will make it more alkaline.

The composting process

The process by which organic matter is broken down in a compost heap relies on the

activity of a number of beneficial, aerobic bacteria and microfungi. To proliferate and work efficiently, these microorganisms need air, nitrogen, moisture, and warmth.

To ensure adequate airflow, first make the base of the compost heap from a thick, open layer of twiggy

material. To maintain good aeration, it is essential that compost materials are never allowed to become either compacted or too wet. Mix fine- and coarse-textured matter when building the heap, if necessary putting fine

---

MAKING A COMPOST BIN

1 To make the first side, lay 2 wood battens (to act as the uprights) on the ground at least 3ft (1m) apart. Nail planks across them, butting the joints together. Leave a 3in (8cm) gap at top and bottom.

2 Make the second side; nail scraps of wood across the top to hold the sides in place temporarily. Nail on the back planks.

3 Nail 2 battens inside each upright (inset) for the front planks to slide between. Fix a piece of wood at the base as a stop.

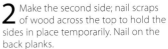

4 Nail planks across the top and bottom of the front panel, to stabilize the bin when the front planks are removed.

5 Check that the front planks slide easily between the battens. If necessary, saw a little off the ends.

Using the bin

Place a thick layer of twiggy material at the base; build up the heap in 6in (15cm) layers, sprinkling each layer with a little manure if any is available.

Manure

Garden and kitchen waste

Twin compost bin system
Fill the first bin (left) with alternating layers of organic matter. When it is full, turn the contents into the second bin (right) to continue rotting, and start refilling the first bin. Keep both bins well covered at all times.

WHAT NOT TO COMPOST

Recycling kitchen and garden waste in the compost heap can provide gardeners with an excellent source of humus to improve soil structure and to mulch beds and borders.

However, take care to leave out waste materials that may not break down and decay or are otherwise unsuitable—cans, glass, plastic, synthetic fibers, and coal ash (wood ash may be added, because it is a good source of potasium).

Home compost bins seldom get hot enough to kill pests, so disease and weed seeds are best consigned to the bonfire, buried deeply, or sent for industrial composting (high temperature) via the municipal green-waste services.

Organic materials that should not be added to the compost heap are:
- Dairy products, oil, fat, fish, and meat waste, which attract rats.
- Used cat litter, dog feces, or disposable diapers, because there may be health implications.
- Laminated cardboard cartons, such as milk and juice cartons, which may contain plastic.
- Glossy magazines, or very densely packed paper, like telephone directories, which rot too slowly.

Cardboard and crumpled-up newspaper, in small quantities, however, are suitable for inclusion in the compost heap, particularly for mixing with quick-rotting vegetable matter.

WORM COMPOSTING BIN

Tight-fitting lid retains warmth and moisture

Brandling worms

Newspaper layers help to retain moisture and warmth

Kitchen waste chopped into small pieces

Worms at work in composted material

Dampened straw or shredded newspaper

Spigot for draining excess liquid

Boards or permeable membrane with gravel or broken clay pots beneath

materials to one side until there is an opportunity to mix it with coarser grades. Turn the compost regularly to avoid compaction and speed up the composting process.

During composting the heap should be damp, but not wet, so water it in dry weather, if necessary. Cover with a tarp, plastic sheeting, or carpet.

The process of bacterial decomposition itself generates a high temperature, which speeds the natural breakdown of organic matter and also helps to kill weed seeds and some pests and diseases. To heat up sufficiently, a compost heap should be at least 1 cubic yard (1 cubic meter) in size but (2 cubic yards (2 cubic meters) is preferable. Compost reaches its maximum temperature in two or three weeks and matures in about 3–12 months.

An ammonia odor indicates that the compost is too rich in nitrogen; add in more carbon-rich material, such as cardboard egg cartons or paper towel rolls. A smell of rotten eggs means that the heap lacks air; turn the heap and incorporate coarse, bulky materials.

Slow composting

Composting may be undertaken in a nonintensive way. Piles of pruning clippings, for example, eventually rot down, even if they are not in a bin. No starter material is added, and the heap is not turned. There will, however, be some material that does not break down fully—this will need to be composted again.

Municipal composting

A number of local entities operate community recycling centers that produce garden compost from "green" waste. This is derived from

municipal parks and gardens and from separated domestic collection by their waste-management divisions. The product is often offered for resale to the home gardener and makes a good mulch material.

Worm compost

Worm-worked compost is highly fertile and is formed when worms consume and digest organic matter, expelling the end-product as fine-textured wormcasts. By far the most productive are small red brandling worms and striped tiger worms. Wormeries are ideal for recycling kitchen waste, and can be purchased in kit form, or as a worm culture for making a homemade worm bin.

To give the culture a good start, introduce the worms into a 2in (5cm) layer of garden compost or manure over a layer of damp straw or shredded newspaper. Add layers of kitchen waste—to a maximum depth of 6in (15cm)—and allow the worms to work most of it before adding more.

The worms work only at temperatures above 59°F (15°C), so store the wormery under cover during winter. Do not allow excess liquid to build up in the bin. When the bin is full, remove the worms from the compost by sifting and use them to start the next culture.

Leaf mold

Although leaves can be included on the compost heap, they are best composted separately because they are slow to break

down. They rely more heavily on microfungi than on bacteria, and need less air and warmth. Stack leaves, as they are collected in the fall, in a wire netting cage or bin, compacting them down firmly each time the bin is filled. Except for watering in dry weather, they

need little further attention while they decompose. Two bins are useful because leaves take so long to break down. Alternatively, use black plastic bags; pack the leaves down firmly, water lightly to aid the rotting process, and leave them.

Using the bin
Leaf mold is an excellent soil conditioner and mulching material. It can also be used as a compost additive when potting plants. It should not be removed from the bin until it has decomposed completely, which is likely to take a year or more. Use one bin while the other is rotting down.

PRINCIPLES OF PROPAGATION

Plant propagation is not difficult once the basic principles are understood, and it is the best and cheapest way to increase plant stocks. In addition, it provides many opportunities for gardeners to exchange plants, thereby increasing the varieties available in cultivation. Techniques range from the simple division of overcrowded perennials to more advanced methods, such as hybridizing in order to create plants with new characteristics, such as novel flower colors. For many people, the transition from a seed into a healthy plant, or the development of a cutting into a new tree or shrub, is fascinating. Successful propagation is well within the reach of any gardener once they grasp the techniques in this chapter.

Seeds

Seed is much the most common way by which flowering plants reproduce in nature. It is normally a sexual method and, as such, always presents the possibility of a variety of genetic combinations, so that the resulting seedlings are variable. Such variation provides the means by which plants adapt to their environment, and enables the breeding and selection of cultivars with new combinations of desirable characteristics. Seeds may more or less breed true but often vary greatly within a species. In horticulture, variation is disadvantageous if the plants raised are to retain particular characteristics, but advantageous when new, improved characteristics are being sought.

REPRODUCTIVE PARTS OF A ROSE FLOWER

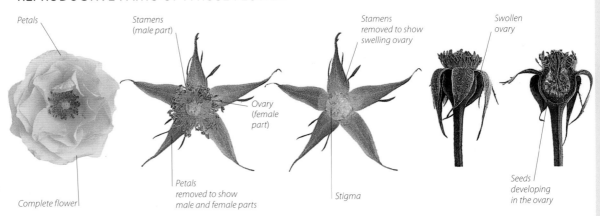

Petals

Stamens (male part)

Stamens removed to show swelling ovary

Swollen ovary

Ovary (female part)

Petals removed to show male and female parts

Complete flower

Stigma

Seeds developing in the ovary

The parts of a flower needed for reproduction are the stamens—the male part, which bears the pollen—and the pistils—the female part, which comprises one or more stigmas, style, and ovary. The petals attract pollinators.

How the seed develops

Most plants are hermaphrodite —that is, each flower bears male and female parts. As the flower matures, pollen is transferred onto one or more stigmas of the same flower (self-pollination) or of a flower on another plant of the same species (cross-pollination) by insects, birds, water, or wind. The pollen grains then produce pollen tubes, which grow down the style toward the ovules in the ovary, and fertilization occurs when the male and female nuclei fuse. From these develop the embryos, which, nourished by adjacent storage tissue in a seed, are capable of forming complete new plants.

Collecting and storing seed

In general, seed should be collected as soon as it is ripe and then stored in a cool, dry, dark, airy place, such as a home refrigerator, until it is used. Certain seeds, however, have special needs. Some are viable for only short periods and should be sown as soon as possible. Others may be stored for very long periods at low temperatures without losing viability. Fleshy fruits should be soaked and softened in water, the seeds removed from the flesh, and then air-dried at 50–68°F (10–20°C). Before they are sown, seeds of most stone fruits (e.g., cherry) and that of some berried shrubs (e.g., *Berberis* and *Cotoneaster*) need to be stratified (see p.630).

As soon as a seed capsule splits, harvest it together with other capsules that are nearing maturity. Dry them in clean paper bags before separating out the seeds. When mature, wind-distributed seed will start dispersing, so quickly cover the seed-bearing branches with fine cheesecloth or paper bags; alternatively, cut one or two seed-bearing branches and place them in water indoors to mature.

How to overcome dormancy

The seeds of some plants have built-in mechanisms to assist in controlling the time of germination; for example, many seeds do not germinate in late fall, when conditions are unfavorable for seedling growth, but remain dormant until the temperature and other factors are more suitable. This dormancy is achieved by a variety of means including the presence of chemical inhibitors in the seed, by hardened seed coats that must rot or be breached before the seed can germinate, or by the need for the seed to experience alternating cold and warm periods. Several methods have been developed horticulturally to overcome this natural dormancy so the seeds will germinate more quickly and are therefore less likely to fail.

Scarification

The aim is to break down the hardened seed coat and allow water to enter, thereby speeding up germination. Large, hard-coated seeds, such as those of the legume family, may be nicked with a knife. Smaller seeds may be shaken in a jar lined with sandpaper or one containing sharp gravel.

SCARIFICATION

Before planting, carefully nick the hard coat on seeds such as *Paeonia delaveyi* var. *delaveyi* f. *lutea* with a clean, sharp knife so the seed can absorb moisture.

Warm stratification

This is used for hard-coated seeds of many woody species (see *Tree Seed Requiring Stratification*, p.79). Place the seeds in a plastic bag in moist (but not wet) standard seed-starting mix, and store for 4–12 weeks at 68–86°F (20–30°C). This is usually followed by a period of cold stratification before sowing. See also "Breaking seed dormancy," p.114.

Cold stratification

Soak the seeds for a period of up to 24 hours, then add them to moist (but not wet) vermiculite in a plastic bag or place them in an open dish on moist filter paper. Refrigerate the seeds at 34–41°F (1–5°C) for 4–12 weeks. If germination has occurred, sow the seeds immediately.

Alternatively for large seeds, place them in a pot containing 1 part seed to 3 parts moist sand. Cover with mesh and leave in a cold frame for one or two winters until they germinate, then sow seed at once.

Requirements for germination

In order to germinate, a seed needs water, air, warmth, and, for a few species, light. The growing medium needs to be a fine soil mix capable of drawing water up to seeds placed near its surface. To aid this

POST-SCARIFICATION SOAK

Before ____ ____ *After*

After scarification, soak seeds such as lupine in water for 24 hours, so they swell slightly, then sow them.

capillary rise, the soil mix is firmed lightly. Without this firming, air pockets occur, and the water columns essential for capillary rise are broken. The soil mix, however, must not be compacted or so damp that air cannot penetrate; seeds will almost certainly fail in such anerobic soil because they cannot obtain the oxygen vital for growth. For most successful results, the temperature for germination of most seeds should be 59–77°F (15–25°C); heated propagators are useful for maintaining a steady temperature (see "Heated propagators," p.637). Some large seeds, such as those of *Hippeastrum*, germinate easily if floated on water rather than laid on soil (see BULBOUS PLANTS, "Tender bulbs," p.246).

Light requirements vary during germination: a few seeds need light (e.g., *Alyssum*, *Begonia*, *Calceolaria*, and *Genista*), but others are inhibited by it (e.g., *Allium*, *Delphinium*, *Nigella*, and *Phlox*). There is no way of distinguishing seeds requiring dark conditions from those needing light by physical examination: if the dark/light requirement is unknown, initially sow the seed in the dark; if it fails to germinate after a period of some weeks, place it in the light.

Sowing and aftercare

After sowing the seed in containers or in open beds, do not allow the soil mix to dry out or become too waterlogged. Cover the containers with ¼in (5mm) of coarse sand or fine grit for fall-sown seeds; for spring sowings, replace the grit with a ½in (1cm) layer of vermiculite: fine grade for small or medium-sized seeds, and medium grade for large seeds. Place the containers in a suitable environment (see "The propagation environment," p.636). The first sign of germination is the emergence of the radicle, or primary root, followed, in epigeal

HOW A SEED GERMINATES

In hypogeal germination (right), the cotyledons, or seed leaves, stay below soil level, while in epigeal germination (far right), they appear above ground.

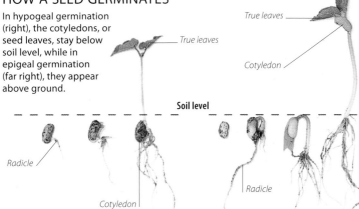

True leaves

True leaves

Cotyledon

Soil level

Radicle

Radicle

Cotyledon

SEEDLING GROWTH

Evenly colored, rich green foliage

Long, thin stems

Healthy seedlings
Sturdy, well-spaced nasturtium (*Tropaeolum*) seedlings flourishing under cover and ready to be pricked out.

Unhealthy seedlings
If not pricked out early enough, the seedlings will become pale, crowded, and etiolated—and may die.

germination, by the cotyledons, or seed leaves, which provide the initial food reserves. The true foliage leaves appear later and generally differ from the cotyledons.

When the seedlings are large enough to handle, they should be "pricked out" (see ANNUALS AND BIENNIALS, "Pricking out," p.217). Failure to do so results in weak growth, because the crowded seedlings compete for light and nutrients and succumb to fungal infection. Once transplanted, return the seedlings to the warm germination environment in order to reestablish; then gradually harden them off by placing the

TRUE LEAVES

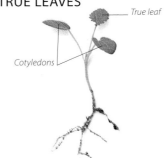

True leaf

Cotyledons

As the cotyledons, or seed leaves, wither, the true leaves gradually take over the process of photosynthesis.

containers in cooler conditions (see "Hardening off," p.638). A cold frame, closed at first, then opened in stages, provides a good environment for hardening off seedlings.

Producing hybrids

When hybridizing plants, it is important to prevent self-pollination. For controlled cross-pollination, petals, sepals, and stamens are removed from the flowers on the proposed female parent and the denuded flowers protected from insects by paper or plastic bags until the stigmas on the female plant are sticky and receptive. Pollen, previously collected from air-dried stamens, is then transferred to the stigmas and the flowers are protected from insects once again until fertilization has occurred. Hybrid seed will develop in the ovaries and should be collected when ripe and according to its requirements (see also ROSES, "Hybridizing," p.168).

F1 and F2 hybrids

For the gardener seeking uniformity and near perfection, F1 and F2 hybrid seed is available for a limited range of plants, mostly annuals. Such seed needs a complex plant-breeding technique and is therefore more expensive.

The first generation derived from crossing two carefully maintained, genetically inbred plants of the same species is termed "first filial generation," or F1, hybrid. F1 hybrids are usually more vigorous than their parents and give uniformity in flower characteristics, such as color and form, that seldom occurs with open-pollinated seed. Sometimes two controlled crosses from four selected lines are used to produce a "second filial generation," or F2, hybrid—retaining some of the vigor and uniformity of the F1 parents but with other favored characteristics less evident in F1s.

Layering

Layering is a natural form of propagation: roots are induced to develop by covering a stem with soil while it is still attached to the parent plant. The rooted portion of stem is then separated from the parent plant and grown on.

The stem to be layered is often cut, ring-barked, or twisted. This interrupts the flow of hormones and carbohydrates, which accumulate and thus help promote root growth. The tissues beyond the constriction are water-stressed, which also favors root formation. Another key stimulus is to exclude light from the stem: light-starved cells become thin-walled and roots form more readily. To stimulate rooting further, use rooting hormone at the layering point.

Methods of layering

Layering methods are classified in three groups: those in which a stem is brought down to the soil (simple, serpentine, natural, and tip layering); those in which soil is mounded over a stem (stooling, trench layering, and French layering); and one in which the soil is brought up to the plant stem (air layering). The word "soil" is used loosely here to mean any growing medium such as peat, sand, sawdust, or sphagnum moss.

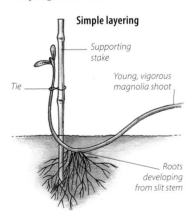

Simple layering
- Supporting stake
- Young, vigorous magnolia shoot
- Tie
- Roots developing from slit stem

Simple layering

This is best carried out between fall and spring. The parent plant must be young and pruned the season before to produce vigorous, flexible stems, which can be brought down to soil level and will root readily. Make a slanting cut on the underside of the stem, and secure it at this point into the soil. The shoot tip is tied to a stake in the soil. If the layer is well rooted the next fall, it can be cut from the parent plant (see also ORNAMENTAL SHRUBS, "Simple layering," p.115, and CLIMBING PLANTS, "Simple layering," p.144).

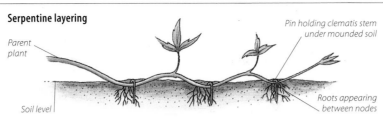

Serpentine layering
- Parent plant
- Soil level
- Pin holding clematis stem under mounded soil
- Roots appearing between nodes

Serpentine layering

This modified form of simple layering is used for plants with pliable stems, such as clematis. Long, young stems are mounded with soil, leaving buds exposed to produce aerial shoots (see also CLIMBING PLANTS, "Propagation by serpentine layering," p.145).

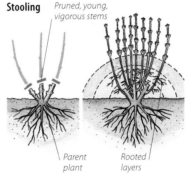

Natural layering
- New strawberry plant
- Runner
- Node

Natural layering

Some plants, such as strawberries, reproduce naturally by sending out a series of runners. These then root at a node, forming a new plant. Once the new plant is fully established, sever it from the parent and grow on (see also "Strawberries: Propagation," p.470).

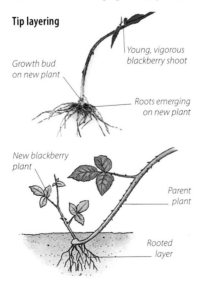

Tip layering
- Growth bud on new plant
- Young, vigorous blackberry shoot
- Roots emerging on new plant
- New blackberry plant
- Parent plant
- Rooted layer

Tip layering

This method is for shrubs and climbers that produce roots from their shoot tips; the blackberry is a common example. In summer, a young, vigorous shoot tip is buried in soil in a hole 3–4in (7–10cm) deep. A new shoot, growing from the tip, appears a few weeks later; the young plant may then be separated from its parent. Grow on the rooted layer *in situ*; transplant it the following spring, if required (see also *Tip Layering*, p.471).

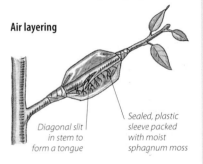

Stooling
- Pruned, young, vigorous stems
- Parent plant
- Rooted layers

Stooling

Used by amateurs for a few woody plants, stooling, or mound layering, is vital for commercial production of rootstocks. Stems of a parent plant are cut back in late winter or early spring to within 3in (8cm) of the ground. Once new shoots are 6–8in (15–20cm) long, mound soil up over their bases, then twice more until summer. On plants that root easily, such as thyme and sage, do not cut back stems before mounding. By fall, stems will have roots; separate from the parent plant and transplant (see also GROWING HERBS, "Mound layering," p.414).

Trench layering

Trench, or etiolation, layering is mainly for fruit rootstocks, usually those that do not root well. The parent plant is planted at an angle, allowing shoots to be pinned down in trenches and covered with soil. The rooted shoots can be detached from the parent to form new plants.

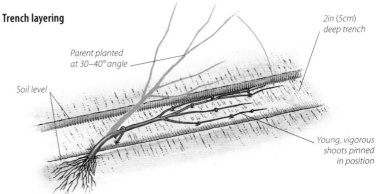

Trench layering
- Parent planted at 30–40° angle
- Soil level
- 2in (5cm) deep trench
- Young, vigorous shoots pinned in position

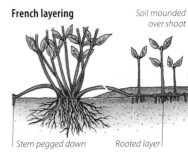

French layering
- Soil mounded over shoot
- Stem pegged down
- Rooted layer

French layering

French, or continuous, layering is a modified form of stooling. In late winter, peg young shoots from the parent stem to the ground. Any new growths are gradually earthed up to a depth of 6in (15cm). New shoots should have rooted by fall and after leaf fall may be separated and grown on (see also ORNAMENTAL SHRUBS, "French layering," p.116).

Air layering
- Diagonal slit in stem to form a tongue
- Sealed, plastic sleeve packed with moist sphagnum moss

Air layering

Use air, or Chinese, layering (also known as marcottage) on trees, shrubs, climbers, and houseplants, such as rhododendrons, magnolias, and rubber plants (*Ficus elastica*). In spring or summer, choose a strong, healthy shoot of one to two years old. Trim off sideshoots and leaves 12in (30cm) back from the tip. Make a slit in the stem and apply hormone rooting compound to it. Keep the wound open by packing with moist sphagnum moss (choose moss from sustainable sources). Then cover the wounded area with more moss and seal with black plastic until roots develop (see *Air Layering a Shrub*, p.116, and INDOOR GARDENING, "Air layering," p.383). Rooting may take up to two years.

Cuttings

Propagation from cuttings is the most common vegetative method. There are three main types: stem, leaf, and root. Stem cuttings produce roots directly from the stem itself or from the mass of thin-walled, wound-healing tissue (callus) that develops at its base. These roots are called adventitious, which means added, or artificial. Some large leaves can be used as cutting material and will develop adventitious roots from near their veins. Vigorous, young roots may also be used for cuttings —propagation by root cuttings is a simple and economical method neglected by most gardeners. Suitable species will produce both adventitious stem buds and roots on the root cutting.

How roots form

Adventitious roots most often develop from young cells produced by the cambium—a layer of cells that generates tissues involved in the thickening of stems. They are usually located close to food- and water-conducting tissues, which provide nourishment as they develop.

Adventitious root growth is also helped by natural hormones called auxins, which accumulate in the base of a cutting. Natural auxins can be supplemented by synthetic auxins, which are available as talc-based powders or as solutions. These aid rooting when applied to the bases of cuttings and are recommended for all plants except those that root very easily. Use only a little hormone, however—too much could harm immature tissue.

Rooting hormones can be bought with low concentrations of active ingredients for soft

CALLOUS PADS

Adventitious roots developing from the callous pad

Protective callous pad

Some plants (here, *Choisya ternata*) form a protective callous pad of wound-healing tissue at the base of a stem cutting, where they have been severed from the parent plant.

SOFTWOOD CUTTINGS

Prepared cutting trimmed below the node

Rooted cutting

The soft, green stem on a softwood cutting (here, *Hydrangea macrophylla*) usually turns brown as it matures and develops its root system.

cuttings and higher concentrations for hardwood material; some contain a fungicide, which helps prevent infections from entering the cuttings through the wounded tissues.

Stem cuttings

Stem cuttings are often classified by the maturity of the stem tissue into softwood, greenwood, semiripe, and hardwood. The distinction is useful, though imprecise, because tissues develop continuously throughout the growing season.

Softwood cuttings

These are taken in spring and are generally made from the tips of shoots (tip cuttings) on the parent plant, but the new, young basal shoots (basal cuttings) of herbaceous perennials are also used (see PERENNIALS, "Basal stem cuttings," p.200). Young material roots most readily, so softwood cuttings often provide the best chance of rooting species that are difficult to propagate. Retain the soft tip if possible, because this is where the rooting auxins are produced. Softwood cuttings need a supportive environment, because they lose water and wilt quickly (see "The propagation environment," p.636).

Greenwood cuttings

These are taken from early to midsummer, from slightly more mature wood, when growth begins to slow. They root slightly less readily but survive better than softwood cuttings, although they still require a supportive environment in which to develop.

Semiripe cuttings

Taken in late summer, semiripe cuttings are less prone to wilting because the stem tissues are firmer and woody (see ORNAMENTAL SHRUBS, "Semiripe cuttings," p.111). Some species with large leaves, for example *Ficus* and camellia, may be propagated more economically by taking a short section from a semiripe stem just above and below a leaf bud, retaining a single leaf (see ORNAMENTAL SHRUBS, "Leaf-bud cuttings," p.112).

Hardwood cuttings

Fully mature, hardwood cuttings are taken at the end of the growing season from fall through to spring, when the tissues are fully ripened. They are the easiest to maintain in a healthy condition but are often slow to root. Hardwood cuttings fall into two categories: leafless deciduous cuttings and broadleaved evergreen cuttings. Growth of many glossy-leaved evergreens, such as holly (*Ilex*) and rhododendron, wilts readily when young early in the season because

SEMIRIPE CUTTINGS

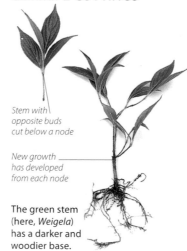

Stem with opposite buds cut below a node

New growth has developed from each node

The green stem (here, *Weigela*) has a darker and woodier base.

LEAF-BUD CUTTINGS

Healthy, green leaf

Leaf bud from which new shoot will develop

A short piece of semiripe stem (here, camellia) provides sufficient food reserves for a leaf-bud cutting, because it produces some food through its leaf.

HARDWOOD CUTTINGS

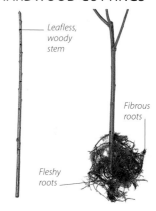

Leafless, woody stem

Fibrous roots

Fleshy roots

Hardwood cuttings (here, *Salix alba*) are the longest type of stem cutting because they need large food reserves while their roots slowly develop.

their protective leaf waxes develop slowly; they are therefore best propagated by semiripe or hardwood cuttings (see also ORNAMENTAL TREES, "Hardwood cuttings," p.76; CLIMBING PLANTS, "Propagation from hardwood cuttings," p.143; and ROSES, "Hardwood cuttings," p.165).

When to take stem cuttings

There are no hard and fast rules about when to take stem cuttings of a particular species, so if cuttings taken in spring fail to root, further cuttings can be taken later in the season and treated according to the relative maturity of the shoots.

Plants that are difficult to root are best propagated early so that the new plants have time to mature before winter. Because the action of root-producing hormones is suppressed by flower-initiating ones, use cuttings without flower buds wherever possible; if cuttings with flower buds have to be used, remove the flower buds.

NODAL CUTTING

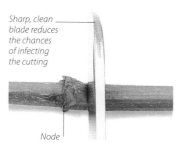

Sharp, clean blade reduces the chances of infecting the cutting

Node

Most cuttings (here, *Hydrangea paniculata*) root most satisfactorily at their nodes and so should be trimmed just below a node.

INTERNODAL CUTTINGS

Internodal cuttings (here, *Clematis montana*) maximize propagating material in an economical way.

Preparing stem cuttings

Stem cuttings are usually prepared by trimming just beneath a node, or leaf joint, where the cambium (the layer of cells involved in stem thickening) is most active. Many easy-rooting cuttings, for example, willows (*Salix*), have preformed roots at the nodes, and these start to develop when the stem is cut from the parent plant. For these and for cuttings with densely crowded leaves on each stem, cut between nodes (internodal cutting).

The cutting length depends on the species but is commonly 2–5in (5–12cm) or about five or six nodes in length. The lower leaves are stripped to give a clean stem for insertion. To help the cuttings root, semiripe and hardwood cuttings are often "wounded" by removing a sliver of bark from the lowest 1in (2.5cm) of the cutting. This exposes a larger area of cambium, stimulating roots to form. Some cuttings, especially semiripe ones, may be taken by pulling a sideshoot away from the main shoot with a small "heel" of bark still attached (see ORNAMENTAL SHRUBS, "Heel cuttings," p.112). A heel may provide a cutting with added protection until it has produced roots, although there is no satisfactory scientific explanation for this response.

With the exception of leafless, hardwood stem cuttings, which contain food reserves from the

PREPARING CUTTINGS

Unprepared cutting

Cutting ready for insertion

To reduce stress from water loss on leafy cuttings (here, rhododendron), remove some leaves, halve others.

previous growing season, few cuttings are able to produce roots and shoots without supplementing their food reserves through photosynthesis. However, active leaves lose water through their pores, which is not easily replaced, and excessive water loss will cause failure. To achieve a balance between retaining photosynthetic tissue and reducing water loss, trim away all but four full-sized leaves, leaving any immature leaves. If the remaining leaves are large, as on many broadleaved trees and large shrubs, reduce each by half to minimize water loss.

Leaf cuttings

For some plants, whole leaves (with or without leaf stalks) or sections of leaves may be taken as cuttings and inserted or secured onto the propagation mix. With whole leaves laid flat, the veins should be nicked at intervals as new plantlets form at the cut surfaces of large leaf veins. Propagate plants such as *Sinningia* and *Streptocarpus* from cut sections of fully expanded, undamaged leaves. African violets (*Saintpaulia*) and *Peperomia* may be propagated from entire leaves

with their stalks (see INDOOR GARDENING, "Propagating from leaves," p.381).

Root cuttings

Root cuttings are taken in the dormant season from young, vigorous roots of about pencil thickness for most trees and shrubs, but the roots may be somewhat thinner for some herbaceous plants, such as phlox.

The length of the cutting

This is dependent on the environment in which the root cutting is to develop: the warmer the environment (within reason), the faster new shoots will appear and, therefore, shorter cuttings with smaller food reserves may be used successfully although these should not be less than 1in (2.5cm) in length. Root cuttings are preferably grown on in a greenhouse. A cold frame is also suitable, but the cuttings may be slower to develop shoots. For *Ailanthus* and lilac (*Syringa*), which can be propagated in open beds, 4–6in (10–15cm) long root cuttings should be used.

Inserting root cuttings

It is important to insert root cuttings the correct way up because the new roots always form at the distal end (the end that was farthest from the crown of the parent plant). Cuttings should be inserted vertically so that their other (proximal) ends are flush with the soil surface; herbaceous root cuttings, however, are often inserted horizontally (see also PERENNIALS, "Root cuttings," p.201).

The rooting medium

Cuttings need air (to obtain oxygen) and water in their rooting medium, but if the medium is too wet, the cuttings rot. Standard cutting soil mix must, therefore, have a more open structure than soil-based

ROOT CUTTINGS

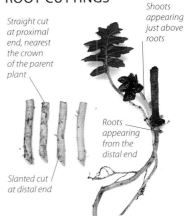

Straight cut at proximal end, nearest the crown of the parent plant

Shoots appearing just above roots

Roots appearing from the distal end

Slanted cut at distal end

To help distinguish the two ends when taking root cuttings (here, *Acanthus mollis*), make differently angled cuts.

PROTECTIVE ENVIRONMENT

Leafy cuttings grow best in a humid environment, such as within a plastic bag secured over a container; keep the plastic away from the leaf surfaces.

potting mix. The rooting medium should also be warm in order to speed up development of the roots: 64–77°F (18–25°C) is ideal for cool temperate species, and up to 90°F (32°C) for those from warm climates. If necessary, use bottom heat (see p.637).

Caring for the cuttings

After insertion, keep leafy cuttings turgid in the humid atmosphere of a closed case, mist unit, propagator, or other similar environment. Leafless cuttings that have been planted outdoors, either direct in the soil or in a container, should be protected by row cover or a cold frame.

Every ten days or so, water the rooting medium lightly if needed, and spray with a fungicide to help prevent disease; at the same time, lift the lights or remove the plastic over enclosed cuttings, to enable air to circulate, for a 5–10-minute period.

Once rooted, cuttings should be potted up individually and those growing under cover gradually hardened off (see p.637).

WOUNDING

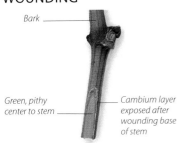

Bark

Green, pithy center to stem

Cambium layer exposed after wounding base of stem

Use a very sharp, clean knife to make a shallow, angled, downward cut at the base of semiripe and hardwood cuttings, such as grapevine (*Vitis*).

LARGE LEAVES

Trimmed leaf cutting

New plantlet has formed where vein was nicked

Large leaves of plants, such as begonia, may be divided into small pieces, each of which will form callous at a nicked vein and then adventitious roots.

SMALL LEAVES

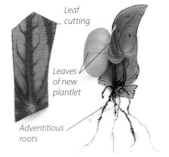

Leaf cutting

Leaves of new plantlet

Adventitious roots

To encourage callous to form, and rooting to occur, small leaves such as *Peperomia* may be trimmed at the edges.

Storage organs

Storage organs have diverse structures, and include bulbs, corms, rhizomes, root and stem tubers, and turions. Most plants with storage organs increase by producing offsets; lift and divide these to avoid overcrowding. Offsets flower faster than seed-raised plants and are identical to the parent, while seed-raised plants can be variable. The main propagation methods apart from division are to cut the storage organs into sections and to stimulate them to produce offsets by wounding; these sections or offsets grow into complete plants if put in a warm, dark place.

BULBS

Bulbs can be propagated by chipping; division of offsets, bulbils, or bulblets; scaling or twin-scaling; and scooping or scoring. For lists of plants appropriate to each method, see Bulbous Plants, "Propagation," pp.244–249.

Wide, fleshy, inner scale leaves

New shoot rising from leaf leaf axil

Membranous, dry, outer scale leaves on Narcissus bulb

Nonscaly, or tunicate, bulb

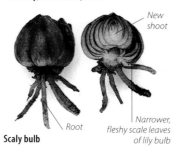

New shoot

Root

Narrower, fleshy scale leaves of lily bulb

Scaly bulb

Chipping

Nonscaly, or tunicate, bulbs, such as snowdrops (*Galanthus*), that do not naturally increase quickly may be multiplied rapidly by chipping. This method involves cutting each bulb into up to 20 pieces, depending on its size. Prompt removal of any rotted or moldy parts is essential to prevent disease because no fungicides are available for protecting the vulnerable sections. The chips can be incubated (see "Chipping," p.248) or placed in vermiculite in a container in a frost-free greenhouse and left undisturbed. New bulbs form usually within 12 weeks, but a few may take almost two years. Separate the bulblets and repot or replant.

Bulblets develop between the scale leaves on a chipped bulb such as snowdrop (*Galanthus*) in air temperatures that do not exceed 77°F (25°C).

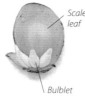

Scale leaf

Bulblet

Scooping and scoring

Some bulbs, such as hyacinths, can be propagated by either scooping or scoring the bulb. This causes a callus to develop, which encourages bulblets to form. For scooping, the basal plate of a mature bulb is scooped out at the center, leaving just the outer edge of the basal plate intact; for scoring, two shallow cuts at right angles are made into the basal plate. Store the bulb, basal plate up, in a warm, dark place, until bulblets have formed; then detach and continue growing (see also "Simple cutting," p.249; "Scooping hyacinths," p.249; and *Scooping and Scoring Trilliums*," p.249).

Shallowly cutting the basal plate of some bulbs (here, hyacinth) stimulates the growth of bulblets.

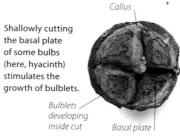

Callus

Bulblets developing inside cut

Basal plate

Scaling

Scaling involves removing bulb scales, which are then induced to form bulblets. It is used for bulbs, such as fritillaries (*Fritillaria*) and lilies (*Lilium*), that are made up of fairly loose scales. Individual scale leaves are pulled away from the basal plate of a mature bulb and left in a plastic bag with moist vermiculite or a peat and grit mix, in a warm, dark place. Bulblets appear at the scale bases, after about two months. Grow from the scales until bulblets are large enough to be separated (see also "Scaling," p.247).

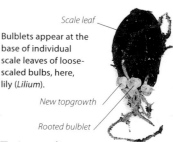

Scale leaf

Bulblets appear at the base of individual scale leaves of loose-scaled bulbs, here, lily (*Lilium*).

New topgrowth

Rooted bulblet

Twin-scaling

Nonscaly, or tunicate, bulbs, such as daffodils and snowdrops, may be twin-scaled, where the bulb is cut vertically into eight to ten sections and each one is divided into pairs of bud scales with a section of basal plate. These are then incubated and grown in the same way as in scaling above. (See also "Twin-scaling," p.248.)

Two leaf scales and a section of basal plate are used for nonscaly bulbs (here, *Narcissus*).

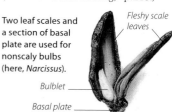

Fleshy scale leaves

Bulblet

Basal plate

Bulbils or bulblets

Bulbils are produced on flower heads or stems; bulblets develop on the bulb itself or on stem roots. Both can be detached and planted to develop into new bulbs (see also Lilies, "Bulbils and bulblets," p.239).

Some lilies (*Lilium*), for example, *L. lancifolium*, produce small, bulblike structures known as "bulbils" on their stems above the ground. Others, for example *L. longiflorum*, may develop similar bulblets on bulbs or stem roots in the soil.

Lily bulblets

Old stem, which has developed roots

Lily bulbils

Division of offsets

Bulbs have wide, fleshy scale leaves, which act as food storage organs. At their base are axillary buds, which may enlarge to form offsets. Lift bulbs at the end of the season, separate offsets, and plant out singly (see "Dividing bulbs," p.244).

Carefully remove each offset from a bulb (here, *Narcissus*) by cutting or pulling.

Offset

Parent bulb

Corms

Corms are reduced, compact, underground stems with a solid internal structure. Most corms produce several buds near the apex; each bud naturally forms a new corm. Miniature corms, or cormels, are produced as offsets between the old and new corms in the growing season (see also Bulbous Plants,

"Gladiolus Cormels," p.244). Larger corms may be increased artificially just before the growing season by cutting them into pieces, each with a growing bud. Prevent disease by removing rot or mold promptly. Place in a pot or the open ground and lightly cover with soil, while new corms develop.

Old corm

New corm

Cormels

Food storage tissue

Thickened stem base

Gladiolus corm

Raising cormels
Separate the new corm and cormels from the old corm when dormant, and plant.

Cormel development
Cormels can take up flowering size. The sequence below shows their development in the first year.

Rhizomes

These consist of a horizontally growing shoot, usually below but sometimes on the soil surface. They are propagated by cutting the rhizome into young, healthy sections, each with one or more growth buds, which are planted individually (see also PERENNIALS, *Division of rhizomatous plants*, p.199; BULBOUS PLANTS, *Scooping and Scoring Trilliums*, p.249; and ORCHIDS, *Division*, p.371).

Root tubers

A root tuber is a portion of root at the stem base that swells during summer and is modified into a storage organ, or tuber, as in dahlias. Propagate plants in the spring by dividing a cluster of tubers into healthy pieces, each with a shoot (see also *Cutting up Bulbs for Propagation*, p.248). Root tubers may also be propagated by basal cuttings of the young, emerging shoots in spring (see DAHLIAS, *How to Propagate by Basal Cuttings*, p.251).

Stem tubers

The stems of some plants (e.g., potatoes) are modified to produce tubers, which act as storage organs. Tuberous begonias, for example, form perennial tubers at the bases of their stems. In spring, prompt removal of any rotted or moldy material is important to prevent disease. Each piece will produce basal shoots, which can be used as basal cuttings (see DAHLIAS, *How to Propagate by Basal Cuttings*, p.251) or grown on to form a new tuber (see *Propagation of Tuberous Begonias*, p.382).

Other types of storage organs

Plants such as *Saxifraga granulata* and some *Kalanchoe* and *Asparagus* species develop round, bulblike buds in their shoot axils. These buds can be separated and grown on individually in the same way as bulblets or cormels (see p.634).

In some water plants, such as *Hydrocharis* and *Myriophyllum*, these relatively large bud structures are known as "turions." When mature, they drop off the parent plant, sink to the bottom, and become new plants.

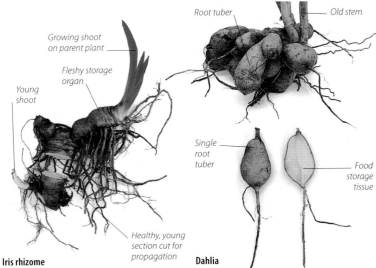

Growing shoot on parent plant

Fleshy storage organ

Young shoot

Healthy, young section cut for propagation

Iris rhizome

Root tuber — Old stem

Single root tuber — Food storage tissue

Dahlia

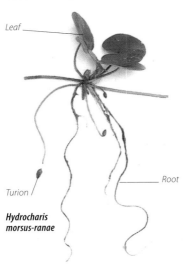

Old stem

Stem tuber

Bud

Food storage tissue

Jerusalem artichoke

Leaf

Root

Turion

Hydrocharis morsus-ranae

Grafting and budding

In a wide range of woody plants and a few herbaceous ones, a budded stem, or scion, is grafted onto a rootstock, or stock, of another species or cultivar, to achieve a composite plant with more desirable characteristics. Most apple, pear, and stone-fruit trees are propagated in this way. The stock may be more resistant than the scion to root disease or more suited to a particular environment. Often, the stock is selected because it controls the growth of the scion to produce a dwarf or a very vigorous plant. Sometimes, a scion cultivar that is difficult to increase from cuttings is grafted onto easily rooted stock. The rootstock also influences the age at which the tree bears fruit and its size and skin quality—trees on dwarfing rootstocks generally fruit earlier. Conversely, the rootstock's growing cycle may be affected by the scion cultivar, which in its turn influences cold hardiness. Reactions to soil acidity can also be affected by interactions between rootstock and scion cultivars.

The scion may take the form of a single bud on a short portion of stem (usually known as budding) or it may be a multibudded length of stem.

When to graft

Field (outdoor) grafting is normally undertaken from late winter to early spring, when the cambium is particularly active, and mild conditions also favor the growth of callous cells. Hot weather later in the season may dry out the thin-walled, cambial cells. Bench grafting, generally done in the greenhouse or potting shed, is undertaken in winter and summer.

T-budding, on the other hand, is most often done in mid- to late summer, when well-developed scion buds are available and young stock material is of suitable diameter. For success, the stock plant needs to be growing actively, so that the bark can be lifted from the wood to allow the bud to be inserted. Chip-budding may be undertaken over an extended season because the chip is positioned beside the stock rather than slipped under its bark.

How to graft

Because grafting cuts inevitably damage plant cells, and the thin-walled cells at the graft union are vulnerable to fungi and bacteria, it is important that knives are sterile and sharp, so that a single cut is sufficient. The propagation environment, prepared plant material, and ties must also be scrupulously clean.

Once stock and scion material have been selected and cut to shape, according to the type of graft, position the two pieces carefully so that there is maximum cambial contact. If the grafting materials are of different widths, ensure the cambium on at least one side of the graft is in contact. Central to the grafting process is the activity of

CAMBIUM LAYER

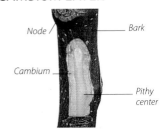

Node

Bark

Cambium

Pithy center

For successful grafting, the scion cambium must be matched as closely as possible to that of the stock.

the cambium—a continuous, narrow band of thin-walled cells between the bark and the wood— that produces new cells that allow stem thickening. Within days of grafting, the region between the stock and scion should fill with thin-walled callous cells. The cambial cells on the stock and scion next to the young callus then link to neighboring cells, so that a complete cambial bridge forms between the two parts. Further divisions of this new cambium produce water- and food-conducting tissue, which functionally joins the scion and stock.

Grafts should be bound with clear plastic tape, which seals the join well. Waxing is not necessary, except in hot-pipe callusing (see p.637). Pot-grown stocks, once grafted, should be kept in a suitable protective environment (see "Greenhouses," p.636, and "Cold frames," p.637).

Regularly examine the graft, and remove the tape once the graft appears to have taken. The following growing season, cut back the stock plant just above the new shoot that has developed from the grafted scion.

Chip-budding

A chip of ripe wood is removed from the rootstock and replaced with a matching chip of similar size from the scion, or bud stick, containing a bud (see "Propagating by chip-budding," p.432).

T-budding

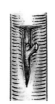

In this technique, just the scion bud is grafted onto the rootstock by cutting a T in the stock bark and inserting the bud beneath (see Roses, "Bud-grafting," p.166).

Spliced side grafting

A short, downward cut through the cambium layer of the stock is followed by a sloping cut down toward the base of the first cut. The chip is removed and then replaced by the scion, which is shaped to match the stock (see Ornamental Trees, "Spliced side grafting," p.80, and Ornamental Shrubs, "Spliced side-veneer grafting," p.117).

Side-wedge (or inlay) grafting

A downward, slightly inward cut is made into the side of the stock. The scion is then prepared by making two oblique cuts at the base. The scion's wedge-shaped base is inserted into the rootstock cut so that the cambium aligns and is bound in position.

Apical-wedge grafting

A ¾–1¼ in (2–3cm) vertical cut is made centrally into the stock; the wedge-shaped scion is inserted into this (see Ornamental Shrubs, "Apical-wedge grafting," p.118).

Saddle grafting

The top of the stock is saddle-shaped, with upward-sloping sides. The scion is then shaped so that it fits closely over the top of the rootstock (see Ornamental Shrubs, "Saddle grafting," p.117).

Whip grafting

Cut back the stock at an oblique angle to 2–3in (5–8cm). Then prepare the scion to match. If the scion is thinner than the stock, first cut the stock horizontally, then obliquely to match.

Flat grafting

Both the stock top and scion base are cut horizontally (see Cacti and other Succulents, "Flat grafting," p.351).

Whip-and-tongue grafting

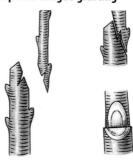

Make matching sloping cuts on the rootstock and scion, then cut shallow tongues along the sloping cuts, so that the scion interlocks securely with the stock (see Growing Fruit, "Whip-and-tongue grafting," p.433).

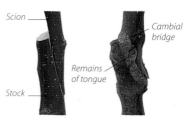

Scion — *Cambial bridge* — *Remains of tongue* — *Stock*

Whip-and-tongue graft
The rootstock and scion gradually unite to function as one plant.

The propagation environment

During propagation, plants are at their most vulnerable and their environment is, therefore, vitally important. The choice of environment depends on which propagation method is chosen and on the relative maturity of the plant material itself. Propagation from leafy cuttings, for example, requires a more closely regulated environment than for leafless cuttings.

Greenhouses

It is important that a greenhouse has adequate ventilation and, in the growing season, appropriate shading (see "Creating the right environment," p.573). From spring to early fall, apply a shading wash to the outside of the glass so that plants are not stressed unnecessarily by extreme weather conditions (see "Shading washes," p.576). Additional protective shading can be provided by mounting shade cloth on wire runners across or along the length of the bench or greenhouse. The curtain can be withdrawn during cloudy weather.

Protecting leafy cuttings

Because leafy cuttings, initially, have no roots and cannot easily take up water to replace that lost from the leaves, they must have further protection within the greenhouse.

Clear plastic sheeting or a plastic bag placed over a tray of cuttings and tucked under is perfectly

HARD-TOPPED PROPAGATOR

When the vents are closed, moisture is retained within the unit. Cuttings therefore remain swollen, and so are more likely to root quickly and healthily.

satisfactory if appropriate shading is provided. The water vapor that condenses on the inside of the plastic helps to protect the cuttings against desiccation. Soft cuttings may succumb to disease if the plastic touches them; insert a framework of split stakes or wire in the potting mix to keep the plastic off the cuttings. In such closed systems, however, excessive air temperatures may build up in very hot conditions and the containers of cuttings should be kept in a shaded but light place out of the sun.

Hard plastic propagators need similar shading to plastic sheeting. Initially keep the vents closed, to maintain a moist atmosphere. Once rooting has taken place and the cuttings are ready to be hardened off, the vents should be opened.

A mist unit provides the best system for summer propagation,

but for winter and early- and late-season propagation, it should be combined with bottom heat. Ideally, the mist unit should maintain a constant water film on the leaf surfaces; some water will still be lost from the leaves by transpiration but this is amply replaced by "applied" water from the misting process. The mist is applied in bursts, so the greenhouse humidity fluctuates and so, inevitably, the water film on each leaf is imperfect, and some water loss occurs. Complete mist systems include supply pipes, water filter, nozzles, and a solenoid and sensor to regulate the misting frequency (see "Mist units," p.580).

For softwood cuttings, which wilt easily, the best system is to arrange a low, clear plastic tent just above the misting nozzles. This ensures a higher ambient humidity between mist bursts

SHADING GREENHOUSES (TEMPERATE CLIMATES)

To prevent the greenhouse from overheating when propagating, add one or more layers of shading, depending on the weather conditions and season. Greenhouses in open, sunny sites are particularly vulnerable to overheating.

		Spring	Summer	Fall	Winter
Cloudy days	Whitewash	▬▬▬	▬▬▬	▬▬▬	
Bright days	Layer of shade netting	▬▬▬	▬▬▬	▬▬▬	▬▬▬
	Additional shade netting	▬▬	▬▬		
	Shade paint	▬▬▬	▬▬▬		

EFFECTS OF BOTTOM HEAT

*Long, strong,
healthy roots*

**Cutting grown
without heat**

*Poor,
short roots*

Cutting grown with heat

than does open mist. It is important to shade such a closed mist system in bright weather.

Bottom heat

Most biological processes are speeded up when temperatures are higher, and so raising soil mix temperature tends to increase the rapidity with which seeds germinate and cuttings root.

Cables or heating mats are most convenient for small greenhouses (see "Propagation aids," p.580). The temperature is controlled by a rod thermostat or electronic controller. If they are used in closed mist systems, excessive air temperatures may build up in sunny conditions, during which heating must be switched off.

Hot-air grafts

Hot-pipe callusing applies thermostatically controlled hot air to a grafted plant to speed the formation of callous tissue, which is the first sign of a successful graft union. A soil-warming cable is threaded twice through a length of plastic drainpipe, 3in (8cm) across, in which slots have been cut—1in (2.5cm) wide for bare-root stock; 3in (8cm) wide for container-grown ones. The pipe is then positioned just above ground level. Each scion and graft is sealed with melted wax, so it is less likely to dry out, and then taped and placed in a slot within the plastic pipe. Any bare roots are covered with soil, to keep them cool but moist, and then the whole pipe is wrapped with insulating material. If the temperature within the pipe is set to 68–77°F (20–25°C), callusing should occur within a few weeks.

Heated propagators

These self-contained units are very useful for extending the propagation season (see "Heated propagators," p.580). The units have heat loadings well in excess of the 15 watts/sq ft (160 watts/sq m) recommended for mist systems, so they must be fitted with working thermostats, otherwise high temperatures may damage cuttings in sunny weather.

Cold frames

Cold frames provide a valuable gain in soil and air temperatures while maintaining high humidity and providing adequate light for young plants. They can be used to raise seedlings early in the season, protect grafts, and propagate leafless and leafy cuttings. They may also, if required, be fitted with bottom heat (see left).

USING A MIST BOX

A mist box can be used to maintain the high humidity needed for softwood cuttings. Attach plastic sheets to a homemade frame and place a cool-mist humidifier inside. Do not run the humidifier constantly, or moisture levels will rise too high.

A cool-mist humidifier

Because such low structures have no great volume, they will easily overheat in sunny conditions unless ventilated and shaded well (see "Cold frames," p.581). Conversely, when temperatures fall below 23°F (-5°C), it is important to insulate frames with thick layers of burlap, coconut matting, styrofoam tiles, or bubble plastic.

Cloches and row covers

Glass and clear plastic cloches and row covers are most often used to give seedlings an early start in the season in the vegetable garden. A wide range of easily rooted cuttings also do well in such an environment (see "Cloches," p.582). Additional shading, such as shade netting, is required in bright, sunny weather.

Growing the propagated plant

To propagate plants effectively, a gardener needs not only to prepare the material properly but also to care for and grow the young plants in a suitable environment until they have developed sufficiently to thrive in the garden. At key stages in propagation, practical inexperience or carelessness can kill well-rooted plants.

Caring for the plants

Most forms of propagation involve cutting various parts of the plants being increased, so plant tissues are exposed to possible disease infection; it is therefore important to maintain hygienic conditions in the propagating area. Tools and benches should be regularly and thoroughly cleaned (using a mild disinfectant if necessary), and dead and damaged plant material removed. Potting mixes must

FIRMING THE POTTING MIX

Ensure that seeds are germinated in evenly pressed, level potting mix so that capillary action and therefore seedling growth are not hindered by air pockets in the mix.

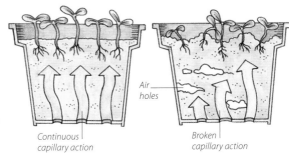

Continuous capillary action

Air holes

Broken capillary action

always be fresh and sterile. Copper fungicides or biological control materials may also be applied to protect seedlings and leafy cuttings, following the manufacturer's instructions.

When preparing pots or flats of soil mix for sowing seed, lightly firm the mix using a presser board, especially around the edges of the container. Water is drawn up through the soil mix by capillary action and, without this firming,

air pockets occur and the water columns needed for capillary rise are broken. However, do not firm soil-based mixes: a medium filled with roots must be well aerated and have an open structure for optimal plant growth.

The composts in which propagated plants are growing should be moist, but not wet, at all times. Too wet a medium will reduce the oxygen available and the roots may die or succumb

to disease. It is also important to maintain the correct environment until the young plants are sturdy enough to be hardened off (see "The propagation environment," opposite). Prick out seedlings to avoid their becoming overcrowded, because unless air is allowed to

DAMPING OFF

Seedlings are more likely to damp off if they are overcrowded, especially if grown in damp, poorly ventilated conditions, or if they are allowed to suffer cold damage.

NURSERY BED WITH RAISED EDGES

Edging boards can be used to enclose a nursery bed. Woven fabric is placed directly onto well-drained soil.

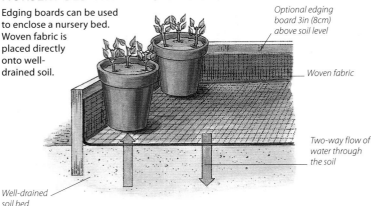

Optional edging board 3in (8cm) above soil level

Woven fabric

Two-way flow of water through the soil

Well-drained soil bed

SAND BED

With this type of nursery bed, woven fabric can be placed over an enclosed bed of coarse sand.

Edging board 3in (8cm) above soil level

Sand bed

Two-way flow of water through the sand

Soil bed

Plastic sheeting cut 1in (2.5cm) below the top of the edging boards

---

circulate freely around the young plants, stagnant conditions may arise and cause damping off (p.658). Remove fallen leaves and dead matter immediately.

Most organic potting mixes are acidic, that is, with a pH value of less than 7, and the ideal range for an organic mix is pH 5–5.5. Simple test kits are available to measure the pH. A very alkaline soil or potting mix reduces the amount of phosphorus, iron, manganese, and boron available to the plant, while too acidic a soil means that calcium and magnesium may be in short supply. For feeding the plants, apply a commercial liquid fertilizer strictly in accordance with the manufacturer's instructions.

Hardening off

Hardening off the propagated plants, the process where the young plants are acclimatized to the outside air temperature, must not be rushed, because, over a period of days, the natural waxes coating the leaves need to undergo changes in form and thickness to reduce water loss. The stomatal pores on the leaf also need to adapt to less supportive conditions.

First, turn off the heat, if appropriate, in the propagator or mist unit. Then, during the daytime, raise the covers for increasingly long periods. Finally, the covers may be removed for both day and night. If the plant has been in the protective environment of a greenhouse and eventually needs to be planted outdoors, move it next into a cold frame. This, too, should be closed at first, then opened in stages. Alternatively, place in the shelter of a wall, fence, or hedge and cover with horticultural fabric, gradually lifting it first during the day, and then at night. The hardening off process may take two to three weeks.

Outdoor nursery beds

Large numbers of new plants and seedlings in containers can be grown in an outdoor nursery bed, once hardened off. At its simplest, this can be an area of cleared and leveled ground covered with water-permeable woven fabric, black plastic, or weed matting, which will suppress weeds, provide a clean growing environment, and help to isolate plants placed on its surface from soil-borne diseases. The plants are placed on the fabric and gain access to soil water through capillary action. Edging boards can be added (as above) to contain the plants neatly and reduce the effect of drying winds, making watering more effective. The fabric should be sterilized regularly to maintain a clean growing environment.

The nursery bed can be of any size, but it must be on free-draining soil. If your soil is a

heavy clay, raise the nursery bed by first laying down plastic sheeting, and then adding a layer of coarse, lime-free sand, 3in (8cm) deep. The entire sand bed will need to be enclosed by edging boards (see above). The boards and plastic sheeting will retain moisture and ensure that watering is effective, while the drainage afforded by the sand will prevent a waterlogging. A covering layer of water-permeable woven fabric can be added to prevent erosion of the sand by wind, and also disturbance by domestic animals, keeping the sand cleaner and more hygienic.

A sand bed has the advantage over a basic nursery bed of reducing the amount of watering necessary, minimizing the risk of potting mixes drying out. More complex sand-bed designs incorporate drainage pipes and automatic watering systems.

■ MICROPROPAGATION

Micropropagation uses explants, tiny pieces of young plant material. Each is grown on in a medium containing organic nutrients, mineral salts, hormones, and other elements needed for growth, and kept in a controlled environment. The explant multiplies to form shoots or complete plantlets, which are rooted as microcuttings

or, if already rooted, weaned to greenhouse conditions. Sterile conditions are vital, and transferring plant material from the culture to a greenhouse is difficult. Micropropagation is used for high-value plants, for example to rapidly introduce new cultivars, plants hard to propagate by other means, and to produce disease-free stock.

A microscopic portion of plant tissue is extracted from a plant under sterile conditions. This portion, or explant, is then divided (right) and grown in test-tube conditions (far right). Once sufficiently large, these embryo plants may be further divided or grown to form plantlets.

Embryo plant

Sterile, test-tube conditions

GENETICALLY MODIFIED PLANTS

Genetic modification (GM) uses DNA technology to identify and extract genes from plant cells and introduce them into other cells, not necessarily of the same species or genus. This makes it possible to recombine genes of fundamentally changed parents in the breeding process, resulting in completely new plants. Potentially, GM techniques could extend the range of flower colors and scents; enhance fruit flavors; increase tolerance of drought and low temperatures; and produce medicinal compounds. GM methods also engender resistance to pests and diseases, such as cucumber mosaic virus in lettuces, tomatoes, and peppers, or herbicide resistance in tobacco plants.

Fundamental interference with the natural order by manipulating genes raises public concern. Questions are asked about potential risks to the environment. Could progeny arising through GM introduce genes into natural plant populations through normal cross-pollination, with deleterious consequences? Might GM plants show undesirable traits, such as invasiveness and produce "superweeds"? Are there potential hazards to human health through consumption of GM food crops? Ethical issues also arise including freedom of choice, dominance of commercial influence, and the nonreversibility of the basic procedures.

As opportunities and challenges presented by genetic modification unfold, gardeners should be aware of the facts. Statutory regulations govern the development of the technique and mechanisms are in place to evaluate both the benefits and the potential risks.

PLANT PROBLEMS

Even the most experienced gardener may encounter problems caused by plant diseases and disorders, the ravages of pests, and competition from weeds. By following the principles of good cultivation and garden management, however, it should be possible to keep these problems to a minimum. When problems do occur, it is important first to diagnose them correctly before deciding on the appropriate course of action required to remedy the situation. Treatments include a wide variety of organic and biological methods. Synthetic pesticides are a last resort.

Pests, diseases, and physiological disorders

Most plant problem symptoms are easy to see. A tree, shrub, or plant may wilt or become discolored, or it may fail to come into leaf or to bloom at all. Pests, which may be the cause of the plant's poor health, may be seen on part or all of the plant. Sometimes an infestation or disease in the roots may be noticed first through symptoms in the leaves. This chapter gives detailed information on how to prevent and control the pests, diseases, and physiological disorders that can cause such problems.

Disease
Apples and pears are particularly susceptible to brown rot (above).

Disorder
Brown blotches on leaves often indicate potassium deficiency in plants (left).

Pests
Aphids can quickly colonize globe artichokes and other vulnerable plants (far left).

What is a pest?

Pests are animals that cause damage to cultivated plants. Some, such as slugs, snails, and rabbits, are well known; most, however, are small invertebrates, such as mites, nematodes, earwigs, and millipedes, which are less evidently plant pests. The largest group by far in this category is insects. Pests may damage or destroy part of a plant or, in some cases, the whole plant. They feed in various ways— by sap sucking, leaf mining, defoliating, or tunneling through stems, roots, or fruit. Sometimes they cause abnormal growths known as galls. Some pests also indirectly damage plants by spreading viral or fungal diseases, while others coat plants with a sugary excrement that encourages the growth of sooty molds.

What is a disease?

A plant disease is any pathological condition caused by other organisms, such as bacteria, fungi, or viruses. Fungal diseases are commonest; bacterial diseases are relatively rare. The symptoms that these organisms produce vary greatly in appearance and severity, but the growth or health of the plant is almost always affected and, in severe attacks, the plant may even be killed. The rate of infection is affected by factors such as weather and growing conditions. In some cases, the disease-causing organism (pathogen) is spread by a carrier, such as an aphid. The pathogen is sometimes visible as a discoloration, as with rusts. Symptoms such as discoloration, distortion, or wilting are typical signs of disease infection.

What is a disorder?

Plant disorders usually result from nutritional deficiencies or from unsuitable growing or storage conditions. An inappropriate temperature range, inadequate or erratic water or food supply, poor light, or unsatisfactory atmospheric conditions may all lead to physiological disorders. Problems may also be caused by deficiencies of the mineral salts that are essential for healthy plant growth.

Weather, cultural, or soil conditions may affect a range of plants. The problems become apparent through symptoms such as discolored leaves or stem wilt. A plant that lacks water, food, or the right environment will not only appear unhealthy but will also be less able to resist attack from insect pests or diseases caused by fungi, viruses, or bacteria. Unless problems are diagnosed and treated, affected plants may die.

How to use this chapter

This chapter begins with a description of plant problems and their possible controls. Then there is a visual guide to plant problems, followed by a more comprehensive A–Z list describing each particular plant problem, its symptoms, causes, and control. Within the visual guide, plant problems are organized by type, so that leaf problems are grouped together, then flower problems, and so on. You can use the visual index to identify the name of the problem, and then look it up in the A–Z list. Alternatively, if you have already diagnosed the problem, you can go straight to the A–Z list to find it.

Guarding against problems
A combination of defenses protects these strawberry plants. Netting prevents attack by birds, while a layer of straw keeps fruit dry and discourages mold and rot.

Integrated pest management

The phrase "IPM" describes the approach widely used by farmers, landscapers, and gardeners in the limitation and management of pest and disease problems. It aims to do everything possible to prevent problems from occurring, but then, should this be inadequate, to consider all the options for preventing problems—for example, using biological controls or organic sprays—before resorting to synthetic chemicals. Gardeners practicing IPM combine the best aspects of all methods of controlling problems, with a preference for cultural controls. They choose resistant plants and maintain high standards of garden hygiene, ensuring plants are healthy and have the best chance of resisting attack; they practice crop rotation, when possible. They seek to prevent pests from landing on plants with the use of traps, barriers, and repellents. Plants are inspected often to spot problems early, and care is taken to ensure an accurate diagnosis. Chemicals are used correctly, and only when warranted by serious pest or disease attack.

Prevention of problems

Always buy strong, vigorous plants that look healthy. Do not purchase plants that are showing dieback or discolored stems, that have leaves that are an abnormal color for the time of year, or that are wilted or distorted. Do not buy plants showing significant pest infestations or disease. Check the root ball of container-grown trees and shrubs: do not buy them if they are either potbound or showing poor root development.

Check that the plant is suitable for its intended location, taking into account the type, texture, and pH of the soil, the exposure of the site, and whether the plant is prone to frost damage. Plant carefully, making sure that the ground is well prepared and that the roots are properly spread out. Follow the individual plant's requirements for watering, feeding, and, where appropriate, pruning.

Garden hygiene

Maintaining a neat and well-managed garden is one of the most important ways to reduce the risk of pest and disease attack. Examine plants regularly to identify any new problem as soon as possible—a well-established infection or infestation is always far more difficult to deal with than one that is identified and treated early.

The regular removal and disposal of diseased parts of plants, and some pests, such as imported cabbageworms, may be laborious but certainly helps to control problems. Debris from infested or diseased plants should in many cases be discarded or burned (check local regulations before doing any open burning); otherwise the pest or pathogen may survive over winter and reinfect plants the following spring.

If a plant is badly diseased or infested by pests, it may be impossible to revive it. Such plants should be removed, especially if there is a risk that the trouble might spread to healthy plants nearby.

Crop rotation and replant problems

Rotating vegetable crops, usually on a three- or four-year basis, can help prevent soil-borne pests and diseases from building up to a damaging level. For further details on planning a crop rotation system, see Growing Vegetables, "Crop rotation," p.498.

Although rotation is more commonly used for vegetables, it is also worth rotating annuals and bulbs where feasible, because this reduces the buildup of diseases like foot and root rots and tulip fire. Growing a particular kind of plant in the same ground for a number of years can also lead to problems. If a disease such as foot or root rot becomes evident, remove all the plants and grow unrelated, nonsusceptible plants on the site.

Resistant plants

Some plants are resistant to attack by pests or diseases. Plant breeders have produced cultivars with a higher-than-average resistance to some pests or diseases. Cultivated plants resistant to pests include sweet corn varieties with thick husks that earworms can't penetrate. Plants resistant to disease include some tomato cultivars, which resist tomato leaf mold, and the climbing rose 'Maigold', which shows some resistance to diseases such as powdery mildew, rusts, and black spot.

In some cases, the resistance appears to be total, but even a resistant plant may succumb to a given disease if its growing conditions are poor, for example, or if other factors, such as the weather, weaken the plant. Before buying plants, check if there are disease- or pest-resistant cultivars readily available. The range of resistant plants varies from year to year, so check catalogs annually for this type of information.

Correcting cultural disorders and deficiencies

Unsatisfactory growing conditions may result not only in poor general growth, but also in some very specific symptoms that closely resemble those caused by pests and diseases. When problems manifest themselves and an obvious cause—such as pest infestation—is not immediately apparent, it is worth considering the plant's growing environment as a whole—recent weather conditions, for example, or the health of your soil, or even whether some aspect of plant care was not provided. At best, the plant may be restored to complete health by some simple measure—the addition of a mineral supplement, for example, or less frequent watering. At worst, you may have to accept plant losses caused by freak extremes of weather—or learn that certain plants simply are not suited to the conditions you are able to provide.

It is also worth remembering that the risk of certain pest and disease problems can be minimized by altering growing conditions. Liming in the vegetable garden (see p.625) is a classic example; by increasing the alkalinity of the soil, it reduces the risk of clubroot affecting cabbage-family crops.

Preventing buildup of disease
Practicing good hygiene prevents problems from building up. Remove and compost yellowing and fallen leaves regularly.

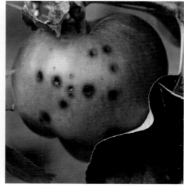

Symptoms of cultural disorder
Bitter pit in apples, caused by a lack of calcium, may be triggered by dry soil that, in fact, does contain sufficient calcium levels.

BENEFICIAL CREATURES

Bumblebees
work as expert pollinators

Garden spiders
trap numerous harmful insects

Lacewings
the larvae eat aphids and other plant mites

Ladybugs
feed on many types of aphids

Frogs and toads
reduce slug and snail populations

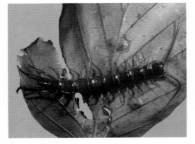

Centipedes
prey on pests that live in the soil

Birds
keep insect pests in check

Shrews
eat slugs and snails as part of their diet

Cultural controls

Organic pest and disease controls use natural methods to help plants both resist and recover from attacks. Such methods have long played their part in gardening, but in recent years they have attracted an increasing level of interest, especially as some harmful organisms have become immune to chemicals that once controlled them. Gardeners have become increasingly aware of the damage that the widespread use of synthetic chemicals can do to the environment, and especially to creatures that are the gardener's natural allies—those that are predators or parasites of plant pests.

Attracting pest predators

Insects and other animals found in gardens are by no means all destructive. Many are not only useful to the plant but are also actually necessary for its survival and extremely beneficial; for example, a large number of fruits, vegetables, and flowers rely on pollinating insects, such as honey bees, to carry pollen from one flower to another to enable fertilization to take place.

In other cases, some species of natural predators can help to control certain types of pests and should therefore be encouraged to visit the garden. A natural balance between pests and predators may take a few years to accomplish but,

once established, such a garden will be much healthier than one that relies on chemical remedies and solutions.

Undisturbed areas will attract beneficial animals, especially if planted with a wide range of native species. A stone or wood pile will attract toads and snakes, and a pond will attract dragonflies. Predators such as flower flies and ladybugs can be encouraged by introducing colorful flowers, especially if flat or open-centered in form, so they, too, will help keep pests at bay.

Recognizing beneficial garden animals

Shrews, frogs, and toads feed on many ground-dwelling plant pests such as slugs and snails. Birds may be the cause of some damage in the garden, but this disadvantage is usually far outweighed by the enormous quantities of insect pests that many devour. Some invertebrates, for example, centipedes, prey on soil-dwelling pests. It is possible to distinguish centipedes from the somewhat similar millipedes (which can very

occasionally cause minor damage) by the number of legs that are carried on each segment of their bodies: centipedes have only one pair per body segment, whereas millipedes have two pairs.

Spiders are also useful allies— their webs trap countless insects. Certain insects, however, may be invaluable in the garden. Lady beetles (ladybugs) are a familiar example nearly everywhere, and both the larvae and the adult beetles feed on destructive pests, such as aphids. Lacewing larvae,

Earwig trap
An inverted flower pot filled with dried grass and placed over a stake attracts earwigs. Examine the pot and remove pests daily.

Bird deterrent
Homemade scarecrows are easily constructed with a little imagination and can be useful to deter birds from crops.

CONTROLLING SLUGS AND SNAILS

Gardeners who prefer not to use slug pellets can try various alternative methods of control. Do not underestimate the value of picking the pests off individually, especially when several pairs of hands are available to help. Slugs and snails are most active at night, and can be readily spotted by flashlight, especially on a damp evening. Gather up the pests and kill them by dropping in a solution of soapy water.

■ Apply an iron phosphate bait to the soil surface around plants. It kills the slugs but is nontoxic to people and pets.

■ Lure slugs and snails into hollowed-out grapefruit or orange halves placed open-side downward, on stones just above the ground. Slugs and snails attracted by the citrus scent will move under the fruit skin and are likely to remain there, until morning at least. They can then be drowned in soapy water.

■ Fill a jar halfway with beer or milk and almost sink it in the ground. The rim should be about ¹⁄₂in (1cm) above the surface to prevent useful predators, such as ground beetles, from falling in. The smell of the beer or milk will attract slugs and snails, which should fall in and drown. Specially designed slug "traps" are available from garden centers.

■ Create a wide, physical barrier of a coarse material, such as sand, grit, wood ash, soot, pine needles, or broken eggshells, around special plants. These can sometimes deter slugs and snails from crossing if they are not bridged by vegetation.

■ Cover or surround vulnerable seedlings and small plants using plastic bottles that have had their tops and bottoms cut off. Press the bottles into the soil so that they encircle individual plants.

■ Place diatomaceous earth, or copper bands, as a barrier around plants that need protection. However, such barriers are less effective in wet conditions, when pests are most active, and if bridged by leaves or soil.

too, have a voracious appetite for aphids, and they can be encouraged by planting flowers, such as pot marigolds (*Calendula*), and the provision of a nesting box in which they can overwinter. Wasps, whose activities might damage some plants, can still help the gardener by preying on other insect pests. Ground beetles are voracious consumers of many pest species.

Companion planting
Certain companion plants grown in association with a crop may help to reduce pest attack. For example, some strong-smelling herbs, such as, mint and garlic may repel pests that are attracted to plants by smell, keeping them away from nearby plants. Deliberate planting of host plants may deflect pests away from other plants or attract predators to feed on the pests: nasturtiums (*Tropaeolum*) are susceptible to aphids, so plant French marigolds (*Tagetes patula*) nearby as these attract flower flies, which have larvae that feed on the aphids.

Traps, barriers, and repellents
These work by stopping pests from getting near plants. Many can be constructed from everyday items. Earwigs may be trapped in inverted flower pots, and wireworms in old potatoes or carrots speared with a stick and buried. In the greenhouse, saucers of water under bench legs will foil ants and pillbugs. Pillbugs are not in themselves pests of established plants, but partial to delicate seedlings. Greenhouse whiteflies, being attracted to the color yellow, may be caught on strips of yellow plastic covered in petroleum jelly or commercial sticky product. Place these near the top of plants and move them up as the plants grow. Introduce biological controls (see opposite) quickly if an infestation is found.

Pheromone traps can be purchased from some garden centers and by mail order. They release the chemicals used by specific insects, such as the codling moth, to attract a mate. The trap captures the males by luring them onto a sticky sheet, which reduces the mating success of the remaining females. Such traps also allow gardeners to monitor infestation levels, and determine whether and when further control methods are needed.

Traps and barriers can be useful to warn of significant numbers of slugs and snails (see "Controlling slugs and snails," left). Larger barriers, from row covers to fruit cages, can be erected around and over plants to deter winged insects,

Companion planting
French marigolds (*Tagetes patula*) often attract flower flies, which feed on aphids that may attack nearby plants. The root secretions of these marigolds can reduce root-knot nematodes, a common pest in hot regions and occasionally in greenhouses.

such as carrot rust fly and cabbage maggot fly, as well as birds, rabbits, and deer. Sticky bands stop pests from climbing up trees and pots, and protective collars fashioned from carpet or carpet pad, will prevent female cabbage root flies from laying their eggs around young brassica plants (see p.656).

Repellents, such as garlic sprays or humming tapes, are often used to protect plants against cats, deer, and birds, which may be encouraged to move or feed elsewhere. However, animals have varying sensitivity to sounds and while bird-scaring devices and repellent sprays may work initially, they need to be changed frequently as the animals become familiar with them.

Acceptable organic treatments
Several effective insecticides and fungicides originate from natural sources; pyrethrum, for example, is derived from the pyrethrum daisy. Other organic treatments are fatty acids and plant oils, and these may be obtained from garden centers as ready-made powders or liquid sprays. Most are effective only on direct contact or for short duration, which necessitates regular and thorough applications.

Organically "acceptable" insecticides are nonselective and may kill nontarget insects as well as the pests for which they are intended. Their short-lived efficacy does, however, make them less likely to kill nonpest organisms, such as lady beetles.

Wasp traps
A jar containing water and honey in a tree will trap wasps and provide some relief for a small area. The jar should be covered with paper with small holes punched in it.

Pheremone traps
Hang a pheromone trap in apple and pear trees in late spring. It will catch male codling moths by using the scent of the female moth and help reduce mating opportunities.

Pest	Biological Control
Aphids	Fly larva predators (*Aphidoletes aphidimyza*)
Caterpillars	Bacterial disease (*Bacillus thuringiensis*)
White grubs	Pathogenic nematode (*Heterorhabditis megidis*)
Fungus gnats larvae	Predatory mites (*Hypoaspis miles*)
Mealybugs	Ladybugs (*Cryptolaemus montrouzieri*)
Spider mites	Predatory mites (*Phytoseiulus persimilis*)
Soft scale insects	Parasitic wasp *Metaphycus helvolus*
Thrips	Predatory mites (*Amblyseius* spp.)
Leafhoppers	Fungal disease (*Beauveria bassiana*)
Black vine weevil grubs	Pathogenic nematode (*Heterorhabditis megidis*)
Whitefly	Parasitic wasp *Encarsia formosa*

Biological control

Some of the most troublesome pests, especially spider mites, whiteflies, and many caterpillar pests, can be dealt with very effectively using biological controls. The term biological control describes the limiting of pest damage by the deliberate introduction of natural enemies, such as predators, parasites, or diseases. Biological controls are living organisms, usually nematodes or small predator insects or mites, which have no detrimental effects on nontarget species. They are bred and supplied under controlled conditions, and because they are alive, they must be introduced onto your plants or into the soil as soon as they have been obtained. These tiny creatures can prey on their host or target pest during a specific stage of its development, or they

Biological control at work
Minute *Encarsia formosa* wasps attack and parasitize whitefly larvae, causing them to blacken and eventually die. This is an effective form of control in a greenhouse.

may spread disease among them. For example, the microscopic pathogenic nematode *Steinernema carpocapsae* is watered into the soil, where it infects pests including cutworms, onion maggots, and sod webworms with a fatal disease, while the predatory mite *Phytoseiulus persimilis* feeds on the eggs, nymphs, and mature forms of spider mite. Not all pests and diseases can yet be countered by appropriate biological controls; however, producers are developing improved strains, better delivery methods, and new organisms.

Most of the biological controls require daytime temperatures of at least 70°F (21°C) and good light intensity in order to breed faster than the pests. They can therefore be introduced into a heated greenhouse earlier than an unheated one or the open ground. Another key to successful use is to ensure that the pest has been correctly identified and therefore the appropriate specific control measures adopted. If you are not sure what pests you have, see pp.650–673 for a visual guide and descriptions of symptoms.

Biological controls may be obtained from mail-order specialty suppliers. These generally advertise in gardening publications and on the internet. Good garden centers will also be able to provide advice on where to buy useful controls.

Greenhouse controls
Some biological controls are suitable for use only in the greenhouse or conservatory. Introduce the control before plants are heavily infested, because it may be a number of weeks before it becomes effective. Restrict the use of pesticides, since most are harmful to biological controls. The least harmful are insecticidal soaps and plant oils, which control a range of small insects and mites.

Open-garden biological controls
Use of biological controls is less predictable in the relatively uncontrolled conditions of the open garden, especially if pesticides are also used, because they may kill the biocontrols as well as the pests. Of the controls listed in the table (above), only those for white grubs, caterpillars, black vine weevil, and leafhoppers are suitable for use in the open garden.

Chemical control

Chemical control is the term used to describe the action of destroying plant pests and diseases by applying synthetic substances to plants or soil. As the widespread environmental impact of the use of pesticides is better understood, responsible gardeners are shifting to organic control methods and minimizing their reliance on synthetic pesticides. Seek advice on nontoxic and organic alternatives before choosing to apply a chemical control product.

Pesticides and fungicides
Most pesticides and fungicides either work by being brought into contact with the pest or disease organisms, or are systemic.

Contact pesticides kill pests when the pests crawl over a treated surface or when they are directly hit by the chemical (when sprayed, for example). Contact fungicides may kill germinating fungal spores and prevent further infection, but they have little effect on established fungal growths.

Systemic chemicals are absorbed into the plant tissues and are sometimes transported by the sap stream throughout the entire plant. Fungicides of this type kill fungi in the plant tissues. Systemic pesticides are predominantly used against certain sap-sucking pests but will also control some pests that have chewing mouthparts, such as black

---

NON-NATIVE PESTS AND DISEASES

Canada is always under threat from pests, diseases, and invasive plant species not native to this country. While the Canada Border Inspection Agency prevents the importation of known problems, insects can fly across the border or be carried on returning vehicles, disease spores can float across on the wind, and invasive plants seeds can also arrive by a variety of routes.

Once identified, local and provincial governments bring into effect measures to try and limit the spread of the problem. For example, the presence of the emerald ash borer (*Agrilus planipennis*), which has spread into Ontario from an initial outbreak in New York State, has resulted in a ban on the movement and use of firewood in Ontario Parks, and the culling of thousands of ash trees in the infected areas. Norway maple, (*Acer platanoides*), originally introduced as an ornamental tree, is now invading woodland, and its use should be discouraged.

USING PESTICIDES SAFELY

Following the instructions precisely—that is, only in the way and for the purpose that the manufacturer describes—is essential to minimize risks and maximize effectiveness of sprays, whether organic or synthetic. It is illegal for gardeners to use pesticides other than in accordance with the instructions. Always take the following precautions:

- think before you spray: is it really necessary, or could you use cultural or biological controls instead?
- choose the product carefully—make sure it is the right one for the job.
- apply the preparation at the rate and frequency stated on the label.
- never use any type of pesticide on plants in ponds.
- never mix different chemicals unless the manufacturer recommends this.
- always observe any suggested precautions.
- always spray when the wind is still, or almost still, to avoid damaging adjacent plants.
- always spray in the evening, when there are fewer bees and flower flies around.
- do not spray on hot, sunny days; such weather increases the risk of scorching plants.
- avoid contact with the skin and eyes by wearing goggles, rubber gloves, and long-sleeved clothing.
- do not inhale dusts or sprays.
- make sure that the product does not drift into other people's gardens.
- keep pets and children away during treatment.
- never eat, drink, or smoke when applying a pesticide.
- dispose of any excess according to label instructions; clean equipment thoroughly.
- do not use equipment for anything other than pest-control substances.
- store products out of reach of children and animals.
- store chemicals in their original containers with their original labels, and keep any instructions with them.

Garden safety
Make sure that watering cans used for watering plants are kept completely separate from those used for herbicides.

Chemical spray
Some products can be bought ready mixed in small quantities; they cost more but avoid the need to handle concentrated chemicals.

Formulation of chemical preparations

The active ingredient of a chemical preparation kills the organism, and the way in which a preparation has been formulated determines its efficacy and use. Pesticides and fungicides are available as concentrated liquids, dusts, powders (with which a surfactant may be incorporated to ensure thorough penetration of the active ingredient), baits, and ready-to-use diluted liquids. These are formulated for maximum effectiveness and safety, for gardeners and also for the environment.

Phytotoxicity

A few plants suffer adverse reactions to fungicides and insecticides. This is known as phytotoxicity. The manufacturer's instructions often list those species that should not be treated. However, such lists cannot be complete, because

vine weevil grubs and some beetles and caterpillars. Thorough spraying of affected plants, especially on the undersides of leaves, is essential if these pesticides are to work effectively.

Pesticide-resistant strains can occur, particularly with persistent greenhouse pests, such as

whiteflies and spider mites. Fungi that are frequently treated with systemic fungicides may also develop strains that are resistant to treatment. Development of pesticide resistance is just another reason to seek out alternative methods of control, such as biological controls (see p.643) and pest barriers.

the reaction of many ornamental plants to certain synthetic and naturally-derived pesticides and fungicides may be unknown. If in doubt about whether a certain product is suitable, first test the fungicide or pesticide on a small area of the plant before undertaking treatment of the whole plant. Wait five to seven days before undertaking treatment of the whole plant if no adverse reaction is seen.

Various other factors, including the stage of growth and the environmental conditions surrounding the plant, can increase the likelihood of a plant being damaged by pesticide or fungicide treatments. For example, young seedlings, cuttings, and flower petals are much more sensitive than mature foliage to variations in the growing conditions, and may therefore be adversely affected by the application of some treatments. Similarly, it is best to avoid treating plants that are suffering any stress.

In order to avoid problems with side effects on plants, never spray when they are in bright sunlight, or when they are either dry at the roots or have been exposed to unusually high or low temperatures.

COMMON GARDEN PEST CONTROL PRODUCTS

Bacillus thuringiensis (BT) Various forms of this bacterium kill a variety of common garden pests, including chewing caterpillars, fungus gnat larvae, and some types of beetle grubs. Be sure to buy the correct strain for the pest to be controlled. Some pests have developed resistance to this control.

Beauveria bassiana This product is a naturally occurring fungus that can infect and kill a variety of pests when applied as a spray. Applications can help fight aphids, chinch bugs, cutworms, leafhoppers, and other pests.

Iron phosphate A natural pelleted bait for controlling slugs and snails. Also acts as a natural iron fertilizer. Nontoxic to people and pets.

Kaolin Clay A natural clay product mixed with water and sprayed on plants to deter egg-laying and feeding of many pests, including codling moth, plum curculio, cucumber beetles, flea beetles, and Japanese beetles. Must be reapplied after rain for continued effectiveness

Spinosad A natural insecticide derived from a bacterium, this product is toxic to caterpillars, thrips, sawfly larvae, and some

other pests. It is also toxic to bees and beneficial insects.

Insecticidal soaps These fatty-acid based products are effective against a wide range of small pests, including aphids, whiteflies, spider mites, thrips, scale insects, and mealybugs. They will also kill many types of beneficial insects, so limit sprays to plants that are infested.

Plant oil sprays Extracted from plants, including aromatic herbs and rapeseed. Available as sprays for use against a similar range of pests as insecticidal soap. Formulations are also available that act as herbicides.

Horticultural oil Spray for deciduous fruit trees and bushes during the dormant months to control overwintering eggs of aphids, mussel scale, and other pests. Also available in a growing season dilution for use against a variety of pests.

Citrus oil sprays These products are toxic to various types of insects including aphids, mites, and wasps. They are labeled for use on ornamentals only, not food crops.

Pyrethrum/pyrethrins Extracted from the flowers of *Pyrethrum cinerariifolium*. Available as sprays and dusts for controlling aphids,

whiteflies, leafhoppers, ants, small caterpillars, thrips, and other small insects.

Neem Extracted from seeds of the neem tree, this is effective as an insecticide to fight aphids, leafminers, mealybugs, whiteflies, and other pests. Breaks down quickly, so repeat applications may be needed.

Potassium bicarbonate Also called baking soda spray, this product is effective at preventing fungal diseases, including anthracnose, black spot, and powdery mildew. The spray can damage leaves of some types of plants, so test the spray on a small area of foliage first.

Bacillus subtilis A biocontrol product containing a bacterium that acts to help prevent fungal diseases by suppressing the activity of harmful fungi. Can help prevent downy mildew, fire blight, powdery mildew, and other diseases. Requires reapplication on a regular basis.

Copper
Copper products have been used for centuries and help control a wide range of bacterial and fungal diseases, but they are toxic and should be used as a last resort only.

UNDERSTANDING PRODUCT LABELS

All pesticides sold in Canada are registered by Health Canada, and there are particular requirements for the product labels. Pesticide manufacturers are required to list a product's active ingredients on product labels. Labels also specify on which types of plants a product may be applied, and for control of which specific pests or diseases. Special precautions will also be given (for example, avoid breathing vapor or spray mist), and instructions for proper disposal of the product. There will also be first aid information in case of poisoning, and a description of any adverse symptoms that may occur.

Be sure to read labels carefully and make sure you are applying the product correctly for a listed use. Many synthetic insecticides and fungicides are labeled for use only by people who are licensed pesticide applicators (which involves taking training courses and passing an exam).

Weeds and lawn weeds

Weeds are, quite simply, plants that grow where they are not wanted. They have important features in common: they are usually fast-growing and invasive, competing with cultivated plants for food and water; they are able to grow in almost any soil or site; and they often show a marked resistance to control. Weeds may occur in almost any part of the yard. Cultivated plants may be placed in the weed category in certain circumstances, depending on their habit. If they prove too invasive for their site and overwhelm their neighbors, or if they self-seed freely throughout the landscape, they may properly be classified as "weeds."

Categorizing weeds

Annual weeds complete their entire life cycle within one year. They set seed that germinates freely; occasionally, as in the case of groundsel (*Senecio vulgaris*), they may even produce several generations in just one season. It is very important, therefore, to remove annuals at the seedling stage, before they are able to produce seed.

Perennial weeds, by contrast, survive from year to year. Some grow readily from seed, like annuals, but more usually persist by means of various storage organs, such as rhizomes, bulbs, bulbils, tubers, and thick taproots. Many perennials are able to proliferate because of poor cultivation techniques that leave small pieces of rhizome or root in the soil when digging or rototilling. These then produce new plants.

Controlling weeds

Weeds may be controlled in two main ways: they may either be discouraged from growing by the use of good, basic gardening techniques; or they may be removed by manual, mechanical, or chemical means.

The choice of how to remove different weeds depends on various factors: the habit of the plants themselves, the preference of the gardener, and the location of the weeds—whether in borders, lawns, paths, or neglected sites.

Annual weeds

In common with other annual plants, annual weeds grow, flower, set seed, and die all within one growing season. They occur most frequently in regularly cultivated areas, such as vegetable gardens or annual borders, where frequent digging deters perennial kinds.

Their strong, rapid growth makes them troublesome among plants raised from seed *in situ* because they smother slower-growing plants and reduce the yields of others by competing for moisture, nutrients, space, and light.

Garden invader
Some groundcovers can be weedy and hard to eradicate once they get a foothold, like this periwinkle (*Vinca minor*). The trailing stems root wherever they touch the soil.

Aquatic thug
Garden ponds are an ideal environment for the yellow flag iris (*Iris pseudacorus*), which thrives in very wet conditions and can outcompete other plants in the ecosystem.

The need for control

It is important to destroy annual weeds before they produce seeds, because many seeds are small, light, readily wind-borne, and quick to germinate. Quick-maturing species like shepherd's purse (*Capsella bursa-pastoris*) may produce several generations in a single season. Common chickweed (*Stellaria media*) smothers nearby plants and is another weed that should be controlled at the seedling stage. Its seeds start to germinate in the the fall and continue growing in a mild winter to form dense mats.

Many seeds may be buried once they are shed, and lie dormant for many years until they are brought to the surface during site or crop cultivation. The weeds then germinate and grow rapidly. If a site is heavily infested with weeds, it should be cultivated regularly when it is crop-free in order to kill germinating seedlings.

Annual weeds may be controlled either by hand, mechanically, or by chemical means (see "Preventing weeds," p.646).

COMMON ANNUAL AND BIENNIAL WEEDS

Groundsel
(*Senecio vulgaris*)

Dward nettle
(*Urtica urens*)

Shepherd's purse
(*Capsella bursa-pastoris*)

Catchweed bedstraw
(*Galium aparine*)

Hairy bittercress
(*Cardamine hirsuta*)

Annual bluegrass
(*Poa annua*)

Tansy ragwort
(*Senecio jacobaea*)

Common chickweed
(*Stellaria media*)

Perennial weeds

Perennial weeds persist from year to year, surviving and resting through winter cold and summer heat by storing food reserves in fleshy roots, bulbs, rhizomes, or tubers.

They may be divided into two groups: herbaceous kinds and woody-stemmed kinds. Herbaceous perennials die back to ground level in the fall. They survive the winter by storing food in their roots and then reappear in spring. Examples are the perennial stinging nettle (*Urtica dioica*), broadleaf dock (*Rumex obtusifolius*), and field bindweed (*Convolvulus arvensis*). Also included in this group are the stemless herbaceous perennials that have leaves arising directly from their roots or rhizomes, for example, dandelion (*Taraxacum officinale*) and goutweed (*Aegopodium podagraria*).

Woody-stemmed perennials, such as Norway maple (*Acer platanoides*) and *Rosa multiflora*, survive the winter by storing food in stems and branches. The woody-stemmed, evergreen, English ivy (*Hedera helix*) can also be an invasive weed.

The need for control

Perennial weeds have underground fleshy roots, rhizomes, and other storage organs that are not easily controlled. Hoeing and digging, along with machine cultivation, tend to break the roots and rhizomes into sections without killing them; many survive to grow and increase

the problem. With most perennial weeds, use of long-term mulches or weedkillers is the most effective approach.

Preventing weeds

Both annual and perennial weeds may be prevented from establishing in various ways. This will avoid the need for tedious weeding later on, especially if you adopt methods that rely on the principle of depriving light from the soil surface. Without light, plants cannot grow.

Before planting, clear the site of all weeds. This can be done either by hand, with a hoe or similar tool, or with a rototiller or other cultivator. Another approach, which requires weeks or months, but can be very effective, is to cover the ground with an impermeable layer, such as sturdy black plastic sheeting, heavy cardboard weighted down with an organic mulch, rocks, lumber, or old natural-fiber carpeting. Using herbicides is also an option, especially to eliminate weeds that are hazardous to handle, such as poison ivy (*Rhus radican*) or wild parsnip (*Pastinaca sativa*). Weeds are often difficult to eradicate from among established plants, which may need to be lifted and the weeds extracted from the root system.

Neutralizing very acidic soils with lime will deter some lawn weeds, as well as many kinds of moss, which thrive where the soil is acidic.

Cultivating healthy plants

Vigorous, healthy plants are able to compete more effectively with weeds than poor, weak specimens. Plants with spreading foliage and habit, such as *Pachysandra*, provide a dark cover over the soil that discourages weed germination under the canopy.

Some vegetable crops, for example, potatoes, compete well with annual weeds and may be grown to help maintain clean ground for a subsequent crop (see GROWING VEGETABLES, "Crop rotation," p.498).

Mulch materials

Covering the soil with black plastic mulch after planting prevents annual weeds from establishing. Such materials can also be effective in suppressing perennial weeds: horsetail (*Equisetum arvense*) and field bindweed (*Convolvulus arvensis*) are both less likely to grow if the area is left undisturbed for one or two growing seasons. There are also paper-based mulches that are generally permeable, allowing water and nutrients to pass through to the roots. Cover plastic mulch with a bark mulch to improve its appearance. Black plastic mulch is particularly useful in fruit and vegetable gardens; make slits in it through which the crops can grow.

In early spring, apply a mulch 2–3in (5–8cm) thick of weed-free, organic material, such as straw or bark chips, to stop weed seeds

from germinating and to smother weed seedlings. Do not use garden compost or insufficiently rotted manure; they often contain weed seeds.

Established perennial weeds may grow through the mulch but, because they tend to root into the loose material, they are easy to remove.

Groundcover plants and grassing down borders

Some plants grow in dense carpets that suppress the germination of weed seeds. They are useful for areas where, because of shade, or very wet or dry soil, weeds thrive. Choose groundcover plants carefully—some are invasive (see PERENNIALS FOR GROUNDCOVER, p.180).

Some persistent perennial weeds, such as horsetail (*Equisetum arvense*) and oxalis (*Oxalis corymbosa* and *O. latifolia*), may resist repeated attempts to eradicate them with weedkiller or to dig them out. An alternative approach is to grass down any badly infested borders and maintain them as close-mown turf for several years. Given time, this treatment will generally eliminate most of the infestation of persistent perennial weeds.

Controlling weeds

Once weeds are present, they may be eradicated in one of three ways: hand-weeding, mechanical control, and chemical control. There are

COMMON PERENNIAL WEEDS

Hedge bindweed
(*Calystygia sepium*)

Canada thistle
(*Cirsium arvense*)

Oxalis
(*Oxalis corniculata, O. corymbosa, and O. latifolia*)

Perennial stinging nettle
(*Urtica dioica*)

Dandelion
(*Taraxacum officinale*)

Goutweed
(*Aegopodium podagraria*)

Dock
(*Rumex* spp.)

Creeping buttercup
(*Ranunculus repens*)

three different types of weedkiller: those that act on the leaves, those that act on the soil, and those that act on specific types of plant.

Hand-weeding, hoeing, and digging are often the only practical ways of removing weeds in flower beds, the vegetable garden, and small patches of ground where weedkillers cannot be used safely without risk of harming nearby garden or crop plants. Small patches of perennial weeds, such as goutweed and quackgrass, may be forked out, but great care must be taken not to leave in the soil any sections of rhizomes, roots, or bulbils that will grow again. Check a month or so later and remove any regrowth.

Hand-weed or hoe in dry weather, if possible, so that the weeds shrivel and die rapidly. In wet weather, remove uprooted weeds from the site to prevent them from rooting back into the soil. Hoe only lightly around cultivated plants to prevent their surface roots from being damaged.

Commercial gardeners often use rotary cultivators with hoeing or cultivating attachments for annual weed control between rows of vegetables, but they may be unsuitable for perennials—they simply cut the rhizomes of weeds, such as bindweed and quackgrass, into many pieces that will continue to grow as new plants. Wherever possible, avoid tilling areas where persistent perennial weeds are established.

Weedkillers

Postemergent weedkillers, or leaf-acting products, enter the weeds through leaves or green stems and are applied with a sprayer or watering can and fine nozzle or dribble bar. There are two different types: systemic and contact. The first acts by translocation, moving from the leaves to the roots, and so destroys both annual and perennial weeds. For best effect the weeds should be in vigorous growth.

The second type works by contact killing only by direct touch. They destroy annual weeds and the green leaves and stems of perennial weeds, although not the roots of perennials, which will usually regrow strongly. Some weedkillers act through both the leaves and the roots.

Soil-acting products are applied to the soil and are absorbed by growing weeds. They move to the parts above ground, killing the weeds by interfering with their metabolism. They remain active in the soil, sometimes for months, killing weeds as the seeds germinate. They kill established annual weeds and may also kill or suppress many established perennial weeds. When planning to use areas that have been treated with soil-acting weedkillers, check the manufacturer's literature for details of residual activity and do not sow or plant anything until the recommended period has elapsed.

Selective weedkillers will kill broadleaved weeds but not narrow-leaved grasses, provided they are applied at the correct rate. They can just as easily kill your garden plants, so apply carefully.

Range of chemicals

Over time the range of weedkillers available to gardeners changes—a new product is introduced or an existing one withdrawn. When buying weedkillers, always check within the range currently available that the products can be used safely and effectively in the situations where weeds are troublesome.

Glyphosate (translocated, foliage-acting) is one of the most useful weedkillers for controlling perennial weeds. It is a foliage-acting weedkiller that moves down to the roots, killing or strongly checking even the most difficult weeds. It is not selective and should be kept away from all garden plants, especially raspberries, roses, and other suckering woody plants.

Organic weedkillers

Some weedkillers based on natural products, such as acetic acid (vinegar), pelargonic acid, and fatty acids (herbicidal soap) are now offered to control weeds. They are based on natural materials, so these controls are more acceptable to some gardeners than synthetic chemicals. These work by contact action, and they may need to be reapplied more frequently.

USING WEEDKILLERS SAFELY

Care must always be taken when applying weedkillers:
■ Wear protective clothing, for example, rubber gloves and long pants and a shirt with long sleeves, when mixing and applying weedkillers.
■ do not apply weedkillers in windy conditions when there is a risk of spray being blown across to nearby plants, which may suffer serious damage.
■ use only for appropriate purposes as recommended on the product label, for example, do not use a path weedkiller to keep down weeds in a rose bed.
■ always dilute soluble weedkillers according to the manufacturer's instructions.
■ always apply weedkillers at the recommended rates on the labels.
■ always keep in original containers and make sure that the labels are well secured to the containers so that contents are known and no errors in usage occur.
■ never store diluted weedkillers for future use.
■ store away out of reach of children and animals, preferably in a securely locked cupboard in a garage, workshop, or shed.

Bramble
(*Rubus* spp.)

Lesser celandine
(*Ranunculus ficaria*)

Japanese knotweed
(*Fallopia japonica*)

Field bindweed
(*Convulvulus arvensis*)

Horsetail
(*Equisetum arvense*)

Quackgrass
(*Elymus repens*)

Willow herb
(*Epilobium* spp.)

OTHER PERENNIAL WEEDS

Virgina buttonweed (*Diodia virginiana*)
Oldfield cinquefoil (*Potentilla simplex*)
Creeping bellflower (*Campanula rapunculoides*)
Ground ivy (*Glechoma hederacea*)
Horsenettle (*Solanum carolinense*)
Blue lettuce (*Lactuca pulchella*)
Milkweed (*Asclepias syriaca*)
Broadleaf plantain (*Plantago major*)
Pokeweed (*Phytolacca americana*)

Lawn weeds

Various perennial weeds can be troublesome in lawns. Their common survival factor is their ability to grow and thrive in the adverse conditions of short, regularly mown grass. They usually originate from seeds carried by the wind or by birds. Once lawn weeds have germinated, most are then rapidly spread by the action of mowing and early treatment is necessary if they are to be eradicated.

Among the most troublesome lawn weeds are: annual bluegrass (*Poa annua*), crabgrass, (*Digitaria sanguinalis*), dandelion (*Taraxacum officinale*), creeping Charlie (*Glechoma hederacea*), and plantains (*Plantago* spp.). These persistent weeds seldom respond to treatment by lawn weedkillers, and need other forms of treatment.

In lawns where the grass is too sparse to offer adequate competition, moss may also become a problem.

Preventing weeds and moss

Good lawn care is an effective preventive measure. The presence of numerous weeds in a lawn usually indicates that the grass is not growing sufficiently vigorously to prevent weeds from establishing. Lack of regular feeding and drought are among the most common reasons for poor growth. Soil compaction and mowing the grass too closely and too regularly may also lead to the spread of moss. For further details on lawn care, see THE LAWN, "Routine care," pp.395–400. Coarser weed grasses such as barnyard grass (*Echinochloa crusgalli*), may remain a problem, and clumps may need to be removed and the cleared patch returfed or reseeded.

Raking before mowing and lifting creeping stems may help to check the spread of creeping weeds, such as trefoils (*Trifolium* spp.) and creeping Charlie (*Glechoma hederacea*), if the grass is mown right afterward and the clippings picked up by the mower.

Moss may be killed with moss control preparations or lawn sand. However, unless the original conditions that encouraged the moss are identified and corrected, the problem will usually recur. The best course of action may be to encourage the moss as a lawn alternative instead.

Removing weeds

There are two main ways of treating lawn weeds, depending on the severity of the problem. They may be removed by hand or treated with an appropriate weedkiller.

Hand-weeding is an effective method of removing a few, rosetted, scattered weeds such as daisy weed (*Bellis perennis*), dandelion (*Taraxacum officinale*), and plantains (*Plantago* spp.). Use a hand fork to lift the weeds, then firm back any displaced turf.

Removing weeds with chemicals

Weedkillers intended specifically for lawns work by translocation—moving within the plant from the leaves to the roots—and the weeds begin to distort and shrivel within a few days of application. The chemicals are selective and do not harm lawn grasses at normal dilution rates, but do not use them on seedling grasses within six months of germination.

You should also avoid using lawn weedkillers on a newly laid turf, until one growing season has passed after laying.

Corn gluten meal

One effective and nontoxic way to combat lawn weeds is to apply corn gluten meal to the lawn. Corn gluten meal is a natural byproduct of the production of corn syrup. When spread lightly over the lawn it inhibits the germination of seeds. It can be quite effective for controlling crabgrass. As a secondary benefit, it is also a source

---

LAWN WEEDS

Slender speedwell
(*Veronica filiformis*)

Common white clover
(*Trifolium repens*)

Lesser yellow trefoil
(*Trifolium dubium*)

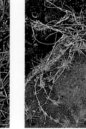

Pearlwort
(*Sagina procumbens*)

Sheep's sorrel
(*Rumex acetosella*)

Creeping buttercup
(*Ranunculus repens*)

Broadleaved plantain
(*Plantago major*)

Self-heal
(*Prunella vulgaris*)

Yarrow
(*Achillea millefolium*)

Common mouse-ear chickweed
(*Cerastium fontanum*)

Mouse-ear hawkweed
(*Pilosella officinarum*)

OTHER LAWN WEEDS

English daisy (*Bellis perennis*)
Large crabgrass (*Digitaria sanguinalis*)
Creeping charlie (*Glechoma hederacea*)
Prostrate knotweed (*Polygonum aviculare*)
Yellow nutsedge (*Cyperus esculentus*)
Narrow-leaved plantain (*Plantago lanceolata*)
Hoary plantain (*Plantago media*)
Annual bluegrass (*Poa annua*)
Dandelion (*Taraxacum officinale*)

of nitrogen, so applying it will green up your lawn as well. It is nontoxic, and is even used as an animal feed.

Corn gluten meal is available in powdered and pelleted forms, and it can be applied with a drop spreader. It can be most effective to apply it in early spring and again in late summer. The spring application will prevent the germination of annual and perennial weed seeds; the later application will prevent the germination of winter annual weeds. It may take up to four years of applications to check weed growth entirely. It is also helpful to combine the use of corn gluten meal with applications of compost or compost tea to strengthen lawn grasses, and mowing high to shade out existing weeds. Keep in mind that corn gluten meal suppresses the germination of all kinds of seeds, so if you plan to overseed your lawn or reseed patches, wait at least six weeks after applying corn gluten meal before sowing seed.

Buying and applying weedkillers

Lawn weedkillers are sold as a concentrated liquid and therefore need to be suitably diluted. They may also be obtained in the form of soluble powder, ready-to-use spray, aerosol, or in combination with liquid or granular lawn fertilizers. Feed the lawn at the start of the growing season, applying weedkiller two to three weeks later when grass and weeds are growing strongly. In the spring, creeping lawn grasses soon colonize any bare patches left as weeds shrivel and die. Great care should be taken when applying weedkillers (see the recommendations on p.647).

Wait two or three days after mowing before applying weedkiller, so that weeds have time to develop new leaf surfaces to absorb the chemicals. Do not mow grass for two or three days after spraying to allow time for the weedkiller to work down to the roots. Also, do not put grass clippings on the compost heap for the first few cuts after applying weedkiller (check label for details).

Some lawn weeds, such as daisy weeds, are killed by one or two applications of weedkiller; others, such as the trefoils, may need two or three applications, at four- to six-week intervals.

Where a weed shows no response to various weedkillers, remove it by hand. This will either mean removing and replacing infested areas of turf or, alternatively, feeding, scarifying, and aerating turf to strengthen it and weaken the weed.

Neglected sites

Different treatments need to be adopted according to how long the area has been neglected and how great a hold the weeds have taken. Sites that have been neglected for some time may take a season, or even longer, to clear for vegetable growing.

Short-term neglect

On sites that have been neglected for up to a year, most of the weeds are likely to be annuals. One option to clear annual weeds is with a weedkiller. But if you'd prefer to avoid using chemicals, you can clear the site by covering it for a few months with black plastic sheeting. For speedier results, a medium-power rototiller prepares the soil satisfactorily in dry spells with two to three cultivations at two-week intervals. Alternatively, planting a smothering crop of mustard, potatoes, or pumpkins can suppress weeds and clear the ground.

Winter clearance

If the site is being cleared during winter, remove overwintering top growth of annual weeds with a rotary mower. Then dig out any perennial weeds by hand, if possible, before cultivating the area. Clear neglected vegetable plots progressively, beginning at the warmer, sunnier end, where the earliest sowings of crops are to be made and the seedbeds sited.

Longer-term neglect

After a second year of neglect, perennial weeds will become well established, competing vigorously with annual weeds. If the site remains neglected for a further year, by the end of the third growing season, the weed population will usually be largely, or entirely, strong-growing perennial weeds. Badly infested sites are difficult to clear by hand or by use of a rototiller (the latter may do no more than turn the weeds back into the soil again). Control can be achieved with translocated weedkillers, allowing a full growing season for treatment to take effect.

Cutting down weeds

If beginning clearance in spring, cut down weeds with woody stems, for example, brambles or multiflora rose, to within 12–18in (30–45cm)

Weed-infested ponds
In the absence of herbicides, control weeds, such as azolla and duckweed, by dragging, raking, or netting. Use bags of barley or lavender straw to treat algae.

from the ground, and then treat the stumps with glyphosate products with a recommendation on the label for stump treatment.

To remove weeds from a neglected area without weedkillers, cover the site with opaque plastic sheeting and leave for one, ideally two, growing seasons. After this, cultivation will be relatively easy, but woody stumps may need to be grubbed out.

Deep digging is the traditional means of clearing neglected ground, but is laborious for all but small areas. For speedier results, a high power rototiller makes the soil workable in dry spells in summer, and repeated rotavation can eliminate many weeds. However, follow-up action, either by cultivation or covering with opaque sheets, may be necessary the following year.

Summer spraying

Another method is to cut the weeds back in spring and then allow them to grow unchecked until midsummer; then spray the site with glyphosate, which acts more effectively on the vigorous young growth stimulated by the spring cut. It is a translocated weedkiller, and it usually takes three to four weeks to show any effect; it leaves no active residues in the soil and as soon as weeds are dead, the site can be cultivated and planted.

Persistent weeds, such as horsetail and bindweed, may need subsequent spot-treatment, again with glyphosate, possibly for a further two or three growing seasons, in order to control them fully.

Uncultivated ground

Where previously cultivated land is to be left uncultivated, and is free from perennial weeds, it can be kept clear by regular light cultivations, at intervals throughout the year, with a hoe or with a mechanical tool, such as a rotary cultivator. Alternatively, at intervals, developing weed seedlings can be killed by application of glyphosate.

If perennial weeds are infesting the site, let them grow untreated until midsummer, then spray them with glyphosate.

Weeds in cracks and crevices

Weeds in the cracks in paths and brickwork are hard to remove by hand, so chemical control is normally required.

In early spring, apply a commercial path weedkiller. Such weedkillers are mixtures of contact and soil-acting chemicals, the latter usually remaining active in the soil for several months. They may also include a foliage-acting, translocated herbicide to deal with any established perennial weeds not usually controlled by the low-strength, soil-acting chemicals in these mixtures.

Perennial weeds growing in paths may be spot-treated or sprayed with vinegar-based herbicides. If there is regrowth, repeat applications will be needed. Pouring boiling water over weeds in paths can also be effective.

Visual guide to plant problems

Use these pages to help identify the cause or causes of damage to plants in your garden

LEAF

Slugs under leaves *see p.669*

Slug damage *see p.669*

Pillbug *see p.670*

Leaf cutting bees *see p.663*

Flea beetles *see p.660*

Black vine weevil damage *see p.655*

Black vine weevil *see p.655*

Viburnum beetle *see p.672*

Red lily beetle *see p.667*

Earwigs *see p.659*

Sawfly larvae *see p.668*

Asparagus beetle *see p.654*

Cabbage caterpillars *see p.656*

Whiteflies *see p.673*

White rust *see p.673*

Powdery mildew *see p.667*

Millipedes *see p.664*

Aphids on stem *see Aphids, p.654*

Leafhoppers *see p.663*

Pear slugs *see p.665*

Psyllids *see p.667*

Rust *see p.668*

Leafminer damage *see p.663*

Viruses *see p.672*

Silver leaf *see p.669*

Bacterial leaf spots/ blotches *see p.655*

Leaf and bud nematodes *see p.663*

Corky scab *see p.658*

Shothole *see Blossom blast, p.655*

Scale insects *see p.669*

Scab *see p.668*

Lily leaf blight *see p.663*

Plant bugs *see p.666*

Tulip fire *see p.672*

Fungal leaf spots *see p.660*

Mealybugs *see p.664*

Fire blight *see p.660*

Insecticide/fungicide damage *see p.662*

Contact weedkiller damage *see p.672*

Spider mites *see p.670*

High temperature and scorch *see p.662*

Drought *see p.659*

Gall midges
see p.661

Potassium deficiency
see p.667

Magnesium deficiency
see p.664

Phosphate deficiency
see p.666

FLOWER

Plant bugs
see p.666

Daylily gall midge
see p.659

Gall midges
see p.661

Edema
see p.659

Peach leaf curl
see p.665

Hellebore leaf spot
see p.662

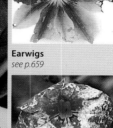

Earwigs
see p.659

Gall mites
see p.661

Nitrogen deficiency
see p.664

Gall wasps/cynipid wasps *see p.661*

Smuts
see p.670

Rhododendron bud blight *see p.668*

Thrips
see p.671

Azalea gall
see p.655

Rust
see Tree rust, p.672

Camellia leaf gall
see p.657

Hellebore black death
see p.662

Viruses
see p.672

Petal blight
see p.666

Leek moth
see p.663

Nematodes
see p.664

Low temperatures
see p.664

Late blight
see p.663

Tomato leaf mold
see p.672

Drought
see p.659

Tulip fire
see p.672

Leafrollers
see p.663

Irregular water supply
see p.662

Leafroller
see p.663

Pollen beetles
see p.666

Proliferation
see p.667

Clubroot
see p.657

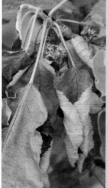

Tent caterpillar
see p.671

Phytoplasmas
see p.666

Andromeda lacebug
see p.654

Hormone weedkiller damage *see p.673*

Winter moth catepillars
see p.673

Boxwood blight
see p.656

Blossom blight
see p.656

Gray mold/*Botrytis*
see p.661

652

FRUIT, BERRY, AND SEED

Scab
see p.668

European apple sawfly
see p.659

Bird damage
see p.655

Gray mold/*Botrytis***
see p.661

Raspberry fruitworm
see p.667

**Calcium deficiency
(bitter pit)** see p.656

Brown rot
see p.656

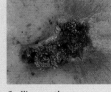
Oriental fruit moth
see p.665

Blossom end rot
see *Calcium deficiency p.656*

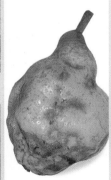
Codling moth
see p.657

Viruses
see p.672

Shanking of grapes
see p.669

Irregular water supply
see p.662

Thrips
see p.671

Pea moth
see p.665

Late blight
see p.663

High temperatures/scorch
see p.662

Powdery mildew
see p.667

ROOT, TUBER, BULB, CORM, AND RHIZOME

Damping off
see p.658

Waterlogging
see p.672

Foot and root rots
see p.660

Clubroot
see p.657

White grubs
see p.673

Storage rot
see p.671

European crane fly larvae
see p.660

Parsnip canker
see p.665

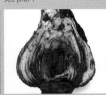
Wireworms
see p.673

Crown rot
see p.658

Phytophthora root rot
see p.666

Iris soft rot
see p.662

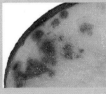
Internal rust spot
see p.662

Onion neck rot
see p.665

Crown gall
see p.658

Slugs
see p.669

Onion white rot
see p.665

Carrot rust fly
see p.657

Bacterial rot
see p.655

Common potato scab
see p.657

Late blight
see p.663

Potato spraing
see p.667

Narcissus nematode see
Stem and bulb nematode p.671

Black vine weevil grubs
see p.655

Root rot
see p.668

Rodents
see p.668

Onion maggot
see p.665

STEM, BRANCH, AND LEAF-BUD

Verticillium wilt
see p.672

Dutch elm disease
see p.659

Dutch elm disease
see p.659

Bacterial canker
see p.655

Low temperatures
see p.663

Sclerotinia
see p.669

Scale insects
see p.669

Forsythia gall
see p.660

Gray mold/*Botrytis***
see p.661

Slime flux/wet wood
see p.669

Spur blight/cane blight
see p.670

Adelgids
see p.654

Woolly aphid
see p.673

Irregular water supply
see p.662

Cutworms
see p.658

Foot and root rots
see p.660

Boron deficiency
see p.656

Spittlebugs
see p.670

Fungal brackets
see p.660

WHOLE-PLANT

Seiridium canker
see p.669

Drought
see p.659

Waterlogging
see p.672

Blackleg on potatoes
see p.655

Pruning mistakes
see p.667

Nectria canker
see p.664

Rose dieback
see p.668

Crown rot
see p.658

Armillaria root rot
see p.654

Clematis wilt
see p.657

**Replant disease/
soil sickness** *see p.667*

Rabbits
see Small animal pests p.669

Damping off
see p.658

Black vine weevil grubs
see p.655

Coral spot
see p.658

Peony wilt
see p.666

**Golden nematodes
(on roots)** *see p.661*

Fungus gnats
see p.661

LAWN

Snow mold
see p.670

Gelatinous patch *see Algae and lichens p.654*

Cats and dogs
see p.657

Slime molds
see p.669

Green slime *see Algae and lichens p.654*

Dollar spot
see p.658

Red thread
see p.667

Toadstools
see p.671

A–Z of pests, diseases, and disorders

Adelgids

Plants affected Conifers, particularly *Abies*, pines (*Pinus*), spruces (*Picea*), *Pseudotsuga menziesii*, hemlocks (*Tsuga*), and larches (*Larix*).
Symptoms A fluffy, white, moldlike substance appears on the leaves and stems. Knobbly swellings develop on *Abies*, and swollen stem tips (pineapple galls) appear on the young shoots of spruce.
Cause Adelgids, or conifer woolly aphids (for example *Adelges cooleyi*), are small, grayish-black, aphidlike insects that suck sap from the bark or the leaves. The bark- and leaf-feeders secrete white, waxy threads.
Control Handpick galls. Apply horticultural oil in early spring. Hemlocks badly infested with hemlock woolly adelgid should be removed.

Algae and lichens

Plants affected Lawns and other grassed areas.
Symptoms Slippery patches of green or greenish-black form on the surface.
Cause Gelatinous lichens and algae, which, in particular, are commonly found on any poorly drained, poorly aerated, or compacted sites.
Control Try to improve the drainage, and also aerate the lawn. Prune back any trees or shrubs that noticeably overhang the area and create densely shaded, damp sections.

Andromeda lacebug

Plants affected Broadleaf shrubs, including *Andromeda*, *Kalmia*, *Cotoneaster*, *Rhododendron*, *Pieris*.
Symptoms Foliage has a coarse pale mottling on the upper surface and rusty brown excrement spots on the underside. Adults, nymphs, and cast skins can be found on the lower leaf surface.
Cause A sap-sucking insect, *Stephanitis takeyai* (other species in this genus are also pests). The adults are 1/8 in (4mm) long with blackish-brown bodies. The transparent wings are carried flat in the insect's back and have a distinctive black

X-shaped marking. The wingless nymphs have spiny bodies.
Control Avoid growing plants that are susceptible in full sun. Wash lacebugs off leaf undersides with a strong spray of water.

Anthracnose

Plants affected A wide range of plants, especially trees, shrubs, and vegetable crops.
Symptoms Dark, elliptical, rough cankers, about 1/4 in (6mm) long, on the stems; small, dark brown leaf spots turn yellow, curl, and fall early. Small sunken, dark spots on fruit, sometimes with spore masses evident. The disease is rarely fatal.
Cause Various fungi cause anthracnose. The disease is usually encouraged by mild, damp weather. Spores produced from the cankers and foliage lesions are spread by rain splash.
Control Prune out and burn or destroy the cankered shoots. Rake up and destroy infected leaves.

Ants

Plants affected Many annuals, low-growing perennials, and woody plants.
Symptoms Plants grow slowly and have a tendency to wilt. Heaps of soil may also appear, sometimes burying some low-growing plants.
Cause On plants, various species of black, yellow, or reddish-brown ants (e.g., *Lasius* and *Formica* spp.), which disturb the roots as they construct their nests. They do not usually feed on the plants, however, and cause relatively little damage.
Control Ants can be controlled by pouring boiling water over the nest where this will not damage nearby plants (e.g. in a path), but it must be done with great care. Seek advice from experts before attempting this. Common ants are often abundant and impossible to eliminate; their presence should be tolerated as far as possible. Where nests have been made under prized plants, traps filled with boron may be effective over time. The material is taken back to the nest and kills the developing larvae. Call in a professional pest control company if ants are invading the home.

Aphids

Plants affected Most plants.
Symptoms Leaves are often sticky with honeydew (aphid excrement), or blackened by sooty molds; stems and buds may also be covered. Leaves may also be stunted and distorted.
Cause Aphids cluster, sometimes by the hundreds, on stems and the undersides of leaves, sucking the sap; some attack roots. They are up to 1/4 in (6mm) long, and green, yellow, brown, pink, gray, or black; some, such as the woolly apple aphid, are covered in a fluffy, white wax. Aphids may transmit viruses.
Control Encourage ladybugs and lacewings. In greenhouses, introduce biological-control *Aphidoletes aphidimyza* and *Aphidius* spp. Apply horticultural oil in winter to destroy aphid eggs on deciduous fruit trees and bushes. Wash aphids off of foliage and stems with a strong spray of water. As a last resort, apply insecticidal soap or neem.

Apple maggots

Plants affected Apples, hawthorns.
Symptoms Brown tunnels wind through the fruit. Larvae may be seen in or on fruit. The fruit surface is distorted and pitted, and the fruit may drop early.
Cause Larvae of the apple maggot (*Rhagoletis pomonella*), a black fly 1/4 in (6mm) long, with zigzag black bands on its wing. The larvae emerge from fallen fruit and pupate in the soil over winter, emerging as adults early the following summer.
Control Hang two red sticky sphere traps per tree from early to midsummer to trap the flies. About one month after petal fall, cover young fruit with small nylon bags and leave on until harvest. Pick up and dispose of fallen fruit daily.

Armillaria root rot

Plants affected Trees, shrubs, climbers, and some woody perennials; most commonly affected are fruit and nut trees on the West Coast.
Symptoms A creamy-white mycelium develops under the bark at the base of the trunk or the stem, sometimes it also extends

upward; tough, black rhizomorphs (i.e., fungal strands) appear. In the fall fruiting bodies grow in clusters and die back after the first frost. Gum or resin exudes from cracks in the bark of conifers. Plants deteriorate and finally die; prolific flowering or fruiting may occur shortly before death. Fruiting bodies also sometimes develop in clusters on underground roots.
Cause The fungus *Armillaria* (principally *A. mellea*) spread either by rhizomorph movement from an infected plant or stump, or through root contact.
Control Destroy affected plants, stumps, and as much of the root system as possible; if necessary, have the stump ground out. Avoid susceptible plants; choose those with some resistance, e.g., yew (*Taxus baccata*), *Cornus*, and beech (*Fagus*).

Asparagus beetle

Plants affected Asparagus.
Symptoms Leaves are eaten; the epidermis is removed from stems, causing the upper growth to dry and turn brown. Damage occurs between late spring and early fall.
Cause Both the adult and larval asparagus beetle (*Crioceris asparagi*) and spotted asparagus beetle (*C. duodecimpunctata*). The adult beetles are 1/4 in (6mm) long, with yellow and black wing cases and a reddish thorax. The larvae are grayish-yellow.
Control Remove old fronds and plant debris from garden in fall. Pick off light infestations by hand. If serious, spray with pyrethrum.

Aster yellows

Plants affected A wide range of plants; China aster (*Callistephus chinensis*) is one of the most commonly infected.
Symptoms Leaves turn pale yellow, plants become distorted, and flowers change color often turning green, then brown. New growth takes a "witches-broom" form. Aster leafhoppers may be noticed on the undersides of leaves. Roots are covered with tufts of fine hair. Plants do not die.
Cause A phytoplasma spread by the aster leafhopper (*Macrosteles quadrilineatus*) and other

leafhoppers through feeding on infected plants. Aster leafhoppers are greenish-yellow with six black spots on the front of the head; they meaure about 1/8in (3mm) long
Control Pull up and dispose of infected plants as soon as seen.

Azalea gall

Plants affected Rhododendrons and azaleas, especially Indian azalea (*Rhododendron simsii*) grown as an indoor plant.
Symptoms Fleshy, pale green swellings (galls) develop on the foliage or flowers, later turning white.
Cause The fungus *Exobasidium azaleae*, which is encouraged by high humidity. The spores are insect- or airborne.
Control Remove and destroy the galls as soon as they are seen, before the fungus produces spores.

Bacterial canker

Plants affected *Prunus*, in particular cherries and plums.
Symptoms Flat or sunken, elongated cankers develop on the stems; droplets of golden or amber-colored gum ooze from the affected area. The stem starts to deteriorate, and the foliage and flowers may wither and die, or the buds do not break, (see "Blossom blast," right). Foliage may show symptoms of blossom blast.
Cause The bacteria *Pseudomonas syringae* pv. *syringae* and *P. syringae* pv. *morsprunorum*.
Control Remove cankered branches back to healthy wood. Copper sprays will probably not be effective due to resistance developed by the bacteria. Some cultivars are resistant and 'Myrobalan' rootstock offers some resistance.

Bacterial leaf spots and blotches

Plants affected Trees, shrubs, roses, perennials, annuals, bulbous plants, vegetables, fruit, and indoor plants.
Symptoms Various spots or patches develop. They may appear water-soaked, and are often angular with a yellow edge or halo ("halo blight"). Black spots appear on delphinium leaves.

Cause *Pseudomonas* bacteria, spread by insects, rain splash, or windborne seeds.
Control Avoid wetting the foliage. Remove all infected leaves. Practice good sanitation; plant resistant cultivars. Preventive sprays of Bacillus subtilis may help avoid problems.

Bacterial ring rot

Plants affected Potatoes and zonal geraniums (brown rot); tomatoes (Southern wilt); potatoes (ring rot).
Symptoms Similar for both diseases—plants may wilt but symptoms are mainly seen in the tubers or roots. Initially, a brown ring just beneath the skin when the tubers are cut in half. Later decay sets in. Plants may develop cankers at the base of the stem.
Cause Bacteria *Ralstonia solanacearum* (brown rot) and *Clavibacter michiganensis* subsp. *sepedonicus* (ring rot).
Control Use only certified disease-free seed.

Bacterial rot

Plants affected Potatoes.
Symptoms The tuber is rapidly reduced to a slimy mass that has a strong smell, while growing or in storage.
Cause Bacteria enter the tuber either through wounds or through damage caused by infections.
Control Maintain good growing conditions, and harvest potatoes carefully in order to avoid injury. Remove all affected tubers as soon as they are found.

Birds

Plants affected Fruits, vegetables, and flowers; some trees and shrubs.
Symptoms Flower buds are pecked from trees and shrubs; outer bud scales are left scattered on the ground. Seedlings, especially corn, beans, and leafy crops, are pecked or eaten. Peck marks leave ripe fruits susceptible to infection from brown rot (see p.656); soft fruit, such as cherries, are often completely consumed.
Cause Blackbirds, starlings, and crows in vegetable gardens; many types of birds may eat fruit or tree and shrub buds.
Control Netting, fine mesh, or a bird-proof cage is the only certain way of preventing damage. Scaring devices, e.g., humming tapes,

scarecrows, or aluminum foil strips, are effective only initially; birds soon lose their fear.

Black knot

Plants affected Plums, cherries, apricots; many other species
Symptoms Large galls—swellings that are generally sausage-shaped—develop on shoots. They may spread toward the crown. Initially brown, they turn black as they develop reproductive structures called fruiting bodies. Infected trees will lose vigor and productivity.
Cause The fungus *Dibotryon morbosum* (also called *Apiosporina morbosa*), which attacks and eventually kills young shoots.
Control Remove any old, infected trees near new plantings. Inspect susceptible trees and shrubs each fall for new galls, and prune them off to prevent the formation of fruiting bodies. Make cuts 2–4in (5–10cm) below the galls. Destroy the prunings.

Black vine weevil

Plants affected Yews (*Taxus*) and many shrubs, such as rhododendrons, hydrangeas, *Euonymus*, and camellias; also strawberries, grapes, and many herbaceous plants.
Symptoms Notches in leaf margins, often near the ground, from mid-spring to mid-fall.
Cause Adult black vine weevil (*Otiorhynchus sulcatus*), a grayish-black beetle 3/8in (9mm) long, with a short snout and a pair of elbowed antennae. It feeds at night and hides by day.
Control Damage occurs over an extended period, and control is difficult, although good hygiene and the removal of plant debris reduce the number of its hiding places. Use trap boards to attract the weevils, then gather and destroy hiding weevils. Use a biological treatment to control the grub stage, watering *Heterorhabditis* nematodes into the soil in late summer. Once established, plants can tolerate damage to their leaves.

Black vine weevil grub

Plants affected Shrubs, perennials, bulbous plants, and indoor plants; fuchsias, begonias, cyclamen, *Impatiens*, *Sedum*, and

strawberries are commonly affected. Yews (*Taxus*), rhododendrons, and container-grown plants are also particularly vulnerable.
Symptoms Plants grow slowly, wilt, collapse, and die. The outer tissues of seedlings and cuttings are gnawed from the stems below ground.
Cause The plump, white larvae of the beetle *Otiorhynchus sulcatus*, which are up to 1/2in (1cm) long and slightly curved, with brown heads and no legs. The adults lay eggs in spring and summer, and damage occurs from fall to spring.
Control Maintain good hygiene to avoid providing shelters for the adults. Biological-control treatments using *Heterorhabditis* nematodes are available; watered into the soil in mid- and late summer, these treatments kill the larvae.

Blackleg on potatoes

Plants affected Potatoes.
Symptoms The stems collapse, blacken, and rot at the base, and the foliage discolors. The disease usually occurs at the start of the season, but any tubers that have formed may also rot. Most of the crop remains healthy; only a few plants show symptoms.
Cause The bacterium *Pectobacterium atrosepticum*, which is usually introduced on slightly infected seed tubers that do not show any symptoms at all when they are being planted.
Control Plant certified disease-free seed potatoes. Avoid overwatering, especially early in the season. Remove affected plants immediately. Inspect tubers on lifting and do not store any that are suspect.

Blossom blast

Plants affected Edible and ornamental cherries (*Prunus*), peaches, nectarines, plums, and *Prunus laurocerasus*; also other trees, shrubs, and woody perennials.
Symptoms Blossoms turn brown and limp and cling to tree, especially during wet weather. Discolored (usually brown) spots develop on the foliage; the dead leaf tissue then falls away, leaving holes. This symptom is called shothole. In severe cases large areas of leaf are lost.

Cause Various forms of the bacterium *Pseudomonas syringae*; see also "Bacterial canker" on p.655.
Control Try to improve the general growing conditions and the overall health of the affected plant. Copper sprays will probably not be effective due to resistance developed by the bacteria. Some cultivars are resistant and 'Myrobalan' rootstock offers some resistance.

Blossom blight

Plants affected Ornamental and fruit apples, pears, and *Prunus* spp.
Symptoms The flowers turn brown and wither, but remain tightly clinging to the stem. The adjacent leaves then turn brown and die, and in severe cases the spur may be extensively damaged. Many tiny, buff-colored spore masses appear on the affected areas, and in winter pustules form on the bark.
Cause *Monilinia* spp., which flourish in damp conditions and also cause brown rot in fruit. The spores are carried on air currents and infect the plant via the flowers.
Control Remove and destroy all infected parts. Do not leave brown-rotted fruit on the trees. Prune regularly to maintain good air circulation. An application of sulfur shortly before blossoming may be effective.

Boron deficiency

Plants affected Root crops, carnations (*Dianthus*), lettuce, celery, and tomatoes; also all fruit. The condition is fairly rare.
Symptoms The roots are of a poor shape and texture, and are grayish in color. They may split longitudinally and sometimes contain cavities. A brown discoloration—known as brown heart—may occur in the lowermost sections, often in concentric rings; it is found mainly in turnips and rutabagas, and makes them poor-tasting and fibrous. Beets show internal discoloration and may develop cankers. In other plants, the growing tips die, causing the plants to become stunted and bushy. Celery stems start to develop transverse cracks and the exposed tissues turn brown; lettuces fail to develop a head. Pears become distorted and dimpled with brown, flecked flesh (very similar symptoms to those of the virus disease called stoney pit). Plums are misshapen

and may show gumming. Strawberries are small and poorly colored.
Cause A lack of boron in the soil, or an inability of the plant to take up the trace element owing to unsuitable growing conditions. Most common on very alkaline or heavily limed soils, those that have been very dry, and those where the boron has been leached out. It rarely affects greenhouse plants.
Control Maintain correct soil moisture levels and avoid excessive liming. Before introducing a susceptible plant to a problem site, apply borax at 1oz/20sq yd (35g/20sq m), mixing with horticultural sand for easy and accurate application. Apply trace elements.

Boxwood blight

Plants affected *Buxus* spp.
Symptoms Similar for both fungi. Leaves develop brown spots, then go completely brown and fall. *Cylindrocladium* causes black streaks down the stem and small stems may also be killed.
Cause The fungus *Cylindrocladium buxicola*. Volutella blight caused by *Volutella buxi* shows similar symptoms. *V. buxi* infects wounds or stressed plants.
Control Boxwood blight was introduced in North America in 2011; it is present in some eastern states and may be spreading into Canada. Inspect new plants carefully for symptoms of the disease and buy only from reputable sources. Keep new boxwood plants isolated from other boxwoods for several months to ensure they are disease-free. Ensure good garden sanitation. Inspect all of your boxwood plants weekly. If you find any blight symptoms, dig up the entire affected plant, immediately seal it in a plastic bag and discard it.

Brown patch

Plants affected Lawns.
Symptoms Leaf blades develop tan lesions with a brown margin. Circular areas of grass turn brown and die. It tends to appear in hot, humid conditions.
Cause The soilborne fungus Rhizoctonia.
Control Avoid overfertilizing or mowing the lawn too closely. Boost lawn health by applying compost or compost tea. Treat diseased lawns with a potassium bicarbonate fungicide or a fungicide containing *Streptomyces*.

Brown rot

Plants affected Cultivated fruit, especially apples, plums, peaches, nectarines, and pears.
Symptoms Soft, brown areas develop on the skin and penetrate throughout the flesh. Concentric rings of creamy-white pustules then start to appear on the surface. Affected fruit either fall or may become dry and remain on the tree.
Cause The fungus *Monilinia* (*M. fructicola* and *M. laxa*). The pustules produce spores, and these are then carried by wind or insects to other fruits; infection occurs through wounds or blemishes on the surface of the fruit.
Control Prevent injury to fruits (e.g., that caused by pests), and pick off and destroy those affected. Prune regularly to maintain good air circulation. An application of sulfur shortly before harvest may prevent fruit rot in storage.

Bulb flies

Plants affected Daffodils, *Hippeastrum*, hyacinths, lilies, tulips, and other bulbs.
Symptoms Bulbs fail to grow or produce only a few grasslike leaves. Maggots may be found in the bulbs.
Cause The large narcissus bulb fly (*Merodon equestris*), which resembles a small bumblebee, has larvae that usually feed singly inside healthy bulbs. The females lay eggs on the bulbs at soil level in early summer. The plump brownish white larvae are up to ¾in (18mm) long and they fill the center of the bulbs with muddy excrement during summer to spring. Small bulb flies (*Eumerus* spp.) are black with white crescent markings on their abdomens. Their larvae are up to ⅜in (8mm) long and feed in bulbs already damaged by other pests, diseases, or physical injury. There are often several small bulb fly larvae in the same bulb.
Control Avoid planting in warm, sheltered places, which attract adult flies. Discourage egg-laying by firming the soil around the necks of bulbs as they die down, or cover with row cover in early summer.

Cabbage caterpillars

Plants affected Mainly brassicas, including cabbage, cauliflower, and broccoli. Some perennial and annual ornamentals, e.g., nasturtiums (*Tropaeolum*).

Symptoms Holes appear in the foliage between late spring and early fall, and caterpillars may be found in the hearts of brassicas and on leaves.
Cause Caterpillars of the imported cabbage butterfly (*Pieris rapae*) and the cabbage looper moth (*Trichoplusia ni*). Both species of caterpillar are green and up to 1½in (4cm) long.
Control Pick off the young caterpillars by hand. Spray young larvae with *Bacillus thuringiensis* or garlic oil spray.

Cabbage root maggot

Plants affected Brassicas, including cabbage, cauliflower, Brussels sprouts, turnips, rutabagas, broccoli, and radishes.
Symptoms Plants grow slowly and wilt; seedlings and transplants die; tunnels appear in root crops.
Cause Root-feeding larvae of the fly *Delia radicum*, white, legless maggots up to ⅜in (9mm) long. Several generations occur between mid-spring and mid-fall, causing damage mainly to young plants.
Control Place collars made of aluminum foil, heavy paper, or heavy cloth, about 5in (12cm) in diameter, around the base of transplanted brassicas to prevent the female flies from laying eggs in the soil. Alternatively, grow under row covers or insect-proof mesh. Sprinkling a repellent, such as wood ashes or hot pepper, around young plants may deter flies from laying eggs.

Calcium deficiency

Plants affected Apples (the condition is known as bitter pit), tomatoes, eggplant, and sweet peppers (the condition is referred to as blossom end rot).
Symptoms The flesh of apples is brown-flecked and tastes bitter; the skin is sometimes pitted. Bitter pit may affect fruit on the tree or in storage. Tomato, eggplant, and pepper fruit develop a sunken, blackish-brown discoloration at the flower end.
Cause A lack of calcium, possibly in combination with other nutritional imbalances, resulting from an irregular or poor supply of moisture to the roots, preventing adequate calcium uptake. Groups of cells deprived of calcium collapse and discolor.

Control Avoid very acidic growing media. Apply lime according to soil test results. Water regularly and, where feasible, mulch plants. Choose resistant varieties of tomatoes and peppers.

Camellia leaf gall

Plants affected Camellias.
Symptoms Creamy-colored swellings (galls) develop during summer in the place of leaves. Usually just a few galls are found, with the rest of the foliage appearing normal. Shriveled pieces of leaf sometimes remain at the tips of the galls. These may be up to 8in (20cm) long, rounded or forked. They develop a white "bloom" as spores develop. Plant vigor is not affected. It thrives in wet weather conditions.
Cause The fungus *Exobasidium camelliae*.
Control Galls should be removed and destroyed as soon as they are seen. Repeat infection is less likely if this can be done before the bloom of spores develops on the gall.

Carrot rust fly

Plants affected Mainly carrots, parsnips, parsley (*Petroselinum crispum*), and celery.
Symptoms Rusty brown tunnels are bored under the outer skin of mature roots. Small plants develop discolored foliage and may die.
Cause Creamy-yellow maggots, larvae of the carrot fly (*Psila rosae*), which feed in the surface tissues of the larger roots; in fall they may bore deeper. They are slender, legless, and up to ½in (1cm) long.
Control Enclose susceptible plants within a clear plastic barrier at least 24in (60cm) high, or grow with row covers immediately after planting to exclude the low-flying female flies. Drench soil with a solution of parasitic nematodes to kill larvae. Lift carrots for storage in fall to limit damage.

Caterpillars

Plants affected Many garden plants.
Symptoms Leaves, and possibly flowers, are eaten.
Cause Caterpillars of various species of butterfly and moth, which feed on plant material. The most common in gardens are cabbage caterpillars, tent caterpillars (see p.671), and leaftiers and leafrollers (see p.663). Leek

moth caterpillars (see p.663) can also cause significant damage.
Control Pick off caterpillars by hand, if practical, and cover crops with row covers. For serious infestations, use appropriate sprays when feasible.

Cats and dogs

Plants affected Lawns, seedlings, garden plants.
Symptoms Lawns and other grassed areas are fouled with droppings; grass and foliage are scorched with urine; and newly sown areas are scratched up.
Cause Cats and dogs. Cats prefer dry soil and newly cultivated areas.
Control When cats and dogs are seen urinating on plants, wash the plant off immediately with water, to avoid scorching. Repellents are available, but these often give only temporary protection. Lay chicken wire flat over newly sown areas to keep cats off for the short term.

Cedar leaf blight

Plants affected *Thuja* species, particularly Western red cedar (*Thuja plicata*) in British Columbia. In other parts of North America, the blight is found on northern white cedar (*T. occidentalis*) and Oriental arborvitae (*Platycladus orientalis*).
Symptoms Individual scale leaves turn yellowish and then brown in late spring and early summer. The fungus can be seen as black bodies on the dead leaves, later falling out to leave cavities. Dead leaves can persist on the tree throughout the winter. Heavy infections can lead to widespread browning of leaves, and sometimes twig dieback. Susceptibility diminishes with age.
Cause The fungus *Didymascella thujina* (syn. *Keithia thujina*).
Control Remove and dispose of any twigs that are shed as a result of infection. Avoid planting seedlings and young plants in areas where air circulation is poor.

Chinch bugs

Plants affected Lawns.
Symptoms Brown spots, often with a yellowish halo, appear on the lawn and expand slowly. Grass does not pull out. Bugs are visible on leaf blades.
Cause Chinch bugs (*Blissus* spp.), which feed on the crowns and leaf bases. Adults are ¹⁄₃₂in (0.79mm)

long, and are black with red legs. Nymphs are even smaller and are orange to red. To detect the bugs, part the grass and watch for movement, or push a bottomless can into the lawn and fill it with warm water; the bugs will float to the surface.
Control Reduce damage by watering lawns well during drought periods. Avoid this problem by planting endophyte-enhanced grasses. Apply *Beauveria bassiana* to reduce chinch bug population.

Clematis wilt

Plants affected Clematis, mainly large-flowered cultivars, e.g., 'Jackmanii'.
Symptoms The terminal shoots wilt, starting with the youngest foliage, and the petioles begin to darken where they join the leaf blade. A small spot of discoloration may develop under the lowest pair of wilting leaves. Whole sections of the plant may start to die back.
Cause The fungus *Phoma clematidina*, which produces spore-releasing, fruiting bodies on the older stems. Other, nonpathogenic causes of wilt (e.g., drought, poor drainage, and graft failure) may be mistaken for this disease.
Control Cut back any affected stems to healthy tissue, below ground level if necessary. Species *Clematis* are regarded as resistant to clematis wilt.

Clubroot

Plants affected The family Brassicaceae, especially brassicas (for example, cabbage, Brussels sprouts, and radishes), and some ornamentals, including candytufts (*Iberis*), wallflowers (*Erysimum*), and stocks (*Matthiola*).
Symptoms Swollen and distorted roots; stunted and often discolored plants; wilting in hot weather.
Cause The slime mold *Plasmodiophora brassicae*, which thrives in poorly drained, acid soils and is also found on manure and plant debris. It is easily spread on boots and tools, and the spores remain viable for 20 years or more, even in the absence of a host plant. Weeds susceptible to this disease (e.g., shepherd's purse and wild mustard) may be a source of infection. In dry summers it may not occur, because moist conditions are needed for spores to germinate.
Control Remove and destroy affected plants at the first sign of

disease. Clear weeds; improve drainage where feasible. Lime the soil to increase it to a pH of 7.2 because the fungus needs acidic soil conditions. Before planting susceptible crops, solarize the soil, or grow a cover crop of winter rye in early spring and till it under about 3 weeks after it germinates.

Codling moth

Plants affected Apples, apricots, peaches, walnuts (*Juglans*), and pears.
Symptoms Holes are tunneled in ripe fruits.
Cause The caterpillars of the codling moth (*Cydia pomonella*), which feed in the core of the fruit; when they are mature, each caterpillar makes a frass-filled tunnel to the outside of the fruit.
Control Hang pheromone traps in the trees from late spring to midsummer to catch the male moths, reducing egg fertilization. Use of traps will also indicate when females are flying, so sprays can be timed more accurately to control caterpillars as they hatch. Spray kaolin clay to deter egg-laying moths; cover fruits with individual barrier bags.

Colorado potato beetle

Plants affected Potatoes, tomatoes, eggplant, peppers, flowering tobacco (*Nicotiana*).
Symptoms Leaves are eaten, leaving only the main vein. Crop yield is greatly reduced.
Cause Adults and larvae of the Colorado potato beetle (*Leptinotarsa decemlineata*). Adults are bright yellow and black striped beetles; larvae are orange-red grubs up to ½in (1cm).
Control Cover plants with row cover and leave it in place until midsummer or later. Handpick beetles and larvae. Remove the orange egg masses from leaf undersides. Mulch crops deeply with straw. Treat soil with parasitic nematodes to kill larvae. Apply *Beauveria bassiana* or spinosad if problem is worsening.

Common potato scab

Plants affected Potatoes.
Symptoms Raised, scabby patches develop on the skin, and these sometimes rupture. Damage may be superficial, but in some cases

the tuber becomes extensively cracked and disfigured. The flesh is not generally damaged and is safe for eating.

Cause *Streptomyces scabies*, a bacteriumlike but mycelium-producing organism, common in soils that are sandy and light with a high lime content, and those only recently cultivated. Disease development is most common during hot, dry summers, and when soil moisture levels are low.

Control Improve soil texture and lower soil pH to 5.3 or below, if feasible; water regularly. Choose resistant cultivars, but be aware that even they may develop symptoms if soil conditions favor the disease. Some varieties show a degree of resistance, such as 'Ontario', 'Cayuga', and 'Seneca'.

Coral spot

Plants affected Broadleaved trees and shrubs, especially *Elaeagnus*, elms (*Ulmus*), beeches (*Fagus*), maples (*Acer*), magnolias, and currants.

Symptoms Affected shoots die back, and the dead bark becomes covered in orange-pink pustules about 1/16in (1.5mm) in diameter. Until recent years, the disease was most commonly found on dead branches and woody debris, but it has become more aggressive and now affects living shoots as well as dead.

Cause The fungus *Nectria cinnabarina*. Spores that have been released from the orange pustules are spread by rain splash and on pruning tools. They enter the wood through damaged or dying areas and wounds, and infect the plant.

Control Clear away all woody debris. Cut back affected branches to a point well below the obviously infected area. Sterilize pruners.

Corky scab

Plants affected Cacti and other succulents, especially *Opuntia* and *Epiphyllum*.

Symptoms Corky or brown, irregularly shaped spots appear. These areas later become sunken.

Cause Either extremely high humidity or excessively high light levels.

Control Take measures to improve the growing conditions of the plant. In extreme cases, however, the plant must be discarded, after having been used for propagation purposes, if desired.

Corn earworm/tomato fruitworm

Plants affected Corn, tomatoes, and many other vegetables, fruit, and flowers.

Symptoms Tunneling and brown excrement present at the tips of corn ears; holes in tomato fruit and large holes in tomato leaves.

Cause Medium-size striped caterpillars are the larvae of tan moths (*Helicoverpa zea*) that lay eggs on leaves or at the tips of developing ears of corn. Larvae feed for 2 to 4 weeks and then drop off plants to pupate in soil. Up to four generations per year.

Control Choose corn varieties with tight husks. Apply drops of vegetable oil to corn silks just after they begin to dry. Apply *Bacillus thuringiensis* var. *kurstaki* or spinosad to plants if fruitworms are visible on leaves and fruit.

Crown gall

Plants affected Trees, shrubs (most commonly cane fruits and roses), woody and some herbaceous perennials.

Symptoms Irregular, rounded swellings develop on the roots; occasionally the whole root system is distorted into a single, large swelling. These swellings can also occur on or burst from the stem, but plant vigor is not seriously affected.

Cause The bacterium *Agrobacterium tumefaciens*, prevalent in wet soils. The bacteria enter the plant through wounds made on the surface and cause cells to proliferate.

Control Avoid damaging plants and improve soil drainage. Cut out and destroy any affected stems in order to prevent secondary infection. A biological control product (NoGall) is available.

Crown rot

Plants affected Mainly perennials and indoor plants; also trees, shrubs, annuals, bulbous plants, vegetables, and fruit.

Symptoms The base of the plant rots and may smell unpleasant. Plants may wilt, wither, and die.

Cause Bacterial and fungal organisms entering the stem through surface wounds; overly deep planting also leads to infection.

Control Avoid injury to the stem base and keep the crown free of

debris; do not mulch right up to the plant. Ensure that planting depths are correct. Complete removal of the affected area may prevent disease spread, but frequently the whole plant is killed and should be dug up and destroyed.

Cucumber beetle

Plants affected Cucumbers and other squash family plants, beans, peas, corn, and flowers of many garden plants.

Symptoms Seedlings may be covered with beetles, which chew on leaves and shoots. Plants may die or be seriously stunted. Beetles also feed in flowers and may transmit diseases that can seriously impair or kill plants. Larvae feed on plant roots, which may weaken or kill plants.

Cause Spotted cucumber beetles (*Diacritical undecimpunctata*) and striped cucumber beetles (*Acalymma vittatum*) cause very similar symptoms and attack largely the same group of plants. Their ranges overlap, although striped cucumber beetles are not found in the far western part of the U.S. or Canada.

Control Dig all squash and cucumber vines into the soil at the end of the season or remove them completely from the garden. Cover young seedlings with row cover. Spray young plants with kaolin clay to deter beetles from feeding and reapply it twice a week. Handpick beetles. As a last resort, spray beetles with pyrethrin in the evening.

Cutworms

Plants affected Low-growing perennials, annuals, root vegetables, and lettuce.

Symptoms Cavities appear in root crops, and taproots may be severed, causing plants to wilt and die. Stem bases and leaves of low-growing plants are visibly gnawed, causing plants to grow slowly, wilt, and die.

Cause The caterpillars of various moths (e.g., *Peridroma* and *Agrotis spp.*), usually creamy-brown in color and up to 1¾in (4.5cm) in length. They eat roots and the outer tissues of stem bases, feeding above soil level at night.

Control Where damage is seen, search for and destroy the cutworms. Protect young plants with a paper or foil collar pushed

into the soil. Keep the growing area frees of weeds, which might attract egg-laying moths.

Cyclamen mite

Plants affected In greenhouses, cyclamen, African violets, and many other types of plants. Outdoors, strawberries.

Symptoms Plants flower poorly; some flowers may be converted into rosettes of small leaves. Grayish-brown scars appear on stunted stems. Strawberry fruit are dwarfed, with an unusual appearance.

Cause The cyclamen mite (*Phytonemus pallidus*), a microscopic mite that feeds in flower buds and shoot tips.

Control Discard infested plants, or dip them, including the pot, in hot (110°F/51°C) water for 15 to 30 minutes. Insectical soap sprays may be effective in the greenhouse.

Cytospora canker

Plants affected A wide range of deciduous and evergreen woody plants, including fruit trees, spruces, and pines.

Symptoms Small cankers form. Needles turn brown; new shoots of deciduous plants turn yellow. Branches die. Resin drips from the the cankers, crystallizing into white deposits. Symptoms of bacterial canker are similar.

Cause Various species of Cytospora fungi cause the disease, depending on the species attacked. Disease is spread by rain splash but enters plants via wounds.

Control Plant resistant cultivars, if possible. Care for trees well to stimulate vigorous growth. Avoid damaging the lower trunk. Remove infected branches when conditions are dry; disinfect pruners after each cut. Do not apply wound dressings.

Damping off

Plants affected The seedlings of all plants.

Symptoms Affected roots darken and rot off, causing the seedling to collapse and die. The disease often starts at one end of the seed flat, spreading rapidly to the other. A fluffy, fungal growth may appear on the potting mix surface as well.

Cause Various fungi—including *Pythium ultimum* and some *Phytophthora*, *Alternaria*, and *Rhizoctonia*—which are soil- or waterborne and attack seedlings

via either the roots or the base of the stem. They flourish in moist and unhygienic conditions.
Control There is no effective control once the disease is established. To prevent it, sow seed thinly, improve ventilation, maintain strict hygiene, and avoid overwatering. Use only good-quality sowing mix, clean water, and clean flats and pots. When sowing seeds, use a thin top layer of sand or perlite to prevent waterlogged conditions at the soil line of seedlings.

Daylily gall midge

Plants affected Daylily (*Hemerocallis*).
Symptoms Flower buds become abnormally swollen and fail to open. The problem occurs between late spring and midsummer.
Cause The daylily gall midge (*Contarinia quinquenotata*), a tiny fly that lays its eggs in the developing buds. Affected buds contain white maggots, up to ¹⁄₁₆in (1.5mm) long, feeding between the petals.
Control Pick off and discard galled buds. The late-flowering cultivars escape damage.

Deer

Plants affected Most plants, especially trees, shrubs (including roses), and herbaceous plants.
Symptoms Shoots and leaves are eaten; tree bark is rubbed, frayed, and eaten.
Cause White-tailed and other species of deer, which eat shoots, leaves, and bark. Bark is frayed when males mark trees with scent glands or rub the velvet from their new antlers.
Control Protect gardens with wire mesh fences at least 6ft (2m) high, or place wire netting around stems and trunks. Repellent sprays or scaring devices, such as hanging tin cans, provide only short-term protection from deer.

Dollar spot

Plants affected Lawns, particularly those containing fine-leaved bents and creeping fescues.
Symptoms Small, straw-colored patches develop in early fall. At first they are 1–3in (2.5–7cm) in diameter, but coalesce to form larger areas, and darken as they age.
Cause The fungus *Sclerotinia*

homoeocarpa, encouraged by heavy or compacted soils and high pH; alkaline soils or those treated with lime may produce symptoms. It often appears in mild, damp weather.
Control Improve soil aeration and remove thatch in the lawn.

Downy mildew

Plants affected Annuals, perennials, vegetables, bulbous plants, and some fruits, including brassicas, stocks (*Matthiola*), lettuce, and flowering tobacco (*Nicotiana*).
Symptoms A fluffy or mealy, white fungal growth develops on the lower surface of foliage, while the upper surface is blotched yellow or brown; the older leaves are usually the most seriously affected. Growth is stunted and the plant is prone to secondary infections such as gray mold (*Botrytis*; see p.661).
Cause Mostly species of *Peronospora*, *Plasmopara*, and *Bremia* fungi, which are encouraged by humid conditions. The fungus can survive in the soil.
Control Sow seeds thinly and do not overcrowd plants. Improve ventilation, air circulation, and drainage; avoid overhead watering. Remove affected leaves or plants. Replant in a new site and do not compost infected material. Potassium bicarbonate sprays may slow the spread of downy mildew.

Drought

Plants affected All plants, especially those that are newly planted, container-grown, or in light, sandy soils; lawns.
Symptoms Buds fail to develop fully, and flowers are small and sparse. Fall coloration develops early, and defoliation, followed by dieback, may occur. Plants wilt and growth is stunted. Flowering and fruit set may decrease markedly. Fruits may be small, distorted, and of a poor texture. On lawns, yellowish-brown, strawlike patches of variable size develop; in extreme cases the whole area may become discolored.
Cause Chronic (prolonged) or repeated drought due to inadequate or unavailable soil moisture; excessive water loss from the leaves of plants on exposed sites; injured or restricted roots; or soil compaction. Plants in small containers are vulnerable during hot weather, and potting media that dry out too much are extremely difficult to rewet. Dry, brown

buds on certain plants, such as camellias and rhododendrons, are the result of a water shortage the previous year during the period of bud initiation.
Control Water plants regularly, and frequently check those in hot or sunny locations. Plants raised from seed resist drought better than transplanted ones. Mulch, where appropriate, to improve moisture retention. On lawns, to improve drought resistance, water deeply and infrequently. Avoid mowing too closely. It is easier to prevent drought than to treat it: plants exposed to prolonged water shortage are less likely to recover than those suffering a sudden, short drought.

Dutch elm disease

Plants affected Elms (*Ulmus*) and *Zelkova*.
Symptoms Notching appears in twig crotches, and young twigs may be crook-shaped. Longitudinal, dark brown streaks develop under the bark. Leaves in the crown wilt, yellow, and die. The tree may die within two years.
Cause *Ophiostoma ulmi* and *O. novo-ulmi* fungus spread by elm bark beetles as they feed on the bark. Infected trees may pass the disease to healthy ones via common root systems.
Control The disease cannot be prevented or eradicated. Remove diseased trees as soon as identified; consult with an arborist about breaking root grafts from diseased trees. Clonal cultivars of American elm that are resistant to the disease are available.

Earwigs

Plants affected Shrubs, perennials, and annuals, most commonly dahlias, chrysanthemums, and clematis. Also apricots and peaches.
Symptoms Young leaves and petals are eaten in summer.
Cause Earwigs (*Forficula auricularia*)—yellowish-brown insects up to ¾in (18mm) long with a pair of curved pincers. Earwigs hide during the day and feed at night.
Control Place inverted pots that have been loosely stuffed with hay or straw, on stakes among susceptible plants; earwigs use these as daytime shelters, from which they can be removed and destroyed. Apply *Steinernema carpocapsae* nematodes to soil in earwig-infested areas.

Edema

Plants affected Potentially all plants, but particularly zonal geraniums, camellias, *Eucalyptus*, and succulents.
Symptoms Raised, warty patches appear on the foliage. These are initially of a similar color to that of the rest of the leaf but later turn brown.
Cause Excessively high moisture levels in either the air or the growing medium, which give the plant cells an unusually high water content. As a result of this, small groups of cells swell, forming the outgrowths, and later burst, leaving brown patches on the leaves.
Control Improve air circulation around the plants by increasing ventilation and ensuring correct plant spacing. Decrease the amount of watering, and wherever possible, try to improve drainage. Leaves affected with this condition should not be picked off; new leaf growth will be normal.

Etiolation

Plants affected Seedlings of all garden plants, and soft-stemmed plants.
Symptoms Stems are elongated and often pale, and the plant may grow toward the available light source, developing a marked lop-sided habit. The leaves are chlorotic, and flowering is often somewhat reduced.
Cause Insufficient light, often due to poor siting of the plant or shading from adjacent plants, buildings, and similar structures. Overcrowded plants are susceptible to the condition.
Control Choose and site plants carefully. Ensure that adequate light is provided for young seedlings as soon as germination has occurred. Plants only slightly affected should recover if conditions are improved.

European apple sawfly

Plants affected Apples.
Symptoms Fruitlets are tunneled and drop off during early to midsummer. The damaged fruit will sometimes remain on the tree and become mature, but they are misshapen and have a long, ribbonlike scar on the skin.
Cause The larvae of the European apple sawfly

(*Hoplocampa testudinea*), white caterpillarlike insects up to ½in (1cm) long with brown heads. They are less widespread than codling moths (see p.657).
Control If sawflies have been a problem in previous years, drench the soil under trees with parasitic nematodes in spring. A spinosad spray can be effective when applied at the appropriate time.

European crane fly larvae

Plants affected Young annuals, bulbous plants, vegetables, lawns and other grassed areas.
Symptoms The roots are eaten, the stems are severed at ground level, and plants turn yellow, wilt, and may eventually die. On lawns, brown patches in spring and summer, and maggots are sometimes visible.
Cause The larvae of European crane flies (*Tipula* spp.), which feed on roots and stems. The larvae are up to 1½in (3.5cm) long; they have tubular, grayish-brown bodies with no legs. This is an introduced pest found mainly in the Pacific Northwest.
Control Use good lawn care practices to maintain a healthy lawn. Avoid pesticide use to encourage natural predators and parasites. Where damage is seen on the plants, search for and destroy the larvae, or in late summer apply parasitic nematodes (*Steinernema feltiae*) to moist, warm (54–68°F/12–20°C) soil. On lawns, soak affected areas with water, and cover with black plastic for a day to bring the larvae to the surface; they can then be removed and killed. For severe infestations, seek a recommendation for an appropriate insecticidal treatment.

Fasciation

Plants affected All plants, most commonly delphiniums, forsythias, *Daphne*, and *Prunus subhirtella* 'Autumnalis'.
Symptoms Peculiar, broad, flattened flower stems develop. The main stems are also broad and flattened.
Cause In many cases, early damage to the growing point is caused by insect, slug, or frost attack, or improper handling; it may also be due to microbial infection or genetic malfunction.

Control Fasciation does no harm; affected areas may either be left on the plant or pruned out.

Fire blight

Plants affected Members of the family Rosaceae that bear pome fruit, e.g., pears, apples, some *Sorbus*, cotoneasters, and hawthorns (*Crataegus*).
Symptoms The leaves generally turn blackish-brown, shrivel, and die, and they remain clinging to the stem. The leaves of some *Sorbus* and hawthorns may turn yellow and fall. Fruit turn black and cling on the branches. Oozing cankers appear on the branches, and it is possible that the whole tree could eventually die.
Cause The bacterium *Erwinia amylovora*, which is produced from the cankers, attacks via the blossoms. It is carried from plant to plant by wind, rain splash, insects, and pollen.
Control Remove the affected plants immediately or prune out affected areas to at least 24in (60cm) past the damaged area; remember to dip the saw in garden disinfectant to avoid spreading the disease, both between cuts and before using it on another tree. Applying *Bacillus subtilis* may provide some protection against the disease.

Flea beetles

Plants affected The seedlings of cabbage-family crops, leafy vegetables, tomatoes, eggplant, potatoes, and some ornamentals.
Symptoms Small holes and pits are scalloped from the upper leaf surface; seedlings may die.
Cause Small, black, brown, or bronze beetles (Family Chrysomelidae) sometimes with a yellow stripe running down each wing case. They are usually ¹⁄₁₆in (1.5mm) long, with enlarged hind legs that enable them to leap off plant surfaces when disturbed. They overwinter in plant debris. Larvae feed on plant roots.
Control Clear plant debris, particularly in the fall. Sow seed under row cover or insect netting and water seedlings regularly to help rapid growth through the vulnerable stages. Spray seedlings with kaolin clay or garlic spray to deter beetles from feeding or with spinosad to kill flea beetles.

Foot and root rots

Plants affected A wide range, especially petunias, and other bedding plants, tomatoes, cucumbers, peas, beans, and young, container-grown plants.
Symptoms The stem bases discolor, and rot or shrink inward. This causes the upper parts of the plant to wilt and collapse; the lower leaves will usually show the symptoms first. The roots turn black and break or rot.
Cause A range of soil- and waterborne fungi that flourish where growing conditions are not adequately hygienic. They are often introduced through the use of unsterilized soil mix and contaminated water, and build up in the soil, especially if susceptible plants are repeatedly grown on the same site.
Control Rotate susceptible plants. Maintain strict hygiene and only use fresh soil mix and fresh water. Remove affected plants and the soil in the vicinity of their roots.

Forsythia gall

Plants affected Forsythias.
Symptoms Rough, woody rounded galls form on the stems of this shrub. They persist from year to year but rarely have adverse effects.
Cause Unknown; possibly bacterial infection.
Control No action is strictly necessary but the unsightly galled stems may be removed.

Fuchsia gall mite

Plants affected Fuchsias in California and other areas in the far West.
Symptoms Severely distorted foliage and flowers, with new growth coming to a halt when the shoot tips are converted into lumpy, pale yellowish green or reddish swollen tissues.
Cause A microscopic gall mite, *Aculops fuchsiae*, that sucks sap from the developing tissues at the shoot tips and flower buds. Chemicals secreted into the plant cause the deformed growth. The mite can be transferred to new plants through bees visiting the flowers.
Control Choose mite-resistant varieties. Cutting down infested plants and disposing of the cuttings

may encourage healthy regrowth but plants may soon become reinfested. Soap or oil sprays are somewhat effective in killing the mites.

Fungal brackets

Plants affected Mainly trees, and especially mature or overmature specimens, but also shrubs and woody perennials.
Symptoms On roots, fungal fruiting bodies, often bracket-shaped, may appear above ground, following the line of the roots; they are attached to the roots by tiny fungal threads. They vary in appearance, often according to weather conditions. The roots may become hollow and eventually die, making the tree extremely unstable in the ground. On stems, fungal fruiting bodies commonly appear on the lower trunk, but also on the upper section or on the crown, sometimes near branch stubs or other wounds. Either short-lived or perennial, they vary in appearance, often according to weather conditions. General growth is slow, and the tree may develop an excess of dead wood and a thin crown.
Cause Various fungi, e.g., *Meripilus* or *Ganoderma*.
Control Seek professional advice, particularly if the tree poses a potential hazard. Removal of fruiting bodies will not prevent further decay, and does little to reduce the chances of spread to other trees.

Fungal leaf spots

Plants affected Trees, shrubs, perennials, annuals, bulbous plants, vegetables, and fruit, as well as many indoor plants.
Symptoms Discrete, concentrically zoned spots appear on the leaves; close inspection may reveal pinprick-sized, fungal, fruiting bodies. Spots may be a range of colors but are often brown or slate gray. In severe cases they coalesce. Early leaf fall may occur—for example, black spot on roses—but in some instances there is little damage or effect on overall plant vigor.
Cause A wide range of fungi.
Control Remove all affected parts of the plant, and rake up and discard or burn any leaves that have already fallen. Prune to improve air circulation. Apply preventive sprays of potassium bicarbonate or fungicidal soap.

Fungus gnats

Plants affected Plants grown under cover. Seedlings and cuttings are more susceptible than established plants.
Symptoms Both seedlings and cuttings fail to grow; grayish-brown flies run over the compost surface or fly among the plants. Larvae may be visible.
Cause The larvae of fungus gnats (for example, *Bradysia* spp.), which feed mainly on dead roots and leaves but may also attack young roots. They are slender, white-bodied maggots up to ¼in (6mm) long with black heads. The adult flies are of a similar length. They do not cause any problems on healthy, established plants, but are a nuisance in the house.
Control Keep greenhouses tidy, and remove dead leaves and flowers from the soil surface to avoid providing shelters. Use sticky yellow traps suspended above plants to trap the adult flies. *Bacillus thuringiensis israelensis* may be drenched onto infested soil to control the larvae.

Fusarium wilt

Plants affected Perennials, annuals, vegetables, and fruit; most commonly affected are China asters (*Callistephus*), carnations (*Dianthus*), sweet peas (*Lathyrus odoratus*), peas, tomatoes, peppers, and melons.
Symptoms Black patches develop on stems and foliage; these patches are sometimes covered with a white or pale pink fungal growth. Roots turn black and die. Plants wilt, often suddenly.
Cause Various forms of the microscopic fungus *Fusarium*, which are present in the soil or on plant debris, or are sometimes seed-borne; they may also be introduced on new stock. They will build up in the soil when the same type of plant is grown in the same site year after year.
Control There is no cure for affected plants. Remove them and the soil in their vicinity, and destroy the plants. Avoid growing susceptible plants in the area. Propagate only from healthy stock; if possible, grow resistant cultivars.

Gall midges

Plants affected Many garden plants, especially violets (*Viola*), honeylocust (*Gleditsia*), and roses.
Symptoms Violet leaves thicken and fail to unfurl. *Gleditsia* leaflets swell and fold over to form podlike galls. Young shoots on roses become deformed and die, and flower buds fail to open.
Cause Whitish-orange maggots up to ¹⁄₁₆in (1.5mm) long that feed within the galled tissues; three or four generations may occur in a summer. These are the larvae of three species of midge: the violet gall midge (*Phytophaga violicola*), the rose midge (*Dasineura rhodophaga*), and the honeylocust podgall midge (*D. gleditchiae*).
Control Remove and destroy affected leaves. The larvae are well protected inside the galls; sprays are not effective.

Gall mites

Plants affected Trees and shrubs, including plums, pears, walnuts, grapevines (*Vitis*), maples (*Acer*), lindens (*Tilia*), elms (*Ulmus*), hawthorns (*Crataegus*), mountain ashes (*Sorbus aucuparia*), broom (*Cytisus*), beeches (*Fagus*), and ash (*Fraxinus*).
Symptoms These vary according to the species of mite, and include: whitish-green or red pimples or spikes on foliage (maples, elms, lindens, and plums); creamy-white or pink hairs on lower leaf surfaces (maples, lindens, and beeches); raised, blistered areas on upper leaf surfaces, with pale hairs underneath (walnuts and grapes); thick, curling leaf margins (beeches and hawthorns); pale leaf blotches, later turning brownish-black (mountain ashes and pears); and stunted leaves (broom). Plant vigor is not affected.
Cause Microscopic gall mites, or eriophyid mites, secreting chemicals that induce abnormal growth. Adults are tiny, creamy white mites with tubular bodies and two pairs of legs.
Control Remove affected leaves and shoots if desired. Control is seldom needed, but if desired, apply horticultural oil in spring, just before bud break.

Gall wasps/cynipid wasps

Plants affected Oaks (*Quercus*) and roses.
Symptoms Symptoms on oaks include: flat disks on the lower surface of leaves in fall; benign, spherical, woody growths (marble galls) or pithy oak apples on shoots in spring; yellowish-green or red bunches of currant galls on the catkins; and yellowish-green, sticky "knopper" galls on acorns. Species rose stems and hybrid rose suckers develop swellings covered in yellowish-pink, mosslike leaves ("bedeguar" galls or "Robin's pincushions") in late summer. Damage to these plants is minimal.
Cause The larvae of gall wasps, or cynipid wasps; as they feed, they secrete chemicals that induce galls.
Control Prune out and destroy galls when young. No other control is usually needed.

Golden nematodes

Plants affected Potatoes: found in New York State and parts of Canada.
Symptoms Plants yellow and die, starting with the lower leaves, and potato tubers remain small. Roots of lifted plants show numerous white, yellow, or brown cysts up to ¹⁄₁₆in (1.5mm) in diameter.
Cause Root-dwelling nematodes, which disrupt water and nutrient uptake. Mature females swell and their bodies (known as cysts) burst through the root walls. Cysts contain up to 600 eggs; these remain viable for longer than 30 years. Cysts of the golden nematode (*Globodera rostochiensis*), also called the potato cyst nematode, change from white through yellow to brown as they mature; those of *G. pallida* change directly from white to brown.
Control Crop rotation discourages the buildup of infestation. Some resistant varieties are available. Solarizing the soil can reduce populations. No control products for this problem are available to home gardeners.

Grasshoppers and crickets

Plants affected Many garden plants; most severe damage to flowers of beans, squash, and other cucurbits.
Symptoms Holes in flower petals; entire flowers may be devoured.
Cause Grasshoppers and crickets (Family Acrididae) cause similar damage. Grasshoppers feed during the day; crickets at night.
Control Handpick the pests; cultivate the garden in fall to kill eggs; natural enemies often provide good control.

Gray mold

Plants affected Trees, shrubs, perennials, annuals, bulbous plants, vegetables, fruit, and indoor plants. Soft-leaved plants are particularly vulnerable, as are soft, thin-skinned fruit, e.g., grapes, strawberries, raspberries, and tomatoes.
Symptoms Dead and discolored patches develop on the stems and leaves. Rapid deterioration may occur, causing the upper parts of the stem to die. A fuzzy gray fungal growth may appear on flowers first, then spread elsewhere. Fungal spores develop on decaying plant material. On fruit, a gray, fuzzy, fungal growth develops on a soft, brown rot. The damage spreads rapidly and the whole fruit may collapse. Unripe tomatoes may develop "ghost spot," where a pale green ring appears on the skin but the rest of the fruit colors normally and does not rot (the unaffected parts may be eaten).
Cause The fungi *Botrytis cinerea* and, on snowdrops (*Galanthus*), *B. galanthina*, which thrive in damp conditions and where air circulation is poor. Fungal spores are spread on air currents or by rain splash; infection is most likely where plants are damaged. Fruits may also become infected by contact with those already diseased. Hard, black, resilient sclerotia (fungal resting bodies), produced on plant remains, fall to the ground and may cause later infections.
Control Avoid injury to plants, clear up dead and dying plant material, and provide good air circulation. Remove and discard or burn any affected areas (and in the case of snowdrops the entire clump) immediately. Spray with a Bacillus subtilus product, which may prevent the disease from spreading.

Ground bees

Plants affected Lawns.
Symptoms Small conical heaps of soil with a hole in the top appear on lawns, especially in spring. Small bees fly over the lawn and enter or leave the nest cones.
Cause Several species of solitary bees. Each female digs her own nest tunnel in the soil and excavates soil onto the lawn surface. When the nest is constructed, the female bee collects nectar and pollen as a food store for her larvae. These solitary bees are not aggressive and will not sting unless roughly handled.
Control Like other bees, ground bees are beneficial pollinating insects, so should be tolerated. Their nest tunnels do not damage the lawn.

Gypsy moth caterpillar

Plants affected Many deciduous trees and shrubs, especially apples (*Malus*), hawthorns (*Crataegus*), oaks (*Quercus*), and lindens (*Tilia*). Conifers occasionally attacked.
Symptoms Leaves are eaten; entire plants may be defoliated. Repeated attacks kill plants.
Cause Larvae of the gypsy moth (*Lymantria dispar*), which hatch from overwintering egg masses laid on tree bark. Young larvae spin silken thread that act as parachutes and carry them from tree to tree. Larvae are black with two white lines down the back and red and blue spots. They are covered with tufts of long hair. Reaching 2in (5cm) when mature, they are voracious feeders that can defoliate an entire tree in a few days.
Control Scrape off egg masses from tree trunks. Set out pheromone traps to catch males and prevent them from mating. Spray larvae with *Bacillus thuringiensis* var. *kurstaki* as soon as noticed. Wrap trunks with burlap bands to trap wandering caterpillars; collect and destroy caterpillars daily.

Hellebore black death

Plants affected *Helleborus* spp. especially *Helleborus* × *hybridus* (syn. *H. orientalis*).
Symptoms Black streaking and mottling of the tissues along or between the leaf veins. The black marks may be in a ringspot pattern or in lines, which pass down the leaf stalks to the main stem of the plant. Flowers may also be affected. Leaves and stems may be distorted and stunted.
Cause Helleborus net necrosis virus.
Control It cannot be eradicated and currently is not well understood. Affected plants should be dug up and destroyed. Spray nearby hellebores with insecticidal soap to reduce the transmittal of the disease by hellebore aphid.

Hellebore leaf spot

Plants affected *Helleborus* spp. but is not so damaging on the tougher leaves of *H. argutifolius*. *H. niger* is particularly susceptible.
Symptoms Large, irregular brown or black spots appear on the leaves and stems. These often coalesce, resulting in yellowing and death of the leaves. Spots also occur on the flowers and lower stems, and infected stems may wilt above the point of attack so that flower buds fail to open.
Cause The fungus *Coniothyrium hellebori*.
Control Pick off and destroy all affected leaves and flowers. Propagate only from healthy material.

High temperatures and scorch

Plants affected In particular plants with fleshy leaves or flowers, those near glass, and seedlings; also trees, shrubs, perennials, annuals, bulbous plants, vegetables, fruit, and indoor plants. Also soft fruit, tree fruit, tomatoes, and apples, especially green-skinned cultivars.
Symptoms Leaves wilt, turn yellow or brown, become dry and crisp, and may die; the tips and margins are often affected first. In extreme cases the stems die back. Scorching produces brown patches on the upper or exposed parts of the plant; foliage close to glass is very susceptible. Affected leaves may shrivel completely. Scorched petals turn brown and become dry and crisp. Roses may show "balling" (as the outer petals dry up, they restrict the bud). On fruit, discolored patches develop on the skin, particularly on the uppermost surfaces of fruits, or on the ones that are more highly exposed.
Cause Very high or fluctuating temperatures in a closed environment (e.g., a greenhouse); scorching is caused by bright, but not necessarily hot, sunlight. Shade-loving plants, such as *Impatiens*, scorch badly if sited in a bright, sunny spot. Grapes, tomatoes, and some other fruit may scorch if plants have sparse foliage due to disease or poor growth.
Control Where possible, shade greenhouses, provide adequate ventilation to keep temperatures down, and move plants away from any faults there may be in the glass. Locate shade-loving plants in a site with at least dappled shade.

Insecticide/fungicide damage

Plants affected Some indoor and garden plants.
Symptoms Discrete spots or patches, often bleached or scorched, appear on leaves, which may fall; the plant usually survives.
Cause Often chemicals used at the wrong rate or interval, applied during hot, sunny weather, or when plants are under stress. Some plants are damaged by fungicides or insecticides applied correctly, and susceptible species may be noted on the packaging; check carefully before using.
Control When using commercial insecticides/fungicides, always follow the manufacturers' instructions regarding dosage and permitted uses.

Internal rust spot

Plants affected Potatoes.
Symptoms Rust-brown flecks develop throughout the flesh.
Cause High soil temperature while tubers are developing. Cultivation either in sandy, acidic soils that are low in organic matter, or in soils that are generally low in nutrients, in particular potassium and phosphorus.
Control Incorporate humus into the soil before planting and apply a balanced fertilizer in spring. Water regularly.

Iris borer

Plants affected Irises, particularly rhizomatous types such as tall bearded and *Iris tectorum*, but also *I. sibirica* and Louisiana irises.
Symptoms Sawtooth edges appear on leaves in late spring/early summer. As borers feed inside rhizomes, foliage gradually yellows. Flowers in bud turn brown and watery. Plants eventually collapse
Cause Larvae of a small gray moth (*Macronoctua onusta*), which lays eggs on old foliage in late summer. The following spring, larvae hatch and tunnel into the leaves a few inches above the ground. Fully grown borers are about 1¼in (3cm) long, white with a reddish brown head. Their tunneling often introduces iris soft rot (see right).
Control Clean up dead foliage and stems in fall or early spring to remove eggs. Dig up and destroy infested rhizomes. Apply spinosad just as eggs hatch. Drench rhizomes with beneficial nematodes shortly before flowering and again one week later. Pinch fans to kill borers as they move down the leaves.

Iris soft rot

Plants affected Irises.
Symptoms The base of outer leaves decays and the rot then spreads into the rhizome, attacking the youngest parts first. The infected area is reduced to a foul-smelling mass.
Cause The bacterium *Pectobacterium carotovorum*, which thrives in waterlogged soil. The bacteria enter the rhizomes through wounds or other damaged areas.
Control Check all rhizomes for any kind of damage before planting, and be extra careful to avoid injuring them. Plant the rhizomes shallowly, and always in good, well-drained soil. Take steps to ensure that iris borers (see left), which may be the cause of injury to rhizomes, are kept under control. The prompt removal of any rotting tissue may help to check the problem temporarily, but in the long term the whole rhizome is best discarded.

Irregular water supply

Plants affected Potentially all plants, especially those in containers.
Symptoms In trees, the outer stem layer or bark of the stem or trunk may split or crack. Leaves and flowers become puckered and distorted or are undersized. Fruit is misshapen and undersized, and a sudden availability of water may cause the skin and flesh to crack, leaving the fruit vulnerable to the diseases that cause rotting.
Cause An irregular supply of water, leading to irregular growth and distortion in the upper parts of plants. Sudden availability of water after a drought or a prolonged dry period due to erratic watering brings rapid swelling, which causes stems to rupture and crack. It may also cause the skin and flesh of tomatoes to crack, leaving them vulnerable to diseases that cause rotting.
Control Provide a regular and adequate supply of water, especially during hot or windy weather, and pay particular attention to any plants that are growing in containers. Do not suddenly overwater plants after drought conditions. Mulch, where appropriate, to conserve as much moisture in the soil as possible.

Japanese beetles

Plants affected Flowers and leaves of many types of plants; soft fruit such as raspberries.

Symptoms Adult beetles chew on leaves, producing a characteristic skeletonized appearance. They may also chew holes in soft fruit, leading to development of rot. Larvae also feed on roots.
Cause Japanese beetles (*Popillia japonica*) are metallic blue-green insects about ½in (1cm) in length. They are found throughout the United States and some parts of Canada.
Control Cover plants with row cover to protect them from beetles. Spray fruit and vegetable crops with kaolin clay to deter beetle feeding. Handpick beetles and drop them in soapy water.

Late blight

Plants affected Tomatoes (in the open and occasionally under cover), potatoes.
Symptoms Brown discoloration develops on the leaf tips and edges; in damp conditions these may be ringed with a white, fungal growth. The leaf tissue is killed, and where the patches coalesce, the entire affected leaflet may eventually die. In tomatoes, the fruits first develop a brown discoloration and then start to shrink and rot. Even fruit that seem healthy when picked may begin to deteriorate rapidly within a few days. In potatoes, dark and sunken patches begin to develop on the skin, and there are reddish-brown stains in the flesh beneath. The tubers start to develop a dry rot and they may also be affected by secondary, soft-rotting bacteria.
Cause The fungus *Phytophthora infestans*, which thrives in warm, moist conditions. Spores produced on tomato and potato foliage, and on potato haulms, are carried by wind and rain; they may be washed into the soil to infect potato tubers.
Control Search out and destroy any potato tubers that may have survived winter in the soil. Avoid overhead watering. Grow tomatoes under cover rather than in the open. Hill potatoes deeply to provide a barrier for the tubers against spores, and choose resistant cultivars. Protect both tomatoes and potatoes by spraying thoroughly with a suitable copper-based fungicide according to label instructions. Remove and burn or destroy infected plants as soon as they are noticed, and clean up fallen foliage in the fall.

Leaf and bud nematodes

Plants affected Annuals and many herbaceous perennials. Most often attacked are chrysanthemums, begonias, and *Anemone* x *hybrida*.
Symptoms Brownish-black patches appear on leaves as islands or wedges between the larger veins.
Cause Microscopic nematodes (*Aphelenchoides* spp.) that feed in large numbers inside infested leaves.
Control Destroy all affected leaves or destroy the whole plant as soon as the infestation is noticed. For chrysanthemums, dip the dormant plants in clean water held at 115°F (46°C) for five minutes to obtain clean cuttings.

Leaf-cutting bees

Plants affected Roses mainly but also trees and other shrubs.
Symptoms Lozenge-shaped or circular pieces of uniform size are removed from the margins of the leaf.
Cause Leaf-cutting bees (*Megachile* spp.), which use the leaf pieces to build their nests. They are up to ½in (1cm) long, and have orange hairs on the underside of their abdomen.
Control Leaf-cutting bees are of some benefit as pollinators and, unless plants are heavily damaged, control is not necessary. If they are a persistent nuisance, swat them as they return to the leaf.

Leafhoppers

Plants affected Trees, shrubs, perennials, annuals, vegetables, and fruit. Rhododendrons, zonal geraniums, primroses, roses, potatoes, and tomatoes are usually most vulnerable.
Symptoms A coarse, pale, spotting appears on the upper leaf surface, except on rhododendrons, where damage is restricted to the spreading of rhododendron bud blight.
Cause Leafhoppers, such as the rose leafhopper (*Edwardsiana rosae*) and potatoe leafhopper (*Empoasca fabae*), are green or yellow insects 1/16–1/8in (2–3mm) long that leap from the plant when disturbed. Their bodies are widest just behind the head and taper back. The rhododendron leafhopper (*Graphocephala fennahi*) is turquoise-green and orange, and ¼in (6mm) in length. The creamy-white, immature nymphs are less active.

Control Cover plants with row cover if possible. Spray plants frequently with a strong stream of water; spray with insecticidal soap, pyrethrin, or neem.

Leafminers

Plants affected Trees, shrubs, perennials, and vegetables, especially birch (*Betula*), hollies (*Ilex*), apples, spinach, *Aquilegia*, and chrysanthemums.
Symptoms White or brown areas within the leaf, often of characteristic shape for the particular leafminer, e.g., linear, circular, or irregular.
Cause Larvae of various flies, e.g., columbine leafminer, and spinach leafminer (*Pegomya hyoscyami*); moths, e.g. arborvitae leafminers (*Argyresthia* spp.); beetles, such as the willow flea weevil (*Rhynchaenus rufipes*); and sawflies, e.g., the birch leafminer (*Fenusa pusilla*).
Control Remove and destroy affected leaves if the plant is lightly infested. Cover susceptible vegetable seedlings with floating row cover. Some birch and holly cultivars are resistant.

Leaftiers and leafrollers

Plants affected Trees (ornamental and fruit), shrubs, perennials, annuals, and bulbous plants.
Symptoms Two leaves may be bound together with fine, silky threads, or one leaf may be either similarly attached to a fruit or folded over on itself. Brown, dry, skeletal patches appear on the leaves.
Cause The caterpillars of moths such as *Archips argyrospila*, which feeds on apples, oaks, quinces, and roses, and *Pandemis limitata*, which attacks many trees and shrubs. They graze away the inner surfaces of leaves. They are up to ¾in (2cm) long, and are generally dark green or yellow with brown heads. The caterpillars wriggle backward rapidly when they are disturbed.
Control Squeeze bound-up leaves to crush the caterpillars or pupae. In winter, scrape leafroller egg masses off trunks and branches. As a last resort, spray with pyrethrin.

Leafy gall

Plants affected Perennials, especially dahlias, zonal geraniums, and chrysanthemums.
Symptoms Tiny, distorted shoots and leaves develop on the stem at or near ground level.

Cause *Rhodococcus fascians*, a soil-borne bacterium that enters host plants through small wounds. It is easily spread on tools or through propagating from infected plants.
Control Destroy affected plants and remove the soil in their immediate vicinity, and wash after handling them. Maintain strict hygiene, sterilizing tools, containers, and the greenhouse regularly. Do not propagate from infected plants.

Leek moth

Plants affected Leek, onion, shallots, garlic, chives in some areas of Canada and areas of New York and Vermont. Range may spread.
Symptoms Small caterpillars mine the foliage, causing white patches, and bore into the stems and bulbs. The pupae are in netlike silk cocoons outside the leaf or stem.
Cause Caterpillars of leek moth, *Acrolepiopsis assectella*, are up to 1/16in (1.5mm) long and are creamy white with pale brown heads. There are two generations with larvae feeding during early and late summer.
Control If you live in or near areas where leek moth has been found, examine seedlings for signs of infestation before planting. Cover plants with row cover just after planting to prevent egg laying. Covers can be removed during the day to tend the plants, because the moths are active only at night.

Lightning

Plants affected Tall trees.
Symptoms Bark may be stripped, and a deep furrow may appear on one side, often following the spiral grain. The heartwood may be shattered, leaving the tree susceptible to disease. Dead wood increases in the crown and the upper crown dies.
Cause Lightning.
Control Lightning conductors may be attached to valuable tall trees, but this is unlikely to be feasible.

Lily leaf blight

Plants affected Lilies (*Lilium*), especially *L. candidum* and *L.* x *testaceum*.
Symptoms Dark green, water-soaked blotches develop on the leaves, later turning a pale brown;

the foliage then withers but remains on the stem. Where the pathogen enters a leaf axil, the stem may rot. Black sclerotia (fungal resting bodies) may form on dead tissues.
Cause The fungus *Botrytis elliptica*, which is encouraged by wet weather. Spores produced on the leaf lesions (or, in spring, from the sclerotia) are spread by rain splash and wind.
Control Grow on a well-drained site; clear away affected debris.

Low temperatures

Plants affected Trees, shrubs, perennials, annuals, bulbous plants, fruit, vegetables, indoor plants; seedlings; young plants and container-grown plants are most vulnerable.
Symptoms Leaves, especially those of seedlings, are sometimes bleached, and brown, dry patches develop; evergreen foliage may turn brown. Cold injury results in puckered, withered, or discolored (often blackened) leaves, and a lifting of the lower leaf surface, giving foliage a silvered appearance. Rotten patches, brown and dry or dark and soft, develop on petals, especially on exposed flower heads. Frost injury may leave petals withered or discolored and kill the whole flower. Brown, dry patches also develop on the stems—especially those of maples. Stems may blacken, wither, and crack or split, giving access to various organisms that cause dieback. The cracks become enlarged if moisture accumulates within them and then freezes, and this may lead to the death of the whole plant.
Cause Low temperatures or occasionally great fluctuations in temperature. Plants in exposed locations or frost pockets are likely to be affected.
Control Check the plant's suitability for the site. Provide winter protection for young, tender and exposed plants. Harden off plants raised under protection and/or cover with row cover.

Magnesium deficiency

Plants affected Trees, shrubs, bulbs, perennials, annuals, vegetables, and fruit; also many indoor plants. Tomatoes, chrysanthemums, and roses are most often affected.
Symptoms Distinct areas of discoloration, usually yellow but

occasionally red or brown, develop between the leaf veins (interveinal chlorosis), and affected leaves may fall early. Older leaves are usually affected first.
Cause Acidic soils; heavy watering or rainfall, both of which leach out magnesium; or high potassium levels, which make it unavailable. Plants given high-potassium fertilizers to encourage flowering or fruiting (e.g., tomatoes) are susceptible.
Control Treat plants and/or soil with Epsom salts in fall; either add them dry to the soil at a rate of 1oz/10sq ft (25g/sq m), or apply a foliar spray of 7½oz Epsom salts in 2¼ gallons of water (210g/10 liters), adding a non-detergent dishwashing liquid.

Manganese/iron deficiency

Plants affected Trees, shrubs, perennials, annuals, bulbous plants, vegetables, fruit, and indoor plants.
Symptoms A yellowing or browning starts at the leaf margins and extends between the veins. The overall leaf color may also be rather yellow. Younger leaves affected first for iron.
Cause The cultivation of plants in unsuitable soils or mixes; acid-loving plants, in particular, are unable to absorb adequate trace elements from alkaline soils. Regular watering with very hard water, buried debris (e.g., construction debris), and rain runoff from mortar in walls are all possible causes of a locally raised soil pH.
Control Choose plants compatible with the soil type and clear the area of any construction debris. Use rainwater, not tap water, for susceptible plants. Acidify the soil before or after planting, and apply acidic mulches. Apply a chelated iron or seaweed foliar spray.

Mealybugs

Plants affected Indoor and greenhouse plants, cacti and other succulents, grapevines (*Vitis*), some tender fruit, *Citrus*.
Symptoms A fluffy, white substance appears in leaf and stem axils. Plants may be sticky with honeydew (excrement) and blackened with sooty molds. Roots can also be affected.
Cause Various mealybugs (e.g., *Pseudococcus* and *Planococcus* spp.); soft-bodied, grayish-white, wingless insects up to ¼in (6mm)

long, often with white, waxy filaments trailing from their bodies. Root damage is caused by root mealybugs.
Control Outdoors, lady beetles provide biological control. Spray infested plants with a strong stream of water. Indoors, wipe with a swab dipped in a solution of half water, half rubbing alcohol. Discard heavily infested plants.

Mechanical wounding

Plants affected Potentially all plants.
Symptoms A neat-edged wound is visible on the stem or bark. Sap from the injured area may ferment into a slime flux, and pathogens entering the wound cause dieback or even death. A healed wound may leave a raised area.
Cause Careless use of garden machinery and tools.
Control Remove severely damaged shoots or stems. Wounds on woody plants should not be dressed or painted.

Millipedes

Plants affected Seedlings and other soft growth, strawberry fruit, and potato tubers.
Symptoms Seedlings and soft growth are eaten; slug damage on bulbs and potato tubers is enlarged. Roots and stems may be damaged in dry periods. Damage is rarely serious.
Cause Millipedes (e.g., *Blaniulus*, *Orthomorpha*, and *Spirobolu* spp.), black, gray, brown, or creamy-white animals that feed below or at soil level. They have hard, segmented bodies with two pairs of legs per segment (centipedes, which are beneficial predators, have only one pair per segment). The spotted snake millipede (*Blaniulus guttulatus*) is the most damaging species. Its slender, creamy-white body is up to ¾in (2cm) long with a row of red dots along each side. Millipedes are encouraged by soils that have a high organic content.
Control Cultivate the soil thoroughly and maintain good hygiene. Be careful not to overfertilize or apply too much mulch in areas where millipedes are a problem. Grow strawberries in raised containers. Millipedes are difficult to control but are rarely a problem in their own right; place board traps around plants and during the day, gather and destroy

the millipedes that congregate under the boards. Sprinkle wood ashes near rows of seedlings.

Moles

Plants affected Lawns, seedlings, young plants.
Symptoms Heaps of soil (molehills) appear on the lawn and cultivated areas. Roots of young plants and seedlings are disturbed.
Cause Burrowing moles.
Control Moles may be trapped, but instead they can be deterred by barriers that cut off their tunnels. Push metal sheets about 1ft (30cm) into the ground, through active tunnels. Repellents have limited effectiveness.

Nectria canker

Plants affected Woody perennials, shrubs, trees, especially apples, flowering crabapples (*Malus*), beeches (*Fagus*), poplars (*Populus*), *Sorbus*, mulberries (*Morus*), and hawthorns (*Crataegus*).
Symptoms Small areas of bark, often close to a bud or wound, darken and sink inward; the bark cracks, forming loose, flaky, concentric rings. Enlarged cankers restrict nutrient and water flow, and lead to stem and leaf deterioration. In extreme cases the whole shoot becomes ringed and dies back. White pustules appear in summer, red pustules in winter.
Cause Spores of the fungi *Nectria cinnibarina* and *Neonectria galligena* infect wounds caused by pruning, leaf fall, irregular growth, frost, and woolly aphids.
Control Prune affected branches or, on larger limbs, remove the entire cankered area. Ensure good tree health by regular watering, fertilizing, and good pest and disease control.

Nematodes

Plants affected Onions and garlic; some other vegetable crops and ornamentals, alfalfa, and clover.
Symptoms Plants may be stunted, with narrow shoot-tip leaves and swollen stems; onion and garlic leaves and stems are swollen and soft, bulbs are soft and misshapen. Plants may be killed by a heavy attack.
Cause Microscopic nematodes (*Ditylenchus dipsaci*) feeding in the plant tissues. Host-specific races of the nematodes attack specific crops. See also p.671.